Images following pages:

Jean Tinguely, letter to Pontus Hultén, 1987.

Klaus Rinke, "Pontus, Listen," portrait, 1989.

Pontus Hultén with Joseph Beuys and Karin Bergqvist Lindegren, Moderna Museet, Stockholm, 1971.

Hultén as boxer Primo Sportycuss in Claes Oldenburg's and Coosje van Bruggen's legend performance "Il Corso del Coltello," Venice, 1985. Costume by van Bruggen.

Mother Elsie Vougt Hultén with bear, Kamchatka, 1922.

Niki de Saint Phalle, Jean Tinguely, Per Olof Ultvedt, *hon, she*, Moderna Museet, Stockholm, 1966.

Niki de Saint Phalle and Pontus Hultén working on *she*, Moderna Museet, Stockholm, 1966.

Sample of Pontus Hultén catalogs.

Andy Warhol and Pontus Hultén, Moderna Museet, Stockholm, 1968.

Don Cherry and others in *Utopias and Visions*, Moderna Museet, Stockholm, 1971. Costumes by Moki Cherry.

Pontus Hultén with Rico Weber at La Commendarie, Dannemois, in Niki de Saint Phalle's film "Nana Island," 1971.

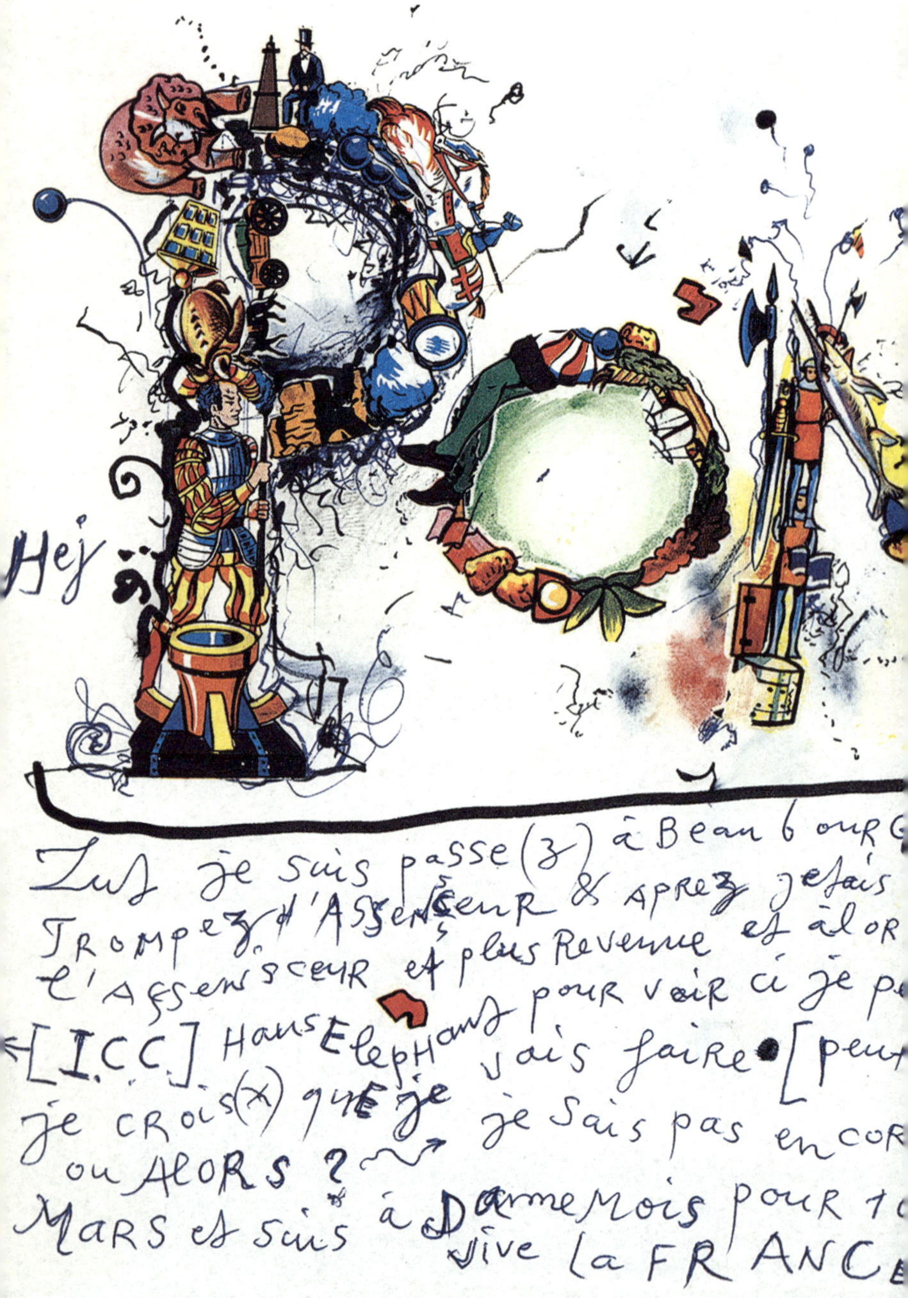
Hej
Zut je suis passe (3) à Beaubourg
Trompez d'Assenseur & aprez je fais
l'assenseur et plus Revenue et alor
pour voir ci je
[I.C.C.] Hans Elephant vais faire • [
je crois (x) que je je sais pas encor
ou ALORS ?
Mars et suis à Dammemois pour
vive la FRANCE

Acclaim for Swedish original of Claes Britton's Pontus Hultén — Commander of Modern Art.

Nominated for Sweden's leading literary award The August Prize 2022. Jury motivation: "Pontus Hultén today is probably unknown to the broader public, though he was the art pioneer who during the 1960s put Moderna Museet on the world map. In his almost 900-page chef d'oeuvre, Claes Britton provides a nuanced portrait of the controversial museum man. He was passionate for modern art and wanted to make it accessible to all. Now, in addition, the reader is educated with a good deal of the art history of the 1900s in this lively and entertaining biography."

Awarded the Royal Swedish Academy's Axel Hirsh Prize for best biography/life narrative 2022–2023.

VOICES ON THE BOOK:

"A lot can be said about Pontus Hultén — and this book does. Brilliantly! But first and foremost it makes it absolutely clear that he, without any doubt, was the curator/director who in the post-war era most radically changed the idea of what an art museum could — and perhaps should — be. For the benefit of the artist. And the public."

LARS NITTVE, FORMER DIRECTOR MODERNA MUSEET STOCKHOLM AND LOUISIANA, DENMARK. FOUNDING DIRECTOR TATE MODERN LONDON AND M+ HONGKONG

"Curator legend Pontus Hultén was a non-conformist and artist friend. He almost single-handedly made contemporary art accessible to a larger audience, with a huge impact on today's scene. Claes Britton now has written the biography he deserves: a tour de force through his curatorial assignments and relationships with the art people of his time. Elucidating, full of informative details and stories, and brilliantly written. If you wonder why contemporary art is as it is, you must read this book."

CARSTEN HÖLLER, ARTIST

"Pontus Hultén was the modern art museums' greatest visionary. During the second half of the 20th century, he transformed the museum into an experimental power center where new contemporary artistic expressions came to involve an ever expanding audience. In this grand biography, Claes Britton portrays him in full figure. It's a groundbreaking work that for the first time gives us the true picture of Hultén's international influence."

DANIEL BIRNBAUM, FORMER DIRECTOR MODERNA MUSEET, STOCKHOLM

"Claes Britton's rich biography builds on a monumental research work, with hundreds of interviews, countless archive hours and an almost ten-year writing process, and is powered by a straight, journalistic prose. It is in every aspect a groundbreaking work (...) an equally impressive and well written monument over the Titan Hultén."

BO MADESTRAND, DAGENS NYHETER, SWEDEN'S LEADING DAILY

"What Hultén did after leaving Sweden in the mid 70s is less well known. Britton, who is an author, journalist and creative director, has made a great and important contribution by documenting this in his more than 800-page book. (...) Britton has not just traveled to Paris, but continued to follow in Hultén's footsteps. He has visited museums around the world where he was director: in Los Angeles, Venice, Bonn and Basel. He has interviewed a couple of hundred persons: artists, museum professionals, collectors and friends of Hultén. He has plowed through archives and the long suite of catalogs that accompanied the exhibitions. In addition, he has succeeded in creating structure in all this material. Interestingly, the story has come to encompass not just Hultén's life and work, but also the story of how museums for the art of Modernism were created and operated in an era before the accelerating commercialization of the art world. Britton portrays how Hultén's driving force was his vision of how artists should contribute to shaping society and how he mourned the increasing focus on art's monetary value. (...) In his text he succeeds in painting the picture of the powerful, charismatic, multi-talented and unruly Pontus Hultén as I myself remember him."

ANN NITTVE, SVENSKA DAGBLADET, LEADING STOCKHOLM DAILY

"Claes Britton doesn't hold back on the gun powder or the anecdotes in this mighty biography with its glittering cover. You are given a powerful feeling of what a wonderful spirit of freedom that blew through the 1960s. Paradoxically, most all was already said. An entertaining and consciousness-expanding read."

JAN EKLUND, DAGENS NYHETER

"It's obvious that this book is the result of an enormous endeavor (...) It's a tremendously solid work that will be referred to for many years to come, also filled with great anecdotes. (...) The Brillo chapter is among the most interesting, containing a critical standpoint by Britton (...) who wrestles with his subject in invigorating manner (...) All this and much more can be found in Claes Britton's ambitious biography, leaving it to the reader to connect the dots."

AGRI ISMAIL, EXPRESSEN, LEADING NATIONAL TABLOID

"Thus Hultén became the most groundbreaking exhibition maker we have ever seen (...) It's an adventure which I now follow very carefully in Claes Britton's massive, magnificent biography. (...) 800 pages packed with energetic desire for knowledge and compassion in every nuance. (...) It is in several ways a colossal book — mighty and overwhelming, but no objections on my side. Two hundred people in eleven countries are said to have been interviewed. The pearl string of anecdotes we are given us as a bonus.

Alas, Britton is extremely meticulous in portraying Pontus Hultén's life from beginning to end. With all this material he constructs a monumental image of a man who lived animated by controversy, single-minded stubbornness and traveling restlessness. It is in fact a mighty chunk of art history which we are gifted, but primarily it's of course not about the substances and particularities of the art world, but about the main character's life and career. As Britton stresses — intuition and chance were Hultén's constant companions. Even when he was on the verge of buying a false Mondrian. At the bottom, all is driven by an unrestrained passion. (...)

Among the book's many strengths is that Britton really makes the social contexts in which Hultén operates come alive again and again — he paints the scenarios, the drama, the politics, the wars with a strikingly agile and entertaining pen. (...)

Claes Britton writes with powerful vigor and lust. He maximizes Pontus Hultén to larger than life and he seems completely tireless. It's a brilliant life journey he gives to the reader (...) Britton's portrait is, again, mighty rich with information. A horn of plenty."

MIKAEL VAN REIS, GÖTEBORGS-POSTEN, SOUTHWEST SWEDEN'S LEADING DAILY

"That Pontus Hultén in his 'soul' was not a museum director but an artist — as the artist Niki de Saint Phalle said — is completely clear for the reader of this book. As geniuses do, he broke the frames, creating new ones: defined art movements, created a new kind of museum and rewrote art history in grand exhibition projects (...) But it actually breaks new ground, too, in its thorough recount of Pontus Hultén's international career, from which his important achievements — contrary to those at Moderna Museet — has unjustly fallen from memory. And above all, Britton's meticulous journalistic relentlessness makes for a nuanced portrait of a complex, whole human being. That is beautiful." MÅRTEN ARNDZÉN, SWEDISH STATE RADIO

VOICES ON PONTUS HULTÉN:

"Pontus Hultén is one of a handful of people, Duchamp and a few others, who, in the 20th century, contributed most to transforming modern art from a small clique phenomenon into a huge force and part of everyday life and references for the broader masses." CALVIN TOMKINS, AUTHOR

"Before him, French curators and museum people were traditional, pro-painting, Cézanne, Picasso, Matisse. Pontus Hultén was a readymade director."

BERNARD BLISTÈNE, FORMER DIRECTOR MUSÉE NATIONAL D'ART MODERNE, CENTRE POMPIDOU PARIS

"Pontus had a unique knowledge and insight into the historical, intellectual and artistic contexts and an equally unique ability to tell this story in his exhibitions. In his broad perspective and his total view of art in the world and in life, I must say that it is he who has influenced me most."

SUZANNE PAGÉ, FOUNDING DIRECTOR FOUNDATION LOUIS VUITTON PARIS

"I envy you this project. Pontus Hultén is such an important part of 20th century art history, in so many ways."

SIR NICHOLAS SEROTA, FORMER DIRECTOR TATE GALLERY, LONDON

"It was Pontus Hultén who created the model for exhibitions we have today, and most specifically here at the Centre Pompidou. I often call them 'oceanographic' exhibitions. You dive into them and have the impression of discovering whole new worlds. Each gallery is a surprise. There is a scenario, a narrative. The only problem with Pontus Hultén's exhibitions was that they were too successful. Today, we speak somewhat melancholically about them as a golden age. But his exhibitions should instead be seen as an opportunity to look forward, as models for the future. Today's profession of curator has persons like Pontus Hultén to thank for everything."

LAURENT LE BON, PRESIDENT CENTRE POMPIDOU PARIS

"Pontus invented a whole new totality in art." GERMANO CELANT, CURATOR

"Not quite everything interesting was created by Pontus."

HARALD SZEEMANN, CURATOR AND MUSEUM DIRECTOR

"With his deep political and historic perspective, he invented a new model for the modern museum and art exhibition."

KASPER KÖNIG, CURATOR AND MUSEUM DIRECTOR

"Pontus Hultén's miracle was not in radically transforming the art system, but rather in capturing the spirit of the time through artistic freedom, granting curators the courage to suggest daring projects and innovation within institutions. (...) He always seemed to prefer to risk allowing instinct and nonsense to interfere with rationality. Doubtless, this explains why he was the greatest executor of the role of the curator as interpreter of the present."

CHIARA PARIS, DIRECTOR CENTRE POMPIDOU-METZ

"The queen of the Nanas was 'Hon' (...) built by her (Niki de Saint Phalle) for a show at what was then the coolest museum on the planet, Moderna Museet in Stockholm." JASON FARAGO, THE NEW YORK TIMES, 8 APRIL, 2021

"The memory of a visit at the Beaubourg will not be simply the impressions of this artwork or the other, a painting, a book or an exhibition, but a play of reflections, contradictions and sparks of inspiration, spanning from the latest works, sometimes shocking and difficult to comprehend, to older, better known works. This perspective of course demands a cross-disciplinary scientific approach, with the need to mirror, on the one hand, art history in multiple media, devoid of hierarchy, and, on the other, the necessity of attracting new audiences by integrating contemporary expressions priorly deemed illicit. To this day, this doctrine is a corner stone in the DNA of the Centre Pompidou, nourishing the presentation of the collections as much as the design of exhibitions, while still being just one of the pillars of the multi-facetted strategy of Pontus Hultén."

ANNE HORVATH, CURATOR/INTENDANT CENTRE POMPIDOU-METZ

"Pontus' generosity and constant readiness to claim a radical artistic position and to professionally — and institutionally — engage in and fight for this standpoint, was a decisive contribution by him to the art world, ever impulsive, provocative and innovative through decades."

-KASPER KÖNIG, CURATOR AND MUSEUM DIRECTOR

"Pontus Hultén isn't bound to a country. He lived a nomad's life. He's often seen as a sailor, a navigator. I think he was one of the first curators who crossed frontiers — frontiers of disciplines, frontiers of countries. I think he wanted to show that art is global. Today it's self-evident, but fifty years ago it was more difficult, so here too, he opened a new road."

LAURENT LE BON, PRESIDENT CENTRE POMPIDOU PARIS

"Pontus put us in touch with the world and art history. He was a powerful figure and left a great legacy. There is no such figure in art today. He was popular here but had a rebellious way of running the museum that led to confrontation with the board members. He had an open heart, a curiosity and sensitivity, and was in touch with all these sacred figures in the art world. I was very sad to see him leave the party."

ED RUSCHA, ARTIST

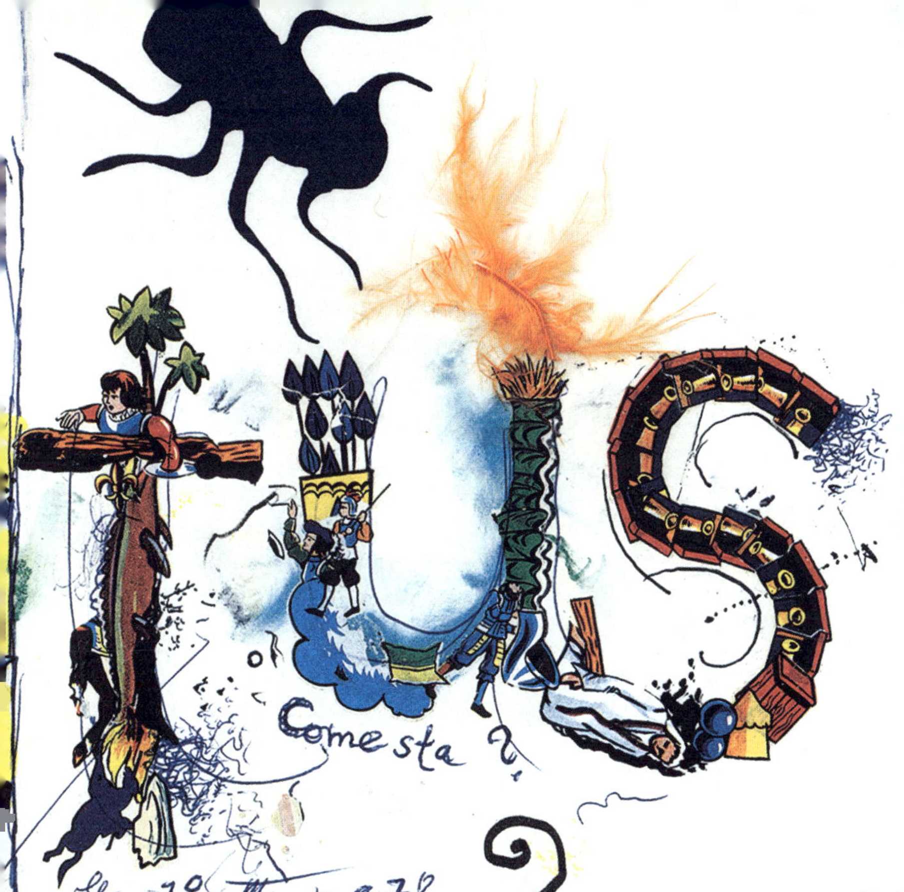

le 10 III 1978

→ Ja été chez KASIMIR et je me suis
CAVE & C + ERA j'ai du pissez & APRES
Filez à BERLIN et la aux Neue KONGRES
AIRE quelque chôse ? DARÏGOLO
des LAMPES ! ¿ ?] en Mouvement !
→ NiKi revient Mardi le 14
eRS mes ont's se VERRA – Alora
amitiés : Jean

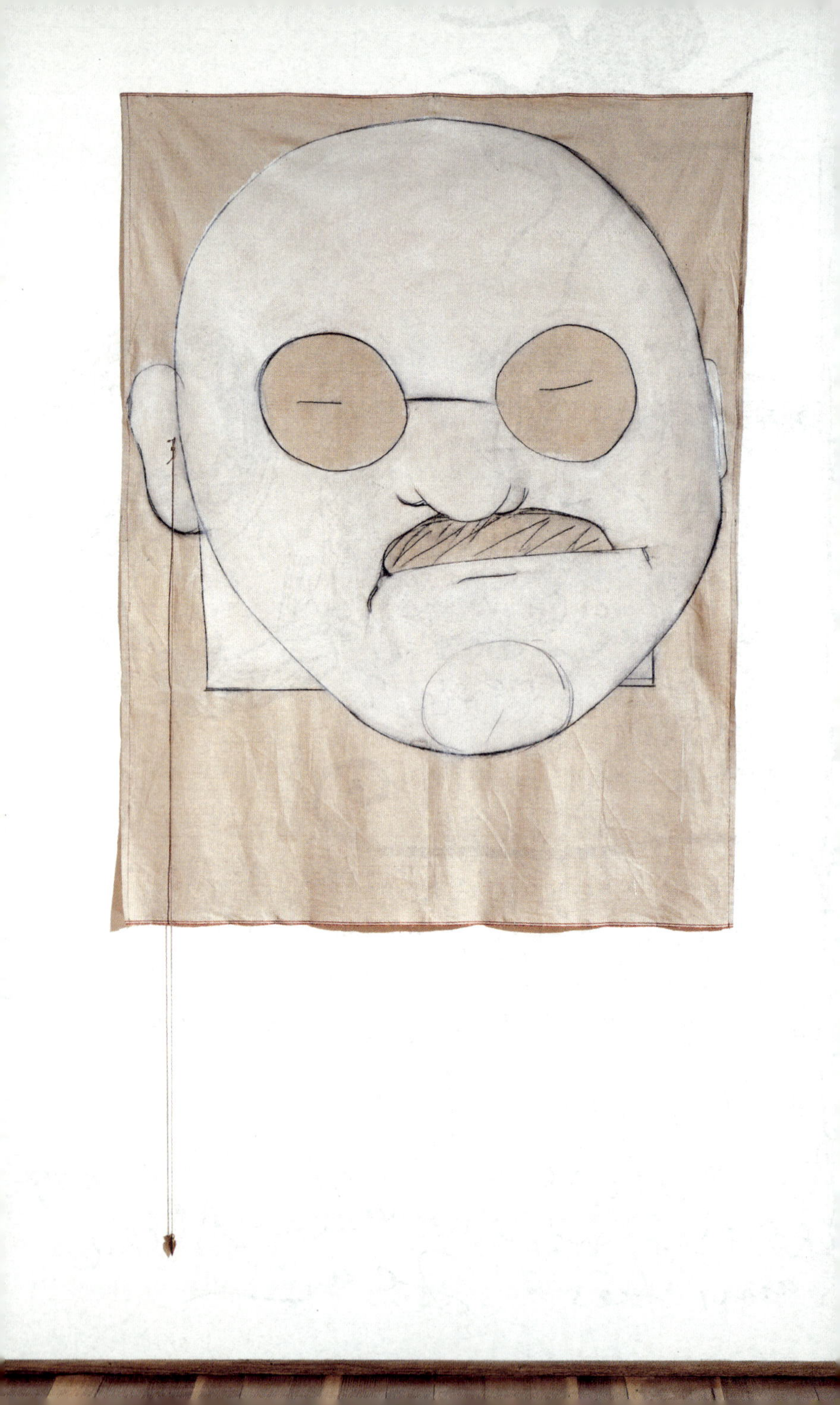

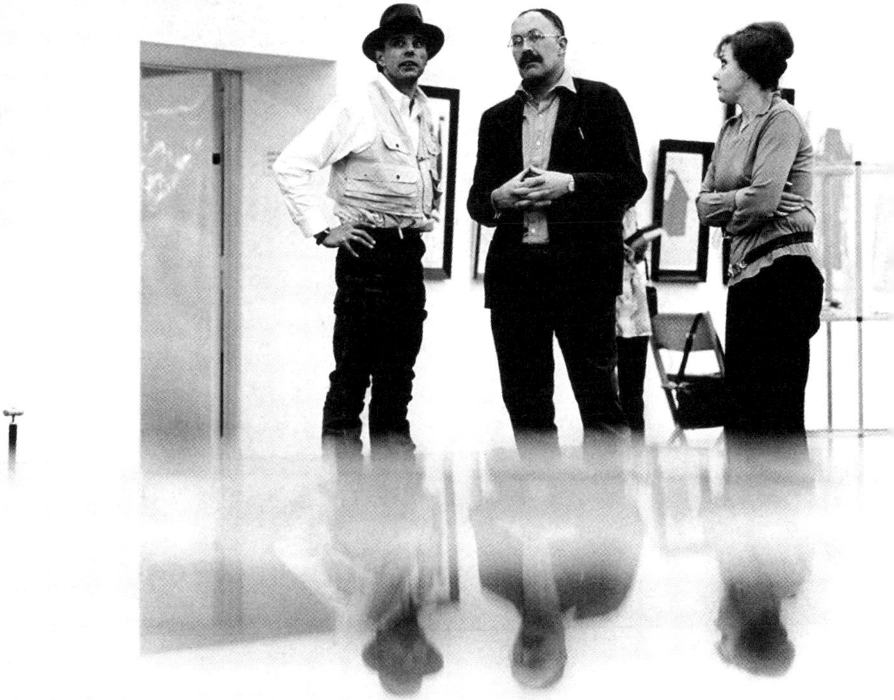

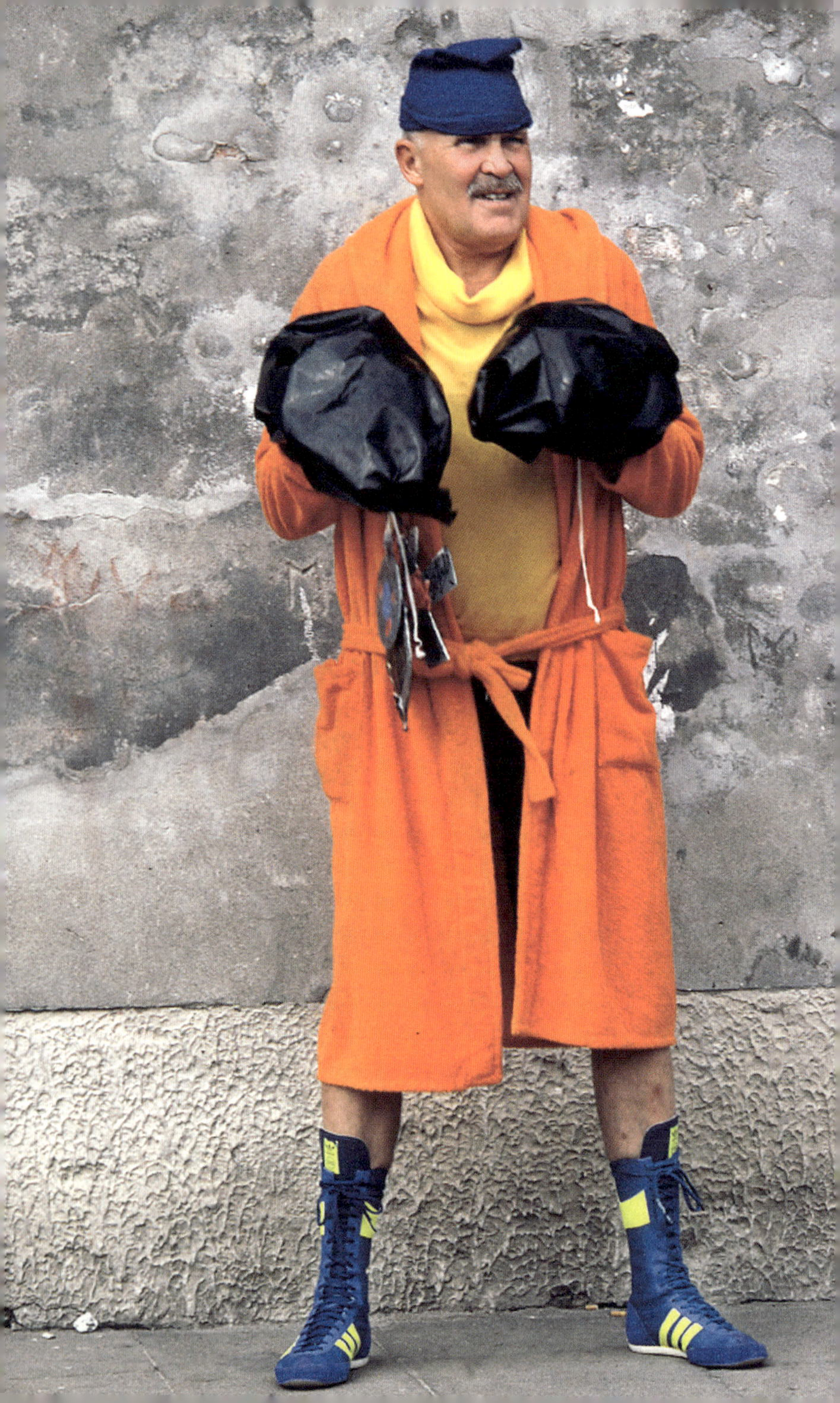

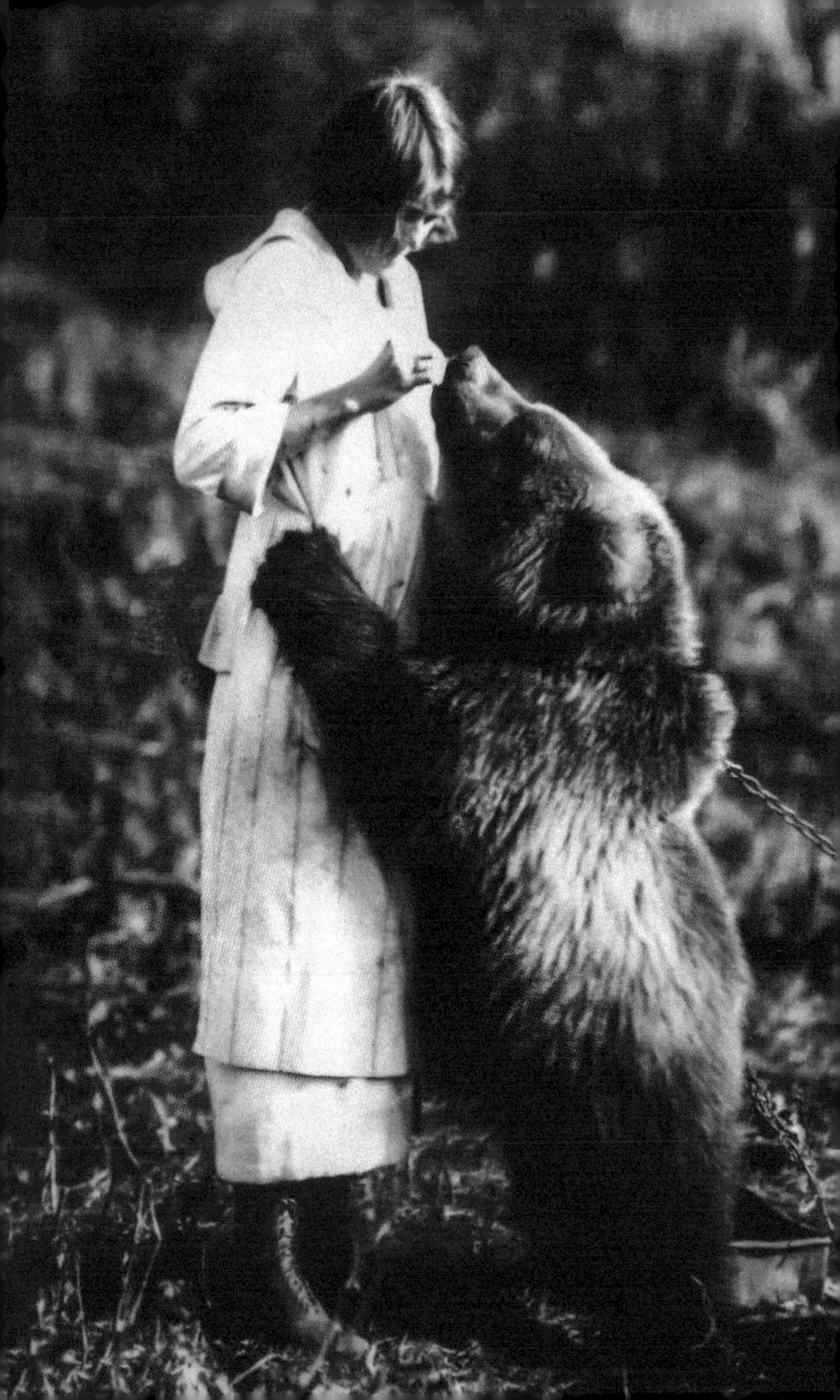

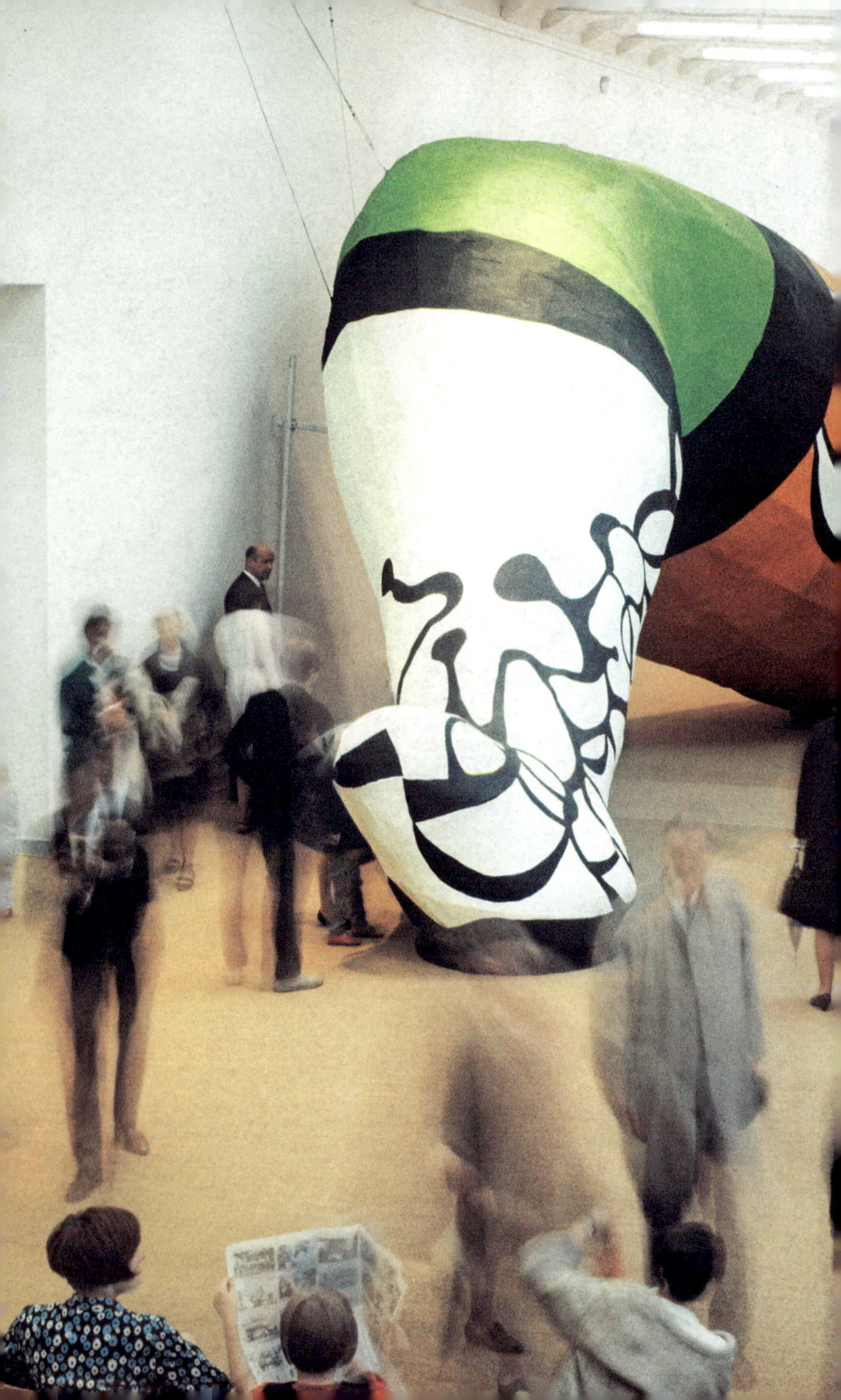

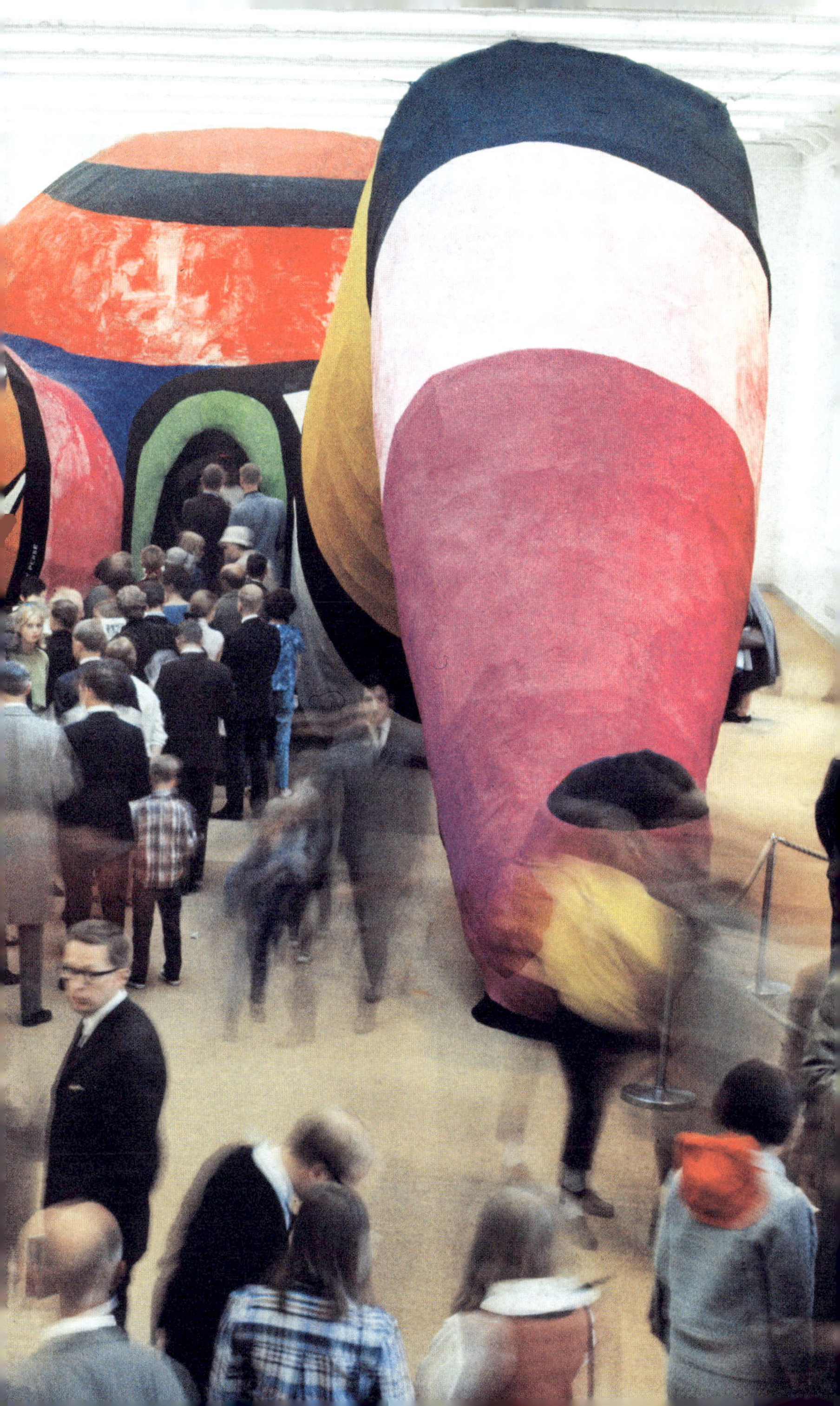

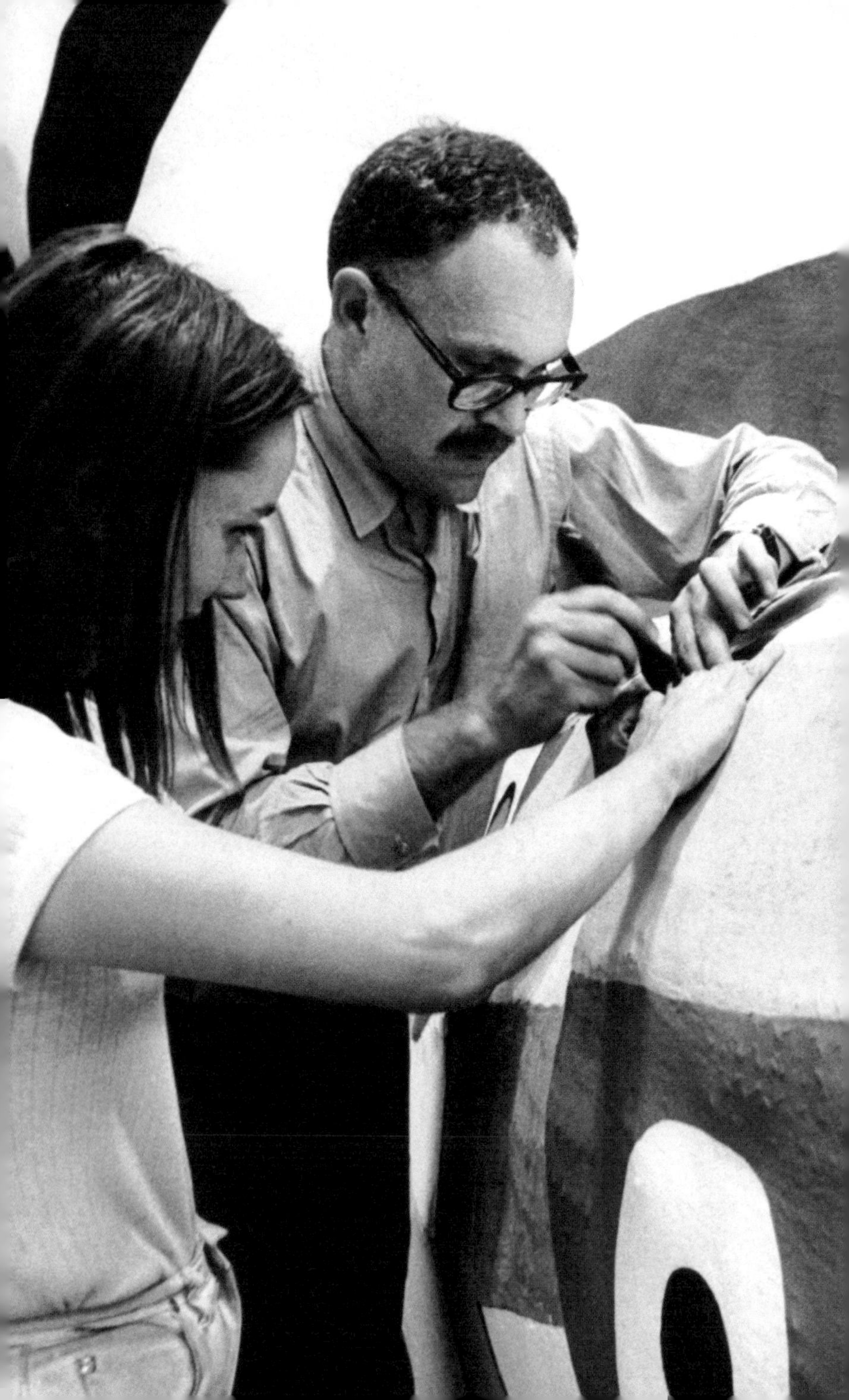

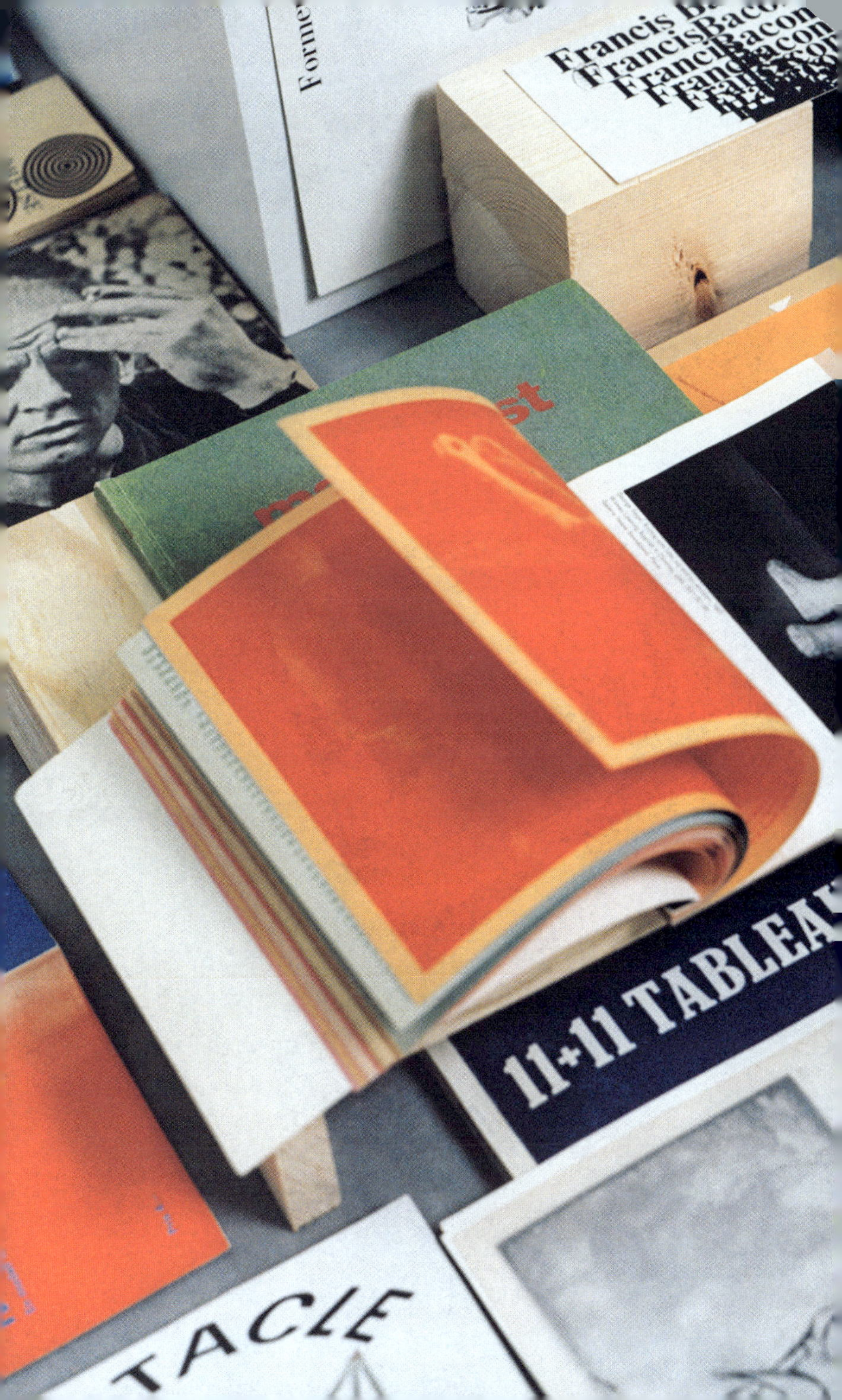
Francis Bacon
11+11 TABLEA
TACLE

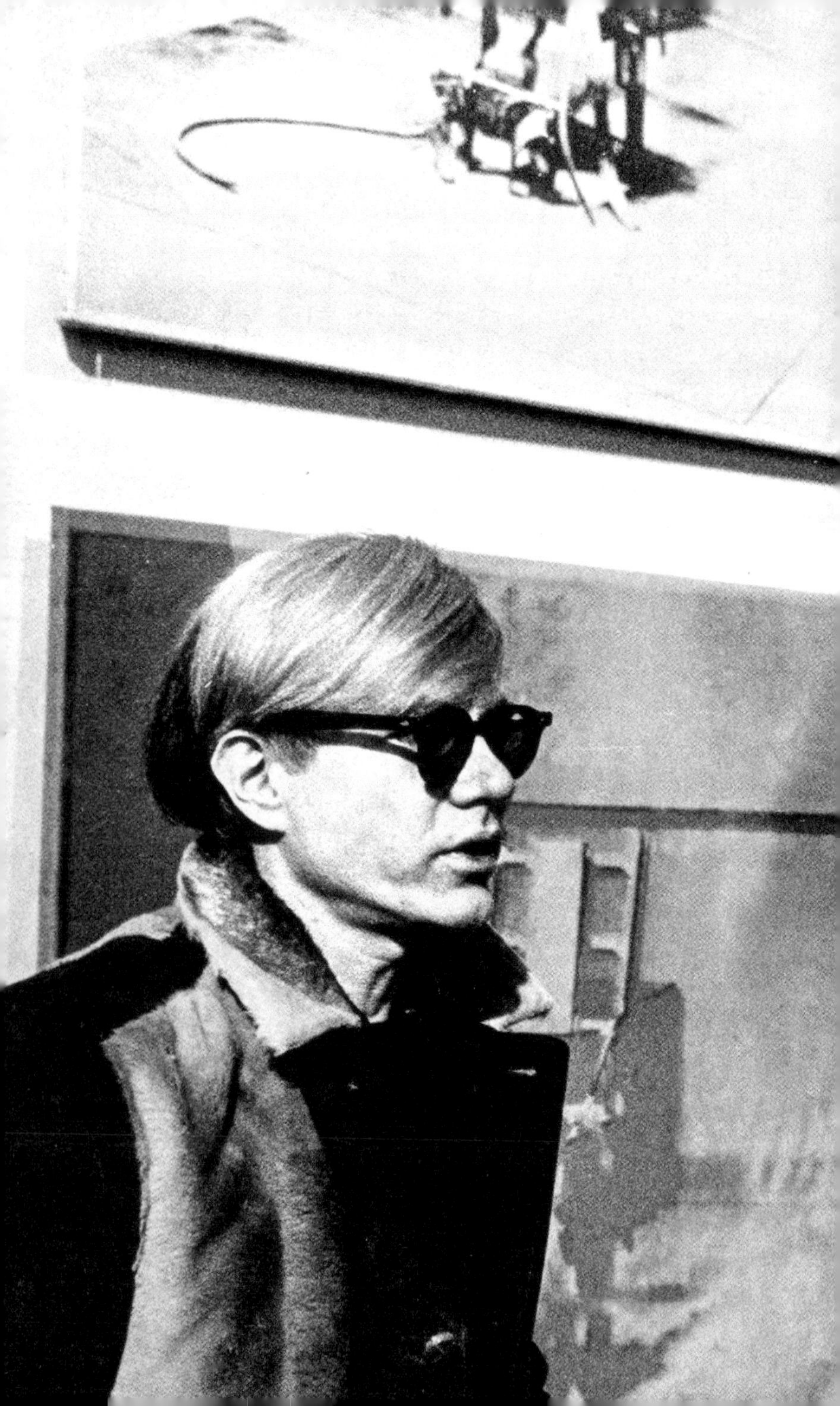

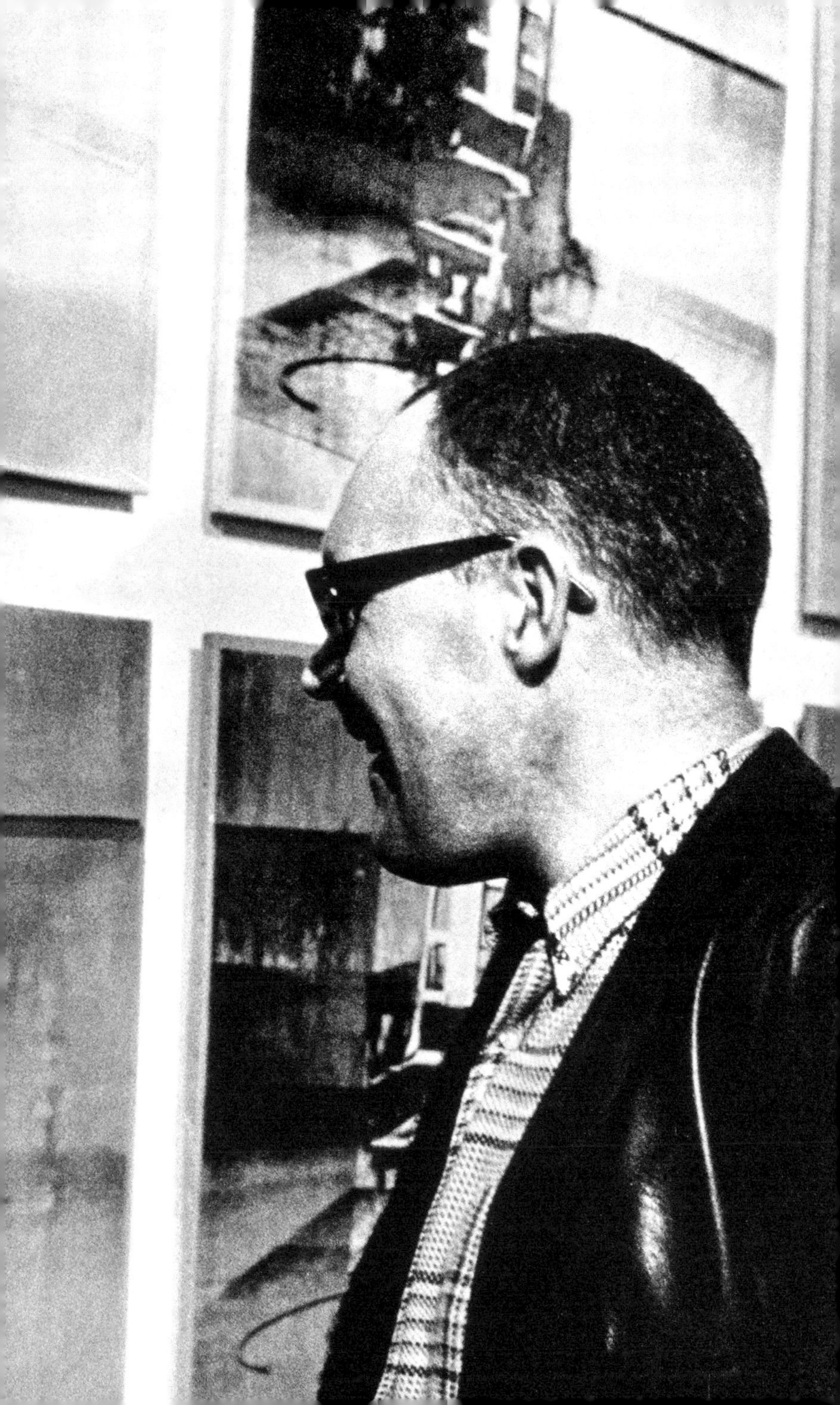

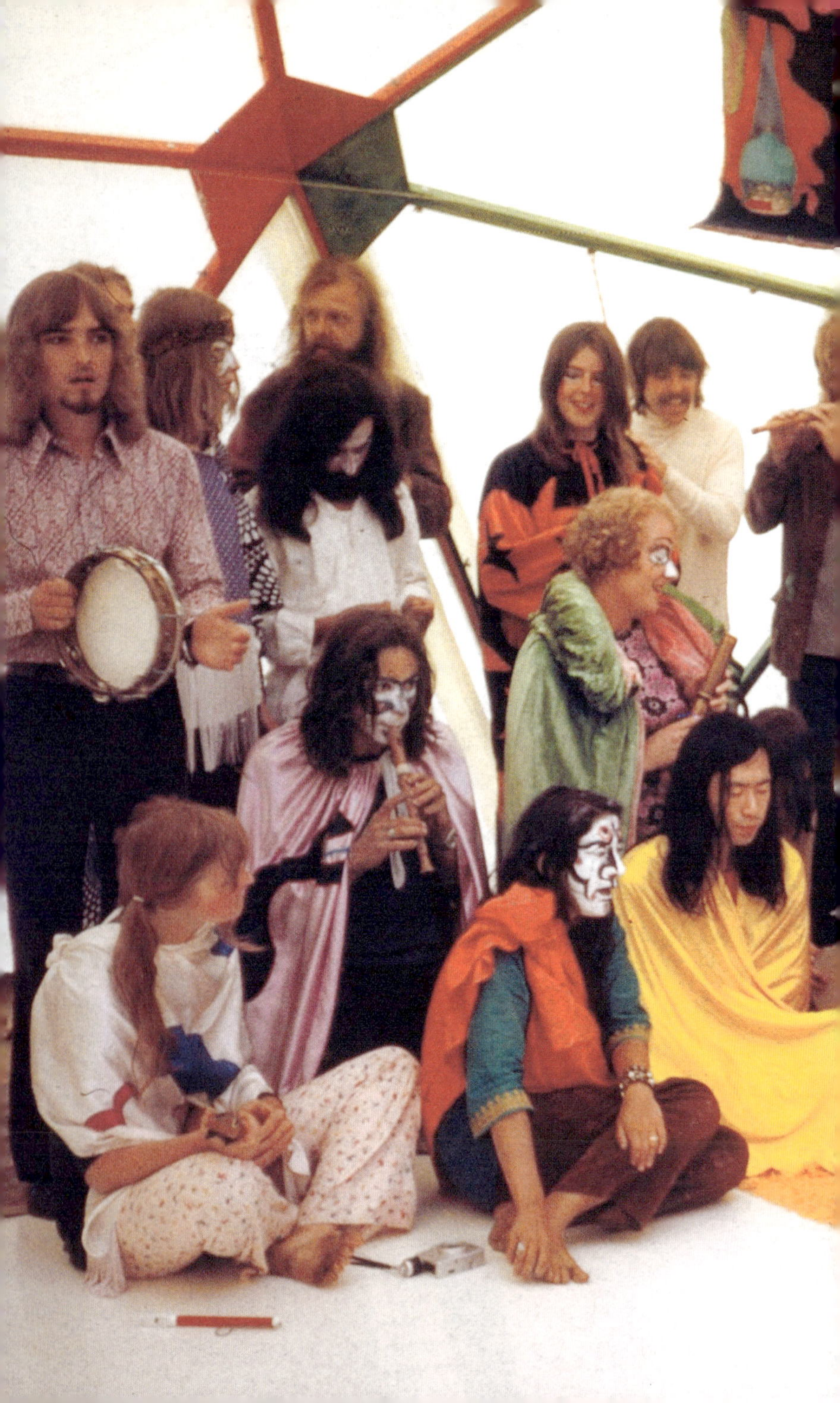

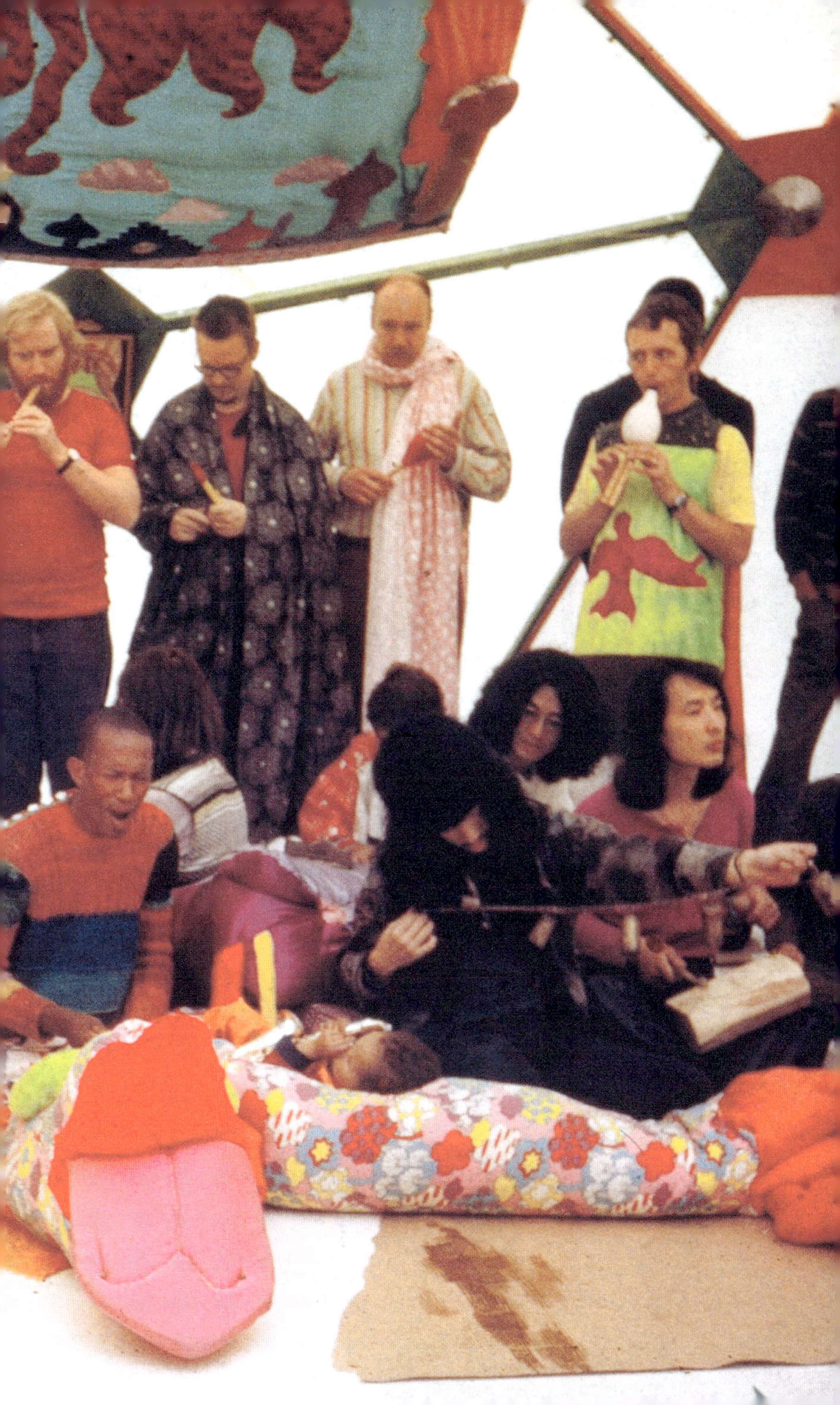

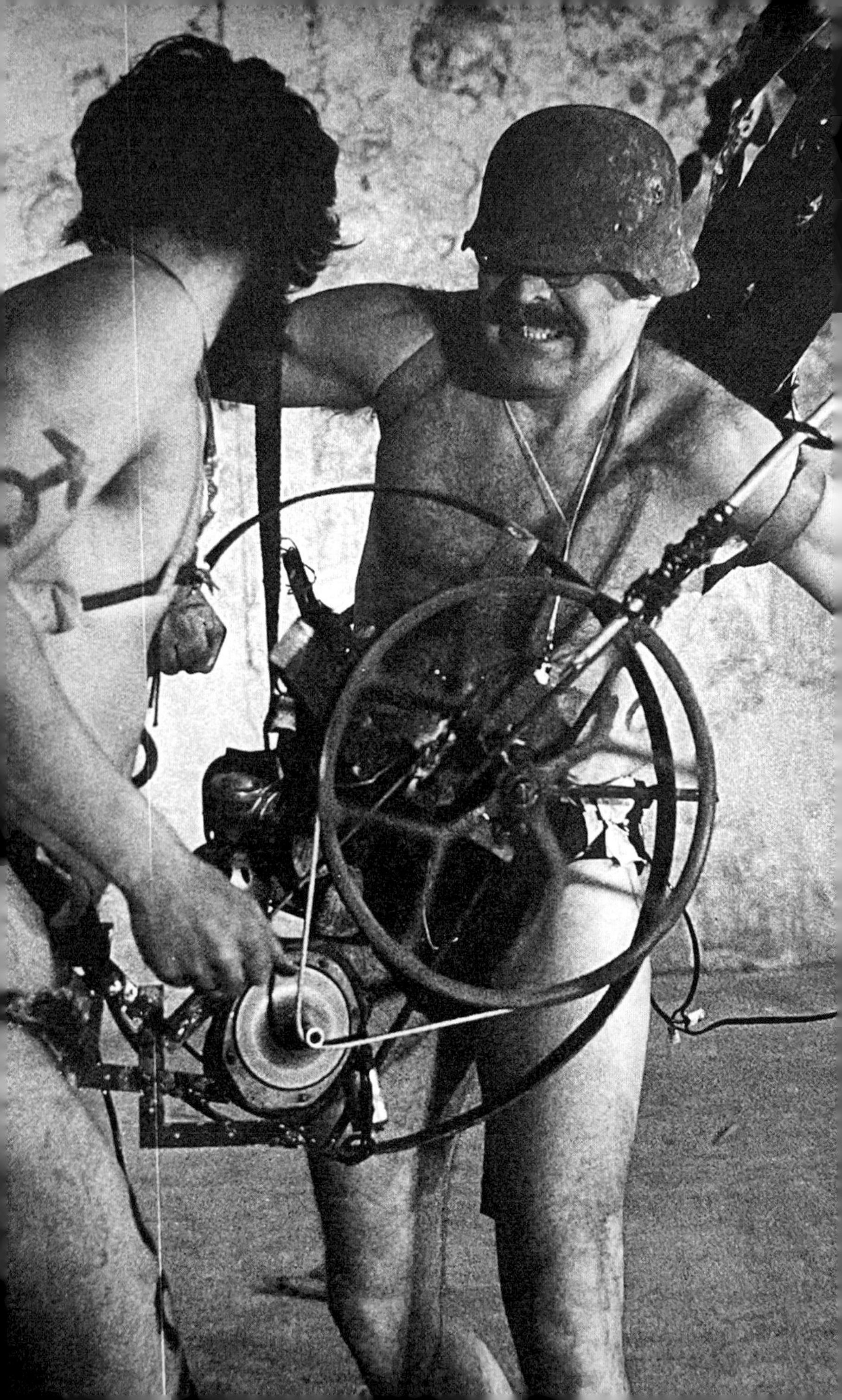

PONTUS HULTÉN

CLAES BRITTON

COMMANDER OF MODERN ART

Contents

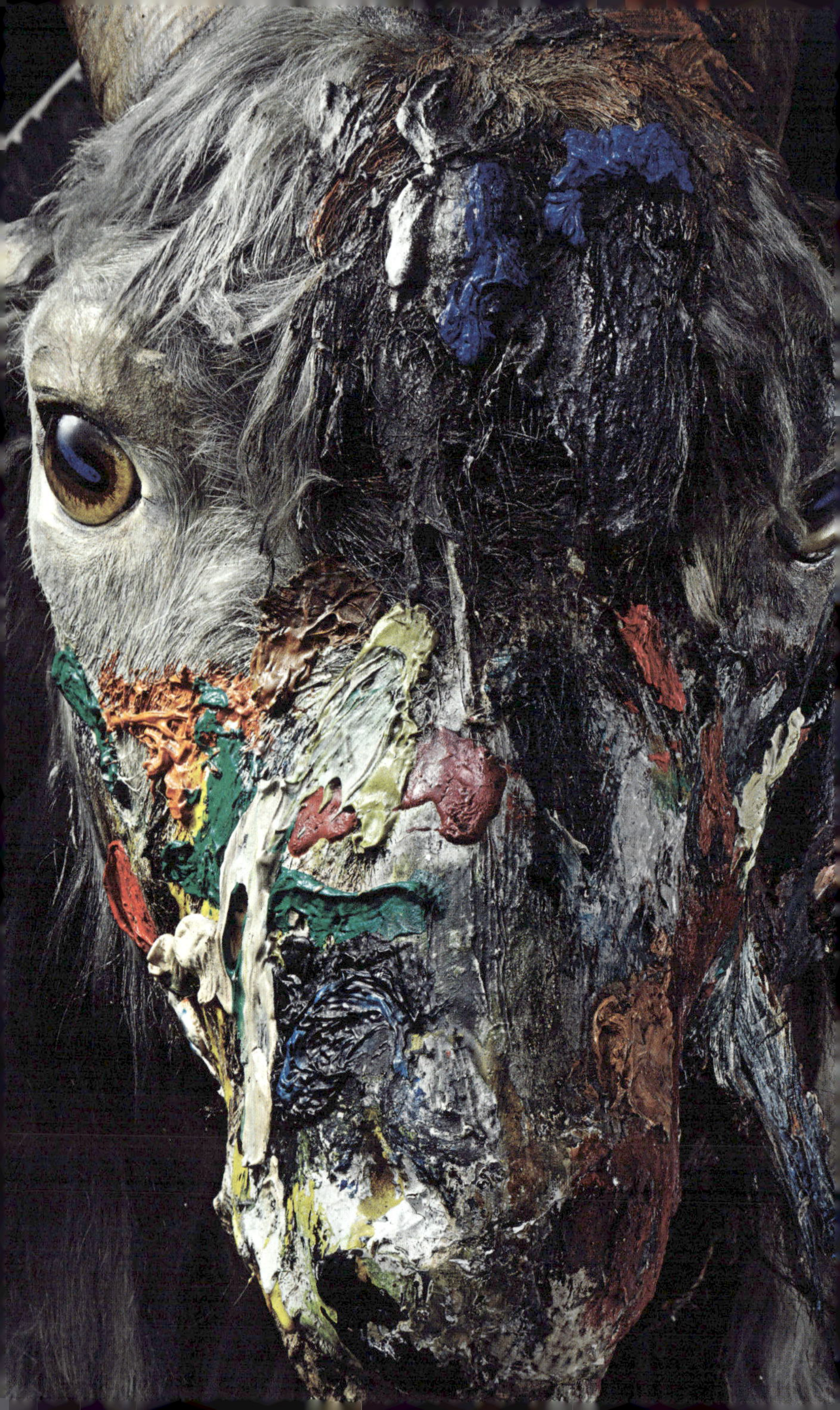

Preface

I'll never forget the feel of the coconut rug under my bare boy's feet. We ran as fast as our child muscles would allow through the halls, skated on our socks across the parquet floor which I remember expanded in another, inner part of the museum. Unforgettable are the light, the smell and the voluminous acoustics in these halls. Not to mention the art itself, which appeared magical — thrilling, mysterious, terrifying — to my young mind.

There was Nils Dardel's "Jealousy Drama," with the nobleman in silk pyjamas; shot, blood gushing from his temple over a bearskin on the floor, the woman with the smoking gun. Salvador Dalí's "Wilhelm Tell's Riddle" dominated the inner gallery, with the old man who I learned much later, from Pontus Hultén himself, is Lenin, with his grotesquely elongated buttock on top of which something bloody, liver-like slimes. Edward Kienholz's "The State Hospital" terrified me, arousing unconscious death anxiety with its stench of suffering, madness, annihilation; the poor bastards lying there in fetal positions in their wretched double bunk with fish bowls for a heads.

In the center of it all, a real Formula 1 car glimmered. A racing car in the midst of the art — how was that possible in a museum, an institution I associated with boring adult propriety and obligation? Niki de Saint Phalle's and Jean Tinguely's sculpture group "Paradise," then sitting in its proper site at the bridge abutment of the Skeppsholmen island, defiantly signaled that we were departing the decent, rational, well-combed world, entering the domain of fantasy. Still, the main attraction was Robert Rauschenberg's "Monogram," just inside the museum entrance, then free of its armored glass cage, surrounded only by a rope; the poor goat with its sad eyes, trapped and humiliated by us

Robert Rauschenberg, "Monogram," 1958–1959, detail.

humans and our industrial civilization, with a car tire like a millstone around its body, its face desecrated with oil paint — that's how I naturally interpreted the artwork as a child.

The whole scene offered a fabulous insight into all the evil, sorrow and pain, violence and lust that awaited in the adult world; enigmatic yet somehow understandable; all that was concealed in the future, which I perhaps already sensed — the sexuality, the violence, the suffering, the anxiety, the class struggle, the humiliation, the rock'n'roll, the madness, the ubiquitous death — that whole bunch of extreme human conditions with which I would soon enough become acquainted.

My aunt and her friend[1] operated the children's cinema at Moderna Museet. As I recall, I spent almost every weekend during the winter months with my cousin and my younger brother[2] at the museum. In the cinema, we laughed our heads off at movies with Chaplin, Laurel & Hardy, Buster Keaton and my favorites, the Marx Brothers. My first certain memory is from 1968 when the museum was taken over by *The Model*, a colossal playground for us kids. What a wild feeling of freedom it was to plunge from a platform into the sea of foam rubber that filled the main museum hall! The feeling, the smell of the foam is unforgettable. Of course, it was a bit scary with the other children landing on and near you. Security policies were far from as developed in those days, least of all at Moderna Museet. After the exhibition, the children's workshop remained, where you could paint and scribble, knead clay, destroy old appliances and dress mannequins with the droves of old clothes, wigs, makeup and accessories that were available for free use. What a paradise for a growing young imagination!

I remember vividly the flaming controversies that surrounded the museum at the time. I was born and raised in haute bourgeois Östermalm district, where I was an ideological stranger as my father was a publicly known left-wing rabble-rouser. None of my schoolmates set foot in Moderna Museet, known as a "communist nest" — a blood-red beacon of the upper-class right amongst which we lived.

Of course, I realized not then, but much later, that what we had experienced during my childhood weekends was something extraordinary — the later phase of Pontus Hultén's fifteen-year era as the first director of Moderna Museet. As a young man, I came to realize the uniqueness of these memories, which led me to take an interest in Pontus Hultén, the man who above all others, as I understood, had made all this possible. I started reading what I could find about him, which was surprisingly sparse. In the Swedish press, Hultén was mentioned remarkably rarely.

Much later, in December 1996, when we published our fashion and culture magazine Stockholm New, I had the opportunity to meet Pontus Hultén, who I had increasingly come to see as a spiritual father figure. Prior to the museum's reopening in its current premises in 1998, we were working on a theme issue about Moderna Museet and its history. I contacted Pontus Hultén in his castle La Motte in the Loire in France and asked if he would be willing to come to Stockholm for an interview. To my surprise, he immediately agreed.

One freezing cold winter morning, I met him there in the entrance of the Grand Hôtel — a heavy appearance dressed in a long black greatcoat and a black fur hat. I interviewed him for two full days. During copious cognac consumption by both of us, Pontus generously poured from his well of art historical contexts, dramatic developments and fabulous anecdotes, all narrated in the same concise, laconic tone, always with an undertone of dry sardonic humor. After this encounter, I kept in touch with Pontus for a number of years — unfortunately not to the end, which saddens me now. My interest grew to fascination — perhaps even obsession.

It turned out that I was the only person in Sweden who had bothered to contact Pontus Hultén before the reopening of the Moderna Museet to hear his stories and opinions. No other Swedish newspaper or magazine interviewed him. This surprised me. I couldn't see the picture in any other way than that Pontus is one of our greatest Swedish international cultural figures of all time. Only Ingmar Bergman and Astrid Lindgren could be compared in our time. Otherwise, we had to go back to Strindberg. While these were ever-present, Pontus was so erased that my own generational peers, even those interested in art and culture, only vaguely if at all knew his name — a man who had been the founding director of seven museums and institutions in six countries, including our own Moderna Museet and the Musée National d'Art Moderne at the Centre Pompidou in Paris, the world's most spectacular art museum. This was incomprehensible to me. Only much later would I understand the explanations.

After our issue with the Moderna Museet special had been published, and the magazine *Månadsjournalen* later had published a Swedish translation of my interview, I was repeatedly told, in reproachful terms, by people of an older generation in cultural circles that I should "beware" of having too close contact with Pontus Hultén and listening too much to his versions of reality. I understood more clearly just how controversial Pontus was in the generation that had experienced the heyday of Moderna Museet under his leadership. This didn't diminish my fascination for Pontus and his work, quite on the contrary.

It was during Lars Nittve's time as director that we were commissioned to design and produce Moderna Museet's fiftieth anniversary book — a heavy coffee-table piece, published in 2008. We had no influence over the actual content. It was decided in advance. My surprise grew when I noticed Pontus' conspicuous absence in this content. His colleagues and collaborators Carlo Derkert and Billy Klüver were more prominent than Pontus Hultén, their superior and the museum's world-famous founding director. I repeatedly pointed this out to the project management and was answered with evasive, half-stifled songs about wanting to "get away from the anectdotic sixties." In *The History Book*,[3] as the fiftieth anniversary book is called, several colleagues told different versions of important events than those that Pontus had shared with me eleven years earlier — with the difference that they themselves took credit for achievements under Hultén's leadership.

During our work on the anniversary book, the Brillo box scandal broke. Now the dead Pontus was transformed into a simple fraudster and counterfeiter. Even today, the Brillo boxes are the only matter that many of my own and younger generations associate with Hultén, if they know his name at all.

My fascination continued to grow. I did some unplanned research, including several interviews with Ulf Linde, Pontus' colleague from the early years of Moderna Museet. Unlike Hultén, Linde was a local hero, idolized in cultural coteries for his work with Marcel Duchamp which I knew that Pontus had initiated after introducing Linde to Duchamp, Hultén's great hero and mentor, whom he had met in Paris in the 1950s. I also had the privilege of befriending Billy Klüver, Hultén's partner in New York.

It all just got stranger. The complexity of Pontus' person and work became increasingly apparent to me. Yet I had never thought of writing a biography of this spiritual father figure of mine — or of any other person at all for that matter. I had assumed myself too self-absorbed to devote so much time and energy to another human being. The idea was surprisingly presented to me by a young friend[4] one evening while we were browsing books. As soon as he presented the suggestion, I realized that this was a calling for me — and also that the task was urgent. Pontus Hultén's contemporary friends, colleagues, collaborators and contemporary artists, those who were still alive, were getting on in years. I embarked on an odyssey around the world in Pontus Hultén's footsteps.

After twelve years of traveling, interviewing more than two hundred people in eleven countries, a significant proportion of them aged between eighty and ninety-five — artists, friends and colleagues, many of them big names — my image of Pontus Hultén has grown into a monument. It has been a rare privilege to hear all these stories about Pontus and the post-war art world.

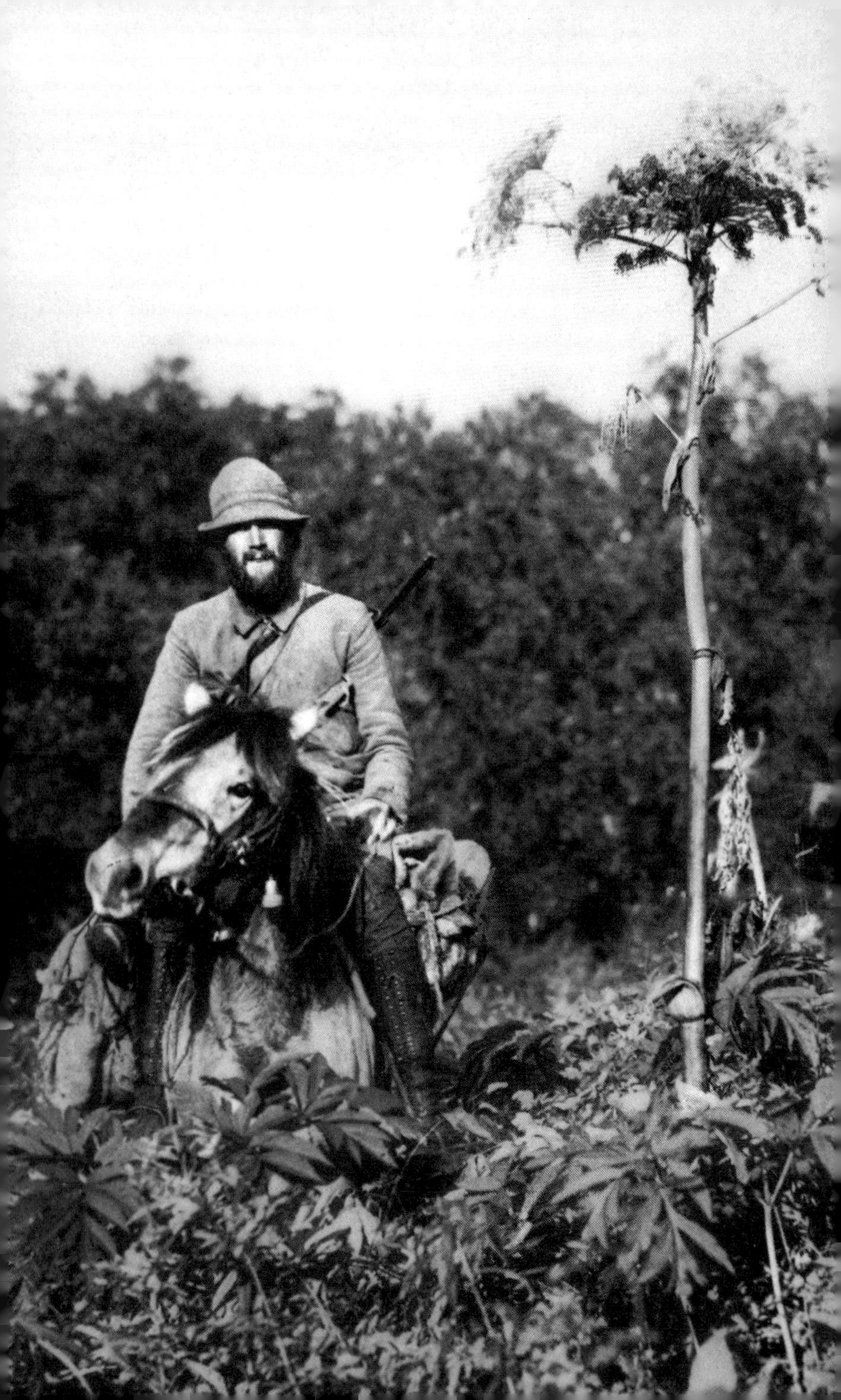

Origin

In his father Eric Hultén, Pontus had a heritage as a museum man. Eric Hultén was an eminent botanist and biologist. From 1945 until his retirement in 1961, he was professor and director of the botanical department at the Swedish Museum of Natural History in Stockholm. He was a member of the Swedish Academy of Sciences and well known in the small international botanical research community, in the USA and not least in Russia, the latter a legacy that would become important to Pontus Hultén.

In 1973, Eric Hultén published his memoir *Men roligt har det varit* (*But It Has Been Fun.*)[1] The book is a captivating read — like a real-life picaresque novel rivaling Voltaire's *Candide* and other classics of the genre, packed with breathtaking adventures, matter-of-factly rendered with an undertone of sardonic humor. Adventurousness and risk-taking were qualities that characterized Pontus Hultén. You don't have to wonder where these inclinations came from when you read *But it has been fun*. In comparison with his father's book, Pontus Hultén's hazardous picaresque through the art world appears, after all, as a comfortable and safe journey.

Eric Hultén was born in 1894 in the Björklunda vicarage in Halla parish in Strängnäs diocese. His father, Pontus Hultén's grandfather, was vicar in Vrena and Halla parishes. His mother had previously been a housekeeper in the home, before his father became a widower the year before Eric Hultén was born. From his father's first marriage, Eric had four half-siblings and a foster brother from Abyssinia (now Ethiopia) who was raised by his father as a missionary. The family lived in humble circumstances. Pontus Hultén's grandfather, the vicar, was

Eric Hultén, Kamchatka, c. 1922.

strict and ascetic. His upbringing would make Eric Hultén a convinced atheist, which was passed on to his son Pontus.

In the book, Eric Hultén recounts how, growing up, his family had just enough to eat. "The whole youth was spent under the cold star of scarcity"[2] as he writes. No extravagances beyond the bare necessities were on the minds of the family, who lived on the father's meagre clergyman's salary in the poverty-stricken Sweden of the early twentieth century.

Eric Hultén met his wife, Pontus Hultén's mother Signe Elisabeth "Elsie" Vougt, at Stockholm University, where Eric studied biology and Elsie chemistry. Elsie came from a well-established family of academics and public officials in Stockholm. Her father was Carl Fredrik Vougt, chancellor at the Ministry of Education. Her younger brother Allan Vougt became editor-in-chief of the newspaper Arbetet in Malmö and a prominent Social Democratic MP. He became historic as the Swedish Minister of Defense in 1945–1951, during the last year of the war and the tense beginning of the Cold War. Allan Vougt would have a major impact on Pontus Hultén's career choice and life direction. Hultén has said[3] that it was his uncle who encouraged him to cultivate his artistic and intellectual interests. He is said to have inherited from his uncle his interest in history and world politics and an insight into how a country was maneuvered in a dangerous world. As Eric Hultén describes it in his memoirs, Allan Vougt became increasingly radical in his views over the years. Perhaps Pontus Hultén also inherited some of his radical mindset from his beloved and admired uncle.

As a newly graduated biologist, Eric Hultén was ready for adventure. The twenties were a time for Nordic explorers. Much of the world still remained to be discovered and mapped. Men (only men, of course) like Roald Amundsen and Fridtjof Nansen (North and South Pole), Otto Nordenskjöld (Northwest Passage), Sven Hedin (Silk Road and India) and others made history. Together with zoologist Sten Bergman, Eric Hultén planned an expedition to Kamchatka, the most remote, least explored part of Russia. Here Eric and his fiancée Elsie would embark on expeditions to collect and catalog the flora of the Siberian peninsula.

The members of the expedition took several months to reach northern Japan via Egypt and elsewhere, where, despite the lack of space, they managed to board "a beautiful little 500-ton boat with a sharp bow"[4] from Vladivostok. *Commodore Bering* was bound for the only town in Kamchatka, Petropavlovsk, where the Russian Revolution had finally reached during the winter. The ship sailed on June 9, 1920. On board was a new government of Bolsheviks who would establish Soviet power in Kamchatka. The Hulténs and the other members of the expedition had to lash their equipment to the masts on deck and sleep in the lifeboats.

For three years, the Hultén couple stayed in Kamchatka, whose magnificent, unexplored wilderness Eric Hultén depicts in succinct terms. When summer arrives, they set out — Eric, Elsie and a local companion, riding sluggish Manchurian horses through the four-meter-high alpine thickets that ring volcanic mountains with glacier-shrouded peaks. They ax their way with machetes through the dense vegetation. The horses keep tripping. There's no possibility of bringing more than minimal provisions such as a little flour and sugar. The expedition members live on salmon from the rivers and bear, ducks, eagles and wild reindeer that Eric shoots with his Winchester and Elsie grills over the campfire. The abundant bear population provides the main staple. They move laboriously through uncharted wildernesses and primeval forests, up mountain ridges, down boiling volcanoes surrounded by glacial ice, through ravines, along rivers and deserted seashores, across yellow volcanic deserts and along lakes lined with these perpetually unforgiving brushes; falling with horses down river cliffs and cheating death again and again in a series of ordeals reminiscent of literary figures such as Baron von Münchhausen and Robinson Crusoe, all rendered in the same matter-of-fact style.

After their years in Kamchatka, the Hulténs return to a financially strained existence at home in Stockholm. Elsie's family, who had previously supported their livelihood, had fallen into financial difficulties. Both Eric and Elsie miss the freedom of the wilderness. Staying months in the same place seems unnatural to them. The couple cope by Elsie getting a job as a math teacher. Eric, on the other hand, realizes his unsuitability as a teacher. He acquires temporary income through writing assignments and substitute work at the botanical department of the Swedish Museum of Natural History while he works on his Kamchatka flora. The couple's first home is a two-room apartment with a kitchenette at Linnégatan 15, above the backyard.

In his memoirs, Eric Hultén briefly mentions the birth of the son who would become known as Pontus Hultén only as an adult. In three impersonal sentences, Eric summarizes his son's entire existence: "A few years after returning from Kamchatka, a son was born, who was baptized Karl Gunnar Vougt, the latter after my father-in-law. To the priest's obvious surprise. 40 years later, under the name Pontus, a name by which his uncle Allan used to call him, but which he was not christened with, he would become famous and controversial as the director of the Moderna Museet on Skeppsholmen in Stockholm, where art of highly varying quality is exposed."[5] In the same passage, Eric Hultén mentions that he has bought his first radio. There is a picture of Pontus as an infant, perhaps one year old, smiling blissfully as he listens to the sound in the headphones of the set — a picture that father Hultén proudly reports won a prize competition in a weekly magazine. The frosty words bear testament to the strained relationship between father and son — a lifelong burden for Pontus Hultén.

It has been suggested[6] that Pontus Hultén was conceived in a tent in Kamchatka, but this romantic whim can hereby be refuted. The Hultén couple returned to Stockholm on January 9, 1923. Karl Gunnar Vougt, later known as Pontus Hultén, was born on June 21, 1924 at Allmänna BB maternity clinic in Stockholm.

In his memoirs, Eric Hultén then quickly returns to the thirst for travel and adventure that continued to govern his life, for a time satisfied insufficiently with trips to Russia and Berlin to study the Kamchatka flora. Soon he sets out on longer expeditions, first to the Kola Peninsula, then to Mexico, where dramatic expeditions among bandits in the thin mountain air at five thousand meters altitude alternate with wild partying and gorgeous young carmencitas.

Apparently, his wife Elsie is now at home with their son Karl Gunnar while Eric collects plants from around the world. Soon he is ready for bigger challenges: an expedition to the Aleutian Islands, a sparse belt of remote, fog-shrouded polar islands in the stormy, treacherous Bering Sea, between Alaska and Siberia. The island belt is the remnant of what is thought to have been a tongue of land between the continents through which plants, animals and people migrated. Eric Hultén's writings on the flora and its distribution across this island belt became his most famous work as a botanist, plant geographer and scientist. During his expedition to the Aleutian Islands, Eric Hultén had time for a solo trip north in a small cutter to the even more arctic and remote Pribilof Islands, St. George and St. Paul, the main colonies of the fur seal, the so-called sea bear, which breeds there in the tens of thousands. After suffering a seizure, an omen he assumes, Eric Hultén receives a telegram from his wife with the message: "Big beautiful girl. Elsie."

On his return three months later to his new home town of Lund, one evening in late November 1932, Eric sees his daughter Maj Anita, Pontus Hultén's eight years younger sister, for the first time. There is no trace of Pontus' early childhood in the book. Eric Hultén applied for a position as conservator, later called first museum superintendent, at Lund University's Botanical Museum. Another applicant was appointed, but Eric Hultén appealed the decision, which was reconsidered. Eric Hultén describes receiving the first month's salary of SEK 482.50 as wonderful.

In the summers, the family moved back to Stockholm and their summer home in Trolldalen on northern Lidingö, where Eric had bought a cottage. The house was built as a model for the new concept of "sport cottage,"[7] in a new area with summer housing for workers and lower officials. From here, the family explored the islands of the archipelago in an open mahogany motorboat. In a brief account of the settlement in Lund, the son is mentioned for the second and last time in his father's four hundred and fifty-page memoirs: "This change between Stockholm and Lund had a beneficial effect. Maj, who learned to speak Scanian from her friends, became bilingual and could speak Stockholmian or Scanian at will. Gunnar, also called Pontus, who was 8 years old when we moved to Lund, on the other hand, never learned to speak proper Lundese, a difficult handicap for a schoolboy."

After a brief log of the status of his family life, Eric Hultén returns to the main subject of his book: his flower-hunting mission over our planet, especially its northern Arctic wastelands. With the Canadian Air Force, he travels along the country's vast Arctic coastline. His "Shangri-La" Alaska and the Bering Sea he continues to explore. He crashes a helicopter on a mountaintop and ends up hanging over a precipitous glacier crevasse, socializes with grizzly bears and survives new dangers like something out of an adventure novel, never returning to the sanctity of family life in the latter part of the book. Neither his son, his daughter, nor his wife are mentioned again before his life story ends in a strangely bland finale.

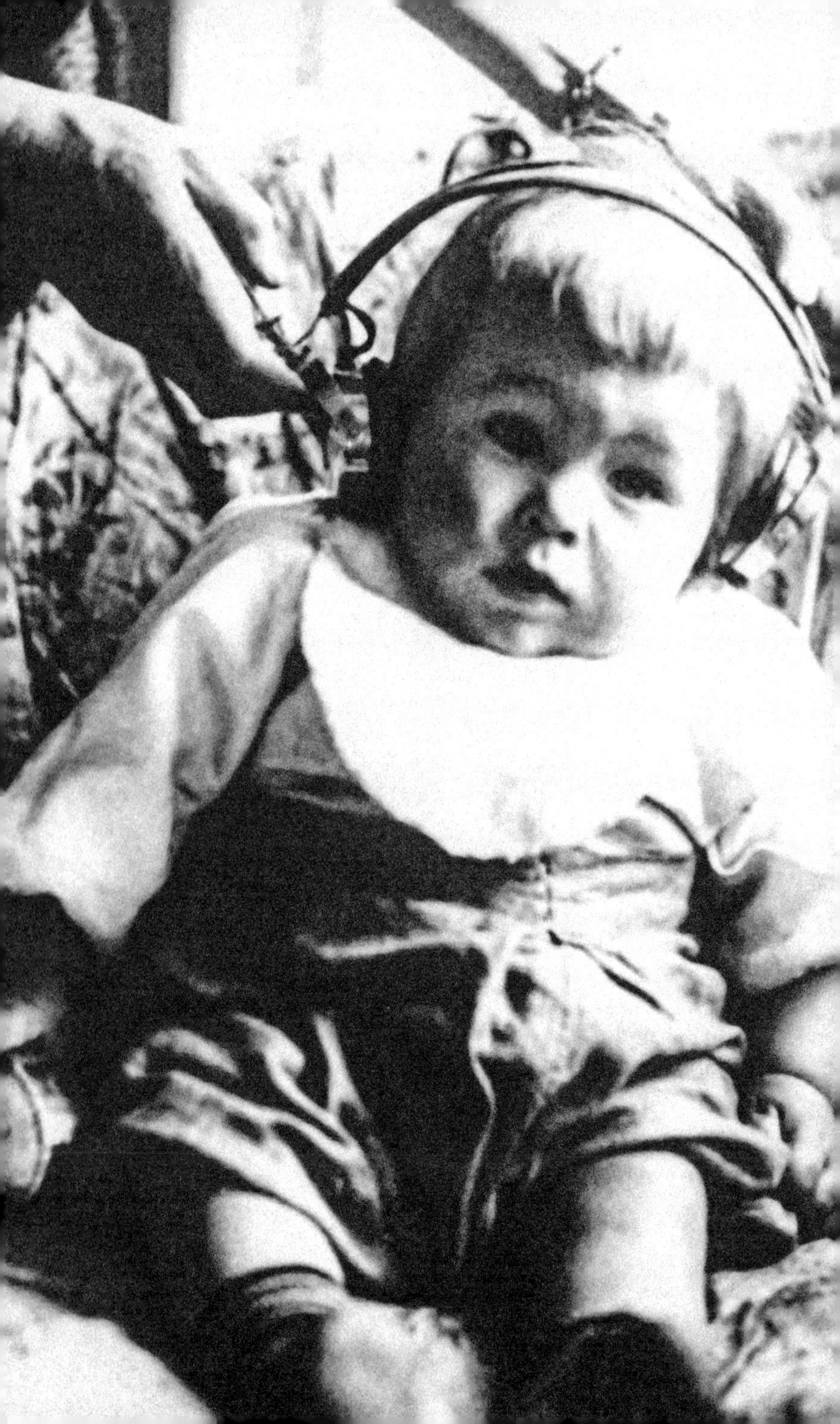

2

Childhood, youth and education

There is not much available information about Pontus, or as he was still called, Karl Gunnar or just Gunnar Hultén's childhood. I have not been able to locate any of his childhood friends from Stockholm. Pontus Hultén told his family and friends little about his childhood years. He offered only occasional snippets. During his early years, the family lived on Linnégatan in Stockholm. Gunnar was often alone with his mother Elsie while his father Eric continued his expeditions to the Arctic.

When he was not traveling, Eric Hultén continued to work on his Kamchatka flora before moving to Lund, alongside his temporary position at the botanical department of the Swedish Museum of Natural History. His mother Elsie took the main responsibility for the family's livelihood as a teacher of mathematics, physics and chemistry at various secondary schools in Stockholm. Gunnar is said to have attended the private Olofskolan on Humlegårdsgatan, which was started in 1927 by Carl Malmsten,[1] something that I have not been able to confirm. If true as likely, the choice of educational institution was radical, as Olofskolan was a school inspired by Montessori where children would learn through creation, with artistry and crafts as important tools of learning. This is where Stockholm's progressive intellectuals in the late twenties enrolled their children.

Pontus Hultén's creative interests seem to have been awakened early. His archive at Moderna Museet contains fine drawings of sailboats, motorboats, ships and soldiers, as well as several almost architectural studies that imply that Pontus Hultén's first career dream was indeed to become an architect. One of these drawings is signed: "Drawn by architect Karl Gunnar Hultén."[2] Hultén has mentioned in

Karl Gunnar Vougt, later known as Pontus Hultén, aged one, 1925.

several interviews that his uncle Allan Vougt encouraged his "cultural tendencies."[3] There was also a professional artist in the family, the folkloristic painter and designer Jerk Werkmäster, married to Pontus Hultén's aunt Ninni, also called uncle, which confuses the references to him and Allan Vougt. Werkmäster had his home and studio on Gumshornsgatan in the Östermalm district, which Hultén sometimes visited with his parents. There is unconfirmed information that Pontus as a boy helped Werkmäster organize exhibitions in his hometown Rättvik in the Dalarna region.[4]

His father Eric himself seems to have harbored an artistic streak. In his memoirs *Men roligt har det varit* there is a skillfully engraved portrait of a teacher from his youth. Eric Hultén both engraved and drew for amusement even later in life. It has been said that Eric himself secretly nurtured unfulfilled artistic dreams. "My father was very talented artistically, but didn't get use of it in his work," says Pontus' younger sister Maj Hultén.[5]

As mentioned, the Hultén family moved to Lund in the fall of 1932, when Pontus was eight years old. Maj was born there while his father Eric was traveling and left the responsibility for the birth, the move and the establishment in the new house in Lund to mother Elsie. In Lund, the young family had the privilege of living a financially stable life for the first time. Eric Hultén earned a decent salary as head of the botanical garden. His wife Elsie, for her part, immediately found work as a teacher in Malmö, where she commuted. Pontus Hultén attended the Högre allmänna läroverket school and then secondary Lund Cathedral School. Throughout his schooling he was at best a mediocre student.

In his relationship with his parents, Pontus Hultén is unanimously told to have loved his mother. Several family members, relatives and close associates describe his mother Elsie as more gifted than his father Eric,[6] to whom she had to submit herself completely. Elsie Vougt Hultén is pictured as considerably eccentric. When spring approached, she was in the habit of traveling to the roadless wilderness of Sarek in Lapland, to camp in the wilderness with the family's king poodle Filippa as her sole companion. The dog was loaded with carrier bags like a donkey. Elsie stayed out in the wilderness for weeks and months on end. Eric is said to have disliked his wife's solitary mountain excursions, worrying about her — unnecessarily, it seems, as Elsie was an experienced alpinist, hardened from the wastelands of Kamchatka. "It's fine until February, but then Elsie starts rattling the tent pegs," Eric used to complain.[7] Eric Hultén said of his wife that she lacked capacity for fear; that the emotion was unfamiliar to her.[8]

One story that Pontus Hultén recounted to confidants, testament to his mother Elsie's unusual form of motherhood, is that when he was sick at home as a young boy, his mother Elsie went to buy lobster to cheer him up. "You can imagine what it was like to grow up with a mother who was so unworldly that she could do such a thing, even though he loved her," says a close friend of Hultén.

The relationship with the father is just as consistently testified as tense and highly charged. Father Eric, who lived for his work, is portrayed as hard, strict and demanding, unable to give his son love, appreciation or understanding. Several witnesses have said that Pontus, or Gunnar, was afraid of his father. Some claim that Pontus Hultén even hated him. "He was a child of his time and growing up as a boy in those days was hard — the upbringing of boys was brutal," says Gunilla Palmstierna-Weiss, the artist and stage designer, who acquainted Pontus Hultén in Stockholm in the late forties when her aunt was a pen pal of his mother Elsie.[9]

Another person close to Pontus Hultén has a theory about the relationship between Eric Hultén and his son Pontus: "I think the father was jealous of Pontus' greater endowment. Both the father's and mother's different talents had been combined in Pontus into something that just burned to something so enormous. I don't think the father could quite tolerate that his son would become something greater than himself."

The Hultén family entertained a limited social life, both in Stockholm and in Lund. Only once a year did they invite friends and acquaintances to their home. Even major anniversaries were celebrated in a minimal family circle. Eric, the father, socialized on behalf of his service at official events, while Elsie, the mother, is said to have largely lacked social interaction. In the summers, the family moved to the summer cottage in Trolldalen, where the whole days were spent in the open air, except during heavy rains, out on the boat or on the small island off the cliffs below the summer cottage.

Between Pontus and his eight years younger sister, another sister was born who died in infancy. This subject was taboo. According to Maj Hultén, the dead sister was mentioned on only one occasion during her childhood, when a photograph was shown. "Her name was Inger or Ingrid, but that was so traumatic and strange that they never talked about it," says Maj.[10]

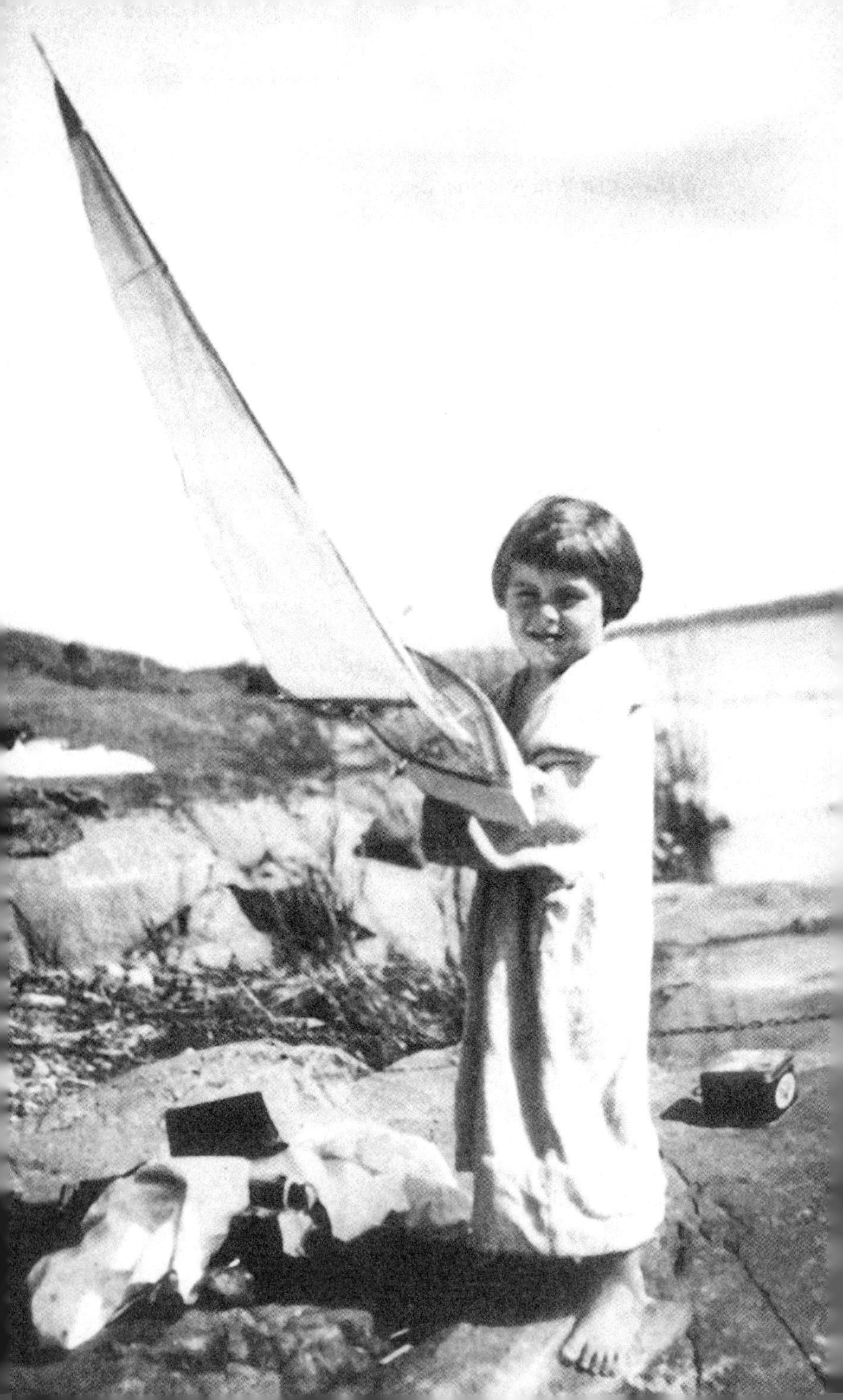

Maj Hultén was born with an impairment that left her partially disabled. According to relatives, Pontus Hultén suggested that his parents' care for his sister made him feel neglected. Some speculate that this relationship may have contributed to tensions between the siblings. While Maj is said to have admired her brother as a child, their relationship deteriorated over the years, to be terminated in adulthood after their parents decided to bequeath the summer house in Trolldalen to Maj, something Pontus could never forgive.

Like her older brother, Maj Hultén nurtured dreams of becoming an artist, but ended up studying medicine instead. She became an internationally renowned geneticist, specializing in chromosomes, and a professor of genetics at the West Midlands Regional Genetics Laboratory in Birmingham, UK. Like her father and brother, she traveled the world throughout her career on behalf of her profession. Her artistic dreams were realized by her daughter Sofia Hultén, a Berlin-based artist.

In retirement, Maj Hultén has returned to Sweden. I meet her on a frozen winter morning in her home in the family's old summer house in Trolldalen, the remote cottage area on the steep north slope of Lidingö island outside Stockholm. It's obvious that Maj Hultén has mixed feelings talking about her brother. "Pontus was a real loner," she says. "He mostly sat silent and never ever brought friends home. He had a terrible temper. He read and drew all the time, even when he was eighteen or twenty years old. He discouraged me from my artistic ambitions. I used to draw and paint all the time too, and I was going to be an artist, but he told me 'don't bother, they've got goddamn electric sockets in the middle of their faces.'"[11]

In general, Maj Hultén has no warm words to say about her family. "Dad was very egocentric and only cared about his job, and Pontus was the same. My mother, on the other hand, was not at all egocentric and much smarter." Maj Hultén describes her older brother as uninterested in school work and intellectual activities. "It was very uncertain whether he would pass his exam. I remember that the cakes were ordered to celebrate but that they could be canceled if he failed," she says — a rare glimpse of her brother in the financially conscious Hultén home from the time when the family still lived in Lund.[12]

According to his sister, Pontus Hultén's main talent was his stubbornness. "If he had an idea, he was just hellbent on implementing it. He didn't care about anything else like social responsibility and so on.

Pontus with Princess Svanevit, Stockholm's archipelago, 1928.

Then he was very lucky to end up in management positions where he had the power to realize these ideas, at a time when there was a lot of movement and it was possible and opportunistic. He had no idea what I was doing, and he didn't give a damn about it."

Maj Hultén points to the small island off the coast below the Trolldalen cottage area, separated from the mainland by a twenty-meter strait, known in the family as The Morning Cliff. "Mom and dad had long summer vacations that we mostly spent here. Then mom and dad rowed out every morning to The Morning Cliff and stayed there all day. Mom then rowed home to get lunch and sometimes even dinner." Maj Hultén says that the family went out by boat to a headland on Bogesundslandet and sometimes further out to an island they called Fulvädersön (Fould Weather Island),[13] near Finnhamn in the outer archipelago. Pontus Hultén was rarely in Trolldalen as she recalls. When he was at home, there were often stormy conflicts with his parents.

"There were wretched arguments and screaming. I don't know what it was about as he was already an adult then. Then he just disappeared one day and said he never wanted to see us again. Then he took the whole inheritance too, but there was an envelope saying that Trolldalen would go to May."[14]

Though their relationship was strained and complicated, his father Eric's influence on Pontus Hultén seems obvious. Many of the legacies in his life appear derived from his father's interests. One was the inherited lifelong love of the sea and boats. There is a story about how Pontus, already at the age of eight, had saved money to buy a wooden rowing boat on Riddarholmen island in Stockholm, and tried to persuade his father Eric to contribute the missing money, but that his father refused. In the end, he is said to have managed to assemble the money to buy his vessel, said to still remain in seaworthy condition.[15] The love of the sea is also said to have been a reason why Karl Gunnar Hultén chose to call himself Pontus from his early twenties. The name is believed to originate from póntos, the Greek word for sea.

Pontus Hultén himself has spoken of his struggles at school during his childhood.[16] A report card from Högre allmänna läroverket in Lund from 1935 in the archive at Moderna Museet shows weak grades — B, Ba, B, Ba, B and B?[17] In the same and other interviews, Pontus Hultén has confided that he was saved by the outbreak of war. The school was closed for a year in 1940, which gave him respite to mature so that he later just about managed to graduate.

Many have claimed that Pontus Hultén suffered what was then called reading and writing disabilities — that he was dyslexic, which made school work difficult for him. He didn't talk about this himself, but it's common knowledge that he needed help with his manuscripts throughout his career.

In upper secondary school, at Katedralskolan in Lund, two of Pontus Hultén's classmates were Ingvar Holm and Sven-Gunnar Bråhammar, with whom he formed a trio of friends throughout his school years. "We found each other in a strange way — we liked to fight and had common intellectual interests," says Ingvar Holm, a literary scholar, professor at Lund University and television talkshow host.[18]

Pontus Hultén has said that he and Ingvar Holm were encouraged by their drawing teacher to organize small exhibitions of local artists from Lund and Malmö.[19] According to Hultén, these exhibitions were staged at school. Ingvar Holm says that they also exhibited at historic Tuna Castle.[20] They were then fifteen to sixteen years old. From that age, Pontus Hultén began working on organizing art exhibitions in various forms, although it would be many years before he consciously chose a career as a museum man.

Pontus Hultén revealed[21] that at this time he was reading all the texts of the Finnish-Swedish art historian Bertel Hintze — including a major encyclopedic work on nineteenth-century art and one on twentieth-century art, "not so well known but most remarkable," as he put it.[22]

Already in his early teens, Pontus Hultén seems to have made his own way into the art world. As high school students during the war years, the trio of Hultén, Ingvar Holm and Sven-Gunnar Bråhammar were frequent guests at exhibitions in Malmö and precocious players on the southern Swedish art scene.

From the beginning, Pontus Hultén's early love of art was combined with an equally keen interest in history, world politics and anthropology, reportedly stimulated by his admired mother's uncle Allan Vougt. Having grown up in the pre-war years and during the Second World War, it's not surprising that the experience of war, and the realization of the self-destructiveness that humanity and its machines are capable of, more than anything else came to animate Hultén's perspective on the world and art. "It goes without saying that the war shaped us all," says his friend Ingvar Holm. "Gunnar had the shadow of war over him always."[23]

It's impossible to avoid speculating about whether growing up during the war was a reason for the interest that Pontus Hultén himself has repeatedly stated was awakened already during his high school years in Dada,[24] the early Modernist artistic movement that more than any other came to distinguish his work as a curator and museum official.

Dada, or Dadaism, was an essentially anarchist artistic movement whose birth can be officially dated: February 5, 1916, the opening of the Cabaret Voltaire in Zürich. The loose-knit movement was founded by German artists Hugo Ball, Hans Arp and Marc Janco, and writers Emmy Hemmings and Tristan Tzara, the Romanian-French avant-garde poet who would become the movement's spokesman and ideologist. It was no coincidence that Dada emerged during the most bestial phase of the First World War. The mass slaughter of the Somme and Verdun began at this time. Nor was the location a coincidence — Zürich in neutral Switzerland, a haven for artists, intellectuals and dissidents from the surrounding belligerent nations. Dada was born out of disgust with the entire civilization that had made the madness of war possible. In boisterous, violent soirées at the Cabaret Voltaire, Dada's revolutionary manifesto was proclaimed, mocking capitalist society and the logic and rationality of industrialism. Dada celebrated irrationality, intuition, spontaneity, improvisation and nonsense as its ideals.

The breakthrough of Dadaist art came later with a series of gallery exhibitions in Zürich and elsewhere. The message was spread around the world through *Dada* magazine and other publications. Small but influential groups were founded in Berlin, Cologne, Hanover and Paris, where Tristan Tzara stood in close contact with Cubism's spokesman Guillaume Apollinaire and Surrealism's André Breton, and not least in New York, where the exiled French artists Marcel Duchamp and Francis Picabia joined Dada along with Man Ray, "Baroness Dada" Elsa von Freytag-Loringhoven, and others in the circle around master photographer Alfred Stieglitz's Gallery 291.

The representatives of the Dada movement saw art as part of the corrupt society against which they revolted. They called their art "anti-art" and worked with techniques such as collage, photomontage and experimental typography, combining anarchist poetry and radical visual expressions. Dadaism was rooted in Cubism, particularly in the collages of Pablo Picasso and Georges Braque, also drawing influence from Futurism, a controversial movement with links to fascism that, with its Italian origins, was an oddity among the early Modernist art and literature movements.

The early Modernist movements were all connected to each other in the then tiny international art world, whose undisputed center was and long remained Paris. It was in Paris that Dada dissolved into Surrealism in the early twenties.

It is in its anarchism and nihilism that Dada had its lasting, still active influence on contemporary art, primarily through Pontus Hultén's beacon Marcel Duchamp.

Another influence of Dadaism on the development of modern art was what is known as "total art." In Cabaret Voltaire, poetry, music, theater, visual arts, costume and graphic design were integrated in multicreative experiences. The concept of Gesamtkunst and the view of the different art forms as a whole would deeply influence Pontus Hultén.

For Hultén, Ingvar Holm and their art-loving friends in Lund in the thirties and forties, Paris was the magnet towards which their interests and youthful dreams were drawn. "We were real Francophiles and big fans of Baudelaire and Rimbaud," says Ingvar Holm.[25] "The music of words and Verlaine interested us a lot. Of course we were interested in Dada. We were not geeks. We knew our stuff. Total art fascinated us greatly."[26]

It was probably during his school years that Pontus Hultén developed the political conviction that colored his view of art and his work as a museum director and curator: anarchism, then a relatively strong movement worldwide — a libertarian, utopian, anti-hierarchic alternative to the communism, fascism and capitalism that had led the world to disaster. Throughout his career, Pontus Hultén proudly emphasized his anarchist beliefs. His hero was the prince and nobleman Peter Kropotkin[27] and his more peaceful branch of anarchism, which contrasted with the militant faction led by Mikhail Bakunin.[28] From a young age, Hultén would engage in endless arguments with artists and other friends who advocated Bakunin's version of anarchism, in which violence was justified.

Some have sarcastically called Pontus Hultén a salon anarchist. There is truth in this label, as he would work in institutions throughout his career — and in positions of power, which may seem to contradict this ideology. Nevertheless, it is evident that the anarchist philosophy of life was a central part of Pontus Hultén's personality and professional oeuvre. It characterized many of his exhibitions and was shared by several of their contributing artists. In the spirit of Dada, Hultén resented every form of establishment, not to mention bureaucracy, which he detested. He became something as unusual as an executive with contempt for hierarchies. A basis in his view of life was the vision that without hierarchies and authority, man is capable of organizing his life and society for the best.

"Pontus was a revolutionary romantic on a grand scale — that was an important part of him," says Olle Granath, Hultén's young colleague and later successor as director of Moderna Museet.[29]

During Pontus Hultén's youth, the war made all travel impossible. Lund lay within sight of occupied Denmark. Pontus Hultén himself was called up for military service as a minesweeper in the Navy in Stockholm. He was utterly unhappy in the military. It was something he didn't talk about as an adult, other than to say that it was cold, with poor food and little sleep, generally unpleasant, even dangerous. He managed to obtain a medical certificate that released him from military service. "That's the only time I remember him from Trolldalen — when he came in uniform having deserted from the army," says Maj Hultén.[30]

Ingvar Holm recounts the tale of how the two friends, after the end of the war but before peace had been formally proclaimed, that is what must have been the spring of 1945, when they were both twenty years old, set off, filled with wanderlust and desire for adventure after the isolation of the war years. According to Holm, they lacked exit visas but made their way across the strait to Denmark, where they managed to acquire the travel documents. From here they hitchhiked with military jeeps through occupied Germany all the way to Paris. They hiked to Lausanne in neutral Switzerland where they exchanged money. The exchange rate for Danish crowns had not yet been registered, so instead they were given back the equivalent of Swedish crowns of much higher value. Suddenly the boys Holm and Hultén were stacked with travel cash. They smuggled the money, wrapped in picture frames, back to Paris where it was enough to live on for months. Pontus Hultén has revealed to friends that in the years following the war, he added to his coffers by illegally smuggling and exchanging currency during his travels in Europe.

Ingvar Holm says that in Paris they encountered many legends. Picasso they met in Montmartre, at an opening for Max Ernst. "He had stood looking out over the crowd observing that everyone looked the same except for two persons who stood out from the crowd, Gunnar and me, so he came up and said hello. He noted that he was forty-six years older than me. Gunnar was otherwise tired of Picasso. He thought there was too much money involved."[31]

I must point out that I have found no reference elsewhere to this trip to Paris, nor to any meeting with Picasso. However, many have testified that Pontus Hultén was considered "anti-Picasso" — even "anti-painting" — during his career as museum director. Pontus Hultén's view of art was Dadaist and anarchist from the outset, anti-establishment and anti-tradition; in a contradictory way perhaps even anti-art, in Duchamp's words. "He was a readymade director,"[32] to quote Bernard Blistène, director of the Musée National d'Art Moderne at the Centre Pompidou in Paris 2013–2021.

In summer of 1945, Pontus Hultén began his studies in art history in Copenhagen. I haven't found any further information about this, not even at which institution he studied. Later in the fall, the Hultén family moved back to Stockholm as Eric Hultén had been appointed director of the botanical department at the Swedish Museum of Natural History. The Hultén family moved into a stately villa at Odinsvägen 21 in prestigious Djursholm in the northern outskirts. Pontus Hultén enrolled at Stockholm College, now Stockholm University, where he continued his studies in art history.

Hultén turned twenty-one a month after the peace in May 1945. At the time, his dream was to become an artist himself and would remain so for several years. He drew, painted, sculpted and worked on Dada-inspired collages alongside his studies. At the university, Pontus Hultén's main teacher was the well-known doctor of philosophy and lecturer Henrik Cornell, who helped him on his career path.

Art history was a minor specialty at the time in Stockholm. Among Pontus Hultén's fellow students were several people who would become his collaborators and who would be involved in Swedish art life in the decades to come: Katja Waldén, Hans Eklund[33] and the ten years older Carlo Derkert, who would become a colleague at Moderna Museet, were schoolmates with Hultén. The artist Oscar Reutersvärd, nine years his senior and a future creative collaborator, was a teacher at the department. Ulf Linde, five years younger, joined the faculty a few years later. For most of the art history students, work was available in the Swedish museum world, where the National Museum was still the only art museum, representing the entire history of art, including modern and contemporary art.

Pontus Hultén's focus was initially classical. He was interested in Gothic arches and older Italian painting. After a few years of study, Hultén began working as an amanuensis and assistant to Henrik Cornell, who seems to have appreciated his talents and abilities. Hultén has recounted how he quickly befriended Cornell. "He was certainly not a modern art historian, but a fine and sensitive person," as he phrases it.[34] Pontus Hultén was appointed as an assistant tour guide on student excursions to France, Switzerland and mainly to Italy and Rome, to study church art from the Middle Ages and the Renaissance in March and April 1948, when the group experienced a historic event, the first free elections in Italy after fascism.[35] Pontus Hultén's archive contains neatly arranged, carefully typed documents on, among other topics, festivals in Florence in 1556, Giorgio Vasari (the sixteenth-century Italian artist, architect and writer), opera stage design from the sixteenth and seventeenth centuries, and the stage designer Bernardo Buontalenti, who worked in the Renaissance tradition in various fields, as an architect, military engineer, artist and designer.[36] The interaction and relationship between different art forms and other disciplines, in particular science, architecture and engineering, was a subject that interested Hultén early on and would come to occupy and characterize him as a curator and museum director.

In a late interview[37], Ulf Linde reminisces Pontus from this time, when Linde was a freshman student in art history at Stockholm University and Hultén a lecturer and licentiate at the same institution. Linde recalls when he first met Hultén at a dinner for the Art History Society: "Suddenly there was a roaring noise and in came Pontus on a motorcycle, dressed like a modern Gattamelata.[38] And it was really something to see. He was very grand (...) It was striking that he was extremely vital, with enormous physical energy. He could do anything. One evening I was talking to him about Romanesque arches and suddenly he showed all kinds of erudition on this subject. He spoke brilliantly and I thought that here must be something more than a motorcycle. I was impressed by him. On the other hand, I had the feeling that 'watch out, this man could be dangerous.'"[39]

Already during his studies in art history, Pontus Hultén began to make a name for himself at Nationalmuseum, the National Museum, where he was first hired as a temporary in the painting department in the summer of 1949.[40] Here he was apparently appreciated, as the temporary appointment was followed by several others. Among other duties, Pontus Hultén was responsible for a new presentation of the museum's modern collections, a towering responsibility for a young substitute, one might think, even though the modern department was small and low in priority at the museum. After the exhibition, he received high praise from Folke Holmér, the head of modern painting, who wrote: "His extensive and solid knowledge, practical outlook and good aesthetic judgment have been of the greatest value to the department. In a short time, he has prepared a clear and comprehensible tableau of a very extensive material, a work that forms a good basis for further processing."[41]

Even before moving back to Stockholm, Pontus Hultén had worked in the capital during the summers and made contacts among young intellectuals and artists. As a student at Stockholm University, he was an eager participant in an intense social life in cafés, pubs and at friends' homes. During these years around 1950, Hultén was engaged in a relationship with the translator Gunilla Ekelund. In 1951 he met Kerstin Ehrenberg, then Kerstin Olsson, through her friend Katja Waldén, Hultén's classmate and later colleague at Moderna Museet. Shortly afterwards, Ehrenberg became pregnant with their son Felix, who was born on 23 December 1951. The couple married on 14 September 1951, with the intention of "legitimizing" their son.[42] When Kerstin Ehrenberg first met Pontus Hultén, he was still living partly at home with his parents in Djursholm. The couple later moved with their newborn son into an apartment on Surbrunnsgatan in Vasastaden in Stockholm. "The nicest little two-room flat you could imagine, with high ceilings and tiled stoves," as Kerstin Ehrenberg says.[43]

In his third year as an art history student, Pontus Hultén began work on his licentiate thesis. He started a study on Johannes Vermeer and his painterly perspective, and one on Inuit art, "Eskimo art" as it was called then, an interest he had inherited from his parents. Later, his idea of exploring the relationship between Vermeer and the philosopher Baruch Spinoza was born. The two were contemporaries and, according to Hultén's paper, both lived for a time in the Dutch city of Delft, even on the same street.[44] Hultén's assumption was that they must have known each other. They were both unknown to the wider world during their lifetimes. Spinoza didn't publish any texts under his own name in his lifetime. His theories were banned by his Jewish community and by the Catholic Church. Vermeer was known locally as an artist during his life but was struck by poverty and died in obscurity. His art was forgotten for more than two centuries before being rediscovered in the 1800s. Pontus Hultén's bold theory was that Spinoza, who worked as an optician, had a camera obscura and that it was from here that Vermeer had derived his famous perspective.

Immediately after signing off on their settlement loan as future parents, the young couple Pontus Hultén and Kerstin Ehrenberg went to Cook's travel agency in the Opera House to cure Hultén's wanderlust.[45] "We didn't call it a honeymoon, no way — we were radicals," says Kerstin Ehrenberg.[46] The journey took them to Italy via Frankfurt am Main, where Hultén studied a painting by Vermeer. He had previously made mathematical calculations about the floor of this painting and its tiles and angles, a work that his mother Elsie, the math teacher, had assisted him with.[47] The young newlyweds spent a month in Italy. From Rome they traveled by train to towns and villages in the surrounding districts. Hultén showed his newlywed wife the art in the Eternal City and in the churches of many towns and villages where he had guided younger art history students as a tutor for Henrik Cornell. There was no doubt that art was the great love and driving force in Hultén's life. "Art was a part of him; it wasn't something you questioned or talked about. It was just a matter of course," says Kerstin Ehrenberg.[48]

The painting for which Pontus Hultén made calculations with the help of his mother was "The Art of Painting," the artist's self-portrait of himself painting a model, considered one of Vermeer's most groundbreaking works. In 2023, in the catalog for the great Vermeer retrospective in Rijksmuseum in Amsterdam — one of the most successful art exhibitions in history — Hultén was acknowledged for his findings, likely without the authors knowing they were writing about Pontus Hultén, due to his changed name. The text reads: "Among the first to examine the perspective structure of the painting was the Swedish art historian Karl Gunnar Hultén, after discovering the hole made by Vermeer with a pin to mark the vanishing point. (...) The Danish Vermeer expert Jørgen Wadum then addressed in detail the question of pictorial composition in Vermeer's work, mapping the perspective lines of The Art of Painting." (Vermeer. Thames & Hudson, London, 2023, p. 268)

Ehrenberg offers a portrait of Pontus Hultén at the time when she first got to know him. Hultén, then twenty-five years old, was already a prominent member of the young artistic and intellectual inner circles of Stockholm, where he enjoyed natural authority and respect. In addition to art history, he had also studied ethnology at Stockholm University. "I was very impressed by him, I must admit," says Ehrenberg. "I think we fell a little in love right away. He had a radiance of action. There was an aura around him. He wasn't one to talk excessively. He was interested in art, history and film in the same way, especially the practical aspects of art and film. It was just natural."[49]

In Stockholm at this time, Pontus Hultén made contacts that would be important for his career. He befriended Per Olof Ultvedt and Öyvind Fahlström, who moved to Paris at a young age and who opened doors for Hultén there and later in New York. Another artist friend was Olle Baertling, who was thirteen years older and worked as a bank clerk at Gustaf Adolfs torg. In Baertling's apartment on Kommendörsgatan, with a studio in the living room, artists and intellectuals gathered for alcohol-fueled social sessions. The circle of friends included artist Lars Rolf and the art historian Rolf Söderberg. Söderberg wrote monographs on a number of Swedish artists. His last work was *Mina konstnärsänkor och andra konstminnen* (*My Artist Widows And Other Art Memories*) from 1999,[50] with mini-portraits of a number of people from the Stockholm art scene of the 1950s, including Pontus Hultén. Söderberg recounts how they were four art historians who used to meet at the Cattelin restaurant in the Old Town — himself, Hultén, Hans Eklund and Oscar Reutersvärd. What united them was their interest in modern art, which they were quite alone with in the "medieval-obsessed" art history faculty at Stockholm University.[51] After the Cattelin dinners, the quartet used to visit artists' studios or go to the movies.

For Pontus Hultén, film was an interest as early awakened as art. He was active in the student film club at Stockholm University. Here, in the early fifties, he befriended several people of importance in his life and career. One was Hans Nordenström, who studied architecture at the Royal Institute of Technology and shared Hultén's interest in film and art. Nordenström was Pontus Hultén's closest friend, creative partner and travel companion throughout the 1950s. The two were regarded by those around them as twins.

Another technology student with a passionate interest in film whom Pontus Hultén got to know was Johan Wilhelm "Billy" Klüver, who studied electrophysics at the Royal Institute of Technology. Alone among his classmates, he ventured to Stockholm University for the film club gatherings. With his unusual combination of technological knowledge and artistic interest, Klüver was to be an indispensable collaborator for Pontus Hultén and for Moderna Museet for many years, as a problem solver, creative partner and link to artists, in Paris but above all in New York, where Klüver moved in 1954, after completing his studies.

As an aspiring artist, Pontus Hultén produced skillful if not strikingly talented drawings and watercolor studies at a young age. He later turned to Neo-Dadaist collages and abstract paintings, as well as smaller mechanical sculptures inspired by artists such as Wassily Kandinsky, Olle Baertling and Alexander Calder. He also produced commissioned paintings using the Jackson Pollock action painting technique. From what I have seen of Hultén's production, it seems that he was searching for his own artistic expression.

As with numerous other issues, even those close to Pontus Hultén are divided on the conviction of his artistic ambitions. "I don't know how serious he really was about that," says Kerstin Ehrenberg. "With Per Olof Ultvedt and Öyvind Fahlström, it was very clear that they were artists and nothing else. I never really had that feeling with Pontus. He was always more interested in the whole apparatus around it all."[52] Pontus Hultén's later life partner Anna-Lena Wibom takes a different view: "Anyone who doesn't understand that Pontus saw himself as an artist understands nothing about him and his work. I remember how proud he was when the Tinguely Museum in Basel was about to open: 'At last, one of us is getting his own museum,' he said. That's how he always saw himself — as one of the artists."[53] Björn Springfeldt, Pontus Hultén's friend, colleague and later successor as director of Moderna Museet, twenty-four years his junior, says: "All of us museum men are probably really failed artists, but Pontus really could have been an artist. Both his collages and his abstract paintings were at that level."[54]

Already at this time, Pontus Hultén was described by many as a ruthless careerist, ready to sacrifice anything and anyone to achieve his goals. Gunilla Palmstierna-Weiss, who had known Hultén since the 1940s and later moved in the same circles in Paris and New York, describes the young Pontus in unforgiving terms: "I always found him very brutal, not only verbally but also physically. He often fought. Among others, he beat up Ultvedt and Fahlström. This of course had to do with their alcohol consumption, which was absolutely macabre. He was a brutal womanizer, though not one of those who needed a new woman every night. He was handsome, with a rough charm that women fell for. He used his friends in every way he could and then threw them away when he had no further use for them. He lost interest in Peter Weiss, for example, until Peter was suddenly lucky to become world famous. Then he picked up the contact again."[55]

Kerstin Ehrenberg, and others, take different, almost opposite views on Pontus Hultén and his career dreams. "Pontus was simply resourceful, a man of action," says Ehrenberg. "He was not the one to sit around playing bridge, he was always doing things. People wanted him involved in various projects. For example, I remember that they wanted him to write for Dagens Nyheter [Sweden's leading daily], but he wasn't interested. He avoided many such requests. I never perceived him as a careerist even though he became one. I think you can say that he was a reluctant careerist."[56]

Gunilla Palmstierna-Weiss is far from alone in expressing hostility. Hultén seems to have acquired antagonists early on. They would become manifold over the decades. Palmstierna-Weiss repeats the word brutality in her portrayal of Hultén's personality. She is not alone among all those I have met in using this word about Hultén either. His powerful physical presence is emphasized by most. He was a big, barrel-chested young man with a masculinity of the Hemingway variety. He appeared macho and seemed to like that image himself, although the reality was more complicated. He boxed, at the classic club Sparta in Södermalm together with the author Stig Claesson, Slas. It was an image that he liked to emphasize, posing for pictures with boxing gloves after training sessions. The myth of the boxer Hultén would later spread in the art world.

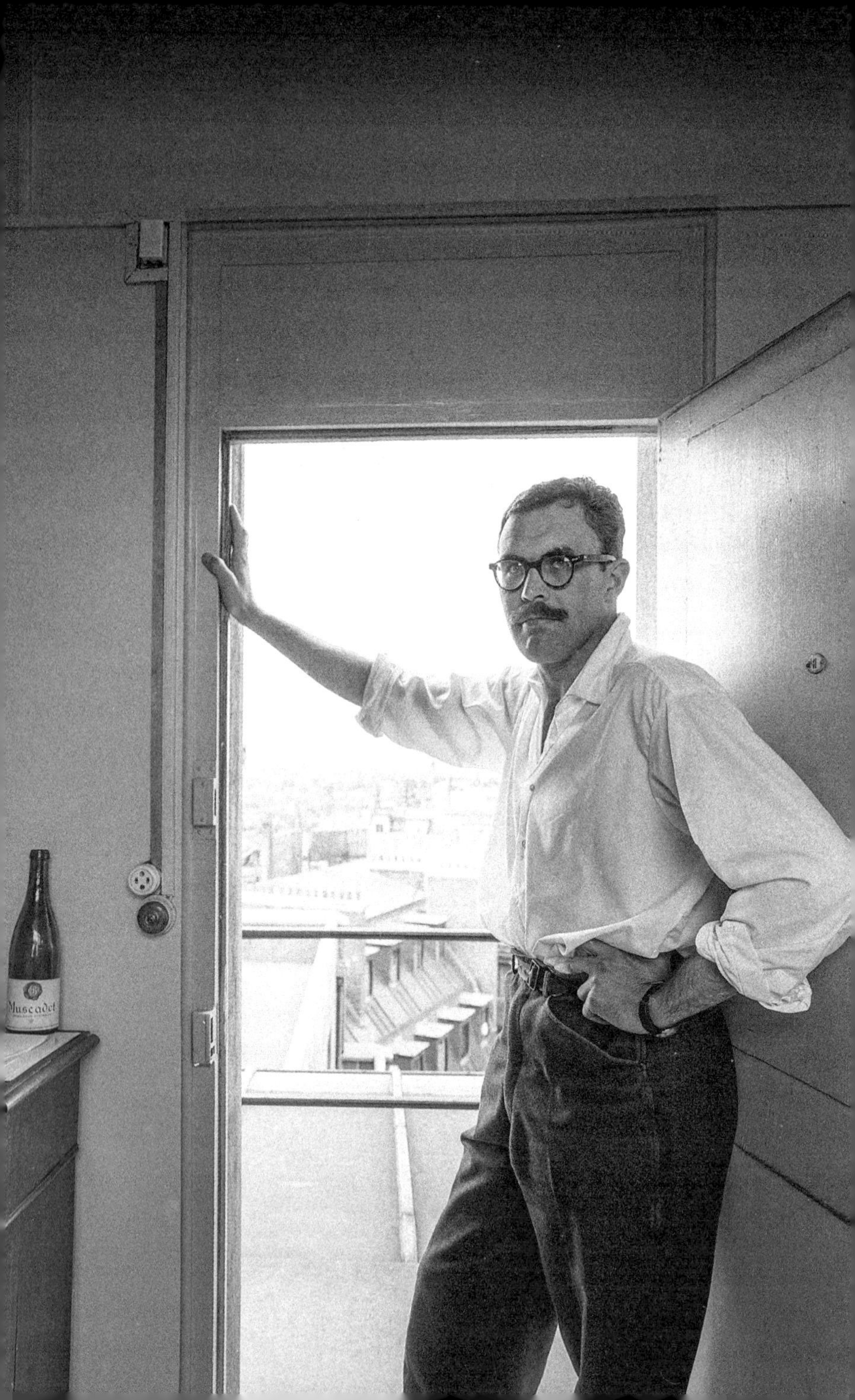
Muscadet

3

The career sets off in Stockholm and Paris

As a new parent, Pontus Hultén's artistic dreams were still alive. By this time, though, he was already becoming increasingly involved in the organizational side of art. With Kerstin Ehrenberg, he talked about opening an art gallery where little Felix could crawl around on the floor. "But that was not something I was interested in," as Ehrenberg ascertains.[1]

There would be none of such beautiful young family dreams. Family life was not, and would never become, any major part of Pontus Hultén's life. Instead, he gravitated to another pole: the art in Paris. Not much time passed with little Felix in the two-room apartment before his father traveled to the world capital of the fine arts, to work on his essay on Vermeer, as he claimed, which he had begun thinking about expanding into a doctoral thesis. Kerstin Ehrenberg was left with the responsibility of caring for their son on her own, with some help from Hultén's parents in Djursholm.

Pontus Hultén's archive contains a number of approved applications for scholarship money, tracking the course of his studies at Stockholm University.[2] Before embarking on the subject of Vermeer, where he had originally planned to write a thesis on the artist and the Delft painting school, Hultén had begun to devote his licentiate work to the so-called paragon question, a doctrine of the mutual ranking of the arts, originating from antiquity. On this scale of value, poetry and drama are ranked highest together with music, while painting is rated below and sculpture even lower. It's a status scale that can be observed practically applied in the various movements of Modernism, where the ideological leaders were poets, philosophers and writers. Pontus Hultén was advised by his teacher Henrik Cornell to drop the paragon

Pontus in his attic apartment at Boulevard Raspail, Paris, 1954.

question, as he considered it difficult to achieve any valuable results.[3] Instead, Hultén eventually came to devote himself to his sensational thesis on Vermeer and Spinoza.

Hultén presented his licentiate essay in 1951. The text has been publicized, mainly because of Hultén's later fame but also for its drastic, typically Hulténian theory. It was published half a century later as a book in French[4] (but not yet in English or Swedish). To me, the text appears to be carefully and academically written, high-brow, complex and intricate, packed with quotations in the original languages Dutch, French, Italian and German. The author, as far as I can judge, takes generous liberties in his thoughts. That two such celebrities as Johannes Vermeer and Baruch Spinoza were assumed to have lived at the same time in the same small town, perhaps on the same street, is certainly remarkable. Still I can find nothing in the paper that proves Hultén's theses about Spinoza's camera obscura and its connection to Vermeer's perspective, or even makes these assumptions more credible beyond the alleged temporal and geographical coincidence. Pontus Hultén himself has suggested that it was time that hindered him in his ambitions to prove these theses.[5] Bold theories of historical context and efforts to show the conformity of the terrain with the vision of the map are elements that would recur time and again in Pontus Hultén's activities as a museum director and curator.

Grades from Stockholm University show that Pontus Hultén had a good pass in art history and a pass in ethnology.[6] He seems to have devoted limited energy to his thesis work during his frequent trips to Paris in the first half of the 1950s. Unlike many of his colleagues, Pontus Hultén was never an academic or classical intellectual by nature. He never did pen a doctoral thesis. However, the fact that he was working on, or as his later life partner Anna-Lena Wibom claims, "pretending to write his doctoral thesis,"[7] was of importance for his future career. Academic credentials were a prerequisite in the Swedish museum world where Hultén would soon make his entrance.

Pontus Hultén himself has revealed that it was in Paris during this period that his interest shifted definitively from classical to modern art.[8] In the 1950s, Paris was still the world's undisputed center of contemporary art. After many European artists, among them Hultén's heroes Marcel Duchamp and Francis Picabia, had moved to New York to escape the war, a reverse movement emerged after the end of the war, when thousands of Americans moved to Paris where they benefitted from so-called GI Bills, pensions for war veterans, on which they lived large with the weak French franc, among them many artists, writers and intellectuals.

The Parisian art establishment at the time was generally conservative and nationalistic. Modern art was still dominated by Picasso, the Cubists and the circle around Picasso's gallerist and dealer Daniel-Henry Kahnweiler. The avant-garde scene was diminutive, with just a few small galleries showing Post-Cubist modern art. Most important of these were two galleries both operated by women.

Parisian Denise René, née Bleibtreu, initially ran a successful fashion studio, Societé Denise René, with her sister "Lulu." After meeting Hungarian artist Victor Vasarely at the Café de Flore, she transformed the studio into the Galerie Denise René, opened in 1944 on rue de la Boétie with an exhibition of Vasarely's designs and prints. By the mid-fifties, the gallery was one of the world's most famous for avant-garde art, with a repertoire that interspersed the new with classical Modernism. "She was wise enough to show not only the abstract avant-garde but also Picasso and Max Ernst," as Pontus Hultén explained Denise René's exceptional success.[9]

Galerie Denise René became a stronghold of contemporary Scandinavian art in the early 1950s. René showed the Danish abstract painters and sculptors Richard Mortensen and Robert Jacobsen as well as Olle Baertling. It was probably Baertling who introduced Pontus Hultén to Denise René, a key figure along his path to the center of the art world. The friendship and professional exchange between Pontus Hultén and Denise René would continue over the decades.

In the circle around Denise René, Pontus Hultén began to build his international network. Here he met Sam Francis, the Abstract Expressionist from Los Angeles, and the American painter and experimental filmmaker Robert Breer, an economically independent heir like many of the players in the bohemian art circles of Paris. Both Francis and Breer became lifelong friends of Pontus Hultén. Another of the many artist he befriended during his time in Paris was the equally affluent William Copley.

In addition to Olle Baertling, his Swedish friends in Paris included the future architect Per-Evert Taube and the writer and adventurer Olle Strandberg and his partner/protector Bibbi Elfwén, as well as the writers Pär Rådström and Stig Claesson. Photographers Christer Strömholm, Lennart Olson and Lennart Nilsson also spent time in

Paris during this period and were part of the social circle, which they documented photographically. Pontus Hultén emphasized how fortunate the Scandinavian connection in the circle around Denise René was for him during the years when he made a name for himself in Paris. "It was important because otherwise I would have risked being isolated, especially since my self-taught French was not viable," as he admitted.[10] For several years in the early and mid-fifties, Pontus Hultén divided his time between Stockholm and Paris. There is a popular story he often repeated of how he sometimes made the trip on his Vespa scooter without setting foot in the hated Germany other than to urinate. In Stockholm, he now began his work in earnest as a producer, or organizer as he himself called it, of exhibitions and editor of magazines.

During Pontus Hultén's sojourns in Paris, Kerstin Ehrenberg was left alone to care for their son. At times during Felix's childhood, mother and son lived with grandfather Eric and grandmother Elsie in Djursholm. "My mother died at the same time, so of course it was hard," says Kerstin Ehrenberg. "I had to support myself, so I took a job as a clerk and had to do my studies in the evenings. I got a lot of help from Eric and Elsie. When Pontus later met Anna-Lena, I stepped back because I thought it was her turn. But grandfather and grandmother wouldn't allow it. 'No, you belong to us,' they said. It was a difficult time, of course, but I would never speak ill of Pontus for this. What good would it do? I've always been used to making the best of the situation and never demanded too much of things."[11]

Between trips to Paris, Pontus Hultén continued his temporary work at the National Museum, where the first exhibition he mentions in his CV bore the now barely writable title *Negro Art*, art by anonymous African tribal artists, in the spring of 1953 — a subject that interested the small modern art clique of the time, as African sculpture had inspired Picasso and Cubism.

Around the same time, in the spring of 1953, Pontus Hultén made his debut together with Oscar Reutersvärd with an exhibition at Galerie Denise René in Paris, *L'Art abstrait en Suède*, ("Abstract Art in Sweden"), or *L'Art Suédoise* ("Swedish Art") for short. The exhibition was a broad exposition of artists from several generations, with works by Gösta Adrian-Nilsson (GAN), Otte Sköld, Christian Berg, the only woman Siri Derkert, Otto G Carlslund, Baertling, Olle Bonniér, Karl Axel Pehrson, Lennart Rohde, and others. The ambition was to provide a comprehensive overview of Swedish Modernism.

L'Art Suèdois was an exhibition that seems to have been well received by the discerning Parisian art public, probably due to the prestige of the gallery Denise René in avant-garde circles. Sales, unfortunately, were almost non-existent. As the savvy Denise René had made a deal that the two young Swedish organizers would cover the expenses, and projected income was minimal, the show was an economic blow for Hultén and Reutersvärd. They had sought support from the Swedish Embassy and from the Tessin Institute in Paris but had been coldly rejected, something that Hultén had not forgotten when he became director of the Centre Pompidou twenty years later.[12] *L'Art Suédoise* still made an impression and helped to establish Pontus Hultén's name on the Parisian art scene.

Officially, Hultén continued working on his planned doctoral thesis on Vermeer and Spinoza at the time. Hultén himself gave as his reason for finally abandoning the work the realization that he would have to learn Dutch and spend a lot of time in Holland, which seemed too complicated.[13] In his archives, there are records of grants awarded for renewed scholarships to support him in Paris, for Vermeer and for other thesis topics.[14] By the time Hultén gave up his academic ambitions, he had already established himself in the museum sphere.

1954 stands out as a crucial year for Pontus Hultén's career in the art world. He had moved into a small apartment he rented on Boulevard Raspail, in the university district of Montparnasse, in an attic with a view of the Parisian rooftops.

In his autobiographical novel *Om vänskap funnes* (*If Friendship Existed*), the famous Swedish writer and artist Stig Claesson, also known as Slas, portrays an unnamed Pontus Hultén in a twenty-below cold Paris in January 1954: "The only significant acquaintance I made, apart from Shirley Lee, was a mildly insane countryman who lived in a very small rented room high up on the roof of Boulevard Raspail and we often met and drank cognac and ate hard-boiled eggs. He used to make little collages out of various tickets and torn pieces of newspaper seemingly unnecessarily and just for his own amusement. And he was interested in something called *Art in Motion*, which he would launch as a museum director. He was funny and fearless and Shirley Lee liked him a lot. In the first week of January he was seriously ill and he thought he was talking to both Churchill and Hitler. Shirley Lee and I often visited him when he was feverish and when he recovered and I told him what he had been talking about, he said it was not so strange.

The idea of an exhibition with the theme of Hitler and Churchill, and also the American commander-in-chief and president Dwight D. Eisenhower, as amateur painters, and Joseph Goebbels as an art critic, was something that Pontus Hultén returned to in conversations throughout his career, including in my own interview, but never realized. Another such "accompanying" unrealized exhibition idea was that of the different branches of anarchism.

He would write a thesis, he said, about Hitler and Winston Churchill as painters and Goebbels as an art critic. He didn't think I should attend art school at all."[15]

Hultén's orbit of friends among artists and other stakeholders within the Parisian avant-garde had widened. During this year, he made several acquaintances decisive for his career.

In a text published several times in different versions, Hultén himself described the life-changing encounter with Marcel Duchamp's world of ideas that took place at the Bibliothèque Sainte-Geneviève near the Panthéon, where Hultén ordered Duchamp's "La Boîte verte" ("The Green Box") from the storage — the former bookbinder Duchamp's beautifully green-bound box from 1934.[16] In this box, the artist had gathered ninety-four documents containing notes, puns, sketches and more from his work on "La mariée mise à nu par ses célibataires, même" ("The Bride Stripped Bare by Her Bachelors, Even"), also known as "The Large Glass," the enigmatic mixed media masterpiece that Duchamp worked on for eight years.

According to Duchamp himself, the documents in the green box were necessary to understand "The Large Glass" — a work with which the artist wanted to appeal to and challenge the recipient's brain rather than just the eye, to move beyond the purely "retinal"[17] eye candy. The green box would later, in 1941, be followed by an even more remarkable box in the form of a briefcase, "La Boîte en valise" ("The Box in the Briefcase"), containing Marcel Duchamp's entire production of works in miniature, also handmade in a numbered edition. It's believed that he crafted these boxes, copied and varied by numerous artists in later times, in an ambition to preserve his work for history in a troubled, war-torn world and at a time when his art had been forgotten for decades. In texts and interviews, Pontus Hultén relates how he was shocked when studying Duchamp's "La Boîte verte" in the library: "Afterwards, I was so stunned that I thought I had been dreaming. I had to take a friend, a Swedish artist, there the next day to confirm that I wasn't hallucinating. My friend was able to confirm

Gallery owner Agnes Widlund with Pontus Hultén in front of Hultén's collage "Le bac á journaux" ("The Newspapers' Tub"), signed with Hultén's sobriquet Bo Ek, in the studio in Vaxholm shared by Hultén and friends at the time, c. 1952.

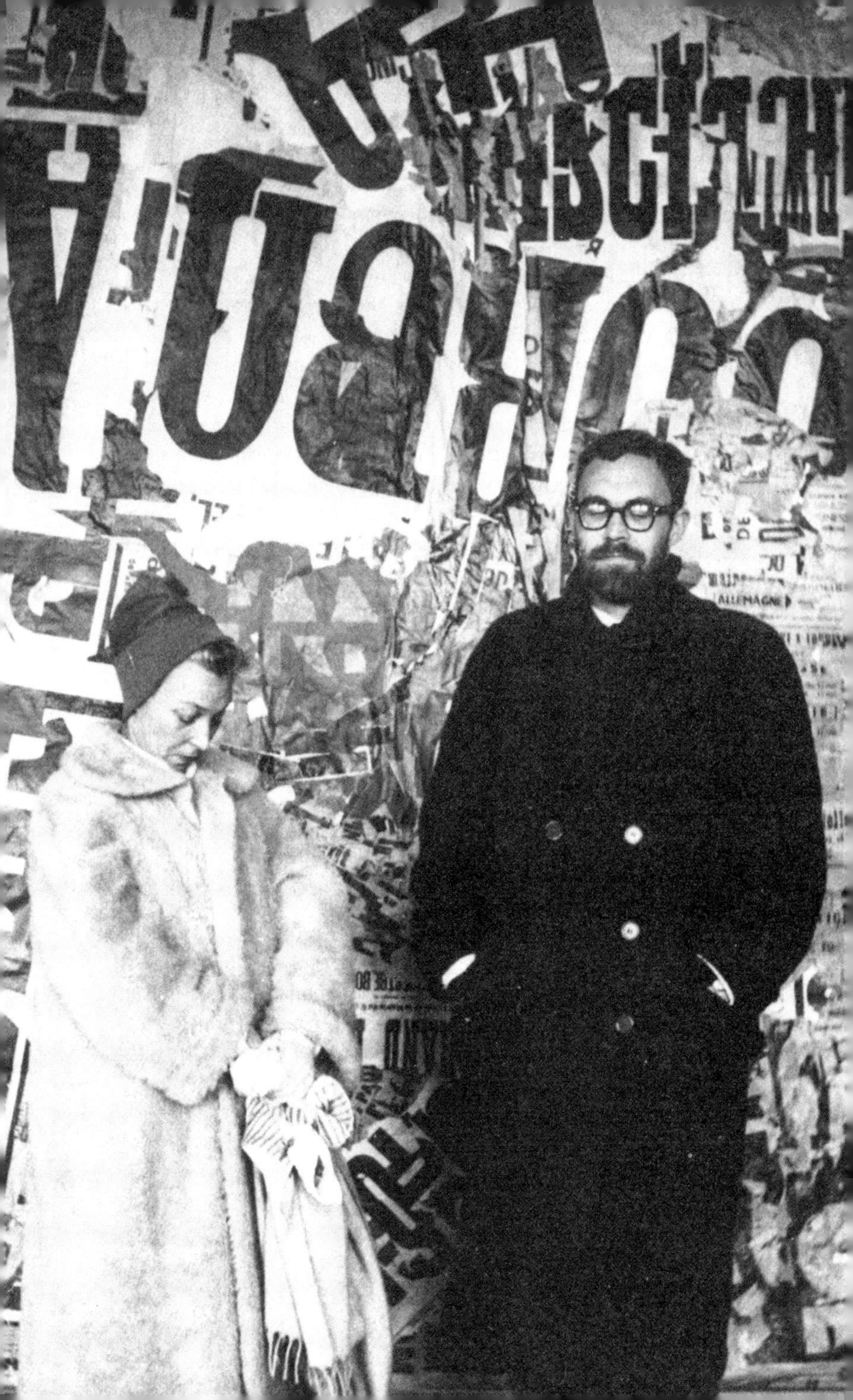
ALLEMAGNE

that it was reality. He himself was not particularly impressed by what he saw."[18]

Although Pontus Hultén himself claimed to have discovered Marcel Duchamp as a teenager in Lund, almost two decades before the artist's "second breakthrough" at the turn of the 1960s, the encounter with the box in the library seems to have been the moment when this interest turned into unreserved adoration. Hultén would go on to elevate Marcel Duchamp above all other artists as his lifelong most important mentor. He has referred how his view of art changed after the revelation.[19] Hultén now once and for all gave up the classics, Vermeer and Spinoza. Avant-garde modern art took possession of him. As he mused, it was Duchamp who explained him the riddle: "Many questions that I had often asked myself in the past were suddenly answered with great clarity."[20] Pontus Hultén has stated that he wrote to Marcel Duchamp, who was living in New York at the time but visited Paris annually, shortly after this crucial encounter with "La Boîte verte," and that he received a friendly reply.[21] He remained in contact with the artist until his death in 1968.

Another physical encounter that occurred in this year, 1954, was with Jean Tinguely, the contemporary artist who would become Pontus Hultén's main collaborator, closest friend and something of an idol — a relationship that has been called a bromance and would last until Tinguely's death in 1991.

Hultén has recounted[22] how one day he saw an exhibition by Tinguely in a small, unassuming but beautiful room in the bookshop of the Galerie Arnaud, at the time the second avant-garde scene in Paris alongside Denise René. The gallery, specializing in "lyrical abstraction," was located near the dilapidated hotel where the poor, sometimes near-starving Tinguely lived with his first wife, the fellow Swiss artist Eva Aeppli. The simple exhibition of Tinguely's small mobile sculptures in the spirit of Alexander Calder made such a powerful impression on Hultén that he wrote a message to the artist and left it at the gallery. Tinguely replied a few days later. From that day on, Pontus Hultén and Jean Tinguely were close friends. They seem to have found each other instantly in a common view of art and in the anarchist, libertarian philosophy of life they shared, with a mutual disdain for everything established, formal and bureaucratic.

Pontus Hultén's contact network in Paris continued to expand from the circle around Galerie Denise René. He also made acquaintances in the film world that would be important in the future, including in the

Cinémathèque française organization for experimental film and with its founder Henri Langlois.[23]

Pontus Hultén has spoken of how Galerie Denise René became a breeding ground where he had the chance to cultivate his newly developed view of art, "a place for meetings, mutual inspiration and exchange of ideas."[24] The gallery circle has been compared to that of the Surrealists around the magazine Littérature[25] in the twenties. In an interview, Pontus Hultén commented on this comparison with a tableau of the atmosphere around the gallery: "Unlike the Surrealists, we didn't exclude any members, although our discussions were infected by politics. There were big debates about how we should deal with Stalinism and capitalism. Some seemed to think that Trotskyism was a viable alternative. There were people like Jean Dewasne (then considered a young Vasarely) who took a Trotskyist position. He was practically excluded from our group. He later left the gallery. We also had many debates about abstraction, which was central to our discussion. Sometimes great Modernist figures came by, like Alexander Calder, when he was in Paris, Auguste Herbin, Jean Arp and Sonia Delaunay. It was very exciting to meet them."[26]

At home in Stockholm, there was a counterpart to Denise René in the gallerist Agnes Widlund, née Horvath, of Hungarian Jewish origin. Before marrying the diplomat Gunnar Widlund and moving to Stockholm, she had studied cultural journalism at the Sorbonne in Paris, where she had acquainted with many artists, as well as her colleague Denise René. Agnes Widlund founded her gallery, konstsalongen Samlaren (The Collector Art Salon), at the prestigious address Birger Jarlsgatan 1 during the war, in 1943. In the early years, the focus was more traditional. Widlund was one of the gallerists who introduced artists such as Henri Matisse, Pablo Picasso, Fernand Léger, Joan Miró, Marc Chagall, Henry Moore and others to the Swedish public. From 1950, Widlund distinguished herself by launching the new abstract geometric art. The focus in the early fifties was on Concrete Realism, with Olle Baertling as a particular favorite. Agnes Widlund was an advisor to Theodor "Teto" Ahrenberg, the scandal-ridden, flamboyant financier and art collector whose dizzying business dealings are detailed in his memoirs *Jag har ju ändå ägt en Picasso* (*But Still I've Owned a Picasso*).[27] Widlund consulted Ahrenberg on his art purchases, and Ahrenberg in turn financially supported Widlund's art salon. In my interview, Pontus Hultén called Teto "the madman Ahrenberg," describing him as the only international style art collector in Stockholm at the time.[28]

Agnes Widlund is portrayed as a firm, "fierce" woman.[29] "I didn't like her at all," says dealer and art collector Jeanette Bonnier, who met Agnes Widlund as a young art enthusiast at the Samlaren gallery. "She was a harsh, mean lady who had married for money, who walked over corpses and didn't give a damn about people she couldn't use."[30] Bonnier's friend, the gallerist William Aronowitsch, is more conciliatory: "I had no problem with her, because I think she liked me as a sweet and kind young Jewish man."[31]

Pontus Hultén, together with Oscar Reutersvärd, Hans Nordenström, Per Olof Ultvedt and others, had been organizing exhibitions at Agnes Widlund's gallery since the early 1950s. Rolf Söderberg summarizes the background in a mini-portrait of Widlund in his book *My Art Widows and Other Art Memories*: "In the 1940s, Widlund's salon Samlaren on Birger Jarlsgatan did not yet have a distinct profile. When she made contact with the highly established French artists in the 1950s, she became a threat to the Swedish-French Art Gallery and Blanche. Between the noble events, she could offer the space for experimental exhibitions of a guaranteed non-commercial nature. You could say that Pontus Hultén could play with ideas on a small scale here, which he could then realize in full format at Moderna Museet ten years later."[32]

At the art salon Samlaren, Pontus Hultén, together with Oscar Reutersvärd, organized, in 1954, the exhibition *Objects and Artifacts. Reality Realized*.[33] The exhibition is exceptional as it was dedicated to Marcel Duchamp, the artist who would have to wait another decade to be rediscovered internationally. The initiative seems even more far-sighted as the subject was Duchamp's readymades, the impersonal objects that Duchamp placed in artistic contexts and that would eventually revolutionize the art world.

The catalog, which is a fold containing a loose leaf, was claimed by Pontus Hultén and his friends to be the world's first seven-page printed matter and was cataloged with a page count of seven by the Royal Library.

For the exhibition, Hultén and Reutersvärd had selected a number of Swedish creators — not only artists but also architects Bengt Lindroos and Sven Markelius. They were each tasked to select an object to be displayed in the gallery spaces. A small, simple but ambitious catalog was produced for the exhibition, for which Pontus Hultén wrote an often-quoted text on the concept of readymades, the utility objects with which Duchamp punctured the heroic myth of the freely creative, ingenious artist. The catalog was also the first issue of Hultén and Reutersvärd's magazine Kasark, published in four issues from 1954 to 1960, an influential publication in the Stockholm art world in the 1950s.

The name Kasark is taken from Mark Twain's short story. "Captain Stormfield's Visit to Heaven" from 1905, where Kasark is a measure of weight equal to that of the world and everything it contains.

In the Swedish cultural elite, and within parts of the international cult of Marcel Duchamp, it's not Pontus Hultén but his younger colleague Ulf Linde who has come to be hailed as the Duchamp connoisseur above others — despite Linde admitting in interviews towards the end of his life that it was through Hultén that he had fallen under the spell with Duchamp.[34] In an article in the influential magazine Konstrevy, the then twenty-five-year-old Ulf Linde wrote disparagingly about *Objects and Artifacts. Reality Realized*, which he called a replay of the Dadaist manifestations of the 1920s. In 1954, Dada had been consigned to history and was no longer able to shock anyone or challenge people's dreams of beauty, Linde proclaimed. This was many years before he himself, through Pontus Hultén, took a fanatical interest in Marcel Duchamp.[35]

Ulf Linde's assessment of the exhibition and its reception by the Stockholm audience is contradicted by the "fashion artist" Mette Prawitz. At the time, in the winter of 1953/1954, she was studying art history at Stockholm University, with Oscar Reutersvärd teaching ancient art. One day, Reutersvärd told her class that he was producing an exhibition at the art salon Samlaren. He asked if there were any volunteers among the students who wanted to serve as assistants, an offer that the then eighteen-year-old Prawitz accepted together with a friend.[36]

According to Mette Prawitz, *Objects and Artifacts. Reality Realized* was the talk of the Stockholm art crowd, arousing great indignation in the press and among traditionalists, something that Pontus Hultén and Oscar Reutersvärd seemed to cherish. "It was hugely controversial. There was a lot of buzz and many people came because it was so crazy. There were beer cans on display, a tree root and things you'd never seen in Stockholm. I think they were very pleased with the attention and controversy."[37]

Mette Prawitz relates an anecdote that reflects the idyllic tiny Stockholm art scene of the time: "It was a Sunday when I suddenly saw the king [Gustaf VI Adolf] looking in through the big display window. He was out on his usual art stroll. I told this to Pontus who immediately said 'you take care of this,' then disappeared with lightning speed upstairs where he remained. The king walked around for quite a while and looked carefully at everything. The gallery charged admission on Sundays and the king made no sign of paying. After a while I walked up and shyly pointed out that we charged a crown. The king looked a bit surprised but signaled to his adjutant who quickly handed over the coin. When the king had left, Pontus came down the stairs furious and scolded me. 'You must realize that you can't charge the king!' he bellowed. Then I actually got angry though I was raised to stay in the background. He could be a coward. It was his exhibition and I thought it was wrong to let me take responsibility for the king."

I ask Mette Prawitz why she thinks Pontus Hultén escaped instead of basking in the royal glory. "I don't know, of course, but I can guess that it was because he didn't know how to treat the king. Otherwise, when people came in and objected, Pontus and Oscar always responded by sneering and making fun of reactionary people and their narrow-mindedness. I can guess that he thought that he couldn't respond to the king in that way had he been upset by what he saw."

Mette Prawitz didn't make closer acquaintance with Pontus Hultén during her internship. She describes him as taciturn and "rather stern." Another observation she made during her first meetings with Hultén deserves to be quoted as it concerns Pontus Hultén's view of women, an area where, as with so much else concerning Hultén's personality, there are differing opinions: "There are many who speak ill of Pontus and say that he was grumpy, irate and selfish," says Prawitz. "But one thing you have to say is that there was never any hint that he didn't think women should come forward. It was something you were very used to as a young woman, but with Pontus you never had the feeling that he looked down on you as a woman. He was equal before equality, without having it as a program."[38]

4

A first breakthrough as exhibition maker

By the mid-fifties, the thirty-plus Pontus Hultén had begun to make a name for himself in the art world, not only in Stockholm but also in Paris, both within and outside the establishment — a dual strategy[1] that came to characterize his career. In 1955, Hultén laid the groundwork for a breakthrough in the larger context. It was the year when he initiated the first of the "cycles" of exhibitions that followed one another throughout his career as an exhibition maker and museum director. His interest had by this time been absorbed by "kinetic" art, i.e. moving art, to which he would devote the next thirteen years, with a series of historical exhibitions, and which remained a lifelong love.

It was the meeting with Jean Tinguely that sparked Hultén's immersion in moving art, a trend that was in vogue in the avant-garde during this period, when painting and sculpture had for the first time begun to be challenged and questioned by a genre of younger artists that we may call Neo-Dadaists. In Paris, Jean Tinguely was a leading figure in this movement alongside his dear and admired friend Yves Klein. In New York, a few years later, a similar pair of Neo-Dadaist artists experienced their breakthroughs: Robert Rauschenberg and Jasper Johns. Hultén knew nothing about this at the time.

Until then, the modern art debate had, according to Pontus Hultén's own testimony,[2] largely raged between representatives of figurative and non-figurative, i.e. abstract art — a tedious and protracted discussion, as Hultén phrases it, that had been ongoing ever since the breakthrough of Cubism at the beginning of the century.[3] Kinetic Art was based on Duchamp and other Dadaist artists. The Neo-Dadaists, or Les Nouveaux Réalistes as they were called in Paris, fundamentally questioned painting, sculpture and tradition, thus foreshadowing the

Conceptual Art that would increasingly take over the art world in the coming decades.

At Galerie Denise René in 1955, *Le Mouvement* (*The Movement*) was the first ever exhibition to present a comprehensive survey of Kinetic Art, an art form that could be claimed to have been practiced since the 1910s. There are different accounts of the origins of *Le Mouvement*. In his book *Méta* on Jean Tinguely from 1972[4], Pontus Hultén quotes the American author and art writer Calvin Tomkins from The New Yorker in 1962,[5] where he writes: "On a rainy spring evening in 1955, when K.G.P. Hultén, Jean Tinguely and Robert Breer, a young American painter who had recently started making abstract films, were sitting on the roof of the apartment Hultén was renting on Boulevard Raspail, they came up with the idea of doing an exhibition on movement in art. They easily persuaded Denise René and the first 'movement exhibition' was shown at her gallery in April." In the next paragraph, however, Hultén writes: "In fact, the plans had already been made in the fall, when Vasarely had expressed the need for an exhibition of this kind."[6]

It seems obvious that Denise René and Victor Vasarely had gained confidence in Pontus Hultén and his abilities. They asked him to contribute a text for the catalog sheet published with the exhibition, in which Hultén outlines the history of Kinetic Art, presenting his own analysis of this art form and its reflection of contemporary society.

The exhibition itself bore the signature of Pontus Hultén in its selection and design. He explains it as being divided into three elements: "a historical section with Marcel Duchamp and Calder, Vasarely's paintings on glass in two layers, one in front of the other, which made the paintings "move" as the viewer moved around the room, and works by four younger artists: [Yaacov] Agam, [Pol] Bury, [Jesús Rafael] Soto and Tinguely."[7] Hultén forgets to mention Danish artist Robert Jacobsen, who was represented by several moving iron sculptures.

Alexander Calder was an obvious starting point for the exhibition. With his mobiles from the 1920s and 30s, he was widely regarded as a pioneer of Kinetic Art.

On the contrary, Marcel Duchamp's participation was controversial. At the time, Duchamp had not yet experienced his second breakthrough and was unknown in Paris outside a small exclusive coterie. His participation was questioned within the circle of the Galerie Denise René. In an interview the year before, in 1954, Duchamp had reiterated his dismissive view of decorative art, primarily painting, which he classified as "retinal" (roughly "for the eye").[8] His reasoning provoked many artists, including Richard Mortensen, Denise René's companion at the time. The Dane took Duchamp's comment as an insult.[9] Pontus Hultén insisted on presenting, alongside Calder, Marcel Duchamp's 1924 "Rotative demisphère" and his 1935 "Rotoreliefs" — rotating circular discs with patterns that create optical phenomena — as pioneering works of Kinetic Art.[10]

Ultimately, Hultén's faction got its way. Duchamp's "Rotoreliefs" were presented in the gallery on Rue la Boétie in an arrangement by Tinguely on a black wall panel, driven by hidden rubber bands from 78 rpm gramophone motors. Marcel Duchamp was unable to visit the exhibition himself, but had met and befriended Jean Tinguely the year before, introduced by Hultén.[11]

The fact that Hultén was in a position to exercise such influence on an important exhibition like *Le Mouvement* seems to be explained not only by Denise René's and Victor Vasarely's confidence in his talent and sense of the spirit of the time, but also by their realization that the gallery was in need of renewal. In Hultén's words: "Geometric abstract painting had reached a dead end. Vasarely was the brain behind the gallery and I'm sure that the exhibition could not have taken place without his approval."[13]

Although Denise René had already established itself as one of the leading galleries for avant-garde art in Paris in the first half of the 1950s, it was *Le Mouvement* that elevated the gallery as the premier venue for new art, in the same year that its competitor Iris Clert opened. The exhibition attracted large crowds and was much publicized and debated, not only in Paris but also internationally. It was the first time that new alternatives to painting and sculpture were presented cohesively, and emotions ran high. Pontus Hultén noted in retrospect: "At this time, art was actually taken seriously, almost as it still is in the Soviet Union."[14]

In his book on Jean Tinguely, Pontus Hultén lists the qualities that he believes made *Le Mouvement* such an innovative exhibition: "What distinguished *Le Mouvement* from other exhibitions and gave it a wide reputation was that it presented a new attitude in art. Much of the art of the 1950s had been pessimist, defeatist and passive. The revelation that there was a different kind of 'modern art,' which was dynamic, constructive, joyful, deliberately confusing, ironic, critical, mischievous and aggressive came as a surprise to many."[15]

Le Mouvement was experienced by the audience as provocative but above all liberating, with several qualities that characterize Pontus

Hultén as an artistic storyteller: the disarming humor, the relaxed, good temper and the open, welcoming atmosphere. The show broke with the rigid solemnity and intellectual snobbery of geometric abstraction. In a Dadaist/Duchampian spirit, *Le Mouvement* invited viewers to interact with the art works, as with Tinguely's "art machines." One of Duchamp's wisdoms is that it is the viewer, as much as the artist, who "creates" the art, through her/his viewing — a thesis he pushed to the limit with his readymades.

Just one year after they met for the first time, the friendship and exchange between Pontus Hultén and Jean Tinguely had deepened so much that Tinguely traveled to Stockholm in the summer of 1955. Here he quickly got to know the circle of friends and artistic collaborators around Hultén. A solo exhibition of Jean Tinguely was staged at Agnes Widlund's art salon Samlaren, which opened in October. Here Tinguely showed sculptures that he had made during the summer in the editorial offices of Blandaren (The Blender), the classic humor magazine produced by students at the Royal Institute of Technology, in whose editorial staff Hultén and Hans Nordenström were collaborators. Blandaren's premises on Drottning Kristinas väg served as a studio for Hultén, Nordenström and others. In addition to the wall reliefs, Tinguely for the first time exhibited graceful free-standing sculptures with brittle gears that drove monochrome plates. One sculpture was mounted in Oscar Reutersvärd's Dalacarlean grandfather clock, with a percussion of pots and other household utensils and objects that produced a deafening "concrete music" that, at the exhibition at Samlaren, caused a lady to threaten to call the police.[16] The sculptures were soldered together from scrap and objects that Tinguely, with the help of Hultén, Nordenström and Per Olof Ultvedt, had collected in Stockholm and the surrounding area, after far more effort than Tinguely was used to. The artist was amazed at how tidy and free of rubbish and junk Stockholm was in the 1950s.[17]

For this exhibition, Hultén, Nordenström, Ultvedt and Oscar Reutersvärd published the second issue of their art journal Kasark, entitled "Om rörelse i konsten" (On *Art in Motion*), with a text "solemnly signed K.G. Hultén."[18] Although the young comrades worked together freely, in anarchistic rejection of formal hierarchies, Pontus Hultén increasingly emerged over the years as the group's de facto leader. He was the one with the main pen.

The Jean Tinguely exhibition caused a sensation on the Stockholm art scene. Kinetic Art was the hot new movement of the international avant-garde and Jean Tinguely its foremost exponent, regarded by many as a new, "mechanized" Duchamp. That he showed newly produced art in a solo exhibition in distant Stockholm as early as 1955 is remarkable. Over the next decade, Tinguely would cause a stir and scandal in a global conquest with his anarchic "anti-machines," dysfunctional in their clamorous futility, mocking the basic idea of rationality and efficiency of industrialism and capitalism.

In our digital age, it can be difficult to comprehend the indignation that Jean Tinguely's art and its ridicule of industrial development evoked at the height of the post-war society's worship of industry, mechanics and technology. Two quotes can give an idea, the first from Tinguely's own mother, in a letter from 1960, after she and his father had visited his son's first exhibition in his home country: "Your father was very angry that people can make money from the likes of this. I cannot understand how an intelligent boy like you can do such things."[19] The second is from an article published in the Soviet Izvestia (News):[20] "Tinguely is a prophet and showman of a self-destructing nature. This means the products of a sick brain: the fantasies of a madman who should be wearing a straitjacket. Tinguely and his supporters spit on the human race and the achievements of civilization. They are akin to the nuclear lunatics in American uniform."[21]

While Tinguely was in Stockholm to produce his exhibition at the art salon Samlaren, Pontus Hultén and Hans Nordenström were simultaneously working on their experimental short film *A Day in the City*, named in reference to the Marx Brothers but modeled on their mutual idol Sergei Eisenstein.[22] In the film, Oscar Reutersvärd plays a civil servant and Jean Tinguely a policeman. *A Day in the City* begins with beautiful views of the Royal Castle and other Stockholm settings on a bright sunny early summer morning and then, after a series of surrealistically interconnected scenes over fifteen minutes, ends in the total destruction of the city. In his texts too, as well as in his collages, Pontus Hultén used a Dadaist-inspired "cut-out" method at this time, with intuitively joined elements. The film was shown at screenings in cinemas in Stockholm and at independent international events of avant-garde film. The film cannot be claimed to have been a major success, at least not financially. Pontus Hultén said in an interview much later that he was seriously considering a career as a film director at the time, but that after the setbacks with *A Day in the City* he realized that the 1950s was the wrong time to choose film.[23]

In the spring of 1955, Pontus Hultén, Hans Nordenström and others worked simultaneously on a special issue of the satirical magazine Blandaren called "Tvångsblandaren" ("The Forced Blender"), openly inspired by Marcel Duchamp's "La Boîte verte" and "La Boîte-en-valise," here in a prankish incarnation. The satirical magazine was published in an edition of no less than forty thousand copies, each with a unique work of art and other objects accompanying the magazine in a cardboard box. The popularity of the Blandaren at the time is demonstrated by the fact that the entire edition sold out on the very first day. The issue is now a sought-after collector's item. The importance that Pontus Hultén himself attached to this publication is evident in that many years later he referred to it in texts as an early tribute to Duchamp.

In his fantastic memorial article "Preludes in the 1950s," published in Moderna Museet's memorial book for the museum's twenty-fifth anniversary in 1983,[24] Hans Nordenström remembers the work on the magazine issue: "In late winter 1955, we produced the Boulevard Carton Tvångs-Blandaren. It had the shape of a cardboard box and contained 35 items of printed matter, some objects and four short films (...) Each Boulevard Carton contained an original painting. The edition was 25,000 copies and the 25,000 original artworks (plus overprinting) were produced by six people in four hours. On a Saturday afternoon we walked through the damp Brunkeberg tunnel's tiled pipes to a printing house on Tunnelgatan, (...) We were not there to print but to paint. The printing rollers of the precision machine were out of action. The paper web ran freely over the machine. We were equipped with buckets of paint and brushes, brooms, hands and feet. (...) The paint splashed over the paper, over the floor, the machine and ourselves, eventually forming a shiny black film over the stage (...) The machine cut the paper into pieces, two to three per second, folded them in pairs into pictures measuring 50 x 60 cm and signed with a text stamp. (...) We calculated that if there are 2,000 painters in Sweden and they join forces in groups of six each and paint for one day (eight hours), then with our method they produce 7 million paintings, one for each Swedish citizen, and in 365 days 3,000 million, one for each citizen of the world (...) In ten months you reach the moon. Sweden's 100 billion linear meters of residential wall area can be filled in five weeks so that each room has six paintings, two per long wall and one per short wall. These are not utopias."[25]

In this text, Hans Nordenström draws a beautiful picture of the life he lived with Pontus Hultén, commuting between Stockholm and Paris, with adventurous excursions elsewhere in Europe. No one else has given such a vivid and detailed account of Hultén and their shared circle of acquaintances during those important formative years in the early and mid-fifties — of the spirit of the times and the roots of creativity. In his text, Nordenström offers several mini-portraits of his friend's personality and qualities, such as this: "Pontus was a mixture of cheekiness and awkwardness, stingy and helpful, sometimes unreasonable in his opinions, with a desire for the idiosyncratic and a remarkable sense of the fruitful. He never made a story weaker."[26]

5 Moderna Museet begins

Although he would continue his own artistic activities for a few more years, the question is whether 1956 should not be considered the year when Hultén abandoned his own artistic dreams. According to several confidants, it was his friendship and collaboration with Jean Tinguely that made him give up these ambitions. Hultén simply realized that his own talents were inadequate in comparison with this Swiss virtuoso with the unfit anarchist scrap machines as his instruments.

Hultén himself has downplayed the seriousness of his youthful artistic ambitions. In an interview, Pontus Hultén claimed that he never really had any more serious artistic dreams of his own — that it was his artist friends who encouraged him to practice art himself.[1] Instead, Hultén claimed that he became interested in Marcel Duchamp's curatorial activities at an early age.[2] I choose to trust his word and take the liberty of digressing on this lesser-known aspect of Duchamp's oeuvre, which I believe was of great importance to Hultén's career choice and actions as an exhibition maker and museum director.

Duchamp, along with his older friend, collector and benefactor Katherine Dreier, founded the Société Anonyme,[3] the first modern art museum in the United States, in a suite of rooms at 19 East 47th Street in New York, as early as 1920. It was Dreier who initiated and financed the museum, based on her own collection, and hired Duchamp to help her realize her idea. He was appointed director of the museum, and in turn hired his friend Man Ray as treasurer (a Surrealist in charge of the accounts — a true Dadaist gesture!). Duchamp was responsible for rebuilding and decorating the galleries, removing stucco, covering the walls with white oilcloth and turning a large closet into a reference library. In a newspaper interview on the occasion of the launch of the

Société Anonyme, Duchamp emphasized the importance of a more light-hearted, carefree approach to art: "People took modern art very seriously when it first came to America because they thought we took ourselves very seriously. Much of modern art is meant to be entertaining."[4]

Société Anonyme means anonymous company, but is also the French term for the English Public Limited Company, or "incorporated." The name was suggested by Man Ray, limited in French language skills, who liked its mystical charge. Marcel Duchamp thought it was a good name for a modern museum. To his and Man Ray's surprise, Katherine Dreier accepted. As an extra Dadaist gesture, the museum's full name was extended to Société Anonyme Inc.

Interest in modern art had waned in the United States by the end of the decade, after being shocked-started by the first presentation of avant-garde European modern art at the old Armory[5] in New York in 1913. The exhibition was a gigantic presentation that brought Matisse's Fauvism and Picasso's Cubism to American audiences for the first time, and made Marcel Duchamp famous with his Cubo-Futurist painting "Nude Woman Descending a Staircase, No. 2." With the Société Anonyme, Katherine Dreier was determined to revive interest. The museum opened on April 30, 1920, with a small survey of modern art from van Gogh to Brancusi. Visitors were few, but Dreier and Duchamp stuck to their plan of opening a new exhibition every six weeks. During its twenty years of existence, the Société Anonyme held eighty-five exhibitions, most of them featuring advanced avant-garde modern art.[6]

For much of his career, Marcel Duchamp doubled as an art dealer and broker of artistic contacts. He also staged three legendary Surrealist exhibitions on commission by André Breton.

The Surrealists had presented numerous group exhibitions, but the *Exposition Internationale du Surrealisme*, which opened in Paris in early January 1938, was something new. For several years, the group had been planning a creative event in which individual artworks would serve as elements in a total Surrealist experience. The opportunity arose when the Galerie des Beaux-Arts offered its premises at Breton's disposal and gave him a free hand. Breton persuaded Marcel Duchamp to put aside his other activities to become the creative director and principal designer of the Surrealist exhibition. Officially, he was called the "chief negotiator" of the exhibition. The term was relevant as Duchamp, with his neutral, dead-pan stance, "the beauty of indifference" as he called it, acted as a mediator in the constant heated discussions and conflicts among the Surrealists. I borrow descriptions of the exhibition largely from Calvin Tomkin's classic 1996 biography *Marcel Duchamp*.[7]

Duchamp approached the task of artistic director of the event with a playful attitude. The result was a visually and suggestively shocking exhibition. The gala-dressed guests at the opening, three thousand in number, were greeted in the lobby by Salvador Dalí's "Rainy Taxi," an old-fashioned Parisian taxi cab outfitted with piping that produced a persistent rain inside the car. In the driver's seat sat a shark-headed figure, in the back seat a mannequin with a blonde wig wearing a party dress adorned with heads of lettuce and crawling Burgundy snails. Across the lobby was "Surrealist Street," a corridor with over twenty-five female mannequins along both sides, dressed and designed by various Surrealist artists. The corridor led to the main gallery of the exhibition, which Marcel Duchamp had transformed into an underground cave. Twelve hundred coal sacks hung from the ceiling, with coal dust streaming like a fog from the bags. Dry leaves and grass covered the floor. Next to one of four luxuriously dressed beds in the room was a water basin. The scent of roasting coffee beans filled the room in accordance with the young Modernist idea of the total work of art, where even the sense of smell should be addressed. On the evening of the opening, the gallery was illuminated only by a dim bulb inside a coal bin that had been hoisted up under the sacks below the ceiling. Works by sixty artists from fourteen nations hung on the dark walls and on the rotating partitions that Duchamp had constructed as swinging doors. Guides with flashlights showed the art to visitors.[8] The opening was a grand scandal of the kind Breton and his allies liked to orchestrate.

During the war, when Duchamp, André Breton and most of the leading Surrealists were exiled in New York, the *First Papers of Surrealism* exhibition was staged in the fall of 1942 at the Whitelaw Reid Mansion in Manhattan. There, Duchamp had installed a cobweb-like structure of wires that guided visitors among the artworks. As late as 1947, when the movement was disintegrating, Breton returned to Marcel Duchamp with a commission for a new international event at Galerie Maeght in Paris, *Le Surréalisme en 1947*, which proved to be the movement's last gasp. It featured a "hall of superstition" and an egg-shaped chamber with works by Surrealist artists such as Joan Miró, Yves Tanguy and others.

Duchamp's unceremonial attitude towards his own and his colleagues' art, with the individual artworks serving as elements in a larger overall experience, can be traced in the style that Pontus Hultén was about to develop into his signature: a method of using art and other components to narrate wider contexts, conscious and subconscious, where the holistic experience is greater than the sum of the individual works. It's thus about the exhibition in itself as an art form — a new concept that challenged the strict, pedagogical, ready-to-view ideal of the classical museum, artist by artist. At this time, in the mid-fifties, the exhibition maker, or curator, was an unknown concept. It would be decades before the role of the director of a modern museum was transformed from an anonymous civil servant and administrator to a public star, an artist of artists.

As mentioned, Pontus Hultén was already by this time a well-known name in the small but influential avant-garde art circles in Paris. He participated in the background when Iris Clert opened her minimal gallery on Rue des Beaux-Arts in 1955 and quickly established herself as a more experimental competitor to Denise René, with a series of high-profile, controversial exhibitions of Yves Klein and Jean Tinguely.

Yves Klein was an artist who took the legacy of Duchamp and Dadaism to his own extreme. At Iris Clert, Klein would open his legendary *Propositions Monochromes* ("The Blue Exhibition") in 1957 and *Le Vide* ("The Empty Exhibition") in 1958. The radically conceptual manifestations at the Iris Clert gallery were presented as holistic experiences, backed up by innovative public relations campaigns. Blue invitation cards with blue stamps were distributed. One thousand and one blue balloons were released at the opening. Blue drinks were served that were said to make guests urinate blue. Klein also had plans to light up the obelisk on the Place de la Concorde in blue. The campaigns whipped up hysterical interest. Three thousand visitors queued to enter the empty little room of the *Le Vide*, through the door guarded by two gendarmes in gala uniforms of the Republican Guard.[9]

Correctly pronounced Klän, French, not Klajn, as English/American.

Yves Klein was the leader of the generation of French artists who saw their breakthroughs in the late 1950s and early 1960s and who, in 1960, would form the group Les Nouveaux Réalistes, the New Realists, led by the critic and philosopher Pierre Restany. Klein formed the core of the group along with Tinguely and Arman.[10] The other original members were Daniel Spoerri, François Dufrène, Martial Raysse, Raymond Hains and Jacques Villeglé. Mimmo Rotella, Niki de Saint Phalle, Christo[11] and Gérard Deschamps were later admitted to the group. This contemporary generation of Parisian artists would have an impact on Pontus Hultén's entire career, but especially during its peak — the years as director of the Musée National d'Art Moderne at the Centre Pompidou. Internationally, his association with this group is less well known than that with Robert Rauschenberg, Andy Warhol and the American Pop artists.

Les Nouveaux Réalistes rejected the unworldliness of abstract art, aspiring to create a new realism beyond painting and sculpture, using everyday objects and scraps from capitalist consumer society as artistic materials. Neo-Realism is a cryptic classification, as I believe you'll rarely find something less grounded in reality than Yves Klein's art. Klein, whose parents were both artists, traveled to Japan in his twenties where he earned a fourth dan black belt in judo, unusual for a Westerner. His art is said to have revolved around Zen Buddhist musings. He proclaimed he was pursuing a detached, Nirvana-like state, what he called "Le vide" ("The Void"), where the mind is freed from worldly impressions and can leave its "representative" self, to be reborn into its real, i.e. "realistic" estate. Therein lay Yves Klein's interpretation of the concept of realism, however seriously one chooses to take such artist's philosophizing.

Pontus Hultén entered the circle of Yves Klein and the Iris Clert gallery through his new friend Jean Tinguely. The artist remained one of his personal favorites and an important point of reference, although curiously, Hultén would never present a solo exhibition with Klein.[12]

Pontus Hultén was not formally involved in the exhibition program at the Iris Clert gallery, but indeed as an informal creative advisor. Hultén has revealed that Klein and Tinguely had discussions with him about him becoming artistic director of the gallery. This manifests how established Hultén had become in the avant-garde scene already in the mid-fifties.

In the same interview, however, Pontus Hultén states that he was not interested in this proposal. The other pole in his life, Stockholm, had gained the upper hand. In his home town, plans to open a museum for modern art had begun to take concrete form after decades of discussion. It seems a given that Pontus Hultén would be involved in its creation. After new temporary appointments, in 1957 he was offered a permanent amanuensis position at the National Museum to work on the new museum. Returning to Stockholm doesn't seem to have been a difficult decision. The fixed salary was alluring. During his years of commuting between Stockholm and Paris, Hultén had lived on a shoestring. The "allowance" that Rolf Söderberg writes that Hultén had from "his mother"[13] was supplemented by smaller incomes, scholarships and many hand loans, as can be seen from the accounts and receipts in Pontus Hultén's archive.[14] His exhibition activities in Paris had cost him money rather than earning him any.

Söderberg writes: "I believe that a prerequisite for Pontus' remarkable international career was his mother's strong belief in him. Her allowance made possible his long stays in Paris around 1950. In this way he built up a network of contacts that would last for the future. He had a tougher time with his father, whose memoirs pass him by in silence and who in the 1960s, when the Moderna Museet was flourishing, said to his colleagues at the Museum of Natural History: 'I don't understand what my son is doing.' Pontus is the only person I have known who has managed to realize his ambitions. But maybe he doesn't think so himself, he probably would have preferred to be a great artist."

Plans for a museum of modern art, meaning twentieth century art, or more precisely art starting from 1909, the breakthrough year of Cubism, with Matisse and the "men of 1909,"[15] had been discussed in Stockholm ever since the thirties. Ideas were drawn from the Folkwang museums in Hagen and Essen in the Ruhr area of Germany and the Museum of Visual Culture in Moscow.[16] Certainly the opening of the Museum of Modern Art in New York in 1929, the first large-scale museum of modern art in the world, was an important inspiration for Stockholm's plans.

Within Stockholm's small but vibrant art circles, persistent forces that had been working for the creation of the museum over the years. An association of friends for the museum had been formed in 1953. Through fundraising, it purchased art for the future institution. Throughout the 1950s, Nationalmuseum's director, the artist Otte Sköld,[17] had discussed the venture with influential stakeholders, including gallery owners such as Gösta Olsson, Gustav Engwall and Agnes Widlund. The leading sponsors for a modern museum also included book publisher Gerard Bonnier and collector Teto Ahrenberg.

There was even some basic funding. At Nationalmuseum, money had been set aside for a modern museum. A "Miss" Emma Spitzer[18] had donated a large sum for the establishment of such a museum in the 1930s. As Pontus Hultén writes in Moderna Museet's twenty-five year anniversary book, the "malice" suggested that Miss Spitzer was not at all interested in modern art, but on the contrary eager to get this art out of Nationalmuseum. According to Hultén, the decision on the new museum was a question of lack of space rather than a vision of the benefits of a modern museum. The modern department at Nationalmuseum was cramped with only one gallery and five small cabinets at its disposal.[19]

Pontus Hultén praises Otte Sköld for having been the first of Nationalmuseum's directors to understand the crucial difference between a modern and a classical museum — that those who work with living artists must behave in a completely different manner than those who deal with remains. As a practicing artist, Otte Sköld understood this difference very well, Hultén argues, adding that this was surely one reason why Sköld was able to lead the establishment of the new museum with such vigor.[20]

Otte Sköld was a gifted artist in the traditional modern style, initially a Cubist with futuristic elements, somewhat in the style of Gösta Adrian-Nilsson (GAN). He later switched to what was called "the New Objectivity"[21] with detailed everyday motifs. He was best known for his café and street scene paintings from Paris. Much later, Pontus Hultén described Otte Sköld's art as "initially promising but then without international breakthrough."[22] Sköld was a professor of painting at the Royal Institute of Art, where he distinguished himself with his administrative and diplomatic talents: handsome, elegant and sophisticated with a slightly bohemian Parisian artist's touch, frequently sporting a chic silk scarf at the neck. Sköld was appointed director of the Royal Institute of Art in 1941 and hired fellow artists Sven Erixson, Erik Grate and Ragnar Sandberg as professors — recruitments that aroused the displeasure of an older generation led by Isaac Grünewald.[23] Throughout his career, Sköld was drawn further and further into the administrative bureaucracy of the Stockholm art world, away from his own painting, a constant source of discomfort for the brooding artist.[24]

Several buildings were discussed as potential sites for the new museum, or the branch of Nationalmuseum, as the planned institution was classified. Pontus Hultén writes in 1983 that in the mid-fifties, Stockholm was in the first phase of a period of intense development. Many old-fashioned activities had ceased. Others moved out of the inner city, including military units. Large, well-planned buildings became available for other purposes. One that was proposed was the so-called stone shed in the cholera cemetery above the end of Strandvägen, a corridor-shaped stone building from the nineteenth century that was later appropriated by Swedish Television. Hultén writes that Otte Sköld was able to reject the proposal when it turned out that the building that had originally been his first choice would become available — the so-called Drill House on the top of Skeppsholmen. The island was then still Stockholm's naval station, but the Navy was in the process of moving out.[25]

The Drill House was a T-shaped edifice largely built in the mid-nineteenth century. The oldest parts are thought to have been designed by "Skeppsholmen architect" Fredrik Blom.[26] Pontus Hultén returns in his writings to the luck and timing that blessed Moderna Museet in its early years. He mentions the good fortune of ending up in almost ideal premises, where especially the entrance room, the old naval drill hall, had strangely perfect dimensions and, as it turned out, almost magical qualities.[27] The connection to Skeppsholmen was natural, within easy walking distance of Nationalmuseum.

Pontus Hultén's text in the twenty-five year anniversary book clearly reveals how consciously he and his friends had worked for quite a few years with the aim of creating a museum for modern art in Stockholm. Hultén writes that shortly after Otte Sköld's appointment as director of the Nationalmuseum, in 1950, he and Oscar Reutersvärd approached him and proposed a campaign among Sweden's art collectors in support of a modern museum. They would all be asked to donate works from their own collections for this purpose. Hultén and Reutersvärd were "naturally" told how unrealistic the plan was, writes Hultén, adding that in retrospect it seems perfectly reasonable.[28] Nothing came of the initiative, but the meeting led to Pontus Hultén, who had already distinguished himself at Nationalmuseum, getting in touch with Otte Sköld and becoming part of his plans for the new "branch." Some time later he was commissioned by Folke Holmér, head of the modern department, to make a proposal for what a modern museum could contain and how it would function.[29]

After a period of reflection, Hultén writes, he came to the conclusion that the whole thing would be too abstract without a concrete building in mind. He decided to locate the museum at Liljevalchs gallery on the park island of Royal Djurgården. He notes that the Liljevalchs proposal was not particularly politically astute, as the gallery is owned by the City of Stockholm while Nationalmuseum is a state institution. "So it could appear as if I was proposing that the state should annex a municipal building."[30] Hultén explains that he outlined the project in all its parts: cutting out pictures of works of art that he thought should be included and inserting them into a model of the art gallery, which he submitted to Folke Holmér along with a theoretical text. "I have the impression that there was never any real discussion about the project," Hultén writes. "Nothing was heard from Folke Holmér or Otte Sköld. It was not until several years later that Nationalmuseum's collections were presented at Liljevalchs in preparation for the opening of Moderna Museet. And later, parts of Moderna Museet's collections were displayed there, in summer showings, so perhaps the idea was not entirely unrealistic."[31]

In his text in the museum's anniversary book from 1983, Hans Nordenström writes about something that Pontus Hultén does not mention — how in 1956[32] the friends used Liljevalchs as an experimental workshop for a future museum, with Hultén still a practicing artist, at the behest of the new director of the art gallery, the same Folke Holmér who had left Nationalmuseum. Here they created installations that foreshadowed two of Moderna Museet's most classic exhibitions. "In the late summer, Pontus, P. O. Ultvedt and I started building an exhibition at Liljevalchs gallery," Nordenström writes. "Tinguely, Öyvind Fahlström, Oscar Reutersvärd and Lars Rolf were also invited to participate. We used the art gallery as a workshop. The plan was to build large temporary structures on the site, open the exhibition in the fall and then demolish it. Ultvedt made a wooden machine that filled one of the high halls and Pontus and I built a hanging volume, a mesh collage. Tinguely contributed the large machine he built in the Blandaren studio. In addition, there was an extensive plan for moving and fixed devices that would invite visitors to participate. (...) The work was abandoned. The material was stored in a shed at Karlaplan square, but the ideas would later be developed in exhibitions such as Rörelse i konsten [*Art in Motion*] and HON."[33]

When Pontus Hultén joined Nationalmuseum's modern department, he became a colleague of his older classmate from Stockholm University College, Carlo Derkert, who had been hired in 1945. This gave a staff of three in total, including the head of the department, Bo Wennberg, who replaced Folke Holmér when he moved to Liljevalchs. The planning of the new modern museum was developed in this group, under the leadership of Otte Sköld. One is served with the impression of a plan that could be crafted under the political radar — as often with innovative initiatives the fruit of the efforts by a few committed individuals. Bureaucracy could be kept to a minimum. Otte Sköld had an energetic partner in Gunnar Wekje, chief architect of the State Construction Board.

In the mid-fifties, architect Per-Olof Olsson was commissioned to transform the old dilapidated Drill House into a museum for modern art. "Everyone involved in the Moderna Museum building was infected by Otte Sköld's and Gunnar Wekje's commitment to the issue," writes

Olsson in the museum's anniversary book from 1983. Otte Sköld is characterized by Olsson as "smooth, with the right connections." He praises the skill of Sköld and Wekje in negotiating access to the Drill House even before the Navy had evacuated. At the government ministry, the new museum enjoyed the dedicated support of the Minister of Ecclesiastical Affairs, Ragnar Edenman, even before he took office in 1957. On the whole, once the decision was made, the process of creating the museum seems to have advanced swiftly in the positive spirit typical of the development-optimistic fifties, when Sweden and Stockholm were imbued with a desire to break the isolation, tedium and boredom of the war and post-war period.

The money allocated at Nationalmuseum, around one million SEK, was not enough to fully transform the Drill House to suit the demands of the new museum. The architect Per Olof Olsson writes that Sköld and Wekje raised the remaining four hundred thousand needed to complete the building through state lottery funds.[34]

The old drill compounds were in poor condition after a century of military wear and tear. Repairs and reinforcements proved more expensive than expected. Plans to open the ceilings of the galleries for skylights were scrapped. The art had to make do with ceiling inlets from a few small lanterns combined with artificial ligtning fixtures — fluorescent tubes of various colors that cast light up to the ceiling and then back down mixed into the gallery. The museum's radical, groundbreaking style of flexible interior solutions was also motivated by limited financial resources, explains Per-Olof Olsson. Dividing the large exercise halls into smaller rooms would have been too costly. Instead, a solution with movable wall modules was designed, which, as Olsson writes, "corresponded well with our idea of what a museum for today's art should look like, exhibition galleries with the possibility of rapid changes and rearrangements, less solemn than the 19th century museum type." Olsson adds: "This outward-looking, propagandistic ambition became strongly dominant in the planning at the expense of more practical, less interesting needs. The office and storage facilities were deliberately underdimensioned in the hope that new premises would later be acquired in an extension or in existing buildings adjacent to the museum."[35]

Among the original ideas for the new museum were rollable screens with tightly hung art not exposed on the walls, which visitors could pull out themselves to see the artworks. I remember these huge screens myself. Per-Olof Olsson writes that the solution was a feature that was appreciated by the audience but that the screens unfortunately wore down after a few years and could not be repaired until the renovation in the seventies. Pontus Hultén would try this idea, which was part of his utopian vision of the maximum accessibility of art, several times later in his career, each time with the same disappointing practical results.

Per-Olof Olsson further notes that the most drastic of the old Moderna Museet's logistical solutions, the entrance leading directly into the museum's main gallery, without a cloakroom or other obstacles, was "a successful if somewhat impractical approach."[36] The experience of stepping from the open air straight into the midst of the radical art enthralled and disarmed the visitor. Many spectators' skepticism about modern art was instantly overcome in this abruptly surprising encounter, as Olsson reflects.[37] This immediacy in the encounter between the street and the art was an ideal that Pontus Hultén would continue to strive for throughout his career, but never again achieve as impactfully as at Moderna Museet.

The inauguration of Moderna Museet was scheduled for 1958. The museum's magical timing, luck and savvy continued when, during the renovation of the Drill House in 1956, the management learned that Picasso's monumental canvas "Guernica," together with the ninety-three sketches that accompanied the painting, was touring Europe. I have no evidence but I believe I can trace Pontus Hultén's spirit in the decision to seize the opportunity when it arose, despite what seemed like insurmountable difficulties; in the radicalism of simply halting construction to display the seven-and-a-half meter long canvas hanging from a self-made frame amidst scaffolding and tarpaulins, which, as Hultén himself relates, created a dramatic and congenial setting for Picasso's powerful anti-war monument.[38]

Hultén's influence over this brazen false start for Moderna Museet is confirmed by the fact that he and Bo Wennberg designed the exhibition in collaboration with Per-Olof Olsson.[39] Hultén and Wennberg were commissioned by Nationalmuseum to produce the simple catalog. It is indeed Pontus Hultén, unmistakable with his round glasses glinting in the darkness of the railway car, who, together with a carrier bell boy in a gilded peaked cap, retrieves "Guernica" rolled up in its wooden box from the railway carriage at Norra Station[40] in the fabulous pictures that I myself had the pleasure of finding in the Moderna Museet picture archive during my inventory for the museum's fiftieth

Pp. 87, 88–89: Pablo Picasso, "Guernica", Moderna Museet, 1956.

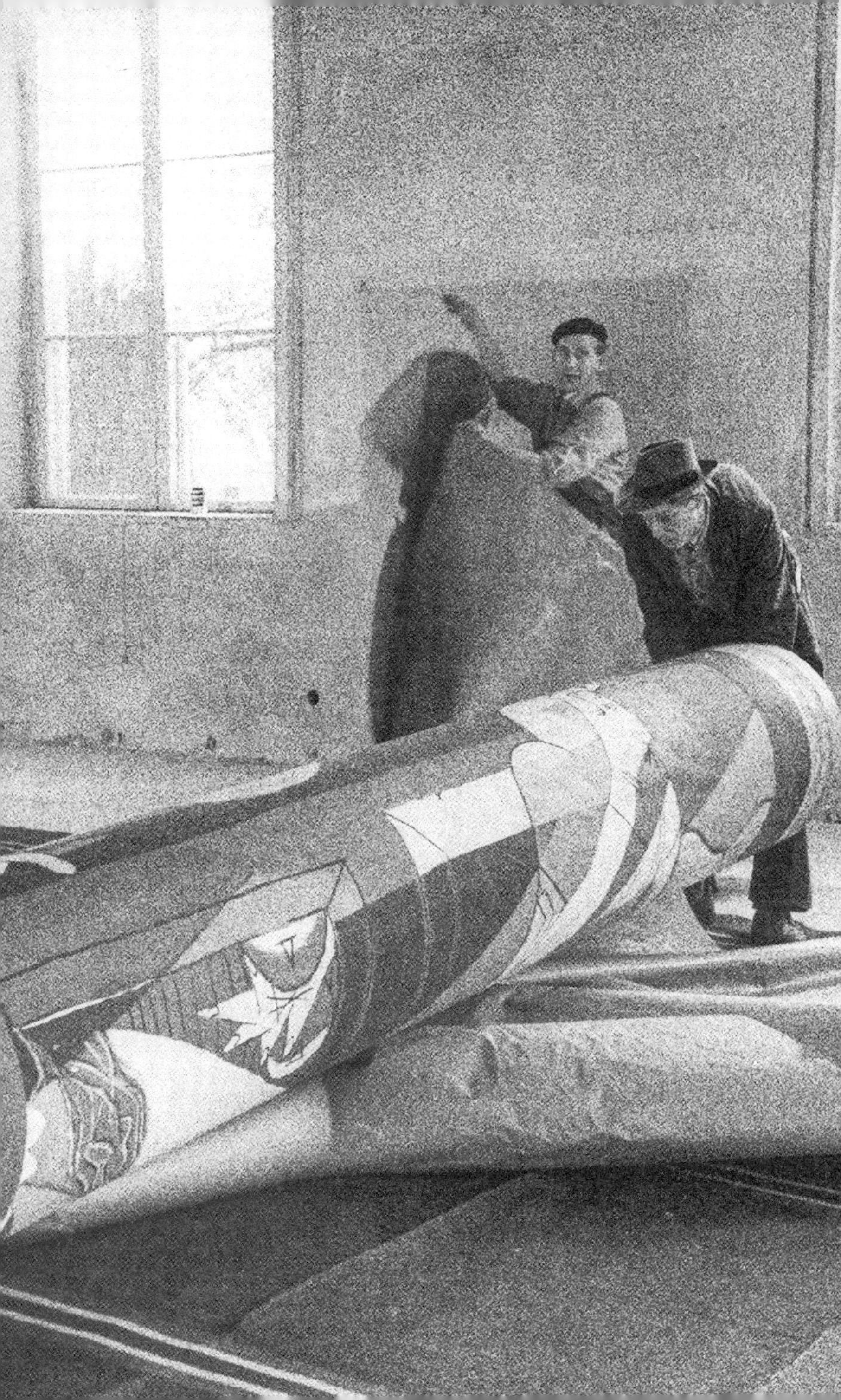

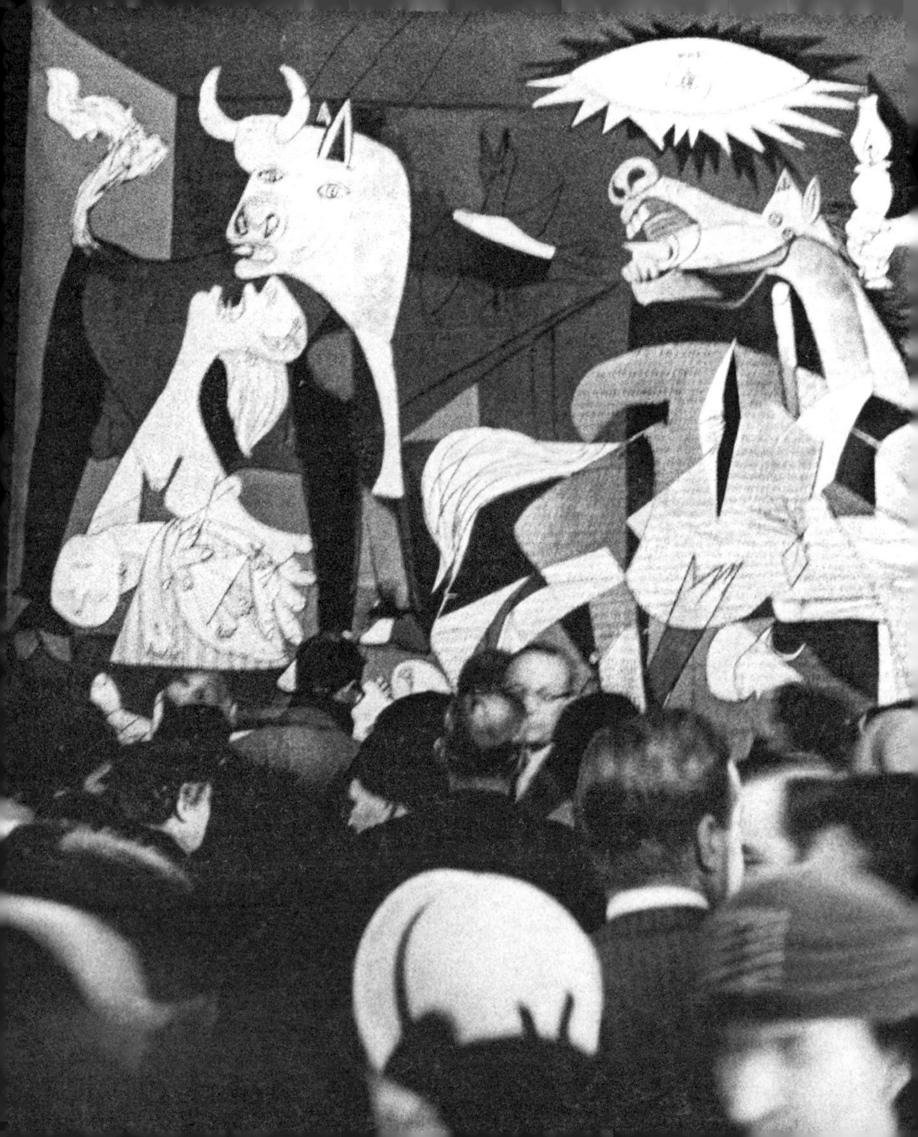

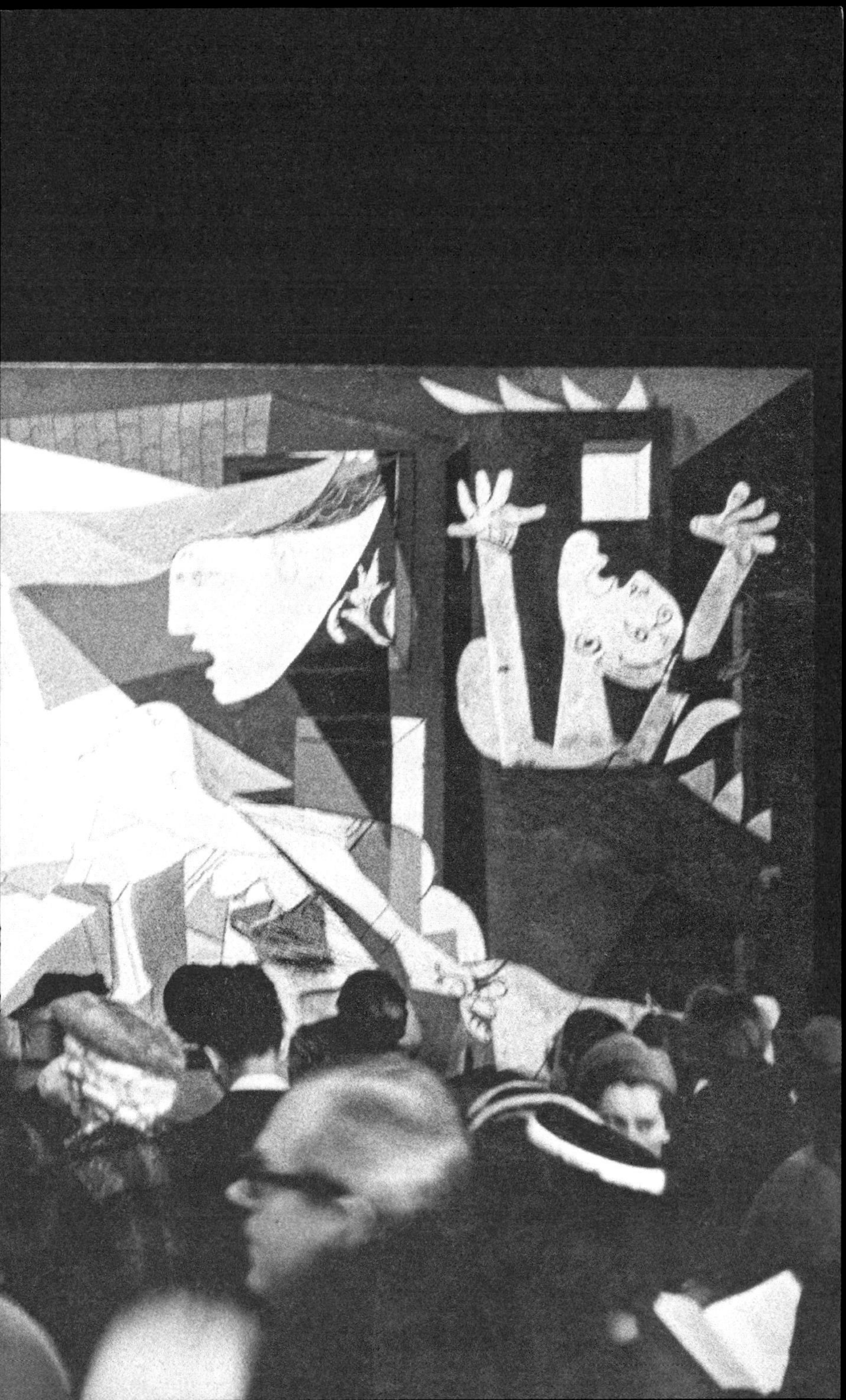

anniversary book.[41] When I interviewed Hultén in 1996, he used "Guernica" as an example of how simple and unbureaucratic the art world of that time worked: "We picked up the painting in a box at Norra Station and threw in in the back of a lorry and that was it. I remember being disappointed at how small the box was."[42]

The *Guernica* exhibition at the construction site in the Drill House on Skeppsholmen caught Stockholmers off guard. In his text in the anniversary book from 1983, Öyvind Fahlström remembers: "The first time I came to Moderna Museet was in 1956 and they had just moved into a naval exercise house from the early 19th century. Two halls, the size of airplane hangars. In the first, you were led through a labyrinth of brown burlap walls, you understood nothing. Then suddenly you were faced with Picasso's 'Guernica,' large and gray-white, filling the short side of the hangar."[43]

Large crowds wandered out to the future museum, which instantaneously established itself in the minds of the capital's cultural audience and even in the wider public. Pontus Hultén writes that especially the new media, television, and Dagens Nyheter, the leading daily, were most sympathetic and positive to the event. The newspapers reported almost daily, in the spirit of curiosity and optimism of the time. "It was an tremendous opportunity to introduce the museum before it existed," writes Hultén.[44]

Pontus Hultén notes that a list of the fortunate decisions from the time of the museum's inception must include its name: "The unbureaucratic, slightly aggressive tone that the two words Moderna Museet (The Modern Museum) set had long been the informal name of the project in the press, but how easy it would have been to lump the name with some 'clarification' or addition. At the opening of the museum, the name sat in stainless steel letters above the entrance door."[45]

To me, it seems characteristic of Pontus Hultén that he understood the significance of what many would dismiss as a detail: nuances in the wording of the name itself. Moderna Museet is a Dadaist name in that it appears at first glance to be official, but on closer inspection, with its definite singular form, becomes something else, "slightly aggressive" and provocative.

Moderna Museet was inaugurated on May 9, 1958, a sunny and beautiful spring day, by King Gustaf VI Adolf, with a long series of speeches initiated by Otte Sköld. Pontus Hultén writes that the spirit of optimism and joy that prevailed at the time around the opening was, for his part, somewhat disturbed by the continued series of ceremonial speeches during the ensuing gala dinner in the Grand Hôtel's marble hall. He mentions the artist Sven Erixson, "Xet," Otte Sköld's old friend and colleague, who "gave a speech that could confuse the most inaugurated, we actually didn't know that what we had created was intended to be a museum for Swedish art of the thirties."[46] The younger staff, Hultén continues, "that is, myself," didn't care much anyway, "because no one really understood what was said, and it soon turned out that what threatened the new museum more than nationalist activism or complicated art-political manipulations was lack of staff, lack of funds, indifference and forgetfulness."[47] Hultén recounts that during the ceremonial speeches, threats were made to eventually take back the older art from the new museum to Nationalmuseum, as the artworks reached classic status. This, he writes, "was of course part of the creation of a system of dependence, which was partly psychological, partly economic, partly practical. But despite this dependence, the general indifference of the slumbering Swedish art world was probably the greatest threat."[48]

For my inner view, I can clearly picture the scenes from the opening ceremonies of Moderna Museet, with solemnly dressed artists and bureaucrats of the old tribe believing that they had created a branch as an extension of their territory, blissfully unaware that they had in fact given life to an entirely new kind of institution that would soon eclipse them and the National Museum itself, helmed by the soon-to-be thirty-four-year-old man who listened to these gala speeches with a plan for this new museum radically different from anything these folks could have envisioned in their wildest fantasies.

Pontus Hultén goes on to write about an important "specialty" for the newly opened museum: something as priceless as the faithful regular audience that existed from the outset in the museum's film club.[49] As we know, Hultén had a passionate interest in film since his adolescence, an art form that he emphasized as equal to painting and sculpture, with his own background as an experimental filmmaker.[50] He had been active since the mid-fifties in the Stockholm Film Club, and before that in the students' film club. The Stockholm Film Club had shown non-commercial films in various venues during the 1950s, including at the Terrassen cinema on Birger Jarlsgatan[51] and at Skandia on Kungsgatan. The club, with several thousand mostly active members, now became the Moderna Museet Film Club.[52] This group formed, as Pontus Hultén phrases it, a core of Stockholm's most energetic, vocal and influential cultural audience, starved of new impressions.[53] The new museum had also entered into a partnership with the experimental music association Fylkingen, led by its chairman, the Norwegian-Swedish composer Knut Wiggen. This further expanded the museum's core audience.

The idea that Moderna Museet would become something much more than an art museum — an unprecedented multimedia cultural center for film, music, dance, design, architecture and other creative expressions, and a meeting place for socializing and partying, all with art as the unifying force — seems to have been clear to Pontus Hultén from the outset. It's unlikely that Nationalmuseum's management was aware of this plan. The parent museum was a traditional institution where service outlets such as a café or a shop were unthinkable distractions. Nothing would be allowed to interfere with the sacrosanct contemplation of art. In my interview in 1996, Pontus Hultén told me that on one occasion before Moderna Museet was established, he had suggested to his superiors at Nationalmuseum that they arrange a film screening, but was told: "Film? But that's for chambermaids!" Otte Sköld's initiative with an exhibition of Dadaist Viking Eggeling in 1950, where the artist's films were also shown, had been a controversial exception.[54]

Already during *Guernica*, Moderna Museet began its work with film as part of the museum's program, in "dialog" with the visual arts, as the museum's representatives emphasized. Among other features, a series of films by Luis Buñuel, the Spanish Surrealist who was and remained an idol for Hultén, were shown. He expressed a controversial opinion at the time when he wrote that Buñuel "is in many ways Picasso's equal," and that "The purpose of the screenings is to present to the public the two greatest Spanish artists, Picasso and Buñuel, in a single context, and to take advantage of the opportunities for deeper understanding of both works that this confrontation can provide."[55]

It was thus no coincidence that the first international event organized at the new Moderna Museet during its opening year in 1958 was the film series, or "film festival" as it was called, *Apropå Eggeling* (*Apropos Eggeling*), named after the same Viking Eggeling, the artist and filmmaker, our Swedish Dadaist.[56] With its program, which also included art and music, the series, organized in collaboration with Fylkingen, offered a foretaste of the many multicultural happenings and events that would be staged at the museum throughout the sixties. That Pontus Hultén, who was obviously the organizer even though he was not yet formally the director of the museum, would open with an element of Dada seems inevitable. For the "film festival," Hultén produced his first catalog for the new museum, if we exclude the small brochure for *Guernica* — an art form in itself, which he would develop to mastery.

Pontus Hultén writes that the lack of resources, and the new museum's unchartered fundamental situation, provided considerable freedom.[57] Expectations were low. These were good conditions for taking the establishment "with its pants down,"[58] presenting it with a fait accompli. At the opening, the staff referred to by Pontus Hultén consisted of a total of four people — himself, the head of the department Bo Wennberg (in practice the director of the museum), the secretary Kerstin Stenberg, and the Nationalmuseum's chief janitor Sture Johansson. In the fall of 1958, Carlo Derkert was transferred from Nationalmuseum, which Hultén notes was an important addition.[59]

Otte Sköld had long kept secret that he was suffering from cancer. Pontus Hultén claims in his text in the anniversary book that the work with the opening of the museum took a toll on Sköld's diminished strength and that he couldn't fight the disease any longer.[60] He fell ill during the autumn and died on November 7 after seeing his life's work completed.

Pontus Hultén was entrusted with the honorary task of organizing Sköld's memorial exhibition. He writes: "It was the first major retrospective exhibition I got to work on and I think I learned a lot from devoting myself exclusively to Otte Sköld's paintings for a few months. I think the exhibition was a beautiful tribute to his very multifaceted art."

Sköld was replaced as director at the Nationalmuseum by Carl Nordenfalk, a classically educated art historian, expert in Chinese antiquities, and former head of the painting department.[61] Nordenfalk is portrayed by people in art circles of the time as an aristocratic, rigid and formal executive of the old school. He was a financially independent nobleman who lived in a stately apartment on Karlaplan square full of art and antiques. I've learned from a later descendant[62] that in his own family, Nordenfalk was not regarded in this way at all, but rather as a slightly eccentric intellectual and bookish scholar, uninterested in hunting and other pastimes popular among aristocrats. It's been claimed that Pontus Hultén and Carl Nordenfalk disliked and distrusted each other. Hultén has made several statements that can be interpreted in this way, including in the anniversary book.[63] Their relationship appears to have been more complex. Pontus Hultén also writes positively about his new boss in his texts.

Moderna Museet opened with the optimistic tailwinds of the time in its back. The curiosity among the Stockholmers was great, attendance good. Initially, the museum displayed the Nationalmuseum's own "rather poor" modern collection, as Pontus Hultén objectively rated it.[64] It was decided that the museum would also produce temporary exhibitions, but no money was allocated for this purpose. Apart from the film series *Apropå Eggeling*, a retrospective of Le Corbusier's[65] architecture, paintings, sculptures, tapestries and drawings, produced by a Swiss architectural firm, was the only international presentation during the museum's opening year of 1958.[66]

Le Corbusier, who was Swiss, had previously, at least in France, been admired as the great leader not only of architecture but of Modernism as a whole. By this time, his star had begun to wane, his ideals questioned in progressive art circles. Hultén writes that there was concern among the museum staff that Le Corbusier would be conservative and difficult to deal with[67] (though this was long before Le Corbusier was posthumously accused of anti-Semitism and fascist sympathies). The architectural pioneer had been lured to the opening with a fine royal medal, like so many celebrities who have been enticed to Stockholm flattered by royalty and the Nobel Prize aura over the years. Once arrived for the opening on August 29, 1958, Le Corbusier, impeccably dressed in his trademark dark pinstripe suit and bow tie, surprised everyone with his boldness and humor. A popular anecdote bears repeating. By this time, the Navy had, apparently reluctantly, evacuated the Drill House, but remained in other facilities at the old naval station. In the midst of the press conference, a deafening machine gun volley erupted, shocking the journalists. The regiment was holding a shooting exercise in the courtyard outside (the officers reportedly took pride in disrupting the activities of the "art Bolsheviks"). Only Le Corbusier remained unmoved, dryly commenting when the gunfire ceased: "No alarm. It's just the museum management shooting some bad artists."[68]

The Le Corbusier exhibition was a success, attracting over fifteen thousand visitors to the new museum — a surprisingly good figure for the time. Together with the film festival *Apropå Eggeling*, the exhibition gave the museum an international flair in what was otherwise initially a program dominated by the Swedish and the Nordic, in line with the more limited ambition that the National Museum seems to have harbored for its new branch. Pontus Hultén writes that Carl Nordenfalk, as the newly appointed superintendent of the National Museum, wanted to be involved in the management of Moderna Museet as well, and that the result of Nordenfalk's involvement, and by implication Bo Wennberg's weak leadership, was a series of "curious compromises."[69] Bo Wennberg, de facto director of Moderna Museet at the time of its opening (no director had been appointed as the museum was still formally part of the National Museum), is portrayed as a kind and friendly person, knowledgeable about art but as a manager weak, inept and provincial. It's said that Wennberg went by the name of "Blindberg" and that he was conspicuous by his absence. He is said to have kept a pair of shoes and an extra jacket in his office to give the impression of being out only temporarily ...[70]

Studying the provincial program from Moderna Museet's opening year, one gets a picture of what this new institution, or branch, would certainly have become under the leadership of men like Carl Nordenfalk and Bo Wennberg — a development that would have been considered normal, what could have been expected.[71]

From the following excerpt from Otte Sköld's academy speech of May 31, 1956, we can conclude that the founder of Moderna Museet was also a traditionalist: "I need only mention the words color organ, objet trouvé, mobiles and moving paintings drawn by electric motors and many other amusing things. It is of course perfectly legitimate to play experimentally and seek aesthetic effects in new forms and materials, but the aesthetically pleasing should not be easily confused with art that has, dare I say it, a higher purpose."

In the fall of 1959, Pontus Hultén conducted two journeys that would prove decisive, for his own career and for Moderna Museet. The first of these went to Paris in the company of Carl Nordenfalk. The purpose was to visit leading art dealers in the art world capital. Hultén writes in the anniversary publication that "in Nordenfalk's opinion, these people held the secrets of the future of art."[72] He goes on to state that what proved more important was that from these dealers, they were able to extract knowledge of where available important works from historical Modernism could be found and, moreover, what they should cost. Pontus Hultén was acutely aware of the urgency of expanding and strengthening the museum's "rather poor" collection. Masterpieces of classical Modernism were still available on the market. Hultén had understood early on that even if the prices of these works appeared high, they would seem as bargains once the major art nations and their museums finally emerged from the post-war lull, which hadn't yet happened at this time.

An important meeting in Paris for Pontus Hultén and Carl Nordenfalk was with Roberto Matta, the Chilean late Surrealist painter, also named Sebastian, often referred to simply as Matta. Matta was born in Santiago and trained as an architect and interior designer in his home country before traveling and devoting himself to Surrealist drawing. In his mid-thirties, he came to Paris where he became good friends with artists such as Le Corbusier, Salvador Dalí and René Magritte, as well as with Surrealist leader André Breton, for whom Matta became a favorite. Hultén's interest in Matta was likely influenced by the artist's close friendship with Marcel Duchamp, also a clear inspiration in Matta's idiosyncratic, politically radical form of Surrealism. Pontus Hultén met Roberto Matta as early as 1954 in Paris, where he was then living with his fourth wife, Malitte (née Pope), seventeen years his junior. The Mattas' home on Boulevard Saint Germain was a well-known locus for the Parisian avant-garde, where Pontus Hultén was a frequent guest. "We knew Pontus very well from way back," says Malitte Matta.[73] "We got to know him through Öyvind Fahlström, who was very good friends with Matta. We liked Öyvind a lot. He always borrowed Matta's studio when he was here in Paris. Nordenfalk was also a nice man, not as rigid as some people thought."[74]

Pontus Hultén writes sarcastically that Carl Nordenfalk — who himself had a background and contacts in Paris, in traditional academic art circles — was so excited that they immediately agreed to organize a solo exhibition of Matta's art, his first in Europe. So frivolous was Nordenfalk's mind, according to Hultén, that he allowed himself to be persuaded to select Matta's largest monumental canvases, fifteen in all.[75] *Sebastian Matta. 15 Forms of Doubt*, opened on October 24, 1959,[76] just a few months after Hultén and Nordenfalk's visit to Paris, was Moderna Museet's first major self-produced international show. The exhibition was well received by the press and became another box office success for the young museum.

Carl Nordenfalk's memoirs[77] and other information give the impression that it was during the trip to Paris that he became convinced that Pontus Hultén, and no one else, was the future director of Moderna Museet. Nordenfalk chronicles how Bo Wennberg was promoted to make room for Hultén: "Actually, I would have preferred to keep them both. However, Hultén declared himself unwilling to continue under Wennberg's leadership. As I was reluctant to see him go, I made a decision that would be highly decisive for the future of Moderna Museet and would also have major repercussions on my continuing life as museum director. In the end, Hultén was the person I most wanted to see as leader of Moderna Museet. With this in mind, I wrote to Wennberg, who was on a long study trip in the United States, and informed him that it was not so sure that he could count on a permanent appointment as director of Moderna Museet (...) I therefore wondered whether he would not rather take over my old position as head of the classic painting department, which had now become vacant. I also thought that if he agreed, his acknowledged skill as an exhibition organizer and painting hanger would be of great benefit to the old National Museum."

Nordenfalk continues: "I had probably expected greater resistance to my proposal from him, dedicated to modern art as he was. But in his reply he accepted without discussion. He later gave me to understand that he thought it was at the request of the Ministry that I had acted as I did. But that was by no means the case; the initiative was entirely my own. I felt that I had made a good choice, even though at the time I could not foresee that within a few years Hultén would emerge as the brightest star of the Swedish, and soon enough the international, museum world."[78]

It's certainly poignant to read how Carl Nordenfalk writes Bo Wennberg out of art history while chivalrously praising his abilities as a "painting hanger." When Nordenfalk proclaims that this was a decision that would have great importance for the future of the museum, he's not exaggerating. It's characteristic of Hultén that, at such an early, decisive stage, when the goal towards which he had apparently been striving for several years was imminent, he didn't hesitate to put all this on one card by declaring to Carl Nordenfalk that he refused to continue with Wennberg as director.

Bo Wennberg's assumption that Pontus Hultén was appointed at the Ministry's request heralds recurring suspicion of Hultén for his good, and as often implied, overly friendly relations with the government and its officials. It's doubtless that the contacts, patronage and support that Pontus Hultén enjoyed from powerful social democrats not only facilitated but was a precondition for Moderna Museet to develop under his leadership into what it became, even though the same social democratic regime would also cause Hultén and the museum major problems.

Already here we can observe that, as the anarchist he always prided himself on being, the ability to interact with those in power high up in the hierarchies he claimed to despise must be included in the arsenal of talents that made Pontus Hultén the global art leader he became.

It was not until the beginning of 1960 that the bureaucratic obstacles were removed and Pontus Hultén was formally appointed as Moderna Museet's first director. Nordenfalk writes that Hultén "was given a six-year mandate as head of the museum."[79]

What Carl Nordenfalk subsequently reveals in his memoirs may well originate in yet another demand from Hultén. Nordenfalk writes that, according to Otte Sköld's suggestion, Pontus Hultén set up "an artists' committee for the purchase of living Swedish artists, one painter and one sculptor, each appointed for two years." Nordenfalk continues: "Otte Sköld had intended that the superintendent should have veto power, but I preferred to let the new purchasing committee act on its own responsibility as far as possible." This is an early example of how Pontus Hultén throughout his career had the habit of working once he had obtained a mandate from those in power on whom he was dependent: "Only when the museum director and the artist members had different opinions would I enter with a casting vote," Nordenfalk writes. "As Hultén worked from the very beginning to free the Moderna Museet from the Nationalmuseum, he made sure that the purchasing committee was always in agreement, so that I would never have to be consulted."[80]

Little more than a year after the inauguration of Moderna Museet, after having been employed at Nationalmuseum as late as 1957, Pontus Hultén had in practice not only succeeded in getting himself appointed as the new museum's first director (his official nomination as museum director was delayed until May 1, 1963, as Moderna Museet was still administratively a branch of Nationalmuseum), but also started to free his museum from the institution that trusted him with this position. These were bold achievements for a young man untested in institutional contexts, with merely a licentiate as an academic qualification, hardly impressive in the academic-based museum world of the time.

Throughout the years, and well into the writing of this story, I have wondered who it was in the Stockholm art establishment that had the courage and foresight to choose the young Hultén, unknown to all outside a small coterie, for this assignment, over all possible established candidates. It has always struck me as a remarkable choice. None of the many people I have asked over the years have been able answer who actually made the critical decision to employ Pontus Hultén — no more precisely than vague assumptions such as "it was probably Otte Sköld." Carl Nordenfalk's story is the clearest I have found of how this crucial selection process actually emerged.

Over time, my understanding has become clearer of how Pontus Hultén at the age of thirty-five had managed to get as far as having a national state museum at his disposal to realize his radical vision of art and its role in society. It's obvious that, although unknown to the public, he had built up a position as a leading figure within the younger group that would become the new museum's core audience. He simply knew the avant-garde art world better than anyone else and already anchored this knowledge in a deep learning of art as well as human history. It appears inevitable that Hultén would reach a position at the new museum. The actuality that he would soon be granted almost absolute power over this institution, nevertheless, remains a bold decision and it was apparently taken by Carl Nordenfalk. Allow me a wild speculation of my own. I wonder if Nordenfalk's aristocratic upper-class background may have made it easier for him to appreciate Pontus Hultén. I have seen other examples, also in this story, of similar kinds of aristocratic or otherwise elevated power holders who have had the confidence to allow reign to strong, controversial players of a kind that intimidate many less confident superiors. Pontus Hultén was without any doubt such an imposing, contentious figure, with his renowned almost brutal physical presence, which alone frightened many.

Another matter is that Hultén had not yet played his hand when he seized control of the new museum, as you may see it. If the power officials in the art establishment of the day had sported the faintest idea of what he and his colleagues were about to create, they would never have allowed him to come to the fore, of this I am fully convinced. My impression is that there was an element of the famous Trojan horse in Pontus Hultén's strategy to get to the helm of this new ship, and I believe that the naval analogy is justified for the sailor and captain that Pontus Hultén was and liked to see himself as: Pontus the seafarer.

6 The New York Connection

The second trip on which Pontus Hultén embarked in the fall of 1959, of even greater importance for the future of the museum and his own career, was his first visit to New York.

This art-historical North American visit was in fact a stop on a trip home from São Paulo, where Hultén had organized the exhibition in the Swedish pavilion at the biennial, funded by the Swedish Institute. As Hultén notes, the initiative was part of the institute's recurring attempt to market Swedish art internationally,[1] with a larger selection of contemporary Swedish artists, including Öyvind Fahlström, who was enthusiastic about exhibiting in what was actually his birthplace.[2] The fact that Pontus Hultén had been appointed commissioner, or "inspector" as the position was called, for this official Swedish appearance is another testament to the position that, despite his weak formal credentials, he had already established for himself even before he was appointed director of Moderna Museet.

Öyvind Fahlström was born in 1928 in São Paulo to Swedish-Norwegian parents. His mother was a Swedish gymnastics instructor, his father a Norwegian businessman and translator living in São Paulo. As their only child, Fahlström lived in Brazil until he was ten years old, when he was sent to visit his aunt and grandfather in Stockholm. The war intervened and Fahlström stayed behind in Sweden.

After the opening of the exhibition in São Paulo on September 21, 1959, Pontus Hultén took the opportunity to travel to New York where he stayed for almost a month. He also visited Harvard, Yale, Connecticut, Washington and of course Philadelphia, where most of Marcel Duchamp's most important works are collected. This was five years before the European art world really took notice of New York and the American metropolis quickly and unexpectedly replaced Paris as the art capital of the world. This only happened after Robert Rauschenberg was sensationally awarded the Gran Premi, the Grand Prize, at the 1964 Venice Biennale, a shock that changed the balance of power in the art world.

In the late 1950s, exchanges between New York and Europe were still sparse. Suspicion of the United States was rampant in the European art world. The first the European public had ever seen of contemporary American art was an exhibition of Jackson Pollock and his generational peers that had toured Europe in 1958–59. The exhibition was organized by the Museum of Modern Art in New York, in collaboration with three progressive European institutions with which Moderna Museet would later collaborate: Stedelijk in Amsterdam under its legendary director Willem Sandberg, Bern Kunsthalle under Arnold Rüdlinger, and Le Palais des Beaux-Arts in Brussels under Robert Giron. These three pioneers of the post-war art world were the only European museum directors who, before Hultén, had made the effort to travel to New York to experience the city's contemporary art scene first-hand.[3]

Pontus Hultén himself revealed that he had no idea of the new art that was developing in New York, although he had met Robert Rauschenberg and Jasper Johns in Paris, in the entourage around Yves Klein, Jean Tinguely and Iris Clert.[4] The reason he stopped in New York was to see the older generation of Abstract Expressionists, the big names of which were Jackson Pollock, Willem de Kooning, Mark Rothko, Franz Kline, Clyfford Still and Sam Francis, the latter being something of an outsider in the group as he came from Los Angeles, although he was living in New York at the time.[5] Despite Francis being one of Hultén's best friends, this heroically masculine, deadly serious, large-scale bombastic abstract style of painting was an art movement that was never one of Pontus Hultén's passions, although he made many attempts to approach it.[6]

Instead, Hultén to his surprise discovered what he has often proclaimed that he immediately recognized as a new focal point in the international art world: the emerging American Pop Art scene.[7] Hultén has also frequently depicted the revelation that the city of New York imposed on him: how he was positively shocked and inspired by the city's aggressive energy and vitality.[8] Despite these strong impressions, neither

In the early years, Hultén exhibited Jackson Pollock, in addition to Sam Francis (1960), at Moderna Museet, in 1963. However, his skepticism towards Abstract Expressionism is widely known. Among other testaments of this reluctance, he is said to have opposed the purchase of works by Willem de Kooning for *The Museum of Wishes* in 1964.

New York nor the United States would ever become true loves for Hultén. He remained European in nature and temperament, keeping Paris as the city closest to his heart alongside his native Stockholm, although in a broader international consciousness he has come to be associated with New York art.

West of the city, in New Jersey, at this time lived Billy Klüver, Pontus Hultén's friend from the student film club in Stockholm, who had moved there in 1954. Klüver had already made his mark as an engineer in Paris, where he had been involved in spectacular projects such as installing a television antenna at the top of the Eiffel Tower and developing underwater cameras for oceanographer Jacques-Yves Cousteau's expeditions. In Paris, Klüver had acted as a contact for the Stockholm Film Club. After a brief interlude in Stockholm, Klüver and his first German-born wife Hill Geber moved to the United States, where Klüver earned a record-breaking doctorate at the prestigious University of California at Berkeley. The couple now lived in Murray Hill, New Jersey, where Billy had been employed at Bell Laboratories, then the world's leading electronics research industry. For many years Klüver would serve, more or less unsalaried, Moderna Museet as its New York liaison, making invaluable contributions to the museum. He would become an important player in the American Pop Art movement.

It's unclear how well Billy Klüver knew Robert Rauschenberg and Jasper Johns at this time, in the fall of 1959.[9] It's more likely that Pontus Hultén's link to these two future stars and to the New York avant-garde art scene was Öyvind Fahlström.

Fahlström was long our most internationally renowned Swedish modern artist, if we disregard Claes Oldenburg, who although he was born in Stockholm must be considered an American artist — until the overlooked Hilma af Klint became a world sensation and emerged as perhaps the greatest figure in Swedish modern art. In the international museum world, Fahlström has been deemed as somewhat too inaccessible to reach a wider audience.[10] However, he has always been an artist's artist, highly respected around the world. Fahlström was close personal

Jasper Johns writes himself: "I don't remember how I met Pontus. He was friendly with a group of people in New York who were my friends, including Billy Klüver and Öyvind Fahlström, and in Europe with the Duchamps, St. Phalle and Tinguely. He was director of the Centre Pompidou when they showed an exhibition of my work in 1978. He sometimes stayed in my apartment when he visited New York. We remained friends, and saw each other from time to time, until the end of his life." (Jasper Johns, e-mail, October 2, 2014) friends with most of the leading avant-garde artists in both Paris and in New York, where he moved in the early 1960s.

Although Fahlström may have been the contact link, Billy Klüver quickly became well known in these circles. During his visit, Pontus Hultén stayed with Klüver in Murray Hill. Taking a hotel was not an option with the museum's minimal budget. Each morning, Klüver drove him into Manhattan in his small car, a convertible, where Hultén visited artists' studios and exhibitions throughout the day. After his day at Bell Laboratories, Billy Klüver returned with his car. The two had dinner and partied with the artists until early morning, when they drove back to New Jersey.[11] Alcohol controls were not a concern in the United States in the 1950s.

At the time, Robert Rauschenberg and Jasper Johns were a couple living and working together in Manhattan's then rough and dilapidated blue-collar Lower East Side, where they rented two full floors at the top of a condemned, now demolished building on Pearl Street for housing and a studio each.

Robert Rauschenberg had left his home and fundamentalist Christian parents in Texas at a young age to eventually attend the seminal art school Black Mountain College in North Carolina during its heyday in the late 1940s and early 1950s. Here he had met John Cage, the experimental composer and sound artist, and Merce Cunningham, the dancer and choreographer, both of whom had been on the school's staff of visiting teachers in various disciplines.

Black Mountain College can be considered an American offshoot of the Bauhaus in Weimar. The school was founded in 1933, the same year that the artist couple Anni and Josef Albers arrived as teachers fleeing Germany after the Nazi regime closed the Bauhaus school (which had moved to Dessau and then to Berlin). During its twenty-four-year existence, Black Mountain College made its mark on modern American cultural history. Like the Bauhaus, the remotely located school was founded on a free, non-hierarchical, transnational, interdisciplinary pedagogical concept. The faculty included artists, poets, directors, composers and designers, as well as scientists such as Albert Einstein, who served on the school's board for a time. Among Black Mountain College's many famous alumni are artists such as Rauschenberg's classmate, friend and lover Cy Twombly, John Chamberlain, Kenneth Noland, Robert de Niro Sr. (yes, father of Robert de Niro Jr.), poet Joel Oppenheimer, film director Arthur Penn and artist Susan Weil, Rauschenberg's then-girlfriend and later wife, with whom he enrolled.

Here, many creative constellations and ideas emerged that would influence American cultural life for a long time to come. At Black Mountain College, composer John Cage staged his first "happenings" in 1952, a term coined much later by Cage's student Allan Kaprow, in 1958.[12]

Jasper Johns grew up in Georgia. After high school he moved to New York where he first attended Parsons School of Design. After the Korean War, during which Johns was stationed in Japan, he returned to New York where he met Robert Rauschenberg in 1954. The two worked together on their art while earning their living decorating shop windows, most notably the famous luxury women's fashion store Bonwit Teller on 5th Avenue, which had commissioned Salvador Dalí to design its windows in 1929. Like Andy Warhol, who was originally an art director, graphic designer and also a window dresser, both Johns and Rauschenberg were well acquainted with the medium of commercial art and advertising — an important component in their art as well as in Warhol's and other Pop artists'.

At the time of Pontus Hultén's first visit to New York, Rauschenberg and John were neighbors and close associates of John Cage and Merce Cunningham. This quartet and their clique of other artists, musicians, dancers and performers on the Lower East Side were spearheading the New York avant-garde at the time. Hultén, along with Billy Klüver, had the good fortune to meet and befriend them in the years before Rauschenberg, Johns, and eventually the entire Pop Art group experienced their international breakthroughs. The personal connections within this coterie have never been entirely official but are worth noting, as the group constituted a creative subculture to itself. When I asked their colleague Claes Oldenburg about his relationship with Rauschenberg, Johns and their group, Oldenburg replied briefly: "Those guys were all homosexuals."[13] (The reticence about the gay element in the group is not surprising — same-sex sexuality was only officially legal in New York in 1980 and in the whole of the United Sates as late as 2003).

While Oldenburg was one of the Pop artists — although he himself, like many of the group's members, dislikes the term[14] — a distinction is made between them and their predecessors Rauschenberg and Johns, who form a two-man movement referred to by art historians as Neo-Dadaism. The influence of Dada is palpable, in some people's view bordering on plagiarism. Jasper John's idol was Marcel Duchamp while Rauschenberg in his collages and Combines (his combinations of paintings and sculptures of which Moderna Museet's "Monogram" goat is the most famous) leans heavily on Kurt Schwitters, the Dadaist one-man force from Hannover. Ulf Linde, among others, argued that Rauschenberg had borrowed too blatantly from Schwitters to be taken seriously as an artist.[15] Although this does not detract from the greatness of Rauschenberg's art, Linde's criticism must be acknowledged. It is indeed similar, not to say copied — but bigger, more powerful and brash than the original, like all New York art in relation to its European counterpart.

Pontus Hultén was at this time well acquainted with the corresponding movement to American Pop Art that was being contemporarily formed in Paris, Les Nouveaux Réalistes, the New Realists. There was also a similar group in London, including Richard Hamilton, Peter Blake, David Hockney and Eduardo Paolozzi, so we can speak of a global movement. The common features were many. It was about breaking down barriers between art and reality in the spirit of Duchamp and the Dadaists — uniting art and life, as Robert Rauschenberg's credo proclaimed. The art of the related movements incorporated everyday objects, advertising, graphics, consumer goods, film, celebrity cult, junk and rubbish. Here American art stood in a relationship to its European equivalent similar to that between a Cadillac and Citroën.

During his highly charged visit to New York in the fall of 1959, Pontus Hultén established contacts with a large number of artists, museum colleagues, dealers and other key players in the New York art world — a vast expansion of his professional network, and his horizons, that would shape the museum and his own career. The scene made such a strong impression on Hultén that, according to his own account, he immediately decided to stage exhibitions of the new generation of American artists at Moderna Museet.[16] During this first visit, however, he was looking for artists and works primarily for the first of the major thematic, multidisciplinary exhibitions that would make him famous and set a precedent in the art world: *Art in Motion*.

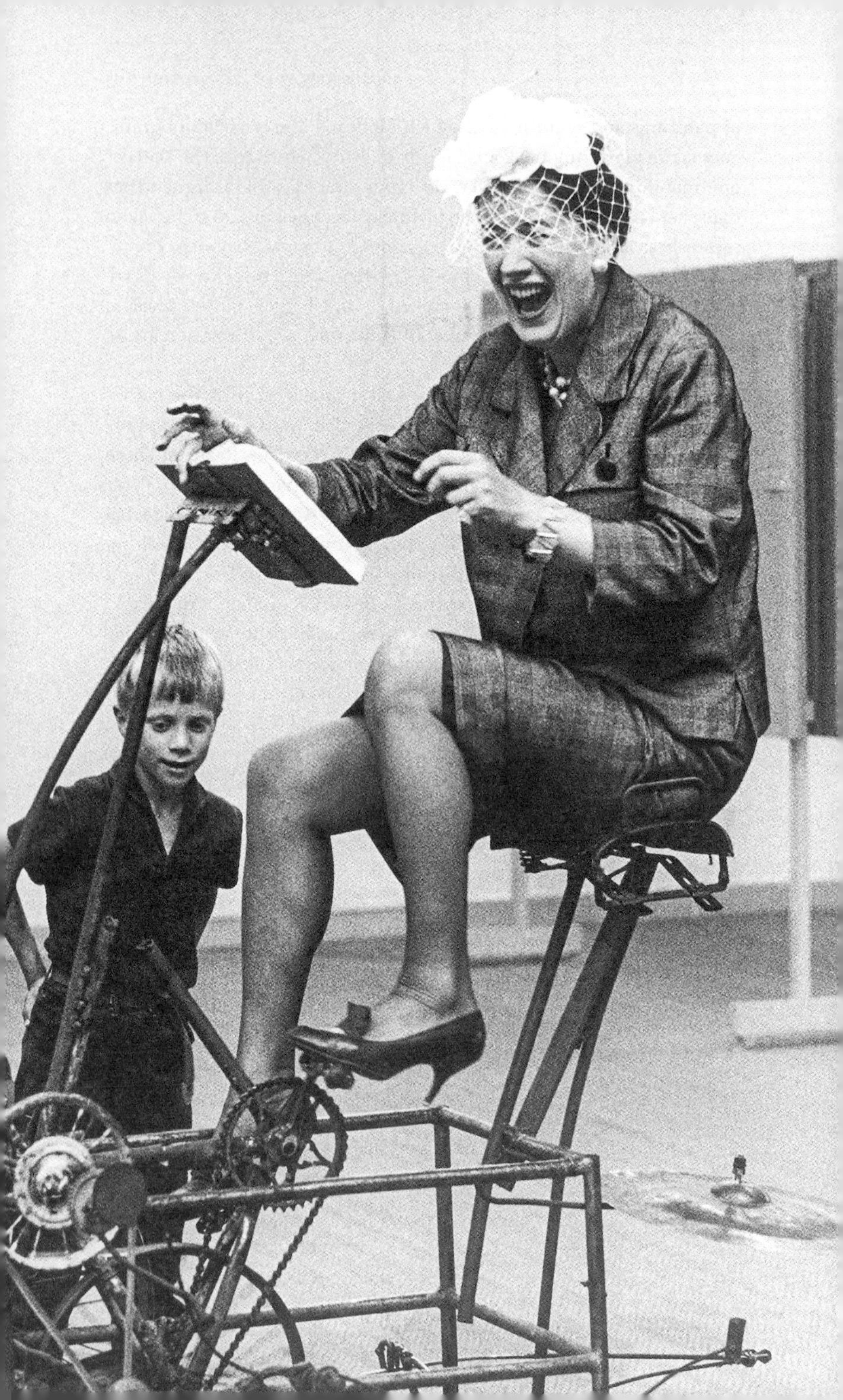

7 Towards Art in Motion

1960, the year in which Pontus Hultén was appointed the first director of Moderna Museet, was another year in which the museum's activities were initially characterized by compromise. Nationalmuseum and its new superintendent Carl Nordenfalk exercised influence over the choice of exhibition themes, which, according to Pontus Hultén, declined rapidly since the exhibitions initiated by the mother institution invariably failed to attract an audience.[2]

As the last exhibition in this spirit of compromise, Pontus Hultén names the retrospective with Jacques Villon, Marcel Duchamp's eldest brother, which opened on February 3, 1960.[3] Duchamp came from an upper middle class family in Rouen, Normandy, where all four siblings became artists. His two older brothers Jacques Villon and Raymond Duchamp-Villon were both famous Cubists. Contrary to his twelve years younger brother, Jacques Villon was a big name during his lifetime, but his reputation has declined since his death. Pontus Hultén writes: "Jacques Villon had long been the special fixation of the Swedish-French Art Gallery (...) and it felt strange to spend so much time on Jacques Villon. Especially when one knew so well that his art in the wake of Cubism was really quite insignificant, and when one suspected that his

Happy spectator on Jean Tinguely's sculpture "Le Cyclograveur" at *Art in Motion*, Moderna Museet 1961.

Marcel Duchamp's older brothers Jacques Villon and Raymond Duchamp-Villon are both considered founders of the so-called Puteaux Cubists, the third grouping of Cubism alongside the Montmartre and Montparnasse Cubists. Marcel Duchamp was a member of the group — also known as the Section d'Or (Golden Section) — which met mainly in 1911–1914 at Villons and Duchamp-Villon's home and studio in Puteaux on the outskirts of Paris. The group included Albert Gleizes, Jean Metzinger, Robert Delaunay, Fernand Léger and Marie Laurencin. The group caused a scandal with its exhibition at the Salon des Indépendants in 1911, where Cubism was presented to a wider audience for the first time.

brother Marcel Duchamp — whom I had organized an exhibition of at Bok-Konsum on Wallingatan a few years earlier — would probably become the most influential artist of the century."[4]

After the Villon concession, Pontus Hultén explains, the museum came to fulfill its main mission: to present hitherto unknown art to the Swedish public.[5] I find it interesting that two of the artists he chose to show as newly appointed museum director, and which he doesn't mention among the compromises he was forced to accept, were two older Swedish women. Siri Derkert, then aged seventy-two, mother of the museum's curator Carlo Derkert, was honored with a large and surprising retrospective.[6] According to Hultén, Derkert was unknown to a wider audience.[7] Most of the works in the exhibition were never previously shown. The exhibition gave Siri Derkert a late breakthrough and heralded her masterpiece in the design of the Östermalmstorg metro station.[8] In the fall, a retrospective of the Swedish-Finnish textile artist Anna Casparsson, ninety-nine years old at the time, was presented.[9]

Posterity, not least in female Swedish art circles, has often accused Pontus Hultén of being part of, or even a leading force behind, the crushingly male-dominated art world that, according to many, has distorted the true picture of art history. By and large, one must agree with these commentators. Pontus Hultén's younger colleague and later successor Olle Granath admits: "Pontus was probably guilty of it just like the rest of us. We were simply blind to that perspective. It seems incomprehensible today, but that's the way it was."[10] In view of this period's oblivion to the gender dilemma, the exceptions that Hultén and his colleagues nevertheless made in the homogeneously male program are worth noting. Hannah Ryggen (1962),[11] Sigrid Hjertén and Barbara Hepworth (both 1964)[12] were three more female inroads into the male domination of the early years.

The big exhibition for Pontus Hultén in 1960 was otherwise the one with his friend Sam Francis' monumental canvases, hanging on the walls and freely from the ceiling, in the first retrospective of the artist in Europe.[13] Francis' star has probably fallen somewhat, but at this time he was a big name in contemporary art circles. The exhibition is described as powerful and beautiful, with Francis' abstract paintings influenced, according to Hultén, by the perspective from which Francis saw the landscape as a fighter pilot during the Second World War — a typically Hulténian observation.[14]

In 1960, Moderna Museet began a tour of guest appearances at and from other museums in northern Europe, which was part of a conscious strategy to make the museum known, establish contacts and initiate collaborations for the future. The first to receive a visit from Moderna Museet was, appropriately, its "little sister" Louisiana in Denmark, founded as a private museum in 1958, the same year as Moderna, by the cheese wholesaler and art collector Knud W. Jensen. Louisiana and Hultén's good friend Jensen would become important partners with Moderna Museet throughout Pontus Hultén's era.

The Louisiana Museum of Modern Art, as the museum is known in English, was founded in 1958, the same year as Moderna Museet in Stockholm, by the Danish cheese wholesaler, art collector, publishing director and patron Knud W. Jensen, in his later expanded summer villa in Humlebaeck by the Öresund sound, thirty-five kilometers north of Copenhagen. Jensen took the museum's style-defining name from the villa's first owner, the officer Alexander Brun, who had the house built in 1855 and named it after his three wives, all with the first name Louise.

Yet 1960 was a year of preparation. Pontus Hultén and the rest of the museum's staff, which didn't yet number ten employees, were highly preoccupied with the first of Hultén's major art historical thematic exhibitions: *Art in Motion*. In fact, he had been working on this collective exhibition of Kinetic Art since 1954, when he met Jean Tinguely and began planning *Le Mouvement* at Galerie Denise René, to be regarded as *Art in Motion* in its first experimental incarnation. Hultén had since returned to his favorite theme in several already mentioned exhibitions. Now the time had come for his full-scale manifestation of moving art.

The scale and ambition of *Art in Motion* still fascinates today. Hultén traveled the art world in preparation. He made full use of the network of contacts that he had built up during his laboratory years, rapidly expanding this sphere in his capacity as museum director. The exhibition featured two hundred and thirty-three works by eighty artists from nineteen countries. Much of the art was created exclusively for the exhibition, including several works on-site in the museum. These facts and figures are mind-boggling given the minimal resources available in terms of staff, time and money. They become even more difficult to comprehend when you browse the museum's archives through stacks of telegrams and letters with instructions for insurance, boat transport, travel expenses and other logistics. Pontus Hultén himself handled correspondence on matters such as alleged damage in transportation, insurance premiums and airline ticket prices. Throughout this correspondence, Hultén, and occasionally Billy Klüver, reiterate that the museum lacks resources for any overhead costs beyond the absolute minimum.[15]

During the preparations for *Art in Motion*, a complication occurred which, due to the art historical dignity of the exhibition, requires some background.

I've already mentioned Daniel Spoerri. He is the Swiss ballet dancer who turned artist and brought Jean Tinguely and his then wife Eva Aeppli, with whom Spoerri according to his own account lived in a strange form of ménage à trois,[16] to Paris, where he moved from his hometown of Bern in Switzerland in 1950. Pontus Hultén and Spoerri got to know each other through Tinguely and began socializing in Paris in the mid-fifties. Over the years they would develop a more complicated relationship.

In addition to his dancing, acting and art, Daniel Spoerri was also active in the fifties as a curator, or organizer of exhibitions as it was then called, which would become a source of rivalry, triggered in the prelude to *Art in Motion*. Like Hultén, Spoerri idolized Marcel Duchamp and became personal friends with the master — another straining factor in Hultén's and Spoerri's relationship as I understand it. Yet another was that they both competed for the favor of Jean Tinguely. Their relationship did not become less intricate when Pontus Hultén later became the companion of Spoerri's former partner Marie-Louise von Plessen. To all this we must add the most sensitive of all: that Pontus Hultén was hardly a great admirer of Spoerri's art and chose to refrain from staging a solo exhibition with him.

In the spring of 1960, Pontus Hultén, as the newly appointed director of Moderna Museet, had arranged for Daniel Spoerri to show his portable exhibition *Édition MAT*[17] at Galleri Wallingatan 42 in Stockholm, an annex to the bookstore Bokkonsum, owned by the labor movement in the nearby headquarters of the nationwide labor union LO. The exhibition featured duplicated replicas of kinetic works by artists such as Dieter Roth, Josef Albers, kinetic pioneer Bruno Munari, Man Ray, Victor Vasarely, Pol Bury, Jesús Rafael Soto, Jean Tinguely and others, as well as Duchamp's "Rotoreliefs" mounted on stands designed by Tinguely.

A few weeks after the exhibition in Stockholm in the spring of 1960, Daniel Spoerri showed *Édition MAT* at the Museum of Decorative Arts in Zürich. On the occasion of the opening, Spoerri was invited to a reception where he met Willem Sandberg, the legendary director of the Stedelijk in Amsterdam, Europe's and the world's leading museum of cutting-edge modern art at the time. In the Stedelijk, Sandberg had created the first museum in Europe that was not content to passively display art but functioned as an open cultural center for various creative and even political expressions, with a radical program of exhibitions and events.

After being introduced to Sandberg by his host, Spoerri jumped at the chance and pitched his idea of staging a major exhibition at the Stedelijk on the theme of Kinetic Art. "By the time I got to Zürich, I had decided to quit *MAT*," Spoerri tells me when we meet at his home and studio in Vienna. "It became very laborious and expensive to travel around alone with the exhibition and I didn't sell anything, although the objects were very cheap. There were only one hundred and fifty people who understood what I was doing. The idea I presented to Sandberg was a dream we all had at the time to do the giant exhibition of Kinetic Art."[18]

Willem Sandberg asked Daniel Spoerri to write back with a presentation of his idea, which Spoerri did at the beginning of June 1960.[19] Spoerri discusses whether the exhibition should present a selection of real, historical machines alongside contemporary art. He gives examples of astronomical clocks, automata from Neuchatel that can play chess, Chinese dragons, perpetual motion machines, particularly beautiful mechanical devices from the nineteenth century, and early examples of machines such as the airplane, which Spoerri thinks resembles a giant bat.[20] In the end, he concludes that it is probably wiser to reject these ideas and focus on the present.

Art historian Andres Pardey, co-curator of the Museum Tinguely in Basel and colleague of Pontus Hultén during his time as founding director of the museum in the late 1990s, has written a study of the prestige struggle between Pontus Hultén and Daniel Spoerri over the copyright for *Art in Motion*, detailing the correspondence between the various parties involved.[21] Pardey notes that it is apparent from this first letter that Spoerri sees himself in the role of creator and inspirer of the exhibition, while Sandberg and Stedelijk are supposed to be responsible for the actual production.[22] Spoerri himself lacked experience of organizing exhibitions on a larger scale.

Daniel Spoerri did not receive a reply to his letter to Willem Sandberg. Two months later, he sent a postcard with what Andres Pardey calls an "indignant reminder."[23] This time he received an immediate reply from Sandberg in a letter dated August 15, in which he assures him that he wants to carry out the project together with Spoerri.[24] In his letter, Sandberg comments in detail on Spoerri's ideas about the exhibition. Spoerri tells me that he took the train to Amsterdam and was shown, with "horror-mixed delight," the eight large rooms that Sandberg had set aside for him to fill with his exhibition. On his return to Paris, he revealed the news about his visit to the Stedelijk to Jean Tinguely, who was thrilled at the prospect of having a whole room at his disposal.[25]

Matters became less cheerful when Tinguely passed on the news to Pontus Hultén. Spoerri says that Hultén was furious and declared that "you can't do that," whereupon he immediately traveled to Paris to talk some sense into his friends. Spoerri describes a charged meeting at La Méthode bar in the Latin Quarter. "Pontus was furious and said you absolutely can't do it in that boring museum," says Spoerri. "He said we have to be first in Stockholm. We have to do something revolutionary, something that explodes. He said that Stockholm must be blown up. But Tinguely knew that exhibiting at the Stedelijk, which was the number one museum in the world together with the Museum of Modern Art, would give a completely different credibility and publicity than exhibiting at a small shitty museum in Stockholm."[26]

It seems that Pontus Hultén contacted Willem Sandberg in connection with the above mentioned trip to Paris, claiming the copyright to the idea of a large exhibition of movement for himself and Moderna Museet. In a letter to Sandberg on August 28, Spoerri writes about Hultén's plans and about his intention to expose real working machines alongside art, "a Bugatti will be shown"[27] — the idea, alas, that Spoerri himself had discussed but rejected in his first letter to Willem Sandberg. Here Andres Pardey speculates that one can assume that Spoerri had discussed his idea with Tinguely and his confidant Hultén, and that Spoerri's and Hultén's visions for the exhibition had "drifted apart." He further notes that such an assumption still leaves unanswered the question of whose original idea it was — apart from *Le Mouvement* 1955, as Pardey appropriatelly adds.[28]

Whatever the case, the rivaling stakeholders seem to have soon negotiated a compromise solution. It appears likely that Tinguely, who had interests in both camps and was equally indispensable in each, may have acted as a mediator, advocating collaboration rather than confrontation. It was decided that the parties would co-produce the exhibition in both cities.

Already in his letter to Sandberg on August 28, Spoerri writes about the exhibition being divided into two parts, Amsterdam and Stockholm. The discussion subsequently focuses on where the exhibition should open first, and how the content should differ between the two cities. In a letter to Sandberg on October 4, Spoerri declares that he has "full authority" to "design the exhibition in Amsterdam."[29] Andres Pardey reflects that Spoerri's role is no longer limited to that of an inspirer, but that he now sees himself as the organizer and designer of the exhibition. Spoerri points out to Sandberg what distinguishes his exhibition from Hultén's: "the essence is that I don't see any point in weighing down the exhibition with toys, dolls, old cars and amusement park junk, because the whole thing can be much more powerful if it moves only under the name of art (...) this is a point on which I don't agree with hulten," Spoerri writes, like Sandberg without capitalization. He rejects the idea of showing a mobile by Calder in the exhibition, as Hultén had apparently suggested. "The idea of building a monument when you want to show something young and alive is somewhat strange," he continues.[30]

Daniel Spoerri concludes by urging Willem Sandberg to ensure that the exhibition is shown first in Amsterdam and then in Stockholm: "i have the support of all the artists here in paris in my opinion that the exhibition will have more power if it starts in your museum. you are recognized in god's name as the best museum in europe and as far as the matter is concerned it is best to start where the best chances are for the matter to spread. on the other hand, i agree, and even think it right, that hulten should carry out his idea in stockholm and extend the exhibition if he sees fit." Willem Sandberg replies in a letter dated October 10 that he prefers the exhibition to open in Amsterdam but that he had noted in a conversation with Pontus Hultén that he wanted the premiere. He left it to Spoerri to negotiate with Hultén but, as Andres Pardey notes, writes in support of his partner Spoerri that "I too want above all to show works of art and to emphasize today — historicism interests me less."[31]

On October 14, Pontus Hultén writes a sharp letter to Sandberg stating the opposite position, on paper with a letterhead reading "International exhibition on *art in motion*" in five languages. Hultén points out that "they" have agreed that the exhibition will be shown first in Stockholm in May and then open in October in Amsterdam. He emphasizes how important it is that this timetable is kept. Hultén writes that he wants to involve Spoerri in the Stockholm exhibition as a contact in Paris, but insists that he himself is the leader. Hultén reports indignantly: "We have worked four people on this for ten months now, and written 300–400 letters about this exhibition. It is meant to be our biggest manifestation in three or four years in this building. I have only been contracted for six years so maybe it's the biggest exhibition I'll ever do."[32]

Just five days later, however, on October 19, after negotiations between Spoerri, Tinguely and Hultén, Willem Sandberg receives a letter from Paris, written in French by Spoerri, in which he announces: "we have agreed to begin the exhibition with you in the month of march, taking into account that this exhibition is presented already in amsterdam as a manifestation organized by the modern museum in stockholm by the working committee hulten, sandberg, spoerri, tinguely." The letter is signed by Pontus Hultén, Daniel Spoerri and Jean Tinguely.[33]

The overtures to *Art in Motion* are indeed intricate. In retrospect, it appears that Pontus Hultén emerged victorious from the negotiations. Although he had been forced to leave the premiere to Amsterdam, in exchange he had managed to make himself and his museum responsible for a major operation, with an exhibition in several locations. Later that fall, Louisiana was added as the third museum to host the show.[34]

In his correspondence, Hultén then begins to discuss the exhibition catalog, for which he has "offered" to take responsibility — another way of claiming copyright for, and, as it would turn out, writing the history of the exhibition. Here it becomes clear to what crucial degree Pontus Hultén's vision differs from Daniel Spoerri's. What Pontus Hultén is planning is an epic exposé in which he uses art as a starting point to tell the story in a larger historical context, which, in addition to involving other art forms, also sheds light on political, economic, industrial and historical connections and phases of development. Furthermore, Hultén envisions detailed lists with information about works and artists, a text on the history of Kinetic Art 1909–1960 (unlike Spoerri, Hultén regards Cubism and the Futurist Manifesto as the starting point of this art movement), and a section with excerpts from important texts on movement in art. He exemplifies with the first Futurist Manifesto, the Realist Manifesto by the Russian artist brothers Naum Gabo and Antoine Pevsner, the Hungarian artist and Bauhaus teacher László Moholy-Nagy's text on light, an essay by the Italian Bruno Munari, and a "strange" piece by the sixteenth-century German philosopher and mathematician Gottfried Wilhelm von Leibniz.[35]

With this publication, designed in collaboration with the designer, or "printer," as he is often called, Hubert Johansson, Hultén took a major step in the development of the exhibition catalog as an artwork in its own right, as well a source of art historical knowledge, a field in which he became a pioneer. Towards the end of his letter to Willem Sandberg, Pontus Hultén writes, as in passing: "The format I propose for the catalog may seem fantastical but I think it fits very well with the general layout of the whole. I would be glad if you have confidence in me to choose it."[36]

The format selected by Pontus Hultén for the catalog for *Art in Motion* was indeed "fantastical" — 57 × 11 centimeters. Not unexpectedly, the odd extreme vertical cover was adorned with graphic reproductions of Duchamp's bicycle wheel from 1912 and his "Rotoreliefs" from 1935. Hultén liked to proclaim that the catalog could serve as a club to defend oneself with against upset visitors to the exhibition.[37] Another anecdote stated that the catalog was the equivalent of a French baguette loaf and would be seen on the streets promoting the exhibition when visitors carried it under their arms, as the classic Parisienne carried her bread.[38]

The content of *the Art in Motion* catalog outlined by Pontus Hultén clearly showed how Hultén's vision differed not only from Spoerri's but also from Sandberg's. The latter had declared that "historicism interests me less." Hultén's letter shows that Spoerri was by now involved in selecting works and organizing transport. The production of the catalog, though, he was not allowed to interfere with. During a visit to Stockholm, Spoerri worked with the museum's team on compiling the final list of artists and works, but was kept in the dark of the plans for the catalog, ins spite of repeated requests, which Spoerri has spoken bitterly about in later interviews.[39]

Another feature that distinguished Hultén's exhibition from the one Spoerri had sold to Sandberg was its global reach. While Spoerri envisioned a content based on art from the contemporary Parisian avant-garde, Hultén had a sensational trump card in the American element — but also Kinetic Art from other parts of the world that Hultén and his working group had endeavored to seek out, with artists from Brazil, Argentina, Venezuela, Japan and Israel represented. Pontus Hultén was a pioneer in this global perspective on the art world, original in the early sixties.

In his study, Andres Pardey observes the differences between the catalogs for the Amsterdam and Stockholm exhibitions in terms of the sender.[40] The Dutch catalog lists K.G. Hultén (Hultén would for many years sign his writings with the initials of his baptismal name Karl-Gunnar), Daniel Spoerri, Willem Sandberg and Jean Tinguely. The exhibition is presented here as a collaboration with Moderna

Museet in Stockholm. K.G. Hultén is the sole editor of the catalog. In the Stockholm catalog, Sandberg and Tinguely are removed from the production committee, replaced by Carlo Derkert. Stedelijk is not mentioned at all; the exhibition is presented as a production of Moderna Museet.

Pontus Hultén has later offered an alternative historical account of the origins of *Rörelse i konsten* (*Art in Motion*).[41] In this version of the story, he doesn't mention his dealings with Spoerri and Sandberg, but claims that he himself made the decision to show the exhibition in Amsterdam first, as he felt that the Stockholm audience was not yet ready for this revolution. Therefore, it was appropriate to stage a "warm-up" in Amsterdam where the art public would be more receptive to the new.[42] We can conclude from the above that this is a distortion of history of a kind that I have found Pontus Hultén habitually guilty of. He didn't hesitate to correct history for his own purposes when suitable.

Art in Motion, with the Dutch title *Bewogen Beweging* (roughly "Moving Movement"), opened in Amsterdam on March 10, 1961. Pontus Hultén himself pronounces the exhibition as having shocked even Amsterdam's more jaded art audience, that it was a great success with the public, and that Willem Sandberg was very pleased with the results and the reception.[43] Although it was Pontus Hultén who became known as the originator of *Art in Motion*, the exhibition is considered one of the classics of Stedelijk's heroic post-war era.

The show that opened at Moderna Museet in Stockholm just two months later, on May 15, 1961 (exhibitions were generally shown for much shorter periods than today), was a considerably expanded version of the one presented in Amsterdam. The most extensive additions had been made to the historical section.

Art in Motion can be viewed as an expansion of the "pilot exhibition" *Le Mouvement* at Galerie Denise René in Paris six years earlier. Most of the artists who had exhibited there were also represented in *Art in Motion*. In addition, a whole lot more had been added. The sheer overwhelming scale and diversity of new and little known art was a sensation in the art world at the time.

The historical section featured movement-themed painting and sculpture from the early Modernist movements of Futurism, Dadaism and Surrealism, many on loan from museums, galleries and collectors worldwide. The hero, of course, was Marcel Duchamp, represented by ten works, including "Nude Woman Descending a Staircase" in its third version, which Pontus Hultén had persuaded the Philadelphia Museum of Art to reluctantly lend. Of the other artists represented in the older section, most were household names for Hultén, many of whose works would form a core in Moderna Museet's classic Modernist collection — Francis Picabia, Man Ray, Hans Bellmer, Alberto Giacometti, Bruno Munari, the Futurist Giacomo Balla, Kazimir Malevich, Naum Gabo, László Moholy-Nagy, El Lissitzky and, of course, Alexander Calder.

A substantial part of *Art in Motion* consisted of works by Russian and Eastern European artists. The Russian and Eastern European avant-garde of the tens and twenties was a somewhat later love for Pontus Hultén than Dadaism. The Russian avant-garde would henceforth become one of the main focal points in Hultén's oeuvre. Its utopian, technology-glorifying visions, its machine romanticism and complex relationship to the Russian Revolution — these were the qualities that appealed to the utopian and revolutionary romantic Pontus Hultén, to use Olle Granath's expression. Hultén always had a penchant for art at the frontiers of architecture, engineering and technology.

So much more spectacular and sensational than the Russian element of the exhibition, which was appreciated mainly by connoisseurs, was the American contribution. In the time since Hultén's visit, Billy Klüver had developed the New York contacts they had established together. Works were sent to the exhibition by the artists Hultén and Klüver had met during their visit in 1959: Robert Rauschenberg, Jasper Johns, Richard Stankiewicz and Alfred Leslie. The happening pioneer Allan Kaprow also participated. None of these artists had been shown in museums or even outside the United States before. Much of Klüver's work had been devoted to the bureaucracy and transportation of the many loans of older art from American institutions.

That Alexander Calder would be represented with several works in the exhibition, as in *Le Mouvement* 1955, was part of the fundamental concept. Calder was a maverick in the history of modern art, trained as an engineer. As a young man he was fascinated by circus. Calder's breakthrough work was his wire circus, an ever-expanding miniature ring with mechanical figures constructed from steel wire. Calder then invented the mobile, lightweight sculptures that move by air currents. He met many Cubists and Dadaists and is said to have been captivated by abstract art during a visit to Piet Mondrian's studio. The influence of Mondrian can be seen in the coloring of the abstract

Pp. 118–119: *Art in Motion*, Moderna Museet, Stockholm, 1961.

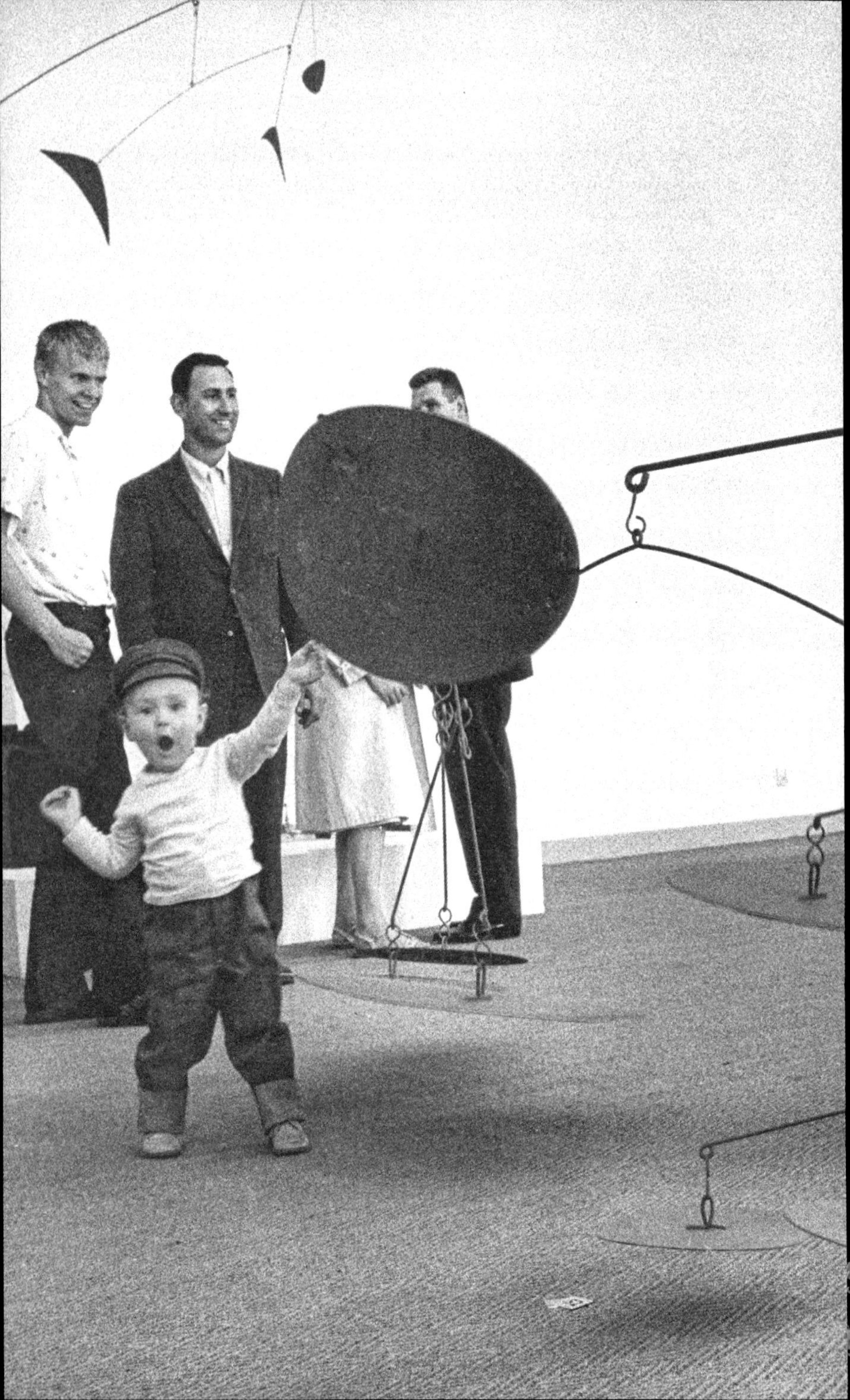

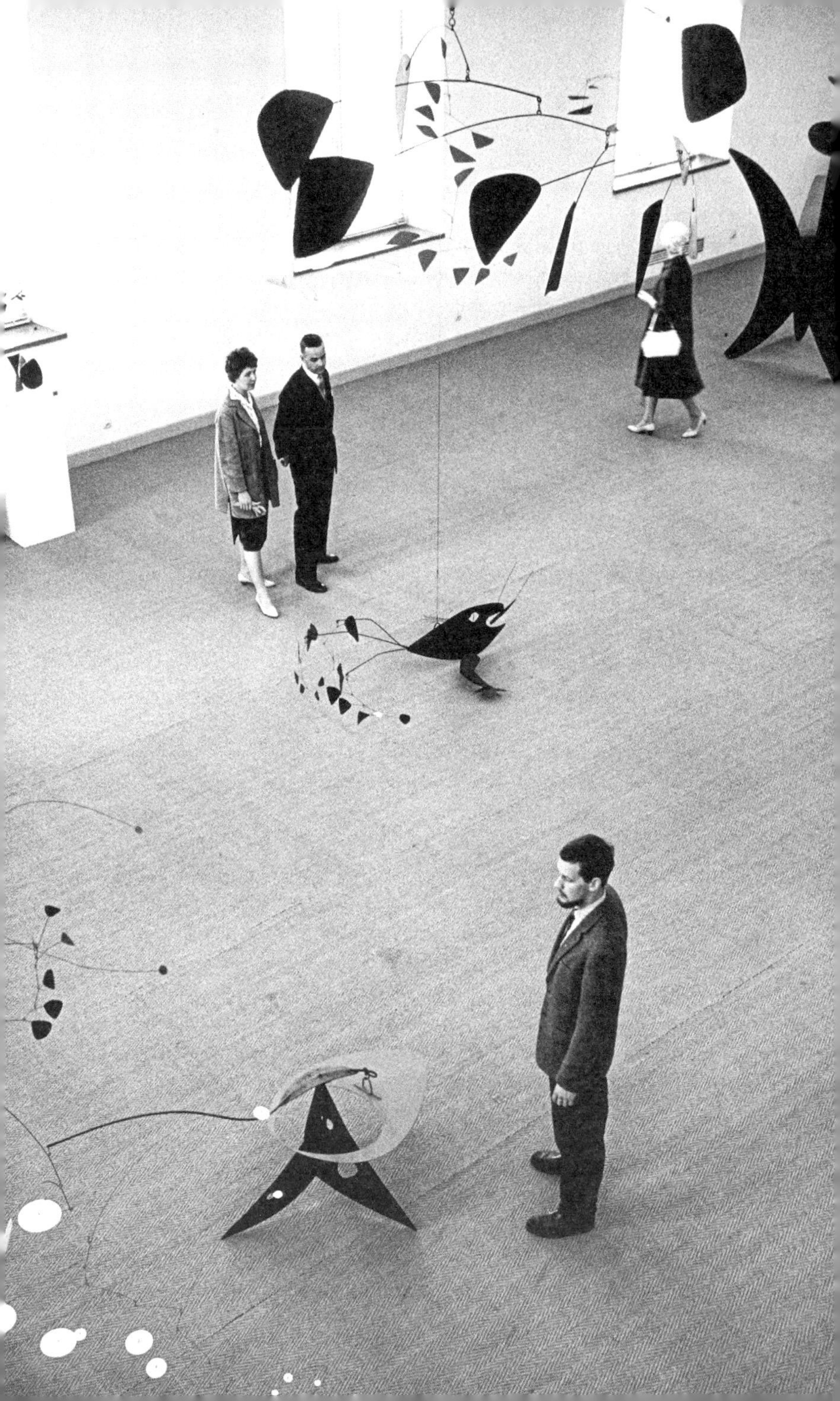

mobile sculptures in increasingly large formats that Calder created later in his career.

For *Art in Motion*, Pontus Hultén had an idea to show something on a larger scale by Calder. On a visit to the artist's home in Connecticut during his visit to New York, the story goes, he asked Calder if he had any larger works, whereupon the artist went and "rooted out" a miniature model of a mobile, "The Four Elements," designed for the 1939 World's Fair in New York but never erected in full scale. Hultén immediately said he wanted to produce the sculpture group and brought the miniature model back to Stockholm.

By this time, Pontus Hultén and Anna-Lena Wibom had been a couple for some years. After first living in the apartment on Stora Nygatan in Gamla Stan that Hultén's mother Elsie had bought for him and his sister Maj, the couple had moved into a larger apartment on Kungsholmstorg in the late 1950s. Their daughter Klara was born in 1960. As Anna-Lena Wibom told me: "When we met, Pontus got not only me but a large, muscular family."[44] Wibom came from an affluent family of construction industry magnates, which now came of service for far from the last time. The museum lacked the resources to construct Calder's monumental mobiles. This did not stop Pontus Hultén. He became known early on for always being able to find money and other resources when needed. Wibom's uncle, construction company executive Allan Skarne, was persuaded to pay for the production of the sculptures that still, more than sixty years later, adorn the courtyard in front of Moderna Museet's entrance as a logo for the museum — and which I remember so vividly from my childhood when you could still ride around in the giant, beast-like mobiles. The sculpture group was planned to decorate a new residential area built by the Skarne company at Kevinge waterfront in Danderyd. After the exhibition and some time thereafter, the group was to be moved to the quay in front of the new area. It later turned out that the tenants were not interested in this abstract artwork. The sculptures remained at Moderna and entered the collection as a donation from Skarne and Calder himself.[45]

The bulk of the *Art in Motion* exhibition was cast from Paris, where Jean Tinguely was the shining star — the contemporary counterpart to Marcel Duchamp in the historical section.

At the time, Tinguely was the hottest name in the international avant-garde. He journeyed to New York for the first time in the winter of 1960, where, on March 17, 1960, he staged his legendary happening

"Homage to New York" — a monstrous giant machine that destroyed itself in the sculpture garden of the Museum of Modern Art. Pontus Hultén was involved in the preparations and put Tinguely in touch with Billy Klüver as a technical collaborator. Robert Rauschenberg helped with the design and contributed a mechanism that threw silver dollar coins.[46] The mechanical suicide of the machine was not completed. Tinguely had to finish the job with an axe while the fire brigade intervened to extinguish an uncontrolled fire. Part of the sculpture came loose and collided with an NBC camera crew.

"Homage to New York" made art history and was a highly inspiring experience for the many artists from the New York avant-garde in the audience, including Rauschenberg, Jasper Johns and the young Andy Warhol, who had not yet become an artist but was still making a living as a fashion and advertising illustrator. Pontus Hultén was present, of course. Marcel Duchamp, as usual, did not come but was also involved. In the small program pamphlet produced by MoMA, where Hultén, in prominent company, wrote one of the short texts,[47] a precious collector's item, Duchamp contributed a priceless poem, printed in the artist's handwritten original: "si la scie scie la scie / et si la scie qui scie la scie / est la scie qui scie la scie / il y a Suissside métallique" ("if the saw saws the saw / and if the saw that saws the saw / is the saw that saws the saw / then there is metallic suicide" — note that "Suissside" also alludes to Tinguely's Swiss nationality). The artist also made a classic Duchampian comment about Tinguely's MoMA happening: that it was a "healthy idea" to "destroy art before it's too late."[48]

"Homage to New York" caused sensation and scandal, a shock effect that quickly spread across the art world. Jean Tinguely's anarchist happening has been called the kick-off to the revolutionary sixties, the decade after which there was no return to the classical ideals of art.[49]

In *Art in Motion*, Tinguely was surrounded by a court of his generational peers in Paris. In addition to Spoerri, his colleagues from the newly formed group Les Nouveaux Réalistes included Raymond Hains, as well as the Paris-based Yaacov Agam and Jesús Rafael Soto. Also participating for the first time was an artist who would play a major role in Pontus Hultén's life and career, and in this story. Enter Niki de Saint Phalle, who would become the sole female member of the New Realists — de Saint Phalle joined the group in the same year, 1961, to the chagrin of some of the original members[50] — and the world's most famous female artist of the 1960s and 1970s.

Contemporary artists and art historians have underscored that Niki de Saint Phalle was one of only eight women among the eighty-three artists represented in *Art in Motion*. It will always seem incomprehensible that even radical young men so committed to class struggle and equality could remain illiterate for so long in the face of the most basic of class injustices.

Niki de Saint Phalle, whose full birth name was Catherine Marie Agnès Fal de Saint Phalle, was of high aristocratic descendance, born in posh Neuilly-sur-Seine on the northwestern outskirts of Paris. After the family bank in Paris collapsed in the Depression, the family moved to New York. At the age of eighteen, de Saint Phalle married the American poet Harry Mathews, whom she had known since childhood. The couple moved to Cambridge, Massachusetts, and had their first child, daughter Laura, in 1951. The bourgeois life of a new mother in a small town idyll, combined with Niki de Saint Phalle's distressing memories of her childhood, contributed to her psychosis and forced admission to a mental hospital. Niki herself has explained that art literally saved her life; that without art she would have been dead or locked up in a mental hospital for the rest of her life.[51] Her two younger siblings both committed suicide in adulthood. The family moved in the mid-fifties to Deià in Mallorca and on to Paris where de Saint Phalle met Jean Tinguely. Niki abandoned her husband and their now two children to live and work with Tinguely in his studio on Impasse Ronsin. This glamorous and controversial couple would impact the international art scene of the sixties and seventies. "The Bonnie & Clyde of art" was just one of the terms used in the media. As an artist, Niki de Saint Phalle made her debut in 1956 with small-scale naive paintings. She moved on to collage, often with themes of violence, knives and guns.

In 1961, the year of the *Art in Motion*, Niki de Saint Phalle won her first breakthrough with her "Tirs," "shot paintings": assemblages of objects such as dolls, household utensils, knives, guns, stuffed animals, religious symbols and much more attached to monumental canvases covered with plaster. Hidden under the plaster were bags of paint that exploded and "bled" across the canvases when Niki fired guns at the paintings in a kind of militant commentary on Jackson Pollock's action painting. It was after seeing one of the first of Niki's "Tirs" in Paris that Pierre Restany decided to include the artist as the only female member of the newly formed "New Realists" group. As part of the program for *Art in Motion*, Niki staged a filmed performance of one of her early "Tirs" on a "backyard in Stockholm" and another in a quarry on Värmdö island.[52] (The painting from Värmdö was acquired for the museum's collection.[53]) de Saint Phalle also created several works on site for the exhibition.[54]

An addition to the Stockholm version of *Art in Motion*, compared to the exhibition that had opened in Amsterdam two months earlier, was a Bugatti Type 35 roadster from its premiere year of 1924, a revolutionary, unbeatable sports car of its time, considered a technical masterpiece — a vehicle that Pontus Hultén himself, in the spirit of Duchamp, considered to possess such beauty and mechanical perfection that it could be considered a work of art.

Art historian Anna Lundström writes: "For a long time, the ambition was also to show, alongside mobile art, what is described as its 'periphery.' Older vending machines, mechanical devices, fireworks and toys were intended to make the exhibition attractive to a wider audience and link Kinetic Art to wider technological developments. Although these types of objects were not included, with the exception of the car, the discussion shows that *Art in Motion* presented a collection of objects whose identity as art was not entirely clear."[55]

Anna Lundström reasons on how Pontus Hultén, by presenting industrially produced objects as art, took the same audacious liberty as his role model Marcel Duchamp when he revolutionized the art world with his readymades in the early decade: "Rather than displaying objects that artists identify as art, along the lines of objet trouvé or ready-made, it is the museum director himself — without the artist as an intermediary — who wants to present everyday objects with the claim that they should be seen as art."[56]

This observation highlights an important aspect of Pontus Hultén's approach as a museum director and exhibition organizer. It has been stressed by several artists and colleagues, most famously by Niki de Saint Phalle,[57] that Pontus Hultén didn't think like a museum man but like the artist he had long dreamed of becoming.

Anna Lundström writes that the preparations for the exhibition and the selection of works presented were considerably less structured and more random than has been assumed — a judgment that applies to Moderna Museet's entire first era of greatness in the 1960s: "In light of the effect that the exhibition had on the art scene of the early 1960s, it may appear to be a well-directed launch of a certain faction of contemporary art. However, correspondence and notes reveal that what became *Art in Motion* was the result of a rather searching process. The archive at Moderna Museet contains countless letters in which Hultén writes, as if at random, to museum directors, collectors and artists, asking if they have any works with moving parts that might be suitable for the exhibition they were planning. A large number of the works presented also seem to have fallen into place at a relatively late stage."

Lundström notes that *Art in Motion* was largely based on three stars — Duchamp, Calder and Tinguely, supported by "a handful of artists:" Munari, Bury, Agam, Moholy-Nagy, Man Ray, Gabo, Pevsner, Ultvedt and Nicolas Schöffer.

Lundström's analysis can serve as a general description of Pontus Hultén's method as an exhibition maker. Based on his favorite artists, he constructed his own historical contexts that he narrated to the audience, focusing on the broad strokes, unconcerned about whether his assumptions were waterproof in every detail. He thus wrote his own art history. Kinetic Art as a whole has subsequently been classified as a movement invented by Hultén himself.[58] As an exhibition organizer, it seems that Pontus Hultén followed the old journalistic principle of never over-checking a good story. He had a consistent talent for adapting the terrain to his own map.

Another innovation that Hultén introduced to the wider public was the art exhibition as the hub of a multicultural mega-event. In addition to sculpture and painting, the show itself contained elements of architecture, engineering, photography and graphic design. The art was accompanied by a rich program of other cultural events. A highlight was a series of experimental films by artists and filmmakers such as Viking Eggeling and Robert Breer. Fylkingen gave a series of concerts. The museum and other institutions organized lectures, debates, happenings, artistic installations and performances.

The museum's library offered a generous selection of literature and magazines related to the theme of the exhibition. Pontus Hultén and his staff brought art to the streets of central Stockholm, including sculptures/installations on Nybroplan square — another inventive initiative to bring the exhibition and the museum to the people of Stockholm.

Yet another novelty was the idea that many of the works would be created on site. Jean Tinguely, together with Niki de Saint Phalle, came to Stockholm in advance to once again collect scrap and junk, for his mobile "The Poor Man's Ballet," one of the most buzzed and scandalized works of the exhibition, which hung from the ceiling of one of the galleries. Robert Rauschenberg arrived from New York, also venturing out around the city on a scrap hunt accompanied by Billy Klüver. Part of Pontus Hultén's vision was for the museum to serve as an artist's studio. This, too, was a trend at the time, for which Hultén was a pioneer.

Pontus Hultén would later say that he should have patented his concept of the multicultural, interdisciplinary exhibition that would become commonplace in the art world.[59] Predecessors existed in various respects, including the Stedelijk under Willem Sandberg. The Museum of Modern Art in New York, under its founding director Alfred H. Barr Jr. was the first to introduce art forms such as photography and architecture in separate sections of a modern art museum in the 1930s. Bauhaus and Dadaist revues were other constant references for Hultén. More surprisingly, Hultén also mentions as a source of inspiration his friend Peter Weiss and how he was influenced by his artistic work as a writer, director and artist.[60]

Although there were precedents, no museum had ever before mixed art forms, objects and events in this unrestrained, free, anarchic spirit — creative expressions and historical eras intersected, classical art and Modernist masterpieces presented alongside new works by young, unestablished contemporary artists created on site, many of these works in progress that developed throughout the exhibition. Following Duchamp's doctrine, the audience was invited to participate in the exhibition and in the creation of many of the works. The rattling, noisy, overwhelmingly rich mass of impressions and experiences was something completely new not only in Sweden but also in the international art world.

Art in Motion was harshly criticized by for presenting art as a circus, a carnival. For those who were interested, however, there was a wealth to learn from all of this, with plenty of opportunity for in-depth study. Here, for the first time, was unveiled what I would call the hallmark of a Pontus Hultén exhibition: a surface so exciting, provocative, pleasurable and spectacular that it attracts an audience even without any knowledge of modern art — but underneath the seductive surface, deep historical roots for those who let their curiosity lead further.

It was a splendid, striking experience that was presented to the Stockholm public on May 16, 1961, a "wonderfully sunny spring day,"[61] expressing myself moderately. The sensation of the avant-garde of the modern art world from six decades coming to visit little northern Stockholm seems hard to comprehend. I can imagine the shock that hit the Stockholm audience when Pontus Hultén played out the hand he had built up over many years.

The opening party wrote its own piece of art history. The hand-scrawled invitation card hinted at the explosion to come, with the title KOLOSSALKALAS (Collossal Party) thickly inked across the top. Guests at the opening were greeted by a barrage of unseen impressions. Jean Tinguely demonstrated his "Méta-Matic" drawing machine, which spat out hundred crown bills. After the official dinner, served in the museum's main gallery, where Ulf Linde played the vibraphone in Arne Domnérus' jazz orchestra, various happenings ensued, including "anti-fireworks" with Tinguley and Per Olof Ultvedt shooting rockets into the water from a rowing boat off Skeppsholmskajen. The guests were shipped by ferry to Arenateatern on Djurgården island,[62] where the American jazz legend Thelonius Monk (who had given a concert at the Konserthuset music hall earlier in the evening) performed and where Rauschenberg, de Saint Phalle, Tinguely and Ultvedt gave a performance, followed by dancing on the theater stage. The party was still going strong as the early summer morning dawned over the Stockholm water expanses to the enchantment of the many foreign guests.

In my favorite read, Moderna Museet's twenty-fifth anniversary book from 1983, Robert Rauschenberg and Billy Klüver draw a joint memory of the opening of *Art in Motion* and the time before and after, in a transcribed recorded conversation between the two friends.[63] Their memories convey a lovely tableau of the time and of the exhibition that jump-started Moderna Museet's "heroic years."

In the conversation, Billy Klüver says: "Rauschenberg had made 'Black Market' for the exhibition, a 'combine' consisting of a painting attached to a suitcase lying on the floor. The lid (...) was open and inside it were four objects (...) The spectator was to choose an object, remove it, and add something of his own in exchange. In April, after the Amsterdam exhibition, Pontus had written to me. 'One thing is very important. All the objects in the 'Black Market' have disappeared. Nothing is left. Can you ask Rauschenberg to make new ones? People have taken them without adding anything in exchange.'"

Robert Rauschenberg responds regarding this one of his most famous "combines," which Pontus Hultén tried but failed to get a mandate to purchase for the collection: "(...) 'Black Market' was intended to be an active cultural attaché with an endless flow of art for anyone. (...) Unfortunately, the artwork is still ahead of its time and basically speaks to the darker side of human nature. I am still disappointed that one cannot accept a gift and give something else in return (...) I have not given up hope."

Billy Klüver discusses another of the exhibition's interactive elements — Allan Kaprow's "environment" built with cardboard boxes, which Klüver was commissioned to install on the museum's newly built mezzanine floor: "(...) Allan had written precise instructions for the spectators of how to behave: take a paintbrush, dip it in one of the cans of paint on a table, and paint any way they wanted on any cardboard box. Each person could only dip the brush once. (...) I went to NK and collected all the boxes I could carry. It took me several days to hang the boxes and set up Allan's environment. (...) Rauschenberg arrived a few days after me and installed the 'Black Market'. He saw that I was working on Allan's room and suggested that he prepare a door. He built a construction of cardboard boxes on both sides of a real door, and at the bottom of the door he attached a wire cage in which he placed half a dozen live chickens."

Robert Rauschenberg responds: "One of the new ideas in art at this time was collaboration and unconditional participation. I don't think art has ever been so truly democratic before or since — or at least tried to be. (...) Since I had no other wishes in Sweden, I offered to help in doing something. One of these activities was to make a door for Kaprow's room. Whatever was going on in the exhibition galleries, the cafeteria was the most popular place in the museum. So when I found myself short on materials, I used eggshells and stale bread that I sprayed with plastic. No chickens."

Billy Klüver reveals the fate of Allan Kaprow's "environment" at the opening: "Allan had made all sorts of predictions about what he thought would happen: (...) Photographs would be taken showing that the Dutch painted like Mondrian, the Scandinavians like Munch, and so on. When I glanced in the door, not a single cardboard box was left hanging. In less than an hour, people had torn the boxes down, splashed paint on them, kicked them around and stomped on them. The room was a complete ruin."

Klüver goes on to relate how he helped Rauschenberg create yet another improvised new work for the exhibition, in the unassuming democratic spirit of collaboration described by the same: "From Pontus I learned that whatever you do, you have to do it properly, whether it's emptying ashtrays or correcting signs, and from Bob I learned that you can't stand by and watch other people work. When Bob finished the door, he wanted to do another painting. But unlike New York, the streets of Stockholm didn't provide him with any useful material — Stockholm's streets were clean and empty. Instead, we drove to a house that we had heard was being demolished (...) We left with old swaths of fabric, chinks of wood and pieces of scrap iron — things that I wouldn't have seen even if I had been looking at them. We took everything to the museum and Bob spread it all out on the floor and got to work. The next day the painting was finished and hung."[64]

I must also quote from Klüver and Rauschenberg's exchange about Alexander Calder, another of the artists who traveled to Stockholm for *Art in Motion*. Klüver: "Pontus, Tinguely, Ultvedt, Linde and everyone else worked frantically to get everything in place. Calder arrived. Just 18 months earlier I had been with Pontus in Roxbury where Calder gave him the 22-year-old model of 'The Four Elements' — Calder's contribution intended as the symbol for the 1939 New York World's Fair — and granted him permission to build it on a full scale. Pontus had placed the 13-meter-high motorized sculpture outside the museum. I will never forget when Calder got out of the car and saw the big sculpture in motion for the first time. It worked perfectly. He walked around it alone, amazed and completely absorbed."

Rauschenberg: "What I remember of the incident is that after a massive Swedish lunch, Calder really walked around it and grunted something, and then he came and sat down — I sat very close to him — and his wife sat down next to him. When the journalists came, he was already dozing off, and she was the one who answered all the questions. I couldn't believe my eyes — all these people — they didn't turn to Louisa with their questions, they kept addressing them to him and yet he was even snoring."

A work of art was exclusively created during the wild opening party. Pontus Hultén and Niki de Saint Phalle had, as Billy Klüver says, intended "to end the evening by unveiling the world's largest 'instant work of art.'" A theater backdrop was stretched across the stage floor to which Niki had attached hundreds of paint bags, covered by a plastic sheet and a carpet. As guests danced, they created an abstract Pollockian monumental painting. Billy Klüver and Robert Rauschenberg explain how they "finish" Niki de Saint Phalle and Pontus Hultén's painting — a shimmering snapshot of the early sixties and the flourishing of Moderna Museet.

Klüver: "I don't remember any details of the performance of the four musketeers in tail coats, nor of the dance afterwards, but at three o'clock in the morning Bob and I discovered that we were completely alone in the theater. Everyone had disappeared. Even Pontus and Niki. The painting was still under the carpet, and no one had bothered to look at it. Bob and I felt very responsible and rolled up the carpet and the plastic cover. (...) The sun was shining and the birds were chirping in Allmänna Gränd. Bob had never before experienced a Swedish summer morning and was amazed. Of course there were no cars, no taxis. No way for us to get home. We would have to walk the four kilometers to Kungsholmstorg where Pontus and Anna Lena lived. We tried to hitchhike, but no one stopped. Then Bob had the idea that we could improve the painting and at the same time call for attention and help. So we rolled out the painting on Djurgårdsvägen and let the cars drive over it, which they did without slowing down at all. (...) There was nothing to do but roll up the painting and put it over our shoulders. (...) At Nybroplan we finally got a taxi, stowed the painting in the trunk and bribed the driver to take us to Pontus and Anna Lena. They were sound asleep and refused to wake up. So we attached the top edge of the painting high up on a wall and let it drape itself all over the living room. Then we went to the kitchen and finished a bottle of whisky."

Rauschenberg: "I can't remember the performance either, which makes me hope that no one else can either. I remember a lot of dancing and drinking, and a rather noble exit by Pontus after he had delivered an unofficial and much-needed punch to one of the biggest 'assholes' among the artists in the exhibition. And I remember the surprise I shared with Billy when we suddenly found we were the only ones left. The shock of a premature dawn that held none of the night's information. The desolation was emphasized by the birds and it was up to us to give the night the understanding that the light had deprived it of. (...) I don't want to sound depressed when I talk about this time. It was a youthful sunset over our optimism."

The monumental painting so vividly described is now part of the Moderna Museet collection, donated by Pontus Hultén, titled "Painting made by dance," measuring 207 × 413.5 centimeters, attributed to Niki de Saint Phalle and Robert Rauschenberg.[65]

Art in Motion attracted a large audience to Skeppsholmen from the opening day. The reactions from the visitors were surprise, excitement and pure joy. This can be seen in pictures of the audience, mostly dressed in the formal style of the 1950s and early 1960s, in contrast to the anarchic mechanical sculptures. "It was a complete shock of joy to visit the exhibition, like a bolt of lightning from a blue sky," says Björn Springfeldt, later Pontus Hultén's younger colleague and eventual successor as director of Moderna Museet. "The exhibition made me and many others realize that this is what we wanted to do."[66]

Initial reactions in the press were cautious, as is often the case with anything as new and revolutionary. Soon the debate picked up, with strong opinions and feelings for and against. The exhibition was called a "carnival," "prank," "slapstick," "madhouse" and other derogatives. Many called for censorship and bans. There were loud demands that the exhibition should simply be closed. To appease the most outraged moralistic opinion, Carl Nordenfalk ordered that Robert Müller's sculpture "The Cyclist's Widow," with a dildo penetrating the bicycle saddle as the guests pedaled, should be removed — a slightly pathetic gesture of half-hearted authority from the good Count, it seems.

In August, an antagonist emerged who had presented himself already at the museum's ceremonial opening dinner three years earlier: the artist Sven "Xet" Erixson, who made himself the spokesman for the scandalization of *Art in Motion*. In an article in Dagens Nyheter, Erixson wrote that "the rattle on Skeppsholmen should have been interrupted" to make room for a traveling collection of Italian paintings. If there were problems attracting people to such a more traditional exhibition, "some beautiful female amanuenses" could have been hung from the ceiling "for people to spin," Erixson suggested. "The screams would certainly have attracted a large audience."[67]

Other younger artists and commentators defended the exhibition, including Öyvind Fahlström in an article in Expressen. A crucial help in this stormy debate came from an unexpected source. *The Grand Old Man* of Swedish art, as Pontus Hultén calls him,[68] Bror Hjorth, the folkloristic master painter and sculptor, mounted the stage, also in an article in Dagens Nyheter, where, in implicit polemic against his contemporary colleague "Xet," he praised the exhibition in lyrical terms: "One needs to thank the museum's management in some way for organizing this exhibition, so charitably healthy," Hjorth wrote, and went on to state about Tinguely's "The Poor Man's Ballet": "To succeed in this, he must, in addition to being a great artist, also be a technical genius (...) One is stuck as if before another of the masters of color, Delacroix. (...) You find the same superb artistry and the same vitality of color. (...) These old broken objects, fox furs, trays, buckets, clothes, etc., achieve the miracle of having the same effect on you as Delacroix's Arabian horses and riders, tigers and lions, and exotic landscapes painted on canvas and with oil paint (…) Certainly the exhibition of so-called moving art at Moderna Museet is something remarkable and something to be grateful for."[69]

According to Pontus Hultén, Bror Hjorth's article silenced all talk of closing the exhibition.[70] Instead, after the summer vacation, visitors flocked to Skeppsholmen in numbers that no one could have predicted. The small team had their hands full trying to keep the exhibition in reasonable condition and prevent it from being torn down.[71] Over seventy thousand visitors saw *Art in Motion* — a sensational figure that shattered all records in the Stockholm of that time, with a population considerably smaller than today. News of the exhibition quickly spread throughout the art world, with substantial international publicity.[72] In response to "Xet" Erixson, a picture of the artist was hung among the "rattle" of the "The Poor Man's Ballet" — an insult in the eyes of many antagonists.

After the roaring box-office success of *Art in Motion*, there was no more compromise, as Pontus Hultén writes in the twenty-fifth anniversary book.[73] For a number of years in the sixties, the period known as "the heroic years," usually counted from 1961 through 1968, he and his staff were able to develop their museum into something unprecedented, pushing full steam ahead through a never-ending storm of controversy. "We were able to come up with something new because our opponents were not organized and had no idea what the museum should be," Pontus said. "We caught them off-guard and once the exhibition opened, the crowds soon became our strong protection."[74]

With the triumph of the exhibition, from what can undoubtedly be called a difficult and precarious position, Pontus Hultén had also won the power struggle against the National Museum. Even though it would take until 1999 before Moderna Museet was formally separated from the mother institution, Hultén and his colleagues could subsequently practically design their program with creative freedom. Pontus Hultén had succeeded in his brazen coup and established a museum that the entire art world would henceforth keep under close surveillance, at the age of just thirty-seven.

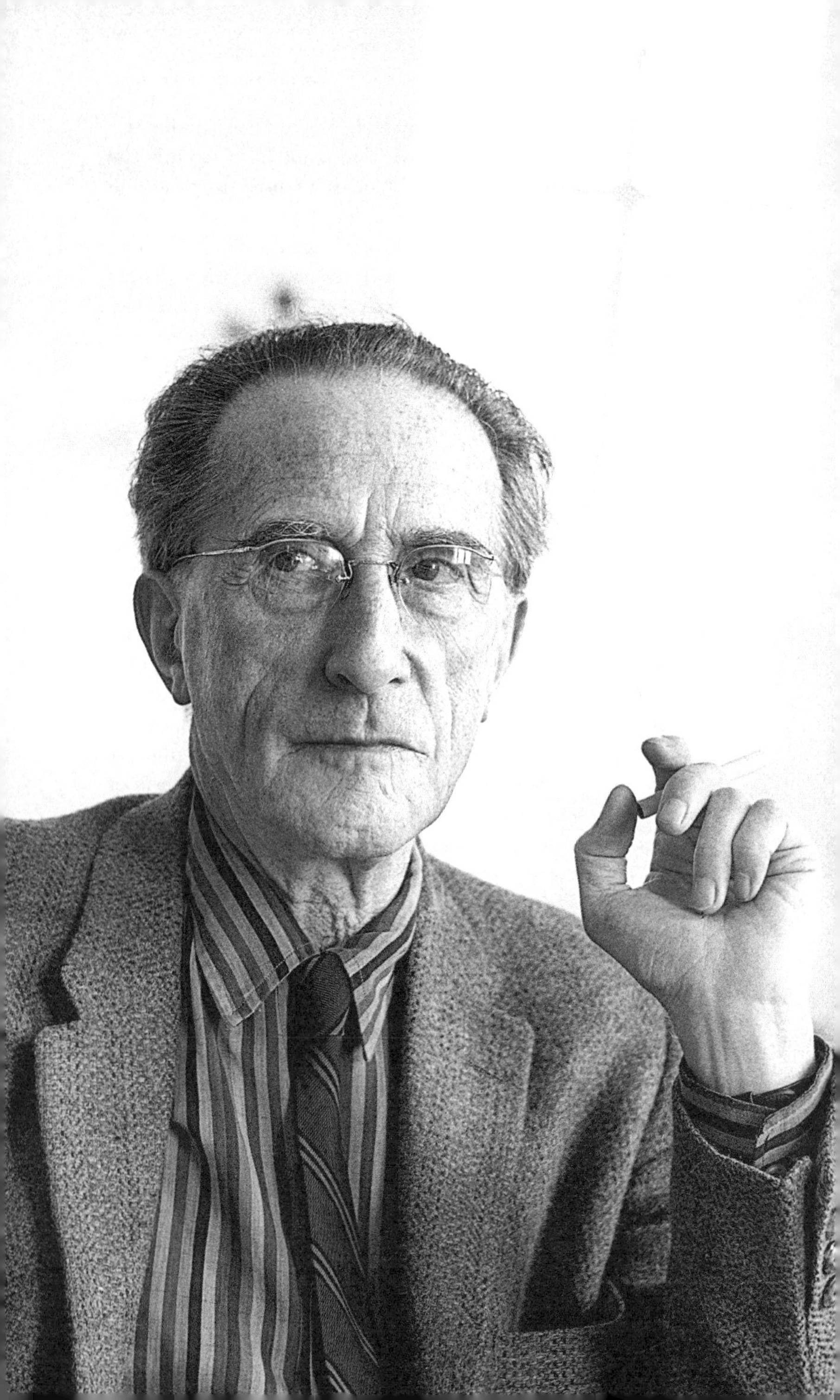

8

Marcel Duchamp in Stockholm: a new breakthrough for an ageing artist and an invaluable friendship for a young museum

Pontus Hultén's great idol Marcel Duchamp's visit to Stockholm for the *Art in Motion* exhibition had a lasting impact on modern art history. In Duchamp circles, and in the art world at large, it's widely recognized how important Hultén's exhibitions with Duchamp in the 1950s, and especially his participation in *Art in Motion* in 1961, were for Duchamp's second, total breakthrough towards the end of his life.

Some has been written about the "Stockholm connection" by international Duchamp connoisseurs.[1] In 2016, a two hundred and fifty-page issue of Étant donné Marcel Duchamp, the Duchamp Foundation's own journal, was dedicated to this theme, entitled "Marcel Duchamp en Suède. Ulf Linde, Pontus Hultén & Friends."[2]

The main author and editor Paul B. Franklin bases substantial parts of his history on nearly nineteen hours of interviews with Ulf Linde.[3] In his texts, alternating between French and English, Franklin does his best to give Linde credit at Hultén's expense, despite the fact that Linde admits in several contexts, even in Franklin's own interviews, that it was Hultén who aroused his own interest in and later infatuation with the artist.[4]

After their first contact in 1954, Pontus Hultén had met Duchamp several more times. Since then, he had corresponded with the artist. The Duchamp Foundation's journal mentions that Hultén first raised the question of participation in the forthcoming *Art in Motion* show at a dinner with the Chilean Surrealist Roberto Matta and his wife Malitte Matta in the summer of 1959, at the couple's summer residence in Boissy-sans-Avoir, west of Paris.[5]

There is no doubt that Pontus Hultén was among the first of his generation to realize the enormous importance that Marcel Duchamp

Marcel Duchamp, Moderna Museet, Stockholm, August 1961.

already had and, above all, would achieve. Already before the mid-fifties, Hultén predicted that Duchamp, at that time still completely unknown not only to the public but also to the art world in general, would become the most influential artist of the twentieth century — a role that had previously been obviously reserved for Picasso, as Hultén phrases it.[6] With *Le Mouvement* at Galerie Denise René in 1955, he made art history when he persuaded René and Victor Vasarely to include Duchamp in the exhibition as a pioneer of mobile art.

In the spring of 1960, a year before *Art in Motion*, Hultén, together with Per Olof Ultvedt and other friends, initiated two exhibitions on a modest scale in Stockholm at a small gallery alternately called Galleri 42 and Galleri Wallingatan 42, an exhibition space that was a branch of the labor movement's bookstore Bokkonsum in central Stockholm. The bookstore was run by Conny Andersson, an ardent socialist idealist who had fought as a volunteer in the Spanish Civil War, the Finnish Winter War and against Nazi Germany's invasion troops in Norway. In the Duchamp journal, the editor Paul B. Franklin for some reason makes a point of emphasizing that it was Per Olof Ultvedt who "around 1958"[7] had been hired by Conny Andersson to lead the artistic activities at Galleri 42 and that it was Ultvedt, not Hultén, who was responsible. Hultén himself has said and written in several contexts that "I,"[8] or "I together with some friends"[9] arranged these exhibitions.

The first of the two short successive displays in the spring of 1960 was the Stockholm version of Daniel Spoerri's previously discussed touring exhibition *Édition MAT*, with duplicated kinetic works by a selection of mainly Parisian artists. Paul B. Franklin admits in his text that it was Pontus Hultén who had urged Spoerri to send *Édition MAT* to Stockholm, and put him in touch with Ultvedt, but points out that the exhibition was produced by Ultvedt and Spoerri, without Hultén's involvement — certainly true as Hultén was busy with Moderna Museet at the time. Nevertheless, the origin is evidenced in that Hultén, Ultvedt, Hans Nordenström and Oscar Reutersvärd simultaneously produced the fourth and final issue of their magazine Kasark, which doubled as an exhibition catalog.[10] The connection with *Le Mouvement* from 1955 was obvious in Spoerri's *Édition MAT*. Many of the artists involved were the same.

Duchamp participated in the traveling exhibition with his "Rotoreliefs," wall-mounted on stands of the same model that Tinguely had designed for *Le Mouvement*. Before the premiere in Paris, Duchamp had unhesitatingly sent Spoerri thirty-five copies from a 1953 edition, with the advice to sell them for the equivalent of ten dollars each.[11] Spoerri had not dared to ask Duchamp to sign the sculptures. It was the artist himself, ever helpful and free of prestige, who, discovering in the catalog that the "Rotoreliefs" were "numbered only," had sent Spoerri some forty signatures with the instruction "to affix, either by pasting or with a fairly hot iron for ten seconds."

Despite ridiculously low prices, Daniel Spoerri sold few of the works in his traveling exhibition. In Stockholm, exceptionally, all four copies of Duchamp's "Rotoreliefs" were sold for two hundred and fifty crowns each.[12] One of these was bought by Moderna Museet at Pontus Hultén's behest.[13]

In the spring of 1959, Hultén was contacted by the Paris-based Anglo-American publisher Arnold Fawcus, who had recently published *Sur Marcel Duchamp*, the first biography and catalogue raisonné of the artist, written by Duchamp's friend Robert Lebel in close collaboration with the artist himself.[14] Fawcus offered Hultén to show and sell in Stockholm the exclusive deluxe edition of the book, for which Duchamp had also created three new artworks. The publisher drew Hultén's attention to the exhibitions presented on occasion of the launch of the deluxe edition in Paris, New York and Zürich, and suggested that Hultén plan a similar one for Stockholm.[15]

After Hultén's introduction, there was correspondence between Ultvedt and Fawcus in which various elements of the presentation were discussed, including the Stockholmers' idea of producing a miniature reproduction of "The Large Glass."[16]

The exhibition organizers had originally intended to manufacture the eighty-eight-centimeter-high miniature glass in an edition offered for sale. The idea was abandoned when production proved so complicated that all the time was spent on completing a single copy for the exhibition, which was gradually postponed from February. The miniature, known in the Duchamp world as "The Small Glass," is a well-known cult object, which after long detours was incorporated into the Moderna Museet collection in 2011.[17]

The exhibition makers were not satisfied with this. "To make the presentation a bit more attractive," as Pontus Hultén put it,[18] it was later decided to produce replicas of two readymades: "The Bicycle Wheel," the first of them all from 1913, whose original had been lost since Duchamp moved from Paris to New York in 1915, known only from a photograph, and "Fresh Widow" from 1920, Duchamp's diminutive French window with panes covered in black leather, a symbolism that, with the pun of the title, has been seen to allude to the recent war and its harvest of "fresh widows,"[19] with the inscription "COPYRIGHT ROSE SÉLAVY 1920" — the first time Duchamp signed one of his works with his androgynous alter ego.

The replicas were manufactured with the help of local craftsmen by Linde and Ultvedt, the bicycle wheel with the clearly visible flaw that the fork on which the wheel spun was curved, not straight as in Duchamp's original, mounted on a stool that was also markedly different. In addition, the team commissioned Daniel Spoerri to acquire a bottle rack similar to Duchamp's from 1914, the first fully serialized object among his readymades. Spoerri bought the bottle dryer at the same market at the Bazar de l'Hôtel de Ville in Paris where Duchamp had purchased the original — though not similar to it, as Ulf Linde noted — and had it sent it to Stockholm.[20] All of these initiatives were apparently initiated by the young Stockholm exhibition producers, without consulting the artist. Requests for replicas were made to the publisher Fawcus, who reported that Duchamp had enthusiastically agreed to the idea once it was brought to his attention.

These freshly produced readymades, and "The Small Glass," were exhibited in the gallery on Wallingatan together with reproductions of Duchamp's new works from the book *Sur Marcel Duchamp*, as well as a display case with four copies of the deluxe edition of this newly published first catalogue raisonné. Despite persistent requests, also from Duchamp himself, it proved impossible to obtain a copy of the artist's "mini-museum" "La Boîte-en-valise." Instead, Hultén's copy of the deluxe edition of "La Boîte verte" ("The Green Box") was displayed. In addition, Albert Fawcus had managed to borrow probably three (the number varies) original drawings from private collections in Paris to further enhance the exhibition's appeal.

Paul B. Franklin goes to great lengths in presenting the small Duchamp exhibition, which finally opened on May 7, 1960 on Wallingatan, as the work of Per Olof Ultvedt and Ulf Linde. Still, my impression of who was behind it is reinforced by the fact that it was Pontus Hultén who wrote the prophetic short text about Duchamp on the invitation card printed for the exhibition, signed "K.G.H." Here, a year before *Art in Motion*, Hultén once again expresses his view of Duchamp as the most important artist of the twentieth century, with a stylishly acidic slap at Picasso, when he writes: "Few artists have been as inspiring for twentieth century art as Marcel Duchamp. The question is whether, in the end, he is not the one who will matter most of all. It has been possible to steal from his pantry with impunity for a long time. He is not the one who claims his copyright or calls the police. And his work has been so relatively unknown that those who have shoplifted haven't risked being slapped on the fingers (...). Picasso complains that his followers are pissing on his heels. Duchamp hasn't complained, it almost seems as if he has been happy not to be completely forgotten. (...)"[21]

Like Daniel Spoerri's immediately preceding *Édition MAT*, the *Marcel Duchamp* exhibition attracted moderate attention in the Stockholm art scene, with no newspaper reviews. In Moderna Museet's collection, "The Small Glass" is cataloged as a "preliminary study" for the full-scale glass produced for *Art in Motion*. The two readymades manufactured for the exhibition on Wallingatan were also shown in *Art in Motion*, along with "Rotoreliefs" from Spoerri's *Édition MAT*, as well as a replica of "Rotative plaques verre," Duchamp's larger, equally hypnotically optical, rotating sculpture from 1920, which Pontus Hultén had commissioned together with Ultvedt and Anna-Lena Wibom's brother Magnus Wibom, and which was donated to the museum after the exhibition.[22] ("Rotative plaques verre" is, according to Olle Granath and general knowledge, a "deadly sculpture." There have been incidents where the rapidly rotating glass plates have come loose and turned into projectiles.[23]).

The centerpiece of the Duchamp collection on display at *Art in Motion* was thus neither the painting "Nude Woman Descending a Staircase," which had been borrowed, nor the readymades that had been commissioned, but Duchamp's magnum opus "The Large Glass" — an abstract picture constructed with lead wires, engravings and other techniques, enclosed in glass panels contained in an aluminum frame.[24]

Duchamp worked on "The Large Glass" between 1915 and 1923 in his New York studio, having developed the ideas for the work during his stay in Munich and elsewhere. He left the work "definitively unfinished," as he himself proclaimed, since the work no longer "amused him," Duchamp's favorite expression when talking about his art. "The Large Glass" is the name commonly used for this work whose title must be one of the most inscrutable in art history: "La mariée mise à nu par ses célibataires, même ...," "The Bride

Marcel Duchamp, then twenty-five years old, lived and worked for about three months in Munich in the summer of 1912, widely regarded as a creatively important period in the artist's development.

Stripped Bare by Her Bachelors, Even ..." (this translation misses the point that the "bachelors" are also virgins, célibataires). The little additional word "même," "even," shrouds this title in another veil of mystery, in one of those puns that Duchamp, more than anything else in his art, liked to "amuse" himself with. With this small addition, he gave scores of academics and Duchamp fanatics something to theorize about to this day and certainly for the foreseeable future.

"The Large Glass," or "The Bride Stripped Bare ...," can be classified as a Conceptual artwork, a complex assemblage executed with high precision in mixed techniques. The glass is divided into two sections, which Duchamp himself calls the domains of the bride (the upper section) and the bachelors. The "bride" is an abstract figure reminiscent of something smeared with acid, designed in lead foil, while the "bachelors" are nine painted figures similar to components in Duchamp's previous machine paintings. The bride and bachelors are complemented by other motifs. One is the chocolate grinder in the bachelors' domain, a machine that Duchamp had seen in a shop window in his home town of Rouen, and which he painted in a first version in 1913 in a stripped-down architectural style, fascinated as he said by the sexual symbolism of the rotating mill heads, here executed in lead wire, then hand-painted before being sealed in the glass.

The "engine" of the work is, according to the artist himself, erotic. Duchamp must have entertained peculiar fantasies. Who else would think of symbolizing the role play and sexual act between man and woman by mechanical devices? If I may empty my tiny vessel into the river of Duchamp theories, I guess the deeply ironic artist was amused by the automaticity of this ancient game, the origin of humanity. A basic premise of "The Large Glass" is that the aluminum frame dividing the 2.77-meter-high glass sculpture precludes any contact between the bride and her bachelors. In Duchamp's play on words, the group of bachelors, seemingly rotating around an axis, are called "Moules Malic," roughly translated as "male forms," or "male types." Together they form the so-called bachelor machine, frozen in perpetually fruitless rotating pursuit of female gratification ...

In a creative process that lasted more than eight years, Marcel Duchamp allowed chance, a factor which he revered, to interfere. For example, he had left the artwork untouched in his New York studio for so long that the glass had accumulated mounds of dust. Man Ray immortalized this thick layer of dust in his classic photograph "Dust Breeding,"[25] an extreme close-up study. Duchamp became so fond of the dust that he encased some of the dust particles in the glass. With "The Bride Stripped Bare ..." Duchamp had invented a manner to depersonalize his art, akin to the method he used with his readymades. His desire was to keep the idea of the artwork as "pure" as possible. He preferred, as he said, "the idea without the interference of the hand's work," a legacy that has been carried on by Duchamp-inspired artists such as Andy Warhol and Jeff Koons, to name just two of the most obvious.

By his own account, Duchamp never intended to show "The Large Glass" publicly. The work was purchased in 1921 by Katherine Dreier, Duchamp's friend, patron and collector. When Dreier wanted to exhibit the work in 1927, Duchamp agreed in his usual cooperative style. After the end of the exhibition, the fragile giant artwork was transported poorly packed by truck. Only five years later, when Dreier prepared to install the piece in her Connecticut home, was it discovered that the glass panels were shattered.[26] Katherine Dreier was understandably distraught, but Duchamp retained his usual equanimity ("beauty in indifference" was his ideal). After being persuaded almost ten years later to spend months of painstaking work joining the shards and reconstructing the glass,[27] the artist, true to his dead-pan philosophy, asserted that the repaired glass's myriad of cracks had only made his portal work "a hundred times better."[28]

"The Large Glass" is part of the collection of the Philadelphia Museum of Art, where Duchamp's patron Walter Arensberg had been determined to ensure that the bulk of Duchamp's output was collected. The reason why Arensberg, and Duchamp — apparently keen on his artistic legacy despite expressing disdain for such vanity — chose this prestigious yet provincial museum was that the leading institutions that had been offered the collection, the Museum of Modern Art, the Art Institute of Chicago and the Guggenheim, had only been willing to promise a short-term display, while Philadelphia guaranteed that it would be on permanent show for at least ten years. Since the collection was installed in Philadelphia after the 1950 donation, it has never been dismantled, becoming the museum's major attraction for art lovers from all over the world and a pilgrimage site for Duchamp fans, artists and art historians.

Borrowing "The Large Glass" from Philadelphia for *Art in Motion* was out of the question. The delicate work has never been lent by the museum. After the "scheme" with the miniature for the exhibition at the Bokkonsum gallery the year before, Hultén now had the bold idea to produce the first full-scale replica of "The Bride Stripped Bare By Her Bachelors, Even ..." for *Art in Motion*. I've never quite understood what "The Glass" has to do with Kinetic Art, even though the work is said to portray "the erotic automatism" and its figures are collectively called the "love machine." Here Hultén allowed himself, as was his wont, a generous interpretation of his own theme, all in the honorable ambition of presenting as interesting an exhibition as possible to the public.

Pontus Hultén wrote to Duchamp, who encouraged his plans to produce the copy.[29] The commission went to Ulf Linde, with a fee of ten thousand crowns.[30] In my interview, Hultén said that he "persuaded" Linde to take on the full-scale replica of the glass.[31]

As I've mentioned, Ulf Linde is a complicated character who played an important role in Pontus Hultén's early career. Linde did not hold a formal position at Moderna Museet at this time other than as a member of the Friends of Moderna Museet, where his partner Bertha Lundgren was the secretary, highly regarded by Pontus Hultén and everyone else at the museum for her personality and work capacity. Bertha Lundgren was one of the original staff of Moderna Museet. Her salary wasn't paid by the museum but by the Friends, which meant that she, and her partner Linde, who was also the editor of the Friends' magazine, could be used as much-needed free extra manpower.

In his professional life, Ulf Linde, who was originally a jazz musician, something as odd as a vibraphonist, was also an art writer and critic for Dagens Nyheter, much later a distinguished member of the Royal Swedish Academy. It seems inconceivable nowadays how Linde could review the exhibitions that he himself was more or less involved in for Sweden's leading newspaper. This dual role was beneficial to the museum. For example, Linde wrote one of the important texts in defense of *Art in Motion* in the heated debate that followed the opening, when the future of the exhibition and the museum management was at stake.[32]

The work of crafting the replica of "The Large Glass" was conducted in Moderna Museet's workshop on Skeppsholmen where Ulf Linde, as I understand it, assumed the mantle of artistic director in a work that in practice was carried out by Moderna Museet's, or rather the National Museum's carpenters and hired experts. Per Olof Ultvedt, who had made the miniature for Bokkonsum's gallery, participated in the work, as did Bertha Lundgren's son Lars Lundgren and a couple of other Swedish artists.[33]

There are various alternative accounts of how Marcel Duchamp and his wife Alexina "Teeny" Duchamp came to travel to Stockholm in August 1961, three months after the opening of *Art in Motion*. Paul B. Franklin claims that the replica of "The Large Glass" and positive reviews of the exhibition from the artist's friends had contributed to Duchamp's urge to see the show and the work with his own eyes.[34] Linde's replica had been presented at the opening of the exhibition, albeit in an incomplete form.[35] Work on improvements and additions continued during the course of the exhibition, in dialog with Duchamp. Pontus Hultén told me: "Linde and Duchamp talked on the phone daily. It was most amusing to listen to descriptions of subtle color nuances. After a while Duchamp said 'that's enough of this, I'll come up and help you instead.'"[36]

Duchamp's visit is well documented. After an exchange of letters with Hultén, Duchamp and Teeny booked the trip from Paris. It's illustrative not only for the museum's scarce resources but also for Duchamp's simple habits that the couple didn't stay in a hotel but in the small one-room chamber that Ulf Linde used as a study next to his and Bertha Lundgren's apartment in a functionalist building on the western outskirts of the city.

In his 1986 book *Marcel Duchamp*, Ulf Linde recounts how Duchamp, upon arriving at the museum, stood for a long time looking at his copy in every detail, commenting that it was "funny, but he had never thought of the glass as unbroken," as he had become accustomed over the decades with the shattered original. He asked if Linde had come to the same conclusion as himself: "that only madmen would sacrifice so much time for so much lead wire."[37]

During his five-day visit, Duchamp worked with Linde, Ultvedt and janitor Sture Johansson at the museum, where the exhibition was in its final phase, on corrections and additions to "The Glass." The whole was impressive, but the differences from the original were conspicuous. Linde and his collaborators had relied on black-and-white photographs, reproductions with questionable color schemes, and Duchamp's hand-colored photographs in the book *Sur Marcel Duchamp* as models. The artist painted a figure called "The Strainer" in "verona green," using his finger instead of a brush, as Linde observed.[38] Duchamp, Linde and others then worked for two days with a master glazier on a subtle batch of glass panels called "The Bride's Clothes" that the Swedes had missed because it was not visible in photographs.[39]

Pp. 142–143: Carlo Derkert, Pontus Hultén, Marcel Duchamp and Ulf Linde during work on "The Large Glass," Moderna Museet, Stockholm, August 1961.

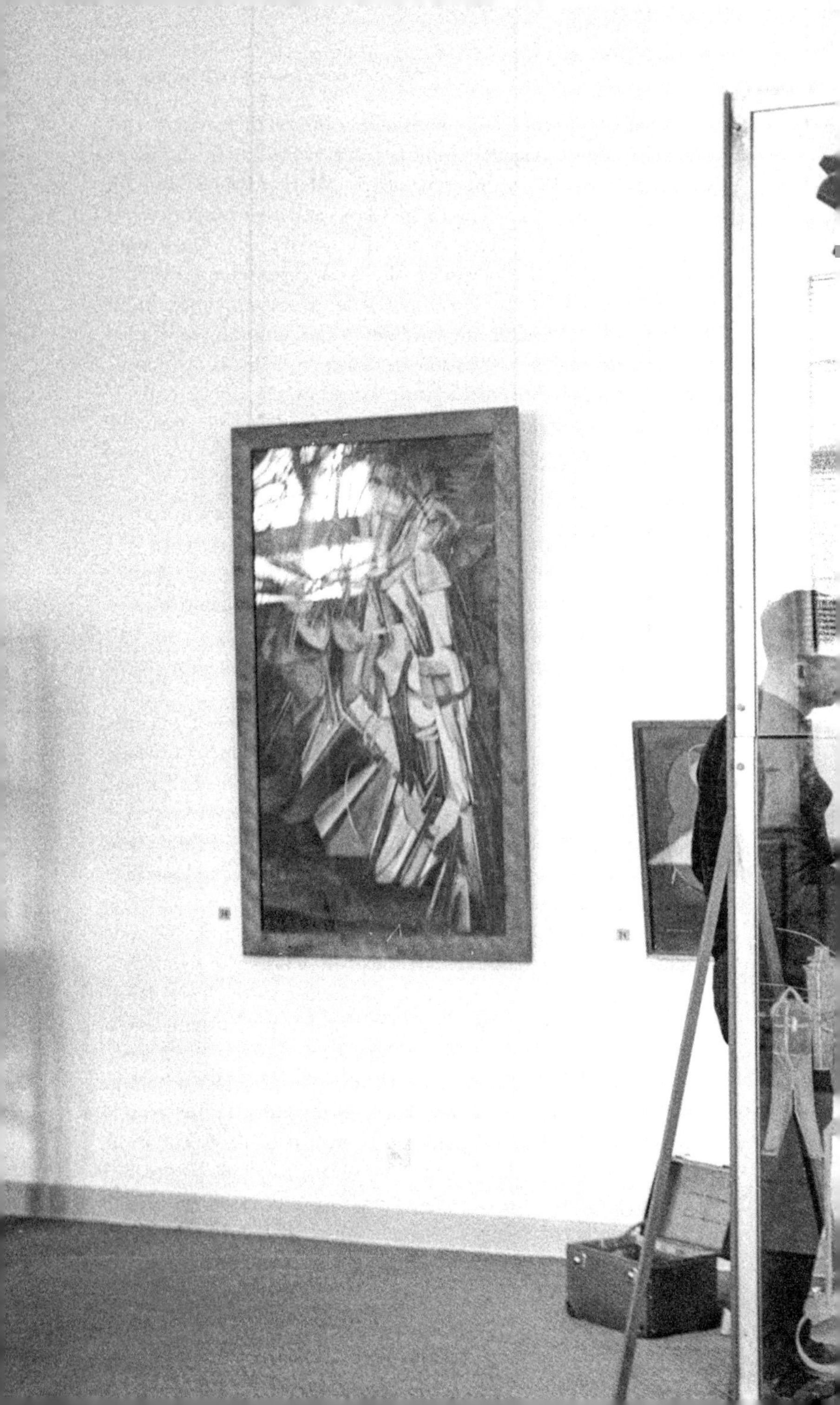

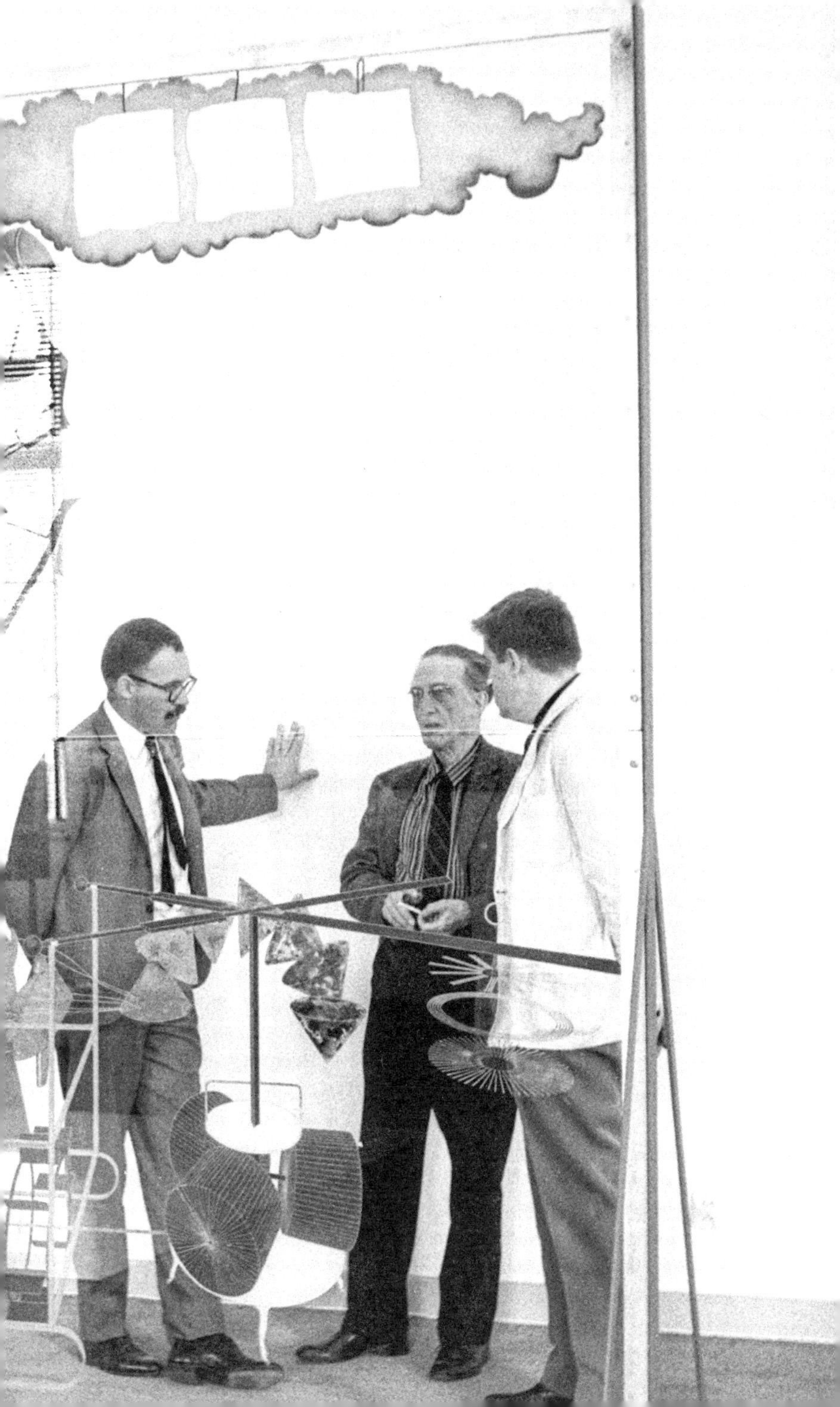

Duchamp declared himself satisfied — "bewilderingly satisfied"[40] — with the result and signed "The Glass" without hesitation with an inscription in white paint on the back of one of the "bachelors": "certifié pour copie conforme ["certified true copy"], Marcel Duchamp, Stockholm, 1961." The replica of "The Bride Stripped Bare By Her Bachelors, Even ..." has since been one of Moderna Museet's most internationally attractive works, a world-famous centerpiece that was constantly on loan to leading museums globally before the copy was "retired" in the early nineties, like the original in Philadelphia, and banned from traveling.

In addition, Hultén cunningly seized the opportunity to ask Duchamp to sign the readymades that he and his colleagues had commissioned for the exhibition at the Bokkonsum gallery the previous year, as well as his own, Ultvedt and Wibom's "Rotative plaques verre," made in 1960–1961. All these works were officially donated by the artist, entering the museum's collection.

Certainly, we must adore the nihilistic radicalism of signing copies of one's own works, even those that were markedly different from the originals. With his relaxed, unpretentious stance, Duchamp effortlessly stripped bare the cult of the godlike artistic genius and the sacred value of the unique work of art.

During his visit to Stockholm, Duchamp had lunch with Oscar Reutersvärd at the Lyktan restaurant on adjacent Blasieholmen island. During the lunch conversation, the artist confided that he had effectively felt "finished" with his work in art as early as 1930, even though he "contradicted himself sometimes." By then, Duchamp told Reutersvärd, he had "created all sorts of artistic images and objects, for all experiences and thoughts, for all senses and units of perception — sight, touch, temperature, imagination." "One day I had the idea of being the pioneer and inventor of all possible forms of sensory and intellectual art," Duchamp explained "with a shy smile" to Reutersvärd. The Swedish artist asked his illustrious older colleague how he could be so pleased and satisfied with Ulf Linde's copy of "The Large Glass," even though it differed in so many ways from the original. His answer was a development of the artist's inimitable philosophy of art. "According to his quantitative aesthetics," Duchamp explained, "all discussion, all varieties of interpretation, and even negative views, were something desirable that made his works and ideas grow and be enriched." Duchamp assured Reutersvärd that "even the cracks in the Glass, which were the result of 'damn negligence,' were an improvement on it."[41]

In my interview, Pontus Hultén spoke about the crucial services that Marcel Duchamp rendered to the museum, including providing contacts for the acquisition of two of the most important pieces in Moderna Museet's collection a few years later, after the museum had received its sensational one-off grant of five million crowns from the Swedish government (see Chapter 10).

The first of these stories is the legend, well known in the international art world, of the purchase of "The Child's Brain," the 1914 masterpiece by the Italian "Pre-Surrealist" Giorgio de Chirico. From the outset, Hultén and the museum had chosen the strategy of focusing their purchases on a limited number of key works that would ideally mark progress and important moments in the history of modern art. de Chirico's painting readily meets this criterion, as it is considered a point of embarkment for Surrealism, Pontus explained to me.[45]

"The Child's Brain" was owned at that time, in the early sixties, by André Breton himself. This was during the war in Algeria. The communist Breton was an agitator for the side of freedom and an object of hatred for the French extreme right and its militant secret nationalist resistance movement, the OAS. An attack had already been made against Breton,[46] Hultén claimed. Duchamp, in his usual concern for his friends and for art, perhaps also in his instinct as an art dealer, thought that "The Child's Brain" was unsuitable to be kept in Breton's home and that the painting should be given a safe public residence, introducing Hultén to the Surrealist leader.[47] The world's major museums were passive in their acquisitions at this time, and tiny Moderna Museet, with its magnificent money bag from the state grant, was able to act as virtually the sole buyer on a market where modern masterpieces were still available.

In Hultén's words, a "funny thing" was the occurrence that the price of a masterpiece at this time was fixed: two hundred thousand crowns, "whether it was a Klein, a Giacometti or whatever."[48] Then there were exceptionally important cornerstones that were more expensive, Pontus said, such as the "figurehead", the de Chirico painting. "I had prepared a long ceremonious introduction but as soon as Breton entered the room he asked 'how much do you want to pay,'" Hultén recounted. "I was a bit flabbergasted but quickly regained my composure and replied: 'We'll pay like a Nobel Prize,' which was five hundred and fifty thousand at the time. Breton knew by then that he was not going to be awarded the Nobel Prize and I think he found my comment somewhat amusing. In any case, the deal was later sealed."[49]

"When I was waiting in his studio, I saw that he had fabulous masterpieces by all his Surrealist friends," Hultén added. "He had magnificent Dalís but I knew that was out of the question because of their conflict. I saw a great Miró that was hanging quite high. When we had settled the first deal, I tactfully remarked that this nice painting was hanging very high indeed. 'How much do you want to pay?', Breton asked immediately. So I came up with my usual two hundred thousand and walked away with another deal."[50]

Ulf Linde provides a completely different version of the events that led to the acquisition of "The Child's Brain." Linde relates a visit to Paris with Bertha Lundgren where he encountered Arturo Schwarz in the revolving door of his hotel, "an Italian art dealer who, for a curious fee, I had published a text I had written about Duchamp the year before, and who also in other respects had shaken my confidence in the 'art world.'"[51] Linde continues: "Arturo had once invited my wife and me to a fabulous dinner on the outskirts of Milan and then, over the liqueur, done everything to convince us that he was André Breton's closest confidant in the world, 'now that Trotsky was dead'. Bertha, my wife, came up with the excellent idea that Arturo should have the pleasure of proving that he had spoken the truth, and we quickly took another half turn on the revolving door to catch up with him in the street (...) Can you arrange for the Modern Museum to buy 'The Child's Brain', she asked."[52]

Linde writes that Schwarz was taken aback but came to his senses and said yes, and that the following morning he, Linde, was surprised to receive a call from Breton's lawyer who had arranged a meeting with the author in the hotel bar, suggesting that a sale might not be out of question. Linde states that he called Hultén, who gave him a free hand, and continues: "While we were talking, André Breton himself came down the stairs to the bar, descending silently like a heavy cloud, a cloud that immediately filled the whole room — everyone fell silent, even Sartre who was sitting with some admirers in a corner. Breton (...) made it quite clear that he didn't want to talk business, that he just wanted to hear something about Ingmar Bergman. The next day the lawyer called and confirmed that the purchase was complete."[53]

Pontus Hultén's second story about Duchamp's, as I assume unsalaried, efforts as a broker of sales contacts concerned Salvador Dalí. Dalí was ousted from the Surrealist group by André Breton in 1939. It was widely believed among the Surrealists and the left that Dalí was corrupt, a slave to capital. Suspected of fascist leanings (rightly so, as he was on friendly terms with the dictator Franco, although Dalí was certainly not a fascist), he was contemptuously referred to by Breton as "Avida Dollars" (roughly "lust for dollars") with his commissions for the fashion industry, Hollywood and Walt Disney. In the highbrow art society, Dalí carried a stigma of cheapness that to some extent still afflicts the artist today.

For Pontus Hultén and Moderna Museet, Salvador Dalí was a main priority, as his importance in modern art history was indisputable, as was his popularity. Marcel Duchamp knew that Dalí's monumental painting "The Enigma of Wilhelm Tell"[54] from 1933, now among Dalí's most famous works and one of Moderna Museet's star attractions, was available. "The painting was controversial in more orthodox communist Surrealist circles because, as you know, the person pictured is Lenin," Pontus said in my interview. "All the agony had caused Dalí to simply roll up the painting. It had been in his studio for twenty years but now Duchamp knew that it was currently exhibited in Tokyo where it was hanging without a frame. So I traveled to Tokyo and got the painting for my usual two hundred thousand."[55]

There is at least one alternative truth about the Dalí painting as well. In Moderna Museet's fiftieth anniversary book *The History Book. On Moderna Museet 1958–2008*, Billy Klüver relays that it was he himself, and no other, who settled the deal for "The Enigma of Wilhelm Tell" in New York, through contacts with Dalí's wife Gala.[56]

Pontus Hultén's accounts of these affairs, and Linde's and Klüver's alternative recollections, illustrate the difficulty of finding an unequivocal truth among the anecdotes in so many of these events. The common denominator of the different versions of reality is usually that the narrator him/herself claims credit for the exploits. "My experience is that different versions can all be true, in whole or in part," says Olle Granath. "Frequently different contacts that were maintained in several locations."[57]

Pontus Hultén's, Ulf Linde's and other friends' impudent copying, or replicating to use the more forgiving term, of Duchamp's "The Large Glass" and the readymades, and the artist's even more audacious approval of these replicas with his signature, would prove to be of major art historical impact — for Moderna Museet and even more so for the global awareness of Duchamp and his readymades, for the artist's second breakthrough and, by extension, for Duchamp's dominance of contemporary art.

In 1963, Ulf Linde continued the quest of constructing copies/replicas in an exhibition for the gallerist Eva af Burén, at her Galerie Burén on Sturegatan. af Burén was a well-known figure in the Stockholm art scene, described as elegant and sophisticated, "unforgettable," according to Linde.[58] She was one of several Stockholm gallerists at the time with good connections in Paris. According to Linde, he and the gallerist had begun talking after af Burén had consulted him about how to display her copy of "La Boîte-en-valise" — discussions that evolved into the idea of staging an exhibition with all thirteen of Duchamp's readymades reproduced. Duchamp enthusiastically agreed in a letter to Linde.[59] Pontus Hultén's presence in the background is apparent in that the readymades produced for the exhibition would not be for sale, but incorporated into the Moderna Museet collection after the exhibition — something that Duchamp, as is evident from correspondence, was keen on realizing.[60]

It's now considered a more or less established truth about "Fountain" that this readymade, the most famous and scandalous of them all, the urinal, was in fact presented to Duchamp by "Baroness Dada," Elsa von Freytag-Loringhoven. The Baroness is said to have pointed out to Duchamp that the urinal resembled a female genital organ. Duchamp submitted "Fountain" to the Society of Independent Artists, signed "R. Mutt," where it was rejected, even though the idea of the salon was that everything that was submitted, after payment of a fee, would be shown. The Duchamp/von Freytag Loringhoven urinal disappeared at the exhibition and lives on in art history only through a photograph by Alfred Stieglitz.

Together with the artist Elis Eriksson, Ulf Linde hired craftsmen in various workshops in and around Stockholm to make a further eleven readymades. For the price of two hundred and twenty crowns, a stone company on Sankt Eriksgatan carved the four hundred marble cubes to the size of slightly oversized sugar cubes for one of my personal favorites, "Why not sneeze, Rrose Sélavy?" (1921), a lacquered birdcage filled with these "sugar cubes" in which the sensory surprise effect is achieved by the object having a radically different weight than expected. The artist Carl Fredrik Reuterswärd was in New York and, after visiting Philadelphia, was able to assist Linde with observations of details in the original works — such as each marble sugar cube in 'Why not sneeze ...' being stamped "Made in France," which Linde arranged by ordering a rubber stamp.[61]

A popular legend, described by Ulf Linde in his 1986 book *Marcel Duchamp*, is that of "Fountain" (1917), the urinal, which caused particular problems. No one could find a urinal that resembled the original until Linde himself stepped into the men's room at the classic restaurant Tre Remmare on Regeringsgatan and discovered a "picture-like" specimen. Linde managed to convince the restaurateur to sell the ceramic piece in exchange for a plumbing company installing another in its place. According to Linde, the stinking urinal was then flushed and scrubbed clean by the gallery owner Eva of Burén herself, dressed in a Chanel suit and rubber gloves, in the gallery's backyard — a chic memory, perhaps even true.[62]

As these readymades arrived at the gallery, Eva af Burén became increasingly enthusiastic but also increasingly worried. She finally concluded that the whole thing was "incomprehensible," which Linde admits she was probably right about.[63]

The exhibition at Galerie Burén was vigorously discussed in the Swedish press. Ulf Linde was praised for his reproductions and for his learned catalog text. Afterwards, an agreement was reached whereby the Moderna Museet Friends Association, led by Bertha Lundgren, paid Eva af Burén four thousand crowns for the eleven newly produced replicas, which were officially cataloged in the museum's collection in 1965.

Hultén's, Linde's and the museum's new collection of replicas, with "The Large Glass" as the center piece, immediately embarked on a world tour, much in demand with the newly awakened global interest in Duchamp that had accelerated with *Art in Motion*. In the fall of the same year as the Galerie Burén exhibition, "The Large Glass" and several of the museum's freshly fashioned readymades made a legendary appearance in the exhibition *By or of Marcel Duchamp or Rrose Sélavy*, presented by the young curatorial whiz kid rebel Walter Hopps at the Pasadena Art Museum in Los Angeles. Incredibly, this was the then seventy-six-year-old Duchamp's first ever retrospective (see Chapter 25).

Through contacts with Pontus Hultén, Hopps had already secured the loan of "The Large Glass," a main attraction in the Pasadena exhibition. After the Galerie Burén show, Hultén/Ultvedts/Wibom's "Rotative plaques verre" and three of Linde's readymades were sent to Pasadena where these replicas complemented the originals and older reproductions borrowed from Philadelphia and elsewhere. While in Pasadena, Duchamp signed Linde's three new readymades from Galerie Burén for Moderna Museet.[64]

On its way back from Pasadena, "The Large Glass" stopped in over Paris, where it was shown in a group exhibition for Surrealism on the occasion of the movement's fortieth anniversary. In correspondence, Hultén personally wrote instructions on how to handle the fragile glass, adding "we trust you" (he personally supervised the dismantling and packing on site in Paris).[65] It was the first time that the Paris audience saw the piece that was only then beginning to be widely regarded as Duchamp's most important. The work attracted a great deal of attention in the exhibition, which was extended over the summer to satisfy strong public interest.

With their bold copying of Marcel Duchamp's work, sanctioned by the artist, Hultén, Linde and their friends spawned a small movement in the art world. In London, British Pop artist Richard Hamilton made his own replica of "The Large Glass" in 1965–1966, after visiting the Duchamp retrospective in Pasadena where he had studied Linde's version in detail.[66]

In Milan, Arturo Schwarz would become notorious as perhaps the most extreme Duchamp fanatic of them all. Schwarz was inspired by Hultén and Linde, emboldened by the occurrence that the artist had allowed the Stockholmers to make replicas of his works.[67] He managed to persuade Duchamp to allow him produce his own edition of eleven readymades in an edition of ten copies each, all for sale.[68] Arturo Schwarz, like Pontus Hultén and Ulf Linde, continued to produce copies of Duchamp's art even after the artist's death in 1968.

Arturo Schwarz's theories about Marcel Duchamp's art are controversial. In my conversation with Duchamp's stepson Paul Matisse, he told me that as a young "know-nothing" he once asked the artist how he could tolerate Schwarz claiming that symbolism in his art was based on his incestuous relationship with his sister. "But Paul," Duchamp replied, "it's not me who says that, but him. It's not my business." (Paul Matisse, telephone interview, February 2, 2016)

In the art world, I've been told that there was a rivalry between Pontus Hultén and Arturo Schwarz. Schwarz did not want to acknowledge this when I met him in April 2016. Like most of the other contemporaries I have interviewed, he spoke well of Hultén. Schwarz had some difficulty with his memory but said: "He was a very nice man — a real gentleman. We often met in Paris and Milan and went out to dinner and so on. We were united by our strong interest in Duchamp. I don't remember which of us started making copies."[69] Here, forgetfulness helps Schwarz. It's well established that he followed the Swedes' example.

Pontus Hultén and his friends were not the first to produce copies of Duchamp's work. Already in the early fifties, the New York dealer Sidney Janis, in collaboration with Duchamp himself, produced replicas of "Fountain," the urinal, and "Bicycle Wheel," the two readymades that had been lost. Still, it's evident from history that Hultén was the one who initiated the duplication of Duchamp's work on a larger scale ten years later. Thus, it can be argued that he helped to realize Duchamp's vision that "art needs its Gutenberg." There's no question that these new replicas, often shown in various exhibitions around the world, helped bring Duchamp's art and ideas to a wider audience that was no longer confined to the museum in Philadelphia.

Duchamp's first breakthrough in the 1910s had been caused by his paintings, notably "Nude Woman Descending a Staircase." His second, half a century later, in the early sixties, highlighted his conceptual oeuvre, through "The Large Glass" and his readymades — the side of Duchamp that revolutionized art.

To conclude, Marcel Duchamp, Pontus Hultén's early "discovery" of him, the replication of his art and Duchamp's visit to Stockholm were of inestimable importance not only for the knowledge of Duchamp but also for Moderna Museet. No other museum besides the Philadelphia Museum of Art has a collection of the most influential artist of the twentieth century that even compares to that of Moderna Museet — a world attraction created at a cost of a few thousand dollars in the years around 1960.

The connection to Duchamp donned the young museum an important status for the future, especially among contemporary artists of the international avant-garde, who, unlike the establishment at the time, understood Duchamp's importance. The whole affair is, to me, a rather incredible, radical achievement by a group of young Stockholmers with methods not so distant from the Blandaren pranks of the mid-fifties. Certainly, Ulf Linde may be the name most people at home associate with Duchamp and these replicas. *À la bonne heure*, as the Frenchman says, Linde's efforts were no doubt important. Personally, I have no difficulty in seeing who was the brain behind these operations — who was the quarterback of this brilliant little offense, if I may use an American football analogy.

Pontus Hultén's research on Marcel Duchamp at this time would have a piquant aftermath much later, reminiscent of certain other less flattering events in Hultén's career, as Paul B. Franklin discusses in the Stockholm issue of Étant donné Marcel Duchamp. In the mid-2010s, many years after Hultén's death, it was discovered that he had possessed a number of sketches by Duchamp that could be traced back to the archives of Yale University in New Haven, Connecticut.

Pontus Hultén had paid a visit there during his 1959 journey to the United States for *Art in Motion*, to study some of the legacy that Katherine Dreier had donated to the university, including the original for the optical sculpture "Rotative plaques verre." Paul B. Franklin reveals that Hultén "seems to have absconded" with "at least five" notes and diagrams, written on detached pieces of paper and flaps of envelopes, with Duchamp's instructions for assembling the sculpture. "Hultén probably found these documents in one of the boxes in which the artwork was packed," Franklin writes. Hultén gave one of these "diagrams" to Ulf Linde as a birthday present much later, apparently without any questions asked about provenance.[70] Three others are said to have been previously sold in Paris.[71] The information available in this case is scarce. After the embarrassing revelation, which was noted on a smaller scale in the press, the sketch received by Linde as a gift was returned to Yale.

9 New York goes Stockholm

In Pontus Hultén's mind, plans to organize exhibitions of American, more specifically New York artists had already begun to take shape during his first visit to the American metropolis in the autumn of 1959. According to Hultén, he had intended the exhibition that would be called *4 Americans* for the spring of 1962, but decided to postpone it until the fall because he sensed that the audience was not yet ready.[1]

The selection of artists was given. The museum would show a group exhibition of four of the young artists Pontus Hultén had encountered and befriended during his visit to New York: in addition to Robert Rauschenberg and Jasper Johns the sculptor Richard Stankiewicz and Alfred Leslie, a painter who also worked with experimental film and who, together with the great documentary photographer Robert Frank, had recently directed the acclaimed short film *Pull My Daisy*,[2] a "beat film" with Allen Ginsberg in one of the roles and Jack Kerouac as the narrator; something that impressed the avant-garde film aficionados Hultén and Klüver. As Pontus replied to my question about this selection: "In those days you didn't make such a fuss of everything. I simply thought it was a good selection and that was it. I had gotten to know Rauschenberg and Johns when they lived together. I saw Stankiewicz as a great innovator of sculpture and Leslie as a typical New Yorker, with plenty of aggressiveness."[3]

Whatever the reasons for the delay, Pontus Hultén confuses the seasons. *4 Americans* opened on March 17, 1962. Again, It must be impossible for a younger audience to imagine how sensational and controversial this exhibition was. The American element in *Art in Motion* had already caused controversy and agony. Now Pontus executed what he had decided to do already during his visit in 1959: present the new New York art for the first time in a museum in Europe.

The title and structure of the exhibition *4 Americans* alludes to the survey show *16 Americans* at MoMA in New York at the turn of 1959/1960, the fifth in a series of exhibitions of American art presented by the radical curator Dorothy Miller, where Robert Rauschenberg's Combines, Jasper John's Targets and also works by young artists such as Frank Stella, Ellsworth Kelly, Alfred Leslie and Richard Stankiewicz were shown for the first time in a museum. Yet it would be several more years before the American museum world and art establishment began to take seriously the movement that had not yet been named Pop Art.

Many argue that despite all his later achievements, this is what Hultén is most famous for in the larger international art world. As one of the first Europeans, he understood the explosive power of this art, which five years after his first New York visit would do what no one thought possible: knock Paris out of its position as the art capital of the world.

Of the four artists featured in the exhibition, Alfred Leslie and Richard Stankiewicz are, if not forgotten, then considered less important on the scale of art historical value. Robert Rauschenberg and Jasper Johns, on the other hand, both rank, as we know, among the greatest names in post-war art.

In modern art history, Rauschenberg and Johns are not labeled Pop artists but Neo-Dadaists. The explanation for this name, as mentioned, is that they were unashamedly inspired by their predecessors among the Dadaists of the 1910s and 1920s.

What was new about New York art was its scale and its violent attack in approach and execution. It was art derived from television, Hollywood and rock'n'roll culture, with the volume cranked up to the max. If this small group of New Yorkers, rooted in a tiny gay coterie on the Lower East Side, had borrowed liberally from the predecessors of European Modernism, they "gave back" through an opposite influence on their contemporary European counterparts.

In Europe in the early 1960s, the United States was about to assume its position as the Great Satan of the left that dominated the cultural circles of the time. Dislike of the US became a unifying force in the

P. 155: *4 Amerikanare, 4 Americans*, Moderna Museet, Stockholm, 1962.
P. 156: Roy Lichtenstein, poster for *Amerikansk popkonst ..., American Pop Art ...*, 1964.
P. 157: Robert Rauschenberg in his performance "The Elgin Tie" in *5 New York Evenings*, Moderna Museet, Stockholm, September 13, 1964.

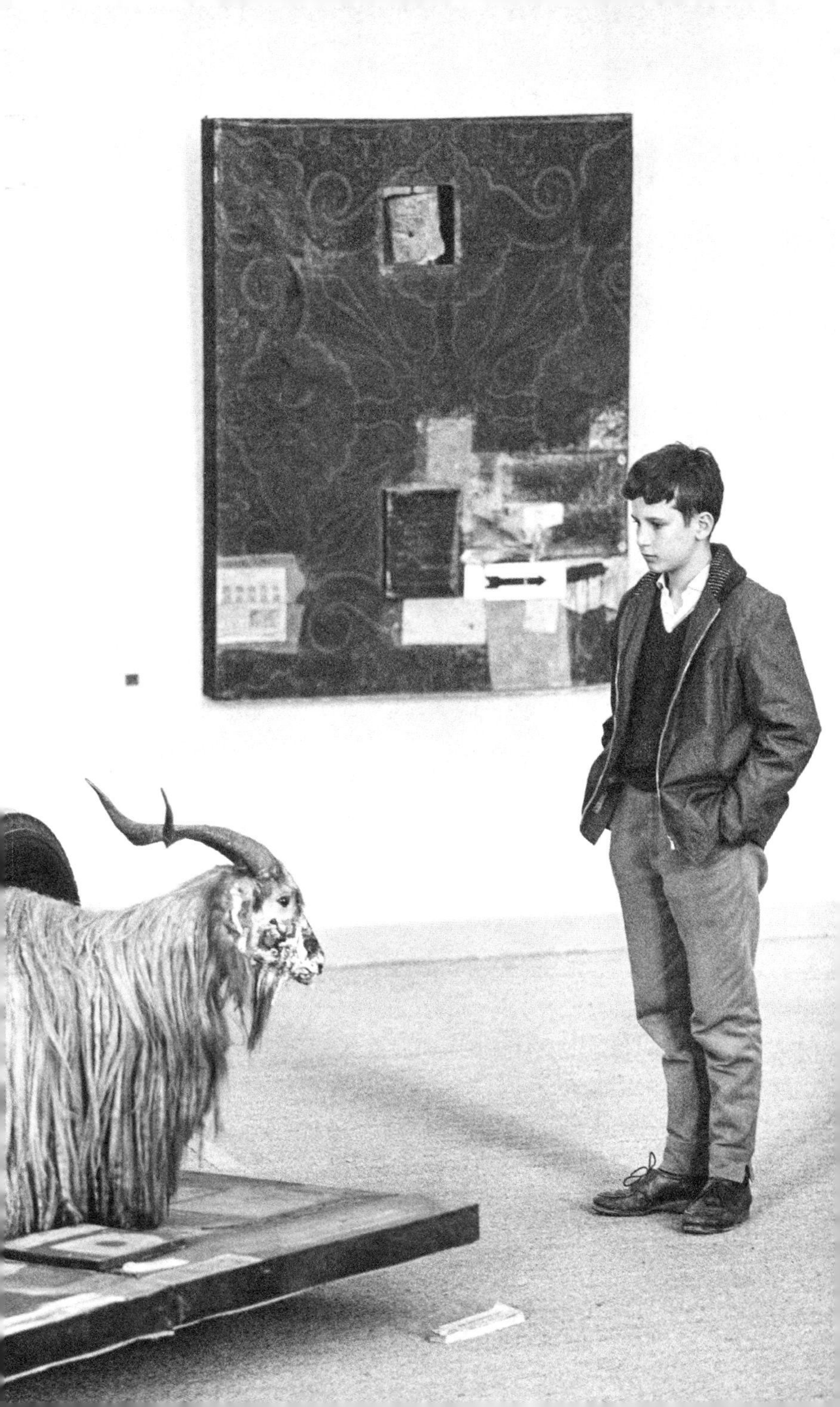

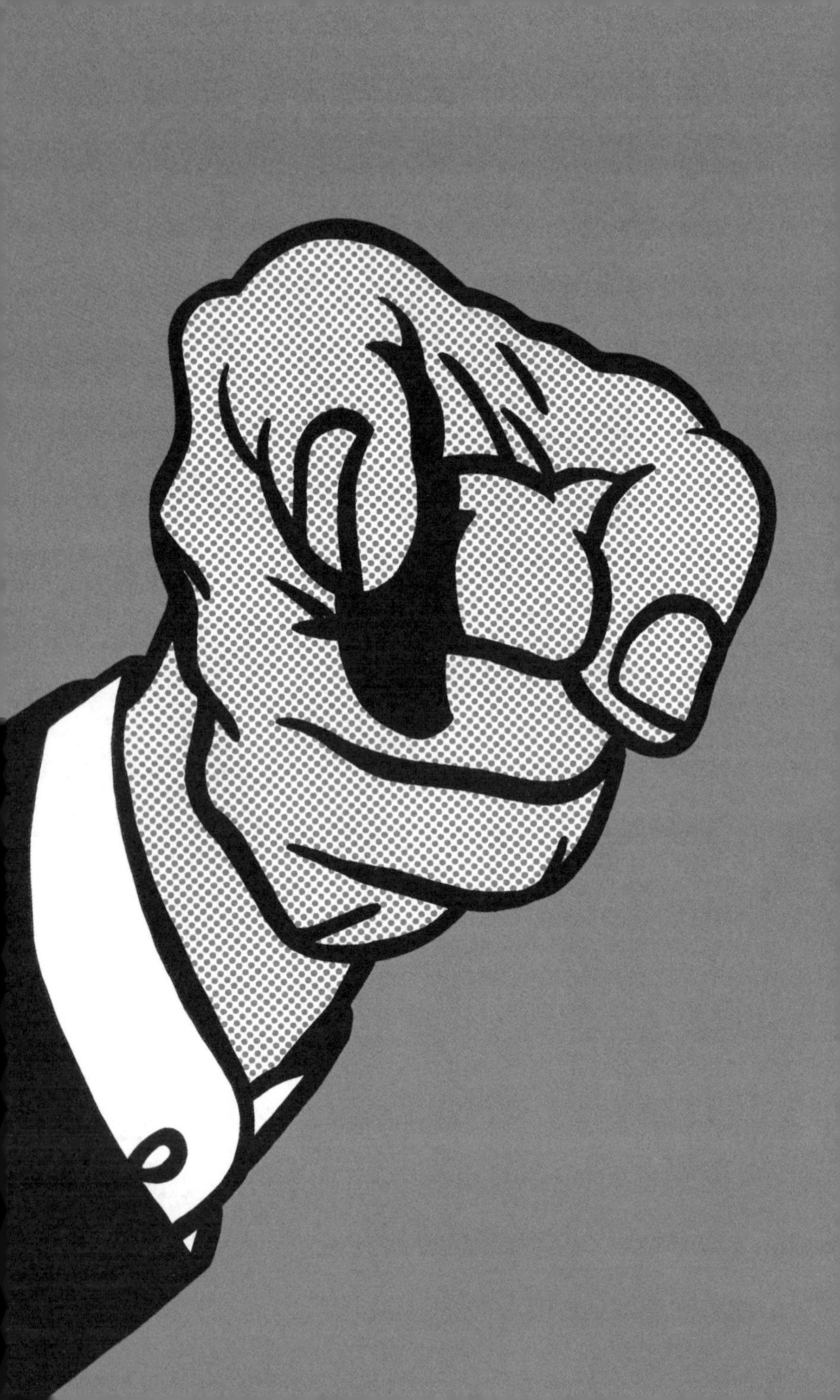

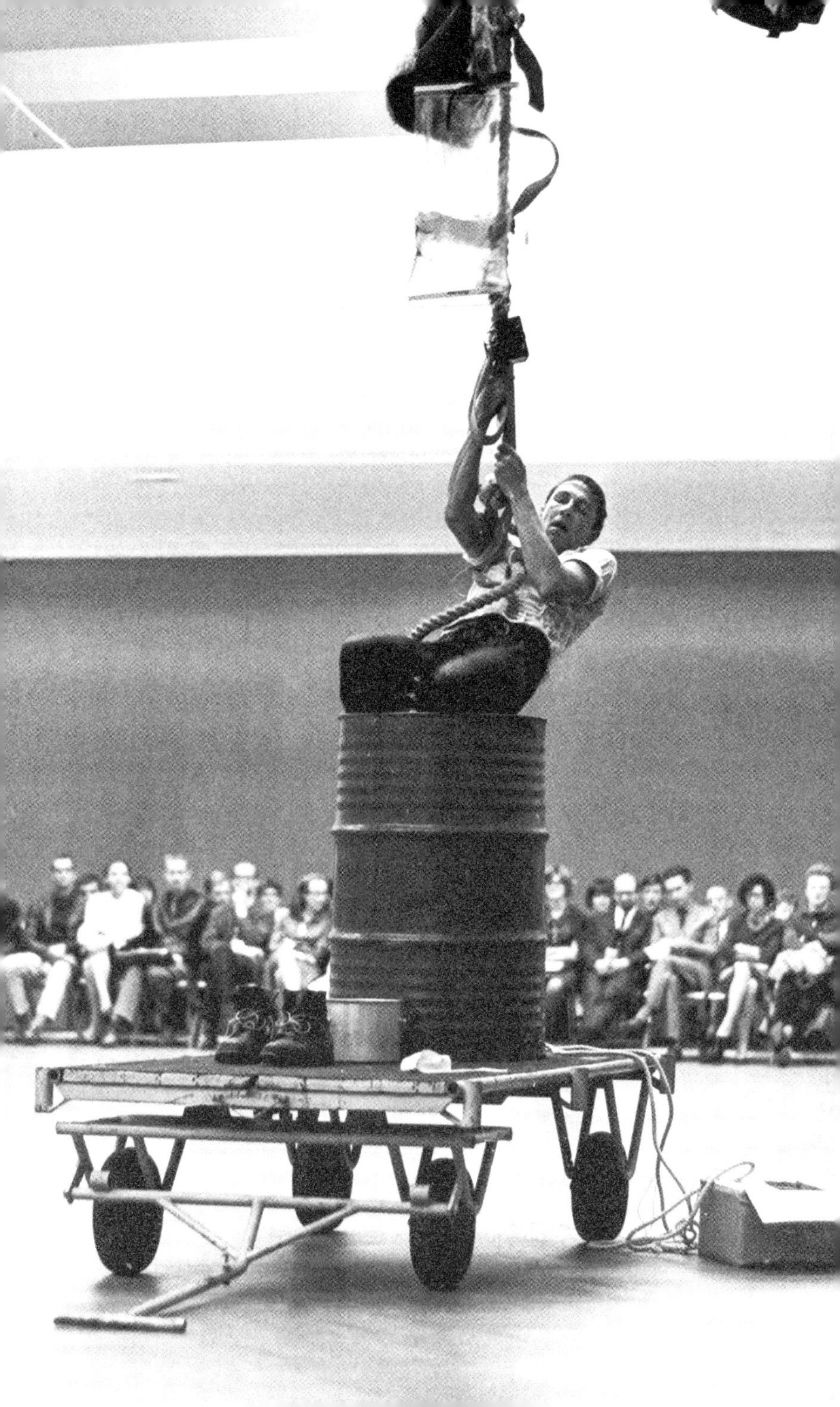

emerging global leftist movement. Post-war gratitude for the Americans as liberators and chewing gum distributors had been replaced by dismay at the US's incipient war in Indochina. The Vietnam movement, a left-wing mobilization unequalled in our post-war history, was on the rise. The left was also motivated by a disgust with the capitalist commercialism represented by the United States. To a large extent, of course, the incentive for this leftist movement consisted of the usual conservative knee-jerk reaction to the new.

The contradiction between Moderna Museet's radicalism and function as an arena for the Swedish and also the international left-wing movement of the 1960s on the one hand, and the museum's repeated exposure of new American art on the other — this was a conflictual relationship that from the outset constituted a witch's cauldron of constant strife. The reality that most of the American artists were anarchists and/or far left, and convinced opponents of predatory capitalism and imperialism, was a context too complicated for the Swedish left-wing movement to digest.

4 Americans was another multimedia extravaganza that included film screenings, performances and events in addition to paintings, sculptures and installations in the museum's galleries.

If *Art in Motion* had kicked off Moderna Museet's heroic years, establishing the museum as a flashpoint for the new and subversive, *4 Americans* reinforced the institution's newfound position as the main arena not only for cultural life but also for Swedish social debate. The term scandal success sums up the effects of the exhibition. *4 Americans* drew huge crowds, sparking a polarized debate in the press and other forums that echoed far beyond Swedish borders.

Among the works shown in *4 Americans*, several are key pieces in the history of post-war modern art, such as Jasper John's targets and American flags, and Robert Rauschenberg's "Combines," assemblages combining sculpture and painting, including "Monogram," commonly known as "The Goat," which later would become a logo for Moderna Museet. Some of these works would eventually be incorporated into the museum's collection — though not in connection with this exhibition. Pontus Hultén told me that, for the most part, there was a consensus on the museum's purchases: "I rarely had to persuade the others in the purchasing committee, but when it came to Pop Art I sometimes had to be quite convincing," Pontus said. "The others thought this was fun and good for temporary exhibitions, but nothing to collect for the future. We were missing out on unique opportunities and here we weren't talking about prices of two hundred thousand crowns per work, but rather five thousand."[4] "Gerard [Bonnier] and I thought that there should be a limit to all that was international and fashionable," Ulf Linde confirmed to me when I interviewed him in 2008.[5]

The story of how Robert Rauschenberg's "Monogram," the sad Angora goat shackled, smeared and humiliated in his car tire, finally made it into the collection of Moderna Museet is yet another legend with several alternative truths.

At this time, Italian-American dealer Leo Castelli, together with his first wife Ileana, née Shapira, later Ileana Sonnabend, had launched his Leo Castelli Gallery. He came to represent virtually all of the leading Pop artists, with Robert Rauschenberg and Jasper Johns as his first clients. The importance of Leo Castelli and Ileana Sonnabend in the conquest of Pop Art should not be underestimated. Like other women in similar positions, Sonnabend, later a world-famous dealer and gallery owner herself, is considered to have been Castelli's mentor in art. Her Romanian family's wealth had enabled Castelli to establish himself as a gallerist, first at Place Vendôme in Paris and much later in New York, where the couple, with the help of Sonnabend's family, had fled at the outbreak of the Second World War.

Leo Castelli was the first super-dealer and pioneer of our current cash-strapped global art market: a slick, tough New York-style businessman. He, or as it has been argued, his wife Ileana, was the first to recognize the commercial potential of Pop Art. Although the art market interaction between gallerists and museums was not nearly as developed as it is today, Leo Castelli and "his" artists fully realized the value of legitimizing the new art through showing it in a state museum — even if that institution was located in a northern province on the other side of the Atlantic. From the start, the contacts between Pontus Hultén and Leo Castelli were crucial to the arrangement of the American exhibitions. The Moderna Museet archives contain voluminous correspondence between the two. Castelli himself was the contact person when it came to transportation, insurance and financial dealings, down to the level of detail in dollars and cents.

About "The Goat," Rauschenberg's "Monogram," it's said that Pontus Hultén simply refused to return the work to New York and Leo Castelli after the exhibition concluded in May, even though he had failed to obtain the mandate and resources for an acquisition. According to Pontus Hultén's partner at the time, Anna-Lena Wibom, the sculpture stood for a period of time in the furnished entrance hall of her and Hultén's apartment on Kungsholmstorg, where the children enjoyed riding it, including the couple's daughter Klara, who had been born in 1960.[6] This story is dismissed as a myth by other people with memories and knowledge of the period. What is certain is that "Monogram" made an interlude in its native New York in the spring and summer of 1963, when the sculpture was a main attraction at Robert Rauschenberg's first solo retrospective at a museum.

Surprisingly, Rauschenberg's exhibition was presented at small Jewish Museum on Fifth Avenue under its new museum director Alan Solomon, a lesser-known key figure in New York's early 1960s art scene, opened with a legendary release party on March 29, 1963. Solomon was a friend and collaborator of Pontus Hultén who contributed a text to the catalog for *American Pop Art* ... in 1964.

In 1963, Moderna Museet continued to present American art in two more traditional solo exhibitions at the beginning of the year, first the forgotten Ben Shahn, then a major exposé of a forerunner of Pop Art, the heroic pioneer of Abstract Expressionism, Jackson Pollock. The exhibition, which was shown at several venues in a European tour, was a sensation and box office success that has been overshadowed by the international breakthrough of Pop Art at Moderna Museet.

At the beginning of the following year, 1964, Pontus Hultén and his colleagues followed up *4 Americans* with a wide-ranging survey show of what Hultén in the catalog refers to as the "second generation of Pop artists" — *American Pop Art. 106 forms of love and despair.*[7] One hundred and six works were shown by Jim Dine, Roy Lichtenstein, Claes Oldenburg, James Rosenquist, George Segal and Andy Warhol. The selection was a hundred percent accurate in its precision. All have gone down in art history and all were at the upstart of their careers, unknown at the time to a wider audience even in their home country. It was far from certain that the exhibition would be the public success it became. Here it's worth reflecting on what Pontus Hultén said about the relationship of the museum and its director to its audience: "As a museum director, it's your duty and privilege to build a loyal audience. People won't come to see an artist called Robert Rauschenberg who they have never heard of unless they have confidence in the museum and know that what we choose to show will be something interesting."[8]

Like *Art in Motion* and *4 Americans*, *American Pop Art* ... was accompanied by a rich program of films, happenings, music, dance, literature and various events, in collaboration with Fylkingen. *The New American*

Cinema[9] series featured films, many of them scandalous, by artists and directors such as Andy Warhol, Jack Smith, Stan Brakhage and others. Pontus Hultén had once and for all embarked on the path that became his hallmark: epic, overflowing multidisciplinary manifestations with accompanying programs that placed art in a larger context — creative, historical, political and philosophical.

In connection with *Art in Motion* and *4 Americans*, Moderna Museet had missed a golden opportunity to buy masterpieces such as Rauschenberg's "Black Market" and "Monogram," Jasper John's flags and targets, and others, at bargain prices. Neither with *American Pop Art …* did Hultén succeed in persuading his colleagues in the newly established purchasing committee to make acquisitions.[10] The museum thus lost the opportunity to acquire many modern classics before prices skyrocketed. Through fortunate circumstances, Moderna Museet was later able to compensate to some extent for what was missed in connection with these early exhibitions. The museum's collection of Pop Art is among the finest in the world, incredibly considered by many as superior to MoMA's.[11] If Pontus Hultén had gotten his way, and the museum would have purchased these works directly in connection with the exhibitions, Moderna Museet's collection of American Pop Art would have been even more superior in the world. The deep traces left by the American exhibitions of the sixties and early seventies can perhaps be detected in an observation that has been shared with me by several foreign observers — that in Sweden our view of art generally seems to be focused on the American and Pop Art tradition.

The artistic expression now known collectively as performance art reached its peak at this time, in 1964. Pioneers include the composer and artist John Cage and his student Allan Kaprow, who had participated with an installation in *Art in Motion*. Kaprow began his artistic career as an action painter in the spirit of Jackson Pollock. In the late 1950s and early 1960s, he refined the action element into an art form in itself. Kaprow developed the expressions then known as "happening" and "environment," authoring theoretical underpinning for these.[12] Pontus Hultén is said to have attended Kaprow's legendary first happening at the Reuben Gallery in Washington Square in New York on his first visit in 1959.[13] Kaprow was part of the circle around Cage, Cunningham, Rauschenberg and Johns on the Lower East Side.

In the late summer and fall of 1964, Merce Cunningham was on a world tour with his dance company. His partner John Cage accompanied him, as did Robert Rauschenberg, who had joined the tour for which he designed stage costumes, created the lighting and set design, and also participated in his own happenings.[14] Pontus Hultén saw the opportunity to lure Cunningham and his company to Stockholm with the promise of a vacation in the archipelago.[15] Cunningham arrived in early September with an impressive ensemble of artists, composers, choreographers and dancers including Cage, Rauschenberg, Steve Paxton, David Tudor, Carolyn Brown, Alex Hay, Deborah Hay, Robert Morris, Yvonne Rainer and Trisha Brown. Öyvind Fahlström also participated. During their stay, the company enjoyed an archipelago vacation at Per Olof Ultvedt's summer house in Roslagen.

5 New York Evenings[16] was a series of happenings, concerts and dance performances that can be considered as linked to *American Pop Art*, organized in close collaboration with Fylkingen, involving local musicians and actors, including from the Royal Ballet. Stockholm audiences were treated to the latest avant-garde performance art straight from downtown Manhattan. Many of the happenings were spectacular, but the one that has come to symbolize Moderna Museet's sixties is Robert Rauschenberg's "The Elgin Tie," in which the artist descended himself on a rope from a skylight in the gallery hall while performing various "chores" with objects attached to the rope, such as changing socks, eating a sandwich, and untying a string knot. Rauschenberg "landed" in a water barrel on a wheeled cart and stepped, dripping with water, into a pair of oversized boots nailed to the floor of the cart. He tied a white tie — the "Elgin tie" — which signaled the entrance of a cow accompanied by Gösta Wibom, a farmer and landowner, brother of Anna-Lena Wibom. The intention was for the "unusually large" heifer to pull the carriage out of the hall. This maneuver could not be executed because of the slippery floor; an assistant pulled the wagon instead while the cow marked her exit by releasing a magnificent pile of dung to the cheers of the audience.[17] One reason why Rauschenberg's performance — which was unrehearsed as the artist proclaimed he was too afraid of heights to perform the rope trick more than once[18] — made art history is that, unlike so many other storied events, it was extensively documented with powerful black-and-white images by photographer Stig T. Karlsson.

Anna-Stina Malmborg and Gunnar Höglund, an art-loving medical doctor couple who much later became major donors to Moderna Museet, provided me with a testimony to the star status that Pontus Hultén's pioneering work rendered him in the new art world capital,

New York. From the beginning, the couple were among the museum's most frequent visitors, devotedly engaged in the Friends' association, of which Anna-Stina Malmborg later became the long-term chairman.

Malmborg and Höglund portray Pontus Hultén as a distant, taciturn person who kept to the background and for whom they had the greatest respect. He paid little notice to the Friends Association and its representatives. The couple says that at openings, the museum's and the Friends' Association parties were held separately, divided by a screen wall. Pontus Hultén rarely if ever came over to visit the Friends' section. "He didn't see us," says Gunnar Höglund. "The most you could expect was a nod and a muttered hello. He was not a socially outgoing person like Carlo Derkert, who was a kind of front man who talked to everyone and was very popular. Pontus didn't see much of his surroundings at all. Gerard Bonnier, yes, the artists, yes, and the Ministry of Culture, yes, but little else. Yet it was obvious from the beginning that he was the power behind getting the museum going."

Anna-Stina Malmborg and Gunnar Höglund donated SEK 50 million to Moderna Museet in 2015 — the largest single donation to the museum in "modern times." With this donation, the museum purchased art by Louise Bourgeois, Olafur Eliasson, Günther Förg, Michel Majerus, Sigmar Polke and Rosemarie Trockel. The Malmborg-Höglund couple also donated works by Cy Twombly and Lucio Fontana to the museum.

The Malmborg-Höglund couple recounts memories from a visit to New York with the Friends' Association in 1963, where Anna-Stina Malmborg served as tour guide and the participants benefited from Hultén's reputation. "It was absolutely unbelievable," says Anna-Stina Malmborg. "All doors swung open like magic at the mention his name. We were received as guests of honor by the biggest collectors. People opened their private homes to us, with big Matisse paintings and an elevator that went straight up in a huge foyer with a big pond with carp and carnations and Brancusi's bird. From Washington, I remember a big dinner banquet with black tablecloths. We came from Stockholm which stood for Pop Art and Hultén and were welcome everywhere."[19]

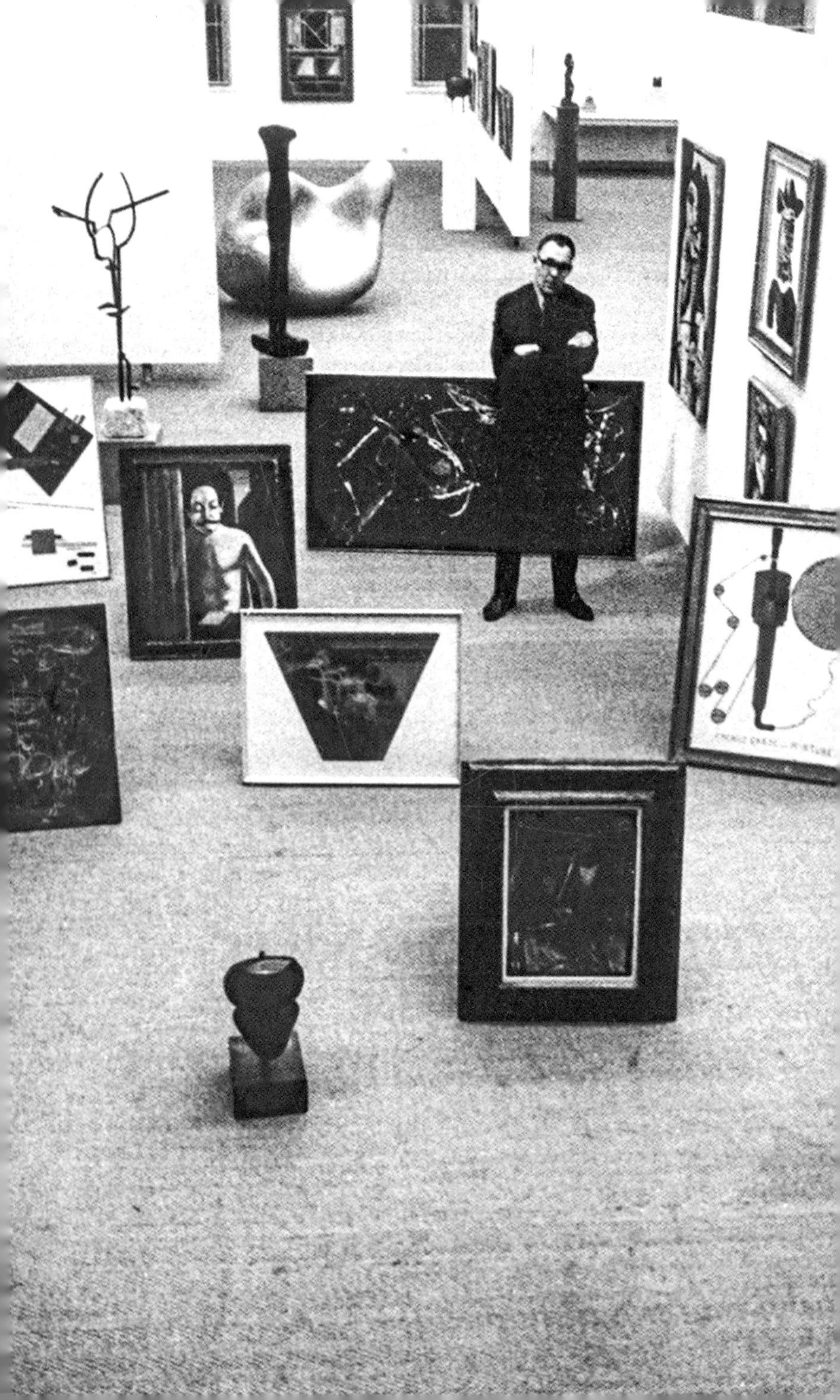

10

The Museum of Wishes — a unique opportunity gives an outstanding collection

Pontus Hultén is most famous for the many art historic exhibitions he staged in museums and other institutions around the world. Informed connoisseurs, however, such as Calvin Tomkins, emphasize an equally important part of Hultén's achievement: his efforts in creating, expanding and strengthening the permanent collections of the museums he directed, most prominently in Stockholm and Paris but also in Los Angeles and, for that matter, at the Museum Tinguely in Basel[1] (Palazzo Grassi in Venice and the Bundeskunsthalle in Bonn, two other institutions of which he was founding director, both lacked collections and should therefore be classified as art galleries rather than museums).

Pontus Hultén himself constantly stressed the crucial necessity of the collection as a "collective memory" and historical anchor for contemporary art — but also for work with temporary exhibitions. In the museum world, the collection functions as a bank for barter. A museum that lends masterpieces can expect to borrow them in return for its own exhibitions. "A good collection is like having money in your pocket," as Hultén expressed it.[2] Without a collection, the organization of exhibitions is more laborious, complicated and costly, as money becomes the only means of payment.

In the twenty-fifth anniversary book from 1983, Pontus Hultén made the oft-quoted judgment "rather poor"[3] about the collection that was part of the new museum's initial capital, that is the art transferred from the modern department at the National Museum, supplemented by donations from, among others, the Friends of Moderna Museet.

Art historian Maria Görts wrote an essay about the "rather poor" collection that Moderna Museet received as a dowry from the parent institution in the museum's fiftieth anniversary book *Historieboken*

Pontus Hultén in *The Museum of Wishes*, Moderna Museet, Stockholm, 1963.

(*The History Book*).[4] As Görts explains, Moderna Museet's collection initially consisted almost exclusively of two elements: Swedish and other Nordic art and purchases from France. German, Italian, English and of course American and Russian art were almost completely absent. In the 1950s, avant-garde modern art from these countries was viewed with skepticism, even considered by some as "subversive."[5]

Our neighboring nations were all the more richly represented: "The collection then contained as many Finnish as French artists, with acquisitions of works by Danish and Norwegian artists in joint third place. (...) The interest in Nordic art appears to be a lively tradition from the 1870s, when the Scandinavian artists formed their own colony in Paris and developed an in many ways similar view of art."[6]

Görts notes that Dada and Surrealism were "considered to be on the fringes" at Nationalmuseum and that no art from these sister movements had been purchased before 1960, while works by "Modernist icons" such as Pablo Picasso, Georges Braque, Fernand Léger, Wassily Kandinsky, Edvard Munch, Oskar Kokoschka[7] and Marc Chagall had been acquired before 1950. Görts further declares that Otte Sköld, as director of the Nationalmuseum, "promoted" the French modern tradition but "was alienated" from the post-war art that Bo Wennberg, as head of the museum's modern department, attempted to acquire. "Occasionally Wennberg succeeded, and Sköld wrote acidic comments in his diary: 'Wennberg on purchases at the Salon de Mai. Germaine Richter and others, can't help but smile at the stupidity of believing that everything 'mother cake' is expressive.'"[8]

Oskar Kokoschka's 1910 portrait "Bildnis eines marquis – Joseph de Montesquiou-Fezensac," purchased by the Nationalmuseum in 1934 from Galerie Axel Vömel in Düsseldorf, was restituted, i.e. returned to surviving relatives, by Moderna Museet in 2018. The painting was sold shortly afterwards at Sotheby's in New York for $20.4 million – a record for the artist.

The shift from the fifties to sixties marked a sharp contrast in the museum's focus. This also applied to the Friends of Moderna Museet's purchases and donations. Having previously purchased and donated exclusively Swedish and Nordic art, with one single exception (the Paris-based Spanish Cubist Juan Gris' "Man with a Violin" from 1953), the Friends switched to focusing on international art, with Alexander Calder's mobile "The Forest is the Best Place" from 1945 as the first acquisition in this new purchasing strategy.[9]

After reading Maria Gört's description of the initial situation for Moderna Museet, it's hard to disagree with Pontus Hultén's assessment of the collection as "rather poor." One can, again, imagine what the new museum would have become if the task of leading the new "branch" had been entrusted to a more traditional academian in the Swedish museum world. There seems to have been no vision whatsoever on the part of the National Museum as to how this collection should be developed.

The young museum management, on the other hand, had the highest possible ambitions. From the very beginning, Pontus Hultén and his colleagues refused to settle for the position of a local or regional museum. Instead, the bold mission was to create an international arena where visitors could survey the history of modern art while strolling through the galleries. The world's leading modern art museums, the Museum of Modern Art in New York and the Stedelijk in Amsterdam, served as role models.

In the twenty-fifth anniversary book, Ulf Linde summarizes the situation in which the museum found itself in the early sixties, during the prelude to *The Museum of Wishes*, the famous exhibition that was presented from December 26, 1963 to February 23, 1964 and which resulted in a sensational expansion of the museum's collection of masterpieces from modern art history: "In 1961, the museum's support association, the Friends of Moderna Museet, had emptied its resources to buy — with additional contributions from private individuals — Brancusi's 'The Newborn'[10] from the legendary Rolf de Maré, who used to keep the sculpture lying on his sofa in his residence (a newborn baby should lie softly ...). The price was SEK 181,000, and the journalists — who always know best — sounded the alarm about an outrageous waste of money. Twenty more works of equivalent magnitude were needed if the museum was to become what it should be: a single purchase had almost broken its neck, and also turned public opinion against it — what was to be done?" [11]

At this time, Linde held no official position in the Friends Association other than as a deputy board member and editor of its journal, but as mentioned, he played an important informal role as an unpaid resource at the museum and later as a member of its purchasing committee, while continuing to write art criticism in Dagens Nyheter. Linde is widely praised as the initiator of the *The Museum of Wishes*. He writes: "At a meeting of the board of the Friends of Moderna Museet, one of the members, Östen Fagerlind, came up with the idea

P. 168: Salvador Dalí and "L'Énigme de Guillaume Tell" ("Wilhelm Tell's Riddle"), 1933. Photograph from the artist's press conference at Musée Galiera in Paris, May 18, 1960.
P. 169: Giorgio de Chirico, "Le Cerveau de l'enfant" ("The Child's Brain"), 1914.

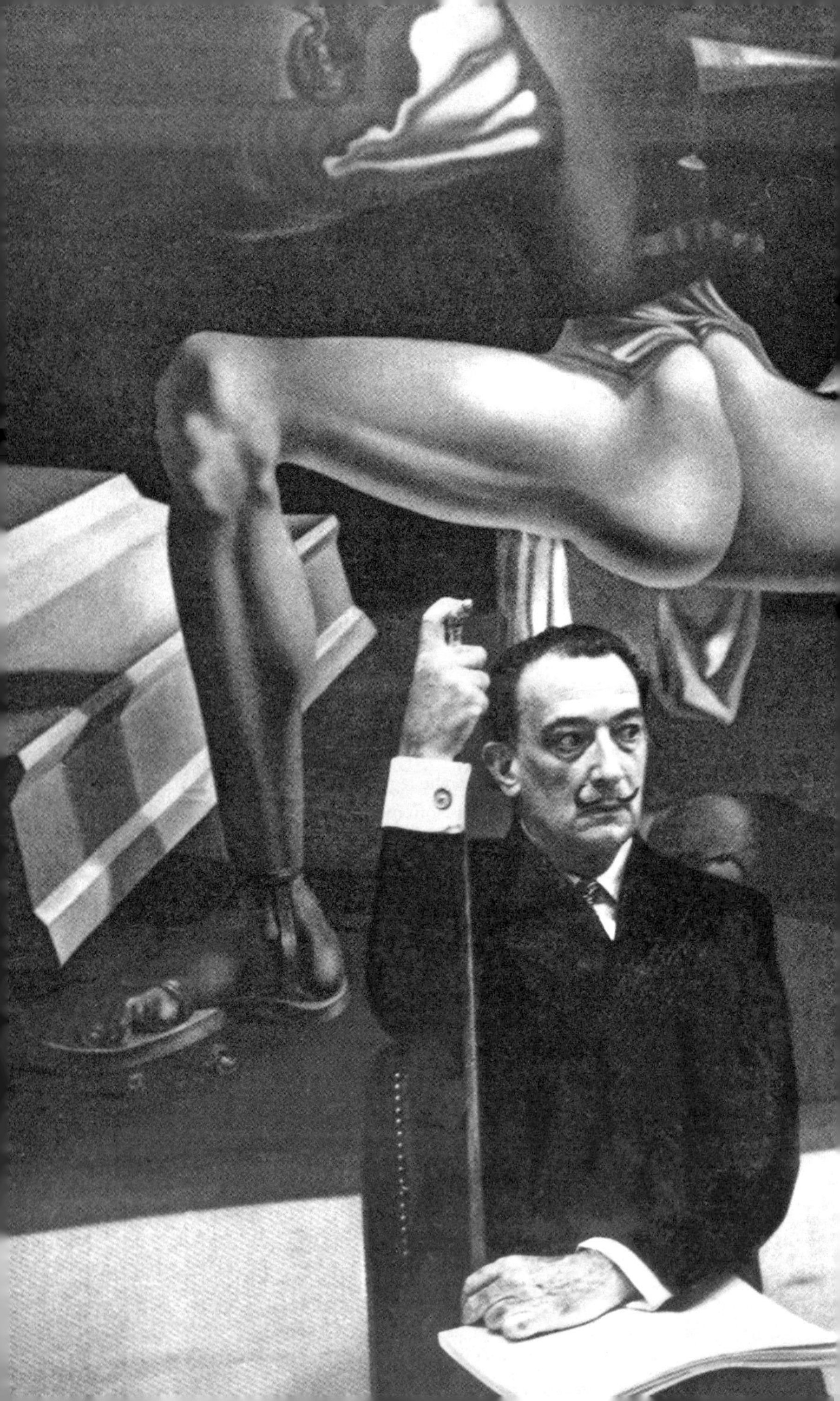

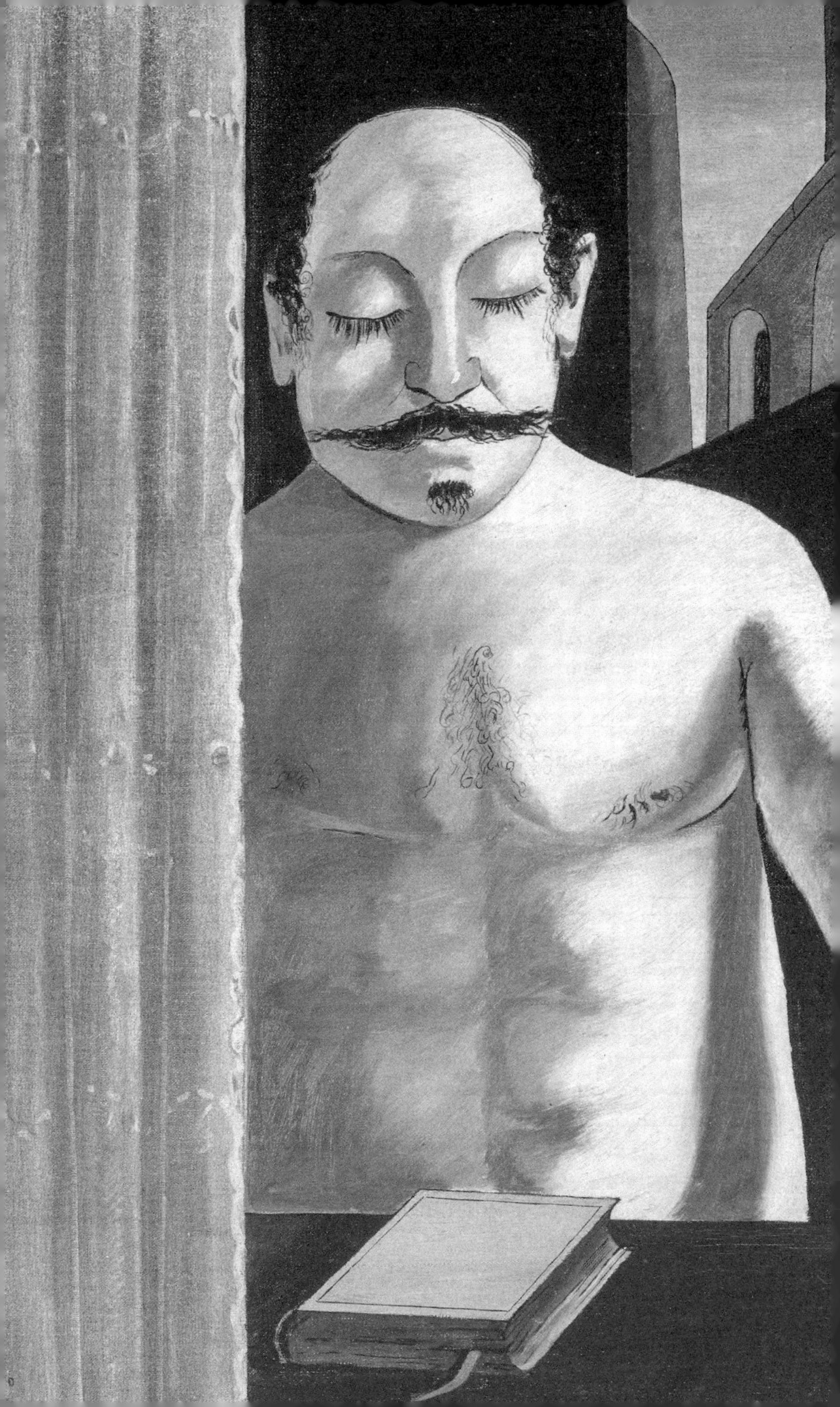

of borrowing a work that the museum needed from the art market, hanging it in the museum and starting a collection among visitors to buy it. I thought the idea should be implemented on a larger scale: borrowing everything that was needed and for sale to show what the museum should look like."[12]

The exhibition *Önskemuseet* (*The Museum of Wishes*) featured around one hundred and forty works by the most influential artists of Modernism. A third of the works were from the museum's own collection, the rest were on loan from the Swedish and European art trade. On display were paintings and sculptures by Cubists Pablo Picasso, Georges Braque, Raymond Duchamp-Villon and Julio González, Dadaists and Surrealists such as Max Ernst, Giorgio de Chirico, Alberto Giacometti, Salvador Dalí, Francis Picabia, Joan Miró and René Magritte, Futurist Giacomo Balla, abstract pioneers such as Wassily Kandinsky, Piet Mondrian and Kazimir Malevich, Expressionists the likes of Jackson Pollock, Ernst Ludwig Kirchner and Francis Bacon, contemporary avant-garde artists Jean Tinguely, Yves Klein and Robert Rauschenberg, among others.

The exhibition, which preceded *American Pop Art ...*, was organized and funded entirely by the Friends of Moderna Museet, who raised additional funds for the acquisition of the artworks through admission, catalog and poster sales. The hanging was pedagogically divided into sections for Fauvism, Cubism, Futurism, Surrealism, Dadaism, Suprematism and other movements to give the audience an overview of modern art history.

The Museum of Wishes was another great public success for the museum with fifty-five thousand visitors, and was well received by the press. Despite the recurring controversies, which essentially still consisted of the debate about whether modern and abstract art was art at all, the young museum enjoyed a tailwind. The spirit of the times was strong and positive.

In his text in the catalog for *The Museum of Wishes*, Pontus Hultén writes about how art patrons in general during the first half of the twentieth century had been alienated from the development of modern art: "One would like to be a patron, but one did not want to support rabble-rousers. Most large collections of modern art were created only after the end of the Second World War."[13] In this catalog preface, Hultén elaborates his view of the crucial importance of the museum collection in contemporary cultural life. In the text, he appeals implicitly to the state to invest money in international art and not to rely on donations from private collectors, i.e. affluent capitalists, who rarely support the subversive or innovative. His words have become classic and can be read as a program statement for the young Moderna Museet:

"It is becoming increasingly clear that modern art is one of the most important carriers of the myths of our time, of all the contents of time that cannot be explained or unambiguously formulated, of what is time itself. (...) A country must have a capital of this myth-bearing material, a system of reference and a source of inspiration. Especially in a country on the periphery, where major art events are rare and the import of foreign art is limited, where there is a risk of being completely out of touch with what is happening in the center (...) Even if the price of art is high, one must invest in acquiring a collection of the pioneers of modern art before it is too late. It is legitimate for a museum to pay a high price for a work of art. (...) The cultural history of the 20th century is full of examples of how the visual arts have inspired other art forms. The core of cultural life, which a good collection of contemporary visual art naturally represents, cannot be dispensed with.

With this exhibition, the Friends of Moderna Museet are taking a large-scale initiative. The time has come for Moderna Museet to make a serious attempt to build up a representative collection of international art. Let us wish each other success in this endeavor."[14]

No one will object if we name *The Museum of Wishes* as the single most important initiative for the future of the museum among the many bold ventures in the early years.

The one-off sum of five million kronor awarded to Moderna Museet by the government as a result of *Önskemuseet* has been called a "bolt from the blue," "miracle," "wonder," "jackpot" and other similar expressions. On closer inspection, though, chance, that element so revered by Pontus Hultén, does not seem to have been a particularly active factor this time.

Hultén himself told me about his ties to the government and the patronage the museum could rely on due to these contacts. He readily admitted that it would have been impossible for the museum to become what it did without this political support.[15]

Two social democratic officials who were both instrumental in obtaining the one-off grant were Ragnar Edenman and Roland Pålsson. The elder Edenman was a political scientist from Uppsala. He was recruited to the Ministry of Ecclesiastical Affairs (then the Ministry of Education, which included the future Ministry of Culture) where he became one of the main architects of social democratic education and culture policy. Edenman had a decisive influence on the realization of Otte Sköld's plans for a modern museum.

In 1963, Roland Pålsson was appointed head of the newly established cultural department at the Ministry of Ecclesiastical Affairs. He would do Pontus Hultén and Moderna Museet great service and act as an indispensable ambassador within the political and bureaucratic machinery. He was part of a network of friends in the cultural social democratic sphere of power that also included people like business man and Film Institute director Harry Schein and future foreign minister Hans-Krister Wickman. The museum official Åke Meyerson[16] was also part of this group of social democratic power brokers in cultural life, an expert at the Ministry of Ecclesiastical Affairs from 1963 and departmental secretary from 1965.

An informal leader within this network was Olof Palme. I have no evidence that Palme was involved in the events surrounding *The Museum of Wishes*, but in my interview, Pontus Hultén particularly emphasized Palme's great influence on Swedish cultural life and his importance for the museum "long before he became Prime Minister"[17] (Palme was secretary of the Prime Minister's cabinet from 1954, Member of Parliament from 1958, Consultative Minister from 1963 and Ragnar Edenman's successor as Minister of Ecclesiastical Affairs from 1967, before he became Prime Minister in 1969).

Raised in academic circles in Stockholm and Djursholm, Hultén was a trusted member of this bourgeoise cultural left-wing establishment, with roots in the universities of Stockholm and Uppsala. I think this Stockholm perspective is important to remember, as well as how much smaller Stockholm was at that time. It goes without saying that Pontus Hultén made sure to use all his friendships and other liaisons to the utmost for his and the museum's purposes. Anything less would have been alien to his personality.

In his text in the twenty-fifth anniversary book, Roland Pålsson relays how the sensational one-off appropriation was pushed through, which appears to have been the result of the skillful lobbying by Pontus Hultén and his team.[18] In today's money, the sum of five million crowns allocated to the museum corresponds to about fifty-five million. This does not sound like much for the purchase of art historical masterpieces, but the prices for modern art were fractions of today's fantasy amounts. By comparison, Pontus Hultén had at the time managed to negotiate the museum's annual purchase allocation from thirty thousand to one hundred thousand kronor. Here the government suddenly granted the museum half a century's worth of annual funding in one swoop.[19]

Pontus Hultén explained to me the uniquely favorable situation in which the museum found itself after the miraculous lump sum payment from the government — a result of the museum's magical timing and luck during its "formative years": "To begin with, competition in the market was very limited during this time. The Museum of Modern Art was in a period of stagnation. The museums in Germany had not taken off after the war, nor those in France or England, so there were few buyers. When we showed up with our money, we were well received everywhere. We were unknown, of course, but sometimes that can be an advantage. Then there was the lucky circumstance that there were still modern masterpieces available in the market — a situation that soon changed when availability, not price, became the problem. There were masters from two generations, the Cubists and the Surrealists, still alive. Several of them and their families were in situations where they were about to leave the cities to buy large houses in the countryside, which made them inclined to sell."[20]

Pontus Hultén talked about how important it was that these acquisitions could, for the most part, be decided in complete agreement within the acquisition committee set up to ensure the government some control over its disbursed funds, with Hultén, Ulf Linde, Gerard Bonnier and the newly appointed departmental councilor Åke Meyerson as members. Nationalmuseum, which was still formally the parent institution, seems to have had little to say about the selection. "The thirty-six works we bought for the money might have seemed like a very small number from a political perspective, but that question never even came up in our group," Hultén said. "We all agreed on quality, not quantity."

The collection acquired for the museum's collection for the state grant included works by Picasso, Braque, Balla, Picabia, de Chirico, Bacon, Dalí, Ernst, Giacometti, Magritte, Miró, Mondrian, Calder, Pollock, Rauschenberg, Klein and others.[21] It's an historical disgrace that none of the works purchased for the state's five million had a female artist as author.

Ulf Linde is not modest when he reviews some of the milestones that make up the core of Moderna Museet's collection:[22] "We immediately agreed that we would not focus on representative masterpieces from the artists' 'mature' periods, but that we would look for works where the fire was burning, where a new idea had been expressed — in short, where adventure was palpable. And I think we succeeded. The Tate

Gallery, the art museum in Basel, the Sammlung Nordrhein-Westfalen are certainly richer in 'heavy' works, but if you want to get an idea of the creative fever in art of this century, of the graceful moments, the excitement and happiness, then Moderna Museet is still superior. (...) Take for example the museum's collage by Picasso. It marks the most brilliant moment of Cubism, when Braque and Picasso summed up five years of work and suddenly realized what they had done. (...) Despite its unpretentiousness, the museum's collage is one of the works by Picasso that has had the greatest impact on the development of art in our time. (...) Or take the museum's de Chirico, once owned by André Breton. It was 'Le cerveau de l'enfant,' 'The Child's Brain,'[23] precisely the museum's painting, that turned the mediocre Cubist Magritte into the Surrealist Magritte, one of the great painters of the century. (...) And our Dalí,[24] the most scandalous of all scandalous Dalí's paintings, provocative not only to the public but also to the Surrealists themselves — it was painted for the Salon, hence the large format."

Ulf Linde describes how, in connection with and after *The Museum of Wishes*, the museum's collection could be supplemented even beyond the purchases for the one-time grant: "*The Museum of Wishes* was a great success, the public really came and for the entrance fee — which went entirely to the Friends of Moderna Museet — the association was able to buy Kurt Schwitter's perhaps most important work, the large collage 'Arbeiterbild' from 1919.[25] (...). The museum has been lucky. But the five million was not enough to complete the collection of Cubism. We had to forget that opportunity, it would have cost too much — but just then the museum received three wonderful early paintings by Braque from Rolf de Maré's collection. And finally, the classicist 'La Source' by Picasso, donated by Philip Sandblom.[26] This filled the last really annoying gap — apart from Malevich, apparently an impossibility. (But maybe once ...)."[27]

It's noteworthy that Robert Rauschenberg's "Monogram" was the only work from the new American art movement to be purchased with the post-*Museum of Wishes* grant. According to Pontus Hultén, he argued in vain for the acquisition of more Pop Art, which at that time could be acquired at minimal prices: "Among the others there was also this notion that American art threatened to overshadow the more low-key European counterpart, the Neo-Realists, with Tinguely, Klein and so on. There were elements of truth in that argument, but I thought the timing was wrong for such delicate reasoning when we had the chance to expand our collection."[28]

11

A Dutch intermezzo: almost lost to Amsterdam and the Stedelijk — or not ...?

In his text in the twenty-fifth anniversary book, Roland Pålsson recalls how he first encountered Pontus Hultén, shortly after Pålsson's appointment in 1961 as the first head of the cultural department of the Ministry of Ecclesiastical Affairs: "One of my first tasks was to interrupt a family dinner in order to use all available persuasive power for a few evening hours to persuade Hultén to stay at Moderna Museet instead of accepting a flattering international offer," writes Pålsson.[1]

The offer he refers to came from Moderna Museet's "big sister" Stedelijk in Amsterdam, widely regarded the world's leading modern art museum at the time, where Pontus Hultén's mentor Willem Sandberg wanted Hultén to succeed him when he stepped down after eighteen years as the museum's innovative, celebrated and controversial director. Like so much else in Pontus Hultén's life and career, on closer inspection the truth seems less simple than one might first assume.

I have no definite information about when Pontus Hultén first got to know Willem Sandberg. It was probably in Paris in the fifties. Like Hultén, Sandberg wanted to be an artist. He was accepted at the Amsterdam Academy of Fine Arts but dropped out, realizing over time that painting was not for him. Instead, he learned typography and began working as a graphic designer and illustrator, influenced by De Stijl and Bauhaus. His style was modern, radical and minimalist, characterized by strong, bright primary colors, jagged edges, "torn" and painted typography, colored texts without capitalization or traditional punctuation, and a repetitive, non-representational use of images. As director of the Stedelijk, he created the museum's visual identity and designed hundreds of catalogs and posters.

Sandberg was a legendary war hero in the Netherlands. His skills as a graphic designer had come to highly dramatic use during the German occupation, when the communist Sandberg was a member of the resistance movement, part of an underground cell of writers, artists and performers who defied the brutal censorship imposed by the Nazi regime. The group manufactured false identity documents for Jews and other persecuted people, saving many from the Holocaust. A German report stated that the documents were of such high quality, including the watermarks, that SS experts could hardly distinguish them from the originals. "The best piece of typography I have ever worked with," as Sandberg said.[2] The Gestapo tracked down the false identity documents. To hinder the work of the Nazi regime's security police, the resistance group carried out a heroic bombing of the Amsterdam registry office, destroying thousands of personal files and saving many from certain death. Most of the conspirators were captured and executed, but Sandberg himself escaped arrest. He managed to stay in hiding for the rest of the occupation, first in the Stedelijk archives, and later with Vincent Wilhelm van Gogh, Vincent van Gogh's nephew and intendant for the museum's van Gogh collection. Sandberg recounts how he moved around Amsterdam by bicycle wearing gold-rimmed glasses and a green cap that concealed his famous blond bangs. He never got off his bike as his characteristic gait would have given him away.[3]

Shortly after liberation in 1945, Willem Sandberg was appointed as Stedelijk's director — a museum official recruited from outside the entrenched art establishment, which was a prerequisite for the innovative renewal he immediately initiated.

When reading in Sandberg's interview memoirs about his vision for the new museum, it's striking how these coincide with Pontus Hultén's — that is, the extent to which Hultén borrowed and developed his ideas from Sandberg. One of his chief ideals was to open up the museum to society and the "man in the street." Among his first moves was to replace the museum's heavy solid wood entrance doors with a glass section through which visitors and passers-by were offered an overlook into the museum.

Stedelijk's new wing, opened in 1954, gave Sandberg the opportunity to realize ideas he had developed during his first decade or as director. The wing was built in a Bauhaus-inspired style almost entirely in glass, which Sandberg explains was not primarily for the sake of the visitors' view, but to offer passers-by maximum insight into the museum. Sandberg's ambition was for the museum to function as an open cultural center for many different art forms, a dream that was in vogue in Europe during this period. "And we brought music into the museum with concerts (...) The Film Museum also made great use of the auditorium, because there was a projection booth at the back. That was in 1952; four years later, the restaurant and terrace were completed, replacing the garden room. It gave visitors convenience and service. But we didn't have dancing or theater, which you really needed to have if we are to talk about a 'mouseion.'"[4]

Sandberg was a predecessor to Hultén in his close relationship with artists, far from a given for a museum director in the museum world of the 1950s. He interacted with artists, architects and other creators and involved them in the design of his exhibitions: a close personal friend of Gerrit Rietveld, who designed the rebuilding of the Stedelijk and the new wing, as well as of the Modernist pioneers Mies van de Rohe, Walter Gropius and Le Corbusier. His personal artist friends included Picasso, Mondrian, Brancusi, Giacometti and many more of the great names of Modernism.

According to Willem Sandberg's ideals, the museum should not content itself with being a passive mediator of art for the already initiated. The mission of a modern art museum was not to reflect but to drive the artistic, cultural and even political debate; to stimulate, even provoking and challenging its visitors with new impressions, thoughts and ideas — a vision shared, or perhaps more accurately adopted, by his disciple Pontus Hultén.

The term mouseion originates from antiquity, meaning "a home of the muses." The muses provided humanity with memories and expression, the conditions for intellectual and artistic traditions, thus inspiring dance, music, song and poetry, and the preservation of these traditions in schools and cults. The original mouseion, which included the famous library, is said to have been founded in Alexandria around three hundred years before Christ.

Still, the question is whether the restaurant and its accompanying terrace were not the most revolutionizing feature of Sandberg's Stedelijk. The museum was the first in Europe to offer museum visitors the opportunity to enjoy food, drink and socializing in conjunction with the art experience. Recall Robert Rauschenberg's words from *Art in Motion*: "Whatever was going on in the galleries, the cafeteria was the most popular place in the museum."[5]

The Stedelijk became the leading global arena for avant-garde modern art. Artists, gallery owners, dealers, museum directors, architects and others from all over the world flocked here to see, learn and socialize under Cobra artist Karel Appel's mural in the restaurant. Willem Sandberg speaks devoid of false modesty about this "tourism" in his interview memoirs: "From 1954, when our new wing opened, I was overrun by museum directors and architects who wanted to build new museums. (...) They all came to the Stedelijk to see how it was done and adopted the principle either in whole or in part."[6]

It's interesting to note that this larger, more active and public model of the modern museum as a "house of culture" was developed in what might be called the peripheries of Europe — Holland, Sweden, Switzerland, Belgium, Austria, Denmark, and German and French provincial cities. Only much later would the heavyweight institutions of the major metropolises follow suit.

It is unclear how often Pontus Hultén visited Amsterdam and the Stedelijk in the years before and after the opening of Moderna Museet, but it was on many occasions. In addition to the ideas he absorbed there, his appreciation for several artists seems to have been elevated through inspiration from Sandberg.

Most important of these was Kazimir Malevich — considered the great pioneer of abstract art alongside Wassily Kandinsky and Piet Mondrian. Hultén's interest in the Russian avant-garde, with its connection to the Bauhaus, was of older date but appears to have deepened in his encounter with Stedelijk and Sandberg.

Among the many acquisitions of masterpieces that Sandberg made for the museum, by far the most spectacular was the intricate operations that enabled him to acquire the German architect Hugo Häring's collection of twenty-four Malevich paintings, which the artist had left behind in Berlin on his last trip outside the Soviet Union in 1927. The Malevich collection was first shown at the Stedelijk in 1958. Pontus Hultén jokingly remarked that he was "practically the only one" who saw the premiere of this collection,[7] through which the contemporary European avant-garde discovered one of the great inspirators of modern art.

Willem Sandberg was well acquainted with the historic Russian avant-garde and its history. He traveled to Leningrad in 1968 and saw in the basement storage of the Russian Museum a series of paintings by Malevich that matched in "time and ideas" those in "his own" collection — works that would remain unknown to the outside world until they were shown by Pontus Hultén in Paris eleven years later (see Chapter 21).

If not before, then in connection with *Art in Motion*, Willem Sandberg appears to have gained great confidence in his younger colleague and, it seems, protégé Hultén. It's undisputed that Sandberg saw

Hultén as his crown prince, but the information about the circumstances is more contradictory. Hultén himself said: "I got close to Sandberg. He came to visit me in Sweden and we got along very well. He sort of adopted me, but our friendship ended in a rather sour note. He wanted me to take over from him in Amsterdam, but my wife didn't want to move, so I decided to decline."[8]

At the time of the "offer," in 1962, Sandberg's final year at the Stedelijk, Pontus Hultén was living with Anna-Lena Wibom and their young daughter Klara. In our 2014 conversation, Wibom told me about Sandberg's attempt to recruit Hultén to the Stedelijk. She and Hultén had traveled to Amsterdam together, where they were met at the museum by artists with placards reading "Hultén Go Home," a manifestation of nationalist opposition to Hultén as a foreigner, according to Wibom.[9] She asserted that the protests had made Pontus hesitate. In Wibom's account, he also felt conflicted about the idea of succeeding such a major figure in Holland as Willem Sandberg: a national war hero, nobleman, friend of the king and married to a woman from a famous affluent family, etcetera. Pontus was not keen on administering someone else's legacy, preferring instead to build something of his own, as Wibom proclaimed.[10] For her part, she hated what she saw of the conservative Dutch society that met the young couple during their "recruitment visit" to Amsterdam, where all of Hultén's prospective colleagues had housewives who cooked lunch for them.[11] According to Anna-Lena Wibom, all this combined to make Pontus Hultén decide to turn down the offer from Amsterdam.

In contrast to this story there is an unofficial recount that Pontus Hultén confided to his friends and which I have been told by, among others, the great Italian curator Germano Celant. At our meeting in Milan in spring 2016, Celant assured me that he had heard the story from Pontus himself. During the visit to Amsterdam where his "candidacy" was officially announced, Hultén had given an interview to a local journalist one morning. Thirsty as he was, during the interview he ordered a beer which he swiftly downed, immediately ordered another one and quickly gulped that one down as well. In his article, the journalist wrote that Hultén was an alcoholic and therefore unsuitable for the job, causing the offer to be withdrawn.[12]

Swedish press reported on the Stedelijk's plans to recruit Pontus Hultén and later on how Hultén's candidacy was "stormed" with protests to the Amsterdam city council from local artists, critics and others in the local art community.[13]

During a visit to Amsterdam and the Stedelijk in the spring of 2017, I sought out Ad Petersen, Willem Sandberg's informal second-in-command and intended candidate for the same position under Hultén, also a graphic designer. In his version of events, the main explanation for why Pontus Hultén's candidacy as director of the Stedelijk was ultimately terminated was more prosaic: "The Amsterdam city council[14] was a very conservative body at the time," Petersen said. "They had been forced to tolerate Sandberg, whose political views they detested, because he was such a high-profile person with a powerful position in Holland. I don't think they were interested in another radical in that position, and a foreigner who didn't speak Dutch. What Sandberg and Hultén had in common was that they liked to provoke. Perhaps this was what united them. I don't think he was ever seriously considered."[15]

Whichever of these versions was closest to reality, Pontus Hultén would not have been Hultén had he not taken maximum advantage of the situation in achieving his own purposes. With the help of the "flattering international offer" from Amsterdam, Pontus Hultén was able to extract "all kinds of promises" from Moderna Museet, including the conversion of his six-year contract into a mandate of indefinite duration, of course a higher salary, more generous resources and even greater freedom of action for himself and the museum. A few new positions were added to the small staff and the annual allocation for art purchases was tripled. After two years as director, the Stedelijk intermezzo helped Hultén create the necessary preconditions for an even bolder future at Moderna Museet.

12

"The Grobian on the Pea": Pontus and Moderna Museet in full swing

A few years into the 1960s, after a series of sensationally successful, widely publicized, wildly controversial exhibitions, with the expansion of the collection enabled after *The Museum of Wishes*, and with the new, larger, freer conditions that Pontus Hultén had managed to negotiate, the young Moderna Museet was riding in full stride. The pace was something new and alien to the museum world which, in Hultén's words, had been caught with its pants down by the new museum and its program.

Hultén's creation was so much more than a museum. The old Drill House on Skeppsholmen had been transformed into what was really a cultural center, or what Willem Sandberg called a "museion" — an arena for all kinds of cultural events. The program of film, music, dance, theater, happenings, debates and other events was extensive and extremely ambitious, enhanced by a huge amount of partying and spontaneous actions inside the art galleries. Moderna Museet became the obvious focal point for several generations. The loyal core audience, based on the members of the film club and Fylkingen, had expanded to include all of Stockholm's intellectual and artistic communities.

The question is, once again, whether Robert Rauschenberg wasn't spot on when he observed that regardless of what was shown and happening in the galleries, the restaurant, with its leafy south-facing terrace, was the most popular section of the museum. Consumption of the era's meager selection of cheap red wines like Alger and Vino Tinto was copious, of this I am a personal witness. Was this where the term "red wine left" was coined?

Indeed, to be more precise, Moderna Museet was the dominant locus for far from everyone, but primarily for the overwhelming majority of the intellectual establishment of the time which stood politically to the left, far to the left.

As the sixties progressed, the museum became an increasingly politicized institution — polarizingly politicized. I would like to know the percentage of the museum's visitors who were left of center politically or left of the Social Democrats. I'm sure the numbers would be astonishing. As I mentioned in the introduction, I vividly remember the hatred that "Moderna" provoked in the conservative right wing among which I grew up. The museum was even worse than the "Bolshevik" Olof Palme.

It wasn't just that upper-class people loathed and despised all those wretched red-wine-spewing hashish beards and wind witches who were known to frequent Moderna Museet and who, after *Art in Motion*, would come to increasingly scare away most of the neatly dressed, well-behaved bourgeoisie who still populate the pictures from the events in the early sixties. We must remember that at this time, say until the late seventies, there was still a politically motivated distrust of the entire concept of modern art within the conservative right — a suspicion that the upper class shared with the "broad masses."

Modern art was a concern almost exclusively of the left — "for communists" as the right-wingers phrased it — with the exception of a clique of bourgeois collectors and art lovers. The new art stood for subversion. This seems inconceivable in our time, when contemporary art has become the new golf — the prestigious pastime of choice among financial tycoons and oligarchs, at least in the more sophisticated layers of these communities; testament, if anything, of art's contemporary political castration.

In my 1996 interview, Pontus Hultén compared the situation of the sixties with that of the nineties. He emphasized money, elephantiasis and bureaucracy as curses in the development of the art world. On the other hand, he saw the growing public interest in, and knowledge of, modern art as an enormous advantage compared to the reality at the beginning of the museum's history. "Nowadays, when you're seated next to someone at a dinner, for example, you can have a conversation where it turns out that this person actually has some knowledge," Hultén said. "That was unthinkable back then. At that time, you had to constantly defend yourself against people who thought that the entire concept of modern art was one great humbug, that Picasso was a charlatan and so on. It was most tiresome."

One of the main principles of Pontus Hultén's model for the modern art museum was accessibility, a buzzword of our own present time.

Together with his staff, he did his outmost to remove obstacles and disturbances in the public's encounter with art. The museum's surprising entrance directly into the main gallery was one part of this vision, as were the restaurant, the many public events and the marketing.

Another was the opening hours. While traditional museums such as the National Museum maintained opening hours that made it virtually impossible for anyone other than retirees and non-working people to visit these institutions except on Saturdays (Sundays were closed), Moderna Museet introduced the novelty of night opening, until eight o'clock on weekdays and weekends, and one evening a week until ten o'clock. In actuality, there number of visitors in the late evening hours were few, and the evening shifts were frowned upon by the undermanned staff. Still, Pontus Hultén stuck to the generous opening hours. These were important for the museum's image as a new kind of free and open arena where the public was welcomed instead of being met with patronizing formality and bureaucratic obstacles. In the same vein, the museum made a point of opening an exhibition on Boxing Day — a cheeky intervention in the traditional family holiday. The posters promoting the museum's accessibility, designed by graphic designers John Melin and Anders Österlin, are classics of modern Swedish graphic design and marketing.

At times, Moderna Museet was open until ten in the evening, seven days a week.

A revolutionary new element in Moderna Museet's activities, which contributed to the experience of boundless openness, was the way in which we children were welcomed to the museum — kids who, within the museum world, had by and large been treated as a disruptive element to be shushed and disciplined. Again, Pontus Hultén and Moderna Museet were not pioneers. The Museum of Modern Art had opened a children's section already in 1942. Willem Sandberg's Stedelijk and several other museums held special tours for children. What was new was that Hultén's Moderna Museet developed children's activities in new dimensions.

Carlo Derkert had already held popular tours for children at the National Museum. At Moderna Museet, he quickly became known for his engaging children's shows, where he used his vivid imagination and intense body language to talk and discuss the works of art with the youngsters. The basic principle was that no prior knowledge, only desire and imagination were necessary to absorb the art.

A couple of years into the sixties, the previously mentioned Mette Prawitz, artist and costume designer, began to give tours for all of

Stockholm's fourth grades at the museum, employed by the Swedish National Agency for Education (free resources were, as always, welcome). Prawitz had heard of a museum in Jönköping that had opened a children's section. She had also been inspired by the Stockholm City Museum's children's activities, Hyllan, and by Carlo Derkert's views on children's education. Prawitz plucked up courage and pointed out to Pontus Hultén that it was a shame that Moderna Museet would allow a provincial museum to take the lead when it should be spearheading development by opening its own children's department. With his usual promptness, Hultén agreed immediately. The very next day, Prawitz recalls, carpenters were on site and "slammed up" two partitions for the first smaller children's section in one of the museum's inner halls, opened in 1967.[1] In 1968, an expanded children's workshop was made permanent.

As early as 1959, the Children's Film Club had been founded by Pontus Hultén's life partner Anna-Lena Wibom and Louise O'Konor. Films by Charlie Chaplin, Laurel & Hardy, Buster Keaton and others were shown here, initially on Saturdays. Due to the popularity of the screenings, the program was expanded to two screenings on Saturdays and one on Sundays. My aunt Maud Jacobsson and her friend Anita Englund took over the business in the late sixties, with a repertoire that in addition to those mentioned also included the Marx Brothers, my own favorites.

The tangible presence of children in the museum contributed to the defusing of the excessive respect for art. I was not yet there when the children were allowed to ride Rauschenberg's goat, as legend has it that they were at first, but the intoxicating sense of freedom in that we children were permitted to do pretty much what we wanted in the museum is unforgettable. It contrasted with everything we had been taught to expect from the adult world. The combination of the children's workshop, tours and films for the children, and the restaurant for the adults, was an ingenious "unique selling point" for the museum. Here the young adult cultural personalities could sit with a clear conscience guzzling red wine for hours on end, engaged in fiery discussions and romantic intrigues with friends and acquaintances, safe in the knowledge that their offspring were simultaneously being educated in the fine arts, culture and, as a bonus, edifying political pedagogy.

In all its novelty and its atmosphere of dizzying freedom, with a tingle of anarchy, the young Moderna Museet went further than any of its predecessors in realizing Marcel Duchamp's thesis that art is made in common with the viewer. The barrier between art and life was razed as in Rauschenberg's vision. One of Pontus Hultén's fundamental philosophies was that prohibitions and restrictions should be kept to a minimum. Visitors were encouraged to participate and interact with the art, in some cases helping to create the artworks, as in the interactive installations in *Art in Motion* and in many other exhibitions and events. In his anarchist, libertarian worldview, Pontus Hultén cherished the blurred boundaries between art and the audience, what was allowed and what was not. The idea of the direct accessibility of the art itself was a principle that became increasingly difficult to adhere to over the years, as the demands for security and care of the artworks grew in step with escalating economic values.

The world-famous era known as Moderna Museet's "heroic years," usually counted from 1961 through 1968, can be described as a prolonged creative explosion. The list of exhibitions and events offered during this mythical era is more than impressive. A number of these have since become part of modern art history and are the subject of an ever-increasing stream of Swedish and international studies. More than half a century later, a growing number of these exhibitions are also sources of inspiration for contemporary museum directors, curators, artists and other creators. Several of Moderna Museet's classic 1960s exhibitions have been the subject of "meta exhibitions," meaning art exhibitions inspired by art exhibitions, in various institutions around the world.

"The first eight years were magical and wonderful," says Björn Springfeldt.[2] He was hired as a curator in 1968, but was a frequent visitor from the outset at the museum, where he journeyed as a young art devotee from his hometown of Västerås to see everything starting with *Art in Motion*, the exhibition that he describes as a "shock of joy" and a revelation.

Björn Springfeldt and Olle Granath, the latter of whom worked on and off for the museum from 1962, in addition to his duties as art critic at Dagens Nyheter, editor of art magazine Konstrevy and teacher at the Royal Institute of Art, can be considered Pontus Hultén's disciples and crown princes from the laboratory years of Moderna Museet. They both succeeded him. It feels natural to let Springfeldt and Granath portray the museum and what it was like to work under Hultén during this stellar era. "No one has ever contributed to the Swedish art scene like Pontus during these years — not even close," says Springfeldt. "He just poured everything onto the museum floor — the Surrealists, Duchamp, the Americans, all that slightly dangerous and titillating stuff."[3]

Björn Springfeldt explains that as a probationary curator, he was assigned the task of "keeping an eye out for new artists." Almost immediately after his appointment, he was asked to hang the Nordic collection, an area that was never a priority for Hultén. Springfeldt responded in surprise by asking how he should go about it. "I don't know how you usually do it," he said to Hultén. "No, that's exactly the point," Pontus replied, giving the young Springfeldt a free hand.[4] Springfeldts had not completed his bachelor's degree and was therefore unable to obtain permanent employment at the museum. His temporary appointment was extended for three-month periods — twenty-seven of them.

The relationship between Pontus Hultén and Björn Springfeldt has been likened to that of father and son. The latter does not hide his admiration when he lovingly portrays the boss he befriended there in the sunny sixties.

"To me, Pontus was a very gentle, extremely loyal person," Springfeldt says. "We called him the 'Grobian on the Pea' because of his combination of power and tenderness. He was completely driven by his convictions but was not a political person. He had a tremendous love and desire to transcend himself, to summon all his intelligence and the subconscious, all that is down there. He wanted to free himself from the system and conventions — and then grab the opportunity quick as hell when chance offered the opportunity, without asking for permission. It was insanely fun to work with Pontus, very physical, we dragged and carried, climbing ladders. He had an absolutely enormous ability to create. In the hangings, he had a simple basic rule. The lower edge of the frame should line up here," says Springfeldt, pointing his thumb with his hand nonchalantly tucked into his trouser pocket. He relays a beautiful anecdote with a whiff of the idyll that prevailed at the museum even in the late sixties: "We got into his car one day, a Volvo PV called the 'flying cave.' It was the summer of 1968. We were going to visit some artist or whatever but suddenly we were at a boat, a Laurin Koster. There was beer, vodka and a leg of mutton hanging from a hook on the mast. I was the navigator. Suddenly we found ourselves in Åland island. We later made many such trips together, also down in Venice when Pontus was the director of Palazzo Grassi."

Björn Springfeldt describes Pontus Hultén's method for exercising his leadership in terms that recur in many later employees' characterizations: "As long as everything progressed smoothly, he never bothered with any details. The demands were of course high. If you hadn't lived up to the expectations, you would quickly have been kicked out. It was something that was just in the air. He was my mentor and I learned so much from him."

Olle Granath joined Moderna Museet for the first time as a young art historian for the exhibition *4 Americans* in 1962, an experience he describes as "a baptism of fire."[5] Pontus Hultén was obviously pleased with Granath's efforts, as he continued to use his services for various exhibitions and events. In his descriptions of Pontus Hultén, a mentor to Granath as well, he is not as unequivocal in his praise as his colleague Springfeldt. In our many sessions, Olle has emphasized Hultén's great, brilliant sides but also the less lovable, darker aspects of his personality: "Pontus was a great optimist, very dynamic physically. He was a person with rare gifts in his exceptional visual ability combined with his great historical knowledge. This unusual combination of talents enabled him to grasp the big scopes in his exhibitions. He had an iron grip on it all. His dyslexia was a handicap, but with help he was still a good writer with great ideas."[6]

Like Björn Springfeldt, Olle Granath highlights passion as Pontus Hultén's main engine, as well as his pragmatic, results-oriented style as a leader and museum director. "He was a very passionate person. Because of that, he was ruthless. Many have fallen along the way. Not everyone made it. The cultural difference between him and many others in the museum world was that he was a practitioner, not a theorist or intellectual primarily. The success of the museums was the most important and he didn't care much about anything else. He was not very good at giving credit to his staff, which created some enmity and dissatisfaction."

Olle Granath, Björn Springfeldt and everyone else I have spoken to praise the composition of Moderna Museet's still minimal staff at the end of the sixties. In addition to Carlo Derkert, the museum's staff of permanently employed curators had been expanded in 1961 with Karin Bergqvist Lindegren, an art historian and wife of celebrated poet Erik Lindegren. Springfeldt and others commend Bergqvist Lindegren as a knowledgeable and competent art historian and exhibition organizer, always well read, a reliable backup to Pontus Hultén, who had great respect for Bergqvist Lindegren. After Pontus Hultén's move to Paris,

Bergqvist Lindegren later became his successor as well, 1977–1979, after four years with the artist and professor Philip von Schantz as director. Until recently, she was Moderna Museet's only female director. "Karin had a rather thankless role," says Olle Granath. "The first violin was played by Pontus, the second by Carlo. If there was a third violin, Karin was left with it."[7]

The museum's permanent staff, which in the late sixties still numbered fewer than ten, further included the secretary Märta Sahlberg and the indispensable Sture Johansson, the janitor and jack-of-all-trades who lived in a basement apartment in the Nationalmuseum with a view from the street. Pontus Hultén had learned already during his time in the mother house that if you wanted to get anything done, you had to get on well with Sture Johansson. With his goodwill, most any problem could be solved. One person was employed to handle the cash register and bookkeeping. In addition, there were extra resources such as the Friends' secretary Bertha Lundgren, who had her office at the museum.

The staff was housed in what architect Per-Olof Olsson called deliberately undersized administrative premises. As much space as possible had been invested in the gallery halls, in the hope of an early expansion, which would, however, be postponed until 1975. Pontus Hultén himself was seated with his secretary Märta Sahlberg in a narrow passageway, with a jammed noticeboard above his desk. The unpretentiousness of this the director's own workplace surprised foreign visitors, accustomed to prestigious director's rooms, contributing to the young museum's atmosphere of freedom from hierarchy, bureaucracy, tradition and convention.

Although the young Moderna Museet conveyed the impression of being non-hierarchical, there was never any doubt about who was in charge. Pontus Hultén was an authoritarian boss who never hesitated to make the necessary decisions alone or to implement them as quickly as possible. He ruled with silence rather than with words.

Olle Granath's image of Pontus Hultén as a "constitutional anarchist," a characteristic confirmed by others in varying formulations, included his outward appearance. Hultén differed from his admired artists and most of his other friends and colleagues in that he always appeared neatly groomed and well-dressed, with a conscious, accomplished personal style. Hultén was, if not vain, then careful with his appearance. In Paris, too, he made himself known for his style, a feat in the capital of fashion. He had his jackets made to measure by a tailor in

Södermalm and wanted them, and his trousers, to be tight and short, unusual at the time, preferably tailored in soft, exclusive flannel. He liked to wear tight shirts, thick crocheted ties and the carefully selected round glasses that became his signature. His thin hair was cut short and neatly trimmed, as was his moustache. His air was that of a French or perhaps even more so an Italian intellectual, with the Nordic gruff primal force mentioned by so many southern and central Europeans delighting in the feathers of his suits and ties — that's the impression I get. His image was macho, with a dose of the eternal Hemingway.

Pontus Hultén was no friend of sloppiness. Things had to be orderly, clean and tidy. He was rigorous with his accessories, papers and personal belongings. Many of Hultén's colleagues talk about his attention to detail, whether it was light bulbs or art. Mette Prawitz recalls an incident: "He rarely spoke to me, but one day when I was wiping stains off a glass wall, he came up to me and said 'you can't do it like that.' Then he showed me how to do it properly with spray and paper instead so that there were no traces left."[8] I want to argue that Pontus Hultén's impeccable style, his experience of conducting himself in international contexts and, of course, his bourgeois academic upbringing in Stockholm and Lund, contributed to his ability to communicate his radical message more effectively than if his appearance had resembled those that many of his friends and colleagues in the red wine left would increasingly adopt — indeed, that without these attributes Hultén would hardly have succeeded in gaining the positions of power he came to command. He really appears as the constitutional anarchist described by Olle Granath: a smart player who, instead of trying to blow up the system, uses this system to promote his revolutionary message.

Everyone who was involved at this time testifies that Pontus Hultén kept himself in the background in official contexts. Appearing in public, giving speeches and presentations, was never his natural element. Perhaps it was his paradoxical shyness that made him prefer to abstain. Many colleagues have talked about how Hultén was completely focused on the practical staging of his exhibitions and projects and that when the assignment was completed and the exhibition opened, he wanted to get the ceremonies over with as quickly as possible, moving on to the next endeavor. He entrusted the role of the museum's public face to Carlo Derkert, the virtuoso educator who was a master of the art of captivating an audience of adults or children, full of imagination and whimsy, but who suffered paralysis when he had to put his thoughts on paper. I wish I could honestly say that I myself remember Carlo Derkert's legendary, well-directed monologues around works of art and discussions with children. Perhaps in a distant haze I can see the outline of an intensely gesticulating figure in a corduroy jacket with glasses on his nose.

The friendship between Derkert and Hultén would not endure. Like many of Hultén's old friends and colleagues, I have the impression that the explanation was to be found in prestige and the notion that Hultén had exploited Derkert, claiming credit for his achievements. Hultén peeled off, so to speak, his old comrades and creative partners from the "struggle years," leaving behind sentiments of disappointment.

Märta Sahlberg, Pontus Hultén's assistant, joined Moderna Museet in 1963 after a career as a secretary at the Court of Appeal and with Professor Arvid Lundborg in Vienna, a right-wing intellectual and journalist who was notorious for advocating the deportation of Jewish students during the war — a tough school. She was attracted to the position because she was interested in art and fascinated by the world of museums. In addition to her secretarial duties, she was immediately called upon to assist with other tasks, such as ironing stage clothes for *5 New York Evenings*. Märta Sahlberg has three passions in life, she tells me when we meet in spring 2014: dance, France and Formula 1. She speaks fondly of her memories of Pontus Hultén as her boss: "He was wonderful — one of the few people I met who knew his job. He was incredibly professional. I was so impressed by him and Carlo Derkert. Derkert did a huge amount for the understanding of the art but it was a mess. I had to keep order, as he had frequently promised himself simultaneously in different places. He saw me as a right-wing girl. Pontus appreciated me for who I was, but was uninterested in me. He only bothered with important people. He, Gerard Bonnier and Ulf Linde were strong. My job was to answer the phone and take care of the practicalities. I worked constantly, including weekends, and hardly took any vacations. In the summers Pontus often disappeared sailing in Greece with Anna-Lena."[9]

Märta Sahlberg explains that her duties included helping Pontus Hultén compile his texts for catalogs and other publications. Hultén was, allegedly because of his dyslexia, but as I suspect as much due to lack of time, dependent on help in producing his texts throughout his career. Secretaries and others have recounted composing articles from mixed components in the form of scribbled notes and dictation. Later in Paris, he would often have others write texts on his behalf.

Hultén was meticulous in shaping the final formulations and allowed no changes that he had not approved. "One didn't dare," as Märta Sahlberg says.

"Those were wonderful years at the museum," she continues, "a great school after Arvid Lundborg. You met so many wonderful people. The artists often came in to use the phone. They were very nice. I remember Warhol because he wore eighteenth century clothes."[10] "It was an insanely fun time with Pontus, Carlo and Karin Bergqvist," says Mette Prawitz. "Stuff happened every day, incredibly funny things. There was no limit to how crazy it was. Pontus was very active. He wanted the museum to appear in the newspaper every day. He was always conducting, receiving people and deliveries. I saw him all the time and heard how he sounded — determined and often angry, except when the artists came. He was often angry at the National Museum, which he thought was small-minded. He was most sarcastic, laughing jovially at opiniated bourgeoise people from Östermalm who didn't understand art. He was somewhat reserved, you had respect for him. I preferred to go to Carlo Derkert if I had any business. I loved him. He was kindness itself. Many people backtalk Pontus, calling him sour, irate, selfish, buffoonish and stingy. Many disliked him. I think much of that was because he was busy with other matters. The museum should stay open until ten and everyone was welcome. It was child-friendly and everything was allowed, no prohibitions. There was something very generous about this, which I think people forget when they say he was buffoonish and stingy."[11]

From the get-go, controversies of various kinds shrouded the young museum's activities, as much as the animated partying. Modern art itself, its spirit of emancipation and political radicalization contributed to making the museum the red flag above all others for the conservative powers of Swedish society.

These forces, highly active also within the governing social democratic government party, did their utmost to get at the museum and Pontus Hultén. In the twenty-fifth anniversary book, Hultén writes about the investigation that the government commissioned in 1965, "with the frivolous name MUS 65," officially to review the purchasing activities of all museums, but in reality as a concession to demands that Moderna Museet's purchases of incomprehensible and political art be limited. This was a debate that had flared up already in connection with the

MUS, Swedish for mouse, is a slang term for female genitals.

purchase of Brancusi's "The Newborn" in the early 1960s, recurring regularly throughout the decade. Moderna Museet's purchasing strategy and exhibition activities were attacked from multiple angles — for the incomprehensibility of the art and the left-wing message, and for the high proportion of foreign, mainly American artists displayed and purchased (here our local Swedish artists were of course chief antagonists). The very raison d'être of abstract art was questioned not only by the right but also from the extreme left, within which non-politically edifying art was regarded by some factions as bourgeois decadence, as defined by Stalin.

In the early 1960s, when Moderna Museet was newly opened and its future in flux, writers Torsten Bergmark and Ingemar Hedenius led a campaign in Dagens Nyheter against the museum and its view of art, in polemic against Ulf Linde, who in the same newspaper defended and promoted the institution he represented through the Friends of Moderna Museet. Torsten Bergmark in particular became a tormentor for Pontus Hultén. Bergmark was himself an artist, described by Björn Springfeldt as "a bad artist," by Olle Granath more diplomatically as "representative of a very Swedish form of Expressionism."[12] Bergmark can be said to have made himself the spokesman for a widespread envy of the new and international within the Swedish art establishment.

More than half a century later, reading *Is Everything Art?*, a book published by Bonniers in 1963 as a summary of what was called "The Great Art Debate," which had been raging through that year, is a thought-provoking time warp. The debate began with a ceremonial speech at the Royal Academy of Fine Arts by celebrated Swedish-Finnish elder poet Rabbe Enckell, which was published in Bonnier's literary magazine, BLM, with the title "Icarus and the tightrope walker: A defense of classicism." The speech is a long, pompous text that attacks modern art in general and Moderna Museet in particular, with special focus on Ulf Linde and his positive writings in Dagens Nyheter about the new art. Ulf Linde and Pontus Hultén, under the signature of K.G. Hultén, defended themselves, opening a floodgate for contributions from twenty-five learned men and a single woman, Moderna Museet's own Karin Bergqvist Lindegren (the latter's text naturally caused outrage, with inadequately masked sexist condescending undertones).

The first impression that strikes you is how the cultural debate of the time was reserved for a few venerable gentlemen, unwilling to even attempt to reach a wider readership. The length of the posts is fascinating. Getting through the texts is laborious. No matter how many times you read these musings, their meanings often remain inscrutable. When you peel back the verbiage, heavy with references to antiquity and other bygone eras, the main lines of criticism become clear. It is partly a rejection of the whole idea of modern art, partly envy of the international, particularly American, elements of the museum's exhibitions, represented by artists with obvious self-interest.

As one cuts further through the verbal foliage, it becomes apparent, as Pontus Hultén concludes in his first of three entries in the debate, that the anger that burned in these thinkers, as once in the Pelidian Achilles, was in actuality directed exclusively at two of the twenty-four exhibitions that the museum had presented at the time: *Art in Motion* and *4 Americans*. Even more specifically, two artists in particular, Jean Tinguely and Robert Rauschenberg, made the scholars' blood boil — most notably the latter's "unbedded bed," one of the artist's most famous combines, exhibited in *4 Americans*.[13]

In hilarious formulations, the debaters argue that there should be absolute, timeless measures of quality for art, based on the tradition of art history. The works of Tinguely and Rauschenberg in particular — it's apparent, though their names are rarely mentioned — are referred to with pejorative invectives such as "rubbish," "fairground," "amusement park," "dormitory spirit," "boyish," "ingenuity," "practical jokes," "purile" and many others. The mass of argumentation constitutes grandiosely worded wounded vanity from an older generation of intellectuals against these pubertal hippies who have the gall to question their interpretive primacy. Torsten Bergmark posthumously ridicules himself with an incomprehensible idea of fashioning some kind of quarantine system to determine whether these works of art could, in the unlikely event, survive the test of time. Only after a prolonged examination of years would the art be allowed to enter the collections permanently. Reading these meandering flusterings, which time has mercilessly scrapped, feels embarrassing.

Of all the debaters, one stands out from all the others in his simple, factual arguments and modern, concise, effective style: K.G. Hultén, of course. In his commentary on Rabbe Enckell's ceremonial speech, he writes: "Must art academies necessarily always be reactionary institutions? Can it never be changed? This is the second year in a row that shit is being thrown at modern art from the rostrum of the Academy of Fine Arts on the closing day (...) I have read Enckell's speech but have not understood much of it. It seems to me to be full of contradictions and confused style flowers. I felt a little sick, perhaps it was the lack of habit, this is a type of text you don't normally read."[14]

Hultén's crass observations triggered smoldering indignation. Several of the haughty academic knights drew their blazing verbal lances in heroic defense of the archaic Rabbe Enckell, whom the young, unaffiliated, academic lowlife Hultén had so gallingly insulted. The "philosopher" Ingemar Hedenius writes, in one of countless examples: "If one wants to imagine how far the aforementioned terror extends in the current situation, one should consider how BLM has behaved towards Rabbe Enckell, perhaps the only living Swedish writer who has a depth dimension in the truly grand style. The magazine asked him to print his speech, and he allowed it. Without letting Enckell get the slightest inkling of the matter, they then employed one of the most rabid and unintelligent propagandists of the 'present day,' who in a postscript to the speech was allowed to call this 'shit' and also to utter a number of other offenses in the same boyish style. No writer, young or old, small or large, should be treated in this way, and it follows logically that Rabbe Enckell should also have been spared such harassment."[15]

In a second entry, Hedenius resorts to invectives that reveal his aversion to Pontus Hultén personally — the epithets that would give rise to Hultén's colleagues' joking nickname for their boss, "The Grobian on the Pea": "This Hultén is beginning to assume fantastic proportions in my mind. A Grobian he undoubtedly is, and yet a prince on the pea."[16] Reading *Is Everything Art?* gives an idea of the resistance that Pontus Hultén and his colleagues had to combat from a cultural establishment of a kind that has long since ceased to exist.

"The Great Art Debate" was a concerted attack by the reactionary forces of the cultural establishment — many of whose representatives, like Torsten Bergmark, stood far to the left in their political views — on the new, radical, international art presented by the young Moderna Museet. In the museum's twenty-fifth anniversary book, Hultén writes about "The Great Art Debate": "But the attack came too late. The museum had already developed a new audience that wanted the museum to continue along the same path, i.e. to offer a wide range of information about everything that was happening in art, in the broadest sense of the word. This new audience was younger than the traditional museum audience, it was curious, innocent, dynamic, it represented the very best of the optimistic 60s."[17]

As we have seen, Pontus Hultén's activity in the international art world was intense from the very beginning and only increased over the years at Moderna Museet. In addition to exhibiting new art from around the world to the Swedish public, Hultén and the museum were energetic in their efforts to promote Swedish art and the museum's brand in the international art world. Throughout the 1960s, Pontus Hultén virtually single-handedly determined and shaped Swedish representation at the Venice and São Paulo Biennials and in other international foras. Several of the museum's exhibitions traveled on to museums such as the Stedelijk, Louisiana and, over time, an increasing number of other institutions with which Moderna Museet established creative exchanges and collaborations. The museum's so magnificently upgraded collection was sent on tour among European "sister museums," of course in exchange for showing other museums' collections in Stockholm.[18]

The Danish cheese magnate and art collector Knud W. Jensen, who opened his wonderful Louisiana in the same year as Moderna Museet, 1958, became something of a "little brother" to Pontus Hultén, even though he was eight years older. Jensen's and Louisiana's lot was often to take over ready-made exhibitions from Moderna Museet, Stedelijk and other museums, rather than breaking their own ground in art history. Knud W. Jensen's admiration and respect for Pontus Hultén was pure and unsullied, while Hultén seems to have held a less elevated view of Jensen as a merchant and capitalist, also with a reputation tainted by suspected swooning for "high German" national romanticism and Wagner during the war, as a member of the Nazi-affiliated youth organization "Ringen." In interviews, Hultén speaks favorably but perhaps somewhat condescendingly of Jensen as "particularly interested in design." Jensen, on the other hand, elaborates touchingly on his younger colleague in the book *Das gedruckte Museum von Pontus Hultén*, in his text about a journey with Hultén and other colleagues from the museum world in Japan around this time. He calls Hultén "You great sheriff of the prairie," and "the wildest of us all," portraying his colleague as a leader in the movement of European museums and museum officials who, during the innovative years of the sixties, developed a new, expanded model and a role for the modern art museum.[19]

Pontus Hultén's travel schedule, which became ever more extreme over the years, increased in frequency during his years at Moderna Museet. He was involved in myriads of international commitments, events and exhibitions outside the museum. From the mid-1960s, Leningrad and Moscow in the former Soviet Union became recurring stops on his perpetual world tour, as the Russian avant-garde had become one of the main poles in his art historical landscape.

Looking back at Moderna Museet's series of groundbreaking exhibitions and events from these young, still relatively innocent years in the early and mid-sixties, it may appear that Pontus Hultén and his diminutive staff were working according to a long-term strategy. Consistent statements from those involved, especially Pontus Hultén himself, have firmly contradicted that this was the case. On the contrary, throughout these creative glory days, Hultén and the museum operated with quick reactions, little foresight, short lead times and a high degree of improvisation. "It was always very improvised," says Olle Granath. "Things happened all the time that you had to take a stand on and solve on the spot with imagination."[20]

When Pontus Hultén summarized the museum's function in Swedish society, he was modest in his assessment of the innovative nature of his own work. Instead, he emphasized the museum as part of the Swedish zeitgeist and social development: "It was a fantastic time of great optimism. Sweden was far ahead in all areas: equality, women's and children's rights, sexual liberation, awareness of the third world and much more. The museum became a natural part of that development. In those days, we didn't think too much. We showed what interested us and did what was natural, such as bringing children into the museum. It wasn't something we particularly thought about. We had children ourselves. It was only natural."[21]

The Inner and the Outer Space and she — two art historic exhibitions at a Moderna in peak form

When Pontus Hultén writes in the museum's twenty-fifth anniversary book about the mid-sixties, the peak of Moderna Museet's young primetime, he mentions two exhibitions in particular — *The Inner and the Outer Space* 1965/1966 and *hon* (*she*) 1966.

I find it justified to follow his example and address these specifically. While *hon* made history as a box office triumph and global scandal sensation, *The Inner and the Outer Space*, in Pontus Hultén's words, "never became really popular" during its run from Boxing Day, December 26, 1965, to February 20, 1966.[1] More than half a century later, the exhibition is attracting increasing interest from Swedish and international art historians, as a source of inspiration for curators and artists. This is probably due to the fact that Kazimir Malevich, and also Yves Klein, two of the three main objects in the exhibition, are artists whose share value has risen sharply on the art world's prestige stock exchange, combined with the growing international interest in Moderna Museet during Pontus Hultén's era.

The Inner and the Outer Space followed the same concept, and the same high level of ambition, as *Art in Motion* and *American Pop Art*, with a program designed in collaboration with Fylkingen, including Dada evenings on the theme "Dada and Space," films about Yves Klein, lectures by Pierre Restany, Klein's friend and founder of the group Les Nouveaux Réalistes in Paris, who also contributed a text about Klein to the catalog, and a visit and presentation by Naum Gabo, the only living of the three main artists in the exhibition. Hultén writes about *The Inner and the Outer Space*, subtitled *an exhibition about a universal art*, that "It was an attempt to draw a thematic line through the history of modern art in a similar way as with *Art in Motion*."[2] Space was a topic of the time, as the first space walk was carried out in 1965 by the Russian cosmonaut Alexei Leonov.

A crucial difference between *The Inner and the Outer Space* and *Art in Motion* was its much more abstract nature. As Hultén describes it, "the theme this time was the image of space, an art whose motifs are emptiness, space and the experience of space, silence, stillness, contemplation, transcendence, simplicity."[3] This sounds considerably more inaccessible than the clattering, boisterous amusement park that *Art in Motion* had offered the audience.

Like *Art in Motion, The Inner and the Outer Space* was built around a few artists, with a theme invented by Pontus Hultén himself. The initiative seems to have originated in Hultén's deepened interest in the Russian avant-garde of the 1910s and 20s in general, and in Kazimir Malevich in particular.

The link between Malevich and Yves Klein is in retrospect brilliantly obvious. Klein, Tinguely and their friends among the Neo-Realists had been among the first to rediscover Malevich after Willem Sandberg and the Stedelijk's collection in the late 1950s had made the artist visible on a larger scale for the first time in post-war Europe. The focus of *The Inner and the Outer Space* was the Stedelijk's Malevich collection, supplemented by other loans.

From Yves Klein, who had been suddenly snatched away at the age of thirty-four in 1962, Pontus Hultén was able to quickly assemble a collection of first-class works, paintings and sculptures, through his contacts in Paris, including the gallerist Iris Clert and Klein's widow, the German-French artist Rotraut Klein-Moquay (née Uecker).[4] Three of the works from the exhibition were later purchased for the Moderna Museet collection, where they are now frequently displayed.[5] It was the first time Klein was presented on such a large scale in Northern Europe and the only time in his career that Pontus Hultén staged a major exhibition of this much-admired artistic whiz kid.

Naum Gabo, the third main artist in the exhibition, younger brother of the sculptor Antoine Pevsner, was a key figure in the Russian avant-garde. Together, the brothers had authored

The artistic prodigy Yves Klein, one of the great pioneers of Conceptual Art, a dear friend of Pontus Hultén, died shockingly at the age of only thirty-four on June 6, 1962 after suffering a heart attack during a film screening at the Cannes Festival in May, followed by two more attacks. I'm not alone in wondering whether post-war art history would have been different if Klein had not been lost so young. Perhaps Yves Klein could have been to the Neo-Realists in Paris what Andy Warhol was to Pop Art in New York?

The Realist Manifesto in 1920.[6] Gabo is best known for his abstract architectural sculptures and as a pioneer of Kinetic Art. Both Gabo and Pevsner had been represented in *Art in Motion*.

Malevich, Klein and Gabo were each presented in separate sections with as many as fifty works each. In addition, there was a fourth gallery with thirty-five selected works by as many different artists from all over the world, from the museum's own collection and on loan from artists, museums, dealers and collectors in Sweden and internationally, including Mark Rothko, Donald Judd and Barnett Newman.[7] An interesting female exception to the male dominance was Yayoi Kusama, then living in New York, with her fantastic sculpture from "One Thousand Boats Show" from 1962–1965, decades before the Japanese artist's long delayed major global breakthrough. The exhibition catalog was extremely ambitious, a classic with high collector's value, with a rich, exclusive selection of historical texts and manifestos.[8] Another common denominator between Malevich, Klein and Gabo, in addition to their "esoteric" qualities, was that they were all accomplished writers. Their texts were featured as important elements in the exhibition and catalog.

Like *Art in Motion*, *The Inner and the Outer Space* took up almost the entire museum. From Pontus Hultén's anniversary book text, and from statements in other contexts, one can sense disappointment that the exhibition didn't cause anywhere near the sensation or indignation that *Art in Motion* and the American shows had stirred up. *The Inner and the Outer Space* seems to have been close to Hultén's heart. He himself describes it as "beautiful." According to Olle Granath, one of the reasons why the crowds that Hultén and his colleagues had anticipated did not materialize was the weather: "That exhibition froze in. It was below minus twenty for the entire time it was on display."

For *The Inner and the Outer Space*, Pontus Hultén collaborated for the first time with the Danish art historian Troels Andersen, who henceforth became his permanent, indispensable collaborator in all exhibitions with a Russian connection at several museums. Andersen is a leading international expert on the Russian avant-garde and on Kazimir Malevich in particular. He came to Moscow for interpretation training during his military service in 1960 and remained in the city as an art history student. As one of the few "capitalist students" in Moscow during this time, Andersen made art historical discoveries, including texts by Malevich, who was banned in the Soviet Union, after having become interested through the exhibition of Stedelijk's collection at Louisiana in 1958. Andersen copied and smuggled out documents found in the city's libraries and archives. He married a Russian in 1964, allowing him to live and work in the Soviet Union.

On his way home in 1963 after seven months in Moscow, he stopped in Stockholm where he met Pontus Hultén and Ulf Linde. The young Danish student must have seemed providential to Hultén, who by this time had evolved his interest in Russian art. Troels Andersen recalls his first meetings with Hultén in Stockholm: "It was most interesting and stimulating to discuss with Hultén and Linde. We talked about the Russian avant-garde and the reactions after *Art in Motion*. Olof Lagercrantz[9] had written about Moscow after his visit there in 1961, but I didn't recognize myself in his impressions. I had a different picture that was less positive. We talked a lot about the relationship between Malevich and Tatlin, who was even less known in the West. As I remember it, Pontus had not yet been to Russia."[10] According to Troels Andersen, one background to *The Inner and the Outer Space* may have been when Pontus Hultén in 1965 in Leningrad gained access to a collection of previously unknown drawings by Naum Gabo. "I think that he really wanted to show these things and that he found a suitable context," says Andersen.

The reception of *The Inner and the Outer Space* may have disappointed Pontus Hultén, but sixteen years later he is well aware of its art-historical impact when he writes in the twenty-fifth anniversary book: "The exhibition was important both because of its very solid historical component and the way in which it introduced so much that was then emerging, Conceptual Art, Minimalism, Spatial and Environmental Art, etc."

The Inner and the Outer Space is remarkable precisely since it harbingers the more unworldly art that came to dominate the 1980s and 1990s — as opposed to the political art that was taking over at the time — which makes the exhibition seem so modern in our times. *The Inner and the Outer Space* is a milestone in Pontus Hultén's career, as it was his first exhibition with a predominantly Russian theme, for which he traveled to the Soviet Union, enhancing his interest in the Russian avant-garde and developing the Russian network of contacts he had begun to build in connection with *Art in Motion*. From this exhibition onwards, Russia was a mainline of his program.

If *The Inner and the Outer Space* was, or became, a low-key, poetic, contemplative emprise, then *she* (consistently spelled with a minor case s by the museum when the exhibition was on display, but not always in our present time), which opened just over three months later, was its exact opposite: a colorful, scandalous, outrageous gala performance; a mythical crescendo of Pontus Hultén's entire era at the museum.

she is by far the most publicized, depicted and storied exhibition in the now sixty-four year history of Moderna Museet — no mean feat in competition with all the museum's art historic shows and events. We can without exaggeration call *she* one of the most famous exhibitions in the international history of modern art. The image of the crowd pouring in through the giant woman's womb has become a logo for the museum and a symbol of the entire freedom-frenzied sixties pre-1968 — that brief, blessed spell when anything seemed possible.

As with *Art in Motion*, *she* too emerged from a collaboration between Pontus Hultén and his mentor Willem Sandberg. Both her predecessor, *Dylaby* at the Stedelijk in 1962, and *she* were part of a series of so-called labyrinth exhibitions, which from the late 1950s had been organized in various venues around Europe, where artists collaborated to create spatial installations, holistic artistic experiences akin to the Surrealist exhibitions curated by Duchamp in Paris and New York a few decades earlier.

Already around 1960, Sandberg and Tinguely had come up with the idea. Hultén, Tinguely, Hans Nordenström, Per Olof Ultvedt and others had been experimenting with similar initiatives since the late 1950s.

The plans that eventually took shape included many of the leading names from the avant-garde art scenes on both sides of the Atlantic, with the Parisian Neo-Realists and the New York Neo-Dadaists, the combined basis of the emerging Pop Art movement. The final constellation became Tinguely, Spoerri, Ultvedt, Robert Rauschenberg, Martial Raysse and Niki de Saint Phalle. The plans for *Dylaby* were developed by these artists, Sandberg and Hultén, in a brainstorming session at the Stedelijk in Amsterdam on September 8, 1962. Construction began two days later.[11]

Dylaby, which opened on September 30, 1962, at the Stedelijk, presented nine room installations by the six participating artists (Tinguely, Spoerri, and Ultvedt contributed two rooms each), grouped in a labyrinthine arrangement throughout the museum.[12] Spoerri, as usual, had built a room angled at ninety degrees, with the paintings on the floor. Ultvedt had constructed an "interactive" labyrinth where the spectators' moves had consequences; Rauschenberg a spatial installation in the form of a giant Combine, inspired by his idol, the Hanoverian Dadaist Kurt Schwitters, and the strange houses, called "Merzbau," that German artists created in his homes. The installation, which was scrapped after the show, is claimed by visitors to have been one of Rauschenberg's greatest works.[13] A good part of the show was stolen by Niki de Saint Phalle and her "Shooting Gallery," where visitors were invited to shoot bebee guns at bags of paint forming random "action paintings" à la Pollock — a "happening" in the "Tirs" series that had made de Saint Phalle the buzz around Europe.

Dylaby caused sensation and indignation in Amsterdam, no doubt to the satisfaction of Willem Sandberg. Predictably, the exhibition was denounced in conservative camps, accused, like *Art in Motion*, of turning the art exhibition into an amusement park, a carnival.

It was to *Art in Motion*, *Dylaby*, the labyrinth exhibitions and other initiatives at the turn of the 1960s that Robert Rauschenberg referred in his previously quoted statement about the strong collective spirit of the time in art: that art "had never before or since been so truly democratic — or at least tried to be."[14] Conflicts between artists eventually arose, according to Rauschenberg because of prestige, mainly between himself and the European artists.[15]

For Pontus Hultén, the idea of artists creating works directly on site in the museum had been under development since before Moderna Museet was established. He had abundantly applied the concept in *Art in Motion*.

Unlike Willem Sandberg and other colleagues, Hultén was not content with having the artists create in collaboration. His intention was to create himself together with the artists.

This is what makes *she* particularly interesting. Hultén's original dream was to become an artist. Niki de Saint Phalle, Hultén's collaborator in *she*, the exhibition that would become the tour de force for this superstar of the sixties and seventies, wrote in her oft-quoted phrase that "Pontus in his soul is an artist, not a museum man." It's here that Pontus Hultén goes further than his predecessors and contemporaries, prefiguring the situation of our time, where the boundaries between artists and curators have been blurred, where artists curate and where curators are sometimes bigger stars than the artists. In no other exhibition during his career did Hultén's talents as an "artistic curator" find such spectacular expression.

As with *Dylaby*, a number of artists' names were discussed, many of whom had experienced international breakthroughs by this time. Jean Tinguely and Niki de Saint Phalle had launched themselves as the power couple above all others in contemporary art. Robert Rauschenberg, another prospective collaborator, had shocked the art world when he sensationally won the Grand Prix in Venice in 1964. These were no small names that Hultén, still in his early forties, had in his stable of artists and friends, whom he had followed from the beginning of their careers, but the cutting edge of the international avant-garde — a group in Paris and New York that was still not too big to function as a creative family. Among the other artists who were "involved and interested" in *she*, an initiative which had been gradually postponed since 1964, Pontus Hultén mentions Claes Oldenburg, Öyvind Fahlström and Martial Raysse, in addition to Rauschenberg. The final selection was limited, after Raysse had dropped off at a late stage, to Tinguely and de Saint Phalle, supplemented by the ever-present Per Olof Ultvedt.[16]

Niki de Saint Phalle and Jean Tinguely arrived in Stockholm on April 27, 1966, just as our northern nature was about to burst into spring after a record-long, bitter winter, as described.[17] The five-plus spring weeks that passed before *she* was finally laid out on the museum floor, compose a sun-shimmering, soot-black, glue-reeking legend that is narrated in detail in diary form in the catalog *she — a history*, published posthumously, richly illustrated with images by several photographers, including Hultén himself.[18]

Per Olof Ultvedt joined de Saint Phalle and Tinguely for an introductory creative session at the museum, from which there are wonderful pictures of the group gathered around champagne bottles standing on scribbled paper tablecloths in the restaurant. As I understand it, Ulf Linde also participated from time to time in these creative discussions. It's indicative of the tight time frames, and of the improvised method by which the museum worked, but also of the self-confidence and risk-taking of Hultén and the young museum, that they dared to gather just five weeks before the opening of the exhibition, without any idea of what this show would contain. The lack of foresight and predetermined ideas was part of the vision and premise of the project. Hultén and the Tinguely/de Saint Phalle couple, who by this time had become his closest and most important friends, were utterly convinced of their ability to fill a large part of the museum with something interesting enough to attract an audience of a size that had come to be expected with the museum's early history. "We were in peak form," as Hultén expressed himself in several contexts.

Various proposals were discussed, including an idea from Niki de Saint Phalle that was tested on the theme of "women taking power," with a machine-driven sculpture of a man at a woman's feet. None of these proposals generated much enthusiasm. Gloom set in among de

Saint Phalle and Tinguely. The latter started talking ominously about going to Leningrad.

Pontus Hultén has later written in various texts, without contradiction from the other participants, that it was he himself who, when creative stress was becoming acute, "suggested" that they build a monumental reclining, heavily pregnant, fetal Nana (French slang equivalent, roughly, to a "broad," or the contemporary slang expression "goding" ("goody"), the term used by the Swedish press — the voluminous, colorful female figures that had recently replaced the shooting ranges as the hallmark of de Saint Phalle). Hultén's idea was that visitors would enter this giant Nana through a portal in her womb.

Niki de Saint Phalle herself has recounted that the idea for the sculpture was Pontus'.[19] This means that the most impactful artistic and visual idea in Moderna Museet's more than sixty-year history came not from an artist but from the museum's own director. In *she — a history*, we learn that Hultén hatched the redemptive idea at the abutment of the Lidingö Bridge in the car on the way to Per Olof Ultvedt's home for lunch, and that the paralysis immediately subsided. During the lunch with grilled chicken drumsticks in Ultvedt's garden, the artist team started planning the sculpture in a creative outburst.[20]

Unambiguous testimonies claim that Pontus Hultén's actual abilities as a craftsman were limited. Some claim that he was gifted with outright poor practical skills. He reportedly liked the idea of working with his hands but was essentially dependent throughout his life on other more practically gifted people to perform the more advanced tasks.

The famous images from the work with *hon*, *she*, the minimally effectful name coined instantly by Per Olof Ultvedt, show that Pontus Hultén also played a very practical, hands-on role in assembling the giant Nana, with spray cans in hand and sparks flying from the grinding blade.[21] A twenty-five-meter-long, eleven-meter-wide and six-meter-high skeleton made of wood, steel pipes and rebar was erected with the Nana's torso, legs, arms, gigantic breasts and strikingly undersized head.[22] Much of the material was taken from Nationalmuseum's stock of discarded construction timber and exhibition props. The scaffolding was covered with chicken wire over which tapestry linen soaked in glue was stretched. Then Niki, aided by two assistants, painted the entire giant sculpture within a couple of weeks. Ultvedt admired the professional confidence with which de Saint Phalle approached the painting. Several participants have described how the giantess's ghostly apparition turned into joyful glory as *she* had her skin made up and tattooed with de Saint Phalle's colorful designs.

Internally, the sculpture was spray-painted black, using a constantly malfunctioning machine. In *she — a history*, the different phases of the work are referred to as the "Iron Age," the "Glue Age" and the "Black Age." The catalog reports how the painters, led by the brave Ultvedt, initially tried to resist but gradually lost the battle against the paint. One hundred and eighty kilograms of carbon black were consumed in the mixture. Poor Ultvedt is likened to a Chinese worker wearing a mask, not as in Mao's China to protect from insects and viruses, but from the black paint that darkened his body and soul. Awareness of health hazards was not what it is in our times. Only when the painting was finished could Tinguely and Ultvedt install their machine sculptures. The largest of these was, of course, a mill by Tinguely, first painted in silver but at the last moment re-coated in black to blend into the background as the sculpture's mechanical internal organs.

Legend has it that one day in the Moderna Museet restaurant, Tinguely discovered his young Swiss compatriot Rico Weber, an upholsterer, decorator and art student who was traveling in Europe and happened to be working temporarily in the kitchen. The dishwasher was immediately employed as an assistant in the construction of the giant sculpture. After the show, Rico Weber joined Tinguely and de Saint Phalle, working as their assistant until their deaths and living with them for long periods. Weber himself became a prominent artist.

Jean Tinguely was concerned about whether parts of the sculpture, particularly the Nana's knee, would withstand the strain from large crowds of visitors. The structure was reinforced after impromptu technical consultations. A humidifier was hired to counteract the cracking of the glue casing, which had to be continually repaired. Ventilation inside the sculpture was provided by two large fans sponsored by the Svenska Fläkt company. A skilled acquaintance installed an electrical panel. Claes-Göran Wanning from the music association Fylkingen was consulted for the rigging of three different sound systems: one inside the sculpture, where Bach was played, one that transmitted sound from the sculpture to the audience outside in the museum gallery, and a third that recorded conversations from the so-called lovers' bench, airing them in the bar/restaurant in another part of the sculpture.

Working days with *she* at the museum were long. Often they lasted until midnight and beyond, and eventually through the night. Each evening, the team enjoyed a "big nightly feast" in the museum's restaurant, which was apparently open especially for the purpose, as you were "always served in the best spirit by the restaurant staff."[23]

The team actually consumed two dinners in the restaurant, the first at normal Swedish dinner time, the second at the nightly wake described above. I need hardly add that the wine was flowing throughout.

It's ever intriguing brooding over how this small makeshift team consisting of the artists, the museum director and a few unpaid assistants improvised this construction in less than five weeks, themselves acting as artists, architects, engineers, builders and painters.

The work was conducted in secrecy. It has been said that no one but the participating artists, Hultén, Linde, Weber and the other assistants had access to the museum's main gallery, the entrance hall, where the mastodont sculpture was constructed behind a curtain of art-hung screens. In his media strategy, Pontus Hultén was careful to ensure that nothing was leaked to the press, aware of the potential risks of the uproar that would ensue if details of the sculpture were released in advance. True to form, he opted to put it all on one card and present the press and the establishment with a fait accompli.

In the midst of production, Jean Tinguely and Pontus Hultén suddenly disappeared to Monte Carlo to watch car racing. In *she — a history* it says that it was to the Monte Carlo rally, but I suspect that this is a misnomer and that what was meant was the Monaco Grand Prix in Formula 1. Jean Tinguely's third passion as expressed, besides his art and, of course, women, was fast cars and car racing, Formula 1 above all. The general impression is that it was Tinguely who aroused this interest in Hultén as well, and made him start to regard the racing car as a work of art.

The surprise departure of Hultén and Tinguely in the most critical phase of the construction process was not appreciated by Per Olof Ultvedt, who complained about this impertinence. It's understandable that Ultvedt did not approve of his old youth buddy escaping with his new, higher-priority friend, the international celebrity, to Monte Carlo of all places, leaving him to slowly fade to black like a medieval slave in the interior of the sculpture. In the relationship between Ultvedt and Hultén, and the latter's friends among international artists, there appears to have been a problem of the classic type that arises during childhood when the best friend finds a new and more attractive companion.

In content, *she — a cathedral*, as the full title read, emphatically fulfilled the condescending characterization of the art exhibition as an amusement park or vice versa — a deliberate achievement from Tinguely, who loved amusement parks. In one of Nana's legs was a staircase, in the other a slide with walls hung with fake paintings by artists such as Paul Klee, Jean Fautrier, Piet Mondrian, Jackson Pollock and others, made by Ulf Linde and Ultvedt. In one arm was a cinema theater where Greta Garbo's first film, *Luffar-Petter* from 1921, was screened in perpetual loop, a fragmentary copy that Anna-Lena Wibom had arranged through her new workplace, the newly founded Film Institute. One of the giant woman's breasts contained a bar adorned with a neon halo and refrigeration units, as well as a restaurant with a 500-kilogram food vending machine that Tinguely had discovered at the Central Station and which, after great effort, could be requisitioned and dragged up into the sculpture by ten men. During the exhibition, the restaurant and bar were serviced by the museum's restaurateur, Robert Michels. For this bar/restaurant, Tinguely had constructed a glass grinder that crushed the bottles emptied by the guests under deafening noise. The second breast was a planetarium with illuminated ping pong balls suspended by Tinguely as stars. "The love bench," which was indeed used as such, was upholstered in red velvet, housed in a secluded alcove (the sense of intimate privacy was an illusion as all conversations between the lovers were broadcast live in the bar). From a platform at the top of the sculpture's belly, visitors could look out over *she's* magnificent vista. Inside the installation, in the torso and chest, rattled thirteen mechanical sculptures by Tinguely, and ten by Ultvedt, as well as various other devices. Tinguely's mill, the Nana's heart muscle, spread its mechanical veins out into both legs. Another of Tinguely's sculptures was "Radio Stockholm," a sound installation of a kind he had previously exhibited elsewhere, with a transmitter that randomly "chirped" in different languages from international radio stations. Ultvedt's most prominent work was a mechanical man in front of a television set. At Tinguely's request, a phone booth was installed in the Nana's trunk, with the phone plugged in by the Swedish Telephone Company technicians. "It rang from time to time," as it was reported. Goldfish swam in a pond.

A decisive difference between *she — a cathedral* and *Dylaby* was that while the artists in *Dylaby* were free to create their own room environments, Tinguely's and Ultvedt's sculptures and other elements inside de Saint Phalle's giant Nana formed a whole with no boundaries between the artists or their works. *she* was a collectively produced total installation, as it could be called today.

P. 208: Pontus Hultén, *she*, Moderna Museet, Stockholm, 1966.

P. 209: Niki de Saint Phalle, *she*, Moderna Museet, Stockholm, 1966.

Pp. 210–211: Niki de Saint Phalle at *Paradise*, Skeppsholmen, Stockholm, 1973.

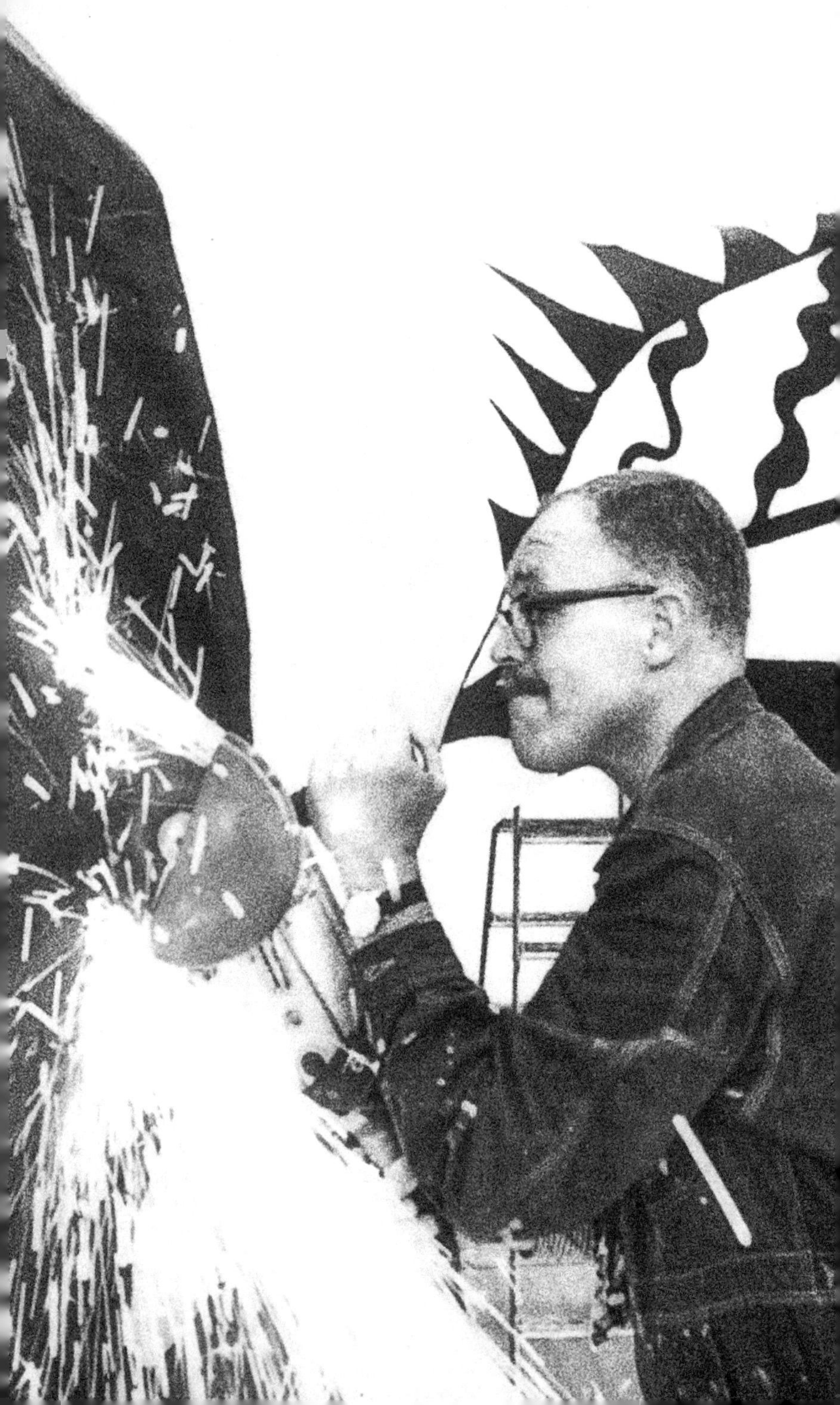

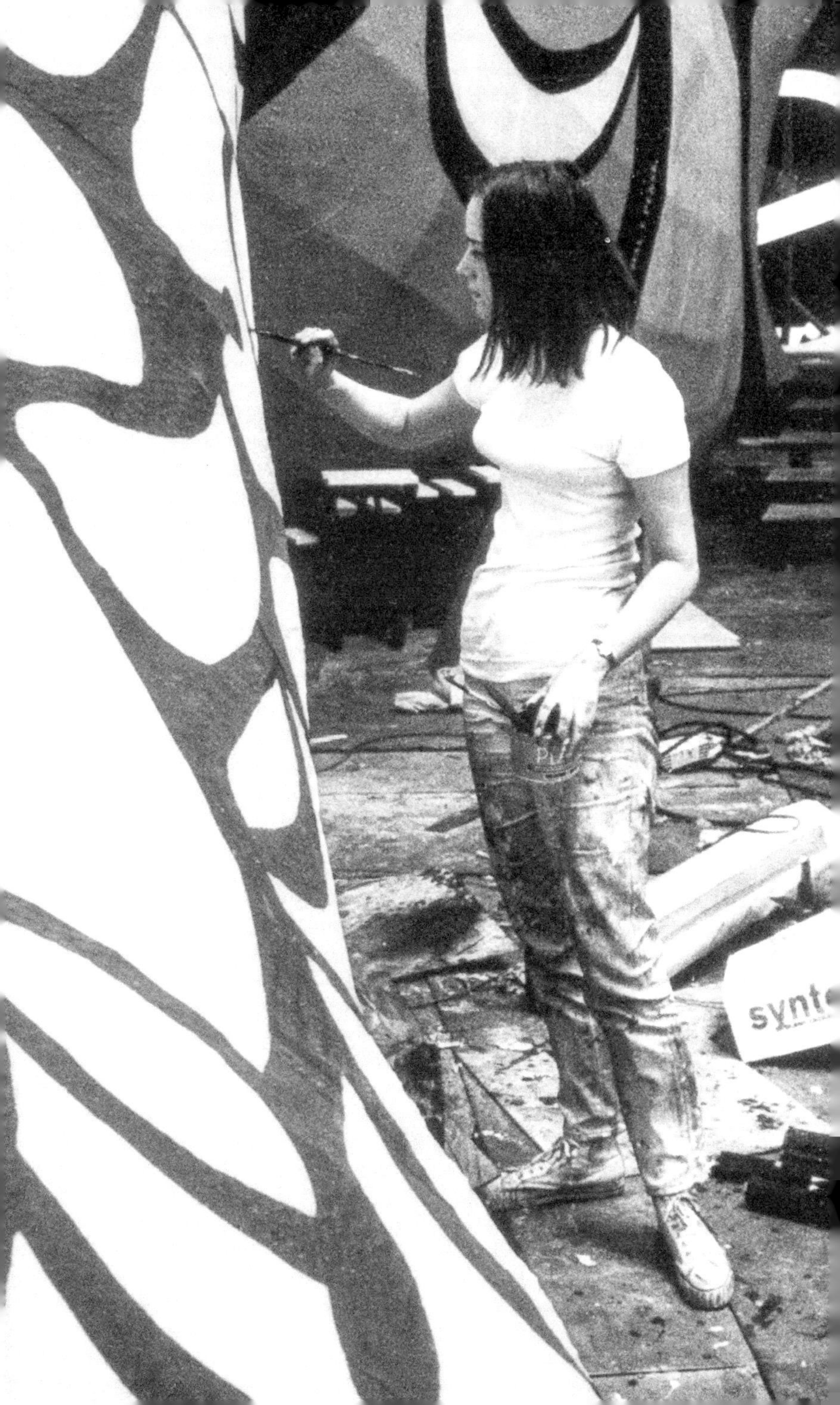

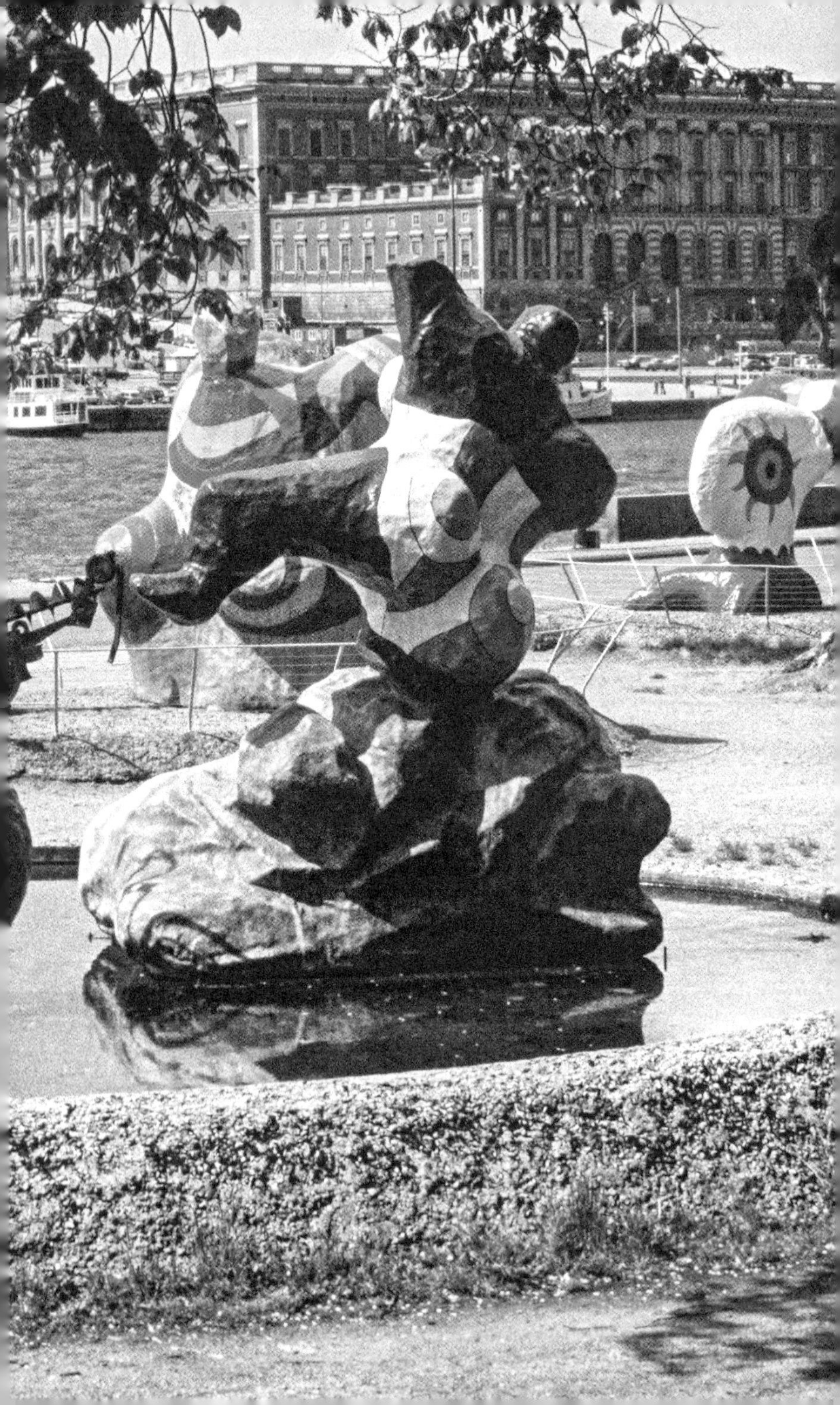

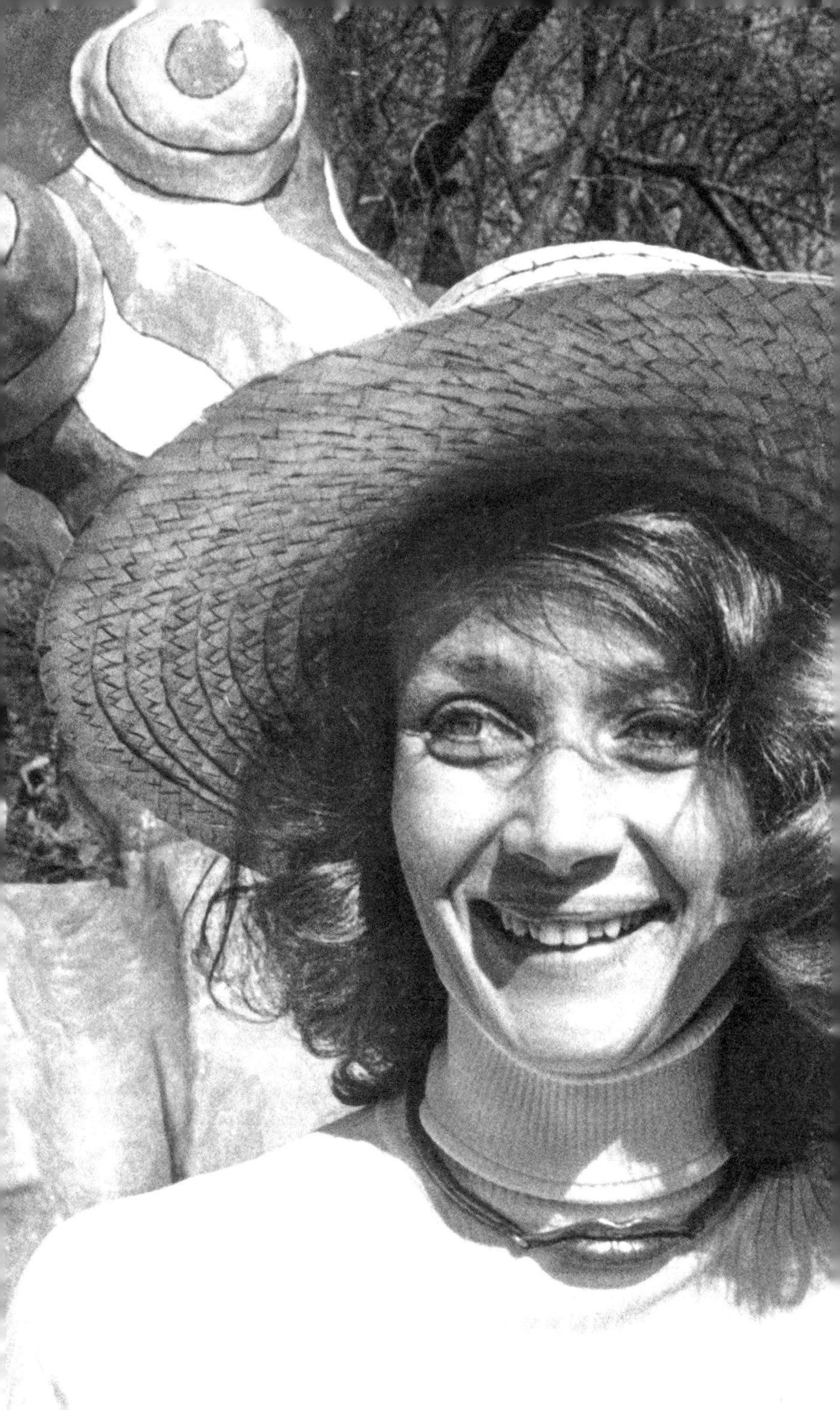

The effort to finish *she* in time for the opening became a frantic race against the clock. This was the case with virtually every exhibition throughout Hultén's career. In the days before the opening, the team worked non-stop around the clock without sleep. During the final night, the protruding pipe ends inside the sculpture were covered with foam rubber, no doubt an appropriate last-minute safety measure to ensure that visitors should not have to spill blood in their confrontation with the art.

The opening of *she* on June 4, 1966, was preceded with viewings the night before, first for the press, then for the Friends of Moderna Museet, followed by a late dinner for the exhausted crew at the Opera Cellar. Of course, the giant Nana caused quite a sensation among the visitors where *she* lay with her legs spread wide in all her colorful splendor. Pontus Hultén has recounted how he eagerly tore open the newspapers the next morning, anxious to see what had been written about the exhibition, only to find — nothing ...

With *she*, the museum had encountered a phenomenon frequently observed in the media when something radically new is presented. As the assessors don't know how to react, they often remain silent.

According to Pontus Hultén, a wakeup call came when the American magazine Time published an article about the crazy little state museum in the northern European periphery that displayed a giant sculpture of a naked pregnant woman ready to give birth, which visitors could explore from the inside after entering through her womb. The news magazine reporter had interviewed Hultén by phone in advance, as he had made an exception to his principle of what the Italians call "silenzio stampa," silence to the press.[24]

Subsequently, the Swedish press began to write volumes about the exhibition, accompanied by extensive amounts of visuals, including in the colored weekly press where the Nana appeared in all her striking color might, with the strong pink accents. *she* attracted sensational international media attention, with major articles in leading newspapers and magazines in the United States, France, the United Kingdom, Germany, Italy, Spain and other countries. The Times in London called *she* a female Gulliver.[25] The Statesman and others referred to Rabelais. If *Art in Motion* was a breakthrough for Moderna Museet in international art circles, *she* made the museum known to a broader art-loving audience worldwide.

Crowds flocked to the exhibition throughout the summer. Summer in Stockholm 1966 — how idyllic it seems, in the calm before the storm, when the positive spirit of the sixties still prevailed and the growing radical political activist and hippie movement was no more than an exotic element. In audience photos from the exhibition, the ladies' hats sand neat suits still hold sway. The long hair is styled after Paul McCartney in the early sixties rather than John Lennon ten years later.

The image of *she* heralded the global myth, or, in the case of men, the dream/fantasy, of Swedish sexual liberation, i.e. that notorious "Swedish Sin," perhaps our strongest international brand, which is considered to have been launched with *Jag är nyfiken gul* (*I am Curious Yellow*)[26] and other films in the following years. The exhibition was a public success of a caliber that no one could have predicted. Queues stretched long down the hill at Skeppsholmen. Somewhere between eighty and up to a hundred thousand visitors (figures vary) saw the exhibition — a remarkable figure in a city the size of Stockholm at the time, especially in the summer. *she* became a must-see far outside the regular museum audience.

Stories abound about what visitors got up to in the narrow corridors and rooms in the giant Nana's interior. Visable in pictures is that visitors, like the artists, had one hell of a time at this exhibition. Its aura shines idyllically like a crown of innocence, after all, atop the museum's heroic mountaintop, curiously largely free of the clouds of controversy that had shrouded *Art in Motion*. Though many cried scandal and some haughty academic writers condescended, with repeated comparisons to neighboring Gröna Lund amusement park and its Fun House, these voices were drowned by the storm waves of joyful and positive reactions. As box office figures soared, critical voices succumbed. As we know, few dare challenge success.

We can assume, without drawing too bold conclusions, that the main reason for its unprecedented popularity, and for *she*'s immortality in modern art history, is the "sexual nature" of the exhibition. Surprisingly, *she* was not widely attacked by the radical feminist forces forming as part of the approaching sixty-eight movement. Such reactions, though they occurred, were certainly neutralized by the fact that the Nana's creator was a woman, Niki de Saint Phalle, who became a hero in the Swedish and international women's movement, albeit a controversial one in her glamour. With all due respect to Tinguely's and Ultvedt's contributions, *she* was above all Niki de Saint Phalle's show. The exhibition became the artist's major global public breakthrough, cementing the Nana as her signature, her logo, which would forever not only represent her art but also serve as a symbol for the entire joyous, optimistic sixties.

Another of the Nana's qualities that likely helped mitigate the outrage that Pontus Hultén and his colleagues had surely anticipated, I believe, was that the giantess's aura was more maternal than sexual. To more sensitive viewers, it was apparent that *she* was about the exploitation of women and the female body by a patriarchal society.

Regardless, the sexual charge was hardly lost on the audience. Openness about sexuality was still something of a novelty in Sweden in the mid-sixties, though we were far ahead of the rest of the world, as Pontus Hultén stressed,[27] in our sexual liberation. I'm convinced that Hultén's later successor Lars Nittve, who was thirteen years old when he visited *she*, speaks for many of his teenage contemporaries when he says: "I can say that it was a very special experience indeed for a boy on the verge of puberty to enter there ..."[28].

At the mother institution, Nationalmuseum, understandable envy flourished over the extravaganza that eclipsed their own major initiative with a jubilee exhibition on Queen Christina. Some even expressed conspiratorial theories that *she* was deliberately mocking this exhibition. Even though the National Museum's officials from that time with whom I have spoken have played this down,[29] I've been told from several quarters about how the museum's staff grimly viewed the parade of Stockholm's young culture enthusiasts marching past them on their way up to the madness on Skeppsholmen.

In *she — a history*, the demolition of the sculpture is duly documented. Perishability was part of the concept. It was agreed that everything would be destroyed so that no part of the sculpture would reach the commercial art market, so hated by Pontus Hultén and also, at least at this time, by Tinguely and de Saint Phalle. Some exceptions were made. Among other fragments, the strange little head ended up in what was then the Östermalm district's old women's prison next to Engelbrektskyrkan church, eventually returning to the museum's collection, frequently displayed and on loan in later years. A few relics have also appeared on the auction market over the years. Just the anti-commercial idea of having some of the world's most celebrated artists build an installation for five weeks and then destroying it all a few weeks later seems alien in this day and age.

In *she — a history*, an anonymous author, most certainly Hultén, writes that the temporary nature of the exhibition is indeed the reason why the museum later published the book/magazine as documentation for posterity, albeit printed on perishable newsprint. The magazine, a kind of posthumous catalog, has survived the test of time despite the cheap paper and is sold at high prices at international book forums. Like most of Hultén's catalogs, *she – a history* is fascinatingly ambitious, with extensive text and image material on the history of the exhibition, detailed artist biographies, a text by Sigmund Freud, newspaper articles from around the world, and even a background on Niki de Saint Phalle's sources of inspiration. A clever move, no doubt prompted by the fierce international interest, was publishing the text in both Swedish and English, with some parts also translated into French and German, contributing to the exhibition's astonishing impact on international art history.

Further testament of the international height that Moderna Museet reached in the golden year of 1966 was that *she* was followed by a solo exhibition, the first in a museum in Europe, by Claes Oldenburg. The Stockholm-born Pop artist, who had already been represented in *American Pop Art …* in 1964, was another star of the international avant-garde at the time.

In the museum's twenty-fifth anniversary book, Pontus Hultén writes about the Oldenburg exhibition: "After *Hon* [here he spells it with a capital H] came a magnificent exhibition in the entrance hall that he concentrated on the cool, shiny 'water' side of his art, in contrast to the sticky 'food' sculptures he had shown at the Pop exhibition two years earlier."[30]

In our conversation in New York in 2014, Oldenburg recalled the experience of working in the shadow of *she* sensation: "When we arrived in Stockholm, we were told that Pontus was out sailing. Well, we thought, that's how much he cared about this exhibition. He was away for many weeks and could not be reached in the meantime. We had to work on the exhibition ourselves as best we could."[31]

Claes Oldenburg and his then wife and artistic partner Patty, who crafted his soft textile sculptures, worked on their exhibition in the mezzanine floor of the museum. Through the large glass windows, they had a view of the giant sculpture throughout the summer, when around two thousand visitors a day were constantly queuing to get inside the Nana. In our conversation, Oldenburg spoke briefly about how it felt to be next in line to fill the gallery space after *she*: "It was no fun," as he confessed, smiling. After the euphoria surrounding *she*, Oldenburg's exhibition was a more modest success with a third of the visitors of its predecessor.[32]

During their stay in Stockholm, Patty and Claes Oldenburg also staged a performance, or happening as it was called at the time, entitled *Massage*, over four evenings, as befits the apex of this art form. In *she — a history* there is a text by Claes Oldenburg in which he elaborates his impressions of *hon* from the upper echelon, laced with what Americans call "explicit language": "I, a passionate anti-American, believe that it is good to accept and take a closer look at the Cunt, an entrance, an exit. (...) In the USA, there is always something in the way. (...) From my studio in M.M., I looked straight up into *Hon's* Cunt. Every day, very clearly, I saw citizens going in and coming out. It seemed to me that this moved things forward a bit. More body art always helps."[33]

Some years later, *she*, this exhibition that was so important to Pontus Hultén, to the international brand of Moderna Museet, to Niki de Saint Phalle and as a symbol of an era, would posthumously indeed deliver her babies, in the form of Tinguely's and de Saint Phalle's masterpiece sculpture group "Paradiset," or "Le Paradis fantastique" as the work's original French title reads, this permanent three-dimensional logo for the museum that the artwork instantly became, and still is to some extent, with its history of heated political controversy. de Saint Phalle and Tinguely regarded "The Paradise" sculptures as the offspring of *she*. They chose to donate the sculpture group to Moderna Museet "so that the children could come home to their intellectual environment of origin."[34]

she brought a global breakthrough especially for Niki de Saint Phalle. During the late sixties and most of the seventies, de Saint Phalle and Tinguely were among the superstars of art. Niki's "Nanas" were in demand all over the world. The year after *she*, in 1967, Tinguely and de Saint Phalle were commissioned to create a group of sculptures for the roof of the French pavilion at the World Fair in Montreal. The result was "The Paradise," a group of sixteen large sculptures, nine of Niki's Nanas in fiberglass and plastic pursued by seven murderous black-painted Tinguely iron monster machines. "Le Paradis fantastique" was the first in a series of sculpture groups featuring Tinguely's machines and fountains interacting with Niki's Nanas that the couple would construct around the world over the next decades, including "Fontaine Stravinsky,"

I've been wondering if I'm the only one who's been struck by the similarity in subject matter between "The Paradise's" Nanas being attacked by Tinguely's machines and Duchamp's "Large Glass," where the bride is "chased" from below by "her" suitors in the "bachelor machine" ...

the "Stravinsky Fountain," in Place Igor Stravinsky next to the Centre Pompidou in Paris, installed in 1983.

When the World Exhibition in Montreal ended, there were no plans for the survival of the sculpture group. At home, there was no interest in hosting the group, let alone paying for its transportation. The time was far from ripe for such radical art in Paris or anywhere else in France. Instead, "The Paradise" was temporarily placed first in the garden of the Albright Knox Museum in Buffalo, then for a year on a lawn in New York's Central Park, at Fifth Avenue and One Hundred and Twenty-Second Street, just south of Harlem, where it attracted a great deal of attention and appreciation, not least among Harlem's black population.

Naturally, Pontus Hultén saw the opportunity to acquire the group for the museum in Stockholm. Tinguely and de Saint Phalle were in on the idea, as none of the major museums showed any interest. Once again, Anna-Lena Wibom's relatives came to help with various efforts in the realization of the plan. Transportation was arranged through the shipping company Svenska Amerika Linien, which frequently provided the museum free shipping of art and artists across the Atlantic. Pontus Hultén's well-oiled contacts in the machinery of power were utilized to remove bureaucratic obstacles. The state also contributed a small amount of money. The chairman of the Skeppsholmen committee, which was responsible for transforming the old naval station into an island of the arts, was, conveniently, the political spin doctor Roland Pålsson, the museum's benefactor. Pålsson allocated a plot of land for the sculpture group on an old drill ground, which was then a parking lot, to the left of the bridge abutment when crossing the bridge from the National Museum. The sculpture group was assembled with great difficulty in the Navy's old torpedo workshop below Moderna Museet, which the museum and its influential friends had barely managed to at least partially save from the demolition frenzy of the 1960s, intended for a future expansion of the museum. The work to arrange and install the group took almost a year to complete.

Despite all efforts by Pontus Hultén's contacts, the relocation of "The Paradise" to Skeppsholmen would not have been possible without "a very substantial donation" from Parisian-American patrons John and Dominique de Menil, oil industry magnates in Houston, Texas.[35] Dominique de Menil, who survived her husband by a quarter of a century, was a friend of Niki de Saint Phalle and of the president's wife Claude Pompidou — three women who together exerted substantial influence in progressive Parisian cultural life and who all played major parts in Pontus Hultén's international career.

As Hultén writes, the surroundings of the site that became available were perhaps not ideal, as "The Paradise' was intended to be housed in the greenery.[36] Here it was placed on a gravel field. On the other hand, the group's location could not have been more spectacular. Scattered less than fifty meters from the quayside, "Paradise" became an extravagant landmark which in its loud, rebellious color euphoria stood out in Stockholm's grey-brown marine silhouette, next to the National Museum and opposite the Royal Palace. When the sculpture group was installed in 1971, "The Paradise" immediately became the most public symbol of Moderna Museet, of modern art, which many still detested, and of the even more despicable left-wing movement that dominated Swedish modern culture at the time, with Moderna Museet as its "headquarters." Pontus Hultén phrases it moderately when he writes: "The Paradise' sculptures have of course not been able to avoid being attacked by the Association for the Preservation of Boredom."[37] As an expression of the anger against the sculpture group, "Paradise" was repeatedly vandalized by drunken conscripts (the Navy had not yet completely evacuated Skeppsholmen) and others. Parts of Nanas were found floating in the water as far away as the Slussen waterlocks across the bay. The museum hushed up these sabotages to avoid inspiring more. Hultén concludes the paragraph in the anniversary book with a pious wish: "If they manage to survive a few more years, they will surely be regarded as a small but enjoyable monument to the happy sixties, which for the museum was a very rich and varied time."[38]

The sculpture group did indeed survive, but not in its original location. The heavy duty as standard bearer of the vocal action group fighting for the downfall of "The Paradise" was heroically shouldered appropriately by an aging former lawyer, business manager, reserve officer and right-wing politician involved in cultural affairs, a certain Erik Trägårdh. In his obituary in Dagens Nyheter, old brothers in arms declared that the uprising against "The Paradise" was the main feat that made his name famous.[39] The location of "Paradise" opposite the Royal Palace was, for these brave activists, a question of breach of majesty, a deadly affront. In defense of decency and the honor of fair maidens they rode out, prepared to bide their time. The fact that old King Gustaf VI Adolf passed away in the course of the struggle and was succeeded by Carl XVI Gustaf did nothing to diminish the determination of these veteran warriors. Reading clippings and letters from furious friends of order in the museum's archives is as startling as it is amusing.[40]

Just when it was thought that the danger had passed, when society had begun to get used to the concept of modern art — to the extent that nouveau riche stockbrokers had begun to collect it, well into the eighties — these forces finally achieved success through the slowly grinding bureaucratic machinery. Moderna Museet's director at the time, Olle Granath, negotiated an agreement with the government that allowed "Paradise" to be moved as late as 1986 from the quayside to its current, inconspicuous location on the grassy slope below the museum. Here the group of sculptures got the green surroundings it was intended for, but no longer fulfills its function as a beacon for art. So unfortunate is this new location that the sculpture group, a world attraction, has been largely forgotten here at home. In my inventory of the Moderna Museet's photographic archives in our work on the museum's fiftieth anniversary book, I found fateful black-and-white images of the sculptures being carried away by cranes under the supervision of the drama's victorious hero Erik Trägårdh, who stood with a grimly satisfied expression, the belt of his trench coat firmly tightened, the by this time decidedly retired business executive, right-wing man and reservist. The friend of order emerged triumphant from the fifteen-year war of attrition.

In the twenty-fifth anniversary book, Pontus Hultén could not refrain from a dig at his successors and at Stockholm's powers-that-be when he wrote: "The group is a significant addition to Stockholm's public sculptures, like Calder's 'Four Elements' and Picasso's 'Breakfast in the Greenery.'[41] Stockholm's decorative arts have not otherwise been characterized by a strong spirit of innovation." Hultén never forgave Olle Granath for what he saw as his betrayal in selling off "The Paradise." Olle Granath himself, who during his decade as museum director in the 1980s constantly battled with insufficient funding, says: "I never thought it looked good on that gravel field and when this action group offered to finance the move, I thought it was a good deal for the museum."[42]

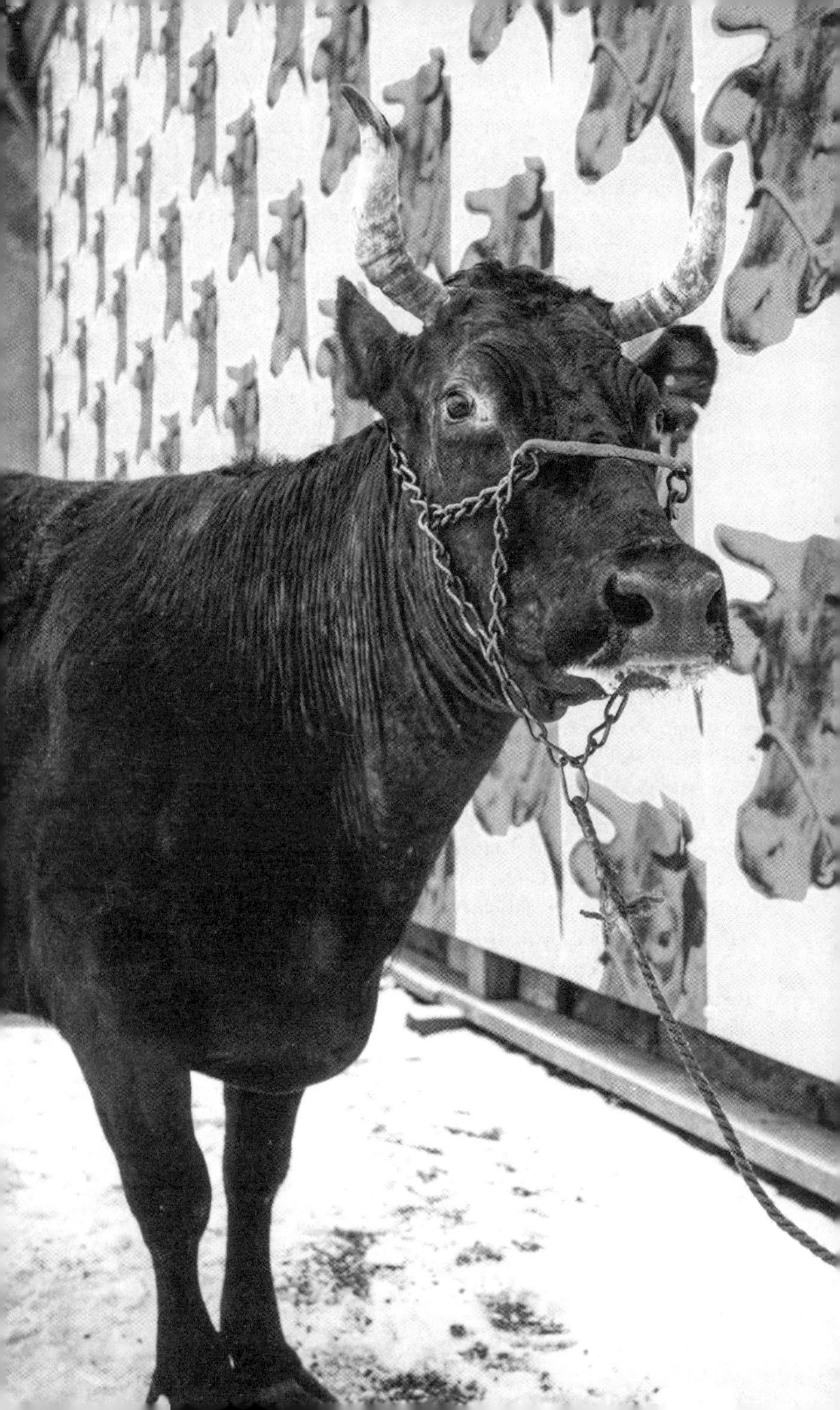

14

Making art history with Andy Warhol

The assessment that Marcel Duchamp has come to be regarded as the most influential artist of the twentieth century, as Pontus Hultén prophetized,[1] a role previously presumed for Picasso, is one that few would now question.

Indeed it was Picasso who, together with Georges Braque, inspired by Cézanne's "geometric" development of Impressionism and by African tribal sculptures, broke with centuries-old rules and perspectives of painting by inventing Cubism, the movement that has been called the greatest artistic revolution since the Renaissance. Picasso's 1907 "Les Demoiselles d'Avignon," the painting that influenced developments from the earliest years, when Picasso kept the monumental canvas in his Montmartre studio, reluctantly showing it only to confidants, is usually cited as the point of embarkment of Cubism.

If Picasso revolutionized painting, Duchamp can be said to have shattered the dominance of the art form. Having been the predominant artistic technique since antiquity, after the rediscovery of Duchamp, painting has never returned as more than an element in the universal palette of artists. It was Duchamp who, with his devastatingly simple readymades like the bicycle wheel, the bottle rack and the urinal, stripped bare the solemn artistic tradition, opening the floodgates to the Conceptual Art that characterizes our contemporary scene.

Guillaume Apollinaire, the Modernist poet, originally an art critic, in his short life not only wrote himself into literary history in the proud tradition of Baudelaire (also an art critic) and Rimbaud. He became the foremost spokesman for young modern art, one of the leading literary figures who put into words what the artists expressed

Andy Warhol, Moderna_Museet, Stockholm, 1968.

visually. Among his friends and artistic collaborators in the circle of the cafés of Montmartre, Saint Germain and Montparnasse were Picasso, the Leo, Sarah and Gertrude Stein siblings, André Breton, Max Jacob, André Derain, Erik Satie, Jean Cocteau, Marc Chagall and many others — as well as the young Marcel Duchamp.

Duchamp is featured in Apollinaire's influential book *Les Peintres Cubistes* (*The Cubist Painters*), which he worked on from 1905, published in a first edition in 1913.[2] That Apollinaire even featured Duchamp in the book is exceptional — he was the youngest artist in a selection that otherwise included Picasso, Braque, Juan Gris, Fernand Léger, Duchamp's two older brothers, and others. The artist's breakthrough Cubo-Futurist painting "Nude Woman Descending a Staircase," inspired by Eadweard Muybridge's photographic experiments with movement, was first exhibited in 1912, though not at the Salon, where it was rejected. Apollinaire realized Duchamp's importance and added him to his book at a late stage. The poet's brief statement about Duchamp in the book is mysterious in its clairvoyance: "Perhaps it is a destiny reserved for an artist so free of aesthetic considerations to reunite art with the people." How Guillaume Apollinaire could predict so early on something so far-reaching about the then twenty-six-year-old, newly established Duchamp is incomprehensible. The question is whether he himself was aware of how far-sighted the formulation was. Duchamp would certainly contribute to bringing art from its isolated, elitist salons out to the broader masses.

However, Duchamp did not achieve this historical "reunion" by himself. He was primarily, and has remained, an artist's artist. Although his name is known in our times in wider circles, Duchamp's art will never appeal to, let alone be understood by, a mass audience. For this, it's too introvert and inscrutable.

Instead, it would be Andy Warhol, the most famous artist of the 20th century alongside Picasso, who clarified, simplified, amplified, modernized, packaged and marketed Duchamp's ideas to a global mass audience; who popularized modern art. Just taste the word that describes Warhol's art like no other artist's — Pop Art, a term derived from the word popular. Warhol became the Gutenberg of art that Duchamp called for. This is how I have always seen it and how Pontus Hultén also regarded Andy Warhol — as a later, more cynical and commercial incarnation of his beacon Duchamp. This has been confirmed to me by Anna-Lena Wibom and several others, as well as in Hultén's own texts.

In Stockholm's contemporary art scene and left-wing movement, Andy Warhol was a so-called watershed. In his interest and understanding of his art, Hultén had strong-voiced opponents even among his own colleagues, especially Ulf Linde. "Ulf did not give much to that generation's interpretations of Duchamp," as Olle Granath says.[3]

I'm surprised that more hasn't been written about Warhol's apparent mission as Duchamp's apostle in the age of television, advertising and rock'n'roll. As the brilliant advertising and fashion guru he was — the greatest of all time? — Warhol brought Duchamp's anarchist message to the masses. That the majority of those masses didn't understand a damn thing about the anarchist, or rather nihilistic, message is another story. They liked the soup cans and Brillo boxes as they were. Warhol himself refused to acknowledge that there was any such message in his art. Even his patented deadpan indifference is a pose that Warhol borrowed from Duchamp, it seems obvious to me. Warhol traveled from New York to Los Angeles to see Marcel Duchamp's first ever retrospective in 1963, two years after Duchamp had come to Stockholm for *Art in Motion*, in Pasadena, of all places (see Chapter 25). It was the same year that Warhol abandoned his commercial commissions as a fashion illustrator and advertising creative to devote himself entirely to his art.

Pontus Hultén became acquainted with Warhol and his art in New York in the early sixties, although it's unclear exactly when and where. There is conflicting information about whether or not Hultén visited Warhol's first exhibitions at the Stable Gallery. He included the artist in the Pop Art exhibition in 1964, notably early, the same year as Warhol's breakthrough "supermarket exhibition" at the Stable Gallery. By 1968, Warhol had reached stardom and established his studio, the Factory, with its flow of myth and legend; this image industry from which Duchamp's Dadaism in modernized, commercialized guise spread across the world.

In Europe, Andy Warhol had not yet become more established in 1968 than that Moderna Museet's exhibition was the Slovakian miner's son's first European solo retrospective. Being the first to show Warhol on a full scale in a museum in Europe or anywhere in the world is a badge of honor on Pontus Hultén's shield of art historical merit.

The "supermarket show" was Andy Warhol's second and last at the Stable Gallery, before he joined Castelli, who had previously rejected him. The exhibition (April 21-May 1, 1964) featured hundreds of boxes for Brillo Soap Pads, Kellogg's Cornflakes, Del Monte Peach Halves, Campbell's Tomato Juice, and Heinz Tomato Ketchup.

The decision to invest in a solo exhibition with Warhol, which was to open in February 1968, seems to have been taken by Hultén and his colleagues at a late stage, in the summer or fall of 1967, an interim year for Moderna Museet after the glorious 1966 and before the turbulent 1968. About 1967, Hultén writes in the twenty-fifth anniversary book that "some more conventional exhibitions were shown." The museum's level of ambition is demonstrated by the packed program of exhibitions "of a more conventional kind" during this year, including, among many others, Peggy Guggenheim's collection from Venice and solo exhibitions with Emil Nolde, Wilfredo Lam, Meret Oppenheim, Lucio Fontana, John Heartfield, René Magritte, Raoul Hausman and Bror Hjorth.

In 2008, for its 50th anniversary, Moderna Museet, under the direction of Lars Nittve, presented a spectacular Andy Warhol retrospective to commemorate the forty-year anniversary of the 1968 Warhol exhibition. For the catalog[4] of this overwhelming box office success,[5] entitled *Andy Warhol. Other Voices, Other Rooms*, produced in collaboration with the Stedelijk in Amsterdam, Olle Granath wrote a frequently quoted text about the work on the historic and, in retrospect, controversial exhibition. In the text, Granath relays that it was "sometime during the fall" that Pontus Hultén contacted him to request his help once again, to manage the Stockholm part of the production of the Warhol retrospective — a few months before the exhibition was to open. Granath was not offered any payment for his services this time either. As always, resources for production were minimal. As Granath writes: "Considering what Moderna Museet had accomplished in its ten years, the staff was also unimaginably small and definitely not sufficient to handle a large production with a lot of time-consuming practical work."[6] In New York, the production team consisted of Warhol himself and his Factory, Hultén's and by now also Warhol's friend Billy Klüver, that constant trouble-shooter, and the twenty-four-year-old German curator Kasper König.

At the time, König was a whiz kid of modern art. He had already visited the museum in Stockholm twice on his own initiative. He was one of the international connoisseurs who understood that this small northern museum was where the most interesting contemporary art in the world was shown. As the hungry young art player he was, König had relocated to New York where he had acquainted Andy Warhol and the rest of the small New York avant-garde. It was Billy Klüver who had suggested to him the idea of offering his services to Moderna Museet in order to acquire the Green Card he needed to work in the US. Pontus

Hultén was immediately on board, always looking for smart deals that could help the museum without burdening its budget. König was hired as Moderna Museet's official New York representative, with a business card but of course without a salary. This way he obtained the coveted work permit. His first assignment for the museum was in 1966, at the age of twenty-three, when he helped Claes Oldenburg in New York with the production of his exhibition (see previous chapter).

The concept for the Stockholm exhibition was rapidly conceived in the fall of 1967 by Warhol and Hultén, assisted by König and Klüver. Olle Granath only came into the picture when the exhibition was to be transported to Stockholm. The theme was repetition, Warhol's signature as Hultén saw it. Three motifs were selected: Marilyn, roses and the electric chair, the latter two in unusual color schemes. Series of screen-printed paintings were to be displayed in the museum galleries, in monumental formats for maximum visual impact, along with film screens of the same size on which loops from Warhol's most famous films such as *Eat*, *Sleep* and *Empire* were to be projected. "The revolutionary novelty, although I didn't realize it at the time, was Pontus' idea to give the film the same dignity as the art in the exhibition," says Olle Granath. "It was something that was still not comme-il-faut in the art world. Warhol himself made no distinction between film and art. He was equally deadpan about the whole thing."[7]

In addition to paintings and films, some spatial installations conceived more as scenographic props would be featured, to reinforce the effect of repetition. "Clouds" helium balloons in metal foil would float around the museum. The whole thing was high-tech for its time. Pontus Hultén wanted to emphasize the modern, slick commercial impact that was new in Warhol's art. Billy Klüver's technical inventiveness was put to the test. Olle Granath describes how Billy had intended to weld the helium balloons in New York, but the gas proved too expensive. As usual, the museum had to improvise. The solution was clear plastic bags filled with air and placed on the museum floor. "Through their static electricity, they attracted all the dust on Skeppsholmen. With these bags on their feet, the audience had to trudge up to the paintings. I wonder if such 'clouds' have appeared in any Warhol exhibition before or later," as Granath writes.[8]

The solution chosen for the much later herostratic Brillo boxes (see Chapter 36) was also the result of improvisation due to time and budget constraints. Shipping Warhol's boxes across the Atlantic was unreasonably expensive and complicated. According to unanimous reports, it was Warhol himself who suggested that the museum should instead have the boxes made in Sweden, with a customary laconic comment, "why don't you make them over there?," which he is said to have uttered to Pontus Hultén, according to the latter's often repeated statement. This too proved costly and time was short. During the process, "someone" came up with the "ingenious" idea of contacting the Brillo factory's printing plant in Brooklyn instead. Five hundred corrugated cardboard boxes were shipped across the Atlantic in flat, folded format. In his text, Olle Granath recounts how he and the museum's janitor got very skilled at folding up cardboard boxes, which were stacked into a mountain in the exhibition gallery. This was how exhibitions of the world's leading artists could be produced as late as 1968. In the museum's film room, *Chelsea Girls* was screened from twin projectors.

The most difficult technical challenge was the films to be presented alongside the paintings on the walls of the museum's main gallery with its "violent" light flow. Rendering films projected from sixteen-millimeter projectors clearly visible in broad daylight was far from easy with the available technology. There was no pre-planned solution. As Granath recalls, "a whole battery" of discarded spotlights was requisitioned at a low cost from Swedish Television, to compensate for the daylight that the paintings were absorbing. From "the big photo company in town" they managed to acquire a new type of silver film screen that gave "pretty good reproduction in bright rooms," writes Granath. The screens were mounted on frames of the same format as the paintings and hung side by side with these on the gallery walls.

Granath recites in his text — and Hultén and Klüver in other contexts — how delivery of films was delayed due to what was assumed to be a rights problem, although the Factory blamed the film lab. As the opening approached, the team was forced to realize that no films would arrive. Their habitual working method improvisation was once again honored. Through Anna-Lena Wibom and Hultén's friend Nils-Hugo Geber, a scholar at the newly established Swedish Film Institute, they obtained a clip from a circus film from the nineteenth century with the great advantage of having no author and thus no rights. Among other features, the clip showed an endless loop in which an elephant is seen climbing up onto a stool but never down again.

There were understandable concerns among the staff about what Warhol and not least "his film guy" Paul Morrissey would think of this

Andy Warhol 1968, poster. The first time the famous quote was printed.
Pp. 228–229: Andy Warhol and Viva, Moderna Museet, Stockholm, 1968.

In the future everybody will be world famous for fifteen minutes.

Andy Warhol

Moderna Museet, Stockholm Sweden 10/2–17/3 1968

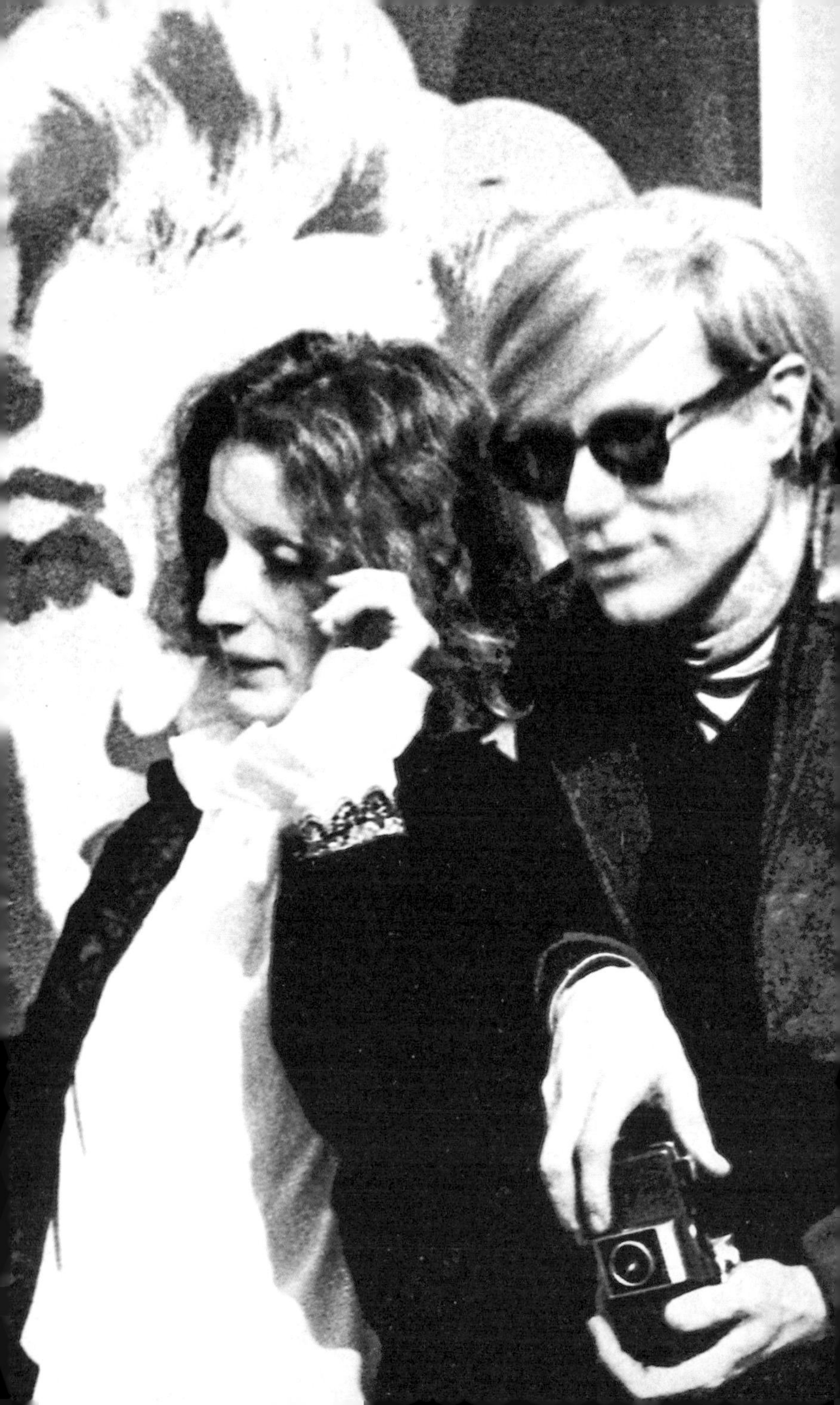

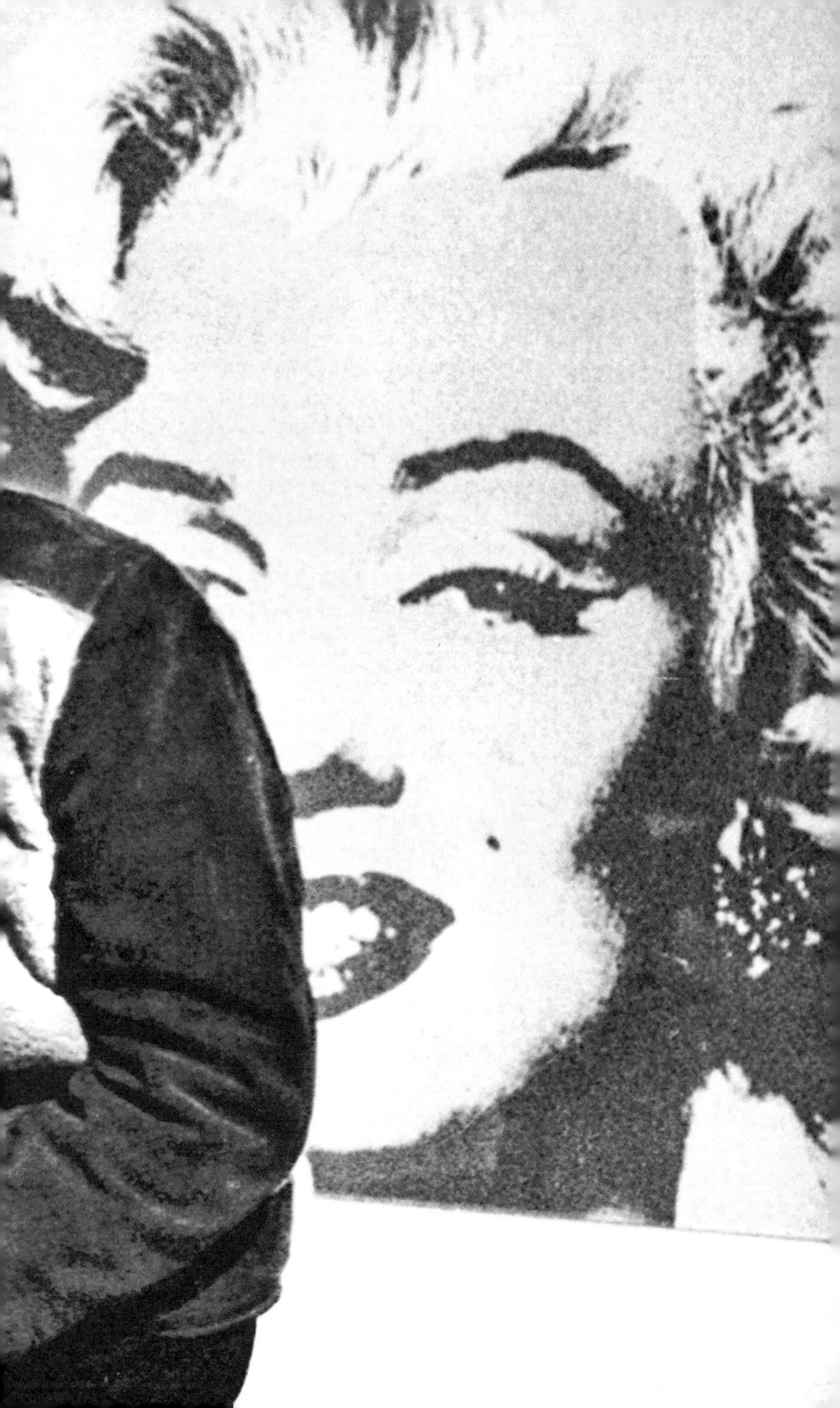

creative solution when they arrived in Stockholm for the opening. There was no need to worry. Warhol liked and approved the idea without further ado and stood fascinated watching the poor elephant climbing up and up on his stool, over and over again, writes Granath.

Kasper König offers a very different version of the reason for the non-delivery of the films when we meet in Cologne: "At the time, Warhol was interested in pursuing a career in Hollywood," König says. "He was worried about what Hollywood producers would think of a movie with a sleeping person — that he would appear too uncommercial."[9]

Most sensational in Olle Granath's 2008 account is a tale of the production of the famous 1968 exhibition catalog, or book as Granath calls it, a desirable collector's item in our time and considered one of the most style-defining exhibition catalogs in modern art history.

Many Andy Warhol quotes were made famous by the catalog and posters for the 1968 Moderna Museet exhibition, including "In the future everybody will be world famous for fifteen minutes," "I like boring things," "All is pretty," "and I don't really believe in love," "I never read, I just look at pictures," and "If you want to know all about Andy Warhol, just look at the surface of my paintings and films and myself. There's nothing behind it."

Like the exhibition, the idea of the catalog was based on repetition. Reproductions of works were repeated alongside documentary images from the Factory and the life of Andy Warhol, with no commentary other than quotes from Warhol. For posters, a solution was chosen without the usual image, with only various Warhol quotes. Olle Granath was entrusted by Pontus Hultén with the task of selecting these quotes and translating them into Swedish. In his text, Granath recounts how Pontus came to him one day with a box "barely Brillo box-sized," containing what he said was everything that had been written about Warhol so far. "The equivalent today would probably be some truckloads," as Granath notes. A few nights of work later, Granath handed a manuscript to Hultén and waited anxiously for his reaction. Granath writes: "'Excellent,' Pontus said when I called him, 'but I'm missing a quote.' 'Which one?' I asked. 'In the future everyone will be world famous for fifteen minutes,' Pontus replied. 'If I had seen it in this material I would have noted it,' I replied. There was silence at the other end of the phone line, then Pontus said: 'Well if he hasn't said it, he very well could have. We'll include it.'"[10]

It's an intriguing thought that Andy Warhol's most famous quote could in fact be an invention of Pontus Hultén. In my research and inquiries to The Andy Warhol Foundation for the Visual Arts in New

York and The Andy Warhol Museum in Pittsburgh, I have not been able to find any information about the origin of the quote, other than that it has a background in the prophetic thinking and theories of the "media philosopher" Marshall McLuhan in his book *The Medium is the Massage*.[11] What is clear is that it was in the catalog for Moderna Museet's Warhol exhibition that this quote was first published. Overall, the solution with the quotes in the catalog and on the posters can be said to have contributed to Andy Warhol becoming such a quote machine, on par with Churchill, Kennedy and Oscar Wilde.

Pontus Hultén's abilities as a market communicator came to further use in the idea of using the museum building itself as an advertising pillar — an early pilot for the "big image marketing" of our time. Hultén, likely in consultation with graphic designers John Melin and Anders Österlin, had decided that the south facade of the museum should be covered with Warhol's cows printed in an aggressive pink and yellow color scheme. The realization of this idea required ingenuity. After experimenting with various techniques, the team, supported as usual by unpaid technical consultants, concluded that the simplest solution was to clad the building with scaffolding, which in turn was covered with standard-sized Masonite panels on which the images were wallpapered. "When the facade was fully clad, two and a half cows remained. The thumbtack had apparently worked. The wallpaper on the facade glowed. In the defoliated spring winter, the cows could be seen all the way from Slussen," Olle Granath writes.[12] Pontus Hultén's brother-in-law, as he was called, Gösta Wibom, Anna-Lena's brother, helped transport a couple of cows to the museum for the second time, to be immortalized in famous photographs while looking at their printed counterparts.

The exhibition catalog, like the *hon* catalog printed on daily newsprint, was a blockbuster that was reprinted in ever new editions, to which new images could be added. An exclusive bibliophile's edition of the catalog with gold trim in a Plexiglas box was produced in an edition of one hundred copies — a batch that was forgotten only to be found in the storage room by Granath years later, now a precious rarity.

About Andy Warhol's days in Stockholm for the visit to the exhibition in the company of his manager Paul Morrissey and Viva, one of Warhol's preferred "superstars" at the time, there are several, partly contradictory stories, some text and a few famous images that together form a modern Stockholm legend.

"Superstars" was the term Warhol used for the various "stars" of the New York underground culture that hung around the Factory, acting in his films and embellishing his entourage.

Some contemporaries even claim that Warhol was in Stockholm twice for the exhibition. The Brillo scandal forty years later has made this information controversial and disputed. According to Anna-Lena Wibom, Warhol and his party stayed at the Hotel Esplanade, while Olle Granath, who had been trusted with the main responsibility by Hultén to take care of Warhol, is certain that it was the Grand Hôtel. "I see myself walking the corridors there to pick him up," as he says.[13] Wibom remembers that they had to wait a long time for Warhol in the hotel lobby before going out to dinner as he first had to apply careful makeup, complexified as he was for his skin scarred by youthful acne. According to Wibom, Warhol wanted to return to what he called "The torch joint:"[14] the grill of the Opera Cellar, where gas torches flanked the entrance. Olle Granath recounts in his text that the group went to see Vilgot Sjöman's *Jag är nyfiken gul* (*I Am Curious Yellow*), the movie that launched "the Swedish sin" globally, which Warhol followed with interest while Paul Morrissey, jet-lagged, slept through the entire screening.

As Warhol's cicerone in the Stockholm night, Granath in turn employed the young jazz and rock drummer Bill Öhrström, still a well-known profile in the Swedish music industry. Öhrström had come to New York as something as surprising as a golf scholarship holder, where he became acquainted with the jazz and beatnik scene. Direct American experience, language skills and contacts were still rare in the Stockholm music world, so Bill became a link to the New York underground scene, renowned for his sense of the new. Öhrström made a name for himself when he urged music producer Simon Brehm to take a chance on releasing the Velvet Underground's self-titled breakthrough album with Warhol's banana on the cover in 1967, a first in Europe for the Swedish EMA record company. None of the label's other European offices understood this band from Greenwich Village with song titles like "Heroin" and Andy Warhol as their manager. "I wasn't a good musician but I had a hell of a feel for how things should be put together and designed," as Öhrström says.[15]

According to Olle Granath, the ciceronage covered several nights, but Bill Öhrström only remembers one evening and night with Warhol and his entourage. He says that he found Morrissey to be an odd character. "He didn't fit in somehow. He was far too ordinary, with a corduroy jacket, almost like a school teacher or something." Viva, on the other hand, was flamboyant to the max, says Bill Öhrström, loudly proclaiming her desire for a fix of heroin for the night. I ask Öhrström if he got the impression that the crew was on heroin. "I don't know, I think so, but not in that hysterical Swedish way, more in a mixed addiction, I think," he replies. The narcotic staple, Bill confirms, was otherwise "acid," LSD, for the circle around the Factory as well as for the entire art, rock and hippie scene on both sides of the Atlantic at the time.

I am, of course, interested in Bill Öhrström's impression of Andy Warhol himself and receive a delightful mini-portrait in response: "He was pretty much what you'd expect — taciturn, secretive, staying in the background and letting the others take up space and attract attention. His glasses were neither shaded nor transparent."[16] Olle Granath chuckles when I relay Öhrström's characterization. "Yes, he may be right," says Granath. "He wasn't exactly a man of surprises, Warhol, that he wasn't."[17]

Bill Öhrström can recall only one comment from Warhol himself during the night in Stockholm. It was when someone mentioned that the Australian brother trio Bee Gees were performing at Konserthuset that evening, and asked if the company was interested in seeing the concert. The Bee Gees would later during the disco era of the seventies, and well beyond, make their triumphant return to the world's dance floors, but at this time the band was marketed as the new Beatles. In Swedish music circles and in the progressive movement, the Bee Gees were branded with a deep geek stamp, a mark of Cain similar to that with which ABBA was later stigmatized. A silence spread in the company at this request, Öhrström says, whereupon Andy Warhol spoke up for the first and only time (Bill Öhrström pitches his voice up to a whimsy squeak): "I want to see the Bee Gees!" "I remember it clearly because that comment was just so damn wrong there and then, in that situation," says Öhrström.[18]

Andy Warhol's visit to the Bee Gees concert and afterwards to the jazz club Gyllene cirkeln (The Golden Circle) in the ABF building on Sveavägen is documented in a book about Stockholm's musical life in the sixties, published in 2002 by the jazz department of the Swedish Song Archive. There is a chapter entitled "With Warhol from Moderna to The Circle,"[19] in which the author and gallerist Bo A. Karlsson[20] writes about this evening in a text that conveys a charming snapshot of Stockholm in the late sixties, when the model society was at its peak and our capital was a meeting place for progressive artists, performers, writers and other creators from all over the world. I can't guarantee the accuracy of the text, which unsurprisingly offers a somewhat different version of reality than Bill Öhrström's, but what Bo A. Karlsson describes seems perfectly possible with knowledge of Stockholm's fantastic little global cultural scene at the time.

"Stockholm in the 1960s was the city where everything was possible," Karlsson writes, "a world center of cultural events." He accounts his attempts to interview Warhol for Se magazine that evening, observing that Warhol bore a strong resemblance to Chet Baker, whom Karlsson had previously met and interviewed, with the same way of dominating the room despite a low profile. Karlsson pointed out the similarity to Warhol, who said he had never heard of Baker. At the Golden Circle, according to Karlsson, Warhol ended up in the company of Diana Ross, who was in town to join the Prince, our current Swedish King, and who visited the Circle to listen to another American artist.

In retrospect, the Andy Warhol exhibition is seen as another "scandal success" for Moderna Museet, far from a foregone conclusion given that Warhol was not yet a big name in Europe and that the idea of a solo show of the artist was a daring initiative. Warhol's "mass-produced" art, as American as could ever be, naturally aroused indignation in the inflamed spirit of the times. The exhibition was seen by more than twenty-four thousand visitors, thirty thousand according to other reports,[21] a good figure considering the harsh winter and the fact that the exhibition was overshadowed in the press by the drama of the students at Stockholm University occupying their own student union building in the sixty-eight spirit of youthful rebellion.

Andy Warhol, I repeat, was still at this time an artist who split opinions even within Moderna Museet's inner circle. Purchasing art by Warhol was politically impossible. Nevertheless, Hultén was not about to miss the opportunity to add this key modern artist to the museum's collection. He settled a typically informal arrangement with Warhol and the Factory. The museum would pay for the production of the silkscreen paintings for the show. In return, the museum would receive a flower and an electric chair, as well as a copy of the film *Chelsea Girls*. Olle Granath writes: "In retrospect, it is easy to see that this was one of many brilliant deals that Pontus Hultén made for Moderna Museet. There were some indications that Warhol's American gallerists were not as satisfied with the deal made over their heads."[22]

This is the official, frequently repeated story of how the main works in the museum's Warhol collection were incorporated. However, concerning the course of the acquisition of these two Warhol paintings, worth easily a billion Swedish crowns and often displayed in the museum's permanent collection, there are of course several alternative versions of the reality/truth. According to Kasper König, Warhol had offered one of the paintings to him personally, in return for his services in the production in New York. In König's account, he had unselfishly suggested to Warhol that he donate two paintings to the museum instead, to which the artist is said to have agreed.[23] König and Daniel Birnbaum talked about these twists and turns during the discussion in connection with the museum's archive exhibition *Andy Warhol 1968*, in fall 2018, where Birnbaum joked that his friend Johann König, Kasper's son, used to say that one day he would "come and get his painting."

I find it hard to fully believe König's version of events. The definitive truth is, as usual, difficult or impossible to ascertain. Nonetheless, there is written evidence that a serious dispute, as Granath suggests in his text quoted above, arose with Andy Warhol's gallerist Leo Castelli. In Moderna Museet's archives I have found two letters in which Castelli writes to Pontus Hultén after visiting Warhol's 1970 retrospective in Pasadena, Los Angeles, where Moderna Museet had apparently lent at least one of the paintings the museum had "received" two years earlier. Castelli expresses surprise that Warhol would have donated a Flower screen painting to the museum.

In his first letter, dated May 21, 1970, the New York gallerist writes: "Dear Pontus. / No doubt you have already heard how very beautiful Andy's show looked on opening night in Pasadena; it was a glorious event. Among the works on loan are eight of the large FLOWERS that were first shown in Stockholm; I noticed that the dark purple one was credited to the Moderna Museet, which puzzled me somewhat, as I was unaware that you had acquired this work (I knew, of course, that Andy had given an ELECTRIC CHAIR as a gift to the museum at the time of the show.)/ Andy himself was also quite surprised. During the initial discussions for the California exhibition, an inventory of various works was undertaken and it was discovered that one of the FLOWERS paintings was missing. Andy could not recall what might have happened to it until he saw the painting again in Pasadena, when it arrived from Sweden. / Andy was at the gallery today and expressed extreme concern about the case, as he had no memory of giving this particular work to the museum. To somewhat alleviate his anxiety, may I ask you to be so kind as to wire me an explanation of how the disposition of the painting was determined at the end of the '68 exhibition. / Sincerely, Leo Castelli."[24]

In the margin of this letter, Pontus Hultén has, in clearly recognizable hand, scribbled what is obviously the text of the telegram requested by Castelli, dated May 25, 1970, in two different text groups. I don't know whether both were sent with the telegram. The first reads: "I thought Andy had given us Flowers stop sorry if it was a mistake stop." The second text group is not apologetic but more offensive: "Andy must have been aware that we had it because he specifically asked Coplans[25] to ask about it stop love Pontus."[26]

Neither Leo Castelli nor Andy Warhol was apparently satisfied with this answer. This is evidenced by a second letter from Castelli to Hultén, dated June 17, 1970, in which the demon dealer writes: "Dear Pontus: / I am so sorry for the misunderstanding between you and Andy regarding his FLOWER painting. / I spoke to him again today, and he seems to really feel that he only donated the ELECTRIC CHAIR to the museum. / I hope to see you somewhere in Europe next month. / All my best / Leo." Here someone, not Hultén, probably Märta Sahlberg, has written in the top margin of the letter: "(Not to be replied according to Pontus.)"[27]

I'm surprised that these events do not seem to have been investigated. No one in the museum administration today knows about these letters and entanglements, not even Olle Granath, the only person left from the working group for the Andy Warhol exhibition in 1968, together with Kasper König. How the affair continued to develop is unknown to me. Some kind of agreement must have been reached, because according to Moderna Museet's website the painting "Ten-Foot Flowers" was incorporated into the museum's collection six years after this exchange of letters, in 1976, as a "donation from the artist."[28]

Either way, I sense behind the operation Pontus Hultén's strategic thinking and manipulations in order to expand the museum's collection — efforts in which he never hesitated to make use of tools such as half-hearted, sometimes non-existent promises or loose pledges, never asking for permission unless absolutely necessary. Then still, I'm phrasing it in forgiving terms. The pattern is recognizable from many undertakings throughout his career. In any case, the result can be admired annually by hundreds of thousands of museum visitors: the foundation of a Warhol collection that was built without a penny of funding for acquisition.

Kasper König himself did not get to see the exhibition he had helped produce. "I got a plane ticket to Stockholm but I sold it," König told me. "Because SAS sponsored the museum, it was a first-class ticket so I got a good price for it. I couldn't afford not to sell it. That was the payment I got for my job."[29]

The Stockholm exhibition marked the end of Andy Warhol's first era as an artist. A few months after his visit to Stockholm, on June 3, 1968, the artist was shot and critically wounded by Valerie Solanas at the Factory in New York, an event that was a turning point for Warhol. When he eventually returned, his art would, as Olle Granath puts it, "move in partly new directions."

In the fall and winter of 2018-2019, the above-mentioned "archive exhibition" *Warhol 1968* was shown at Moderna Museet for the fiftieth anniversary of the 1968 exhibition. The exhibition was presented in the lower gallery, in a modest format, with works of art and other material from the museum's own collection, as well as textual information on signs.[30] The show attracted much interest internationally, with crowds of spectators growing throughout the exhibition period. In a symposium organized as part of the program, Kasper König, Olle Granath and others participated in a panel discussion.

On the occasion of the symposium, I met König again and spoke in more detail about the organization of the 1968 exhibition. He described the idea behind the show as far ahead of its time, assembled only with works produced exclusively for the occasion, in a powerful, coherent concept, more like a large-scale gallery presentation. König gave part of the honor for this exhibition's legendary status to the catalog and specifically to the designer John Melin, or "the guy in Malmö" as he called him, who according to König has not been duly credited. "That catalog became a model for how to make catalogs for exhibitions," König said, claiming that the publication has sold three hundred and twenty thousand copies over the years.[31] König has previously reported that when Warhol, who was not involved in the production, was shown the first draft, he flipped through the catalog slowly and carefully, without comment, then flipped through it again in silence, whereupon he tore out two images and then said, "Okay, you can print it."

Curiously, Kasper König, like Pontus Hultén in writing,[32] stated that the 1968 exhibition was never shown elsewhere — that there were proposals from Louisiana and the Stedelijk but that Warhol and the production team had not considered this compatible with the concept. In fact, parts of the Warhol exhibition did indeed go on tour to Amsterdam, Oslo, Bern and Berlin.

In the contemporary industry of Andy Warhol's art and rights, and in official history, the 1968 exhibition in Stockholm is acknowledged as one of the milestones in the artist's career. In the international art world, Pontus Hultén is naturally associated with Warhol. It's well documented that at the time of the exhibition, Pontus Hultén already considered Andy Warhol to be the most important of the Pop artists, in a class of his own — a realization which it would take the art world and American institutions twenty years to arrive at, until after Warhol's death in 1987.

Double Vision, the biography on patrons Dominique and John de Menil, major collectors of Warhol's art and close associates of The Andy Warhol Foundation of Art, recounts a conversation between Dominique de Menil and Pontus Hultén in New York in January 1979, after the two friends had attended the premiere of Warhol's *Shadows*, the massive suite of abstract "shadow paintings" owned by the de Menil family's Dia Foundation. "In the taxi on the way back uptown, Hultén told Dominique that he was convinced that Warhol was a deeply religious artist," writes the de Menils' biographer William Middleton. "He had gotten the idea when he curated Warhol's first European retrospective, a legendary exhibition presented at Moderna Museet in 1968, and had to defend the show against criticism. Although he said it was difficult to put it into words, he sensed a strong spiritual quality in Warhol's work. The repetitive nature of the work — 'even Campbell's soup cans, even dollar bills' — felt like litanies to Hultén. 'Of all the Pop artists, Warhol is the one who touches me the most, who may be the most important,' the museum director told Dominique. 'Every time, he goes all out. He holds nothing back — he risks everything.'"[33]

15

The Machine — interlude at the Museum of Modern Art in New York

On July 3, 1968, the exhibition *Vladimir Tatlin* opened, famous in art history primarily for the reconstruction of the model of Tatlin's never-realized utopian tower "Monument to the Third International" from 1919. The model of the tower was manufactured also for the exhibition *The Machine* in New York, but entered the collection of Moderna Museet where it is a central piece, frequently loaned to other museums around the world over the years.

The *Vladimir Tatlin* exhibition was important in that it was the second, after *The Inner and the Outer Space*,[1] in a long cycle of Russian-themed art historic exhibitions that Hultén would stage at various institutions throughout his remaining career — an international contribution to Russian art and culture that makes him unique among Western art players.

The Constructivist artist and architect Vladimir Tatlin, who at the time was far less known internationally (and still is today) than his alleged rival in the Russian avant-garde, Kazimir Malevich, became yet another of Pontus Hultén's household gods after he had discovered this artist at an even slightly later stage than Malevich, as it seems to me, since his interest in the Russian avant-garde had steadily deepened.

Vladimir Tatlin can be characterized as the most utopian, and the most large-scale, of all the utopian artists of the Russian avant-garde — a quality that was irresistible to the arch-utopian Hultén. Tatlin's philosophies were fundamental to the Bauhaus art school in Weimar, where the Russian influence was strong through the exiled Russian teachers. Tatlin began as an iconographer, trained in painting and sculpture in Moscow. An encounter with Picasso during a visit to Paris in 1913 was crucial to his Modernist orientation and his ideas on geometry.

Dedicated to the service of the young Soviet state, he became increasingly involved in architecture, engineering and industrial design.

After the 1917 revolution, during a few years when the future of the new communist state was still uncertain, a narrow historical "window" opened for the artists of the Russian avant-garde, most of whom were utopian anarchists in their political beliefs. Malevich, Tatlin, Antoine Pevsner, Naum Gabo, Aleksandr Rodchenko, female pioneers such as Lyubov Popova and Aleksandra Ekster, and others, put their art in service of the revolution to varying degrees. For a while it seemed that artists would be able to influence the construction of the new ideal state. This brief historical exception is probably the closest that any society has come to Pontus Hultén's own cherished ideal of the artist as a constructively creative primordial force, acting in conjunction with science and engineering, superior to lowly politicians and capitalists; not only with the cramped studio but with the entire social order as his workshop and stage — this beautiful dream that he would later in his lifetime, to his bitterness, see demolished.

It was during this fleeting post-revolutionary period that Vladimir Tatlin, the artist in the Russian avant-garde closest to the communist revolutionary leadership, developed a vision that pushed the symbiosis of art with industry, architecture and engineering further than any of his colleagues. Tatlin's philosophy, related to Futurism, the movement that gave rise to Constructivism, was that artistic expression should be subordinated in every respect to the material and its properties. Like the Futurists, Tatlin believed that beauty lay in the power and function of materials pushed to their limits by the arts of technology and engineering, hence devoid of the Futurists' youthful fascist worship of violence and destruction.

In Tatlin's theory, the most beautiful forms were the most economical. Troels Andersen, Hultén's long-time partner in all projects with a Russian connection, told me in Copenhagen[2] that he and Hultén had extensive conversations about Tatlin already during their first meeting in Stockholm in 1963.[3] Hultén has revealed[4] that it was Andersen who, in these conversations, made him interested in organizing an exhibition with Tatlin and who, through his technical knowledge, gave Hultén the idea of recreating the mythical tower in the form of a model.

Tatlin's "Monument to the Third International," or "Tatlin's Tower" as it's known, was intended to be erected in the former capital of the Tsars, Petrograd, later Leningrad, now once again Saint Petersburg. The tower was designed as a monument to and headquarters for The

International, the organization formed in 1919 as a union of the world's communist parties, tightly controlled from Moscow, with the aim of spreading the revolution across the world, by force if necessary. The tower was intended to be over four hundred meters high, a hundred meters higher than the Eiffel Tower, which of course was the benchmark in the eternal showdown between megalomaniac men of all persuasions around the world.

The construction of the tower was based on a double spiral of steel which would rise cone-like as a futuristic Tower of Babel almost half a kilometer, into the clouds. Around this structure, visitors would be transported by various futuristic technological devices. This enormous framework would house four geometrically shaped glass pavilions. At the bottom was a cube-shaped assembly hall for congresses, lectures and the International's decision-making body, with room for tens of thousands of participants. This cube would rotate at a speed of one revolution per year. The next plateau was a pyramid-shaped pavilion for executive meetings, designed to rotate one revolution a month. Above this was a cylinder-shaped chamber intended to house an information center from which news bulletins and manifestos would be sent out over Petrograd and the world via loudspeakers, radio and telegraph (an idea that we shall see recurring in Hultén's utopian visions). This would rotate one turn per day. At the top, a hemispherical terminal for radio transmission gear towered. Tatlin had plans for the facades of the cylinder (the information center) to function as a giant three hundred and sixty-degree screen for film projections, and for light cannons to project messages and manifestos onto the cloud shield on overcast days. These were not exactly modest plans.

In communist reality, there was ultimately no room for the realization of this mammoth vision, either politically or financially. Tatlin and his colleagues constructed a model of the tower — intended to be built entirely from the industrial materials of steel, glass and concrete — in wood. So prosaic was the post-revolutionary reality that even the model was lost after it was seized by the French craftsmen who made it, as a pledge for non-payment of wages. All that remained were some blurry black and white photographs of the model.

Through the Ministry of Foreign Affairs, Pontus Hultén and Moderna Museet made a request to the Soviet Ministry of Culture to lend some of Tatlin's preserved paintings, sculptures — his so-called counter-reliefs in wood and metal — architectural drawings and other material from museums in Moscow and Leningrad, where all this was kept in storage. The request was denied, on the grounds of alleged ongoing work on a "comprehensive documentation" of the artist. In the late 1960s, Tatlin was still far from being politically approved in the Soviet state. Hultén's disappointment was considerable but, as always, the ingenuity was greater. Hultén, Ulf Linde and Per Olof Ultvedt's passion for copying found its most extreme expression in the idea of producing, for the first time, an exhibition exclusively of replicas, without any originals.

The main piece of the exhibition would be the tower. Troels Andersen knew that one of Tatlin's assistants who had helped build the model was still alive. There was renewed disappointment when, as claimed for health reasons, it wasn't possible for the elderly technician to leave Moscow.[5] Thankfully, through Andersen, the Moderna Museet team was able to obtain important information from Tatlin's old assistant. The duo of replica makers Linde and Ultvedt went to work under Hultén's direction, supported by Troels Andersen and backed up by the museum's carpenters and janitors. As habitual in the museum's lucky streak, the team was incredibly fortunate when a previously unknown photograph of the model, of higher quality and with greater clarity of technical detail, was published in a Czech magazine during the course of the work.[6] Thanks to this photograph, it was possible to correct some fundamental errors in the design. When a first smaller model was completed, Nationalmuseum's carpenters Arne Holm and Eskil Nandorf constructed a model more than six meters high — about the same size as Tatlin's own lost structure — in wood. It was the first time that Tatlin's tower, previously known in the West as little more than a legend, had been recreated. "It was almost like a scientific experiment where small mistakes had big consequences — a real detective reconstruction," as Pontus Hultén enthusiastically told the German artist and curator Stephan Andreae.[7]

The Tatlin exhibition was a modest public success that received limited press coverage. In part, I assume that this was due to the niche subject matter — a completely unknown artist, a difficult one at that, not from the enticing United States but from the gray, depressing Soviet Union; a display with no original works, consisting only of photographs and documents in addition to the tower, and a set of other replicas, a couple of which had been borrowed from the Universities of Newcastle and Portsmouth in the UK, where they had been made for study projects.[8] Four replicas, three sculptures and Tatlin's "bird" "Letatlin," a utopian glider, were crafted on commission by the museum in Munich, as shown by documents in the archive, which are now part of the Moderna Museet collection.[9] Tatlin's famous costume was, of course, tailored in Pontus Hultén's size. It's unclear from the catalog and archival documents whether all of these replicas were actually exhibited or if some were added afterwards. Archive documents show that the tower was immediately requested for loan from numerous institutions around Europe.[10]

After the exhibition in Stockholm, the model of Tatlin's tower was straight away shipped, in deconstructed form, to New York, where Nationalmuseum's master carpenter Eskil Nandorf supervised its erection in MoMA's sculpture garden. In a letter dated March 1967, more than a year before the exhibition opened in Stockholm, Hultén writes almost apologetically in a letter to MoMA's legendary founding director Alfred H. Barr Jr. that what he and Troels Andersen are preparing "is probably one of those exhibitions that exist more in the form of a catalog than as things on the walls." In the same letter, he calls Moderna Museet's exhibition a "preparation for the Tatlin part of *The Machine* exhibition at MoMA," which Hultén had been working on for more than a year at the time.[11]

In December 1965, Pontus Hultén had been contacted by MoMA director René d'Harnoncourt with the proposal to stage an exhibition in the capacity of "guest director" at the museum, on the theme of Kinetic Art, moving art, the movement that he himself had arguably invented, five years after *Art in Motion*.[12] In the following correspondence with d'Harnoncourt, Hultén reasons that this motif is "too vast." As a counter-proposal, he presents the more limited theme of the machine, which MoMA accepted, despite initial objections from d'Harnoncourt that it was doubtful whether this was suitable for the American market.[13] It seems that after Hultén's ensuing New York visit, MoMA had at least partially accepted other firm counter-demands posed in his response letter, including a considerably higher fee than offered, longer production times, more generous resources, a full-time assistant, and more.[14] The exhibition, eventually given the simple title *The Machine*, was endowed with a subtitle — "*As Seen at the End of the Mechanical Age*."

The Machine can still be viewed as a sequel to *Art in Motion*, building on the Futurists' romanticization of the machine, the Russian Constructivists' worship, the Surrealists' fear and the Dadaists' mockery of it as a benefactor/god/destroyer of humanity.

Many of the exhibited artists were the same, what had become Hultén's usual guard — Duchamp, Picabia, Calder, Tinguely, Rauschenberg,

Léger, Moholy-Nagy, and many more. Unsurprisingly, Duchamp was particularly prominently represented, with two versions of "Nude Woman Descending a Staircase," his first "machine painting" "The Coffee Grinder" (1911), "The Bride" (1912), and Linde/Ultvedt's replica of "The Bride Stripped Bare by Her Bachelors, Even," the "Love Machine" as it's called in MoMA's press material.[15] The exhibition featured works from as far back as the Renaissance — a woodcut of a gear-driven machine by Albrecht Dürer, utopian machine drawings by Leonardo da Vinci, Italian and French machine-themed paintings from the seventeenth and eighteenth centuries, and more. In total, two hundred and twenty works by over fifty artists were displayed. As with *Art in Motion*, many of the pieces were interactive in nature. According to Pontus Hultén's philosophy, the audience was invited to participate in creating the art — to be artists themselves, like with Tinguely's painting machine "Méta Matic No. 8" and a machine sculpture, "Rotozaza," which, according to the press release, "mocks the practical side of production machines and echoes the notion of overproduction by eating its own production — balls — when the visitor throws them back into the machine." The latter became one of the most publicized, discussed and ridiculed works of the exhibition.

A difference from *Art in Motion* was a greater element of real machines, presented as art in the spirit of Duchamp. Hultén had identified two specific devices which he considered to be works of art by virtue of their technical precision and special significance for humanity and art — the car and the camera. In the press release, and in his catalog text, Hultén justifies this choice: "The car and the camera are machines that people feel strong emotional connections to, as intimate extensions of their bodies. The car not only serves a practical function but has become a symbol, an object of our fantasies, hopes and fears. The camera, along with some photographs and films, has been chosen because it is an image-making, mechanochemical device that has provided a basis for much of our seeing and is therefore particularly relevant in an art exhibition."

The camera, the image and photographic technology were represented by the Lumière brothers' cinematograph from 1895, in which some of the brothers' earliest motion pictures were screened, enlarged stills from Chaplin's *Modern Times*, and films by Léger and Moholy-Nagy, while four cars adorned the exhibition, all utterly utopian in character. The oldest was a 1931 Bugatti Royale, designed by the former artist, as the catalog points out, Ettore Bugatti, and an "anachronism" even at its launch — useless, superfluous machines were a particular passion of Hultén, Tinguely and other like-minded friends — seven meters long, absurdly heavy and grotesquely expensive on the brink of the Depression, manufactured in only seven copies between 1927 and 1932. Ultra-radically presented vertically mounted on a gallery wall, Swedish driver Joakim Bonnier's McLaren race car from the 1968 Formula 1 season must have taken the visitors' breath away. Who else before or since has come up with the idea of presenting a racing car as a painting, I wonder?

An even more spectacular example of the car as an art object was designed by the American architect/engineer/inventor/artist Buckminster Fuller, another hero of Pontus Hultén's, which he showed here for the first time and would later return to. Fuller's three-wheeled vehicle "Dymaxion Car No. 2" from 1933 was part of the inventor's plan to improve the standard of living of the world's population by extracting maximum performance per unit weight of material resources consumed (the kinship with Tatlin is recognizable — in ideas relevant to our own time). The car prototype, or rather minibus, was designed in collaboration with a naval architect, streamlined according to aircraft aerodynamic principles in lightweight materials such as aluminum sheet, front-wheel driven and steered like a boat with the only rear wheel as a rudder, capable of rotating on its own axis and of reaching speeds with a V8 engine that would have required many times the power in a conventional car of the same dimensions, but difficult to steer at higher speeds (up to two hundred kilometers per hour) and sensitive to wind. The first prototype crashed, resulting in a lawsuit. Fuller produced two more. All three prototypes had been presumed lost but the second, featured in *The Machine*, had been discovered just a year earlier in Tempe, Arizona. A student at the University of Arizona had read an article about Buckminster Fuller's creation, which he linked to a vintage car he had seen in a storage shed in his local area.

Still, the prize was taken by the fourth vehicle, car builder Ray Fahrner's "Boot Hill Express," an outrageous rebuild of a more than hundred-year-old horse-drawn hearse, equipped with a 500-horsepower Chrysler engine, parts from many other cars, a steering wheel from a T-Ford, headlights in the shape of Indian kerosene lamps, and chrome-plated machine parts. The antique wooden chassis was gilded with thirty layers of gold paint. Only Pontus Hultén could have dreamed of placing such a contraption, a hillbilly homebuild, among

Andy Warhol with unknown woman, gala opening of *The Machine*, MoMA, New York, November 1968.

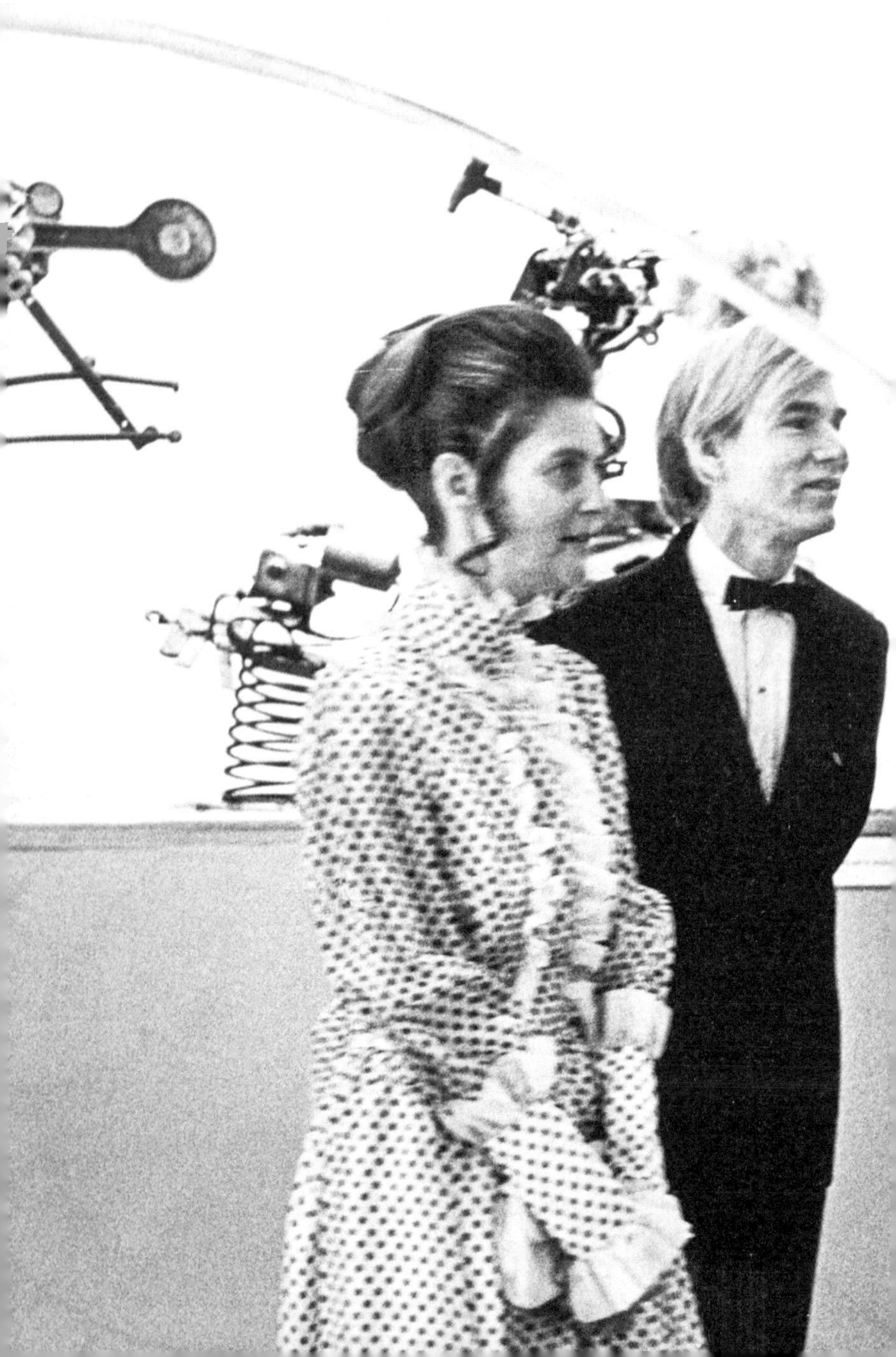

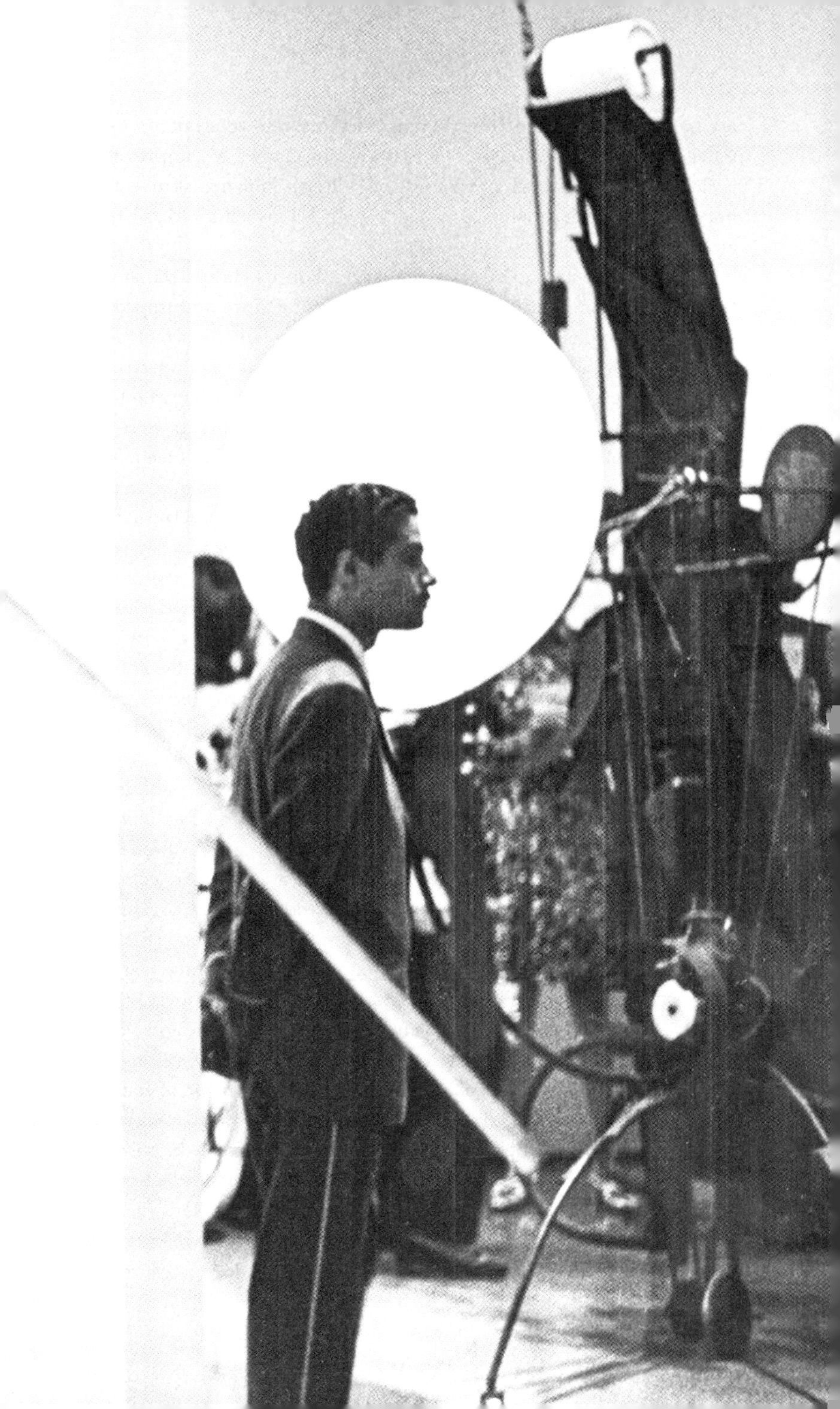

art by artists spanning from Renaissance masters to students — a move that naturally aroused the irritation of many.[16] My impression is clear of the boyishness of this side of Hultén's showmanship — the nerve to play with cars in art museums, which I myself loved as a boy at Moderna Museet.

Although the arena was so much larger, Pontus Hultén remained true to his habit of using his favorite tools of chance and improvisation. He supplemented his selection of artists with a set of new contemporary names, more or less randomly selected, as I understand it. One of these was Thomas Shannon, then still a teenager, who told me that Hultén had come to visit his art school in Chicago. Here he had seen a robot sculpture that Shannon, at the age of nineteen, had entered in a competition at the Art Institute Chicago, displayed in the school's corridor. "Pontus liked the sculpture and immediately decided to include it in the exhibition," says Tom Shannon. "It was surrreal, my first experience of a major museum. It was typical of Pontus to dare to mix the greatest artists with completely unestablished ones."[17]

The Machine was a full-scale effort by MoMA, the major wide-ranging survey show of the year. The exhibition was accompanied by a rich program of film screenings, including computer-animated films, lectures using innovative technology, electronic music concerts, special screenings for children, and more. In addition, it featured an exhibition called *Some More Beginnings* at the Brooklyn Museum, with entries for a Kinetic Art competition for young artists and engineers, organized by Experiments in Art and Technology (E.A.T.), the association founded the previous year by Billy Klüver, Robert Rauschenberg, Robert Whitman and Klüver's engineering colleague Fred Waldhauer, with the utopian vision of uniting art and technology for the advancement of society and humanity. Three winners were selected, their entries presented in the main exhibition at MoMA. A total of nine works from the E.A.T. competition were displayed in *The Machine*, including a computer graphics sculpture, a mechanical fountain, and a red dust installation activated by visitors' heartbeats.

Pontus Hultén says in the interviews with Stephan Andreae that the E.A.T. Foundation was established in connection with the work on *The Machine*. A press release sent out in January 1967 is usually regarded as the starting point of the foundation. Other sources claim that the foundation was already formed in connection with the legendary event *9 Evenings: Theatre and Engineering* at the 69th Regiment Armory in Manhattan in October 1966, where Pontus Hultén was involved in the creative process together with Billy Klüver and Robert Rauschenberg, among others.

The catalog for *The Machine — as Seen at the End of the Mechanical Age* was something far beyond the ordinary, now a coveted collector's item and art historical reference work. Despite strong opposition, Hultén managed to push his idea through with a cover by Anders Österlin printed on beer can tin at PLM's factory in Malmö. The catalog itself too was printed in Malmö. Convincing MoMA's management that the catalog should be printed in an unknown location in Sweden, designed by Gösta Svensson, John Melin and Hultén himself, was an achievement. However, Hultén failed to realize his vision of selling the catalog for one dollar, a price similar to that charged for the Warhol catalog in Stockholm, in order to make it available to a wider audience. The basic principles of American capitalism were untouchable even for Hultén's machinations. The price was set at seven dollars. The catalog thus became another luxury product reserved for the museum's core audience in upper Manhattan.

The encyclopedic catalog opens with what I consider a masterful preface signed K.G.P.H., also presented on a wall panel in the entrance to the exhibition, with one of his strange, poetic prophesies, echoing Marshall McLuhan, the great media philosopher of the time. Consider that these lines were written as early as 1968: "We are surrounded by obvious manifestations of the culmination of the mechanical age. Yet, at the same time, the mechanical machine — which can be defined most simply as an imitation of our muscles — is losing its dominant importance to humanity; while electronic and chemical mechanisms — which imitate the brain and nervous system — are becoming increasingly important."[18]

In the press release, Hultén offers another grandiose sample of his utopian vision of the future, in the spirit of Tatlin and Buckminster Fuller, on the vocation of art in the emergence of the ideal society: "By the year 2000, technology will undoubtedly have advanced to such an extent that our world will be as different from today's as our present is from ancient Egypt. What role will art play in this change? (...) Clearly, if we believe in either life or art, we must achieve total domination over machines, submitting them to our will and directing them to serve life in the most efficient way possible, with the totality of human life on the planet as our criterion. In planning, and in helping to bring it about, artists are more important than politicians, and even than technicians."[19]

In the 2020s, Hultén's vision, which he shared with his mentor Willem Sandberg and many other like-minded predecessors and contemporaries, is both wistful, forward-looking and hopelessly outdated: the dream of the importance of art in the construction of society. This utopia seems distant nowadays when the art world, albeit much larger and above all more money-saturated than then, has been deprived of political and revolutionary potential, influence and importance, returned to its decorative, entertaining, at best poetic and contemplative but primarily social and economic functions, with the most expensive art serving as the ultimate of luxury and status symbols. Who knows what our world would have looked like if development had been led by artists instead of capitalists and technicians — certainly an intriguing, if naive, thought in the light of history. From Hultén's catalog text, and from some of his comments on the exhibition, I get the impression that by the time *The Machine* was launched, he himself had begun to realize that time was running out for these dreams — that he was not entirely comfortable presenting this, after all, modified repetition of *Art in Motion* from seven years earlier. This was a long period in his own development as an artistic storyteller, where he had long since moved on. For the paradoxically conservative and conventional New York art establishment, on the contrary, *The Machine* was something new, radical and controversial, almost revolutionary, far behind Europe in their tastes and views as New Yorkers on the Upper East Side were.

The Machine opened on November 27, 1968, at the height of the New York art scene's peak season. In the days preceding, a press preview and VIP opening was hosted for no less than three thousand two hundred invited guests, including all the museum's trustees and all manner of celebrities in tuxedos and evening gowns, followed by a gala dinner in the museum's penthouse for three hundred guests. Among the many famous artists in attendance were several of the biggest names from the older generation of Abstract Expressionists who had placed American modern art on the world map, as the tired old cliché goes. In this generation of artists, and even among the younger Minimalists, there was a hostility to the Neo-Dadaist art presented in *The Machine*. Mark Rothko and Donald Judd were among those said to have condescended to the exhibition. Even Andy Warhol, still recovering from the near-fatal shooting less than six months earlier, attended the gala dinner.

Pontus Hultén himself described *The Machine* as a success.[20] As such, and as a milestone, the exhibition is considered in a historical perspective.[21] The box office numbers were impressive, if not sensational. The exhibition was especially loved by younger audiences. In New York, *The Machine* was something new also in its completely open and, as it would be called in our time, "inclusive" presentation, with Hultén's usual minimum of barriers to the audience and between the different sections of the exhibition and the various artists.

Within the conservative, snobbish, and more than a little bigoted New York art establishment, much of the criticism of *Art in Motion* in Stockholm was repeated in New York seven years later, perhaps about as far behind as the New York art audience of the time lingered behind its European counterpart. It was the whole song and dance about art as a circus performance, adolescent antics, etcetera, which the influential judge of taste Hilton Kramer in The New York Times, among others, denounced.

A cultural dilemma was the fact that the exhibition's socially critical, subtly ironic, complex political message was largely lost on the American audience. At best, the potentates understood that it seemed to be some damn European communist propaganda. It's said that their elegant Upper East Side wives found Tinguely's pointless ball-spitting machine and other plebeian amusement park devices repugnant to the fine "European" cultural status they had so painstakingly achieved, and for which their interest in art was the ultimate expression. For most of these wealthy museum patrons and donors, an art audience of a kind that was and still is lacking in Sweden and Europe, Cézanne, Matisse, and Picasso were still considered daring taste and domestic American Abstract Expressionism the height of radicalism.[22] Pontus Hultén, however global he became, was profoundly European in his view of art, life, society, and politics. In the United States, this perspective on art and his way of communicating his vision would never be understood or appreciated in the same way as in Europe. Here the rules were simpler, more brutal and so much more conservative and commercial.

I consider the person who has most wisely analyzed Pontus Hultén's difficulties in comprehending and making himself understood in the United States to be his arguably most important collaborator of all time in his career, including in the work on the exhibition *The Machine*: Billy Klüver, of course, the incomparable electrical engineer and cult figure on the international art scene. Klüver disliked the subtitle of the exhibition *American Pop Art* ... at Moderna Museet in 1964 — *106 Forms of Love and Despair*. He believed that this view of Pop Art was attributing messages to the art that were not there. Klüver argued the simple truth that Pop artists, like their friends among performance artists of the Lower East Side, Allan Kaprow, John Cage and others, did not hide any deeper, more intellectual philosophies but simply produced and performed their artistic acts for the sake of these expressions — an insight that Hultén soon "absorbed." In *The History Book*, Moderna Museet's fiftieth anniversary book from 2008, Klüver comments on these cultural differences: "At the time, it always manifested itself in how materialistic America was, with cars and televisions. Physiologically, that attitude was obviously related to the fact that Europeans themselves were only interested in cars and televisions, whereas people here had kind of outgrown that. The cars were commodities and the TV was an everyday thing, so nobody saw cars and TVs as status symbols worth talking about at the lunch table, as they did in Paris when I worked there for a year."[23]

Richard Armstrong, director of the Solomon R. Guggenheim Museum in New York since 2008, is more bluntly American in his assessment. Armstrong, who became somewhat acquainted with Pontus Hultén as a young art historian and curator in Paris and New York in the seventies and eighties, was, I think, speaking of a general attitude in the American art establishment of the time when he talked about the exhibition which he visited at MoMA as a nineteen-year-old: "I didn't understand it. People here hadn't even had time to digest Pop Art properly. It was too complicated. An artist like Tinguely never really worked in America. There was a lot of prejudice against him. Even Calder was mostly seen as a clown, funny but not to be taken seriously. These kinds of shows were not done here. This criticism of industrialism — it's not popular in America. People with intellect are not interested in machines. They just found it unattractive."[24]

From MoMA, the exhibition traveled to Houston and the San Francisco Museum of Modern Art (SFMoMA) in the spring and summer of 1969. About Houston, Pontus Hultén told Stephan Andreae thirty years later that it was Dominique de Menil, the oil heiress and the great French-American patron who a few years later would become Hultén's benefactor and ally in Paris, who had been so enthusiastic about the exhibition that she had decided to show it in the oil metropolis of Texas, the hometown of the de Menil oil gear company, even though there was no museum there yet.[25] At the time, patrons Dominique and John de Menil, with Dominique as curator, were staging exhibitions at the University of St. Thomas. Solely for the purpose of showing *The Machine*, the couple commissioned the construction of a simple "art barn" on campus, appropriately called "The Art Barn" for short, in a radical design by architect Eugene Aubry, where many other exhibitions were presented in the following years. In Houston, *The Machine* caused a sensation and became a great public success.[26] According to Pontus Hultén, it was de Menil's exhibition of *The Machine* that sparked Dominique de Menil's much later realized idea of opening her own exquisite museum The Menil Collection in Houston, built with Renzo Piano as architect (see Chapter 28).

The Machine was an exhibition that markedly divided the New York art world into two camps. With the perspective of time, it has been elevated to the ranks of MoMA's classics, listed by ArtNews magazine as one of the museum's nine most "iconic" 1960s exhibitions.[27]

I'll leave the summary to Calvin Tomkins, who is qualified to judge the exhibition's importance in art history and in New York after writing about art and the art world for The New Yorker for more than six decades: "*The Machine* was a bombshell," says Tomkins, "a real eye-opener, hugely influential, very popular and well attended. I think it was seen by many artists who were inspired by it. Unfortunately, the message of the exhibition was lost on the audience. People here had learned what they knew about modern art from MoMA and Alfred Barr's recognition of Cubism and Abstract Expressionism. They couldn't absorb this kind of complex philosophical message and total openness in the same way as in Europe. It wasn't possible."[28]

An inevitable question is whether *The Machine* was to be regarded as an advanced exam that Pontus Hultén was subjected to in order to investigate whether he could be a possible new director of the Museum of Modern Art?

There is no doubt that Hultén was a strong candidate to this the most prestigious post in the art world. Calvin Tomkins writes in his portrait of Pontus Hultén in The New Yorker in 1978, after the opening of the Centre Pompidou, that "it is no secret that Hultén was considered for the job" after René d'Hanoncourt's death in a car accident shortly after *The Machine*. Tomkins adds that the "job offer" never reached the stage of formal negotiations as "Hultén made it clear that he would take the job only on the condition that ownership of the museum be transferred from the board of trustees to the City of New York." "I'm totally against private museums. Art belongs to everyone and that's the way it should be," Tomkins writes that Hultén is said to have explained, whereupon the board of trustees, understandably, seems to have lost interest. Further on in the same text, Calvin

Tomkins refers to Hultén's late assistant at MoMA, Jennifer Licht, who says she believes that Pontus Hultén was "very disappointed" by the exhibition's reception as "just another MoMA spectacle, with an emphasis on the aesthetic qualities of the exhibited objects."[29] In the article, Hultén himself denies that he was disappointed. He says that the collaboration with MoMA was "everything he could have asked for," but still offers modest criticism: "I like MoMA a lot. But I still thought, to myself, that it is absolutely devastating to continue in that direction, to sanitize art, to create a place where it can be explained and controlled."[30]

Billy Klüver recounted that New York Governor Nelson Rockefeller wanted Hultén to become director of MoMA, where his family had great influence.[31] A few years later, when he was recruited to MNAM in Paris, Hultén himself responded to questions in the Swedish press that it was true that he had been offered the position of director of MoMA but that had turned it down, as Anna-Lena Wibom also claimed in our conversation.[32] None of the others I have spoken to recognize this story and all doubt its veracity. "He would never have said no to MoMA," as Billy Klüver's wife and partner Julie Martin says.[33] The actual course of events will never be clarified. As Daniel Birnbaum, Moderna Museet's former director, says: "Such things are always difficult to know. It rarely works out in the way that you get a direct request; it's usually more ambiguous."[34]

A factor that may have influenced the outcome is that it appears that the one person who most forcefully advocated for Pontus Hultén was René d'Harnoncourt himself, a sophisticated director who was more "European" in orientation, born in Austria, by whom Hultén had first been approached about *The Machine*. With his short-lived successor Bates Lowry, who according to testimony was more traditionally American, and with the rest of the MoMA management, Hultén reportedly found it difficult to communicate.

According to Björn Springfeldt, however, the matter is clear: "If *The Machine* had been a success, Pontus would have become the director of MoMA."[35]

Whatever the nature of any "offer," there is a consensus among those I have discussed the topic with that Pontus Hultén would not have been suitable as director of MoMA — and also that the museum management can hardly have been fully serious about recruiting him. Eli Broad, the business tycoon and multi-billionaire, often referred to as the world's greatest art collector and the leading patron and duke of the Los Angeles art world, had long been on the board of MoMA when we met in Los Angeles in the fall of 2014. I raised the question of whether Hultén could have been seriously considered as MoMA director. Broad replied: "I can't imagine that. In any case, I can say that it would never have worked. In that position he would have had to deal with people like David Rockefeller and that would have been impossible."[36]

Again, I'll leave the last word to Calvin Tomkins, who, in our conversation in New York, gave the shortest, simplest and, I think, truest answer to my question about whether Pontus Hultén could really have become the director of MoMA when he shook his head and said, "No no. Too much of a lefty."[37]

16

The father rebellion in the magma chamber: Pontus, Moderna, Stockholm, House of Culture and the "68 revolution"

Much can be said about Pontus Hultén's political beliefs, and quite some I've already written. Like most matters concerning this man, it's complicated and often contradictory. Hultén loved to call himself an anarchist, to almost parade and of course to provoke with this extreme political philosophy, already marginalized in Hultén's time. Hultén's anarchist conviction stemmed from Kropotkin's school, in simple terms a more peaceful, idealistic, humanistic and of course utopian branch of Russian anarchism, in contrast to Bakunin's militant, agitational camp, in which violence was justified. On the merits of Kropotkin versus Bakunin, he would engage in nightlong, boozy discussions with Tinguely and other friends.[1] The German post-Hegelian philosopher Max Stirner, considered a precursor of nihilism and individualist anarchism, was another of his ideological mentors.[2]

Some have doubted the sincerity of Pontus Hultén's anarchist beliefs. I've heard the term "salon anarchist" used by several spokespersons. I prefer Olle Granath's more appreciative "constitutional anarchist."[3] Hultén stayed within the constitutional boundaries — although he never hesitated to exceed these borders, often with substantial, more or less well-calculated measures of risk, if it served his purposes and he could get away with it. Within this framework, he operated in a highly anarchistic or, even more so, Dadaist manner. Few have been able to play so virtuously with the state apparatus as an instrument for such provocative, not rarely downright subversive purposes. I myself do not doubt the authenticity of Hultén's anarchist philosophy. A contempt and disgust for any form of bureaucracy and hierarchy was fundamental to his personality — although he never hesitated to act authoritatively, if necessary autocratically, from his position of power at the top of these hierarchies. "Freedom was fundamental to him," as Olle Granath says. "He was the kind of person who could be infuriated by waiting at a red light at a crosswalk."[4]

Yet, Hultén was no more consistent in his ideology than that, when he really wanted to provoke, he could also call himself a Stalinist, a political stance that, while not as impossible in the sixties as it is today, was more than enough to achieve its purpose of stirring up emotions. He undoubtedly had a penchant not only for the Russian but also for the Soviet.

He was indeed a "lefty," Pontus Hultén, and well out to the left at that. As he himself conceded: "They accused us of being extreme to the left and in a way they were right. We took a position on the left, that we did, and we were a bit extreme."[5]

I've been fascinated by how Hultén was able to combine this at least slightly extreme left-wing political conviction with his prolific ability to socialize and do business with, or obtain money from, some of Sweden's and later in his career some of the world's most wealthy and famous magnates and patrons.

In the winter of 2014, I met Maja Oeri, heiress to Hoffmann-La Roche, the world's largest pharmaceutical company and one of the world's most important art patrons, who worked with Pontus Hultén at the Centre Pompidou. I took the opportunity to ask about this — how the radical Pontus had been able to socialize so comfortably with her relatives and so many other moguls around Europe. I think Maja Oeri spoke the truth when she broke into a smile and replied: "But you know, Pontus was a communist in the *Italian* way!"[6].

I would argue that the politicization of the museum was one of the most sensational, innovative and of course burningly controversial aspects of Pontus Hultén's entire career at Moderna Museet. Certainly, there was a legacy from his mentor Willem Sandberg and other radical museum managers of an older generation, and of course it was something that was in vogue in the sixties. Almost all of Hultén's contemporaries among curators and museum officials stood, like the artists, more or less far to the left. Still no one, before or since, with a state institution as a powerful instrument, had pushed such a radical, sometimes borderline revolutionary political agenda nearly as far as Pontus Hultén during his fifteen years at Moderna Museet.

The provocative political note was struck already with the drastic, fateful presentation of *Guernica* in 1956, to be launched on a full scale with *Art in Motion* and intensified with the American exhibitions and related events, as well as *she — a cathedral*. From the early sixties, Moderna Museet became center stage for the predominantly bourgeois intellectual left in Stockholm and throughout Sweden — the movement whose growth increased in volume and intensity with the expansion and beastly brutality of the Vietnam War from the mid-sixties.

It is nonetheless of the utmost importance in understanding Pontus Hultén, his work and his time to emphasize that the political radicalism of this still relatively innocent primetime lay exclusively in the art itself, in its politically and otherwise radical and provocative content, and in how innovatively this was presented to the audience.

Pontus Hultén was the first to encourage and spur on the rising extremism of the left. From 1966 onwards, one can see how the museum was gradually radicalized in line with the left-wing movement, to the point where one wonders what was the chicken and what was the egg. All of the museum's events, happenings and performances grew increasingly wild and unruly. Pontus Hultén's Dadaist-inspired ideal that it was the audience who, by seeing and acting, completed the artists' works was taken to ever more extreme forms by the audience and the artists themselves. A new explosive dynamic had been generated. All the boundaries and barriers that Hultén had sought to remove were now being spontaneously transgressed from all sides. I myself remember from my childhood the thrilling notion that anything, at any time, could happen at the museum. Already in 1964, the experimental pianist and composer Karl-Erik Welin wrote himself into the legend when he sawed up his grand piano with a chainsaw, seriously injured his leg and finished the concert bleeding profusely. The audience, used to rough goings even then, laughed, convinced that the blood flow was part of the art.

Towards the end of the 1960s, all these actions and happenings, often more or less spontaneous, became increasingly difficult for the museum to control. Among the most extreme was the incomparable Norwegian artist Kjartan Slettemark who, when threatened with eviction from his studio in Stockholm in 1970, simply had his belongings transported up to the museum. Slettemark said that when he arrived with his truck, Pontus Hultén gave him permission to store his belongings in the museum's basement. "But I wanted to exhibit my art. By the time we finished arguing, the movers had already unloaded all the stuff and placed it in front of the big Matisse painting. My fridge and everything."[7] According to Slettemark himself, he took a room at the Grand Hôtel. He claimed to be an Icelandic artist exhibiting at

Moderna Museet. The bill was sent to the museum, which also paid. "They knew how difficult it was for us artists. They were themselves involved in the debate and probably saw my occupation as a happening," said Slettemark. His "occupation" lasted two weeks. When the wild Norwegian finally had to be evicted by the police, Pontus Hultén found himself in a dilemma typical of the time. He was mocked by the most radical factions of his audience, including my father and aunt, for representing the state and capital when it came down to it, while Kjartan Slettemark was the true anarchist and revolutionary.

1968 was the year in which Pontus Hultén and the museum transcended its own boundaries and began to stage exhibitions and organize events that were pure agitational political statements, in which art was no longer always the chief priority.

Andy Warhol was followed by *The Language of Revolution*,[8] with communist, socialist and anarchist propaganda posters from around the world plastered on the museum walls, a selection from a larger exhibition in Warsaw the previous year. Coincidentally, the exhibition was shown in Stockholm during the May Revolution in Paris, when the barricades were burning and the possibility of a real revolution spreading across Europe and the world seemed plausible. We can see how far the rebellion against the museum had already advanced from the incident that this exhibition was not praised but criticized by the extreme left. Pontus Hultén wrote fifteen years later in his sardonic style about these reactions: "[The exhibition] showed a plethora of unknown material, also from countries such as China (the Japanese invasion in the 1930s), Hungary, Italy, South America. The museum faced a lot of criticism from political radicals. It was argued that such material should not be institutionalized as it would lose its saltiness and impact. It was historicized. Little thought was given to the reality that without the museum's intervention these images would almost certainly have remained unknown. One must admit that in the wake of goodwill at this time there was a good deal of messiness of thought."[9]

The Model, opened on September 30, 1968,[10] kicked off a series in which activists were invited to stage exhibitions and events at the museum. Led by Danish artist, activist and, unsurprisingly, anarchist Palle Nielsen, a group of artists, pedagogs, psychologists and other specialists were assembled to conduct a "full-scale experiment." *The Model. A Model For a Qualitative Society*, commonly referred to as

The Model, was aimed "primarily" at children. This is how Pontus Hultén himself depicts the exhibition: "A large frame construction and lots of materials were made available. There were boards, paper, paint, fabric, nails, etc. in large quantities. There were also hundreds of discarded opera costumes, make-up, wigs and other theatrical paraphernalia, cameras and recording equipment. In the center of the gallery, a large foam rubber pool was built into which one could jump off a bridge."[11]

The purpose of the exhibition was to study how the children behaved in the face of the unlimited availability of materials and almost total freedom to act. "The experiences were almost exclusively positive," writes Hultén. "Many interesting observations could be made, for example about how a 'fashion' arises, develops and passes away. It also became apparent how extraordinarily labor-intensive such a project is for those in charge of it. The children's activity was thoroughly studied by a group of psychologists and the exhibition was filmed."[12]

One feature of the exhibition, or "experiment," that may seem slightly uncomfortable in retrospect, was that the parents, many of whom were sitting in the restaurant drinking wine while the children played, could follow the activities of their offspring on television monitors.

Yet it's the exhibition itself that made art history and claimed its place of honor among my own fondest childhood memories. I vividly remember all the details that Hultén mentions in his text and the intoxicating, unreal feeling of freedom and creative euphoria of being able to rummage around in all this without any prohibitions, rules or restrictions — scribbling with finger paint, drawing and painting, dressing up as pirates, eighteenth-century noblemen, Charlie Chaplin or whatever, breaking down electric appliances to construct little machine sculptures and, above all, throwing ourselves off the bridge into the sea of foam rubber, again and again, with that thrilling, forbidden, slightly dangerous feeling in the pit of our stomachs. From *The Model* there are famous pictures of Olof Palme, the museum's patron and supporter, then still Minister of Ecclesiastical Affairs, soon to become Prime Minister, who in shirt sleeves and tie dives from the pier into the foam rubber wave and comes up smiling like a happy schoolboy. For me, these images represent Sweden's model society at its peak, this experimental social construction, so admired worldwide — and feared and loathed by the global right.

In their catalog texts, Pontus Hultén and Palle Nielsen write polem-

The Model, Moderna Museet, Stockholm, 1968.

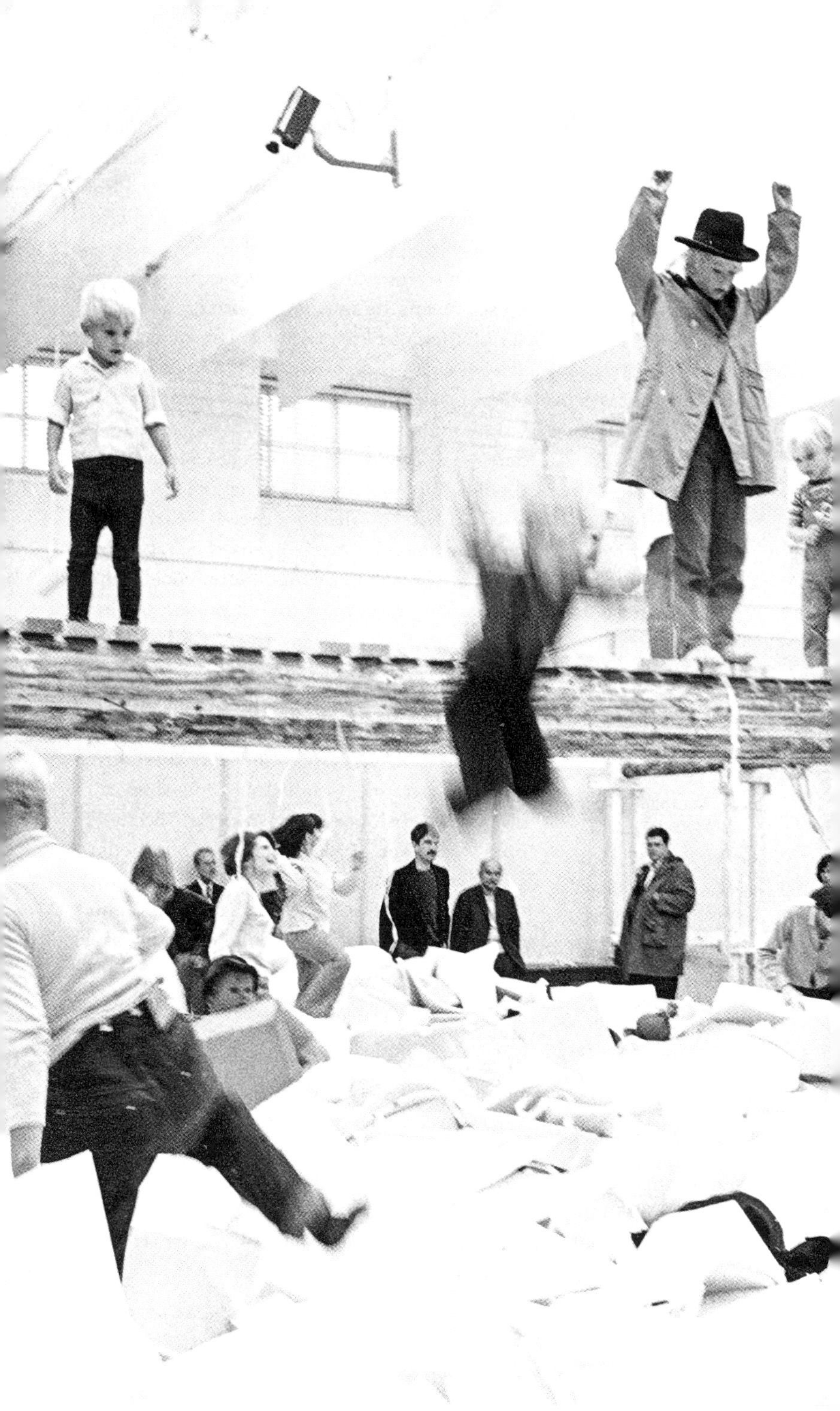

ically about *The Model* as an educational alternative to school. Hultén proclaims that school is dedicated to "gathering knowledge, encouraging uniformity, grading success based on adaptability." He accuses the current education system of being a "reactionary element" that ignores the creative and artistic aspects of human beings. Hultén concludes with a paragraph in which he offers a programmatic explanation of his view of the "new museum" and its mission in society: "We have seen very few models for a different type of school. This model is of course secondarily a model of a new form of society. It must be one of the urgent tasks of the new museums to offer a place for this kind of experimental model."[13]

With *The Model*, there was no doubt that Moderna Museet was taking a direct, radical political position in the social debate. It was a long road that the museum had traveled in a decade — from the antiquated halls of the National Museum to the arena of agitation for the radical left, to a degree where the museum director could claim that it "must" be the task of the "new museums" to present models for an alternative society.

The Model had an impact that can only be described as enormous, in terms of attendance and attention in the Swedish and international press. The exhibition indeed did serve as a model for alternative learning, carefully studied by educators far beyond Swedish borders. As Anette Göthlund, professor at Konstfack art college in Stockholm, writes in the museum's fiftieth anniversary *History Book*: "*The Model* was echoed not only in the press, but also in public discourse as a whole. In particular, it gave rise to a discussion about children's play environments. Seminars and debates were organized, not only by the museum. Dagens Nyheter, for example, organized a 'cross-debate' between various professional groups with the aim of generating 'new thinking about how kindergartens, playgrounds and other children's environments should be planned.' Anyone who attended kindergarten in the early 1970s will remember how playrooms and workshops were installed, and outdoor play areas were created. These are tangible 'remnants' of *The Model*."[14]

In 2023–2024, the MUDAM Luxembourg contemporary art museum staged a trilogy of exhibitions titled *A Model*, curated by its director Bettina Steinbrügge. The exhibitions, showcasing the work of a large number artists and other creatives from the globe, reflected of the role of the museum in the early twenty-first century, "inspired in part" by *The Model* in Moderna Museet in Stockholm in 1968.

Olof Palme, then minster of education and culture, at *The Model*, Moderna Museet, Stockholm, 1968.

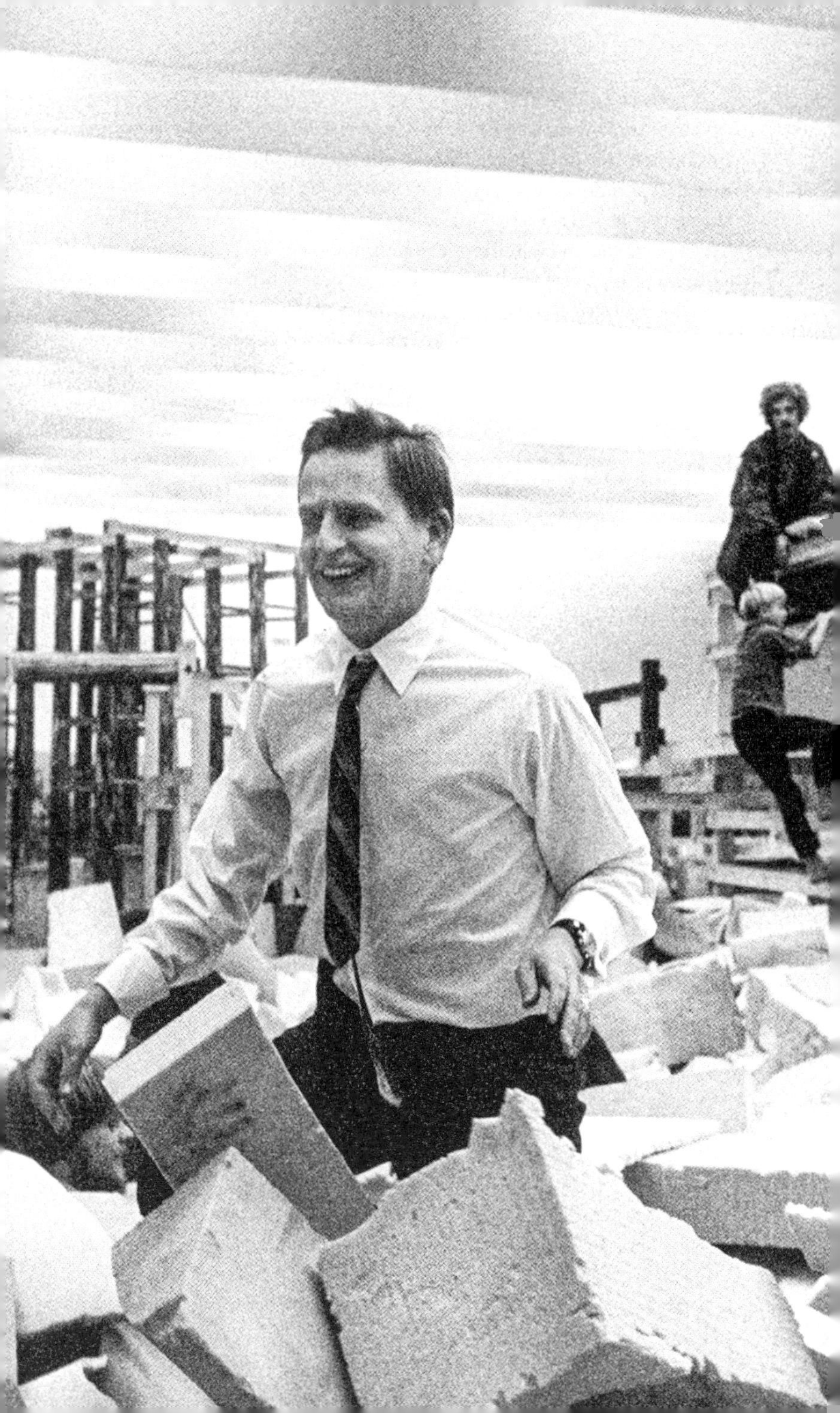

That's no mean feat for a museum exhibition to make such an impression not only in art history but also in educational development, especially considering that Sweden in turn became a model that inspired and served as an example for the rest of the world. With *The Model*, Pontus Hultén and the museum truly did achieve concrete positive results with their vision of art, or in this case the art museum, as a constructive creative force in social engineering of society.

In the wake of the exhibition, an expanded children's workshop was made permanent. With *The Model*, Moderna Museet consolidated its position within the international avant-garde of creative children's education, with inspiration, ideas and methods drawn from the art historian Herbert Read, Reggio Emilia, Montessori and the Egyptian architect and teacher Ramses Wissa Wassef. The latter was a pioneer in his belief in the innate artistic and creative ability of every child — an inspiration for the museum's own pedagogic guru Carlo Derkert. Works from his Ramses Wissa Wassef Art Center in Harrania, south of Giza, where young villagers were taught to create arts and crafts, were displayed in three exhibitions at Moderna Museet, two of these during Pontus Hultén's tenure.[15] Again, it must be noted that hardly any other art museum has gone so far in involving children in its activities or in using the museum for children's artistic and creative education — a proud tradition for which the museum has received international recognition and a legacy that it is honoring in our own time.

Sir Herbert Read was a British art historian, poet, philosopher and literary critic, known for his work on the role of art in education and human development. Herbert Read's ideas had a major influence on the post-war modern art world. He also co-founded the Institute of Contemporary Art in London, opened in 1946, an important precursor to cultural centers such as Kulturhuset (House of Culture) in Stockholm and the Centre Pompidou in Paris.

In 1969, Pontus Hultén's era at Moderna Museet reached its peripeteia, that fatal turning point in the Greek tragedy from which the hubris of success carries the hero downhill. In the museum's unofficial history, this point of no return is usually marked by Hultén's encounter with the young radical activist Pär Stolpe.

Pär Stolpe, who grew up in the academic upper middle class in the Stockholm suburb of Bromma, began his career as a poet and artist. In the mid-sixties, in his early twenties, he became increasingly involved in politics as part of an inner core of young left-wing activists in Stockholm. Pär Stolpe told me how he early on abandoned his artistic dream in favor of a radical political commitment to society. His story is representative of the predominantly bourgeois Stockholm sixty-eight movement in which art, culture and politics were inseparable. "I had spent a lot of time in Finland and published books as a poet and writer, but I felt uncomfortable selling myself to publishers like Bonniers and the like,"[16] says Pär Stolpe. "Through relatives I had contact with hunting, fishing and coastal culture. Instead, I became more interested in ethnology and folk culture."[17]

Like his friends and peers, Pär Stolpe was a frequent visitor to Moderna Museet from the start. Here he had been inspired by several of the museum's most unconventional exhibitions, those that went beyond the confines of art. In 1966 he had been deeply impressed by *Hej stad! (Hello City!)*, the inaugural exhibition of the Museum of Architecture, which moved into the museum that year,[18] with projected images of urban environments accompanied by an electronic music soundtrack by composer Ralph Lundsten from forty loudspeakers.[19] "It was like a revelation, a huge kick," says Pär Stolpe. "It was about urban planning. I saw it as a starting point for the modern exhibition — a way of staging and visualizing an idea instead of just showing rich people's ability to acquire expensive objects. It went far beyond anything that had been done in the museum — a liberation from form that showed how you could convey an idea three-dimensionally which really moved people."[20]

Pär Stolpe explains that protest against the Vietnam War was of course important to him and his group, but that their opposition was just as much about disgust with the social democratic hegemony of power as it had manifested itself in the demolition of Stockholm's city core and virtually all of our Swedish small town centers — a mass destruction brutally illustrated by the "Riksgropen" ("The National Pot Hole") that the area around Sergels torg square, Hamngatan avenue and the Klara neighborhood in downtown Stockholm formed at the time. The devastated site, reminiscent of the bombed-out European cities during the war, was a consequence of the infamous Cityregleringen (The City Regulation) urban development scheme, when seven hundred older buildings were demolished to make way for the modern metropolis that was intended to be the crown and hub of the new ideal society.

"It was obvious that something was devilishly wrong with the development of the Social Dems, and it was manifested by 'The National Pot Hole,'" says Pär Stolpe. "All traces of the past had to be wiped out. It was called sanitizing. I remember a debate at the City Museum where

Hjalmar Mehr (1910–1979) was for decades a leading Social Democratic politician in the City of Stockholm, the equivalent of a mayor in the 1960s. Mehr is usually portrayed as the villain chiefly responsible for the demolition of Stockholm's old city core, regarded as an historic disaster.

Hjalmar Mehr was red in the face, shouting: 'You young people don't understand what the people of Stockholm have endured!' One or more universities should really research this. It hasn't been sufficiently investigated. It was a transformation that changed conditions for people in the countryside even more than for us in Stockholm. The resistance to this whole development was an important denominator. In line with this, I found artistically active people and others — artists, writers, architects, physicians, educators. Together we created a center of rebellion."[21]

Pär Stolpe confides that the *Hello City!* exhibition enhanced his and his group's interest in urban transformation. In the same year, Stolpe and his friends discovered that a late nineteenth-century brick gas mill, called a "gas bell," by famed architect Ferdinand Boberg in western downtown Stockholm, was marked for demolition. The idea was soon developed to create what came to be called an "all-activity house" for various creative expressions, with music at the center — but also for the political activism of the youth movement. A plan was designed to accommodate five thousand visitors simultaneously. The main idea was to make culture, political debate and activism accessible to a maximum number of people, not primarily to the bourgeois clientele that usually consumed culture, but to all social classes. "There was an underground movement of music and culture that had nowhere to go," says Stolpe. "Moderna Museet was the only venue that was somewhat open. For us, the political aspect was crucial. Politics and culture were the same thing for us. We also wanted the community center to be for the old folks on the streets, the poor who were actually visible everywhere in the city at the time. Everyone would be welcome. In City Hall and in the press, it was said that it would be impossible to gather five thousand people like this — that there was a danger of a riot, but that was exactly what we wanted."[22]

Stolpe and his friends outlined a program for the all-activity house, known simply as Gasklockan (The Gas Bell), and managed to engage an ambassador for this venture in Bo "Bobo" Lagercrantz, city archivist and director of the Stockholm City Museum. Even Olof Palme was enthusiastic about the project. Lagercrantz, Palme and other culture political leaders of the time were concerned about culture being predominantly reserved for the upper class. According to Pär Stolpe,

Palme led the "struggle" against Stockholm City Hall, which was dominated by the chief executor of the demolition frenzy, Hjalmar Mehr, the de facto mayor. Patroned by Bo Lagercrantz, the group presented a proposal, complete with architectural plans, to the city council, which initiated an inquiry into the matter. In the end, nothing came of it. "The investigation came to the conclusion that it would be best to preserve the gas bell, but the decision of the politicians was: tear the crap down," as Pär Stolpe remarks.[23]

In parallel with Gasklockan, official plans were being developed for a venture based on partly the same ideas — what was to become Kulturhuset (The House of Culture) on the new Sergels torg square, then still ground zero in Riksgropen, The National Pot Hole. As Pontus Hultén ironically writes in the jubilee book, the very name Sergels torg can be considered a "peculiar band-aid" since the studio of the eighteenth century sculptor Johan Tobias Sergel, which had been located in the area, had been liquidated in the urban harakiri.[24]

The idea of simply moving Moderna Museet on Skeppsholmen to a new cultural center on the south side of Sergels torg was raised as early as 1963 in an article in Aftonbladet by the cultural writer Kurt Bergengren, a close ally of Pontus Hultén. The debate about the planned cultural center, and Moderna Museet's relocation to this new institution in the absolute logistical and economic center of the modern metropolis and all of Sweden, was subsequently carried on in the media more or less continuously until the turn of the decade 1970, while the vision for the new Moderna Museet at Sergels torg square developed and finally collapsed. Much has been written about how these plans developed. Kurt Bergengren himself described the process in his book *När skönheten kom till City* (*When Beauty Came to City*) from 1976.[25] The process is documented in detail in the German architecture professor Christoph Grafe's frequently cited study "People's Palaces" from 2014.[26] These writings in turn form part of the sources for Kim West's acclaimed dissertation "The Exhibitionary Complex" from 2017,[27] in which the Swedish art historian provides a detailed account of the events surrounding Moderna Museet's planned move to Kulturhuset, as well as the development of ideas in the related plans for the Centre Pompidou in Paris a few years later.

In his study, Kim West concludes that it was manifest that Pontus Hultén was very much behind and supportive of the ideas presented by Kurt Bergengren in his article in early 1963. From this time, if not before, Hultén and his colleagues planned to move the museum to the city core, as the dominant institution in a cultural center with a completely new, expanded function based on interaction between the arts, the artists and the audience. In the ensuing debate through the early and mid-sixties, Moderna Museet's premises on Skeppsholmen were called "temporary." It was common knowledge at the time that the cramped museum needed more space — an issue advocated for by Olof Palme and the political network around the museum.

In early 1965, Hultén himself entered the stage with an article entitled "Moderna museet i centrum" (Moderna Museet in the center") in Dagens Nyheter,[28] signed by K.G. Hultén. Here, he argues that the museum, by virtue of its collection, is superior to all other institutions as an organizer of exhibitions and cultural events. Located in the center of the city, the museum would have the opportunity to reach new, larger target groups beyond the traditional bourgeois cultural audience, Hultén argues, urging that society should "be able to afford" to let the museum lay the foundation of such a new, powerful cultural nucleus. He introduces the concept of "Stockholm's cultural living room," which recurs in several articles. Furthermore, Hultén advocates that all or part of the premises on Skeppsholmen could be retained for storage and production of exhibitions, in order to save precious exhibition space.

A key player who was initially positive about the idea of Moderna Museet's move to Sergels torg was the same Hjalmar Mehr, the powerful municipal head of finance and de facto mayor, who as early as March 14, 1963, enthusiastically supported Kurt Bergengren's ideas in an article in Aftonbladet. As Kim West and others have noted, it's doubtful how genuine this commitment from Mehr and his colleagues in the city administration really was. Mehr and others seem to have found the idea of Kulturhuset and Moderna Museet as a useful instrument to counteract the growing public opinion that criticized those in power for the imbalance in that only bank palaces, department stores and hotels were rising from the ruins of the war-like demolitions. In one of his subsequent articles, Hultén writes beautifully in proudly utopian terms that "One wants to be able to offer spiritual manifestations with the same efficiency that commercial and material life provides."[29]

The vision for the new Kulturhuset at Sergels torg square and the relocation of Moderna Museet developed in the press debate formed the basis for two architectural competitions. The latter was announced in December 1966, also including Riksbanken, Sweden's National Bank, two theaters and a hotel, the result of a complicated game of real estate negotiations between the city and the state. Finally, Peter Celsing was commissioned to design the new building complexes on the southern front of Sergels torg. His idea for Kulturhuset (The House of Culture) was a building vertical to the Sveavägen esplanade, forming a radical backdrop to what would become the new Sergels torg. "Most of Stockholm's important streets run north-south, starting from the Royal Castle," says Peter's son Johan Celsing, also a prominent architect. "Dad's idea was to break this with a building that ran parallel to the Strömmen waterway and instead looked outwards, towards the suburbs. Vällingby was new at that time and Kulturhuset was aimed in that direction."[30]

Peter Celsing's main competitors were the trio of Ralph Erskine, Léonie Giesendorf and Anders Tengbom, whose proposal had many supporters. Erskine had the idea of taking up the old vision from the seventeenth century of a parade route from the Royal Palace to Haga, by letting Sveavägen continue as a "garden boulevard" past Kulturhuset down to Gustav Adolfs torg. Celsing partly incorporated this proposal by adding the portal through Kulturhuset with a passage to Brunkebergs torg square.

In the spring of 1969, Pär Stolpe was one of the organizers of an exhibition produced on behalf of the Swedish Institute on the image of Sweden abroad, which was to be shown at the opening of the Sweden House at Kungsträdgården, designed by Sven Markelius. The exhibition turned out to be far from what its patrons had envisaged. Stolpe and his co-organizers had sent reporters around the world to present a critical picture from a radical left perspective of how companies such as the mining multinational Lamco in Liberia were exploiting the countries and local populations in the third world. The presentation featured equipment such as teleprinters that allowed visitors to communicate directly with the outside world. TV2, the newly founded second state television channel, which had a more progressive political profile than the original TV1, aired a report on the exhibition.

There was great indignation within the Social Democratic leadership, both in the government and in City Hall. According to Pär Stolpe, demands were made by the national trade union organization LO and Volvo,[31] among others, that the politically agitating elements in the exhibition be removed before it could open. Stolpe and his fellow activists defied orders and opened the exhibition in its original condition. An occupation situation ensued. The organizers managed to keep the show open for two days before it was closed by the Swedish Institute.

The authoritarian actions of the authorities gave rise to what Pär Stolpe calls a "huge backlash." Among others, author Per Olov Enquist, in Expressen, entered the cultural debate in defense of the exhibition organizers. Olof Palme gave a speech on freedom of expression in which he used the exhibition at Sweden House as an example of the kind of social criticism that an open democratic society must be able to afford. The turmoil, which in retrospect seems farcical but at the time was fraught with tension, ended with the solemn official opening of Sverigehuset being held as planned, with the allegedly subversive exhibition intact. During the opening ceremony, Pär Stolpe and his supporters were locked in their offices by the police, citing the safety of the royals, connected to the press, to whom they reported in real time on developments.[32]

According to Pär Stolpe, it was at the height of the occupation of Sweden House that Pontus Hultén, invigorated by the drama and controversy, approached him and said: "That's enough of this. Now you come up to us at the museum instead."[33] Hultén had secured resources to reinforce the museum's staff with a "counselor." His aim was to introduce the sixty-eight movement into the museum and in Pär Stolpe he had identified the right representative. In the twenty-fifth anniversary book, he describes Stolpe as "imaginative, energetic and expansive."[34]

Several of Pontus Hultén's colleagues and other contemporaries have claimed to me that Hultén recruited Pär Stolpe in order to appease the sixty-eight movement and neutralize the growing opposition to the museum from the left. This would soon prove to be a move that had the opposite effect. I believe that Hultén's motives were more complicated and find Pär Stolpe credible when he shares his version with me: "Pontus was completely enthralled with the revolutionary power of the sixty-eight movement. He was damn tired of all the happenings and spectacles up at the museum, with Staffan Olzon at the Pistol Theatre[35] and a lot of other naked people in Hall 1 and such like. It was good fun but not based on anything, just empty provocations. He had exhausted the revolutionary power of art and was looking for the next anarchist move."[36]

Pär Stolpe was formally employed as a "counselor" at Moderna Museet in the spring of 1969. "It was a big step for me to cross the Skeppsbron bridge and enter this institution," Stolpe says. "I had been an independent artist, working with poetry and doing exhibitions inspired by Moderna. I wanted to continue to be the point of contact with the movements I had been active in."

Stolpe serves up some striking interiors of Moderna Museet as a workplace and its still minimal staff, eleven years after its opening, which consisted of Hultén, Carlo Derkert, Karin Bergqvist Lindegren, secretary Märta Sahlberg, secretary of the Friends of Moderna Museet Bertha Lundgren, and the key figure Sture Johansson, Nationalmuseum's chief janitor. Björn Springfeldt had started the year before, in 1968, and his wife Emilia "Milla" Trägårdh Springfeldt had shortly afterwards been employed as Hultén's personal assistant.

"Pontus was rarely present, he was usually traveling," says Pär Stolpe. "He was completely uninterested in formal requirements, working hours, rules, unions and such. When he came back after his long professorial leave in the summer, it was a hell of a rush with work until four or five in the morning. Then he was a real fixer, like a sub-sergeant in the war. It was supposed to be fun to work and it really was. Carlo was there more often. Pontus had no respect for him whatsoever, treated him like air. When I first arrived at the museum and Pontus introduced me, Bertha Lundgren fell to her knees and screamed: 'Oh no, not him, please! I knew it would be him! He's an art hater!' I quickly realized that there were strong contradictions with the Friends and all the rich people there who hated the radicals that Pontus let into the museum. I kept to myself and had nothing to do with the others, just worked directly with Pontus."[37]

Pär Stolpe's first task for Moderna Museet, the assignment for which he had been recruited, was to represent the museum, alongside Pontus Hultén, in the planning of the new Kulturhuset at Sergels torg, which at the time occupied much of Hultén's focus and energy. "The reason they brought in Moderna was because of the international reputation the museum had gained," says Pär Stolpe. "Palme was in the background and I think he was interested in the positive image that the museum could communicate internationally, and in the idea of bringing culture to the people."[38]

In practice, the planning group for the Kulturhuset venture consisted of Pontus Hultén, Pär Stolpe and the architect Peter Celsing, with Carlo Derkert "as usual in Pontus' wake," as Stolpe relates. Hjalmar Mehr's colleague Åke Hedtjärn was chairman of the building committee. "It's unbelievable that I was tolerated there," says Stolpe. "I was completely blacklisted in all contexts. I think Pontus ensured this. He was very interested in Gasklockan (The Gas bell). He didn't care so much about what Hedtjärn said. We tried to implement Celsing's vision. Eventually, they came to the conclusion that they were dealing with a bunch of lunatics."[39]

From the beginning, the project was fraught with a fundamental problem: Kulturhuset was a City of Stockholm building while Moderna Museet was a state institution. The matter was further complicated by the circumstance that the Swedish Parliament was interested in Kulturhuset as temporary premises during the impending renovation of the old parliament building. Johan Celsing and others argue that the plans for the parliament were in actuality probably the reason why Kulturhuset was built at all, instead of joining the list of many other unrealized municipal prestige projects.[40]

Pär Stolpe is full of contempt when he talks about the Kulturhuset building and its history. "It's Sweden's largest illegal building," he says. "Hjalmar Mehr just decided that it should be like this because he wanted to manifest himself. He possessed such total power. Celsing was a sensitive artistic soul. He had won the competition by drawing a line across Sveavägen boulevard and that's how it would be from then on. He didn't give a damn about the content that Pontus, me and Carlo were working on, just his aesthetic ideas. He started crying when he had to remove some detail like a lamp or something, teardrops fell. Kulturhuset is a terrible building. It has no backside. no connection to anything around it. I don't understand why he didn't want a context. It may look cool from the outside, but for those who have to work there, it's not cool. None of the requirements we demanded regarding room configurations, technical solutions and so on were implemented."[41]

The program outlined by Pontus Hultén, Pär Stolpe and Carlo Derkert for Kulturhuset was, to say the least, radical and, of course, insanely utopian, with ideas borrowed from Gasklockan and its international sources of inspiration, and obviously from Vladimir Tatlin and E.A.T., Experiments in Art and Technology.

In this vision, the Kulturhuset was completely open on the street level facing Sergels torg. Here, soup kitchens and sandwich carts would lure the street's proletariat into the warmth of culture — and, in Stolpe's and, I believe, Hultén's dream vision, also the community of revolutionary political ideology. This entrance level was conceived as a vast "social space" for spontaneous activities, artistic, political and others — so open that trucks could drive right into the interior of the building, where the street and its population, the building and culture would intermingle without any physical or mental barriers. "We imagined gathering young lost people, old drunkards and others who would never think of visiting such a madly bourgeois environment as a museum — everyone would be welcome," says Pär Stolpe.[42]

On this floor, Hultén and Stolpe wanted to offer the public access to teleprinters that were connected to the entire world. Here everyone would be able to follow "how news is formed," a utopian idea at the time to counteract the capitalist and imperialist indoctrination that the left-wing movement believed people were being force-fed by big business and state-controlled news reporting. By receiving and evaluating information directly from the source, citizens would build their own worldviews, independent of these oppressive forces. This was in line with the thinking of Pär Stolpe and his group of activists, and also with Pontus Hultén's and the museum's collaboration with Billy Klüver and his newly founded E.A.T. "If Pontus was a revolutionary romantic, Billy was an information romantic," says Olle Granath. "He was always a few decades ahead in his thinking. His ideas were basically the internet before the time of the internet. It was already there in his head. It was just that the technicians hadn't had time to tinker it out yet ..."[43]

From this entrance level, the audience would gradually "wind up" as if unconsciously through Celsing's monumental staircase serpentine, originally intended to be much wider, placed in the center of the building with views in all directions. The middle floor was planned for artists' studios, workshops and research laboratories. Here, temporary exhibitions and, according to Pär Stolpe, political manifestations would be presented — "here we would prepare protest marches," as he says.[44] Art forms such as film, dance and theater would be accommodated, as well as a library, reading salons and restaurants. The building would make technology and practically skilled people "of the Sture type," in Stolpe's words, available to artists and audiences.

As Pontus Hultén has declared, the type of institution they outlined was completely new, with no international precedent, built to an extreme degree on boundless interaction between the museum/culture house, artists, activists and the public. "The technical solutions we proposed for the street level sections of the building were based on the assumption that most of the installations could be swiftly altered to accommodate various initiatives. One could adapt the spaces to public studios for music, theater, dance, film experiments, etc. We frequently used the word flexibility, which would later become a buzzword for architects."[45]

From the street scene "with its openness and chaotic universality,"[46] via the temporary installations and manifestations of artists, other creators, activists and the public, and a flow of news and information, the visitor would work her/his way up the building, physically, mentally and intellectually, to the upper levels where the museum's collection would be presented. Hultén poetically envisions how the visitor would emerge from chaos into "the relative clarity, solemness, luminosity, intelligence of the art collections, an environment of contemplation and intimacy. 'The collective memory bank' is what we called the art collections in the light-hearted frenzy that characterized the elaboration of the project that we would present during the coming year."[47]

The House of Culture's spectacular all-glass facade facing Sergels torg Square was to contribute to the ambition of erasing boundaries between culture, art, the street and outside society — a gigantic display window for art and the free creativity in revolutionary defiance of all the surrounding bastions of capitalism and commercialism; or a "television screen of art" as the building was also called in the debate, where television was still the major topic of the time.

These plans appear today as so touchingly utopian and blue-eyed romantic that one wonders whether they could ever have been implemented even in the spirit of the times. Pontus Hultén admitted: "We were a bit naive, but not nearly as naive as it may seem in retrospect. Had we gotten started a couple of years earlier, it's quite possible that we could have pulled it off."[48]

According to Pär Stolpe and others, including Pontus Hultén himself, the vision for Kulturhuset could be seen as an experimental application of the cultural policy that Olof Palme and his associates had pursued in their ambition to bring culture to the people, which had included support for Moderna Museet and its programs. "Palme was complicated," says Pär Stolpe. "He saw all these opportunities for culture. He had initiated a movement to change cultural policy that led to the great cultural bills of seventy-four and seventy-five and the new national cultural policy. No other country had devised such a cultural policy before. It was about formulating a new definition of the concept of culture. The basis was the idea from the thirties that culture should reach all layers of society and be part of people's everyday lives. The idea of fairness was important — why should miners in Kiruna pay for people in Engelbrekt to go to the opera?"[49].

Pär Stolpe emphasizes that the Kulturhuset project must be viewed as a child of its time — the culmination of our Swedish welfare society's so-called "record years." 1969 was the absolute apex of the welfare state. That year, no differences in health status could be measured between the different social classes. "Almost all markers of class affiliation had been wiped out and it actually seemed that we were moving towards a more equal society," claims Stolpe.

Until the autumn of 1969, it seemed that the vision for the new Kulturhuset, with Moderna Museet as its dominant institution, had a good chance of being realized. According to Pär Stolpe, Olof Palme personally engaged in intensive negotiations with the city's leadership at this time, in support of the initiative.[50] Pontus Hultén was hotly involved, publishing, together with a number of co-authors, a large article in Dagens Nyheter in May, a manifesto on the plans for the new institution.[51]

Despite the Prime Minister's support, the planning of Kulturhuset was dogged by constant political and bureaucratic tribulations. The city stubbornly demanded the use of one floor to exhibit its models for the new greater Stockholm. The National Parliament claimed its share of the building for its plenary hall and other functions. According to Pär Stolpe, Pontus Hultén was initially intrigued by the idea of sharing premises with political decision-makers, talking about blowing up the walls to the parliament,[52] but the project gradually grew increasingly politically infected. At a late stage, the city management wanted a large part of the entrance floor facing the square to be used for public restrooms. This prompted Pontus Hultén to issue an ultimatum, supported by Olof Palme. The proposal was withdrawn and the toilet compound moved to the subway entrance,[53] where so many heroin users met their fate in overdoses in the following decades. From all evidence, there was little support for the ideas presented by Hultén and his group in collaboration with Peter Celsing from the municipal leadership in Stockholm City Hall.

As the negotiations dragged on, the museum issued a new ultimatum in late autumn 1969 to be allocated eighty percent of the premises — "in this position we were discreetly supported by the government," as Hultén writes.[54] When the demand could not be guaranteed, Pontus Hultén claims that the museum withdrew from the negotiations. According to Pär Stolpe, though, it was Olof Palme himself who called the museum one day, probably in early 1970, and said that "there will be nothing."[55] In late February/early March 1970, the project's demise was a fact when the city leadership rejected Moderna Museet's ultimatum and accepted its own "compromise proposal," in which the city, not the museum and thus the state, gained control of Kulturhuset.[56] In the press, Hultén and others lamented a missed opportunity for a unique cultural and social experiment.

In the museum's twenty-fifth anniversary book, Pontus Hultén writes in resigned, merciless terms about what he regards as the project's, and the spirit of the times', breakdown — provocative words, no doubt, for many who have subsequently worked in Kulturhuset: "The rest of the story is a series of compromises, a rape by bureaucracy — among other things on the architecture of the building, a mishmash of various programs, budget cuts and confusions, but also the story of a changed time, an optimism that is tormented to death, the overwhelming return of demagogy and moralism; the disintegration of what was originally an original and promising project. Peter Celsing did not live to see the building finished.[57] The parliament decided to take part of the building for its plenary hall and its commissions, leaving a part for culture that we could do with or without. Politics once again dominated over art."[58] He adds a typical marine metaphor: "Kulturhuset at Sergels Torg sank with its bottom valves open in this not even agitated sea of moral collapse."[59]

Pontus Hultén's disappointment at the ultimate failure of his vision for Kulturhuset was considerable. It undoubtedly contributed to his motivation and energy for his work at Moderna Museet, after nearly fifteen years, beginning to wane sometime around 1970. In a typically drastically simple formulation, he summarized how he saw the collapse of the Kulturhuset plans as a symptom of a changing zeitgeist: "Time was running out of breath."[60]

Olle Granath, who periodically worked closely with Pontus Hultén during the years when the Kulturhuset was being planned, has a more stark view of the vision: "I found it difficult to share his enthusiasm for the project. I was most measured. Pontus was dazzled by his dream of placing art firmly in the center of the village. It would never have worked to move the museum there. It's far too small and impractical. We couldn't even have fitted Matisse's 'Apollo' in there. I'm glad the museum didn't move there."[61]

Personally, I can't help imagining what might have happened if Pontus Hultén and his group, with Olof Palme's support, had succeeded in pushing through their plans for Kulturhuset — if, as Hultén said, they had gotten started a couple of years earlier, when the optimistic spirit of the sixties was still dynamic. Certainly, on rare days when the temperature is pleasant and there is no wind, it's nice to take a walk out to Skeppsholmen island, but that's an excursion reserved for the already convinced — those who have been motivated to see art from home, school or elsewhere. Skeppsholmen is a nook that no one ever passes by. For me, it remains frustrating to think about the opportunity that was lost and how different and exciting the urban energy of Stockholm city could have been with Moderna Museet at Sergels torg instead of the half-measure that Kulturhuset eventually became.

Olle Granath and several others have told me that Pontus Hultén in retrospect regarded the recruitment of Pär Stolpe as the biggest mistake he made as director of Moderna Museet. "He tried to get a foot in the door of the left but quickly realized his misjudgment, regretting it almost immediately,"[62] says Granath.

I myself wonder whether this interpretation is correct. I believe Pär Stolpe when he relays in thoughtful, sometimes loving, sometimes uncompromisingly harsh formulations his and Hultén's, as it sounds, almost intimate interaction during this first period, including in the "prison," the Navy's old detention building near the entrance to the museum. I'm convinced that Hultén was infatuated with Pär Stolpe and initially saw him as a younger soul mate and colleague of a kind that he was constantly on the lookout for. "Most of the time Pontus didn't bother to go home to Anna-Lena, instead sleeping in his cell in prison," Stolpe confides. "There we talked and drank whisky at night. He lay on the bunk while I sat on a chair. There were many late nights. We were often out with PO Ultvedt on Lidingö too, he was good, PO. Carlo was rarely around, his wife kept him on a tight leash. We had a lot of fun. Pontus and I had a lot in common. We were both interested in social networks. We talked about ideas and politics, planned for different projects. When we were in the cell, he often complained and talked about how hard it was at home. He was an unhappy boy — the kind of child whose father had been tough with him, one that no one had believed in. There was always a desire for revenge. He never talked about his father. I always thought it was great fun talking with him."

"That's how he worked, Pontus, that's where his real entrepreneurship lay," adds Stolpe. "He drank in the cell with Tinguely and others and then got them to do what he wanted. He was a real innovator in finding those people that he could milk for ideas that were profitable. This often led to conflicts. Sparks were really flying at the museum."[63]

After some time, probably quite soon, it seems to have dawned on Pontus Hultén where the unbridgeable gap opened between him and the museum and the radical left-wing youth movement that he, in the guise of Pär Stolpe, had let across the bridge. It was in the view of art, the core of the museum's activities and its raison d'être.

Hultén's dream of art as a bearer of revolutionary messages stood against Stolpe's and the sixty-eight movement's contempt for art as a whole. Here we were talking about "anti-art" in a different sense than in the Dadaist definition. As Olle Granath states: "Pontus had an unfailing faith in art. When he made a political exhibition, art would always be central. For him, art had a revolutionary potential. He was totally alienated from the new generation of leftists who viewed all art was bourgeois crap."[64]

Pär Stolpe confirms that there was a divide between his and Pontus Hultén's perception of art in relation to politics and social criticism. "For me, it was about image rather than art," says Stolpe. "I had become interested in the new image — video technology, the space image, and later also the development of medical images. I was interested in how ideas and messages could be communicated through images. Pontus always stressed the importance of engaging artists to harness their creative power. He had a strange idea about artists as researchers that I found nonsense. Of course I thought it was important to engage artists, but also people with other purposes, in my case political goals."[65]

With Pär Stolpe on board, the radicalization and politicization of Moderna Museet's activities accelerated, just as expected and as Pontus Hultén had apparently sought. Stolpe opened the museum to the various "free groups" of activists who were part of his network. The young, know-it-all revolutionaries drove the eccentric artists out of the museum, and with them all the joy and humor, according to unanimous reports. The degree of controversy and hostility rose far above the level that Pontus Hultén was comfortable with, as the provocateur he was.

At the end of 1969, the museum opened another revolutionary-themed exhibition in collaboration with activists, this time British art critic Ronald Hunt, another anarchist-minded kindred spirit of Hultén's, *Poetry Must Be Made by All!*, with the subtitle *Transform the World!*.[66] The exhibition, which had been planned without Pär Stolpe's involvement, was based on a convoluted idea of art as part of society; the notion, so cherished by Hultén, that everyone was an artist. The title was borrowed from the famous battle cry of Count de Lautréamont, the avant-garde eighteenth century French poet who inspired the Surrealists. The theme was called "art outside the frame," that is, outside the institutions and the establishment, with a variety of images, posters, architectural sketches and models, pamphlets, protest signage and photographs from five different eras and cultures. Of these, we recognize four from Pontus Hultén's immediate areas of interest — the golden day of Constructivism after the October Revolution in Russia, Dada, the "Surrealist revolution," and the May uprising in Paris in 1968. The fifth "example," the Lamu people of New Guinea, can be attributed to Ronald Hunt and his anthropological interests. *Poetry Must Be Made by All! Transform the World!* has been portrayed by many as a plotty, messy and confusing exhibition. I've been told that Pontus Hultén himself was not overly involved in the production and not particularly pleased with the outcome. The collaboration with Ronald Hunt is said to have been conflictual.

In recent years, the exhibition, like this entire period at Moderna Museet, the transitional time of the late 1960s and early 1970s, has attracted increasing interest among Swedish and international art historians, researchers, curators and artists. In 2015, Daniel Birnbaum, with his friend Hans Ulrich Obrist as guest curator, among others, staged *After Babel. Poetry Will Be Made By All! 89 plus*, an exhibition inspired by its predecessor, with the year 1989, when the communist bloc collapsed and the internet was born, as the "year of revolution."[67]

Even more than the exhibitions, it was the events and actions at the museum that were radicalized after the arrival of Pär Stolpe. Many think it was during *Poetry Must Be Made by All!* but it was in fact later in the summer of 1970, on the American National Day the Fourth of July, that the museum took a decisive step across the border into revolutionary activism. On Pär Stolpe's initiative, the Black Panthers, a militant African-American liberation movement outlawed in the United States, were invited to an "evening of solidarity" with "dance, music, poetry and film."[68] Images of shirtless black activists with clenched fists surrounded by young enthusiastic Swedish hippie girls echoed far beyond Sweden's borders. Even American deserters, considered traitors in the United States, were invited to the museum. The loud Stockholm chapter of the North Vietnamese Liberation Front (FNL), consisting mostly of idealistic bourgeois youth, of which my father and aunt were active members, impressed increasing influence on the museum. It even went so far as to trigger a diplomatic complication in the strained relationship between the United States and Sweden. The American Embassy sent an envoy to the museum to formally protest the negative image of the United States that the Swedish state institution was spreading. Pontus Hultén had undoubtedly succeeded

Pp 280–201: Solidarity evening for the Black Panthers, Moderna Museet, Stockholm, July 4, 1970.

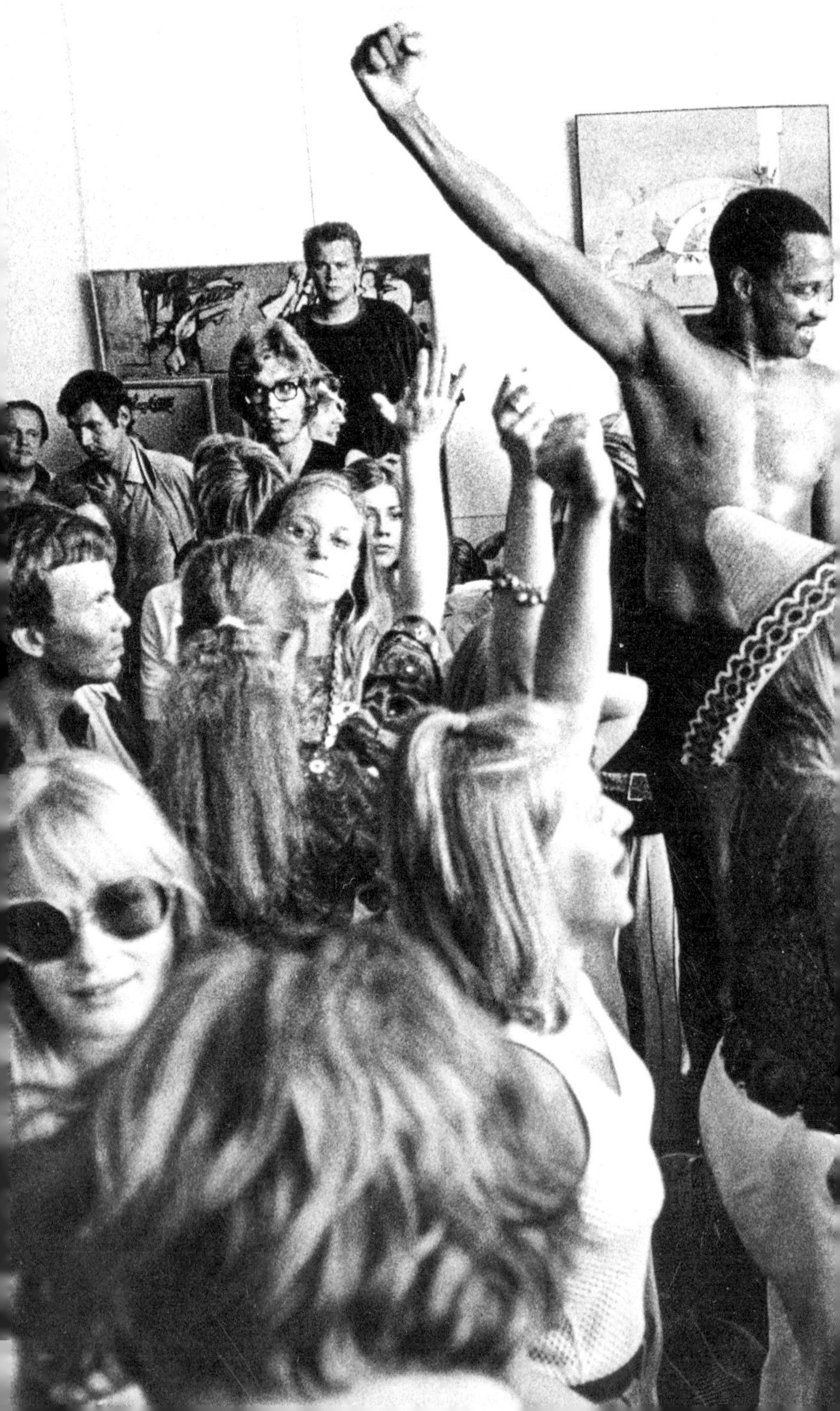

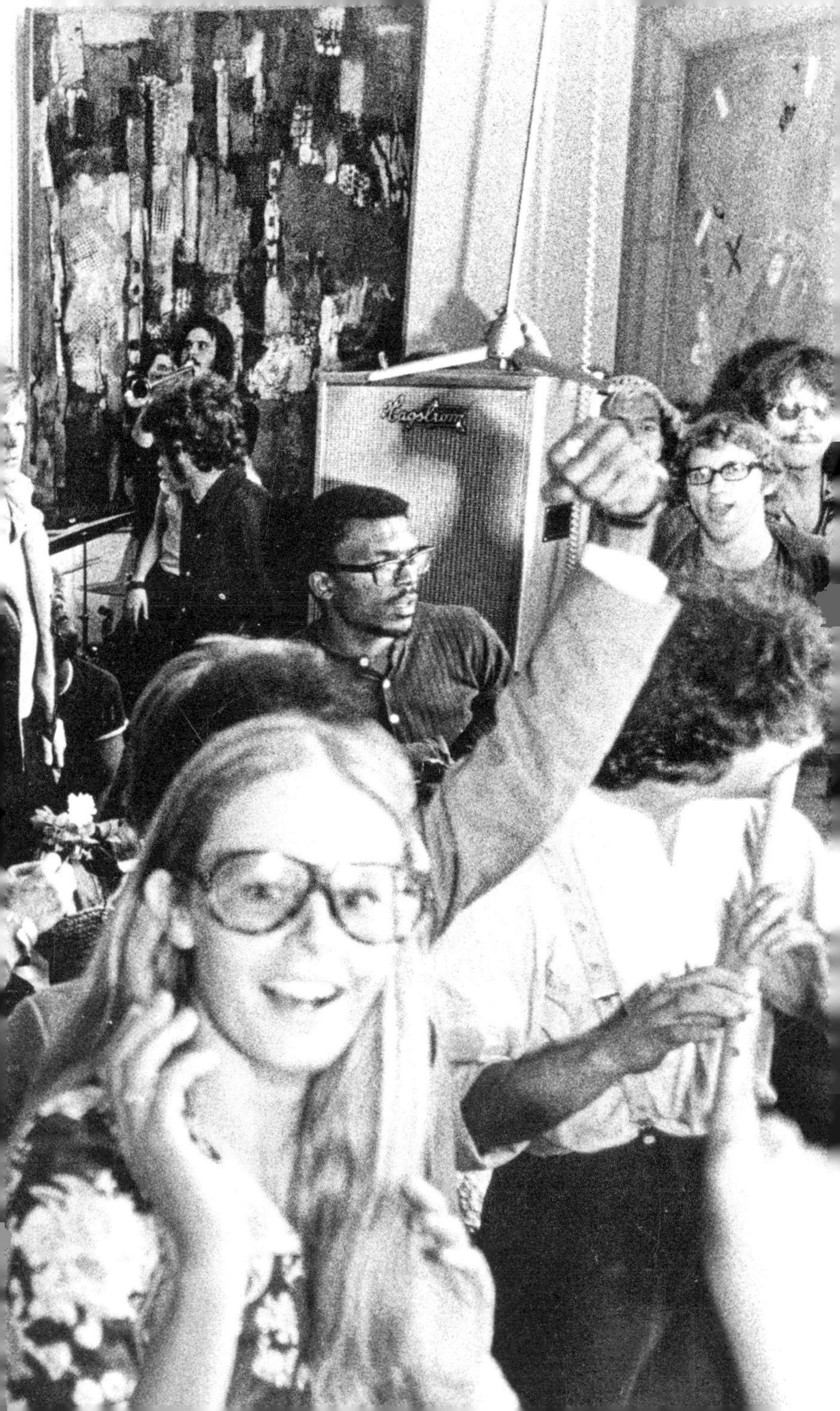

in his ambition to make the museum a player in the public debate — a daringly provocative one at that. "When he let the Black Panthers in, Pontus really crossed all boundaries," says Olle Granath. "It felt desperate and was almost like the nail in the coffin."[69]

It didn't matter how far the museum went in its radicalization in order, as has often been claimed, to appease the increasingly militant radical left. The youth movement showed no gratitude, on the contrary becoming ever more hostile — to the museum, to society and amongst each other. Controversies boiled over all around, but the main source of the hottest antagonism, the "magma chamber" in Björn Springfeldt's words,[70] remained the Vietnam War. The museum's conspicuous display of American art was a blood red flag for the extreme left movement — no clichés are exaggerated. "To them, the museum represented American imperialism," says Björn Springfeldt.[71]

In the winter of 1971 at the latest, his mistake in recruiting Pär Stolpe seems to have dawned on Pontus Hultén, with all that this entailed in turning the museum even more into a headquarters for various "free activist groups" within the radical left. On March 1 of that year, the museum opened "Filialen" ("The Appendix") in the old naval cafeteria in Barracks III, which Hultén had managed to claim on behalf of the museum. Under the direction of Pär Stolpe, the premises were to be used for "experiments with new forms of image communication." The branch was to be "a forum for the collection, documentation and discussion of new visual messages."[72]

According to several of Pontus Hultén's colleagues at the time, this was a measure he undertook to get Stolpe and his entourage out of the museum. Pär Stolpe denies that this was Hultén's motive: "People talk about wanting to get rid of all this by moving it to the old cafeteria, but that's not what it was about at all. Pontus wanted to conduct a large-scale experiment. Throughout the sixties and much of the seventies, Moderna was an innovator. The Appendix was an experimental arena where the audience itself would create exhibitions that would be displayed alongside professional art."[73]

Pär Stolpe explains that The Appendix was an initiative that instantly faced strong opposition, mainly from Nationalmuseum, still the mother institution of Moderna Museet. Stolpe was obliged to make use of the trust he had won from the chief janitor, Sture Johansson. Despite the opposition, he was able to launch a frenetic, ultra-radical program in The Appendix. During its brief run, The Appendix really did come to operate as something of a disruptive revolutionary resistance cell within the institution.

Pär Stolpe himself adamantly denies that he and his friends in the activist groups were left-wing extremists, let alone "lunatic lefties" as some claimed — an epithet he uses instead to describe the opponents in the left-wing movement of the time, where internal ideological disputes and power struggles raged ever more relentlessly. "We had nothing to do with the lunatic left, not with Lenin or Mao," Stolpe asserts. "It did enormous damage. It was mainly the KFML(r) and the Maoists, there was a group in Uppsala, all academics. Those I associated with were mostly free left, single-issue groups. Our basic demand was to crack up that damn social democracy. I don't understand why they thought we were communists."[74]

For those who read the program from The Appendix's two years of activity, it's hard not to perceive the institution as pretty way out there on the left. Here' s a selection: 1971: *People's Images: My Home is Palestine* by Odd Uhrbom; *The People and the Towers of Power* by Gun Kessle and Jan Myrdal; *Albania* by the Swedish-Albanian Society. 1972: *Women* by Group 8; *Vietnam Exhibition* by Stockholm's FNL group; *Chile — an alternative?* by Adolfo Herrera.[75]

In the perspective of the debate of latter decades on the one-sided male dominance during the legendary first era of Moderna Museet, it's noteworthy that the feminist movement and its radical activist group Group 8 used Moderna Museet as a main stage for communicating their message. Together with the FNL, Group 8 became the political right's primary hate object, the symbols above all of the communist propaganda with which Moderna Museet in their opinion, at taxpayers' expense, was indoctrinating its audience.

The basic concept of many of The Appendix's exhibitions and events was audience participation. The inaugural show *Folks bilder* (*People's Images*) began with empty walls that were gradually filled with thousands of pictures hung by visitors. Many of the exhibitions were pedagogically angled from a stern left-wing perspective, such as how television and advertising distorted people's perception of reality in the interests of commercialism and multinational finance.

The museum itself also presented several exhibitions with political activist and alternative content in the early 1970s. A major multimedia initiative of the Hultén model was *Utopias and Visions 1871–1981* in the summer of 1971, dedicated to the centenary of the Paris Commune of 1871. The "Commune," as it's called — "the only utopia realized in modern times," as Pontus Hultén writes in the catalog — was a consequence of the Franco-German war of 1870–1871, when a utopian anarchist socialist society similar to the one Hultén dreamed of was allegedly established over a short period of time — seventy-two days to be precise, which was also the time frame of the exhibition. The reportedly messy exposition, which was staged outdoors on the old naval firing range next to the detention unit adjacent to the museum, featured photographs, paintings, drawings, posters, texts and other material from the Paris Commune, mainly from everyday life in the city during this "ideal state." The year 1981 referred to the second part of the exhibition — a vision of what might await humanity a decade hence. The structure seems to be intricate and intuitive in the same way as in *Poetry Must Be Made by All!* — an interesting development of Hultén's and the museum's activities in the increasingly delirious zeitgeist, where the psychedelic element had broken in on a broad front by the turn of the decade in 1970.

In the production, Pontus Hultén collaborated with the future artist Tonie Roos, who at the time was working at the museum as a guide and study leader in the children's workshop — a collaboration that became the beginning of "a lifelong friendship between two twin souls," in Tonie Roos' words.[76] Roos' friends, artist Monika "Moki" Cherry and Don Cherry, the New York star jazz trumpeter, were invited to participate in the production immediately after Moki Cherry had introduced herself to Hultén.

In addition to the material from the Paris Commune, the program was to include elements from Hultén's new favorite utopian Buckminster Fuller's "World Game," which illustrated "the insanity of shipping goods around the planet for the sake of profit." The program had to be largely canceled due to communication problems. Fuller's "geodesic" climate-regulating dome was erected as a miniature model in white plastic, designed and constructed by the architect and artist Bengt Carling, next to the detention center in front of the museum, with a roof that opened "like lotus leaves"[77] to the summer sky. With clear symbolism, Carling also blew a hole in the prison wall as the entrance to the exhibition. The content of the show was initially an open question, soon filled by the Cherry family. There are classic images of the family sitting on the floor playing music with their children Neneh and Eagle-Eye, both later internationally accomplished artists. The family lived in the museum throughout the summer, keeping their household in the jail. Hosted by the Cherry couple, musicians, artists, performers, activists and creators of all kinds gathered with audiences, adults and children, in the Fuller climate dome, richly decorated with Moki Cherry's draperies and textile sculpture sets. There were daily impromptu concerts with Swedish jazz musicians and Japanese Taj Mahal Travellers on tour in the Nordic countries, spontaneous happenings, performances, socializing and parties, with many of the participants dressed in Moki's amazing creations. On the floor of the Dome, the artist painted a mandala formation that evolved over the course of the event.[78]

According to Tonie Roos, Pontus Hultén was most pleased with the exhibition, which he found beautiful and poetic.[79] Immediately after the press preview, she recalls, Hultén set off on a sailing trip, with the instruction: "Now you take care of this."[80] "No one else at the museum cared about that exhibition, so I did pretty much what I wanted," Tonie Roos continues. "With Olle Granath's good memory, I organized concerts in the galleries as well."[81]

As a third part of the exhibition, visitors were offered telex connections with Bombay, Tokyo and New York, where the audience, when the technology was working, could ask questions about the future to "experts," the latter a collaboration with Billy Klüver and his E.A.T.[82] Olle Granath, who as acting intendant was delegated responsibility from Pontus Hultén when he disappeared on his sailing vacation, followed by leave of absence, says: "There wasn't much of an exhibition before it was filled with content from visitors. It was very improvised. Suddenly Billy Klüver came with a Japanese rock band and wanted to be paid. I also remember Don Cherry coming in one day and saying that Louis Armstrong was dead and wanting to go to the funeral in New York."[83]

Judging by the images, stories and texts, *Utopias and Visions* appears to me as Stockholm hippie culture of the noblest kind, as I remember it from my childhood. I can smell the scents too. This exhibition is among to the initiatives from Pontus Hultén's "late" era at Moderna Museet that have attracted growing international interest

The "World Game," also known as the "World Peace Game," was introduced by Buckminster Fuller in 1961 as an alternative to military war games, with the intention of developing new solutions to deal with overpopulation, overexploitation and unequal distribution of the earth's resources. Using Fuller's "Dysmaxion Map" as a game plan, groups of players solve problems based on a holistic "total view" of the world. The motto is to "make the world work for 100% of humanity in the shortest possible time through spontaneous cooperation without ecological damage or disadvantage to anyone," with the reward being improved quality of life for all people.

in recent years. Moki Cherry has, unfortunately after her death, had an international breakthrough, which began with a compact, powerful exhibition of her art, textiles and fashion design at Moderna Museet in 2016–2017.[84] In recent years, several well-publicized and acclaimed exhibitions and events have been presented in the United States featuring Cherry's art and documentation of her and her husband Don Cherry's life and artistic collaboration. Moki Cherry herself heralded her memories of the exhibition in her diary, describing how she, after the day's non-stop "life performance" ("life as art") in the dome, went in exhausted to cook dinner in the prison while her children Neneh, six years old at the time, and Eagle-Eye, two and a half, ran out into the museum to "play in the collection." Even the task of daily cleaning of the dome was left to Moki herself ...[85]

Moki Cherry struggled to make a living from her art, but more than ten years after her death, her work and life story are in demand throughout the art world. Cherry's textile works and her entire broad artistic production are coveted by international collectors. I dare claim that we have a new Swedish female international star artist, sadly posthumously. I'm surprised that this gratifying development has not received more attention here at home — especially since Moki Cherry is one of the few exceptions to the male dominance among all the artists highlighted at Moderna Museet during Pontus Hultén's era.

Although several of Moderna Museet's initiatives during this critical final period of Hultén's tenure crossed the boundaries of politics and activism, this did not mean that the museum neglected art. It continued to produce more traditional exhibitions in parallel. *Poetry Must Be Made by All!* for example, was preceded by a retrospective with an old acquaintance, Sven "Xet" Erixson, the older generation Expressionist painter who had lashed out against *Art in Motion.* "A lot of water had flowed under the bridges in the eleven years since the museum opened," as Hultén noted.[86]

Among other initiatives that can be mentioned during these years were a retrospective on Max Ernst (1969),[87] an exposé on Surrealism and its ideological background and philosophy (*Surrealism?* 1970)[88] and *Svenskt alternativ* (*Swedish Alternative*),[89] with some sixty works by eight young Swedish artists, an all-male crew of course: Dick Bengtsson, Ola Billgren, Lars Englund, John-E Franzén, Lars Hillersberg, Einar Höste, Olle Kåks and Ulrik Samuelson, produced in collaboration with the Musée d'Art Moderne de la ville de Paris, where the exhibition was also shown.

After the turn of the decade in 1970, the museum introduced Stockholm audiences to two new radical artists of the highest caliber, both pioneers of installation art.

The first was Los Angeles artist Edward Kienholz. Frequently regarded as a Pop artist, he was much more brutal, uncompromising and openly political in his message than his cooler contemporaries in New York. He and Pontus Hultén became close friends. Even before the exhibition[90] — which traveled to the Stedelijk and other European museums — Hultén had secured the acquisition of the 1966 masterpiece "State Hospital," my own poignant childhood memory: the tableau of the two poor bastards in their double bunk in the asylum, strapped down naked with belts, their genitals hanging, with goldfish bowls for heads, chemically impregnated with an eternal ooze of filth, degradation and death (the installation, a world attraction, is based on Kienholz's memories from working in a mental institution in the forties.[91]) Though not a blockbuster, the brutally powerful show was relatively well attended. "At that time, the museum's visitor numbers were declining," says Olle Granath. "The audience in the sixty-eight movement turned their noses up in the air and thought it was nothing new. It could not provoke sensation like *4 Americans*. I think many also found Kienholz a bit heavy to take in. But nobody could settle down with that exhibition. It brought the relay forward, definitely."[92]

In early 1971, Björn Lövin's *Konsument i oändligheten* and *Herr P:s penningar* (*Consumer in Eternity* and *Mr. P:s Money*) was shown, the first museum exhibition of this pioneer of installation art. Lövin was one of Hultén's personal favorites who he exhibited again at the Centre Pompidou in Paris in 1981 (see Chapter 22). The artist was long forgotten by the wider public. In the spirit of the time, he saw his installations as scenographic illustrations of ideas, not as something to be preserved for the future. In 2022, Björn Lövin made a posthumous comeback when Moderna Museet opened *The Surrounding Reality*, with reconstructions of the artist's consumerist installations from Stockholm in 1971 and Paris in 1981.

The second of the great masters, pioneers and ideologists of postwar art to be presented in an art historic exhibition in the early 1970s was Joseph Beuys, after the turn of 1971.[93]

Hultén stood in a notoriously ambiguous relationship with Beuys, which had to do with Beuys' German origin and background as a fighter pilot during the war. Kasper König told me that this skepticism was the reason why Hultén did not go for a solo retrospective with Beuys, but exhibited him together with another more forgotten German contemporary Conceptual artist, Günther Uecker.[94] "He thought that Beuys was a charlatan," says Pontus Hultén's later life partner, the

German art historian and artist Marie-Louise von Plessen. "But when he was told that Beuys' story about how he was shot down during the war, rescued by shepherds who smeared him with fat and wrapped him in felt was just a fairy tale that he had made up himself, Pontus got more respect for him. He thought that was Dadaistic."[95] A more likely explanation for the arrangement with the two German artists shown in parallel is the official one reported by Olle Granath and others, namely that the initiative was partly financed by the West German embassy in a program for the international dissemination of German culture, and that the federal state was prevented by its statutes from supporting individual artists.

The Beuys exhibition, entitled *Joseph Beuys. Actions/Aktionen*, was the artist's first museum exhibition in a non-German speaking country. This was the year before Beuys' global breakthrough at the most influential post-war art biennial, Documenta in Kassel in 1972. By this time, Beuys, who turned fifty during the Stockholm exhibition, was known outside Germany only in small avant-garde coteries, not primarily for his own visual art but for his actions as a "shaman" and as a controversial professor at the Düsseldorf Academy of Art.

Documenta 5 in Kassel in 1972, under artistic direction of Pontus Hultén's main international rival Harald Szeemann, is generally considered the most influential art biennial in the late twentieth century, a breakthrough for Conceptual Art. Documenta is often referred to as a biennial but is a quinquennial, as the event is only held every five years.

Pontus Hultén was, according to unanimous reports, marginally involved in the Beuys exhibition, which was an initiative of his colleague Karin Bergqvist Lindegren, who was of German origin, mastered the language and had good contacts in the German avant-garde. Moderna Museet's archives contain extensive correspondence between Beuys and Bergqvist Lindegren in which the latter initially addresses the artist as "Herr Professor," eventually changing to "Lieber Joseph," with greetings to his family.[96] The exhibition was based on a collection that had been built up over decades by Beuys' old friends, the brothers Franz Joseph and Hans van der Grinten, with thousands of drawings and objects stored in the brothers' "outwardly inconspicuous house in Kranenburg," as Pontus Hultén writes in his catalog preface.[97] Joseph Beuys, together with the van der Grinten brothers, was personally involved in the selection and design of the exhibition, spending months compiling an almost complete photographic documentation of his most famous actions. Most of the one hundred and ninety-three objects in the exhibition had never been shown before. In addition to drawings, paintings, photographs, sculptures and objects, a key piece was the now legendary installation "The Pack"[98] from 1969. The catalog cover was adorned with Beuys' painting with the text "Marcel Duchamp's silence is overrated," from a live Fluxus action of the same name from 1964.[99] The message has been interpreted as a criticism by Beuys of Duchamp's silence and withdrawal from art and political debate. "That painting as a cover was of course like swearing in church in that environment," says Olle Granath.

Joseph Beuys traveled to Stockholm with his family, where he worked on the installation of the exhibition for about ten days. This visit and the exhibition, unlike so many of Moderna Museet's art historic events of the early period, are fully documented photographically. Accompanying Beuys was his friend and collaborator, photographer Lothar Wolleh, who captured over six hundred images of the artist's Stockholm visit, featuring stunning portraits of Beuys in his usual outfit as an art adventurer, with the boots, work pants, vest, wide-brimmed felt hat and sheepskin coat that inevitably bring to mind Operation Barbarossa. The idea was that these images would be published in an exclusive artist's book that Beuys planned with Karin Bergqvist Lindegren, printed in an edition of two hundred copies on PVC plastic, a sophisticated printing exercise. Something went wrong in the binding of the book. The project was abandoned, with thousands of sheets of PVC plastic already printed. Over the years, these have gradually been released on the market by dealers, at prices that have risen as Joseph Beuys' status in the art world has only continued to grow since the 1980s. The unpublished book is also famous because Beuys used the unbound plastic sheets in his sculpture "Unterwasserbuch"[100] from the following year, 1972, with a flashlight illuminating the book in a water-filled box. Lothar Wolleh's images have been shown in leading German museums over the years.[101]

The Joseph Beuys exhibition was far from a success. According to Olle Granath's description, the by now spoiled, jaded museum audience was not impressed. The fact that the Düsseldorf master was still waiting for his breakthrough outside of Germany is evident in that the show was met with unanimously negative, even hostile criticism — so bad that Karin Bergqvist Lindegren refrained from sending the Swedish press clippings to the artist.[102] Olle Granath distinguished himself with a review that was more benevolent than the others, but which can still be classified as neutral at best.[103] "I could have been more generous, but I was a little hesitant, trying to read the mood," admits Granath. "Beuys was a hard nut to crack for the sixty-eight audience. He was Europe's most radical artist, but at the same time he was doing abstract art, which was bourgeois decadence. They couldn't figure out which leg to stand on."[104]

To me, these final years, which in the museum's and Pontus Hultén's own historiography have been portrayed almost as a phase of decline — this turbulent, conflict-ridden period when the museum operated in a state of flux between art, culture, politics and revolutionary activism — seem at least as exciting as the creative explosion of the early 1960s. Hultén had a constant attraction to "all that slightly dangerous stuff," in the words of Björn Springfeldt. During this last phase, he took his museum out on hazardous adventures in his experimental zeal to realize his vision of the expanded role of art in society. Hultén himself said: "Today when utopias are dead, it can be hard to phantom the optimism and dynamism that existed in the sixties, but then we really believed that it was possible to create a different kind of society where culture would play a much greater role."[105]

Like his mentor, Hultén's younger colleague Björn Springfeldt sees the radical sixties movement, in which he himself was involved in many respects, as a brief glimpse of historical possibilities that were just as quickly forlorn. "For a time it actually looked as if brain and abdomen could be united and one could enjoy life," says Springfeldt, "but it quickly became a sect, Maoist, moralistic, intolerant and puritanical."[106]

In one of his texts in the twenty-fifth anniversary book, Hultén summarizes the experiences of the collaboration with the sixty-eight movement: "Moderna Museet as an institution had been responsible for the intensified and expanded cultural situation in Stockholm. The museum had shown the new film, opened the doors to new music, provided a clear and coherent picture of the new art, and collaborated with activist groups like the one that made *The Model*. The collaboration had been interesting and rewarding. But it had also revealed its weaknesses. The moralizing and the vanity, the neo-bureaucratic paralysis behind the altruistic facade that these groups presented, which seemed more false than the frank egoism of the artists."[107]

Unsurprisingly, the new radical left's attacks on Moderna Museet included unholy alliances and intrigues with other, older enemies. Among these was the Artists' National Organization (KRO), which, under radical auspices, repeated the old criticism of the museum's "one-sided" focus on international art at the expense of local talent. By purchasing and displaying American art, the museum was part of American imperialism, and so on.

A symbolic and for Hultén personally utterly disappointing proof of how far the alienation had gone between himself and the "revolutionary" movement he had fostered was when Per Olof Ultvedt himself, Hultén's old friend, collaborator and comrade-in-arms from Djursholm, allegedly without warning, joined this resistance, in direct confrontation with his old companion. "Suddenly, 'Hante' [Ultvedt's nickname] was going around with a list that Pontus should be deposed," says Björn Springfeldt. "It was really a completely unreal situation, a huge antagonism."[108]

"Ultvedt and KRO must be one of the strangest alliances imaginable," says Olle Granath. "It was not his world at all. He moved into the Academy of Fine Arts and turned against all of us. At the Academy, he used the landscape school's money for a voyage to Albania. I think it was a father's rebellion against Ulf [Linde]. They had been very good friends. I also think there was something about the international artists — that they were considered more remarkable than him. Ultvedt was that way — a brawler who often ended up in conflict."[109]

The radicalization of the museum naturally intensified the antagonism from the right. The hatred from the upper echelons was one thing. More serious was the growing hostility from the conservative factions of the Social Democrats. Olof Palme, the cultural visionary, found it increasingly difficult to defend his protégé from the forces within the party who thought that the museum was engaging in subversive propaganda at the expense of the state. In 1971, the parliamentary auditors set up an inquiry into the museum's use of its allocated tax money. The investigation demanded a flood of detailed information from the museum that largely paralyzed its small organization. The auditors' questioning of the museum's activities echoed "The Great Art Debate" from a decade earlier. "When the parliamentary auditors attacked the museum, it was really far beyond the limits of parody and cast a shadow over social democracy," says Olle Granath.

Pontus Hultén candidly summed up this lengthy campaign of political scrutiny: "They claimed we were left-wing extremists and in a way they were right. We took a position on the left, that we did, and we were a bit extreme. Our critics were probably good and well-meaning in many ways, but these constant inquiries became most strenuous and eventually threatened the whole museum. It went so far that I had to go up to Olof Palme and say that this good cause must come to an end, which it then did."[110]

In the long term, the most damaging consequence of politicization was probably how this development catastrophically deteriorated the museum's relationship with its most loyal supporters, represented by the Friends of Moderna Museet. Pär Stolpe revealed how he had immediately experienced the tension between Pontus Hultén and the Friends. Stolpe's own attitude is clear when he uses an infamous anecdote to illustrate his point: "The Friends Association consisted of a lot of rich people and luminaries in the state administration. Pontus had no love for them. When I organized our solidarity evening for the Black Panthers, it just so happened that the Friends hosted a reception in the adjacent gallery. Pontus moved between the two, making sure that the passage was open so that all the rich people could see in properly. It was obvious that he enjoyed it."[111]

Alienating one's friends' association and thus the institution's core audience is a mortal sin for a museum director. The museum paid a devastating price for this conflict. Within a few years, the membership of the Friends plummeted from five-six thousand to five-six hundred — a collapse that would take decades for the museum to recover from. "We were among the few who remained during that time," says Anna-Stina Malmborg, later chair of the Friends and now a major donor to the museum along with her husband Gunnar Höglund.[112] Pontus Hultén summarized the experience of that strife-ridden era in one sentence: "It was a new generation that wanted to make its voice heard, which was admirable in many ways, but it damaged the museum."[113]

A crucial difference for me between the sixties movement, in which I grew up, and later fashions is that, despite all its madness, the movement was propelled by a collective political message as its driving force, in contrast to later contemporary trends where self-realization is the sole engine. I'm grateful for the privilege of having grown up in a Sweden and Stockholm that at the time composed the world's most advanced social experiment, where we at least wanted to appear as if we cared more about others than ourselves and our closest family — about the weak, also in other parts of the world. Of course the sixties movement bred a self-destructive force within itself. Many, perhaps most, of its utopian ideas were impossible to realize, for which we should in many cases be grateful. Equally apparent is that several of the fundamental ideas of the left-wing movement are firmly anchored in our Swedish social system and our public consciousness in real time, as corner stones that no political forces, not even the extreme right, have yet dared to question or disrupt — all these public preschools, parental benefits, Medicare, social security and various other welfare systems.

The development of Moderna Museet in the sixties and early seventies must be viewed as a consequence of this social movement, which to a large extent was born and developed at the museum, in the complex symbiotic relationship between art and politics during this time up here in our provincial north — a short dynamic era that shaped our modern society and continues to fascinate.

Personally, I persist in seeing the sixties movement, with all its self-destructive excesses, as an overwhelmingly positive, pathetically heroic force — this cavalry that rode out in hopeless defense against the armored, motorized modern forces of egoism and commercialism. Although we have now lived for forty years under the totalitarian rule of the market and materialism, in this "communism of capitalism" as the condition has been called, I retain my faith in the eventual return of more idealistic, utopian, optimistic forces.

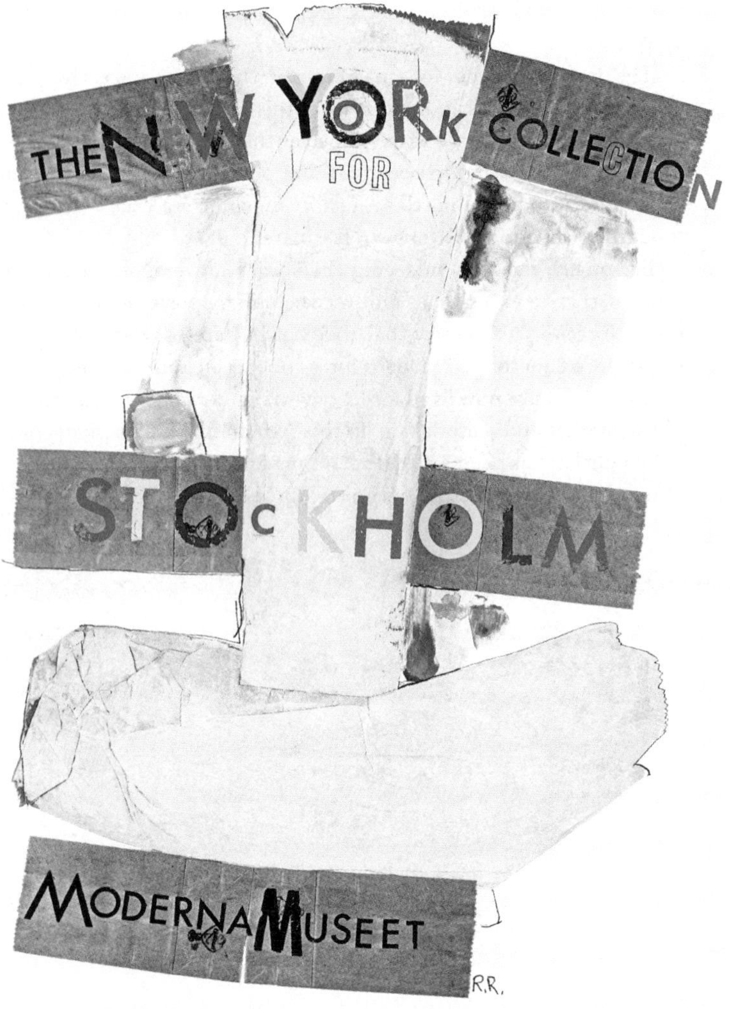

FOR MARK RAUSCHENBERG 73

The New York Collection for Stockholm — grand finale in triumph and agony at Moderna Museet

After the summer of 1971, following the opening of the exhibition *Utopias and Visions 1871–1981*, Pontus Hultén took a year's leave of absence to write and produce a book about his admired friend Jean Tinguely, which also served as the catalog for the museum's Tinguely retrospective in the fall of 1972.[1] Carlo Derkert filled in as museum director. Hultén worked on this magnificent publication — a massive volume presented in a cardboard briefcase, complete with a handle, no doubt inspired by Hultén's and Tinguely's mutual idol Duchamp and his ingenious "La Boîte en valise" — in Torpedverkstaden, The Torpedo Workshop, below the museum. The catalog is a classic, considered to be style-defining and crucial to the knowledge of Tinguely's art.

Like Filialen, The Annex, the Torpedverkstaden workshop can be seen as a project that was part of Pontus Hultén's ambition to expand the museum's activities and premises after the plans for Kulturhuset had derailed. The utopian vision for the venture was grandiose. Here, artists and technicians from all around the world would create innovative art together, in collaboration with Billy Klüver and his E.A.T. Little of this was realized. It became increasingly clear that time was running out for utopias. Resources were lacking and, as I understand it, so was energy. The only international guest who came to make use of the Torpedverkstaden workshop to any great extent was the Japanese Conceptual artist On Kawara, a good friend of Pontus Hultén, who stayed here during the summer of 1971 with his wife, a sojourn that contributed to Kawara's donation of parts of his now classic postcard suite to Hultén and the museum.[2] "Otherwise, not much more than a rousing opening party came of Torpedverkstaden," says Olle Granath.[3]

Robert Rauschenberg, poster for *The New York Collection for Stockholm*, 1973.

The then thirty-one-year-old Granath, who was appointed temporary intendant during Hultén's leave of absence, describes how apparent it was to everyone at the time that Pontus Hultén had tired of the museum and all the conflicts surrounding him. "All he wanted to do was work on his Tinguely book. When I tried to talk about the museum, he was gloomy. I tried to engage him in our exhibition with Paul Thek, which he had commissioned.[4] Thek came to Stockholm with his crew and built his 'Pyramid.' Harald Szeemann visited the museum in the summer and decided to bring the entire exhibition to his classic Documenta in Kassel. Pontus' only comment was that he had expected a small exhibition. It was like he didn't really care, as if he had already left. I remember another time when Katja Waldén and I had made an effort to assemble an exhibition called *Pictures of the 1910:s*,[5] with art and photography, a lot of unknown material, which we had displayed on screens, not unlike *Poetry Must Be Done By All!* When I showed it to him, he just muttered 'goddamn ABF exhibition' [ABF — the Swedish national labor union's educational association]."[6]

Olle Granath recalls a walk in the company of Pontus Hultén, it must have been sometime in the spring of 1972, before Hultén was to resume his position as museum director. "I remember so vividly when we crossed the Skeppsholmen Bridge," says Granath. "He was generally unconcerned, not enthusiastic about any ideas. I asked if he wouldn't do an exhibition with On Kawara, who had been living at the museum anyway. He replied that there was no point — it would be cheaper to charter a plane and fly to New York with the few people who were interested. I remember clearly thinking that now — now it's time for you to go ..."[7]

Pontus Hultén was offered an escape of the most spectacular kind. In the winter of 1973, Robert Bordaz, one of French President Georges Pompidou's most trusted officials, in charge of the new cultural center in Paris that the President had initiated and which after his death would be named after him, Centre Georges Pompidou, traveled to Stockholm to meet Hultén. Pontus told me about his first meeting with his future boss: "He came to the museum one day and we went to lunch at the Opera Terrace. When we finished, he said 'I'll see you in Paris.' I wrote a letter a few weeks later to find out a bit more but he called me back immediately and said 'you might as well come right away.' The building was being designed and they needed someone to answer the architects' questions."[8]

I harbor a personal, unsubstantiated suspicion that Robert Bordaz's visit to Stockholm may not have been so unexpected after all. My notion is that his old reliable companion chance may have been aided by a measure of lobbying by Hultén and his friends in Paris, the city that Hultén had never quite left and which I wonder if he had not maintained the ambition to one day return to. He spoke of the liberation he experienced in coming to Paris, where the controversies would be no less intense, but of a different nature, leaving behind the "magma chamber" that Moderna Museet had become. "Sure, there were rich people who were pissed off and all that, but there wasn't the constant nagging that is so tiresome in Stockholm."[9]

Pontus Hultén's emotion was shared by his colleagues. "I think we all breathed a collective sigh of relief," says Olle Granath. "It was really in the air that it was time. We had also known for a long time that Pontus wanted to broaden his horizons."

Fate, or chance, Hultén's ally, again with the support of Pontus himself, characteristically designed this exit to occur not in silence but with a burst of equal shares of triumph and antagonism.

In New York in the early seventies, the perpetual motion machine Billy Klüver, backed by Robert Rauschenberg, his friend and partner in E.A.T., had developed the idea of creating a collection of works as a memorial to the New York art scene of the sixties, that decade of Neo-Dadaism and Pop Art when New York took the art world by storm. Robert Whitman, one of the twenty-nine artists who participated in and contributed works to the project, co-founder of E.A.T. along with Klüver and Rauschenberg, tells me that it was natural to ask Pontus Hultén to make the selection of works for the collection, since, according to Whitman, Hultén was widely regarded among the artists as the curator and museum official who had done the most for, and best understood, the new art that had developed so sensationally in New York during the sixties.[10]

According to Pontus Hultén himself,[11] Whitman and official history, the idea from the beginning was to donate this collection to an American museum. However, none of the major institutions showed any acute interest. Hultén writes in the twenty-fifth anniversary book that "it was not difficult to persuade" the group[12] that the collection should instead go to Stockholm and Moderna Museet, the museum in the world that had undoubtedly been most important for the breakthrough of the New York art. I suggest to Robert Whitman that Pontus Hultén may have had an ulterior motive in building the collection from the very beginning, to seize this treasure for his own museum. "I think so too," Whitman replies. "But I remember that there was also talk that it could end up at Beaubourg, where he was going."[13]

Be that as it may. Pontus Hultén and Billy Klüver, representing the participating artists, managed to negotiate a deal whereby a unique collection of key works from the height of New York art from the sixties was donated to Moderna Museet. A prerequisite for this advanced operation was that the Swedish government, reportedly unlike the American museums, was prepared to pay for the realization of the donation, specifically one hundred thousand dollars, at that time about half a million Swedish crowns. We art-loving Stockholmers and Swedes should be grateful to the politicians for pushing through support for this initiative. In the inflammatory cultural climate of the time, it's hard to imagine anything more controversial, less timely than yet another direct government grant to purchase more American art ...

The government grant was far from enough to fully fund the donation's transportation, insurance and other costs associated with the transaction. It's indicative of the spirit of the times, of the limited resources available, but especially of the collective loyalty among the artists, that the group therefore agreed that each artist would also donate a work for an edition of prints to be sold in order to provide additional much needed funds. There were also contributions from a number of American patrons, including of course Dominique and John de Menil. I have not been able to fully investigate exactly how the financing was organized or what compensation the contributing artists received.

Jeanette Bonnier, then living in New York, where she later opened a gallery, was engaged by Billy Klüver to assist him, Robert Rauschenberg and the dealer Leo Castelli with the project, along with other volunteers. Bonnier was asked to work primarily on "fundraising," that archaic American concept. "I was completely inexperienced and begging for money was not my thing," says Jeanette Bonnier. "The project was entirely Billy's idea. He was absolutely amazing in his madness. Bob Rauschenberg was unusual as an artist in that he was committed and helpful to younger colleagues, with a strong social sense. Leo Castelli made the collection of lithographs. He and Pontus were in close contact. Pontus was the first to do this with Pop Art and Leo respected that. It was *4 Americans* that had made him famous. It was quite complicated. Some artists broke up because they wanted a share of the profits. The dealers still demanded their commissions. The edition of lithographs stood packed in boxes in Leo's basement, selling nothing. Finally, I told Leo that we must do something about this. I bought half the edition for six thousand dollars."[14]

Jeanette Bonnier related that Pontus Hultén, whom she had known since her youth, when he and Ulf Linde had often been guests of her grandfather Tor Bonnier at the Bonnier family's residence Nedre Manilla in the Royal Djurgården park island, visited New York during work on the collection. She confided to me that she found Hultén attractive, "handsome to look at, powerful, confident and nonchalant, with elegant, crisp attire, tweed, flannel — he really stood out from most people around him who were not elegant at all. When he came to New York, I told him that so and so is missing, we have to pay the artists," Bonnier continues. "Now you have to get that money. But he replied 'no, that's your business.' I also remember that he told the board of the National Museum that 'it's not you who decide, it's I who decide.' He couldn't bear the thought of them having a say."[15]

The donation of *The New York Collection for Stockholm* finally comprised thirty works by twenty-nine artists, as well as the accompanying graphic collection. The contributors included not only Pop artists but also Minimalists and Conceptual artists. The list of names speaks for itself, notably with Louise Nevelson and Lee Bontecou as the only women among twenty-seven men.[16]

In the twenty-fifth anniversary book, Ulf Linde delivers a sweeping assessment of *The New York Collection for Stockholm*: "When it came to foreign art — when the means of purchase were considerably more limited — Pontus Hultén himself decided what to buy. At least in practice. Thanks to his excellent relationships with international artists of his own generation, he was able to acquire many of their works early and at cheap prices: this is how the museum's collection of 1960s art was built up, drop by drop — until the New York Collection waterfall came along. Time will tell whether the *New York Collection* was an important project or not. For the time being, one can refrain from assessing the whole and — as far as possible — see the individual works without prejudice. Then it seems to me that the museum has received one of the best paintings Ellsworth Kelly has made, a very beautiful Kenneth Noland, an extraordinary Roy Lichtenstein and a good Dan Flavin — at least four works that I would envy any other museum. That's enough."[17]

The future invoked by Linde, the arbiter of taste, transformed into history, has revealed who among himself and Hultén was right and who was wrong about American art, and revealed his prophecy to be highly ungenerous. Many of the works in *The New York Collection for Stockholm* have achieved canonical status and are among the most frequently shown, in demand for loans and popular in Moderna Museet's collection. For Pontus Hultén, the *New York Collection* was a belated compensation for being prevented from purchasing works from the museum's early American exhibitions.

In his text about the New York connection in the twenty-fifth anniversary book, Hultén, in a passage about the conflicts surrounding the *New York Collection* and the criticism of the misuse of state funds — the Department of Education's grant of one hundred thousand dollars — cannot restrain from noting that the thirty works of art in the collection "would already today [1983] be worth 100,000 dollars each, if they could be acquired at all, which is not the case."[18] Not even Pontus Hultén, as late as in the 1980s, could have foreseen the continued increase in value since. Further zeros can be added. The collection is invaluable in our time.

Hultén concludes his New York text with a proudly self-conscious summary of the museum's acquisitions of American art from the sixties — or rather, art by artists active in New York during the 1960s — as usual with a modest reference to his faithful old partner, chance: "Thus, through a series of more or less random circumstances, Moderna Museet acquired a large and significant collection of the most important and innovative art from the 1960s. (...) Only Count Panza di Biumo's collection in Varese[19] and the Ludwig Collection in Cologne can be compared to that of Moderna Museet, and these have been acquired with completely different pecuniary resources. In the United States, no museum collection can be compared in terms of quality to that of Moderna Museet with regard to this area of collection and this time period."[20]

The exhibition *The New York Collection for Stockholm* opened on October 27, 1973. The catalog cover and poster were designed by Robert Rauschenberg. The opening was surrounded by protest rallies. The Vietnam War was in its most bestial phase and New York art was linked to the atrocities of the American war machine. Many of the participating artists had traveled to Stockholm for what became a full-fledged last feast with the gang, after having first celebrated their departure with infamous partying in New York.[21] In the press, the museum and Pontus Hultén were subjected to what Olle Granath calls "a slap in the face" in gratitude for the donation. The museum,

Opening of *The New York Collection for Stockholm*, Märtha Tallroth, Julie Finch and Donald Judd, Moderna Museet, Stockholm, October 1973.

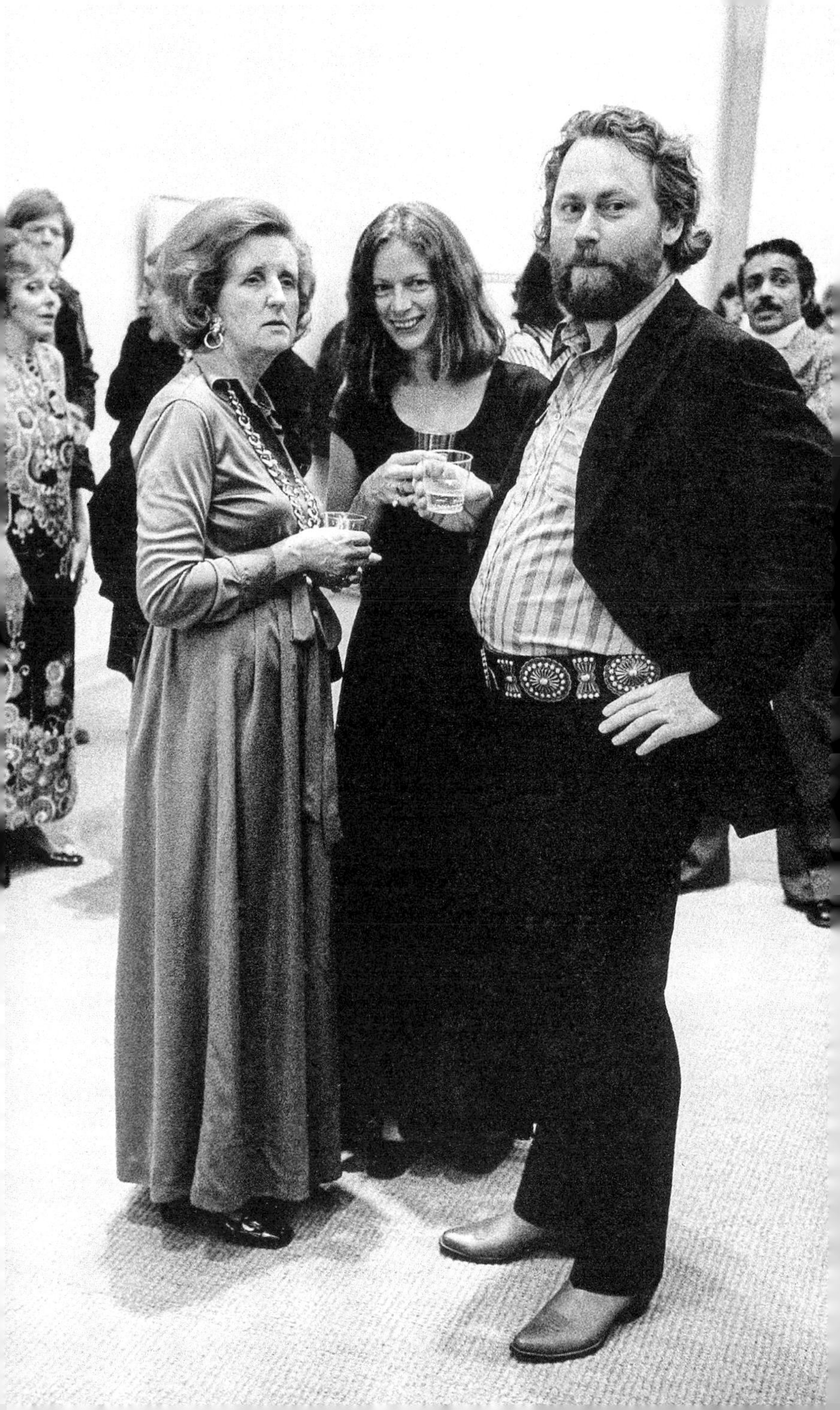

and Hultén personally, were attacked in spiteful terms in a debate that raged mainly in Dagens Nyheter. It was of course particularly painful for Hultén that Per Olof Ultvedt was one of the museum's most unreasonable critics. Ultvedt was among the signatories, along with representatives of KRO and the Royal Swedish Academy of Fine Arts, to several articles questioning the initiative to acquire more art from New York, and the government grant.[22]

For Pontus Hultén, the experience was bitter. The resistance and hostility he encountered in his efforts to secure this art treasure on behalf of the museum and the nation he had already left behind, the value of which he recognized, unlike the rabid public opinion — this was something Hultén never forgot. Björn Springfeldt refers a story from the press preview that illustrates how Hultén's patience had reached its limit. "I knew there would be trouble when I saw Torsten Bergmark there," says Springfeldt. "There was an experimental film-maker there, Emile de Antonio,[23] known as 'De,' who was a well-known leftist. I tried to par Bergmark with 'De' to divert attention, but soon he was standing there with Pontus, explaining to him how reprehensible it was to support imperialism. I saw how it boiled in Pontus, how he clenched his fists ... his knuckles whitened ..."[24]

I have been brooding for decades over the hot negative feelings that Pontus Hultén aroused and in many cases still triggers among Stockholmers of the sixty-eight generation — people with backgrounds similar to his own, ten or twenty years younger than himself, for whom he was such a father figure. I'm certain that our tiresome old Lutheran "Jante Law" (don't ever imagine yourself better than others) has once again played the first fiddle. Hultén's habit of speaking his mind in a straightforward manner, without bothering to conceal his contempt for stupidity, I think also played a part, as did something as simple as his habit of wearing a suit and tie.

I find it so true to style, so consistent with Pontus Hultén's nature, that his exit from the museum that he had created against all odds was preceded not by the laurel-wreathed triumph that one might think would have been warranted, but by a final discharge of the flaming controversies that he and the museum had struggled their way through from the beginning in their climb to world fame. I would strongly argue that controversy was an inevitable part of Pontus Hultén's greatness and of what he had created at the museum — and one of the explanations why Hultén has not reached an undisputed position among Sweden's leading cultural personalities of all time.

It must be ascertained that the farewell was bitter on both sides. Pontus Hultén left behind conflicts, broken friendships and animosity, which to some extent still exists today.

"Pontus had a ruthlessness that was linked to him being such a passionate person," says Olle Granath. "Ruthlessness often pays off, but people have fallen along the way. For those who didn't measure up, there was no mercy. Many felt hurt, of course."[25]

According to Billy Klüver's wife and business partner Julie Martin, the reason why Pontus Hultén was, and has remained, so controversial in his home country is not primarily a consequence of his management style, but cultural: "He was always very easy to deal with and not at all one who bulldozered people, as many claim," says Martin. "That people in Sweden didn't like him was simply because Swedes don't appreciate people who stand out and are different. Billy always said that. That's why he left Sweden."[26]

Pontus Hultén also left Sweden in the fall of 1973, more or less for good. He would not return for more than occasional visits until the end of his life, when his career was over. I'm convinced that this circumstance, that Hultén chose to leave Sweden forever, is yet another explanation for why his legacy in the Swedish collective consciousness is so remarkably weak or non-existent — why he must be considered largely forgotten by a broader public, even in culture-minded groups.

In my conversations with Pontus Hultén, it was apparent that he was disappointed in his home country. He felt that he had not received the appreciation he deserved. Hultén's sense of injustice was expressed in his frustration over the pension from the National Museum that he claimed to have been cheated out of, something he kept coming back to. "He never stopped talking about that," says Olle Granath. "They claimed that he had worked too short a time, but he insisted that he had been promised one by the then director Bengt Dahlbäck."[27]

"Pontus knew the value to Sweden of what he had created with the museum," says Björn Springfeldt. "He rightly felt that he was entitled to a pension for this."[28]

I experienced that Pontus Hultén's betrayed love of his country was a sadness for him, because a passionate love for this country he did most definitely hold. He was a Swedish patriot of the highest order and would always carry the loss of his homeland with him for the rest of his life.

In terms of art history, it was the next chapter of Pontus Hultén's career, the biggest stage of all in Paris, which made him one of the greatest museum directors of the twentieth century.

In a small international circle of initiates, however, Moderna Museet during Hultén's era is considered to have been one of the most influential and style-defining art venues in the post-war world. For the rest of his career, Pontus Hultén always retained a special respect for those who had made the effort to travel to Stockholm to see what was happening at this strange, storied northern provincial museum.[29] Few if any in the art world would disagree that Moderna Museet during Hultén's era was indeed, as the New York Times wrote in 2021, "the coolest museum on the planet."[30]

What I myself consider the most advanced of all the daring experiments that Pontus Hultén staged at Moderna Museet is the politicization of the museum, this in many respects successful attempt to intervene in society. This expanded role for the museum he would never again achieve in quite the same way at the institutions he would later lead, although conflicts and controversies, including highly political ones, would continue to mark Hultén's career to the end.

Once again, Calvin Tomkins sums it up brilliantly. He first traveled to Stockholm and Moderna Museet in the early sixties to meet Pontus Hultén, on the firm advice of several people in Paris where he was living at the time, including Jean Tinguely, whom Tomkins had first portrayed in The New Yorker in 1959.[31] "Moderna Museet was like nothing else," Tomkins says. "It was just two rooms and totally open — a completely open field that I had never experienced before. It was the idea that art could be anything, the accessibility, that everyone was welcome, everyone could be an artist — that art could be linked to philosophical and political themes. All this was completely new."[32]

Other books can be written about the half century plus that has passed at Moderna Museet since Pontus Hultén departed in 1973. I myself will be brief.

Hultén is partly to blame for the unfortunate reality that, when he left the museum, his creation entered a decades-long gray period of decline, as we must call it, in sad contrast to Hultén's fifteen years of constant spotlight and glamour.

He was succeeded as director by the artist Philip von Schantz, a conventional figurative painter who in retrospect seems a surprising choice. Hultén had not chosen a successor himself. The question is whether he would have had the mandate to appoint one in the inflamed political climate that prevailed.

von Schantz was in turn succeeded in 1978 by Pontus Hultén's colleague Karin Bergqvist Lindegren, whose two years as director are described as conflict-riddled. With several of her exhibitions, Lindegren continued on the path laid out by Hultén to address the activists of the left-wing movement. One can suspect that Lindegren's gender may have played a role in judgments about her as "weak," etcetera.

The whole of the rest of the seventies must be likened to a desert march for the museum, even though many interesting exhibitions were presented during these years. "There was a hangover after Pontus and a hangover after sixty-eight that was devastating," says Olle Granath. "There was a tremendous indifference that affected the museum from all sides. It didn't matter what you did. The radical left held primacy in the media. I was a lone voice in the desert in Dagens Nyheter when I tried to write positively about what was happening at the museum."[33]

Granath, who took over the helm in 1980, was forced to devote much of his energy during his decade as director to restoring the museum's ailing finances, as government funding and visitor numbers had stagnated. He did this most conspicuously with the three super exhibitions of Chagall (1982),[34] Matisse (1984)[35] and Picasso (1988),[36] each of which drew hundreds of thousands of visitors. In all these cases, Granath had good help from Pontus Hultén. "Especially with Chagall and Matisse, the exhibitions would never have been what they were without his efforts and contacts," says Granath. "We presented loads of of interesting exhibitions, but everyone talks only about these classics. It was something we had to do for the economy but also to bring back interest in the museum. I thought the press was going to have a field day when we showed Chagall and was very surprised when they fell flat."[37]

Granath reflects over how the art world changed in the 1980s and how this affected the museum. "It became very different when money came into art in the eighties. Trends also came into the picture, which changed the way exhibitions were made."[38]

In all the years that followed, the museum's "heroic years" and its founder Pontus Hultén were an unpopular, almost taboo topic of conversation among the staff at Moderna Museet. Monica Nieckels, who joined the museum as a communications officer in 1972, the year before Pontus Hultén's exit, serving until 1996, says: "I personally heard every one of his successors try to disparage Pontus. I sat in many big meetings with different directors where they said that 'now we are finally free from the legacy of Pontus Hultén.' I never understood why it was something they wanted to free themselves of — why they weren't proud of this legacy instead?"[39]

When Olle Granath resigned as director in 1989, many people thought, and still think, that the choice of successor should have been the young Lars Nittve, who had made a breakthrough with the highly intellectual postmodern exhibition *Implosion* in 1987,[40] as curator under Granath. The strongest advocate of Nittve was Granath himself. The other main candidate was Dagens Nyheter's art critic Ingela Lind, with support from, among others, the Social Democratic government's women's association but not from the museum staff. According to Olle Granath, the then Minister of Culture, Bengt Göransson, chose Björn Springfeldt instead as a compromise candidate.[41] Springfeldt himself offers a different analysis of the situation: "Granath wanted Nittve, whom he admired boundlessly, but the government chose me because they thought I had a broader competence. My assignment was to create opportunities to build a new museum because the old one was a machine for the destruction of art."[42]

Bengt Göransson largely confirmed this version of Springfeldt's in our conversation. "I have been involved in appointing a number of managers and I have always believed that the most important thing for a manager is to make it work internally in order to be able to fulfill his mission," said Göransson. "Spectacular appointments that the media like usually don't even get access to the manager's room if they don't have the staff with them."[43] Several people I have spoken to in the international art world have asserted that Pontus Hultén acted on behalf of his friend Björn Springfeldt and that this gave rise to a disappointment on Nittve's part towards Hultén, something that Lars Nittve himself firmly denies.

Frankly, I think it is fair to argue that it was only under Lars Nittve's, in some people's opinion, fifteen-year delayed tenure at the museum — after a long detour via the Rooseum, Louisiana and Tate Modern — and later under Daniel Birnbaum's leadership, that the museum managed to break out of the shadow of Pontus Hultén and the legacy of the sixties. The inferiority complexes and tensions in relation to this heritage that I have experienced over the years at the museum have finally begun to subside. The museum has also finally been given at least slightly increased resources and better conditions to defend its position as one of the world's leading museums of modern art and one of our capital's most important destinations and meeting venues. "I never felt any complexes towards Pontus, I just found the legacy inspiring," says Daniel Birnbaum. "I think it has to do with the old truth that it's easier to relate to your grandfather than your father, and Pontus is more like a grandfather to me."[44]

As an afterword to Pontus Hultén's era at Moderna Museet, I must briefly discuss another exceptional exhibition that was presented on a large scale throughout the museum and its surroundings in 1976, three years after Pontus Hultén had left the museum for Paris, during Philip von Schantz's watch as director.

I'm referring to *Ararat*,[45] another manifestation organized in collaboration with a group of activists, this time from the environmental movement that at the time, fueled by the resistance to nuclear power, had begun to grow strong in Stockholm and Sweden. I was captivated by the images from this exhibition during my inventory of Moderna Museet's photographic archives in preparation for the museum's fiftieth anniversary book, *The History Book*, in 2007 and 2008. The photographs depicted hippie culture in peak form, with activists in clogs and beaked boots carving, forging, weaving, knitting, juicing, pickling and brewing in glorious fashion. I could even smell the rich aroma of the seventies as I sat there transfixed by these images. It seemed like a fairy tale that such a spectacle could be staged in a modern art museum. The courtyard in front of the entrance was filled with experimental buildings and greenhouses constructed from discarded wood and other construction elements, with energy sources such as solar panels and windmills, and organic food and drink production from locally cultivated produce.

In the main gallery hall, a monumental structure was erected based on the four elements. A workshop for alternative, sustainable manufacturing techniques and a "recycling laboratory" were also featured, among a plethora of other elements. The exhibition addressed a spectrum of man-made threats to the Earth's survival. It presented a wealth of alternative, ecologically sustainable technologies that were already well developed at the time: in addition to solar and wind power also wave power, geothermal, ocean and waste heat, micro-hydro plants, various engines, generators and means of transportation, recycling and reuse technologies, organic farming methods, alternative technologies for the production of clothing and furniture based on recycling, waste management, water purification, energy flows and holistic life cycling, and much more.

Studying the catalog for *Ararat*, presented in a loose-leaf system, is fascinating and sad. In essence, the texts could have been taken from our contemporary climate debate. It's inevitable to ponder what the health of our planet would have been like if society and industry had listened to this knowledge and its advocates; taken them seriously instead of dismissing them as "forest wonks," "tree huggers," "hippies" and other derogatory epithets that I've heard repeated countless times in the decades since. Then, almost half a century ago, the winters were cold and the freight train of ecological disaster, now blinding us with its headlights, was still only visible on the horizon, for those who wanted to see.

The exhibition title *Ararat* is an E.A.T.-like abbreviation for *Alternative Research in Architecture, Resources, Art and Technology*,[46] but also the name of the mountain where Noah's ark was stranded after the flood in the Old Testament story. How about this statement in the catalog, about the progress of Western industrialism and capitalism in the last century: "The preconditions for this enormous development have been that the rulers of the West have played masters of nature in a way that was previously unthinkable. Industrial and economic progress depended entirely on the ruthless exploitation of the new forms of energy. Predation was primarily focused on the exhaustible fossil fuels. The fact that the world's resources of coal, oil and gas may be exhausted has only recently been recognized. But the environmental poisoning that accompanied this development was known early on. First locally around the coalfields and large industrial areas. Finally, we have observed the global poisoning of the entire biosphere — which in turn causes climate change and deposition even in the most remote wastelands."[47]

It all seemed so far, far ahead of its time, so visionary, utopian and political that I immediately sensed Pontus Hultén's brain in the background. I found it particularly interesting as I have been told by several spokepersons that environmental activism was a movement within the political left that never really engaged Hultén.

Over the years, I therefore asked several people at and outside Moderna Museet about Pontus Hultén's possible involvement in *Ararat*, but no one was aware of any such engagement. Hultén does not list the exhibition in his CV. I have never seen or heard him speak about it. "I can never imagine that he was involved in that exhibition," says

Olle Granath. "For Pontus, art was always the main event, but in this exhibition art was completely overshadowed by all the other stuff."[48]

I was content with these answers until the fall of 2018, when I met in a social context the set designer and director Jan Öqvist, one of the activists behind *Ararat*, along with old acquaintances such as Hans Nordenström and Bo "Bobo" Lagercrantz. "Of course it was Pontus!" said Öqvist. "It was he who commissioned the exhibition from us while he was still at the museum. Then it took three years to produce it."[49]

Öqvist's depiction is confirmed by several other participants and surviving relatives.[50] The general picture is that *Ararat* emerged from an idea by Hans Nordenström, which he discussed and developed with Pontus Hultén. The production collective, initially seven or eight people, including several architects, was allocated space at Torpedverkstaden, next to the studio that Hultén kept for himself until he moved to Paris after the summer of 1973. Over time, the collective grew to more than three hundred volunteers. "It was incredibly dynamic and so timely," says architect Varis Bokalders, one of the original production group members.[51] "We were inspired by the environmental conference in Stockholm in 1972, where many new insights had been raised." The exhibition was based on a journey to the United States by Hans Nordenström and his wife Monica Nordenström, together with other stakeholders and students, funded by research grants. Here the group studied the latest environmental technology, with many new inventions that were then unknown in Sweden. "The US was a leader in environmental technology in the seventies — a position it lost completely in the eighties," says Varis Bokalders.[52]

Björn Springfeldt and his wife Milla Trägårdh Springfeldt, registrar and close associate of Pontus Hultén, were also part of the original *Ararat* team. "I remember that there were two camps in the working group — one that sought to show how destroyed the earth was and one that wanted to demonstrate the possibilities," says Milla Trägårdh Springfeldt. "Pontus was of course attracted to highlighting the utopian possibilities. That's what he wanted to focus on."[53]

After the initiation phase, Pontus Hultén had little to do with the preparation and production of *Ararat*, other than, presumably, as an

The United Nations Conference on the Human Environment, also known as the Stockholm Conference, June 5–16, 1972, was the first international environmental conference. The conference is widely regarded as a starting point for global awareness of the environment. The historic conference was commemorated in early summer 2022, when the fifty-year anniversary conference UN Stockholm +50 meeting was held.

informal interlocutor. After the exhibition, which was a tremendous box office success, had closed in Stockholm, Hultén arranged for parts of *Ararat* to be shown at the newly established Architecture Biennale at the Venice Biennale, for which he had been appointed as an consultant. Hultén served as creative advisor for a relaunch of the Biennale, the world's oldest, which had been languishing after conflicts triggered at the 1968 Biennale. Jan Öqvist recounts a terrifying anecdote: in the Italian pavilion near the Swedish pavilion, the organizers were about to install Alexander Calder's famous 1937 mercury fountain. Öqvist was horrified to see tubes of mercury stacked in the exhibition hall, ready to be poured into the fountain. He explained to Hultén that the fumes from the openly exposed mercury would be absolutely lethal and cause irreversible damage to visitors. Hultén immediately understood the gravity of the situation and stopped the installation.

With all this information, *Ararat* must be added to Pontus Hultén's list of achievements. Placing the museum at the disposal of the environmental movement and the new alternative ecological thinking in this way — as he had done for children, the left-wing, peace, and women's movements, the fight against racism, activists for the Third World and others — appears, in our times of climate crisis and environmental collapse, to be magnificently visionary, contradicting, as do several of his own statements, claims that the environment had been a "blind spot," like feminism, in Hultén's political commitment.

18 A new horizon in Paris

How in hell did it happen that the founding director of the world's first mega-museum for modern art, at the Centre Pompidou in Paris, that sensation that echoed far beyond the art world, was a bloody *Swede*; a brute of the barren northern backlands from where those fish-stinking Vikings once came roaring in; and such a deeply controversial, political and in every way contentious person as Pontus Hultén?

This was the question I asked myself already during Pontus Hultén's tenure as director of the Musée National d'Art Moderne at the Centre Pompidou in the late seventies and early eighties, when as a teenager I frequently visited to Paris, serving as a helper, farmhand and family member of a count and countess at a chateau northwest of the city, and becoming familiar from the inside with the animated French nationalist chauvinism and superiority.

Regrettably, I wasn't mature enough to even consider waiting my way through the crazy queues that constantly snaked throughout the Place Beaubourg to any of Hultén's landmark exhibitions. During those years I saw the museum, or the cultural center as it is properly labeled, only from the outside, with the incomparably sparkling scene of street performers, jesters and folk life in the courtyard in front of its fabulous facade, on the face of which the crowds continued to flow in escalators and on "outdoor streets" among the building's monstrous ventilation pipes, electrical installations and all. These impressions were more than enough to arouse a strong attraction for the building whose equivalent I have still not seen, despite its long succession of more or less impressive "logotype" edifices for the arts. I still remember my first encounter with the center as one of the most awesome urban shocks of my youth. Appearing without warning, right smack in the heart of old Paris, it made an otherworldly impression. The radicalness of daring to erect such a monstrous creation in this setting — where Paris has a powerful tradition since the Eiffel Tower and before — heightened my admiration for the metropolis' creative culture.

The most important part of the answer to the question of how Pontus Hultén could be chosen for this pioneering task is self-evident. It lies, of course, in the history of Moderna Museet, at that time undisputed among international connoisseurs in its position as the world's most progressive and innovative museum for modern art. This background is far from sufficient as explanation. It is, after all, Paris, where the degree of complexity is of different proportions than in Stockholm. It therefore requires a longer account, starting appropriately at the highest level, with President Georges Pompidou, regarded in French history as one of the Republic's greatest post-war statesmen.

Georges Pompidou came from a modest background in the small town of Montboudif. He was educated as a literature teacher at the École Normale Supérieure in Paris. During his studies, Pompidou met his wife Claude, who would become almost as important to Pontus Hultén's career as the President himself, also from an upper-middle-class family. Claude Cahour, her given name, studied law at the same university in Paris.

Pompidou worked as a literature teacher at secondary schools in Marseilles and Paris before the outbreak of the war, when he enlisted. In 1944, Pompidou's life changed dramatically when, after writing a request, he was introduced to the leader of the French Resistance, General Charles de Gaulle, the future President and very symbol of heroic French nationalism.

Shortly after this first meeting, Pompidou joined de Gaulle's staff. He seems to have immediately gained the general's unbounded confidence. Without any political experience, he proved to be the one who best understood de Gaulle's ideas and how to translate them into realpolitik. He soon rose to become one of the future president's most trusted advisers. Pompidou remained a member of de Gaulle's shadow cabinet after the general unexpectedly resigned as head of government in 1946.

In 1955, Georges Pompidou abruptly changed careers a second time when he was recruited by Baron Guy de Rothschild for the Rothschild Bank. He must have been an unusual high school literature teacher because in this position too, again with no experience, he quickly rose to become the bank's managing director in 1959.

Charles de Gaulle had maintained close contact with Pompidou. When the general returned as head of government in the summer of 1958 during the Algerian crisis, he hired Pompidou as his personal assistant. Pompidou would play a historic role as a negotiator in the process that led to the end of the Algerian War of Independence a few years later, where de Gaulle finally realized not only the defeat but also the course of history and went against the ultra-nationalist far right. When de Gaulle was proclaimed president in 1959, Pompidou returned to his civil service at Rothschild, but without giving up politics. In 1961, he was resummoned by de Gaulle to hold the crucial secret final negotiations with the Algerian Freedom Front (FLN), which eventually led to an armistice, peace and the liberation of Algeria in 1962.

When Michel Debré resigned as Prime Minister in protest at the peace settlement, de Gaulle proved his complete confidence in Pompidou by appointing him as his successor — a head of government who still had hardly any political experience. The appointment was politically controversial as Pompidou was not a member of the National Assembly. He was rejected in a vote of confidence, but de Gaulle dissolved Parliament and Pompidou was reinstated as Prime Minister. In this position, Pompidou instantly proved his worth. He retained this hot chair for seven years, making him the longest serving Prime Minister in modern times and the best French Prime Minister of the post-war era.

With the sixty-eight revolution, Pompidou's skills as a negotiator were put to a new crucial test. In Paris, unlike in Stockholm, the term revolution is justified. Barricades were burning and cobblestones broken up in the Latin Quarter. Curiously, workers across the country joined the spontaneous student revolt, which can be defined from the outset as a rebellion against the conservatism, rigidity and moralism, not least sexual, of de Gaulle's economically prosperous post-war France (the revolt was triggered by a demand from students to be allowed to share rooms with their opposite-sex partners). Eight million workers defied their own unions and went on a wild strike. Pompidou's younger colleague and later successor Jacques Chirac carried a revolver in his coat pocket when negotiating with the strikers' representatives. The government is said to have prepared an evacuation at the most critical time at the end of May 1968.

This crisis led to a conflict between de Gaulle and Pompidou. Pompidou could not forgive de Gaulle for having secretly traveled to

Baden-Baden in what was then West Germany at the height of the revolt on May 29. Wild rumors abounded that de Gaulle had been deposed in a military coup, but in fact the purpose of the President's trip was to meet with France's top military leadership to ensure its loyalty in order to crush the rebellion by force if necessary. Meanwhile, Pompidou and his staff negotiated the explosive conflict through the crisis to a peaceful resolution.

When the then 79-year-old de Gaulle stepped down as president in 1969, the year before his sudden death, he was succeeded by Pompidou, who won a landslide victory over the opposing candidate from the center democrats, interim president Alain Poher. As President, despite representing de Gaulle's political camp, Pompidou pursued a more pragmatic, less bombastic nationalist policy than his grandiose predecessor and former boss. Pompidou inscribed himself in history for, among other achievements, breaking with de Gaulle's hard-line nationalist doctrines and improving strained relations with the United States, as well as enabling Britain's entry into the EU, which de Gaulle had blocked for fear of jeopardizing France's strong position and "authority" in the European Community. Pompidou pursued and expanded de Gaulle's investment in infrastructure during an era of runaway growth and urbanization, when the number of farmers in France from the end of the war to the mid-sixties fell from seven to three million (now about half a million). The modernization of the capital, Paris, where the future Centre Pompidou was the most spectacular prestige project, also rank among Pompidou's many accomplishments as Prime Minister and President.

After being elected president, Georges Pompidou declined to move into the Élysée Palace. The presidential couple opted to remain in their apartment on the Quai de Béthune on the Île Saint-Louis, the discreetly elegant "little sister" of the Île de la Cité, the most exclusive district of Paris, and as far as possible maintain their private social life, especially in cultural circles. They themselves had built a fine, if not opulent, art collection that included mainly paintings from the broad Post-Cubist movement "École de Paris"[1] but also more experimental elements. Claude Pompidou's personal favorite artist was Yves Klein, the prodigy leader of the Parisian avant-garde of the 1950s and 1960s.

"The Pompidous' interest in art was really genuine — they weren't at all like all those people in power who just think it looks good to be seen in an art context," says curator and museum official Jean-Hubert Martin, Pontus Hultén's younger colleague and later successor as director of the Musée National d'Art Moderne at the Centre Pompidou (1987–1990). "When we worked at the old Musée National d'Art Moderne in the Palais de Tokyo and guided Pompidou on a tour, he would ask us about young artists that we ourselves had not heard of but had to look up afterwards."[2]

Georges Pompidou's idea of creating something new in the old market district around the Les Halles, The Halls, on both sides of the Boulevard de Sébastopol thoroughfare, was conceived already during his time at the Banque Rothschild in the 1950s. The area was dilapidated, stinking and downright unhealthy, populated only by rats, thieves and whores, as the Parisian saying went. Pompidou passed the area every day as his chauffeur drove him between his home on Île Saint-Louis and the bank's headquarters on Rue du Faubourg Saint-Honoré. Pompidou, like many others, considered the whole area a disgrace to the capital of the French Republic. When he left the bank to enter politics as Prime Minister, he was determined to do something for this disreputable area in the center of Paris.

Pompidou's original idea was reportedly a new kind of combined library and art salon, inspired by the reading rooms that existed in Britain in particular. At the time, there was no public library in Paris or in France as a whole. When Pompidou became president in 1969, he immediately began the planning process, having pushed through the decision as Prime Minister to move the food markets from the center of Paris to Rungis in the southwestern suburbs. Pompidou's determination to do something positive to channel the frustrated energy of the sixty-eight movement that had recently risen in revolt intensified the President's commitment to this venture.

Over time, the vision for the new cultural center evolved. In addition to the French national museum of modern art, Musée National d'Art Moderne (MNAM), and the library, Bibliothèque publique d'information (Bpi), much later named Bibliothèque Kandinsky — the first major public library in France — the industrial design center Centre de Création Industrielle (CCI) was also included. A fourth institution added during the planning process was the Institut de Recherche et Coordination Acoustique/Musique (IRCAM), led by the later world-famous French composer and conductor Pierre Boulez.

Originally, the new cultural center was to be located at the current location of the Les Halles hub, which was lowered into the ground with the new metro entrance. Various considerations prompted the decision-makers to change the location to the east of Boulevard de

Sébastopol at Place Beaubourg, or Plateau Beaubourg as it was then called, at the time a parking lot surrounded by dilapidated buildings with bars, brothels, cheap hotels and murky housing. The blighted area was adjacent to the old historic Marais quarter dating back to the 1300s, for centuries a fashionable neighborhood among royalty and nobility, which by this time had long lost its chic status and fallen into disrepair.

An often repeated misunderstanding, even in writing, is that Pontus Hultén became director of the Centre Pompidou. This was not the case. He was appointed as the first director of the French national museum of modern art, the Musée National d'Art Moderne (MNAM), in its new, expanded form at the Centre Pompidou. With its success, the museum became dominant within the new center but was administratively only one of the four institutions to be housed in the new cultural center. In the original vision, the museum and the library had roughly equal priority.[3]

The new National Museum of Modern Art would be a merger of the old MNAM, then located in a wing of the Palais de Tokyo building on Avenue du Président Wilson, near the Jardins du Trocadéro on the right bank of the river, and the Centre National d'Art Contemporain (CNAC), an art gallery founded in 1967 on the initiative of André Malraux, de Gaulle's Minister of Culture, to exhibit and purchase contemporary art on behalf of other institutions, without a permanent collection of its own, housed in the Hôtel Salomon de Rothschild, a private palace on Rue Berryer near the Champs-Élysées. In addition, the new MNAM incorporated the contemporary art exhibition program previously hosted at the Musée des Arts Décoratifs in the Louvre.

The old MNAM in the Palais de Tokyo was a sclerotic museum with low attendance. The museum had been surrounded by scandal since its creation just before the Second World War. The gloomy, remote neoclassical wing building was delayed and flawed when it was finally completed. The basement included a cinema that had never been used and other oddities. In summer, the museum became unbearably hot. At the turn of the 1970s, modern art was still a phenomenon outside the everyday life and perception of the "ordinary Parisian," not to mention the Frenchman — a matter concerning only a small clique. Within this isolated establishment, modern art still primarily meant Cubism and its predecessors, especially Matisse, Picasso and Braque.

There were gaping holes in the museum's collection for movements such as early abstract art, the Russian avant-garde, and most conspicuously for Surrealism and Dadaism, where the two great French Dadaists, Marcel Duchamp and Francis Picabia, were blatantly absent. In the early 1970s, Duchamp was still a forgotten, neglected artist in Paris, represented by only one work[4] in a museum collection in his home country. His friend Picabia was utterly discredited. Neither was taken seriously by the Parisian art establishment. Post-war international avant-garde art, primarily American, both Abstract Expressionism and its successors Neo-Dadaism and Pop Art, had been almost entirely ignored by French institutions.

The MNAM had finally been opened at the end of the war, after wartime delays, with resistance hero Jean Cassou as its first director. The museum had been important and vital at first but then gradually stagnated during Cassou's twenty years as director. Hultén himself spoke about Cassou, who became a sworn enemy of him and everything he stood for: "Cassou was a strange man and a strict Stalinist. I met him in 1962 at my Strindberg exhibition[5] but he was always alien to me. Then, when I came to Paris, he did everything to oppose me, not only in the museum but also outside. (...) I think Cassou's reservations were mainly about my nationality."[6]

According to Jean-Hubert Martin and many others with whom I have spoken, it was President Pompidou himself who recognized the stalemate which modern art had been lulled into in the former world capital of the arts. He understood the importance for the country as a whole of breaking this deadlock.

The planning of the building itself, the Centre Beaubourg, or Centre national d'art et de culture Georges-Pompidou as its full name came to read (in telling contrast to what Pontus Hultén called the unbureaucratic, "slightly provocative" name of Moderna Museet in Stockholm), began a couple of years before the recruitment process for the management started. As the newly appointed founding director of the new MNAM in 1973, Pontus Hultén thus entered the project too late to decisively influence the building's exterior or its location. He was only able to exert significant influence on the museum's interior solutions — something he later pointed out and regretted on several occasions.

Although the museum was only one of the institutions of the planned cultural center, the ambitions were grandiose in the spirit of the French superpower aspirations. The new museum was to be the largest in the world for modern art (which it still is, with the largest modern art collection in Europe[7]), comparable only to the Museum of Modern Art in New York, which was of course the new museum's main benchmark. Georges Pompidou may have been toned down in his chauvinism compared to his predecessor de Gaulle, but certainly the grand nationalist pride was a factor behind in the quest to regain a position of strength that France had lost. There was also an intricate global political agenda at play — one that seems remote in an age when the political potency of art has been drained away — as presidential son Alain Pompidou pointed out when I met him in Paris: "Art was a tool of the Cold War. Both the CIA, the KGB and the French security services were interested in having leading roles in international art. My father was part of that game."[8]

In August 1970, Robert Bordaz, one of the leading French political officials, was appointed as "delegate for the realization of the Centre du Plateau Beabourg." In 1972, Bordaz's position as president of the "public establishment Centre Beaubourg" was formalized.

Robert Bordaz belonged to an exclusive elite of the French political administration. He also held a high position in Masonic circles, which would prove helpful for the Centre Pompidou. Bordaz had access to the innermost closed rooms of the Parisian power elite where many decisions were made in secret. His background in the Resistance was an asset in this sphere of power. In the 1950s, he had come to know and be influenced by Le Corbusier. In the early 1960s, he was appointed Director-General of the French state radio and television. He was one of the organizers of the French exhibition in Moscow in 1961 and political officer of the French pavilion at the Montreal World Fair in 1967, where Niki de Saint Phalle's and Jean Tinguely's "Paradise," which later ended up in Stockholm, was erected on the roof.

In connection with this event, Bordaz was acquainted with Pontus Hultén for the first time, which may have played a role in Hultén being chosen a few years later as the new museum's first director, although this is not something I have confirmed. When the Centre Pompidou opened in 1977, Robert Bordaz was its first president. In his loathing of bureaucracy and bureaucrats, Hultén made an exception for Bordaz — and for the French bureaucracy in general: "Centre Pompidou was a unique project where the strength of the political vision was matched by the power of the administrative implementation," he said. "Bordaz was an extremely nice and sophisticated man. He and his colleagues were incredibly skilled. In France, in a completely different way than in Sweden, bureaucracy can really be a fine art."[9]

Georges Pompidou and his trusted chief official Robert Bordaz (and Pompidou's wife Claude) had many unusual qualities and characteristics. One of the most important was the global perspective they shared with Pontus Hultén, so much rarer at those times, especially in nationalist France. In 1971, when the newly founded institution "The Public Establishment Centre Beaubourg" announced an architectural competition for the new building complex, it took the extraordinary step of inviting architects from all over the world to submit entries.

Launching an architectural competition for such an assignment at all was unusual. The global invitation was sensational. It was the first time in French history that an international architectural competition had been organized, with a jury that was also international. The initiative was, of course, highly controversial, not only among French architects, who soon organized a protest movement, but also in the media, in the dreaded French trade union movement, in public opinion and, in particular, in the sixty-eight movement. The President and his staff were aware that French architecture, like the country's creative culture in general, was in a deep slump.

The jury appointed to judge the six hundred and eighty-one entries received from all around the globe — a staggering number — was unprecedented. Presiding over the nine-man group (of course, the jury was one hundred percent male — the international window may have been opened slightly, but the feminist one was still firmly shut) was Pompidou's confidant Jean Prouvé, the great self-taught French interior and industrial designer, and architect, a leading figure in French Modernist design and architecture. With his name and aura, Prouvé donned the jury and the competition unquestionable authority.

The three international jury members were all superstars. Two of them were architects. The first was Philip Johnson, the great American post-war Modernist and the designer of many of the most famous skyscrapers and other historic buildings in New York and other American cities. Johnson was deeply connected in the art world, in the US and also in Europe, with roots going back to the Bauhaus, and close ties to the Museum of Modern Art, where, as curator, he had organized the museum's first architecture exhibitions in the 1930s. The other was the Brazilian Oscar Niemeyer, the creator of the largest realized utopian urban development project in world history: the Brazilian capital Brasilia, a brutally futuristic tropical metropolis unparalleled in either architectural or world history.

So there was nothing wrong with the utopian level of the international part of the architecture jury. It was further elevated by its third non-French member: an old acquaintance, Willem Sandberg, the pioneer and nestor among post-war museum directors and curators; Pontus Hultén's own mentor.

Of the competition's sensational winners, British architect Richard Rogers was thirty-seven years old when the competition was announced in July 1971. His Italian partner Renzo Piano was thirty-three. Rogers had started his career in London partnering with his later world-famous compatriot Sir Norman Foster. He had made a name for himself among architects for some smaller buildings, including the house in south London that he had designed for his parents in 1967 and which, with its radical flexibility and innovation, is considered one of the starting points for the Centre Pompidou. Rogers came into contact with Renzo Piano, born and raised in Genoa in a family of builders and engineers, trained as an architect in Milan, after Rogers had admired his younger colleague's Italian industrial pavilion with its high-tech lightweight steel and aluminum construction at the 1970 Osaka World Expo. This exhibition pavilion, inspired by naval architecture and his father's construction sites in Genoa, is another of the Centre Pompidou's core references, with parts of its light steel structure clearly visible outside the building's facade. The two founded their partnering architectural practice in London in 1971.

The Rogers-Piano duo's first joint building was the prestigious Italian interior design company B&B Italia's headquarters in Novedrate near Como in Lombardy, northwest Italy, completed in 1973. The B&B Italia building is a single-story structure evocative of the Centre Pompidou, with eye-catching, aggressively colored elements of the building's construction and technical infrastructure positioned as eye-catchers along its facade.

At the time of the Centre Beaubourg architectural competition, Rogers and Piano were working in their small, newly formed architectural office in London with another Italian architect, Gianfranco Franchini, as a third partner. During our conversation in London, Richard Rogers tells me that he himself was reluctant to enter the competition as he thought the chances of winning were non-existent. "We were young and completely unknown, none of us had built a structure with more than one floor," Rogers says. "I didn't think there was any point in spending time on this. But I was outvoted by the others."[10]

It's common knowledge that Rogers, Piano and Franchini did not come up with the idea of submitting an entry to the competition themselves, but were persuaded by the Danish-British engineer Ove Arup, founder of the young architects' partner, the London-based engineering firm Ove Arup & Partners,[11] who stood behind the entry together with the architects.

Ove Arup's role in the realization of the project should not be underestimated. The Centre Pompidou has made history as a building with an extreme combination of architecture and engineering. Arup was the world's foremost post-war structural engineer, with a more than impressive list of architectural milestone buildings and infrastructural installations to his credit. Legend has it that Arup paid for the production of Roger and Piano's competition entry — and that this entry was posted at the very last moment after the architects at the post office had been forced to frantically cut their sketches down in size to fit into the tubes minutes before closing time. Parts of the item were later returned due to insufficient postage; Piano managed to persuade the post office to take back the package with the original postmark after adding stamps ...

The proposal submitted by the tiny, untested firm in competition with the leading architectural bureaus of France, Europe and North America was ultra-radical in every aspect.

Richard Rogers and Renzo Piano shared with Pontus Hultén the utopian dream of art and architecture as tools for achieving higher political and cultural purposes — a vision harking back to Tatlin and Constructivism, among other mutual references. The young architect partners were, of course, both politically radical, anarchist-minded members of the sixty-eight movement which greatly influenced the design of their building.

The sources of inspiration for Rogers and Piano's design for the Centre Pompidou have been the subject of voluminous analysis. It's given that the influence of the British avant-garde architecture of the 1960s, represented by the Archigram collective and its unrealized sketches and models of future cities and societies, is striking.

The most obvious and direct reference, though, is Cedric Price and his "Fun Palace," an edifice that was actually seriously proposed for construction by this architectural pioneer who built very little but whose innovative sketches and ideas influenced Rogers, Rem Koolhaas and many of the greatest architects of the late twentieth and twenty-first centuries. The "Fun Palace" was Cedric Price's solution to a proposal of creating a "laboratory for fun" in East London. Price's vision was to offer maximized flexibility and freedom for creative expression and human interaction through innovative technology. The complex would include spaces for theater, dance, film and fireworks (!). Conspicuously reminiscent of the Centre Pompidou in its design, Price's 1964 proposal was even more uncompromising than the epochal building it came to inspire: an open steel structure with no facades or internal floors, ceilings or walls, inside and outside of which construction cranes would lift visitors and various building elements to create an infinite variety of new spatialities and venues for different, ever-changing purposes, contexts, events and manifestations. Some architectural historians and critics have called the Centre Pompidou a plagiarism of Cedric Price's "Fun Palace," arguing that Price's fate would be the all-too-familiar lot for the eccentric visionary — to see his ideas exploited in due course by other driven, more opportune players.

Richard Rogers is not too enthusiastic talking about these role models when I ask about them during our conversation — questions that he has, of course, been asked countless times in the four decades since he and Piano (Franchini was involved in the competition entry but fell away during the execution of the building) shocked the world with perhaps the most canonized, controversial and transformative building in modern architectural history. Rogers has acknowledged that he and Piano "stood on the shoulders" of Archigram and Cedric Price,[12] but in our conversation doesn't mention these known connections, reluctantly citing instead a few other historic buildings, including The Palm House in Kew Gardens[13] and Crystal Palace,[14] both in London.

Rather than detailing architectural references, Richard Rogers has talked about how the building's design was influenced by the sixty-eight movement of which he, Piano and the whole project were a part. In a 2013 interview, Rogers highlights how the revolutionary spirit of the movement shaped the building and its architecture: "That time almost changed history, definitely for Europe. It looked like it was going to be a revolution. In the end, it never happened. But we captured something of it in the building."[15]

It has been written that Renzo Piano's and Richard Roger's Centre Pompidou flipped the world of architecture upside down. Others have noted that the correct depiction is that they turned it inside out. The building's architectural solution set the stage for what became known as "inside-out architecture," or, more graphically, "bowels-out architecture."

One of the conditions of the architectural competition was a building that would be flexible for different types of exhibitions and events — partly because the program for the cultural centre had not yet been developed when the competition was announced. In their proposal, Piano and Rogers spectacularly met this requirement by simply turning the building inside out and placing its supporting framework and technical infrastructure on the outside of its all-glass facade — "a glass box enclosed in a steel skeleton" as the center has been called. This achieved, in addition to the building's shockingly monstrous exterior, double football field-sized floors[16] free of vertical barriers, within which screen walls could be swiftly moved around to create spatialities for various purposes.

The construction's engineering solution was at once simple and high-tech, based on a system of prefabricated steel tubes, beams and couplings bolted into a sophisticated grid as the supporting structure. A stroke of genius was the idea of placing the glass facade three meters inside the steel skeleton, thus preserving the unbrokenness of the facade while making room for a transport infrastructure on its exterior, with the trademark glass tube-enclosed escalators and open corridors, or "streets," from which audiences are offered panoramic views of Paris, as well as a system of elevators for the transport of goods at the back facing Rue Beaubourg. The building has been likened to a giant mechanical kit and was conceived as such, with new units that could be added to the structure — an advanced form of kit construction of the kind Piano had presented with his industrial pavilion in Osaka, though never used for extensions in practice.

Piano's and Roger's proposal was radical in yet another crucial quality, beyond the building's interior solutions and exterior appearance. The young architectural duo's competition entry was the only one of the six hundred and eighty-one in which the authors chose to place their structure not in the center of the site provided by the city of Paris and the French state, but along the eastern front of that site, forming a monumental wall against the adjacent historic Marais district with its network of narrow streets and alleys, leaving a generous sloping open space in front of the submerged building, the urban stage Place Beaubourg, called the "Piazza."

In his massive article on Pontus Hultén and the Centre Pompidou in The New Yorker in January 1978,[17] Calvin Tomkins quotes Richard Rogers as saying that the young architects decided from the beginning to

P. 324: President Georges Pompidou, Paris, 1970.

P. 325: Centre Pompidou under construction, c. 1975.

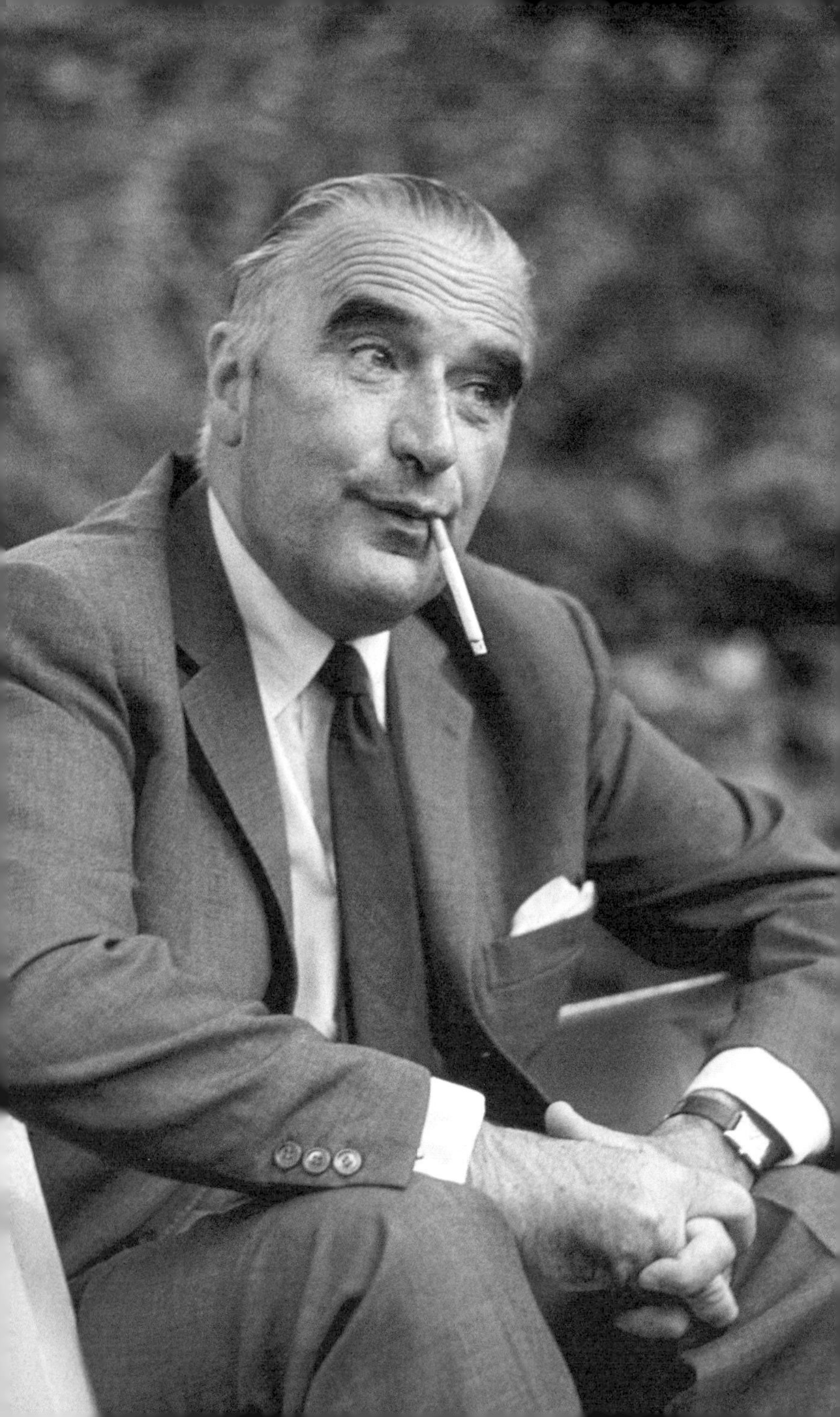

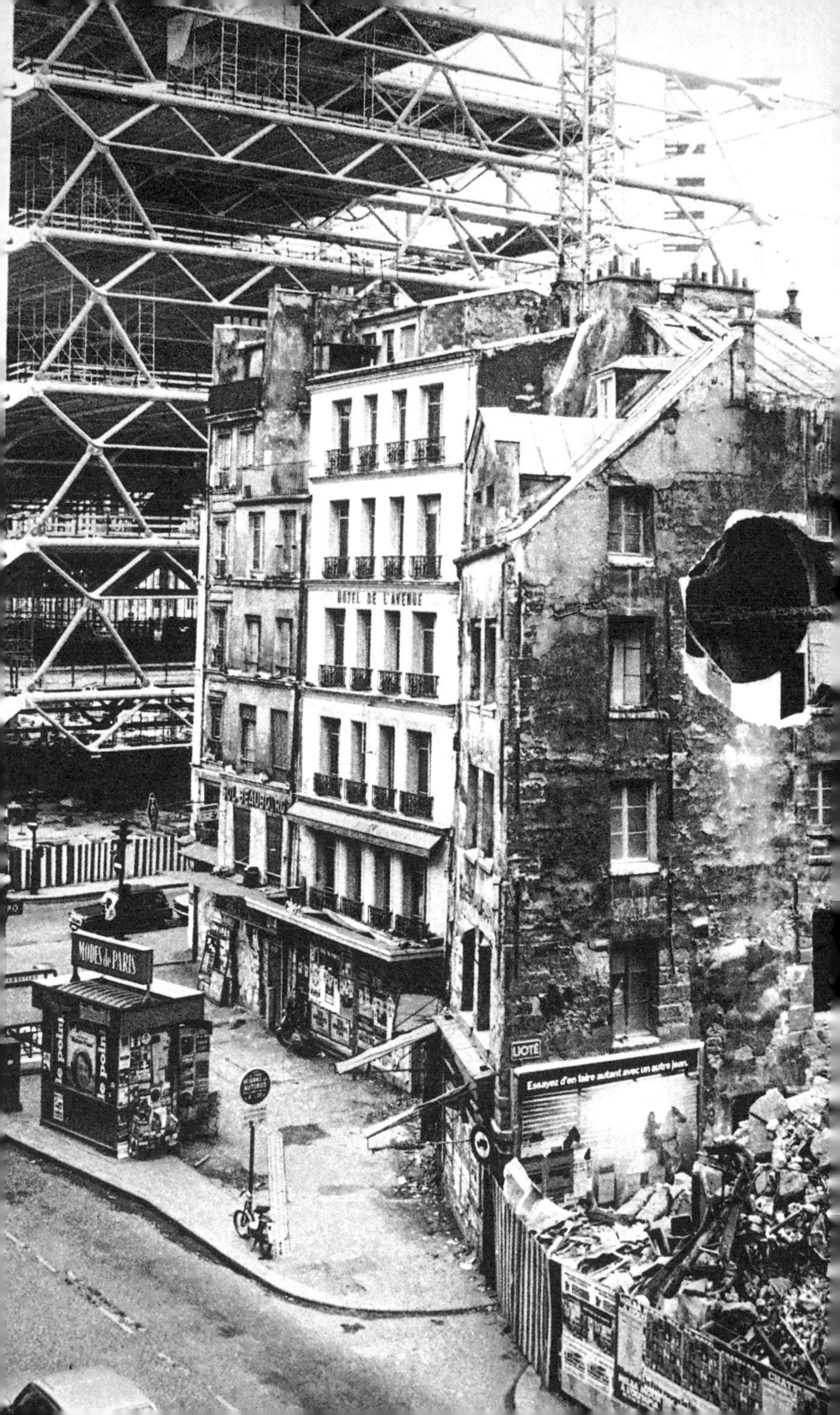
HOTEL DE L'AVENUE
MODES de PARIS
le point
LIOTÉ
Essayez d'en faire autant avec un autre jean.

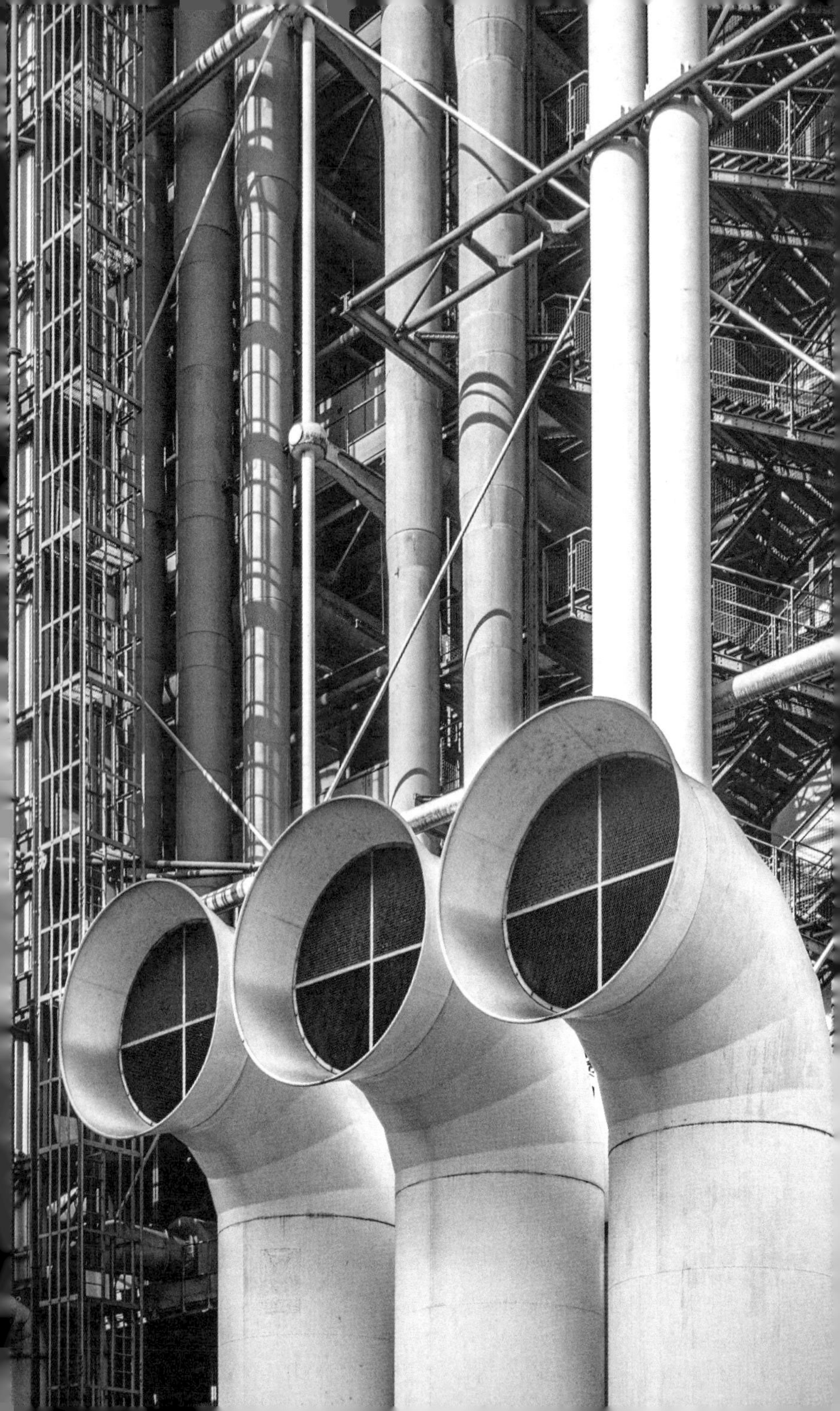

expand the future center's function as a home for a number of cultural institutions to include an additional element of "entertainment," in order to broaden the center's target audience and increase its appeal. Initially, a budget was set aside for the center to stage various events on the piazza. This ambition fell by the wayside during the project's production, but was fulfilled through an endless array of spontaneous performances, happenings, events and more by Paris's army of street performers, jugglers, fire-eaters, impersonators and other actors and entertainers.

I've always been intrigued by how the layout of this glass building and its relationship to the open piazza in front is reminiscent of Peter Celsing's architecture for the Kulturhuset and Sergels torg a few years earlier, for which Celsing was unable to fully realize his vision. At my meeting with Richard Rogers, I asked him about this. He admitted that he had seen Kulturhuset before the Beaubourg building was conceived, and that he liked the architecture, but denied that what could have become the sister institution in Stockholm was one of his and Piano's sources of inspiration. Instead, he does mention an obvious common reference for both complexes, the Piazza del Campo in Sienna, with the sloping piazza in front of the fourteenth-century town hall.[18]

In the interview quoted above, Rogers explains his and Piano's vision with its contemporary counterpart in Paris: "When we did our first studies, it turned out that there were no public spaces in the area," says Rogers. "We created the big piazza. (…) It's really central to the function of the Pompidou. We said we would not put the building in the middle but on one side, because it gives people a place to meet. The idea was to have a public space, and then you go up the facade on streets in the air, with escalators floating above it, so the whole thing is very dynamic. People come to see people along with the art: people come to meet people. We wanted to stage this as a theater."[19]

In an interview in 2017, on the occasion of the 40th anniversary of the Centre Pompidou, Renzo Piano states that they wanted to create "not a building but a city where you could find everything you were looking for — lunch, great art, a library, great music." In the same article, Piano reveals that part of the reluctance to enter the architectural competition had been due to the fact that Rogers in particular had assumed that the building was intended to be "a rhetorical gesture of grandeur," something which they, in their sixty-eight spirit, did not want to participate in, but that they had changed their minds after studying the composition of the jury — in particular that this jury

Centre Pompidou, Paris, 2022.

included Jean Prouvé, a man "who cared more about low-cost housing than about monuments." Piano says in the interview that "we saw that it could also be about ethics, people, society. We were young but not stupid. We saw some sign of a possible miracle."[20]

The contrasts could hardly be starker between the visions of this "city," this "popular theater," this wide-open public arena, and the closed, elitist French museum world of the time, which catered exclusively to the already initiated.

One usually mandatory requirement specification that was conspicuously absent from the instructions for the Centre Beaubourg architectural competition was the budget. Contestants were not required to specify what their proposal would cost to realize. The project was allowed to cost as much as required out of state money — a unique condition for a venture of this kind that also shows the importance President Pompidou attached to this personal life project.

It's a testament to its competence, vision and integrity that the jury dared to select as the winner, from the overwhelming number of proposals from France's and the world's most renowned architectural enterprises, by far the most radical of all, from a constellation of young, unknown Italian architects (Richard Rogers was also born and raised in Italy) based in London.

Consensus seems to have ruled among the architects and other members of the jury that Piano and Rodger's proposal was simply superior to all others. In my interview, Richard Rogers told me that it was Philip Johnson, whom he had met in other contexts before the competition, who had championed their proposal, as Johnson had later confided to him.[21] Johnson is also said to have ensured that the winning proposal would actually be built, with his idea that the jury would not award a second prize but twenty-nine third prizes.[22] What President Pompidou personally thought of the building I have no record of, but he accepted without question the jury's decision with the oft-quoted laconic comment "My God, it will cause a lot of screaming"[23] — a prophecy that would come true in spades.

Architectural historians have incorporated Piano and Roger's Centre Pompidou in a trend in the late 1960s and early 1970s called "megastructures" — a kind of extreme version of the late functionalist movement of brutalism; building complexes of a kind reminiscent of Futurism's fantasy of urban mega-organisms encroaching on the urban fabric. The idea of placing the building along the flank of the plot rather than in its center also has British precedents, such as the

1968 Byker Wall housing estate by the British architect Ralph Erskine, who spent most of his career in Sweden, where the long building with a closed north facade shields the Newcastle housing estate from cold North Sea winds, creating a sheltered environment with its own favorable microclimate for the residents on the inside.

Another epithet that has frequently been used to classify the Centre Pompidou is high-tech. The building is seen as a source for the stream of high-tech buildings still flowing, especially museums and other "logotype" buildings. Renzo Piano rejects this classification, depicting the complex in poetic twists and turns, complete with the maritime references as the Genoa son and high sea sailor that he is: "Beaubourg is a joyful urban machine," he says in the interview, "a creature that could have come from a Jules Verne novel, a sort of bizarre ship in a dry dock. (...) It is a double provocation, a challenge to academia but also a parody of the idealized image of technology in our time. To regard it as a high-tech object is a mistake."[24]

Inevitably, Piano's statement brings to mind a specific affinity — of course, Pontus Hultén's, Jean Tinguely's and their admired Dadaist predecessors' obsession with industrialist technological developments and machine romanticism, with their own "ironic machines." In my interview, Renzo Piano smilingly confirmed that he and Rogers joined Hultén and Tinguely in this peculiar passion for large-scale "machine humor." "We loved *useless* machines," as he declared.[25] In actuality, the entire fabulous creation of the Centre Pompidou can be seen as just that — something as glorious as a monstrously elegant parody of industrialist developmental optimism, an enormous Neo-Dadaist installation embedded in the historic center of Paris.

Unsurprisingly, Piano and Roger's winning proposal immediately upset a hurricane of fierce negative reactions when it was presented to the media and the public in 1971. The shock to Parisians was enormous. The building was popularly dubbed "the oil refinery," a nickname — among many — that the center retained throughout its construction. The choir of negative criticism of the new cultural center and its architecture would continue resounding in all tunes and media through the planning and construction process, and long after the building was inaugurated. Le Figaro wrote that Paris had created its own monster, "just like Loch Ness" while Le Monde called the building "a rape" and an "architectural King Kong." In several interviews, Richard Rogers has said that "not a positive word" was uttered about the building before its opening in 1977 when it was seized by Parisians. In the 2013 interview quoted above, he recounts an anecdote: "I remember once standing outside on a rainy day and there was a little lady with an umbrella offering me shelter," Rogers says. "We started talking, as one does in the rain, and she asked 'what do you think of this building?' I foolishly said that I had designed it and she hit me on the head with her umbrella."[26]

Remarkably, Piano and Rogers were able to guide their building through the entire Parisian planning and construction process without major compromise of their basic ideas, although compromise is the norm in projects of this kind. The complex as it was realized looks essentially like Studio Piano & Rogers' first model, which I admired in the small model museum in Rogers' London office. That the revolutionary architecture was able to survive the storm that surrounded the building and the entire venture from the get-go, including several lawsuits and legal proceedings, is generally explained by the political and administrative skill and determination with which the young architects were backed from the highest level. The project's director, Robert Bordaz, was partnered by senior political officials from the Ministries of Culture, Education and Finance, who gave the architects their full support at all times, without yielding to public opinion. When needed in particularly critical phases, Bordaz untied the knots in the Masonic Lodge.

Ultimately, of course, the project was protected by President Pompidou himself, radical as he was in his views on architecture and urban development, influenced like Bordaz by the Modernist visions of Le Corbusier. Probably, part of the explanation as to why, despite all the protests, the building was eventually accepted by the Parisians also lay in the French mentality that Pontus Hultén described in my interview, in contrast to our Swedish mindset. When the protests failed to yield results, the Parisians finally accepted the new center instead of continually "nagging." There was a tradition of accepting the radically modern in contrast to the historic and traditional, albeit under passionate protest. After all, a building can hardly be more radical than the Eiffel Tower, not even the Centre Pompidou.

Although there is a case for considering the Centre Pompidou as something as outrageous as an ironic architectural installation, indeed the greatest Neo-Dadaist manifestation of all, the main quality of this architectural masterpiece lies not in this, but in the majestic elegance with which this enormous "bizarre ship in a dry dock" inserts itself into the surrounding historic Parisian buildings like a futuristic imperial palace.

An analysis in Architectural Review likens the building to "a man in full armor in a room of civilians."[27] The same article praises how the building's backside facing the Rue Renard/Rue Beaubourg thoroughfare and the Marais district — here the resemblance to an oil refinery is striking — paradoxically harmonizes with this traditional Parisian streetscape from the second half of the nineteenth century; how the facade of the center, with its brutally exposed, aggressively colored structural elements and infrastructural installations, actually appears to be at the same height as the surrounding traditional nineteenth-century buildings, when in fact it is twice as high.

Another peculiarity of the Centre Pompidou building is that while from its galleries, from the restaurant and from the exterior escalators and corridors it offers some of the most spectacular views of Paris available, the building itself, despite its proportions, is visible from only a few locations in the surrounding neighborhoods. Optically navigating to the Centre Pompidou through the Paris street network isn't possible. You don't see the building until you are surprised by it — still today a shock to visitors experiencing it for the first time.

It is precisely in the sensational contrast and strange harmony between the traditional surroundings and the futuristic building that the magic of the Centre Pompidou lies. As architecture critic Rowan Moore writes in The Guardian: "A radical building in a radical city plan, or a conventional building in a conventional one, would not be so powerful."[28]

Thus, the recruitment of the management of the new Musée National d'Art Moderne (MNAM), which would occupy the lion's share of the new Centre Beaubourg cultural center, began somewhat later than the design of the new building, while the planning of the content of the new cultural center developed.

The very thought of hiring a non-Frenchman for the post as founding director of the new museum, the person who would launch and shape this entirely new form of national institution, was even more far-fetched and controversial within the French cultural establishment than the idea of choosing foreign architects to design the building. Would a bloody foreigner, *un étranger*, a rough-hewn Viking at that, come and teach the French something they didn't know about art? That such a recruitment could even be considered was the result of the natural French candidates for the position disqualifying themselves, one after the other.

The old MNAM in the Palais de Tokyo was headed at this time by Jean Leymarie, successor to the museum's founder Jean Cassou, a traditional French museum official — a "pleasant and sympathetic man."[29] The museum under Leymarie's leadership was negative, even hostile, to the whole concept of the new center, which in conservative circles was initially associated with the sixty-eight movement, and to the idea of moving the museum's collection to this new building in the plebeian quarters on the wrong side of the Boulevard de Sébastopol — an unreasonable idea for many in the Parisian art noblesse. I've been told that Jean Leymarie took a good eighteen months to respond to a letter from President George Pompidou inquiring about the planned new institution.[30] Leymarie's second-in-command, Dominique Bozo, who would become Pontus Hultén's most dangerous rival in the Paris museum establishment, was loyal to his boss and the camp that opposed the new initiative and therefore unthinkable for the task as well.

The resistance from the old museum management can likely be explained in part by the background that they themselves had for many years been planning a new museum of twentieth-century art, a project initiated by André Malraux and developed by Cassou and his staff, to be housed in a building by Le Corbusier in La Défense, the now Manhattan-like district in the Champs-Élysée's extension. This project had fallen through after Le Corbusier died in 1965 while swimming outside his cabin at Cap Martin on the French Riviera.

The contemporary art museum, the Centre National d'Art Contemporain (CNAC), with which the MNAM was to be merged in the new cultural center, was headed by Blaise Gautier, a respected art historian, curator and museum official who was, however, notorious for his drinking habits and who never seemed quite up to the challenge of the new, much expanded mission. At these two state institutions for modern art, there were a number of younger, ambitious "conservateurs" who later joined Pontus Hultén's staff and several of whom would succeed him as directors of the museum (which has not yet had a female director). At the time, they were all too young and unexperienced to be considered. Claude Mollard, a high-ranking cultural official who at the time worked as assistant and right-hand man to Robert Bordaz in the organization of the Centre Beaubourg, describes the situation: "There was a wide gap between the older and younger generation of museum officials in Paris and no one in between who was the right person to take us into the future."[31]

One candidate for the new director's position outside the two modern art institutions was François Mathey, director of the Musée des Arts Décoratifs, the design and crafts museum housed in the Louvre, where he had been acclaimed for a series of progressive exhibitions on architecture and other subjects. Mathey, whom Pontus Hultén knew well and had collaborated with,[32] is portrayed as a jovial, slightly eccentric and creative museum man. Under his leadership, the Musée des Arts Decoratifs had taken more and more initiatives in contemporary art in the void left by the passive MNAM. Many saw Mathey as an interesting prospect for the new directorship, but as he was an outsider in the art establishment, the management of the future Centre Pompidou needed proof that Mathey was up to the task, so he was subjected to a proper exam. In 1972, Mathey was commissioned to organize an exhibition of French contemporary art at the Grand Palais. The exhibition was called *72/72*, with a selection of seventy-two artists to show Parisians where contemporary art stood at the time. The opening of the exhibition was chaotic as artists who were not selected demonstrated outside the Grand Palais in the best spirit of the revolutionary sixties. Some took matters into their own hands and hung their works in the exhibition, while others removed theirs. The protests degenerated into chaos when the police intervened violently against the demonstrators at the Grand Palais during Queen Elizabeth of England's state visit to Paris. "Mathey was given the chance, but that scandal showed that it wouldn't work," as Claude Mollard notes. He says that the management team also searched for possible candidates elsewhere in France without finding anyone considered qualified.[33]

Many argue that President Pompidou himself was intent from the beginning on recruiting the head of the new institution from abroad, recognizing how far behind France and Paris had fallen in the development of modern art. In any case, the management of the Centre Beaubourg began to search in earnest for its new director on the international market as late as 1972, after the Mathey fiasco. That Pontus Hultén was among the main candidates was obvious. According to Calvin Tomkins, it was, as one might have suspected, Willem Sandberg who had advocated Hultén to Bordaz.[34]

I have not been able to investigate the true nature of the Pompidou couple's mythical visit to Stockholm in 1964. His son Alain Pompidou confirmed at our meeting in Paris that his father had indeed been in Stockholm that year, then as Prime Minister. During this visit, the future French President is said to have been given a tour of the Moderna Museet by Pontus Hultén in the company of Olof Palme, then Minister for Ecclesiastical Affairs. I have received information from various sources that this visit and meeting between Hultén and Georges Pompidou was the origin of the process that eventually led to the recruitment of Hultén. However, the Swedish Foreign Ministry has no documentation of such a visit. It's certain that Pompidou as president was hosted in Stockholm during a state visit on May 15–19, 1972, when Olof Palme was Prime Minister, which coincides with the future recruitment of Hultén. Even from this visit, however, I have not found any documentation of a visit to Moderna Museet in either writing or photographs. I have not even found any more precise information or testimony that Pontus Hultén ever did meet George Pompidou in person — not a single reference to such an encounter having taken place in Hultén's texts or in any interview.

It is certain that people in President Pompidou's orbit were well aware of what Pontus Hultén had achieved in Stockholm. Unlike Richard Rogers, Claude Mollard acknowledges that Stockholm, Moderna Museet and above all Kulturhuset were the most important source of inspiration in planning for the new cultural center in Paris,[35] which in many ways would evolve into a more large-scale metropolitan incarnation of the original vision for Kulturhuset that Pontus Hultén and his collaborators, together with Peter Celsing, had presented. Mollard explains that the team of planners visited Stockholm, Moderna Museet and Kulturhuset three times on the research tour they undertook during the devising of Centre Beaubourg, studying institutions such as the Design Center in London, the public library in Birmingham and several institutions in the United States, including Lincoln Center in New York, as well as in Canada. "The House of Culture in Stockholm was a model, no doubt, with the large library and the other activities in the house," says Mollard.[36]

In addition to Pontus Hultén, two other main international candidates for the post of founding director of the new supermuseum are said to have been on the management's shortlist: Willem Sandberg's successor Edy de Wilde at the Stedelijk in Amsterdam and Thomas M. Messer, then director of the Guggenheim Museum in New York. I have heard various accounts as to why they were both dropped, in Messer's case a story of links to the CIA. A fourth candidate, according to several people I've spoken to, was Harald Szeemann, the Swiss demon curator who is the one contemporary colleague to whom Pontus Hultén is most frequently compared and who is generally regarded as the most influential curator of the post-war era alongside Hultén. Szeemann is said to have been rejected because of his lack of museum experience. It is claimed by some that Szeemann never got over being passed by in favor of his constant rival Hultén.[37]

Whatever the truth of these various claims, Claude Mollard asserts that his boss Robert Bordaz returned to Paris after his visit to Stockholm and announced: "I have found our director." According to Calvin Tomkins in his 1977 New Yorker article, Bordaz himself expressed himself more firmly: that the planning group had concluded that Hultén was the only candidate capable of realizing their vision of the center and that President Pompidou had accepted this analysis without objection, despite the controversy he knew such a recruitment of *un étranger* would cause.[38]

Mollard recalls Bordaz enthusiastically narrating how he arrived at the museum in Stockholm on a morning when it was closed, opened an unlocked door and was greeted by "a janitor" climbing a ladder. It was, of course, Hultén. In the evening the two of them had dinner, Bordaz said, and he immediately realized that Hultén was the right man for the job. Hultén himself has recounted how Bordaz carefully studied him during the meal — how he ordered his food, what he ordered, how he conducted himself.[39] Hultén went on to say that Bordaz asked Hultén to stage two exhibitions at the future culture center, but that he sensed something bigger in the background. According to Claude Mollard, Robert Bordaz and Pontus Hultén immediately connected personally and began a close, trusting relationship and collaboration. This picture is confirmed by what Pontus himself told me and by all others with whom I've discussed the matter.

Robert Bordaz himself talks about the recruitment process and his first meeting with Pontus Hultén in a "conversation book" published with Renzo Piano: "Monsieur Leymarie had no ambitions and I could find no one in France who seemed perfectly suited to the task. For this reason, I set out with the pilgrim's stick. I traveled through Denmark, Sweden and the Netherlands. Finally, my meeting with Pontus Hultén in Stockholm was decisive. I felt I had met the man who could do it. He had a shyness and an extreme kindness but also a capacity to execute difficult projects. Moderna Museet was animated, fun, alive. In the park I saw works by Tinguely and Niki de Saint Phalle placed in a most special environment. I got the impression that he would act in the spirit of President Pompidou. When I returned, I proposed him to the President. President Pompidou chose him without worrying about the political consequences of appointing a foreigner. It was a very happy decision for the center because he was an exceptional man of action."[40]

The circumstance that Hultén was a well-established name on the Paris art scene since the 1950s was undoubtedly another factor in his favor. Olle Granath specifically mentions that Hultén had a good relationship with Pierre Restany, the founder of the group Les Nouveaux Réalistes and a leading figure in the more progressive art circles of Paris.[41] The relationship between Hultén and Restany is, however, controversial. Several contemporaries I've spoken to claim that Restany was actually seeking the post of director for himself, scheming against Hultén ("He was a very jealous man" as the artist Jacques Villeglé, one of the original members of the New Realist group, said of Restany at our meeting in Paris[42]). A contemporary colleague and rival of Restany, the artist, critic and poet Alain Jouffroy, whom Hultén, like Restany, had invited to Moderna Museet in Stockholm, took credit at our meeting for having initially recommended Hultén to Pompidou and Bordaz.[43] As habitual in this story, there are many emphasizing their own contributions to history.

Most definitely, in the background in the Parisian cultural arena lured a double force working with great energy for Pontus Hultén: the Bonnie & Clyde of the art world, of course, Niki de Saint Phalle and Jean Tinguely. As Daniel Abadie, art historian, curator, dealer and editor, a good friend of de Saint Phalle and Tinguely, at the time a young "conservateur" at the CNAC and later on Hultén's staff at the Centre Pompidou, relates: "Niki and Jean were called the nutcracker. One came from one side and the other from the other. You were crushed in between if you didn't do as they pleased."[44]

From the perspective of modern art history, the choice of Pontus Hultén as the founding director of the new Musée National d'Art Moderne at the Centre Pompidou, the world's first "mega-museum" for modern art, seems logical and natural despite all these complexities. Hultén was undoubtedly the most qualified candidate in the world for this epoch-making task. Equally, it was a bold, untimely choice that could not have been made by decision-makers without strong personal conviction and integrity, with firm support from the very top.

19

"Hugely impressive to see him conquer Paris with Picabia": The new museum before the Centre Pompidou

Pontus Hultén moved to Paris to begin his work as the newly appointed director of the future museum in August 1973, three and a half years before the museum's opening on January 31, 1977. He left Stockholm without his life partner Anna-Lena Wibom and thirteen-year-old daughter Klara, and without his son Felix from his marriage to Kerstin Ehrenberg, then twenty years old, with whom he entertained only sporadic contact. With the move, he chose conclusively between his career and his family, and he was once and for all a man who lived for art, not family. From now on, he would see Anna-Lena Wibom and his children mainly during the summer vacations. "I had a black hole in my relationship with my father between 1973 and 1995," as his son Felix Hultén confides.[1]

It was in connection with the relocation to Paris that Karl Gunnar Vought Hultén definitively abandoned his birth name, including the signature K.G., and once and for all became Pontus Hultén — the nickname his admired uncle Allan had used and by which he now became famous in the wider art world.

Several of his friends and collaborators in Paris who were there from the start have told me about the lonely impression Pontus Hultén made when he first arrived in the city to take up his new post. The first period was tough for him, as he himself testified.[2] His first office was in temporary premises on Boulevard de Sébastopol, where Bordaz also had his "bureau," with a minimal staff and a secretary with no knowledge of English or other necessary skills.[3] Hultén said that he found it difficult as his French language skills were inadequate despite his Francophilia and his years in Paris in the 1950s and 1960s.[4] It wasn't until the following year when Annick Boisnard was hired as secretary and assistant that it became easier for him to communicate with his new surroundings. "She was nervous at first, but that changed immediately when she understood the importance of her position," states Pontus Hultén.[5] Annick Boisnard herself remembers: "Pontus was very friendly and sweet. It was clear that he had had a hard time in the beginning. My English was poor but I learned quickly because I had to."[6]

As could be expected, Pontus Hultén was viewed with suspicion from the art establishment and the press, which was almost exclusively skeptical and negative. Hultén had been preceded by his reputation from Moderna Museet for his radicalism and even more so for his frivolity. In an article in the conservative Le Figaro, reliable in its hostility to the whole Centre Beaubourg initiative, Hultén was called "the Swedish pornographer," of course mainly because of *she — a cathedral*, an epithet that stuck.

Almost everyone of those who were there and with whom I've spoken in Paris have vividly portrayed the powerful physical impression imposed by Pontus Hultén. "He was like a colossus but very sweet, attentive and smiling," as Annick Boisnard describes her first meeting with Hultén for her job interview in 1974.[7] There are recurring associations with the great Viking: taciturn, somewhat shy and awkward as many describe it, with heavy physical authority and a massive presence in the room, which inspired respect. The press, too, was full of comparisons with Vikings and other exotic northern phenomena. Jean Cassou, the Stalinist leader of the old establishment's reactionary resistance to the new, weighed in with an infamous article in Le Monde entitled "Lohengrin descends from his swan," which Pontus Hultén said he found, after all, "quite flattering."[8]

Even though Hultén himself was fascinated by Vikings and ancient Nordic mythology, he never liked the kind of parables and observations that haunted him in Paris — understandably, since in such metaphors with the big, rough-hewn Nordman, stomping awkwardly in the sophistication of the Parisian salons, there is a well-dosed measure of condescension of the good old French brand. It's a bit like the poor old peasant tromping awkwardly, spinning his greasy old hat between soiled thumbs on huge, meaty paws in the landlord's foyer; a superiority and a xenophobic/chauvinist distrust in certain environs that Pontus Hultén never quite escaped during his years in Paris.

"The French never accepted Pontus because he was a foreigner, Swedish, almost German," says Jean-Yves Mock,[9] the curator and art collector who joined Pontus Hultén's staff in late 1973 as public relations officer and press contact, assistant and ghostwriter, not surprisingly on the recommendation of Niki de Saint Phalle and Jean Tinguely. Mock was recruited for the written and spoken English skills he had acquired while working at the Hanover Gallery in London in the 1960s, but also for his network of contacts and social skills. "The French are like that," Mock adds. "They think they know better than others because they are French but they are stupid. I am French, nothing else, but I have never understood the French."[10]

Pontus Hultén's most pressing task was the construction, which had begun with groundwork in April 1972. Richard Rogers and Renzo Piano had reinforced the image of wild young rebels that the press had already conveyed by opening an inflated portable office on a barge on the right bank of the Seine.[11] They had caused a minor scandal when, in the democratic spirit of sixty-eight, they arrived at the solemn official announcement banquet hosted to present their winning entry with all six architects from their office, dressed in denim jeans, T-shirts and miniskirts among all the Parisian potentates in tuxedos and evening gowns.

Rogers, Piano and Hultén seem to have become immediate friends during the planning of the building's interior solutions, with Hultén being able to influence and change many of the original, often extreme ideas. Although Hultén was more than a decade older, they were children of the same spirit. Both Rogers and Piano had the anarchist in them, always essential for true friendship with Hultén.

Despite the consensus and shared utopian visions, they had many heated conflicts where Hultén's role was to say no when he felt that the architects' ambitions had taken over at the expense of art and the museum's functions. The idea of movable floor plans disappeared at an early stage. Another idea the architects had to drop was that toilets and other service functions should also be flexible and movable, in a system of portable balloons.

In Calvin Tomkins' previously cited major portrait of Pontus Hultén and account of the opening of the Centre Pompidou, a meticulously researched article of over twenty dense pages in The New Yorker from February 1978, Tomkins writes about these conflicts. This is how he depicts Hultén's entry into the Parisian scene: "In the intricate Parisian art world, he was a refreshing, if somewhat unpredictable, new player, and for a time no one really knew what to expect from him. (...) The kind of center that Rogers and Piano wanted Beaubourg to be was in many ways close to Hultén's ideal museum. He liked the emphasis on openness and flexibility, and he liked the populist ideas behind it — the idea that someone who had never been to a museum before could walk in off the street, look around without preconceived notions, and draw their own conclusions. What he liked most, he said in 1974, was that the builders had no 'museum mentality' and that Beaubourg would be 'not so much a museum as a platform for sensibilities.'"[12]

Tomkins writes that in the many conflicts that arose with Rogers and Piano, Pontus Hultén revealed himself to be "a more conventional museum man than he sometimes appeared." Hultén was against and did his best to stop one of the building's canonized features. Tomkins quotes Hultén as saying: "'What I didn't agree on was that it would be a very showy building' (...) 'I was very much against those strong colors, because they didn't seem to me to take into account the light in Paris. That was our main argument for a long time. I tried to introduce brown, silver and gray. For a while they wanted to paint the whole building bright orange. I just thought it was ridiculous.'"[13]

Calvin Tomkins informs that the architects managed to push through their aggressive primary colors on the exterior but not as intended on the interior — that Pontus Hultén made sure that all of "his" galleries were painted completely white. Displaying the art not on conventional screens but on "floating panels" suspended from the ceiling was another of Rogers/Piano's ideas that Hultén managed to scrap. "Hultén said that if there was one thing he hated, it was seeing other people's legs under paintings."[14] The architects were "visibly disappointed" by the compromises Hultén forced them to make, Tomkins notes, adding: "'They wanted something much more open,' Hultén has said. 'They wanted you to really feel the interior space. But we had the problem that we had to show eleven hundred works of art, and to make recent art history understandable. Some of these works are very intimate and cannot compete with all this architecture. We had big discussions about this for a year.' 'Pontus didn't see flexibility and change in the same way as we did,' admits Richard Rogers. (...) 'Sometimes Pontus can seem a bit fuzzy, but he knows exactly what he wants and he's very sharp about it — which for us was a disadvantage (...) We had many battles and Pontus won most of them.'"

"Piano and Rogers were two young cowboys who liked to have fun on boats," as Jean-Yves Mock says. "Pontus' job was to make sure that the boys didn't become too eccentric."[15]

Interacting with the architects and planning the building seems to have been an enjoyable if stressful part of Pontus Hultén's first time in

Paris. Both Piano and Rogers paint a picture of free and creative collaboration at a furious pace within a small group of young men in exile in Paris, under the "masterful" leadership and patronage of Robert Bordaz. "We were a group of foreigners who knew no better than to do what we wanted," says Renzo Piano. "We were not established in the business, but still young guys who liked to have fun and play tricks. We were bandits, but good bandits … no guns …"[16]

Pontus Hultén summarizes his early collaboration with Richard Rogers and Renzo Piano as follows: "It was a rather complicated situation. The architects were very young and unfortunately had no experience of constructing a large building, with many large systems (…) Despite all their often fantastic ideas, I perceived Renzo Piano in particular as a realist. The first contact was mainly with Rogers and his assistant. In 1974 the whole team came to Stockholm to visit me and see the Moderna Museet. We went all around Stockholm on a tour with my boat and I think they were quite impressed (…) The French authorities had difficulty dealing with foreigners. It wasn't even possible for them to open an office so that's why they were mainly based on a barge in the Seine. The relationship between Bordaz and the architects was not warm at first. It was usual in Paris for construction to be delayed and for there to be various problems. When he was most worried, Bordaz confiscated the architects' passports so that they couldn't leave France. On another occasion when an important decision had to be made, Piano was unreachable on his boat in the Mediterranean. Bordaz called in the French Navy who actually found him in northern Corsica. The inhabitants of Saint-Florent remember this to this day."[17]

Much of Hultén's first time in Paris was spent getting acquainted with the two institutions that were to be part of the new museum and their staff, the Musée National d'Art Moderne (MNAM) and the Centre National d'Art Contemporain (CNAC). According to Hultén, Bordaz and Pompidou felt that the CNAC worked better and was more dynamic[18] with its team of young, hungry curators. He was therefore instructed to focus particularly on the MNAM. Hultén led an itinerant existence between the two museums, the construction site and his temporary office, as well as traveling in his incessant tour of the art world.

Long before the building was completed, Pontus Hultén and his staff moved into the museum. A widely circulated legend is that Hultén set up his office in one of the construction elevators for a period of time, where he received visitors while construction traffic was ongoing.

Jean-Hubert Martin recalls the expectations and trepidation with which he and his colleagues encountered their new boss. "We knew very well what he had done in Stockholm, of course," says Martin. "He had a great reputation and name, almost like a god. When he arrived, he didn't say much. You almost had to drag his thoughts out of him. We were all very worried in the beginning because we were convinced that he would fire the entire staff the first thing he did."[19]

Pontus Hultén had no such plans. Nor, as far as I've understood, had he even thought of bringing any of his staff to Paris, but was focused on building his team mainly from the younger staff members at the two institutions, most of them between ten and twenty-five years younger than himself, forty-nine years old as he was when he took over as director of the new MNAM. Over time, Pontus Hultén began to build this team of curators and other collaborators who would make art history. With the exception of his successor Dominique Bozo, the short-serving Bernard Ceysson and the newly appointed Xavier Rey, every MNAM director in the museum's history has served under Hultén at the beginning of their careers.

Pontus Hultén himself has relayed how his "foreignness" was a strength rather than a handicap when he first familiarized himself with the two institutions that would form the new museum: "I considered it an advantage both for me and the museum. As a foreigner, I could see old defective structures, intrigues, gangs and the like, obviously built up over many years, which paralyzed the mobility of the institutions and could not be ignored. The strange rigidity and dryness that used to characterize national museums remained. (...) It was exciting to see the two teams starting to work together, but it was quite successful. To reduce mutual suspicion, I summoned them all for a gathering in Jean Cassou's old office, which was very strange. It was round and there was a dome in the middle which gave a strange acoustic. Behind the director's chair was a staircase hidden in the wall where he could miraculously disappear when he didn't want to talk to someone."[20]

In Paris, Pontus Hultén ushered in a new era in that he was what Bernard Blistène, MNAM's director from 2013 to 2021 — who began his career as an intern at the end of Hultén's time at the Centre Pompidou — calls a "readymade director."[21] That is to say, he stood for an artistic vision based on Duchamp, not Picasso, if I may simplify. This was the dividing line between Hultén and the traditional Parisian museum world. In this establishment, modern art remained essentially painting and sculpture, with the backbone of the old trio of classic Parisian modern masters, Matisse, Braque and Picasso. While the traditional Parisian coteries continued to regard art as something refined and aesthetic, an entity reserved for the initiated that required considerable prior knowledge, Pontus Hultén represented a radically broader vision, developed at Moderna Museet, of infusing the world into art and vice versa, in order to reach and interact with a maximum number of people.

The younger generation of curators, or "conservateurs," at both MNAM and CNAC were, as Jean-Hubert Martin recounts, mostly products of the sixty-eight movement, politically radical and focused on the freer vision of art that Hultén had pioneered. There was great desire to break out of provincial isolation and enter the international art arena in earnest. "The situation was very bad for us," says Germain Viatte, one of the young curators from the CNAC who would join Pontus Hultén's team at the Centre Pompidou and who also became director of the MNAM (1992–1997). "We were very dynamic with the sixties movement but the problem was the state, the system. Even the directors knew how bad our modern museums were. Everyone who was interested in contemporary art knew about Moderna Museet and what they had done. It was considered the most important museum along with the Stedelijk and represented the new developments in art along with Harald Szeemann at the Kunsthalle in Bern and also the Kunsthalle in Düsseldorf. At the CNAC we had the idea of collaborating with Moderna Museet. It simply wasn't possible for us to work like the progressive European museums with the system we had."[22]

Jean-Hubert Martin says that there was considerable uncertainty among his colleagues about Pontus Hultén's attitude towards the political left they represented. "Pontus was suspicious and wary of the left," says Martin. "He didn't trust it. I think he hated the Swedish left."[23]

Martin recalls that Pontus Hultén was taciturn in their communication when he and his colleagues first got to know him — that he rarely elaborated on his ideas but expected his colleagues to draw their own conclusions and understand the matters. Certainly, Hultén's brevity during his early days in Paris could be partly explained by his difficulties with the French language. Martin remembers that after a lengthy presentation, Hultén confided to him that hadn't understood a damn thing of what had been said.[24]

The young staffers soon became acquainted with another of Hultén's strategies that contrasted drastically with the hierarchical management style of their former management — how he always gave full confidence to his younger colleagues even in difficult and crucial matters, expected them to figure out how to solve problems themselves, never interfered with details but intervened personally only if absolutely necessary, but then with great efficiency. "That he gave you such total confidence was fantastic, but you also had a constant fear of not being up to the task," says Jean-Hubert Martin.[25]

He relates an anecdote that reflects Pontus Hultén's way of conveying his vision of art by means other than the verbal: "It was one evening when we were sitting in the office in the old museum in the Palais de Tokyo that he came in and said that we should go for a tour in the galleries. He liked to go and look around at what was in the collections and in the storerooms, and discovered a lot of things that people hadn't realized the value of. Of course, we soon ended up in the small Dada room. He stopped in front of a sculpture by a Russian Dadaist and said that this was a nice piece, though not remarkable. I happened to have read up on that particular work so I said that it might not seem so special but then started telling him about various publications where it had been depicted and such. Pontus said nothing but let me talk. When I was done, he was silent for a while and then burst into a huge laugh. It was a lesson for life for me. He was right. The work had no direct major aesthetic value and it was pointless trying to compensate for this with theoretical explanations."[26]

Leaving Stockholm for the biggest stage in Paris was of course a triumph for Pontus Hultén. However, coming to the city as the outsider he was considered by many was like rising from the ashes into the fire, even though Hultén was spared the "constant nagging" from Stockholm. Several of those involved have portrayed the palpable "us-versus-them" atmosphere that prevailed within the small working group led by Robert Bordaz, with the architects and the team of collaborators that emerged under Pontus Hultén.

It seems typical of Hultén's dramatic career that this already tense situation was suddenly struck by a blow that instantly placed the whole project in an all new hazardous situation, on the verge of total disaster, when President George Pompidou fell ill with lymphatic cancer after New Year's Day 1974. Pompidou, who had hitherto kept his disease secret, died on April 2, 1974, a situation similar to that which had affected the Kulturhuset project in Stockholm, when the architect Peter Celsing had fallen ill during the construction process, but much more critical as the Centre Beaubourg project in Pompidou lost its initiator and highest patron.

Hultén describes how the president's death changed everything about the project overnight: "I was in New York meeting with the Institut Français and the Museum of Modern Art when we suddenly received the news of Pompidou's death. I immediately returned to Paris and found that the atmosphere had completely changed. In the press there were terribly inflammatory articles against the center, full of lies and distrust, at the lowest level. Bordaz was most worried, but kept his nerves under control very well."[27]

Worse still, in the presidential election two months after Pompidou's death, centrist Valéry Giscard d'Estaing narrowly defeated socialist candidate François Mitterrand. d'Estaing, or Giscard as he was more commonly known, was a traditional French statesman, icy formal with the classic French aristocratic hauteur. His view of culture was distinctly conventional, decrying the prevailing view still held in conservative circles of the whole phenomenon of modern art as a humbug invented by bearded communists. "Giscard was a stupid asshole who was not interested in any culture at all, except for playing his accordion," as Jean-Yves Mock summarizes.[28]

Valéry Giscard d'Estaing shared the conservative establishment's view of the whole new cultural center initiative. Shortly after taking office at the end of May 1974, he declared his intention to shut down the entire project, as he did with several other state ventures initiated by Pompidou. "It was not his project, not his style at all," as Pontus Hultén said. "We had to play hardball for project to survive."[29]

In the critical predicament in which the Centre Beaubourg suddenly found itself, with the controversial construction underway, the project's management under Bordaz would use its full range of contacts and skills to navigate with precision through the labyrinths of French politics and bureaucracy. Pontus Hultén's "hustler skills" would also prove useful in the vicious game of intrigue that played out after Giscard d'Estaing became president. In my interview, Hultén said: "We managed to convince them that it would be more expensive to shut down the project than to go ahead with it, which I am sure was not true."[30]

The most immediate threat to the project lay in the building itself, which had been loathed in conservative camps ever since the winning proposal was presented in 1971. The project management's first line of defense against the new political regime was therefore the expected one. With references to investments already undertaken, contracts that had been signed and damages that could be claimed in the event of closure, they managed to produce the calculation referred to by Pontus Hultén, which showed that it would be "cheaper" to continue building than to terminate the project — a familiar trick from developers in similar situations then, now and probably throughout history.

Nationalist indignation weighed heavily in the establishment's aversion to the Centre Beaubourg. As if the Italian-British architectural duo, the Danish-British engineering firm and the Swedish director weren't enough, Bordaz turned to a German construction company as there was little interest in the new cultural center from the French construction industry. Moreover, the structural steel elements of the building were to be supplied by the German company Krupp, despite the brand's historical burden of the Big Berta doomsday gun and other weapon systems that had cost countless French lives, as no French supplier was deemed capable of producing high-quality steel at a competitive price.[31] Apparently, the French were no match for the creation of the new French national cultural center — so the indignant voices cried. "Someone wrote that with Italian architects and a German construction company, you might as well bring in some Japanese too, to revive the Axis powers while you were at it," as Richard Rogers says.[32]

A creative financial estimate was far from the only defensive measure taken to save the project from the new president's desire to simply wipe the slate clean. Shortly after President Pompidou's death, Robert Bordaz performed the simple act of genius of renaming the new cultural center from Centre Beaubourg to *Centre Pompidou*, or *Centre national d'art et de culture Georges-Pompidou* as its full official name reads. Pontus Hultén has revealed that this was something Bordaz had kept to himself, that the name had suddenly been changed overnight.[33] This action not only made it much more difficult for Valéry Giscard d'Estaing to cancel the project, but also provided him an escape for his personal prestige, as the new name would clearly associate the cultural center with its predecessor and not with Giscard himself. Almost half a century later, both names are still used for the center — Centre Pompidou and Beaubourg.

The question is whether even this would have been enough to avert d'Estaing from stopping or mutilating the building and the project beyond recognition. It's widely believed that the decisive event that definitively saved the Centre Pompidou was the intervention of Jacques Chirac, who, as a result of the political game that preceded the presidential election, had become Prime Minister under Giscard d'Estaing. The President was indebted to Chirac for his support in the election campaign. Now Chirac showed his loyalty to his former boss and elder Gaullist party brother by telling Giscard that he would resign if the President liquidated the cultural center. With what is described as disgusted reluctance, the president was forced to allow his predecessor's initiative with the new national cultural center to proceed.

Although the Centre Pompidou barely survived this crisis, the death of Pompidou and the arrival of Giscard d'Estaing rendered the venture in a more precarious position. The "open budget" honeymoon was over. Now all costs were scrutinized. There was a huge difference between working with the originator of the initiative as its supreme patron and negotiating with an enemy as president in a predominantly hostile environment.

Maneuvering the building itself through this emergency without major compromise was a particular achievement of the late president's task force. The main features of the building were rescued with a few symbolic pawns sacrificed. As a demonstration of power, Giscard d'Estaing wanted to cut off the top two of the building's five floors. The management team dodged this snub by playing the tried and tested card that reducing the height would be more costly for technical reasons.

One prominent feature of the building's exterior that had to be abandoned was the huge screen for films, information and messages from other cultural institutions worldwide envisioned to dominate the facade facing the future piazza in front of the cultural center, making the cultural center's appearance "a cross between an information-oriented, computerized Times Square and the British Museum."[34] "The facade of the building, if you look closely, was very much about the riots and very much about Vietnam," said Richard Rogers. "Everything was going well until Pompidou died and Giscard came in and brought it all down. He said: 'That's a political weapon, and I don't want that.' So that part died."[35]

Though opinions within the creative team often differed, Pontus Hultén and his well-known unscrupulous ingenuity in problem solving came of use in defending Piano and Roger's architecture against the new hostile clients. Renzo Piano amusingly recounts how Hultén became a senior associate in their "gang of bandits" under Bordaz's patronage. He relates a fantastic story about the building's exterior color scheme, which Hultén himself had opposed. The bright, aggressive colored elements of the building's infrastructure are perhaps the most distinctive feature of the Centre Pompidou. This color palette is typical of the British architectural avant-garde of the 1960s, rooted in Futurism. As related in the architecture forum ArchDaily's 2010 feature:[36] "The different systems on the exterior of the building are painted in different colors to clarify their different functions. The structure with the largest ventilation components was painted white, stairs and elevator structures were painted silver-gray, ventilation was painted blue, sewage systems and fire protection piping were painted green, electrical elements are yellow and orange, the elevator motor rooms and shafts, or elements that allow movement through the building, are painted red."[37]

Renzo Piano laughs when he talks about the Centre Pompidou's famous "color system." "The color thing was very controversial and the politicians demanded that we change it," says Piano. "Then we realized that we had to convince them that there was a carefully calculated system that related to the functions of the building and safety — blue for water pipes, red for electricity and so on. These were arguments that the bureaucrats could understand and respect, so we managed to get it through. In fact, there never was a system. I don't know who came up with the idea for that. You shouldn't think like that when you work together with friends in a group, but it was probably Pontus."[38]

Another major battle Pontus Hultén had to fight was the conflict with the artists, donors and artistic families who had contributed to the collection in the old museum — the core of the Parisian art establishment with representatives of the Picasso, Braque, Matisse, Léger and other families. This society, represented in the Friends association of the museum, controlled a major part of the collection. The group was loyal to the old management, representing the conservative view of the new cultural center "at Sébastopol," as they condescended to say. In their view, moving the national art treasure to this location would mean a vulgarization of art. In such groups, the new center was the subject of explicit epithets — "brothel," "supermarket," "amusement park," "flea market" and, of course, "oil refinery," "nuclear plant," and so on. The collectors and artists' families of the MNAM's friends association protested against the Centre Pompidou by simply declaring that they would refuse to allow the art they controlled to move to the "brothel." The Russian-French master Marc Chagall, living in Paris since 1910, hardly one of Hultén's own favorite artists, personally threatened to take back the fifteen paintings he had donated to the old MNAM.[39]

Here Bordaz, Hultén and the Centre's management team were faced with a delicate dilemma that simply had to be resolved before the opening of the Centre Pompidou: a war of position with people of a kind that Pontus Hultén detested, which would require highly advanced diplomacy. Leaders of this resistance were the son (actually not the son, as Hultén notes[40]) of Henri Laurens and the daughters of Georges Rouault, typically the offspring of two École de Paris artists of limited art historical importance. "This group met, had dinner in posh Parisian style and created a lot of confusion," as Hultén phrases it. He states that the situation was extremely difficult for him and Bordaz.[41] For several years they had to pay continuous personal courtesy calls on these potentates in their attempts to flatter them.

In this fatiguing game, Hultén and Bordaz had an important ally in Dominique de Menil, with her younger sister Sylvie Boissonnas as backup. Pontus Hultén's friendship with Dominique de Menil became lifelong. The widely revered patron reportedly held warm feelings and complete confidence in Hultén and his knowledge and judgment.

Indeed, it has been emphasized by many that one of Hultén's specific talents was his "good rapport" with elder women, especially elder rich and powerful women. It is undeniably striking how a series of senior, more or less wealthy and influential women had a great impact on Pontus Hultén's career from the very beginning. Dominique de Menil was undoubtedly one of the most important of these female patrons. In addition to the respect she enjoyed, the family's then still ample (though not inexhaustible) resources, and de Menil's advanced taste and openness to radicalism, she and her family were of crucial importance to the museum also through their American connection. Anti-Americanism in Paris at the time was massive, uniting the conservative cultural establishment with the sixty-eight movement.

French political suspicion of the United States played well into the conservative establishment's opposition to anything American. Essentially, however, the hostility was rooted in protectionist — and justified — concerns that blazing American iconoclasm would drown out and displace the more sophisticated, subtle French art, as represented by the abstract painting of Jean Dubuffet, Jean Fautrier, Pierre Soulages, and a host of other French artists of the École de Paris, the more cautious French version of American Abstract Expressionism that had long dominated contemporary French art. Hultén was generally not overly fond of this amorphous, historically somewhat downgraded school, sometimes referred to as Tachisme or "the informal style." One reputation that had preceded him, alongside the frivolity and political rabble-rousing, was, of course, his passion for American art. Wild rumors abounded. There was widespread concern that Hultén would simply throw out, even sell, French in favor of American art. This fear was part of the view of the new Centre Pompidou as a "supermarket" for art. French artists in particular took this position.

Hultén was more than aware of this public opinion. To counteract the suspicion that he would focus his purchases exclusively on American art, Hultén went so far as to decide not to buy any American art at all in the early years, when he began to complement the collection and patch up its many holes. Jean-Hubert Martin relates a comical incident involving an interview that Hultén gave after a period of this purchasing policy: "The journalist accused Pontus of buying only American art," Martin says. "Pontus then asked the journalist to name a single American artist that he had bought for the collection. He was silent for a long time and finally said ... Joseph Beuys."[42]

For the necessary acquisitions required to create an American collection, in Hultén's declared intention to transform the MNAM from a French to a global museum, he relied heavily on Dominique de Menil and other patrons in New York. Jean-Yves Mock, a good friend of the de Menil couple since the 1950s, took credit in several of our many conversations in Paris for having urged Hultén to create an "American Friends of the Museum" on the model he knew from the Tate in London. The strategy was for American mecenates to provide donations and funds for the necessary American purchases, as these were politically impossible for Hultén with the museum's government funding. While Dominique de Menil was influential in the MNAM's friends association, her sister Sylvie Boissonnas became a key member of this new American Friends. Their older sister Anne Gruner Schlumberger was also involved in the support of the museum.

Jean-Hubert Martin explains that Pontus Hultén had a clear picture from the beginning of the most important priorities in the acquisitions needed to complete the collection with the declared ambition of becoming Europe's Museum of Modern Art and challenge the American model as the world's leading modern art museum, and that he acted decisively and purposefully to realize these acquisitions. Martin mentions four specific priorities. The first was Surrealism, where there were large gaps for artists such as Salvador Dalí, never accepted by the Parisian art establishment, and many others. René Magritte was also missing from the collections of the French state. "Magritte was barely considered a painter in Paris," says Jean-Hubert Martin. "It was bad taste to like Magritte." Another artist who left an embarrassing gap despite the fact that, like Magritte, he had worked in Paris for part of his career was Piet Mondrian, a priority that would become almost an obsession for Hultén. The "New York School," meaning post-war American art starting with Abstract Expressionism, was an obvious third priority. The fourth was to establish contact between the museum and the contemporary avant-garde.[43]

With donations from the de Menil family and other American and international collectors and patrons, Pontus Hultén and his staff were able to strengthen the collection on a broad front in a series of complicated operations and negotiations in the years before and after the opening. The de Menil family donated Jackson Pollock's last painting "The Deep" (a gift for which Dominique de Menil was criticized even within the family) and two important works by Andy Warhol. Among the Surrealists, de Chirico's magical portrait of Guillaume Apollinaire from 1914[44] and key works by Dalí and Magritte were acquired. There were no opportunities for Duchamp, that train was long gone, but the Dada section was strengthened with, among others, George Grosz's masterpiece "Remember Uncle August" (1919). The New York School collection was enriched by donations of works by Barnett Newman, Sam Francis, Robert Rauschenberg, Jasper Johns, Larry Rivers, Claes Oldenburg, Dan Flavin, and others.

Among contemporary artists, works by international stars such as Germans Joseph Beuys and Gerhard Richter were acquired, and of course the French Neo-Realists, including Jacques Villeglé, and in particular two major works by Yves Klein. Hultén also acquired art by old Swedish and Scandinavian friends with Parisian connections such as Olle Baertling, Öyvind Fahlström, Richard Mortensen and Robert Jacobsen. The extensive renovation and expansion of the French National Museum's collection of international masterpieces could be crowned with Mondrian's "Composition en rouge, bleu et blanc II" from 1937, and Malevich's Black Cross from 1915, donated in 1980 after complicated maneuverings.[45]

In these efforts to strengthen the collection, the price tag as well as the degree of complexity was considerably higher than ten years earlier, when Pontus Hultén and his colleagues had expanded Moderna Museet's collection after *The Museum of Wishes*. As previously discussed, the collections function as bank accounts on the international art market and in the production of exhibitions. A museum with global ambitions must be able to offer visitors an "encyclopedia" of the most important milestones in the history of modern art. Here, the prestige for donors and collectors of having their works and names represented in the French national collection was a major trump card for the museum. "Pontus was very good at buying," says Jean-Hubert Martin. "He knew exactly how the market worked and had an incredible network of contacts. He knew every trick in the book and was great at raising the money needed."[46]

The reason why Pontus Hultén and his colleagues were able to act independently at all, in a creative stretching of the law and its appropriations, as customary with Hultén, was due to another anticipatory measure taken by President Pompidou.

Under the old regime, the state museums had been directly subordinate to the government, with purchase funds even for individual acquisitions allocated directly by the minister in charge. One legend is that of André Malraux, who sat with a Mondrian painting on the wall of his office for a period of time in order to personally assess whether it was worthy of purchase, before deciding that, no, it was not something the French state should invest in. The bureaucracy of the old system was paralyzing. The MNAM was prohibited by law from acquiring art by living artists. All purchases were managed centrally by a committee responsible for all French state art museums, including the Louvre, Versailles and so on. "Pompidou realized that with that system it would never be possible to build a new kind of museum," says Jean-Hubert Martin. "So he turned the center into a new kind of institution, a public company, which was responsible for its own budget and decided its own purchases without needing the approval of the ministry. It was the first such institution in France. Without that freedom, we could never have done what we managed to do under Pontus."[47]

Pontus Hultén hardly had a planned program for the new museum when he arrived in Paris. Despite the larger context, he kept his way of working with improvisation, fascinatingly short lead times and a constant death race with deadlines, in the borderlands between the possible and the impossible.

Some of the main features of the exhibition program he would develop at the Centre Pompidou indeeed seem to have been clear in Hultén's mind from the beginning in Paris. His eras of movement and Americanism were behind him. Instead, his epic perspective had for several years been increasingly focused on the Russian and Eastern European, which came to characterize his work at the Centre Pompidou. Restoring the honor of his heroes Marcel Duchamp and Francis Picabia — and the whole of Dada and Surrealism — in their old hometown was another proud main priority from the outset for Hultén.

A quality that would characterize Hultén for the rest of his career was his method of taking the museum's geographical location, in this case Paris, as a point of embarkment for his program, which may seem obvious but was far from it. Paris as part of the world, and its role in international art history — this became a nucleus of Hultén's program during his years at the Centre Pompidou. It's widely regarded as one of his achievements as director of the MNAM that he opened up the former "world capital of the arts" to the wider world, awakening its art scene from a slumbering false self-image. "He made us understand that Paris was not the center of the world but just a bus stop on the Moscow-Berlin-New York route," says art historian and writer Gérard Régnier, better known by his authorial alias Jean Clair, renowned Duchamp expert and collaborator of Pontus Hultén at the Centre Pompidou, now a member of the French Academy.[48]

As Pontus Hultén declared, in the early years, before the center opened, it was crucial for the new organization under his leadership to promptly demonstrate its professionalism and what it stood for. "The best way to do this is in my opinion through some good exhibitions," he said.[49]

Hultén began his program in Paris with some more modest stagings in the old MNAM premises in the Palais de Tokyo. The first major effort was a critically acclaimed exhibition of Matisse's sculptures and drawings in the spring of 1975. Henri Matisse can be seen as a tactical soft launch as the artist was one of the key figures of the Parisian art establishment, a member of the master trio in the canon of classical Parisian Modernism alongside Picasso and Braque, with the pioneering Cézanne in the background. By opening with Matisse, Hultén countered fears that he would make a clean sweep of sophisticated good taste and fill the "art supermarket" with vulgar American junk. He had exhibited Matisse in Stockholm and befriended the artist's surviving relatives through Alexina "Teeny" Duchamp, who had been married to Matisse's youngest son Pierre, with whom she had three children, before meeting Marcel Duchamp. In an interview some years later, Pontus Hultén himself said of the fauve master: "One should probably be careful when making judgments. For example,

The phrase is taken from Matisse's own 1908 book *Notes d'un peintre*, in which the artist writes that he strives for art to have "a calming effect on the mind, something like a good armchair offering rest from physical fatigue."

when I was much younger I found Matisse too soft an armchair, but my attitude has changed completely since then; now I see him as a more radical artist than Picasso. His transposition, his humanism, is for me more subtle and much deeper."[50] In connection with the Matisse exhibition, Pontus Hultén and his colleagues also managed to enrich the collection with a number of additional works by the Modernist master, several of which were donated by the family.

Soon after his arrival, Pontus Hultén began the work on Russia and the Soviet Union that would occupy much of his time and energy during his years in Paris, with countless trips to Moscow, Leningrad and other parts of Russia, Eastern Europe and the Balkans. His passion for Russian and Slavic had only grown stronger over the years.

The subject of the first exhibition in the Russian-themed suite that Hultén staged under the auspices of the new MNAM may be considered surprising, since he was not primarily a visual artist: Vladimir Mayakovsky, the revolutionary avant-garde poet, a Futurist from the start — a tragically heroic figure of Hultén's taste. Mayakovsky, also an important cartoonist, graphic artist and agitator, was presented in early 1975 at the CNAC in the Hôtel Salomon de Rothschild in an exhibition of classic Hulténian multimedia style, with texts, paintings, graphic works, posters and more. Pontus Hultén himself describes the Mayakovsky exhibition at CNAC as a first step in the mammoth *Paris–Moscow* initiative — a "preparation for what was developing in my head."[51]

The Soviet authorities had "for reasons unknown" allowed a reconstruction in Moscow of the exhibition that Mayakovsky had presented in the city shortly before his suicide in 1930.[52] The exhibition included restored films from the twenties and thirties by the Soviet documentary film director Dziga Vertov. Hultén explains that his first contacts in Moscow were taken by his partner Anna-Lena Wibom, at the time head of the Cinemateket film club in Stockholm. As a Russian speaker, Wibom was important from the start in Hultén's Soviet contacts. She had attended the opening in Moscow together with Dziga Vertov's widow, where they had managed to get invited after Mrs. Vertov had found an original invitation from 1930 in her archive.[53]

With the help of Louis Aragon, the Surrealist poet admired by Pontus Hultén, it was finally possible to obtain permission for his sister-in-law, Mayakovsky's beloved Lilya "Lili" Brik,[54] writer and legendary muse of the Russian avant-garde, to visit Paris for a few days in conjunction with the 1975 CNAC exhibition.[55] Hultén recounts how he was driving Lili Brik around Paris when the widow suddenly exclaimed, "Don't run him over! That would be the day of judgment." Hultén barely managed to avoid hitting who if not Aragon, who "drunk and flamboyant as usual" stepped out into the street. As Hultén notes: "It would have made great newspaper headlines: Lili Brik and Pontus Hultén run over Louis Aragon in Place Saint Sulpice."[56]

The Mayakovsky exhibition was well received in the press and in art circles, where, according to Germain Viatte, it marked a real new beginning,[57] but did not attract a large audience. Pontus Hultén observes that it was "not very smart" to organize exhibitions at the existing institutions MNAM and CNAC as this did not serve the purpose of demonstrating the capacity of the future new museum, since the change was not palpable to the public.[58] The museum management therefore looked for other venues to present larger exhibitions under the auspices of the museum while waiting for the new building, and settled on the Grand Palais[59] on the Champs-Élysées — as grand as could be. In a typical observation, Hultén depicts the imposing exhibition palace, a crown jewel of the Parisian so-called Beaux-Arts style from the turn of the century: "The building reminded us of what we had in mind for the new center, namely an optimistic and very imaginative building, though almost a hundred years older."[60]

The first exhibition that Pontus Hultén and his staff presented at the Grand Palais in the name of the new museum was a major Max Ernst retrospective opened in the spring of 1975. The popular, much-loved and relatively accessible Ernst seems a strategic choice for this "sneak preview" — one of the pioneers of early Modernism, representative of both Dadaism and Surrealism, the two movements that Hultén was determined to "re-establish" in Paris. Hultén had shown Ernst in Stockholm[61] and knew the artist well from Paris, where the Jewish German Ernst had moved back in the mid-fifties after belonging to the group of exiled artists in New York during the war, where he inspired Abstract Expressionism. Max Ernst was also important to Pontus Hultén as an art diplomat with an extensive global network of contacts in Germany, France and the rest of Europe, Russia and the USA.

Ernst, eighty-four at the time of the exhibition, had led an adventurous life. At the outbreak of the Second World War, he had been rescued from the Gestapo and taken across the Atlantic by Peggy Guggenheim, and out of gratitude, as it is said, entered into a brief marriage with the mecenate. At the time of the exhibition, Ernst was living in Paris and on the Riviera with his third wife, the artist Dorothea Tanning, twenty years his junior, dependent on her help after being paralyzed by a stroke. Hultén reports that he often visited Ernst at his home and large studio in Paris and that the "maestro," as he called him, was always in good spirits, albeit unable to move.[62]

For the production of the Max Ernst exhibition, the first retrospective of the artist in France, Pontus Hultén engaged German art historian Werner Spies, considered the world's leading Ernst expert (though later questioned[63]) and a close friend of the artist. The exhibition at the Grand Palais was well received by the still hostile press and attracted a large audience by the standards of the time. Speaking about his first exhibitions under the auspices of the new museum, before the opening of the center, Pontus Hultén says, with stark disapproval of his predecessors' program: "We attached great importance to a clean and conscious hanging, completely contrary to how it had been done before — confused, disorganized, with a lot of carelessness. We tried to show the opposite."[64]

What Pontus Hultén himself calls his baptism of fire in Paris[65] was the second exhibition at the Grand Palais, a full-scale retrospective of one of Hultén's all-time favorite artists: Francis Picabia. "I knew from the beginning that we would open by showing the two great French Dadaists, Duchamp and Picabia, who were both forgotten in Paris," said Hultén. "I decided to start with Picabia at the Grand Palais in 1976 and then Duchamp when we opened the new museum the following year."[66]

If Duchamp was disregarded and forgotten in Paris, Francis Picabia was arguably disgraced. This wealthy, flamboyant, hard-drinking, hash- and opium-smoking dandy and playboy, who himself seemed to refuse to take anything seriously, was indeed never taken seriously by the Parisian art establishment in his own time, much of which, like Duchamp, he spent in exile in New York. If anything, his reputation had further deteriorated after his death. In his late period, Picabia, curiously like several Modernist pioneers, including Malevich, turned to representational painting. Picabia's late production of kitschy, semi-pornographic Neo-Realist nudes had further degraded the artist. Like Magritte and others, Picabia was not considered to be in *good taste*, still an indispensable mark of quality in the snobbish Parisian art world. "There were even rumors that Picabia had painted portraits of Hitler," says Olle Granath. "He was not at all comme-il-faut in Paris."[67]

(Jean-Hubert Martin confirms that Picabia did indeed do "a small drawn portrait" of Hitler, adding that "very few people knew about it."[68])

For the Picabia exhibition, scheduled for early 1976, Pontus Hultén introduced the new working method he would develop at the Centre Pompidou, with teams of curators assembled to work in parallel on different exhibitions. This may seem obvious with today's star curators and guest curators. At that time, however, the very concept of a curator was new, not yet commonplace in the museum world. The same applied to the idea of independently operating working groups within an institution. Pontus Hultén is recognized as the inventor of this method, which is now commonplace in modern art museums, as the New York Times noted in its memorial text about Hultén.[69] Hultén told friends and family about the new opportunities that opened up for him here in Paris, compared to back in Stockholm, with access to this staff of hungry, ambitious, well-educated younger employees, trained to conduct research in a different and more thorough manner than he was used to.[70]

Evidence of Hultén's early confidence in Jean-Hubert Martin is that he chose him as his closest collaborator for the production of the key Picabia exhibition. As third curator, Hultén boldly appointed, on Martin's initiative, the only woman on the original staff of the new institution, Hélène Seckel, now Hélène Klein, an art and literature scholar from Strasbourg who had joined the MNAM at the age of twenty-three. When I meet her in Paris, Klein tells me about the enormous responsibility of working on this exhibition as her first assignment with Martin, who was only a few years older. Hultén followed his method of interfering as little as possible as long as everything went according to plan, although Klein confides that he may have engaged a bit more than usual in details in his particular love of Picabia.[71]

The Picabia exhibition was a huge production involving a large number of institutions and collectors on both sides of the Atlantic. Like Duchamp, Picabia's work was more recognized in the United States than in Europe. Here, Pontus Hultén's network of contacts and reputation in New York was a precondition for the dignity of the exhibition. Lenders and partners included MoMA, the Philadelphia Museum of Art and many other leading American and European institutions and private collectors, including Moderna Museet and also the Dansmuseet (The Dance Museum — the Rolf de Maré collection) and Gerard Bonnier in Stockholm. The Louvre itself was engaged in the complex operation of assembling a larger selection of Picabia's dispersed output than had ever been shown before.[72] Dominique de Menil was, of course, in the background. Among the lenders were also note younger artists such as Jasper Johns, Arman and Carl Fredrik Reutersward, reflecting the importance of Picabia to the avant-garde of the sixties.[73]

Most important among these lenders and collaborators was Picabia's widow Gabriële Buffet-Picabia,[74] a key figure in the early Modernist avant-garde. Pontus Hultén had long cultivated a good relationship with her, as with so many elder women in the art world.

The exhibition was a massive exposé that also included films and an ambitious documentation of Picabia's texts. Among the many commonalities between Picabia and Duchamp were their love of language, puns and riddles. In her catalog text, Gabriële Buffet-Picabia mentions that her husband wrote constantly but never spoke about it. Martin reveals that the team was proud of the discovery made during the production of the exhibition, as a contribution to Picabia research — that the artist had taken his puns from lines in the pink pages of the Larousse dictionary.[75] Jean-Hubert recounts that the decision was made to include Picabia's late work, the kitschy nudes of the forties, which were controversial not only in the Parisian art establishment but also in international Picabia circles.[76]

According to Hélène Klein, the design of the exhibition emphasized, not surprisingly, the avant-garde and anarchist aspects of Picabia's work. Klein reveals that she and Martin were inspired by the epoch-making Documenta biennial in Kassel in 1972.[77] Martin says that Pontus Hultén "naturally" wanted to include a boat in the exhibition, the day cruiser that Picabia lived in on the Riviera. The idea proved impossible to realize. The team had to settle for a Delage, a French sports car from the 1920s of the kind in which Picabia was known to make an entrance, as an alternative to the Bugatti.[78]

The catalog from the exhibition at the Grand Palais is a classic. The textless cover is adorned with a machine painting that was not shown in the actual exhibition, which Pontus Hultén notes was "strangely enough" not discovered by anyone — "everyone thought they had seen it."[79] The reason was that the owner of the work, Peggy Guggenheim, who had previously lent the same painting to Stockholm,[80] now unexpectedly suddenly refused and could not be persuaded, even though she and Hultén knew each other well. Guggenheim — yet another of the elder women with whom Pontus Hultén had great exchange with and use of during his career — was "capricious, very capricious" in Hultén's words.[81]

One of Hultén's old friends from Paris, the wealthy American artist William Copley, contributed a delightful text to the catalog. By now, Hultén had moved into Copley's penthouse on Rue Beaubourg behind the future new center (after initially staying with his friend Per-Evert Taube), a charming, modest-sized attic apartment that had the unique quality of a generous terrace with a magnificent view of the Parisian roofscape. Copley did not use the apartment, allegedly as his wife did not like it. He first rented and later sold it, allegedly reluctantly, to Hultén who, with this purchase, made one of the best private deals of his life.

Pontus Hultén's own introductory text in the Picabia catalog, only one page long, is among the most quoted and best I have read by him. In this affectionate text, he describes Picabia as the least known and respected of the pioneers of early Modernism. Hultén offers his explanation for this: the artist's flamboyance and nonchalant dandyism, his "persona" as we say in our time. Hultén writes about how many had always been provoked by the fact that Picabia had everything — that he was beautiful, rich and supremely talented, but even more so that he had the audacity not to take these rare gifts or even his own art seriously. Hultén observes that the artist's extravagance hardly reached the bottom of Picabia, but that there was something else — a mysterious darkness that is visible in the artist's eyes, Hultén writes, in all the surviving photographs, many of them Man Ray's portraits.[82] There is reason to suspect that Picabia had had less pleasant experiences growing up in his family of wealthy Cuban immigrants in Paris. Throughout his adult life, he was plagued by recurrent deep depressions for which he repeatedly committed himself to mental hospitals and health resorts.

Pontus Hultén concludes his text with perhaps his three most famous written sentences — the statement of his artistic taste that made Jean-Hubert Martin wonder how Hultén, at the age of eighteen, had managed to achieve such refinement[83] (this one may ask oneself, especially as Hultén, in the words of Hans Nordenström, "never made a good story weaker"): "Quand je avais 18 ans, je avais de sentiments très différents pour les deux Picas. Picasso je admirais. Mais Picabia je adorais." ("When I was 18 years old, I had very different sentiments for the two Picas. Picasso I admired. But Picabia I loved.")[84]

At one of our many meetings, Jean-Hubert Martin shares with me a wonderful anecdote that I have never heard told or read in writing in any other context: that of Hultén's meeting with Picabia.

Jean-Hubert says that Hultén had recounted how he had sought out the artist in Paris. Since Picabia died in 1953, this meeting must have taken place in the early fifties. Towards the end of his life, Picabia had moved back to the city of his birth, where he lived in the family building on Rue Danielle Casanova near the Tuileries. Hultén told Martin that one day he went to this address. Outside the gate, a fat old concierge of the typical Parisian type was asleep in a chair when Hultén arrived. He told the man that he was there to see Picabia and was asked: "Are you sure you want to see him?" Hultén assured him that he was sure. "Are you really sure?" the gatekeeper asked again, to which Hultén explained that he was indeed really sure. The old man pointed to a staircase and told Hultén to go up and knock on the door, which he did, without getting an answer. The doorman was of course Picabia himself, aged and ravaged to the point that Hultén had not recognized his idol. The master's health and energy may not have been the best, but the old playboy's anarchic Dada spirit obviously remained intact ...[85]

Jean-Hubert Martin confides that on one occasion, while working on the exhibition, he told Pontus Hultén that "we must not betray Picabia," receiving an amused look of questioning in response. The day of the opening arrived and no one could question the magnitude of the exhibition. Not even the many enemies of the prospective new center could argue otherwise than that the exhibition was outstanding. Although some critical voices were heard, after this exhibition no one could further question Francis Picabia's position among the pioneering masters of classical Modernism. Hultén had achieved crucial success already the year before the new museum opened. Olle Granath, who traveled to Paris to experience his teacher's baptism of fire, says with undisguised admiration: "It was truly fantastic and enormously impressive to see how he conquered Paris with Picabia."[86]

At the opening of the gala at the Grand Palais, Pontus Hultén spent an hour, as was his custom, chatting with dignitaries, patrons and potentates. As soon as the ceremonies were over, he grabbed Jean-Hubert Martin and said they should go to the bar on the other side of the Champs-Élysées for a beer. "We drank many, of course," says Jean-Hubert with a broad smile. "After a while, he took out two cigars and gave one to me. When he lit it, he said: 'So what do you say, we didn't betray Picabia, did we?'"[87]

20
Grand Opening

After being a gigantic pit, with three underground levels drilling down to a depth where the lowest basement floor was practically floating on the groundwater of the Seine surface level, as it were, the Centre Pompidou began in 1975 and 1976 to rise majestically like a stranded futuristic Poseidon from the abyss. A key moment in the Centre's transition from crater to building was the erection of the long steel beams that formed the monster's backbone in a much-publicized operation. The professional sailor and boat builder Sven-Olof Hellström, who designed several boats for Pontus Hultén and sailed with him in the Stockholm archipelago and in the Adriatic Sea, says that in response to his question, Pontus laconically described how the street lights had to be dismantled when the beams arrived at night with a motorcycle escort through the streets of Paris, but that "everything went well on the whole," a typical Hultén formulation.[1]

Then, as the skeleton of the building towered ever higher over the future new piazza, after dark bathed in the flood of lights like an alien Jules Verne monster teeming with tentacles, an unspoken phenomenon described by Calvin Tomkins in his New Yorker report occurred: the Parisians, whether they wanted/dared to admit it or not, began to embrace, even love, the "oil refinery."[2]

Meanwhile, for Pontus Hultén and Robert Bordaz, "the war of the many long dinners" continued, this struggle of attrition they had to fight, knives and forks in hands, to secure and expand the old museum's collection for the opening of the new one. Hultén has recited one of many visits to the home of a reluctant donor — the widow of the Constructivist Russian sculptor Antoine Pevsner, who controlled an important collection. During the conversation, Mme Virginie Pevsner asked why the French government intended to sell donated works from the collection in connection with the move to the new center (a persistent, baseless myth among the museum's opponents — French state museums were forbidden by law to sell from their collections). Bordaz seldom lost his temper, but this time he broke into a half-hour lecture to the widow Pevsner on the honor of the French state and his own obligations as a civil servant, ending with the phrase: "And now, my dear madame, I bid my goodbye."[3] Mme Pevsner later became one of the heirs whom Hultén and Bordaz managed to "turn" — a victory of the will that affected other donors as well.[4]

The "donors" had no formal authority over the MNAM collection. The works belonged to the museum and the state. Therefore, as the case continued to drag on, Pontus Hultén, not unexpectedly, advocated simply overruling the donors. Michel Guy, the Minister of Culture, forbade such a confrontation — everything had to be resolved in a salon-like manner so as not to hurt important feelings in the Parisian establishment. It remained for Hultén and Bordaz to continue the series of visits, dinners and soirees with these potentates.

An idea launched as an alternative by opponents of the new center, with support in the art establishment and in conservative political orbits, was that the new Centre Pompidou would become the world's largest art gallery, with temporary exhibitions and contemporary art, while the pride of Fauvism, Cubism and other older Modernism would remain at the old MNAM, which was to be renovated. This was a scenario that was not at all unreasonable but which Pontus Hultén categorically opposed, probably to the extent that he already played his frequently used card of threatening to resign. Hultén was relentless in his conviction that a modern art museum of this caliber needs the older Modernism, this "collective memory" in the form of a permanent collection. The starting point for Hultén and his staff was 1905, the year of the breakthrough of Fauvism with Matisse.

During the grueling negotiations, Hultén and Bordaz won a few more partial victories that helped to settle this protracted power showdown in favor of the new center — a final triumph of the new era over the old. Max Ernst's heirs were among those who were convinced early on, in connection with the 1975 exhibition at the Grand Palais (Ernst himself died in 1976).

A particularly complicated case concerned one of Hultén's personal heroes, Constantin Brancusi, the enigmatic Romanian sculptor, forerunner of Minimalism, and beloved friend of Duchamp; the great cook and coffee maker whom Hultén had studied and admired/spied on from afar in the 1950s, walking among his beloved sculptures in his studio on Impasse Ronsin, wearing his white Romanian peasant clothes, visible from the studio of Jean Tinguely and Eva Aeppli.

The meals that Constantin Brancusi served to friends like Duchamp, Eric Satie, Henri-Pierre Roché and others are legendary: homemade specialties from the Romanian peasant kitchen prepared on the wood-burning stove in the artist's studio on Impasse Ronsin, finished with Brancusi's famous strong coffee. It was said that Brancusi had cured sickness with his cooking.

Brancusi's *estate*, a concept encompassing the inheritance and rights, was controlled by two younger Romanian artist friends of the sculptor, Natalia Dumitrescu and Alexandre Istrati, who had sought out Brancusi when they arrived in Paris after the war, moved into a studio next to his on Impasse Ronsin, and helped the artist at the end of his life when he was alcoholic and unwell. The unmarried, childless master sculptor had bequeathed his studio and all its contents to the French state on the condition that it be restored in its entirety. For Brancusi, the studio was a work of art in itself. At the end of his life, he had stopped sculpting and exhibiting his art. Instead, he devoted himself to his studio and the interrelationship of the sculptures in the group (every time he sold a sculpture, Brancusi made a plaster copy so as not to disturb the harmony).

A condition for the heirs to agree to allow the new center to take over the Brancusi collection was that the artist's most famous sculpture "The Endless Column" could be displayed at its full height of seven meters. Dumitresco and Istrati also had plans for the reconstruction of the studio from Impasse Ronsin, where the master sculptor had lived and worked from the time he came wandering to Paris in 1904 until his death in 1957. According to Pontus Hultén, when the buildings on the cul-de-sac were demolished, parts of Brancusi's studio had been preserved, stored in an incomplete state in the basement of the old MNAM[5] (Jean-Hubert Martin, who worked extensively in the storerooms, denies that any such thing existed in the warehouses.)[6]

Here was a seemingly unsolvable problem. The ceiling height in the galleries of the future Centre Pompidou was far from sufficient for "The Endless Column," let alone the studio. However, the concept of unsolvable did not exist for Pontus Hultén when such a good cause was at stake. He soon came up with a typically simple and drastic solution: they would build the studio on the piazza in front of the center. The idea of a small, primitive building, a shed, built of plaster and wood, without electricity or running water, in front of the futuristic new complex did not appeal to Piano and Rogers — but all the more to Hultén, who waxed lyrical about the beauty of the little free artist in his hut in front of the palace of high-tech Modernism.[7]

Hultén had to overcome a nationalist opposition to the idea, as Brancusi was non-French and had not been a friend of Pompidou, as Hultén said.[8] Once again, he managed to win the battle against Piano and Rogers and other opponents by convincing Bordaz that a solution would also have a positive impact on the other donors. Everything was ready to recreate the studio on the piazza and construction was underway when it was suddenly stopped by the mayor of the third arrondissement. As Hultén describes it, Bordaz had forgotten to apply for a building permit — "or perhaps not forgotten but thought it best not to ask."[9] Such a permit would take years to obtain, the mayor reportedly informed Hultén and Bordaz, and "quite rightly" demanded the demolition of the already half-finished studio.[10]

The acute crisis required extraordinary measures. Hultén admits that he himself was "absolutely desperate." He says he sought out a Florentine sculptor, Roberto Lardera, who had been Brancusi's "only student." The next morning, Hultén says, Robert Bordaz came up to him and asked "Pontus, what have you done?" "And he never otherwise got personal with me!" says Hultén. "I thought I had done something terrible, but then he told me that the mayor was no longer a problem. Everything had been cleaned up. It turned out that someone high up in the authority was a member of the Freemasons. The Masons consider Brancusi their artist, even though Brancusi was not a Mason. With this argument, Lardera had managed to convince this person. Maybe Bordaz was also a member of the Freemasons and was involved. At least I think so. The Masons are a secret society. Many politicians were members there and that was the reason why the problem was solved without further demands for anything. The thing was saved, and we were extremely relieved. The execution of the command had put us in a deep crisis."[11]

Pontus Hultén expresses himself carefully when he says that Bordaz was "perhaps" a member of the Freemasons. His high position within the secret brotherhood was a well-known fact in Paris, where I have heard other versions of this story according to which Bordaz himself solved the matter the same evening in the lodge. The turmoil surrounding Brancusi ended with his estate being secured for the new Centre Pompidou. An exact replica of Brancusi's studio, but built with more modern techniques and materials, was completed in the opening year of 1977 with Renzo Piano as architect. According to Jean-Hubert, Hultén was not fond of this building, which he considered too perfect. Located south of the cultural center, the studio was moved to the north side of the piazza during a renovation at the turn of the millennium.

Another critical partial victory won by Pontus Hultén in those years before the center's opening was the agreement with Nina Kandinsky, the "godmother of the Centre Pompidou" as she is known.

Nina Kandinsky, born Andreevskaya, grew up in Moscow. She studied history and philosophy at university before meeting the abstract pioneer in 1916, when she was twenty-three and Wassily Kandinsky fifty. Other accounts claim that Nina was only seventeen when she first met Kandinsky. He is said to have fallen in love with the young Nina over the phone and to have painted a canvas of the beloved voice that very evening.

Nina Kandinsky was maliciously considered a fortune seeker by many but her marriage to Kandinsky lasted twenty-eight years, the rest of the artist's life. The couple had a son in Moscow who died early. Children were then a taboo subject between the couple. They moved together to Paris in 1933, after the Nazi regime forced the closure of the Bauhaus, where Kandinsky taught after fleeing Moscow and communism. The artist became very rich in the latter part of his life, a fortune that Nina managed well, never selling from the priceless collection Kandinsky had left behind except for domestic purposes. Ever since her husband's death in 1944, Nina Kandinsky lived as a widow in the couple's penthouse in posh Neuilly-sur-Seine, filled with art by Kandinsky and his contemporaries, antiques and other precious items. In the late seventies, Nina Kandinsky had been a well-known figure in the Parisian art world for more than forty years, with her extravagant style of dress and her famous collection of large rattling jewels. Jean-Yves Mock, who had known Nina Kandinsky since the 1950s, describes her with the native Parisian's unfailing sense of degrading nuance and tone: "She liked to wear extravagant clothes and a lot of makeup. She wasn't beautiful but she did her best. She had done her facelifts, not very good jobs. I met her on the Champs-Élysées where she was standing in the street with her jewelry after visiting a gallery and waving for a taxi in the evening. I tried to tell her she couldn't do that but she didn't care. She took taxi drivers up to her appartment in Neuilly to drink vodka. It was inevitable that she would be murdered eventually. It was bound to happen sooner or later."[12]

Pontus Hultén was well acquainted with Nina Kandinsky's collection, with many masterpieces in addition to those she had already donated to the museum. He had known her since the Kandinsky exhibition of mainly her works at Moderna Museet in 1965, when Nina had spent several weeks in Stockholm. In Paris, he cultivated contact with the widow in order to convince her to bequeath her art to the museum and the French state. Jean-Yves Mock relays that Hultén regularly dined with Nina Kandinsky at various fancy restaurants and that he himself accompanied him at these dinners. According to Mock, Hultén found Nina Kandinsky "a bit long-winded." He would excuse himself after a while by saying that he needed to make some calls, after which he would leave Mock alone with the widow while he himself relaxed with a couple of beers in the bar. "Pontus is very busy," Mock says Nina Kandinsky observed.[13]

One such evening in the spring of 1976, Hultén had decided that it was time for his tactical move. Jean-Yves Mock says that Hultén had asked him to come along as usual for dinner with Mme Kandinsky.[14] Pontus Hultén himself has said that this important dinner took place at the luxurious Lasserre restaurant near the Grand Palais and that Paris was at its best, "which helped."[15] Some way into the dinner, Jean-Yves Mock says, Hultén locked eyes with Nina Kandinsky and said: "Nina, if you don't write your will now, the Russians will invent a nephew and take everything you have."[16]

Early the next morning, still according to Jean-Yves Mock's account of the events, Nina Kandinsky called Hultén and said, as usual referring to herself in the third person: "Pontus, Nina has been crying all night. Bring the Minister of Culture with you and we'll meet at Mme Pompidou's at noon." Hultén, who knew that Nina Kandinsky was capricious and that it was important to seize the opportunity, succeeded in getting the Minister of Culture to come at short notice to Claude Pompidou's home on Île Saint-Louis, where Nina Kandinsky signed her will, by which the French state and the Centre Pompidou inherited her entire estate.

Four years after the will was settled, on September 2, 1980, Nina Kandinsky was robbed and murdered in her chalet in Gstaad, Switzerland, a homocide that remains unsolved. When the apartment in Neuilly was to be evacuated, Pontus Hultén demonstrated his psychic abilities, an anecdote that I have been told in several slightly different versions. After emptying the residence, Kandinsky's legendary jewelry collection had still not been found. "Look behind the stove" was Hultén's request (or behind the gas meter, in another version). Sure enough, there was the storied collection. Hultén explained his intuition by saying that Nina Kandinsky had grown up in Russia and that he knew that it was common in revolutionary times to hide one's valuables by fireplaces.

Fifteen oils and fifteen watercolors by her husband were donated in 1976, After Nina Kandinsky's death, more canvases from her husband's studio in Neuilly, his collection of works by artist friends, and even his entire fortune including his antiques collection followed — an inheritance worth billions of dollars. It was by far the largest single donation to the new museum, a treasure in the collection of the Musée National d'Art Moderne. In recognition of this invaluable gift, the center's library was later renamed the Bibliothèque Kandinsky (Kandinsky's library and archives were also included in the donation).

The ultimately victorious outcome of the the longstanding negotiations with donors and artists' families was crucial to the new museum's collection and position in the international art world. Niki de Saint Phalle is one of many who, like Richard Rogers, have praised this exceptional ability of Hultén's to break down resistance and impose his will: "He convinced people because his knowledge and convictions were simply greater than theirs," writes Niki de Saint Phalle in the 1996 book *Das gedruckte Museum von Pontus Hultén*. "Like when he persuaded Nina Kandinsky to bequeath her inheritance and Madame de Menil to donate her Jackson Pollock to Beaubourg. He had an amazing ability to get people on his side."[17]

Formally, these politically sensitive negotiations ended with a compromise solution. Works by the artists Braque, Laurens and Rouault — whose families were the informal leaders of the donor resistance — as well as André Dunoyer de Segonzac, another French Modernist who had not tampered with paint, would remain in the old MNAM premises, while the rest of the collection would be moved to the new museum. A number of galleries in the old building would be set up under MNAM's administration for the aforementioned artists, while the rest of the building, after renovation, would become a museum for art from the late nineteenth and early twentieth centuries, subordinate to the Louvre. It was, as Pontus Hultén commented, a typical French compromise: "devilishly complicated, probably impossible to make work and guaranteed to satisfy no one."[18]

This compromise solution would never be put to the test of reality. Once the Centre Pompidou opened, the lamentations of the old establishment were drowned out by its vulcanic success. As people flocked to the new center, the halls of the old Palais de Tokyo were emptier than ever. The administrative house of cards collapsed without much fanfare. It was a decisive victory for the "entertainer," "circus director," "pornographer," "Viking" and all the degrading nicks by which he was called, Pontus Hultén. His willpower had overcome the old Parisian establishment. Hultén and Bordaz's triumph in the protracted tug-of-war also marked the breakthrough for a broader, more popular definition of modern art, at the expense of the old forms of expression such as painting and sculpture. Time was on Hultén's side. Art would never again be what it had been.

That Pontus Hultén would open the Centre Pompidou with his guiding star above all others since his youth, Marcel Duchamp, seems a given. It was a matter of pride for Hultén to once and for all restore the honor of his teacher in his old hometown. At this time in January 1977, nine years after the artist's death, Duchamp's obscurity in Paris was still compact. The city's museums had managed to ignore the revival of interest in Duchamp brought about in the international art world by Neo-Dadaism, Pop Art and, not least, Hultén's own efforts. So little was known about Duchamp in Paris, according to Hultén, that many considered him an American artist associated with the loathed New York scene.[19] Duchamp expert Jean Clair, who was appointed to work on the exhibition, reveals another typically Parisian aspect of the disdain for Duchamp: "He was seen as a strange provincial character from Rouen, not to be taken seriously."[20] Robert Bordaz's comment when Pontus Hultén announced that he had decided to open the center with a Duchamp retrospective, the first in France, is telling: "Good, but who is that?"[21]

In the production of the Marcel Duchamp exhibition, Pontus Hultén mobilized the entire network of contacts he had built up over more than twenty years of working with this artist, which must be considered the very foundation of his oeuvre as a curator and museum director. Over two hundred works by Duchamp, almost all of the artist's surviving production, were collected mainly from the United States. In Paris and the rest of France there was not much to be found. Almost the entire exhibition had to be borrowed from outside. Most important among the lenders was Anne d'Harnoncourt at the Philadelphia Museum of Art, where, after persistent persuasion, the museum reluctantly agreed to lend even sensitive key works such as

"Nude Woman Descending a Staircase, No. 2" and several of the early machine paintings.

In these negotiations, Pontus Hultén had his most important ally in Duchamp's widow Teeny Duchamp, another of those elderly women so essential to Hultén's career, with whom he had carefully nurtured his relation since their first meeting in Stockholm in 1961. Hultén was a frequent guest with Teeny and her children Paul and Jacqueline Matisse from her first marriage to Pierre Matisse, Henri Matisse's youngest son, and their families, at their house in the village of Villiers-sous-Grez near Fontainebleau, an hour's drive south of Paris. At the time of the preparations for the opening exhibition at the Centre Pompidou, the artist's widow was recovering from a traffic accident. "Pontus was very protective of Teeny," says Jean Clair, who attended several Sunday visits to Fontainebleau during the production of the exhibition. "It was touching and somewhat amusing to see how he wanted to protect little fragile Teeny from the outside world with his large body shell."[22] In the negotiations with the museums, Teeny Duchamp was not fragile. With her on his side, Pontus Hultén got almost all the loans he wanted for the show. "Who could say no to Teeny?" as Jean Clair says.[23]

Some of Duchamp's works, like the original of "The Large Glass" and his last installation "Étant donnés," could not leave Philadelphia, as Hultén and his staff knew from the beginning. The copy of "The Glass" was of course borrowed from Stockholm, as were several other replicas built by Ulf Linde, Per Olof Ultvedt and their associates. For "Étant donnés," Hultén entertained far-reaching plans to recreate the mysterious installation, as yet unknown to the wider art public, that had only been shown to the world after Duchamp's death in 1968. These plans had to be abandoned due to the level of complexity.

In his mobilization of Duchamp expertise, Hultén also engaged Ulf Linde. Linde wrote a text in the extremely ambitious catalog, which contained a great deal of new material on Duchamp. The catalog was produced in the form of four volumes bound in green faux suede in a box of the same material, referring to Duchamp's "La Boîte verte." One of the volumes was an unfinished novel by Duchamp's good friend Henri-Pierre Roché,[24] a key figure in the early twentieth-century Parisian and New York avant-gardes, with a portrait of Duchamp as the novelist-author Victor — a text published here for the first time.[25]

Ulf Linde and Jean Clair found each other while working on the exhibition and remained friends. They represented similar approaches to their common idol Duchamp, a worship of genius and an eternal interpretation of Duchamp that united them with many others in the then still limited but growing coterie of Duchamp followers, but which was not shared by Pontus Hultén. To put it simply, while Hultén took Duchamp at his word, or pun, and thought it was enough for his works to speak for themselves, Linde and Clair, and many of their peers, aspired to read all conceivable and inconceivable secret sentences and messages into the master's art and texts. "Ulf and I agreed that Duchamp was a highbrow intellectual," says Jean Clair. "He read Mallarmé and was highly educated, even if he pretended not to be."[26] In this ongoing battle of words between different schools of Duchamp scholarship around the world, where the proliferation of advanced theories is rampant, I personally think it is enough to listen to Duchamp himself, who had nothing but indifference to any form of genius cult. Duchamp did not regard artists as intellectual geniuses, but rather as craftsmen. He believed that success was largely determined by chance, while the majority of artists, including many of equal or greater talent, remained unknown.

It was typical of Hultén that in addition to the established Duchamp experts, if one could call them that at the time, he also included a joker in the game. Jacques Caumont was a former film technician whom he, like so many others, had met through Niki de Saint Phalle and Jean Tinguely. Caumont is now a maverick in Duchamp circles, distrusted in more literalist circles. Nevertheless, his contribution to Duchamp science is undeniable. Hultén seems to have taken an immediate liking to Jacques Caumont, a colorful personality with a characteristically long wispy beard and hair whip, whom I met and got to know in Paris.

Caumont says that Duchamp was unknown to him when he met Hultén, but that the artist immediately piqued his interest.[27] Hultén started talking to him for the simple reason that Caumont, like Duchamp, is from Normandy. When Hultén began planning the exhibition, he commissioned Caumont, despite his lack of knowledge and experience of both Duchamp and art exhibitions, to research the artist in their shared Normandy home, a task Caumont undertook with his then wife, the British photographer Jennifer Gough-Cooper. According to Hultén, he and Caumont were united in an intention to "re-Frenchify" Duchamp by creating a link to the artist's Normandy roots.[28] Caumont had the idea that there was nothing more French than Normandy's markets, so it was decided to build a typical wooden market hall as an entrance to the exhibition itself, which filled the entire top floor of the new center. For this creation, the artist André Raffray, with a background as a set painter in the film industry, later renowned for his ability to copy masterpieces from art history — another new acquaintance Hultén made through Caumont — painted tableaux on glass with scenes from Duchamp's life, which were placed as backlit ceiling paintings in the "market hall." A booklet was printed with these images. This surprising, generally considered kitschy installation provoked criticism and confusion in Duchamp circles, in the art establishment and also internally among the museum staff and the team of curators, where Ulf Linde, Jean Clair and others were negative. Teeny Duchamp did not like the move either, calling Raffray's pictures in the booklet, now a collector's item, "the ugly pictures."[29]

The *Marcel Duchamp* exhibition is described as beautiful, with great impact. It must have been a magnificent experience with the two hundred works presented across the two thousand five hundred square meters of completely open space. The success of the exhibition is more questionable. Pontus Hultén himself explained that it was both a good and bad decision to open with Duchamp.[30] On the negative side, the exhibition of Duchamp's never easily accessible art was drowned out by the sensation of the building's inauguration. Press coverage was limited and visitor numbers to the exhibition were modest in relation to the huge crowds that streamed through the Centre Pompidou building (access was initially free to the giant entrance hall and to the facade's escalators and viewing areas — it was only for the exhibitions on the upper levels that visitors had to pay admission).

At the same time, the *Marcel Duchamp* exhibition, although overshadowed by other events, fulfilled Pontus Hultén's ambition of re-establishing Duchamp in Paris once and for all. Jean Clair states that the reception of the exhibition in the press was mixed, but that the respected art historian André Chastel wrote a large and important article in Le Monde[31] which helped re-establish the artist in France. "After the exhibition, it was no longer possible not to take Duchamp seriously," says Clair.[32]

It was a forceful entrance into Paris by "Lohengrin" — opening by restoring order, dragging the city's two super-Dadaists, Picabia and Duchamp, out of the closets of oblivion and placing them at the front of the stage from which Duchamp in particular has dominated contemporary art ever since. Although Duchamp's comeback was, as Hultén himself said, inevitable,[33] it was hardly destined that the artist would have such an unlimited influence on the development of modern art well into the twenty-first century, when contemporary artists continue to recast his more than a century-old ideas in more or less strained "interpretations." Pontus Hultén's importance for Marcel Duchamp's remarkable comeback is undisputed.

A far more populist exhibition that helped shape the image of the new MNAM and the Centre Pompidou was *Le Crocrodrome de Zig et Puce*, the gigantic crocodile-like machine dragon by Jean Tinguely and others that greeted visitors just inside the entrance to the vast submerged Forum arena. The monumental sculpture (more than thirty meters long, fifteen meters wide and ten meters high[34]) can be seen as another monster child of *Dylaby* and *she*; the idea of mastodon sculptures incorporating other art that Tinguely, with the help of his artist friends, was simultaneously developing in "Le Cyclop" in Fontainebleau, the life's work that occupied all of Tinguely's free time during this period.

Tinguely's co-artist in the *Crocodrome* was his Swiss friend Bernhard Luginbühl, an underrated artist for whom I have a soft spot and whom I would describe as a heavier, more brutal version of Tinguely in his machine sculptures. Niki de Saint Phalle and Daniel Spoerri also participated. If *she* had been Niki's show, *Le Crocodrome* clearly bore Tinguely's signature. The interior of the sculpture included the miniature "Musée Sentimental," by Spoerri and his then companion, the German art historian Marie-Louise von Plessen, who would later become Pontus Hultén's life partner: a cabinet of curiosities including a number of "memorabilia" from the history of France and Paris, such as Marie-Antoinette's knitting needles and the keys to the Bastille, in cases welded with bulletproof glass. Inside the dragon was a roller coaster. One of its hind legs was lined with chocolate, donated by the German chocolate magnate and major art collector Peter Ludwig, one of Hultén's benefactors, from which children could chop chips (hygiene and safety requirements were not what they are nowadays, apparently). No lone adults were allowed here, only those accompanying children. Between the dragon's legs, a new version of Tinguely's "Poor Man's Ballet" from *Art in Motion* 1961 and Luginbühl's pinball machine for giants in rusty iron, which was later moved to the "Le Cyclop" in the Fontainebleau forest, rattled and made noise, accompanied by a thundering steel ball track running along the monster's "dorsal fins." The success and popularity of the *Crocrodrome* was instantaneous — a frantic continuation of the show that had already begun with the crowds, the jesters, the musicians, the fakirs and the constant spectacle on the piazza outside the entrance.

There are many stories about the creation of the *Crocodrome*. Pontus Hultén of course made sure that as often as he could, almost every night as I understand it, he assisted his friends with drinks, advice and action during Tinguely's usual manic round-the-clock work. On one of these nights, Tinguely, industrious as ever, with Hultén's approval, staged the theft of a conspicuous Centre Pompidou feature, one of the huge curved ventilation pipes rising from the concrete across the piazza. The pipe was transported to the Fontainebleau forest where it congenially adorns his own then rapidly growing "Le Cyclop" monster. The anarchist prankster spirit, if one wants to use a forgiving expression, was intact in both Tinguely and Hultén when they now made their entrance on the main stage.

Le Crocodrome was scheduled to be completed in its lair for the opening of the Centre Pompidou, but the schedule fell through. This only added to its appeal, as Tinguely and his team continued to expand the monster sculpture throughout its life, until it was dismantled in the fall. Obituaries in Paris newspapers announced the "demise of the Crocodrome."

The presentation of the museum's collection was, of course, a major concern for the inauguration of the Centre Pompidou and the new MNAM — and a litmus test for Pontus Hultén as museum director. It's impressive how he and his team had managed to strengthen the collection in the three and a half years that Hultén had worked with the museum before its opening. In addition to the important donations, the generous purchase budget of thirty million francs a year had allowed for a great deal of additions. Although prices had risen considerably, far above inflation, it was still possible in the seventies to acquire contemporary and even older masterpieces by artists such as Klein, Magritte and Dalí.

Among the international contemporary artists purchased were the Germans Joseph Beuys, Gerhard Richter and also Sigmar Polke, this advanced artist with his own personal version of what we might call German Pop Art. Jean-Hubert Martin tells the story of how, during an exhibition of Polke's work at a gallery in Paris, he selected a canvas

Pp. 374–375: Seppi Imhof, Rico Weber and Jean Tinguely working on *Crocodrome de Zig et Puce*, Centre Pompidou, Paris, 1977.

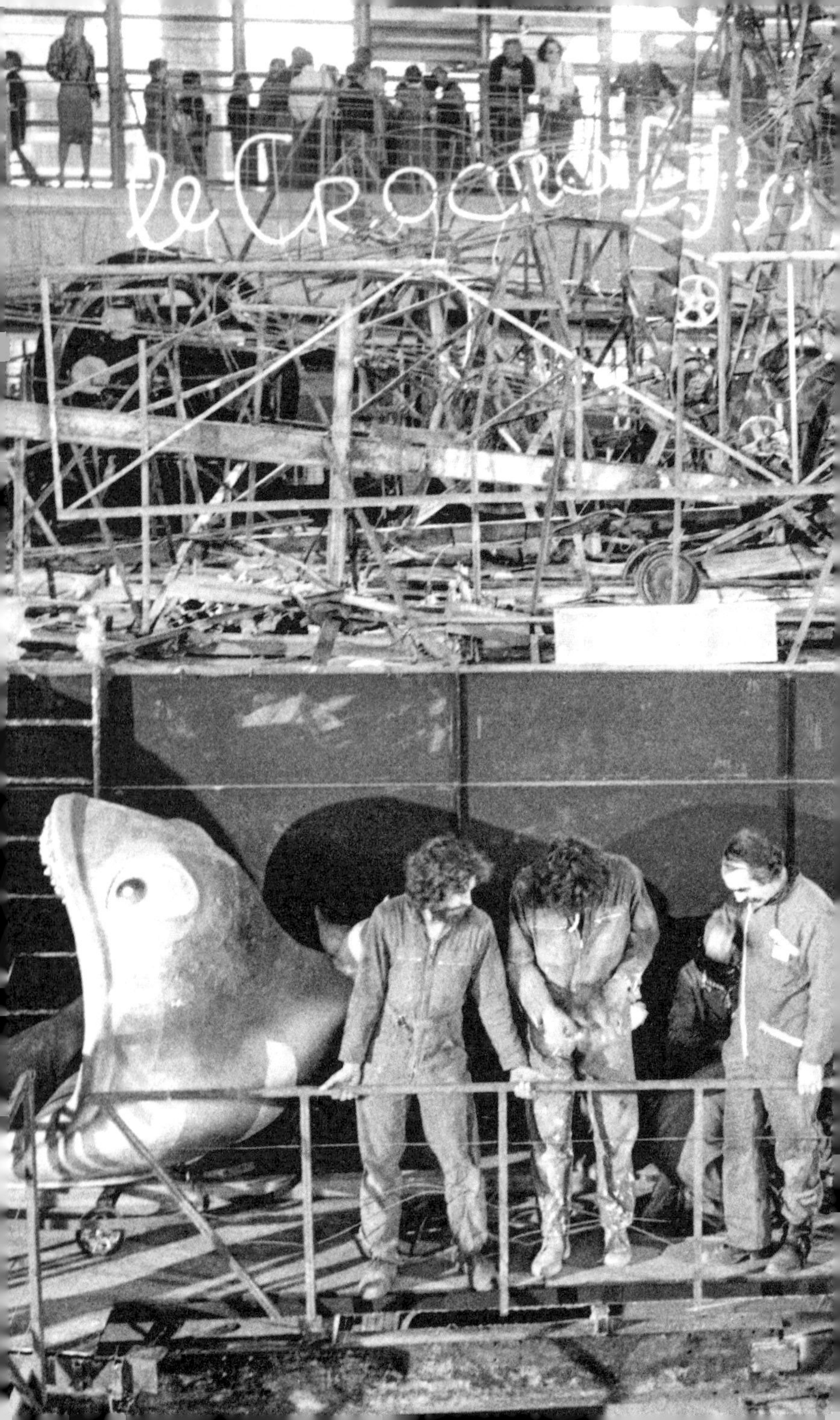

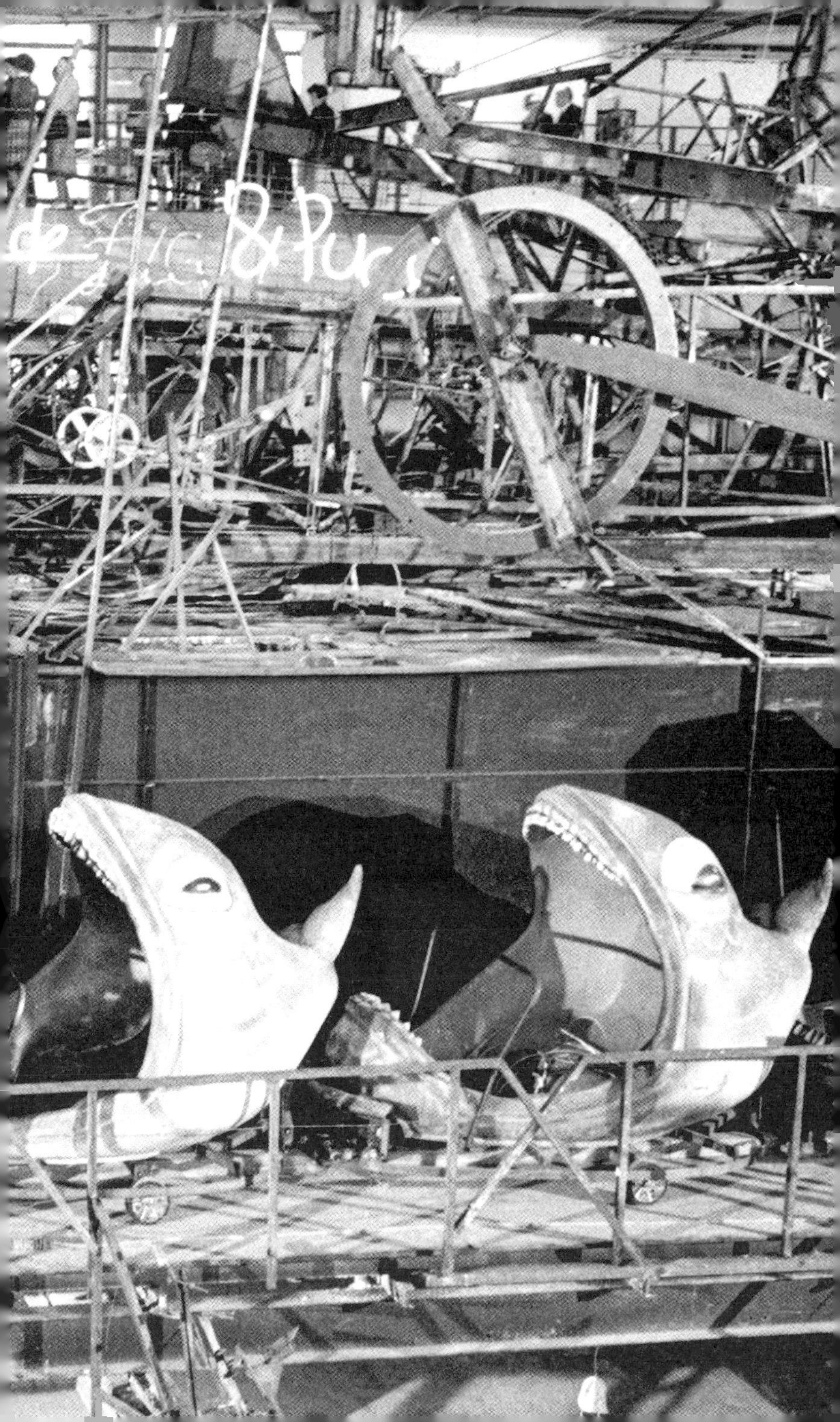

that he recommended to the purchasing committee but was rejected on the grounds that there were better artists in the genre in France. Hultén then visited the gallery himself and selected a much more radical painting which he personally presented to the committee and which was then of course accepted.[35]

Hultén followed the same strategy as in Stockholm. The purchase committee had to be unanimous, otherwise no acquisition. Among the more oddball works Hultén purchased, which gave the collection an eccentric and crowd-pleasing accent, was the record shop of Nice artist Ben[36] from his hometown, "le Magasin," where Yves Klein and other Neo-Realists had used to gather and hang out, complete with its interior and assortment — "an anthropologically interesting thing," as Hultén told Jean-Hubert Martin when he, surprised, inquired.[37]

To further enhance the glory of the collection and the prestige of the museum at the opening, Pontus Hultén also took more unconventional measures. From the Soviet state, he managed to secure the loan of a number of Constructivist portal works. The collection of Dadaism, American Neo-Dadaism and Pop Art, where he had been particularly scrutinized by the Parisian establishment, was strengthened by a long-term loan from Peter Ludwig's collection of works by Kurt Schwitters, Jasper Johns, Andy Warhol, Roy Lichtenstein and Cy Twombly, among others. Throughout his career, Pontus Hultén nurtured his relationship with Peter Ludwig, for whom he also acted as an advisor. Ludwig, whose fortune was based on his chocolate empire, was considered the world's greatest art collector at the time. His reputation in the museum world was questionable, especially in Paris where suspicion of Ludwig as a German was considerable. After Pontus Hultén left the museum, his successor Dominique Bozo returned this collection to Ludwig. "An idiotic mistake," says Jean-Hubert Martin. "Everyone knew that the Ludwig did not usually ask for its loans back but instead donated them after some time."[38]

Peter Ludwig is considered not only the world's greatest private art collector of his time, but one of the greatest ever. He was also the largest donor to museums in Germany and other countries. No less than thirty museums in Germany and other countries have been named after him as a result of his donations. Ludwig was controversial, criticized by some for the uneven quality of his purchases and for using his art collection for business purposes.

To broaden the presentation beyond the classical art forms, the museum borrowed a collection of two hundred photographs from the French national library Bibliothèque national. There was no photography in the old MNAM's collections. Pontus

Hultén's personal interest in photography is disputed, but he saw photography as a natural part of the offerings of a modern art museum. During his tenure as director, the museum established a national French photographic collection. Another dimension that Pontus Hultén, well ahead of his time, was keen to emphasize was the global dignity of the museum. He borrowed works and objects from the anthropological museum Musée de l'Homme ("Museum of Man") and from other parts of the world, with the ambition to show art not only from Europe and the United States but from all continents.[39] "He was very adamant that we should include works from Africa, South America and Oceania, for example, and not just some African sculptures to show the inspiration for Picasso's cubist sculptures, which had been done before, but as art hung with the collection, to show that we were really serious about being a museum for the whole world," says Jean-Hubert Martin.[40]

Germain Viatte was responsible for the presentation of the classical modern collection on the third floor. He explains that the hanging was conceived as an Alsatian village, with an open landscape where walls of screens formed streets and squares, with secondary works from different art historical movements grouped around the central pieces — an informal, open, intuitive display that broke with the French museum tradition of presenting the different artistic works separately. Entering this art-historical landscape, visitors were greeted by a disarming overture: the self-taught maverick Henri Rousseau's (called "Le Douanier," "The Customs Officer," after his profession) monumental canvas "La Guerre" from 1894, depicting a riding sword-wielding female warrior, borrowed from the Louvre's then Impressionist branch Jeu de Paume, hung on a back wall that screened the view before entering the collection itself. "It was a very good idea to put visitors in the mood and prepare them mentally for what they were about to see," as Jean-Yves Mock says.[41]

The contemporary collection on the fourth floor was presented under the direction of Jean-Hubert Martin. It featured an exhibition of Gerhard Richter, another bold choice given the artist's nationality. Pontus Hultén was ambivalent about Richter's production of abstract and photorealistic paintings, but accepted without question when his colleague suggested the German virtuoso for the opening exhibition.[42] In addition to the various exhibitions, there were several other features in and around the museum, such as Claes Oldenburg's colossal ashtray on one of the terraces.

In the run-up to the official opening on January 31, 1977, nervousness grew among the museum's management and staff. Although curiosity about the new center was palpable, resistance remained aggressive. Among numerous other controversies, Pontus Hultén was forced to defend the new center before an auditorium of nearly one thousand outraged French artists from the sixty-eight movement at a mass meeting in the cultural center in the suburb of Créteil, led by the French Pop artist Gérard Fromanger.[43] The artists' critical perspective was the socialist one espoused by much of the cultural left — the center as an elitist colossus which, by swallowing up resources, would undermine the idea of bringing art to the people, according to André Malraux's vision of local cultural centers around the country. Such centralist initiatives were outdated according to many on the left. Instead, art should infiltrate the people in a guerrilla strategy. There was no end to the number of angles from which Centre Pompidou could be attacked by representatives of different political camps and special interests. Here, long before the opening, Pontus Hultén had fulfilled his old goal from Stockholm that something would be written about the museum in the newspapers every day — almost exclusively negative and hostile articles.

Few dared to express any opinion other than that the new center could not possibly attract the crowds needed to justify the large and controversial investment. Modern art was still generally considered too marginal to attract a wider audience. In its calculations, the museum management had anticipated up to five thousand visitors a day — a figure that far exceeded the combined numbers of the institutions that would be part of the new center. The most optimistic observers hoped for up to eight thousand visitors on public holidays. The Ministry of Culture had repeatedly summoned the museum management to justify and defend their estimates of attendance.

A measure of *how* low the expectations of the new cultural center were in the market is that no restaurateur was prepared to take on the task of operating the center's restaurant at the opening.[44] The management was forced to take the creative provisional measure of hiring Air France's catering department as restaurateurs at the opening. Annick Boisnard describes the tense atmosphere among the staff, who of course worked around the clock in the run-up to the opening. Only one person was calm — Pontus Hultén. "Pontus kept saying: 'Don't worry. People will come,'" says Annick Boisnard.[45] Unlike his Parisian colleagues, Hultén's experience made him well aware of the potential appeal and popularity of modern art.

Over three thousand five hundred guests were invited to the opening. Boisnard recounts how the museum staff had devised a method of manipulating the response lists to accommodate more guests than their allotted quota, at the expense of the other institutions, in order to avoid turning away all the important guests who would be traveling from all over the world — artists, donors, patrons, lenders, gallerists, and other potentates from the United States in particular.

The opening day was a gigantic event. Around eight thousand guests were waiting when the doors opened — more than double the number invited. For Pontus Hultén himself, the opening began with the task of guiding President Giscard d'Estaing through the entire museum and the Duchamp exhibition before the formal opening ceremony, while all the thousands of guests, including "some fifty"[46] royalty and heads of state, waited without champagne in their glasses or even access to water or toilets on the floors to which they were directed by the color coding on their tickets.[47]

About Giscard d'Estaing, Pontus Hultén says that he got to know him well, that while the President was never unfriendly at their meetings, he never seemed to make any effort to understand what Hultén was trying to say, "probably because I wasn't born in France."[48] In Calvin Tomkin's article in The New Yorker, Hultén reveals he was "furious" at the President's lack of interest in the Duchamp show. "I have guided three generations of Swedish royalty at Moderna Museet and they all knew what they were seeing," as he says in the article.[49] Giscard d'Estaing's opening speech is remembered for its cold, contemptuous tone. Neither Pontus Hultén, Robert Bordaz nor anyone else was thanked. "Giscard said: 'We see here before us the seed of President Pompidou,'" says Jean-Yves Mock. "Can you imagine anything so offensive and rude?"[50] Jean Clair reveals that he and Ulf Linde sat drinking beer in a café on the piazza outside the museum, watching the crowds, refraining from indulging. Pontus Hultén himself confided that, unsurprisingly, he found time during the opening to slip away for some drinks "in a secluded room in the office area" with his old friends Billy Klüver and Jean Tinguely.[51]

When the new museum and the entire Centre Pompidou opened to the public a few days later, all the dams broke and, like a spring tide, washed away all the negativity that had overwhelmed the building, the center and the entire initiative from its inception. The whole of Paris flocked to the Marais and the center, as if in a prolonged mega version of the Stockholmers' migration to *she* just over a decade earlier. Day after day, week after week, month after month and year after year, the queues filled the piazza in front of the center, with attendance ranging from ten to twenty-five thousand people on weekdays and up to fifty thousand a day on weekends — five times higher than the most optimistic hopes.[52]

The art world had never seen anything even close to this sensational, chaotic shock success. Certainly the building itself was the biggest crowd magnet, with the views of Paris that visitors could enjoy free of charge through the glass tubes of the escalators. The library also attracted a large number of visitors.

Yet Pontus Hultén's role in this historic triumph should not be underestimated. The museum he and his colleagues had created was in many respects the full-scale realization of the vision of the active, multidisciplinary, extremely accessible function of the modern art museum that he had developed in Stockholm and that coincided with the ideas of Piano and Roger — something as exclusive as a realized utopian dream. It was striking how many of the ideas from Kulturhuset materialized here in Paris almost ten years later.[53] Into the Paris night, the monster building bathed in the spotlight like a giant luxury cruiser for art and culture.

The new Centre Pompidou was completely unprepared for its own colossal popularity, which presented the building, staff and organization with acute problems. Almost immediately, the total openness that had been an important part of the original vision had to be severely curtailed — to a degree that only one of the center's twelve entrances could be used. Queues became ridiculously long and audiences had difficulty moving between floors because of the congestion.[54]

Over time, the center and the museum would be forced to gradually restrict access further. The public success of the Centre Pompidou was of a magnitude that no one could have predicted. Nor, as many had foreseen, did the attendance decline when the novelty wore off, but continued steadily year after year. Understaffing on all fronts was a constant problem. The wear and tear and the strain on the building, which in the early years was plagued by technical "teething problems," forced management to close down the museum as early as 1981 for renovations and rebuilding to control the flow of visitors.

The opening of the Centre Pompidou marked a dramatic shift in the position of modern art in society and on the Paris street scene. The modern mega-museum was born. All modern art museums that have opened in the world since then have directly or indirectly related to the Centre Pompidou.

According to Calvin Tomkin's analysis, perhaps the most important part of Pontus Hultén's impact on art history lies in this epochal popularization, as the impresario of modern art that he was. The vision that a modern art museum should not be reserved for a classical cultural audience, but accessible and inviting to all, with no prior knowledge required, had been Hultén's stated ideal from the beginning of his career as a museum manager. As Calvin Tomkins wrote in his article in The New Yorker, the MNAM was not only the largest modern art museum in the world, but also the first to be designed from the outset for a mass audience.[55] "Pontus was undoubtedly one of a handful of people, like Duchamp, Warhol, and a few others, who contributed most to transforming art from a small clique phenomenon into something of huge impact — a part of the everyday life of ordinary people," as Tomkins said in my interview.[56]

In the weeks, months and years after its opening, visitors flocked to Paris to see the new monster museum, including heads of state, business leaders and all the dignitaries of the art world. Renzo Piano, who showed the building to many celebrities, says that some cautiously asked if the building was finished. "But Mr. Honda liked the building because he thought it looked like a motorcycle," says Piano.[57] Paris had a new attraction comparable to the Eiffel Tower. Pontus Hultén had become a leading figure in the international museum world, publicized and interviewed by media from all over the world. Renzo Piano and Richard Rogers were no longer young and unknown but the new enfant terrible superstars of international architecture.

The urban vision behind the creation of the Centre Pompidou, too, was instantaneously realized. Even before its opening, new cafés, shops and galleries began to move into the area around the new cultural center, which ultimately contributed to the Marais district's regaining of its chic status and ensuing gentrification. Much has been written about how the new cultural center generated this metamorphosis in central Paris — a process that has been repeated in various cities around the world over the decades. The Centre Pompidou and the MNAM were the first modern art museum in the world to perform this "magical" function in the urban dynamic. As the British architectural critic Rowan Moore phrased it in an article on the occasion of the Centre Pompidou's fortieth anniversary, calling the Centre Pompidou "probably the most important post-war building in the world": "It is in this way, as a magically transformative cultural building, with an appearance both popular and progressive, and the power to lift a city

On a visit to Amsterdam, I met master architect Rem Koolhaas, who revealed that he too had entered the architectural competition for the Centre Pompidou at a very young age. "I'm very happy that I didn't win," Koolhaas added. "Why?" I asked. "Because I could never have done anything as good as that." I asked if it's correct to consider the Centre Pompidou as the beginning of Postmodern architecture. "Yes, the beginning – and the end," Koolhaas replied. "Why the end?" "Because it's not possible to make anything as good as that." (Conversation February 4, 2017)

and change its image, that Pompidou has been most influential (...). Pompidou's descendants include the grandiose projects — the Pyramid in the center of the Louvre, the Arc de Triomphe in La Défense — that later presidents built in Paris and that ambitious mayors built in French cities. Then the Guggenheim in Bilbao and the very many aspiring icons, from the brilliant to the disastrous, that followed. (...) At its best, Pompidou is about celebrating the life of cities and energizing their centers — and in the 1970s, as a result of a combination of suburban flight and destructive planning, the traditional city appeared threatened and in need of such support."[58]

We must regard the realization of the Centre Pompidou as something of a miracle — a final test of this uniquely progressive era, the sixties and early seventies, which in the late seventies came to an end. Renzo Piano, who forty-five years later divides his time between Paris, New York and his native Genoa, with offices in all three cities, calls himself in an interview "Beaubourg's Quasimodo." He has given hundreds of interviews about the building, which he says will live for two thousand years. "For every bolt in the structure, I have a sense of why it's there."[59] Piano smiles broadly at our meeting in his Paris office, a block from the center, as he tells us, "About once a month, I take my family for lunch in the restaurant at the top of the Centre Pompidou. Every time, I think to myself: how the hell did we do this ..?"[60]

21

Pingpong with the world and art history

Jean-Hubert Martin clearly remembers that from the beginning Pontus Hultén had decided to highlight three artists, Duchamp, Picabia and Malevich, at the new MNAM. He is unsure whether he also harbored the basic vision for the large-scale, epic, multidisciplinary trilogy of artistic manifestations that would become not only the focus of his work as founding director of the new MNAM, but the crowning achievement of his entire career — the so-called Pingpong exhibitions: *Paris–New York* (1977), *Paris–Berlin* (1978), *Paris–Moscow* (1979) and *Moscow–Paris* (1981). (*Paris–Paris*, 1981, on the theme of international art in Paris in the first half of the twentieth century, is classified as a separate part of the series, not included in the Pingpong suite but in many respects related to the other exhibitions).

Never before or later would Hultén have the opportunity to play out his visions of art and its role in world history on such a scale, in a cycle of art exhibitions that in its dimensions is more comparable to a Russian epic novel or a romantic symphony suite.

Pontus Hultén himself has claimed that the idea of tracing these "axes" through art history in exhibitions had already begun to develop in his mind in Stockholm.[1] This seems natural, as the Pingpong exhibitions contain many of the perspectives, ideas and artists that he had immersed himself in over the years. Pingpong can be seen as Hultén's true masterpiece — a mastodonic examination of all the knowledge, insights and beliefs he had built up over his more than twenty-five-year career.

Judging by Hultén's own statements, and information from others, New York seems to have been the starting point for the transatlantic art historical axis that the exhibition trilogy would draw: his own experiences in Paris in the fifties with the many American artists who had settled in the city after the war with the GI Bills, and the New York art scene earlier in the century with the French and other Europeans who had come there to escape both world wars, including his idols Duchamp and Picabia of course, but also the Surrealists, Mondrian and others; how these European artists had inspired the development of American modern art with movements such as Abstract Expressionism, Neo-Dadaism and Pop Art. It was a scenario of artistic and cultural cross-fertilization that may seem conspicuous in retrospect, but was an original product of Pontus Hultén's unique insight into the symbiosis of art with history and social development, and the global nature of artistic development. In the interview with Hans Ulrich Obrist, Hultén says that in the 1960s he had proposed an exhibition on this theme to the Guggenheim, but received no response.[2]

There is, though, a contradictory version of the background to *Paris–New York*, narrated by Jean-Hubert Martin, namely that the exhibition had its roots in an idea by Blaise Gautier, the former director of the CNAC, for an exhibition on the theme of artistic exchange between Paris and New York.[3] "What I remember is that later on, after he became alcoholic, Gautier once came up to Pontus and accused him of having stolen the idea of *Paris–New York* from him and then left him by the wayside," says Jean-Hubert Martin.[4] Germain Viatte, who was Gautier's second-in-command at the CNAC, does not remember any such idea from Gautier but concedes that he can imagine that Gautier may have discussed such ideas because of Pontus Hultén's reputation as a proponent of New York art.[5]

Determining the truth, as in so many other similar cases in this story, is impossible or at least impractical. With my knowledge of Pontus Hultén's personality and management style, it does not seem unlikely that the story with Blaise Gautier could be wholly or partly true. Hultén was known for that kind of ruthlessness. If so, Gautier would be far from alone in having been shoved aside during Hultén's career, in which collaborators could be sacrificed to achieve visions (remember Daniel Spoerri and *Art in Motion*, Hans Nordenström, Oscar Reutersvärd and others). Certainly, Blaise Gautier, praised by all as a kind, intelligent and capable museum man in the old French tradition, was left out of the team at the new museum.

Fairly soon after arriving in Paris, Pontus Hultén's vision seems to have expanded to include the eastern art metropolises of Berlin and Moscow to form the art historical axis where Paris was merely a "bus stop," not the center of the art world as the French had imagined, in Jean Clair's depiction.[6] Once Hultén started thinking in broader geographical and art historical horizons, the choice of cities seems to have been natural — in particular Moscow with its beloved avant-garde, and the treasure of early French Modernism built up by some wealthy Russian collectors before the First World War and the revolution. In Berlin, there was the link to the Bauhaus and the German art scene before World War I and during the Weimar Republic, with Expressionism, Berlin Dadaism and other pioneering modern movements.

In Pontus Hultén's basic vision, *Moscow–Berlin–Paris–New York* is said to have been conceived as one giant production. Malitte Matta, who was recruited to the museum to work on the exhibition, according to Hultén because of her excellent contact networks in artistic circles in both Paris and New York,[7] is one of those who have told me about how the plans for the exhibition cycle took shape. Matta describes that on a wall in her study she had a large number of images, texts and other materials arranged under the headings of the different cities. According to Matta, it was she herself, and no other, who first suggested dividing the exhibition into several parts.[8] Be that as it may, the giant exhibition was soon splitted into first two, then three stages, chapters or whatever we want to call them. The reasons were partly the enormous, unmanageable volume of material and partly that the reality of the Cold War made it politically impossible to unite Moscow and Berlin in the same exhibition, something that Hultén and his colleagues could have foreseen.

True to his new habit, Hultén commissioned the tasks of preparing and producing the various exhibitions among teams of art historians/curators on his staff, most of them young or very young, aged between twenty and thirty. After drawing up the guidelines, Hultén, as was his custom, handed over the responsibility to his colleagues with full confidence. In addition to Malitte Matta, Hultén chose the trio of Alfred Pacquement, Daniel Abadie and Hélène Seckel (later Klein), all just over twenty years old, as the *Paris–New York* team.

All of the actors I have spoken to have vividly pictured the major difficulties in the production of *Paris–New York*, in particular the extremely tight production time of just over six months. The sparse production budget contributed to the arduous nature of he operations. "Checking into a regular hotel was out of the question," says Hélène Klein. "In New York, we stayed with friends or in horrible little rooms in the cheapest possible boarding house — I still remember the cockroaches and the smell, yuck!"[9] Klein shares a glimpse from the work on the exhibition that says a lot about Hultén's trust in his collaborators and also about his outlook on the art world and his exhibition making. "I once complained that it was difficult to find some material I was looking for on Alfred Stieglitz," Klein says. "'No, it's not difficult at all,' Pontus said, 'You just go to New Mexico and meet his widow Georgia O'Keeffe, who is very nice.' To me it was an unimaginable that one could seek out such a famous person in this way, but to him it was the most natural thing."[10]

In the production of the exhibition, Pontus Hultén, as the representative in New York, naturally engaged Billy Klüver. *Paris–New York* was a complicated global operation in which Pontus Hultén again mobilized his by now superior network of friends and contacts all over the world. The Museum of Modern Art, the Guggenheim and the Philadelphia Museum of Art (with its Duchamp collection and other works of Dadaism and Surrealism) would be among his most important partners throughout the Pingpong cycle. The lenders included numerous leading North American art institutions, collectors, patrons and galleries. The list fills more than one densely written full page in the catalog.

In addition to painting, sculpture and installations, *Paris–New York* would present film, photography, music, dance, architecture, industrial design and literature in an expanded version of the multidisciplinary shows at Moderna Museet and *The Machine* in New York. While working on the literature section, Hultén came into contact with Serge Fauchereau, who would become a close collaborator at several institutions in different countries. Fauchereau had a background as a literature teacher with a degree from the University of Texas in Austin. He recounts that he was still wearing cowboy boots and pink shirts with large collars, recently returned from Texas, when he and Hultén first met on a walkway at the Centre Pompidou some time after the opening in 1977.[11]

Moreover, *Paris–New York* would feature five reconstructed environments of particular significance to the cross-fertilization of European and American art in Paris and New York in the early twentieth century: Gertrude Stein's salon on Rue de Fleurus in Paris; Katherine Dreier's and Marcel Duchamp's Societé Anonyme museum on 47th Street in Manhattan; master photographer Alfred Stieglitz's small gallery 291 on Fifth Avenue; Peggy Guggenheim's Art of This Century on 57th Street, with futuristic interiors by artist and architect Frederick

Kiesler; and Piet Mondrian's basement studio where, during his New York period, the artist developed his extremely simplified painting in new forms. It was typical of Pontus Hultén that, by recreating historical environments, he wanted to enrich his exhibitions with additional spatial, intellectual and anthropological dimensions in order to offer the audience, even the uninitiated, alternative entrances to the overall experience.

A new feature of *Paris–New York* was Hultén's initiative to invite the other institutions of the Centre Pompidou — the library, the music institute and the center for industrial design — to participate with their own content, which all of Hultén's fellow directors enthusiastically accepted. The collaboration helped boost the exhibition to even greater dimensions, setting an international precedent in the process.

Daniel Abadie, one of the curators of *Paris–New York*, relates a dramatic story that illustrates the tense atmosphere during production and the hothead temper for which Pontus Hultén soon became notorious in Paris.

In the course of production, communication with representatives in New York had revealed that something was wrong with the plans for the replica of Mondrian's studio that they were about to construct. "I think it may simply have been a confusion of centimeters and inches," as Abadie says.[12] In his own interpretation of Pontus Hultén's "democratic" working method, with a great deal of freedom and responsibility for employees, Abadie, known for his independence, had himself taken the decision to remove the Mondrian studio from the show. "It was a necessary move," says Daniel Abadie. "We would never have had time to finish it and it could not have been fitted into the exhibition."[13]

So confident was the young Abadie in his professional position that he had "forgotten" to inform his boss Pontus Hultén of this decision. He recalls an afternoon close to the opening, when they were working against the clock on the hanging over the entire fifth floor of the center, when Pontus Hultén, who no longer participated in the work on the hanging at the same tangible level of detail as in Moderna Museet's pioneering years, came up to the gallery in the company of his friend Edward Kienholz, who was represented in the exhibition (the fact that Kienholz was a Los Angeles artist was no obstacle, as the exhibition's interpretation of the concept of New York was the broadest possible). "He had been drinking all day with Kienholz, I'm sure, and was in a hell of a mood," says Abadie. "He asked to see the Mondrian studio. I had to tell him that we had to cancel it. He was absolutely furious and pushed me up against a wall with his big fists on both sides of my head and his face very close to mine and said: 'You little bastard, you don't respect me and don't do what I say just because I'm not French. You like Blaise Gautier and are against me. We're paying for this exhibition and you're going to do what the hell I say'! I saw then that he was not so sure of himself really. He saw himself as a poor lonely and misunderstood child. A few months later I met him at a dinner with Jean and Niki. He had been drinking and came up to me and accused me of badmouthing him to others. After that I was in the freezer for six months with nothing to do."[14]

When we meet in Paris forty years later, Alfred Pacquement, another of the young curators in the *Paris–New York* team, and later himself a long-serving director of MNAM,[15] is even more critical than Abadie of the organization of the exhibition and the conditions provided by Hultén. "There were far too many art historical errors because we didn't have time to check everything properly," says Pacquement. "It was too imprecise. Pontus was very difficult to read. He gave some information but not more than that. It was also unclear who was responsible for what. Maybe that was the way he wanted it. The lack of precision frustrated me as the exhibition was such an important political statement."[16]

Paris–New York was the only one of the Pingpong exhibitions with an art-historical theme extending to the present day, while the other two were purely historical. A starting point was, appropriately, the Armory Show of 1913, the massive exhibition that in one mighty bang introduced the innocent American public, not yet accustomed to anything other than realist painting and sculpture, to European modern art, from van Gogh, Gauguin, Cézanne and Impressionism to Fauvism, Cubism, Futurism and Cubo-Futurism, represented by the show's most scandalous painting by the youngest participating artist, Marcel Duchamp's "Nude Woman Descending a Staircase, No. 2." The Armory Show caused outrage in New York and throughout the United States, even up to former President Theodore Roosevelt who proclaimed the eternal truth that "this is not art," but inspired generations of American artists and became the starting point for modern art in North America. *Paris–New York* showcased many of the masterpieces that were the American art public's first exposure to Modernism.

The *Paris–New York* exhibition and catalog clearly demonstrated the impact of New York in the development of French avant-garde art — how American gallerists, collectors and patrons such as Walter Arensberg, Katherine Dreier, Peggy Guggenheim, Alfred Stieglitz and others, as well as MoMA, had invested in Parisian and European movements such as Dadaism and Surrealism while they were still ignored by the French art establishment. Alfred H. Barr and MoMA were way ahead of Paris even with Cubism, which was only purchased for the French national collections after the Second World War. It became clear that during and after the war, American artists enjoyed access through MoMA to a much more complete picture of young Modernism than their Parisian colleagues.

In his preface to the catalog, Pontus Hultén proclaims that it had been"clear early on" that a series of exhibitions would explore the importance of the city of Paris for the development of modern art.[17] He argues that Fauvism and Cubism did not leave a deep mark on modern American art, while Dada, Constructivism and Surrealism had a decisive influence on the first American art movements. He complements this observation with a vintage Hulténian thesis that this has to do with the American visual perspective being more vast than the European one, and that American culture lacks references to the Renaissance theory of perspective that Cubism had broken down, thus revolutionizing art.

A major part of the exhibition was Abstract Expressionism, with works by Pollock, de Kooning, Rothko, Franz Kline, Sam Francis and others, juxtaposed with its French counterpart, Tachisme, the "informal style," represented by Jean Dubuffet, Jean Fautrier, Michel Tapié and others.

The influence of Duchamp, Kurt Schwitters and other Dadaists on Neo-Dadaism and Pop Art was one of the main points of the exhibition. Paris was represented not only by the French, but also by artists from other countries who had lived and worked in the city and who are classified under the broad concept of L'École de Paris, such as the Italian Futurist Severini, the Surrealists Dalí and Magritte, the Dutch Expressionist Karel Appel, the Argentinian "spatialist" Lucio Fontana and many others.

The *Paris–New York* catalog is a mighty art historical document of the intellectual and creative exchange between Paris/Europe and New York/USA in various artistic fields. At over seven hundred pages, this piece ushered in a new era for the modern exhibition catalog as an art form in its own right, often as important as the exhibition itself. The contributors were of the highest caliber. Writers included a cavalcade of big names such as film historian Henri Langlois, Jean Prouvé,

Daniel Cordier is a legend in France as he was a close associate and assistant to the resistance hero Jean Moulin, whom he met in 1942. Cordier got his interest in modern art from Moulin, an art collector who used an art gallery as a cover during the war. After the end of the war, Cordier began painting, collecting and trading art. He opened his first gallery in Paris in 1956, where he showed the French Neo-Realists and was the first in France to exhibit American Pop artists. In 1959, he opened the Cordier & Ekström Gallery together with Swedish-born American diplomat Arne Ekström. Cordier was a member of the MNAM's acquisitions committee, where he was an important ally of Hultén. From 1973, in collaboration with artists and others, Cordier was among the largest donors to the Centre Pompidou, with a total of over one thousand works of art and objects donated to the French state collection.

Duchamp biographer Robert Lebel, philosopher Claude Lévi-Strauss and American Surrealist/Abstract Expressionist artist Robert Motherwell. The text on Pollock and action painting was penned by Harold Rosenberg, the influential art historian who coined the term. Pierre Restany writes about the exchange between the Neo-Realists and Neo-Dadaists in Paris and New York, where the Chelsea Hotel was the focal point. Restany states that Neo-Dadaism's bigger and stronger baby sibling, Pop Art, later crushed this fragile collaboration. The importance of galleries in the exchange between cities is discussed in an interview by Malitte Matta with Leo Castelli, Ileana Sonnabend and Daniel Cordier. Matta also contributed a lengthy interview with Gabrièle Buffet-Picabia about her and Picabia's first visit to New York for the Armory Show in 1913. Matta's colleagues had been critical of her lack of formal experience, but Hultén knew what he was doing when he included the artist's widow in his team because of her first-class contacts in both the Paris and New York art circles. "We initially saw her as a 'femme du monde,' but she immediately proved her quality," says Jean-Hubert Martin.[18]

Pontus Hultén's friend and benefactor William Copley contributed a wonderful text under his signature CPLY about being introduced to Surrealism by his brother-in-law in Los Angeles, a cartoonist at Disney Studios, and how they both opened the Copley Gallery in Beverly Hills where they tried to sell Surrealist art to collectors among the city's movie moguls — a difficult and thankless task. For the literary section of the exhibition, legendary publisher Maurice Girodias, founder of Olympia Press, which published the scandalous successes of Vladimir Nabokov's *Lolita* (1955) and William S. Burroughs' *Naked Lunch* (1959), wrote about the literary scene in Paris in the twenties around bookseller and publisher Sylvia Beach and her bookshop Shakespeare and Company.

Paris–New York catalog, 1977. Cover painting by Larry Rivers.

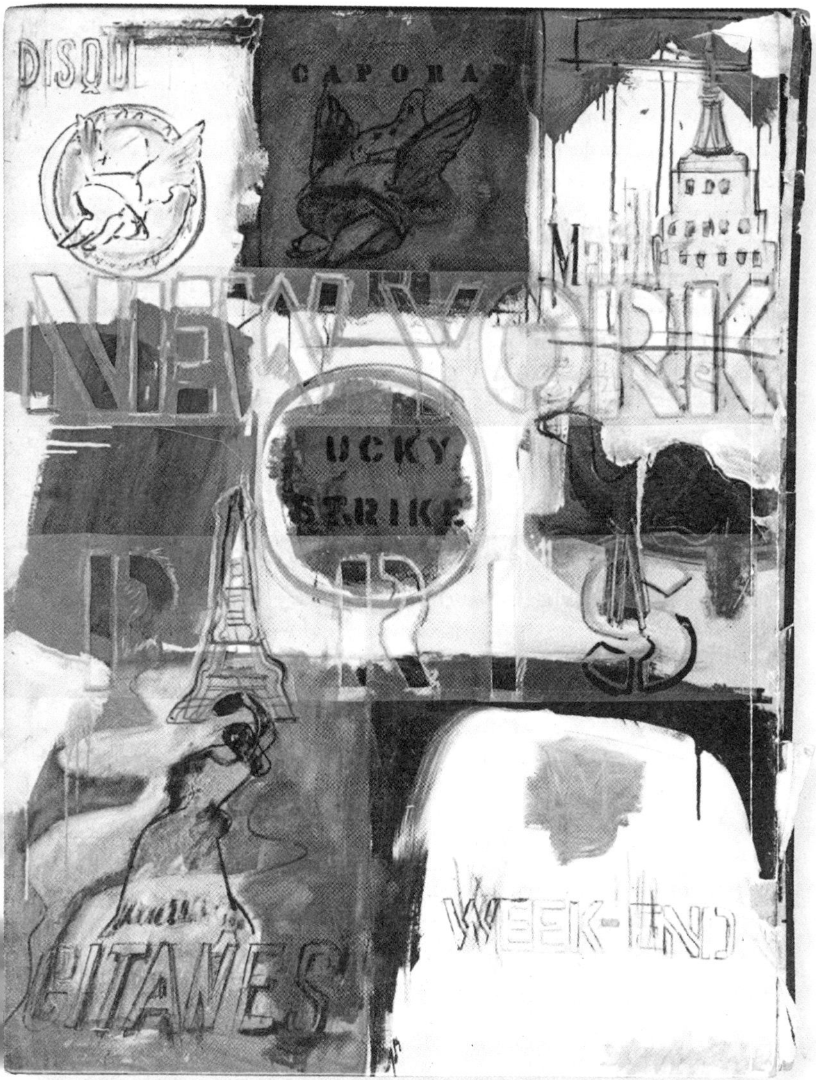
DISQU
CAPORA
UCKY
STRIKE
WEEK-END

The list of famous collaborators in the directory could be made considerably longer. There was no limit to the level of ambition. Most of the texts are long winding essays packed with facts and names. It seems incomprehensible that the team managed to produce both this catalog and the exhibition itself in just over six months production time, also in view of the limited technical aids available compared to our own time. Almost as alien is the fact that this massive, to put it mildly advanced, deep-drilling printed matter, the exhibition catalog as an art historical treatise in coffee table format, with a volume of text equivalent to one or more doctoral theses, was sold in an edition of over one hundred thousand copies.

According to Alfred Pacquement, the problems with *Paris–New York* lay mainly in the contemporary section, where Pop Art was given too much of an advantage. Several of the leading French contemporary artists were left out, which was severely criticized. "We also made too many dubious parallels, with Rauschenberg, Jasper Johns, Poliakoff, Soulages and de Kooning in the same room and so on," says Pacquement. "We fell into the trap. But the worst thing was that the Neo-Realists weren't given enough space."[19] He argues that Hultén's exhibition consolidated New York's dominance in the global art arena. As an outsider studying at the catalog and other documentation forty years later, it appears that the contemporary French artists were simply unable to stand their ground against more powerful and driven American colleagues such as Rauschenberg, Johns, Warhol, Lichtenstein and others.

The *Paris–New York* exhibition was an overwhelming experience for visitors to the new cultural center when it opened in October, nine months after the inauguration, presented across the entire fifth floor and elsewhere in and around the center, with a rich program of events offered in the center's other institutions as well. A few years later, Pontus Hultén himself said of *Paris–New York* that the exhibition "probably went over the heads of the audience, even though it was perhaps the best in the series."[20] He has also called *Paris–New York* the most beautiful in the trilogy of Pingpong exhibitions and particularly emphasized its high technical level.[21]

In summary, *Paris–New York* received a mixed reception. Attendance was good, with over one hundred and eighty thousand visitors. The press was largely critical.

Daring to challenge his many conspiratorial opponents in the opening year with a show that confirmed the prejudice against Hultén as a

Paris–Berlin catalog, 1978. Cover and graphic design by Roman Cieślewicz.

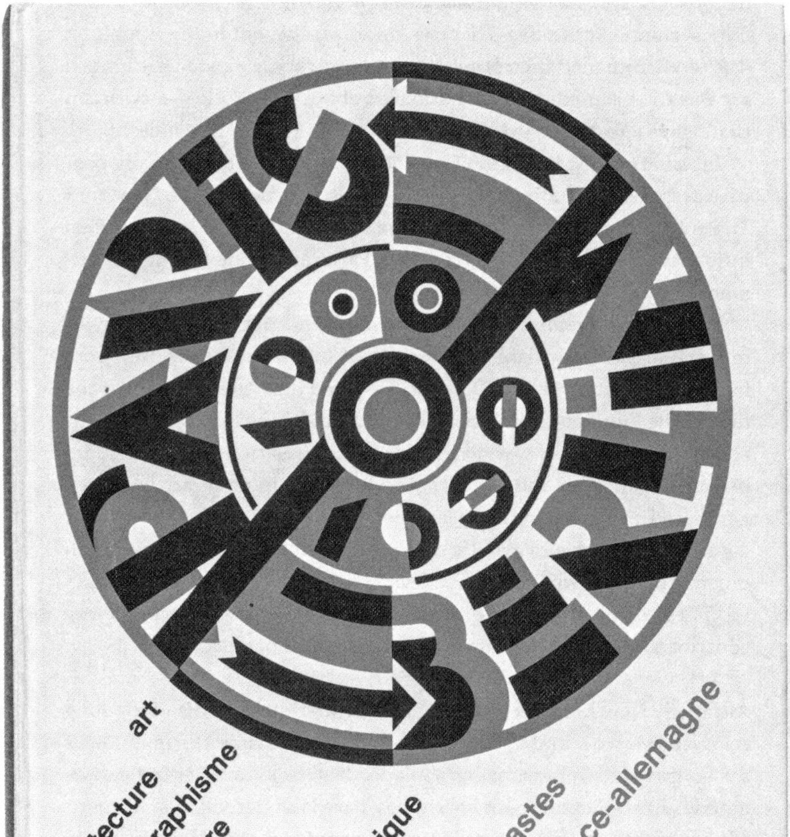
art
architecture
graphisme
littérature
objets industriels
cinéma
théâtre
musique
rapports et contrastes
france-allemagne
1900-1933
centre georges pompidou
12 juillet - 6 novembre
1978

champion of New York and American art was a bold, not to say provocative, move, controversial both within the sixties leftist movement and in conservative, protectionist art camps. As Hultén chronicles, many critics' point of attack was that the American element in the exhibition was too dominant, while others, on the contrary, claimed that French art was too prominent in an exhibition about New York — a criticism that "gave a confused overall impression," as Hultén concludes.[22]

Internationally, the exhibition received a more unequivocally positive response, including a large, enthusiastic review in the New York Times that praised *Paris–New York* for highlighting the lesser-known influence New York had exerted over Paris, alongside the well-documented inverse relationship.[23]

While *Paris–Berlin* and *Paris–Moscow* stand out in the history of modern art as undeniable successes and milestones, *Paris–New York* had some question marks. These have faded over the years. Even the first of the Pingpong exhibitions has come to be regarded as an epochal high point in post-war art history — a revelation that opened up brand new insights into how the evolution of modern art had been generated in exchange between metropolises; how older ideas had continued to evolve in artistic dialog between the continents — even during the wars, when many believed that artistic progress had halted. These connections were made clear to audiences on many levels, contributing to a globalization of art historical perspectives.

Although New York seemed an obvious first stop for the Pingpong triptych, Moscow and the Soviet Union soon became the main focus for Pontus Hultén personally. While for New York and Berlin he delegated the production to his colleagues, here Hultén took more responsibility for the details. It was clear from the start that Moscow would be the most difficult challenge. No one had previously undertaken the kind of cooperation with the Soviet authorities that Pontus Hultén envisioned, not in art and hardly in other contexts either. Here the entire arsenal of knowledge, contacts and skills in intrigue that Hultén had built up would be put to full use.

Pontus Hultén made his first trips to Moscow and Leningrad on his own, shortly after taking over as museum director in 1973.[24] Soon he began to bring along with him on his eastward commute the team he had formed for *Paris–Moscow*, including Jean-Hubert Martin, Serge Fauchereau, and Stanislas Zadora, a young Polish art historian specializing in Slavic art who would become one of Hultén's closest friends

Paris–Moscow catalog, 1979. Cover and graphic design by Roman Cieślewicz.

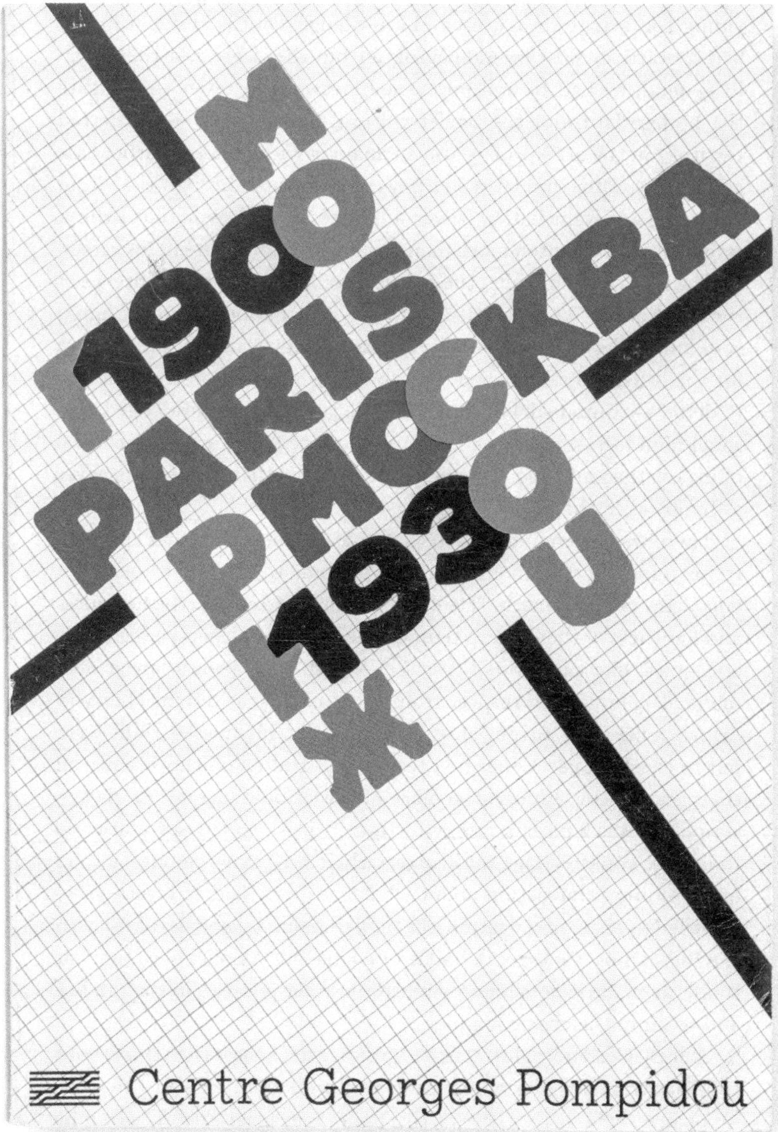
1900
PARIS
MOCKBA
1930
Centre Georges Pompidou

and who possessed the Russian language skills crucial for the project. Troels Andersen, the Danish art historian and expert on Russia and the Soviet Union, was also deeply involved in the production, providing contacts, information and knowledge. Pontus Hultén initially had contacts in Moscow and Leningrad, but they were relatively few.[25] In general, he had to build up a new network in order to navigate the nomenclature of the Soviet cultural bureaucracy — uncharted territory in the art world, to use an analogy with Hultén's father Eric and mother Elsie and their journeys of discovery through the virgin wilderness of Kamchatka. It was a hazardous endeavor that I think satisfied Pontus Hultén more than perhaps anything else in his career.

The degree of difficulty, the political complexity and the absence of the rules of the Western art world were explanations for why Hultén could not delegate responsibility to his colleagues in the same way as for the other exhibitions, but had to engage himself on the spot and in detail — combined, I'm sure, with the generally acknowledged personal high level of pleasure he found in these trips to Russia. Several of his relatives and friends have vividly told me that Hultén was never as happy as in the Soviet Union.

There was much in the Eastern and Slavic mentality that appealed to his mind. "It was enough for him to come to Finland to be enlivened," says Olle Granath. "He loved the sorrow and joy, the heaviness and lightness of the Eastern temperament."[26] His physical appearance and poise, like that of a "Prussian general,"[27] or even a Soviet field marshal, commanded respect from the Russians, as did his ability to drink vodka with anyone. Just as manifestly, his hustler skills were put to excellent use. Colleagues testify that Hultén quickly learned all the tricks to cut through the maze of Soviet bureaucracy. As always, simplicity was a basic strategy for him. Tip-Ex to the secretaries so that they could change and correct their scripts were one method of obtaining information about what had been said at meetings — knowledge that gave Hultén the upper hand in negotiations with the Russian bureaucrats. A bottle of cognac for a political commissar suddenly made it possible to publish ten color pictures in the catalog, and so on in the classic manner.

Stanislas Zadora claims that the group made no less than thirty trips to Moscow during the preparation and production of *Paris–Moscow*. According to Serge Fauchereau, this figure is exaggerated: "Divide it by half."[28] Jean-Hubert Martin says he never counted the trips. Whatever the exact number, the eastern expeditions were numerous, long and arduous. Wonderful pictures exist of the team, with Jean-Hubert in classic bearded sixty-eight style, trudging along the winter streets of Moscow, Hultén with his characteristic fur hat to protect him from the Winter War cold. They stayed in large state hotels where no food was available. The evening meal often consisted of pepper vodka and sardines. In the evenings, the team sat drinking in vast, desolate Russian restaurants with a single dish on the menu. "Pontus loved those places," says Stanislas Zadora. "There would be two hundred kilo ladies dancing and drunken soldiers singing. It was like Dadaist revues, truly Surrealist experiences."[29] Hultén's love of Dadaism can make one forget how close Surrealism was to his heart as well. In Russia it was offered in abundance. The mills of the Soviet bureaucracy grinded slowly. There was no way to speed up the process — hence many long days and nights of waiting in Moscow, Leningrad and other Soviet cities, welcome to Pontus Hultén. With each new trip, the number of contacts at museums and institutions grew. Stanislas Zadora says that during each stay in Moscow, Pontus Hultén himself visited the Soviet State Museum of Natural History and Anthropology, an institution he loved in its magnificent antiquity, where he was always drawn to the Arctic section. His parents' field of expertise remained a strong interest for Hultén throughout his life.[30]

As representatives of the French National Museum of Modern Art, Hultén and his team had a historical tradition to draw on, fundamental for the realization or even initiation of this gigantic undertaking. Hardly any other Western country would have been able to realize something similar. de Gaulle's relationship with the Soviet state was unique during the Cold War, with the President's bold third position of keeping the US at a distance in order to build his own relations in many areas with the Soviets. In Paris, exhibitions and cultural events in cooperation between France and the Soviet Union had been organized in the sixties and early seventies. Here, trust was established as a necessary foundation for this new collaborative project. The strong French Communist Party, within which Hultén and his staff established secret contacts, was deeply rooted in the Soviet state, which benefited Hultén and his team.

I have also heard from several sources that Pontus Hultén himself emphasized that he had an important personal advantage in his contacts with the Soviet authorities precisely because of his father Eric's Russian history. The world-renowned Russian artist

Sergei "Afrika" Bugaev, a disciple of Pontus Hultén, is one of those who have told me that his father's contacts and reputation were important, perhaps even decisive, to Hultén's cooperation with the Soviet authorities. Pontus Hultén also confided to Bugaev that he had some elementary knowledge of the Russian language — something that Hultén of course concealed in his Russian contacts and which I have not seen any other information about. According to Bugaev, Hultén said that his parents used to speak Russian to each other when they didn't want their son to understand what they were saying and that through these secret conversations he had built up some rudimentary understanding of the language.[31]

At the beginning of the *Paris–Moscow* project, important contacts were established with the long-time (more than half a century!) director of the Pushkin Museum in Moscow, Irina Antonova[32] and her colleague Alexandre Khaltourine, the museum's artistic director. In their first exchanges with these officials, the idea of a triple axis exhibition, Moscow-Berlin-Paris, was still alive — an idea that Antonova and Khaltourine immediately rejected as politically unfeasible. Instead, they proposed only *Paris–Moscow*.

During my December 2019 conversation with Irina Antonova, then ninety-eight years of age, still active at the museum, she denied that political considerations were behind her reluctance to include Berlin in the exhibition. "It was because I was afraid that the importance of Russia for the development of Western art, which was our main focus, would be overshadowed," Antonova said.[33] Jean-Hubert Martin dismisses this "alternative truth." "I think Antonova is lying," Martin writes in an email. "She was NOT part of the initial discussions about the exhibition. They took place at the Ministry of Culture with Khaltourine. The decision was political."[34]

This abrupt change in circumstances presented Pontus Hultén and the museum with a formidable challenge. This was in the fall of 1977. A major manifestation was planned for the summer of 1978. The team realized that it would be impossible to produce an exhibition in such a short time with the Soviet bureaucracy as a partner. After the meeting at the Pushkin Museum, Hultén and his colleagues immediately made the decision to postpone *Paris–Moscow* until 1979 and instead insert in a new exhibition, *Paris–Berlin*, 1978. Less than ten months were available for the production of this presentation, also historically and politically charged of course, as the wounds of Franco-German relations after three wars were still far from healed. The sequence of events shows the extent to which Pontus Hultén, at the height of his Paris career, was still working according to his old methods, with short lead times and considerable scope for new thinking, improvisation and innovation.

For *Paris–Berlin*, Pontus Hultén had a trump card in the aforementioned Werner Spies, the Paris-based German journalist, art historian and curator with whom Hultén had collaborated on the production of the Max Ernst exhibition at the Grand Palais in 1975. Spies would later succeed Pontus Hultén as MNAM's only foreign-born director to date (1997–2000) alongside his predecessor. Hultén had known Spies since the 1960s, when he had visited Stockholm, and was well aware of his network of contacts in the German-speaking art world. "*Paris–Berlin* was a really high-risk project," says Jean-Hubert Martin. "It's incredible that we managed to complete it in such a short time. Without Werner Spies' excellent contacts, it would have been impossible."[35]

According to Werner Spies himself, Pontus Hultén called two weeks before Christmas 1977 with the task of producing the *Paris–Berlin* exhibition, which was to open on July 12 in the summer of 1978. Despite the extremely tight time frame, Spies accepted the assignment and, in his own account, was the one who insisted that an ambitious catalog as well as a film be produced for the exhibition. Spies says he immediately started calling his contacts in the museum administrations of Berlin, Munich, Stuttgart, Hamburg and other German cities, MoMA and the Guggenheim in New York and other institutions, as well as his friends among artists, artists' families and collectors. The project instantly caught a favorable tailwind. "All the colleagues were very positive and enthusiastic about finally showing German art in Paris," says Spies. "They almost all said that you can borrow anything you want. There were only a few rare exceptions who refused loans because of jealousy."[36]

In just a few months, Werner Spies, in a team that also included Jean-Hubert Martin, responsible for the French part of the exhibition, Serge Fauchereau, Marie-Laure Bernadac and Maja Oeri, succeeded in compiling a magnificent exposition of German art and other creative expressions from the turn of the century to the National Socialist takeover in 1933. The texts for the catalog poured in. Fauchereau, responsible for the literature section, describes the struggle against the deadline: "I was writing around the clock in a country house in the last days. I looked like a fucking bear when they came to collect the manuscript for printing. I hadn't had time to shave or anything else for weeks."[37]

The spontaneously initiated exhibition was blessed from the start with a rare stroke of luck, or let's call it momentum. Pontus Hultén's team at the new Musée National d'Art Moderne, or Département d'Art Plastique as the museum was then called within the Centre Pompidou, was already sailing at full rig.

Most of the art shown in *Paris–Berlin* had never been seen in France. The exhibition was the first ever with the theme of German art from the early twentieth century, as Pontus Hultén notes in his preface to the catalog.[38] Several German artistic movements that were poorly known in Paris and the rest of the art world and that were important for the international development of art were extensively presented in *Paris–Berlin*.

In full splendor, the image of a cosmopolitan, bohemian scene in Berlin and other German cities during the interwar period was a new revelation for most of the exhibition's visitors. In addition to Expressionism, Berlin Dada, with Richard Huelsenbeck, Raoul Hausmann, Hannah Höch, Johannes Baader and John Heartfield, with its more political, partly communist-agitating version of the movement, was of course one of the heavyweight sections of the exhibition, along with Kurt Schwitters in Hanover and Max Ernst, Hans Arp and Johannes Baargeld in Cologne (like the other Pingpong exhibitions, *Paris–Berlin* interpreted the concepts of Berlin and Paris in the broadest sense).

Two other art-historically influential movements were presented in detail in the exhibition and catalog. One was "Der Blaue Reiter," "The Blue Rider," a movement led for a short period, mainly 1911–1912, by Wassily Kandinsky during his time in Munich: a school of painting in which Kandinsky, together with the German Franz Marc and other more loosely connected German and exiled artists, including Paul Klee and August Macke, pushed Expressionism in an abstract direction. One of the co-founders of the Expressionist group was Gabriele Münter, the artist who studied under and lived with Kandinsky. Another important female member of the group was the Russian-German Marianne von Werefkin (born Marianna Vladimirovna Verevkina), whose Munich salon gathered artists from the Russian and German avant-garde during the early days of the movement. *The Blue Rider* is also the name of an almanac published by Kandinsky and Marc in 1912, with one hundred and forty paintings and some thirty texts. The philosophy of the movement, which heralded the breakthrough of abstract art, was about the spiritual dimension of art freed from the yoke of reality; that art should appeal to the soul on an inner level, beyond logic and rationality. For Kandinsky and Marc, blue was the highest of colors. The color represented the spiritual, quasi-religious dimensions of art — sometimes called the fifth dimension of art. Here the Russian-German movement emerges as a precursor to Yves Klein forty years later.

The other less well-known movement presented was the "Neue Sachlichkeit," a current in which a group of avant-garde painters, after the end of the First World War, returned to a realism with a socialist political message and a dark satirical edge. The two main representatives of this school, which had counterparts elsewhere in the world, were George Grosz and Otto Dix, the former (and to some extent also the latter) originally a Dadaist, with Max Beckmann, Rudolf Schlichter and Christian Schad as other names. Grosz and Dix were particularly highlighted in the exhibition and catalog, both represented by several magnificent works; two Modernist masters who had previously been relatively unknown to the French and international art public but who had a breakthrough with *Paris–Berlin*. As mentioned, Pontus Hultén made sure to purchase George Grosz's Dadaist masterpiece "Remember Uncle August, the Unfortunate Inventor"[39] from 1919 for the collection. Jean-Hubert Martin confides that Hultén, on the other hand, was dismissive of suggestions to purchase German Expressionism and "Neue Sachlichkeit."[40]

It is a far from bright or cheerful picture that these artists — or, judging by the catalog, the exhibition as a whole — paint of Germany and Berlin in the early twentieth century and during the Weimar Republic: a decadent cosmopolitan scene whose desperation, darkness and elegance Grosz and Dix depict so unvarnished, with the raw eroticism, violence and other naked human urges hung out in a dirty, dripping manner. In his catalog preface, Pontus Hultén asks whether the impending catastrophe can be read in this art. Judging from the catalog, the answer is undoubtedly yes. The Berlin portrayed by Grosz, Dix and others reflects the gasp-inducing feeling that Richard Huelsenbeck, the writer and poet who is considered the founder of the Berlin Dada, describes in a famous quote: "Berlin was a city of knotted stomachs, of thundering hunger, where hidden rage was transformed into a boundless money-lust, and people's thoughts were concentrated more and more on questions of mere existence. Fear was in everyone's bone marrow."[41]

In terms of art history, *Paris–Berlin* demonstrated how the ideas of Fauvism, Cubism, Futurism and Surrealism had quickly taken hold in Germany through a series of astonishingly ambitious exhibitions across the country organized by, among others, the magazine Der Sturm, founded in 1910, under the leadership of editor, publisher, composer, poet and artist Herwarth Walden. A catalog text by the Hungarian art historian and avant-garde expert Krisztina Passuth highlights how the avant-garde movements in almost all Central European countries were represented by corresponding literary leaders. The group of exiled German artists in the Paris avant-garde before the First World War and the pre- and inter-war exchanges between German and French artists are also discussed, as are the functions of Berlin and Munich as hubs for Eastern European artists in the early century.

The Bauhaus and its influence on international art, architecture and industrial design was another key chapter in *Paris–Berlin*. Yet another was German Expressionist avant-garde film, where Fritz Lang was the big name. Literature, photography and political art (and the difficulties of such art under the Weimar Republic) were also given highly interesting sections/chapters, with many unique documents in the literature section. Hitler and Nazism are largely absent, surfacing only here and there at the end of the stories, a menacing spirit brooding beneath the sadly poetic whole. One section of the exhibition, called "Salle Berlin," consisted of a room with enlarged documentary photographs of political events and industrial mass production and how this affected the daily lives of Germans. There is no end to the wealth. The catalog requires weeks to study in depth, with plenty of art history lessons. "It was an exhibition that would be totally unthinkable today, but it was possible to realize at the time thanks to everyone's willingness to help in every way," says Werner Spies.[42]

If *Paris–New York* had been received with mixed reactions, *Paris–Berlin* was a complete success in all respects from start to finish. The reviews were glowing. The exhibition was praised by Europe's most influential cultural writer at the time, the French philosopher Michel Foucault, while setting a sensational attendance record with four hundred and twenty thousand visitors — a previously unthinkable figure for a modern art exhibition. "It really had an outstanding reception," says Werner Spies of *Paris–Berlin*. "The exhibition also had great political influence. It was the first time ever that the French began to understand something of the German soul. They had previously done so in music, poetry and philosophy, but not in art. The public discovered a whole new world of art, innovation and sensibility."[43]

"*Paris–Berlin* was a catharsis for French audiences," says Jean-Hubert Martin. "It was the first time after the war that the French could allow themselves to see something positive from Germany —

something beautiful and sensual. You could really feel the relief and liberation. The exhibition undoubtedly contributed to a new cultural exchange between France and Germany."[44]

Paris–Berlin consolidated the overwhelming success of the new museum, granting Pontus Hultén and his staff more maneuvering space. As Hultén himself describes the blessed state of creative harvest in which the museum found itself in the years following its opening: "These were huge projects. But we weren't particularly scared of them. We had support from all sides and therefore nothing to lose. Nobody knew exactly what to expect from this new cultural institution. These circumstances made us more optimistic than afraid. We worked enormously, almost day and night, but it was a lot of fun, especially because the center was accepted so wonderfully by the public. Every day there were long queues in front of the entrance. It inspired and encouraged us. (...) There was a working environment of complete independence. It was a wonderful time."[45]

While Werner Spies led the *Paris–Berlin* team, Pontus Hultén continued to devote his main efforts to *Paris–Moscow*. Spies relates in warm terms his good cooperation with Hultén, how he gave him full mandate and trust, always ready to back him up when needed with his knowledge, experience and network of contacts.

My Dadaist ideals forbid me to refrain from telling the story of Werner Spies' gift to Pontus Hultén on his sixtieth birthday. Spies had flown on one of the first Concorde departures from Paris to New York. On the plane he had filled in his name as Marcel Duchamp, with his own address in Paris (this was after the artist's death in 1968). Some time later a certificate arrived in the mail with the inscription: "Mr. MARCEL DUCHAMP passed through the Wall of Sound." I do not believe for a moment that Werner Spies is exaggerating when he claims that Pontus Hultén was extremely excited about this gift, which I haven't been able to locate. The certificate would undoubtedly be highly desirable among Duchamp fetishists.

In Moscow, the work of Hultén and his colleagues consisted largely of pure research. Through their gradually established contacts at the Pushkin Museum and other Soviet institutions, the team managed to gain access to the storerooms from which one after another masterpiece of the early 20th century avant-garde could be retrieved, with the help of leading Russian experts. The most remarkable single find was Malevich's black square on a white background from 1915 — a milestone

The full name of the exhibition was *The Last Futurist Exhibition of Paintings 0,10*. The number 0 in the name was the number of the mind, as the vision was that after the destruction of the old world the mind could start from 0 again. 10 was the number of artists originally intended to be shown in the exhibition (they eventually became fourteen). The exhibition was shown in the small Dobychina Art Bureau in Marsovo Polye Park in the center of Petrograd and was the premiere of the Suprematism movement. In addition to Malevich, works by Vladimir Tatlin and "Constructivist Amazons" Lyubov Popova, Olga Rozanova and Nadezhda Udaltsova were exposed.

Amazons of the Avant-Garde was the title of an exhibition at the Guggenheim in New York from September 8, 2000 to January 7, 2001, featuring paintings by Aleksandra Ekster, Natalia Goncharova, Lyubov Popova, Olga Rozanova, Varvara Stepanova and Nadezhda Udaltsova. It was the first time that this group of women artists, unique in the history of art, was shown together in a major exhibition at a leading Western museum.

in art history, first shown at the 1915–1916 Futurist exhibition in Petrograd, which few in modern times had seen in person as it had been hidden in the storeroom of the Russian Museum in Leningrad. Other gold nuggets on display for the first time to the modern art world included Malevich's magnificent figurative "The Red Cavalry" from 1918 and a 1916 "counter-relief" by Tatlin, clearly influenced by Picasso's wood and metal sculptures. A canvas with multi-colored diagonals on a white base by Mikhail Matyushin from 1917–1918 titled "Movement in Space," sensationally modern as it is presented over a full double-page spread in the catalog, was discovered. Among many other finds were also collections of works by the female Russian avant-garde pioneers Lyubov Popova, Olga Rozanova and Nadezhda Udaltsova, "Amazons of the avant-garde" as they have been called.

It was a gold-digging bonanza, reminiscent of old boyhood detective stories. Stanislas Zadora describes how the team smuggled a camera into the storerooms and masked the clicking of the shutter with sneezes as the lady supervising them fetched tea;[46] Jean-Hubert Martin explains how hot it was for a young art historian to work with the mythical Russian avant-garde — about the excitement, euphoria and sense of the unreal that he and his colleagues experienced when they were able to see and touch these art historical treasures that they had only seen depicted in small, poor black and white images in magazines and catalogs, if at all.[47] Many of the works were in poor condition, hidden from the world since the years after the revolution.

The material that was unearthed also included Malevich's futuristic architectural sculptures/models and sketches, his so-called "arkhitektons" and "planits," among many other more or less unknown art, architecture and design history objects, literary documents, film, photography, theater scenographies, political propaganda art and much more. The joy of discovery described by Jean-Hubert Martin is understandable. Malevich caused the greatest excitement. It was the first time his work in Russian museum collections would be shown outside the Soviet Union — or at all since the years after the revolution, as the Russian avant-garde was still officially banned. "Often the Russian experts didn't know what was in the storerooms themselves, so we had to show them," says Jean-Hubert Martin. "But they pretended to know so as not to lose face."[48] Jean-Hubert's Russian-speaking colleague Stanislas Zadora has a different interpretation: "They knew, but they didn't tell the truth."[49]

From 1923 until the early thirties, Kazimir Malevich created a series of experimental three-dimensional models and assemblages; a kind of intermediate between abstract sculptures and architectural urban landscapes, called arkhitektons. The drawings that accompanied the models are called planits.

In their contacts with the Soviet cultural bureaucracy, Pontus Hultén and his group were constantly involved in a negotiation situation which, in simple terms, meant that while the curators prioritized the pre- and post-revolutionary avant-garde — Malevich, Tatlin, Rodchenko and so on — the Soviet authorities aimed to reach out with the Soviet Social Realist, soldier and proletarian romanticizing counterpart to Nazi propaganda, this poster art which in itself had always interested Hultén and had its given place in the exhibition, though not a dominant one.

Hultén's firm fundamental principle, which he had adhered to throughout his career, was that even if the art and the exhibition were political, it was the artistic quality, not the political message, that must determine what was shown to the public. For *Paris–Moscow*, he was interested in the aesthetically stylish revolutionary propaganda art inspired by Futurism, created by the Constructivist avant-gardists in the years around the revolution — but not in the kitschy Social Realism of the dictatorship of later eras.

The political balance between the different elements of the exhibition was negotiated in a lengthy process of wrangling, give and take. For the Russians, the project was a political matter, right up to the Politburo and the KGB. Jean-Hubert Martin recounts a John le Carré/Graham Greene-esque anecdote: "In the hotel room, Pontus made sure we talked loudly and clearly about that if we didn't get this or that piece, or if we had to show such and such a work, we wouldn't open the exhibition. If we were bugged, he wanted us to be able to use it to negotiate with the Russians."[50]

Stanislas Zadora relates the endless tussle with the Soviet cultural bureaucracy: "On Monday, when we came in, we had twenty-five issues and problems to deal with. When we came in on Tuesday, there were still twenty-five issues. Nothing happened and the Russians kept changing the conditions. You had to have endless patience."[51] Zadora portrays his friend and boss Pontus Hultén as "a giant" in this marathon poker game, "tactically but also strategically." By virtue of his independence from the French state, Hultén was able to take a hard line against the Soviet authorities.

"Without the center's new status as an 'établissement public,' which Bordaz had negotiated, with money from the ministry but its own autonomous status, *Paris–Moscow* would have been impossible," says Jean-Hubert Martin. "There had been many Russian exhibitions in Paris before, during de Gaulle's time and later, as part of the political relationship, but then the Soviet regime had basically decided what was shown in contact with the French government. They got some masterpieces and in return had to display other things that the Soviet state wanted to show."

The *Paris–Moscow* exhibition, which spanned the tumultuous historical period 1900–1930, was naturally divided into two sections — before and after the revolution in 1917. In addition to the pre- and post-revolutionary avant-garde — Constructivism and related movements — and Social Realism, there was also a heavy older section of masterpieces representing the artistic exchange between Paris and Moscow in the first two decades of the twentieth century, when many Russian, mainly Jewish, artists lived in Paris.

Moscow at the turn of the century was home to two of the world's foremost collectors of young Modernism, Fauvism and Cubism, Sergei Shchukin and Ivan Morozov, both of whom had accumulated fortunes during Russian industrialization. Their collections were invaluable to the development of modern Russian art. Both visited the Paris Salon purchasing vast amounts of art. Shchukin started buying Impressionism in 1890 but moved on to Modernism from 1906. His incomparable collection came to include fifty-four Picassos, thirty-seven Matisses, nineteen Monets, thirteen Renoirs, twenty-six Cézannes, twenty-nine Gauguins, twenty Derains, seven Rousseaus and four Denis. Shchukin's personal favorite was Matisse, whose works were given positions of honor in his palace, where art hung frame to frame from floor to ceiling. Shchukin met Matisse in Paris in 1906, and three years later commissioned the monumental canvas "La Danse," "The Dance," perhaps Matisse's most famous masterpiece, to be mounted in his stairwell; and later, after seeing the artist's sketches, a second work, "La Musique," "The Music." The paintings were shown at the Paris Salon in 1910 and then in Moscow in 1911, when Matisse visited the city. Morozov's collection was more conventional, with artists such as van Gogh, Renoir, Pissarro, Signac, Sisley, Gauguin, de Vlaminck and others, but was later supplemented by more modern elements such as Matisse and some Cubism.

Both the Shchukin and Morozov collections were confiscated by the Soviet state after the revolution and are now divided between the Hermitage in Saint Petersburg and the Pushkin Museum in Moscow.

Thanks to Shchukin's exquisite taste in particular, many of the most important works by Matisse and Picasso disappeared straight from their studios or after being shown in Paris only once, at the Salon — another example of how international collectors and other connoisseurs were quicker than the Parisian establishment to understand and purchase the new from the avant-garde of modern art. These works by Matisse, Picasso and the others, on loan from the Pushkin Museum in Moscow and the Hermitage in Leningrad, caused a sensation when they were displayed for the first time in Paris during *Paris–Moscow*. Being able to show "La Danse" and "La Musique," as well as little-known key works by Cézanne and Picasso, was a triumph that earned Pontus Hultén much credit in the Parisian art establishment.

In Moscow, contemporary artists and art lovers had been able to see this art as Shchukin and Morozov kept their collections open for visits one day a week. It was here that the artists of the Russian avant-garde drew their inspiration. This influence was evident in much of the Russian art exhibited in *Paris–Moscow*, such as Tatlin's "Matisse-esque" nude studies from 1913.

Another dominant influence in Russian art highlighted in the exhibition was, of course, Futurism, the powerful, aggressive artistic movement that developed more extensively in Russia than in any other country besides its native Italy. Italian and Russian Futurism went their separate ways early on, with the Russian version being less doctrinaire and more rooted in tradition. Visually, the lasting influence of Futurism on Russian art, architecture, propaganda and other expressions is flagrant when browsing the catalog.

A key figure in the exhibition and catalog was the art critic, exhibition maker, ballet impresario, etc., Sergei Diaghilev. Coming from a wealthy and cultured family in Novgorod and Saint Petersburg, he aspired to become a composer but instead began studying law at the University of Saint Petersburg, where he befriended a group of artists and other art lovers who rejected industrialization, united by a romantic view of art, similar to contemporary international movements such as the Bloomsbury Group in England.

In 1906, frustrated by the conservatism of the Russian art world, Diaghilev staged the first major Western exhibition of Russian art at the Petit Palais in Paris. The exhibition was a huge success and resulted in all things Russian becoming high fashion in Paris. The following year, Diaghilev gave concerts of Russian music at the Paris Opera and the year after that a series of opera performances. His first opera season in Paris was such a success that Diaghilev was invited to return with a program of both opera and ballet. His first ballet season was a triumph but the costs were staggering. From 1909, when Diaghilev returned to Paris with his company, he instead presented his ballet at smaller private theaters such as the Théâtre Mogador and the Théâtre du Châtelet. The *Ballets Russes*, the Russian Ballet, was born — a phenomenon that would revolutionize not only ballet, choreography and music but also art, influencing fashion, design and set design, a leverage relevant to this day.

The Ballets Russes originally consisted of an ensemble of dancers on summer leave from the Saint Petersburg Imperial Ballet, with ballerina Anna Pavlova as the shining star. Composers for the ballet included Erik Satie, Igor Stravinsky, Sergei Prokofiev, Richard Strauss and many others. Ballets Russes was an instant sensation in its freedom and vitality, which contrasted sharply with the rigidity of classical French ballet. At least as disruptive as the dance itself was Diaghilev's concept of the ballet performance as a visual and sensual experience for the audience.

In 1917, Diaghilev hired Pablo Picasso for his first commission for the ballet, set and costume design for "Parade" by Erik Satie. Picasso went on to work for the Russian Ballet for ten years. Subsequently, Diaghilev employed many artists and other creators for his performances, which were total works of visual art, dance and music, with elements of circus and cabaret. His collaborators included Henri Matisse, George Braque, Giorgio de Chirico, Jean Cocteau, Max Ernst, Francis Picabia, Joan Miró and many others. The Ballets Russes became a major venue for the Parisian avant-garde. Throughout the decade and much of the twenties, the scene was the chicest meeting place for Paris's advanced cultural circles. "Diaghilev invented Russia for foreigners," as Gabrielle "Coco" Chanel said of the Russian-inspired fashions sparked by the Russian Ballet which she herself was influenced by.

The ballet quickly gained a worldwide reputation with guest appearances in London and a tour of the United States. The Russian Ballet never performed in Russia. After the revolution, Diaghilev chose to stay in Paris. When he could not be persuaded to return, he was banned and written out of Russian history. With *Paris–Moscow* and *Moscow–Paris*, the Russian Ballet was presented to Russian audiences for the first time. In Paris, the ballet was well known, but the exhibition and catalog were able to fill in the knowledge with stage designs, costumes, texts, drawings, sketches and more, much of which was previously unknown or never before shown.

With *Paris–Moscow*, Hultén became a latter-day Diaghilev in that this and the other Russian exhibitions revived interest in the Russian in the international consciousness and among contemporary artists and other creatives.

More surprising, since unlike the Ballets Russes it was largely unknown to the public, was the Russian theater and its corresponding artistic expressions from the same period, before and after the First World War and the Russian Revolution, which was also presented in the exhibition and in a separate chapter in the catalog. During the pre- and post-revolutionary period, the theater was an important stage and source of income for avant-garde artists who otherwise had difficulty reaching out with their art in the conservative Russian art world that Sergei Diaghilev had fled.

After the revolution, the theater became a stage for revolutionary propaganda. A fascinating central figure alongside Mayakovsky was his collaborator, the actor, director and theater producer Vsevolod Meyerhold, who is portrayed in the *Paris–Moscow* catalog. A committed communist, Meyerhold was appointed head of the Theater Division of the Ministry of Education, where he effectively led the nationalization of Russian theaters. Scenographically and visually, Meyerhold's theatrical productions were as revolutionary artistically as politically, with many innovative elements that set a precedent in the world of theater and even film.

Meyerhold, like his friend and collaborator Mayakovsky, was poorly rewarded for his services to the revolution. Mayakovsky shot himself in 1930. Meyerhold met a more unfortunate fate. He was imprisoned in 1938, tortured into confessing to treason and executed after a summary trial. A small consolation was that Meyerhold was acquitted on all counts in the first de-Stalinization in the 1950s. Then it was due time ...

Throughout *Paris–Moscow*, the relatively strong position of women artists and other creatives in the Russian avant-garde, where women were regarded, at least in theory, as equal champions of the world revolution, was presented as a remarkable exception in art history. Until our own time, there has hardly been another period in the history of art when female artists have claimed such a visable position on the stage, even if the main roles were played by men. Lyubov Popova, Varvara Stepanova (who was married to Rodchenko), Aleksandra Ekster, Natalia Goncharova, Olga Rozanova, Nadezhda Udaltsova, Marie Vassilieff, Ekaterina Zernova, Aleksandra Soborova, the sisters Olga and Galina Chichagova, Aleksandra Shchekatikhina-Pototskaya, Evgeniya Leneva and many other female artists and creators were all prominently represented in *Paris–Moscow*. The phenomenon that the Russian avant-garde produced the strongest generation of women artists in the history of modern art up to our present day is worth noting in the midst of the communist misery, even if many of them emigrated to Paris, Munich and elsewhere before the revolution.

Generous space in the exhibition and catalog was allotted to the broad creative territory referred to in the catalog as "applied arts" — architecture and urbanism, industrial design, product design, graphic production, poster and propaganda art, and more. These extensive, dense catalog chapters are treasure troves for architecture and design enthusiasts.

Tatlin's tower was of course displayed once again, borrowed from Stockholm. According to Jean-Hubert Martin, Hultén had the tower completed in Paris. He must have been immensely proud when the geometric inner parts rotated according to the schedule set by Tatlin, driven by a motor at the bottom of the model. Olle Granath remembers that Moderna Museet got its tower back in tatters and that a favorable insurance premium made it possible to have not one but two new towers reconstructed — one for Stockholm and one for MNAM in Paris.[52] I have not been able to comprehend exactly how these events are connected, despite considerable efforts. In any case, the end result was that MNAM's collection was enriched with a model of Hultén's beloved tower.

The industrial and graphic design departments are bewitching. Constructivist and Suprematist artists such as Rodchenko and Popova, Nicolai Suetine, Varvara Stepanova, the Chichagova sisters, the Stenberg brothers, Vasyl Yermylov, the Vesnin trio of brothers and others also worked in the fields of graphic and poster design, industrial design, crafts, furniture design, set design and costume design. There was a goldmine for the Parisian fashion houses to exploit. The impact of the utopian Constructivist unisex costumes on the fashion world is apparent.

The *Paris–Moscow* catalog is a magnificent scrapbook of inspiration not only for artists but equally for architects, graphic designers, furniture and product designers, industrial designers and fashion designers. Its contents were poured into the collective reference banks of the architecture, design and fashion industries. The Russian and Soviet influence on movements such as De Stijl and Bauhaus, and on Western aesthetic and visual culture in general, became evident in the exhibition.

The literature section, for which Serge Fauchereau was responsible, is overwhelmingly massive, with a flood of manuscripts, letters and documents, many of these previously unknown. In addition, a musical program directed by Pierre Boulez was composed for *Paris–Moscow* as well as for the other Pingpong exhibitions.

Browsing through the catalogs for all three of these exhibitions, but especially the *Paris-Moscow* catalog, one is struck by the notion that each of the sections/chapters would have sufficed as a theme for its own exhibition. *Paris–Moscow* was an enormous manifestation — considerably larger in volume than the previous two. As Hultén notes in the catalog, the preparations had lasted five years, while the others had been produced in just over six months each.[53] More than two thousand five hundred works of art, objects and documents were shown in *Paris–Moscow*. So space-consuming was the exhibition that the team of scenographers led by Jacques Lichnerowicz had to construct a temporary mezzanine floor in the gallery. The list of lenders fills a densely typed full spread in the catalog. This catalog, written in equal parts by French and Russian art historians and other experts, is a massive reference and flip book on Russian Modernism, so packed with learning, information and inspiration that it takes your breath away.

As an overture to *Paris–Moscow* in March 1978, the museum, with Jean-Hubert Martin as curator, presented the Malevich retrospective that Hultén had already planned on his arrival in Paris. The exhibition was based entirely on loans from outside the Soviet Union. At the time of production, the museum team had begun to expand its

Russian network of contacts and at the last minute was able to add a few paintings unknown in the West, along with a large number of drawings, from a private Russian collector in exile, but nothing from the Soviet institutions, which meant that there was no overlap with *Paris–Moscow*.[54] "Understanding of Malevich was very limited in Paris at the time," says Jean-Hubert Martin. "His figurative painting was completely unknown. I think it must be said that the Malevich exhibition together with *Paris–Moscow* made many people in Paris aware of Malevich and the entire Russian avant-garde for the first time."[55]

The Malevich exhibition was well received and became a good breeding ground for the audience for *Paris–Moscow*. Preparing and accustoming the audience for a major event in this way was another of Pontus Hultén's strategies.

The same was true of the Kandinsky retrospective shown in the spring of 1979, just before *Paris–Moscow*. By now, the museum's Soviet contacts had deepened, allowing it to add some paintings on loan from the Hermitage in Leningrad.

When *Paris–Moscow* opened on May 31, 1979, the exhibition was a revelation to the entire art world. Hardly any other modern art exhibition has presented such a fortune of previously unknown or poorly known art historical material of the highest caliber to the public. *Paris–Moscow* was an overwhelming public and critical success, with over four hundred and seventy thousand paying visitors, even though the exhibition's content was narrower than in *Paris–Berlin*, where figurative painting had dominated.

The group that appreciated the exhibition most of all were the contemporary artists, as well as architects, designers and other creatives. Suddenly it became apparent how much the Russian avant-garde had influenced the whole of Modernist visual culture. Jean-Hubert Martin quotes Jean Tinguely's statement during a preview: "Well, it's a good thing we didn't know because then we wouldn't have been able to do everything we did in the sixties ..."[56].

It had originally been intended that Malevich's utopian, abstract sculptural models of Suprematist urban panoramas, "Arkhitektons," would also be included in *Paris–Moscow*. An anonymous mecenate had donated to the museum what remained of the artist's little-known models/sculptures that had not been exhibited since 1932. Jean-Hubert Martin explains that the models arrived in small fragments in numerous shoeboxes. Getting them ready in time for the exhibition proved impossible. It took Danish artist Poul Pedersen, a friend of Troels Andersen, two years to recreate the models. They caused an uproar in the art and architecture world when they were shown together with sketches ("planits"), drawings and other material in a separate exhibition in 1980, with Jean-Hubert Martin as the main curator and catalog editor.[57] The models/sculptures are an attraction for the well-informed in the MNAM's collection, which continues to inspire contemporary artists and architects to this day.

Two years after *Paris–Moscow*, in spring 1981, it was time for the second part of the exhibition. Unlike *Paris–New York* and *Paris–Berlin*, *Paris–Moscow* was originally planned as a full-blown pingpong match in that it would be shown in both cities, in Moscow at the Pushkin Museum.

It goes without saying that the exhibition in Moscow was politically even more sensitive to the Soviet state than the one in Paris. Moreover, since 1979, the Cold War had moved from a period of relative détente into a more sinister phase, drastically increasing the level of complexity. After the Soviet invasion of Afghanistan, launched on Christmas Eve 1979, this West-East cooperation project in Moscow suddenly seemed unrealistic. The decision to postpone the exhibition from the planned 1980 to 1981 was made sometime around the turn of the decade.

The Russian art historian, curator and critic Andrei Erofeev,[58] who became one of Pontus Hultén's "guides" to Moscow's artistic underground movement, writes about these critical political conditions in an article for the Russian art magazine Iskusstvo from 2019,[59] on the occasion of the 40th anniversary of *Paris–Moscow*: "The two-part exhibition *Paris–Moscow* and *Moscow–Paris* was a state project. The permission to organize it was given by Leonid Brezhnev himself, since only the General Secretary had authority to make decisions that did not fit the ideological agenda. Brezhnev was guided by political pragmatism, at that time formulated as 'peaceful coexistence.' For the sake of the cause, he was prepared to make some concessions in the least important, in his opinion, part of public life — the cultural sphere (...) For Brezhnev, the *Paris–Moscow* endeavor (...) became a 'gesture of goodwill.' However, during the three years until the *Moscow–Paris* return project, the political situation changed dramatically. Détente[60] was replaced by a new tension. The USSR, referred to by the new American President Ronald Reagan as the 'Empire of Evil,' embarked on a deadly arms race. In the West, the Soviet army prepared an occupation of Poland, in response to the rise of 'Solidarity.' The scholar

Sakharov went into exile, dissidents were re-imprisoned and the persecution of critical voices intensified."

The new tension made *Moscow–Paris* "clearly out of place in time," writes Erofeev. Although the exhibition was sanctioned at the highest level, "Brezhnev's apparatchiks[61] (...) felt the scent of a regime about to swing towards neo-Stalinism." Communist Party functionaries devoted themselves to trying to slow down and diminish the project. Pontus Hultén and the museum were forced to adapt the content in a negotiation game involving the diplomatic corps of both countries. Among other sacrifices, they had to accept a more prominent element of Social Realism. Many conflicts concerned the catalog, over which MNAM was forced to relinquish control. It's said that Hultén was furious when he was confronted with a picture of Lenin in the introduction to the printed catalog. Elements of historical falsification also aroused his rage.

Many who worked on the exhibition testify to the skill with which Hultén conducted the negotiations with the management of the Pushkin Museum and the Soviet authorities, always ready to play his last card with the threat of canceling the exhibition and causing a political scandal. Here Hultén justified the analogy of a field marshal of art.

"The crucial role was played by the director of the Modern Museum at the Centre Pompidou and the project's main curator, Pontus Hultén," writes Erofeev. "In contrast to the traditional aloofness of French diplomats, and their constant readiness to 'take the opponent's position,' Pontus Hultén offered fierce and uncompromising resistance. His Nordic Swedish character, his passion for Bakunin, his anarchist conviction, which allowed him to consider the cultural territory of the 'left' as his own, also helped him."

Erofeev illustrates the politically explosive negotiation games for *Moscow–Paris* with a metaphor: "(...) imagine a scene of a tug-of-war in a market. One end is pulled by the giant, extravagant and terrifyingly grim Hultén together with a flock of French assistants. They are encouraged and assisted as much as possible by liberals and Western-oriented Soviet art historians (...) The other end is drawn by a crowd of ministry officials (...) The curator from the Soviet side, Alexandre Khaltourine, runs between the two sides, trying to reduce the intensity and breadth of the disagreements. The least enviable position was that of the director of the Pushkin Museum. If the other actors were fighting in ernest, Irina Antonova was more concerned with 'playing the comedy,' expressing either support or hard-line principles, pretending to be either a liberal or a hard-core conservative."

In warlike parables, Erofeev goes on to state that Pontus Hultén was backed in this bitter struggle by "underground" resistance forces on the "enemy side;" "saboteurs" who pointed out the bureaucrats' weaknesses to the MNAM team and secretly provided them with information about objects and documents that the authorities wanted to hide. "Unlike the Russian exiles," Pontus Hultén was not ashamed of Social Realism. Instead, Hultén placed the avant-garde in a "semi-disciplinary" exhibition that showed its role in a larger historical event.

Andrei Erofeev explains that Hultén reluctantly accepted certain concessions to achieve his larger goal: "to stage a visual head-on collision between Social Realism and the avant-garde." It was a showdown of which Hultén knew the outcome. "For Social Realism, surrounded by Picasso, Malevich and Matyushin[62]," writes Erofeev, "looked not like a propaganda weapon for the revolution but like a moldy cloak from the attic. In contrast to Lissitzky and Rodchenko, it appeared as old bourgeois images. (...) The audience was met by such an incredible stream of colorful images and forms that 'it was impossible not to drown in it, and then, after swimming, to remain forever in love with this remarkable art' (Kseniya Muratova, art critic)."[63]

One of the most contentious issues in these political negotiations concerned a text related to Lev Trotsky in the literature section of the exhibition and catalog. Trotsky was politically banned in the formally Lenin-loyal communist state. For Hultén and for many of his anarchist artist friends, Trotsky was an important figure who was considered to represent the utopian vision of the expanded territory of art and imagination in a new ideal society. For the Surrealists, Trotsky had been a hero after the break with the Communist International. His ideas had also influenced Abstract Expressionism in New York. André Breton met Lev Trotsky during his trip to Mexico in 1938. He is believed to be the co-author of the "Manifesto for Independent Revolutionary Art," signed by Breton and the Mexican artist Diego Rivera in Mexico that year. Art and creativity as a revolutionary force — this was Hultén's own Crown utopia, if we

The "Manifesto for Independent Revolutionary Art" was signed by André Breton and Diego Rivera in Mexico in 1938 but is believed to have been written by Breton and Lev Trotsky. The document, which rejected the Communist International, established the short-lived organization "Federation of Independent Revolutionary Art," to which Breton succeeded in getting a number of artists, writers and intellectuals to join, including Yves Tanguy, André Masson, Herbert Read and George Orwell.

may call it that. The Manifesto's place in the Franco-Russian cultural and political context was obvious.

For *Paris–Moscow*, Hultén had, after tough negotiations, managed to push through the presence of the manifesto in the exhibition, with a reference in the catalog. For *Moscow–Paris*, he was forced to give in and delete "he whose name must not be mentioned," Trotsky. It was typical of Pontus Hultén that he and his colleagues wore buttons with ice picks (from the French Alpine Club) on their jackets at the official opening, as a reminder that Trotsky was murdered with such a tool.[64] The story may seem hilarious in retrospect, but there and then in Moscow it's easy to realize that the atmosphere was tense. Pontus Hultén has revealed[65] that during the opening event he had a taxi waiting at one of the museum's rear exits in case he and his colleagues needed to leave for the airport in a hurry.

The opening at the Pushkin Museum attracted what is described as "an incredible amount"[66] of guests of honor who crowded the museum's "Italian courtyard." Pontus Hultén had arranged to print, date, sign and distribute his speech in advance to Andrei Erofeev and other trusted collaborators, knowing that the Russian interpreters would not translate his words correctly in all parts. He also knew that the speech, which was openly critical of his partners in the Soviet museum management and cultural bureaucracy, would become a cultural-historical document.

It's testified that *Moscow–Paris* was initially greeted with anxious anticipation by the Russian press and public. What was awaited, of course, were the political "signals." A few weeks[67] after the opening, after the French delegation had gone home, the museum was closed to the public as the head of the government, Brezhnev, arrived with his delegation on his official visit (in Russian official chronicles, the story was later rewritten stating the head of state had attended the opening). Brezhnev made no statements but declared the exhibition officially open and signed the guest book. Word instantly spread that he had liked or at least approved of what he had seen. The next day, huge crowds flocked to the exhibition. *Moscow–Paris* was a gigantic success. The queue stretched twice around the building, longer than that for the Lenin mausoleum. You had to arrive at six o'clock in the morning to have a chance of getting in, as the story goes.[68] Muscovites and visitors flocked to the museum in numbers no one had even dreamed of. Six hundred and fifty thousand is the number of visitors mentioned — an incredible figure. Jean-Hubert Martin describes the reception of the exhibition in historical terms: "If *Paris–Moscow* was a great success with the public, *Moscow–Paris* created historic political and cultural changes," he says. "Brezhnev opened the exhibition and a generations of artists and art lovers suddenly had access to their own avant-garde art history. It marked the beginning of the disintegration and fall of the communist system."[69]

On my journey around the world in this work, during which I have met hundreds of people who were involved at the time — artists, curators, museum directors, art historians, critics and others — almost all have spoken in superlatives about the enormous impact of the Pingpong exhibitions and the new revelations, insights and perspectives they opened. Throughout, it's *Paris–Moscow* in particular that most people speak of in glowing terms.

Nowhere else was the exhibition so crucial as in Russia. Everyone I have met and spoken to in the country mentions *Moscow–Paris* as a ground zero, a rebirth of Russian contemporary art. Several have told me that many Russian artists and art historians experienced great frustration and anger when it suddenly became clear what they had been deprived of — when they realized how much they would have to catch up with modern art history in order to regain their position in the international art world. For many Russians, this meant starting with Fauvism and Cubism. "The heirs of Soviet art collapsed," writes Andrei Erofeev. "The inheritors of Social Realism, the 'Muscovites,' the artists who formed the heart of the Moscow Art League, now turned away from this heritage. (...) In this connection, the mischievous spirit of Moscow Dadaism from the 1910s burst into the 'Muscovite' milieu. But the great subject was Malevich. His authority skyrocketed, relaunching the abstract line, almost completely extinct by the end of the 1970s."

Erofeev lists Russian artists of different generations who, after *Moscow–Paris*, abandoned figurative painting for Abstract and Conceptual Art and were thus able to "re-enter" an international context.

In my conversation with Irina Antonova, the controversial matriarch of modern Russian art, she is clear: "*Moscow–Paris* is undoubtedly the biggest and most important exhibition of my seventy-five years at the museum."[70] In November 2021, the 40th anniversary of the exhibition at the Pushkin Museum was celebrated with an international symposium.

No one can dispute that the Pingpong exhibitions at the Centre Pompidou in Paris and the "sequel" in Moscow were of far-reaching consequence not only in terms of art but also historically and politically. There is consensus on the importance of *Paris–Berlin* for cultural exchange and renewed friendship between the former hereditary enemies France and Germany, as well as on the dignity of *Paris–Moscow* as an icebreaker in the opening of the Soviet dictatorship to the outside world. *Paris–New York* also had political significance, albeit more limited to the art world. Pontus Hultén's utopian vision of art as a political force may seem romantic at times, but with the Pingpong exhibitions he realized his vision of art as a constructive power in social development and history — a unique moment in post-war modern art history.

The fourth exhibition in the Pingpong suite, the one that doesn't quite count, *Paris–Paris*, opened in the spring of 1981, Pontus Hultén's farewell year at the Centre Pompidou, curated by Germain Viatte. The theme was the Parisian art scene in the first half of the twentieth century and in particular the great influence of artists from all over the world who had come to Paris.

Jean-Yves Mock told an anecdote that the title was originally intended to be not *Paris–Paris* but *École de Paris*. As usual, the production of the catalog was a race against the clock. Pontus Hultén came to Mock in the morning of the day the original was to be picked up by courier for the printers later in the afternoon and asked him to write his preface. Jean-Yves had a couple of hours. He said that he bit his wrist so that the blood flowed, splashed the blood on Hultén and said "Here, take this too!," after which he went home and authored the text. Minutes before the courier came to collect the original, Mock claims to have told Hultén that the exhibition could not be named *École de Paris* and that he had suggested *Paris–Paris* instead. At the last moment, the cover was allegedly cut and recopied so that the word Paris from the original title was repeated twice.[71]

Germain Viatte dismisses this story with a smile — still worth repeating as an example of the pace and work routines that everyone clearly says prevailed during Pontus Hultén's time at the Centre Pompidou. "No, no, no," says Germain. "Jean-Yves Mock ... oh my God ... first of all, he would never have had the authority to do something like that ... no, the theme was the foreign influence on the Paris art scene. That the exhibition was in many ways part of the series is clear from the catalog and Cieślewicz's[72] cover."[73]

Everyone agrees that *Paris–Paris* was a beautiful, impressive exhibition that was another blockbuster. However, the exhibition reportedly lacked the sensational, mind-expanding qualities that characterized the other shows, which is one reason why it is not fully included in the Pingpong suite.

There were plans to extend the series with further exhibitions. Mexico was an art country that was discussed as it interested Pontus Hultén (perhaps because of his father's travels in Mexico). There were those on the museum staff who advocated Paris-Vienna, including Jean Clair. Pontus Hultén confided that he was opposed to the idea because he felt that although there had been an important exchange between Paris and Vienna, it was not of art historical importance comparable to the others.[74] Jean Clair himself says: "Pontus' east-west axis was fantastic. The problem is that I myself do not believe in such an axis. I believe more in a north-south connection — from Italy through Vienna and on up to Germany and Holland, even to Sweden."[75] I think it's worth noting that London did not appear in the discussions and plans for these Pingpong manifestations — the city was never really a central hub in the development of modern art.

Given the importance of the Pingpong trilogy, until recently the literature on the "exhibition cycle" has been limited. Yet the shows have lived on, through their catalogs. These up to more than seven hundred pages thick pieces, weighing over three kilograms, set a new standard for art catalogs. All were designed by Paris-based Polish graphic designer and illustrator Roman Cieślewicz, who also designed the covers, with the exception of *Paris–New York*, for which the cover was painted by New York artist Larry Rivers. Rivers was a natural choice as he was one of the earliest Neo-Dadaist/Pop artists of the New York School, considered by some art historians as the "godfather of Pop Art" (a term that has also been used for Marcel Duchamp[76]).

In my conversation with Nicholas Serota, I make the mistake of suggesting that the Pingpong catalogs must have been the first examples of the exhibition catalog as a coffee table book. "I think it's unjust to call them coffee table books," says Serota. "They are rather encyclopedic works of art historical and general historical knowledge."[77]

When I first visited Germain Viatte at his home in Paris, he had prepared our meeting by piling up on the table the Pingpong pieces and the other mighty catalogs published during Pontus Hultén's time as director of MNAM. These art books, this mass of learning and beauty, certainly made a heavy, awe-inspiring physical impression. "I thought I'd collect them so you could feel the volume," said Germain with a smile. "There must be something special about a person who leaves this behind."[78]

Recent years have seen steadily increasing international interest in the Pingpong exhibitions among international art historians. The Centre Pompidou, for example, has organized several events and published texts on the subject, including the seminar "Hommage à Pontus Hultén" during the cultural center's fortieth anniversary year in 2017, and a well-documented symposium with invited international speakers in the autumn of 2019 for the fortieth anniversary of *Paris–Moscow*, both with ambitious special issues of the museum's journal Les Cahiers.[79] In Russia, too, secondary literature on *Moscow–Paris* and on Pontus Hultén's Russian achievements has been increasing.

The publicity surrounding the Centre Pompidou's fortieth anniversary in 2017 highlights the extent to which the Pingpong exhibitions, and in particular *Paris–Moscow*, continue to inspire artists, art historians, curators and other creatives, even in much younger generations. In the monthly magazine The Art Newspaper, a number of key figures in and connected to the art world were interviewed about the impact of the Centre Pompidou on art and creativity over forty years.[80] The article repeatedly refers to Pontus Hultén's pioneering years and in particular to the Pingpong exhibitions and their catalogs. "It's an important moment to celebrate this great building by Richard Rogers and Renzo Piano and also to celebrate Pontus Hultén, because one is connected to the other: the great building and the great program of Hultén's laboratory years," says Hans Ulrich Obrist in an interview. "He used so brilliantly this vision of the building as a radical event, a building as a happening; he played the building almost as an instrument. In the early exhibitions like *Paris–New York* and so on, art, literature, dance, film — and, of course, with Ircam next door, music — were brought together. And this is the history of the avant-garde: those moments always rose above the fear of bringing knowledge together."

Rem Koolhaas talks about how the building and program of the Centre Pompidou during the years of Pontus Hultén came together in a mind-expanding whole: "There were a series of groundbreaking exhibitions right at the beginning when Hultén was director, and as it coincided with my own interests, I was very excited that the Pompidou had a special relationship with Russia, or the Soviet Union.

I remember, for example, when in 1979 or 1980 the Soviet government — or if it was the (Malevich) family and the government — delivered to Pompidou the plaster models — Tektoniks[81] — that had been made by Malevich himself. They were too controversial to show in Russia and then went into exile in Paris. It was an amazing moment to see these things for the first time. The *Paris–Moscow* exhibition was a total eye-opener."[82]

Italian curator Massimiliano Gioni speaks for many of his contemporaries when he talks about what he learned from the Pingpong exhibition catalogs: "For me, it's mainly through books and catalogs that I have come to love the Centre Pompidou (and its ghosts and memories). All the *Paris–Moscow*, *Paris–New York*, etc. catalogs, which you can still see in the libraries of anyone with a decent sense of style and art history: those books were simply incredible. Like the beautiful Duchamp retrospective book (...) I remember always spending as much time in the bookshop as in the exhibitions."[83]

Looking back at the Pingpong trilogy, the "cycle" appears to be the result of a long-term *master plan*. I find it interesting to consider how the exhibition suite, like so many other innovative initiatives, evolved organically through a series of rethinkings and adaptations to prevailing circumstances, with Hultén's old faithful allies chance and intuition still active as driving forces.

Many people I have spoken to around the world complain that it has become impossible to produce exhibitions even close to *Paris–New York*, *Paris–Berlin* and *Paris–Moscow*. This is not only because of outrageous insurance costs, security requirements and the fragility of masterpieces, but also because of the increasing commercial competition between museums, gallerists, dealers, artists' estates and others. Large-scale collective exhibitions with so many major artists have become unthinkable, a development that began in the 1980s. "The only problems with these shows was that they were too great successes," says Laurent Le Bon, President of the Centre Pompidou since 2021. "Today we often speak with some melancholy of this as a Golden Age. Instead, we should look at these shows as inspiration for the future."[84]

Although Pontus Hultén had many years left of his prime as a museum director, the Pingpong exhibitions, as I stated at the beginning of this chapter, must be considered the apex of his career. *Paris–Moscow* in particular stands out as Pontus Hultén's most Herculean achievement as a museum director. The relaunch of Russian Modernism should be placed alongside his efforts for Duchamp and Dadaism and for New York art among Hultén's art historical feats.

Again, I think his old colleague Olle Granath, who of course saw all the Pingpong exhibitions and most other shows by Pontus Hultén during his Paris years, sums it up well: "With *Paris–Moscow* and the other exhibitions in the series, Pontus showed what a fantastic pedagog he was," says Granath. "There he really got to use his extremely broad knowledge of art, history, politics and anthropology and his great vision of the art world."[85]

A final reflection on the historical Pingpong suite is precisely its uncompromisingly historical scope, that the exhibitions focused on art historical movements between fifty and eighty years previously. I ask myself whether it would have been possible, with the more limited historical interest of our present day, to attract such crowds to exhibitions with such complicated, educational historical themes, even if it would have been possible to produce similar ones today? I would like to think so, but I doubt that anyone in our time would even have the ambition to try.

22 Pontus in Paris

Pontus Hultén's persona during his eight-plus years at the Centre Pompidou in Paris appears a lonesome figure. His friends and colleagues from the time return to the descriptions of the great, powerful, silent, inscrutable Hultén; the Viking, the walking obelisk, shy, almost godlike, a giant, a colossus, who ruled with silence rather than words — the epithets lead in the same direction.

Opinions are divided as to whether Pontus Hultén was fully accepted in the Parisian cultural société. Some argue that Hultén was duly appreciated while others claim that he remained an outsider. Jean-Yves Mock is adamant that Pontus Hultén was never recognized by Parisians for the simple reason that he was Swedish, not French.[1]

In his work at the museum, Pontus Hultén formed, in addition to the teams he assembled for the various exhibitions, a private entourage of his most trusted collaborators, with whom he sat and drank in restaurants and bars at the end of long working days. This inner, usually all-male core included Jean-Hubert Martin, Stanislas Zadora, Serge Fauchereau, photographer Jacques Faujour and a few others who came and went, such as designer Roman Cieślewicz and set designer Jacques Lichnerowicz. "We formed a real group around Pontus," as Jean-Hubert Martin says.[2] Serge Fauchereau depicts it more dramatically: "We were like a gang of gangsters. Everyone knew exactly their roles. I was the man with the pistols."[3]

Pontus Hultén's closest friends throughout his time in Paris were Jean Tinguely and Niki de Saint Phalle. It was with Tinguely and de Saint Phalle, by this time no longer a couple in the traditional sense, and their entourage of artists and friends that Hultén was able to relax and live out in his Parisian existence. Hultén always felt most at ease among the artists. He was a regular guest of Tinguely and de Saint Phalle at the Commanderie[4] in Dannemois in Fontainebleau, and of Teeny Duchamp and her family in nearby Villiers-sous-Grez. "Pontus was a permanent installation, a piece of furniture," says Catherine Matisse Monnier, Teeny Duchamp's granddaughter, who tailored garments for the fashion-conscious Hultén.[5] Fontainebleau and the surrounding forest was the weekend gathering locus for the extended art family of which Pontus Hultén was an mandatory member; a much-needed free, bohemian refuge from the harsh, high-pressure life in Paris.

Near the village of Milly-la-Forêt, hidden in the forest from passers-by and the uninitiated, since 1969 Jean Tinguely's life's work "Le Cyclop," the one-eyed machine monster in the forest, grew ever bigger and more fantastically wonderful.

"The Cyclop," too, can be said to be a child of the *she* in Stockholm in 1966 — a giant, overgrown baby. *she* had led both Jean Tinguely and Niki de Saint Phalle to thinking on an ever larger scale. Niki had long admired the Spanish architect and artist Antoni Gaudí and his slowly evolving, organically ornamented buildings in Barcelona. Ferdinand Cheval, known as "Le facteur Cheval," the postman who spent thirty-three years building his own fantasy palace from stones picked up on his mail runs in the village of Hauterives in central France, who inspired the likes of André Breton and Pablo Picasso, was another of de Saint Phalle's and also Tinguely's idols.[6] A further role model was the Italian-American miscellaneous worker Simon Rodia and his magnificent junkyard palace Watts Towers in the slum of central Los Angeles, with its spires and towers — again, curiously, built over some thirty-three years. Cheval and Rodia are categorized as "naive artists," a collective term used for self-taught eccentric artists who live their lives outside the art world.[7] The Hanoverian Dadaist Kurt Schwitters and his mysterious building sculptures Merzbau appears a further reference. Yet another was the Sacro Bosco, the "Sacred Forest," also known as the Parco dei Mostri, the "Monster Park," in Bomarzo, north of Rome, Italy, commissioned by a feudal prince in the sixteenth century with "Surrealist," or proto-Surrealist as they are called, stone sculptures and buildings scattered around the parkscape, "rediscovered" by the art world after Salvador Dalí's visit in 1938.

Reportedly, it was originally Niki de Saint Phalle who inspired Jean Tinguely to create a monumental work, a world of his own, for himself, his family and friends exclusively, not intended to be shown or even known to the public. It was not until a decade later, in the late 1970s, that Niki herself began to build her own fantasy world, the Giardino dei Tarocchi, the "Tarot Garden" (see Chapter 28), outside the village of Capalbio in northern Tuscany, Italy, not far from the Sacro Bosco model.

I had the privilege of visiting "Le Cyclop" for the first time in the company of Bloum Cardenas, granddaughter of Niki de Saint Phalle and main custodian of the artistic legacy of both de Saint Phalle and Tinguely. Since 1994, "The Cyclop" has been a museum owned by the French state, open to the public during the summer months. Pontus Hultén, who was chairman of "The Cyclop's" committee and involved in the project from the beginning, has revealed that the monster sculpture was originally conceived as a collaborative project between several artists, but that the initiator Tinguely soon took command. From 1969 until his death in 1991, Tinguely devoted all his available time to "The Cyclop," with Pontus Hultén visiting, inspiring and advising as often as he could. Twenty-three meters up among the stately deciduous tree tops, the one-eyed monster skull, also known simply as "La tête," "The Head," rises with its tongue outstretched, as in the most famous monster rock sculpture from Sacro Bosco, in the form of a slide leading down into a pond, all silvered with Niki's mirror mosaic. Originally, the monster's face was skinless, its features composed of rusted cast iron like the rest of the sculpture. Bloum confides that during a period when Tinguely was depressed, her grandmother Niki covered parts of the head including the inside of the jaw with her mirror mosaic to cheer up her partner.

On the many floors, platforms and mezzanines inside the head and outside the entrance, there are numerous works and installations not only by Tinguely but also by his friends among the Neo-Realists and their circle: Arman, César, Niki de Saint Phalle, Larry Rivers, Jean-Pierre Raynaud and Tinguely's assistant and colleague Rico Weber; an upside-down room by Daniel Spoerri, a deafening sound sculpture by Jesús Rafael Soto, Bernhard Luginbühl's oversized pinball machine in rusty cast iron from *Le Crocodrome*, a miniature museum with works by Italian artist and architect Massimo Podestà, and much more, all encapsulated in Tinguely's machine sculpture with its myriad of giant pulleys and belts that form the brain itself, reaching out and up among the trunks and branches of the trees in its tentacles, charged by a "bloodstream" of spirals with rolling, thundering bowling-sized steel balls.

At the top of the sculpture is Tinguely and Niki's penthouse apartment, in which Bloum used to hang out as a child, with access to a terrace where rainwater collects in a blue pool, Tinguely's homage to his long-lost friend Yves Klein. At the same level as the terrace on the monster's head, a railway carriage, of the same model and date as the ones that went to Auschwitz, hangs surrealistically among the tree-tops, filled with Eva Aeppli's human-sized dolls, or textile sculptures as they are properly labeled, packed like the Jews on their way to the extermination camps — a powerful, ghostly installation.

Bloum generously shares fabulous interiors from the long growth process of "The Cyclop," when in the summers she ran around naked in the forest and the sculpture among the hippifed team and a steady stream of visitors who came to socialize and participate in the work, usually including Pontus Hultén. She says her friends at school didn't believe her when she asked if they wanted to come along to her grand-folks'[8] monster in the forest where it was so much fun to play ...

In one of the films made about the "The Cyclop," Rico Weber tells the story of its construction — that Tinguely was an even worse welder than himself, and how the professional Josef "Seppi" Imhof, who worked with Tinguely and Weber from the early seventies, was brought in to weld the tower that forms the sculpture's spine. Tinguely's most frequent artistic collaborator on "The Cyclop" was Bernhard Luginbühl. Bloum tells me that as a little girl, she was afraid of Luginbühl, tall and fat with a floppy moustache, often wearing a long leather coat, who used to stand outside "The Cyclop" barbequing whole animals for the many feasts in the forest — a scene that makes me think of Bruegel paintings. As we walk up the winding stairs to the top of the sculpture, Bloum shows me a cast-iron grate where she tells me that Luginbühl once stood barbequing a doll for a movie someone was shooting.[9] "He was actually very nice but looked scary and spoke an even broader Schwizerdütsch than Tinguely," Bloum says. "I didn't know what a Nazi was but wondered if it could be someone like him. I thought, if he can do that to a doll, what could he do to me?"[10]

In Jean Tinguely's enclave in the glade of the Fontainebleau forest, the optimistic spirit and complete freedom of the sixties lived on through the seventies, into the eighties. "Le Cyclop" stands there in the forest as a monument to this exception in the history of our western world.

Hultén's time for socializing was limited by a heavy workload at a furious pace. The long days were packed and his travel schedule ever increasingly hectic. As director of the world's leading modern art museum at the time, Hultén was the most powerful leader in the modern art world, a position he also held formally as president of CIMAM,[11] the International Committee of Museums and Collections of Modern Art. In his position, Pontus Hultén had the entire art world at a phone call's distance. He was consulted incessantly by collectors, patrons, colleagues and others, involved in most of the major events in the art world, constantly surrounded by all those drawn to power and success.

Even during the Paris years, Hultén stayed true to his habit of withdrawing from the world to sail in the Stockholm archipelago and the Adriatic during prolonged summer holidays. Those close to him agree that these sailing escapes were Hultén's exhaust valve that allowed him to cope with his hard work and lifestyle, but the years in Paris, with the pressure and constant travel, took their toll.

By and large, Pontus Hultén was a well-liked and highly respected manager among his staff. Many testify to how much they grew from the boundless responsibility Hultén entrusted them with. He became more personally involved only in the exhibitions closest to his heart, in the later years at the Centre Pompidou with artists such as Öyvind Fahlström (1980),[12] On Kawara (1980), Niki de Saint Phalle (1980), Fernand Léger (1981) and Piotr Kowalski (1981). Other exhibitions in which he was particularly engaged in the later years were that of Malevich's architectural models, drawings, paintings and drawings (1980), the first major retrospective of Ellsworth Kelly[13] (1980), *Sextant*, with six contemporary Swedish artists (Lennart Rodhe, Petter Zennström, Torsten Andersson, Åke Karlung, Göran Hägg and Kjell Ohlin, 1981), an exhibition of eleven copies of famous paintings by André Raffray (1981), and others.

Several of Pontus Hultén's colleagues stress that their boss was always open to new ideas, even those far outside his own personal interests. For these exhibitions, he paid even less attention to the details unless it was absolutely necessary.

In 1981, MNAM presented another Swedish exhibition, *L'Ilac*, Björn Lövin's installation with films about a fictional international life insurance company and its celebrated founder Dr. John Löwenskjöld. Jean-Hubert Martin is surprised when I inform him that the installation has been reconstructed for Moderna Museet's exhibition with Björn Lövin in 2022 (see Chapter 16). "Incredible!," Martin writes. "It took 40 years for Björn Lövin to get an audience! I am very happy for the artist. It also shows that Pontus was right, because he really fought tremendously to get this understood (...) What I remember is that it was a total failure. No reviews, no interest, total misunderstanding ... Pontus was furious: the whole inner circle of the Paris avant-garde accused PH of not showing enough Conceptual Art, but when he showed Lövin, nobody cared because he was not on the list of 'usual suspects.' I must admit that the whole concept was not easy to understand at first sight."

Jean-Hubert Martin relates a story about Joseph Beuys, an artist with whom I have previously discussed Pontus Hultén's ambivalent relationship. On one occasion, Hultén asked Martin which contemporary artist he thought had a moral dimension similar to the one he had experienced with his admired friend Yves Klein — "a very moral artist," as Hultén called him. "I immediately said Beuys, without thinking," says Jean-Hubert. "All right, let's go to Düsseldorf," Hultén replied immediately.[14] Together they visited Beuys in his studio to select works to purchase for the collection and to offer Beuys the opportunity to do whatever he wanted at the Centre Pompidou — a retrospective, an installation, a performance, a manifestation or whatever he preferred; an offer to which the artist never responded. Although the German was not one of his favorite artists, Hultén was well aware of his importance. As early as 1975, MNAM had purchased Beuys' felt-covered grand piano "Homogenous Infiltration for Concert Grand Piano" from 1966,[15] a key work for the artist and a cornerstone of the museum's sixties collection.

Even Jean Clair, whose artistic tastes and interests differed considerably from Pontus Hultén's, testifies to Hultén's willingness to embrace initiatives far beyond his own sphere of interest, such as Clair's own *Les Réalismes* 1980/1981,[16] a wide-ranging exposition on the theme of realist European painting 1919–1939, with a massive catalog and a level of ambition almost comparable to the Pingpong shows. "It must have been about the most boring thing he could have imagined, as far from his tastes as you could get — like going to the doctor," says Jean Clair, "but he accepted without hesitation when I proposed the exhibition and then helped in every way with loans and other matters, coming spontaneously to give me tips and contacts."[17]

A recurring conversation topic with colleagues from most of Pontus Hultén's workplaces is the question whether he gave appropriate recognition to his colleagues. Olle Granath is one of those who have emphasized that Hultén was weak in this discipline, Kasper König another. Jean-Hubert Martin and Daniel Abadie, on the other hand, and several others with them, argue that Hultén, unlike other museum directors, was careful about giving "credit," at least in their own cases. "He was fair to me but not always to others," as Jean-Hubert summarizes. "There were those who had grounds for criticism."[18] It's a fact that the collaborators in the various exhibitions are listed in the catalogs, far from a matter of course at this time. Still, some of his colleagues were and are bitter about what they perceived as ingratitude on Hultén's part, a tendency to make other people's ideas his own — his "big ears" in Serge Fauchereau's words — and to claim credit for them. Several members of his team from Paris would follow Hultén on assignments elsewhere. I've heard it said that there was often talk among them that each mission would be the last precisely because of this "ingratitude" — but that they would pack their bags the next time Hultén called.

Others dismiss complaints of Hultén's lack of generosity as whiny nonsense, including the Italian art historian, curator and museum director Ida Gianelli, who would become Pontus Hultén's close collaborator in Venice. "That's just jealous bullshit," Gianelli said at our meeting in Milan. "Of course he gave credit, more than he needed, even if some people didn't realize it. I personally believe that those who work on exhibitions should not get credit. They are paid to do their job and that's enough. It's the director who must take full responsibility for the exhibitions."[19]

Among the Parisian artist collective, the attitude towards Pontus Hultén can roughly be said to have been divided into two camps, the second of which was considerably larger than the first — the artists who were shown at the Centre Pompidou and those who were not, i.e. much as the situation had been in Stockholm and in all other parts of the world. In the older generation of traditional Parisian Modernists, abstract painters and others, opposition to Hultén remained compact. Even among his contemporaries in the New Realist group, by now no longer avant-garde but well-established artists, Hultén acquired opponents in the simple way that he chose which ones to present prominently in solo exhibitions and which others to show less prominently or not at all. The latter category included big names like Arman, César, Soto, his old rival Daniel Spoerri and others. For a museum director, refraining from exhibiting with artists who expect it is often tantamount to making enemies of them. In the traditional Parisian museum establishment, Hultén was never fully accepted simply because he did not belong to the exclusive family of curators trained at the École du Louvre, as described by Alfred Pacquement and others.[20]

Vivid accounts of Pontus Hultén's physical attributes have continued to recur in all my conversations and meetings with his friends, colleagues and others in Paris. Even though these constantly repeated evaluations of his face and physique may seem derogatory, they are also indicative of the respect that Pontus Hultén commanded from everyone with whom I have spoken. Certainly, it was not just his physical appearance but above all his knowledge that attracted respect. I've heard many stories about how Pontus Hultén could surprise his interlocutors with his reservoirs of knowledge. "Pontus had such a broad knowledge, not only in art, but in history, politics and all other subjects — that's what made him so unique," says Hultén's friend and collaborator Stanislas Zadora.[21] Gérard Fromanger, the French Pop artist who led the group of artists who revolted against Pontus Hultén and the new cultural center on the eve of the opening of the Centre Pompidou in 1977, speaks of Hultén with deep respect almost forty years later: "He was an enormously impressive figure. Even if one had opposed opinions, everyone knew very well that there was no one who could question his knowledge or authority in the arts."[22]

Hultén was careful about who he trusted. Among his closest confidants, he showed other sides. Many tell of how he could be attentive, caring and emotional, almost tender and sentimental. Jean-Hubert Martin remembers an event that moved him and gave a new picture of Hultén. "It was one morning when he was crying in the office. We asked what it was and he said that he had just learned that a janitor[23] whom he had worked with and liked very much at Moderna Museet had passed away. I thought it was amazing that he could show such emotion over something like that."

Daniel Buren, one of the then young, hot French artists that Pontus Hultén promoted during his time at the Centre Pompidou, I think summarizes the multifaceted impression that Hultén made on friends and colleagues in Paris: "He had many contradictory sides. He was shy and reserved and he was loud and aggressive. He was very self-assured and he was deeply insecure. He was stingy and he was generous. He was too quiet and he talked too much. He was complicated, quite simply."[24]

We recall that Pontus Hultén did not take over any office or institution. The Centre Pompidou and the expanded MNAM were new entities, invented and developed from scratch by Robert Bordaz and Pontus Hultén, without direct models or precise instructions, with new legislation that guaranteed an unprecedented independence in the French museum world from its political patrons. When designing the building, flexibility was a demand for the architectural competition for the very reason that the political clients did not have a detailed idea of what type of institution they were planning.

Pontus Hultén has in various contexts praised these open conditions — that the new museum, despite its size and power, could still act as something of an outsider. "Nobody really knew what to expect from us," as Hultén puts it.[25]

In interviews, Hultén has revealed that he had more far-reaching strategic ideas about how the museum should build its organization and recruit its staff — visions that he discussed at length with Robert Bordaz. Hultén and Bordaz advocated making the new institution a public company under the category of "industry and commerce" rather than "culture and education." Such a corporate form would have granted the museum the right to make its own decisions on staff recruitment and to dismiss staff who didn't meet expectations. As Hultén notes, this could have led to a future "PR risk" as the word culture would have been missing from the center's categorization. According to Hultén, such an arrangement would have made "the apparatus more powerful and easier to control."[26] Bordaz was forced to sacrifice this plan after the death of President Pompidou. The center's organization became a less radical institution than its vision. Hultén often complained that the bureaucracy at the cultural center grew relentlessly larger and more heavy-footed over the years.

Hultén mentions that he entertained the idea that the museum could be operated entirely without "employees" in order, as I understand it, to save resources, increase flexibility and efficiency, and reduce the bureaucracy that Hultén always despised. He regretted that the concession on organizational model had devastating consequences in the form of underperforming staff, staff not showing up for work for years, and other common problems among government institutions. The winners, Hultén goes on to say, were the lucky ones who had secure employment contracts at the museum.[27] Hultén, here in the guise of a neoliberal organizational strategist, was certainly a man of surprises, but still in line with his general philosophy of life and work, in which minimizing hassle and bureaucracy remained the ideal.

For the museum itself, unprecedented openness was a fundamental principle and, alongside the building, a key reason for the center's sensational public success. The immediate onslaught of unprecedented huge crowds meant that Hultén had no trouble pushing through his old idea of keeping the museum open until ten in the evening, a plan that had been dismissed as utopian when he first presented it. He was often there himself until closing time. Hultén also managed to pursue his desire to recruit younger people in civilian clothes who were not necessarily art historians, instead of the classic uniformed French museum guards as hosts, in order to further break down the barriers to the public.

Children's activities were also introduced, with ideas from leading contemporary educators — new in Paris and France, which was far behind Sweden in its view of the child and its rights and potential. The cinema was another priority for Hultén, the old film buff, with an extensive program linked to the museum's exhibitions. However, Hultén regretted that during his time, the restaurant failed to reach gastronomic levels that matched the three-star view of Paris.[28]

The entire museum was imbued with Hultén's trademark openness and freedom, with presentations in the wide open galleries and free movement between the different sections of the center. In its pioneering years, the cultural center was very different from the Centre Pompidou of today, where access and freedom of movement have been dramatically restricted for various reasons, security and otherwise. As mentioned, radical crowd control efforts were required already during Hultén's time, with various adaptations and restrictions forced by the public success. Nevertheless, the museum and the Centre Pompidou did indeed emerge as a perpetually open, enticing, light-flowing state-of-the-art department store for the arts, not unlike the horror vision brandished by opponents.

One element in the program of openness that Hultén was unsuccessful in implementing, here as in Stockholm, was the beautiful idea of making the art in the museum's storerooms accessible to the public. Hultén believed that since art was owned by the people, it was a shame that only a fraction of the museums' collections were shown while the bulk remained unseen. The Moderna Museet had installed an open archive with large scrolling screens that visitors could pull out to decide for themselves what they wanted to see — a project that collapsed due to constant technical problems, wear and tear, and a heavy workload for the staff. At the Centre Pompidou, Renzo Piano, at Hultén's request, designed a more sophisticated public gallery where visitors could order screens of paintings to be hoisted from the ceiling. The apparatus met the same fate as its more rustic predecessor in Stockholm. Technical and logistical problems plagued the "open archive" which had to be closed after some years and the idea abandoned.

A substantial part of Pontus Hultén's work at MNAM involved continued efforts to expand the museum's collection. The results he had achieved in just a few years were remarkable. Many important enhancements had enabled the museum to show the mass public the world's foremost modern art collection after the Museum of Modern Art in New York. As Calvin Tomkins says: "When you talk about Hultén, you usually think of his exhibitions. It is easy to forget the contributions he made to the collections of his museums."[29] Pontus Hultén himself expressed his satisfaction with the annual purchase budget of thirty million francs and the fortunate circumstance that this money could still be used to acquire works of art historical importance.[30] He stated that the museum could rely on its old collection of thirty thousand works, but that much of the French art in this collection was of mediocre quality[31] (Jean-Hubert Martin contradicts this description as "ridiculous"[32]). Forty-four years after its opening, the MNAM has over one hundred thousand works of art in its collection.

The quest of strengthening the collection led Pontus Hultén and the MNAM into a protracted, strangely hushed scandal. Piet Mondrian was one of the most embarrassing gaps in the complete encyclopedia of twentieth-century art history that Pontus Hultén was determined that the MNAM collection must provide. The ambition to complete the collection with paintings by Mondrian had become an obsession for Pontus Hultén and Germain Viatte, who, as a somewhat more senior curator than most of his colleagues, was in charge of the collection under Hultén.

Viatte reveals that he and Hultén made the acquaintance of a known Belgian artist and writer with contacts in Mondrian circles. For several years they entertained the acquaintance with regular dinners in the hope of tracking down works by the artist. Sure enough, the man eventually revealed that he actually knew of three unknown Mondrian paintings. Slowly but surely, he released information about what subsequently turned into a deal.

Hultén and Viatte's "Deep Throat" into the Mondrian world had one condition: nothing about their dealings could be leaked to the press, the museum world or anyone else, especially in Mondrian's native Netherlands. If the deal became known, everything was off, the man underscored. Viatte asked Hultén whether Mondrian experts should still be consulted, but Hultén forbade this, nervous that the plan would fail. Eventually, the paintings arrived at the museum's warehouse. Funding was arranged through contributions from several important patrons, including Dominique de Menil and one of the Louvre's most important donors. The purchase contract was signed.

All that remained to close the affair was to transfer the money to the seller, a Jewish widow in Amsterdam whose husband, murdered in the Holocaust, had allegedly bought the paintings from Mondrian himself in the 1930s and then hid them from the Nazi terror, after which they had remained forgotten. The purchase price was to be transferred to the poor beleaguered widow when the banks opened on the Monday after the weekend following the arrival of the works in Paris.

In the midst of Friday night, Germain Viatte recounts, he suddenly woke up and felt that something was very wrong. He decided to go to the Netherlands immediately on Saturday morning, without asking Pontus Hultén for permission.[33] He took a morning flight to Amsterdam to visit an acquaintance who was one of the world's leading Mondrian experts. When Viatte arrived, the acquaintance said, as he opened the portfolio of pictures that Viatte had brought with him, "oh, no, this doesn't feel good, I can tell you that right away." He informed Viatte that the paintings were by no means unknown but of dubious origin. Germain's nervousness increased. He dashed off to Waterloo in Belgium where another expert confirmed the assessment. He phoned the owner in Amsterdam to come and visit, but this was not possible — on the contrary, it was highly inappropriate. Not satisfied, Viatte went to the address given, where no one answered the door, although he noticed that someone was home. The whole thing began to smell like an old movie mystery. Viatte contacted the first Mondrian expert and asked him to come to Paris immediately, to which he agreed. On Sunday, as Pontus Hultén was out of town, Viatte brought Michel Laclotte, the director of the Louvre, to the MNAM warehouse because he wanted a witness when the expert examined the paintings. He concluded that they were forgeries. This was later confirmed by technical analysis of the oil paint and the discovery of a white pigment that had not been used commercially in the thirties. Thanks to Germain Viatte's decisive action, the payment was stopped and the purchase canceled. He thus saved Pontus Hultén and the museum from a major disgrace.

The matter was already sufficiently troublesome. Germain Viatte reveals that, for once, Hultén was caught up in the gravity of the moment. To begin with, it was embarrassing to tell Dominique de Menil and other donors that their money had almost paid for fake art. "But Madame de Menil was very polite and friendly and said it was good that we had acted as we did to prevent it," says Germain Viatte.[34]

The Mondrian affair was a shame that haunted Pontus Hultén. A legal process was initiated that would last for years. The press reported on the developments. The police were convinced that Hultén's and Viatte's friend, the writer, had colluded with the owner of the paintings. In the end, they were unable to prove this. No one was convicted in the forgery case. The "poor woman" who had offered the paintings for sale was thrown into prison but, according to Pontus Hultén, turned out to have had nothing to do with the plot; the two later became friends.[35]

Germain Viatte confides that he had to deal with most of the aftermath of the legal entanglements while Hultén stayed away as much as he could in this matter, which became a stain on his reputation as a museum director. "I have to say that he left me a bit alone," as Viatte says. I ask Germain how the process could go so far without them suspecting anything. The whole set-up seems undeniably shady from the start when relayed. "We were blind, me too," Viatte replies. "It was a classic case of tunnel vision. We were so obsessed with getting over the Mondrian works that we refused to see the warning signs."[36]

In the interviews with Stephan Andreae, Pontus Hultén admits that the Mondrian affair was deeply unpleasant for him and that he failed in his administrative judgment in this case.[37] Buying fake art is a debacle that many museums have suffered throughout art history. Numerous masterpieces hanging in leading institutions are indeed questionable in terms of authenticity. Although the incident is far from unique, it's worth considering in relation to other events in Pontus Hultén's career and life. He was always willing to find solutions to achieve his priorities, if necessary by adapting the terrain to the map — something like the old journalistic rule of thumb of never over-checking a good story. "He could be a bit quick sometimes," as Germain Viatte concludes.

It should be added that Piet Mondrian was hardly one of Hultén's personal favorite artists. He was well aware of the artist's importance, but from what I've heard personally skeptical. Jean-Hubert Martin reveals that Hultén had talked about Mondrian with some Chinese people who did not understand the Dutchman's greatness — something that had increased Hultén's own doubts. "For him, art was global and he thought that if the Chinese couldn't see the greatness, maybe it wasn't there," says Jean-Hubert.[38]

A major setback for Pontus Hultén was the sudden resignation of his boss Robert Bordaz after the inauguration of the *Paris–New York* line in the summer of 1977. Bordaz returned to his profession as a lawyer with an office on Boulevard Montparnasse. He was replaced by an official appointed by Giscard d'Estaing named Jean Millier, who, according to Hultén, had no intellectual or cultural interests, "with one exception — he knew all about Senegalese sugar."[39] Millier proved to be a friendly and pleasant man and the two became friends.[40]

Thanks to the masterly political maneuvering of Robert Bordaz, Pontus Hultén had survived the drama of President Pompidou's death. The museum and the entire center, as we have seen, was very much a product of the collaboration between Bordaz, Hultén and the architects Rogers and Piano. Although Bordaz's departure had no immediate consequences for Hulten — he and the museum continued to surf the wave of success — it meant that he lost his political patronage. It was a weakening of his position that was decisive in ensuring that his era at the Centre Pompidou did not become as long as he and many others thought that it should have been.

Pontus Hultén portrayed it as if the new museum and the entire cultural center, once it had picked up steam from the start, functioned like a machine that spat out a new exhibition every month.[41] It's certainly an evocative image: this art factory, likened to monsters, motorcycles, oil refineries, nuclear power plants, and several other brutal metaphors, pumping art and other culture and creativity, devouring the masses of people from the street into its organism. The Centre Pompidou changed not only the position of modern art in society but also the city of Paris and its urban pulse.

23

Surrealism's revenge: Salvador Dalí breaks records

The density the exhibition program at the Musée National d'Art Moderne during the mere four years that Pontus Hultén remained as director after the opening of the Centre Pompidou in 1977 is testified by the fact that *Paris–Moscow*[1] was preceded and followed by two massive Surrealist retrospectives, the second of which, with Salvador Dalí, still holds the all-time attendance record for an exhibition at the Centre Pompidou.

Salvador Dalí was another artist who had been kept short by the Parisian establishment and the conservative French Academy — an actuality true of Surrealism in general, never accepted in the same elevated sphere as Fauvism and Cubism. Few works by Dalí were in the collections of French state museums, despite the artist having lived and worked in Paris off and on throughout his career. Dalí left a gap that Hultén saw as necessary to fill. In his opinion, Surrealism as a whole constituted perhaps the most troublesome void in the French state's collection, an obvious analysis since Surrealism was a purely Parisian art movement. A significant part of Hultén's efforts to strengthen the collection was devoted to Surrealism, with purchases and donations of works by Ernst, André Masson, Dalí, Magritte, Miró and other masters of the movement.

1979 saw the launch of a wide-ranging retrospective of René Magritte,[2] the other truly popular Surrealist — an artist who had also been neglected by the establishment in the city where the Belgian had lived for a number of years. The exhibition was a blockbuster and further Magritte works were acquired.

Hultén probably knew Salvador Dalí from Paris in the 1950s and 1960s. He states that they had good contacts with the artist and also with Dalí's former friend and collaborator Luis Buñuel, whom Hultén greatly admired. Dalí may not have been one of Hultén's personal favorite artists, but he was well aware of his appeal, position among the Surrealists, and importance in art history. The acquisition of "Wilhelm Tell's Riddle," the monumental painting with the portrait of Lenin, in conjunction with *The Museum of Wishes*, had given Moderna Museet in Stockholm one of its most powerful crowd-magnets, of course borrowed as a centerpiece in the Paris exhibition as well.

Salvador Dalí and Luis Buñuel were youthful friends from their student days in Madrid in the early twentieth century. Dalí helped Buñuel with the script for his 1929 film *The Andalusian Dog*. Buñuel broke off contact with Dalí after Dalí wrote a letter shortly after the dictator Franco's victory in the Spanish Civil War in 1939, rejecting socialism and praising Catholicism and the fascist Falange organization.

Daniel Abadie, the then young curator/intendant who had fallen out with Pontus Hultén during the production of *Paris–New York*, tells me that sometime in 1978 Hultén called and said that he had decided to show a full-scale Salvador Dalí retrospective the following year, the first in France, and that he wanted Abadie to organize this mammoth exhibition.[3] I comment that this must have meant that Hultén had by then forgotten the strife and that he still had great confidence in Abadie's abilities, as I understand he did. Abadie denies this. "He knew Dalí and was aware it was an impossible mission," says Abadie. "He soaped the floor for me so that I would slip."[4]

In Daniel Abadie's account, Hultén knew that the Dalí exhibition would be particularly difficult to execute because of the rivalry between the artist's two "advisors," the photographer/filmmaker Robert Descharnes and the secretary/business manager Enrique Sabater, and, as was commonly known in the art world, with his wife Gala as a further complicating factor — a game of intrigue in which Hultén himself didn't want to get involved, according to Abadie.[5]

Despite the risks, the intrepid Daniel Abadie decided to produce the exhibition on his own. He says that Dalí came to visit Paris and that he met him and his entourage at Le Meurice, a classic hotel on Rue de Rivoli where Dalí always stayed in an apartment during his Parisian sojourns to which he would be driven in his Rolls-Royce from Cadaqués. "I had a good relationship with Dalí," says Abadie. "He was a very nice person. His wife, though, was not. Descharnes was very tricky, mostly keen to get money for something he had never done.

I got close to Sabater who was very helpful because he was an enemy of Descharnes."[6]

Daniel Abadie, whose accord with Pontus Hultén gives the impression of a love-hate relationship, says that the production faced many problems but that despite Abadie's claim that Hultén wanted to "soap the floor" for him, Hultén always "stood behind me like a wall, something you can't say about other museum directors." "Pontus was a real museum director, prepared to take risks and back up his decisions," Abadie adds.[7]

For the Dalí exhibition, the museum managed to assemble the largest collection of works by the artist ever shown, borrowing all the major paintings from museums and collections around the world with one exception, Abadie says: the Cleveland Art Museum in Ohio, where there was a problem with images that had been reproduced without rights.

"With Dalí, nothing worked, you knew that beforehand," says Abadie, explaining that during the artist's visit to Paris, he took him to the Centre Pompidou to see the gallery on the fifth floor where the bulk of the exhibition would be displayed. The entire floor happened to be vacated between two exhibitions at the time. "There was no sense of the gallery, just a vast empty open space," says Abadie. "Dalí was quiet for a while and then suddenly said: 'Now I know how we do it. Let's hang the paintings along the walls and put stargazers in the middle for the audience.' It was always like that with Dalí. He had sudden ideas that changed everything."[8]

Young Daniel Abadie chose to ignore this magnificently surrealist idea from the ageing artist and went on to plan a completely different exhibition. He was nervous when Dalí called from Cadaqués a year later, a week before the opening. The artist was on his way to Paris and told Abadie that it would be interesting to see how this stargazing thing had worked out. Dalí also had a new idea for his "Visage du Grand Masturbateur" ("Face of the Great Masturbator") from 1929[9], which the artist wanted to present in an installation arranged in a certain way. "Yes, yes, that sounds interesting," Abadie replied, knowing full well that such ideas were impossible to implement at this stage.[10]

The Salvador Dalí retrospective was a gigantic presentation. In addition to the fifth level with Dalí's art from more than half a century,

Pp. 440–441: Salvador Dalí retrospective 1979. The exhibition holds an unbeatable attendance record at the Centre Pompidou with around one million visitors. The giant spoon in the Paris installation in the Forum entrance hall is Dalí's tribute to the absinthe drinkers of Boulevard Montparnasse.

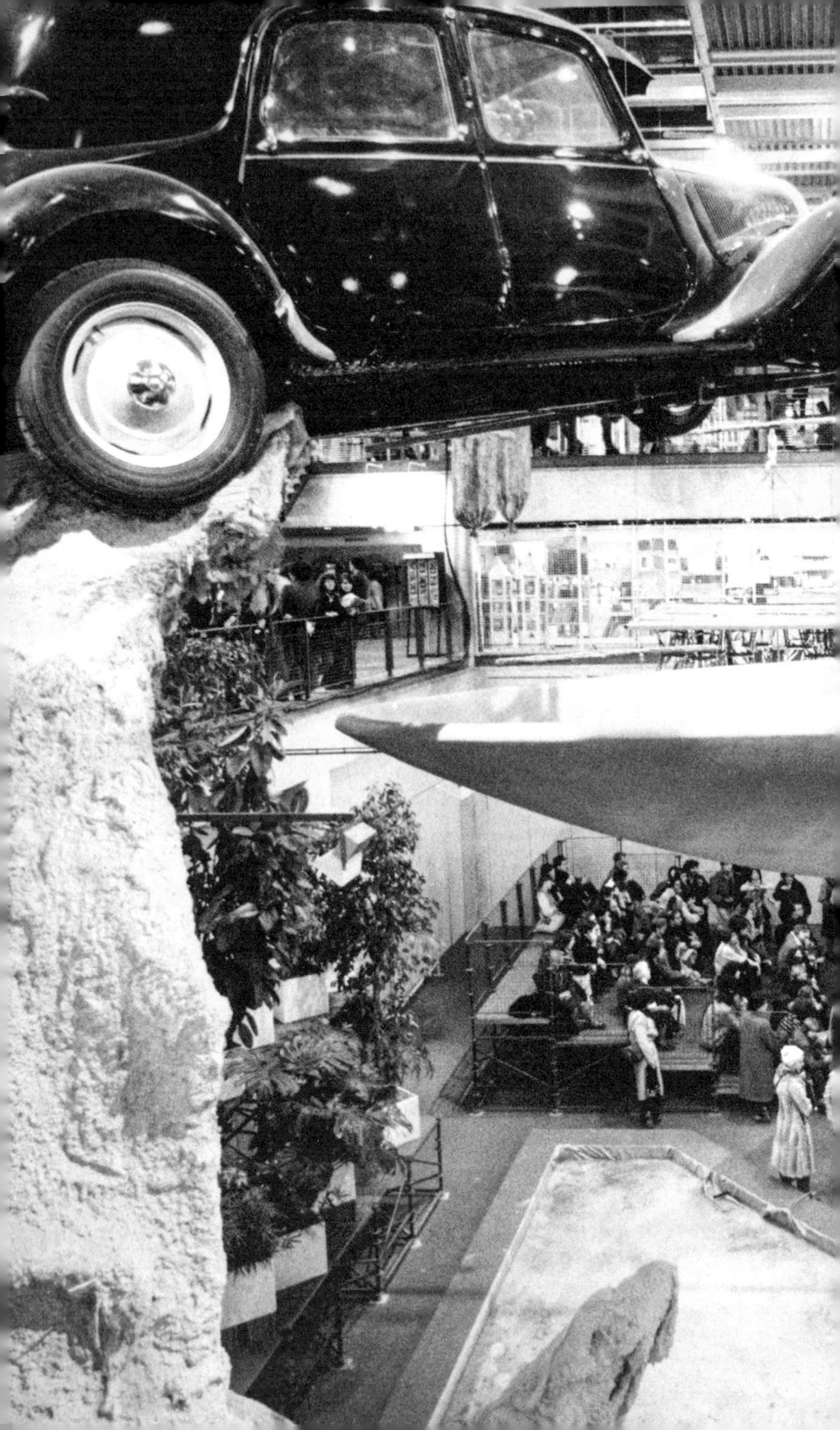

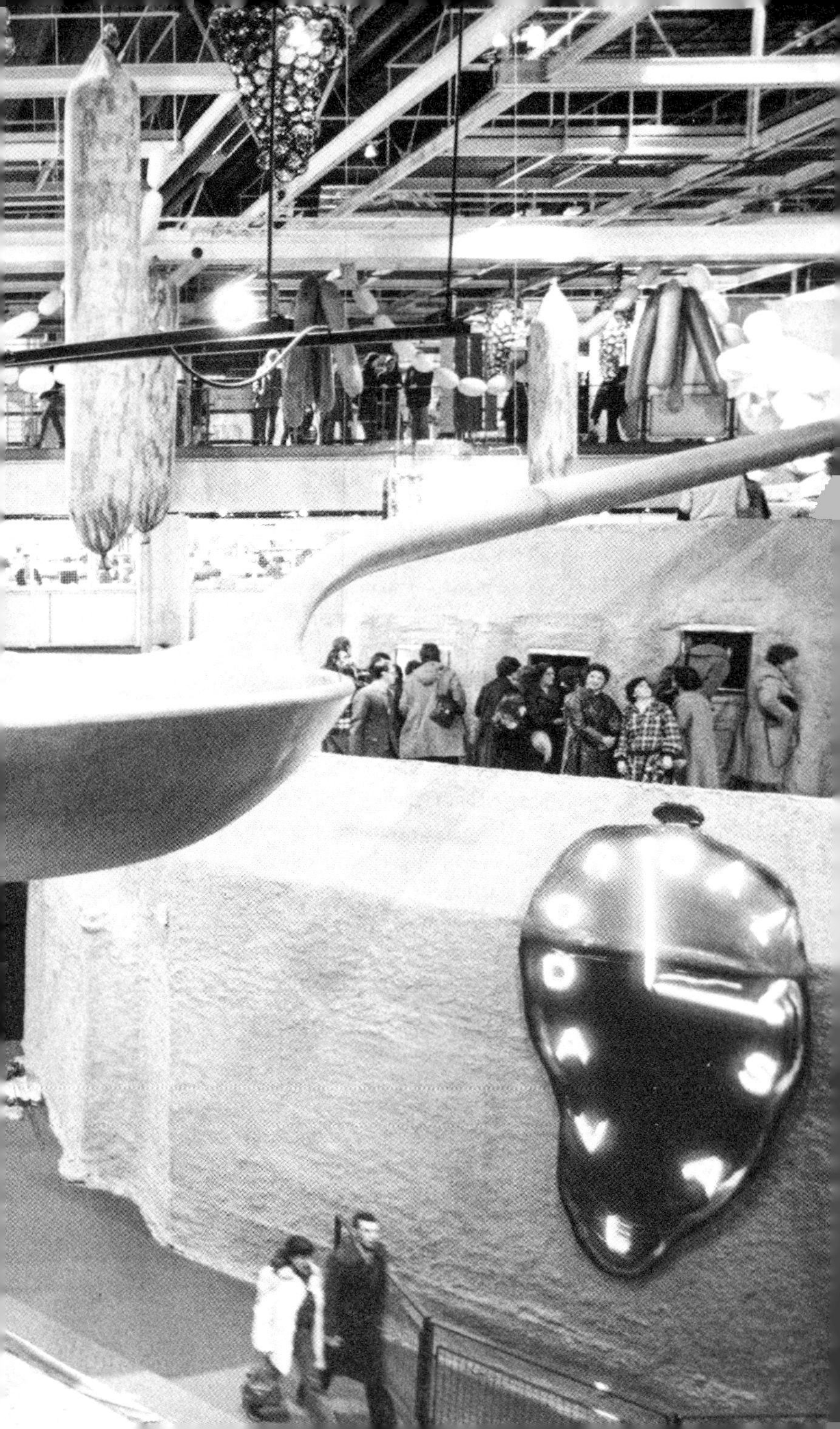

the exhibition included a second part: a giant installation in the submerged Forum on the ground floor. Abadie explains that it was Dalí himself who had the idea of building an "environment"[11] with a Paris theme. In addition to a series of paintings, it included a flying Citroën from the twenties, a twenty-five-meter-long steel spoon (a "nod" to the absinthe drinkers on Boulevard Montparnasse[12]), a set of forgeries of the paintings of the heroic eighteenth-century French artist Ernest Meissonier, a running clock, Elsa Schiaparelli's dress, and windows with various surrealist objects.

Daniel Abadie reveals that he was, understandably, stressed when he went with Hultén, Dalí, Gala and Sabater to see the exhibition a few days before the opening, nervous about how the artist would react when he discovered that his idea for the stargazers had been scrapped. His fears were unfounded. Abadie recounts that when the party arrived on the escalators to level five, Dalí stopped in front of a painting from 1927 that he hadn't seen in forty-five years. Fascinated, he showed the painting to Pontus Hultén and told him about how he had painted over the canvas seven times, meaning that there were six other paintings sealed under the oil surface. The stargazers were forgotten. Dalí made no mention of them. He checked carefully that no fakes had crept into the exhibition and was then satisfied, according to Daniel Abadie.[13]

Hultén's own account of the visit with Dalí is that the party was considerably delayed and that Gala, as usual, created drama when she didn't want to see the show — she already knew the paintings — but preferred to sleep in the Rolls-Royce outside the museum.[14] Hultén says that he spent five hours alone with Dalí in the exhibition and that they then went to the artist's hotel suite on Rue de Rivoli together. He describes Dalí as "extraordinarily pleasant" and sociable, a true humanist bon vivant and a great storyteller, though only when his wife was absent.

During the tour, Dalí told Hultén about his relationships with Buñuel and Breton, among others. "You know," Hultén recalls Dalí saying, adding that the artist was "strangely" personal and familiar in his tone with him: "Actually, I was much more interested in literature than art, but this is how it turned out."[15] Dalí, like many artists, was a wonderful writer and poet with a significant literary output.

The day before the opening of the exhibition, the museum workers at the Centre Pompidou went on a classic French strike, reportedly in protest against Dalí's alleged fascist leanings.[16] The museum was closed and the gala opening with visiting celebrities had to be canceled. Hultén had arranged a Surrealist-inspired dinner at the Natural History Museum in the Jardin des Plantes "with a variety of unusual dishes," but suddenly a large number of guests were missing. When substitutes had been called in at short notice to fill the gaps at the tables, Dalí instead failed to show up because Gala was "indisposed." "It was a strange experience full of bizarre anecdotes," says Hultén. "In the end, many people thought that even the strike was a work by Dalí." He explains that they "went through heaven and hell" in the production of the exhibition and praises Daniel Abadie for his work, adding with satisfaction that the adventure concluded with the successful acquisition of important works by Dalí for the museum's collection.[17]

It was only two weeks later that the exhibition opened. By then Salvador Dalí had long since returned to Cadaqués. Hultén concludes that after the exhibition in Paris, Dalí became increasingly extravagant and that towards the end of his life he was "really very strange."[18]

From the delayed opening, the Dalí exhibition drew unprecedented masses to the Centre Pompidou. An official figure for the number of visitors to the exhibition is seven hundred and eighty thousand. Daniel Abadie and others claim that the real total was 1.1 million.[19] Including the installation in the Forum entrance hall, the exhibition attracted over 1.25 million visitors[20] — a record that stands by a wide margin. Photos and films show the crowds of visitors who were still allowed to walk right up to the paintings without hindrance. Exhibitions on this scale are no longer staged at the Centre Pompidou and hardly anywhere else. "The Pompidou is a regional museum today," says Daniel Abadie. "At the time, we had the ambition to compete and be a counterweight to the United States."[21]

The René Magritte and Salvador Dalí exhibitions were important steps in the breakthrough of modern art in Paris. Both are extremely broad-based artists, which has made them suspect in elitist cliques. Dalí in particular attracted large numbers of Parisians and tourists who had never before visited a modern art museum, or a museum at all. Not least the younger museum visitors were fascinated by Dalí — a quality that Pontus Hultén always appreciated. For him, a hallmark of really good art was that it could be understood even by a child. The question is whether any other artist has the same immediate impact on children and young people. Many little Parisians were sucked into art by the Dalí exhibition in 1979, like myself in front of "Wilhelm Tell's Riddle" at Moderna Museet in my childhood. One of these visitors was Philippe Vergne, an art historian and curator from Paris who much later succeeded Pontus Hultén as director of the Museum of Contemporary Art (MOCA) in Los Angeles. "The Dalí exhibition opened the whole art world to me," Vergne says. "It was an incredibly exciting experience, a shock, to understand that art could be something so amazing. That and the other exhibitions at the Pompidou in the early years made me realize that art was what I wanted to do."[22]

24
Exit Paris: a bitter end to the success saga

Pontus Hultén claimed in various contexts[1] that after his original five-year contract as director of the Musée National d'Art Moderne had been extended to eight years, he decided it was enough.

This assessment doesn't correspond to reality. Hultén's close friends know that the new French socialist government that took office in 1981, with the colorful Jack Lang as Minister of Culture, decided, to Hultén's immense disappointment, not to renew his contract. Hultén also acknowledges this in the interviews with Stephan Andreae, where he says that he was "shown the door" by the Centre's executive director;[2] that while this was "fully within their rights" as the contract had expired, it was "not very elegant."[3]

I have heard a number of different versions of the reasons for the termination, as it must be called, and the people behind it. Some claim that Jack Lang himself made the decision, while others say that he was not directly involved[4] (Lang himself did not respond to my inquiry on the matter). There are reports that Hultén's grandiosity, both financial and otherwise, played a role in the decision not to extend his appointment. The measure appears to have been primarily the result of political gamesmanship in connection with the change of government. Hultén's successor was Dominique Bozo, who had bided his time as director of the new Picasso museum. Some argue that Bozo was close to the left, while others claim that he was politically conservative. It seems ironic that the leftist Hultén survived a conservative government but was brought down by a socialist one. The pattern from Stockholm repeated itself — the left caused him worse problems than the right. Pontus Hultén himself was convinced that outgoing President Giscard d'Estaing was behind his dismissal, which he had certainly wanted to carry out already when he took office.[5]

It seems to me that Hultén's opponents in the Parisian art establishment, who had never given up their opposition, still had the last word after Robert Bordaz, the direct link to President Pompidou and his vision, had disappeared from the center. Bordaz's second-in-command, Claude Mollard, who at the time of Hultén's departure had taken another post, confirms this picture: "Pontus had many enemies, of course, and with Bordaz gone it was more difficult for him to defend his position," says Mollard. "In my new position, I could no longer protect him either."[6]

Jean-Hubert Martin is one of several of Pontus Hultén's confidants who have told me how hard Hultén took his forced resignation. "Somehow he never got over that," says Martin. "It was noticeable in his old age, when he became cynical and sarcastic."[7] Martin is among those who believe that the decision not to further extend Hultén's contract was unfortunate for the museum and for the Centre Pompidou: "It would have been much better if he had been allowed to continue for a number of years. He had much more to give and no one from our generation was ready to take over."[8]

Hultén's successor Dominique Bozo is portrayed as a traditional French museum man, with his heart in the classical art forms of painting and sculpture. It is said that Bozo was involved in the political power play in the cultural world, unlike Hultén who abhorred it. Bozo resigned in 1986 after conflicts, was employed by the Ministry of Culture in 1990 and then returned in 1991, after Jean-Hubert Martin's contract had not been renewed either,[9] as director of the MNAM as well as of the entire Centre Pompidou — an unfortunate double patronage according to many. Under Dominique Bozo's leadership, a rapid "reset" of Hultén's wide-open museum was executed. The optimistic, utopian sixty-eight spirit that had characterized the museum and center from the start was gradually "normalized." The presentation of the collection was divided up with different artists in individual sections. "Bozo brought back the idiotic chicken cages," as Jean-Yves Mock says.[10] Dadaism and Surrealism were toned down in favor of Fauvism and Cubism. "When I became director in 1987, I brought back Dadaism and Surrealism," says Jean-Hubert Martin. "I created for the first time a room for Duchamp and one for Picabia, similar to those for Picasso and Matisse, but smaller. As soon as Bozo came back, he erased them. They're still carrying on like that."[11]

MNAM at the Centre Pompidou is nowadays confidently ranked as one of the world's three leading modern art museums, in a class of its own alongside MoMA in New York and Tate Modern in London. Yet there is a general perception that the museum has never regained the impact in the art world that it enjoyed during Hultén's tenure in the years following its opening. After breaking attendance records with almost eight and a half million visitors in 1984, three years after Hultén's departure, the cultural center now receives around three and a half million visitors a year, a remarkable figure in itself. "I knew when I took office that I could never achieve anything like what Hultén did in his time," says Bernard Blistène, MNAM's director from 1993 to 2021. "Those were the pioneering years — it must have been a great time. Now we live in a different era."[12]

Against this backdrop, it's striking how little Pontus Hultén and his legacy have, until recently, been highlighted by the Centre Pompidou throughout its history. When I began this work in 2013, I had to search extensively on the museum's website to find a small paragraph of text that briefly mentioned Hultén and Dominique Bozo together, as the directors who had led the museum in its early years. Searches on Hultén's name yielded few hits. Most people I've spoken to agree that Pontus Hultén is relatively forgotten in Paris, well known, of course, to an older generation and in museum circles, but at best fleetingly familiar in the broader contemporary art and cultural scene. The pattern is again recognizable from Moderna Museet and Stockholm.

In recent years, we've seen increasing evidence of a renewed interest in Hultén and the pioneering years on the part of the MNAM. The aforementioned international symposiums and the voluminous issues of the museum's journal Les Cahiers du MNAM for the forty-year anniversaries of the museum (2017) and *Paris–Moscow* (2019), respectively, are important contributions to the historiography. In 2021, the Centre Pompidou Metz,[13] the first of the cultural center's branches, in northeastern France, presented *Face à Arcimboldo*,[14] an epic, spectacular exhibition of contemporary art in "dialog" with the sixteenth-century Italian Mannerist master Giuseppe Arcimboldo, inspired by Pontus Hultén's *Effetto Arcimboldo* at Palazzo Grassi in Venice in 1987 (see Chapter 28). In the almost Hulténian encyclopedic catalog, designed by the acclaimed graphic design duo M/M Paris, curator Anne Horvath, producer of the exhibition together with the museum's director Chiara Parisi, writes about how, after forty-four years, the Centre Pompidou continues the tradition established by the first director of the MNAM: "The memory of a visit to Beaubourg will not just be impressions of this or that work, a painting, a book or an exhibition, but a game of reflections created between experiences, contradictions and sparks of inspiration, ranging from the most recent works, sometimes shocking and difficult to understand, to older, better known works of art. In this perspective, of course, interdisciplinarity is required which corresponds, on the one hand, to the need to reflect art history, in several media without hierarchy, on the other hand, and necessary to attract new audiences, by integrating expressions previously considered illegitimate. This doctrine is still today a cornerstone of the Centre Pompidou's DNA, nourishing the hanging of the collections as much as exhibition design, but only one of the pillars of Pontus Hultén's multifaceted strategy."[15]

In 2025, this renewed, expanding interest in Pontus Hultén and the pioneer years of the museum is manifested in grand style when the Centre Pompidou opens its exhibition *Niki de Saint Phalle, Jean Tinguely, Pontus Hultén*[16], an epic survey on the dynamic trio's half a century of artistic collaboration. The much anticipated show is staged at the Grand Palais, as the Centre Pompidou closed in spring 2025 for a total renovation — a nice tribute, one may think, to Hultén's early exhibitions at the same Grand Palais before the museum opened (see Chapter 19). The show can be viewed as part of museum's ambitious historic endeavor in preparation for its fifty-year anniversary in 2027, initiated by Centre Pompidou President Laurent Le Bon, who says of Hultén: "Pontus Hultén was a man without a homeland. He's frequently called a mariner, a navigator. His scope was totally global. I sometimes refer to his exhibitions as 'oceanographic.' You dived into them and had the impression of discovering all new worlds. It was Pontus Hultén who created the model for how we do exhibitions today, and most certainly specifically here at the Centre Pompidou."[17]

Magiciens de La Terre was a gigantic exhibition staged at both the MNAM Centre Pompidou and the large exhibition hall at the La Vilette Science Park from May 18 to August 14, 1989. The exhibition is viewed a milestone as it is considered the first in a leading Western museum to show a "fair" selection of art from around the world, without the usual Western-centric perspective. Fifty Western and fifty non-Western artists were exhibited. *Magiciens de La Terre* related to two famous historical expositions, the controversial *Primitivism in 20th Century Art* at MoMA in 1984 and *L'Exposition Coloniale* in Paris in 1931.

During Jean-Hubert Martin's tenure as director of MNAM in the late 1980s, Hultén returned as an advisor to the museum, also serving as an inspiration for Martin's famous manifestation *Magiciens de la Terre*. Hultén himself has called this comeback as "an idiotic mistake."[18] Jean-Hubert, on the other hand, describes the collaboration as "problem-free."[19] "Pontus started as an advisor when I took over in 1987," says Martin. "In that role he was very reserved, discreet and humble, careful to help only when I explicitly asked him to do so."[20]

Although Pontus Hultén maintained a lifelong respectful relationship with MNAM and the Centre Pompidou, with many collaborations even in later years, he retained a bitterness towards the institution, as well as in many respects towards Moderna Museet. I think, sadly, that's how you have to look at it.

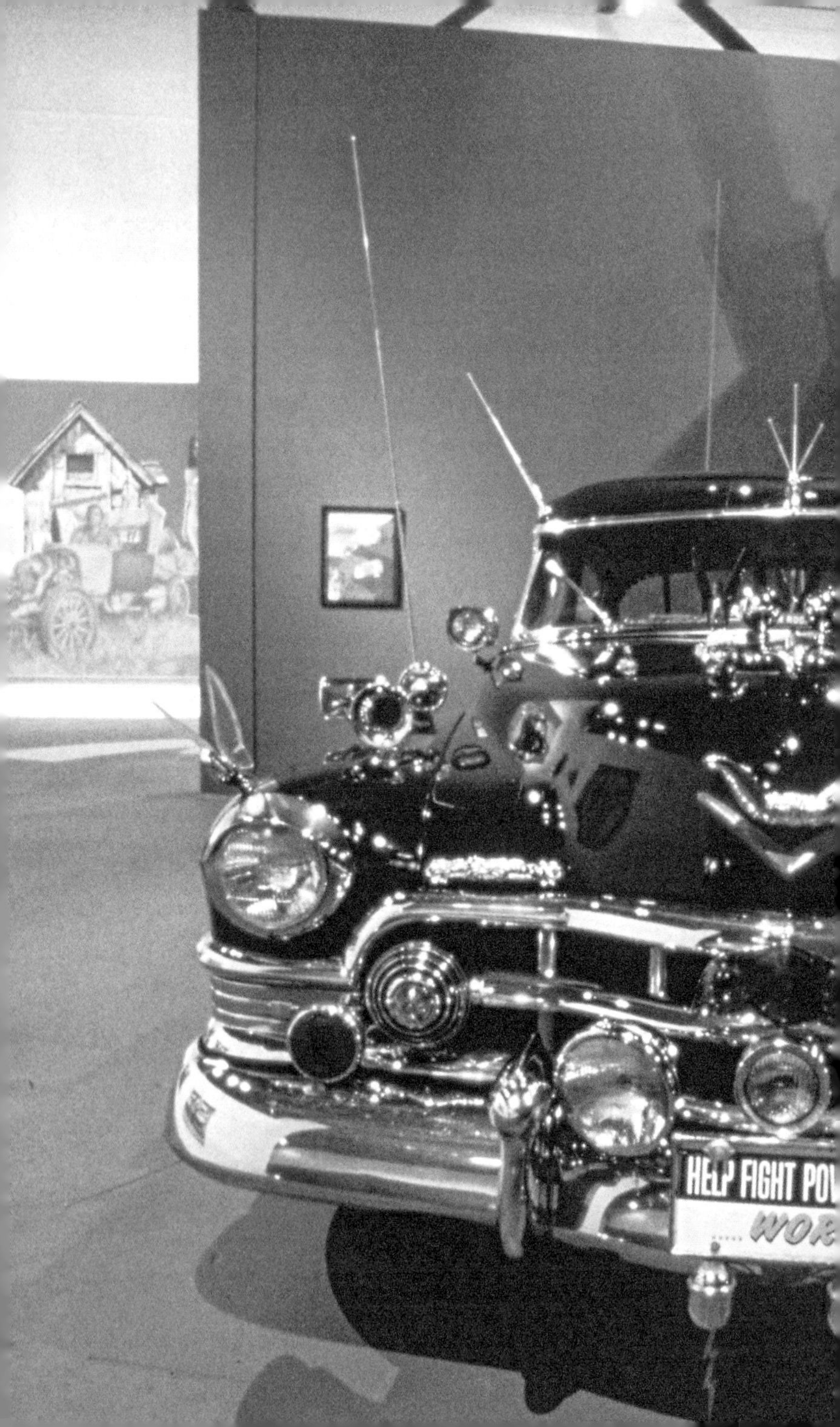
HELP FIGHT POV
WOR

25 MOCA, Los Angeles, California — a defeat in the West?

In my young age, I found it a strange coincidence that the second stop on Pontus Hultén's international career was my own second home town of Los Angeles, where I lived and went to school for three periods from the mid-seventies to the early eighties.

This was long before Los Angeles became the international metropolis it is today, when my old neighborhoods in Santa Monica and Venice have become a new Brooklyn for hipsters from all around the globe, not least from Stockholm and Sweden. In the early eighties, Los Angeles was an exotic destination that few at home had visited. If any city in California was talked about at the time, it was San Francisco. Art and culture were not what I associated with this urban organism — "a hundred suburbs in search of a center"[1] as the city has been called — while growing up in Santa Monica's tough public schools. It sure appeared to me like a big step down in his career.

At the same time, it seemed an exciting and surprising career move in the spirit of Hultén. Through my father's friends and colleagues at the UCLA university, I had come to know the city's radical, thoroughly hippiefied intellectual culture that I had loved as a child and teenager. My father's mad scientist boss was married to an artist who served life-size fetuses cast in jelly with the roast in their outrageously bohemian home. It was a culture reminiscent of that around the Moderna Museet back home in Stockholm but harder, wilder, freer and more relaxed in the Californian sun. In that world, I could see that Pontus Hultén would have thrived.

In the international art world, there is a general perception that Pontus Hultén's two-year-long Californian excursion was a failure. Some have even called it a disaster. There is no doubt that it was a

Automobile and Culture, MOCA, Los Angeles, 1984.

time of conflict that was in many ways unfortunate for Hultén. This is evident from his own statements. In my research, I have found that the historiography is more multi-dimensional — as so often with Pontus Hultén, this master of complicated truths.

When the news was announced in the fall of 1980 that Pontus Hultén was to leave Paris to become the founding director of the new Museum of Contemporary Art (MOCA) in Los Angeles, it caused a sensation and surprise in the art world, not least in New York, where the New York Times noted the remarkable truth that Los Angeles had managed to trump New York in attracting this star from Paris.[2]

The story requires a background on the Los Angeles and California art scene. To help me, I again turn to the great art writer and author Calvin Tomkins, who published his second major profile article on Pontus Hultén in The New Yorker in the spring of 1981, in connection with Hultén's move to Los Angeles for the opening of MOCA.[3]

Tomkins tells the story of a city that, since the 1950s, had seemed on the verge of achieving what Southern California artists dreamed of — breaking through as one of the world's art metropolises. By the mid-sixties, the city had fulfilled the four conditions necessary to achieve such dignity. It had a dynamic colony of contemporary artists, a few progressive galleries, resourceful collectors, and two ambitious modern art museums — the Los Angeles County Museum of Art (LACMA) and the Pasadena Art Museum (now the Norton Simon Museum). There was also a fifth factor cited by some: an internationally acclaimed art journal in Artforum — the world's most prestigious art magazine of our time — which moved from its native San Francisco to Los Angeles in 1965.[4]

The focal point of the art scene that had emerged in Los Angeles in the early sixties was the tiny Ferus Gallery on La Cienega Boulevard in what is now West Hollywood, opened in 1957 by artist Edward Kienholz together with Walter Hopps, the then twenty-five-year-old curator who became the major key and cult figure in the aspiring art metropolis of Los Angeles. Kienholz left the gallery the following year to pursue his own art. He was replaced by art dealer Irving Blum, who had recently moved to LA from New York. In practice, it was Blum who ran the gallery, with the erratic Hopps in a "free role."

In a more far-reaching conclusion, the rise of Los Angeles as an art city can be claimed to have originated with the couple Walter and Louise Arensberg, the foremost collectors of Marcel Duchamp and his most important patrons, who moved from New York to their now famous villa in the Hollywood Hills in 1921 for health and financial reasons. It was in this home that the fifteen-year-old Walter Hopps had his revelation of modern art during a field trip from his highschool in Eagle Rock in Pasadena, northeast Los Angeles.

After this enlightenment, Walter Hopps began visiting the Arensbergs every Saturday in their home, becoming like a son in the house. While in college, still a teenager, he and two friends opened Syndell Studios, an improvised gallery in a shed built from telephone poles in Brentwood, where he showed artists from the small Los Angeles avant-garde, including Edward Kienholz, Craig Kauffman, and the beat artist Wallace Berman, a pioneer of the assemblage art that Kienholz also represented and which can be considered much of a Californian art form.[5] Together with his wife Shirley, Hopps also ran an informal gallery in their Brentwood apartment. In 1954, the couple organized their first major exhibition, *The Merry-Go-Round Show*, a legendary event, considered the starting point of modern art in Los Angeles, that reflects Walter Hopps' anarchic, unconventional style as an exhibition maker. For eighty dollars, he rented the carousel on the Santa Monica Pier, stretched a tarp around the carousel's poles, and displayed over a hundred works of art, most of which he drove down from San Francisco — paintings by artists such as Mark Rothko, Clyfford Still, Richard Diebenkorn, and many more. All the works were for sale, none for more than three hundred dollars. Not a single painting was sold.

The small gallery Ferus (Latin for wild, untamed) quickly established itself as the most dynamic and progressive gallery in the United States outside or perhaps even including New York. Ferus became the breakthrough scene for many Californian artists. The gallery attracted even more attention for its early display of Neo-Dadaism, Pop Art and Minimalism from New York. In 1962, Ferus presented the first Pop Art exhibition of Andy Warhol, which was also the first exhibition of Warhol's Campbell's Soup paintings, thirty-two in number, of which five were sold for one hundred dollars each.[6]

Simultaneously, Walter Hopps began organizing exhibitions at the Pasadena Art Museum, where he had contacts since his school days. In 1962, he was hired as a curator at the museum

Irving Blum later bought back the sold works from their buyers, including the actor and artist Dennis Hopper, after what he described as an experience akin to being in a room of Picasso masterpieces. He bought all thirty-two paintings by Warhol, who did not yet have a gallery, for one thousand dollars, in a package deal. In 1996, Irving Blum donated and sold the intact collection to MoMA for the heavily discounted price of fifteen million dollars.

and two years later, at the age of thirty-two, became the youngest museum director in the United States. In 1963, Walter Hopps made international art history when he staged the world's first ever retrospective of Marcel Duchamp at this small local museum. In New York, the first Duchamp retrospective did not take place until 1973. At the Pasadena Art Museum, Walter Hopps built a program that also included Surrealism, Abstract Expressionism, Pop Art and contemporary Californian avant-garde. The self-taught prodigy Hopps succeeded in transforming the museum into one of the world's most innovative venues for modern and contemporary art in a style that was described as freer, bolder, more laid-back, informal and experimental than the austere museums and galleries of New York. Though his unpredictability disqualified Hopps from the highest posts, he is counted among the great curators and museum directors of the world in the twentieth century. I see him as a younger Los Angeles version of Pontus Hultén, even wilder and more outside the system.

In his article in The New Yorker, Calvin Tomkins writes about how the dreams of Los Angeles artists were shattered when the good conditions that had been built up during the brief period of greatness suddenly collapsed one after the other towards the end of the sixties. The Ferus Gallery closed in 1966. Museums reverted to conservative exhibition programs and Los Angeles artists began exhibiting in New York, where Artforum magazine also relocated. To the despair of the artists, the aspiring art metropolis of Los Angeles was back to square one as a backwater of the art world.

How fragile the illusion of Los Angeles as an international modern art metroplis had been was demonstrated by the fate of the Pasadena Art Museum after Walter Hopps left for a new position at the Washington Gallery of Modern Art. The museum was bankrupt after Hopps' lavish program. It was saved from ruin by patron and collector Norton Simon, a classic Los Angeles benefactor who used his money to buy absolute power over the museum. He moved modern art to the basement, hung his own collection of Impressionism and Old Masters, and renamed the museum the Norton Simon Museum — the final coup de grace for the California artist collective's dream of Nirvana, as Tomkins writes.[7]

The idea of creating a new museum to restore the sunshine state's perennial dream of cultural refinement was sparked by Norton Simon's own sister Marcia Weisman, also one of the city's greatest collectors and patrons. Weisman had undertaken several initiatives for contemporary California art in the 1970s, some of which had become reality. Tomkins writes that the vision of creating a new museum began to take concrete form after Weisman was seated next to then high-profile Los Angeles Mayor Tom Bradley at a "political dinner" at the Beverly Hills Hotel in 1978. Weisman told the mayor that it was time for the city to create a contemporary art museum. She sweetened her sales pitch by offering her own collection — known as one of the West Coast's premier modern art collections — as a foundation for the new museum.

In the spring of 1979, Mayor Bradley appointed a committee of ten prominent members, including Weisman, to find a suitable location for the new museum. Following an article in the Los Angeles Times about the plans, the committee was approached by a group of developers who were planning to exploit an area in Downtown Los Angeles called Bunker Hill.

The restoration of the blighted downtown business district had begun in the mid-seventies, and the developers had broadened their vision to create a truly vibrant downtown — at a time when other American cities were losing theirs. A deal was negotiated whereby, instead of allocating the usual percentage of their budgets for artistic decoration, the operators would invest in the construction and operation of the new museum.

For their part, the patrons of the museum's founding committee would contribute capital and guarantee about half of the museum's operating costs. The rest would be covered by ticket sales, government grants and other sources of income. A basic principle was that no funds would be requested from the City or County of Los Angeles. The new museum would be run entirely privately, accountable only to its "Board of Trustees," the board of representatives of its founders. Eli Broad, a real estate and insurance magnate who was already a major collector of contemporary art at the time, just before the turn of the 1980s, and who later became known as the world's greatest art collector, was appointed chairman of the board.

Eli Broad's wife Edythe was interested in art and discovered the galleries on La Cienega Boulevard shortly after the couple moved from Detroit to Los Angeles in the early sixties. Edythe purchased a Braque print and a Toulouse-Lautrec poster. In an article in The New Yorker, she tells writer Connie Bruck that she had wanted to buy one of Warhol's soup cans to hang in the kitchen but that "I figured if I came

Pp. 456–457: Pontus Hultén with David Hockney, Hollywood Hills, Los Angeles, November 1986.

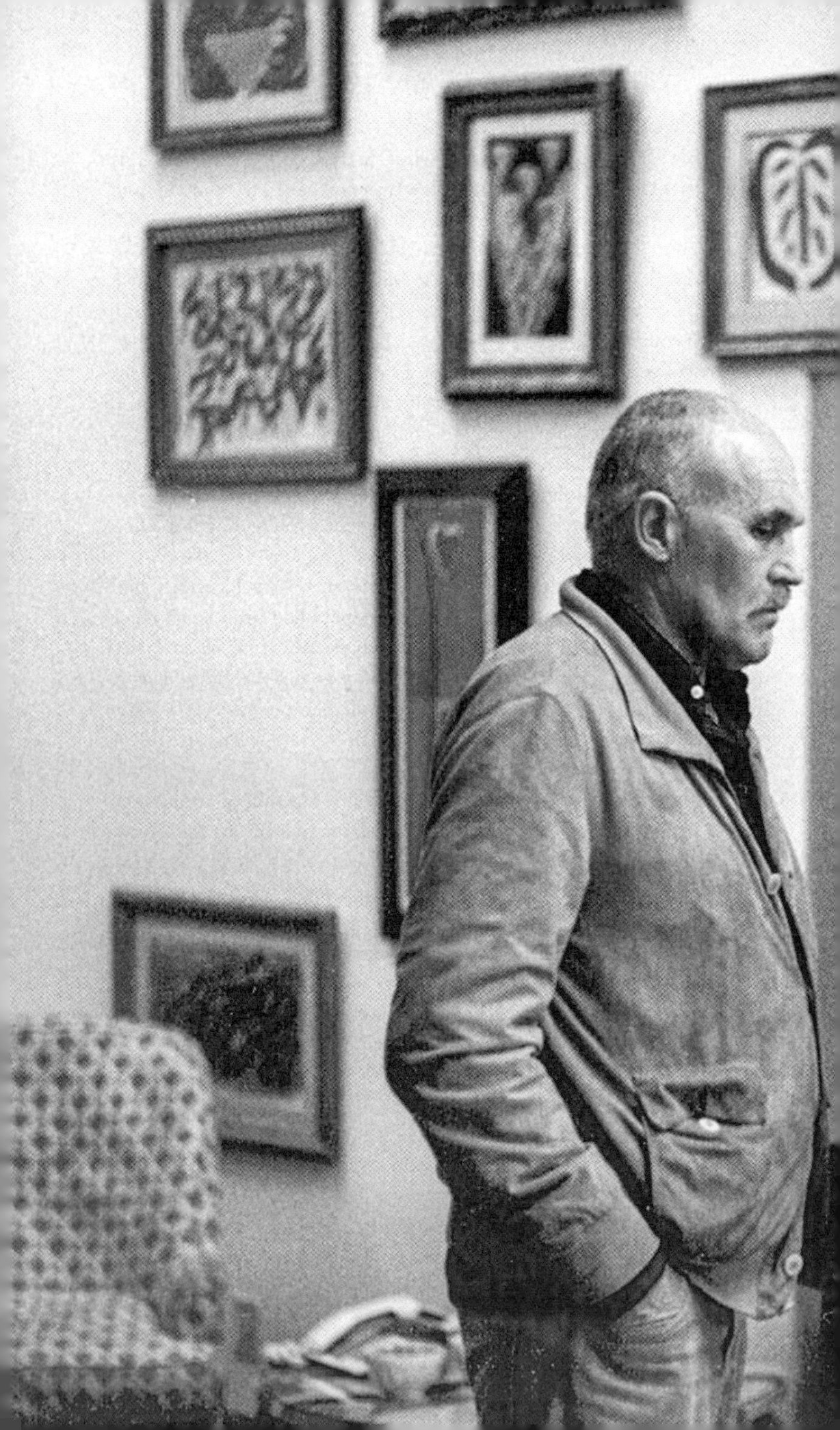

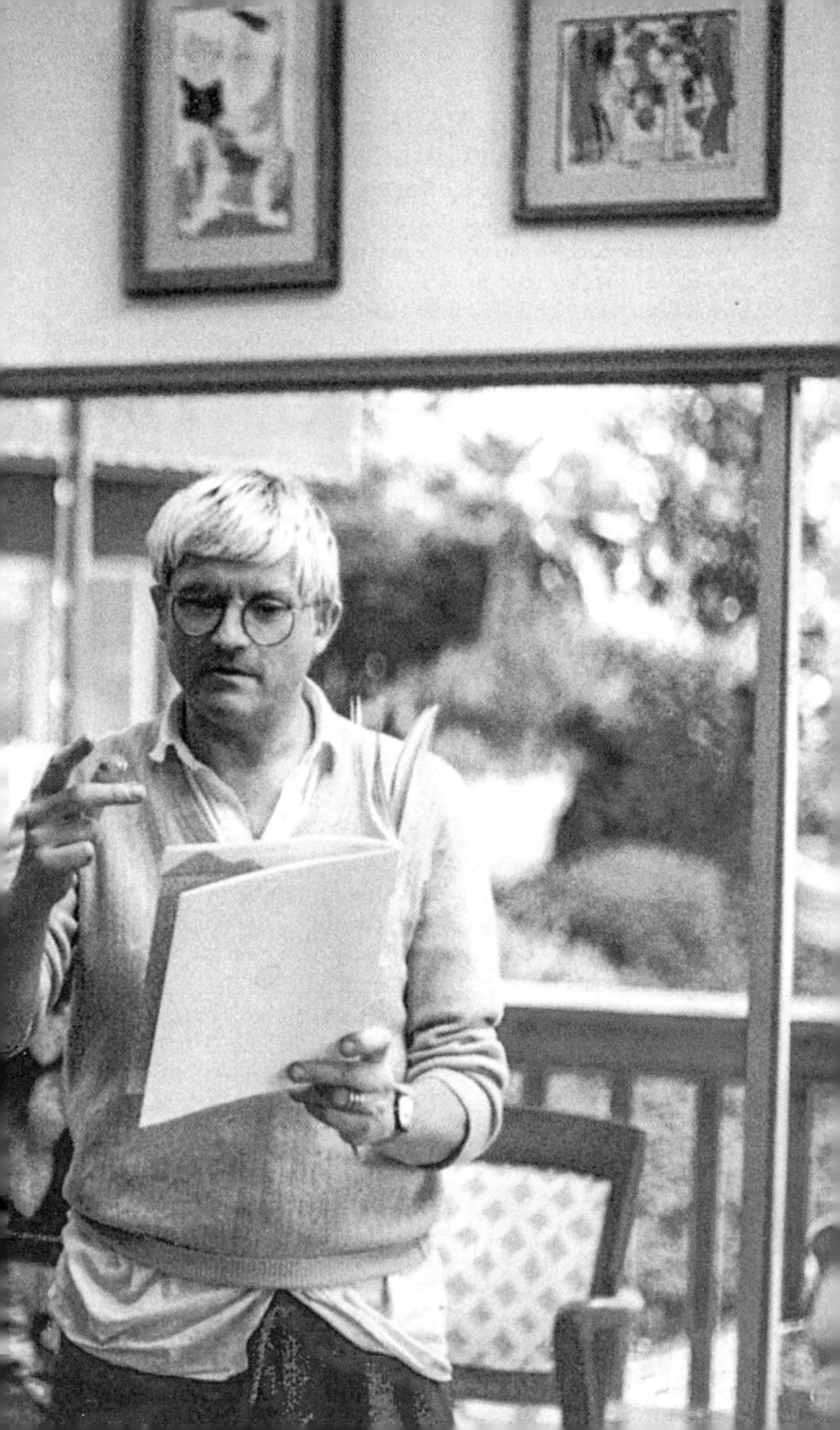

home and had spent a hundred dollars on a painting of a soup can, Eli would have me locked up."[8] Her husband showed no interest in his wife's art purchases at this time beyond asking about their price.

Eli Broad's salvation in art was carefully considered. From a fellow businessman who was an art collector, he came to understand that art provided access to other, desirable, more sophisticated social contexts. As Shelley De Angelus, who worked as a curator for Eli Broad in the eighties and nineties, formulates it with typical American cynicism: "When you have a big house and drive a Jaguar, what separates you from any asshole dentist in the Valley? Art was a way for Eli to distinguish himself."[9]

Once he had reached this insight, Eli Broad soon began to devote more and more of his energy to collecting and patronizing the arts, culture and science. He was clear in that it was a matter of buying maximum social prestige and immortality with his money. In the Los Angeles cultural community, Broad became notorious for never paying more than he needed to achieve his purposes, always being ready to wait out his counterpart, exploiting weaknesses, negotiating hard, and not hesitating to tear up existing agreements when conditions changed in his favor.

Over time, many of Southern California's famous patrons and donors from the 1950s heyday had fallen away, leaving Eli Broad largely alone in an almost imperial position. One of Broads' basic requirements for donations was that the facades and interiors be adorned with signs bearing the names Eli & Edythe Broad. Edythe tried unsuccessfully to persuade her husband to tone it down with his own name. The wife is generally portrayed as the good half of the Broad couple; as possessing the true taste and interest in art, a common role among magnate spouses.

Broad began his art collecting, that most sophisticated of billionaire hobbies, in a haphazard way, crawling before he learned to walk, with purchases including a Van Gogh, a Miró, a Matisse and a Modigliani. He quickly realized that he could never build a major collection of older art — that all great collections are built in their own time. Broad stopped laughing at modern art, sold his van Gogh, bought a Rauschenberg and set about building his contemporary collection with the determination and sensuality of a financial empire builder.

Eli Broad's art collection is considered to be characterized by huge volume but uneven quality. His strategy was based on buying large series of works from various artists at heavily negotiated "bulk discounts." In retrospect, Broad realized that at the beginning of his collecting career he was on the smart side. In the New Yorker article, he acknowledges that one of his collecting competitors in Los Angeles, music magnate David Geffen, thought more wisely and was less stingy in his purchases. "David Geffen bought a Jasper Johns painting for thirteen million dollars — I thought he was crazy," Broad says, adding "as a catechism:" "You can never overpay for a masterpiece."[10]

Broad began building his collection in the eighties, with Los Angeles' own Pop artist Ed Ruscha and his Californian colleagues, as well as Jean-Michel Basquiat, Eric Fischl, Anselm Kiefer and Cindy Sherman — a typical American art collector's collection of the era. Broad filled the couple's Brentwood home with art. His company bought art by Californian artists. He founded an "art library" that lent works to institutions, and stored large quantities of works that he found worth purchasing "but didn't want to look at every day," as Connie Bruck writes. Eli Broad traded art like bonds and his winning stock was Jeff Koons.

In 1995, he bought a number of Koons' sculptures, including the masterpieces "Michael Jackson & Bubbles" and "Rabbit," immediately making him the largest Koons collector in the US. The scandalous publicity surrounding Koons' failed marriage to Italian porn star Cicciolina had by then devalued the American artist's standing on the market, and Broad acquired the unique collection for "about a million dollars, when no one was interested in Jeff's work."[11] Broad visited Koons at his studio in lower Manhattan, where he saw models of sculptures, all now classics, that the artist could not afford to realize on a full scale. He paid in advance at fixed prices, which meant that in some cases Koons made a loss when the works turned out to be more expensive than expected to produce. Many were appalled by Broad's cynical approach to building his art collection, but no one can deny that he was the first to invest in Koons on a large scale at a critical time for the artist.

Whether Eli Broad developed a more emotional relationship with art during his decades as a collector is disputed. His speed was notorious as he marched through museums and galleries on his "death marches," as his wife Edythe calls them, but afterwards he could accurately describe the details of individual artworks.

The founding of The Museum of Contemporary Art (MOCA) was Eli Broad's opening move as a power player in the cultural life of Los Angeles. He became the dynamo from the beginning, contributing one of the ten million dollars that the founders had committed to raise for the new museum. Broad presided over the raising of what eventually amounted to thirteen million dollars. For his own modest contribution, he bought himself the chairmanship of the committee and a dominant position in the project.

A unique feature of the museum construction outlined by the founders was that Los Angeles artists would be involved in the design and administration of this new institution — an idea of the museum project's initiator Marcia Weisman.[12] At a stormy mass meeting in Venice with one hundred and fifty artists, the collective managed against all odds to agree on an agenda for the new museum. Robert Irwin was appointed as the artists' first representative on the museum's Board of Trustees, later supplemented by the older leading figure of Los Angeles art, Sam Francis. For Pontus Hultén, the circumstance that artists would have influence over the new museum was naturally a utopian attraction, in keeping with his old dream of artists as Renaissance gentry and community builders. In interviews, he cited the artists' position of power in the new museum as one of the reasons why he accepted the offer to become the museum's founding director.

Under Robert Irwin's diplomatic, informal leadership, the artists, by maintaining a united front, were able to exercise major influence over the design and strategy of the new museum. They pushed through the idea that the museum should be contemporary, not modern, focusing exclusively on post-war art — something new in the international museum world. Through Robert Irwin and Sam Francis, they were able to convince the committee that the new museum should adopt a leadership structure with two artistic directors — a "superstar" who would represent the museum internationally, and a younger, hungry, more local talent responsible for the operation and administration of the museum and for liaising with the California art scene. MOCA's international ambitions were declared from the beginning.[13]

The two candidates who were the artists' first choice for the dual leadership role were also the two names chosen by the museum management's recruitment committee. Pontus Hultén was a given as the international figurehead of the new museum, a role in which Hultén made his debut here and which he would play at all the institutions he helmed for the rest of his career. For the position of the younger, energetic assistant director, the "doer" as we might call his function, the choice fell to thirty-eight-year-old Richard Koshalek, who had profiled himself as the "brilliantly innovative" director of the Hudson River Museum in Yonkers, New York. Calvin Tomkins lists several similarities between Hultén and Koshalek: "Both are highly unconventional museum men, known for taking risks, for mounting exhibitions that challenge conventional wisdom, and for seeing art in its social, political, and moral context. Both are also known for their belief that museums exist, or should exist, for the benefit of contemporary artists."[14]

Sam Francis was of course appointed to the task of exploring the interest of Pontus Hultén. Francis traveled to Paris in the spring of 1980 and found his old friend "immediately receptive."[15] Robert Irwin contacted Koshalek. Tomkins reports that Hultén and Koshalek met for lunch on July 23, 1980, at the Sky Club restaurant at the top of the Pan Am Building in New York, where Sam Francis joined them. During the lunch, both museum directors found themselves to be in "total agreement" on how the museum should be operated, Hultén told Tomkins. From the restaurant, Francis called Los Angeles where the museum's Board of Trustees was in session and broke the news that Hultén and Koshalek were ready to work together. The board immediately voted to hire them both — Hultén as director and Koshalek as deputy director.[16]

Hultén's acceptance of the offer came as a surprise to everyone, even in Los Angeles. Tomkins writes that after eight years in Paris, Hultén felt ready for a change and that his contract with the Centre Pompidou was "up for renegotiation" in 1981. Tomkins also quotes Hultén on his romantically utopian vision of Los Angeles: "I like Los Angeles very much. There's something about the mentality here, how things are not so worn down by tradition. There is also a very nice ocean." The latter, about the nice ocean, which Hultén repeated in interviews, has often been quoted — perhaps because it did not communicate an acute urge to build a new dynamic art scene in the West, but rather a desire to relax with a whiskey on his sailboat on the waves of the Pacific Ocean.

What Pontus Hultén carefully avoided mentioning in any interview, and even more carefully in negotiations with the museum management in Los Angeles, was that his contract in Paris would not be renewed, something Hultén obviously knew, or at least suspected, when he was first approached by Sam Francis.

Pontus Hultén often argued that the main reason why his time as director of MOCA became so short, conflict-ridden and generally unhappy was his professional obligations as director of a privately funded American museum, the scope of which he had not understood beforehand. His main task was not to produce exhibitions but to act as a corporate executive, using his name to generate resources for the new museum — simply begging money from wealthy Los Angeles residents in an endless series of representative social events. It is hard to imagine anything more alien to Pontus Hultén's personality.

Regardless, it seems unlikely that Hultén didn't initially understand how the American museum system functions. He had worked with the American museum world for twenty years. There is evidence that in his negotiations with the future director, Eli Broad was frank about what the new museum expected. Broad told me at our meeting in his office in Century City, Los Angeles, that he knew Pontus Hultén superficially when he traveled to Paris in the fall of 1980 to negotiate his contract as director of MOCA with him. He had met Hultén for the first time at the opening of the Centre Pompidou in 1977 and later on a few occasions elsewhere in the world. Broad says he was well aware of Hultén's reputation, particularly his political stance, and immediately brought it up in their first conversation, straightforward as ever. "I said to him: Pontus, you're a socialist, are you really ready for this?" says Eli Broad. "I made it clear to him that I expected him to meet with donors and sponsors for breakfast, lunch, drinks and dinner every single day. He said he was ready for it. It was obvious that he wanted the job."[17]

In Calvin Tomkin's The New Yorker article, Hultén is asked about his known hostility to private museums, to which he replies that "eight years at a French state museum changed his mind."[18] The impression is that Pontus Hultén negotiated from a position of weakness with Eli Broad and MOCA.

Once in Los Angeles in the fall of 1981, Hultén seems to have been struck almost immediately by the sheer pallor of reflection out there in the sunshine by the "pleasant ocean." It irritated Eli Broad and the rest of the management team that the newly appointed director started his frenetic traveling immediately upon his arrival. Richard Koshalek reports that in the first month Hultén flew the Concorde twice to Paris — not exactly the best start for a manager concerned with building trust in his new workplace if the story is true.[19]

It's striking how quickly Hultén's utopian enthusiasm for Los Angeles seems to have turned into what appears like hopeless resignation to the task. For Stephan Andreae, he bemoans the meagre conditions: a new museum with no building, no collection and no program. "The only thing that existed was my friendship with Sam Francis," Hultén complains.[20] Apart from the international focus and the limitation to post-war art, there were no clear guidelines for the new museum. For example, it had not been specified how the term "contemporary" was to be defined. What would happen to the works purchased for the collection when art sank back into history? This and many other strategic questions had been left to the museum management to answer.[21]

It seems difficult to explain why Pontus Hultén would not have comprehended the conditions awaiting him. One wonders if Hultén had not only exaggerated his enthusiasm in his eagerness to secure the assignement, but also engaged in wishful thinking on his own part. In some ways, the situation was reminiscent of that when he had created Moderna Museet in Stockholm twenty years earlier, but in the brutally commercial, artificial American reality, with no government behind him. The change of scene from helming the world's leading modern art museum with a large staff of top-notch employees and political backing in Paris, back to an entrepreneurial situation in the far west where no one back home in old Europe could hear you scream — all this seems to have been more of a culture shock for Pontus Hultén than he could have imagined. The youthful entrepreneurial spirit and irrepressible energy of the "struggle years" at Moderna Museet were missing.

Worse than the absence of a building, collection, and program was the new museum's chronic underfunding, which has continued to hamper MOCA until our own times — a perpetual lack of money that seems paradoxical in Los Angeles, already at the time home to many of the world's wealthiest people. The weak culture of sponsorship and "charity" for which Los Angeles is notorious was blatant from the outset for the young museum.

One person who indeed had a calculated plan for the new museum was Eli Broad. His priorities were clear: minimal costs beyond what was absolutely necessary, the most public exhibition program possible to attract visitors and donors, and maximum influence for himself. It is common knowledge that Hultén and Broad were immediately set on a collision course. Hultén told Stephan Andreae that Broad had initially regarded MOCA as his own museum and that this attitude was a source of conflict, "especially intellectually and emotionally."[22] It was a reluctant, cantankerous sidekick that Broad brought along at the begging bowl.

In addition to courting donors, the building was the first major challenge facing Hultén and the new museum. The choice of architect was similar to the recruitment of the museum's management. The artists' committee, led by Robert Irwin, had agreed on three conditions: "flexibility (meaning that the architect would allow them to participate in the design process), a large architectural vocabulary (the absence of a clear style or "signature"), and a proven ability to solve difficult site problems."[23]

Pontus Hultén and Richard Koshalek were invited to join the architectural recruitment committee which had begun its work earlier. The committee started from a list of thirty architects from all around the world, which was trimmed down to six names. I have been told from several quarters that Pontus Hultén himself had recommended Renzo Piano for the commission, but failed in this sales pitch. Certainly the Centre Pompidou's still fresh architectural shock was considered far too radical in conservative Los Angeles.

The six selected architects, all of whom traveled to Los Angeles to present their proposals, included New York star Richard Meier, Los Angeles' own great son (though born and raised in Toronto Canada) Frank Gehry, then in an early stage of his career, and Japanese Arata Isozaki, who had attracted international attention mainly for some industrial buildings but had never built in the United States. Sam Francis' favorite was Isozaki, while Irwin advocated Gehry. Francis and Hultén traveled to Japan to meet Isozaki and, in Hultén's account, decided to hire him there and then.[24]

Calvin Tomkins offers another version in his article — that Irwin, Francis and other members of the recruitment committee argued for Isozaki as he was considered the best qualified according to the criteria they had dictated. The overall impression is that Hultén was persuaded by Francis to choose Isozaki. Frank Gehry being bypassed proved, in general opinion, fortunate for his work in his home town. If he had designed this museum building, with the severe constraints that conditioned the commission, Gehry would not have been considered for what became one of his masterpieces, the Walt Disney Concert Hall, on the neighboring site on Grand Avenue more than twenty years later (inaugurated in 2003).

Arata Isozaki's museum building has not made much of a splash in international architectural history. The complex can be attributed to the major trend of the eighties, Postmodernism, never an easy genre, with its bulky forms and typical flesh-colored facade. The building is anonymous as it lies submerged in a pit, crouching below the futuristic monster skyscrapers that were the end result of the Bunker Hill development. The burial was one of several clever workarounds forced to deal with the lack of space on the site that was eventually made available. The museum has beautiful galleries, with a grand main hall, but was undersized already before it's construction.[25]

To compensate for the lack of space that Hultén and the rest of the museum's management team realized in advance would limit the museum, and to present the new institution to the public during the construction phase, as in Stockholm and Paris, the management team came up with an innovative solution. Nearby, in downtown LA's Little Tokyo area, where several artists had studios, there was an old warehouse complex that had been a hardware store and a garage for police cars. The museum's board managed to persuade the mayor to take possession of the warehouse, which was renovated in a short period of time and on a low budget to designs by Frank Gehry, who was commissioned the assignment as a "consolation prize." While Isozaki's museum building evokes mixed feelings in the architectural community, Gehry's renovation of the warehouse is widely hailed as a masterpiece on a smaller scale.

This annex building was named Temporary Contemporary, as it was conceived as a temporary solution. Here, Hultén, Koshalek and their staff of young curators staged a series of rapidly produced, short-term, guerrilla-style exhibitions and events featuring Californian artists and other creatives that were enthusiastically received by audiences and in the press. Temporary Contemporary struck a bold, free, anarchist tone that shaped MOCA's profile as a progressive contemporary art venue.

In the historiography, Temporary Contemporary is viewed as the sharpest, most groundbreaking part of the launch of the initially troubled MOCA. In our times, when art galleries in raw industrial buildings, guerrilla exhibitions and temporary pop-up galleries are clichés of contemporary art, it doesn't seem very original, but Temporary Contemporary set the standard as the first temporary art gallery in the world. In my conversation with Eli Broad, he said that the idea for Temporary Contemporary was Pontus Hultén's and that it was Hultén who "found the building."[26] This is strongly denied by Richard Koshalek, who himself claims credit for the initiative together with the artists.

Richard Koshalek claims that the choice of architect created animosity between Frank Gehry and Pontus Hultén. Gehry himself writes in a 2021 letter: "I first met Pontus when he came to LA, and I loved him from the moment I first met him. He was grumpy and smart. Regarding his involvement in MOCA, I was very peripheral to these discussions, so I can't comment on this or the choice of architect. Obviously it was not me. We had a lot of fun doing Corso del Coltello in Venice many years ago [see Chapter 28] and I never saw him after that." (Frank Gehry, letter to the author, March 25, 2021.)

A more difficult challenge than the museum building was the collection, as had been the case in Stockholm and Paris. The difference was that in Los Angeles there was nothing to start from. The art that could be begged into the museum from local collectors would not be nearly enough to give it the international weight the founders dreamed of. Problems arose with several of these patrons, including Marcia Weisman, the initiator, who had promised her own collection as a cornerstone but had since gone through a divorce process that complicated the deal. Eli Broad himself was quietly among those who "kept his foot in the door," hesitating, procrastinating and negotiating for donations.

Hultén attacked the problem with methods he had developed in Stockholm and Paris. At MOCA, Hultén and Koshalek decided, "in total agreement," as Koshalek says in Tomkin's article,[27] to focus on a small collection of the highest international quality from the last forty years.

At the end of 1981, the museum's "board of trustees" was reinforced with four names of glittering stardom, with access to art and contacts in the vast art world with which provincial Los Angeles had previously had limited exchange. The four were Hultén's friend and benefactor Dominique de Menil; Peter Ludwig, the chocolate magnate from Cologne; Seiji Tsutsumi, a Japanese industrialist, art collector, novelist and poet; and Giuseppe Panza di Biumo, an Italian count with a magnificent collection of post-war American art. All were players Pontus Hultén had known for a long time and had previously had many exchanges with. All came to bring prestige to the newly formed museum and make important contributions to the development of its collection.

In order to attract additional donors and build new fruitful relationships, Pontus Hultén decided to focus his inaugural exhibition on a presentation of post-war art from eight leading collections from the West Coast and other parts of the United States, including, of course, the de Menil family's collection — a version of *The Museum of Wishes* at Moderna Museet that would eventually become valuable to MOCA and lead to the acquisition of major works. The generosity of the museum's new international patrons also spurred local Californian collectors to make donations and loans to the collection, another intended effect of these initiatives.

Most important and extensive were the transactions negotiated by MOCA with Count Giuseppe Panza di Biumo, heir to a wine distribution company and real estate empire. He was one of the first major private collectors of Neo-Dada and Pop Art. From the mid-sixties, Panza di Biumo steered his focus towards Minimalism and Conceptual Art. In the early eighties, Count Panza began looking around the world for museums to distribute his art. In need of money, he wanted to combine donations with sales at greatly reduced prices to leading institutions. The Turin Art Museum declined because of the American content of the collection. Longstanding negotiations with the Kunstsammlung Nordrhein-Westfalen in Düsseldorf, West Germany, fell through due to a lack of financial resources.

In early 1983, MOCA began negotiations with Count Panza di Biumo, led, of course, from the museum's side by Eli Broad, the negotiator from hell. The museum lacked the resources to pay the amount that Count Panza was demanding. At one point, as Connie Bruck writes in The New Yorker, Eli Broad offered to buy the collection himself and "eventually" transfer it to the museum, a proposal that Broad himself denies.[28] Other members of the board feared that Broad would find a way to keep the collection on his own account, paid for with the radical discount that the museum had been offered.[29] Only after Pontus Hultén had left MOCA could the deal finally be sealed. The museum acquired a unique collection of eighty works of Abstract Expressionism, Neo-Dadaism and Pop Art by artists such as Rothko, Kline, Rauschenberg, Oldenburg and others. The price was eleven million dollars for much of the finest private collection of post-war American art in the world at the time. The deal must be one of the best ever by a museum in post-war art history, comparable almost to the acquisitions after *The Museum of Wishes* in Stockholm. Already in 2010, the The New Yorker article estimated the value of the collection to be over a billion dollars.[30] Twelve more years later, this sum would be vastly inadequate if the works were to become available on the free market — a hypothetical equation as art of this historical dignity can no longer be bought regardless of financial resources.

After the acquisition of the Panza collection and several important additional donations and purchases, MOCA had already created a world-class collection of post-war art within a few years. With this foundation, MOCA became what Los Angeles artists and art lovers had long yearned for but many had thought impossible: a museum of contemporary art at the forefront of not only the national but also the international arena.

In our conversation, Eli Broad states without the slightest hesitation that it was through Pontus Hultén that all the major international names could be recruited to the museum's board and ultimately add invaluable works to the collection.[31] Just as in the case of Temporary Contemporary, he is vigorously contradicted by Richard Koshalek, who claims that the contact with Count Panza di Biumo was entirely Robert Irwin's.[32] Nor does he want to give Hultén credit for the recruitment of Dominique de Menil. In general, it's striking how often Koshalek tries in various ways to belittle Pontus Hultén's contributions to MOCA, even if he mixes these disparagements with praise of his former boss and predecessor.

Other information confirms Broad's version rather than Koshalek's. In a long interview with Count Panza di Biumo in UCLA's "Oral History" series (interviews with cultural figures and others in Southern California), Panza mentions his friendship with Hultén since 1963 as a natural connection to MOCA.[33] Panza di Biumo belonged to the group of sophisticated international art lovers respected by Pontus Hultén who had visited Moderna Museet in Stockholm at an early stage[34] and was an outspoken admirer of Hultén.[35] The 2018 biography of Dominique and John de Menil discusses Dominique's involvement in Los Angeles. It reports how de Menil had lunch with Hultén and her old friend Jean-Yves Mock in November 1980. Dominique had previously declined to become a member of MOCA's board of trustees but changed her mind after Hultén's persuasion during the lunch and wrote a letter to Eli Broad accepting.[36]

No, there can be little doubt that Pontus Hultén's efforts and contacts were crucial in building a permanent collection that is outstanding for a museum founded so late in time and with such limited resources.

Early on, Pontus Hultén also seems to have decided what would be the museum's first major exhibition after *The First Show*, the opening with the private collections — a multidisciplinary historical exposé of the classic Hulténian brand. The subject of the show was typical of Hultén in that it was based on the location of the museum, and what was more characteristic of Los Angeles than the automobile?

The *Automobile and Culture* exhibition was planned for the summer of 1984 when the museum could expect maximum global attention as Los Angeles was hosting the Olympic Games that year. As guest curator, Pontus Hultén engaged Walter Hopps, Los Angeles' own curatorial prodigy — one of several examples during Hultén's career of his tendency to choose strong, idiosyncratic collaborators, unlike some of his colleagues.

Automobile and Culture, opened on July 21, 1984 at the Temporary Contemporary, was a public show of a kind rarely seen in a modern art museum. As we know, Hultén had shown cars in art exhibitions before, but here he took his idea of the car as an art object further. Fifty historic cars were displayed alongside paintings, sculptures and other art forms, including film, architecture, photography, design, posters and advertising, with the car as a theme. Car designs from various eras were juxtaposed with works by artists and other creatives from around the world from corresponding time periods. Pontus Hultén is easily recognized in the impressive selection of paintings, sculptures, installations, photographs, drawings and sketches, presented in interaction with the shiny metallic paint, chrome and leather of the cars in the exhibition and catalog. The traces of *Art in Motion* and *The Machine* are apparent. In addition to Americans such as Ed Ruscha, Edward Hopper, Andy Warhol, Roy Lichtenstein and Buckminster Fuller, classical masters such as Leonardo da Vinci and Albrecht Dürer were represented, along with Henri de Toulouse-Lautrec, Le Corbusier, Marcel Duchamp, Francis Picabia, Umberto Boccioni, Giacomo Balla, Salvador Dalí, Hannah Höch (the only woman in this high-octane masculine context) and many others, as well as contemporary sculptors such as Arman, César and Tony Cragg. The photographic element was prominent, with car-centered art by Lee Friedlander, Alfred Stieglitz, Robert Frank, Jacques-Henri Lartigue, Eugène Atget, William Eggleston, Garry Winogrand and others.[37]

It was impossible not to think of *Automobile and Culture* when MoMA 2021 presented the popular *Automania*, where classic and utopian car models (“rolling sculptures”) were displayed alongside art and other creative expressions from the history of motoring — painting, sculpture, film, photography, architecture, posters, advertising. The artist names are familiar: Warhol, Ruscha, Hopper, Toulouse-Lautrec, Picabia, Balla, Le Corbusier, Robert Frank. Many of the museum’s formulations in texts about the exhibition are similar to those in the catalog for *Automobile and Culture*, about the car as a social symbol, bringer of death, art object and so on.

I have heard wildly varied accounts of the reception of *Automobile and Culture*. Richard Koshalek deems the exhibition a failure, also insisting that the idea was originally Walter Hopps’, and that Pontus Hultén and Hopps did not get along and could not work together. “People in Los Angeles are not interested in going to see an exhibition of cars,” says Koshalek. “Showing fifty cars together with paintings was a bad idea. Nobody came. It was a disaster.”[38]

Others have diametrically opposed memories. Art historian, curator and museum director Kerry Brougher is one of them: “Pontus’ view of the automobile as an art form was very radical for Los Angeles," says Brougher. "That exhibit during the Olympics was the right move to establish MOCA as part of the culture, part of Los Angeles."[39] Artist Gregory Mahoney speaks for many of his contemporary California colleagues — Mahoney was barely thirty years old at the time — when he recalls *Automobile and Culture*: "It was such an amazing show, something completely new for Los Angeles. It was a major exhibition that was so much more than art, that was diverse, educational, inspiring. Many people were provoked because they didn't get it."[40]

Another of those who strongly disagrees with Koshalek's description is Ed Ruscha, the city's most world-famous contemporary artist and its only representative among classic Pop stars. "It was absolutely not a failure in my book," says Ruscha. "I thought it was a great show, just like *The Machine* in New York. It was an exhibition that was well attended and left discussions in its wake, which I like. I think it inspired a lot of artists here in Los Angeles."[41]

Right from the start, Pontus Hultén had also planned a second epic historical exhibition in his signature style,[42] which I regret he did not have the opportunity to realize. The theme was as obvious and site-specific as the car: Hollywood, of course! It would have been exciting to see how the "film nerd" Hultén would have interwoven this phenomenon with art in a contemporary historical perspective. I have not found any more detailed information about Hultén's plans for this exhibition, but the idea is no less tantalizing as he is said to have envisioned a fashion theme for the Hollywood show. Fashion is a subject that I know interested Hultén.[43] "I have a memory of Pontus planning an exhibition called *Hollywood Hollywood — Factory of Dreams, Factory of Style* or something like that," says Kerry Brougher. "He was interested in how Hollywood had influenced style, fashion and how we looked."[44]

To me, Pontus Hultén's appearance in Los Angeles seems like a flying start despite the difficult conditions. Regardless of these problems, it seems that upon his arrival he was full of ideas and motivation for this new challenge in his career and life.

Gradually, however, his energy seems to have waned as he realized that the bulk of his time would be filled with anything but art and producing exhibitions. Soon enough, he appears to have understood that his blue-eyed vision of a freer mind in the West, unencumbered by the ballast of tradition, would be yet another unfulfilled utopian dream.

Richard Koshalek, who frequently accompanied Hultén in representative contexts, recalls that after a while Hultén began to behave in an increasingly openly stubborn and obstinate manner during all those lunches, dinners and drinks with potential donors — that he refused to insert himself into the American social culture of "false flattery and superficial politeness," to quote Guggenheim director Richard Armstrong.[45] "He used to sit with his arms crossed just staring," says Koshalek. "When someone asked a question, he wouldn't answer, but just sit silent and stare at the questioner. The person might then rephrase the question, first once, then a second time, but he would still just sit and stare. For these Hollywood people, Pontus was a celebrity who had been director of the Centre Pompidou and was friends with the French president. At every dinner they always asked Pontus to order the wine, coming from Paris. Then Pontus would sit there with his arms crossed and say 'I want a Bloody Mary.'"[46]

Hultén's recurring duels with Eli Broad are storied. Broad was notorious for calling people to his office or home in Brentwood and lecturing them as if they were his employees. As one might have guessed, Pontus Hultén had a hard time putting up with this arrangement. Richard Koshalek recounts a couple of adrenaline-oozing anecdotes that testify to Hultén's growing frustration with his situation. "I remember one time in Brentwood when Eli, as usual, attacked Pontus for not doing enough. I thought Pontus would get angry and blow up but he didn't say anything. When we came out, he stood and pissed on the house. I said to him: 'Damn it, don't do that, are you crazy? The guy has video cameras that monitor everything.' 'I don't give a damn,' said Pontus. Another time he pulled up newly planted trees in the garden and threw them away. He had enormous anger towards Eli."[47]

Pontus Hultén himself described how the stinginess and indifference of the wealthy patrons of Los Angeles in general and the Hollywood moguls in particular made him disillusioned: "I think I would have continued to work in LA if there had been more commitment from the city. It had been my hope that we could get support from Hollywood. But I was wrong. The 'industry,' as they call filmmaking there, is not interested in museums. It took me a while to realize it, but it's true. Those who work in film in LA do nothing but get up at seven o'clock to work. When they're not making movies, they're not in LA. They go to Europe, to India and who knows where, but they're not in LA. There's no identification of the filmmakers with their city. There's no civic engagement because most of them are not from LA.

There's hardly any social context, so running a museum is an isolated existence. This in a city of twelve million people! It's very interesting and very different from Europe."[48]

We need not doubt that Pontus Hultén was serious about his involvement with MOCA and that he saw the move to California as long-term. He shipped to Los Angeles not only parts of his art collection but also his library, his boat and his car — and certainly not just any car, but a Citroën SM. The interest in cars that Hultén had cultivated under the guidance of Jean Tinguely had progressed. He had come to see the car as an art form and the Citroën SM is a work of art that must have spoken to Hultén's heart — one of the most utopian car models ever put into production and one of the most problematic. Shipping this car to Los Angeles with the intention of using it as a utility vehicle was a very bad idea for various reasons. From the day it arrived at the port of San Pedro, the vehicle caused Hultén constant trouble and horror. There were all sorts of problems with US legislation (including failure to meet California's exhaust emission requirements), tax and import regulations and other bureaucracy, not to mention constant technical problems.

Citroën SM: the luxurious, experimentally high-tech sports model that the French car brand produced in small series in 1970-75 in collaboration with Maserati, which Citroën then owned, with a famous six-cylinder Maserati engine and a wide range of innovations such as power steering and gas-assisted (!) suspension, with exclusive features including the ability to offer comfort during prolonged driving at speeds of over two hundred kilometers per hour, but also with great technical vulnerability. The Citroën SM itself was an anomaly in the market, but many of its innovations later became commonplace in the automotive industry, and examples of the car now command towering prices among collectors.

More serious were Hultén's shortcomings as a driver in this automotive metropolis. Hultén was a distracted and poor driver. This characteristic in this difficult to maneuver car in the heavy traffic pace of the Los Angeles freeway rivers was a lousy combination. Hultén had several more or less serious incidents resulting in damage to his own and others' vehicles. He could be grateful that he himself escaped unharmed. "The problems he had with that car were unbelievable," says Richard Koshalek. "It was scary to watch. He was unattentive. Eventually he got scared."[49]

After some time, Hultén was persuaded by Sam Francis and others to give up his Citroën SM. From then on, he had to rely on being chauffeured to and from work in Downtown and his home in a spectacular ocean-view apartment in a skyscraper on Ocean Avenue in Santa Monica, a journey that can take hours in peak traffic, and to all his commitments around the city. Hultén seems to have nurtured a romantic notion of Los Angeles as the city of the car, but was quickly sobered by reality. He lamented the time wasted and the constant dependence on these cars, and the absence of street life. Sitting in the smog in bumper-to-bumper traffic is a daily psychological torture that millions of Los Angeles residents endure but can quickly drive a person from another culture insane.

His boat, too — an open fishing cutter with sailing rig and antique engine, built in Greece — caused Hultén magnificent trouble. Shortly after he first met Pontus Hultén, the artist Gregory Mahoney was hired by him to work on the vessel. Mahoney is, as he puts it, "good at making things," a talent that Hultén unfailingly sniffed out among younger friends and collaborators around the world. His own handyman skills, by all accounts, left much to be desired.

Gregory Mahoney narrates the tale of the Greek fishing cutter's journey along the Pacific coast, moving between a number of different artists' studios where the boat was parked for endless renovations. For twelve years, Mahoney estimates that he followed the vessel on its land-based cruise, pouring in countless hours of work, before Hultén finally shipped the boat dry-shod back to Europe, nearly a decade after his own return. "I don't think it ever reached the water," says Mahoney. "It was in incredibly poor condition and needed work from scratch on most things. Pontus had a dream to go down to Baja [the Baja Peninsula, the end of the Californian coast in northwest Mexico] and sail among the gray whales. It sounded beautiful but had nothing to do with reality."[50]

No, Pontus Hultén didn't make life in Los Angeles easy for himself, constantly relying on others to get through his daily life. Kerry Brougher was one of the young colleagues who often picked him up and dropped him off in Santa Monica. "For me, it was an amazing assignment — to have access to such a person right at the beginning of my career," Brougher says. "I had him trapped in my little Datsun for several hours every day. There was nothing to do but talk. We talked a lot about art and maybe even more about film. He loved to talk about Eisenstein, Robert Breer, Stan Brakhage and other filmmakers. It was a great university for me. His knowledge and experience was absolutely enormous. I thought every day that I can hardly believe it was true that I got to sit there and learn all this."[51]

For the installation of his library, Pontus Hultén was assisted by another of MOCA's junior collaborators, Ann Goldstein, later an internationally renowned curator who was for a time director of the Stedelijk in Amsterdam. "It was a privilege to help him unpack and sort his library in his Santa Monica apartment," says Goldstein. "I learned an enormous amount from the conversations we had and also from my work with the library itself. I was fascinated by the breadth of his interests. It wasn't just art at all, but books on a variety of subjects. Among other things, I remember he had great books on Innuits."[52]

Through Sam Francis, Hultén was fortunate to meet the then twenty-five-year-old Jerry Sohn, who worked as an assistant to Francis. Shortly after their first meeting, Sohn began helping Pontus Hultén with all sorts of professional, practical and private matters and activities. He quickly became indispensable to Hultén and his close friend and confidant. Sohn is a fitting name because Jerry really became a son in the "chosen family" that Pontus Hultén gathered around him worldwide during his thirty-year international career.

Jerry, now a publisher, multi-tasker and liaison in the Los Angeles art and culture world, told me about his first encounter with Pontus Hultén, when he helped him unpack his art collection after moving to Santa Monica: "When we installed a work by Niki, a small toy figure, a dinosaur, was missing," Jerry says. "Pontus was absolutely devastated by this. To him, things were like people are to others. I went to some toy shops and managed to find a dinosaur exactly the same. Pontus was incredibly grateful and gained confidence in me. After that I helped him for the rest of his life with everything from loans of works for exhibitions to spare parts for his boat."[53]

"Of course, it was wonderful for me as a young person who loved art to be with the likes of Sam and Pontus," Jerry continues. "Pontus was the bridge to another generation, to the big art world. He knew Man Ray, Salvador Dalí. With him I encountered Warhol, Johns, Rauschenberg, Beuys — I met them all."[54] Jerry Sohn and Sam Francis became Pontus Hultén's links to the Los Angeles art collective, in which he thrived, as always among artists.

Sohn says he regularly drove Hultén to visit the studios in Venice and elsewhere of artists such as Ed Ruscha, Robert Therrien and Sarah Perry, as well as the brothers Greg and Jeff Colson and the aforementioned Gregory Mahoney. Together with Sohn, Hultén also visited David Hockney in the Hollywood Hills, where the British gentleman painted the pool motifs that become logos for Los Angeles art. The caliber of the city's artists' collective was far from bad at the time. The city was also a center for Minimalism and the land art movement that had emerged since the late 1960s, with artists such as Robert Smithson, Michael Heizer, Richard Long, Walter De Maria and others. Also in Los Angeles were Hultén's friend Edward Kienholz and his ex-wife Lyn, a key figure in the Southern California art world whom Hultén had known since the Kienholz retrospective in Stockholm in 1970, when Lyn had spent a month in Stockholm installing the exhibition.

Hultén reportedly enjoyed working in the museum's temporary office in Downtown, as part of a team of about twenty young curators, many of whom later became well-known names in the art world. Richard Koshalek and others testify that Hultén liked to sneak off to nearby Korea Town for a few beers and learned to love sushi. In these neighborhoods, Hultén found the closest thing in Los Angeles to the street life he missed so intensely from Paris. Several of his colleagues of the time have recounted that in this environment, surrounded by young collaborators and artists in Korea Town's simple hole-in-the-wall taverns, Hultén relaxed and unleashed his "waterfall"[55] of stories and anecdotes from modern art history, while at official lunches, dinners, and receptions he stiffened and fell silent, filling the rooms with discomfort.

Despite these bright spots in Pontus Hultén's Los Angeles life, the overall picture of his time in the city is darker. In Los Angeles, the portrait of Hultén as a lonely, sad, almost tragic figure with an underlying blackness becomes increasingly sharply defined. Almost everyone I talk to bears witness of the lonely impression that Hultén made — contradictory, perhaps, given what appears to have been an extensive social life in a network of contacts that quickly grew extensive. "When I came up to his apartment, there was always a strange feeling that nobody lived there," says Kerry Brougher. "He always told me to get something from the fridge but there was never anything in it. It was completely empty."[56]

According to Richard Koshalek, the disappointment and frustration that Pontus Hultén experienced in his work and life in Los Angeles could be partly explained by the romanticized image of the city he had nourished. "He felt disconnected from the art world, no longer relevant," says Koshalek. "He had a Mickey Mouse idea of what LA was. It wasn't Paris or Stockholm. He didn't fit in and it never worked for him here. He was often unbalanced, wanted to fire secretaries who didn't do what he said, banging his hand on the table and shouting 'I want her fired' and so on. I remember once on a flight when the pilot said that you could see the Grand Canyon down there and Pontus stood up and shouted all over the plane 'where the hell is that goddamn Grand Canyon?' He was abroad and rented cars that he wrecked. There were legal issues that the museum had to deal with. I saw this many times. His personality had complications — loneliness and a lot of anger."[57]

Richard Koshalek more than suggests that there was a fundamental creative conflict within the artistic leadership of the museum. "Sam and Pontus stood for one view and me and Bob [Robert Irwin] for another," says Koshalek. "They were strong personalities with different views. Bob's perspective was more future-oriented and experimental, with light and space, while Sam was a more traditional painter. We had discussions about different artists and Pontus was hooked on Warhol and Rauschenberg and talked about the likes of Dorothea Tanning, Niki and Richard Stankiewicz. It surprised us, because it was art that wasn't really relevant to what we wanted to do. His intentions were good. These artists were his friends and friendship was important to him. He was a bit tired and disengaged and often wondered why he had to talk to all these people. He liked to go away and have his morning beer and his afternoon beer. I understand that — it's nice. He never worked eight hours a day."[58]

A number of more or less patronizing reviews like these and what I have heard from others make me wonder if one of Pontus Hultén's many problems during his time at MOCA was Richard Koshalek himself. Troels Andersen, the Danish Malevich and Russia expert, says what others hint at: "His second-in-command, whatever his name was, it was clear that he was after Pontus' job. It was an unpleasant feeling."[59]

Pontus Hultén's conflicts with Eli Broad, in particular, became increasingly acrimonious over time. Koshalek says that Broad's suspicion of Hultén went so far that he hired a private detective to find out whether Hultén had really been the director of the Centre Pompidou. This detective is said to have concluded that this had not been the case. Hultén had only been director of the Musée National d'Art Moderne, MNAM. The story is so improbably American that it could be true.

At some point in 1982, the situation became untenable for Pontus Hultén and apparently also for the museum's board. This time it was undoubtedly Hultén who took the initiative to divorce. In the fall of 1982, he informed the board that he was breaking his contract to return to Paris, where he had been recalled by his old friend and client Robert Bordaz. In his resignation, Hultén referred to a letter signed by

French President François Mitterrand asking Hultén to come to Paris to become the artistic director of the world exhibition planned for 1989 as the bicentennial of the French Revolution. Koshalek mentions that Hultén also spoke of a Matisse exhibition in Paris that he "had to" organize.[60] "He showed the letter at the Stanhope Hotel in New York announcing that he was leaving Los Angeles because he had been recalled to Paris by the President," says Richard Koshalek. "Word later spread that it was in fact Bordaz who had put the letter together."[61]

If, as some suggest, Koshalek had acted to outmaneuver Pontus Hultén, his mission was accomplished. He succeeded Hultén as director and led MOCA until 1999.

Hultén's exit from Los Angeles was fraught with conflict. The news that the star director from Paris would break his contract and leave the museum after less than two years, before the new museum building had even been inaugurated, was a scandal that the press made a big deal of — an embarrassing loss of prestige for the aspiring young museum and its board.

Considering this messy, dramatic history, and everything I've heard firsthand here in Sweden over the years about Pontus Hultén's "disaster" in Los Angeles, I'm surprised that almost everyone I meet during my visit to the city, thirty-two years after Hultén's departure, talks about the invaluable contributions Hultén made to the museum and to the Los Angeles and California art scene during his short tenure at MOCA, and the legacy he left behind.

In our conversation, Eli Broad is candid about the problems in his collaboration with Pontus Hultén, especially when it came to contacts with donors. On the whole, nevertheless, Broad is unreserved in his praise of Pontus Hultén and his efforts for MOCA. The generosity of Broad's assessment surprises me. "We wanted a manager with an international reputation who would fly over New York," says Broad. "There were other competent candidates, but Pontus had the respect of the art world. Everyone respected him. We were a young museum without a collection and he gave us immediate attention and credibility around the world. He deserves a lot of credit for that."[62]

Broad continues: "He was irreplaceable, a great impresario. He had tremendous foresight. What he did in Stockholm and at the Pompidou — great exhibitions, great visions. He gave us a great start and it could have been something fantastic but he was not happy here, it was obvious to everyone. He didn't like all this business of raising money and answering to the board. He liked what he had in Paris, where he was the king and only talked to the Minister of Culture. But he helped create MOCA."

Ed Ruscha speaks in similar terms about Hultén's contribution to the Los Angeles art scene: "He put us in touch with the world and art history. He was a powerful figure with his reputation and left a great legacy. He was a writer, able to conceptualize his thoughts, always focusing on the big picture. There is no such figure in art today. He was popular here but had a rebellious way of running the museum that led to confrontation with the board members. He came to my studio several times and bought some works, even when he was still at the Pompidou. He had an open heart, a curiosity and sensitivity, and was in touch with all these sacred figures in the art world. I was very sad to see him leave the party."[63]

According to Gregory Mahoney, Pontus Hultén's difficulties in Los Angeles can be largely attributed to the old reliable force of envy. He argues that the artists understood and easily communicated with Hultén, while the establishment figures felt insecure in his company. "These people were envious of his knowledge and everything he had done and stood for. They didn't understand what we lost when he left."[64]

Richard Koshalek too is, somewhat contradictory, quick to acknowledge Pontus Hultén's importance to MOCA and to Los Angeles as an art city. "Pontus belonged to a special class of museum directors, along with Harald Szeemann and a few others," says Koshalek. "Such people made me feel that being a museum director was a noble profession. This is no longer the case. Creative integrity doesn't exist today, but these people insisted on it. Their bond was with the artists. Now they are loyal to boards and donors. Pontus would be a total anachronism in today's art world. They would just look at him and wonder what the hell this was all about. Art today is driven by fashion and trends."

"What Pontus Hultén had created in Stockholm was nothing short of exceptional," Koshalek adds. "I was very inspired by him — his integrity and his belief that art could change the world and challenge the status quo. He changed the whole dimension of the museum. When I became his deputy director, I felt I was the luckiest person in the world. He didn't get the chance to do what he had done before at MOCA but he brought instant credibility to an institution that had nothing, based on what he had created in Stockholm and Paris. He had enormous respect throughout the art world. Nobody else could have done what he did just because of the reputation he had before. He was absolutely brilliant."[65]

I'm particularly fascinated by the extent to which Pontus Hultén managed to influence the young curators at MOCA during his brief spell in Los Angeles. Through them, his legacy lives on in the city. Ann Goldstein and Paul Schimmel are two now internationally renowned curators who have spoken to me about the decisive impact of Hultén's heritage on their careers and their approach to art and its role in history and society.

A third is Kerry Brougher, who after Pontus Hultén's departure worked as a curator at MOCA from 1983 to 1997, staging several internationally acclaimed exhibitions at the museum. My impression is that Brougher was the one among the young curators at MOCA closest to Pontus Hultén. He is the most detailed in his analysis of Hultén as an exhibition maker and in his accounts of his influence. "Pontus was invaluable to MOCA and Los Angeles," says Brougher. "He gave us the courage to see the museum not from a regional or even national but from an international perspective. For me personally, he meant a lot. He changed my view of how art exhibitions can be done. What he made me understand was that an exhibition can be so much more than painting and sculpture. He made me realize that a cinematic approach could be applied to an art exhibition — that it could be multidisciplinary and narrative and that it could even be about film. Those kinds of exhibitions are not easy to do. They require careful planning and many loans, but it is well worth the price if you can manage it."[66]

"Pontus had the unique capacity to see the big picture and present it in a coherent form," Brougher explains further. "I really regret that he didn't stay longer at MOCA. Having him as a director to take the museum forward was hugely important. We really needed a person with that kind of trust capital and appeal. It made people in the art world understand that this is real, this is going to happen. During its early period, MOCA built its reputation for well-researched, broad historical exhibitions that explored various phenomena such as Minimalism, Conceptual Art, Case Study Houses, *Hall of Mirrors*[67] with the film and others. All this

Hall of Mirrors, March 17–July 28, 1996, was the first exhibition in the United States to highlight the relationship between film and the visual arts. The exhibition featured more than ninety of the leading post-war filmmakers and artists, with one hundred and seventy-five artworks, sixty films, fifteen installations, and a film series organized in collaboration with the UCLA Film and Television Archive. The exhibition traveled to a number of American institutions and also to Rome.

was a legacy from Pontus. He gave us the permission to do very expansive projects. He set the tone. Unfortunately, he was not ready for all the misery it brought. The birth of MOCA was a difficult delivery."[68]

During my visit to Los Angeles, I also meet Robert Irwin, one of the leading forces behind the creation of MOCA. He tells me that he never got to know Pontus Hultén closely, even though the two had much collaboration, with different views on some crucial issues for the museum. "We artists wanted Koshalek," says Irwin. "I had worked with him in Fort Worth[69] where he did a show of seventy-eight big, amazing trucks. Koshalek was a real riverboat gambler. He had big, crazy ideas, took incredible risks and was never afraid to fail. If things went wrong, he would just spit in his palm, pick up the dice and roll them again. We needed such a person, who was in touch with our sensibility, our thinking. Pontus was a character with a completely different level of sophistication. We came to the conclusion that we needed two directors. Pontus was a celebrity to the people in the Hollywood world. His mission was to raise many millions of dollars in a city where you couldn't even raise one million for art. With his eminence, he was able to unlock resources beyond what anyone else could have done, just through the respect he commanded. He was the director of the board. Koshalek, *oh boy*, him those people treated like a janitor."

Irwin says there was much bitterness and anger on the part of Eli Broad and others on the board, and plans to take legal action against Hultén for breaching his contract. "I made the argument that, as a representative of the museum, he had done a better job than anyone else could have, just with his person — all this money and donations coming in, all this great press. I told them that we should send him home with congratulations and flowers instead. He had already done his job and he never liked it here."

"When he left, we were already up and running with MOCA, thanks to Temporary Contemporary," Irwin continues. "By getting started there before the museum building was completed, we were able to create a fast-paced, active museum that was part of the culture and art scene instead of a boring institution where the board members wanted to show their collections. The board had wanted Pontus to be the real director of the museum, but that wouldn't have turned out well. When he disappeared, they eventually realized that Koshalek, whom they had treated like shit, had been the driving force all along and he was appointed director."[70]

Eli Broad himself left MOCA in 1984, the year after Pontus Hultén's official resignation. Other board members and partners had reached their limit with Broad's harsh methods and his pushing his own interests too far on various issues. After being kicked out of MOCA, Eli Broad instead devoted his efforts and donations to the Los Angeles County Museum of Art, LACMA, among others.

In the 21st century, after Richard Koshalek left the museum, donations dwindled and MOCA's finances became increasingly strained. After the financial crash of 2008, the situation became critical. The museum faced bankruptcy. A merger with LACMA was discussed. There was even talk of selling art from the collection for the museum's survival. At this point, Eli Broad stepped in as the savior, with his trademark sense of profitable desperation. In a campaign labeled by his opponents as a hostile takeover, Broad led a fundraising effort among city donors that saved MOCA and ensured its continued operations and independence.[71]

MOCA has not yet become a MoMA for contemporary art, as originally intended. However, despite its constant financial difficulties, the museum has managed to gain respect in the art world as a progressive and dynamic museum, with its small but high-quality and growing collection and an impressive track record of internationally acclaimed exhibitions.

A common suspicion in the Los Angeles art world was that Eli Broad's comeback as MOCA's rescuer in 2010 was a move in a larger plan. Broad never made any secret of his goal to establish a collaboration and ideally merge his own long-planned museum, The Broad, with MOCA. His plans for The Broad were met with skepticism in Los Angeles and the art world. The whole Eli Broad phenomenon is seen by many as an extreme manifestation of the commercialization of art and the museum world.

Still, no one can question that he succeeded in what many deemed impossible — turning Los Angeles' godforsaken, intimidating Downtown into a world-class attraction for art and culture lovers, a feat for which the Broad is almost single-handedly credited even by his opponents and enemies. Even before The Broad opened in 2015, many former detractors began to change their minds. The choice of architect Elizabeth Diller and her museum building have been praised. The museum has become popular and the temporary exhibition program has pleasantly surprised skeptics. The Broad has undoubtedly become a great addition to the Los Angeles art scene and a museum respected throughout the art world.

After Eli Broad's death in spring 2021, his life's work was celebrated in superlatives in major articles across the art world. "It's a little scary to imagine Los Angeles without Eli Broad," as the founder of one of the city's civic groups said in one of several articles in the New York Times after Eli Broad's passing.[72]

BCAM, Broad Contemporary Art Museum, opened in 2008 as part of LACMA, Los Angeles County Museum of Art — a new stand-alone contemporary art museum in a building designed by Renzo Piano. Originally, Eli Broad had promised to donate his collection to the BCAM, a promise he reneged on shortly before the opening, causing a scandal.

With The Broad, MOCA, LACMA, and BCAM, it's hard to contradict Broad's assertion that nowhere in the world can you see so much contemporary art of such high quality in such a concentrated area.[73] If we add to this the Walt Disney Concert Hall, the Los Angeles Opera Dorothy Chandler Music Pavilion, Rafael Moneo's Cathedral of Our Lady of the Angels, and other cultural institutions and architecturally interesting buildings, Downtown Los Angeles has become an attractive destination for art, culture, and architecture enthusiasts. I'm convinced that Pontus Hultén would have been proud, despite all the misery, to have played an undeniably decisive role in the critical beginning of this development process, albeit perhaps primarily as a figurehead rather than a museum man.

From Robert Irwin's studio in Oceanside north of San Diego, I drive with my father as a passenger northwest, over the mountains, into the desert, to Desert Hot Springs near Palm Springs. We want to end our journey in Pontus Hultén's footsteps here in the West by visiting the California memorial he left behind.

The next morning I head into Yucca Valley towards Joshua Tree National Park to visit the "desert cabin" I've heard so much about. We pass through hillbilly towns with names like Pioneer Town in the high desert valleys and take off on a road with the poetic cowboy name Old Woman Spring Road. Once there, we are greeted by stunning beauty. We wander around what is a sculpture and architecture park in this primeval landscape, feeling almost like walking on the moon. There are three concrete "pavilions" by Arata Isozaki designed for different seasons, intended for sleeping in the open air, protected from snakes and scorpions. Jerry Sohn designed the kidney-shaped concrete pool, which on our visit is curiously half-filled with emerald-green muddy water. On the natural terrace in front of the pool, the meter-high glass spheres of British land artist Richard Long's[74] work "Glass Ring" shine in a similar green-blue hue against the backdrop of the rocks of the spacescape and the mountain ridge in the distance. Long has made two other works on the large property: "Tree line," a line of dry logs, branches and twigs, and "Junk Ring," or "Debris Ring," a fantastically strong and evocative circle of similar dimensions to the glass ring, made with rusty scrap metal Long has scavenged from the surrounding area. Two rusted cast-iron ships by Los Angeles artist Sarah Perry stand on tall spider-leg-like stilts.

Jerry Sohn later tells the story of his and Hultén's sensational desert cabin. They traveled to this area to visit Ed Ruscha, who owns a large tract of land in Yucca Valley. On the other side of some hills, Ruscha's young artist friend Jeff Colson was living on land he had bought from Ruscha. It was Pontus who discovered the site of the little cabin, which was then deserted. Much later, Jerry went to the property records of the nearest town and found that the land was owned by Ruscha and his wife Dana. In 1993, they bought the land from the artist. "Ed rarely sold anything but he admired Pontus, so he agreed," Jerry says. "He has been buying up the surrounding land to protect the environment and prevent it from being developed, but the abandoned cottage was already here, which may have worked to our advantage."[75]

Jerry says that Hultén regularly came to Los Angeles to visit the cabin until the last years of his life, alone or with guests. Here he walked, read, wrote and lived on a simple diet of bread, cheese, ham and fried eggs — and whiskey, of course. "Pontus loved the beauty, the silence and the open spaces here," says Jerry. "He came every year and spent one week at the cabin and one down with Niki in La Jolla."[76]

Niki de Saint Phalle, who moved permanently to the beach town of La Jolla, north of San Diego, in 1994, for the sake of her damaged lungs but also, as I understand it, for financial reasons, was certainly one of the forces that attracted Hultén to keep returning to California. Despite the unfortunate circumstances, these parts became a lifelong love for him, something of a second home after all. In his will, Pontus Hultén donated his half of the property to Jerry Sohn who preserves this place where the memory of Hultén lives on under the scorching desert sun of Southern California.

26

The World Expo that was canceled and became a school

After Pontus Hultén's contract at the Centre Pompidou was not extended, there had been talk of making him director of the city of Paris' own modern art museum, the Musée d'Art Moderne de la Ville de Paris, located in the second wing of the Palais de Tokyo. The Paris newspapers speculated about such a move for a few years in the early eighties, and Hultén is said to have been interested in the job. According to several sources, when these plans fell through, there was a sense of obligation to Pontus Hultén among certain influential people — a kind of guilt that he had been poorly rewarded for the services he had rendered to the city of Paris and French cultural life.

Robert Bordaz's close associate Claude Mollard asserts that it was he himself who had raised the idea of organizing a world exhibition in Paris and that this event was to be staged in 1989, to commemorate the bicentenary of the French Revolution of 1789 and to be a worthy successor to the 1889 world exhibition for which the Eiffel Tower had been built.

Claude Mollard writes in a book about his career[1] that as early as 1979, a group led by Bordaz approached President Valéry Giscard d'Estaing with this idea. The President flatly rejected the proposal.[2] I have been informed that Giscard's reluctance had to do with his lack of interest in celebrating the revolution that can be seen as the origin of socialism and communism. Claude Mollard dismisses these theories, although he admits that a distaste for the revolutionary may have been in the background. "But the main thing was that he hated the modern architecture that was to be a major feature of the World Fair. It was absolutely not his style. His ideal was the nineteenth century."[3]

Shortly after socialist leader François Mitterrand defeated Giscard d'Estaing in the 1981 elections and was named president, Bordaz and Mollard presented the idea to him. Mitterrand enthusiastically endorsed the initiative. A budget of fifty million francs was allocated for planning, and a creative team was appointed under the direction of Bordaz. Pontus Hultén and Renzo Piano were hired as artistic directors. It was for this grandiose commission that Hultén was "called back" from Los Angeles, as suggested by an allegedly forged presidential letter.

In Paris, a temporary office for the project was set up in June 1982 at the Musée des Arts Décoratifs in the Louvre. Hultén and Piano recruited a number of other associates to the group, including the Italian architect Vittorio Gregotti and the artist Martial Raysse. Judging by the timing, Pontus Hultén had already started work on the world exhibition before breaking his contract in Los Angeles.

Knowledge of the short-lived revolutionary jubilee project is surprisingly scarce even in Paris. The plans quickly developed by the creative team were hugely ambitious. In essence, the vision was that the World Fair would be staged mainly on land owned by the French state, such as La Villette, La Défense, the banks of the Seine, Tolbiac and the Trocadero.

Most striking was the idea of using the Seine as an exhibition stage several kilometers long. Here the team planned a series of buildings, artistic installations and international pavilions on artificial islands and temporary bridges, as well as on existing bridge abutments.

The plans were monumental, with a grandiose element of urban planning that corresponded well with the 1889 World's Fair and the Eiffel Tower. The production time of six or seven years seems short for everything that was outlined. As a permanent development of the Parisian city center, a covering of the Gare d'Austerlitz was proposed where the group planned to construct a new grand boulevard, a sort of left bank contemporary counterpart to the Champs-Élysées.

It is intriguing to think how Paris might have developed if this world exhibition had become a reality. Claude Mollard writes in his book that fifty million visitors were expected in Paris during the exhibition year.[4] An estimated three hundred thousand jobs would be created. The plan also included new residential areas, public facilities, cultural institutions and artistic manifestations in the exhibition areas planned in the city's periphery. I have never seen any published sketches, but from Renzo Piano's office I received fascinating ones including a long, narrow landscaped island on the left bank of the Seine below the Eiffel Tower, from which monumental stairs would lead down.

The Paths of Freedom is Jean Paul Sartre's semi-autobiographical suite of novels about wartime France and the German occupation, written during the war and published in three volumes from 1945 to 1949. The suite was planned as four volumes but Sartre never completed the fourth book. Some chapters were published after Sartre's death in 1980.

Pontus Hultén's plans for this world exhibition are said to have included a highly utopian design in which the world and its continents would be represented by different districts of Paris, with the tiny noble Île Saint-Louis as the center of Europe. Unfortunately, I have not found any further information about these ideas. Pontus Hultén is said to have written a "white book" on the initiative which I have failed to locate. The working title of the world exhibition was, stylistically, *Les chemins de la liberté* (*The Paths of Freedom*), the title of Jean-Paul Sartre's unfinished novel quadruple.

This heroically utopian, artistically urban juggernaut went down in a political poker game after the initial conceptual stage, before the plans could take more concrete shape. Its bane was the Mayor of Paris, Jacques Chirac, who publicly opposed the project by claiming that it was Parisians who would pay for these grandiose national ambitions — an argument that had also been part of the case against the Centre Pompidou. According to Claude Mollard, Chirac's stance against the planned world exhibition had nothing to do with any aversion to modern architecture or revolutionary ideals. The mayor's motives were political. "It was his way of profiling himself as a main opponent of Mitterrand for an upcoming presidential campaign," says Mollard. "In the end, he was succesful in this."[5]

Realizing that Jacques Chirac's opposition was unwavering, Mitterrand soon understood that the World Expo would be impossible to implement. "Mitterrand had embarked on a number of major modern, controversial building projects such as the glass pyramid at the Louvre, the Institut du monde arabe, La Défense, La Villette, the Bastille Opera House and several others," says Claude Mollard. "It would be too complicated when Chirac chose to side with his opponents. Bordaz had a very good relationship with Chirac and we tried to persuade him, but it was not enough. It was entirely a question of politics and his own plans."[6]

Pontus Hultén called the cancellation of the plans for the World Expo, which was already a fact in July 1983 when the group had been working on the project for just one year, "one of the biggest disappointments of my life."[7]

French Conceptual artist Daniel Buren, who would soon become Pontus Hultén's colleague and who was supposed to participate in the World Expo, offers a drastic analysis of the decision to nip this mammoth macro-utopian project in the bud. "Since then, France has gone downhill," says Buren. "It's a serious sign that something is wrong in a society when you cancel such a project and fail to pursue the vision. Chirac was a fucking asshole."[8]

A year after leaving Los Angeles, Pontus Hultén found himself back in Paris, unemployed. To the rescue came one of his elder guardian fairies. Claude Pompidou, the president's widow, is said to have been the one who, together with Robert Bordaz, wooed Mayor Chirac that the city of Paris had an obligation to Hultén since he had been called back to Paris.[9] As it has been presented to me, Hultén himself could suggest what he wanted to do.

The idea of opening an art school was, according to what I've been told from several quarters, Pontus Hultén's own. The initiative surprised friends and colleagues as Hultén had never taught or shown any excessive personal interest in pedagogy, even though pedagogical ambitions had characterized his activities as a museum man. Annick Boisnard, Hultén's assistant from the Centre Pompidou, whom he had hired on his staff for the planned world exhibition and who was eventually appointed to work on the school instead, claims that the idea was not Hultén's but Mayor Jacques Chirac's: "He wanted to start an art school in Paris and Pontus said, okay, I can create the structure, but it won't be a traditional school."[10]

The vision of the school seems to me to be classic Hulténian utopian. The pupils would not be art school students but young graduate artists from all over the world. The teaching would not even necessarily be artistic. Instead, teachers and guest lecturers, who in addition to artists were scouted from far beyond the realm of art — architects, philosophers, writers, anthropologists, astrophysicists, historians, mathematicians, physicians and so on — would engage the students in day-long mind-expanding conversations on various subjects. It almost appears like an update of the ancient Greek symposium,[11] or something along those lines.

The direct models, however, were drawn from the history of modern art. The first of these was the Cubist's cafés on Boulevard Montparnasse at the beginning of the century, where art evolved through the conversations that flowed over absinthe between avant-garde artists from around the world. The second was the Bauhaus, always a reference for Hultén and one of the pillars of his "total" vision of art. The third, most direct source of inspiration was its American successor, the Black Mountain College in North Carolina, created in 1933 after the Nazis had closed the Bauhaus — the seminal institution where Robert Rauschenberg, John Cage, Merce Cunningham, Cy Twombly and many others developed their artistic expressions in cross-disciplinary collaboration.

The official task of founding the school, which was given the uncharacteristically complicated, pretentious — perhaps ironic? — name L'Institut des Hautes Études en Arts Plastiques ("Institute for Higher Studies in the Plastic Arts"), abbreviated IHEAP, was only given to Hultén by Jacques Chirac in 1985, after a long period of discussion and negotiation. The inaugural season was delayed until the fall of 1988. The grant from the city of Paris seems to have been generous. Hultén was able to recruit a team of permanent teachers — in addition to himself Daniel Buren and Sarkis, an Armenian-French Conceptual artist in the tradition of Neo-Realism, as well as Serge Fauchereau, Hultén's literary collaborator from the museum in Paris.

"The idea had originally been that the institute would be part of the Pompidou, along with the library, Ircam and the design center," says Sarkis. "Now it was a different idea that Pontus was assigned by Chirac to develop. The school was based on the Bauhaus but we were not going to produce objects but create a discussion space for art and ideas. We wanted to increase the space for art through exchanges with science, politics, psychoanalysis, philosophy and so on."[12]

Twenty students were admitted, based on applications from all over the world, and had their stay in Paris financed. No wonder the institute was, in Daniel Buren's words, "drowned in applications" after the first year. The terms, or "sessions," lasted three months in the fall, followed by another month in the spring. Classes, or "talks," were held only three days a week. The school was housed during the first sessions in the MNAM's old desolate vacated halls in the Palais de Tokyo, later in what is now the Jewish Museum in the Marais.

The list of lecturers during the school's seven-year lifespan is impressive, with names such as Harald Szeemann, Claes Oldenburg, Niki de Saint Phalle, Jean Tinguely, Renzo Piano, Jean Nouvel, Ed Ruscha, Michael Asher, Jean-François Lyotard, Tadeusz Kantor, Giuseppe Panza di Biumo, Giovanni Anselmo, Jannis Kounellis, Ilya Kabakov and many more. The arrangement was that the group spent the whole day together, including lunch, in continuous discussions and lectures. The teachers and guest lecturers were responsible for different days, with one discussion topic for each day. The generous offering to the selected students included access to studios, initially in the Palais de Tokyo and elsewhere. However, studio visits were not part of the curriculum. Instead, students were given one day each to present their art in front of the whole group and defend themselves against often fierce criticism from classmates and, above all, teachers.

Many of the then young artists who were students at the school have told me about the horrific experience of being subjected to this inquisition, especially by the teachers Daniel Buren and Sarkis, who could be merciless in their judgments. For artists imperfect in French, these appearances were particularly painful. That all teaching be in French was a basic requirement, which nowadays seems unreasonable for an international school and was already questionable at the time. French nationalism and poor English language skills made English impossible as an alternative. Many of the students learned French to qualify for the school. One Chinese artist was rejected for not knowing a word of French but returned a year later, having become fluent, and was accepted. About half of the students came from France, the rest from many parts of the world — China, Japan, North Africa, South America, the United States and the Middle East. True to his global philosophy, Hultén made a point of having a geographical spread across all continents among the admitted students. In reality, the international element was less than it appeared. A substantial proportion of the international artists came from neighboring French-speaking countries such as Belgium and Switzerland. Others from the rest of the world had already been living in France when they were admitted. The language barrier was a formidable obstacle that limited the global nature of the school.

Several of the school's students have gone on to become globally successful artists, including Philippe Parreno, Dominique Gonzalez-Foerster, Xavier Veilhan, Rebecca Quaytman, Meir Eshel, known by the stage name Absalon,[13] and others. Three Swedish artists, Jan Svenungsson, Sophie Tottie and Anna Selander were students at the school at different sessions.

All of the students I have spoken to remember their school experiences with warmth. Several tell me what these experiences and lessons have meant for their lives and artistic careers. "I am grateful that I had this experience," says Rebecca Quaytman. "It was a very beautiful time, like a time capsule, totally open and free. Besides me, there was only one other American student at the school. It was a generation before the internet and our knowledge of Europe and European art was quite low. It was a privilege to get an insight into this world with a lot going on and great artists coming to the school. I had major language problems and struggled to keep up with all these theoretical discussions. I remember Daniel Buren interviewing me in English and finishing by saying "you said you speak French, right?"[14]

Xavier Veilhan is one of many who confirm that it could be difficult to absorb all the verbal wisdom that washed over the young artists in the moment. "It was a great opportunity for me to come to Paris and have my living expenses paid and be able to do my own work at the same time," says Veilhan. "I grew up in dull suburban areas outside Lyon and in Normandy and suffered a great lack of intellectual debate. Unfortunately, I found it easy to get bored with the discussions at school. The artists who came were fantastic. You could feel that Pontus stood for a view of art that was much more popular than the traditional one, but at the same time always very radical. Harald Szeemann came and talked about his exhibition *When attitude becomes form*, things like that. Many of the artists we discussed were related to the seventies, but I was more focused on the eighties, on Post-Pop Art like Ed Ruscha and John Baldessari, so it was great when Ruscha came to the school. I'd probably die today to be part of much of what we experienced, but back then I was a bit too restless to fully appreciate it, not fully aware of the dignity of the context."[15]

Live in Your Head: When Attitude Becomes Form was Harald Szeemann's major 1969 survey show of sixty-nine artists — mainly American Minimalists and "land artists" — at the Kunsthalle Bern, one of the most influential exhibitions in the history of modern art among contemporary curators.

Dominique Gonzalez-Foerster was twenty-three years old when she attended the school during its first season.[16] "It was a very special, intense time in the ghostly rooms of the Palais de Tokyo," Gonzalez-Foerster says. "It was a great combination, with an interesting Chinese painter and Absalon who had a most intense presence, opposing everything. I remember when Michael Asher[17] came to the school, a very radical artist with a great personality. My strongest memory was when Pontus suddenly took us all one day to visit Teeny Duchamp in her and Marcel Duchamp's house in Fontainebleau. Meeting her, touching her, seeing books with Duchamp's notes — it was unreal to experience art history so directly and physically."[18]

Pontus Hultén, then aged around sixty-five, is consistently portrayed in admiring terms by the school's students as a bridge to older art history. "Pontus was there when it all started so he had always been controversial," says Rebecca Quaytman. "There were great artists he brought to the school. It was clear that he had close friends among these people. He belonged to that generation of men who drank a lot, talked a lot and were a bit sexist. There were no female teachers at the school and no female artists as lecturers. But I remember him as incredibly warm. I liked him a lot and admired him a lot."[19] The sexism is contradicted by Dominique Gonzalez-Foerster, who graduated a few years before Quaytman: "I didn't see him as macho at all, not dominant. I had no problem with that. He was a bit old school but it was rather the opposite — that he made a point of men and women being equal."[20]

Swede Jan Svenungsson had what he calls the good fortune to come to the school during its first session, three months in the fall of 1988 and a follow-up month in the spring of 1989, when everything was new and characterized by a pioneering spirit. "It was Lars Nittve who had recommended me after a request from Pontus. He had asked Nittve to recommend some Swedish artists who spoke French and I simply don't think he could think of anyone else but me."[21]

Svenungsson remembers the admission interview with horror; how the teachers sat grimly on a podium with Pontus Hultén as "Secretary General." With comical points, he describes how the IHEAP school, although founded by a Swede, was archly French in its idea, structure and style: "Daniel Buren was a fantastic example of the hyper-intellectual Frenchman who mastered the entire register of rhetoric in long, elegant speeches, very difficult to follow. Sarkis struggled to be as polished as Buren and his origins meant that he tended to slip into romanticism and sentimentality. Serge Fauchereau on the other hand was not threatening and then Pontus who was the reason for all this — it was a cool feeling to know he was a Swede. He wasn't Olympic like Buren in his speeches either, he didn't have the linguistic ability for that, but he dominated the whole context anyway. Then there were long lunches, of course, with catering and wine."[22]

Jan Svenungsson serves up a couple of wonderful recollections that further illustrate the French mastery of rhetoric on which the school was so heavily based: "Two of the visiting lecturers were Renzo Piano and Jean Nouvel. I saw one as an Italian genius and the other as a

French fool. Piano was friendly and nice. He dwelt at length on a special node connector he had invented[23] and told us about all the problems it had solved — how it actually worked in practice. Jean Nouvel was a snobbish and arrogant intellectual in trendy clothes. He spent half the morning telling us about his building for the Institut du monde arabe where he had designed for the facade light-sensitive shutters, like in a camera, adapting to different light conditions. He ended the long harangue by briefly noting that the shutters had unfortunately not functioned in practice. It was just a footnote, absolutely nothing important. To me, he represented Frenchness in a bad sense."[24]

About Pontus Hultén, Jan Svenungsson, like several of the other artists in the school's alumni, testifies that he was usually friendly and nice but that he had a moody side. "He had a short fuse. His patience wasn't infinite and when he got annoyed it wasn't fun anymore. He could sometimes speak his mind in a very abrupt way. I remember once when I brought up Anselm Kiefer, who was in vogue and interested me at the time, but he didn't want to discuss it. 'He's a Nazi,' he just cut it off and that was the end of that."[25]

Even though all the students and others I have spoken to express themselves reverently, gratefully and effusively, I get the overall impression of some confusion about IHEAP's pedagogical concept — as if these lofty philosophical, theoretical, intellectual, political and art-historical conversations, this rhetorical spring flood of words, seem to have flown a bit over the heads of the young artists. An image of Pontus Hultén as a slightly outdated figure emerges through all the accolades. It appears that in his vision Hultén had overestimated the depth of the young contemporary artists' interest in art history.

Jan Svenungsson snickers when I mention the school's pedagogical model. "There was no pedagogical model," he says. "It was a *vanity project* for Pontus and it's quite wonderful that it could be like that. He provided us with a physical contact with the history of art and made us understand that it is actually about connections between people. I'm very grateful that I was part of that first year because I'm convinced that talk workshop must have soon become routine."

During the school's seven-year run, IHEAP organized two international "guest performances" and associated exhibitions, the first of which has gone down in modern art history. It was staged in Russia, in Saint Petersburg, or Leningrad as the city was still called, in the spring of 1990 — in the brief period of historical upheaval following the collapse of the Soviet Union and the resurrection of Russia, before the old capital was returned to its imperial name.

The artists who took part in the Leningrad adventure all agree on the uniqueness of the experience and the impact of the month in Russia at a time of transition for their artistic careers and personal development. It's remarkable what a lasting impression this visit and the hybrid exhibition it produced made and how the exchange came to influence the development of contemporary Russian art.

Through his contacts established with *Paris–Moscow* and *Moscow–Paris*, the exhibitions that had made Pontus Hultén a legend in the Russian art world, he had arranged for the school to use a floor of the Russian Museum in Leningrad for sessions with fifteen selected young Russian artists. In collaboration with these young local colleagues, a double exhibition was organized where the students' and teachers' art was complemented by masterpieces from modern art history, borrowed through Hultén's contacts and also, not surprisingly, replicas.

The exhibition in Leningrad can be seen as an experimental first part of the vision for a new epic exhibition cycle, Hultén's last, which he had been developing in his mind. Called *Le Territoire de l'Art* (*The Territory of Art* — see next chapter), the idea was to present works of art that had advanced the development of art, claiming new territories.

The school's second international expedition was to Taejon, South Korea, where the art students and teachers organized an exhibition in collaboration with a number of South Korean and international artists, including Nam June Paik. The exhibition was staged as part of the 1993 World Expo, in a pavilion designed by Renzo Piano (who else?), with an artificial island surrounded with water where works were installed in the open air. The trip to South Korea has not become legendary like the one to Leningrad, although the level of ambition was on par and the set-up similar. The name of the exhibition was *Devant, le futur* (*In Front, the Future*) and, judging by the catalog, the content was interesting and the quality impressive. In addition to teachers and students, artists who had been lecturers at the school, including Claes Oldenburg and Niki de Saint Phalle, participated. A selection of former students of the school were also invited, among them Jan Svenungsson.

The nerve of the unique historical moment in Leningrad was missing in Korea. The metaphysical qualities of the exhibition were disrupted by physical circumstances. According to Daniel Buren, the mission to create an art experience as part of the World Expo was hopeless. "The exhibition was nice, but it was a messy environment with incredible noise pollution — impossible to do anything with," says Buren. "The sound invaded everything. It was like presenting an exhibition at an airport."[26] Jan Svenungsson is amused when I reproduce Buren's depiction. "Well, yes, of course, you can chose to see it like that from a perfectionist French snob perspective. Sure, there was sound pollution, and visual pollution as well for that matter, but it was a lot of fun, totally crazy. I've been to a world exhibition another time too, in Seville, and it's completely insane, surreal events where countries try to outdo each other in futuristic installations. The Koreans were incredibly nationalistic, saw themselves as superhuman."[27]

Jan Svenungsson explains that he was invited to participate after having experienced "a small breakthrough" with his sculpture in the form of a factory chimney. He made a modest proposal for a work with plaques on the ground instead, with transport to South Korea in mind, but received no response. On a visit to Paris, he sought out Pontus Hultén at the Marais school and asked what happened to the proposal. "Oh, no, I don't want that, I want a chimney," Hultén replied. Svenungsson pointed out that it would be three times as expensive and that he would have to travel to Seoul immediately. This was no problem. It was arranged for him to travel to South Korea three times — for research, for construction and for the exhibition itself.

Pontus Hultén's fellow teachers Daniel Buren, Sarkis and Serge Fauchereau, with several of his friends and associates, have all confided in me that they were skeptical that Hultén would have the patience to remain at the school and participate in teaching for any length of time. He surprised them by being almost always present and punctual, always well-dressed and elegant, day after day during the years of the school's operation. Even for me this is surprising — not quite like Hultén.

The IHEAP did not become a new Black Mountain College or Bauhaus, and well into the 1990s the school's financial situation became precarious. Hultén was forced to devote more and more time and energy to the art he hated but mastered: begging for money. "He always knew how to get money — until it became too expensive in the end," says Serge Fauchereau. "It was the same every time."[28]

Sometime before the mid-1990s, Jacques Chirac (who was elected president in 1995) finally decided to withdraw the City of Paris' reduced funding for the school, thus sealing the institution's fate. Daniel Buren notes laconically: "I think ultimately we were all pretty happy that it ended."[29]

It's an impression confirmed by others with insight. The school had been an exciting, grandiose attempt to bring something new to the arts. Even so, the institution had failed to establish an indispensable position in the years that the expensive experiment had been conducted. Now this trial period had come to an end. As Serge Fauchereau summarizes: "The City of Paris progressively cut its funding until it became unsustainable. Maybe they were tired of spending money without getting what they saw as a result. I think they also thought there were too many foreigners — Pontus, Sarkis, the students. Eventually they didn't want to hear about it anymore and let's be honest: it was a hell of a lot of work that sucked the life out of us, alongside all the other projects we all had. We were all pretty tired and exhausted."[30]

An aftermath of the school concerned the library of thousands of volumes that the Institute had assembled. Much of the collection consisted of catalogs, artists' books and other publications from art institutions around the world. Bibliophile Pontus Hultén and his colleagues had realized the idea that a vital art library could be quickly created through exchanges with other players. Hultén negotiated with several institutions for the donation of this reference library, both in France and internationally. The choice fell on Marseilles where Hultén was able to negotiate for the library to have its own department and also for publications in two volumes documenting a selection of the school's conversations with students, teachers and guest lecturers.[31]

Opinions are divided on the importance of the school for Pontus Hultén personally. "Of course he would have preferred to lead a large museum, but I think he really enjoyed being with the young artists, at least in the beginning," claims Jean-Hubert Martin.[32] Others close to Hultén have given me a different picture. One of them says pithily: "The school was a disaster, okay?"

As in the case of many of Hultén's exhibitions and other initiatives, the question marks that existed at the time have faded in retrospect. The artists who attended the school all emphasize this experience as a merit in their career lists. The IHEAP has acquired a cult status in the art world. The school is increasingly referenced in international art literature and the media.

It's said that copying is the ultimate compliment. According to this thesis, the dignity of the IHEAP is confirmed by the controversial "recycling" of its brand. Since 2013, the organization that organizes the Paris Biennale[33] runs a school named "Institut des hautes études en arts plastiques," unlike its predecessor spelled with continuous lower case letters. Another key difference is that while the IHEAP paid for students' expenses, its successor is charging theirs expensively. Daniel Buren has taken legal action over what he and others understandably consider to be a gross trademark infringement. "It's a criminal artist who has started this and is making money by scamming young hopefuls who think the school has something to do with what we did," says Buren. "I have spoken to various people involved but no one has been prepared to do anything to stop this or pay a single euro, absolutely zero. So I have had to pay for this process entirely myself. It's really not fun to spend time, money and energy on this. I will never get a cent out of this guy. It's something I feel like a necessary duty, for the sake of Pontus' memory and for what we all did."[34]

27

Saint Petersburg and Pontus' great Russian legacy

The Saint Petersburg artist Sergei Bugaev, known in the art world by his stage name "Afrika," is a legend. When Pontus Hultén and his IHEAP school visited Leningrad in the spring of 1990, the then twenty-four-year-old Bugaev was the "rock star" among the participating Russian artists.

He emerged as a cartoon character, this "Afrika" – an anti-superhero and rebel of the communist dictatorship, a precocious prince of the Leningrad underground who operated with virtuosity in the undergrowth of the post-communist system. "He was a bit like a British punk guy," said Xavier Veilhan, one of the eighteen students from the Paris school who were in Leningrad. "He really knew everything about how the system worked. He could get booze and drugs and open swimming pools at night so we could swim and party. I remember one time when we were way out of town in some suburb in the middle of the night and he arranged for a regular bus from the city center to come out and pick us up, passengers and all. We took the night train to Moscow and drank vodka all night. He knew everyone everywhere. These are really amazing memories — an incredible privilege to have been part of all this."[1]

When I first came into contact with Afrika in 2015, the image of the mythic status that the artist enjoys in the Russian and in the international contemporary art world grew — as did also the realization of the extent to which Pontus Hultén had been a mentor not only to him but to the whole of Russian contemporary art.

Afrika's stories conjured up a new image of *Le Territoire de l'Art* — the messy, substandard exhibition that Olle Granath depicted and about which I had heard others speak disparagingly. Even the young international artists who participated, and the teachers in Paris, had emphasized the primitive conditions — lack of food, dilapidated premises, masterpieces in danger of being destroyed, rivers of vodka, etc. — to the extent that the idea, content, message and reception of the exhibition itself had been obscured for me.

None of the numerous people outside Russia with whom I have spoken had mentioned anything about what Afrika told me about the influence of the exhibition on the development of contemporary Russian art. His description of reality was later confirmed by Jean-Hubert Martin, the Russia expert, who put me in touch with two female Russian art historians and curators, Ekaterina Andreeva and Olesia Turkina. Andreeva and Turkina were young curators at the Russian Museum, where *Le Territoire de l'Art* and the associated student exhibition, *Atelier* as it was called, were shown in the early summer of 1990. In their own words, they had the life-changing opportunity to work with Pontus Hultén, his staff and the Russian and international artists on the production. Both are still with the museum and both, like Afrika and his friends, have been working on as yet unrealized plans to commemorate and clarify the legacy of *Le Territoire de l'Art*.[2]

Pontus Hultén's deep Russian devotion and the contributions he made to Russian art, both the historical avant-garde and post-communist contemporary art, are central to his career, little known in the Western art world. Certainly, *Paris–Moscow* 1979 (but not *Moscow–Paris* 1981) is generally considered to be Pontus Hultén's greatest achievement and one of the most influential exhibitions in the entire history of international modern art, but few outside Hultén's Russian team know much more than that, unable to answer when I ask in more detail what they know about Hultén's Russian connections. It's easy to understand that this ignorance can be explained by the iron curtain that still separates Russian from Western culture. Quite simply, few in the West care about Russia. In contrast, anyone with any historical insight into the modern art world knows what Pontus Hultén did for New York, for Rauschenberg and Warhol. "The cliché with the Pontus and America thing is an unfair picture — almost like a caricature," as Jean-Hubert Martin stresses. "It doesn't correspond to reality at all. He was not overly interested in American art. He talked much more often and extensively about Russian art than American, that's for sure."[3]

When I finally visit Saint Petersburg in November 2019, Afrika meets me at the airport. A slightly chilling sea breeze sweeps in from the Baltic Sea while a soft drizzle falls over the gray urban landscape of the seven-million city where the Western consumer culture as Afrika describes has settled down for good in the form of shopping centers and familiar Western brands. "But behind that is another reality that you don't see here. Seventy-eight percent of the money in Russia is in Moscow," Afrika explains. "There it trickles down from the top, so there's always something coming to the lower layers as well. There are no middle layers here. So people have to go out into the forests and pick berries and mushrooms."[4]

Sergei "Afrika" Bugaev was born and raised on the Black Sea in southern Russia. During the summer seasons, he met vacationing visitors from Moscow and Leningrad, among them representatives of the cities' artistic underground cultures. In 1980, at the age of fourteen, he left his homeland for good, taking the train alone to Leningrad, a two-day journey at the time, where he had made older friends in underground circuits. With his charm, artistic talents, hustler skills, audacity and fearlessness, Sergei quickly became a profile in this subculture of all kinds of creatives who lived outside the communist system where their lifestyles and artistic expressions were strictly forbidden. The young Sergei became a master at maneuvering and navigating the shadowy world of the illegal black market economy that thrived under the crushing bureaucracy and paranoid police state of the communist dictatorship. "I was younger than everyone else, so I took greater risks," as Afrika relates the situation.[5] He acquired his nom de guerre during this time as a street child in the Leningrad underground. "Peter the Great had an adopted son from Ethiopia and there were those who said Pushkin had black blood," says Afrika. "I was only interested in black music and culture, like Bob Marley and things like that. Plus I was from the South. So they started saying 'you must be from Africa.'"[6]

I knew that Afrika had become famous in a wider circle as he had played one of the starring parts in the 1977 Russian cult film *Assa*, which made him an idol and sex symbol in the semi-prohibited late Soviet youth culture. "Afrika was the huge star of the time," says Olesia Turkina, one of the then young curators assisting with the 1990 Leningrad exhibition. "He was bigger and more important than Gorbachev in Russia at that time, that's absolutely no exaggeration."[8]

I've been told that Afrika is a spider in many webs, controversial in some camps, and that he is "good friends" with Leningrad native

Vladimir Putin, fourteen years his senior. "If you want, I can support that rumor by saying yes," says Afrika himself. "I've sat like I'm sitting with you now a few times with him, that I have. But with you, I feel like I've become a bit of a friend. You don't get that with him."[9]

I naively ask what creative expressions Afrika and his comrades in the Leningrad underground engaged in before the collapse of communism — if "street art" was part of the culture. "Wow, there were all kinds of expressions, with performance, film, music, poetry. Poetry has always had a strong position in Petersburg and there were many poets who were leaders."[10]

These underground movements in the Soviet cities are described as late relatives of the Dadaist "cells" and other pioneering avant-garde movements of the early twentieth century, with their total-art approach. Typical of the movement was the free creative exchange over boundaries between art forms. Many of the underground profiles were artists, poets, musicians, actors and performers. It appears inevitable that Pontus Hultén took an interest in this creative culture, unknown in the West. "Here in Leningrad we had no contact with Moscow or anywhere else in the world," says Afrika. "We just had our own world. We were classified as a 'toxic social element.'"[11]

It was in 1986 that the communist regime under Mikhail Gorbachev, the historic last party secretary, began to use the terms *glasnost* and *perestroika*, with the approximate meanings of *openness/transparency* and *reconstruction* respectively. A process of easing communist oppression began, which within a few years led to the collapse of the Soviet state and the entire Eastern bloc. The liberalization brought about by *glasnost* made living conditions more bearable and the opportunities of reaching out with their art somewhat more favorable for members of the Leningrad underground, although restrictions remained harsh and contemporary abstract art was still officially classified as a manifestation of bourgeois decadence.

Afrika informs me that the first time the group of artists to which he belonged, "The New Artists," together with the related "Necrorealists" (the group's overall basic tone is dark) showed their art abroad was in Stockholm, in the exhibition *The New Artists from Leningrad* at the House of Culture (see Chapter 19) in 1988.[12] Diplomatic representatives visited Afrika's studio, from which artworks for the exhibition were smuggled out. Another of the young artists involved was Timur Novikov, Afrika's friend and the informal leader of the underground movement, also a central figure at Pontus Hultén's and IHEAP's "session" and exhibition in Leningrad in 1990. Together with Timur, Afrika received an invitation from John Cage to visit New York in 1989. The duo became the first among their artist friends to travel outside Russia and to learn to speak useful English. Timur had worked as an electrician at the Russian Museum and was familiar with the masterpieces by early 20th century Russian avant-garde artists hidden in the museum's storerooms.

In 1989 the Russian Museum in Leningrad hosted a semi-official exhibition of works by the Necrorealists, the New Artists and other local contemporary artists, from which works were purchased for the museum's collection. The exhibition was not open to the public but only to museum staff and official representatives.

Such was the situation when Pontus Hultén visited Leningrad sometime in 1989. Afrika says that he had met Hultén in the city already in 1987, when he had visited his studio. Naturally, Hultén was well acquainted with the underground movement and its art through the first-class Russian network of contacts he maintained since *Paris–Moscow*.

In early 1990, Hultén's fellow teacher Sarkis, an Armenian and Russian speaker, came to visit the city and the Russian Museum with Hultén's trusted friend and collaborator Stanislas Zadora, also a Russian speaker. As Ekaterina Andreeva and others recall, Sarkis and Zadora didn't reveal any details but "let it be known" that Hultén had an idea for a project in Leningrad and was looking for local artists. "He had started negotiations with the authorities about the exhibition but at the same time also an inventory of the underground scene and art here," as Afrika says.[13]

Ekaterina Andreeva was among those tasked with inviting young Leningrad artists — the rule was that no one could be more than thirty years old, although exceptions were made — to submit art for consideration for participation in a workshop and exhibition in collaboration with the IHEAP in Paris. It was clear from the start that the artists would be drawn only from Leningrad, not from Moscow or other parts of Russia. "Pontus said that he had enough of Moscow while working on *Moscow–Paris*," says Olesia Turkina.[14] Timur Novikov was involved in the selection of artists from the beginning. "I remember Timur asking if it was okay to invite unknown artists," says Ekaterina Andreeva. "It was, which was amazing in a museum.

Pp. 502–503: Sergei "Afrika" Bugaev and friends study a book donated by Andy Warhol in Timur's studio, Leningrad, 1986. Warhol, John Cage, Larry Rivers and other artists in New York supported Leningrad's artistic underground.

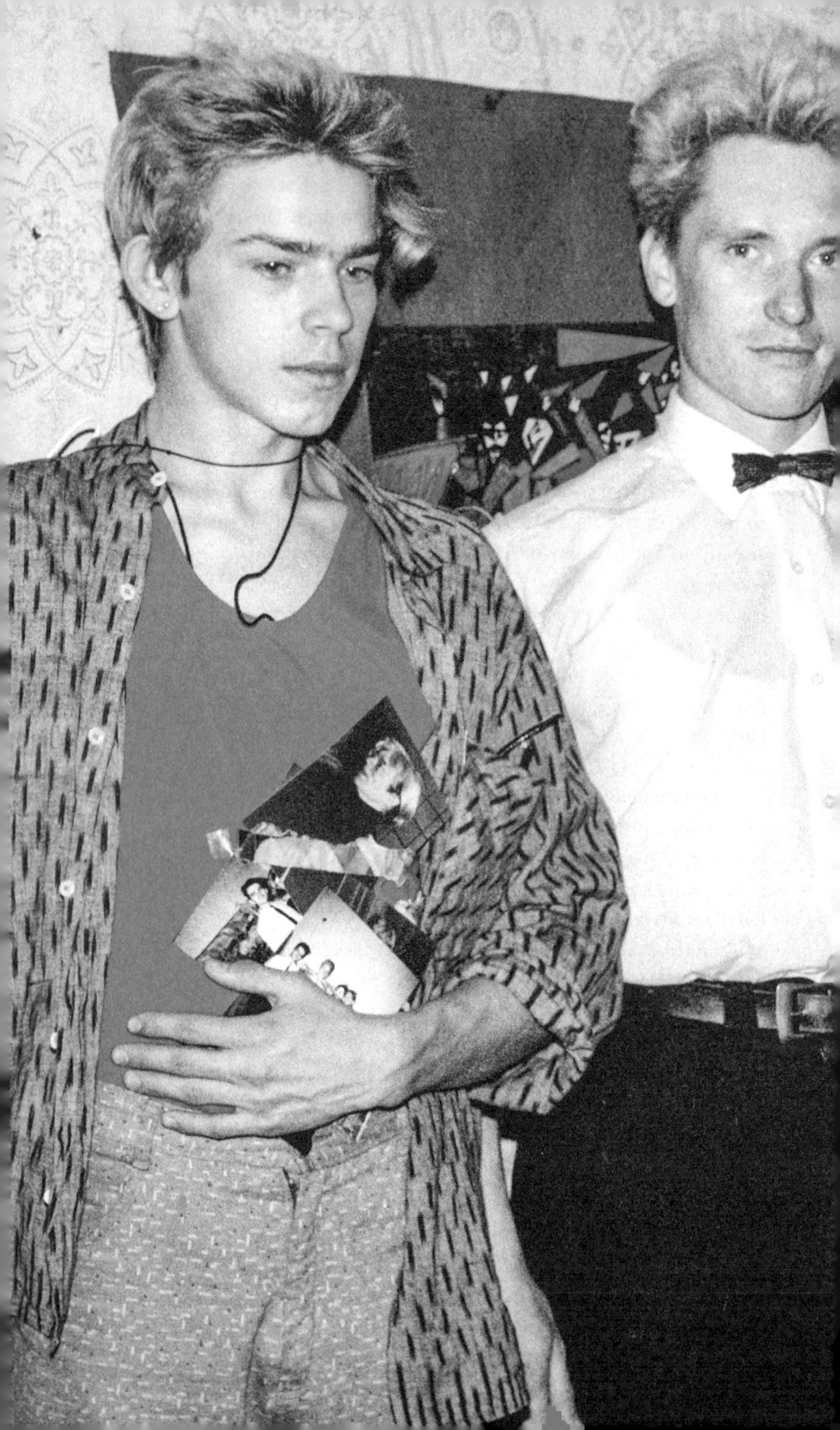

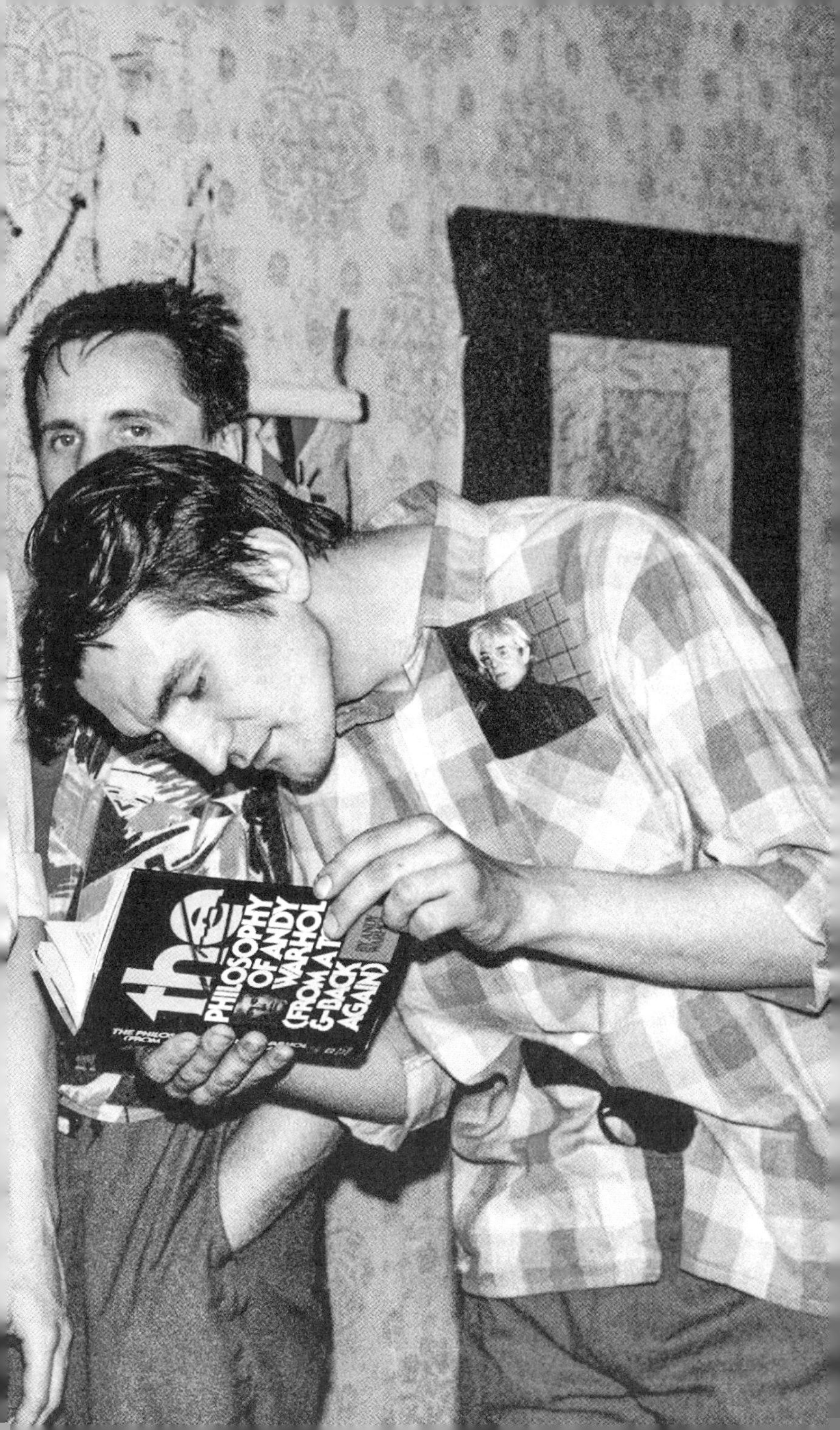
the
PHILOSOPHY
OF ANDY
WARHOL
(FROM A T
BACK
AGAIN)

It meant we could include the trendy underground."[15] Pontus Hultén's main collaborator at the Russian Museum was the French-speaking curator Mikhail Guerman, alone among the museum's experts to have studied European Modernism.[16]

As usual with Pontus Hultén, everything proceeded very quickly thereafter. He, Zadora and Sarkis returned to Leningrad in the spring of 1990 when the selection of Russian artists was made in consultation with a local jury. Of those chosen, most were drawn from the city's post-communist underground, all self-taught, while three came from Leningrad's official art academy, including Elena Gubanova, now a well-known artist still working in her hometown. "I don't know how many were invited, but I remember that the submitted works filled about three galleries of the museum," says Elena Gubanova. "I never thought I would be included because I was a painter and there were rumors that Sarkis in particular was against painting. For me it was something I never thought possible, with total freedom in contrast to the formal education I was used to."[17]

Pontus Hultén then returned from Paris with his full forces at the end of April and beginning of May 1990, a month before the exhibition was due to open. Guest teachers at the "session" in Leningrad were the New York-based German Conceptual artist Hans Haacke, already world-famous at the time, and several other big names, such as the Italian Arte Povera artists Giovanni Anselmo and Jannis Kounellis. Arriving from Los Angeles were Jerry Sohn, Gregory Mahoney and brothers Greg and Jeff Colson, who also participated in the exhibition. "It was absolutely incredible to meet such people," says Olesia Turkina. "No one in Russia had ever been close to contemporary artists from the West."[18] According to Ekaterina Andreeva, many of the Russian artists selected for participation could be referred to in a broader term as Expressionists. In the years before 1990, an increasing number of Russian artists had begun to experiment with assemblage, mixed media and Conceptual Art. "You can see that there were strong similarities with the New Wave movement in New York," says Andreeva. "In the early eight-

New York's New Wave movement took its name from the landmark *New York/New Wave* exhibition that opened on February 15, 1981 at the then P.S.1 Contemporary Art Center in Queens (now MoMA PS1), which featured the work of over one hundred artists, photographers, musicians, writers and directors from New York's post-punk avant-garde, including Jean-Michel Basquiat, Keith Haring and Nan Goldin. Andy Warhol was featured as the "father figure" of the movement. Above all, the exhibition — a sensational public success and hype in New York — made contemporary art history as the breakthrough of the then twenty-year-old Basquiat.

ies, when the New Artists were developing their Neo-Expressionism, they hadn't heard of Basquiat, but in the second half of the eighties they were aware of similar art internationally. There had recently been some influence from Jeff Koons, among others."[19]

The young artists and teachers were housed in an old dilapidated imperial summer palace on the coast outside Leningrad, from where they were picked up by bus for their daily sessions with their Russian colleagues in the so-called Benois Wing of the Russian Museum in the city center. The group worked from morning until the museum closed at six in the evening. A classic Hultén idea was that a substantial part of the works on display would be created on site at the museum. It was the first time that contemporary artists were allowed into a Russian museum in this way. Work on the exhibition was interspersed with discussion sessions at the museum and sometimes in the artists' simple studios. All discussions were held with the help of interpreters. "It was completely new for us that museum staff and teachers had direct contact and worked with the artists in this way," says Elena Gubanova. "Pontus was part of all this, as one of the others, not at all like the big boss. I remember thinking that it was so different that he often sat silent and that as an artist you were expected to explain your thinking — something we were definitely not used to."[20] "Pontus was not like a museum director," says Olesia Turkina. "He was like the father of everything. For me he was a futuristic god — a cross of Mayakovsky, Malevich and Tatlin, ready for discovery and progress."

The month of May in Leningrad with the school from Paris shimmers in a romantic light. As Pontus Hultén himself muses: "It was a very special time, with spring outside the museum window and spring in Russian society."[21] The anecdotes are many, colored by the scarcity of the comforts that Russian post-communist society could offer, but above all by the adventure and an intoxicating anarchic sense of freedom. "There was nothing to eat, but lots to drink," says Olesia Turkina. "Buying a few kilos of cucumbers cost like my monthly salary. I'll never forget a discussion we had with Hans Haacke about the price of cucumbers. Vodka was always available but in those days it was absolutely not safe. There was a lot of bad vodka too."[22]

Sophie Tottie remembers a darker overriding sense of risk and danger that permeated the atmosphere of the newfound freedom of the Russian spring — of the burgeoning mafia making its mark, of nighttime drives in broken-down cars on roads with large unmarked potholes, and of several more or less serious incidents. "You constantly had the feeling that at any moment you could die in some kind of accident," says Tottie.[23]

For Elena Gubanova and the other participating young Russian artists, the discussions about art during the session were transformative. "I remember that one of the first discussions was about Brancusi. We talked for hours about the pedestals of his sculptures. I thought it was incredibly strange. In a Russian art school you would never, ever pay attention to such a thing."

The language barrier was difficult to negotiate and the cultural and economic contrasts stark between the French-international delegation from the Paris school and the young artists and museum officials in Leningrad. Even today, the differences are striking. For the young Russian artists who had grown up and educated themselves in the Leningrad underground, traditional artistic materials were rarely available. Utensils such as oil paints, canvases and classical sculpture materials had been out of reach for most of them. Some of the artworks submitted for judging and created for the exhibition were made using packaging plastic, pigskin and old wallpaper as canvases, and remnants of communist society as materials for assemblages and sculptures. "They had to be very inventive," says Ekaterina Andreeva. "It was the idea that was important when there was no money or materials. The conditions under which artists in the West lived were a completely different world for us. I remember as late as 1998, when I was invited to an artistic conference in Visby on Gotland.[24] The Swedish artists all talked about how they needed more money from the state in order to make a living from their art. I myself was glad that before I left I had been able to buy two kilos of apples that I could exchange for other things, such as cucumbers."[25] A brutal manifestation of the contrasts in living conditions is that barely half of the Russian artists who participated in Leningrad, none of whom are/would have been more than sixty years old today, are still alive. Several are long gone.

In its structure, *Le Territoire de l'Art* seems to have been a complicated, spontaneous, highly Hulténian hybrid. The exhibition consisted of three parts. On the ground floor of the wing building, the works of young international and Russian artists were shown in the student exhibition *Atelier*. The upper level presented installations by the participating teachers — Sarkis, Hans Haacke and Daniel Buren — as well as the third part of the exhibition, a selection of works from the history of modern art, from the advent of Cubism to the present day. The idea was based on topographical thinking typical of Hultén — to offer the Russian audience, unfamiliar with modern international art history, an overview through a collection of works from different eras, all of which, according to Hultén, had broken new ground, expanded the "territory" of art.

The international artists all describe the rugged, dilapidated, dirty premises of the Russian Museum, with filthy, non-functioning toilets, no running water, and electricity coming and going. Borrowing masterpieces from leading international institutions under these circumstances was a feat that tested the loyalty of Pontus Hultén's friends and contacts. Security was not exactly the best.

Hultén's "alma mater" Moderna Museet was, of course, responsible for a good number of the borrowed milestones in art history, and had to accept the temporary loss of a substantial number of its much-loved treasures. That no effort or expense was spared is evident in that Robert Rauschenberg's "Mud Muse,"[26] the magnificent Plexiglas box filled with bubbling, "singing" mud, donated to the museum for the *New York Collection for Stockholm* in 1973, was shipped to Leningrad for the exhibition. "What would you do?" says Olle Granath. "You couldn't refuse to let him borrow the works he had acquired for the museum. Of course he got what he wanted."[27] The Centre Pompidou, led by Jean-Hubert Martin, also lent invaluable works. A trump card, evidently, was the Russian Museum's own collection of the early twentieth century Russian avant-garde, so important in *Paris–Moscow* and *Moscow–Paris*, including Malevich's supremacist paintings and key works by Kandinsky and Rodchenko, among others. Other lenders included the Tate Gallery, the Musée Matisse in Nice, and other leading institutions from as far away as the National Gallery of Victoria in Melbourne and LACMA in Los Angeles.[28] Private collectors from around the world also contributed loans, including Pontus Hultén himself. Hultén's highly personal selection featured art by friends such as Claes Oldenburg, Niki de Saint Phalle, Jean Tinguely and Rebecca Horn.[29] Contemporary works by artists such as Bruce Nauman, Nam Jun Paik, Walter De Maria and Jeff Wall, the innovative photographer, were also shown. It is incomprehensible when you flip through the simple black-and-white catalog and study the list of art historical jewels offered to the virgin Russian art public.

Pontus Hultén would not have been Hultén if he had settled for this. He commissioned his good friend André Raffray to create replicas of some paintings that were inaccessible for loan — of course Duchamp's "Nude Woman Descending a Staircase, No. 2," Salvador Dalí's "Figure

Most infamous of the replicas shown at *Le Territoire d'Art* is of course the pile of, as it turned out much later, brand new Brillo boxes that stood in the stairwell on the upper floor of the museum, at the entrance to the "classical" section of the exhibition. These notorious boxes would become world news with the so-called Brillo scandal that broke seventeen years later, six months after Pontus Hultén's death (see Chapter 36).

paranoïaque" ("Paranoid Figure," 1937) and, most remarkably, Pablo Picasso's "Les Demoiselles d'Avignon" from 1907, the painting Hultén in his catalog text calls "the central work for the birth of Cubism" and "the beginning of the path of subjectivity that characterizes the century."[30] The recently retired director of the MNAM, Bernard Blistène, expresses undisguised admiration for this move: "It says everything about him as a museum man. No one, absolutely no one else in the art world would have the audacity to even think of making a copy of 'Les Demoiselles' …"[31]

Yevgeniya Petrova, a leading Russian art historian and museum administrator, then and still today deputy director of the Russian Museum in Saint Petersburg, Hultén's main collaborator alongside the late Mikhail Guerman in the production of the 1990 exhibition, recalls the installation of *Le Territoire de 'l'Art:* "It was incredibly instructive to see how Pontus and the others worked — even for me, who was working mainly with older art at the time, but especially for my colleagues in the modern department, who were only three people," says Petrova. "Their methods were really different in every way from what we were used to."[32]

I ask Yevgeniya Petrova to specify which elements of Hultén's and his team's approach that were most surprising and instructive to the Russian colleagues. "The speed," says Petrova. "Everything was very fast, which was totally new and unusual for us. We were used to working seriously, carefully and slowly. They were totally intuitive but knew exactly what they were doing. Pontus had a very sure eye for what he wanted to show and narrate. For him it didn't matter if the art came from Russia, the USA, Finland or wherever. The only thing crucial was if it was good art. That is something very unusual."[33]

There are many hilarious accounts of the chaos, cultural differences and practical difficulties that characterized this installation, as the masterpieces arrived at the detoriated museum while the artists completed their works and installations on site. Olle Granath, who, as the largest lender, traveled to Leningrad for the opening, grimaces at the memory. "Ugh, it was awful to see our art in that environment," he says. "I was afraid of the dark and quickly decided that we should go somewhere else. I just had to close my eyes and keep my fingers crossed that nothing was destroyed. The 'Mud Muse' had dried up. Someone was stirring it with a wooden spoon. It's a miracle that the delicate bottom valves didn't clog up and it was completely destroyed. I wonder if we didn't even have de Chirico's 'Child's Brain' there as well. I almost think so.[34] I have tried to repress all this ..."[35]

Olesia Turkina and the other collaborators emphatically confirm Granath's recollections of the precarious circumstances — and in particular the critical dangers for Rauschenberg's poor dehydrated "Mud Muse." "She almost breathed her last when the bottom valves were about to be encased in cement," says Turkina. "It's absolutely true! It was terrible! The problem was that the museum's electricity was turned off at six o'clock and not on again until the following morning. At the last moment, Petrova and the others managed to persuade the administration to leave the power on at night as well, otherwise it would have been destroyed."[36]

Ignorance of the concept of modern art was prevalent outside the small circle of artists and museum officials. In the Soviet state, the entire process of getting used to the history of modern art from Picasso onwards had passed the public by. The tiresome debate about whether modern and abstract art is really art at all remained. "A few exhibitions of Warhol, for example, had been staged between 1960 and 1980, but that was it," says Ekaterina Andreeva. "In the Hermitage's collection of Modernism there was no art from after 1913."[37] The alienation in face of the new and unfamiliar took on comical forms. "I remember a babushka spinning Duchamp's bicycle wheel," says Rebecca Quaytman.[38] "Not many people understood much French, but we learned some expressions," says Olesia Turkina. "One day Pontus started shouting '*arrête, arrête!*' [stop, stop!] He was absolutely furious. It was an artist who had just finished a complicated installation with cardboard boxes that the workers were about to carry out to throw away ..."

According to Sophie Tottie, many of the problems were caused by a lack of cooperation from some of the Russian staff. "There were many who did not believe that *perestroika* would last," says Tottie. "They wanted to be loyal to the old system in case the dictatorship came back, but at the same time they wanted to be part of the new one with Hultén. It made the situation complicated, exhausting and somewhat unpleasant."[39] Sophie Tottie says that this contradictory attitude one day gave rise to one of Pontus Hultén's infamous outbursts of anger. "I remember it exactly — right where he was standing," says Tottie. "Suddenly he started shouting at the staff that they should do what he said. He was terribly angry. Afterwards, the staff were completely white in the face and did exactly what he wanted, they didn't dare anything else. Pontus later explained that he had needed to straighten them out."[40]

Considering that modern art was still inherently controversial in Russia at the time, I ask Yevgeniya Petrova whether the realization of this advanced, often provocative exhibition did not require a complicated game of political negotiation. "Not at all — we had complete freedom to do exactly what we wanted," says Petrova.[41] "After *Paris-Moscow*, Pontus Hultén was a god in the Russian art world. No one questioned his decisions," says Olesia Turkina.

Undeniably, it seems that the "revolutionary romantic" Hultén here experienced his historic moment of freedom after a revolutionary process of a kind that bore clear similarities with his idealized "utopian states of exception" that is said to have arisen in connection with other revolts throughout history — the Paris Commune and so on.

Despite the scarse circumstances by Western standards, the cost of this whole adventure must have been impressive. The financial resources that Hultén had at his disposal for his school, especially in the early years before budgets gradually began to tighten, were exceedingly generous. Grants were provided by several external patrons and institutions such as the Getty Foundation in Los Angeles, where Hultén had good contacts from his time in the city, the Cartier Foundation, and Paul and Leo Goldschmidt. The Canal+ television channel, a major player in the French cultural world at the time, also sponsored the exhibition by paying for some of the art produced for the occasion, a collection that it later intended to sell at auction. The art is said to have been sent to Paris after the exhibition, but my Russian contacts, and I myself, have been unable to clarify what happened to the auction or to some of the works shown in Leningrad (a number of the pieces from the "student exhibition" were included in the collection of the Russian Museum, others ended up in Moscow).

Le Territorie de l'Art was responded to by the Russian public as one would expect — and as so many of Hultén's major exhibitions had been received. It divided the audience into two camps: those who loved it and those who hated it. The attendance was strong and the discussion among the audience often audibly heated and intense, as the story goes. Many of the artworks in the exhibition were difficult for some of the audience to digest, but none more so than Afrika's contribution. "His things were considered the most shocking and outrageous," says Olesia Turkina.[42] "There was a good, strong reaction and a stimulating discussion that followed," says Yevgeniya Petrova, who herself praises the exhibition as fantastic. "It showed in a very effective, clear and powerful way the history of modern art — it evoked powerful emotions. The exhibition was undoubtedly the start of contemporary art in Russia."[43]

Petrova explains why an exhibition like *Le Territoire de l'Art* is so unthinkable in our own time. "It's not primarily about money, insurance, fragile works and so on," she says. "It's mainly a question of mentality. Today, all museum directors have to choose artists to show from a list of names approved by time and trend — otherwise they risk disappearing from the list of hot museum directors themselves. This makes everything very predictable. We actually have more freedom here in Russia than in the West to do something a bit different — although many of our artists and curators also do what they can to get on the list."[44]

As in the case of many of Pontus Hultén's exhibitions, this one in particular, there was a target group that more than others knew how to appreciate and be inspired by *Le Territoire de l'Art* and the "student" exhibition *Atelier*: the Russian artists, of course, especially the younger generation. It was the first time in sixty years that contemporary art had been shown in a Russian museum.

The impact can hardly be overestimated. "The exhibition was the first experience of modern art for several generations," says Afrika. "I have been trying for many years in different contexts[45] to explain the incredible importance of Hultén for Russian art. He made two revolutions in Russian modern art — first *Moscow–Paris*, then *Le Territoire de l'Art*. There are not many people who influence so much."[46] "Russian art before and after *Le Territoire de l'Art* are two completely different things — it changed everything," says Ekaterina Andreeva. "No exhibition can ever have such influence again, it's impossible. Pontus was first. I'm sure he paid a high price for it."[47]

Several of the Russian artists who participated in *Le Territoire de l'Art* were later invited to Paris during the remaining years of IHEAP's existence. Hultén's particular favorites Afrika and Timur both visited the school on repeated occasions as lecturers and guests. "You always knew you were welcome at the Institute," says Afrika.[48] Elena Gubanova was invited to spend a month in Paris during the summer, when the school was closed and she stayed with various artist friends.

"You can imagine what it was like for me from Russia to come to Paris for a whole month ..." she says.[49] According to Olesia Turkina, the self-taught Afrika and Timur always proudly pointed out afterwards that they were not self-educated but "trained by Pontus Hultén at IHEAP in Paris."

Pontus Hultén stayed in touch with Afrika in particular over the years. He became one of the young friends and disciples that Hultén gathered around him in the art world. Marie-Louise von Plessen says that Hultén "admired" the young Leningrad legend, who, like Timur Novikov,[50] is represented in the collection that Hultén donated to Moderna Museet.[51] "He was my spiritual and artistic father," says Afrika himself. "I have been interested in Buddhism, where it's important to honor your teachers. I would like to start a movement of artists all over the world working in the tradition that he stood for and that is missing in art today."[52]

28

A realized dream of Venice?

The teaching role at IHEAP, something of an exception in his career, was far from Pontus Hultén's only professional engagement during these years from the mid-eighties to the early nineties. Hultén himself has said that after the setbacks in Los Angeles and with the cancellation of the World Fair in Paris, he didn't have to worry about his daily livelihood after all.[1] He had already been hired for another large and prestigious assignment, again as founding director of an art institution — the glamorous Palazzo Grassi in Venice.

It's hardly surprising that Pontus Hultén had a long-standing fascination with this unique little diamond of a city whose fame is of such magnitude that on first visits the place appears like a caricature. Venice's historical legacy, with its combination of shipping, trade and art, where the city had its own distinctive Renaissance somewhat later than that of Florence, with artists such as Bellini, Titian, Tintoretto and Veronese, was naturally captivating to Hultén. In modern art, too, Venice's position was well established, with the International Biennale, the world's oldest, founded in 1895, and Peggy Guggenheim, who had moved to Venice in 1949 and opened her home with its incomparable collection as a gallery in 1951.

Pontus Hultén had regularly visited Venice and Italy since early in his career, indeed ever since his Italian art excursions during his studies. He had been involved in continuous exchanges with the city in professional engagements, with the Venice Biennale, where he had been curator of the Swedish pavilion in 1964 and 1966, and with Peggy Guggenheim, lender to several of his exhibitions over the years, whose collection he had shown at Moderna Museet in 1967.

In the mid-seventies, Hultén had been recruited as an advisor by the

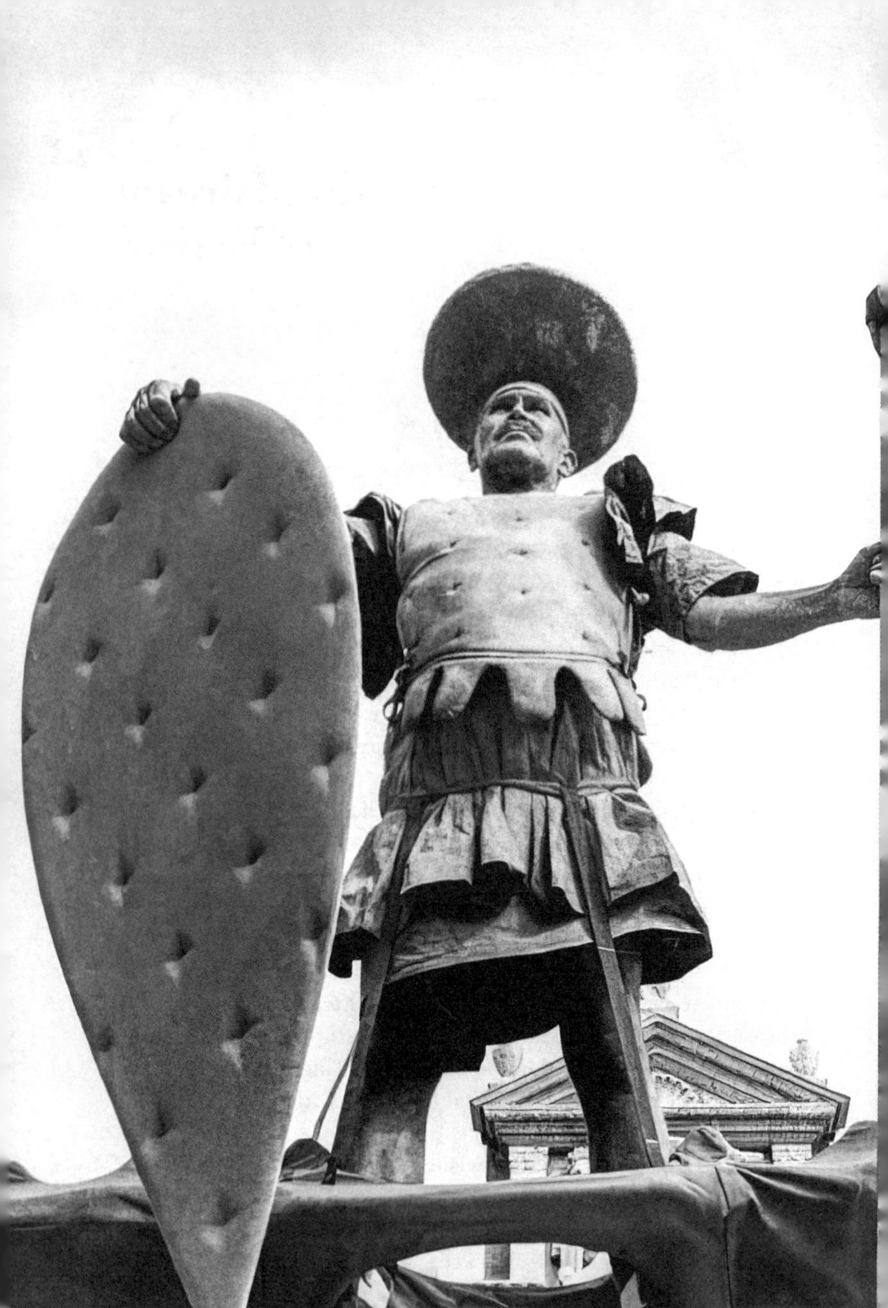

architect and designer Vittorio Gregotti, who at the time was working on a modernization and relaunch of the biennial after the event had almost succumbed in the heated political conflicts of the sixties. Gregotti was part of a team tasked with creating the new and expanded version of the event, which from 1980 included an architecture biennial. Gregotti had been a player in the Italian and international art world since the early 1960s and had met Hultén in 1962 when he visited Moderna Museet during the preparations for *4 Americans*. "The biennal we worked on in 1976[2] was the first real one organized since 1968," says Gregotti,[3] who, like his friend, colleague and compatriot Renzo Piano, was himself part of the sixty-eight movement. "Pontus came for the first time a few years earlier. He stayed in a room at our house in Venice. This was during the time when he was director of Pompidou. Of course he was most important to the Biennale with his name, ideas and contacts."[4]

How beautiful that the fourth country where Pontus Hultén was to help found an art institution[5] was Italy, the home of the Renaissance, where modern art had a weak tradition at the time. With the exception of the Venice Biennale and Peggy Guggenheim's gallery, and smaller avant-garde scenes in Rome, Milan and Turin, Italy had exercised limited influence in the modern art world since the Futurist movement of the 1910s and 1920s. In 1985, when Pontus Hultén took up his position at Palazzo Grassi, the country had few internationally successful artists and no modern museum of international standing. The post-war lull was still in effect after forty years of peace in the Italian museum world. Italy had remained untouched by the revolution that had taken place in Paris with the opening of the Centre Pompidou eight years prior and by the earlier development of progressive modern museums in northern and central Europe. The position of modern art in the wider Italian public was non-existent. Modern art was not included in the curriculum of Italian universities. The collections of Italian museums came to a halt after the beginning of the twentieth century. Since then, there had been no funding for purchases.

The reasons why this institution, Palazzo Grassi, was created in Venice, and why Pontus Hultén was recruited as its founding director,

Pontus Hultén as the knight/patron saint St. Theodore in Claes Oldenburg and Coosje van Bruggen's performance "Il Corso del Coltello," Campo dell' Arsenale, Venice, 1985. Hultén, Oldenburg, van Bruggen, Frank Gehry and the initiator Germano Celant all played two characters each.

can be found in the glamorous circuits of the industrialist and global super-playboy Gianni Agnelli, which included two old acquaintances: once again Jean Tinguely and, above all, Niki de Saint Phalle.

The link between Agnelli and Niki de Saint Phalle dated back to New York in the late 1940s and early 1950s, during Niki's career as a star model. Also living in New York at the time was Gianni Agnelli's wife Marella Agnelli, commonly referred to as Donna Marella. Until her marriage to Agnelli in 1953, she was Princess Marella fascination Caracciolo dei Principi di Castagneto, born in Florence to a father who was Prince of Castagneto, Duke of Melito and Neapolitan patrician, and a mother who was a wealthy American heiress to a whiskey distillery. Marella Caracciolo worked as a photographer's assistant and model in New York, and was immortalized as the youngest of Truman Capote's "swans" — the most glamorous women of upper Manhattan — along with Jacqueline Kennedy's sister Lee Radziwill and Babe Paley in *Breakfast at Tiffany's*.[6] Marella Agnelli, with her famous "swan neck," gave rise to the expression said to have been coined by fashion photographer Richard Avedon after he photographed Agnelli in 1953. Niki de Saint Phalle and Marella Agnelli had been friends ever since.

Donna Marella Agnelli became famous as an interior, garden and fashion designer. She had a deep interest in art and culture, with great knowledge and famously exquisite taste.[7] It's widely believed that it was Marella who, if not aroused, encouraged and developed her husband Gianni's interest in art and collecting. The couple had been well known in the international art world since the 1950s and had built an impressive collection in their homes in Turin, Rome, Marrakech, New York, St. Moritz and elsewhere around the world, ranging from Impressionism, Matisse, Picasso, Modigliani, Futurism and Symbolism to Pop and later contemporary art.

Industrial magnate Giovanni "Gianni" Agnelli, Pontus Hultén's main client in Venice, held a position as the controlling owner and chairman of the Fiat car group, founded by his grandfather, that is difficult to understand today. In Italy, which at this time changed governments at short intervals, where monarchy was abolished and few outside the country knew the name of the president, Agnelli acted for a long period as Italy's informal head of state. He was received at the White House, the Élysée Palace and Buckingham Palace, kept Henry Kissinger as a political advisor, negotiated and conducted business with Muammar al-Gaddafi (for a time a partner in Fiat) and counted among his friends many of the world's heads of states, royalty and

Giovanni "Gianni" Agnelli, also known as "L'Avvocato," "The Lawyer," 1986.

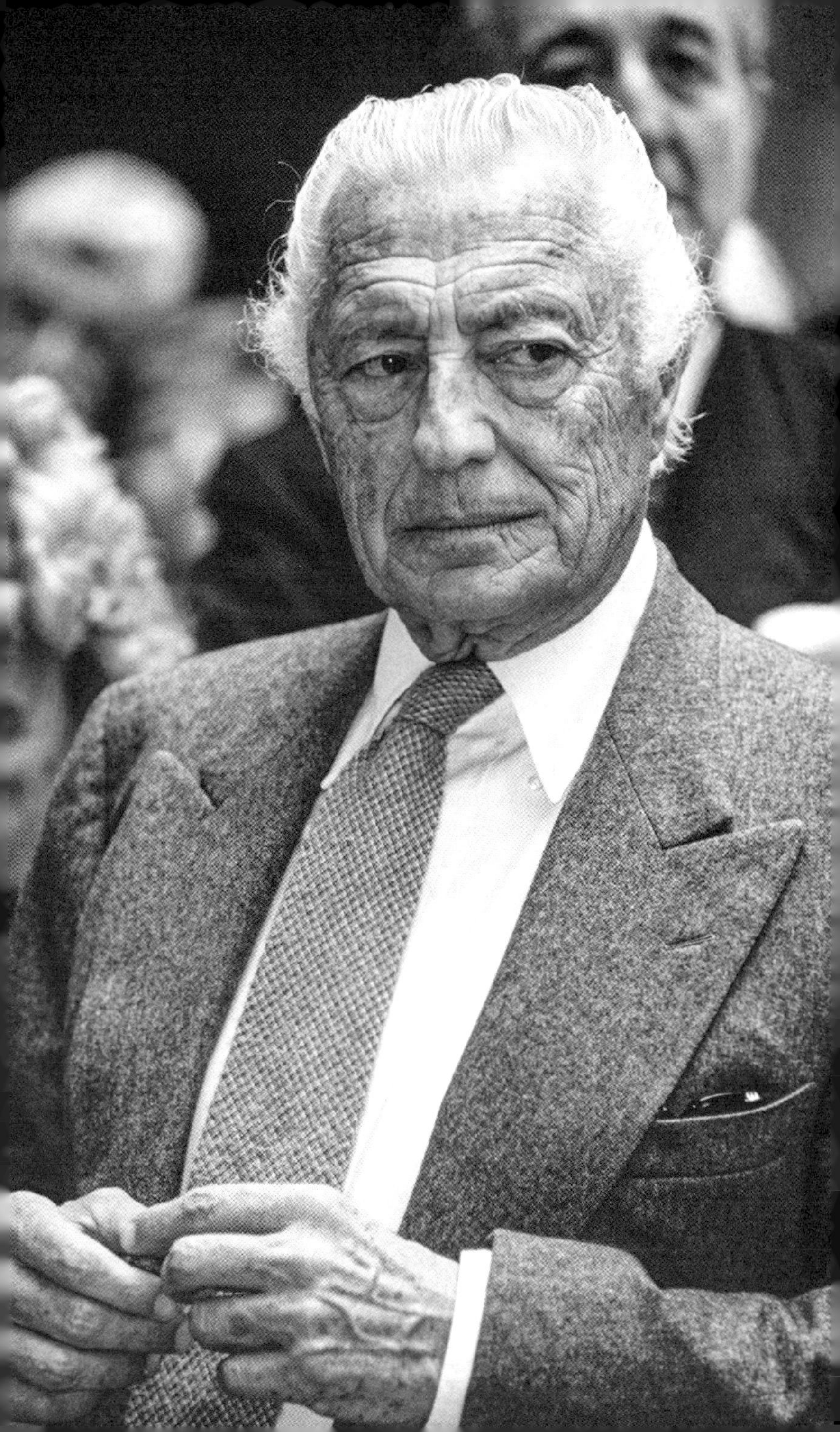

biggest stars. Agnelli commanded influence over the Italian press as owner of the leading daily newspaper La Stampa in his hometown of Turin.

To a wider audience around the world, Agnelli was known primarily as the playboy above all others, notoriously present in the tabloid and celebrity press where he was constantly associated with Ferrari cars, Formula 1, the Juventus football team, yachts in the Mediterranean, his slightly nonchalant yet impeccably formal dandy elegance and a parade of striking mistresses. Gianni Agnelli's taste for the good jet-set life was incurably Italian. Throughout his career, he fought against this media image in his efforts to present himself as a serious business leader, statesman and cultural figure. His interest in art and activities in the international art world are seen by many as part of these efforts. Although his wife Donna Marella was generally considered a more sophisticated art connoisseur, the authenticity of Gianni Agnelli's interest in art could not be questioned. He considered himself a Renaissance man, sporting a habit of displaying detailed expertise in various fields, not least art.

The relationship between Niki de Saint Phalle and the Agnelli and Caracciolo families intensified in the late seventies when Niki began building her sculpture park Giardino dei Tarocchi in 1979. Niki herself has revealed that it was Pontus Hultén who advised her to consider Italy when she started planning this life's work.[8] The artist contacted Donna Marella, who suggested she talk to her brothers Carlo and Nicola, who had summer estates in Garavicchio, the Caracciolo family's private hilltop village in a secluded, exclusive corner of southwestern Tuscany, an hour and a half's drive north of Rome; a haven for sophisticated Roman society since ancient times.[9]

The Caracciolo brothers agreed immediately when Niki approached them with his request. They provided a generous piece of land at the foot of the Garavicchio hill, overlooking the bay, where the artist could realize her dream of a sculpture park from 1979 to 1997.

The Giardino dei Tarocchi, which opened to the public in 1998, is now a discreet destination that attracts over a hundred thousand visitors from all over the world during the open summer months to this part of Tuscany, which otherwise has few foreign tourists. The twenty-two sculptures represent the tarot cards. Visitors can enter several of the largest of these (even the Tarot sculptures can be considered children of *she*), grouped around a square, sparkling and shiny in color and mosaics, with a moon rocket like the one from Tintin's *Destination Moon* in the church's place — a fantasy world where the art joyously borders on the domain of the amusement park. Niki's own apartment, where she lived during her long periods of work in fascination Garavicchio, located in the Sphinx sculpture, is an inspiring architectural and interior design experience — a futuristic/surrealist dream nest clad in mirrored mosaic that evokes associations with sixties James Bond films, *Clockwork Orange* and *2001: A Space Odyssey*. Nicola Caracciolo smiles as he explains: "Niki first came here in 1978. She said from the beginning that she wanted to do something very simple and low-key, without any color and decoration. It had to be so modest and invisible. Then when she started — well, we see how it turned out ..."[10]

Pontus Hultén was a regular guest at Garavicchio, involved from the beginning in the creation and development of Niki de Saint Phalle's fantasy garden. Here he met the Caracciolo family and Donna Marella Agnelli, with whom he was already acquainted and had encountered with her husband Gianni Agnelli in Turin, Paris, New York and elsewhere in the art world. Giardino dei Tarocchi became another entry point into the Italian art world, society and social establishment for Hultén.

The common view is that it was Donna Marella — another important woman in Hultén's career — who raised the idea of a public Italian art scene funded by Fiat. The choice of Venice for such an initiative, rather than the Agnelli family and Fiat's home city of Turin, was controversial among the car company's shareholders and executives. The reason was that in 1983 the Fiat group had swallowed up a bankrupt, sprawling Italian industrial conglomerate called SNIA Viscosa. Among the properties included in the purchase was Palazzo Grassi, a dilapidated eighteenth century palace on the Grand Canal, where the group's president had presented arts and crafts exhibitions, including shows on the history of costume and fashion. Fiat considered selling the palace but decided instead to develop its artistic activities through a major investment in a modern art museum — or indeed formally an art gallery — with high-flying international aspirations.

Fiat and Gianni Agnelli's motivation for creating a new arena for modern art in Italy is said to have been the ambition to elegantly build a positive image for the troubled, strike-ridden group. "Venice was brilliant — as far from the usual advertising as one could get," says Germano Celant, Pontus Hultén's colleague in Venice.[11] Another reason for locating this art initiative in Venice is said to have been that

Gianni Agnelli's sister Susanna aspired to the post of mayor of the city.

Germano Celant, the famous art historian, author and curator[12] who later in his career would become artistic director of the Fondazione Prada in Milan, artistic director of the Venice Biennale and senior curator of contemporary art at the Guggenheim Museum in New York, was hired by Hultén at Palazzo Grassi from the start in 1985. Celant emphasizes that political and diplomatic ambitions on the part of Fiat and Gianni Agnelli played into the plans for the new institution. "It was a damn smart idea to use Grassi for representation and international meetings," says Celant. "It was still during the Cold War and art had become a neutral meeting place for unofficial contacts between the Russians and the West. The Guggenheim was used for international meetings, among other venues. You could use art as a political tool, in secret. You invite someone to participate in an art exhibition and meet through this. Grassi was a pioneer. It was very political. For example, there were meetings between Russia and the Vatican and with Iran."[13]

Once it was decided to create an international art institution in Palazzo Grassi, Pontus Hultén was the obvious and sole candidate for the post of founding director of the new institution. According to some reports, Hultén had been "linked" to the Agnellis even before Fiat acquired Palazzo Grassi. A pattern began to emerge in which Hultén, like a professional football player, was recruited by museum after museum as a figurehead and battering ram, tasked with placing these institutions on the world map of international art, as the old worn-out metaphor goes.

The assignment of contacting Hultén was entrusted to one of Gianni Agnelli's closest associates, a man with the wonderful pseudonym Furio Colombo (actually Marc Saudade). Colombo, a childhood friend of Donna Marella Agnelli, was a journalist for the state broadcaster Rai and for La Stampa in Milan. He moved to New York in the early 1960s to become the paper's correspondent. There, he was recruited to the business world, first to the typewriter giant Olivetti, Italy's largest and most high-profile multinational industrial company after Fiat, where he worked for its heir Adriano Olivetti, before being enrolled back by Gianni Agnelli, now as head of North America for Fiat — a bold career move for a journalist. His friends included international politicians, businessmen, freedom fighters, writers, artists, directors and performers. As the head of Fiat in the US with this unusual background for a business leader, he was the right man to approach Hultén. "I went to Los Angeles and met him for the first time at Temporary Contemporary," says Furio Colombo. "I had only heard of him before, but spontaneously liked him right away. He was nice in the typical Pontus way — very straightforward, no unnecessary small talk. He had something so rare as a serious humor. There was often a serious undertone even when he was joking. He told me about the problems he had in Los Angeles and was immediately very open to discussing a collaboration."[14]

Colombo describes the negotiations with Hultén as uncomplicated. "We hardly talked about money, but almost exclusively about his independence. He was adamant that he demanded to be completely autonomous with total artistic control. I already had a mandate to guarantee him complete sovereignty. For Agnelli and Fiat, it was important for credibility that Grassi should not be directly associated with the company or with Agnelli himself. They didn't want people to suspect that they were influencing the content or wanting to promote Fiat. With Hultén, that was guaranteed. No one would ever suspect him of being controlled. When he agreed to come to Venice, we then planned the operations entirely around Pontus."[15]

Palazzo Grassi became the second consecutive private art institution for Hultén, a former sworn enemy of private museums. However, the contrast with Eli Broad and Hollywood was stark. With enlightened, cultured, politically nuanced European magnates like Gianni Agnelli, Pontus Hultén rarely had any serious cooperation or social problems.

According to Furio Colombo, the Palazzo Grassi institution was thus created on the basis of Pontus Hultén. The benchmark was obvious: Centre Pompidou of course, the mega-cultural center in Paris with the museum that under Hultén's leadership had become the world's most influential art arena. The vision was a Centre Pompidou in miniature — a dynamic cultural center that would also offer a library, cinema/theater, restaurant and other public meeting venues. Like Moderna Museet and Pompidou, the palace would be open every day of the week until late in the evening, as an illuminated, permanently accessible department store for art and culture — another version of Hultén's model with larger, broader, more public venues for the fine arts and more.

Pontus Hultén elaborated how important this expanded function was in Venice, where public meeting places such as cinemas were lacking and where the social life of the city died out in the early evening after which the fabulous alleys and canals lay black and deserted.[16] The ambitions went far beyond Venice. From the outset, it was a stated goal that Palazzo Grassi would become a leading art scene nationally and internationally. With Gianni Agnelli in charge, expectations couldn't be higher. It was the first time that Agnelli and Fiat had become involved in culture, and only the best was good enough. The Italian Ministry of Culture and the City of Venice were also involved and supported the project.

The conditions must have seemed almost optimal for Pontus Hultén to create another unique institution based on his grand vision of art as an engine in a larger cultural, social and political whole — especially since the financial resources seemed unlimited. As in Paris, Pontus Hultén thought he had an "open budget" at his disposal. This time, too, he was deceived. Serge Fauchereau, Hultén's collaborator from the Centre Pompidou and later at the school and elsewhere, who was of course appointed to work on the exhibitions at Palazzo Grassi, recounts: "Pontus said that now boys — now you will see how to spend money! He claimed that there were no restrictions on what it could cost but, as usual, it didn't last. It got a bit expensive in the end ..."[17] There are no public figures for the budget for Palazzo Grassi, but the amounts involved were sky-high for the time, even in comparison with the largest international museum initiatives.

Unfortunately, two constraints dogged the potential of the Palazzo Grassi. The planned combined theater and cinema was postponed indefinitely. The reasons given by Fiat's management representatives were practical and bureaucratic — that the old theater in the palace park was condemned for fire safety and other technical reasons, that it was needed for storage, etc. Hultén regretted that without a theater and a cinema, Palazzo Grassi could not fulfill its intended function as a social public venue for a broader cultural audience.[18]

The second limitation that Pontus Hultén had to reluctantly accept was the decision not to invest in building a collection for the new institution. Palazzo Grassi would thus become not a museum but an art gallery for temporary exhibitions, albeit an utterly extravagant one. Hultén argued with his clients on this crucial issue, advocating his firm belief that the new institution must build its own collection, however costly such an investment might seem. His idea, as in Los Angeles, was to acquire primarily post-war art, especially Italian art. This seemed too expensive for Fiat. Hultén made a different calculation — that the collection would become the museum's capital, which would facilitate and reduce the costs of temporary exhibitions in the longer term. Without an anchor in the "collective memory," the temporary exhibitions would be left hanging in the air and nothing would be left for posterity, Hultén firmly believed. He also repeatedly emphasized that without its own collection, an institution becomes vulnerable and at the mercy of its clients and others.

Pontus Hultén lost this battle. It was hardly any consolation that history proved him right. Palazzo Grassi didn't become a miniature Centre Pompidou. With its own collection, the palace might have continued to function as the cultural center it was intended to be. A foundation could have been Gianni Agnelli's own collection, but the magnate's generosity apparently did not extend that far.

Pontus Hultén moved to Venice in the spring of 1985[19]. He immediately felt at home in the city and in his residence in an elegant penthouse at the top of the palace itself, furnished with precious Venetian antiques. There were handsome apartments for other staff members and visiting artists. Hultén's salary was generous and all his expenses, including his residence, were paid. Of course, he also had one of his boats, the two-masted "Lediga stunder" ("Free Times"), shipped to Venice, in which he regularly escaped for day trips in the lagoon and more distant excursions to the Adriatic and Croatia. It is hardly surprising that the storied Harry's Bar became Hultén's regular haunt in Venice. Here and at the Skipper's Club, where he was a member, Hultén enjoyed sitting with different groups most evenings. He developed a taste for Italian drinks like grappa and Fernet-Branca, downing them in quantities that frightened his colleagues. For me, Pontus Hultén in Venice bears an unavoidable, heavily Hemingwayian association. In pictures where he sails his open boat in the city with his broad chest and mustache, the visual similarities with "Papa" are striking. Only the skipper's beard is missing.

Shortly after his arrival, during the Architecture Biennale in September 1985, Pontus Hultén made a spectacular public entrance in Venice as an actor in Claes Oldenburg's legendary performance "Il Corso del Coltello," together with Oldenburg himself, Coosje van Bruggen, Germano Celant and the architect Frank Gehry. The performance began with Hultén sloped over a table dressed as a boxer, snoring loudly. "The museum management, the Venice city council and the directors of Fiat were very nervous when they saw that and wondered who the hell they had hired," said Germano Celant (Milan interview, April 18, 2016).

During the years in Venice, Hultén's main female relationship was with the famous German artist Rebecca Horn. It's said that Hultén nurtured a dream of retiring to Venice with Horn. Reality would thwart this plan. The reportedly stormy relationship came to a bitter end after six years.

Hultén entertained a generally good relationship with his client Gianni Agnelli. Expectedly, Agnelli is portrayed as a man who did not let anyone get too close to him. Pontus Hultén apparently got along well with Agnelli on a formal level, even though everyone I've spoken to emphasizes that it was with his wife Marella that Hultén had a warm friendship with mutual respect. Ida Gianelli confides that at the beginning of his engagement in Venice, Hultén tried to strike a more personal note with Gianni Agnelli by inviting him for a cruise on his boat. "Agnelli didn't understand what he was doing there. It was very awkward and never repeated," says Gianelli.[20]

A complicating factor was that Palazzo Grassi was not owned by Gianni Agnelli, although he was its initiator and figurehead. The palace and the new art institution were a hundred percent controlled by the Fiat Group. Although Agnelli was chairman of the board and heir to the founding family, there were other major shareholders and power players, including major financial institutions, the city of Turin and even the Italian state. The management included influential patrons who didn't see the big picture in terms of artistic achievements, positive image, representation and informal diplomacy, but looked at Palazzo Grassi in strictly economic terms. One of these was Agnelli's own brother Umberto, who, although interested in art, looked at costs rather than results. "Grassi's operations were controlled by people who were used to counting screws in the car industry," as Germano Celant phrases it.[21]

Although Fiat would not flaunt its brand, Pontus Hultén was actually an employee of the car company. "Pontus never understood that," says Ida Gianelli. "It didn't matter how many times I explained it to him. I tried to make him understand that Agnelli had contributed nothing himself, zero, but that Fiat and its shareholders controlled everything. These people were the kings of Italy and people with a lot of money demand control. There were problems after just six months. Pontus thought he was guaranteed independence but in fact he was not independent at all. His belief that it was a museum was a misunderstanding. It was Palazzo Grassi S.P.A., a subsidiary of Fiat."[22]

One of Pontus Hultén's superiors was Cesare Annibaldi, the right-hand man of CEO Cesare Romiti and head of public relations for Fiat. With him, Hultén was on an immediate collision course. "Annibaldi was more powerful than Pontus and Pontus did not understand that sometimes it's better to play along," says Ida Gianelli. "When these people asked questions, he refused to answer. He refused to cooperate with them. He didn't think he should have to explain himself to them. This led to constant fights and confrontations from start to finish."[23]

Pontus Hultén was forced to yield to Agnelli and the Fiat management when it came to the architecture of the extensive renovation and reconstruction of Palazzo Grassi for the purposes of the new art institution. Hultén advocated Renzo Piano, but the commission for the transformation of the palace went instead to the female Italian architect Gaetana Aulenti, known as Gae Aulenti, the hottest interior designer in the European art world at the time. Hultén already had some history with Aulenti, who became known for her interior design for the Musée d'Orsay in Paris, an architectural solution that many in Pontus Hultén's entourage, including Hultén himself, were critical of for its lack of openness and overview. Aulenti had been commissioned by Hultén's successor Dominique Bozo to rebuild the Centre Pompidou to limit the original total openness of Piano and Rogers' design and introduce more traditional galleries. The choice of Gae Aulenti, who was well-connected in Venice, seems to have been a local affair over which Hultén had little influence. Aulenti's creative partner in the project was the Venetian architect Antonio Foscari, one of Venice's leading patricians. "It was necessary to bring someone from the Venetian aristocracy into the project and Foscari is a count," says Ida Gianelli.[24]

At our meeting in Venice, Count Antonio Foscari, who became a good friend of Pontus Hultén, recounts memories of the renovation and his impressions of Gae Aulenti and Gianni Agnelli, the magnate who does not seem to have excessively impressed this nobleman. "When I was hired for the project, I was a professor of architectural history and involved in the Save Venice Committee," says Foscari. "There was little time, one year, for the reconstruction, and a very big project. Fiat had never done anything like this before. Gae Aulenti was chosen by Donna Marella. She was fascinating, a prince's consigliere. She could be very hard on subordinates, very authoritarian, but she was committed. Mostly she was fascinated by herself. She knew how to make herself public and a star. It suited me well because I don't like to be public. She was afraid of me and didn't want to accept my ideas. She was very interesting as a person."[25]

The distinguished Count Foscari, who during his life in Venice and in the international art world befriended many great artists, formulates a fine portrait of Pontus Hultén: "Pontus talked very little. He was solid. He had an idea and didn't get involved in discussions. He talked a little with The Lawyer [Gianni Agnelli's nickname], that's all. He was completely autonomous and didn't want any contact or exchange of ideas. He had a charm and a power. I once asked him about how to make museums. 'With a smile,' he replied. It was not intellectual. You know what to do and you do it with a smile. Sometimes he would go away with his boat and a bottle of whisky and be gone for two days. We'd go to a restaurant and talk like old friends. 'It's a beautiful day. What would you like to eat? A pasta sciutta?'[26] He had problems with Gae that he talked about. We also talked about music experiences we had."[27]

It is said that during the Venice Biennale it has always been popular with international celebrities to visit Antonio Foscari at his famous Villa Foscari "La Malcontenta" ("The Discontent"), Andrea Palladio's famous late Renaissance villa (1558–1560), where an ultra-radical chandelier by Jean Tinguely adorns the salon.

Pontus Hultén spoke and wrote with polite appreciation of Gae Aulenti's interior solution for Palazzo Grassi.[28] In private, he was less enthusiastic. The plan that he himself and Renzo Piano envisioned was certainly more radical.

It was thus with what were in many ways good but fundamentally compromised conditions and complicating conflicts that Pontus Hultén took up his position as director of the new art venue Palazzo Grassi. He was formally appointed in the fall of 1984, and in the spring of 1985 began working on the planning of the opening exhibition while the reconstruction of the palace was underway, with two hundred and fifty construction workers in a race against the clock.

In recruiting his team of curators and other collaborators, Hultén enjoyed complete freedom from his patrons. The choice of the young radical Germano Celant as his closest collaborator was natural but nevertheless bold and progressive. Pontus Hultén and Vittorio Gregotti had already hired Germano Celant for the Venice Biennale in 1976, but he had resigned due to difficulties in cooperation with other actors at the Italian pavilion[29] — a rebellious move for a young curator. At the end of the seventies, he was again engaged by Hultén to organize the exhibition *Italian Identity. Art in Italy since 1959* at the Centre Pompidou,[30] including the artists of the Arte Povera movement. "It was a fantastic trust he gave me there, with completely free hands at the Pompidou, which was then bigger than MoMA," says Celant at our meeting in Milan. "I was given carte blanche to do whatever I wanted. He didn't interfere with anything."[31]

Pontus Hultén also hired Celant's former long-term life partner, the aforementioned Ida Gianelli, who was responsible for the scientific part of the exhibition activities. "He needed someone who understood Italian culture," says Gianelli. "That's understandable, because it is difficult even for me to understand."[32]

The creative team for the 1986 premiere exhibition was supplemented by Hultén's associates from *Paris-Moscow*, Serge Fauchereau and Stanislas Zadora. Through Ida Gianelli, the young Venetian linguist Clarenza Catullo, who had previously worked as a volunteer at Peggy Guggenheim's gallery, was hired as Pontus Hultén's secretary and assistant. Catullo became a counterpart in Venice to Annick Boisnard and Nathalie Meneau in Paris; Meneau who had been hired as Hultén's personal and professional secretary and assistant and who would work closely with Hultén for the rest of his life. Clarenza Catullo also collaborated with Hultén for many years on assignments ranging from highly complex commissions to constant practicalities such as shipping and travel. Hultén's archives contain copious amounts of correspondence between Catullo and Meneau, garnished with pleasantries, which highlight the complicated practical aspects of Hultén's hectic professional and personal life during the eighties, nineties and early twenty-first century. It was a small but potent team he gathered around him in Venice. "We all became close friends in our group and we felt we were doing something important for the Fiat people in Turin and for Italy," says Germano Celant. "I was the one with the most experience, even though I was young. We were several people from Genoa and we are known for our grumpiness. We were a grumpy, grumpy group."[33]

The subject of the opening exhibition was an open question when Pontus Hultén assumed the directorship at Palazzo Grassi. Options discussed included Pop Art and Claes Oldenburg — quite conventional, one might argue. Soon a more exciting motif was chosen: Futurism, of course.

Very far from being as obvious as it may seem

Curator and critic Germano Celant earned international fame when he named the movement Arte Povera and published its manifesto in 1967 in Flash Art magazine. In Celant's analysis, the differences between this Italian art movement — with artists such as Giovanni Anselmo, Jannis Kounellis, Mario Merz, Michelangelo Pistoletti, Giuseppe Penone and others — and the contemporary American Pop Art movement could be explained by the Italian artists originating from a smaller, later industrialized and commercialized society, closer to nature and inherited traditions. Italian artists were driven by humanism, not by trends, "coolness" and sophisticated image-making like American Pop artists, Celant argued.

Several of his Italian colleagues and friends mention that Pontus Hultén developed a good understanding of the Italian language but kept this secret from his employers and colleagues.

thirty-five years later, this choice of subject matter was explosively charged and controversial. Italy's major contribution to the history of modern art, this pioneering young Modernist movement, remained stigmatized in its home country at the time because of its association with fascism. No exhibition of Futurism had been organized in Italy after the war, and hardly any internationally. Futurism was at this time still a repressed historical art movement.

"Pontus was the only person in the world who could have come to Italy and taken on Futurism, and he knew it," says Olle Granath,[34] who, as director of Moderna Museet, worked closely with Hultén throughout his Venice years.

That the idea to focus on Futurism was Pontus Hultén's own is not undisputed. Some reports suggest that it may have come from Gianni Agnelli himself. Agnelli owned an impressive Futurist collection, mainly by Giacomo Balla, one of the movement's major artists. Still, most people agree that the idea was Hultén's, but that it may have surfaced after he visited Agnelli's home in Turin and saw this collection.

Futurism was a worthy subject for another of Pontus Hultén's epically multidisciplinary mammoth manifestations. "It's self-evident that Futurism was irresistible to him, with its theme of movement and other qualities," as Olle Granath says.[35] Needless to add, the Futurist exhibition, which was named *Futurismo & Futurismi* (*Futurism & Futurisms*), took a far broader approach than painting and sculpture. The exhibition and catalog featured expressions such as architecture — a highly interesting feature/chapter — industrial design, fashion, photography, film, performing arts, graphic design and typography, music and more. Futurism's extreme philosophies on gastronomy were also highlighted, and of course not least the rich, politically compromised Futurist literature and poetry, led by the incomparable Filippo Tommaso Marinetti.

Nor would Hultén have been Hultén if he had confined himself to Italy. The exhibition surveyed the world to trace the movement's offshoots in different continents, including Japan and several South American countries — art that was largely unknown in Italy and the rest of the art world. "It was I who told Pontus that there was a South American Futurism, but of course he made the idea his own," says Serge Fauchereau. "Then we got to travel to South America to look for works."[36] Stanislas Zadora was assigned responsibility for the extensive section on Futurism in the Soviet Union and Eastern Europe, the part of the art world outside Italy where the Futurist movement had the greatest impact and where Mayakovsky became a leader and representative whom Hultén in his catalog preface compares with Marinetti in Italy.[37]

The exhibition and catalog included a historical section, presented on the ground floor of the palace, featuring the precursors, inspirers and contemporaries of Futurism, as well as the works of Futurist artists before Futurism. There were paintings and sculptures by Picasso, Raymond Duchamp-Villon, František Kupa, Alberto Giacometti, Mikhail Larionov, suites of images by Eadweard Muybridge and Étienne-Jules Marey, pioneers of the moving photographic image; but also works by older artists such as Edvard Munch and Georges Seurat.

The Post-Impressionist and Pointillist Georges Seurat, incidentally, was the artist among the Impressionists whom Marcel Duchamp ranked highest — higher than Cézanne. (Pierre Cabanne, *Dialogues with Marcel Duchamp*, Thames and Hudson Ltd, London, 1971, p. 93).

The focus of the exhibition on the first floor was the "heroic years" of mature Italian Futurism, in Hultén's words in the catalog,[38] before, during and after the First World War, with its five main artists Umberto Boccioni, Giacomo Balla, Carlo Carrà, Luigi Russolo and Gino Severini. Filippo Marinetti's violently dynamic cartoon and typographic images and Antonio Sant'Elia and Mario Chiattone's incredible unrealized sketches from the early 1910s of skyscrapers, industrial plants and utopian urban fantasy landscapes were also featured in this section.

The continuation and succession of Futurism in Italy, and the movement's influence throughout the world, was displayed in an extensive section on the upper floor of the palace and in the catalog, with an overwhelming number of masterpieces on loan. Marcel Duchamp was represented by his eternal "Nude Woman Descending a Staircase No.2" (1912), borrowed from the Philadelphia Museum of Art, and "Sad Young Man on a Train" (1911–1912) from the Peggy Guggenheim Collection in Venice, two paintings from the brief, formative period when Duchamp was influenced by Futurism. Picabia and Malevich, the German Dadaists Max Ernst, George Grosz and Otto Dix, and many of the shapers of Modernism were represented with masterpieces in this section. Sweden's sole surviving Futurist Gösta Adrian-Nilsson, GAN, the sailor painter, flew his colors well in this prominent company. Futurism in the "applied arts" — industrial design, performing arts, fashion and more — was also presented on this upper floor. A Hulténian show trick was two Italian airplanes from the 1910s, a utopian plane from 1911 and a World War I fighter, hanging from the ceiling in the skylight. Borrowing all these works and objects from museums, other institutions and private collectors from around the world was a costly endeavor, all the more difficult than at the museums Hultén had previously directed since Palazzo Grassi had no collection of its own to draw on or use for barter. Since there were no works of their own to trade, they had to pay for each loan, in many cases by financing renovations of the works of art,[39] in others in actual cash.

There were also cultural and logistical problems to contend with. At the time, Italian museums and institutions had no tradition of major modern art exhibitions and were not granted international loans as they were not considered reliable. "Pontus thought I was joking when I told him," says Ida Gianelli. "For a hundred letters of inquiry, you got a hundred no's."[40] The systems for insurance, transportation and other logistics were outdated and substandard. Transportation presented a particular challenge as the only way to bring the objects to the palace was by boat, with risks and stresses to the fragile artworks. With the names and contacts of Pontus Hultén and Gianni Agnelli, and Fiat's generous budget, these obstacles were overcome and loans were secured from many of the world's top museums and institutions, including MoMA in New York, with by far the world's finest collection of Futurism.

The Futurist exhibition at Palazzo Grassi was the first in Europe to take a holistic approach to this controversial artistic movement, with a total of nearly four hundred artworks and thirteen hundred objects, including the documents in the literature section.[41] The exhibition is a landmark in art historical knowledge and research on Futurism.

Germano Celant confides that he and his colleagues learned a lot from working with Pontus Hultén in preparing for this gigantic event, with an impossibly short production time of one year. "In Italy there was no culture of organizing modern art exhibitions," says Celant. "Pontus brought a whole new professionalism. He taught us things like how to work with architects and how to deal with lenders and never take no for an answer but keep asking until you get a yes. He once sent Peggy Guggenheim a hundred red roses every three days until she agreed to lend him a Picabia he wanted, he told me."[42]

With the catalog for *Futurismo & Futurismi* — like the other catalogs from Hultén's time at Palazzo Grassi published by Bompiani in Milan — Pontus Hultén and his collaborators wrote another thick chapter in art history. Like the Pingpong catalogs, the Futurist catalog is a brick — the art catalog as a doctoral thesis and coffee table book once again: a massive, more than three kilograms heavy piece of six hundred and forty pages, Italian chic and extravagance, elegantly designed by the Milanese graphic designer and architect Pierluigi Cerri, with soft covers printed on mirrored paper, playfully typographed in bright, gaudy colors. Palazzo Grassi's international ambitions and at least initially muscular financial resources are demonstrated by the fact that this luxurious catalog was published in two separate language editions, Italian and English. The effort and cost of translating this vast material was certainly considerable. The catalog's introduction presents the list of the "Friends of Palazzo Grassi," with names such as Claude Pompidou, MoMA director Richard Oldenburg and Thomas M. Messer — a collection of prominent figures who gave international weight to the new institution. "That association was purely formal," says Antonio Foscari. "All the decisions were already taken when it convened."[43]

In several unusually long prefaces to the catalog, Pontus Hultén begins by explaining that the ambition of the Futurist exhibition was to explore the artistic movements of the early twentieth century and their cultural and historical context — a historiography that had fallen into oblivion as a result of the tragic history of the later century.[44] One of the texts is an interesting essay on the influence of Futurism and its relationship to the other early movements of Modernism, primarily Cubism in Paris. Hultén formulates the theory that Modernism developed differently in different countries but that a pattern can be detected: the closer the countries were to Paris, which was the center, the greater the resistance to the new. The "central" art nations were "forced" to rebel through Dadaism, Hultén argues, while more peripheral countries such as Russia and Italy, which did not have the same visual tradition to break with, were more open to the straightforward message and influence of Futurism — in Italy, Dadaism was completely absent, Hultén notes in his text. I don't know if this is common knowledge, but it reads well and appears most Hulténian. He writes that Cubism and Futurism differed in that Cubism was typically Parisian introverted and snobbishly intellectualized, while Futurism was violently extroverted and more easily comprehended — differences he explains with French and Italian cultural characteristics.

In one of his texts, and in other contexts, Pontus Hultén describes the Futurist exhibition as a continuation of the Pingpong exhibitions in Paris, without mentioning these by name — part of a cycle of exhibitions intended to highlight the avant-garde movements of the young century and their impact on the present.

Hultén narrates the unlikely story of how this movement foreshadowed modern marketing by being single-handedly launched as a brand by Marinetti using all available means. Futurism had its own office in Milan, from which the movement's militant message was pumped out around the world, tracking Futurism's global success in press clippings from Armenia to Japan like a modern PR agency. The movement's amazing international success was largely explained by this advanced branding, writes Hultén.

Pontus Hultén conspicuously avoids the question of Futurism's relation to fascism in these texts. He implicitly writes that the Futurists were not fascists but young utopian anarchists who allowed themselves to be carried away by an optimistic spirit of the times. Here, he manages to squeeze in a quote from his beloved Strindberg, "Here we demolish for air and light," as an expression of industrialism's striving for progress. As he elegantly formulates it, both Marinetti in Italy and Mayakovsky in the Soviet Union in their futuristic idealism fell into the hands of forces they could not control, to the misfortune of both — Mayakovsky who committed suicide and Marinetti who was isolated from intellectual life from the thirties onwards.

Hultén's imaginative interpretations are forgiving to Marinetti and Futurism. He and other Futurists were for years active members of the Fascist Party, "useful idiots" or not, and Marinetti was an energetic cultural-political spokesman for the regime, before he realized far too late that Fascism was an authoritarian system that had unleashed oppressive forces far beyond all control. Marinetti himself was an impossible combination of anti-authoritarian, anarchist and totalitarian-militarist in his philosophy.

The Futurist movement's delicate connection to fascism is intricately illustrated by the story of one of the works Hultén wanted to borrow from Gianni Agnelli's own collection, a monumental central canvas by Balla from 1913, which was built into the wall of a salon in Agnelli's Turin home. The magnate was surprisingly reluctant to lend the painting, arguing that the wall would have to be demolished. Pontus Hultén, who refused to accept no's to loans for his exhibitions, naturally could not accept one from his own client. Eventually he managed to persuade Agnelli. Removing the painting from the wall revealed the real reason for his hesitation. On the back side of the canvas, sometime between 1931 and 1933, Balla had painted a snapshot of Mussolini's march to Rome in a kitschy Social Realist style, probably to commemorate the tenth anniversary of the march.[45]

The ceremonial opening of the Palazzo Grassi and the Futurist exhibition on May 3, 1986 was a gigantic event in Venice, in Italy and in the global art and gala world. Guests traveled from all over the world to attend. No one wanted to miss Gianni Agnelli and Fiat's first ever cultural event. Agnelli had anchored a luxury yacht in the harbor, as the palace could not accommodate all the countless Italian and international celebrities. Olle Granath, who attended the opening, says: "It was really an incredibly lavish opening. Afterwards, while standing on Agnelli's yacht, I suddenly heard a very familiar rolling voice from below. It turned out to be Henry Kissinger. It was that kind of event."[46]

The Futurist exhibition at Palazzo Grassi, widely described as strikingly beautiful, was a huge, formidable success — no adjectives are superfluous. The exhibition was seen by no less than seven hundred thousand visitors — an incredible figure for a city the size of Venice, on a par with the Centre Pompidou's greatest successes. The sales figure mentioned for the giant catalog is two hundred thousand copies — a volume that seems unreal for this extravagant printed matter. The overwhelmingly positive and laudatory press reactions poured in from all over the world. "For Agnelli and Fiat it was a fantastic success," says Antonio Foscari. "Sure, it was an expensive venture, but not compared to the amounts they invested every year in advertising and publicity, where Agnelli himself never appeared."[47]

With *Futurismo & Futurismi*, Pontus Hultén had once again presented an exhibition of historical, cultural and political consequence. The sensational audience and sales figures, and the enormous interest generated, are partly explained by the exhibition serving as a redemptive experience for the Italian public. For the first time, Italian art lovers were offered the opportunity to see and feel pride, not shame, over this unique historical heritage on a full scale. I think the effect can be compared to that of *Paris–Berlin* at the Centre Pompidou in 1978, which was also a catharsis and a corresponding success on all fronts. *Moscow–Paris* in Moscow in 1981 is another relevant parallel.

Overall, as Pontus Hultén himself writes,[48] the Futurist exhibition must be linked to the Pingpong exhibitions in Paris — a venture of the same scale and ambition as these, but less well known in modern art history. That he himself regarded the exhibition in this way is confirmed in a later interview where Hultén is asked which of his own exhibitions he is most satisfied with. Surprisingly, he answers not *Paris–Moscow* or any of the other Pingpong exhibitions, but the Futurist exhibition at Palazzo Grassi.[49]

One of the conflicts between Pontus Hultén and his clients from Fiat was that they were determined to show archaeological exhibitions at Palazzo Grassi in addition to modern art — archaeology was a strong interest of his immediate superior Cesare Annibaldi. Hultén refused to get involved in that part of the program and left Venice during work with these exhibitions. "It was a big mistake on his part," says Ida Gianelli. "The result was that I had to go two years without anything to do."[50] Due to these circumstances, Pontus Hultén's exhibitions at Palazzo Grassi were few and far between — only seven in the years 1985 to 1993.

The subject of Hultén's next presentation was a surprising choice, to say the least: Giuseppe Arcimboldo, the mannerist Italian late-Renaissance artist with the inimitable portraits constructed from fruit, vegetables, animals and various objects — the first ever "solo exhibition" of this then forgotten and little known artist, an oddity of art history who, like Hieronymus Bosch, heralded Surrealism four hundred years later.

The Dutch Renaissance master Hieronymus Bosch (c. 1450–1516), with his incomparable visions of hell, is widely regarded as one of the main inspirations of Surrealism.

I've been informed that the unexpected choice of motif was an attempt by Pontus Hultén to satisfy his clients and other authorities in Venice by showing older art at Palazzo Grassi. Pontus Hultén himself tells Stephan Andreae that his ambition, as with Futurism and Marinetti, was to revive interest in Italy in a forgotten Italian master and to give Arcimboldo, an artist whom Hultén says had long fascinated him, his rightful place in art history. Belatedly, I discovered that Arcimboldo was an idea that Pontus Hultén had carried with him for at least two decades. In his archives, I found an exchange of letters with Dominique de Menil from the spring of 1969, when *The Machine* was shown in Houston. Hultén suggests an Arcimboldo exhibition co-produced for Stockholm and Houston.[51] de Menil enthusiastically accepts the idea, after Hultén has sent her a Swedish book on Arcimboldo from 1957.[52] When I ask Olle Granath whether any bells are ringing and if so, whether he knows why the exhibition never materialized, he replies: "No, my bells are silent, but it confirms what I know — that Pontus carried with him a set of ideas from his youth that he returned to. It was when he ventured beyond these that things didn't turn out as brilliantly."[53]

Giuseppe Arcimboldo was born and raised in Milan, where he worked with his father, also an artist, on stained glass windows in the cathedral. He was a Renaissance artist who also worked as a decorator, designer and costume maker. Arcimboldo was recruited as a court painter for the German Roman Empire, first in Vienna for Emperor Maximilian II and then in Prague for his son Rudolf II, two enlightened despots with advanced artistic interests. It was in Vienna that Arcimboldo developed the Mannerist style that became popular in his own time and that makes him unique, with portraits devised with elements such as fruits, vegetables, tree roots, books, kitchen utensils and other objects that from a distance appear to be ordinary portrait paintings, but which up close "collapse" into their constituent parts in a kind of organic fusion of man, nature and surroundings — a surrealist double effect to Hultén's taste. The fact that Arcimboldo left Italy early and developed his unique expression abroad was one reason why he was unknown in his home country (hardly any of the artist's conventional portraiture has survived). Only one of the twenty plus surviving "object paintings" by Arcimboldo was in Italy. No exhibition had ever been organized with the artist in his home country.

Mannerism was a style that developed during the latter part of the Italian High Renaissance, roughly from 1520. Mannerism reacted against the classical harmonic perfection of artists such as Leonardo, Michelangelo and Raphael. The school emphasized excitement and exaggeration rather than harmony and perfection — an intellectual style of painting demanding to the viewer.

Arcimboldo was forgotten by art history when, during a visit to Vienna in the early thirties, MoMA's founding director Alfred H. Barr, according to legend, discovered in an antique shop a dark illusory landscape painting of Arcimboldo's school that he associated with Salvador Dalí and his bewildering double optical effects. Barr included paintings by Arcimboldo, in the form of photographic reproductions, in his 1936/1937 exhibition and catalog *Fantastic Art, Dada, Surrealism* at MoMA. Through this exhibition, Arcimboldo was rediscovered by modern art history. André Breton highlighted him as one of the artists in the "Pantheon of Pre-Surrealism," including in the Surrealist exhibition in Paris in 1947. Together with Bosch, Arcimboldo had increasingly come to be seen as the most important "progenitor" of the Surrealist movement, the foremost of the "Proto-Surrealists," "deeply modern" in his expression as it has been formulated.[54] Hultén borrowed the work that Barr had bought in Vienna for the exhibition in Venice from Barr's widow. He dedicated the exhibition and catalog to his role model Barr, the first great museum director of modern art.

There was a strong Swedish connection here. During the sacking of Prague at the end of the Thirty Years' War in the 1600s, several paintings by Arcimboldo were part of the treasure looted from Emperor Rudolf's Kunstkammer ("Wunderkammer") in Prague Castle, where works of art and other manufactured objects were mixed with naturalia from around the world. Two of these paintings — the fruit portrait "Vertumnus" of Emperor Rudolf and the stunning "Librarian," a profile portrait of a man made up of books — had eventually ended up in the collection of the imperial palace Skokloster, another in Gripsholm.[55] The National Museum also owns a painting, which of course they were obliged to lend out.[56] Olle Granath helped Hultén with the practicalities of securing the loan of these paintings to Palazzo Grassi. "I had to talk to them at Skokloster because it was very expensive as they wanted the paintings to be accompanied by two members of staff," says Granath. "Of course, they thought it was nice to come to Venice. You had to be a bit careful with such things so that it didn't become a tourist activity."[57]

Wunderkammer, cabinet of curiosities, was a phenomenon that began to develop in the fifteenth century, when it became fashionable among princes and noblemen to furnish rooms in which, in the spirit of the Renaissance, natural finds, archaeological and ethnographic objects were mixed with religious relics and art. The "Wunderkammer" of the Renaissance, with its combination of different objects and ideas, was an important source of inspiration for Dada and Surrealism.

For the production of the Arcimboldo exhibition, Pontus Hultén introduced a new collaborator, Yasha David, a Czech art historian whom he had befriended in Paris. David was known as a handsome ladies' man, famous for his relationship with Brigitte Bardot and for his wide network of contacts and friends among artists and other key figures in the international art world. David would later work on several of Hultén's exhibitions during the remainder of his career and became one of Hultén's closest friends and confidants during the last part of his professional life. "I had visited Sweden in the sixties and seen the paintings that Pontus had seen as a young man," says Yasha David when we meet in Paris. "When he was in Venice, he talked about the program and said, 'Why not Arcimboldo?' I thought about the problems of transportation on the water, climate control and so on. It was very difficult. I was very negative. That the exhibition came about was thanks to Pontus, who said that this we had to do."[58]

It was the first time, not only in Italy but in international art history, that a large number of Arcimboldo's paintings were gathered in one exhibition. Pontus Hultén said they managed to borrow all the canvases they wanted to show, with one exception: a painting in Madrid. Hultén suggested he should have gone directly to the Spanish king and asked — then even that loan would have been resolved, as he assumed.[59] In the hanging and in the catalog — another exuberantly rich piece in double language editions from Bompiani in Milan, packed with scholarly texts in addition to a spectacular imagery — these paintings were juxtaposed with selected works from the history of modern art where the artists, according to Pontus Hultén and Yasha David, had worked in the spirit of the Renaissance master, with humor and surrealistically illusory, surprising visual and symbolic effects, with the human body and nature as "building blocks."

Many of the works and artists in the exhibition are recognized from Pontus Hultén's repertoire and previous workplaces. There was, of course, a collection of classics by Surrealists such as de Chirico, Dalí, Magritte, Man Ray, Victor Brauner and Hans Bellmer. Dadaism was amply represented by, in addition to Duchamp, Picabia, Raoul Haussmann, George Grosz, Otto Dix, Kurt Schwitters, Hannah Höch and others. More unexpected names included Jean Dubuffet, the Filipino-American Abstract Expressionist Alfonso Ossorio, the Japanese Conceptual artist Natsuyuki Nakanishi and the sculptor Tomio Miki. Jasper Johns, Roy Lichtenstein, Andy Warhol and others were also represented.

The Arcimboldo exhibition, entitled *Effetto Arcimboldo* (*The Arcimboldo Effect*), opened in February 1987, was another formidable public and international press success for Pontus Hultén and Palazzo Grassi. To me, *Effetto Arcimboldo* appears a hallmark Hultén show: visually surprising and spectacular in content, with interesting historical context, but accessible to a wide audience without prior knowledge, including children who love Arcimboldo's paintings. Hultén himself, no doubt surprisingly to many, referred to the exhibition as "one of my most important."[60]

The title of the exhibition has a double meaning, referring both to the concept of how the components of the paintings form a completely different whole from a distance, and to the impact the artist had on Surrealism in particular.

The Arcimboldo exhibition, on the other hand, was very badly received by the Italian intellectual elite, who in the press stormed in "blind rage" against the show, which was accused of kitsch and populism, among other ills. Arcimboldo was called a grotesque and secondary "craft artist."[61] Hultén even speaks of a mafia conspiracy that tried to prevent the opening. "Perhaps two successes in a row was too much," he tells Stephan Andreae.[62] Germano Celant has a simpler explanation: "The Italian intellectual elite hated

Pontus and everything he stood for," he says.[63] Hultén himself summarizes the Arcimboldo exhibition as "despite this [hostilities in the press and elsewhere] it was a great success, very well attended, very beautiful and very interesting."[64] There is no doubt that the exhibition fulfilled its purpose of making the domestic and also the international art public rediscover a unique Italian master.

For decades, the Arcimboldo exhibition was one of Pontus Hultén's less internationally known major exhibitions. *Effetto Arcimboldo* is one of a growing number of Hultén's exhibitions that have inspired "meta exhibitions" in our own time. In spring 2021, the Centre Pompidou-Metz, the MNAM Centre Pompidou's branch in northeastern France, presented *Face à Arcimboldo*, a wide-ranging multidisciplinary exhibition in the spirit of Hultén, inspired by its predecessor in Venice in 1987. Many of the artists and works returned from the exhibition at Palazzo Grassi, but the time horizon had been pushed forward by over thirty years in an impressive, popular and well-attended event.

In the catalog, the museum director Chiara Parisi writes: "I had the chance to visit *Effetto Arcimboldo* during a school trip in the spring of 1987 (...) Despite the spatial difference between the eras, I vaguely remember the connection between these heads garnished with fruit, fish or objects, and works by Kazimir Malevich, Jackson Pollock or Nam Jun Paik (...) Pontus Hultén has always seemed to prefer to risk letting instinct and nonsense get in the way of rational thinking. Undoubtedly, this explains why he was the first major practitioner of the role of the curator as creator and interpreter of the contemporary (...) With *Effetto Arcimboldo*, Pontus Hultén's foresight lay not in having radically changed the conditions of art, but in having captured the time by calling for a new freedom for curators, who are inspired to dare innovative and radical projects within institutions."[65]

In the same year as *Effetto Arcimboldo*, in the fall of 1987, a second exhibition directed by Pontus Hultén opened at Palazzo Grassi, the highest frequency during his time in Venice, where he otherwise presented no more than one show a year. Now the turn had come to his old brother-in-arms Jean Tinguely, a natural choice also because of Tinguely's friendship with the Agnelli couple.[66] By this time, in the late eighties, Tinguely had suffered serious heart problems and a general decline in health. It's said that Pontus Hultén wanted to use the exhibition to cheer up his beloved friend and bring back his spirits.

The Tinguely exhibition was conceived as a full-scale retrospective that would include several site-built works, including a monumental machine sculpture dedicated to Venice that Tinguely designed for the Palazzo Grassi's courtyard, comparable in size to *she*, in which the audience, especially children, were supposed to be able to enter a rattling, screeching surrealist carnival with a vast array of moving parts — wheels of all sizes, drive belts, fragments of carousels and other amusement park paraphernalia, etc.: a mechanical marvel that came to life in all its tentacles at the push of a button. Tinguely and Hultén were disappointed when the palace administration decided, certainly wisely, to close the sculpture to the public for safety reasons.

The Tinguely exhibition caused consternation among Fiat's representatives at Palazzo Grassi and in the Venetian establishment.[67] When boatloads of building materials arrived by sea in the form of frightening amounts of rusty, rattling scrap iron, Hultén explains, the concern increased. Many wanted to throw it all into the canal, but Tinguely managed to pour oil on the waves with his charm and cunning psychological skills, switching effortlessly between different languages. When emotions were running high, the artist always had a piece of chocolate that he brought out to calm down the agitated.[68]

Soon the junkyard on the canal quay began to take shape in machine sculptures that filled the palace and overflowed into the surrounding area. Problems arose as the palace was not built to host art exhibitions. As so often before, improvisation was the solution. Many of the components of the sculptures were too large to be brought in through the doors. These had to be winched up and brought in through windows. Hultén recounts that they worked at night so as not to upset anxious people in the museum management and among the Venetians. In four weeks, the tiny team, Tinguely's collaborators reinforced by the institution's technicians, had transformed the palace into the artist's own fantastically rattling, squeaking, howling world of what Renzo Piano calls "useless machines"[69] — a madly anarchic universe of their own that contrasted strikingly with the elegant architecture of the eighteenth-century palace and the serene poetry of the city of Venice.

I think the stories of the Tinguely exhibition and its implementation show the extent to which Pontus Hultén, even this late in his career, was prepared to rely on improvisation and innovation, still open to letting chance rule and true to his habit of never unnecessarily informing his clients in advance but rather presenting them with his old tried and tested fait accompli. Hultén had blind faith in Tinguely's team, this ever-traveling theater company that could always solve any problem and do what was needed, without ever asking for permission, and which was now nearing the end of its long, cacophonous journey.

Tinguely's long-time closest collaborator and technician, Josef "Seppi" Imhof, the master welder who had joined Tinguely during the work on the "Le Cyclop" in the Fontainebleau forest, tells me that the shipments were problematic, especially when the largest wheel of the giant sculpture had to be unloaded and the transport barge almost capsized at the quayside. He shares with me a wonderful anecdote from the production of the exhibition in Venice, a scenario that would make any Surrealist proud.

One of the many new works presented by Jean Tinguely at the Venice exhibition was the large room installation "Mengele-Totentanz" ("Mengele Dance of Death"), as it is called, or "Mengele — danse macabre," the official title of this work, which now occupies its own gallery space in the Museum Tinguely in Basel. The year before, in 1986, after surviving a massive heart attack by sheer force of will, as it is described, Tinguely had built this group of machine sculptures in a frenzied, obsessive outburst of inspiration, from scrap iron and other debris he had found in the ruins of a barn that had burned to the ground after a lightning strike.[70] The stench of burnt animal carcasses reminded him of the Holocaust and the incinerators of the concentration camps, as did the gray film that covered the cast iron scrap from the extreme heat released when huge volumes of hay burned over old machinery and tools. Tinguely worked around the clock on this installation with his vision of apocalypse and his own approaching death, inspired by a fresco of a dance of death in a Dominican monastery near Basel. Tinguely envisioned this group of sculptures as the first in a series of dances of death in different locations titled "Mengele-Totentanz."

It was the artist's idea to install this dance of death in a chapel next to Palazzo Grassi. Tinguely was raised Catholic and had a complicated relationship with the Church, being a convinced atheist. Pontus Hultén had reportedly been reluctant at first.[71] The idea of installing this ultra-radical sculpture group in a Catholic shrine in religious Italy must have seemed provocative in the extreme even to Hultén — or perhaps he just deemed it too difficult politically and practically. He was persuaded and through Agnelli's and Fiat's contacts, permission was obtained.[72]

When the time came to install the "Mengele-Totentanz," Imhof tells me that one that day they saw the vicar emerge theatrically from the church gate draped in his robe, carrying the altar cross over his shoulder. The poor man of God despaired of the blasphemy with which these foreign drug hippies intended to desecrate his shrine. He wanted to save the Holy Cross from this curse. Imhof says that Tinguely and Hultén ran after the priest and stopped him in the alley. A while later, all three of them, the priest, Tinguely and Hultén, were happily drinking together at the local tavern, with the cross leaning against the bar.[73]

Another lavish catalog was produced for the exhibition, although Hultén, as usual, countered the impression of banal luxury by choosing unexpectedly cheaper materials and other unusual details and refinements. The cover of the beautiful black box features Tinguely's brightly painted machine sketches and the handwritten poetic subtitle *A Magic Stronger than Death*. The catalog for Hultén's book on Tinguely, which was published in connection with the retrospective at Moderna Museet in 1972, had been equipped with a handle, like a briefcase. This, even larger and more massive in format, could be carried on a shoulder strap. Hultén was pleased to note that in Venice one could see people carrying this piece over their shoulders in the city's alleys, just as Stockholmers had carried the *Art in Motion* catalog like a baguette under their arm a quarter century before. Hultén said of the catalog that he thought "it was one of my best" — a fine self-assessment of the master cataloger Hultén.[74] In his preface, he writes poignantly that his friend Jean Tinguely, after returning from the dead following his heart attack in 1986, had become more introspective in his art, that the previously ubiquitous humor was no longer present in his sculptures.[75]

The Tinguely retrospective drew crowds that were good but nowhere near the masses that had been attracted to the Futurist exhibition and *Effetto Arcimboldo*. The general consensus was that the exhibition was not a real success, that Tinguely was too much of a good thing for the conservative Venetian audience. Clarenza Catullo, Pontus Hultén's secretary and assistant in Venice, states: "It was too innovative for Italy and our short-sighted perspective on contemporary art."[76] Tinguely's superstar glamour of the sixties and seventies had faded somewhat in the increasingly trend-driven art world of the eighties, but the exhibition at Palazzo Grassi emerges as a powerful finale to the two old friends' more than thirty years of artistic collaboration and constant creative exchange and interplay. The exhibition traveled in modified form to Turin and to the Centre Pompidou in Paris, where it was a success.

The following year, in 1988, Germano Celant returned from New York to Venice to produce, together with Pontus Hultén, the exhibition *Arte Italiana*, another broad, impressively epic art-historical exposé, this time of the whole of Italian art and creative culture from the turn of the 20th century to the end of the war in 1945, with an accompanying seven-hundred-page catalog bible. The "lifestyle" element was generous: film, architecture, design, fashion — art forms in which Italy had excelled more internationally than in modern art. Celant says that for the hanging, Hultén, as usual, engaged only the highest quality — in this case some of de Chirico's enigmatically perfect canvases.

Jean-Yves Mock, Pontus Hultén's close associate at the Centre Pompidou in Paris, uses this word to describe Hultén. In a letter, Mock writes: "One word for Pontus: Lifestyle!"

Arte Italiana was another brilliant audience success for Palazzo Grassi. In retrospect, Hultén himself does not seem to have been fully satisfied. To Stephan Andreae he says self-critically: "In this exhibition I may have gone a bit too far in my love of Italy. At least my catalog text seems to me to be written with too much enthusiasm for this country. I didn't find the way."[77] The exhibition was subsequently shown at the opening of the new Reina Sofia Museum in Madrid in 1992, where construction was still far from complete when the show was installed. The Spanish museum management was worried and wondered if Hultén and his team would make it in time for the royal inauguration, says Germano Celant. "Pontus said 'clean the room and give me twenty technicians and we'll hang it in two days,'" Celant says. "I learned a lot from this — that you can actually install masterpieces in one day."[78]

The last exhibition organized during Pontus Hultén's time as director of Palazzo Grassi was an Andy Warhol retrospective, opened in February 1990, twenty-two years after Hultén's Warhol exhibition at Moderna Museet in Stockholm and three years after the artist's death. This presentation cannot be considered a Pontus Hultén exhibition, as it was produced by MoMA in New York and curator Kynaston McShine, as part of the extensive collaboration between Palazzo Grassi and MoMA. I have been told about the difficulties of collaboration between Hultén and McShine. "It was a conflict between different artistic visions," explains Jean-Hubert Martin. "McShine was a typical MoMA person who only cared about painting and sculpture. Pontus thought that was too limited a perspective and that you couldn't get a complete picture of Warhol as an artist without his films, photography, publications and so on."[79] Hultén made a number of additions to this exhibition, which was shown in various modified versions in leading museums around the world. Apparently, none of the Brillo boxes that Hultén had made in Malmö (see Chapter 36) around the same time (correspondence about this with Clarenza Catullo in Venice is in Hultén's archive) were shown in Venice.

Pontus Hultén failed to realize his dream of a more peaceful and quiet life in Venice. On the contrary, the years in the water city became a period of stress and ever increasingly frenetic travel, with engagements all over the world in addition to the low-frequency exhibitions at Palazzo Grassi. Hultén was at this time the international art world's "elder statesman"[80] above all others, consulted and engaged by institutions, patrons, private collectors and all sorts of players across the art world on various issues and projects. "Everyone sought his advice on the stock market, which he hated," as Marie-Louise von Plessen says.[81]

A major project that Pontus Hultén was involved in during these years was Dominique de Menil's own museum, The Menil Collection, in the de Menil oil industry group's hometown of Houston, featuring the family's exquisite collection of antique, modern and contemporary art. Hultén inspired his friend Madame de Menil, as Dominique was commonly called, to invest in a museum for the collection.[82] When the plans became concrete in the early eighties, Hultén recommended Renzo Piano[83] as the architect for this institution, inaugurated in 1987. Over the years, The Menil Collection has often been classified as the world's most beautiful modern art museum in various rankings.

Hultén demonstrated his sensitivity to the interplay between architecture and art by not only choosing an architect for Madame de Menil, but also by identifying for Piano and de Menil a model and source of inspiration for the new institution: the Mishkan Museum of Art in Kibbutz Ein Harod, Israel's first museum, completed in 1948 in a classic Modernist design by architect Samuel Bickels. The Israeli museum is considered the first in the world to rely entirely on daylight, filtered through skylights, which is what Pontus Hultén believed should be taken into account.[84]

Renzo Piano confided that the first thing Dominique de Menil said to him at their first meeting, after Pontus Hultén introduced him, was "I don't like the Centre Pompidou." "Ouch, that's not a very good start, I thought," Piano said. Mme de Menil then expressed her oft-quoted desire for a museum "that is small on the outside but big on the inside" (Interview Paris January 9, 2015).

Pontus Hultén and Renzo Piano never had the opportunity to design a museum together from scratch, even though Hultén did his best to bring about such a collaboration at several sites after the Pompidou. In the early eighties, both Piano and Richard Rogers experienced a well-known phenomenon in the world of architecture after the completion of a revolutionary building: the big commissions were not lining up, as developers were reluctant to hire the creators of something as subversive as the Centre Pompidou. Rogers and Piano's canonization was decades distant.

Arguably, The Menil Collection was the closest the two friends Hultén and Piano came to collaborating on a museum from the idea stage. Although Hultén's role in the project was unofficial, he was in close creative contact with both Dominique de Menil and Renzo Piano throughout the work on the museum. He also recommended Walter Hopps as artistic director of the museum. There is no doubt in my mind that Pontus Hultén's little-known contribution to the creation of the sublime Houston museum is worthy of attention.

The significance of this collaboration between Hultén and Piano is illustrated in that The Menil Collection has been as important to Piano's stellar career in our own time as the Centre Pompidou, their first collaboration that had catapulted that career. Though Piano's office is responsible for an astonishing number of the world's most high-profile buildings in most segments — skyscrapers, airports, public buildings of all kinds, and more — it is his museum buildings[85] that make Piano stand above all his generational peers among the world's star architects.

In a major portrait interview in the New York Times in 2013, Renzo Piano is reminded by the writer that his office has designed no less than twenty-five museum buildings worldwide (several more have been added since). "It's unbelievable. Is it true?" says Piano.

Hultén played similar informal advisory roles for decades in many projects across the art world. During these years, he held the formal leadership role of president of CIMAM, the association of world curators and museum directors. In Venice, Pontus Hultén was regularly visited by dignitaries from the entire art world, as well as from other international cultural, political, diplomatic and business circles, all of whom welcomed the opportunity to visit the fabled water city. The ambitions of Gianni Agnelli and Fiat to make Venice and Palazzo Grassi an international hub for culture and politics were duly fulfilled during Hultén's years in the city.

Hultén commuted to Paris, where he kept his penthouse on Rue Beaubourg, throughout his time in Venice. He maintained several engagements in the city. In addition to the school, he was also an "advisor to the president" at the Centre Pompidou during Jean-Hubert Martin's time as director.[86] I have received information from several sources that during this time there was also discussion of appointing Hultén himself as president of the entire Centre Pompidou, i.e. overall administrative executive of the entire cultural center with all its institutions. The reason was that visitor numbers had dropped considerably after Hultén's departure. It's unclear to me how far-reaching these plans may have been and why they fell through. Another assignment in Paris was that of artistic advisor for Europe's largest science museum, the spectacularly futuristic Cité des Sciences et de l'Industrie in the Parc de la Villette on the northern outskirts of Paris, one of François Mitterrand's bold culture and architecture endeavors, inaugurated in 1986. Clearly, there were influential people in Paris who were of the opinion that Hultén had disappeared too soon and was still an asset to the city. In recognition of the services he had rendered to France, Hultén was awarded the Commandeur de l'Ordre des Arts et des Lettres in 1984, and in 1991 he was made an officer of the Legion of Honor — the star among the substantial number of orders that the old anarchist had accumulated and which, to the amusement of some friends, he liked to wear whenever the occasion arose, "like a Soviet marshal" as someone likened him to, or "like Gadaffi," to quote the sarcastic Jacques Caumont.[87]

Reading Pontus Hultén's archive of correspondence with the whole world, one gets an idea of the global scope of Pontus Hultén's activities during these years, when his career was still basking in the hot afternoon sun, if no longer burning in zenith. Even taking into account the sparse frequency of exhibitions at Palazzo Grassi, it's hard to comprehend how he managed to do all this, all the more so without access to today's technology.

During these years at the end of the eighties, when he was director of Palazzo Grassi, "headmaster" of the Paris school and advisor to the Centre Pompidou, as well as being involved in a wide range of other projects throughout the art world, Pontus Hultén also found time to make two significant contributions to the literature of art history. In 1987, together with Natalia Dumitrescu and Alexandre Istrati, Constantin Brancusi's younger Romanian compatriots, artist friends and heirs, he published a handsome monograph on the master sculptor and mystic so admired by Hultén. The book[88] is considered to be an important contribution to the literature on Brancusi, although Pontus Hultén's text has been criticized by some experts for his wide-ranging theories on how the artist's simple peasant origins can be read in his art — another of Hultén's anthropological-philosophical theses where one can sometimes wonder what is the map and what is the terrain.

The second literary work that Pontus Hultén published during these years was more unexpected and has become an even more important contribution to art history — a true "labor of love" as it appears, an anthology produced in collaboration with his old friend Sam Francis: the beautiful, refined *The Surrealists Look at Art*.[89] The book consists of Hultén's selection of texts by the leading poets and ideologists of Surrealism, with a longer, perspective-widening introduction by Hultén himself. The authors represented are, in addition to the Surrealist general André Breton, Louis Aragon, Paul Éluard, Philippe Soupault and Tristan Tzara, all of whom Hultén greatly admired. They are not easily read or digested, these dense, enigmatic, politically radical, poetically winding texts by this all-male quintet of Surrealist philosophers. With this book, Hultén and Francis remind us that Surrealism in its time was at least as much a literary as a visual movement.

With his book *The Surrealists Look at Art* — exquisitely illustrated with a series of reproductions of Surrealist visual works that have been lost or altered by time — Pontus Hultén manifests how close the Surrealist movement was to his heart. In his introductory text, Hultén writes about the communist political conviction of the Surrealists, without which he believes the movement cannot be understood.

While editing *The Surrealists Look at Art*, a sophisticated piece of book art, Hultén reportedly spent some good, happy time with Sam Francis and other friends in California. The art collector and gallerist Robert Shapazian, a younger friend of Francis and Hultén in Los Angeles and at the time director of the publishing house The Lapis Press (later founding director of the Los Angeles branch of the Gagosian Gallery), writes admiringly of Hultén's efforts in working on the book in his text in the book *Das gedruckte Museum von Pontus Hultén*: "When we started working on *The Surrealists Look at Art*, Pontus sent me a flood of suggestions for various possible texts and ideas on how to group them. Although I had been collecting Surrealist photography for years, had a good knowledge of the literature of the period, and had even gotten to know Michel Leiris, Maurice Tabard, José Corti and others who shaped this moment in time, I was humbled by Pontus' vivid and vast knowledge. He could immediately pick out the most insightful essays, recall texts that had long been inaccessible, or inform me that a version of a particular text was not quite complete — that I could find the right version in some distant place. He was always right. Working with him was like peering into a wonderful treasure chest, in which beautiful things revealed themselves in their fullest range and in purest color and form."[90]

Ida Gianelli and others have reported that Pontus Hultén's travel schedule during the years in Venice had taken on manic forms, that an obsessive restlessness had increased with age. It's said that at this time Hultén was unable to stay in the same place for more than three consecutive days. "Nor could he concentrate on a subject for more than ten minutes in a conversation," says Ida Gianelli. "People thought he was rude and pretentious, but he simply couldn't focus for longer than that. It's a problem that comes with age."[91]

Ida Gianelli also addresses the sensitive subject that continued to recur with increasing urgency throughout Hultén's career — his drinking habits. "There is one thing and that is that in Italy, you cannot be drunk," says Gianelli, "but in Venice he was very often drunk. And people thought he was even more drunk than he was because of his asthma, which meant he had to go to the window to breathe."[92]

Pontus Hultén's only break from this ever faster spinning squirrel wheel was, as always, his sailing, the short spontaneous cruises in the lagoon and the waters around Venice and the longer ones in the Mediterranean and the Stockholm archipelago. As throughout his career, during the summer he took to the seas for weeks and months with only minimal contact with the outside world. On these voyages, Hultén became a different person, as testified by his crewmates — relaxed and calm, focused on the details of sailing and the pleasures of nature. "I remember once when he was sailing and Madame Pompidou called every day to ask if we had heard from Pontus," says Clarenza Catullo. "It was some important question about the Institute. Finally he did call in, but it was only because the fridge on the boat was broken."[93]

Hultén's problems and conflicts with Fiat's representatives in the management of Palazzo Grassi and other officials in Venice didn't diminish but rather increased, with the archaeological exhibitions as a constant bone of contention. There were many others. Pontus Hultén complained in various contexts that the way in which Venice was governed made it difficult to work and live in the city: conservative, with money as the overriding interest. In practice, according to Hultén, Venice was controlled by seven families.[94] "The relationship between Palazzo Grassi and the municipality of Venice was very complicated," as Vittorio Gregotti says.[95] "I remember one night when we were sitting in a deserted piazza in Venice drinking a lot of grappa and Pontus gave a long monologue about how hopeless it was to deal with these people," says Monica Nieckels, who was working at Moderna Museet in Stockholm at the time.[96]

Although he enjoyed much of life in Venice, with all its Hemingwayian attributes, the image of the lonely, sad and, it must be said, tragic, big heavy figure becomes increasingly distinct. This loneliness recurs time and again in his colleagues' portraits of their boss, as do the accounts of Pontus Hultén's complicated, contradictory character. "Pontus was a bulldozer, he really cleared the way," says Germano Celant. "But in fact he was very sensitive and receptive. If I wasn't paying full attention myself, he noticed it immediately and said 'Germano, are you ok?'. I liked him as a person. He was strong, powerful, but very fragile. When he was hurt, he could tell people to fuck off. He was not for power. He was interested in doing things, the pleasure of doing things, not the power itself, that came after. He was isolated, a kind of an island. He had no social life, was not accepted in the culture."[97]

"Pontus was a very, very generous person but he expected to be recognized and respected," says Ida Gianelli, who stresses a constant source of conflict throughout Pontus Hultén's career: "He wanted to implement his ideas and didn't accept any discussion. He reasoned that 'I'm the director, I'm the one who brought you here, and I'm in charge.' He didn't say thank you to the people in the team. I agree with him, I don't think you should have to thank your employees for doing their job, but people were very hurt by this. It contributed to his isolation. Pontus did not want to be alone. He wanted to go out for dinner and have company."[98]

Pontus Hultén's secretary and assistant Clarenza Catullo offers a Nietzschean interpretation of his loneliness, a version that I have heard several people close to Hultén express in different variations: "To me, Pontus was a UFO," says Catullo. "He was too intelligent. Ordinary people didn't understand how gifted he was. He gave me what no one else has given me — intelligence, humanism, professionalism. He felt exploited. It was the loneliness of genius. He didn't care. Either you understood him or you didn't understand him. Men hated Pontus, only women loved him. He was alone in his intelligence. He was the saddest person I've ever met in my life."[99]

In the years around the turn of the 1990s, several events occurred that affected the physical and mental health of Pontus Hultén, then aged sixty-six. Consistent testimony indicates that from this time onwards his life became heavier and darker in a slow downward spiral. The devastating break-up with his partner Rebecca Horn took a toll on Hultén. At the time, Horn was one of the world's most celebrated contemporary artists, in demand for exhibitions and projects throughout the art world, something that Hultén reportedly found difficult to accept. Rebecca Horn herself says that the trigger that ended their six-year relationship was when she traveled to the United States for the production of the film *Buster's Bedroom* (1991), which Horn directed: "Pontus told me that if you leave now we can't see each other anymore. But I had no choice. I couldn't withdraw but had to go."[100]

The date is uncertain, but it was probably sometime in the fall of 1989 that Pontus Hultén had an accident in Paris with far-reaching consequences for his health. The details are unclear but it was a so-called "Isadora Duncan incident" where Hultén allegedly got his coat stuck in the door of a taxi, fell into the street and suffered a minor stroke. During the 1990s, several leg clots followed, gradually limiting Hultén's mobility and making it more difficult for him to walk. After the accident, Hultén became afraid of traffic in Paris and stopped driving in the city. "After the accident, he was no longer the same," says Ida Gianelli. "In the late eighties he became bitter. It had to do with his health. His body was under too much stress and he was drunk every night. He was also very disappointed with the development of the art world." Pontus Hultén's increasing health problems were a sensitive, taboo subject. "When something was not good, he never wanted to talk about it," as Ida Gianelli says.[101]

Isadora Duncan was a style-defining American ballet dancer who died on September 4, 1927 after her scarf got caught in the wheel of the open Bugatti in which she was traveling and broke her neck — a death that in its tragedy is unparalleled in glamour.

Around the turn of the decade 1990, the conflicts between Pontus Hultén and Fiat's representatives in the management of Palazzo Grassi became untenable. According to Clarenza Catullo, Pontus Hultén left Palazzo Grassi in 1990 because of disagreements over the archaeological exhibitions.[102] An alternative truth, which I've heard from several others, and which seems more credible, is that it was Fiat that terminated his contract. Hultén was "invited to leave," as one insightful person phrases it. According to most of the information I've received, this decision was primarily related to money — it was simply too expensive in the end, as Serge Fauchereau and others have testified. In any case, Hultén resigned as director of Palazzo Grassi in 1990.

Unlike at his previous museums — Moderna Museet, MNAM and MOCA — the exit from Palazzo Grassi was a "soft" sortie. The divorce doesn't seem to have given rise to hostility between the parties. Pontus Hultén remained as artistic advisor to Palazzo Grassi for several years. He continued to return regularly to his beloved Venice until the last year of his life. In his conversation with Stephan Andreae, Hultén says that his departure was without bitterness and that he and the Agnelli couple remained good friends.[103] In private he expressed greater disappointment.

Proof that relations between Pontus Hultén and Palazzo Grassi remained friendly is that he gave his farewell performance at the institution in 1993, three years after he had resigned as its director. What could have been more appropriate as a subject for this Venetian swan song than the greatest idol of his life and career: the ever-present Marcel Duchamp, of course.

The exhibition, entitled simply *Marcel Duchamp*, which had begun to be planned during Hultén's tenure as director, was his second retrospective with his great role model and the fifth in art history. In the early 1990s, Duchamp had come a long way in his return to the art world, but was still far from the dominant position that the artist posthumously commands in our own time.

The Duchamp exhibition at Palazzo Grassi was comparable in size to the one at the Centre Pompidou sixteen years earlier. Virtually all of Duchamp's limited-volume output was on display (Duchamp's *catalogue raisonné* contains around four hundred works, compared to thousands in Picasso's, for example), totaling around two hundred and fifty objects, many of which were shown for the first time — drawings, sketches, models and photographs. There were never-before-seen curiosities such as the amazing toys Duchamp had made as a child. The artist's last work, the installation "Étant donnés," was presented in the form of a series of preliminary studies and a three-dimensional relief model.[104] Borrowing Duchamp's work had become increasingly difficult since 1977. Even

The installation "Étant donnés" has been called by Jasper Johns "the strangest artwork any museum has ever had in it."

more than in Paris, one had to rely on replicas and models, especially of Duchamp's readymades.

The year before, Pontus Hultén had commissioned a new replica from Ulf Linde of "The Large Glass" (not a readymade, mind you), the work that adorned the exhibition poster papered all over Venice, with the city's silhouette seen through Duchamp's glass with its figures. The first copy that Linde and others had made for *Art in Motion* in 1961 had also become too old and fragile for its rigorous travel schedule. Ulf Linde, with the help of the artists Henrik Samuelsson and John Stenborg, created this second copy in the warehouse at the Thielska Gallery on Royal Djurgården island in Stockholm, where Linde and his life partner Nina Öhman were directors for almost thirty-five years and also had their home.[105] It's not clear how this second replica of "The Large Glass," which is now traveling around the world, in constant demand by institutions globally, was commissioned. It was probably jointly financed by Palazzo Grassi and Hultén's new client, the Bundeskunsthalle in Bonn (see next chapter). In any case, the work became part of Moderna Museet's collection — the same smart deal that Hultén had cut with Tatlin's tower for *The Machine* at MoMA in New York in 1968. Evidently, Pontus Hultén still had the interests of the mother museum in mind. A major difference from the first "Stockholm copy" was that this second version was not authorized or signed by the artist himself, as Duchamp had died fifteen years earlier, but, to Jacques Caumont's amusement, by his widow Teeny Duchamp.

Behind Hultén in the production of the exhibition was once again Alexina "Teeny" Duchamp. Hultén had entertained his friendship with the artist's widow throughout the years following Duchamp's death and enjoyed her full confidence. Although Teeny was ill at the time, she became involved in the exhibition assisted by her daughter Jackie Matisse, a close friend of Hultén. When Teeny supported the loan request, it was almost impossible for museums and institutions to refuse.

Pontus Hultén and his co-curators Jacques Caumont and Jennifer Gough-Cooper did not want to call the Duchamp exhibition a retrospective. The presentation was arranged not chronologically but thematically, with sections and galleries for paintings, readymades, "The Large Glass" and others. According to Jacques Caumont, he himself was responsible for the entire design of the exhibition.[106] The stated ambition was to show Duchamp's oeuvre in its entirety, without entering into the kind of advanced philosophical and/or psychoanalytical interpretations that had already become omnipresent in Duchamp coteries.

The exhibition presented a wealth of new, never-before-seen and little-known material, which added much to the overall picture of Marcel Duchamp. The same was even more true of the catalog — another magnificent six hundred page piece, published in double language editions, an important and controversial contribution to modern art history and the hysterical scholarship on Duchamp. The visual material includes many never-before-seen images of works, never-before-seen color images, unknown sketches, letters, private photographs, postcards and other curiosities, and more. Most sensational, however, is the more than four hundred pages of textual material — a "chronology" of the artist's life, admired, criticized and scandalized in the Duchamp conferences of the art world.

Jacques Caumont was unfamiliar with Duchamp when Pontus Hultén introduced him to the artist at the opening of the Centre Pompidou. Since then, having immediately taken a fanatical interest in Duchamp, he had become one of the world's leading experts on the artist, controversial in Duchamp circles. The chronology of the artist's life published in the catalog by Caumont and his partner Jennifer Gough-Cooper was the result of eighteen years of research and contained an overwhelming amount of completely new material — a revolution in the Duchamp world.

The problem was the eccentric, not to say Dadaist, way in which this enormous material had been organized. No less than three thousand six hundred pieces of text, known as ephemerides (kind of astrological "diary entries"), had been sorted by dates in Marcel Duchamp's life, arranged according to astrological signs, without chronology or any other system — the dates could be from any year of Duchamp's life. Caumont, Gough-Cooper and Hultén certainly drew inspiration from Duchamp's own "Green Box," where notes on "The Bride Stripped Bare By Her Bachelors, Even," i.e. "The Large Glass," have been arranged seemingly according to a random principle. The question is how wise it was to choose this method of editing this vast amount of essential research material. What is certain is that it has annoyed Duchamp experts around the world ever since.[107]

Francis M. Naumann, one of the world's leading Duchamp authorities, writes in his review: "... for those who hope to consult this col-

Alexina "Teeny" Duchamp and Pontus Hultén, Palazzo Grassi, Venice, 1993. "Teeny" Duchamp was herself a trained artist but gave up art after her first marriage to the art dealer Pierre Matisse, Henri Matisse's youngest son.

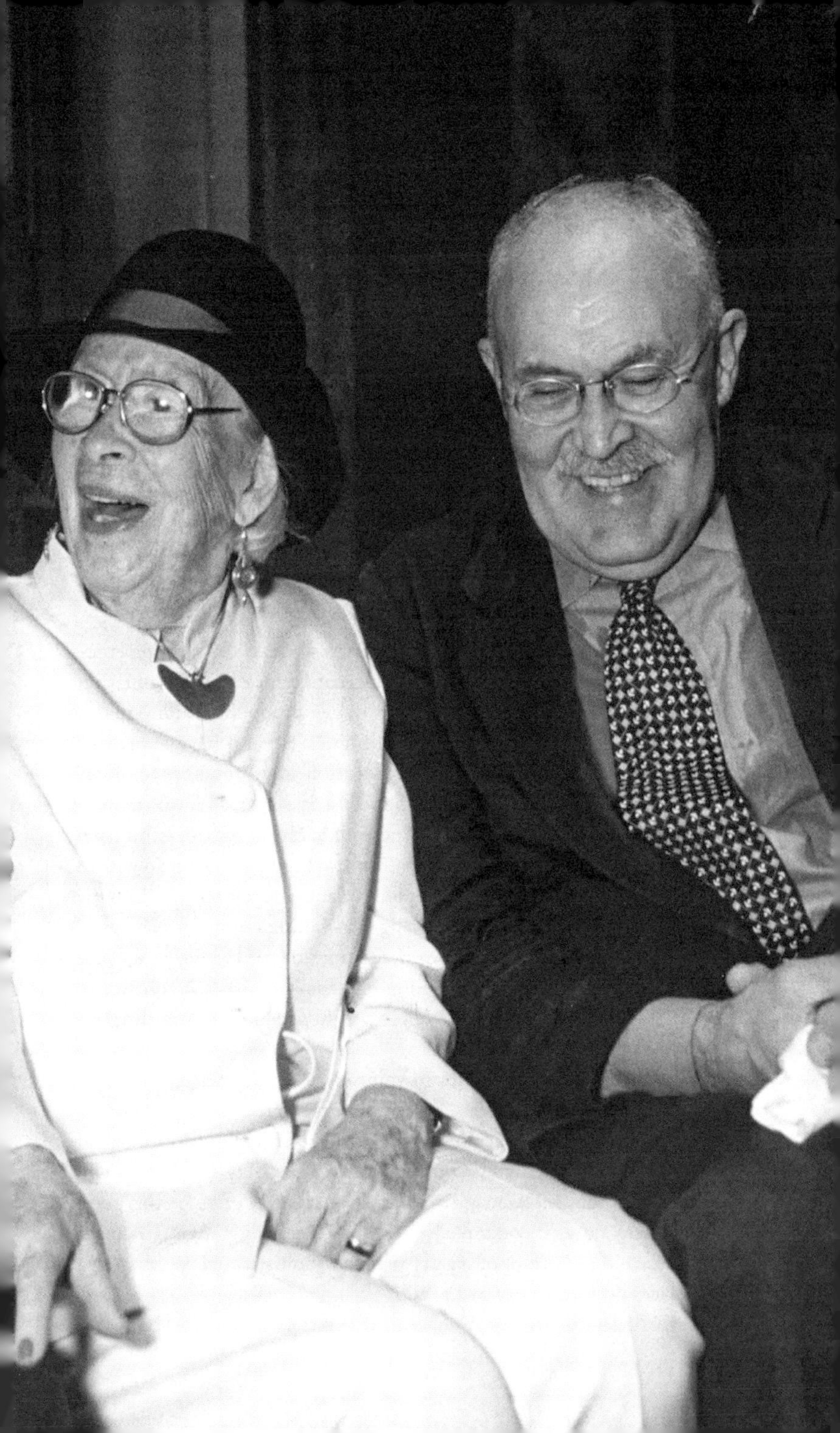

lection as a traditional chronology, a shocking disappointment awaits. If you do not know the exact date of an event in Duchamp's life, you will not be able to find it in the ephemerides, at least not without great difficulty."[108]

After this and other serious objections, Naumann concludes with an admiring verdict: "No future study of the artist that makes any claim to completeness can be undertaken without first consulting this publication. The most ardent Duchamp scholars will learn something new about the artist and his work at every turn of the page. Most of the material is gathered from unpublished sources — letters, diaries, manuscripts, unscripted interviews, etc. — and from countless, otherwise largely inaccessible sources such as newspaper articles, exhibition texts and reviews that have long been buried in obscure publications. Gough-Cooper and Caumont have even managed to locate a number of works by the artist that have never appeared in any catalogue raisonné. All in all, it is a remarkable achievement, one that will influence Duchamp scholarship for many years to come."[109]

The eccentric Jacques Caumont is a person who evokes strong emotions. It's testimony of Pontus Hultén's confidence in Caumont that he hired him again, despite Caumont being unpopular among many, not least Hultén's employers and colleagues. Several have expressed views similar to Ida Gianelli's: "He is a terrible man. You have to follow rules, but Caumont did the exact opposite and spent a lot of money. Everybody went mad at him."[110] The collaboration on the exhibition ended in disagreement between Hultén and Caumont and also within the Caumont-Gough-Cooper couple, as Caumont felt that Hultén, by putting his own name on the catalog, was taking credit for the ephemerides, which he himself had worked on for nearly twenty years, and as Gough-Cooper, according to him, had compromised the quality of the final editing by accepting Hultén's tight schedule for the English language edition of the catalog.[111]

The Duchamp retrospective in Venice was not an unequivocal success, either in terms of box office numbers or in the press. Perhaps the content of the exhibition was too advanced for the still provincial arena. Opinions are divided on its quality. According to Ida Gianelli, Jacques Caumont had a negative impact on the outcome. "It was good but not as good as it could have been," says Gianelli.[112] "Again, Pontus' perspective on contemporary art was too sophisticated for the time and place," argues Clarenza Catullo.[113]

Regardless, the Venice Duchamp exhibition was a worthy *grand finale* for Pontus Hultén in his dedication to his hero and mentor, and a powerful contribution to the knowledge and myth of this unique artist. Undoubtedly, the exhibition and catalog contributed to the outstanding influence that Duchamp exerts on the art world more than half a century after his death.[114]

After Pontus Hultén left Palazzo Grassi in 1990, the art center continued to be operated by Fiat for another decade and a half. In the following years, it hosted many ambitious exhibitions of modern and classical art as well as archaeology, organized by various invited guest curators, including Jean Clair. However, the palace no longer made as much noise in the art world as during the early years. "People didn't understand that Palazzo Grassi wasn't Agnelli or Fiat — it was Pontus," Clarenza Catullo declares.[115] In 2006, the palace was sold "for a ridiculous amount of money," as it is said, to the French super-collector and multi-billionaire François Pinault, to display his extensive private collection. Pinault hired Japanese architect Tadao Ando who erased every trace of Gae Aulenti's and Antonio Foscari's interiors and some of the palace's original ornamentation in favor of a trendy minimalist interior. "Nothing remains — everything is obliterated," says Antonio Foscari.[116] Ando also designed the theater building that had been planned but never realized during Hultén's time, the acclaimed Teatrino del Palazzo Grassi, which now hosts concerts, film screenings, lectures and events. Still, the palace in Pinault's reign can hardly be called a dynamic art scene.

I ask Germano Celant if Pontus Hultén is remembered in Venice and in Italian art and culture. "No," Celant replies. "It's typical. In the eighties there was a shift. Before, art was linked to culture. Now it is linked to money and investment. Pontus was the first curator. Today everyone is a curator."[117]

To Ida Gianelli, I pose the delicate question of whether she thinks that Pontus Hultén was still at the peak of his ability and career during his time in Venice. Ida falls silent and then answers: "Yes, he was. Then it started to go down."[118]

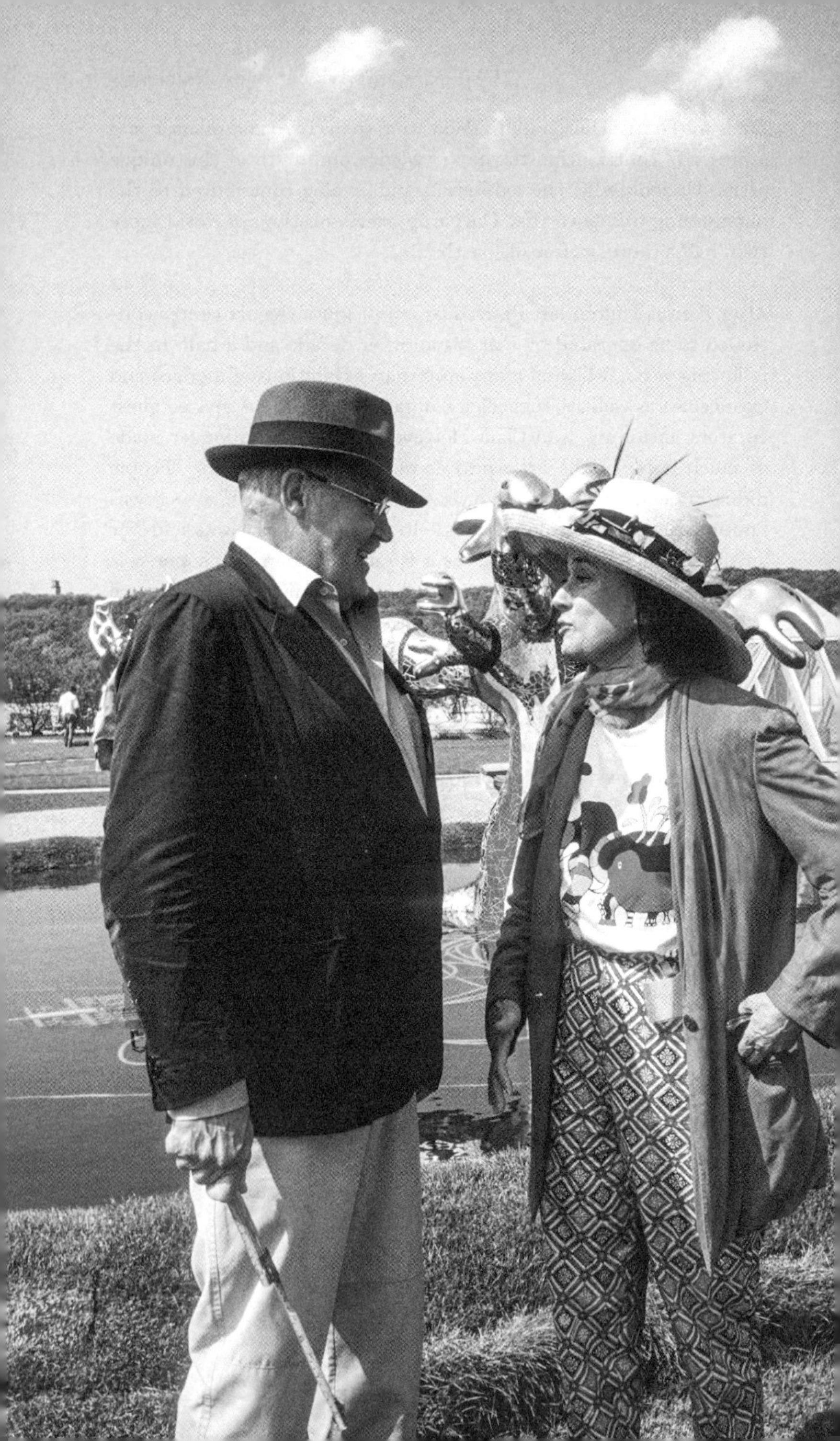

29

Who would have thought? Pontus sets foot in Germany …

It seems ironic that after Italy, Pontus Hultén's odyssey across the art world continued to Germany, the country he had hated with such passion in his younger days, growing up with the Second World War. Hultén was nine years old at the time of the Nazi takeover and fifteen at the outbreak of the war — at his most sensitive age when humanity's madness and dark forces erupted in their worst outburst of self-destruction to date.

Like his heroes among artists of his own and older generations, Pontus Hultén was more influenced by the war than perhaps anything else. As Sarkis, Hultén's younger artist friend and colleague at the Paris school, observes, Hultén's career as an exhibition maker and museum director can be viewed as influenced by the Yalta Conference and the division of the world that resulted from the Armageddon of World War II.[1]

We recall how Hultén took every opportunity to tell his story of how, as a young man, he rode a motorcycle or scooter from Stockholm to Paris without setting foot in Germany except to urinate on German soil. Much of the youthful dislike of an entire nation and its people had faded, but Hultén, as he approached seventy, still retained a dislike and suspicion of Germany, despite having had much interchange with the country throughout his career. Together with Werner Spies, Hultén had made a historic contribution to German art with *Paris–Berlin* and was a big name, indeed a legend in the German museum world.

Hultén admired early German Modernism, including Dada and the Surrealists, but held a more ambivalent attitude towards later German art.[2] He had exhibited and bought art by both Joseph Beuys

Pontus Hultén and Niki de Saint Phalle, Kunst und Ausstellungshalle der Bundesrepublik Deutschland, Bonn, 1992.

and Gerhard Richter without being fully convinced of the greatness of either, as testified. As is well known, he disliked Anselm Kiefer, so much so that he didn't hesitate to call the artist a Nazi in front of his young colleagues at the school in Paris.[3] Nor did he like Georg Baselitz. "I had known Baselitz since I was a child and liked his art, but I knew there was no point in advocating that kind of Expressionism to Pontus," says Kay Heymer, one of Hultén's younger curatorial colleagues and closest associate at the Kunsthalle in Bonn.[4] Undoubtedly, there was something about Germanness itself and any hint of German chauvinism or, worse, sentimentality, that bothered Hultén; something he never "trusted."

"Pontus hated Germany, everybody knew that," says Wenzel Jacob, the then thirty-eight-year-old German art historian and curator who became Hultén's assistant director at the Kunst- und Ausstellungshalle der Bundesrepublik Deutschland (KAH) in Germany's then capital, Bonn, and who was tasked with recruiting Hultén as the new institution's founding artistic director. "We discussed it often. It was good for me to be able to say that my father had fled from the Nazis to France and, because he spoke English and French, managed to get to Bergen, Norway, where they could listen to BBC broadcasts."[5]

The decision to establish a national German modern art venue was taken at the highest level, by none other than the then German Chancellor Helmut Kohl, the powerful, physically imposing Christian Democrat patriarch who for decades played a dominant role in European politics and who had the honor of going down in history as the head of state who ended the forty-five year post-war era by reuniting West and East Germany.

The background to Helmut Kohl's initiative is said to have been the West German Chancellor's visits to French President François Mitterrand in the early and mid-eighties when he had been impressed by the Centre Pompidou. Like other politicians and tycoons around the world, he wanted something similar for his own city and country.

A national modern art institution in the then German federal capital of Bonn was an idea that had been discussed ever since Bonn was designated the capital of West Germany in 1949 as a compromise solution. There had been a consensus from the outset in the German political and cultural establishment that governmental power needed to be complemented and balanced by cultural institutions in order for Bonn to achieve full credibility as the seat of government and parliament of the Federal Republic.

The realization of this vision dragged on for decades. The decision to build a federal art gallery and cultural center in Bonn was only taken in 1982 by the Bundestag on the initiative of Helmut Kohl. An international architectural competition was launched for the plot of land set aside adjacent to the government and embassy quarters, where, in addition to the art gallery, several other cultural institutions were built at the time. In the 1980s, Bonn was a city that, apart from its university, was entirely dominated by politics and diplomacy. The architectural competition was won in 1987 by the internationally less known Austrian Gustav Peichl, with a square postmodern bunker clad in sandstone, with historicizing references to Egypt, Rome and Versailles. The building has a flat roof serving as an exhibition space, crowned by three minaret-like light towers that have become the logo of the complex. It's said that the reason Peichl was chosen as the winner was in actuality that the architect was a neighbor and good friend of Helmut Kohl from his summer residence in the Austrian Tyrol — a far from uncommon explanation in similar cases since the dawn of civilization.

When Germany was divided after the war, the initial intention was to make Frankfurt the capital of West Germany. As the ambition was always that Berlin would eventually regain its privileges in a united Germany, there was concern that Frankfurt, a large and economically powerful city, would be accepted as a real capital. So Bonn was chosen as a more apparent provisional solution. One reason is thought to have been its proximity to Cologne, the hometown of the first West German Chancellor, Konrad Adenauer.

To review Gustav Peichl's winning architectural proposal and to "optimize" it for the purposes of the new art gallery, a committee was appointed with representatives of the German art and museum world, which also had influence over the recruitment of the museum management. The most senior member of the committee and its secretary was Johannes Cladders, who had known Hultén since the early 1960s. It's widely believed that Cladders was primarily responsible for the recruitment of Pontus Hultén as artistic director of this new institution, the only one of its kind in Germany. As the founding director of the model MNAM at the Centre Pompidou, Hultén's name was not difficult to sell to Helmut Kohl and other leaders.

As usual throughout his career, the task for which Pontus Hultén was recruited was controversial. More than forty years after the end of the war, German cultural policy in general, and a federal cultural program in particular, was a subject charged with historical legacy, not least in the arts, where the Nazi branding of "entartete Kunst," "degenerate art," still echoed ominously in the background. In the agreement that was forced on Germany after the war, cultural policy, like many other social issues, was managed at the regional level by the eleven West German states, to counteract the possibility of building a new strong German central power. The vision of a federal German arts and culture center was a sensitive one and was naturally opposed by the museums and political leaderships of the states.

These conflicts and the historical shadow were also reasons why it was decided from the inception that the new federal institution would be an art gallery and cultural center without its own collection. The idea that the federal German government would build its own art collection and thus encroach on the responsibilities of the regional states was a subject too sensitive to even be discussed seriously. In his new position, Pontus Hultén would once again lead an institution that was not a museum, without a collection of its own — something he could not influence and which he later regretted: "The fact that KAH [the abbreviation by which I henceforth refer to the art gallery] did not get its own collection is very dangerous for the institution. If you have a collection, despite conflicts and serious problems of all kinds, you can survive and bounce back decade after decade. The collection provides security. Because what happens when the institution dissolves? Suppose one day it goes bad. Recovering with only temporary exhibitions is very difficult when there is no capital. There will be no reason to continue running a defunct shop."[6]

When we meet in Bonn, Pontus Hultén's colleague and successor Wenzel Jacob recounts the story about how he traveled to Venice to meet Hultén for the first time in April 1989 to formally ask Hultén, on behalf of the museum committee, if he wanted to take on the assignment in Bonn. The committee had come up with an administrative model in which Hultén was offered complete artistic control over the new institution and its activities, with total autonomy, while Wenzel Jacob, as assistant director, would be responsible for all administrative matters — a kind of luxury contract with seniority, in other words, under which Hultén was relieved of most dealings with the politics and bureaucracy he had always detested, as well as of financial responsibility.

"When I arrived in Venice, the first thing he asked me was if I could sail," says Wenzel Jacob. "I could. I myself had an eighteen-meter Colin Archer, a Norwegian boat from 1918 that I had in Turkey. It was the perfect start to our friendship. Early the next morning we sailed out in his nice little open two-masted boat. We sailed in the lagoon and stayed and drank in all the little restaurants. We spent the night in the boat and sailed the next day until evening. We didn't speak a word about art. When we were back in Venice and had cleaned the boat and parted, I turned around after walking ten meters and asked: 'Well, are you coming to Bonn then?' 'Yes, why not?' he replied."[7]

Once again, the timing had proven so favorable for Pontus Hultén that an offer of a new assignment, again as founding director of a new international art institution, surfaced just as he was about to leave a previous assignment. One can almost sense a system behind this synchronization. In Bonn as well as in Paris, Los Angeles and Venice, his name seems to have appeared at the idea stage well before these initiatives were realized. That Jacob's request hardly came as a surprise to Hultén is evident from the above-mentioned anecdote.

Pontus Hultén claimed his post as founding artistic director of the new federal German art gallery and cultural center in Bonn in the spring of 1990. Again, he arrived too late to influence not only the decision to refrain from building its own collection, but also the choice of architect and the physical planning of the museum and its context. Construction was already underway. For his clients, it was embarrassing that Hultén made no effort to hide his low regard for the politically connected architect Peichl and his building. The complex makes an anonymous, vaguely Postmodernist impression where it sits on a wide highway in Bonn's flat urban landscape. The exhibition halls impress with their monumentality: a total of five thousand six hundred square meters divided into five galleries, where the largest halls with their church-like ceiling height give weight and authority to German Conceptual artist Hanne Darboven's repetitive minimalist installations that cover the vast wall surfaces when I walk through them on a weekday afternoon with few other visitors. Pontus Hultén is said to have been pleased with these galleries and the flexible possibilities they offered. "But he was not fond of the building itself, which was very rough at the time," says Wenzel Jacob. "He thought it was too big and not sophisticated enough. I explained to him that he couldn't do anything about the building. I told him that he had to be satisfied with certain adjustments to the interior and focus on the content instead."[8] Hultén himself says that all communication with the architect Peichl went through Wenzel Jacob since Peichl didn't listen to him and never responded to his attempts to contact him.[9]

Jacob goes on to recount that when Pontus Hultén arrived in Bonn, the museum provided him with an apartment in the city where he spent as little time as possible. Instead, he mostly stayed at Wenzel Jacob's home or at a hotel near his house in the village of Rodenkirchen on the outskirts of Cologne, forty kilometers from Bonn. "He didn't want to be alone — not to go out for dinner alone and so on," says Jacob. "So I offered him to stay at my home instead of a hotel — in a penthouse overlooking the Rhine. Right next to my house is a classic old pub from 1645, Zum Treppchen. It became our office during the five years he was in Germany. We had the table in front of the bar. There we sat and drank beer together, discussed the program and did most of the planning for the Kunsthalle."[10]

Wenzel Jacob and everyone else I've spoken to tell me that Pontus Hultén started his new assignment in Bonn and Germany as was his habit — traveling all around the world at a furious pace. He landed in Bonn every two weeks. "He didn't want to travel alone either, so I was usually with him," says Wenzel Jacob. "It was great to meet his network of contacts all over the world. We went to Russia and Saint Petersburg and to MoMA in New York. We had to travel everywhere to secure loans for our exhibitions."[11]

As we know, shortly before Pontus Hultén's arrival, in the fall and winter of 1989/1990, an unforeseen historical convulsion, the most dramatic since the Second World War, occurred, which instantly changed the conditions for the ambitious art and culture initiative in Bonn: the sudden collapse of the Soviet Union, followed by the fall of the Berlin Wall and the reunification of Germany. Although the change of capital did not become official until 1992, it was apparent immediately after the reunification of Germany, decisively pursued by Helmut Kohl and declared on October 3, 1990, that Berlin would most likely be restored to its dignity as the capital of Germany.

It's easy to understand the difference between an art institution of this dimension located in the capital of Western Europe's largest country and economy compared to an ordinary provincial town of just over three hundred thousand inhabitants, which everything indicated that Bonn would soon return to being. Construction of the new culture center was in full swing, but powerful voices were raised in politics and in the press to stop the whole venture now that Bonn would certainly lose its capital privileges. The management of the new art institution was already involved in a life-and-death struggle even before its creation. Pontus Hultén's first assignment was to use his weight, his authority and his deep knowledge of all the tricks in the book to help ensure that the federal art gallery was realized at all and that construction was not interrupted, as influential commentators advocated; immediately drawn once again into the political hot air that he claimed to abhor but had a constant ability to be drawn to like the moth to the flame.

In many ways, the situation was similar to the one Pontus Hultén had faced in Paris after the sudden death of President Pompidou, although perhaps the drama was not quite as intense or the odds as high this time. "It was important for us to build as early, as fast and as large as possible — and to show that we had already spent more than fifty-one percent of the budget so that it would be more expensive to stop the construction," says Wenzel Jacob[12] — a quote echoing the strategy and tactics of Pontus Hultén and Robert Bordaz in Paris sixteen years before.[13]

At the beginning of 1991, the crisis was over when the German Bundestag decided that the construction and planning of the new federal art gallery should proceed as planned despite the changed circumstances. The arguments posed by the proponents were that Bonn, with its location in Germany's most populous state, North Rhine-Westphalia, close to the Benelux and other European countries, was nevertheless a good location for an international art and culture center of this magnitude. Bonn would also retain some government administration, which it still does today. It's not unlikely that Helmut Kohl's personal prestige was another active factor in the decision to go ahead with the venture after all.

Even if the project was saved from being smothered in its infancy, like the Paris world fair, there was no escaping the reality that Pontus Hultén and his colleagues were launching a pre-degraded institution. With Hultén as artistic director, there was no question of adjusting the level of ambition downwards because of these new conditions. Planning continued on the largest possible global scale, as if Bonn had remained the capital of Germany. The preconditions of the Kunsthalle were that the new institution would be multidisciplinary and multimedia, following the example of the Centre Pompidou and, by extension, the Kulturhuset and Moderna Museet. It's safe to state that Hultén had invented a model for the modern cultural arena that had become a successful export product, a franchise concept more or less, with himself as the conspicuous front man.

In Bonn, where the lack of an in-house collection required large amounts of content to fill the nationally dimensioned exhibition spaces, and to attract larger audiences in this small city, the focus was broadened far beyond the realm of art to include scientific, historical, natural history and archaeological exhibitions, with classical art alongside modern and contemporary, as well as architecture and photography. At the turn of the 1990s, the obsession with technology began to increasingly influence social and cultural life. Advanced technical solutions for systems such as lighting and other logistics were part of the gallery's profile, something that Pontus Hultén cursed and which caused problems.

In his conversations with Stephan Andreae, Pontus Hultén is critical of the basic conditions for the new Kunsthalle, sensitive views that were one of the reasons why the minutes of these conversations, invaluable to this story, could not be published as planned in Germany.

Pontus Hultén not only disapproves of Gustav Peichl's architecture and the unnecessarily complicated and expensive infrastructural solutions, but also of the museum's location in this anonymous area between highways, with no natural connection to the surrounding urban area, when, according to Hultén, it would have been possible to build the art gallery complex on the banks of the Rhine instead. "These were practical decisions made by people who were not particularly interested in the issue," he says. "The area lacks the infrastructure of shops, restaurants, etc. that could have attracted people here."[14]

If it's clear that he was not very impressed with the art gallery facility itself, Pontus Hultén was more satisfied with other conditions at his new workplace, such as the staff of young curators recruited by Wenzel Jacob and the museum committee, which Hultén describes as "… these people were very interesting to me. It was nice and much less complicated than what I was used to from Paris. They had a desire to work and listened to me."[15]

Since the nearly six thousand square meters of the new art center, with the thousands of square meters of exhibition space on the roof added, could be divided into five separate galleries, Pontus Hultén and his colleagues decided to open the Bundeskunsthalle with five exhibitions of different natures, which together would show the breadth of the new institution's multidisciplinary array. The idea for this combination of art and popular science, which still characterizes KAH, though partly based on the conditions, was, not surprisingly, largely Pontus Hultén's.

The relationship of art to technology and science had interested him since the beginning of his career as an exhibition maker and museum manager. "The idea of combining art with science was his, it was something completely new to me, even though I had studied mathematics," says Wenzel Jacob.[16]

The new institution also featured, following the example of the Centre Pompidou, a library and an auditorium seating three hundred spectators for concerts, film screenings, lectures and the ambitious program of other events.

The main attraction of the opening program was to be a new and full-scale manifestation of the last of Pontus Hultén's epic historical "exhibition cycles" — a thematic exposé titled *Territorium Artis*, which was a further development of the show he had launched in experimental form with *Le Territoire de l'Art* with the Paris school in Leningrad two years earlier (see Chapter 27). The idea of the exhibition was to highlight artworks and artists who had moved art forward, conquered unexplored ground and marked new territory.

Once again, Hultén mobilized his global network of contacts in the museum world and among collectors and patrons as he succeeded in assembling another outstanding collection of epochal masterpieces of modern art, with an extensive list of lenders in another impressive catalog. As critic Peter Iden wrote in a review: "In the main hall, Pontus Hultén, perhaps the world's most experienced creator and organizer of exhibitions, presents what only he, thanks to his contacts in the international museum world, could have achieved: a collection of exquisite works of art from this century. According to Hultén, each of them marks a point of no return, a milestone that has changed the expression and manifestation of art, from which no path can return and which no one can avoid passing."[17] Correspondence prior to the exhibition shows that Pontus Hultén, in loan negotiations with mainly American museums and institutions, naturally took full advantage of Chancellor Helmut Kohl's personal involvement in the venture, aware of the Americans' thirst for celebrities, of which royalty and heads of state are the most prominent. The Chancellor's personal engagement is demonstrated in that he authored the introductory foreword to the catalog of *Territorium Artis*.[18]

Pontus Hultén's partner as junior curator for *Territorium Artis* was the aforementioned Kay Heymer, one of the young art historians recruited to the staff in Bonn. Heymer recalls her first meeting with

Pp. 566–567: Niki de Saint Phalle's sculptures installed on the roof of the Bundeskunsthalle, Bonn, 1992.

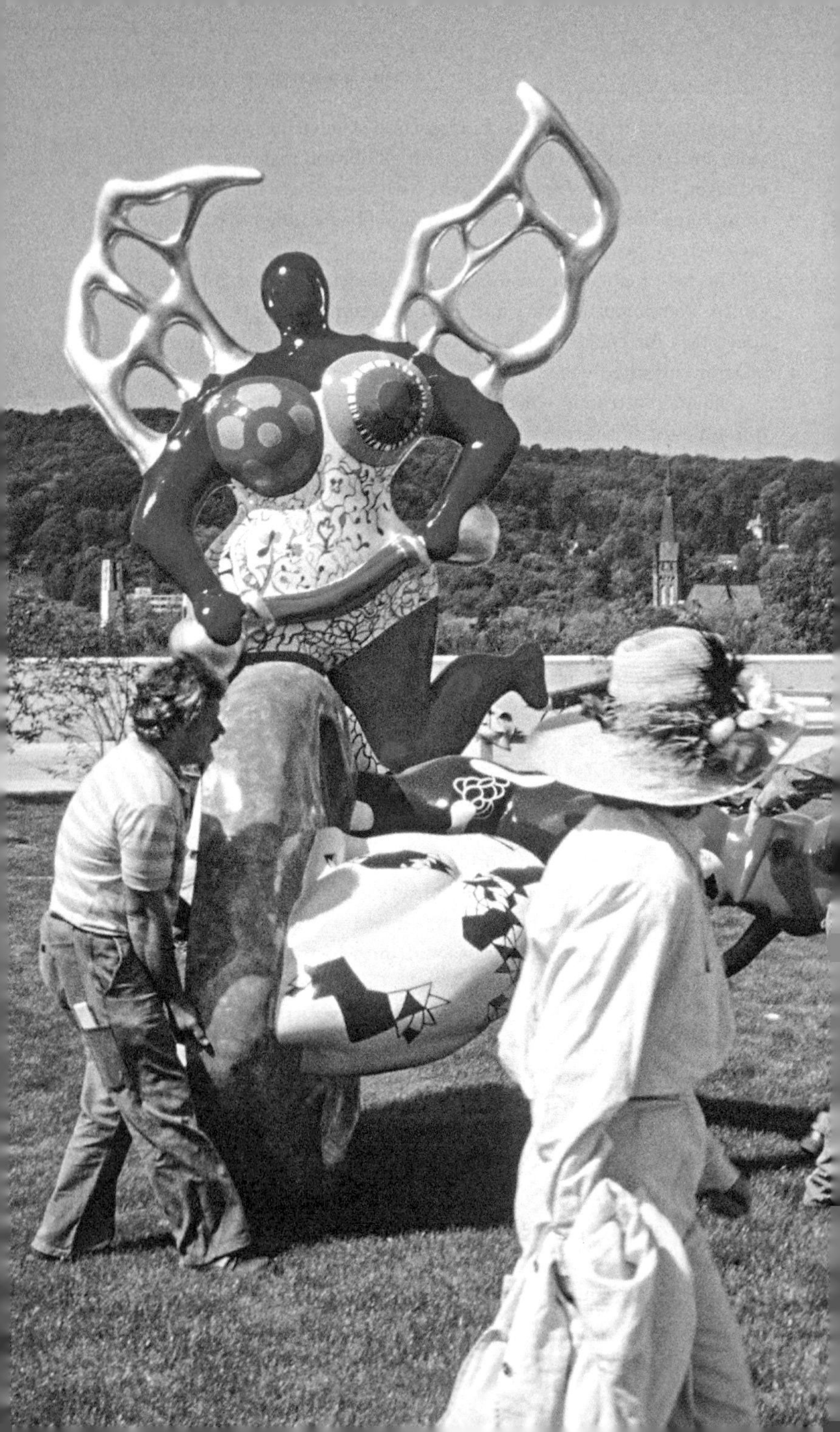

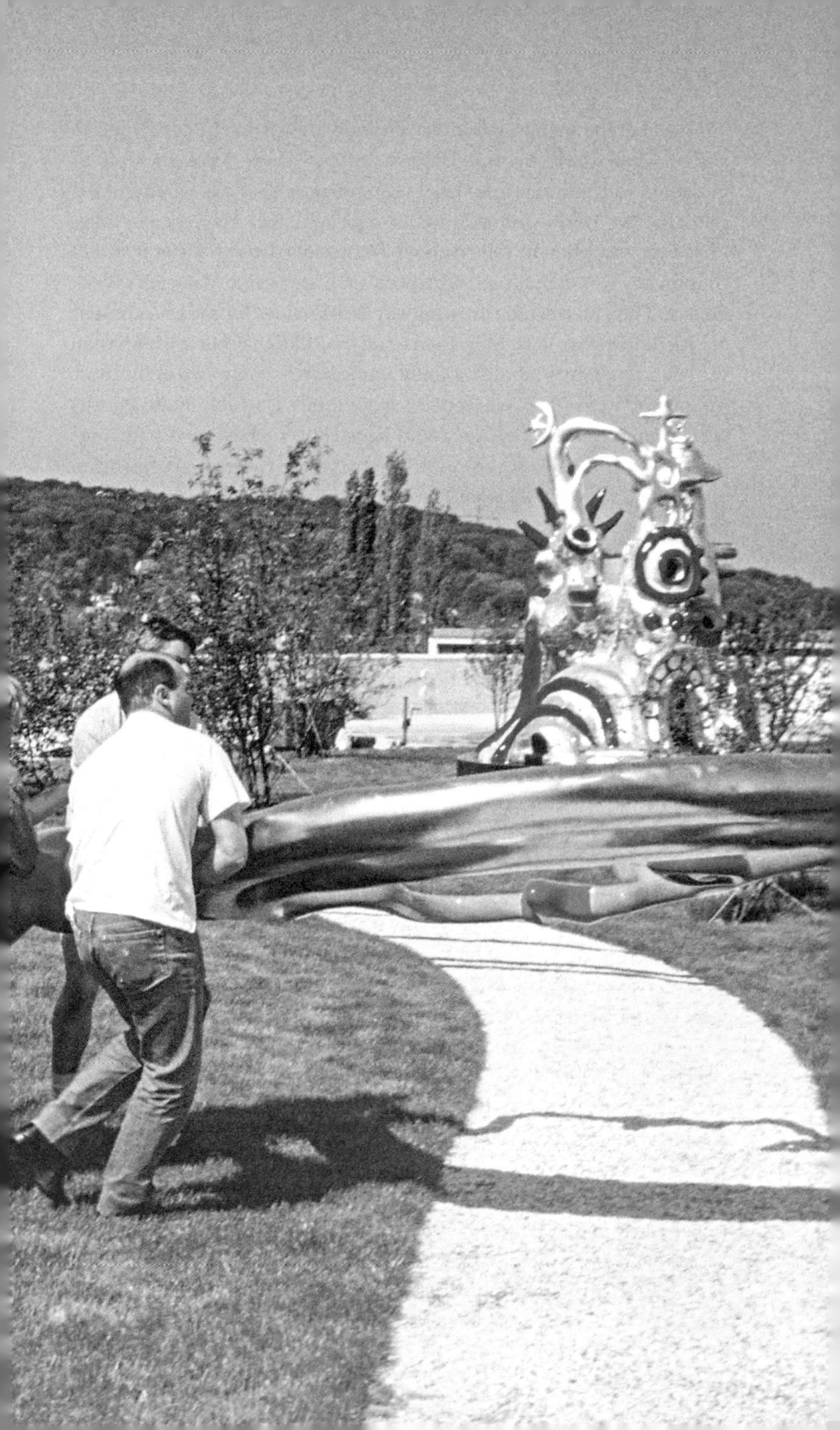

Pontus Hultén during a job interview in a caravan on the construction site of what would become the art center: "There were a couple of moments in the interview that I remember as decisive, when Pontus said that we could probably work together," Kay Heymer confides. "The first was when he talked about *Territorium Artis* and that it would contain key works that had influenced art history, like Malevich's Black Square. Then he started throwing out artist names for me to comment on. He didn't start with Mondrian or anyone like that but with Mikhail Vrubel, a Russian Symbolist. I could immediately name two of his most important works and where they were located, which made Pontus very happy. He said that he could have chosen those two paintings himself. I think he was impressed that a young German art historian even knew who Vrubel was. The second was William Copley. He was not part of *Territorium Artis* but I had translated a very funny text by him, "Portrait of the Artist as a Young Dealer," which had recently been published in Germany. I told him that, completely unaware that he was a close friend of Copley. He asked if I knew the background to the text [Copley's story of his career as a Surrealist art dealer in Beverly Hills]. I didn't know. He then told me that it was he who had commissioned it, for the 1977 *Paris–New York* catalog.[19] I had not read the French original but only the English version that came two years later. He was very amused by this. It appealed to his anarchist streak that it was a random coincidence. After that we never had any problems with one another and we worked very closely together."[20]

Pontus Hultén entertained thoughts of continuing the theme of *Territorium Artis* with further exhibitions, but there were no more in the series. When studying the catalog and the whole idea, the impression is that something is missing in comparison to Hultén's vast epic exhibitions earlier in his career, even though the scale and level of ambition was of mega format and the amount of amazing art is mesmerizing. "For me it was difficult to continue with exhibitions later, because with Pontus we only learned to do mammoth things," says Serge Fauchereau, who was again called in under Hultén's banner for *Territorium Artis* and other exhibitions in Bonn.[21]

The credibility of the selection in *Territorium Artis* could be questioned due to a phenomenon that became increasingly apparent towards the end of Pontus Hultén's career: his preference for choosing artists who were his personal friends and who had been important earlier in his career. In *Territorium Artis*, he selected as art historic milestones works by artists such as Jean Tinguely, Niki de Saint Phalle,

Thomas Shannon, Rebecca Horn, Sam Francis, Claes Oldenburg, Richard Long, Hans Haacke, Daniel Buren, Öyvind Fahlström, Piotr Kowalski, Ed Ruscha, Sarkis and others. It seems extraordinary that so many of his own friends would belong to an objective selection of modern art's most important pathfinders. Although Hultén himself claims for Stephan Andreae that "no one questioned the selection"[22] there is reason to consider what was art-historically universal and what was personal, what was the map and what was the terrain.

Once again, Moderna Museet in Stockholm, where Björn Springfeldt had taken over as director from Olle Granath, who in turn had been promoted to director of the National Museum, was obliged to lend numerous works acquired for the collection by Hultén and nominated as epoch-makers in this exhibition by no one else than Hultén himself. Olle Granath, who attended the opening in Bonn, confirms my impression of *Territorium Artis*: "I think it was probably good that he didn't continue to develop it into one of his major series," says Granath. "It somehow felt like the idea didn't quite work all the way through."[23]

Kay Heymer believes that it is correct to consider *Territorium Artis* as the final of Pontus Hultén's great epic exhibitions, or exhibition cycles, in the tradition he has built up from *Art in Motion*, the American suite in Stockholm, *The Machine* in New York, the Pingpong exhibitions and the Russian series in Paris, Futurism in Venice, and others. Yet he doesn't think the Bonn exhibition is comparable to these. "They all had great art historical content and told complex historical contexts," Heymer says. "*Territorium Artis* was more his personal manifesto. He presented his personal perspective on the twentieth century. I don't see anything wrong with that — following your own sentiments rather than being influenced by what's going on at the time."[24]

Pontus Hultén even managed to squeeze his beloved August Strindberg into *Territorium Artis*. Among the artists from a more contemporary generation represented were Bruce Nauman, Sigmar Polke, John Baldessari, Gilbert & George, Jeff Wall and Jeff Koons with his "Rabbit" from 1986.

The choice of topics for the exhibitions that accompanied *Territorium Artis* at the opening of KAH on June 17, 1992 was in many cases dictated by the Kunsthalle's program. Architecture was "naturally," as Pontus Hultén puts it,[25] represented by an exhibition about the new complex's architect Gustav Peichl and the building. Photography was determined to be another permanent component of the institution's program At the opening, an exhibition designed by Klaus Honnef, Germany's leading authority at the time, *The Pantheon of Photography*, presented a selection from the history of international photography.

In the eyes of some, Hultén reinforced the impression of something akin to nepotism by choosing to present a massive retrospective of his beloved and admired friend Niki de Saint Phalle as a contemporary feature at the opening, both in the upper gallery and with a spectacular outdoor section of twenty-four monumental sculptures in a lush park created on the flat roof of the Kunsthalle with its magnificent exhibition space. The exhibition was accompanied by a huge encyclopedic catalog, in German and English language editions — perhaps the most ambitious publication on the artist to this day.[26] Hultén justified the choice of de Saint Phalle explaining that the artist "(…) fulfilled important criteria. She was not very well known in Germany and, in general, art by women was not very well known. In my opinion, she is a remarkable artist who was also able to show her art in the open air on the roof of the gallery. Niki fulfilled all the conditions to make her right for this opening exhibition."[27] The argument that Niki was not well known in Germany is surprising as German museums, art centers and galleries had shown de Saint Phalle more often than in perhaps any other country early in her career. "I myself was not very fond of Niki de Saint Phalle, although I respected her," says Kay Heymer. "I said this to Pontus as well. It was fantastic working with him, that there was always an understanding that we could have different opinions about what we showed."[28]

Like her partner Jean Tinguely, Niki de Saint Phalle had by then lost some of her superstar glitz from the sixties and seventies. Nevertheless, the exhibition was a major public success and contributed to the gallery's broad impact.

As the popular science element of the Bonn premiere, Hultén introduced a surprising collaboration with the researching Swedish couple Annagreta and Eric Dyring, who had organized the exhibition *Visible and Invisible* at Moderna Museet in 1973.[29] *View of the Surface – Global Change*, a series of satellite images documenting the effects of climate change on our earth, was a high-tech presentation for the time that was a reason why the Kunsthalle was later selected to host international political events on the environment and climate change. Aerial photographs, films and scientific installations were presented alongside works by artists reflecting and associating on images of the earth photographed from space, again several friends of Hultén, such as Thomas Shannon, Urbain Mulkers, Dan Wolgers and Piotr Kowalski.

"The perspective of the exhibition was global change, which was very early," says Annagreta Dyring when I meet her at her and her late husband Eric's home outside Uppsala north of Stockholm. "Eric was a specialist in satellite images and for Pontus it was about showing context through images. We had images that showed things like desert expansion and burning oil wells. The idea of having artists illustrate environmental phenomena was ours, which Pontus accepted. He gave us free reign but was very committed. Before the exhibition, he walked around incognito in a blue blouse. When he interfered and asked about installations, people took him for a talented janitor."[30]

The exhibition opened a series of combined art and popular science ventures at the gallery, including *Arctic-Antarctica* in 1998, an epic exposition of Hultén's lifelong interest in his parents' inheritance — again, the personal, nostalgic touch at this late stage of his career — with Inuit art, historical artifacts from polar expeditions, stuffed animals, archaeological objects, "illustrated anecdotes" and much more. "I featured his parents' expedition to Kamchatka and Pontus was very honored," says Stephan Andreae, who curated the polar exhibition in collaboration with the Dyrings.[31] "Pontus was very involved, but he let us design it. Academic papers were written about the exhibition and it even led to a polar expedition by Arved Fuchs who reconstructed Shackleton's Antarctic expedition from Elephant Island to South Georgia. He wrote a book about it — all because he saw Shackleton's lifeboat in our exhibition and built a replica of it."[32]

For Stephan Andreae, Pontus Hultén, in a discussion about the exhibition *Arctic-Antarctica* — which was planned during Hultén's time but not shown until three years after his formal departure — elaborates on the new art center's broad range of subjects, combining art, history, geography, nature and science. His reasoning becomes a kind of program statement for his entire career as a museum director and exhibition maker: "A completely new type of exhibition was created. They were not categorized as science, geography, history and art, but everything was combined in a way that more closely resembles the totality of human experience at all levels."[33]

Despite Bonn's loss of capital status, the inauguration of the Kunsthalle was a large, grand and glamorous event. The institution was declared open by Helmut Kohl and invited guests included heads of state, European political dignitaries and German and international celebrities. Guests of honor traveled from all over the art world to see the new institution — the first German national modern art initiative.

For the opening festivities, Pontus Hultén had rented a barge on the Rhine where he welcomed his friends and collaborators from his forty-year career across the art world, large parts of his global art family, his court as some prefer to call it. Still, Pontus Hultén remained a prince, an uncrowned king in the still relatively small international modern art world, although his era was obviously nearing its end.

The new German "federal art hall" KAH in Bonn was an immediate storming success. Queues filled the Postmodernist piazza in front of the entrance, outside which a column of eleven pillars representing Germany's eleven states had been extended to sixteen, for the five new East German states. The center and its opening exhibitions were well received by the German and international press. "The press was positive, but should have been even more enthusiastic about the incredible quality of art that the public was presented here in Bonn," as Wenzel Jacob summarizes the media reception of the new cultural institution. "Actually, it was surprising that there weren't more negative reactions given that Helmut Kohl was unpopular with the German cultural left and that there was a lot of jealousy from other museums. With Pontus in charge, no one dared to criticize or question. We got fantastic press internationally. They better understood the level of what we were showing."[34]

Karin Weber, logistics manager and Hultén's close associate during his years in Bonn, sums up her impressions of the opening program at the KAH in retrospect: "With the composition of the opening exhibitions, Pontus showed the breadth of his vision and knowledge," she says. "KAH allowed him to summarize his life experiences, his broad perspective and his vast overview, which was very beautiful. It was a perfect combination of accumulated knowledge, a condensation of his view of art and the world. Unfortunately, in 1992 we probably didn't realize how unique it was. We were too caught up in the opening itself and the new institution to see clearly enough the broad philosophical vision behind it. We were all young and Pontus was mature — not like today when museum directors are getting younger and younger. We probably didn't quite appreciate then how visionary his perspective was, how much wisdom it contained. Now everything moves so much faster. Regrettably, there is no time to look back, only to react to the present. The art world now lives at a completely different pace. It's all about becoming famous and making a living. Pontus had a long breath where he inhaled the future as well."[35]

From the ceremonial opening of the KAH, there are stories about Helmut Kohl's visit and tour of the opening exhibitions. "I think Pontus was amused by how stupid Kohl appeared," says Kay Heymer. "He was completely uninterested in the art and asked only about the insurance value of the works. When we said forty million dollars for Picasso's portrait of Vollard[36] from the Pushkin Museum in Moscow, he was disgusted. He was also very upset about a work by Hans Haacke, 'Homage to Marcel Broodthaers,'[37] with a picture of Ronald Reagan and one of German protests against nuclear weapons on another wall, with a red carpet in between. He thought it did not show the right image of Germany, which is exactly what it did. President Richard von Weizsäcker, on the other hand, was very different. He stopped in front of a box by Joseph Cornell, the American Surrealist, and said 'it's nice to see a Cornell here.' It turned out that he knew Cornell personally and was very interested in art."[38]

It's testified that Pontus Hultén was consciously thinking publicly, if not populist, when planning the content of the exhibition program at the KAH. The idea of borrowing some of the world's most famous art collections for a series of guest exhibitions can be seen as a smart and "simple" initiative in such an ambition. Hultén understood that the major international museums were interested in raising their profile in the reunified German market. The series was a more large-scale version of the exchanges that Hultén had conducted with other museums and institutions in Stockholm and also in Paris. The difference was that the exchange in Bonn, due to the lack of its own collection, was one-sided and thus extremely costly.

Naturally, the first and leading light in this impressive venture, a series called *Die grossen Sammlungen* (*The Great Collections*), was the Museum of Modern Art in New York. Once again, Hultén knew that with MoMA "on board," no other institution could refuse collaboration. He could still benefit from his first-class contacts and friendships with the management of the New York institution. The collaboration was smooth and amicable.[39] MoMA also had a German connection in its tradition. Its founding director Alfred H. Barr, himself of German

MoMA, like many other art institutions, had its origins in a strong interest in art on the part of the wife of a powerful man. The museum was founded by a committee headed by Abby Aldrich Rockefeller, wife of the magnate John D. Rockefeller. Her husband was himself opposed to the whole concept of modern art. For several years he refused to contribute money before finally investing and eventually taking over the project.

descent, visited the Bauhaus during his stay in Europe in 1927–28, which had a decisive influence on his view of modern art for the opening of MoMA the following year, in 1929. The museum's founder, the Rockefeller family, was also of German origin. Wenzel Jacob suggests, not entirely transparently, that the museum had a "debt" to Germany with the legacy of the Holocaust; presumably referring to the fact that many of the masterpieces in its collection had been incorporated during the Second World War, often under dubious circumstances, some stolen from Holocaust victims (a number of which were later returned to survivors).[40]

According to Hultén himself, the guest appearance with the MoMA collection at the KAH in Bonn was a "simple exhibition," with a certain "conventionalism." "MoMA and its collection were pure gold," he tells Andreae. "You could just pick anything you wanted from catalogs and postcards. The exhibition had nothing mysterious (...) no hassle with complicated lenders, just masterpieces that were widely accepted. We only had to deal with one lender and were not dependent on the whims of artists."[41]

What Hultén does not mention is the level of cost. It goes without saying that the sheer expense — money spent, not invested — of borrowing these more than seventy masterpieces was awe-inspiring. Wenzel Jacob confides that the Kunsthalle had an annual budget of seventeen million euros, which together with ticket sales and other revenues amounted to twenty-five million — a sky-high figure in the museum world of the time. As in Venice, Hultén and his staff were forced to engage in negotiations about the cost of renovations and other methods of payment for the loans of the works of art. The priority of the art gallery for Helmut Kohl and the reunified German Federal Republic is evidenced in that the German state guaranteed the then astronomical insurance amount of one billion Deutschmarks for the MoMA exhibition.[42]

More than twenty years later, Wenzel Jacob recounts in excited terms the visit to New York when the agreement was concluded for MoMA's "guest appearance" in Bonn: "It was unreal to be welcomed at MoMA and see what contacts Pontus had there. We went and had a very nice dinner with Dick Oldenburg. Then when we sat at the table and negotiated with them about which masterpieces to borrow, about transportation and insurance, I have to admit that it felt like the building moved a little bit for me when I felt the responsibility. We could negotiate with them because the German state guaranteed the insurance value. I called the person in charge at the ministry from the meeting and he said we should go ahead. Pontus was fantastic in such situations. He had been through everything and was not afraid of anything except the sky falling down."[43]

Richard E. Oldenburg, known as Dick, younger brother of Claes Oldenburg and like him born in Stockholm, was the longest-serving director of MoMA until the current Glenn Lowry, from 1972 to 1995. In our conversation, Claes Oldenburg said of his brother: "He was a good director, but certainly no Alfred Barr."

The exhibition *The Museum of Modern Art New York zu Gast in Bonn* (*The Museum of Modern Art New York Guest in Bonn*), opened on October 17, 1992, was a tremendous public success, attracting some quarter of a million visitors to the newly opened art center, paramount for the success and prestige of the institution. Perhaps it says the most about Pontus Hultén and the network of contacts that he had expanded over four decades in the art world — a veritable work of art in itself! — that he managed to pull off this extravagant show featuring many of the most canonized portal works in modern art history. *The Great Collections* series was to continue long after Hultén had left Bonn, with modern but above all classical and archaeological museum collections — from institutions such as the National Archaeological Museum in Naples, the Russian Museum and the Hermitage in Saint Petersburg, the Prado in Madrid, the Petit Palais in Paris, the Vatican Museum in Rome, the Moderna Museet in Stockholm, and others. Almost all of them were box office blockbusters. The premiere with MoMA, though, was impossible to surpass.

In 1994, Pontus Hultén presented another of his characteristically epic historical exhibitions: *Europa Europa*, featuring art from the Eastern European avant-garde movements of the last half-century, loosely linked, as the title suggests, to the Pingpong exhibitions in Paris. A special focus on Eastern European art, motivated by the historical importance of Germany for Eastern artists, but certainly also by his personal attraction to the East, was part of Hultén's vision for the Kunsthalle. This massive exhibition was curated by two younger art historians, Ryszard Stanisławski, Hultén's Polish friend and collaborator since the seventies, and the German Christoph Brockhaus, in the classic Hultén school, with no less than sixteen hundred exhibits — art, photography, theater, literature, architecture, film and video — including seven hundred paintings, sculptures and installations that filled and flooded all the galleries of the Kunsthalle. Hultén initiated the exhibition and chose Stanisławski as curator but did not get involved in the details of the production. The impression was described in the press with terms like "overwhelming" and "overgrown." "For me, that exhibition was a bit too big," says Kay Heymer. "It's simply not possible, at least not for me, to take in seven hundred works of art at once. Pontus came from a time when these kinds of huge exhibitions were made. You could say that he himself had invented them, together with Harald Szeemann. Today, such exhibitions are not possible. It's fun to have been part of it, but it's over."[44]

Moreover, in Bonn, after the premiere of Niki de Saint Phalle, Hultén staged a series of large-scale monographic retrospectives, defying his own earlier assessment that he saw monographic exhibitions in general as "a bit too simple."[45] Niki was followed by a "very beautiful" mammoth presentation of Sam Francis, with an overwhelming amount of paintings and prints, thirty-three years after Hultén had shown his first Francis retrospective at Moderna Museet in 1960. The meeting for the opening in Bonn was the last between the friends. Francis was exhausted by his cancer and died shortly afterwards. There are beautiful, loving pictures of the two old friends, the big Hultén and the little Francis, together for the last time. Hultén never succeeded in his mission to elevate his friend to the prominence in art history that he felt he deserved as "one of the most important artists of the twentieth century"[46] — a judgment that becomes even more startling in view of the known circumstance that Hultén was otherwise skeptical of this type of "heroic," monumental-scale, masculine, color-rich abstract painting. The exhibition was well received, but it was hinted in the press and in the German art establishment that Sam Francis was perhaps not the most relevant artist of the time. The show was not a public success.

The impression that Hultén was looking back rather than forward — which had become increasingly apparent ever since Los Angeles — was reinforced by what was by all accounts an exquisite and powerful Alexander Calder retrospective on the roof of the Kunsthalle in the same year, 1993, followed in 1994 by Eva Aeppli, Jean Tinguely's first Swiss wife with her inimitable textile sculptures.

The choice of Aeppli surprised many and drew some criticism, more or less explicit. Aeppli is another relatively forgotten artist whose greatness Hultén never quite succeeded in convincing his audience of, which is regrettable (fortunately, Eva Aeppli recently made a posthumous "comeback"[47]). In Bonn, the exhibition included Moderna Museet's fantastic sculpture group "La Table," which has rarely left the warehouse on Skeppsholmen since Hultén's time.[48] Hultén called the exhibition — which did not become a success with the public — beautiful and said that the only thing he was disappointed about was that the reclusive Aeppli did not come to the opening, although he is sure that she saw the exhibition later incognito. The following year, 1995, Hultén's third and last as director of KAH, it was Sarkis who was presented with the major retrospective — another of Hultén's good friends and fellow teacher from the school in Paris, at the time certainly current. The old friends' club was completed with Claes Oldenburg in 1996 and an extensive, celebrated architecture retrospective with Renzo Piano in 1997, two years after Hultén had left Bonn.

The familiarity was further reinforced as Hultén brought to Bonn so many of his old friends and collaborators from previous postings, including Anna-Lena Wibom, who worked on the film program in the auditorium of the Kunsthalle, and Hultén's new life partner, the German Countess Marie-Louise von Plessen, Daniel Spoerri's former private and artistic partner. von Plessen, as an art and cultural historian, was an advisor for the historical exhibitions, also curating her own shows at the Bundeskunsthalle. "Pontus liked to invite his old friends," says Karin Weber. "It was a privilege that he could afford at that stage of his career."[49]

During Pontus Hultén's time as artistic director of the KAH in Bonn, a "film retrospective" of one of his great idols, Luis Buñuel, opened in April 1994, showing the Spanish director's complete oeuvre, in many cases films that had been restored for the exhibition. Buñuel's film art and stills from his films were presented in the context of paintings and sculptures by the director's Surrealist friends such as Salvador Dalí, Giorgio de Chirico, Alberto Giacometti, Hans Bellmer, René Magritte, Max Ernst, Pablo Picasso, Man Ray, Fernand Léger, Francis Picabia, Yves Tanguy and others; along with photography, literature and objects from Buñuel's life, following the principle of many of Hultén's previous exhibitions.

Yasha David, who co-curated the exhibition with Hultén, was known for his indecision and hot emotions. It's said that he repeatedly packed his bags to leave Bonn, as he had done in Venice, before the exhibition was finally completed. "Yes, Yasha was something of a diva, but an absolutely wonderful person, incredibly knowledgeable and skilled," says Karin Weber with a smile. "He worked all the time, all night, very intuitively. It was incredibly intense. Anything could happen."[50] "Pontus and I were in complete agreement about what we wanted to do," says Yasha David himself. "I had a totally free hand. Our ambition was to show the totality of Buñuel's world and the artistic context to give a deeper understanding of his films."[51]

The Buñuel exhibition is depicted as a great experience and was a resounding box office success. Together with the catalog, the retrospective contributed substantially to the knowledge of the Spanish film poet. Anecdotes about the opening night are rich, surrealist tales. Among the many celebrity guests was Catherine Deneuve, who danced with Piéral, the short psychologist from Buñuel's last film *The Dark Side of Desire* — a surreal scene. "It was the best opening ever," says Stephan Andreae. "In the history of the Bundeskunsthalle, the Buñuel exhibition is an unforgettable super highlight."[52] The exhibition traveled to the Reina Sofia in Madrid and to the Palacio de Bellas Artes in Mexico City, the city where Buñuel lived at the end of his life, enjoying great success in these venues as well.

Gerhard Richter was honored with an immense retrospective at the KAH, opened in December 1993. The exhibition was produced by Hultén's former colleague Kasper König, by now a global star curator, in a co-production with the Musée d'art moderne de la ville de Paris under Suzanne Pagé and several other European museums, including Moderna Museet.

The retrospective, which presented the artist's photorealistic as well as abstract oeuvre, with an accompanying magnificent catalog of the thirty-year career of the Dresden-born Richter, was first shown in Paris in the fall of 1993 and, after Bonn, in the fall of 1994, moved on to Moderna Museet in Stockholm. Pontus Hultén had more than a hand in the game when his friend and successor Björn Springfeldt bought Richter's "Bach Suite"[53] of four monumental abstract paintings from the exhibition — a controversial acquisition at the time that can be considered by far the most important single purchase for Moderna Museet's collection since Hultén's own time. Above all, it was Kasper König who negotiated with Richter that the museum could buy the paintings for the heavily discounted price of four and a half million Swedish crowns.[54] At the time, Björn Springfeldt was criticized for the high price, even though it was the Friends of Moderna Museet, led by Gerard Bonnier, who financed the purchase, according to Springfeldt after arduous persuasion.[55] Twenty-five years later, the sum appears a joke for this series, which would likely be worth more than a billion crowns on a free market.

Even the highly acclaimed retrospective of Sigmar Polke, with his sophisticatedly unrestrained German version of Pop Art, opened in June 1997, was planned during Hultén's time in Bonn — an exhibition that consolidated Polke's position as one of the post-war masters. Kay Heymer confirms that of the great contemporary Germans, Polke was the artist Hultén liked best, the only one of these who fully appealed to his own personal taste. "Polke's art was about drugs and also had a strong sense of humor, which appealed to Pontus," says Heymer. "Humor was always very important to him. In his view, self-irony was proof that the artist took himself and his art seriously, but not too seriously."[56]

It's noteworthy that Pontus Hultén, in his own list of exhibitions in his career[57], does not include the Gerhard Richter exhibition, Buñuel, Oldenburg, *Europa Europa* or any of the "science exhibitions" in Bonn. His colleague, deputy director Wenzel Jacob, relates that Hultén got involved in the details of the exhibitions only as long as he found the work enjoyable and constructive: "Pontus was a very serious worker. He worked together with the project managers, together with Kay Heymer and the conservators and got involved in details. He was always very determined that he wanted to shock and entertain the audience. When it became too complicated, he left. When there was no enjoyment or pleasure in the project, he just forgot about it — left it to the project managers or canceled it."[58]

Wenzel Jacob and others say that during his years in Bonn Pontus Hultén learned to speak and correspond in good German, a language in which he had a foundation from his youth. His years in Bonn, when Hultén stayed in the city about two weeks a month, are recounted in admiring, loving stories by his colleagues at the new art institution who had the privilege of working under this living legend, this dinosaur of twentieth century art history, as Karin Weber reverently calls Hultén — stories that I think illustrate Hultén's character at this late stage of his career and life in all its complexity. "The time with Pontus was the most beautiful of my life," says Wenzel Jacob, "a fruitful, happy time of working together. With Pontus you never had the feeling of compromise, of being under pressure or forced not to tell the truth. The trust was total. We had endless conversations and laughed all the time."[59]

Wenzel Jacob, like many others, talks about Pontus Hultén's shyness and even suspicion of strangers — qualities that had always been there, but which seem to have been reinforced over the years, expressed in the way he took a defensive stance at the art gallery's ceremonial openings and other public events, reluctant as ever to enter any major social context. "He had special glasses for immediately spotting who was a real person and who was not," says Jacob. "He stood with his hands behind his back and smiled a little when people approached, saying as little as possible. After twenty minutes he went to the bar. Then all the important people came there. Everyone knew how it worked. After his career it was not necessary for him to participate in the social game. That was also one of the reasons why he chose to stay at my house, as a protection from being disturbed."

Wenzel Jacob brings up a negative aspect of Pontus Hultén's seemingly relatively happy time in Bonn that had recurred throughout Hultén's career: his inability to share credit and express gratitude to his colleagues. Hultén didn't take the time to extend his appreciation as he immediately moved on to the next project. "He didn't show enough attention to those who worked so hard," says Wenzel Jacob. "He made me grow. For others, it was more difficult. He himself had never had the experience of working so deeply into the projects, with all the work involved. He never did. He couldn't imagine how much work it was. It was not malice. Then he hired them again for the next project and the same thing started all over again. There was definitely a problem with his older colleagues, but not in our German team. It was something we could easily discuss in the pub."

"With Pontus, I felt extremely protected," says Karin Weber. "I was very empowered, not necessarily encouraged, but very stimulated. From him, we learned how to exceed limits to achieve more. It worked very well for me. For others, it was a deadly threat. They became 'lame ducks,' paralyzed. Pontus was a very extreme person in every way. He went to extremes in everything he did, in how he worked, loved, ate, drank. He was the bullfighter and the bull in the same person."[60]

Weber, who started working at the Kunsthalle as a young conservator employed by Wenzel Jacob, cinematically describes Pontus Hultén's entrance into Bonn — the aging mythic impresario arriving to take command of a new theater company for a new performance on yet another shore. "Before he came, two technicians arrived carrying a huge coffin, like Pirates of the Caribbean," says Weber. "It was his books. It was a most symbolic entrance. He was a thinker, a man of books. The first thing he asked when he came after himself was 'Where are my books?'"

"Pontus traveled all the time. When he was here, he was very direct in the way he talked about art and problem solving," Weber continues. "He was so focused. His German improved quickly and he soon became fluent. But he remained very Swedish, very shy and intimate. He observed a lot and took his time, then made his decision. He couldn't stand the artificiality of everyday life. He wanted sincere people. We adopted him like a child."

"When he met people he didn't like, it was not pleasant to see — when he sensed someone who might betray him," adds Weber. "It could happen in an instant and he would change completely. He was very intellectual. He got bored with stupidity and could get grumpy. He judged people by whether they were interested in learning. He didn't accept indifference. He could be mean and shake people up. Then when he had a drink, he became a book, the stories poured out. It was so completely natural."

Karin Weber talks about the secret topic during this phase of Pontus Hultén's life, the one he didn't want to talk about, but which contributed to the darkening tone that descended on his personality and character towards the end of his life: his failing health. "His health was extremely fragile. I picked him up at the airport and the first thing he did when he got in the car was to open his leather briefcase and reach for his asthma spray. His health was affecting him. He was losing his breath. He was so extremely restless and never relaxed. He lived under such stress — never being alone, never being at home. He reminded me of a deer with a fatal injury retreating into the woods to die."[61]

Wenzel Jacob, Karin Weber and all of the other colleagues I've spoken to from the time in Bonn express in superlatives all that they learned from Pontus Hultén about the art of exhibition making and the larger, broader perspective on art and its role and function in life, society and history.

"After a long curatorial career, I understood for the first time what selection and presentation means," says Wenzel Jacob. "I learned that from Pontus. He was used to working with mixed media. With the hanging he started a dialog, that was most important. We had a multimedia approach that stimulated discussions, not least with our Eastern European connection. There was no comparable institution that could deal with art, photography, architecture and science as we did. Unfortunately, it went over some people's heads. He was the greatest exhibition maker ever. Not a day goes by that I don't think about what I learned from him."

The colleagues in Bonn, like virtually everyone else I spoke to for this story, are in perfect agreement on one point: Pontus Hultén, and the ideals he represented, became increasingly outdated as the commercialization of the art world began in earnest in the 1980s and has only continued to accelerate since then. "He would have hated the way things are today," says Wenzel Jacob. "He would never have been able to work with the big dealers and gallerists. He would have quit immediately. He couldn't have stomached the big business side of art that he couldn't influence — like the two Frenchmen Pinault and Arnault.[62] When Pinault took over Palazzo Grassi, it was a nail in the coffin for him."

"Pontus was the dinosaur of the twentieth century, but he didn't like the twenty-first," says Weber. "He lost his orientation. He would never have been able to do research on the internet. He was a man of books. Our system today is difficult. Everything is so controlled and regulated. We lack the freedom that was still there then. There's no time or space for his perspective or way of telling stories."

At the end of Pontus Hultén's years in Bonn, KAH and Cantz publishers launched in 1996 what was for a long time the only book written about Pontus Hultén, entitled *Das gedruckte Museum von Pontus Hultén* (*The Printed Museum of Pontus Hultén*).[63] The subject of the book is Hultén's tremendous, often overlooked achievement as a publicist in art. The initiative was taken by Lutz Jahre, head of the library at KAH. "I was fascinated by his catalogs, which were so creative and playful, like artists' books," says Jahre. "He spent a lot of time in the library and brought his own books that we discussed, details such as bindings and repairs. He was a true bibliophile. We talked a lot about books and his catalogs and I developed the idea, which he was very enthusiastic about."[64]

Das gedruckte Museum is an unpretentious but highly ambitious, comprehensive, superior quality and well-researched book of the utmost importance for the knowledge of Pontus Hultén, especially since so surprisingly little had been written about Hultén until recent years. The book covers Hultén's forty-year career as a cataloger, with extensive excerpts and cover images from his most important catalogs from the early fifties onwards, as well as from his books on Duchamp's notes (1980, with Paul Matisse as co-author), the artist monograph on Brancusi (1987, with Natalia Dumitresco and Alexandre Istrati) and *The Surrealists Look at Art* (with Sam Francis, 1990).

Moreover, the book contains many valuable texts. In Lutz Jahre's own interview with Hultén, he talks in retrospect about his own role models Alfred H. Barr and Willem Sandberg and how he wanted to combine the best of what he had learned from these two mentors at Moderna Museet in Stockholm.[65] A large number of prominent guest writers, many of whom are now long gone, contribute most personal texts about Hultén, including the artists Carl Fredrik Reutersward, Niki de Saint Phalle, Claes Oldenburg, Bernhard Luginbühl, Daniel Buren, Jan Svenungsson and Sarkis. Hultén's colleagues Billy Klüver, Jean-Hubert Martin, Germain Viatte and Kasper König, Louisiana founder Knud W. Jensen, Hultén's Los Angeles friends Jerry Sohn and Robert Shapazian, even Harald Szeemann, and others, are also among the contributors. These texts offer a treasure of memories, thoughts, observations, analyses and anecdotes about Pontus Hultén's person and career, and about the history of twentieth century art.

Best known is Niki de Saint Phalle's long personal text in which the artist writes about her, Hultén's and the deeply missed Tinguely's joint adventures in the art world. Frequently quoted in various contexts is Niki de Saint Phalle's statement in the text that Hultén "in his soul is an artist, not a museum director," a judgment that has been used almost ad nauseam in various afterthoughts.[66]

Das gedruckte Museum von Pontus Hultén was launched with an exhibition of books from Pontus Hultén's own library at the University Library in Bonn, as the Kunsthalle's own library was too small for the purpose. Lutz Jahre recounts how he was surprised by the enthusiasm with which Hultén engaged in both the book and the exhibition: "It was a rather unpretentious, modest-scale project. I thought it would be a small thing for such a legend who had done so many huge and world-famous exhibitions and catalogs. But he was incredibly friendly and polite, almost shy. He was grateful that we were doing this and most helpful. You could tell that the book was very important to him. At the opening he said something that surprised me: 'Now I know how the artists feel.' It was almost touching how proud he was."[67]

When it comes to the events surrounding Pontus Hultén's dismissal from KAH and Bonn, there are, as usual, different versions of the cause and sequence of events. After five years in Bonn, Hultén ended his contract in the fall of 1995 — or his contract was terminated. As with his previous posts, the economy seems to have been the deciding factor. Pontus Hultén and his program eventually became too expensive for the institution, although his German colleagues do not say this outright.

These colleagues all agree that regardless of the turmoil surrounding the end of Pontus Hultén's contract in Bonn, his exit was natural — that Hultén gradually slipped away from Bonn and then suddenly disappeared for good. There was no amicable parting of the ways. Once again, Hultén left a workplace with a considerable degree of disappointment and bitterness, at least on his own part but it was apparently mutual. "We had decided from the beginning that Pontus' role would only be needed for the first five years, to get the art center up and running," says Wenzel Jacob. "He had an idea that he would continue a little longer but I wanted to do it myself. I had the intention to involve him with his own exhibitions that he would design, but Pontus just disappeared. That's how it was with him. As soon as a project was finished, he lost interest. He never found a place where he stayed. He never said thank you. He disappeared without coming back."[68]

"Pontus loved creating new things, then leaving," says Karin Weber. "The freedom he needed only exists when you create a new bubble. He was completely uninterested in things like whether you need new parking lots and fire protection. He got bored with budgets and talking to politicians. For him, the challenge was to open the new. Then he lost interest. This is where it ended."

No worse were the clashes with the museum management in Bonn than that Hultén returned the year after his resignation, in 1996, for a grand epilog — the second exhibition in the series of major museums' guest appearances in Bonn, featuring the collection he had to such an extent built up personally at Moderna Museet in Stockholm — a testament to the sensational first era of his career.

Moderna Museet's visit to Bonn in 1996 was well planned as Rafael Moneo's new museum complex was under construction and the museum was temporarily housed in premises in central Stockholm. Moderna Museet's director at the time was still Björn Springfeldt (who later became the Swedish cultural attaché in Germany). Pontus Hultén is said to have been very involved in the exhibition and proud of the result. It was an emotional experience for him to see in a new location the magnificent set of masterpieces that he and his colleagues had almost miraculously assembled. Looking at the images from the exhibition, which was a public and critical success, it's striking in a different way than on its "home turf" that this outstanding collection could come from such a northern outpost — a testimony to Hultén's achievements in the art world that he had so fearlessly embraced in Stockholm and Paris in the early fifties. The exhibition opened in the fall of 1996 and was inaugurated by our German-born Swedish Queen Silvia. Prime Minister Göran Persson also visited the exhibition.

When I met Pontus Hultén in Stockholm in December 1996, the Moderna Museet collection was still hanging in Bonn. Hultén's pride and self-consciousness were evident as he began our conversation about the museum in Stockholm by telling me about the presentation of the collection at KAH. "It looks very good and has been very much appreciated," Hultén said. "When we made the catalog and poster, we toyed with the idea of simply calling it 'The World's Best Museum of Modern Art.' In the end, we didn't, but we actually seriously considered it. Sure, there are many great museums and collections in the world but most of them are so damn boring. What's unique about Moderna Museet's collection is that it is so fresh, with only key works, nothing from the artists' production phases."[69]

Pontus Hultén's years in Bonn are not counted among the highlights of his career. "There was not quite the same energy and intensity there as in Paris and Venice," as Olle Granath notes.[70] This can be partly explained by the Kunsthalle's lack of its own collection and by Bonn's demotion from the city's position as capital. A measure of criticism for a certain nostalgia and obsolescence is, as we have seen, part of the overall picture drawn by Hultén's German posting.

In our time, almost a quarter of a century after Pontus Hultén's departure, the Bundeskunsthalle is an important European art institution that seems somewhat oversized. The number of visitors has dropped from more than a million during Hultén's time and the years after, to around two hundred thousand a year. From an art historical perspective, it's the first five years' attendance figures that stand out as remarkable. Without doubt, Pontus Hultén had once again performed a pioneering act in the international art world. "We were without competition the foremost art center in Germany and that was no mean feat," as Karin Weber concludes.[71]

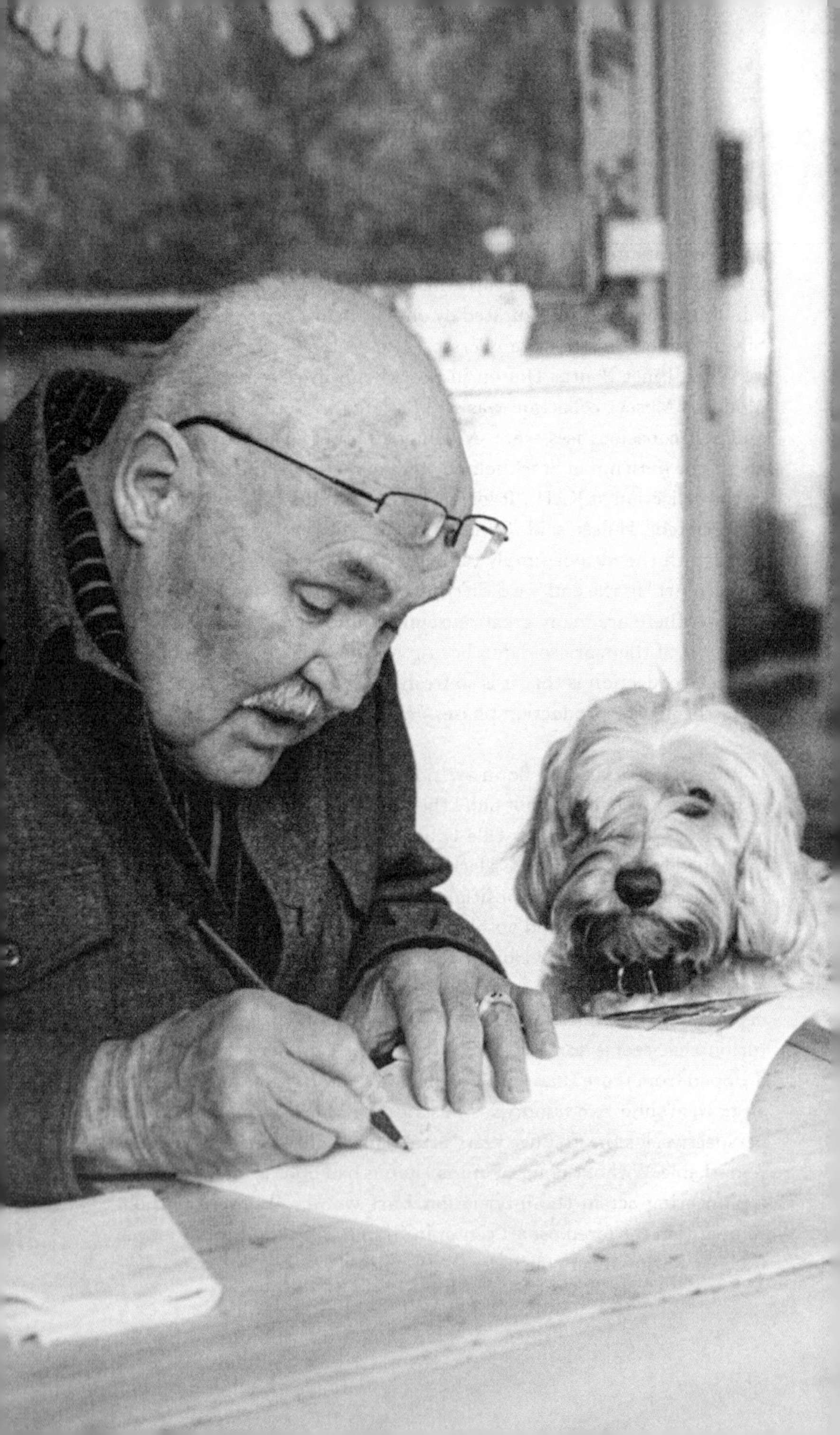

30

Finally a recluse, where to settle down? Pontus becomes lord of the castle in the Loire

I have mentioned several times Marie-Louise von Plessen, the German Countess, Pontus Hultén's friend and rival Daniel Spoerri's former life partner and artistic collaborator. von Plessen, who descends from an ancient North German-Danish noble family with a number of historic castles, estates and manors in northern Germany and southern Denmark in its possession, is a cultural historian and museologist with a doctorate. Since the early seventies, she has collaborated with artists and curators on artistic and historical projects, organizing exhibitions in many countries. von Plessen first met Pontus Hultén in 1976, prior to the work on the first edition of Spoerri's and her exhibition concept *Musée Sentimental*, which was shown in the interior of Jean Tinguely and Bernhard Luginbühl's sculpture *Crocodrome* at the opening of the Centre Pompidou in 1977. They had later met a few times over the years at Teeny Duchamp's in Villiers-sous-Grez and at Spoerri's in Le Moulin Boyard, southeast of Paris. von Plessen met Hultén again in 1990, when the latter had begun his mission in Bonn, at a reception at an international museum fair in the Grand Palais in Paris, where Hultén escorted the German ambassador. He was delighted to see von Plessen again, who at the time was curating the successful Bismarck exhibition that inaugurated the controversial new Historical Museum of Reunified Germany in Berlin. Hultén immediately forgot his official duties. "The ambassador, whose name was Pfeffer, told me that I couldn't bother him because it might hurt the national feelings of the French, but I told Pontus that I would defy orders," says von Plessen. "He was very protective of me, in a touching way."[1]

Marie-Louise von Plessen had been living for a few years in a small chateau in the Loire two hours south of Paris. She had bought the

Pontus and Dolly signing books, La Motte, 2002.

property together with a male German friend and shared the charming little moat-lined castle with him. When Pontus Hultén came to visit, he fell in love with the castle and its surroundings. When von Plessen later told him that her German friend wanted to sell his share and move from La Motte, Hultén said to her great surprise: "I'm moving in." Without hesitation, he bought her friend's share and moved to the Loire, with his art collection and library as luggage to prove that he meant business.

Hultén had long been looking for a place to settle down and eventually retire, a real home, and a stately one at that. He had nurtured a dream of Los Angeles and a hope of Venice. Instead, it became a chateau on the Loire. "He had been looking for years for a retreat from the international art world, not too far from Paris, where he could keep his art and his books," says Marie-Louise von Plessen.[2] The move to the Loire surprised many of his friends and colleagues in Paris. "Castles were perhaps good in the seventeenth century, but not today," says Hultén's old collaborator Serge Fauchereau. "Nobody understood why he moved there, it made him isolated."[3]

I myself have no difficulty appreciating the allures that seduced Pontus Hultén with this little castle and the region where I have had the privilege of frequently staying as a guest of Marie-Louise von Plessen, who still lives at La Motte. The castle is blessed with an enchanting charm, built on an antique Roman-Gallic settlement, surrounded by a rectangular moat between the bank of the Loire and the Briare Canal. The oldest parts date from the sixteenth century. The moat, with its water lilies, and the round towers, lends the castle a fairytale medieval character.

Obtaining a chateau in the Loire is known to be popular with Americans and also with artists. One who belongs to both categories and who already owned a chateau on the Loire was Hultén's old friend Claes Oldenburg — "a chateau that makes La Motte look like a gatehouse," as Marie-Louise von Plessen expresses it.[4] Hultén had many friends who lived in the same direction south of Paris, such as Teeny Duchamp in Fontainebleau, en route between Paris and La Motte, where Tinguely's "Le Cyclop" was also located, Niki de Saint Phalle who had her studio and home in Soisy, and others.

Along the Loire River, Pontus Hultén went for his daily walk, with glorious views of its calcareous sandbanks, which give character to the dry white wines of nearby famous villages and districts. After a couple of kilometers on the riverbank, the walk reaches the Pont-Canal de

Briare water bridge — a green-painted cast iron and sandstone structure that connects two canals in a vast system. During the summer season, the bridge is crossed by a steady stream of tourist barges on tours of the canal system, from as far afield as Holland, passing just behind La Motte. The Pont Canal, which naturally fascinated Pontus Hultén — the bridge, designed by Gustave Eiffel's office and inaugurated in 1894, is a masterpiece of architecture and engineering — leads across to the picturesque village of Briare, where Hultén drank his daily glasses of walking wine at a café at the bridge's abutment. Here he liked to sit and watch the barges gliding by before walking back with his and von Plessen's beloved Pyrenean sheepdog Dolly for company.

Pontus Hultén adorned — filled to the brim is another expression — the castle with the collection that he had amassed during a life in the arts, with works by artist friends from all over the world. For the lower salon, where one of Eva Aeppli's madames permanently reclines in a chaise-longue, he purchased a vast silk carpet from Venice. Many of the household objects were also partly or wholly works of art. Marie-Louise von Plessen is, among many other capacities, a pianist of near professional class. For her, Hultén bought a Steinway grand piano at a reduced price, placed in the upper salon where one wall is still adorned with a monumental collage by Hultén himself, dated as early as 1952 under the signature "Bo Ek," one of Hultén's two aliases as an artist. For Hultén's seventieth birthday, Marie-Louise von Plessen gifted him a gift a pair of peacocks that have since multiplied into a whole family; some individuals from Hultén's time of this incomprehensibly magnificent, shy bird still strut around the castle courtyard and garden screaming dramatically like true gala queens. "Pontus loved them," says von Plessen. "He loved to look at them, their vanity, and was very proud of them."[5]

The other was Kjell Buffington. Hultén chose Bo Ek as it is the shortest Swedish name.

More eccentrically, Hultén had his open sailing cutter "Porto Kalada," with the additional name "Klara," built on the Greek island of Leros and kept in Venice until, through its dry-shod voyage to Los Angeles, it had been renovated and painted in bright colors by Greg Mahoney over many years.[6] The boat was "anchored" in the windowed corridor next to the large salon on the ground floor. Hultén had a hole drilled in the castle wall to let out the diesel exhaust so he could start the laboriously renovated engine, enjoy its sound and fury, and dream himself out on the Adriatic ...

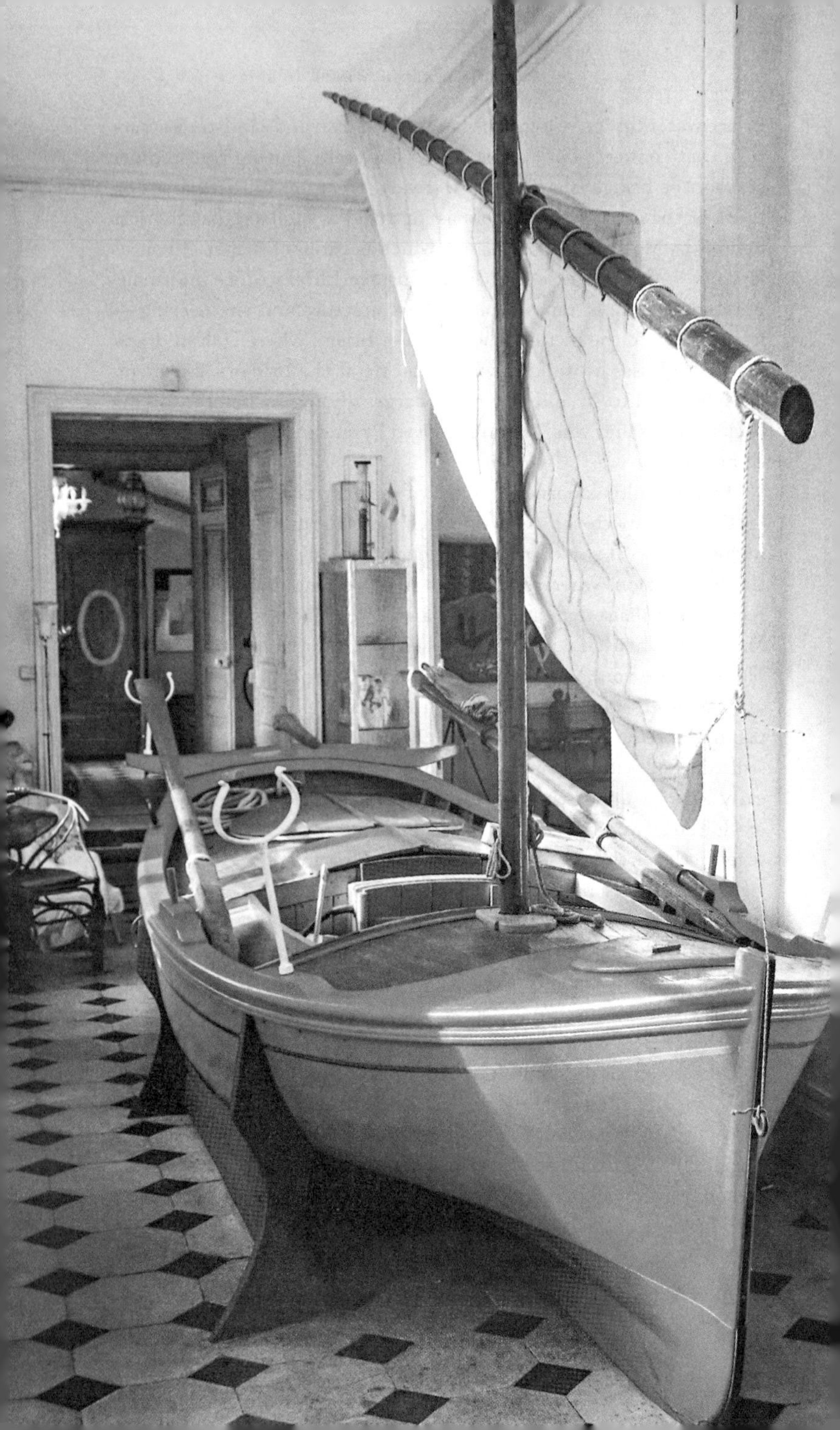

It may all sound extravagant. Back home in Sweden, the image of Pontus Hultén as lord of the castle in the Loire conveyed a lavish impression. In reality, it's not so outrageously grand. La Motte is a small chateau of the kind that abound throughout France, the size of a manor house. Pontus Hultén was careful to stress that he did not live in the distant "chic" Loire,[7] where Oldenburg and many others had/have their castles. Hultén was undoubtedly wealthy, but he had not gathered any great fortune.

During his early years in the Loire, Pontus Hultén was still traveling the world at his usual furious pace, as director first of the KAH in Bonn and then of the Museum Tinguely in Basel (see next Chapter). He commuted to Paris, where he still had his penthouse on Rue Beaubourg, for his assignments at the school and as advisor to the MNAM, among others, and to Venice, where he was still engaged until the Duchamp exhibition in 1993. At the time of his seventieth birthday in June 1994, celebrated at a storied luncheon at La Motte, Hultén was still very much involved in his international career. I've seen wonderful film footage of the celebrations, with the eighty-eight-year-old Teeny Duchamp, the year before her death, Niki de Saint Phalle and so many other familiar faces from Pontus Hultén's global art family.

Marie-Louise von Plessen immediately became not only Pontus Hultén's life companion but also his artistic collaborator and historical source of knowledge, advisor and researcher for his exhibitions and other projects. Among the first of these was *Le Territoire de l'Art* in Leningrad in 1990, where von Plessen was indispensable as Russian is one of the seven languages she commands, with extensive knowledge of Russian history. Marie-Louise adds another description of Hultén's passion for everything Russian, at that time newly post-Soviet — a picture that confirms what several others have reported: that this love was Dadaist-Surrealist in nature. "He was so happy in those palaces in Saint Petersburg," says Marie-Louise. "Everything had just opened up and it was a unique atmosphere. When he spoke about Russia, it was not from a philanthropic perspective. He could be a convinced socialist. He felt a strong kinship with the mentality and it was not at all just about vodka. He loved the people and the rotting, decaying culture. He loved even the catastrophic aspects of it. Everything could come crashing down he would be left standing. He could read the layers of Russian society. It also strongly appealed to his sense of humor. He loved going to restaurants in his cowboy boots, which he

"Porto Kalada" stranded at La Motte.

only wore in Russia. He liked that there were strong, unpredictable minds there."[8]

At the Kunsthalle in Bonn, Marie-Louise von Plessen became a close collaborator of Pontus Hultén. She was part of the creative team along with several of Hultén's old friends and colleagues, herself curating an exhibition of nineteenth-century panoramic photographs here in 1993 — a success that drew two hundred and fifty thousand visitors to the Kunsthalle. Since then, von Plessen has produced exhibitions at the KAH, most recently in 2018, an epic, acclaimed exposé on the history of the Rhine River, featuring everything from relics and remnants from the eleventh century to works by William Turner, Max Ernst, Joseph Beuys, Anselm Kiefer, Andreas Gursky and other artists.[9]

The creative "family" at KAH also included Anna-Lena Wibom. Even during his relationship with von Plessen, Hultén maintained his long-distance relationship with Wibom, meeting her and their daughter Klara mainly during his summer vacations. Marie-Louise visited Sweden with him, but says that there was always a tension about her role in Hultén's relationship with his home country:

"Sweden was so incredibly important to Pontus. He was a true patriot, of the kind which you can only become if you live abroad for so long. He loved the people, strawberries, crayfish, his boat and the people who worked on it — a lot of things like that. It was sacred to him. He often talked about us living in Sweden one day. He took me to the Old Town where he still had his apartment on Stora Nygatan. He was very proud that Carl Jonas Love Almqvist had lived in the house. He was a great admirer of Almqvist and often spoke about him. He saw him as a realist, an observer of a changing society. He showed me Gripsholm and other places. We were supposed to see Birka too, but that didn't happen. But Sweden was always Anna-Lena's territory. She was the bond to his homesickness and when he went to Sweden in the summer he was always secretive. Swedes are like that. They stick to their own. Non-Swedes never really get into that group."[10]

As a life partner and creative collaborator of Pontus Hultén for more than fifteen years, Marie-Louise von Plessen paints a loving, complex portrait of Pontus as a professional, personality and companion. "I felt a deep, deep kinship with Pontus," she says. "He had many faults but I could see his noble sides." von Plessen claims that a fundamental trait of Pontus Hultén as a person and as a professional

Lower salon at La Motte with works by Daniel Tremblay (painting), Eva Aeppli (small sculptures) and Niki de Saint Phalle (large sculpture).

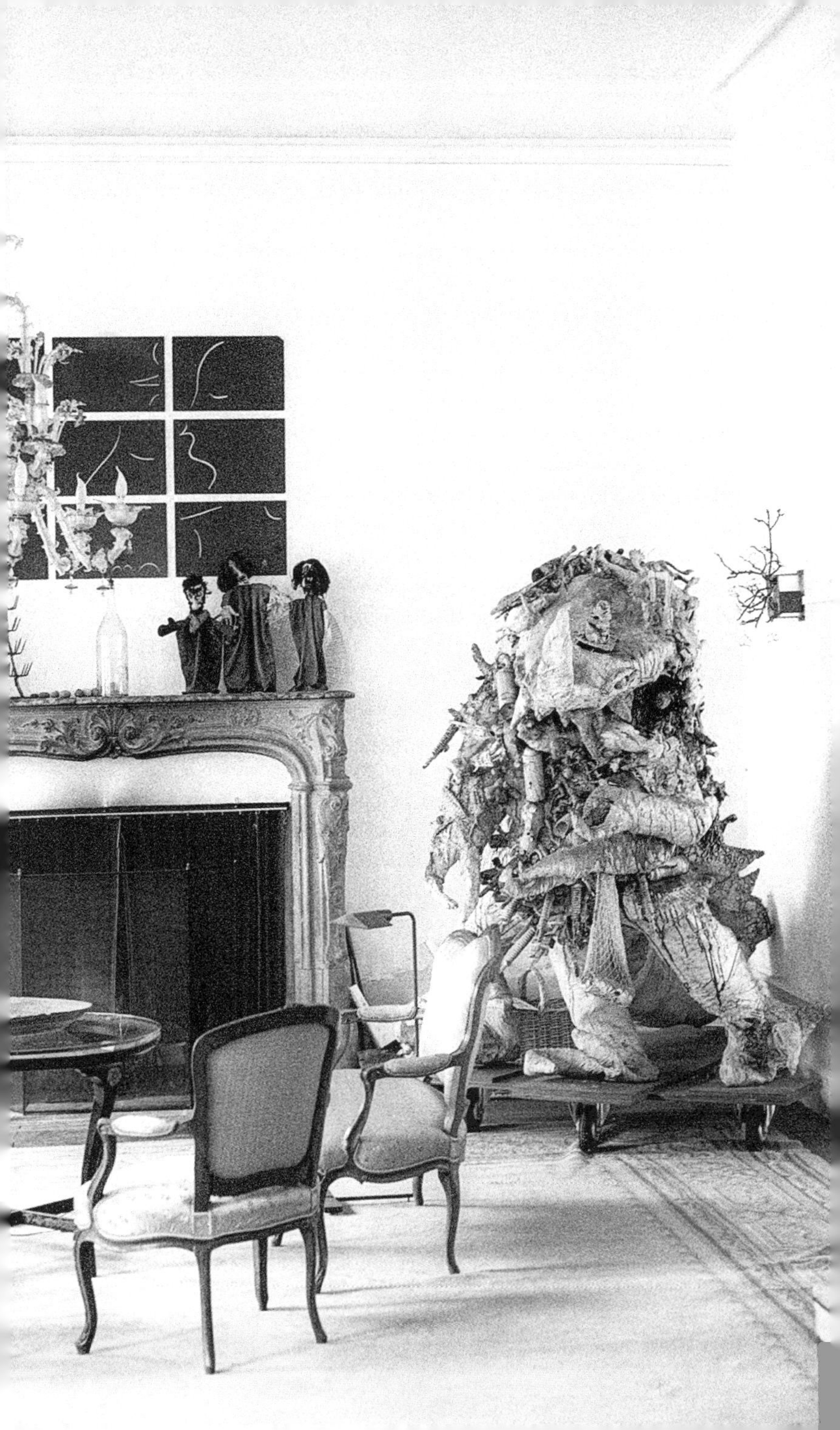

was his refusal to submit to given structures or hierarchies. "He was so totally convinced in his creative approach, never interested in makeshifts or compromises. He would fight or just walk away rather than compromise."[11]

According to Marie-Louise, Hultén's philosophy of life and art was to "expand life and people's ability to enjoy it." "It was built into his whole behavior. He was like a circus director. He wanted to entertain and more than that — he wanted to get people to interact, even though he didn't want to interact himself. That was the only thing that interested him. Compromise and accommodation are part of a power game that bored him. He was completely uninterested in the art market, even though people constantly sought his expertise. He used the tactic of letting others tear each other apart without saying anything. When they were done, he just said 'we'll do it like this.' He was a real leader, not a manager. He could take a flame and blow it up into a fire, like with the Pingpong exhibitions. It was like Niki said: He was a failed general who should have been commanding armies."[12]

In my opinion, von Plessen expresses the essence of Pontus Hultén's view of art when she talks about his desire for art to delight and entertain — and to stand for a political message and a critical stance towards society. "But not in a philanthropic way," Marie-Louise emphasizes. "For him, it was about a philosophical attitude, not about driving smaller cars. That's what he loved about Tinguely — that he took waste from industrial society and turned it into art that was critical of consumer culture. What made Pontus unique was his great general knowledge. He was a utopian and believed in anarchic change. He also saw art as a way to achieve equality, in the Swedish way, with children's workshops and so on, although he himself was not interested in such things."[13]

Marie-Louise elaborates on Pontus Hultén's natural aura of power and authority, and how he used this asset: "Pontus didn't exercise his power. He was just very powerful. He didn't do it by talking. He was demanding without opening his mouth. He was not easy. On many people he had a paralyzing impact. Like my family, for example. Coming from the aristocracy, they had never heard of Pontus or what he had done, but when they met him they were immediately like yapping lapdogs. He was almost godlike, but not in his own mind. He always doubted himself. He was very conscious of this effect he had on people and he used it. He behaved completely differently towards men and women. He was a real *womanizer* and he utilized it."

As a life companion, Pontus Hultén was by no means easy or uncomplicated, says Marie-Louise von Plessen, hardly surprisingly. "In the morning he would say 'see you later.' I never knew whether I would see him in the evening or much later. Either he was there or he wasn't. He wasn't romantic but always provocative. He liked to tease and poke and provoke, that was part of his love."

In his views on gender, as with almost everything else, Pontus Hultén was contradictory. He gave Group 8 a platform at Moderna Museet, launched Niki de Saint Phalle and in many contexts professed a feminist approach, although he would never have thought of calling himself a feminist. In his private life, he preferred traditional gender roles, confirms Marie-Louise von Plessen: "Pontus was not a modern man who cleaned and washed dishes," she says. "He could cook a few simple things, like what you do on a boat, like an omelette, but here at home he asked every day: 'what's on the menu?' Otherwise, his contribution was to buy the wine, often Sancerre and Pouilly-Fumé."

Marie-Louise recounts how Pontus Hultén constantly used her historical knowledge in his work. Their mutual interest in the historical and anthropological contexts of art and social development was a strong bond between them. "Pontus had a unique holistic approach in his intellectual outlook and view of the world — a bit like I think André Breton had. It was great to learn from his insights. He had a subtle understanding of the big picture — a way of understanding the world and the development of technology, as in studying the emergence of railway stations for example. As a 'documentary researcher,' I had to replace the teams of skilled collaborators he had under him, which was not easy. I was like a retrieving bird dog for him. When I came back from traveling, he expected me to bring him something beautiful and interesting. He used me as his Google, constantly asking me for information that he expected me to find out for him."

After 1997, when Hultén, at the age of seventy-three, completed his last brief posting at the Tinguely Museum in Basel (see next Chapter), he retired, largely and more or less voluntarily. The intensity of his travel and work schedule declined, partly out of self-preservation due to his declining health.

The career of Marie-Louise von Plessen, who was twenty-six years younger, continued to develop at an ever-increasing pace, with trips for exhibitions and other projects. As a consequence, Hultén became increasingly lonely at La Motte over the years. In von Plessen's absence, he was assisted by his secretary Nathalie Meneau, whom he paid as a private employee and who had settled nearby. Her Russian husband Sergei Serp, or Serge as he is sometimes called, a necrorealist artist from the Leningrad school exhibition, where he and Meneau had met, was on hand as a kind of "handyman." Meneau and Serp's daughter Marie, whom Hultén was very fond of, was often a guest at the castle during von Plessen's absence.

Marie-Louise von Plessen is a person who evokes strong emotions. Some of Pontus Hultén's friends and colleagues from Paris portray von Plessen in terms of fear. Some go so far as to claim that Hultén himself eventually became afraid of von Plessen, referred to by some as "Panzer Countess," a nickname alluding to her alleged kinship with Bismarck, a myth that Marie-Louise herself dismisses. Germanophobia and gender bias seem to characterize many of these assessments.

Some of Pontus Hultén's close friends say that when they wanted to visit him at La Motte, they first checked with Nathalie Meneau that von Plessen was away and "the coast was clear." In any case, visits from Paris and elsewhere were not particularly frequent. They decreased over the years. Although some claim that Marie-Louise von Plessen scared Hultén's friends and drinking companions away, it's generally agreed that the main reason for his increasing loneliness was of a different, more crassly human nature. "He no longer had the power he once had, so people didn't have the same interest in seeking him out," says Daniel Abadie. "That's the harsh truth, unfortunately."[14] According to von Plessen, Pontus Hultén himself was well aware of this state of affairs: "He knew very well that this was how it worked and he accepted it. He became a private person. When there were openings in Paris, he often said 'you go, I'll stay here.' He enjoyed the simple life. Basically, Pontus hated the consumer society. He would rather sit on a couch and eat a piece of goat's cheese with local olive oil than attend a fancy dinner with famous people."

I point out to Marie-Louise that Pontus, in his aversion to materialism and consumerism, made some exceptions, such as with his own wardrobe, selected accessories and other items: "Yes, it's true that he was very particular about his clothes and some personal possessions," she replies. "He had a great interest in different materials and details of the craft. He would search all over the world to find the right fabric."[15]

Some of Hultén's friends and colleagues may express negative views about Marie-Louise von Plessen, but many had opposing opinions.

Niki de Saint Phalle became a close friend and confidante of von Plessen. “We were like real sisters,” says Marie-Louise. “We shared the experience of growing up in the aristocracy with all that it entails and that bonded us.”

No, La Motte didn’t become Pontus Hultén’s long longed-for retreat to the end of his life either, but close enough. For fifteen years, the chateau in the Loire was his main residence — his most enduring permanent home in life. His relationship with Marie-Louise von Plessen was also, as Marie-Louise notes, by far his longest with a woman. His friends in Paris could say what they wanted. There was no doubt that Hultén loved life in the Loire. “When he came back after being away, he always said that he was coming back to paradise,” says von Plessen.

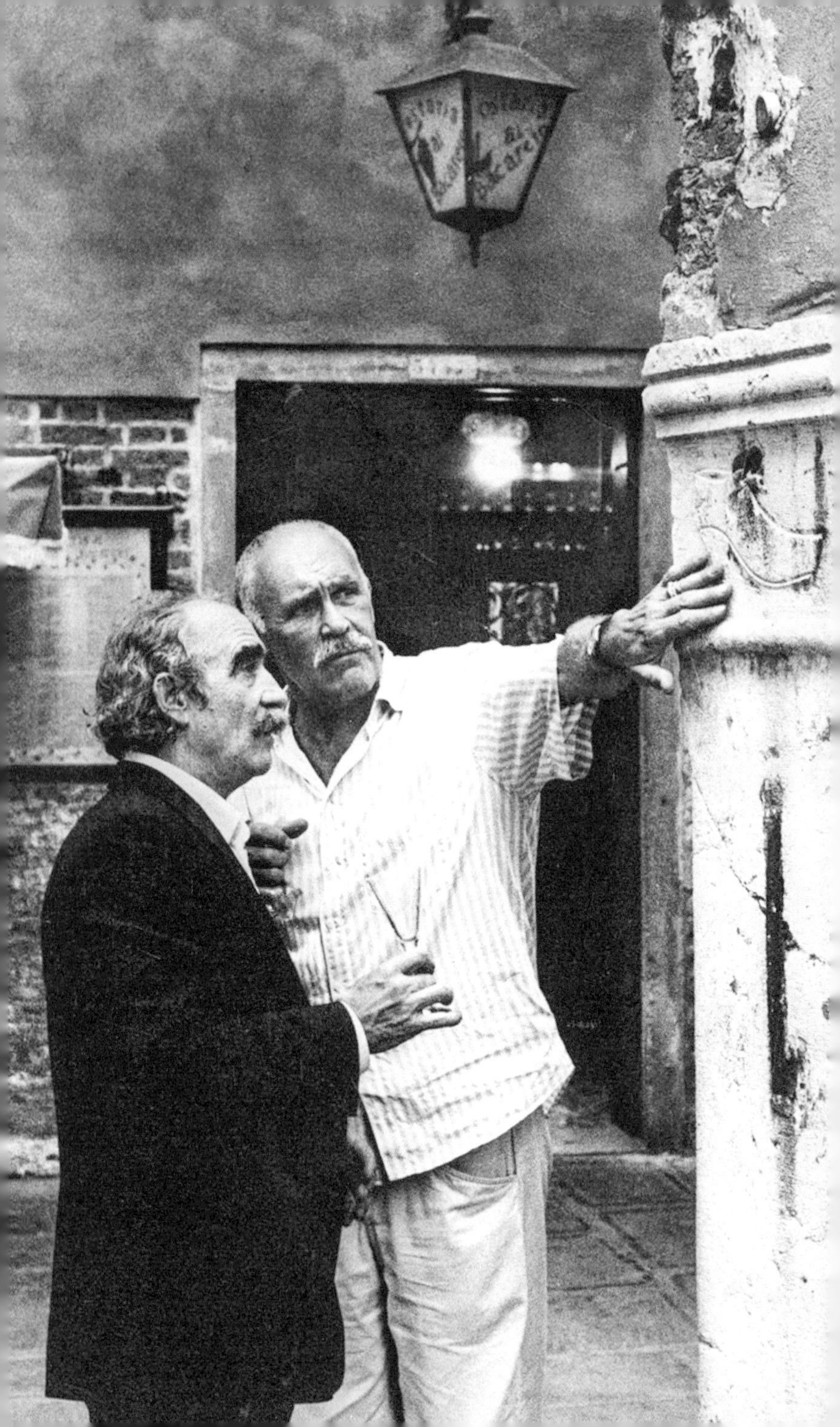

31

Finale in the museum world with Jean Tinguely

On August 30, 1991, Pontus Hultén suffered a loss that would shadow the rest of his life when his old friend and artistic partner — accomplice is another word — Jean Tinguely's rattling, clamoring, howling, steaming, smoking, squeaking, hissing, sputtering, roaring, ever-rotating tour of the art world came to an end. Tinguely died at the age of sixty-six in a hospital in Bern as a result of the heart problems that had plagued him for a number of years, without slowing down the artist's frenetic pace of life or copious production.

Jean Tinguely, actually named Jeannot, said he was descended from the Jener, a Central European nomadic people, and was proud of his heritage. "He told it to me, which doesn't necessarily mean it's true," as Niki de Saint Phalle's granddaughter Bloum Cardenas says of her "step-grandfather."[1] Adventurousness, impetuosity, rebelliousness, death-defying bravery, audacity, constant movement, refusal to conform to or be constrained by convention — qualities that have been associated in myth with various tribes of wandering peoples — characterized his person. An adventurer and rebel from boyhood, he was born in Fribourg and raised under humble circumstances in the working-class neighborhood behind the railway station in German-speaking, Protestant-dominated Basel, the only child of a French-speaking Catholic family. His father was a warehouse worker, his mother a maid. Tinguely has recounted how the family faced discrimination and struggled to fit into the social patterns of the city.

A childhood experience that made a decisive impression on Tinguely and, together with the war and car racing, became a driving force in his art, was the famous Fasnacht carnival in Basel, a wild seventy-two hour pageant with strong surrealist elements. The carnival has ancient

Jean Tinguely and Pontus Hultén, Venice, 1987.

Catholic roots but was transformed during the Reformation in the fifteenth century and is considered the sole Protestant carnival in the world. In a radio interview, Tinguely describes his encounter with the carnival: "For me as a Catholic, Basel Fasnacht was forbidden. And I was very frustrated. But when I saw my first Morgestraich [the dawn procession that opens the festival], I was as frightened as when I saw my first grand prix at the Bremgarten in Bern. The Morgestraich thing is weird. And it has this power, a channeled power, the military, the uniforms, with masks, and the terrible heads, that's heavy and Basel Fasnacht is something that affected me deeply, that's for sure."[2]

At the age of thirteen, Tinguely reportedly left the Church after the Pope blessed Mussolini's troops on the eve of the invasion of Albania on Good Friday 1939. During the war, he joined a socialist youth organization that was later outlawed. For Tinguely, as for Pontus Hultén and so many of their contemporaries, communism was the obvious alternative in the fight against fascism. At the age of fourteen, Tinguely was determined to put his position into action when he attempted to cross the Italian border at Chiasso to make his way to Greece, where he hoped to join the resistance movement against the fascist Italian invasion forces.[3]

During the final year of the war, 1945, Tinguely served for thirty-nine days as a machine gunner in the Swiss army where he met several lifelong friends, among them the jazz musician Lukas Burckhardt, later a member of Basel City Council, and Corporal Eberhard "Ebi" Kornfeld, who became one of Switzerland's foremost art dealers, a leading expert on Rembrandt, Picasso, Giacometti and on Tinguely himself. Together, the friends became part of the so-called Kuttlebutzer clique, which for forty years organized its own anarchic and artistic carnival during Basel Fasnacht, where Tinguely, together with other artists, craftsmen and performers, created outrageous actions and performances with music, dance, costumes, machines, fireworks and other elements. The influence of Basel Fasnacht is apparent in the Swiss artist's work. The popular festival was one of his ideals and an environment he loved.

After the war, Tinguely became a partisan in art, eternally rebellious and subversive, anarchist to the core, a daring rebel and risk-taker, constantly parodying the capitalist industrial and consumer society that had been born out of the war. He harbored a dualistic relationship with technological development and industrialism. He was captivated by the power of industry and technology, which he considered superior to that of art, especially the virtuosic, extreme engineering that found expression in racing and, in particular, Formula 1, Tinguely's great passion. At the same time, Tinguely regarded the consumerist machine and industrial overproduction as frightening and "grotesque." He refused to accept, let alone respect, its alleged logic and rationality.

Tinguely literally built his own enormous artistic production out of the discarded waste that this production apparatus incessantly spews out — scrap, rubble, used building materials, worn-out consumer goods and other things that he bought cheaply and often received as gifts from suppliers in Paris and elsewhere. The variety of his material palette was limitless — machine parts, plywood, plastic, glass, industrial textiles, light bulbs, cables and electrical installations, ceramics, concrete, insulation materials, discarded vehicles, tools, toys, furniture and, above all, discarded iron and steel in every conceivable variation.

In his sculptures, Tinguely never used traditional artistic materials, only those offered by chance. He had learned this method in Basel's vocational[4] art and design school from his teacher Julia Eble-Ris, who taught her students the philosophy of using found everyday objects, known as objets trouvés, and who influenced the artistic avant-garde of the city and Switzerland, where the anarchist tradition was strong.

Along with Yves Klein in Paris and their contemporary friends and colleagues Robert Rauschenberg and Jasper Johns in New York, Tinguely personifies the concept of Neo-Dadaism, born out of the Second World War as the Dadaists were products of the First. Tinguely himself said that "my affinity for Dadaism was given to me by nature."[5]

I think we can add Pontus Hultén to the small group of Neo-Dadaists. Even though he was not formally an artist, I believe that Neo-Dada is the epithet that best summarizes Hultén's artistic and philosophical approach to life. He was spiritually, artistically, politically, intellectually, humorously and in other ways related to Jean Tinguely and entangled in his career from their first encounter in Paris in 1954. At our meeting in Basel, Josef "Seppi" Imhof, Tinguely's longtime collaborator, confirms that it was Tinguely who extinguished Hultén's own artistic dream as the two spiritual brothers embarked on their joint adventurous expedition into the art world. "Pontus wanted to be an artist himself, but he realized that Tinguely was better," says Imhof. "They made a deal that Jean would make the art and Pontus would write about it. Both were equally dependent on the other."[6]

Seppi Imhof, who spent more time with Tinguely and Hultén together than any other living person, says that the relationship between the friends was far from uncomplicated, that they were often quarreling brothers. "There was a lot of yelling and screaming when they met, these two machos. The relationship between them wasn't always close. When Pontus came, there was often something he wanted. It was the same with Jean. He also often wanted something when he met Pontus."[7]

Since the late 1960s, Tinguely had been developing plans for a museum of his own to house his phenomenally extensive output. Towards the end of his life, Tinguely gradually moved from France back to his native Switzerland, which he had previously cursed for its provincial conservatism and petty bourgeoisie. In 1988, he bought an old glass factory in the village of La Verrerie, not far from his home in Neyruz outside his native Fribourg, with industrial halls huge enough to house his largest movable sculptures. Tinguely expected Pontus Hultén to head this museum, which he intended to call the Torpedo Institute, in homage to Hultén and the Torpedo Workshop at the Moderna Museet in Stockholm. Tinguely also knew which artists would be represented besides himself — his old friends and life companions: Niki de Saint Phalle and Eva Aeppli, Bernhard Luginbühl, Daniel Spoerri, his late friend and hero Yves Klein and a few more Neo-Realists, of course. "Pontus didn't like that," says Seppi Imhof. "He didn't want to be told what to do."[8]

Pontus Hultén and other friends of Tinguely were skeptical about the idea of the museum. The old factory was remote and lacked daylight. Nor did Tinguely envision the museum as public, but as an "anti-museum" in the Dadaist spirit, to which guests would be invited for special tours and events. Tinguely clearly had no urgent desire to reach out to the broad masses with his art. At the time of his death, plans to open the hidden "Le Cyclop" to the public had not materialized, as the sculpture was not yet completed. Although Tinguely made a fortune from his art, creating public decorations and interiors on commission for high fees, he remained in many respects an anti-commercial artist who liked to work with his friends in collective actions and manifestations. He produced many of his most famous works and exhibitions outside the commercial market, not available for sale and often not intended to last, but destroyed at the end of the events or worn down by time.

Jean Tinguely's museum plans died with the artist. Daniel Spoerri, Tinguely's compatriot and one his longest-standing artist friends along with his first wife Eva Aeppli, recalls an unforgettable image from his friend's deathbed in the hospital in Bern; how the perpetual motion machine finally stopped and fell silent like once his self-destructing machine sculpture in MoMA's garden at *Homage to New York* in 1960: "It was like watching an express train slowly slowing down and stopping," Spoerri says.[9]

At the time of his death, Jean Tinguely was an immensely popular and in every way successful artist. In his native Switzerland, he was a modern national artist, at least since his major retrospective at the Kunsthaus Zürich in 1982, which traveled to Geneva, Brussels and London. With this exhibition, Tinguely finally received the broad recognition in his conservative homeland that he had earned internationally twenty years before. The previously controversial Tinguely became a popular figure, not least among children, who loved his unreasonable, fantastic machines. "Any child can understand my art," was Tinguely's motto.

The artist's funeral in his native Fribourg on September 4, 1991 was like an anarchic state funeral or a mechanized medieval carnival. In the Museum Tinguely in Basel, I saw amazing film footage of the funeral procession through the medieval alleys lined with more than ten thousand spectators, with a procession of the artist's rolling, rattling, smoking machine sculptures escorting the coffin on its way to the cathedral.[10]

Although Jean Tinguely and Niki de Saint Phalle had not lived together since the early 1970s, and even though they had both had many other partners, they remained each other's closest friends and confidants, artistically and privately. They had remained married and, as Tinguely's widow, Niki had inherited his estate and artistic rights. The mammoth task of taking care of huge volumes of art and other property and belongings was an overwhelming task for Niki de Saint Phalle, whose own health was failing at the time. Pontus Hultén became her most important assistant in this work. Tinguely's old friend Ebi Kornfeld, the art dealer, was also involved.

A first challenge concerned "Le Cyclop." At the time of Tinguely's death, the mega-sculpture in the forest lacked security arrangements and had been severely vandalized. The need to do something was urgent. During Tinguely's lifetime, there had been discussions about moving "The Cyclop" to Saint-Cloud on the outskirts of Paris, but these plans had not materialized. French President François Mitterrand had visited "Le Cyclop" in 1985 and Tinguely had donated the

Pp. 604–605: Jean Tinguely, "Grosse Méta-Maxi-Maxi-Utopia," installation for Tinguely's 1987 retrospective in Venice. Museum Tinguely, Basel.

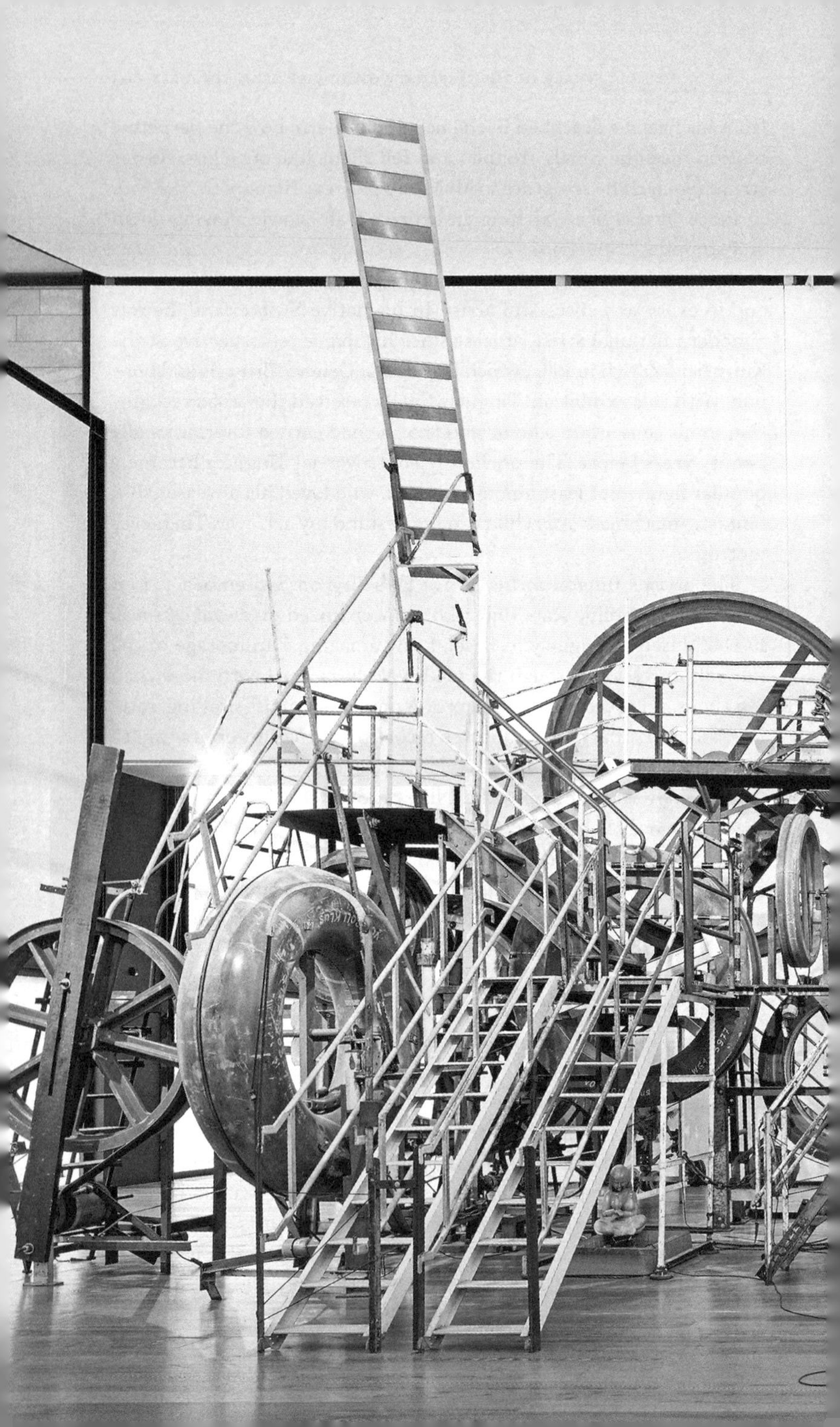

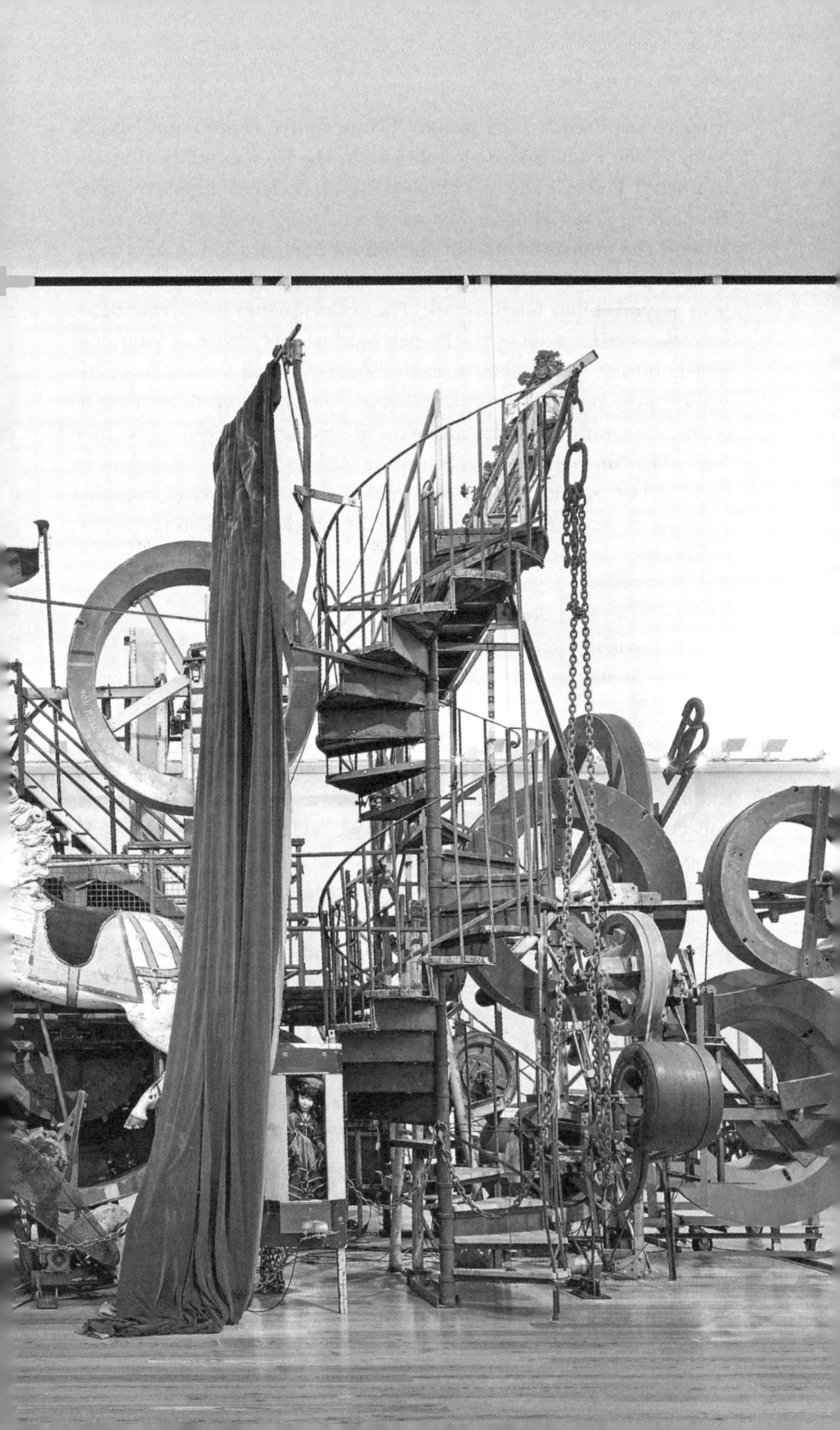

work to the French state in 1987.[11] Now Pontus Hultén and Niki de Saint Phalle mobilized their contacts in the French political establishment. The work was completed and declared finished under Niki's direction.[12] Hultén was proud to show President Mitterrand around the monster's head at the official inauguration in May 1994, as chairman of the "Cyclop's" association, after the state had taken over responsibility for the work. The sculpture and its surroundings are now administered by the French Ministry of Culture as a museum which, during the summer season, attracts visitors from all over the world to the remote forest glade outside the village of Milly-la-Forêt, with a program of events and exhibitions in the forest park. Like Niki's Giardino dei Tarocchi Sculpture Park in Tuscany, directions to the "Cyclop" are discreet, as is the marketing. "The Cyclop" retains a measure of its secrecy and inaccessibility, tucked away in the forest, as Tinguely wanted.

The museum that Jean Tinguely had dreamed of was more complicated, requiring substantial financial resources to realize. Fortunately, there was a natural financier with bottomless resources in Tinguely's old hometown of Basel — a solidly wealthy city, as it is the capital of the Swiss pharmaceutical industry and of the Hoffmann-La Roche Group, the world's largest pharmaceutical company. The Sacher-Hoffmann-Oeri family belonged to the exclusive group of industrialists, collectors and patrons of the arts with whom Hultén was friendly and dependent on throughout his career.

Paul Sacher was another character in this story with a unique history in culture and business, born in Basel and trained as a conductor in his home town. As such, he had a brilliant career before marrying Maja Hoffmann-Stehlin, widow of Emanuel Hoffmann, in 1934. Her late husband's father, in turn, was the Basel industrialist Fritz Hoffmann-La Roche, founder of the pharmaceutical group F. Hoffmann-La Roche AG, one of the world's most profitable companies of all time, with brands such as Valium, Rohypnol and Librium in its extensive drug portfolio. After the Second World War, the modest and low-key Sacher managed to usurp control of this profit machine. Once in possession of this fortune, Sacher could devote himself to patronage. The family's foundation is one of the world's largest supporters of culture.

Niki de Saint Phalle has said that already during Tinguely's funeral in Fribourg in September 1991, she asked Paul Sacher, who was marching alongside her in the procession, whether he and Roche, as the Hoffmann-La Roche group is known for short, would consider financing a Jean Tinguely museum in Basel. Sacher is said to have agreed on the spot. Together with his late wife Maja Sacher, Paul Sacher was himself a great collector of Tinguely's art. The artist's anarchist-communist view of society had never prevented him from associating with liberal-minded, culturally invested big-time capitalists, the richer the better, just as Pontus Hultén's similar political convictions had not inhibited his socializing in such cultivated social circles. Despite his appearance, Tinguely had a taste for the good life. The at first glance shabby suits he wore and disrespectfully abused could on closer inspection prove to be tailored in exquisite fabrics.

A few years before his death, the artist had approached the Sachers with the idea of building a chapel for his 1986 Mengele Totentanz sculpture group, which was owned by Hoffmann-La Roche, on their property on Mount Schönenberg. The installation in the chapel in Venice had given Tinguely, who became increasingly obsessed with death towards the end of his life, a taste for the sacred. In the artist's late work, his Catholic heritage becomes increasingly apparent. Together with the Swiss architect Mario Botta, Tinguely had presented sketches to Paul Sacher. The project had remained unrealized. Now, de Saint Phalle and Sacher reached an agreement whereby Niki would donate fifty-two of Tinguely's sculptures, along with large volumes of other material such as drawings, sketches, letters and so on, to this museum in return for Roche fully financing the construction and operation of the museum, in what became the pharmaceutical group's largest single cultural initiative.

The Tinguely Museum was not funded by the Sacher-Hoffmann-Oeri family foundation but has been wholly owned by the Roche Group from the start. It was decided that the museum, which in Sacher's vision consolidated Basel's position as a city of art and culture, would be ready for Roche's centenary in 1996, which put the project under time pressure. That Pontus Hultén would be the founding curator of the new museum was a given. Museum Tinguely would thus become the sixth museum, or sixth art institution if we're picky (seventh if we include the school in Paris) in a sixth country, that Hultén would help to found; the last or penultimate of his career, depending on how you count. Once again, he would head a privately owned museum — the kind of institution that in his early career he had been a sworn opponent of.

Yet again, Pontus Hultén was denied the opportunity to influence the fundamental decisions on the location and design of the museum building. The original idea was to build the museum on the grounds of Schönenberg, where the "Mengele Chapel" had previously been planned. Hultén tells Stephan Andreae that he and Renzo Piano discussed a museum building on this site, but that Mario Botta, who was close to both the Sacher-Hoffmann-Oeri family and Niki de Saint Phalle, was instead chosen for the assignment, in Hultén's analysis because it was "bureaucratically easier" to hire a Swiss than an Italian architect.[13]

Mario Botta designed a circular museum building to be mounted on the crest of Schönenberg Hill. The plan was abandoned when it became clear that the solution would not work for various reasons. The miscalculation added to the time pressure. The date for the inauguration and anniversary celebrations was fixed in advance for October 1, 1996. In 1993 Roche concluded an agreement with the city of Basel for the lease of a plot of land in a park on the banks of the Rhine. Construction only started at the end of 1994, with less than two years to go before the scheduled opening date. Such was the stress that much of the museum's interior architecture was developed during construction.

Museum Tinguely's location is brilliant in many ways, overlooking the river and the park with its towering old deciduous trees, but also complicated as the site is sandwiched between a busy highway and the equally busy river. Botta's solution is a postmodern building that turns a blind facade towards the highway to generously open up to the beautiful park. A colonnade leads to the museum entrance where one of Jean Tinguely's water fountain sculptures spreads its refined cascades. Fountain sculpture is an art form that Tinguely developed to mastery. Two of the most famous are the "Fontaine Stravinsky" on Place Stravinsky south of the Centre Pompidou in Paris, built in 1983 in collaboration with Niki de Saint Phalle, and the masterpiece "Fasnachtsbrunnen," Basel Carnival's own fountain, erected in 1977 in front of Basel's Stadttheater — a water machine that with great precision splits jets of water into artistic patterns, seemingly defying gravity, which in cold winters freeze into fantastic ice sculptures.

During my visit to Basel, deputy director Andres Pardey confides to me that Pontus Hultén didn't think much of Mario Botta's architecture. Pardey shows me around the three-story building, with over three thousand square meters of exhibition space, explaining the result of the exchange between Hultén and the architect. "Look at this," Andres says as we walk from the Postmodern round stairwell into one of the upper floor's stripped-down white galleries, where beautiful daylight streams in through generous windows overlooking the park. "This is Botta," he says, pointing to the stairwell, "and this is Pontus," he adds as we enter the white space of the gallery. "Pontus only cared about the galleries, lighting conditions and how the collection would be presented. How the galleries are planned, the beautiful daylight — all that is thanks to Pontus. He did all that. Then he completely ignored details like stairwells, toilets, shops, the restaurant and so on. He let Botta realize himself there."[14]

As a newly graduated art historian, Andres Pardey became assistant to Hultén and Margrit Hahnloser, an older colleague who was hired as curator and administrative director of the museum. Hultén had no influence over this recruitment either. Hahnloser lived in Tinguely's birthplace, Fribourg, and was a good friend of the Sacher-Hoffmann-Oeri family who had hired her. Pontus Hultén calls the situation with Botta, Sacher and Hahnloser "very Swiss."[15] The confrontation between Hahnloser and Hultén was immediate. Conflict arose, for example, over the catalog for the premiere exhibition, where Hahnloser advocated a feature on Tinguely as a Swiss artist — a subject that interested Hultén little. Other causes of dispute were purely practical, and Hahnloser's opinions on Hultén's "behavior." "It was a matter of misunderstanding," says Andres Pardey. "Margrit Hahnloser thought that Pontus would be involved in the administrative side of things, planning the program, budgets, staff and practical details. She was also very interested in the social game. Pontus was completely uninterested in all that and refused to take part in it. His only interest was in getting the museum up and running and making sure the art was properly installed."[16]

As usual, Pontus Hultén swiftly gave up on finding a way to cooperate with Margrit Hahnloser. Instead, he set up a work routine where he needed to have as little to do with his colleague as possible. "When Pontus was in Basel, he came in quite late in the morning, took his mail and went to his room," says Andres Pardey. "After half an hour he came out and said to me 'let's go for lunch.' I took all the papers with me and we walked or took a taxi to Restaurant Brauerie on Grenzacherstrasse. There we sat and drank until three-thirty when Pontus went to his hotel around the corner and I went back to the museum. Sometimes we had dinner in the evening too. The actual work was done in half an hour or so. Pontus was very efficient. I ran through the list with all the decisions to be made and he instantly answered yes or no. The rest of the time we sat and talked about art history. He was completely open and I could ask him anything. I learned a tremendous lot."[17]

For the opening exhibition, Niki de Saint Phalle's donation was complemented by loans from museums, institutions and private collectors around the world, including Pontus Hultén himself, who owned an exquisite collection of Tinguely's art, particularly from the early period of the artist's career, which was otherwise lacking in the new museum. The majority of Niki's donation consisted of late works on a larger scale, including Tinguely's largest and most important machine sculptures. The collection was further supplemented by several other donations from, among others, the Sacher-Hoffmann-Oeri family itself.

Unlike Niki de Saint Phalle, the Sacher-Hoffmann-Oeri family and other affluent donors, Pontus Hultén had no intention of donating his Tinguely collection to the new museum where he was appointed director. Hultén's personal finances were strained after his purchase of half of the La Motte estate, and in need of cash.[18] The wealth he had managed to accumulate during his career was mostly tied up in his La Motte estate, the apartment in Paris and the desert cottage in California (the apartment on Stora Nygatan in Stockholm, which he still accessed with his sister Maj, was a rental). At least that's how the notoriously "financially aware" Hultén himself described his financial situation.

Eventually, Hultén sold most of his Tinguely collection to the museum in Basel, a deal that was finalized in 1999. Ever since he left Sweden in 1973, Hultén had tried the patience of his Swedish friends by complaining about the pension he felt he had been promised but cheated out of by the Swedish state.[19] Now, as payment for his Tinguely collection, Pontus Hultén finally received the pension he had longed for and which meant that, however concerned he was with his assets, he no longer had to worry about his personal finances for the rest of his life.[20]

A sensitive subject is that this sale led to a schism between Pontus Hultén and Niki de Saint Phalle. The artist felt betrayed that Hultén forced Roche to pay for the collection. de Saint Phalle and Hultén did not completely break off contact and reconciled in the last years of Niki's life.

I don't know the value of the pension insurance policy that paid for Pontus Hultén's Tinguely collection. Certainly, from an art historical perspective, it was a ridiculously low price for a unique collection of works mostly from the first phase of Tinguely's career, when he was one of the pioneers of the international avant-garde.

Hultén hardly charged a full market price for this treasure that so clearly belonged in a museum. Several of the works Hultén sold to Museum Tinguely had been shown at *Le Mouvement* at Galerie Denise René in 1955, where Hultén and Tinguely had together anticipated future movements such as Conceptual and Installation art. In many of these works, Tinguely engaged in a "dialog," as it were, with his heroes among the abstract pioneers such as Malevich and Kandinsky. With his art, Tinguely set these austere idioms in motion, contributing like few others to the radicalization of art. "I was born to motion," Tinguely himself said.[21]

This is what Museum Tinguely writes in its massive collection catalog about the acquisition of Pontus Hultén's collection: "The most important purchase, by far, was made in 1999 when we succeeded in acquiring a large number of Tinguely's early works from Pontus Hultén, our museum's first director. Again from Hultén, three years later we were pleased to acquire a total of 760 letters, letterheads, papers and documents, and prints. As a major reinforcement of our collection of works on paper, these form a necessary base in our archive and document department."[22]

These sales were part of a series of business transactions that Pontus Hultén conducted during the last almost ten years of his life in order to exchange parts of his collection into a small fortune for his own old age and as an inheritance to leave to his son Felix and daughter Klara.

The exhibition staged by Pontus Hultén for the opening of Museum Tinguely was divided into themes for the three floors of the new museum building. The emphasis was on the main galleries on the ground floor with beautiful daylight which, according to Andres Pardey, Pontus Hultén had persuaded the architect Mario Botta to design for Jean Tinguely's largest machine sculptures, among them "Grosse Méta-Maxi-Maxi-Utopia" from 1987, where visitors were now, unlike when it was first shown in Venice, allowed to walk around inside the giant sculpture's machine labyrinths — the museum's main piece with its rattling, noisy monumentality, a veritable mobilized scrap cathedral.

On the upper level, Hultén presented Tinguely's collaborations with his artist friends. Also exhibited were drawings, sketches, films, photographs and models from exhibitions, actions and events around the world, along with Tinguely's remarkable series of "portraits" of political and philosophical thinkers, nine in number. No "likeliness" to the subjects can be detected in these wonderful machine sculptures. On the basement level, the sculptures that required darkness were on display, such as the hysterical 1984 Formula 1 installation "Pit Stop," made from two of sponsor Renault's Formula 1 cars, and the 1986 "Mengele Totentanz."

The formal opening of the Museum Tinguely on October 1, 1996, an event that simultaneously celebrated the centenary of Hoffmann-La Roche, was a grand, ultra-glamorous affair that brought together the artistic and financial societies of Switzerland and the art world — the last major gala event of its kind in Hultén's now nearly forty-five-year career. In the magnificent catalog published for the opening, Hultén made use for the third time of his text from his 1972 book *Jean Tinguely Méta*.

With this opening, Hultén's mission for the museum was essentially complete, although his contract wasn't terminated until 1997, when the museum had been open for a year. It had never been Hultén's intention to continue leading the museum. Over the years, his interest had become more and more focused on the visionary idea stage, the design, planning and launch of the new institutions. As operations took over, his commitment waned. Hultén sums up his penchant for pioneering with a not-so-common aside about his colleagues: "My advantage is that I love working on projects from scratch. I know that some of my colleagues don't like to get involved in things that don't exist, but for me it's the opposite, as I find what you can dig out of nothing particularly interesting, but of course I share that experience with many others."[23]

There is certainly something beautiful in that Pontus Hultén's finale in the international museum world was at this museum for the artist who, alongside Marcel Duchamp, had been the most important in his life's work in art. It's said that Hultén felt a sense of pride in the museum almost as if it had been his own.[24]

Parts have been redesigned, but the main features of the presentation of the permanent collection remain when I visit Museum Tinguely. The museum has been in operation for nearly twenty years at this point and is a well-established and respected institution with an ambitious program of temporary exhibitions, events, research and education with annual figures of over a hundred thousand visitors, around a quarter of them international. The collection has been greatly expanded through purchases and donations. In part, it has functioned as *The Museum of Wishes* at the Moderna Museet in Stockholm in 1963–1964, as many of the works loaned by Pontus Hultén for the opening exhibition have over time been purchased by Roche — which still wholly owns and operates the museum — or donated by other Tinguely collectors. In addition to its permanent collection, Museum Tinguely runs an exhibition program with other artists, historical and contemporary, working in the spirit of Jean Tinguely.

In the museum, visitors can study Tinguely's three main periods: the "mobilization" of geometric abstract painting in the 1950s and early 1960s, with reliefs and simple, initially Calder-inspired mobiles and machines; the black machine sculptures of his mid-career and the "baroque," multicolored, mastodon installations of the late period. It's the latter in particular that inspire awe — gigantic mechanical mega-organisms that startle into noisy, rattling, howling life at the touch of a button from the visitor; the effect is surreal.

A "death pilot" he undoubtedly was, Jean Tinguely, fascinated by death and drawn to live and work in its presence. In the late phase of his career, as his own death inevitably approached, this fascination grew to bewitchment. From the early eighties, Tinguely began to consistently use animal skulls — and occasionally human skulls — skeletal parts, rust and twisted, deformed wreckage as memento mori symbols in his sculptures, along with parts of dolls, toys, amusement park paraphernalia and other objects ominously discarded by consumer society in these inept monster machines of transience. The influences of his Catholic heritage are evident in Tinguely's late art, when he produced a series of "altar pieces" and became obsessed with the idea of creating his own chapel. The highlight of this death cult is the previously discussed "Mengele Totentanz," with Bernhard Luginbühl's hippopotamus skull as the choir's centerpiece, now installed in its own windowless, dimly lit hall. The constant presence of death is balanced in almost all of Tinguely's works and installations by his other hallmark, the equally palpable, defiantly anarchic humor and irony.

Another striking feature of Jean Tinguely's life that is well represented in the museum, and part of the death cult, is of course motor racing. Tinguely was an incurable racing aficionado who aligned his life and artistic program with the Formula 1 season. Racing in the mid-twentieth century was incomparably more dangerous than in our time, a gladiatorial game that regularly claimed victims. Formula 1 drivers who survived their careers were almost exceptions. The hellish crash Tinguely witnessed at Le Mans in 1955, when more than eighty people, most of them spectators, were massacred by flying machine parts and torched in burning gasoline in the worst disaster in racing history, became a source of inspiration for Tinguely, something of his equivalent to what the bombing of Guernica had been for Picasso, visible in several of his works.

Tinguely himself was involved in several serious car accidents (as well as work accidents), in Paris and elsewhere, was badly injured and narrowly escaped death on repeated occasions. Being a passenger in Tinguely's car was described as a near-death experience. The artist drove fast, very fast, and, according to Seppi Imhof, less well.[25] That he was a hundred percent sober at all times behind the wheel could hardly be guaranteed. "He crashed a lot of Ferraris, that's for sure," says Imhof.[26]

The museum's collection catalog includes Tinguely's letter to Hultén from 1970, in which he urges his friend to buy the historic Formula 1 car for Moderna Museet — one of hundreds of unique works of art for letters, with Tinguely's partially capitalized typography, with a nod to his and Hultén's mutual friend Joakim Bonnier, who died in a crash two years later:

> *I will be / in / EUROPe iN 20 DAYS*
> *ViVA la / Lotus / 25 / : JosepH SiffeRt / has a 25-33 oNe*
> *to seLl / With the one from / SCHlumpf in AlSAce / 600*
> *CaRs (2 Royal) / 64 BUGAttis / clOsed To the public / &*
> *Mine / it's the laSt / of these masteRpieces / BUY it / foR*
> *the / Muséet / MODERNA / There areN't anY / IN the USA*
> *Or in / Great BRitAIN / PS = doN't Ask / Jo BONNieR he'S*
> *a / cRaftY deVil = He / will / SelL you / hiS / old BRM-Mc*
> *LAReN / witH/ no HistoRical Value / If your mind is made*
> *up / tel Jo SiffeRt / 037 27710 / in FRibouRG / I hope / that*
> */ you / will BUY it / ?*
> *greetings = Jean*[27]

Like his American contemporaries Robert Rauschenberg and Jasper Johns, and Andy Warhol, Jean Tinguely began his career as a freelance window dresser. In this profession, the artist developed mastery as a draughtsman, painter, graphic designer and calligrapher. Later in his career, Tinguely unhesitatingly alternated anti-commercial artistic projects with commercial commissions as an interior designer, decorator and product designer, and with a large number of public works around the world. This part of his production is well represented at the Tinguely Museum in Basel. It includes a Kyoto café interior with lamps and chandeliers made from crashed Japanese motorcycles (!), and many of the stunning chandeliers and lighting installations Tinguely created for friends and collectors, combining artistic and practical functions. The culmination of this production is the four-ton light monster "Luminator" from the last year of his life in 1991, with six hundred and thirty-five light bulbs in colors chosen by Tinguely, created to illuminate friend and curator Klaus Littmann's exhibition in a factory hall at the Art Basel event that year. The work was purchased by the Swiss Bankers Association and for many years greeted visitors in the arrivals hall of Basel's railway station, as a memorial to the city's great artist son.

In this context, I cannot refrain from recounting an anecdote that reflects the anarchic-nihilistic spirit that characterizes Jean Tinguely as an artist and a human being. It was when Richard Rogers designed his famous building for the headquarters of the world's leading insurance broker Lloyds of London in London's financial district — a radical twelve-story complex with clear parallels to the Centre Pompidou in Paris, built in 1978–1986. Rogers asked Jean Tinguely to create a monumental clock for the building's facade. The artist agreed — on one condition. The clock would show the wrong time. The idea was a nut too nihilistic to swallow for this group, for which rationality, orderliness, trust and reliability were conditions of existence, even if its management had shown progressiveness in its commitment to Rogers' uncompromising architecture. One can only agree with Jerry Sohn when he says: "It was a big mistake for them not to go for the clock. Imagine, it would have been an attraction that would have made Lloyds famous all over the world."[28]

Although Jean Tinguely is very far from being forgotten thirty years after his death, it must be admitted that his name does not carry the superstar status that Tinguely enjoyed during his lifetime and especially during the sixties and seventies. Among the younger artists and art students of our time, he's not among the leading references. For a wider public, he's no longer well known outside Switzerland. There are several reasons for this devaluation of Tinguely's work. In the text of the Tinguely Museum's collection catalog, it's argued that Tinguely's many public decorations and commercial commissions, and his status as a celebrity, came to overshadow his artistry in his late career.

Another probable reason why Jean Tinguely hasn't retained his relevance in contemporary art, at least not for the moment, is more blatant. The industrial, mechanized consumer society that Tinguely mocks in his art seems obsolete in today's digitalized world where, as Pontus Hultén writes in his preface to *The Machine* at MoMA in 1968, electronics and chemistry, comparable to the human brain and nervous system, have taken over from mechanics and machines, the counterparts of man's more primitive muscles.[29]

Daniel Buren offers a credible alternative main explanation for why Jean Tinguely's work is not as highly valued today as it was during his lifetime: the general Americanization of the art world.[30] Tinguely made a serious attempt to break into the American market after his first visit to New York in 1960, when he staged his art-historical guerrilla action "Homage to New York." For a time, Tinguely was represented by Neo-Dadaist and Pop Art super-dealer Leo Castelli, who initially believed in Tinguely's great potential in the United States. The relation between the two soon soured. Tinguely told his friends that he refused to become a slave to Castelli and made a drawing with a "New York fly" nailed to a piece of paper, explaining that the work was a portrait of Castelli. Although Tinguely is by no means unknown in the United States, where he made several public works and had many collectors, on the whole, as Guggenheim director Richard Armstrong notes, "Tinguely is virtually nothing here in America today."[31]

According to Daniel Buren, this reality is a consequence of the hegemony that New York and the United States have exercised over the art world since the early 1960s. "Everyone knows that Tinguely is *at least* as important as Rauschenberg — there's no question," says Buren. "Jasper Johns was doing the same thing as Braque long before, but Braque did it better. The reason that they are more famous is simply because they are Americans. It's impossible for artists from other countries to have the same impact as American artists."[32]

While Daniel Buren is surely correct in this analysis, and Jean Tinguely may seem to have fallen out of the mainstream, his impact on modern art history and influence on our own contemporary art is unquestionable — whether contemporary artists are aware of this influence or not. Tinguely's contribution to the development of art in the decades after the war, when he and Pontus Hultén together broke through in the avant-garde of modern art, is above simple opinion. After my visits to the Museum Tinguely in Basel and the "The Cyclop" in Fontainebleau, where the power, energy and vitality of his art silences all doubts, I'm convinced that the museum's catalog text is true in its prophecy of an inevitable future return on a larger scale in our contemporary art consciousness of this, as he is called in the catalog text, one of the most radical, joyfully experimental and subversive artists of the twentieth century. Hopefully, this revival will occur with the centennial anniversary of Tinguely's birth in 2025, when his memory is celebrated in his hometown Basel and with a series of large-scale exhibitions in various European museums and galleries, including the Centre Pompidou show *Niki de Saint Phalle, Jean Tinguely and Pontus Hultén* at the Grand Palais in Paris.

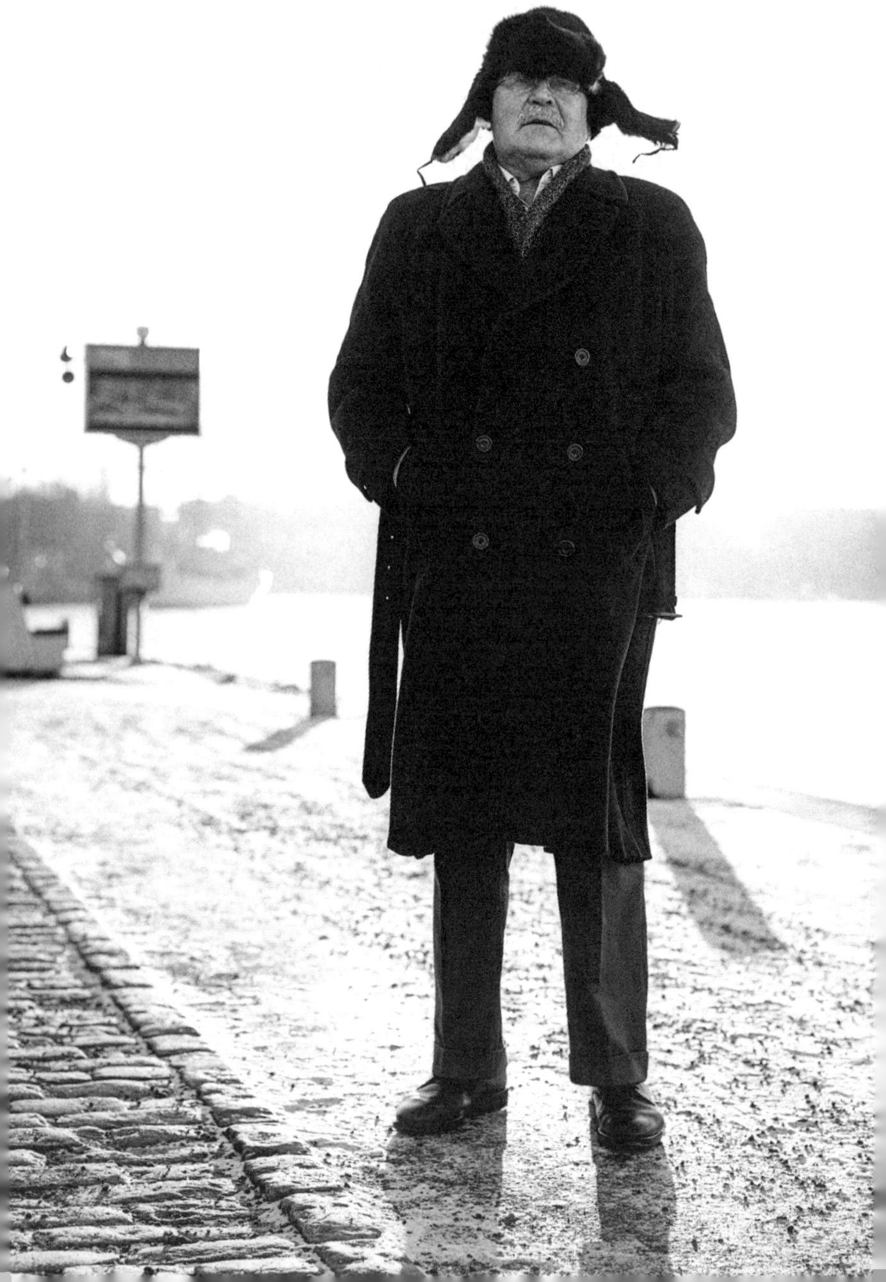

My meeting with Pontus

32

Pontus Hultén had practically left Museum Tinguely, and had recently presented the exhibition with the Moderna Museet collection at the Bundeskunsthalle in Bonn when we met in Stockholm on the veranda of the Grand Hôtel on two freezing cold December days in 1996.

The background to this unforgettable encounter was the new museum building for Moderna Museet on Skeppsholmen. At the time, we were publishing our international fashion and culture magazine Stockholm New and working on a theme about Moderna Museet to mark the new opening. Consequently, I wanted to interview Pontus for this issue. I had long known that Hultén was a controversial figure in Swedish cultural circles, but in the course of the work I realized *how* controversial he was and what strong emotions Hultén still evoked, despite — or perhaps partly because of? — having been away from Sweden for a quarter of a century.

I had obtained the address and telephone number of the chateau in La Motte, mailed material and was surprised when Pontus answered when I then dialed the number — and even more so when he was immediately prepared to travel to Stockholm for an interview and photography session. Hultén's patriotic feelings for the motherland had by this time grown ever stronger. He probably took the opportunity to come to Stockholm to meet friends and family.

Together with master photographer Mikael Jansson and his assistants, I was waiting in the winter morning sun in the entrance to the Grand Hôtel's veranda on a morning with an outside temperature of at least fifteen degrees below zero, when a large, heavy figure stepped through the airlock with dramatically smoky breath, wearing a black longcoat and Hultén's wintry trademark, the Russian fur hat with

Pontus Hultén at Blasieholmskajen, Stockholm, December 16, 1996.

earflaps — a magnificent entrance that could have been a scene from a movie by one of his heroes Eisenstein or Buñuel. The sheer physical poise that so many have mentioned was palpable even to us. My first question after the greeting was whether everything had gone well with the plane ticket and the trip. "Thank you, it didn't work at all," Pontus replied. "I had to buy a new ticket."[1]

When we sat down in the armchairs and I asked Hultén if he wanted something to drink, he replied without the slightest hesitation: "I'll have a brandy." Out of courtesy, I followed his example. Thereafter, we drained many six-centiliter bowls of the noble golden brown beverage during the two long days we spent together there in the leather armchairs on the veranda of the Grand Hôtel.

Like so many others, I immediately found Pontus Hultén to be open, easy to talk to and prepared to answer all my questions in a simple, easy-to-understand manner. The wings of history flapped majestically as he recounted all the anecdotes from Moderna Museet's beginnings and its heroic years in the sixties, about the conflicts associated with the sixty-eight movement, the move to Paris and the construction of the museum at the Pompidou center. Our conversation stopped here because the subject of the interview was the museum in Stockholm, its history and reopening. Some, but far from all, of these stories I had heard before and after and seen published in other contexts.

Pontus Hultén surprised me with his modesty. Even the shyness that many mentioned I could sense. Above all, I enjoyed his underlying sardonic humor, constantly communicated with the same poker face and the heavy, authoritative body language that made such a strong impression and which, according to testimonies, was always an important weapon in the arsenal of qualities that Hultén deliberately used to push through his will. A few times he burst out laughing and then surprisingly, in unexpected instances — also a gesture that I've heard others mention, his way of using laughter as a rhetorical tool.

For me personally, it was an exclusive privilege, an extravagant luxury, to return to my cherished childhood memories of the museum and ask all the questions I had accumulated about how all this had actually been possible. Pontus refrained from claiming ownership of all these achievements for himself, though he didn't hesitate to speak in the first person about many of these historical achievements.

Hultén attributed much of the credit for the realization of Moderna Museet and its unlikely global groundbreaking run to Swedish society and the spirit of confidence and optimism that prevailed in Stockholm during the 1960s, when Sweden, as Hultén formulated it, "was way ahead." He cited sexual liberation, equality, women's and children's rights, the peace movement, and environmental and Third World awareness as examples. I thought it was humble of him to present the museum as a product and integrated part of this political experiment, this attempt at an ideal society that still arouses interest, admiration and antipathy all over the world. Hultén said it was "only natural" to offer all these movements of the new era an arena in the museum.[2]

Much later, while working on this story, it occurred to me that the arch-utopian Pontus Hultén actually had the unique opportunity to kick off his career in what must be considered an outstanding utopian moment in world history, fully comparable to the "states of exception" he romanticized so passionately, when utopia had briefly reigned, with creativity unleashed, at least in myth; such as the Paris Commune of 1870, the Russian post-revolutionary avant-garde, the Surrealist "revolution" and the sixty-eight Paris revolt.

While these historical moments were all linked to revolutionary processes, the revolutionary romantic Hultén was lucky to work in a state of political and cultural exception that had been achieved by peaceful, democratic means. The 1960s was the decade in which the Swedish welfare state was at its height, when everyone, truly everyone, was better off year after year and when there appeared to be no limits to freedom or opportunity. Never before or since has Swedish society — or indeed any democratic society in the world — been so equal. Nor has Sweden ever been so "left-wing." In the 1968 election, the Social Democrats achieved their own majority for the first and only time.

The sixties in Stockholm were an extreme time and place in world history, when the long post-war period was finally over and everything seemed open and achievable; when utopias appeared realistic for a while, before the turning point came with 1968 and, as Pontus Hultén expressed it in our conversation, "time lost its breath," with the subsequent hangover of indifference, bureaucracy, neo-moralism, and devastating internal strife and intrigue. It seems that Hultén is right in his analysis. His own career and the new model he and his colleagues created for a modern museum, which he later single-handedly exported around the world, is very much an offspring of the progressive Swedish welfare state in its best sense, unimaginable in any other geographical, historical or political context.

I asked Hultén how it felt to come from provincial Stockholm to Paris to open the new museum at the Centre Pompidou: "Maybe it was the other way around," Hultén replied. "Maybe it was Paris that was provincial and Stockholm that was ahead of its time."[3]

In our conversations, Pontus Hultén emphasized one of his most important tools: chance, which he thanked for several of the museum's achievements. A recurring theme in his reasoning was simplicity — how most things in the sixties had given themselves easily and naturally, how one thing was allowed to lead to another, more or less at random, opportunities seized in the moment, without well elaborated or long-term strategic plans. To me, as to many others, he expressed his disgust and incomprehension at the unmanageable bureaucracy of the new era, devastating to art and creativity as he saw it. When I asked him about the selection of artists for the *4 Americans* exhibition in 1962, he replied: "In those days you didn't make such a *big deal* out of everything. I just thought it was a good selection — and, it was."[4]

We mostly stuck to the topic, but Pontus also offered a string of bonus anecdotes, one of which sheds light on his storied psychic ability, from the 1950s when Hultén was a young official at the National Museum. "Back then, security at the museum wasn't great," Hultén said. "There were many thefts, and not always did one know exactly what had disappeared. One day we received a message from the Paris police. They had caught a kleptomaniac who told them that he had been on a theft tour in Sweden where he had stolen pieces from the National Museum, a painting attributed to Frans Hals and some other things by a Swedish artist that no one had even missed. He had buried the loot in a place he had marked on a map he had drawn for the police and which they had sent to us. There were only three things on the map: a road, a railroad, and a cross for the spot where he had buried the art. I put that drawing up on the wall of my office. Then, when I was on the phone and people got a bit long-winded, I used to sit and look at that drawing. One day it suddenly struck me: what the hell, it's Albano![5] So we sent a janitor to dig where the cross was in relation to the road and the railroad, and there was the stuff."[6]

When we had finished the second day's conversation, many hours after the midwinter night had fallen heavily over Stockholm's stream and the Royal Palace outside the Grand Hôtel's panoramic windows, I asked Pontus Hultén if he would like to finish with a walk up to the object of our meeting, the new museum under construction on the crest of Skeppsholmen. "Yes, why not," Pontus replied. We walked over the Skeppsholmen bridge, up the hill in a temperature that had fallen to probably more than twenty degrees below zero; a slow ascent

Pontus Hultén at Blasieholmskajen, Stockholm, December 16, 1996.

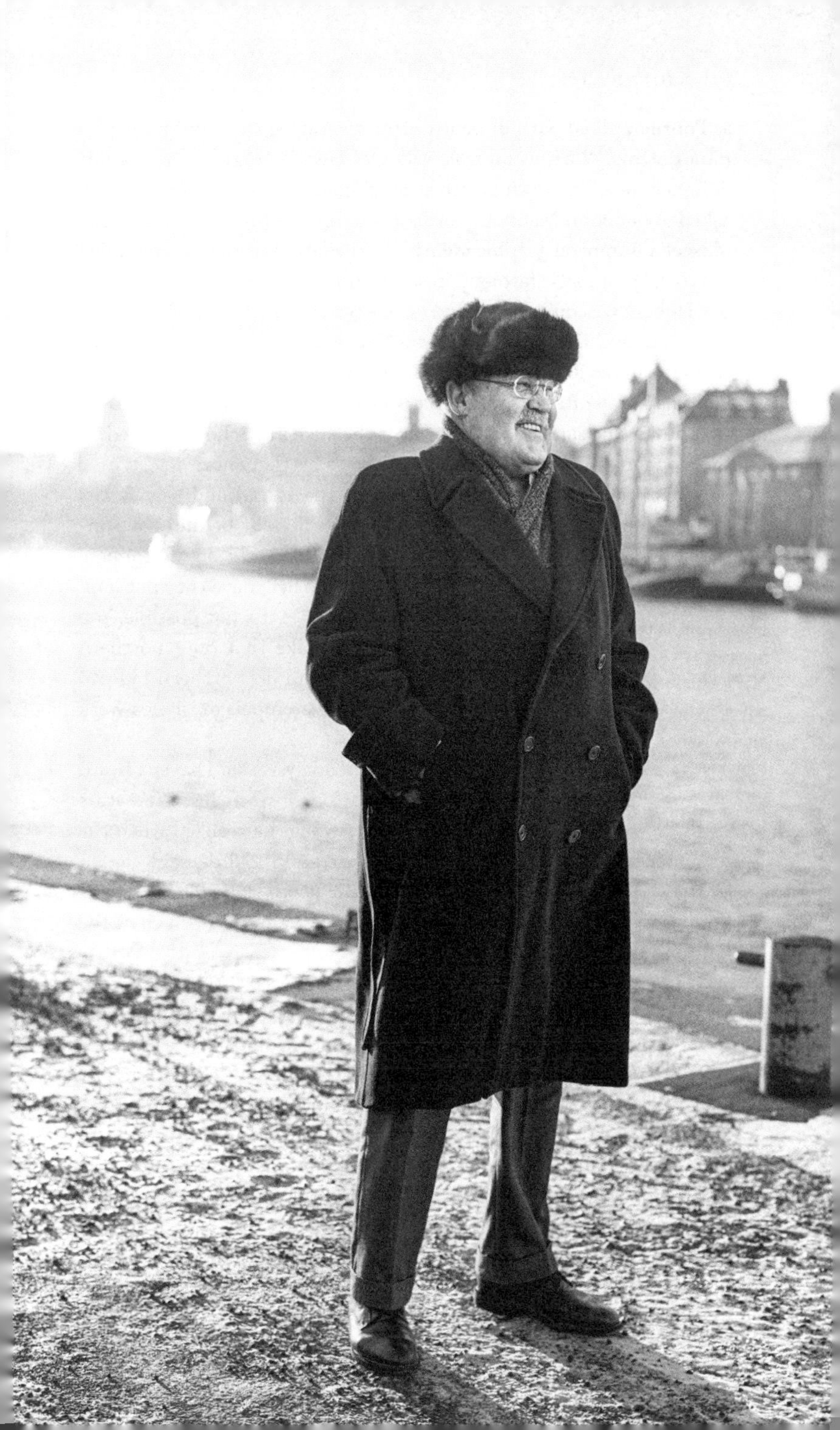

as Pontus walked with difficulty after several leg clots and perhaps a minor stroke. With us on this walk was Henrik Nygren, the graphic designer we were working with at Stockholm New at the time. Henrik asked about John Melin, the brilliant designer who created Moderna Museet's immortal graphic identity in the late sixties. Hultén replied in typical pragmatic fashion: "Yes, we worked with Hubert Johansson, but Hubert was quite expensive, so we brought in John Melin to save some money." During this arduous, bitterly cold walk, when the fur earmuffs of his Russian hat came in handy against the Siberian winds, Pontus Hultén offered several snapshots. "We were always going to tip that down," he said, nodding towards the ancient anchor mounted on the slope in front of Skeppsholm Church's battlements.

When we finally reached the top of the island and saw Rafael Moneo's new museum building, which was floodlit behind the construction site's barriers, Pontus stopped and made the, in my opinion, wingedly simple comment: "No, but what the hell, have they put it on the north side? No, but ... it's not possible. You can't place a building like that on a northern slope like this. I grew up on northern Lidingö and I know how these archipelago islands work on the north side."

"Pontus made that analysis as a sailor," says Marie-Louise von Plessen when I tell her about his views on the north side building. "It was typical for him to see things from that perspective."

It is a self-evident analysis that I haven't heard from anyone else, before or since. Just a few years later, Hultén's fears would be realized when the new museum had to be closed due to harmful mold damage caused by the water flowing down the cliffs of the north slope. The two-year sanitation and evacuation of the museum cost almost as much as the new building.[7]

I missed the opportunity to ask, but I'm convinced that Hultén would have advocated thinking outside the norm and leaving Skeppsholmen to move Moderna Museet into the city center where new and larger audiences could be won. Placing art in the middle of the village had always been his ambition. We remember how he lost his appetite in Stockholm when his and the museum's plans for the Kulturhuset at Sergels torg "sank with open bottom valves on a not even agitated sea."[8]

A number of years seemed to have passed since Pontus Hultén had last visited his mother museum — or maybe he just hadn't noticed the view. He reacted with surprise to the new landmark Vasa Museum, which had been inaugurated seven years earlier, in 1990, with its fake sailing rig adorning the roof. "Disneyland" was his verdict.

He was surprised and dismayed when he asked what would become of the old museum's main gallery, the Navy's excersise hall, where so many historical exhibitions and events had been staged during his time. When I replied that it would be taken over by the Museum of Architecture, he exclaimed: "What? The Museum of Architecture? But it's a world-famous hall for art. The dimensions, the light, the acoustics — everything is perfect, but there is also something else, a magic, something that cannot be explained."[9]

Almost twenty years later, Olle Granath told me that Pontus Hultén never forgave him for having, in his capacity as director of the National Museums of Fine Arts and chief client of the new Moderna Museet, "sacrificed" — as Hultén saw it — the old museum's main hall in a political negotiating game. Together with another incident, to which I will return, Granath's decision was, according to Granath himself, the reason why he was included among the many friends and collaborators with whom, for one reason or another, the acquaintance had ended during Pontus Hultén's life and career. "He grumbled about it and threatened that he had a ready-written debate article," says Olle Granath. "I tried to explain to him that it wasn't possible to climatize the hall or meet the new security requirements — that I had been busy saving it at all for the museum. But he wouldn't listen to that."[10]

I later met Pontus Hultén briefly during the opening ceremonies for the new museum just over a year later, in February 1998,[11] where Hultén gave a speech that was short, just nine words: "A quadruple salute to the world's best museum, salute!"

I talked to Hultén a few more times in the years that followed, the first time when working on a feature I published in Dagens Nyheter in April 1998,[12] on the new museum and its opening ceremonies and about the Stockholm European Culture Capital 1998 event. I called Pontus at La Motte and asked him what he thought of the new museum but he wouldn't answer. "That's a bit difficult for me, as you can understand," he said. "I don't understand anything about this new project, but I'm sure it must have something to do with unemployment. In any case, I can't help thinking that it's about time the government did something for the museum after letting the collection stagnate and neglecting the funding for temporary exhibitions since the seventies."

I also asked about the Culture Capital event. Twenty-five years later, it's rarely mentioned, but the late nineties in Stockholm were a time of event fever, triggered by the infamous Stockholm Water Festival.

A series of major events was to culminate in the 2004 Summer Olympics in Stockholm, for which the city ran a costly, unsuccessful campaign. The European Culture Capital year was a key initiative in that suite. In this capacity, it was a top political priority, planned and managed for many years prior to 1998 by a cabinet of politically connected cultural officials. Major investments were made and the event operation was not questioned, let alone criticized by the media. The event opened doors to political spaces and coffers that culture rarely accesses. As a matter of course, we have Stockholm Culture Capital 1998 and the general event hysteria of the 1990s largely to thank for Moderna Museet getting a new building at all.

"Yes, on that I can say something more," Pontus said when I asked him for an opinion on the Culture Capital, "because I haven't seen a worse dump than Stockholm for a long time. I was in Thessaloniki when it was such a cultural city,[13] and it was the same there — shabby, shitty, no order to anything, but I wouldn't have thought it would be as bad in Stockholm. I've read the program, that I have, and it was boring and uninteresting. Frankly, I have very low respect for the people behind this. Why have they taken this on, really, when they have no particular thought behind it? Nothing is forcing them, is it?"[14]

I published these quotes from Pontus Hultén in my article in Dagens Nyheter. I later realized that the kind of frankness rarely seen in the Swedish cultural debate that Hultén displayed in contexts like this, combined with who he was and what he represented, hardly helped to make him popular among the administrators of our Swedish cultural life. The hostility that I had encountered towards Hultén from such "culture personalities," among them several of those who worked with the Capital of Culture event, became more understandable when Hultén here made a temporary comeback in the Swedish cultural discourse. "To feel that you weren't respected by Pontus, that he didn't think you were up to par — that wasn't fun," as one person who I let remain anonymous put it. "He made a lot of enemies that way."

I saw Pontus Hultén again in 2004, two years before his death, at the opening of the exhibition of his collection. He was sitting in a wheelchair, swaddled of course, with what I thought looked like an ironic smirk on his face. I'm not sure he recognized me. Needless to say, while working on this story, I have had reason to curse myself for not making the effort to stay in touch with Pontus until the end.

33 Vandals, Vandals ...

Although Pontus Hultén had left Museum Tinguely with his long-awaited retirement, jokingly calling himself a pensioner, we know that his career was not over. It was to conclude with an epilog that continues to baffle.

It's uncertain when Hultén's interest was aroused for the Vandals, this little-known ancient conquering people, the Vikings' predecessors and teachers, if we are to believe Pontus Hultén. In any case, towards the end of the nineties, this interest seems to have intensified into an obsession.

Hultén tells Stephan Andreae that already during his time in Bonn, he had become interested in staging an exhibition on the Vandals as part of the Kunsthalle's historical program.[1] According to Marie-Louise von Plessen, these plans were "reactivated" in Hultén's mind after he had been introduced sometime in 1997 by Anna-Lena Wibom to Sven Lundh, a well-known entrepreneur in the furniture industry in the Småland region who had founded and built up the design company Källemo in Värnamo.

Sven Lundh was a pioneer in the Swedish furniture industry as, with Källemo, he had invested in a new generation of Swedish designers during the 1980s, such as Jonas Bohlin with the Concrete chair, Mats Theselius and, in an older generation, the underrated architect and furniture designer John Kandell. Sven Lundh and Källemo set the style with the eighties concept of furniture as art, exhibited in galleries and sold in limited, numbered and signed editions. It can be said that it was Sven Lundh and Källemo who ushered in the renaissance of the Swedish furniture industry and design in the 1980s. Several of the furniture and objects that the company launched during the era are among the few Swedish design objects from the last four decades that have lasting collector value.

Sven Lundh had a burning interest in art and an ardent commitment to the art scene in Småland. Since the 1960s, he had worked to ensure that the Småland Art Archive would have its own permanent building in his hometown of Värnamo in the heart of what is known as Gnosjö, an area widely renowned for its skilled, hard-working, successful entrepreneurs. Sven Lundh was tireless in his fight to found a modern art museum in Småland. But his dreams were more expansive than that.

As I understand it, Anna-Lena Wibom had made the acquaintance of Sven Lundh through her work at the Swedish Film Institute, to which Lundh and Källemo are said to have delivered furniture. The two are alleged to have become close friends.

According to Sven's daughter Karin Lundh, who after her father's death leads Källemo together with her brother Erik, it was with Anna-Lena Wibom that Sven Lundh sometime in the second half of the 1990s began to discuss his vision for a modern art and design museum in Småland with national and even international ambitions.[2] Wibom took the initiative to connect Sven Lundh and Pontus Hultén. In the fall of 1997, Hultén made his first visit to Värnamo in the company of Wibom. He returned several times over the next year.

Karin Lundh says they were all surprised that international superstar Pontus Hultén was immediately willing to discuss the vision. With Hultén's interest, the dream immediately materialized and grew into something that was assured to promptly attract the interest of the major art world. "Sven and Pontus got along well, they were similar in many ways and found it easy to talk to each other," says Karin Lundh. "Pontus instantaneously thought it sounded like an interesting idea and saw possibilities. He said he was tired of the art world and how incredibly complicated and bureaucratic it had become to run museums. He saw this as a chance to do something outside the traditional museum world. I think it appealed to his entrepreneurial spirit. I think he also liked the notion that it would annoy and confuse some people in the art world."[3]

The step between thought and action had never been a long one for Pontus Hultén, even as he approached seventy-five and his health faltered. Hultén soon escalated the museum venture by offering to donate his own art collection to the new museum and by contacting his friend — who else? — Renzo Piano, who was once again on board.

Piano arrived in Småland at the end of 1997, where Karin Lundh picked him up at Jönköping airport. “He was very observant during the trip and fascinated by the forest,” says Karin Lundh. “On the way he asked to stop at a sawmill. He wanted to see the dimensions of the logs. When we arrived at the old barn that stood where the museum is today, which was dilapidated with sparse planks in the walls, he thought it was beautiful in its spaciousness with a roof truss only on one side. We went on to Källemo where he was inspired by John Kandell’s building with the atrium. During the meeting, he picked up a match, which he knew came from Jönköping, and said: ‘This has very beautiful dimensions.’”[4]

Renzo Piano becomes enthusiastic during our conversation in Paris when Vandalorum comes up. He confirms that his and Hultén’s idea was indeed based on the safety match and draws a couple of quick sketches in my notebook of the principles of the barn-like gallery buildings constructed with logs of the dimensions of the matches, intended to create beautiful shadow play in the facades.[5]

With global names like Piano and Hultén involved, the big plans quickly became public. Pictures and interviews were published in the local press in Småland and spread in the national and international media. Sven Lundh was determined to realize these seemingly wild visions for a museum, which Hultén had christened with the outrageous name Vandalorum, a naming that I assume was inspired by Louisiana.

Sven Lundh and Pontus Hultén crossed the Rubicon with a press conference in Stockholm in February 1998. Here Renzo Piano’s sketches were shown for a gigantic museum compound with twelve red-colored barns of four hundred and fifty square meters each, inspired by the existing old drying barn, grouped around an artificial lake and connected by walkways and atriums.

Two of these barns were dedicated to Pontus Hultén’s own collection. The others were intended for the Småland art archive, for temporary exhibitions and for a growing international art and design collection that was to be assembled. With the free-standing barns, donors could have their own galleries — a selling point — and the museum complex could be expanded over time.[6]

Looking back, the plans don’t seem entirely unrealistic. The original vision described the museum’s location where the E4 highway meets two other national routes, halfway between Stockholm and Copenhagen, as well positioned for creating a new kind of Nordic and international arena for art, design and creativity. Louisiana in Humlebaek was an apparent benchmark. So far later, I can see how Pontus Hultén could feel inspired by such an idea, certainly attracted by the underdog position that such a new cultural institution would occupy.

However, when I heard about Vandalorum in 1998, I reacted first with astonishment, then with skepticism and credulity. I was far from alone in these reactions. It all seemed too fantastic, a few measures *too* wild, an impression reinforced by the name Vandalorum. Would the conspicuously aged Hultén and his contemporary Sven Lundh really be able to pull this mastodon rabbit out of their hats at such a late stage of their careers?

As presented, the project had good backing financially and in other forms, locally in Värnamo and Småland but also nationally. Småland County Council guaranteed the design cost of the building up to the start of construction at SEK fifteen million, a fee to Piano that seemed adequate for the time, although the sum included some other expenses. Karin Lundh explains that this money was expected to be around one tenth of the total cost of the museum, which was estimated at around one hundred and fifty million SEK (for reference, the official budget for the Moderna Museet's new building in Stockholm, opened in 1998, was around four hundred and fifty million SEK). The municipality of Värnamo matched the county council's contribution and donated the land for the project, practically valued at fifteen million. Several local sponsors had also committed to invest in the project.

Most impressive was the assurance of financial support that Sven Lundh and Vandalorum had managed to obtain from the Swedish Social Democratic government under Prime Minister Göran Persson. Sven Lundh had engaged Claes Ljung, State Secretary at the Ministry of Finance, who had the Prime Minister's confidence, on Vandalorum's board. It's said that Göran Persson, who had met Pontus Hultén in Bonn, was attracted by the regional policy perspective of this cultural initiative. He became publicly involved in the venture and spoke positively about Vandalorum in the media. In addition, the Ministry of Culture guaranteed an annual operating grant of eight million SEK, a respectable figure for a museum in the countryside that still existed only as a utopian plan.

Pontus Hultén's ideas for a Vandal exhibition took on a whole new life in Småland. As if by chance, he had discovered that the Vandals, a people whose origins are usually assumed to be Slavic in the scant historiography, actually originated in Småland, more specifically in the area around Jönköping. The inclusion of these Vandals in the reporting on the new art museum made it all seem interesting and amusing, but also more than a little bizarre. I must confess that I wondered if Pontus Hultén had lost some of his professional and mental acuity when I first learned of these plans. Another possibility that I and others considered was that Hultén was playing a joke on us all; that it was the anarchist, the Dadaist and the prankster playing one last trick on the art world and the establishment.

Pontus Hultén began his research on the Vandals sometime in 1998, a work that continued for several years, with trips in France and to Venice, Tunisia, England and Uppland north of Stockholm, among other places. This time he had neither an institution nor a team of well-trained, competent, energetic younger collaborators behind him. When Hultén set out on his work on the Vandal exhibition, Vandalorum was an imaginary entity, without a hint of museum bureaucracy. Here Pontus Hultén was backed only by an informal team consisting of his secretary and personal assistant Nathalie Meneau (and her husband Sergei/Serge who, as usual, stepped in when needed), Anna-Lena Wibom in Stockholm and Marie-Louise von Plessen in La Motte, the latter who, willingly or unwillingly, became deeply involved in the Vandal exhibition in her capacity as historian.

I perceive that the enthusiasm for the Vandals was moderate among most of those involved, apart from Hultén himself and possibly Anna-Lena Wibom at first. The exhibition was the price that Sven Lundh and his colleagues in Värnamo had to pay for Pontus Hultén's name and involvement in the Vandalorum dream.

During his international career, Hultén had habitually been called a Viking. He himself had a fascination for these notorious seafarers and for other figures in Swedish history and mythology. His foreign friends and colleagues recount that Hultén often returned in conversation to his native Sweden and its importance in European history. In his interest in ancient Norse history, he had a source of inspiration in the Danish artist Asger Jorn and his vast, forgotten epic historical research on ancient Scandinavian art and mythol-

The Danish artist Asger Jorn, admired by Pontus Hultén, devoted much of his life to collecting a gigantic documentation of over twenty-five thousand images, for which he traveled across much of the Nordic region. Jorn planned a massive book on Old Norse art and history. He envisioned the archive as part of a study center for ancient Nordic art: Skandinavisk Institut for Sammanlignende Vandalisme, the Scandinavian Institute for Comparative Vandalism. Hultén was interested and inspired by this unfinished amateur historical lifework of Asger Jorn's.

ogy. Jorn's work and magnificent artistic perspective on history had interested Pontus Hultén since his youth. Hultén dedicated the catalog for his Vandal exhibition, teasingly titled *The True Story of the Vandals*, to Asger Jorn.[7]

Those close to Hultén, especially Marie-Louise von Plessen, testify that his passion for the Swedish, the Old Norse, the mythical ancestral heritage, grew stronger as Hultén aged. His friends who visited him at La Motte speak of Swedish flags almost as altarpieces, the ones Sam Francis had painted for him[8] and the one on the poster for Öyvind Fahlström's scandalous film *Du gamla du fria*.[9] Hultén was proud of his homeland and revered its traditions, with Midsummer, herring, crayfish, table flags and more. Marie-Louise von Plessen says she sometimes had to drive Hultén from La Motte to Ikea south of Paris, so he could eat meatballs with lingonberry jam. Like most matters concerning Pontus Hultén, his love for his country was complicated. His bitterness and disappointment towards his homeland was considerable. At the same time, several of his friends say that Hultén frequently repeated his portrayal of Sweden as a little *better*, a bit more advanced and civilized than the rest of the world.

During the initial contacts about Vandalorum, Pontus Hultén and Anna-Lena Wibom suffered a tragedy when their daughter Klara died suddenly and shockingly in her apartment in Södermalm, Stockholm, aged only thirty-seven.

Klara Hultén was born with a disability that had made life difficult for her. She had struggled to fit in and live up to the expectations that came with her famous parents and their glamorous life. That's what I've been told in half-baked songs. Few of the people I've met know much about Klara. Even fewer are willing to talk about her. Several of those who have said something have asked not to be quoted. Klara grew up with her mother Anna-Lena Wibom on Lidingö. She had sporadic contact with her father over the years. Hultén's friends and colleagues abroad say that they had little or no knowledge that Hultén had a daughter. They had been surprised when Klara had occasionally turned up.

Klara's death was a devastating blow to Pontus Hultén, an event he reportedly never got over. Klara's funeral in Lidingö church is described as a painful ceremony. Anna-Lena Wibom's friend Gunilla Palmstierna-Weiss, who is hostile to Pontus Hultén, speaks of "an awful event with black anarchist banners and a lot of horrible junkies."[10]

Others depict the ceremony as beautiful with the banners in the color of mourning and anarchism as a dramatic accent.

Klara's death, and indeed her life, is a taboo subject in the story of Pontus Hultén — "the world's poorest daddy," as Anna-Lena Wibom herself called him.[11] Although Hultén rarely spoke about his daughter's fate, it's clear that Klara's death was a turning point in his life — for the worse. "After his daughter's death, he was never happy," as photographer Jacques Faujour says.[12] Hultén confided to Faujour and some of his other close friends that he was plagued by remorse for neglecting Klara. One positive consequence of this tragedy, if such an expression can be used, was that Klara's death led Pontus Hultén to reconnect with his son Felix, after the "black hole," as Felix Hultén himself calls it, that characterized their relationship between 1973 and 1995.[13] From then on, Hultén visited Sweden more often, meeting Felix on sailing trips and in other contexts, and inviting his son and his family — Felix had a daughter Louise with his wife Lillemor in 1995 — to La Motte, Paris, Venice and other places. Louise Hultén recalls early childhood memories of visiting art museums in different cities and places like "Le Cyclop" in the Fontainebleau forest when these venues were closed to the public. "These were my playgrounds, it was normal for me," she says.[14]

According to Marie-Louise von Plessen and others, Klara's death led to a strengthening of Pontus Hultén's ties with Sweden, where his son Felix lived, and with Anna-Lena Wibom. It was as if Hultén wanted to atone for his negligence and his long absence from his homeland with a closer contact with his origins. von Plessen believes that his interest in the Vandals can be explained by this intensified romance with his homeland. "The Vandals were part of his maneuvering to return to Sweden," she says.[15]

For the production of the Vandal exhibition, Sven Lundh and the management of the future museum had asked Pontus Hultén and Anna-Lena Wibom to present a budget, which they eventually did: one and a half million kronor, a considerable sum for the purpose at the time. Through local sponsors and contributions from, among others, Framtidens kultur, one of the forgotten state foundations that managed capital from the scrapped wage earner funds, Lundh and his group managed to finance the venture.

Soon the patrons in Värnamo encountered a phenomenon that I myself have experienced and which can easily occur when a small provincial player gets to scrimmage with stars from the big world: the dizzying feeling of not being able to control the processes that you've set in motion. With partners like Pontus Hultén and Renzo Piano, the Lundh family and their employees were playing in a new league, with all that that entailed — like an invoice for half a million SEK when Hultén and Piano had visited for a weekend.

According to Karin Lundh, Renzo Piano's sketches for the museum were a solid piece of work in which Piano had engaged his old collaborators Arup & Partners in London to calculate light penetration, among other technical details. Financing remained to be raised, so construction had to wait.[16]

Karin Lundh defines her contacts with Pontus Hultén as friendly and positive. "I really liked Pontus," she says, "he was easy to deal with." Eventually, though, the Lundh family became aware of something that was familiar to Hultén's co-workers, especially in the latter part of his career. "He wanted nothing boring, nothing negative," says Karin Lundh. "If there was a problem, he just let it go and left it for others to solve. He was above such matters which is understandable. Why should he concern himself with our problems?" She adds: "Pontus also had an entourage that made it expensive and complicated. Sometimes it was difficult to communicate. I think it was a question of center and periphery. Maybe they didn't take us fully seriously because we came from a small town in the countryside. Pontus didn't have that attitude, but maybe some other people involved did."

While the announcement of the start of construction was delayed, Pontus Hultén and his small family production team, including Karin Lundh as co-curator, continued to work tirelessly on their Vandal exhibition, which they now planned to stage in an old factory for the manufacture of clothespins, "Knäppfabriken," a brick building in central Värnamo. Here, the Vandal exhibition was to be organized under the name Vandalorum and become an unofficial inauguration of the future new museum. After being postponed, the opening was finally set for May 2001.

Pontus Hultén's level of ambition with the Vandal exhibition was the highest imaginable. Anything else would have been an impossibility. The habit of not settling for less than the best was an occupational hazard. Among the institutions around the world that sent priceless historical objects to the old factory building in Värnamo were the British Museum, the Vatican Library, the Bibliothèque Nationale de France and many more. "No one, absolutely no one but Pontus would have been allowed to borrow those objects for such an exhibition in such a place," says Danish art historian Troels Andersen, who saw the exhibition in Värnamo after advising on its production as director of the inspirational Asger Jorn Museum in Silkeborg. "It was a very strange experience to see those objects in that environment, quite amazing," Andersen says.[17]

To help with the production and handling of the borrowed objects, Hultén had enlisted the help of German experts Christian Axt and Stephan Böhmer, with whom he had worked in Bonn and elsewhere. Vandalorum had also recruited Björn Springfeldt as curator. Concern spread when Springfeldt suddenly resigned just months before the Vandal exhibition was due to open. "I think Springfeldt panicked when he suddenly realized that Pontus would actually come here and be here for several weeks to really work on the exhibition," says Karin Lundh. "He couldn't understand it and asked several times — is he really coming *here*? There we were, without a manager, with a huge amount of unsolved problems. It was I who had to take over Björn's tasks and become the exhibition commissioner."[18] Björn Springfeldt himself says: "After a while I realized that there was no order to anything in the project. In the car on the way home from the first board meeting, I decided to resign."[19]

Karin Lundh remembers the excitement that animated the whole community when the shipments of precious treasures began to arrive in Värnamo with couriers from prestigious museums and institutions, and how the local fire brigade was called out to ensure that the rigorous security and other requirements were met. Most sensational of the objects on loan were the so-called Albertine tablets, writings on wooden tablets from fifth-century North Africa that had been loaned for the first time by the Musée national des antiquités et des arts islamiques in Algiers, Algeria. Another headliner, which graced the poster and catalog cover, was a sixth-century mosaic from Bordj-Djedid near Carthage, depicting a "merry" horseman alleged to be a Vandal, called "The Merry Vandal" — a large, outstanding object remarkably on loan from the British Museum. The connection between the Vandals and the historical objects that poured in from different parts of the world was more or less clear and/or well documented by history.

That Pontus Hultén and his team exceeded the budget surprised no one. Still, the painful truth that the exhibition cost three times as much as budgeted, four and a half million according to Karin Lundh, came as a shock to the museum management, which was instantly on the brink of bankruptcy. Only thanks to the support of the county council, the municipality and other local and regional actors and sponsors did they manage to sort out the financial situation several years later. According to Karin Lundh, Pontus Hultén was hardly concerned about this grim economic reality. The conflicts between the museum's management, in practice Sven Lundh, and Anna-Lena Wibom in particular were fierce, the atmosphere tense and nervous.

The True Story of the Vandals is repeatedly portrayed as a strange and memorable experience — an overwhelming amount of art-historical beauty gathered from all these treasure troves, dynamically displayed in the old factory building in small Värnamo. The revelation was something of a miracle for those who understood and even for the uninitiated.

In the exhibition catalog, the two-hundred-page book *The True Story of the Vandals*, designed by Hultén's friend Gösta Svensson, Pontus Hultén tells his story of this people — the result of the research he had conducted with the help of Marie-Louise von Plessen and Anna-Lena Wibom over the years, divided into short paragraphs in a chronology. Hultén's, von Plessen's and Wibom's texts were supplemented by learned academic essays by Swedish and international historical experts, mainly on the various objects in the exhibition.

It's a rich history that Hultén narrates in this catalog, largely without source references, with descriptions that at times become detailed and exuberant. Hultén explains that the exhibition and the catalog aim to restore the reputation of the Vandals — the term vandalism is said to derive from the ravages of the Vandals in Rome. On the contrary, the Vandals were a cultured merchant class, according to Hultén, and "experienced high seafarers." He speculates in the catalog text whether the Vikings had learned their courage and navigational skills from the Vandals. Somehow the three or four centuries of time difference between the peoples must have been bridged. In the texts, he theorizes that blond, blue-eyed Venetians and even blond tribes in North African mountain regions are in fact descendants of our Nordic Vandals.

The idea that beautiful blonde Venetian women were descended from Norse sailors, whether Vikings, Vandals or both, was a theory that Hultén had often propagated to his colleagues in Venice. There is reason to suspect that these theories may have been part of the origin of the idea for the Vandal exhibition. In his catalog preface he writes: "Did they found Venice (Torcello) in the fifth century? It is likely.

Today's Venetians are still blond and blue-eyed, 1,500 years later."[20] When reading such formulations, it's impossible not to wonder what Pontus Hultén's perception of reality was really like during the last part of his life.

It's well known that Hultén's obsession with the Vandals went so far that he himself — who had not appreciated being compared to Vikings — began to consider himself a Vandal, a Vandal King even, a world traveler about to return to his northern homeland as the Vandals once did, after his thirty-year odyssey in the art world. It sounds like a joke. With Pontus Hultén, there is always reason to suspect irony, which many did. That he was serious about this craze, or cult almost, is manifested by his decision to be buried in solitary majesty at Vendel's church on the Uppland plain north of Uppsala, where he believed the Vandals had "returned," as close as he could get to the sixth- and seventh-century ship graves near the church wall. Pragmatist and romantic — this had always been one of many opposites in Hultén's personality. He remains a romantic in his grave.

The True Story of the Vandals at the Knäppfabriken in Värnamo attracted handsome visitor numbers during the summer of 2001, with people traveling from as far afield as Denmark, Germany, Holland and the UK to see the exhibition. The Vandal exhibition was, by all accounts, much appreciated by visitors.

If the exhibition was popular locally, and even aroused some international interest, it was different with the Swedish national press and cultural establishment. Here, one could say that a confused, embarrassed silence spread. The exhibition was not reviewed by the major Stockholm newspapers, much to Pontus Hultén's chagrin. Karin Lundh has a theory as to why: "I think it was because they didn't know if they should take it seriously or if Pontus was making fun of them," she says. "They didn't know how to react and therefore didn't dare write about it."[21]

Instead of reviews, a text by the historian Dick Harrison was published in Svenska Dagbladet after the exhibition had ended, in which he mercilessly, like a verbal Vandal, pronounced judgment on Pontus Hultén's efforts as an amateur historian and anthropologist in the catalog/book — an article that infuriated Pontus Hultén. Harrison writes that Hultén's aim is to restore the cultural reputation of the Vandals and demonstrate their importance to European and Nordic history. He sees this as a worthy cause and agrees with Hultén that the Vandals have been subjected to a "grossly unfair and prejudiced denigration" which has given rise to the expression vandalism. But in trying to prove the historical impact of the Vandals, Hultén goes too far, Harrison writes: "The truth is that we have not the faintest idea where the ancestors of the Vandals lived before they appeared in the midst of Germania in antiquity. Nor do we know where they went after the defeat of Belisarius' Eastern Roman troops in 533–534. The most likely scenario is that they were assimilated into the Roman and Berber ruling classes in North Africa and ceased to exist as an ethnic group with an identity."

Dick Harrison draws what must have been a painful parallel for Pontus Hultén when he writes: "(...) today this way of writing history tends to be reserved for circles of enthusiasts involved in nation-building projects. There are plenty of examples from the Balkans and the former Soviet Union of hypotheses about the ancient super-importance of one's own people."[22]

Dick Harrison's article confirmed the Swedish cultural establishment's perception of Pontus Hultén's Vandal exhibition. There is no escaping the conclusion that the Vandal show, and Hultén's entire involvement in Vandalorum, cast something of a pall over his figure as an aging legend, out of step with the times and perhaps even with reality. In combination with other events and complications during the last period of his life, the venture would affect the image of Pontus Hultén, especially in his native Sweden, where there was no shortage of people who were suspicious and hostile towards him.

Twenty years later, we can choose to view the Vandal exhibition and the Vandalorum museum initiative in a different light — as a rather phenomenal, improbable finale to the old storyteller and raconteur Pontus Hultén's era in the world of art and museums; something as exclusive as an unintentionally Dadaist history exhibition, worthy of this mischief-maker and rebel. No one phrases it better than Hultén himself in his catalog text: "What were the relations between the returning Vandals and the early Vikings? We do not know." He then makes a magnificent prophecy as a historian with self-imposed artistic freedom: "Perhaps a new kind of history that is more oriented towards using the imagination — something that is not in vogue today — will find new contexts."

In his article, Dick Harrison, after stripping the academic credit bare from Pontus Hultén, turns to praise: "I took the opportunity to visit the exhibition in Värnamo in mid-August and could see that there was a lot of interest. T-shirts with the exhibition name were offered for sale. The many visitors were fascinated by the Vendel helmet, King Gelimer's silver bowl and all the other treasures. People of all ages walked in and out of the rooms, up the stairs and out into the parking lot, whispering and discussing what they had seen. We did the same; it's hard not to be fascinated when you come across such a combination of bizarre hypotheses and genuine artifacts from the Migration Period (...) For a short time, the light of great history and culture shone on Värnamo. Hard to understand, but fun!"[23]

In Dick Harrison's text about the book and the exhibition *The True Story of the Vandals*, his opinion, despite the severe academic rejection, appears almost overwhelmingly positive in the end. A reason why Pontus Hultén and others involved took such offense at the article was due to the national press's otherwise collective silence. "Pontus probably thought it was a pity that no other historian seriously wanted to test his theories," says Karin Lundh, who claims that several German historians were interested in Hultén's new historical theses, but could not remember who they were.[24]

The Vandal exhibition in Värnamo strikes me as a travesty of a typical Pontus Hultén exhibition. His propensity to "enhance" historical facts and contexts, and if necessary to adjust the terrain according to the map, as well as his heroization of artists and historical figures, had been part of Hultén's work from the beginning and were instrumental for exhibitions such as *Art in Motion*, *The Machine*, the Pingpong shows and others; Hultén who "never made a story weaker," in the words of his old youthful friend Hans Nordenström, or "mythomaniac" as Olle Granath less coyly calls him. With the Vandals, it appears that these urges to write history with imagination as a superpower have been given free rein, without any moderating staff who could tone down the most advanced theoretical extravagances.

In the aftermath of the Vandal exhibition, after the expensive couriers of the distant international institutions had brought their treasures home from Värnamo, there was, not surprisingly, bitterness and conflict, financial stress on the part of the museum management, and disappointment over what were considered to be unfulfilled promises from Pontus Hultén and Anna-Lena Wibom.

The catalog for the Vandal exhibition reads as a postscript: "Vandalorum is the name given by Pontus Hultén to the museum complex being planned for Värnamo, which is to become a Nordic meeting place for contemporary art and design." An account of the background to the initiative follows, ending with a timetable: "Overall project planning 2001, start of construction 2002, inauguration 2004."[25] These objectives came to nothing. After the Vandal spectacle, the museum management, in practice Sven Lundh as many people describe it, was forced to devote itself primarily to financial "consolidation," i.e. avoiding ruin. The groundbreaking ceremony was still a long time coming. This meant that the promised government grant could not be received either. Vandalorum found itself in a Catch 22 dilemma.

In 2002, an attempt was made for a new start with a symposium in the old drying barn outside Värnamo where the new museum was to be built, in which Pontus Hultén and well-known actors in Swedish and Nordic cultural life participated. Monica Nieckels, Hultén's old friend and colleague from Moderna Museet, was hired as the new director of the Museum Vandalorum, which was still waiting to be realized. "When I got the offer in 2003, I asked Pontus if this was really something you would dare to believe in," says Nieckels. "He didn't answer properly, but just smiled somewhat subtly."[26]

Monica Nieckel's involvement with Vandalorum was short-lived, lasting only six months. Soon after Nieckels' departure, Pontus Hultén himself sent a typed letter from Anna-Lena Wibom's home in Lidingö, where Hultén often stayed during his visits to Stockholm, in which he terminated his collaboration with Vandalorum. According to Monica Nieckels, there was a simple explanation for Pontus Hultén's decision to withdraw: "He thought it was okay that they used his name, but then he wanted to be paid for it," says Nieckels. "When he didn't get any money and it was just a problem, he didn't want to be involved anymore."[27]

With Pontus Hultén, of course, went the promise of the donation of his own collection, intended as the backbone of the new museum, for which two of Renzo Piano's barns had been earmarked. Museum Vandalorum in Värnamo was back near zero as it seemed, without a museum building, with few assets but extensive debts. Karin Lundh describes the contacts with Renzo Piano and his office, that they "could not keep such a world architect on hold."[28] Lundh claims that they therefore agreed with Piano to hire a so-called "second architect" to realize his already completed and paid sketches on the day when the conditions existed to realize the building.

Over the years, Sven Lundh and his family and colleagues confirmed the myth of the stubbornness of Smålanders and had the last word. Vandalorum overwintered with, among other projects, training and seminar activities in design. Sven Lundh lived to see his dream fulfilled. Vandalorum was finally inaugurated in 2011, with two of Renzo Piano's "barns" (the old one had been demolished), after several turns and conflicts finally realized by Magnus Silfverhielm and AIX Arkitekter in the role of "second architect," financed by local investors. 2016, the year after Sven Lundh's death, the museum was expanded with another barn and the glass terrace "Sven Lundh's veranda" with a restaurant.

Against all odds, Vandalorum has managed to establish itself as a successful, respected and popular art and design museum, including the Småland Art Archive in its own barn. Plans are well advanced for further expansion with more barns. The museum has been acclaimed for its exhibition program, has won awards and attracts good and growing audiences.

Opinions are divided as to the extent to which Renzo Piano is behind Vandalorum's buildings. On Vandalorum's website and in official printed material from the museum it is written: "The architect responsible for the extension was Magnus Silfverhielm of AIX Architects, based on Vandalorum's original concept by Renzo Piano Building Workshop." According to Karin Lundh, she herself traveled to Genoa and Paris to meet with representatives of Renzo Piano, with whom an agreement was reached on the above quoted wording. Karin Lundhs claims that the buildings were constructed in accordance with Piano's detailed architectural sketches for the museum.

Renzo Piano himself rejects this description of reality. In response to my question, he says that no agreement was reached and that the buildings are not based on his original concept but "free interpretations." Piano denies that his office provided any finished sketches but only a "preliminary plan."[29]

The closest we get in Sweden to a building by Renzo Piano is in any case Vandalorum. The museum has, as it says on its website, become a meeting venue for Nordic art and design. I've been told by local people how much Vandalorum has meant to the region — to its cultural and business life and to its self-image. To some extent, the spirit of Pontus Hultén hangs over the museum, if only in its name. Hultén's bust (by Arne Jones) can be seen in the museum's foyer and his and Piano's names are, of course, mentioned in museum material. One wonders how far the initiative would have gone without these names. Pontus

Hultén himself called Vandalorum his seventh museum and that is, after all, how it can be seen.[30]

I used to think that the ancient Vandals had made mockery of Pontus Hultén in his old age; that the project, with its rural character and its parodic turns, had tarnished Hultén's reputation as the celebrated museum man in the big art world. I have changed my mind. Now I see Vandalorum as an fascinating epilog to Hultén's unprecedented career — not a sure-fire ceremonial card, but an unexpected final gambit, not an ace but a joker. Hultén left the museum world in confusion. It didn't turn out as planned, but something viable nevertheless emerged from the miasma of ideas. For me, Vandalorum has come to appear as a congenial conclusion worthy of Hultén, precisely because of the unlikely quality of the project. It was rarely boring with Pontus Hultén. He knew the art of surprising to the very end.

34

Escape from La Motte: a tragic drama

Pontus Hultén's gradually deteriorating health had plagued and hampered him since the mid-1990s. Around the turn of the millennium and in the years that followed, his mobility became increasingly poor, as did his fitness. "He hadn't been living very healthily," says Marie-Louise von Plessen. "He tried to be healthy, walk, eat better and not drink so much, but it was difficult for him."[1]

Hultén's friends relate how he made an increasingly unhappy impression. Visits from guests at La Motte became more infrequent and Hultén himself traveled less often to Paris or further, except for stays in Sweden. Flying had become dangerous with his weakened blood vessels, asthma and generally impaired bodily functions. His diminished sense of balance and reaction made him insecure in the traffic and information overload of the city.

Due to von Plessen's travel schedule, he was often alone at La Motte. His friends' recollections of the hermit at the castle grow darker, downright Dickensian, however seriously one chooses to take such testimonies. Colleagues say that Hultén looked for reasons to socialize, something he had never had to worry about during his career. "He invented anniversaries for different exhibitions to have visitors and entertain," says Serge Fauchereau.[2]

Bitterness is a word that recurs in the portrayals of Pontus Hultén during these late years. He was disappointed with the way the world and humanity at large had developed, but mostly with the art world, with money subjugating all other motives, red tape and bureaucracy stifling imagination and creativity. "He said that when a person like Tom Messer[3] can become the director of the Guggenheim, then it's over," says Marie-Louise von Plessen. Ida Gianelli recalls a reception in Venice when a smartly dressed middle-aged gentleman walked in: "'Who is that?', asked Pontus. I told him it was Jasper Johns. 'But he looks like a banker!' he said. He couldn't understand how art had turned out."[4]

"Pontus was tired," says Marie-Louise von Plessen. "Several of his good friends were gone, like Tinguely and Niki [who died in 2002]. He hated the art market and developments in the world. It was moving too fast for him. His curiosity didn't go as far as trying to understand computers. He didn't feel at home in the new era. He knew very well how it worked and accepted it. He gave up."[5]

After the Vandal exhibition and his involvement with Vandalorum, which he ended in 2003, Pontus Hultén had no further major assignments in the art world. One of the last trips he made on behalf of art was to Las Palmas in the fall of 2004, where he came full circle when he attended the opening of an exhibition of Denise René, the Parisian gallerist with whom Hultén had begun his career in the international art world in the fifties, still fit and strong despite being eleven years older than Hultén. That it was a fond reunion is evident from photos of the occasion. (René would outlive Hultén by six years — she died in 2012, aged ninety-nine.)

The day after his eightieth birthday, June 22, 2004, Hultén was honored by the Centre Pompidou with a gala dinner at the entrance to the collection on the third floor. The dinner was also the opening of a documentary exhibition in the Bibliothèque Kandinsky with photographs, archival material, books and catalogs, entitled *Pontus Hultén: un esprit libre* (*Pontus Hultén: a free spirit*). A pamphlet on Hultén's career and influence was published by the the museum. His birthday was the last time many of his friends and colleagues from Paris and elsewhere saw him.

That Hultén was aware of his own end approaching seems obvious. He devoted the last years of his life to caring for his heritage and legacy. In addition to the donation of his art collection, library and archive, which he spent many of his last years contemplating, planning and negotiating, carefully considering a number of different options, his other, never realized project was his own literary autobiography. In several late interviews, Hultén said that he was writing one.

He doesn't seem to have been truthful in these statements. No manuscript of his own — Hultén always wrote by hand — exists that resembles the beginning of an autobiography. It's well known that

Hultén had the ambition to produce such a book at least since the mid-nineties. However, it doesn't seem to have occurred to him that he would write it himself. Throughout his career he had never written any particularly long texts and had usually had help even with shorter ones. Hultén asked several younger friends and colleagues, more or less seriously, if they would write his autobiography.

The one who took up the offer was Stephan Andreae, the artist and curator whom Hultén had taken a liking to in Bonn as they shared interests and perspectives on art. Andreae stayed at La Motte for a number of periods in the years before the turn of the millennium and recorded many hours of interview material with Hultén, which I have quoted extensively throughout this book. The conversations were mostly conducted in French, with some German thrown in. The sessions were held in the mornings, when Hultén was at his best, often with Andreae sitting in a chair next to the big old bathtub with feet painted in bright colors by Marie-Louise von Plessen's late Colombian artist friend Lorenzo Jaramillo. Here Hultén lay splashing while narrating his memories and anecdotes. The project faded out. Stephan Andreae only compiled the transcripts of his interviews in 2013, seven years after Hultén's death.

Pontus Hultén's intended title for his autobiography was "Walking with Giants."

A colleague who visited Pontus Hultén at La Motte in the years at the beginning of the millennium was Lars Nittve, Hultén's younger successor at Moderna Museet. Several people have claimed that the relationship between Lars Nittve and Pontus Hultén was strained, as a result of Hultén's alleged advocacy of Björn Springfeldt over Nittve as Olle Granath's successor as superintendent of Moderna Museet in 1990. Nittve himself denies such tensions. He knew Hultén since the late seventies and the glory years at the Centre Pompidou, where Nittve saw all of Hultén's major exhibitions when guiding art students. "I thought he was dead cool, in every way, in the whole style," says Lars when I ask about his view of Pontus Hultén at the time.[6]

Nittve explains that he got in touch with Hultén before the opening of Tate Modern in May 2000, when Nittve was founding director of the British mega museum. "I received a friendly letter from him in which he thanked me for the invitation and wrote that he was unfortunately unable to attend and that he regretted this as he recognized himself in me," says Lars Nittve. "He wrote that he had difficulty traveling but that I was welcome to visit him at his castle. It's one of those things that people say without necessarily meaning it and it's easy for it not to happen, but I thought it was something I couldn't miss. I'm very glad that I didn't neglect it but went to visit him."[7]

Nittve paints a poignant picture of the big, heavy Pontus sitting alone in his castle, "drinking from some demijohn" and telling his anecdotes from art history — an encounter that Nittve says influenced his decision to leave his post at Tate Modern in 2001, after just three years, to return home to Stockholm and Moderna Museet. "I was very touched to see him there, sitting alone with a big Swedish flag on the wall. He really was the Flying Dutchman for me, a man without a homeland. I asked myself if I wanted to end up where he was, and I didn't."[8]

A lingering question during these late years at La Motte is whether, despite his health problems, Pontus Hultén still retained his mental acuity at the end of his life or if he suffered from some form of dementia, as some suggest. The overall picture I get from Marie-Louise von Plessen and many others is that in his last years, Hultén was still in his right mind in private and in small groups, for short periods, but that he became tired and absent in larger groups. Some doubt whether it was really the same Pontus Hultén in his last years. At our meeting in New York, Catherine Matisse Monnier, Teeny Duchamp's granddaughter, says what others imply: "He went south,"[9] i.e. the untranslatable American expression to go south, in a mental sense, leaving behind the everyday reality of fellow human beings for one's own mental domain.

Although Pontus Hultén's intellectual status at this time is questionable, he was demonstrably capable of orchestrating at least a couple more complicated maneuvers. The first was when he donated his art collection to Moderna Museet.

Hultén had long pondered which institution would receive his collection, which he had essentially kept intact, although he had sold some valuable works and archival material,[10] also in addition to the deal with the Tinguely Museum. In the picture of Hultén's relationship to money and his widely reputed stinginess, this is important to emphasize. Like most things with Hultén, it was complicated. In the last years of his life, he was keen to convert part of his art collection into hard cash for his old age and for his son Felix's inheritance. Still, he never intended to sell most of this collection or leave

Including a collection of letters from Marcel Duchamp to the Belgian art dealer Ronny Van de Velde (see Chapter 36), which the latter says he later sold at auction in Paris.

it to Felix. Hultén wanted to see his art in a museum or other public institution. He may have been stingy in small, but here he was truly generous at large. In our time, the collection he donated would be worth hundreds of millions on the commercial market.

With this art treasure as his dowry, Hultén sought out the institution that had the most favorable terms to offer. At one time he had considered donating his collection to Palazzo Grassi. In later years, he is said to have discussed the donation of all or various parts of his collection, library and archive with Uppsala University, Palazzo Cavalli-Franchetti in Venice, Vandalorum, Louisiana, Oxford University and perhaps even more institutions.

I wonder about Hultén's intentions in these courtships. Did he really seriously consider anything other than his collection ending up where it all began, at Moderna Museet? Knowing his patriotism and how dear the museum remained to Pontus' heart during all his years abroad, how he protected the museum's interests, despite his bitterness, I find it hard to imagine so. After the reopening in 1998, though, the relationship between Hultén and Moderna Museet was almost non-existent, so if nothing had happened, it is still doubtful whether Pontus Hultén's collection and archives would have ended up on Skeppsholmen. Such things are difficult to know with Hultén. He kept his cards close to his chest, as they say in gambling parlance.

Lars Nittve's first visit to La Motte sometime in the fall of 2000 would prove to be a well-invested trip. When the news was surprisingly announced the following year, in the fall of 2001, that Nittve would be leaving Tate Modern to return to Moderna Museet as David Elliott's successor as director — a sensation in art Stockholm — he had a fresh relationship with Pontus Hultén and was well acquainted with the collection after his visit to La Motte, where Hultén kept most of his art. Shortly after Nittve took up his post at Moderna Museet, he began talks with Hultén about the donation.

What made these dealings tragic was that Pontus Hultén chose to keep Marie-Louise von Plessen out of the negotiations about the collection — and, more dramatically, out of his plans to leave La Motte and move back to Sweden in connection with the donation. The conversations and correspondence with the museum in Stockholm took place while von Plessen was away from La Motte, with Nathalie Meneau as the museum's main contact person. For one reason or another, Pontus Hultén was not prepared to confront Marie-Louise von Plessen with the decision he made sometime during those years between 2002 and 2004, after the first exchanges with Lars Nittve in the winter of 2002.

It's uncertain whether the plan for the donation originally included the decision to move home to Sweden or whether this evolved. The former option seems more likely. Why else would Hultén have been so secretive towards Marie-Louise von Plessen? Should we believe the horror stories from Paris about the "Panzer Countess" who kept poor Pontus on a tight leash and regarded his art collection as her own? "I knew very well that he wanted to give the collection to the Moderna Museet and I was all for it as I had told him — I would have encouraged it if he had talked to me about it," says von Plessen herself. "It was a security nightmare with the collection here at the castle and it was far too crowded. There was art everywhere. I didn't even have room for my books."[11]

One fateful circumstance looms at this stage of Pontus Hultén's life: he felt death approaching and did not want to end his life in France but in the Swedish motherland, to which, like the Vandal king he seems to have come to see himself as, he would return. Moreover, it appears that Sweden and Anna-Lena Wibom, not France and Marie-Louise von Plessen, provided the security that Hultén sought in the final stage of his life. To what extent Pontus Hultén himself was able to lead the planning of this operation, and how much was handled by Anna-Lena Wibom and Nathalie Meneau, is difficult for me to assess. The latter, of course, handled the practicalities, such as the correspondence with the museum, with Sergei as their assistant. Nevertheless, I'm convinced that Hultén himself was behind the master plan, no matter his physical and mental state.

In any case, it was an intricate maneuver that was planned over a long time, with the above-mentioned and some others as conspirators. Pontus Hultén's "master plan" included that the collection would first be shown at Moderna Museet in the spring of 2004,[12] which Marie-Louise von Plessen was involved in, and from there be transported back to La Motte — with the exception of a selection of works that Hultén donated to the museum in connection with the exhibition. What Marie-Louise didn't know was that the collection, in collaboration with Moderna Museet, was to be brought back from La Motte to be displayed in a palace in Venice, but not at Palazzo Grassi as Hultén had initially hoped, as the new owner François Pinault made this impossible. Instead, Hultén had made contact with the Veneto District Institute of Science, Literature and Art in Palazzo Cavalli-Franchetti, where the collection would be presented in an exhibition that would open in early 2006, complete with a handsome Italian-language catalog,[13] an initiative supported by the City of Venice. From Venice, the art would then be transported directly to its new permanent home on Skeppsholmen. Moderna Museet would be responsible for all logistics and transportations.

Keeping Marie-Louise von Plessen in the dark with this complex planning operation must have required cunning, accuracy, calculation and acting skills. "I knew something was up," says von Plessen. "Sergei kept asking very interestedly about the dates of my travels. I sensed that something was very wrong but didn't understand what."[14]

The time came in November 2005, when Marie-Louise von Plessen was in Lisbon on an assignment as a senator in the European Parliament of Culture. Everything was prepared. As I understand it, the transport was ready when Hultén's confidants announced one day that the moment had arrived. It was no small logistical operation. Trucks specially built for transporting art arrived at a given time on the small country road, drove the muddy gravel road through the alley, one at a time, and parked for loading on the narrow passage in front of the bridge over the moat. This alone was a precarious maneuver. The art had been packed by the staff of Moderna Museet in advance and was loaded onto trucks that turned around inside the walled courtyard for transport back out to the highway and on down to Venice.[15] There the art was reloaded onto boats to be transported the last bit across the canals to Palazzo Franchetti. Hultén's library and archives were transported directly to Stockholm. The secret operation at La Motte was carried out in great haste, as Marie-Louise von Plessen was only away for five days.[16]

The exhibition at Palazzo Franchetti opened on March 3, 2006. Pontus Hultén was there with his entourage consisting of Anna-Lena Wibom, Natalie Meneau, Felix Hultén and others. The exhibition in the small palace is described as beautiful, but Hultén's old colleagues were shocked by his poor physical condition. "It was painful to see him like that, our hero, our Viking," says Clarenza Catullo.[17]

The deal for the donation also included the most important feature for Hultén: the construction of the "Pontus Hultens Visningsmagasin," ("Pontus Hulten's Study Gallery"), on the second floor of the museum, adjacent to the auditorium, which was only opened in 2008, two years after Hultén's death. There, the collection would always be available to the public, along with Hultén's library and archive, all designed by Renzo Piano, who worked pro bono in honor of his friend.[18] The question was whether it would be the third time lucky when Hultén now tried again what had failed before at the Moderna Museet and at MNAM in the Centre Pompidou — an archive of screens that the visitor could order herself; more sophisticated this time, with a construction powered by engines from the sponsor Volvo, controlled by the push of a button on a panel by the visitor? The answer is no. The solution was a third failure. The screens stopped working many years ago. The collection has mostly sat unseen. Thankfully, in the fall of 2022, the Study Gallery reopened after renovation, with the screens back in operation, and is now once again a vital exhibition space and study for art historians, researchers and visitors.

Keeping his life partner Marie-Louise von Plessen out of all these machinations is a feat, no matter how much help he had, that not only says something about Hultén's personality but also proves that he must have been at least largely sane. It seems to me that when physical strength was failing, judgment was probably clouded, and death was approaching, he "crossed over to the dark side" — as if he knew it was almost over and intended to do what was needed and take what he thought was his. It appears to me that in those last years he no longer cared about the consequences of his actions. A bold audacity and a willingness to transgress all sorts of boundaries when necessary had always been part of the battery of characteristics that had made Hultén what he became. These traits seem to have been accentuated, as it can be when age exaggerates elements of people's personality during the final phase of life.

The scene when Marie-Louise von Plessen returned to La Motte to find Hultén missing and the castle emptied of its art collection is straight out of a Wagner libretto — a legend among all those who knew Hultén and in the wider art world. I've often heard this drama rendered with fervor, even though none of the speakers were present on the occasion.

More than ten years later, Marie-Louise von Plessen recounts with tears in her eyes the shock when, after sixteen years of life together, Pontus Hultén disappeared from one day to the next, never to return. From the day he left La Motte, Pontus Hultén was not available on the phone for von Plessen either. "I almost died," says Marie-Louise. "I lost fifteen kilos and couldn't do anything for six months — no work, no sleep, no reading, no writing, just riding and playing the piano."

Pontus Hultén is said to have been satisfied with both the exhibition and the plan for the Study Gallery, and with the catalog in Swedish and English produced for the donation, designed by Gösta Svensson, which was also part of the agreement. This catalog became a certain substitute for the autobiography that Hultén didn't manage to realize, with his personal texts about the artists represented in the donation, most of them dear friends of Hultén. The book about the collection is also a fragmentary account of his life in art, supplemented with a rich selection of autobiographical documentary images.[19]

As I study this ambitious, luxurious catalog, the varied, personal character of the collection is striking. Many of the works are portraits of Hultén by his artist friends. Among the big names, such as Duchamp, Brancusi, Malevich, Rauschenberg, Warhol, Tinguely, Lichtenstein, Johns, de Saint Phalle, Kienholtz and others, there are many artists unknown to a wider audience, friends of Hultén, whom he highlights in his texts with the same respect as their more famous colleagues. In many ways, the catalog *Pontus Hultén's collection ...* is a "friend's book" — a beautiful account of a life in art. As has been pointed out to me from several quarters, some of the works in the collection are questionable in terms of ownership. "But that's not unique to Pontus," as Lars Nittve says. "That was often the case with museum directors in the past. Often it was hard to distinguish what was theirs and what should belong to the museum."[20]

Much of the art in Pontus Hultén's collection and in this catalog is relegated to the anonymity of storage. Yet many of the works and objects included in Pontus Hultén's donation are art historical gems that have been frequently shown in the museum's galleries in recent years, such as Rauschenberg's coin tosser from Tinguely's "Homage to New York" in 1960 and Warhol's self-portrait from 1967. It was no mean addition to its collection that Moderna Museet received with this gift. The same goes for the archival material, which is a growing attraction for international art historians and researchers. The entire donation has added depth to the museum as one of the most important institutions in the development of international art in the second half of the twentieth century.

For a long time, I thought that Pontus Hultén's Study Gallery was a legacy that the museum had tucked away, difficult to access even with its "un-Hulténian" limited opening hours. I've gotten over this notion. I now see the Study Gallery as a worthy monument to Hultén in the mother museum. The archive is a mini-museum within the museum, with research projects and interesting exhibitions from Pontus Hultén's collection and archive, as well as other content. There is no doubt that the Study Gallery has become famous among art historians and museum professionals, much appreciated by its many international visitors. "It was amazing to sit in the archive," says Michelle White, curator of The Menil Collection in Houston, who visited the Moderna Museet and the Study Gallery for the museum's 2021 Niki de Saint Phalle retrospective.[21] "I was there for a few days, but I would have loved to stay for a month."[22]

Pontus Hultén did not take everything from La Motte. What he left behind — graphics, posters, replicas, objects and curios, as well as some original works — is more than enough to give the castle's interior an incomparably eccentric artistic character. It's hard to imagine how this small chateau must have appeared when it contained the collection. Every hall, room, chamber and space must have been veritable "Wunderkammers," with the boat and its exhaust pipe through the castle wall a bizarre installation in the midst of it all.

When Pontus Hultén arrived in Stockholm in the fall of 2005 after leaving La Motte with his art collection, Anna-Lena Wibom took him to the small, functionally adapted two-room apartment she had acquired on his behalf in a home for senior citizens in a then newly built area by the Hammarby Canal. From the small apartment, Hultén had a view of the canal and its boats, which he appreciated. I've heard it said that when Hultén was wheeled in his chair for the first time into this apartment, he said: "I never want to move from here." Perhaps here he felt a sense of security that he had missed in La Motte, returned to his homeland in smaller, more comfortable, safer circumstances.

To help her look after Pontus Hultén in Stockholm, Anna-Lena Wibom hired Carl Fredrik Hårleman, a well-known figure in Stockholm art circles. Hårleman has told me about the short year he spent with Pontus Hultén — quiet days walking with his wheelchair in the then newly built Hammarby Sjöstad and in Stockholm's inner city, some visits to shops and lunches at restaurants such as Zum Franziskaner on Skeppsbron, Operabaren and Sturehof. Hårleman says that Hultén wanted traditional Swedish home cooking specialities and, of course, beer and schnapps. Hultén met few people other than his family. Journalists, art historians and others tried in vain to get in touch with him. "There were several who wanted a final interview and so on, but Pontus didn't agree to anything like that," says Carl Fredrik

Hårleman. "But he was interested in contemporary art. We visited a number of galleries."[23]

In Hårleman's opinion, Pontus Hultén generally retained most of his mental capacity to the end. "When you met other people and even sometimes otherwise, he could become absent-minded," says Carl Fredrik. "But when you were sitting quietly one-on-one and he was relaxed, he was all in, joking and quick-witted."

Pontus Hultén's collection traveled from Moderna Museet to Helsinki, where it was shown at the Ateneum Museum in an exhibition that opened on September 15, 2006. Pontus Hultén traveled by boat with Anna-Lena Wibom, his son Felix, Natalie Meneau and others to the Finnish capital, a city that had always been dear to him. It was the last trip that Pontus Hultén undertook. From here there are some of the last pictures taken of him by professional photographers, bearded as he had not been since his youth, after which the characteristic mustache, Hultén's trademark, had always been left to its own devices. When I see the pictures of Hultén in a beard, I'm reminded, don't ask me why, of Marcel Duchamp's comment at the sight of his dead eldest brother Jacques Villon, as referred to in Calvin Tomkins' biography: "He is like father, without the beard."[24]

35 End of the earth life

Pontus Hultén died on October 26, 2006, in his apartment on Alsnögatan in Stockholm as a result of a heart attack. His son Felix Hultén, who was at home in Gothenburg, tells me that he was told by the staff at the home that Hultén had gotten up in the night, started "screaming and shouting" and then fallen down dead. I ask Felix if he thinks his father was suffering from death anxiety before his end. "No, I don't think so, because he was so extremely happy with his life," Felix replies. Let's hope that he, who on one level knew his father best, is right in this assumption.[1]

Carl Fredrik Hårleman, Dan Wolgers and others who met Hultén during his time in Stockholm say that he seemed to settle into his quiet, limited life at Hammarby harbor. From Hultén's friends around the world I've heard the opinion that it was tragic that Hultén ended his life in this way, alone in a small service apartment, with only an occasional banal painting on the wall as reported. Judging from the few testimonies, the overall impression is that after leaving La Motte, Hultén still managed to find some kind of peace during these months, with the accounts of his life largely settled, as it seemed at the time. Serge Fauchereau recounts that he traveled to Stockholm after Hultén's death to help prepare for the funeral and that he stayed in his old boss's apartment.

Carl Fredrik Hårleman says that he was told by Anna-Lena Wibom to ask Pontus Hultén to stop signing up for activities at the service home that he had no intention of participating in. Wibom had found that "Bo Ek" had signed up for this and that. It turned out that a man with this Pontus Hultén alias, Sweden's shortest name, lived just a few doors down from Hultén.

"It was a very strange feeling to sleep in his bed and be among his things, as if he was still there, but I got used to it," says Fauchereau. "It was a very small apartment but nice and pleasant with a charming view of the harbor."[2]

The news of Pontus Hultén's death was reported relatively sparingly in the Swedish press. At that time, Pontus Hultén could be said to have been a person unknown to the wider public in his home country. Over the years, I had seen his name and work fall deeper and deeper into oblivion. Few efforts had been made to keep his legacy or memory alive. The donation of the collection and Pontus Hultén's Study Gallery, but above all the scandal of the Brillo boxes, which broke six months after Hultén's death and which I will return to in the next chapter, did bring about a certain "revival" of his memory — a negative one — but by and large the process of forgetting has continued. In a middle-aged audience interested in general culture in contemporary Stockholm, most people have vague or no associations when Hultén's name is mentioned. In younger generations, he is largely unknown even in art circles.

In the international art world, the death of Pontus Hultén was big news. His fame and importance for the development of art in the twentieth century was confirmed by the New York Times' extensive obituary of October 30, 2006, which I have previously quoted. In February 2007, the world's leading art magazine Artforum published memorial texts by Daniel Birnbaum, then professor at the Academy of Fine Arts in Frankfurt, Ann Goldstein and Daniel Buren. In his text, Birnbaum tells of a dinner with Harald Szeemann where a younger artist made the mistake of asking whether *Les Machines Célibataires* (*The Bachelor Machines*), a legendary Szeemann exhibition from 1976 inspired by Duchamp's "The Large Glass," was not a work by Hultén, to which the Swiss, notably irate, replied: "Not quite everything interesting was done by Pontus."[3]

The funeral was held on December 1 in Vendel Church in Uppland, where Hultén had chosen his grave next to the wall of the cemetery, some fifty meters from the monument erected in the 1930s over the ship grave, discovered in the 1860s, which according to Hultén had been so historically revolutionary.[4] Here he was laid to rest in his conviction next to the Vandal kings whom he had apparently come to regard as his at least spiritual ancestors. The ceremony is pictured by Dan Wolgers: "It was atmospheric and solemn with a lot of people but not a brutal amount of people. People were very sad. It was a nice, pretty standard funeral."[5]

A lunch at the Hyllan restaurant in Uppsala followed — a lively event, as witnessed. Many of Hultén's closest friends from around the world had traveled to Sweden to honor his memory. From the later, even livelier reception at Moderna Museet, Olle Granath recalls a memory of Leif Nylén, a longtime art critic for Dagens Nyheter, who, alongside Torsten Bergmark, had been one of Hultén's and the museum's most vehement critics during the turbulent late sixties and early seventies. Nylén approached Granath and said: "I don't think we ever understood what he stood for."[6]

On a nice quiet day in late September 2018, I drive with my father as company to the beautiful, well-kept cemetery on a hill overlooking the vast Uppland plain half an hour north of Uppsala. As revealed in the opulence and diligent maintenance of the graves, and the names on the tombstones, this is a prosperous tract with ancient historical roots; many archaeological discoveries from the Stone Age onwards have been made in the surroundings. Hultén's own tomb is as close to the Vendel monument as you can get; a tastefully modest, meticulously manicured grave with sharply raked gravel, fresh flower arrangements and a medium-high natural stone with the name in a simple inscription without titles.

In a stand in front of the tombstone itself rests the smaller, softly rounded, light-colored stone that I have heard tales about — the one that has been called Pontus Hultén's "care stone," which he is said to have brought with him during parts of his odyssey around the art world. The rock is said to have been the stepping stone from the Hultén family's summer home, the cottage in Trollängen on northern Lidingö, so beloved by the son Karl-Gunnar. Hultén is said to have used the stone as a pillow when he was a little boy. Now it watches over him in eternal rest.

Dan Wolgers relates an anecdote about this care stone, from sometime in the eighties. He helped Pontus Hultén with a refurbishment of his apartment on Stora Nygatan in Gamla stan, which had to be carried out in consultation with the National Heritage Board, including renovation of the old tiled stoves. "Pontus had brought a real doll's house wood stove from his old nursery and we connected it to one of the stoves," says Wolgers. "Then he could lie in bed and make a fire with pine cones in the doll's stove. I remember thinking, 'That's what I want to do when I'm older.'" One evening, Wolgers continues, Hultén called and asked him to come and meet him in front of the house. "When I got there, he was standing in the rain, soaking wet and dirty in his work clothes, with a rental car outside the door, about to lift out a stone. 'I realized that I must have Pålle,' he said. He told me that he had been out on Lidingö and dug up the stone, which was called Pålle [Swedish nickname for horse] because he had ridden on it as a child, and tossed it over the fence. Now he needed help to carry it up to the apartment, four flights of stairs without an elevator."[7]

It finally dawned on me which cinematic figure it is that Pontus Hultén has constantly reminded me of, in the appearance I myself encountered at the Grand Hôtel in Stockholm and in the image that has emerged ever more clearly in the work on this story. It's of course Orson Welles and his *Citizen Kane*, considered by many film scholars to be the best film of all time, about the great, heavy, aged magnate Charles Foster Kane, modeled after the newspaper moguls William Randolph Hearst and Joseph Pulitzer, in Welles' own grandiose role incarnation. The resemblance is striking — Kane lying on his deathbed, uttering his last word, *rosebud*, which those around him try to interpret. As a movie audience, we learn that the word is not a code word for some crucial riddle but the name of the toboggan that the great man played with as a child, which he sees in his mind's eye as he dies. For me, the stone becomes the romantic Pontus Hultén's *Rosebud* — the stone where child he had played, in the words of Swedish national romantic poet Verner von Heidenstam.

Say what you will about his theories on the Vandals, but it is a magnificent external and internal image to me of the old sailor and adventurer, this commander and conqueror of art, who here rests eternally moored after his long journey next to the ship's grave of his supposed ancestors on these sea-like expanses.

In the park at La Motte, next to the moat, Marie-Louise von Plessen had her own tombstone installed: a beautiful simple natural stone, leaning back against another stone, with an engraved inscription in black:

PONTUS

1924–2006

NAVIGATEUR EN MER ET EN ART

MARIE-LOUISE

"Navigator at sea and in art"

The following summer, Renzo Piano, together with Anna-Lena Wibom, Felix Hultén, Nathalie Meneau, Jerry Sohn and his wife Eba, conducted a sailing trip in the Stockholm archipelago in Pontus Hultén's memory, in the open two-masted boat that Hultén had kept in Venice, with Piano as helmsman. "It was something we had talked about for years, but of course it never happened — that I would come to the archipelago and we would sail together there instead of in the Mediterranean," says Renzo Piano. "I felt that it was something I owed him, that it had to be in his memory when it didn't happen in life."[8]

36

Brillo — a posthumous global mega-scandal

So we have arrived at the inevitable, posthumously revealed mess that has cast its shadow over Pontus Hultén's name in the art world and here at home in Sweden; a misery that chronology has allowed me to save for the finale.

It's archetypical of Hultén that after ending his life in a storm, with the breakup from La Motte, six months after his death he returns with a hurricane, in what has been characterized in the international media as "one of the boldest art frauds of modern times"[1] — an embarrassing affair for several of the world's most prestigious art institutions.

Pontus Hultén's actions may seem in line with his entire personality — a character that, in the final phase of his life, as I see it, slipped over to "the dark side." It's regrettable that this fateful chain of events, after all only a fragment of Hultén's long life and career, has come to stain the image of Hultén to such an extent, not least in Sweden, where the Brillo scandal is what many in our time associate with his name. Internationally too, the scandal has severely tarnished Hultén's legacy. I've had contact with several people in the art world who have reacted with dislike and hostility to Hultén's name, even calling him a criminal, partly or entirely because of this scandal.

My own instinctive approach to the Brillo scandal, before I delved deeper into the affair, going through material and talking to many people involved and all of Pontus Hultén's old friends, colleagues and partners, was to minimize Hultén's responsibility and downplay the whole thing. Most people in Hultén's circle have shown the same inclination. In general, the closer these people were to Hultén, the more convinced they were of his innocence — a common human phenomenon.

I even viewed it as if Hultén's actions seemed to be in the spirit of Andy Warhol and Marcel Duchamp, that the whole affair could be seen almost as a Dadaist demonstration — a final kick in the ass of the loathed moneyed art market from the anarchist and rebel Pontus Hultén. Even after I had first read the philosopher and culture writer Thomas Anderberg's well-received book *Den stora konstsvindeln* (*The Great Art Swindle*) when it was published in 2010,[2] based on the revelations of the Swedish newspaper Expressen in 2007, I retained this general view.

In retrospect, I've realized that it was my own emotional attachment to Pontus Hultén that clouded my judgment and prevented me from soberly taking in the indisputable facts presented by Expressen in their elaborate exposé series, which wrote its own chapter in the history of modern art.

I was far from alone in this "blindness." Thomas Anderberg himself maintained an attitude towards Pontus Hultén similar to my own, in which he downplayed Hultén's moral responsibility and advanced the thesis that Hultén's motives were not primarily economic but subversive. Expressions such as "Warhol is smiling in his heaven" have been recurrent, as Anderberg noted in an article in Dagens Nyheter in 2008, which he later expanded in his book.[3] MNAM's former director Bernard Blistène is one of several prominent figures in the art world who use such terms when he not only defends but hails Pontus Hultén's actions in the Brillo affair: "I think it was brilliant!" Blistène says. "It was exactly in the spirit of Warhol and there is no one else but him who would have even dared to think of doing something like that."[4]

I remained in this perception of reality for a long time. As I began to study the information in more detail and was able to accept other arguments, a less flattering picture inevitably emerged. I clearly remember a turning point in my own approach. It was during a lunch with Germain Viatte, Pontus Hultén's colleague and successor as director of the MNAM Centre Pompidou, together with his wife Françoise, also an art historian, at the couple's home in Paris. We got to talking about the Brillo affair. Françoise Viatte and I discussed precisely this, that Pontus, insofar as he had been guilty of fraud, had acted in the spirit of Warhol and Duchamp; that these two subversives of art are laughing in their graves, that one could regard the whole thing as a Dadaist installation, etcetera.

Andy Warhol at his "supermarket show" at Stabe Gallery, New York, April 1964, where his Brillo boxes were first shown.

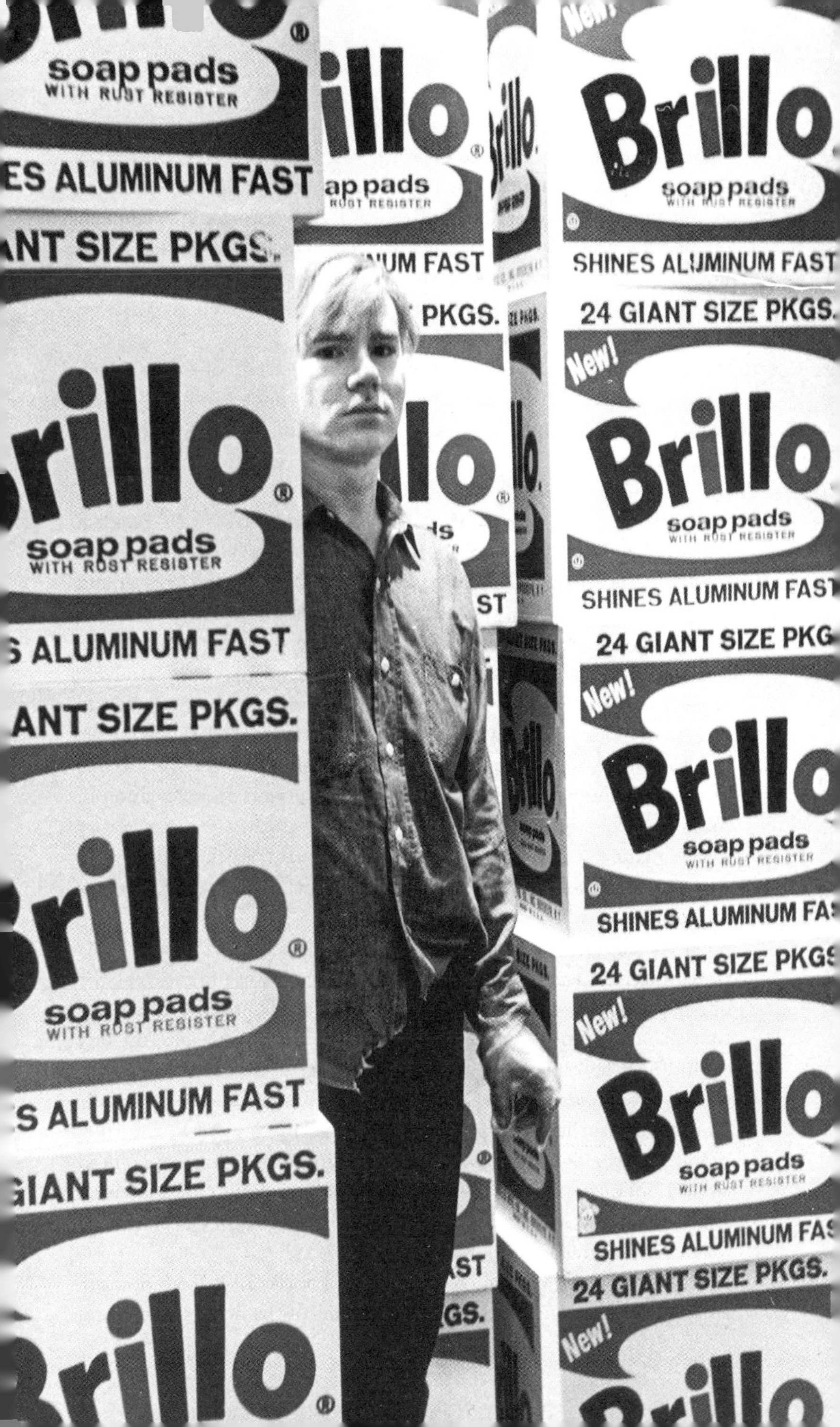

soap pads
WITH RUST RESISTER
ALUMINUM FAST
Brillo
soap pads
WITH RUST RESISTER
SHINES ALUMINUM FAST
24 GIANT SIZE PKGS.
New!
Brillo
soap pads
WITH RUST RESISTER
SHINES ALUMINUM FAST
24 GIANT SIZE
New!
Brillo
soap pads
WITH RUST RESISTER
SHINES ALUMINUM
24 GIANT SIZE
New!
Brillo
soap pads
WITH RUST RESISTER
SHINES ALUMINUM
24 GIANT SIZE PKGS.
New!
soap pads
WITH RUST RESISTER
ALUMINUM FAST
GIANT SIZE PKGS.
soap pads
WITH RUST RESISTER
ALUMINUM FAST
GIANT SIZE PKGS.

Germain Viatte refused to agree with us and said in a serious tone: "No, wait a minute, I have to object. If you write a false certificate for a work of art and sell it and make a lot of money out of it, then it's not an installation but something entirely different."[5] Germain's comment opened my eyes. It was a simple truth. The odd thing was that it had taken me ten years to digest the indisputable facts of the case, so colored had I been by the defensive position I had taken on behalf of Hultén, without being aware of it.

I will do my best to explain the unfortunate chain of events. Many questions will never be answered. Much is shrouded in mystery and ambiguity. All the intricate twists and turns of the story are not all that easy to follow.

On March 30, 2007, six months after Pontus Hultén's death, Swedish daily tabloid Expressen published the first of several large-scale investigative series of articles by journalists Micke Ölander, Leo Lagercrantz and Christian Holmén, with detailed accounts of what became the complicated intricacies of the Brillo scandal — a fascinating read, structured like a crime chronicle, with quotes from those involved, experts and written sources from several countries. The news spread like the famous wildfire across the art world and international media.

The origin was that auction house Stockholms Auktionsverk as one of the main numbers in the catalog for its auction Stora Kvalitén in April 2007 had listed a wooden Brillo box with the provenance that it was made for the Andy Warhol exhibition in Stockholm in 1968 where it had also been displayed. The price estimate was six to eight hundred thousand SEK.

At the last minute, this Brillo box, which had aroused hot international interest, was withdrawn after suspicions were raised that the box had in fact been manufactured much later, in 1990 in Malmö, and that the alleged provenance was thus false. This was despite the fact — and here lay the global impact of the case — that the "sculpture" was reviewed and approved as recently as November 2006 by the Andy Warhol Art Authentication Board, AWAAB, in New York, the then "sphinx-like"[6] highest authority for assessing Warhol's art, appointed by and operating under The Andy Warhol Foundation for the Visual Arts, the foundation that manages the artist's legacy and is one of the major powers in contemporary art.

Respect for the Warhol Foundation, as I shall call it from now on, among collectors and dealers was at the time of the Brillo scandal, and remains today, total — for understandable reasons, as the foundation is the guarantor of the ever-increasing value of their assets. In all the articles and reports I have read in the international media about the Brillo scandal and other disputes involving the Warhol Foundation, descriptions of the silence that afflicts those involved and outside experts are repeated as soon as the Warhol Foundation is mentioned. The foundation consistently refuses to release information or make more than minimal statements. In the few cases where it does speak to the media, interviews are preceded by caveats. Many of the art dealers, auction house representatives, collectors and others contacted for all of these articles do not want to talk about the Warhol Foundation or about Andy Warhol at all. Those who do speak are taciturn and cautious. As described in a 2010 article in The Guardian: "Talking about Warhol to anyone in the international art world is strange. 'Don't tell anyone you met me,' says an east London dealer. A millionaire dealer in New York warns: 'I'll tell you and then deny we've met if it gets out.' A third emails from a specially generated address, with all identifying markers cut out."[7]

Stockholms Auktionsverk had been tipped off about the suspicious provenance and dating of the Brillo box by Per-Olov Börjeson, an art dealer in Malmö who had been dealing in Andy Warhol's art for decades and who had also met and was acquainted with the artist personally. In my conversation with art historian, museum curator and Andy Warhol connoisseur Bo Nilsson, who was director of the Rooseum art gallery in Malmö in the second half of the 1990s, he tells me that he too had warned that the information about the provenance of the Brillo box was phony, in a telephone call to Niclas Forsman, then managing director of Stockholm Auktionsverk auction house.[8] "It was certainly not an easy decision to withdraw the box," says Andreas Rydén, then chief art intendant at Stockholm Auktionsverk. "We had the certificate from the highest authority in New York, but I remember that Börjeson's letter was sharply worded and credible. Börjeson is a rather controversial person, but he had been dealing in art at high values for a long time and was respected as knowledgeable, so we felt that it was something we had to take seriously. I also recall that we posed the question to New York but when we had to wait for a response we decided we had to withdraw the box even though it was one of the main attractions in the catalog."[9]

Per-Olov Börjeson was well acquainted with Malmö's small art world and knew that a number of Brillo boxes made in the city in

1990 had been circulating on the local market ever since. Bo Nilsson and "everyone else," in Nilsson's words, in Malmö's art world also knew about the boxes. "All the printers at Screentrycksbolaget, who had printed the boxes, had boxes," says Bo Nilsson. "I tried to buy one myself from a contact, but of course he wouldn't sell it."[10] Per-Olov Börjeson was acquainted with a carpenter who had made the boxes on behalf of Pontus Hultén, according to information for the exhibition *Le Territoire de l'Art*, shown at the Russian Museum in Leningrad in the spring of 1990 (see Chapter 27). The boxes are said to have been made by this carpenter and his colleague in Malmö Konsthall art gallery's workshop. The contact had been mediated by Björn Springfeldt, director of Moderna Museet at the time, who had been head of Malmö Konsthall in the late 1980s. The assignment with the Brillo boxes is alleged to have been carried out by the carpenters outside regular working hours.[11] "Pontus asked me to help get boxes made for the exhibition in Leningrad and it was natural to do it in Malmö," Springfeldt tells me. "The carpenters in the art gallery were fantastic and in Malmö there was also the designer John Melin, who had done the Warhol catalog and who could help with the decor and printing."[12]

Decisive for the detonation of the scandal was that Per-Olov Börjeson was not content to warn Stockholms Auktionsverk, but also contacted Expressen, where he knew the journalist Micke Ölander, who at the time worked for the paper's investigative reporting group in Stockholm, but who came from Malmö. Ölander recalls a snapshot straight out of a crime noir story by any "hard-boiled" writer: "I remember the scene when my colleague Christian Holmén, who was already head of the investigative journalism group at Expressen, came in with a note with this tip. Christian told me the story of the Brillo box that was supposed to have been made in Malmö in 1990. I then had a feeling of déjà vu. At this time, spring 2007, I had been sober for several years, but around 2000, I was still a practicing alcoholic. Now I remembered how a guy I knew in a bar had told me a story about Brillo boxes that had been made in Malmö around 1990 and sold as genuine Andy Warhol on the market. I contacted this man, who is a very respectable and credible person, even though I knew him from the bar scene. He confirmed that he had told me this story and repeated it exactly as I remembered it. I went back to Christian and we realized that we might be on to something here. I immediately felt it was big, although I never imagined it would become world news."[13]

"I myself had a background that allowed me to immediately relate to Andy Warhol, to Pontus Hultén and that whole world," continues Micke Ölander. "My parents had great interest in art. Even though I'm from Malmö, I grew up with Pontus Hultén and everything he and Moderna Museet stood for. When we got the tip, I could immediately go home to my parents and look up the catalog from 1968, which was worn and torn but could be read. We could go straight to the sources. I knew exactly what Hultén had done and had enormous admiration for him and his incredible life journey. That's why this story is so tragic from a human perspective, because in the end it was all about legal issues."

Journalists Christian Holmén and Micke Ölander, together with colleague Leo Lagercrantz, formed a group within Expressen's editorial team for investigative journalism, which worked on this story for six months. Ölander was sent to New York for research and interviews. It's noteworthy that a tabloid newspaper like Expressen devoted such generous time and other resources to a revelation in an industry as marginal to the general public as modern art.

"Of course, the huge interest had to do with Andy Warhol's enormous stardom," says Micke Ölander. "We were given the time and resources we needed and spent hundreds and hundreds of hours. We went through huge amounts of material flowing in from different sources and followed up on all tips and contacts. One thing led to another and, of course, all three of us made full use of our networks. It was classic journalistic craft and groundwork. We got hold of a guy who had bought a box cheaply from a carpenter, knowing full well what it was, and then sold it on for a lot of money at an international auction. Then it was just a matter of following the trail. We found that everything that had been sold by Warhol had ended up in his catalogue raisonné. We obtained a copy of this catalogue raisonné and started looking at the boxes there."[14]

When the reporters scrutinized the texts in the catalogue raisonné, they were struck by the curiosity that, although the boxes were claimed to have been made at the same time, for the Andy Warhol exhibition at Moderna Museet in 1968, they were made of different materials, in varying sizes and different colors. "It became clear that the information was entered completely uncritically," says Micke Ölander.[15]

When the Expressen reporters requested material from Moderna Museet, they could see from shipping invoices that the museum had bought a consignment of cardboard boxes in New York that had subsequently been shipped to other cities when the Andy Warhol exhibition traveled. Nowhere was there information about any wooden boxes.

"It was incomprehensible when we put the different data side by side," says Ölander. "The more we learned, the clearer it became that something was not right. No matter how hard we tried, we couldn't make sense of it, so we decided to publish. We had to check and double-check everything with lawyers beforehand. There is a clause in the Freedom of the Press Act called 'defamation of the deceased' which meant we had to be even more careful. It was brave by the managing editors to dare."[16]

In the first of Expressen's series of articles on the scandal, Malmö Konsthall's chief technician at the time, Arne Göransson, explains that the boxes were made in the workshop in 1990, with a "high finish" as the work order read, based on a model in corrugated cardboard that had been provided by Hultén.[17] The design was screen-printed at Screentrycksbolaget, a printer with a good reputation for this printing technique in Malmö's art circles, with one cliché for the red typography and one for the blue, certainly designed by John Melin.

When I talk to the eighty-eight-year-old Per-Olov Börjeson in the fall of 2018, he informs me that he himself had worked on what would become a book about the fake Brillo boxes, but that he sold the story to Expressen after he had received a financial offer that was too good to refuse.[18] "I don't know anything about that," says Micke Ölander when I ask him about this purchase price, without denying that such a price was paid when I confront him with Börjeson's statement.[19]

According to the information that Pontus Hultén had given to the carpentry at Malmö Konsthall, the boxes were to be shown in the exhibition *Le Territoire de l'Art* in Leningrad later in the spring of 1990. Why Hultén chose to have the boxes made in Sweden when he was working in Paris and Venice at the time is an unanswered question. He probably found the solution more flexible and the transportation easier than if the boxes had been made in Paris or Italy. Conspiracy theories have been voiced that Hultén already had ulterior motives when he had the boxes manufactured. In his archives, I've read correspondence about the operation from Nathalie Meneau in Paris and Clarenza Catullo in Venice.[20] Hultén's contact in Malmö was John Melin, the brilliant graphic designer behind the epoch-making Andy Warhol catalog and so much else of Moderna Museet's classic graphic communication from the museum's heyday. Melin died in 1992 but his name reappeared in the case in 2007 as the seller of the Brillo box that was withdrawn by Stockholms Auktionsverk turned out to be one of his sons. The father had been among those who by Hultén had rewarded with at least one box as payment for their efforts. It's unlikely that these installments would have been subject to more rigorous accounting or tax reporting.

An inconvenient circumstance for Pontus Hultén, giving grounds for suspicion, is that these newly manufactured Malmö boxes in the simple catalog for the exhibition *Le Territoire de l'Art* in Leningrad, where a small number of the boxes were displayed in a stack in the museum's stairwell, were illustrated with an image from the installation at the exhibition in Stockholm in 1968, for the inaugurator clearly boxes in cardboard, not wood. The choice of this illustration constitutes a "slip with the truth" of the kind that even Pontus Hultén's most staunch defenders admit he habitually allowed himself. The kindest possible explanation for Pontus Hultén is that he and his colleagues wanted to impress the Russian art public by attributing a false art-historical provenance to the installation with the boxes at the Russian Museum in Leningrad. There was no indication that the boxes on display were newly made.

According to Per-Olov Börjeson's information, published in Expressen, Pontus Hultén had ordered one hundred and five or one hundred and eight — the exact number varies — boxes for the exhibition in Leningrad, plus an extra edition for his own use. The carpenters probably also made some extra boxes on their own. In total, about one hundred and thirty Brillo boxes are said to have been manufactured at the Malmö Konsthall workshop, several of which ended up in the carpenters' possession as part payment. (As a parenthesis, it says a lot about the generous budget that Hultén must have had at his disposal from the school in Paris that they could afford to have these boxes made at all — something that had been unthinkable at Moderna Museet in Stockholm in 1968.) Brillo boxes had been seen in various places and homes in Malmö's art circles and had also been sold for small sums between friends and business partners since the early nineties.

In his book about the Brillo scandal, Thomas Anderberg interviews the art and design dealer Kenneth Witt, one of Expressen's sources, who had been interested in Andy Warhol since his youth. Witt, who at the time ran a large art and curio shop in Malmö, says that he was offered to buy a copy by the art gallery's carpenter, which he had done for the asking price of two thousand five hundred SEK. Witt reveals that a few years later, after "nagging," he sold the box on to a friend and fellow dealer for the same price, a "buddy price" — whereupon the friend thanked him for his generosity by selling the Brillo box at Sotheby's in London for four hundred thousand SEK, curiously without Witt having reacted particularly to this.[21]

From the mid-nineties, when Andy Warhol's popularity and market value as an artist only continued to soar — after actually having slumped seriously in the seventies and eighties, until Warhol's surprising death in 1987 — more and more Brillo boxes with provenance from the 1968 Stockholm exhibition surfaced on the international art market. All were sold at skyrocketing prices. Shortly before Expressen's revelation in the spring of 2007, a Brillo box, according to the catalog information shown in the 1968 Stockholm exhibition, had been sold by Sotheby's in London for SEK 1.3 million.

A background to the ensuing events was that not a single Brillo box had appeared on the open international art market from the 1968 exhibition in Stockholm in the more than twenty years that had elapsed until the early 1990s. From 1994, the market was suddenly flooded with boxes stamped with certificates of authenticity from AWAAB, assuring that they had been exhibited in the Moderna Museet exhibition in 1968.

The explanation to this sudden injection of "Andy Warhol's" Brillo boxes into the global art market was to be found in a well-publicized visit by the Belgian art dealer Ronny Van de Velde to Pontus Hultén at La Motte sometime in the autumn of 1994 — an event reported in the Expressen articles, for which Van de Velde had been interviewed.

Ronny Van de Velde is a renowned international art dealer, active since the seventies, specializing in early avant-garde Modernism and artists such as Duchamp, Picabia, Man Ray and Magritte, with whom he has staged museum-like exhibitions. That his and Pontus Hultén's paths had crossed over the years was a given. In various articles, Van de Velde portrays Hultén as an idol, a mentor, "a monument" and "almost a god" in the art world.

Ronny Van de Velde was also interviewed in a documentary broadcast on Swedish Radio on April 15, 2012,[22] two years after the publication of Thomas Anderberg's book. In the radio interview, he says that it was Alexina "Teeny" Duchamp who had urged him to visit her good friend Pontus Hultén at La Motte. The art dealer recounts that he was visiting Teeny (as I assume in her and Duchamp's home in Fontainebleau) to see "some Duchamp books" and that Teeny had told him that he should take the opportunity to visit Hultén while he was in the area, as he probably also had interesting books to show. Van de Velde says in the interview that he didn't think Pontus Hultén would have time as he was "so important" but that as soon as Teeny Duchamp called he had agreed to receive him at La Motte, where Van de Velde marveled over Hultén's art collection.[23]

Van de Velde recalls in the radio interview how he was smoking a cigarette on the sofa in the salon and noticed that the two coffee tables were Brillo boxes, worn ones with cigar burns. He pointed out to Hultén that the boxes were frayed and damaged, but Hultén just laughed and said it didn't matter as he had many more. He asked Van de Velde if he wanted to see them, which of course the art dealer did. Van de Velde says that Hultén took him down to a basement storage room where a very large number of boxes in mint condition, "maybe a hundred," were stacked.

According to the art dealer, Pontus Hultén replied to his question without hesitation that the boxes were made "with Andy Warhol's consent" for the exhibition in Stockholm in 1968, where they had also been shown. Van de Velde goes on to say that he asked Hultén if he would consider selling some boxes and that he gave his typical answer: "Why not?" Van de Velde reveals that Hultén first asked for seven thousand five hundred dollars, which the dealer negotiated down to six thousand dollars each for the boxes. Legend also has it that Hultén told Van de Velde that he "needed money to repair the roof of the castle." A deal was struck whereby Van de Velde bought twenty boxes which he had shipped to Antwerp.

What is serious is that in connection with this purchase, Van de Velde asked Pontus Hultén for a certificate of authenticity, which he, again "without hesitation,"[24] immediately issued, according to Van de Velde, with the text: "These Brillo boxes were made in Stockholm in 1968, in accordance with Andy Warhol's instructions. These Brillo boxes were included in the exhibition *Andy Warhol* at the Moderna Museet, Stockholm, February–March 1968 ..."[25] The certificate, which was used to certify the authenticity of forty Brillo boxes, was signed by Pontus Hultén.[26]

Note that the wording used in this false certificate of authenticity is not one of the more general "in agreement with Andy Warhol" or "in consultation with Andy Warhol," which appear in other contexts, but "in accordance with Andy Warhol's instructions" — a more precise wording that suggests that Warhol would have supervised the production of these boxes in line with his usual working method where he often acted more as a creative director than as a traditional artist and let assistants and sometimes even external collaborators execute works after his guidelines. Neither Pontus Hultén nor anyone else has ever claimed that there were any instructions from Andy Warhol about any wooden boxes, beyond the oft-quoted general phrase "Why don't you make them over there?"

Ronny Van de Velde's customers were excited about the Brillo boxes that the dealer offered with this provenance — "the best one could possibly imagine," as Van de Velde states in several interviews. All twenty boxes were immediately sold out.

Some of the buyers, however, asked for further assurance of the boxes' authenticity, Van de Velde says — a sign that the market still viewed the suddenly appearing Brillo boxes with some skepticism. The art dealer therefore sent the boxes to AWAAB in New York. After just a few weeks, the boxes came back with a certificate of authenticity and the stamp "Approved."[27]

In several interviews, Ronny Van de Velde talks about Pontus Hultén's "godlike" position in the art world. Hultén and his partner Billy Klüver, who had produced the 1968 exhibition in Stockholm together with Hultén, Warhol and the Factory, had excellent contacts and enjoyed the highest respect and trust within the Warhol Foundation and throughout the New York art world. No one seems to have even thought of questioning the authenticity of Hultén's certificate. Ronny Van de Velde's clients clamored for more boxes and he bought another twenty copies from Hultén at the same price, which went the same way as before — authorization by AWAAB in New York and quick sale or vice versa. Van de Velde sold the boxes, according to his own account, for ten thousand dollars each and thus made a swift profit of one hundred and sixty thousand dollars on these transactions. It's easy to calculate that Hultén made two hundred and forty thousand dollars on the sale of the forty boxes. When Van de Velde contacted Pontus Hultén again a year or so later for a third order, he was declined. "He knew by then that they were sold for much higher prices at auctions," as Ronny Van de Velde says in the Swedish Radio interview.[28]

Now the story becomes truly intricate and the evidence of a carefully planned operation increasingly difficult to dismiss. The Expressen article quotes Pontus Hultén's text about the Warhol exhibition in the catalog of his collection, published by Moderna Museet in 2004, in connection with the exhibition at the museum.[29] In a paragraph about the Brillo boxes, six of which he had donated to the museum almost ten years earlier, Hultén writes that for the exhibition in Stockholm in 1968, one hundred wooden boxes had been made. "It was the same there," says Micke Ölander. "We learned that a biography of Hultén's collection had been published and went out to Skeppsholmen and bought the book. When we read the text, we were very surprised to read information that we had not seen anywhere else in all our vast material."[30]

Almost everything in this text in the catalog *Pontus Hultén's collection ...* were sensational new facts also for Hultén's colleagues from the Andy Warhol exhibition in 1968 and the time after. In the Expressen article, Olle Granath is interviewed about how he personally worked on folding and stacking boxes for the Warhol exhibition in 1968, where he was responsible for the production in Stockholm in his capacity as what would now be called assistant curator. Granath says in the interview that he knew with one hundred percent certainty that no wooden boxes had been included in the impressive mountain of Brillo boxes in the exhibition — that he, if anyone, who worked so hands-on with the installation, would have noticed if any had been among the cardboard boxes. Others who worked on the exhibition and the Brillo installation confirmed in Expressen that there were no wooden boxes in the mountain of cardboard ones, which were often blown down by the wind from the entrance doors and had to be re-stacked.[31]

According to Olle Granath,[32] he had later, in the late summer or early fall of 1968 as he remembers it, indeed seen a number of wooden Brillo boxes stacked in Pontus Hultén's office at Moderna Museet — ten, at most fifteen in number.[33] In several interviews, Granath repeats that he believed that Hultén had commissioned National Museum's carpenters to make these boxes "as souvenirs." Hultén is said to have distributed the boxes as gifts to people who had helped with the exhibition. Of course, he had kept some for himself. There is no indication that Hultén at the time, in 1968, attached any economic value to the boxes.

Olle Granath himself received three of these wooden boxes, which he kept in his apartment for a couple of decades before selling them in the early nineties in New York through a London dealer, unfortunately for him before the big jump in value. In a follow-up article, Olle Granath says that, as he remembers it, he received a total of a hundred thousand SEK for these boxes, which are still classified today as genuine works by Andy Warhol, even though this assessment has been strongly questioned.[34] In the Expressen article, Ulf Linde, too, confirms that he saw a small number of boxes in wood in Hultén's room after the Warhol exhibition in 1968. He makes the same estimate as Granath about the number — ten, at most fifteen.[35]

Unlike the boxes that had now been revealed as manufactured much later, in 1990 in Malmö, the Brillo boxes that Olle Granath and others had received and sold were nevertheless to be regarded as genuine goods. They were said to have been made during the exhibition year 1968 in Stockholm, regardless of whether they had been shown in the exhibition or not, which Granath and others insist they had not. These boxes could possibly be claimed to be covered by the "consent" that Warhol is said to have given to have the boxes made in Stockholm. No one other than Pontus Hultén witnessed or heard this "authorization" of the production of the copies.

Whatever the circumstances — we will never know the definitive truth — there was a critical difference between the wooden boxes produced in Stockholm in 1968 and those manufactured in Malmö. By 1990, Andy Warhol had been dead for three years and evidently could not have given permission for anything. To claim that these "late boxes," as they were called even before the revelation by some on the market, were made with Warhol's permission can never be anything but counterfeit or, in an even harsher term, art forgery. "I remember that an eye-opener and a pivotal point in our investigations was when I sat with a lawyer in Manhattan who was an expert in such matters and he said that it's perfectly okay, you can have an oral consent to produce something, but the moment the artist dies, that consent ceases," says Micke Ölander. "Then the rights go to the estate, which was completely unaware that these boxes had been produced."[36]

Later investigations by Moderna Museet, AWAAB and the Warhol Foundation established a number of flagrant technical differences in the execution between the boxes made in Stockholm in 1968 and those produced in Malmö in 1990. The Expressen article interviews a carpenter who worked in the National Museum's workshop at the time of the Warhol exhibition in 1968, who says he doesn't remember any Brillo boxes being made. He would definitely have done so if there had been as many as a hundred copies, which is what Pontus Hultén had claimed in the book about his collection.[37]

Olle Granath, Björn Springfeldt, Ulf Linde and Karin Bergqvist Lindegren unanimously deny in Expressen that they had ever seen or heard of any wooden Brillo boxes[38] that were supposedly stored in the warehouse at Moderna Museet, also according to Hultén.[39]

Pontus Hultén's intricate catalog text about the Brillo boxes contains further sensational details: "The Brillo cartons were stacked quite high in front of the entrance. There were about 100 Brillo cartons made in Sweden according to Andy's instructions ('Why don't you make them there?'). Since a hundred didn't seem enough in the rather large room, a few Brillo cartons in cardboard were added to the back of the top of the carton pile. Those cartons came from The Factory. I still have one of those cardboard cartons."[40]

This small piece of text, which at first sight doesn't seem exceptional, has been scrutinized and interpreted by journalists, art historians, experts and other interested parties since the scandal broke in 2007. A number of questions, which will never be definitively answered, have to be asked and several phrases need to be read closely.

Why does Pontus Hultén start by writing "cartons" and not "boxes"? Several art-historical researchers have taken issue with this formulation. Certainly, the boxes, or "sculptures" as they are now classified, were made on the model of cartons. That may explain this wording, which nevertheless seems confusing in the context. In the English version of the catalog for Pontus Hultén's collection, *Pontus Hultén's collection ...*, "brillokartonger" is translated as "Brillo boxes." There the wording becomes clear. No one who reads the text in English can doubt that the museum in Sweden had hundreds of wooden boxes made according to Andy Warhol's instructions. One interpretation favorable to Pontus Hultén, advocated by some, is that this difference between the two language versions can be explained by a sloppy translation and/or a deficient proofreading by the tired and aged Hultén. A less apologetic reader must suspect that it is instead a linguistic smokescreen laid out to confuse the Swedish audience and those readers who had memories of the mountain of cardboard boxes from the exhibition, who hardly read the English version of the book.

It must be emphasized again that Hultén selects the phrase that the boxes were made "according to Andy's instructions." This choice of words suggests a more active role on Warhol's part than if Hultén had instead written "with Andy's approval," "with Andy's permission" or "in consultation with Andy." By claiming that the "boxes" were made "according to Andy's instructions," Pontus Hultén transforms his Brillo boxes from exhibition props into original works of art by Warhol, following the precedents set by the Warhol Foundation and AWAAB by "authenticating" other works in Warhol's legacy that had been made "off-site," as it's called, on his instructions and otherwise always with his written permission. No one else involved in the exhibition remembers or has heard of any active role on Andy Warhol's part in the decision to order five hundred cardboard Brillo boxes from the Brillo factory in Brooklyn, let alone in the production of any wooden boxes in Stockholm or elsewhere in Sweden.

This doesn't mean that we can rule out the possibility that a conversation between Warhol and Hultén actually took place. Nor will we ever know whether this formulation indicating a more active involvement on Warhol's part was deliberately chosen by Pontus Hultén or more randomly written down. My knowledge of Hultén's personality and other information makes me inclined to believe in the more calculated alternative explanation. The sentence that follows, then: "Since a hundred didn't seem enough in the rather large room, they added a few Brillo boxes in cardboard to the back of the top of the carton pile." This is a description that diametrically contradicts all accounts from Olle Granath and other participants and eyewitnesses, including Pontus Hultén's most ardent defender Anna-Lena Wibom, of the mountain of five hundred cardboard boxes that were folded up, stacked, blown down and restacked. Wibom has long since claimed in various interviews that wooden boxes were used to prop up the cardboard boxes but never the reverse — that the cardboard boxes would have been complementary in a wooden pile.

This is followed by an even more inexplicable phrase: "Those boxes came from The Factory," and the conclusion "I still have one of those paper cartons."

Certainly, the five hundred cardboard boxes that were demonstrably transported from New York, well documented by testimony and by printing and transportation invoices in the museum's archives, came from a factory — from the Brillo factory, or more precisely from the Brooklyn printing plant where the boxes for the steel wool soap pads were manufactured. They had nothing to do with Andy Warhol's "the Factory" (usually spelled with a minor t in the word the). So why on earth did Pontus Hultén choose to write "The Factory" in English, with capitalized initial letters, a spelling that's repeated in the English version? Is it typos and the tired, aged, slightly confused and absent-minded proofreader who is haunting the book, or is it an attempt to mask deliberate forgery after the fact?

Most striking in this for Pontus Hultén so compromising catalog text is still when he, after having discussed other elements of the exhibition in 1968, returns to the Brillo boxes in the closing paragraph where he first writes: "Andy was very pleased with the exhibition and gave the museum the copy of 'Chelsea Girls,' a large flower and 'Electric Chair.'"[41] He concludes with four sentences that deviate from the rest of the text in their details: "Andy gave the Brillo cartons to me. They were kept for many years at the museum. I got them back when I moved to Los Angeles. I don't think the museum has any Brillo cartons in its possession today."[42]

A hundred wooden crates would have taken up almost fifty cubic meters in Moderna Museet's warehouse. That something like this could have remained unnoticed for thirteen years, until Hultén's move to Los Angeles, is out of the question and is not claimed by anyone except Pontus Hultén. Nor have I heard a word from anyone in Los Angeles about any stored Brillo boxes.

Several people, though, including Bo Nilsson, who was appointed curator at Moderna Museet in 1988, recall a small batch of folded cardboard Brillo boxes that were stacked in the museum's storeroom for decades after the Warhol exhibition.[43] As a further complication, these cardboard boxes disappeared without trace at a later date. They were probably thrown away or lost in connection with the move to the new museum building in the nineties.

It's certainly a small masterpiece of ambiguity and confusing information, this short catalog text. It all becomes even more complicated and, for Pontus Hultén, undeniably burdensome.

It turned out later, after the Expressen articles and the publication of Thomas Anderberg's book in autumn 2010, in the final report issued on the Brillo scandal by AWAAB later that fall, that the section on the Brillo boxes was not in fact written by Hultén in 2004, when the book on his collection was published, but ten years earlier, in December 1994. The Danish art collector Peter Hvidberg, who has spent many years researching "the so-called scandal" as he calls it, with the express intention of clearing Pontus Hultén of responsibility, has clearly proved this after archival research.[44]

The text about the Brillo boxes in the English-language catalog, both the first and the final paragraph, is found word for word in a letter dated December 29, 1994 from La Motte, written by Hultén to the Warhol Estate in New York.[45]

After the first shipment of boxes had been sent to New York for certification by Ronny Van de Velde, someone at the Warhol Foundation raised the matter with Kasper König. He had said that the Brillos shown in Stockholm in 1968 had all been cardboard boxes, purchased from the printer in Brooklyn — an operation for which König had been personally responsible. This information had obviously worried the representatives of the Warhol estate, who were just about to certify the first batch of boxes from Pontus Hultén's basement storage. In a letter from the Warhol Foundation to Ronny Van de Velde, the Foundation asks the art dealer whether cardboard boxes had also been shown in the Stockholm exhibition[46] and suggests him to check with Hultén. The 1994 letter to the Warhol Estate was Hultén's answer to this question. The Committee was evidently satisfied with this written explanation. The boxes were certified again and again over the next twelve years without further questions being asked, ninety-four in all.

Pontus Hultén's choice to republish this 1994 letter to the Warhol Estate in the catalog of his collection ten years later, explaining why cardboard boxes had "also" been shown at the Stockholm exhibition, complicates his case and reinforces the impression that the Brillo boxes operation was calculatedly planned.

Firstly, the original text of the letter and the decision to publish it ten years later reveal the long-term nature of Hultén's operations. Second, the dating shatters arguments in Pontus Hultén's defense — the story of the poor, weak, perhaps slightly confused old man at the castle who didn't quite understand what was happening when shrewd art dealers wanted to buy his boxes, who didn't care about the money[47] but wanted to "play a trick on the art market"[48] and so on, and who when the book about his collection was published perhaps mixed up memories. In 1994, when this text was written, Pontus Hultén was seventy years old and undoubtedly in his right mind, active in his career as director of the Bundeskunsthalle in Bonn and not yet suffering from any stroke. It's impossible for me to find any other explanation for why Hultén chose to tell this history than a calculated intention to mislead Andy Warhol's estate and the art market and to cover up the traces of his shady business dealings.

To add to the confusion, the catalog text in the book *Pontus Hultén's collection* ... is illustrated with two pictures of Brillo boxes. The upper of these is a cardboard box with the caption:

> ANDY WARHOL
> *Brillo Box* (*Soap Pad*). Original box
> Brillo box (soap pad). Original box
> ca 1964
> cardboard
> h: 44. l: 44, d: 36[49]

Why the year of origin of this cardboard box, probably one of those that was indeed exhibited in Stockholm and on the subsequent tour, is not given as 1968, when the boxes were purchased for Moderna Museet from the Brillo factory, but as 1964, the year of Warhol's breakthrough exhibition at the Stable Gallery in New York, is another of all the unanswered questions that Pontus Hultén took to his grave. The very act of naming Andy Warhol as the artist of this carton is highly questionable and misleading. The other box depicted is a so-called Malmö box from 1990. Here, the year of origin is not given as 1964 but as 1968. The caption reads:

> ANDY WARHOL
> *Brillo Box*
> Brillo box, 1968
> silkscreen on wood
> h: 44, l: 44, d: 36[50]

I ask Olle Granath if, in 2004, when the book on Hultén's collection was published, he paid attention to the sensational new information presented by his old boss in this text. Granath's answer is not kind to Pontus Hultén: "Of course I did! I read the text when the book came out and couldn't believe my eyes. I can say that hardly a word in that text is true. I thought it was very strange, of course, and raised the matter with Lars Nittve as well. Then I wrote it off as a manifestation of Pontus' usual mythomania. At the time I couldn't have dreamed of what consequences this would have. I knew that Pontus was an unreliable brute, but I never imagined in my wildest fantasies that he would make millions on this, I must say."[51]

It appears that Pontus Hultén became nervous after being asked by Ronny Van de Velde about the cardboard boxes on behalf of the Warhol Estate. The letter to the estate from December 1994 was not the only "diversionary maneuver" he conducted after this request. The 2007 Expressen articles also revealed that Olle Granath, already in 1995, then as director of the National Art Museums, under which organization Moderna Museet at that time was included, had again been confronted with copies of the Malmö-made boxes that he had seen for the first time at the exhibition in Leningrad in 1990.[52]

In the spring of that year, 1995, a few months after the request from AWAAB in New York, Pontus Hultén donated six so-called Malmö boxes from 1990, as investigations later showed, to Moderna Museet.

According to Olle Granath, he explicitly requested that these be immediately cataloged as shown in the 1968 exhibition. Granath says that he firmly opposed the museum agreeing to this cataloging after a request from the intendant Nina Öhman. "I told NÖ that it was impossible, well aware of the price tag attached to this NO when it came to my relationship with Pontus," as Granath writes in an email to me.[53] Nina Öhman tells Thomas Anderberg that she does not remember but that it may have been so.[54] Despite Granath's warnings, the six boxes were received and cataloged as Pontus Hultén had requested with the false information in the museum's collection. Embarrassing for the museum, the boxes with these provenance details were often displayed as part of the museum's permanent collection over the next twelve years until the revelation. The Expressen article states that it was Björn Springfeldt who, as the outgoing director of the museum, made sure to approve the donation of the Malmö boxes with this cataloging. Springfeldt admits to Anderberg that this was a mistake and also that Pontus Hultén's authority would have been difficult to oppose. "He didn't like to be contradicted," as Springfeldt says.[55]

"I immediately thought there was something fishy about that donation and tried to stop it simply because the boxes were so badly made," says Olle Granath in one of our conversations. "I certainly didn't realize at the time that it was part of his manipulations in this affair."[56]

In a conversation with Björn Springfeldt in the fall of 2018, he said: "For me, there was nothing strange about receiving those boxes in the collection. I knew they were replicas, but I was used to Pontus and the museum always working with replicas. We had made replicas of Duchamp's large glass and of Tatlin's tower, among other things. Art in the sixties was about the ideas, not the economic value of the works."[57]

I ask Björn Springfeldt whether, by accepting these Brillo boxes and cataloging them according to Hultén's instructions with the enigmatic year of origin 1967, i.e. strangely not the year of the exhibition 1968, he had not contributed to giving the boxes a false provenance? Springfeldt, who like several others says he is tired of talking about these Brillo boxes, first falls silent for a while and then says, apparently oblivious to the fact that he was already asked about this by Expressen: "I never even thought about it, but now that you say it, it's obvious that it may have been so ..."[58]

Olle Granath reveals that Pontus Hultén became furious at his resistance to accepting and cataloging the six Malmö boxes as instructed and that this incident was one of the reasons why Hultén broke off their acquaintance.

In a 2012 Swedish Radio documentary, Anna-Lena Wibom, Pontus Hultén's main defender in the Brillo affair, tells a different version of the controversial events. According to Wibom, Hultén had a small number of wooden boxes made for the Warhol exhibition, intended as a kind of "rebar" in the installation of corrugated cardboard boxes in the museum's entrance hall. In Wibom's account, the wooden boxes would prevent the mountain of cardboard boxes from collapsing when the winter winds swept in through the entrance gate.

Wibom implies that these "original boxes" were then mixed up with the later Malmö boxes in Hulten's basement storage at La Motte. When Ronny Van de Velde wanted to buy boxes, Hultén had, at Van de Velde's request, issued a certificate of authenticity for the whole bunch, which, as Wibom admits in the interview, "perhaps he shouldn't have done."[59]

In the radio interview, Anna-Lena Wibom returns to how alien Pontus Hultén was to the idea that these boxes could have any economic value, that he regarded them as exhibition props and that if anyone was stupid enough to want to pay for them, they could do so. The illusion Wibom conveys is that of the eccentric elderly art player with a fox behind each ear who allows the process to proceed through the agency of others while he himself watches the spectacle with amusement, pleased to be able to play yet another prank on the wretched art trade, more or less unaware of the sums which as a consequence flowed into some account somewhere. Wibom laughs again and again in the interview but also emphasizes with seriousness in her voice that it is "extremely difficult for us relatives" to see Pontus Hultén subjected to these misconceptions after his death, something she has returned to in various contexts.[60]

The Expressen news broke across the art world after the tabloid's series of articles was published in late May/early June 2007. The story was cabled out by the global news agencies, resulting in a multitude of articles around the world, not only in Europe and the United States but on all continents. "At that time, we didn't translate our main news into English like we do today," says Expressen editor Christian Holmén, "but I remember how fast it happened. Already the day after our first article, they knew exactly its content in New York."[61]

Back home in Sweden, the then director of Moderna Museet, Lars Nittve, immediately told Expressen and other media that the museum took a serious view of the information presented by Expressen and that it had immediately decided to set up its own investigation into the matter.[62] Even more prompt was the decision to remove from the museum's collection exhibition the six Brillo boxes that had been donated by Pontus Hultén in 1995 and which Expressen had now shown "with the utmost probability" were made in Malmö in 1990, not in Stockholm in 1967 as the signs in the exhibition and the museum's computer system stipulated.

Christian Holmén and Micke Ölander at Expressen both underscore that Moderna Museet, and in particular its director Lars Nittve, were open, helpful and accessible in the work with the Brillo revelation, before and after the first publication. "It was also a great help to us and essential that we were able to obtain information from the museum's archives, such as printing and transport invoices and other documents, where we could follow in black and white what had actually happened," says Christian Holmén.[63]

In New York, on the other hand, the other scene of the drama, there was less openness. Expressen and other newspapers and media around the world have consistently reported on the "deafening" silence from the Warhol Foundation and other organizations linked to Warhol's estate, from representatives of the international art trade in general and, in particular, from everyone who was in any way involved or affected by the scandal. This included Christie's in London, where a box had been sold for SEK 1.3 million shortly before the Stockholm auctioneers withdrew their equivalent and the whole story was revealed.

The Warhol Foundation in particular, under which the other Warhol institutions and organizations operated, was under pressure from the moment the Express story broke in New York and elsewhere in the art world. In particular, the art historian Neil Printz, "one of the most influential members"[64] of the AWAAB authentication board and the person who had signed the certificates of authenticity for the box withdrawn from Stockholms Auktionsverk, the one sold at Christie's and, as it later turned out, all the other Malmö boxes, was in the firing line. Expressen reported that they had been promised a comment from Printz, but this was not forthcoming.[65]

The pressure on Neil Printz and the other members of AWAAB, and on the entire Warhol Foundation, was further increased as Micke Ölander had succeeded in seeking out Paul Morrissey, Andy Warhol's filmmaker and manager, who had been in Stockholm in the winter of 1968. On the same day that AWAAB held a board meeting in connection with the unfolding scandal, June 14, 2007, Expressen published an interview with Morrissey. In the text, he claims not to remember that "there was talk of making wooden Brillo boxes." Morrissey becomes "very surprised" when Ölander tells him that after the exhibition "there were 10–15 wooden boxes in the museum." "What are you saying?" Paul Morrissey asks in the text. "There was never any discussion of having any boxes made." Ölander writes that Morrissey is "almost shocked" when he learns that many years later, after Andy Warhol's death, a hundred wooden boxes were made in Malmö. "Yes, I can say with some certainty that Andy would not have given permission for that."[66]

As Micke Ölander writes, Paul Morrissey possessed unique knowledge of Warhol's work and of the 1968 exhibition in which he was involved and which he visited together with Warhol and Viva. If only he had been asked, Morrissey could have provided information on what really happened. A more obvious and accessible person for the Warhol Foundation to check the matter with is unimaginable. In the Expressen interview, however, Paul Morrissey says: "The Warhol Commission has never asked me."[67]

Already at this stage, the facts that have given the Brillo affair its global impact and status as one of the most notorious scandals in modern art history became clear. The statements of Morrissey and others involved (Olle Granath, Kasper König and others) confirmed what was already obvious from the certificates of authenticity issued and the cataloging of the Malmö boxes in Andy Warhol's catalogue raisonné. The "Sphinx-like" AWAAB committee, which arbitrarily, at exorbitant fees and without justifying its decisions, decided whether collectors' works were worth multimillions or nothing — these judges had authenticated and approved nearly one hundred fake works of art without any further factual checks. The same was true of the editorial committee of Warhol's catalogue raisonné, which had the same sovereign power to turn gold into ashes and vice versa.

The revelation disclosed how casually the Warhol Foundation and its hierarchy of subordinate committees in actuality operated in examining objects and elevating glaring fakes to the status of insanely expensive art. This realization, which quickly spread across the art world, shook confidence in the foundation and, by extension, in the entire contemporary art market stock exchange. Enormous economic values were suddenly at stake.

In Andy Warhol's catalogue raisonné, published in 2004 by The Andy Warhol Foundation, ninety-four Brillo boxes attributed to Pontus Hultén were listed. For all these "sculptures," the year of production was curiously not given as 1968 but as 1967, the same year that Hultén had listed in his donation to Moderna Museet in 1995. The material in the boxes was incorrectly cataloged as masonite.

The catalog raisonné listed a total of around three hundred Brillo boxes by Andy Warhol. Ninety-three of these were original boxes from the 1964 exhibition at the Stable Gallery in New York, visually distinct from the other boxes as they were screen-printed by Andy Warhol and his collaborators on a yellow-tinted background. In our time, these boxes would be worth at least three million dollars each or more if they came onto the market. There were also over one hundred boxes made for the Warhol retrospective in Pasadena in 1970, with Warhol's written permission and on the condition that they never be sold or leave the museum. A surplus of about fifteen boxes from this exhibition has been circulating on the market, worth about a million dollars each. Between five and ten boxes — the figures are somewhat vague — in this catalogue raisonné from 2004, characterized as "of the Stockholm type," were later found to have been produced in connection with the 1968 Stockholm exhibition, including Olle Granath's three boxes. The other almost ninety boxes were thus concluded to be what were renamed "Malmö boxes."

It seemed incomprehensible that such a large number of Brillo boxes could have flooded the international art market since 1994, where no Brillo boxes had been sold in the preceding decades, without the Warhol Foundation reacting. The total value of the ninety-four boxes that turned out to have Pontus Hultén as their provenance was estimated at the time, in 2007, at around one hundred million Swedish crowns, as reported by Expressen[68] (converted to today's monetary value, around one hundred and twenty-five million). The authorization from AWAAB and the cataloging in Andy Warhol's catalogue raisonné were the direct preconditions for these "works" to be sold on the market. "I remember that we saw it as another sign that something was not right that the boxes we examined were sold at high prices, but still not at the level of other comparable works by Warhol," says Micke Ölander. "We spoke to experts who felt that this difference in value reflected market skepticism about the authenticity of these boxes."[69]

Through the revelations of Expressen, it became clear that the Warhol Foundation and its subordinate bodies had not only accepted but quickly and smoothly certified these nearly one hundred boxes of forged provenance, thus securing easy profits for dealers and collectors the world over. An artwork that had been accepted in print in the mighty, now five-part, three thousand four hundred page catalogue raisonné, published in its first edition in 2004 after eleven years of production, had been certified with the final stamp of authenticity. In the Warhol industry, this Andy Warhol catalogue raisonné was and continues to be far more than an art book. For collectors with objects represented on its pages, the mammoth catalog is akin to a stock certificate.

When it was now revealed that the editors of this catalog, like the members of the AWAAB authorization committee, had been so easily fooled by the Brillo boxes that had turned out to be blatant forgeries, and had expressed themselves imprecisely in their catalog texts, the credibility of the entire Warhol Foundation and its catalogue raisonné was suddenly called into question. How many other collectors out there had fake works represented in this catalog? Could their paintings worth multimillion dollars actually be worthless?

In order to realize the extent of the doubts raised by the Brillo revelation, we must be aware that Andy Warhol is certainly the world's most forged artist of all time, and also the most easily falsified and difficult to control. A blurring of the boundaries between the freely creative and the commercial, between the unique and the mass-produced, as well as repetition of the same motifs, underpinned Warhol's entire oeuvre — an approach that he had borrowed from Duchamp but developed and enhanced in a new era with his own ingenious insights into the dynamics of modern mass communication.

Andy Warhol's work seems immune to the effects of the brutal overexposure to which he has been constantly subjected, with the copious amounts of "Warhol works" of various dignities flooding the market. After rising steadily since the artist's death, prices escalated further after MoMA's 1995 retrospective, from which the museum purchased twenty-three Campbell's Soup paintings for its collection, thus silencing any doubts about the proletarian Pittsburgh son's status in the canon of modern art history.

Warhol himself proclaimed that he despised the myth of the free, uniquely creating artist. He worked with an explicit ambition to distance his art from his self. In his studio appropriately called the Factory, he produced large series of works using all available means of expression — painting, sculpture, screen printing (Warhol's favorite technique), various other kinds of prints, photography, film, music, performance, magazines, books and other publications. The degree of "authenticity" of Warhol's work is often hard or impossible to determine, a quality that has always been exploited to the full by dealers, especially after Warhol's death, when the artist himself could no longer arbitrate what was "real." Andy Warhol forgeries, particularly in the lower price segments, are a billion-dollar industry.[70] The authenticity of many of the highly valued Warhol works listed in the artist's catalogue raisonné can be legitimately questioned.

It was this extreme market situation, which no other artist has come close to, that made the authorization committee so powerful. To the relatively modest premises of the Warhol Foundation in lower Manhattan, collectors and dealers from all over the world had their works transported, paying expensive fees to have them assessed by this four-man committee, which only gave the message "Approved" or "Denied," stamped on the back of the artwork. Approval from AWAAB meant automatic cataloging in Warhol's catalogue raisonné. Collectors and dealers around the world slavishly followed the directives, fearing that their Warhols would lose the committee's blessing. In its statutes, with numerous clauses to protect the foundation from lawsuits, the AWAAB reserved the right to change previous decisions on authentications at any time and without motivation.

The reason that AWAAB was founded at the turn of 1995, i.e. at the same time as the first batch of Brillo boxes from Pontus Hultén's cellar at La Motte was launched onto the market, was controversies surrounding previous authentications after Andy Warhol's death. Among other affairs, Warhol Foundation founder and first chairman Frederick W. Hughes, Warhol's manager and business partner for more than twenty-five years and executor of the artist's will, was suspected of authenticating several fake, or unauthorized, Warhol works in the years following the artist's death. Fred Hughes was a strong and charismatic figure, well-known throughout the art world, famous for his flamboyant, dandyish elegance and drastic humor, whom Pontus Hultén knew well since the mid-sixties through their mutual friends and benefactors John and Dominique de Menil.

Hughes, who came from an upper-middle-class family in Houston, had the good fortune to encounter the de Menils while studying art history in the city. The de Menils took a liking to the young Hughes and came to trust his eye for art and its economic value. They took him on trips to New York, where they introduced Hughes to Leo Castelli and got him his first job at the famous Alexander Iolas Gallery in Paris. Hughes met Andy Warhol in 1967, an encounter he described in interviews: "I never doubted whether we would get along or not. He knew who I was, and he saw a pot of gold at the end of the rainbow, just as I did. I was called Le Dauphin [French for Crown Prince] because I was so well looked after by Baron de Menil and his beautiful wife Dominique. I bought art for them and was a factor at Castelli in my young years."[71]

Alexander Iolas was a pioneer as a gallerist and an important player in the post-war art world, with whom Pontus Hultén had much collaboration. He was born into a wealthy family in Alexandria, from where he moved to Athens, Berlin and Paris. Iolas was a successful ballet dancer and came to New York as a star of the Metropolitan. He was known as an extravagant, sharp-tongued dandy with unfailing taste. He opened galleries in Paris, New York, Geneva, Milan, Zürich, Madrid and Rome. Iolas dealt with Surrealists Max Ernst, Giorgio de Chirico and René Magritte, Neo-Realists such as Jean Tinguely and Niki de Saint Phalle, and Arte Povera artists. In 1952, he staged Andy Warhol's debut exhibition in New York.

After this first meeting, Hughes and Warhol soon became business partners. Hughes was effectively the managing director of the Factory and publisher of Warhol's magazine Interview. It is widely believed that Hughes played a major role in the whole Andy Warhol phenomenon and the wildly successful industry that the artist's legacy has become. After Warhol's unexpected death on February 22, 1987, Hughes was the executor of the artist's will and organized the landmark auction at Sotheby's in New York where thousands of collectors and Warhol fans queued in vain to get into the auction room where Warhol's legacy — not including his art — was sold for over twenty-five million dollars. Hughes founded the Warhol Foundation shortly after the artist's death and led the organization until 1992, when he was forced out as a result of the questionable authentications, among other controversies.

With the original leadership of Fred Hughes and the Warhol Foundation, Pontus Hultén enjoyed excellent connections — bonds that some believe are part of the background to the Brillo scandal.

To grasp even more of the commercial explosiveness of the Andy Warhol industry, it's essential to understand the staggering financial value of Warhol's artistic legacy, the rights to his works and the Andy Warhol brand.

This bequest includes more than four thousand paintings, over five thousand drawings, sixty-six thousand photographs, more than one hundred films, four thousand hours of video footage, and vast quantities of sketches, notes, Polaroids and other archival material. Warhol's heritage has risen in value faster than gold, stock, or almost any other valuable assets.

Andy Warhol's estate and the Warhol Foundation had a history of recurring financial disputes at the time of the Brillo revelations. Not long after Warhol's death in 1987, a conflict arose over the valuation of the estate. The then directors of the Warhol Foundation, represented by Fred Hughes, argued that the estate should be valued at two hundred and twenty million dollars (over five hundred million in today's money). The general view is that it was in the foundation's interest to undervalue the estate — for a variety of reasons, including to limit scholarship payments. Andy Warhol had dictated in his will that his entire estate should be used for "the promotion of the visual arts." So keen was the foundation to keep the value down that its lawyers publicly asserted that Andy Warhol's art was in danger of falling in value if large quantities of works entered the market.

Fred Hughes, who had been diagnosed with MS shortly after Warhol's death, was opposed by the equally flamboyant New York lawyer Edward W. Hayes. A third key player was Hughes' successor Archibald L. Gillies.

Edward W. Hayes, the star lawyer who became famous for his role in the dispute over the Warhol estate and as a defender of mafia bosses, is the model for Tommy Killian in Tom Wolfe's classic 1987 New York novel *The Bonfire of the Vanities*.

Gillies and the Warhol Foundation emerged victorious when, in a 1993 settlement, the New York Attorney General accepted a valuation of Warhol's estate of three hundred and thirty million dollars, a gross underestimate according to many. The sum was based on the auction house Christie's valuation of Warhol's remaining art treasure, which in addition to his own production also contained a collection of his generational artist friends such as Cy Twombly, Roy Lichtenstein, Jasper Johns, Claes Oldenburg and James Rosenquist, younger artists such as Jean-Michel Basquiat, Keith Haring, and others.

The strategy used by the Warhol Foundation in this bitter, protracted conflict, which it has continued to practice, was to grind the opposition down with unlimited investment in legal fees and to make it clear from the outset that it will never back down and is determined to force the other side to pay every cent of its own legal costs if it loses the conflict. The result of the Warhol Foundation's many legal disputes has been, in each case, settlement on the foundation's terms, as no other party has dared to pursue this "chicken race." Fred Hughes and Edward W. Hayes were both bought out for small amounts in this context. The Brillo scandal was the culmination of a series of conflicts and controversies that raged around the Warhol Foundation during the first two decades after the mega-artist's death, before the foundation and Warhol's estate, one must conclude, emerged victorious.

It's difficult in this day and age to put a value on the Andy Warhol estate, with the collection that remains in the foundation's possession, the funds that has been built up through the sale of art and the income from the rights to the Andy Warhol brand. The Warhol Foundation never discloses information, but it must be an imposing number of billion dollars.

The approval of the Brillo boxes that suddenly materialized on the market in 1994 was one of the first major cases that the authentication board AWAAB — formed as a result of the conflicts referred to above and others — had to deal with. When Expressen revealed that the committee, and thus the Warhol Foundation, had authenticated fake Brillo boxes worth over one hundred million Swedish crowns on apparently loose ends, it was news that sent shock waves over the global art market. The affair became even more embarrassing when it was revealed that the authentication had continued despite warnings from Pontus Hultén's two closest collaborators at the 1968 Warhol exhibition in Stockholm — Kasper König in a conversation with the Warhol Foundation in 1994, and Olle Granath in a letter to the Foundation in 1998.[72]

After vague promises made immediately after Expressen's revelation in late May to investigate the background to the supposedly fake Brillo boxes, the Warhol Foundation's representatives stalled until the end of November 2007 to comment publicly on the matter. As the suspected Brillo boxes had not yet been officially declared fake, or inauthentic, which is the mitigating definition generally used in publicity about the Brillo scandal, collectors, dealers and even several prestigious public institutions were in the meantime in a state of uncertainty. Many in the art world were critical of the Warhol Foundation, although few dared to voice such criticism publicly, for taking so long to act, even though they had known about Expressen's information since April, even before the first article was published.

In the long, exhaustive article in The Guardian in 2010, "a source close to" the Scottish National Gallery of Modern Art in Edinburgh, where Brillo boxes were shown to tens of thousands of visitors in an Andy Warhol retrospective in the summer of 2007, says: "After working closely with the foundation, getting images licensed, a catalog completed and the authenticity of everything we showed checked, it felt like we had been hung out to dry."[73]

Moderna Museet in Stockholm did not wait for the Warhol Foundation but acted on its own. In a press release in November 2007, Moderna Museet presented the results of its own investigation, which it had promised to carry out immediately after the revelations in Expressen, led by the museum's director Lars Nittve and chief technician Lars Byström. Instrumental to this investigation was that the museum had succeeded in obtaining two of the wooden boxes that were allegedly made in Stockholm in 1968.

These wooden boxes deserve the name "mystery boxes." Almost everything about these "sculptures" is unknown: when, where and above all why Pontus Hultén had them made, and who has owned them over the years. The boxes seem to have been passed within a small group of people around Moderna Museet in the years following the Warhol exhibition, much as the 1990 overprint had been exchanged in Malmö's art circles, and eventually found their way onto the global art market.

Not even Olle Granath, who himself received three boxes from Pontus Hultén as "gratitude" for his services during the 1968 exhibition, claims to have any idea of Hultén's motives for having the boxes made.[74] The mystery of these wooden "Stockholm boxes" from 1968, with a current market value of around one million dollars each, will never be fully explained.

When I discuss this with Christian Holmén, mentioning that Olle Granath, Björn Springfeldt and others involved at the time have ensured they were unaware of Hultén's motives for having these boxes manufactured, and of the boxes' subsequent fate, Holmén falls silent for a while and then says: "Yes, it's of course possible that this is the case. Our definite impression, though, was that there were several people who knew more than they wanted to reveal about how this had happened. With the exception of Anna-Lena Wibom, no one questioned our information. We took this as an indication that there were more people who knew, more or less, what it was all about."[75]

Moderna Museet's report identified a number of "obvious" differences between the 1990 Malmö boxes and the two "Stockholm boxes" from 1968 that had been examined. The older boxes were made to a considerably higher standard of craftsmanship. The results of the survey are summarized:

> *Box 1968 Stockholm:*
> *Painted with a brush using oil-based paint. The chipboard has been painted with primer. The surface is "soft and smooth." The edges have been beveled to forty-five degrees. The white color shade is close to NCS 0502-Y.*
> *Box 1990 Malmö:*
> *Painted with water-based acrylic paint. The chipboard has been painted with a roller. The surface is rough to the touch. The edges have not been beveled. The boards are 1 centimeter thick.*[76]

The two Stockholm boxes examined had been requisitioned from two unnamed collectors in Stockholm. In its report, Moderna Museet estimates the number of wooden boxes produced in Stockholm in 1968 to be "at most 15."[77] The report notes that one of the two "Stockholm boxes" examined has a signature, "A.W." In a letter to AWAAB, Moderna Museet suggests that the committee investigate further whether the box could be signed with initials by Andy Warhol. Moderna Museet concludes its analysis by explaining that it is changing the cataloging of the six boxes that had been donated to the museum by Pontus Hultén in 1995. From now on, these Malmö boxes will be classified as "copies or scenography."

It was embarrassing for the Warhol Foundation and its sub-committees that, according to Expressen, it had taken Moderna Museet's experts "only a few minutes" to determine which boxes were made in 1990 and 1968 respectively.[78] The differences were conspicuous. The deficiencies in the Warhol Foundation's control procedures became painfully clear. It appeared obvious that there could have been no careful examination of the boxes, let alone any comparison between the two different types of that had been authenticated as "Stockholm boxes." This even though significant differences were noted in their own catalogue raisonné, and despite explicit warnings. Had the Warhol Foundation simply settled for the "royal" provenance Pontus Hultén?

As Expressen and international media showed, it was evident that this scandal would have far-reaching consequences for the authentication of Andy Warhol's art — far beyond the values of more than one hundred million Swedish crowns that had already surely been lost to the owners of the Malmö boxes that had now almost certainly proved to be worthless.

Any lingering hopes that the whole affair might be a big misunderstanding were extinguished when, on January 7, 2008, more than six months after Expressen's revelation, AWAAB, and thus indirectly the Warhol Foundation, finally spoke out in a first "preliminary report." The committee's assessment confirmed that Pontus Hultén had sent a written statement to AWAAB in December 1994 in which he assured that around one hundred wooden boxes had been made for the 1968 exhibition in Stockholm.[79]

The AWAAB's preliminary report discloses another incriminating circumstance for Pontus Hultén and his defenders: that Hultén had also orally repeated the same information, in an interview with the editorial committee of Warhol's catalogue raisonné on March 3, 1998, more than three years after his first authenticity statement to the AWAAB. In this interview, Hultén had proclaimed that he had ordered these wooden boxes made for the 1968 exhibition not in Stockholm but in Malmö — a statement that doesn't appear anywhere else. I myself have not been able to refrain from speculating whether this may have been another deliberately laid smokescreen. "That may have been the case — or he simply mixed it all up," says Christian Holmén. "In our experience, it's usually difficult to keep track of all the details when you keep telling stories that are not consistent with the truth."[80]

In its report, AWAAB firmly assures that all the information unequivocally shows that Pontus Hultén's statements have been false, that only a few boxes had been produced in connection with the 1968 exhibition and that none of these, but five hundred cardboard boxes directly from the Brillo factory, had been shown in the exhibition. In Expressen, Olle Granath, who of course was one of those interviewed by AWAAB for this report, said: "This is a problem for the Andy Warhol Art Authentication Board, which previously approved Brillo boxes made in 1990 as genuine. It remains to be seen how they will resolve this issue."[81]

For several years thereafter, the Brillo scandal and its aftermath continued to attract regular attention in the international media. 2010 saw a new wave of publicity with the publication of *Den stora konstsvindeln* (*The Great Art Swindle*). Thomas Anderberg's book largely follows the factual basis that had already been presented by Expressen three years earlier, but in addition, the author speculates vividly on Pontus Hultén's motives for his actions.[82]

The most factually substantial information that Thomas Anderberg added to his book was his interview with the London art dealer Brian Balfour-Oatts, who in 2003 had bought twenty-two Brillo boxes from Pontus Hultén. Anderberg had taken the news from the previously quoted article in The Guardian in August 2010, in which Balfour-Oatts said he had been misled by Hultén. "If true, he was a *sneaky old bastard!*" as the art dealer expressed himself.[83]

We recall that Balfour-Oatt's Belgian colleague Ronny Van de Velde contacted Hultén a year or so after the deal with the second batch of Brillo boxes to buy even more, but that this time he was turned down.[84]

Almost a decade after the first deal, the value of the Brillo boxes had risen dramatically, as demand for Andy Warhol continued to snowball. For twenty-two Brillo boxes, Brian Balfour-Oatts paid six hundred and forty thousand pounds, about seven and a half million SEK, or forty-five thousand pounds per box — almost ten times the price Van de Velde claimed he paid in 1994: not a bad increase in value. It was the last major transaction that Pontus Hultén adminsitered with this lot of Brillo boxes in his basement storage at La Motte.

A simple head count shows that over the course of just under a decade, with the first two deals with Van de Velde and the final one with Balfour-Oatts, as well as some smaller private sales in between and perhaps even after, Hultén had earned well over ten million Swedish crowns from the sale of these boxes — a lot of money, certainly, but still a small sum in relation to the enormous global publicity and other attention that the Brillo scandal has aroused.

In the fall of 2018, Brian Balfour-Oatts, now even more successful with his art dealer business Archeus than before the scandal, finally agreed to an interview after years of persistent requests. He explained that the Brillo scandal and its aftermath had affected his business for about seven years, until the last few years: "That's how it works when you are affected by a scandal, even though I knew I had done nothing wrong. It affected me negatively for a very long time. In retrospect, I wish I had acted more forcefully, not so defensively. After all, I had nothing to hide."[85]

One friend who privately bought Brillo boxes from Pontus Hultén was Robert Shapazian, the Los Angeles gallerist and publisher. Lars Nittve says that shortly after the Brillo scandal was revealed, he met Shapazian in Los Angeles. In an email from 2022, Nittve writes: "He knew Pontus well — and wanted to talk about how it came about that Pontus sold him a bunch of Brillo boxes without telling the truth about the provenance ... a disappointed, very educated and friendly man."

In the fall of 2003, Balfour-Oatts had been researching the market for Brillo boxes by Andy Warhol, noting that they had risen sharply in price. The contact with Pontus Hultén was mediated by the Swedish art dealer Fabian Karlsson, a close friend of Balfour-Oatts, who received a commission on the deal for his introduction. Together, Karlsson and Balfour-Oatts visited La Motte in October 2003, the first of several visits for the dealer.

The following year, Balfour-Oatts was invited to Hultén's eightieth birthday dinner at the Centre Pompidou. He depicts with a metaphor how he looks back on the aged Hultén who met them in the Loire: "He was like an old spider who had been sitting there waiting for someone to get caught in his web."[86]

Brian Balfour-Oatts confides that he found Pontus Hultén tired and weak but in his right mind, capable of having an interesting and even entertaining conversation. "He was very fragile. I remember we had to sit and wait for over an hour because he was asleep and the secretary[87] said we couldn't disturb him. But then at lunch he came on, told stories and was very nice. It was of course interesting and impressive to meet him and see his collection with Rauschenberg and other things. I saw an early Ruscha that I later bought from him but unfortunately sold. I'm sure it's worth a lot of money today. Certainly, I was very well aware of what a huge personality he was in art. There is no one who comes close to that stature today."[88]

On his first visit, Brian Balfour-Oatts bought ten boxes. A few months later, he returned to La Motte and settled the deal for the remaining twelve. Pontus Hultén subsequently wrote a receipt on behalf of Brian Balfour-Oatts in January 2004, confirming the purchase of twenty-two boxes "made by Andy Warhol." In an earlier receipt for the first installment, Hultén had written that the boxes "were exhibited at the Moderna Museet in Stockholm, Sweden, in 1968."[89] Balfour-Oatts also sent the boxes to New York where they were immediately stamped "Approved" by AWAAB — to the art dealer's relief as he knew that the board "was known to deny authentication." Balfour-Oatts opted to sell some of the boxes at auction at Sotheby's, others to private clients — all in all a good deal with a profit of over one hundred and fifty thousand pounds, without much effort.

As a bonus in the deal with the twenty-two boxes, some of which were worn and damaged and therefore discounted by Hultén, Brian Balfour-Oatts received a cardboard box, a real Brillo box, which according to what Hultén told him had been given to him by Andy

Warhol at the Factory in New York, with instructions to have a screen made using this as a template to print on the wooden boxes in Stockholm. If the art dealer remembers correctly, this information adds another version of reality. According to Brian Balfour-Oatts, Hultén stated that the cardboard box was made not in 1968 but in 1964, the year of Warhol's breakthrough exhibition at the Stable Gallery — an "alternative" cataloging which, as we have seen, he used several times for later produced Brillo boxes.

One might wonder why Hultén chose to provide these details of information. Thomas Anderberg writes: "The only real thing he has left from La Motte is the Brillo box that Hultén threw in as something of a bonus. And even that has been given a false history. In the above-mentioned confirmation, Hultén states that the box belongs to 'the original set from 1964.' Which could be a lapse in judgment or a red herring, but also an ironic grimace from Hultén: a clue that Warhol would have been flexible in his choice of materials etc. already at the premiere of the Brillo boxes in The Stable Gallery."[90]

Thomas Anderberg's questions are indeed justified. In a benevolent interpretation, it's tempting to go for alternative explanations such as a lapse of thought, an ironic grimace or even a "clue," Personally, I have a hard time believing in such explanations. I find the red herring more likely, more smokescreens. It's possible that Christian Holmén's thesis that those who tell untruths often struggle to keep the different versions apart in the long run may also be valid. At the time of the deal with Balfour-Oatts, Hultén was decidedly aged and weakened, at times even confused according to testimonies.

Another new revelation in Thomas Anderberg's book was that of the already discussed donation of six Malmö-type Brillo boxes from Pontus Hultén to Moderna Museet, which were received and cataloged on bequest by the outgoing director Björn Springfeldt in 1995. After the publication of Thomas Anderberg's book, Springfeldt was asked by Expressen: "Did it ever occur to you that these could be the same boxes that were made at Malmö Konsthall?" — i.e. the boxes that Springfeldt had helped Pontus Hultén manufacture at Malmö Konsthall in 1990. Springfeldt replied: "It may sound incomprehensible but I didn't think about it. I never reflected on when they were made."[91]

In an article in Expressen in October 2010,[92] Micke Ölander and Christian Holmén summarize the press reactions to Thomas Anderberg's book, where several of the reviewers share Anderberg's view when he speculates "that Pontus Hultén probably had a higher purpose with his coup than just to carry out a simple fraud. Namely, to pull down the pants of Andy Warhol and the hysterical development of the international art market." Anderberg himself says in an interview: "Andy Warhol wanted to tear down the boundaries between ugly and fine, folk and genteel. He mass-produced art that people could enjoy for not at all expensive money. But that idea was eventually corrupted by the rise in values. This is how I think Hultén could justify it to himself." Anderberg continues, though: "It cannot be ruled out that a certain amount of greed got hold of him, at least in the case of the latter deal when such large sums were involved. In fact, he also cheated people he respected and knew well."[93]

Among the reviewers quoted is the young culture writer Natalia Kazmierska, who differs from the others in her view of the case. Kazmierska dismisses what she sees as Thomas Anderberg's attempt to "exonerate" Pontus Hultén. The Expressen article reproduces several excerpts from Kazmierska's, as it appears in retrospect, lucid review,[94] long before the MeToo-movement altered certain views on men of power in the culture sphere: "The most fascinating thing is not how much shit powerful men can get away with, but how much effort others are willing to put into defending them." Kazmierska continues with a scathing assessment of the otherwise celebrated Anderberg's efforts: "The DN writer Thomas Anderberg was already there, bobbing with his powder puff, when the Brillo scandal came to light in 2007. Now he's shoveling out the beautybox to restore Pontus Hultén's honor." We have to agree with Natalia Kazmierska's verdict of Anderberg's book when she continues: "*The Great Art Swindle* is based on Expressen's scoop about how the former Moderna Museet director made and sold fake copies of Andy Warhol's piggy banks. It is telling, and dishonest, that Expressen's reporters are mentioned only once, while references to obscure 70s critics like George Dickie abound. Like a cultural theory plumber, Anderberg sets out to find someone else to blame."

Holmén and Ölander also quote extensively from Kazmierska's conclusion to her review — a summary of the whole Brillo affair which seems ahead of its time: "In *The Great Art Swindle* you get a good picture of how such a male network actually works in reality. Pontus Hultén was not alone. For example, the production of the fake boxes was supervised by Björn Springfeldt, then boss of Moderna Museet, who also happily accepted the boxes as a donation to the collection.

His colleague Bo Nilsson, former curator at Moderna, also knew about them, and arranged for them to be exhibited at the Danish Louisiana. Catalog texts attesting to the authenticity of the Brillo boxes turned out to consist of 'memories' signed by Pontus Hultén's friends, the art critic Ulf Linde and Olle Granath — also a former Moderna Museet director. (...) When Anderberg confronts them, they fall silent, or talk about their enormous respect for Hultén. (...) It is precisely this blind faith in authority that creates abuse of power, corruption and rot in the art world. Thomas Anderberg doesn't see the old man's rule because he stands in the midst of it."[95]

In September 2010, three and a half years after the initial revelation by Expressen, AWAAB finally published its detailed final report on the Brillo scandal. Moderately expressed, the committee had taken its time to summarize in its twenty-seven-page report what Expressen had revealed in 2007. In addition to written sources, the report was based on interviews with those involved in several countries, following visits to Stockholm and Malmö, among other places.

AWAAB writes about how Hultén and his colleagues at Moderna Museet, primarily Ulf Linde, worked with replicas of famous artists' works as an instrument in their exhibition activities. The reality that it was Pontus Hultén who had posthumously ended up in this situation was almost a logical, if dark, consequence of his strategy as an exhibition maker ever since the 1950s. No one, before or since, in the higher museum world has had the anarchic audacity to work with copies on a scale that can even be compared with what Hultén "got away with" throughout his career, constantly balancing "on the verge of the criminal," to quote Kay Heymer, Hultén's younger colleague from Bonn.[96]

From his guru Marcel Duchamp Pontus Hultén adapted the philosophy that "art is anything you can get away with."

The two copies, or replicas as they're called, of Duchamp's "The Large Glass" are discussed; the latter, made by artists Henrik Samuelsson and John Stenborg under the direction of Ulf Linde, is a particularly interesting parallel to the Brillo boxes, as this replica was crafted in 1992–1993 for Pontus Hultén's exhibitions at the Bundeskunsthalle in Bonn in 1992 and Palazzo Grassi in 1993, a quarter century after Marcel Duchamp's death. The decisive difference was that this replica, as the report states, was authorized by Duchamp's widow Teeny Duchamp, the heiress to the artist's rights,[97] while Andy Warhol's estate, as noted, had been unaware that Hultén had ordered the new Brillo boxes made in 1990. The Tatlin exhibition, which immediately followed Warhol in the spring of 1968, and the model of Tatlin's tower are also discussed — an exhibition that, in the words of the report, "consisted entirely of reproductions of Tatlin's work, due to the fact that loans from Russian museums were unavailable." The report goes on to proclaim: "The emphasis on documentation and reconstruction led Hultén to describe the project as conceptual." The text quotes Pontus Hultén from Hans Ulrich Obrist's interview:[98] "We reconstructed Tatlin's Tower in 1968 with the help of the museum's own carpenters, without the help of outside experts. This method of installing exhibitions began to create a phenomenal collective spirit — we could complete a new exhibition in five days."[99]

Björn Springfeldt is quoted in a depiction of Pontus Hultén and his working methods — a defense of Hultén with an account of several projects from his time at Moderna Museet, where he worked with "replicas" as "carriers of ideas" under Hultén. The report notes that Springfeldt adds that he "understood" that "the reproductions would be destroyed after *Territorium Artis*[100] — after having fulfilled their function as an idea." Conspicuously, Björn Springfeldt is not asked any follow-up questions in the report about the six boxes made in 1990 that he, as outgoing museum director, received as a donation from Pontus Hultén and had cataloged as made in 1967 and shown in Stockholm in 1968.

In this AWAAB final report, a long chapter entitled "Stockholm type boxes, 1968" first chronicles the entire background with all the information that the committee had collected about the exhibition in Stockholm 1968, with the five hundred cardboard boxes from the Brooklyn factory that were shown in the exhibition, and the wooden Stockholm boxes that Pontus Hultén had made after the exhibition had ended, "sometime in the spring or summer of 1968."[101] The report details the improvisations that Hultén and his small team were forced to conduct, with the films, the clouds and, of course, the five hundred Brillo boxes that were rearranged during the course of the exhibition after "weekly" concerts in the galleries — all "entirely in line with the experimental character of Hultén's curatorial style, with artworks typically integrated into a broader interdisciplinary or documentary project." Olle Granath's statement that Andy Warhol was satisfied with the result when he visited the exhibition is referenced.

AWAAB's report then discusses the fate of the Warhol exhibition after its premiere at Moderna Museet in the winter of 1968. It's curious that Pontus Hultén writes in his catalog text[102] that, as far as he remembers, the exhibition didn't travel — and that Kasper König had the same recollection when we met in Moderna Museet in the fall of 2018. "They wanted to show the exhibition at the Stedelijk and other places, but we didn't want to do that because it wouldn't have been in line with the concept," König told me.[103] As we know, Kasper König was living in New York at the time in 1968, never visiting the exhibition he had helped to produce together with Warhol, Hultén and Billy Klüver, which may explain his erroneous recollection. In fact, the exhibition traveled to five other venues: Amsterdam (Stedelijk), Oslo, Bern, Kassel and Berlin. As the report notes, "installation photographs from Stockholm and the other museums participating in the exhibition tour, as well as museum receipts and transportation invoices, show no indication that wooden Brillo boxes or any material other than cardboard were included with the cardboard boxes. The visual and documentary evidence supports the first-hand recollection of Olle Granath. He has asserted that only cardboard Brillo boxes were exhibited in Stockholm in 1968."[104]

After a recount of the apparent visual differences between the cardboard boxes shown in Stockholm and the wooden boxes exhibited by Warhol himself at the Stable Gallery in New York in 1964, the AWAAB report moves on to Pontus Hultén's wooden Stockholm boxes. The text relays that Hultén, as Granath understood it, had a "special agreement" with Warhol authorizing him to make "some of these boxes" — that crucial, ever-recurring, never-documented agreement that transforms these wooden boxes from worthless props into multi-million dollar sculptures.

Having established that it's unknown whether Pontus Hultén's mysterious wooden boxes were made in Stockholm or elsewhere, the report refers to an accounting entry in the Moderna Museet archives that I and many others have been pondering since 2007. This "ghost invoice" is dated August 28, 1969, more than a year and a half after the opening of the Warhol exhibition in Stockholm, with the text "Brillo-lådor [Brillo boxes]. Screen printing." In its report, AWAAB writes that the invoice "suggests that they were made under the supervision of the museum, albeit not on its premises." The report further speculates: "It is likely that the entry records the date on which the invoice for the screen printing was paid by Moderna Museet, but that the boxes were produced somewhat earlier, probably in the spring or summer of 1968, as Olle Granath has stated on several occasions."[105]

What's sensational about this enigmatic accounting entry is, which AWAAB fails to note, the amount — just over sixty thousand kronor. As everyone understands, that was a lot of money in 1969 — a zero too much at least if it had been for "ten-twelve" or "ten-fifteen" boxes as AWAAB themselves claim a few lines earlier in the same text. Even if the cost had been for printing "about a hundred" boxes — the number that Hultén himself claims in *Pontus Hultén's collection* ... that the museum had produced in Stockholm, or alternatively in Malmö, for the 1968 exhibition — the cost seems excessive. It appears sloppy that AWAAB in its report uncritically notes this accounting entry without reflecting on the amount. There are several such oddities in the report.

In summary, AWAAB concludes that the number of wooden boxes that Pontus Hultén had made in 1968 "is not known" but repeats Granath's and Linde's estimates of about ten, at most fifteen. Interestingly, AWAAB then writes that the board itself has only managed to identify six of these boxes of the Stockholm type. Of these six, three are the boxes that Olle Granath says he received from Pontus Hultén after the 1968 exhibition and which he sold in 1999. The other three, the report states, Hultén had kept for his own use, two of which had been used as bedside tables for "his children." The latter information was obtained by AWAAB from its representative Neil Printz's interview with Anna-Lena Wibom at her home in Lidingö in December 2008.[106]

The report discusses the technical and visual differences between Warhol's original boxes from the exhibition at the Stable Gallery in 1964 and those that Pontus Hultén had produced in Stockholm four years later — in addition to the color of the box they differ in dimensions, production technique and the blue color field with the text "Pad Giant." The Stockholm boxes were made using the exhibited cardboard boxes as a model, a later edition than the one Warhol had used. The Stable Gallery boxes were painted on five sides, while in Stockholm the production was simplified by leaving both the top and bottom sides without the screen-printed decor.

In the AWAAB's first preliminary report from 2007, the authentication board had deemed that Pontus Hultén had been completely unauthorized to manufacture Brillo boxes since no written permission from Andy Warhol for any such production had been found.

On two other occasions, Warhol had granted permission to outside companies to make boxes. For its Warhol exhibition in 1970, the Pasadena Art Museum had obtained permission from the artist to manufacture one hundred Brillo boxes, which Warhol then donated to the museum. The artist's condition was that the boxes remain in the museum's collection and never reach the market. In the same year, the Los Angeles County Museum, LACMA, had obtained permission to similarly produce one hundred Kellogg's boxes with the same conditions. In both cases, Warhol had issued clear written contracts to the museums. The report notes that as many as sixteen Brillo boxes of the "Pasadena type" had found their way onto the market despite Warhol's directives — an "over-production" thus of the same kind as that also manufactured in Malmö in 1990. These Pasadena boxes are authenticated as genuine Warhol artworks despite being produced without the artist's permission.

In its final report, AWAAB states that it has not been able to find any comparable documentation that the boxes Pontus Hultén had produced in 1968 "had been made with Warhol's permission or knowledge." In the text, AWAAB refers to the Moderna Museet's investigation from 2007, in which it's claimed that "these boxes (the Stockholm type) are, according to information and catalog texts, constructed with the artist's permission." The information is, again, apparently based on Olle Granath's recollection of what Pontus Hultén himself is said to have claimed. The report observes that no documentation has been found either in Hultén's papers or in the Moderna Museet archives to support this statement.

AWAAB then formulates a conclusion which, despite the mystical circumstances, approves the few "Stockholm boxes" and thus officially transforms them from props into precious works of art: "As noted earlier, Olle Granath has claimed that when he first saw the Stockholm-type boxes in the spring or summer of 1968, he understood that Hultén had a 'special agreement' with Warhol authorizing him to produce these boxes. Given their personal friendship, the impromptu nature of the Stockholm exhibition, and the earlier dating of the Stockholm type boxes in relation to the Pasadena and Los Angeles type boxes, it is possible that some sort of informal verbal agreement may have been reached between Hultén and Warhol in early 1968. The Authentication Board has been unable to either confirm or rule out such a possibility." The AWAAB adds that it has not yet had time to go through all of the huge number of "time capsules" — boxes of material such as pictures, sketches, notes, etc. — left behind by the manic collector Andy Warhol, in which, according to the report, a written agreement between Warhol and Hultén could theoretically still be hidden.

Like a court, AWAAB opts to acquit rather than convict, as it cannot be ascertained that Pontus Hultén *did not* have Andy Warhol's permission to make "his" Brillo boxes — to the delight of the owners of the enigmatic few precious boxes of disputed provenance that are still out there on the market. About the mysterious signature "A.W." on one of the wooden boxes from 1968 that had been examined by Moderna Museet, AWAAB neutrally states that it's impossible to determine where it came from and whether it could have been made by Andy Warhol, who, as noted, usually signed his works differently, if at all.

Many observers believe that AWAAB and the Warhol Foundation were far too generous in their assessment of the Brillo affair. Andy Warhol's closest associate and manager Paul Morrissey and Arthur Danto, perhaps the world's most respected Warhol expert, both assured in Expressen's first series of articles that Andy Warhol would never have allowed this type of reproduction of his works. Pontus Hultén's operations with the Brillo boxes, both in 1968 and 1990, fall back on this constantly recurring question from Warhol — "Why don't you make them over there?" — uttered only to Hultén himself, according to his own statement, and by Hultén seemingly used it as a general carte blanche to produce "replicas." This was despite the fact that the whole idea of having the wooden Brillo boxes made in Sweden had been dismissed for economic and logistical reasons, which is why Hultén and his colleagues had instead chosen to order cardboard boxes from the Brillo printer in Brooklyn.

In its final report, after all detailed accounts of Pontus Hultén's wooden Stockholm boxes from 1968, AWAAB moves on to the chapter "Malmö type boxes, 1990." The section begins with a thorough background on Pontus Hultén's school IHEAP and the exhibition *Le Territoire de l'Art*, for which, according to his own statement,[107] Hultén had the one hundred and five wooden boxes (as well as an unspecified "spontaneous" over-production) manufactured in Malmö Konsthall's workshop in the spring of 1990. The report calls these boxes "the second and larger edition of Brillo box sculptures produced under Pontus Hultén's direction."

The text reads as follows: "In early 1990, carpenters in Malmö Konsthall's workshop constructed the boxes and painted them white, using one of the cardboard boxes exhibited in Stockholm in 1968 as a model. They were printed by Bengt Andersson, a silkscreen printer who had worked with graphic designer John Melin and his partner Anders Österlin. Melin introduced Andersson to Hultén, who gave him one of the Stockholm type boxes to use as a model for their screens. An invoice from the printer, dated May 7, 1990, to Hultén at IHEAP documents both the date of production and the number of boxes printed: 105 in total. From Malmö the boxes were shipped to Stockholm where they were stored at Moderna Museet."[108]

What is really surprising is the information given without further comment in the last sentence: that the one hundred and five freshly made wooden boxes after production in Malmö in 1990 were shipped to Stockholm and stored at Moderna Museet. This assertion, which according to the report's footnote originates from conversations with the printer Bengt Andersson, has not been confirmed by anyone else involved. There is a mysterious transport invoice but, again, not a single testimony from any employee or other collaborator at Moderna Museet that any wooden Brillo boxes have ever been seen in the museum's storage.

The AWAAB report also contains an analysis of Pontus Hultén's motives for producing this "second edition" of boxes. The text argues that "in contrast to the Stockholm type boxes, Pontus Hultén's motives for producing the Malmö type boxes remain clear." The AWAAB further explains that "for the individuals involved in the production or aware of the production," it was "clear" that "the Malmö type boxes, produced explicitly for *Le Territoire de l'Art*, were exhibition 'scenography.'" "Moreover," the report continues, "they believed that there had been an 'old authorization' from Warhol to Hultén giving him permission to produce copies of the Brillo boxes."[109]

It's fascinating how innocent all the survivors have been in their actions according to their own statements. They have all been deceived by the dead Pontus Hultén. No one involved had any suspicion that there could be any legal or ethical problems with producing "props" in the form of "sculptures" of the world's most famous artist, who died three years before.

In 1968, it's easy to buy the image of such alleged cluelessness. In 1990, after the commercial explosion of art in the 1980s, and the posthumous return of Andy Warhol as modern art's greatest superstar, it's more difficult to understand this blue-eyed innocence. What's clear, regardless, is the interest of those involved that this version — which is uncritically conveyed by AWAAB in their report — gains traction in the historiography. Without this innocence, Hultén's accomplices in the production of the Malmö boxes risk being not "useful idiots," tricked by Hultén, but culprits in a potential art forgery scheme ...

The AWAAB report provides an account of the mysterious fate of the Malmö boxes. To begin with, the report presents a fact that makes Hultén's entire operation with the Malmö boxes and its purposes even more difficult to explain, about the exhibition *Le Territoire de l'Art*: "it seems likely that as few as ten Malmö boxes were included." The text specifies: "This number is based on several exhibition lists compiled by Hultén's secretary at IHEAP, and on the testimony of Olle Granath, who visited the exhibition. On that occasion, Granath noted the differences in workmanship between the boxes he owned and those exhibited in Leningrad. He described the latter as 'poorly executed' and observed that this bothered him as he thought Warhol always cared about the appearance of his work."[110] The report comments that the Brillo boxes in the Leningrad exhibition catalog are not "identified or cataloged" but instead illustrated with an image from the 1968 Warhol exhibition of the mountain of cardboard boxes.

The installation of a smaller stack was placed by a staircase in the Russian Museum where, according to Granath, the "poorly produced" boxes were a "sad sight."

It's surprising that neither AWAAB nor the many who have written about the Brillo scandal have made a bigger deal of the oddity that so few boxes were apparently shown in Leningrad. It's stated in all contexts, including repeatedly in the AWAAB report, as a fact that Pontus Hultén had the boxes made in Malmö "early 1990" to be shown in the school exhibition later in the spring of that year.

The big question then is: why did Pontus Hultén have as many as one hundred and five boxes made if only ten were shown in Leningrad? Could some technical mishap have occurred during transportation? Did Hultén already know in 1990 that he would show all one hundred and five boxes two years later, in *Territorium Artis*, but still let his school pay for the large installation in Bonn?

The AWAAB report then goes on to relate how some thirty of the boxes were shown in a Warhol exhibition at Louisiana in the summer of 1991. This is where the aforementioned Bo Nilsson, the Malmö art gallery director and Warhol connoisseur, comes in. Nilsson was working at Louisiana at the time and tipped off his colleagues that a whole batch of Brillo boxes that were available in Malmö, where they were stored in a warehouse in Malmö Konsthall's workshop. "Everyone in Malmö's art circles knew that these boxes were there," as Bo Nilsson says.[111]

In the Louisiana exhibition, an installation with the then brand new Brillo boxes was one of the central pieces. The cataloging was again cryptic. The year of origin of the boxes was given as 1964 with the provenance "private collection."[112] If the cataloging in Leningrad can be argued with goodwill to be sloppy, it's impossible to consider the information that Louisiana provided its audience with as anything other than a pure falsity. There is a slippage here that transforms the boxes from props to art.[113]

The disinformation was even more blatant in the opening exhibition at the Bundeskunsthalle in Bonn in 1992, *Territorium Artis*. All of the one hundred and five boxes that Hultén had commissioned for the exhibition in Leningrad were displayed here. The catalog does not show any of the newly produced boxes, but instead what looks like one of Warhol's original boxes, with the cataloging information "Andy Warhol. Brillo Boxes. 1964."[114] Unlike in Leningrad, here Pontus Hultén had a resourceful organization at his disposal. I refuse to believe in factors such as carelessness and printing errors.

In summary, AWAAB's final report, despite some harsh wording, is on the whole lenient towards Pontus Hultén in its verdict. AWAAB and the Warhol Foundation had less interest than anyone else in the matter being further magnified.

AWAAB's report did not impress the art world. The criticism of the committee's leniency and lack of precision in its judgments of Hultén's actions was serious, although few dared to express it publicly. AWAAB was dissolved in December 2010, the same year the Warhol Foundation reorganized its authentication system, as considered as a result of the Brillo scandal.

Viewed from an art historical perspective, it's striking how limited the consequences of the scandal were in the end. The high-profile rumors of lawsuits with large sums at stake came to nothing. Remarkably, not a single owner of the ninety-four Brillo boxes (of which five to ten are said to have been Stockholm boxes) sold by Pontus Hultén even tried to recall their purchases. The certificates of authenticity from AWAAB have allowed the art dealers who made money from these boxes to escape

One of those threatening legal action was British collector Anthony d'Offay, who planned to sue Brian Balfour-Oatts and auction house Sotheby's for millions of pounds after buying boxes he later donated to Tate Scotland. Balfour-Oatts confides the lawsuit was withdrawn after d'Offay was asked if he had confidence in Warhol Foundation, which he declared to have. Thus, according to Balfour-Oatts, the case fell because he could not question the certificate of authenticity from AWAAB (Telephone interview, November 22, 2018).

liability as they can claim they acted in good faith. Questions have remained unanswered about what the flaws revealed by the scandal in the Warhol Foundation's authentication procedures mean for other works by Andy Warhol.

Nor were many players in the art market in general keen for more stones than necessary to be turned over. That the art dealers and others involved in the case should have acted in innocent good faith is something that I and others find hard to believe. Experience tells us that as long as money is flowing in to all concerned parties and everything appears to be in order, few people are in a hurry to ask too many questions.

In our conversation, Brian Balfour-Oatts raises another interesting point — how "immunity" to scandal in the art world has spread since the Brillo revelation in 2007. In the opinion of Balfour-Oatts, the affair would probably not have had the same impact if it had been disclosed a decade later. According to Balfour-Oatts and others, as money in the art world balloons, and the number of affluent collectors and investors increases, especially in "emerging" markets such as Russia, China, the Arab world and Asia, while the availability of historically important works decreases, the propensity to conduct unnecessarily in-depth investigations is diminishing. "Take something like the sale of the da Vinci painting for 450 million dollars at Christie's last year," Balfour-Oatts says. "Nobody knows if da Vinci painted that canvas, but there are still buyers willing to pay."[115] Olle Granath laughs when I ask him about this reality — that a laissez-faire attitude has increasingly come to be applied when alleged art historic gems surface on the market. "I bet it has!" Granath says. "Money has no value any more. There are people willing to pay billions for anything today."[116]

The painting "Salvator Mundi" ("Savior of the World"), previously thought to be painted by students or followers of Leonardo da Vinci, later revalued as executed by the master himself, was sold on November 15, 2017 for 450.3 million dollars, the highest price ever paid for a work of art. The buyer is believed to have been Saudi Crown Prince Mohammed bin Salman. The painting was rumored to be exhibited at the Louvre in Abu Dhabi but its current location is unknown. Many experts question the "revaluation" of the heavily restored painting as a genuine Leonardo artwork.

Pontus Hultén's own responsibility in this matter must, in my opinion, be classified as clarified. The amount of sources and evidence is overwhelming. As Christian Holmén at Expressen says: "We have worked with crime journalism for a very long time and have extensive experience in evaluating the overall picture of what can be considered proven, beyond reasonable doubt and so on — things you learn after reviewing thousands of trial protocols and legal documents. For us, it was very clear when we made the overall assessment that there was a carefully thought-out system behind this whole affair and that Pontus Hultén was the one responsible."[117]

The image of Hultén as an aged, slightly confused legend who lived for art and didn't understand money was something the Expressen journalists never accepted. "As a museum director, he was comparable to a business leader or high-level government official," says Christian Holmén. "Such a person is used to managing budgets, certifying invoices for large amounts and conducting negotiations with major financial interests. That such a person would be so naive and ignorant was not credible to us."[118]

Nor do Christian Holmén and his colleagues give much credence to the popular theory that Pontus Hultén's primary motive was not money but the rebellious desire to play a trick on the art market. "No, it's our definite experience that when millions are involved, as in this case, it's usually the money and nothing else that is the main driving force."[119]

The Brillo affair is far from the only financial transaction that Hultén carried out during these years. I and others I have spoken to believe that it can all be linked to the lack of a pension that Hultén nagged his friends about and which he felt he had been cheated out of by the Swedish state. He had finally received a pension from Hoffmann-La Roche, as payment for his Tinguely collection. To supplement this income, he made sure to build up a modest fortune in other ways during the last decade of his life, probably in order to leave a legacy to his son Felix, whom he had neglected for so much of his childhood. A person close to Pontus Hultén, who wishes to remain anonymous, agrees with this analysis and confides in me: "Pontus became bitter towards the artists. He rightly felt that he had helped create their fortunes while he himself had always had to make do with a modest salary. When he helped Niki to clean up after Jean's death and they found sacks of cash in the attic, it upset Pontus. I think he decided to take the money he felt he deserved, for his own old age and for Felix."

Even though the question of guilt has been settled as far as I'm concerned, I still feel obliged to present some of the arguments and historical accounts that several people have put forward in Pontus Hultén's defense.

Anna-Lena Wibom has been at the forefront of these from the start. Wibom has contributed several different stories in order to whitewash Hultén. During my conversation with Wibom in the winter of 2014, she told me that she had discovered that Andy Warhol had been to Sweden not once but twice in connection with the 1968 exhibition. On his first visit, which is unknown in art history, Warhol is said by Wibom to have arrived in Copenhagen and then traveled on to Malmö, where he and Hultén together had the wooden boxes made "according to Andy's instructions."[120] This visit was not mentioned to AWAAB's representative in 2008, nor in the radio documentary from 2012. In these conversations, instead, Wibom insisted that Warhol had been a guest at her and Hultén's home on Lidingö during his visit to Stockholm for the exhibition. Here Warhol is said to have seen the wooden boxes that Hultén had commissioned and "liked them."[121] Neither any second trip to Sweden nor the visit to Lidingö has, to my knowledge, been mentioned by any other source.

Over the years, Anna-Lena Wibom's estimate of the number of wooden boxes Pontus Hultén had made for the 1968 exhibition has grown. In early interviews after the revelation, Wibom like others spoke of a few boxes, but in the radio documentary from 2012 the number has increased. These boxes from 1968 she suggested had been mixed up with the Malmö boxes from 1990 in the storage room at La Motte, from where Pontus Hultén had sold them to art dealers who insisted on buying them, not caring about the money but amused with "tricking the art market."[122]

In an interview with the Danish art collector Peter Hvidberg, in November 2017, Anna-Lena Wibom provides more sensational information about Warhol's first visit to Sweden that has not been presented by anyone else. This time, unlike in my interview in 2014, the visit didn't take place in Malmö but in Stockholm: "It started in 1967. Pontus was in NYC where he was in discussions with Andy about doing an exhibition in Stockholm. Andy came here in November 1967, I think it was. He wanted to see the facilities. Pontus had seen boxes in NYC and wanted the same thing for the exhibition here. We had some cardboard boxes. Some with white and blue and red and some in yellow with red and blue I think. Maybe brown. Andy wanted to show Brillos so Pontus took a cardboard box to the National Museum. They had a carpentry shop. And he said 'You can make this out of wood.' The head carpenter said sure. I think they made fifty or a hundred."[123]

Another person who has devoted great efforts to exonerating Hultén is the aforementioned Peter Hvidberg, the Danish art collector and dealer living in Copenhagen. His collection now also includes the notorious Stockholm box with the cryptic signature "A.W.," purchased from the printer Bengt Andersson.

Hvidberg became interested in the "so-called Brillo scandal," as he consistently calls the affair, after he picked up Thomas Anderberg's book *The Great Art Swindle* on a vacation with his girlfriend in the Mediterranean sometime in the early 2010s. "I was absolutely fascinated and read the book twice in one sitting, I couldn't stop," says Hvidberg. "The woman who was with me was very nice, we had just met, but I neglected her because I couldn't put the book down. I immediately felt that something was not right."[124]

After returning home, Peter Hvidberg began researching the Brillo affair. He spent the next four years or so writing a book about the scandal — a three-hundred-and-thirty-page manuscript, an unpublished version of which I have studied.[125]

Hvidberg's manuscript contains many previously unpublished documents and new findings. The book is well researched, carefully constructed and credible — although I think Hvidberg seems to have stuck to his theory of Pontus Hultén's innocence, which he has consequently devoted himself to proving. His reasoning is largely convincing, with hard-to-contradict evidence in written documents — the fruit of many hours of archival research. "They're lying — all of them," as Hvidberg summarizes the whole matter in an email to me,[126] one hundred percent convinced as he is that the whole "so-called Brillo scandal" is the result of an international conspiracy in which Pontus Hultén has been made a scapegoat to protect powerful interests.

Peter Hvidberg's basic thesis, which he formulates in general terms in his text, without detailed factual information, is that Pontus Hultén had an excellent relationship with Andy Warhol, with his estate, with the original Warhol Foundation and above all with the founder of the foundation, Fred Hughes. Hvidberg pleads that it's likely that Hughes, who was suffering from MS at the time, was well acquainted with Hultén's production of the one hundred and five boxes in Malmö in 1990. Hvidberg believes that this edition was actually sanctioned and approved by Warhol's estate and the Warhol Foundation under the direction of Fred Hughes, even though no contract has been detected — Hultén and Hughes were both of the "old school" who were accustomed to working without one.

In implicit, more conspiratorial reasoning, Hvidberg suggests that several other representatives of the Warhol Foundation must also have been informed of this background — that the foundation under Fred Hughes had sanctioned the production of the boxes — but that they had hidden motives, such as their own sales of boxes, to make the dead Pontus Hultén the sole culprit. Hvidberg presents the far-reaching hypothesis that the Warhol Foundation under Hughes collaborated with Pontus Hultén in the production of Brillo boxes — that Hultén produced the boxes more or less on behalf of the Foundation and other interested parties, with the aim of exhibiting them in museum shows around the world.

Things get even more complicated when Peter Hvidberg involves MoMA in New York. In Pontus Hultén's archive, Hvidberg has found a letter from the previously mentioned MoMA curator Kynaston McShine. In the letter, dated November 3, 1987,[127] eight months after Andy Warhol's death, McShine proposes a collaboration for future exhibitions. McShine is planning MoMA's major Warhol retrospective and wants Hultén to show it in Palazzo Grassi in Venice. Peter Hvidberg has focused on the wording on the last page of the letter where Kynaston McShine writes to Pontus Hultén:

"Warhol's interest in art as 'decoration' and in what an artist represents and what he may intend to present must be considered weighed by 'recreating' some of his special installations, such as for example:

Brillos, Heinz 1964
Del Monte, Mott's
Campbell's and Kellogg's
boxes

The estate has signaled its willingness to cooperate fully ..."[128]

The wording of this letter leads Peter Hvidberg to conclude, never really stated in his manuscript but in our correspondence, that Pontus Hultén acted in collaboration with two of the most important institutions in the modern art world, the Museum of Modern Art and the Warhol Foundation, in a never documented plan to have exhibition props, Brillo boxes and other of Warhol's most famous "sculptures" produced for a traveling exhibition produced by MoMA, but also for other purposes.

The connection to MoMA and, through the museum, to the Warhol Foundation is interesting. It's no less intriguing considering that Hvidberg fails to mention: that Pontus Hultén did indeed show

MoMA's Warhol retrospective at Palazzo Grassi in Venice, opened in February 1990. The traveling exhibition, which was shown in a number of museums worldwide, was essentially a finished product supplied by Kynaston McShine and MoMA. The presentation at Louisiana, curated by Steingrim Laursen, where some thirty of Hultén's Malmö boxes from 1990 were added, was also part of this MoMA tour. Indirectly, the world's most prestigious modern art museum can thus also be said to have been affected by the Brillo scandal. It's noteworthy that Pontus Hultén was involved in a collaboration with a Warhol retrospective during the very time when the fateful boxes were being manufactured in Malmö, in the spring of 1990. Undoubtedly, this connection makes me wonder even more about Hultén's purpose with having the boxes made in Malmö in spring 1990.

However, according to the catalog and testimonies, no Brillo boxes were shown in Venice — perhaps for the simple reason that the boxes were not yet manufactured when the exhibition at Palazzo Grassi opened in February 1990, but were probably only completed a few months later? This is only speculation.

In his book manuscript on "the so-called Brillo scandal," Peter Hvidberg implicates another of the world's leading art institutions, namely MNAM at the Centre Pompidou, when he uses shipping documents to show that as many as sixty of Pontus Hultén's newly manufactured boxes were transported from Louisiana to Paris and the Centre Pompidou. Apparently, a small number of these boxes were shown here in MoMA's traveling Warhol exhibition when it moved on from Venice to Paris in the spring of 1990, this time with 1964 given as the year of production. A "European collector" was listed as the owner. I have asked Jean-Hubert Martin, who was the director of MNAM at the time, about this. Jean-Hubert sent me a picture of a stack of about fifteen wooden boxes in the exhibition. He doesn't remember anything about the origin of these boxes.[129]

Peter Hvidberg has hired handwriting experts and believes it to be proven that it is Hultén who has scribbled "Répliques," the French word for replicas, on the loan document he has found in the archive. On Hvidberg's behalf, this note absolves Hultén of any responsibility for falsely stated provenance and cataloging. According to Hvidberg, the note proves that Hultén was sincere all along about his boxes being later replicas, even though he ostensively had no objection to the boxes repeatedly being cataloged with different years of origin, alternately 1964, 1967 and 1968.

How the operation fits together in terms of time is difficult to understand. The exhibition at Louisiana was shown after the one in Paris. If Hvidberg's information is correct, the whole lot must have been transported first to Louisiana, from where sixty boxes were then shipped to the Centre Pompidou, while the other forty were kept at Louisiana for the museum's own upcoming exhibition.

The information I have on the Malmö boxes in the Warhol exhibition at the Centre Pompidou is scant. We cannot even consider it one hundred percent clear that the boxes were actually shown in Paris. The Centre Pompidou does not appear in the later reports of Expressen, Thomas Anderberg or the world press. If this was the case, it was embarrassing for both MNAM and MoMA.

Peter Hvidberg returns repeatedly to the same argument in Pontus Hultén's defense — that money was not of interest for Hultén; that if he had needed financial resources to repair the roof of La Motte, he could have sold a few works from the collection that he chose to donate to Moderna Museet instead; that Hultén would be something as rare as an altruist, a free-floating art god above lower human inclinations, mindlessly signing the papers handed to him by money-hungry art dealers, selling old and new boxes all mixed up, mostly as a favor to others while his own thoughts were occupied by art as an idea and philosophy, and so on. We can dismiss this whole picture of Hultén with the knowledge of his personality that this story has built up. If there was one thing Hultén was *not*, it was oblivious to money. His donation of a collection worth a great fortune was grandiose and contradictory, as usual when it comes to Hultén, but hardly affects the evaluation of his motives. More than ten million Swedish crowns in non-working earnings would seem to be sufficient reason for anyone familiar with Hultén's attitude to money.

After all these sad and sordid turns and revelations, I wish to end this long chapter, and almost the whole story, with my own defense of Pontus Hultén.

I still think there is something anarchic, nihilistic, Dadaist and Duchampian about the Brillo affair, although, like Christian Holmén, I have reached the conclusion that it was the money, not the prank, that seems to have been Pontus Hultén's main motivation in his actions with the Brillo boxes.

Hultén really did loath the art market and art dealers in general. He felt that the galloping prices and the flow of money on the market were devastating for art. He was deeply saddened and bitter about the death of utopias and that art had lost the political, social and philosophical power of the glory days of the Moderna Museet in the sixties and beyond. He was disgusted to see art transformed into a fashionable pleasure for the nouveau riche and an investment object for speculators. There are many testimonies to the hatred Hultén had for people who profited from art.

Pontus Hultén's close friends agree that he was far from an immoral person. On the contrary, he is said to have upheld high moral ideals, with which he never compromised. This moral code was strictly his own. It didn't follow laws, rules, conventions or the opinions of others. According to this personal morality, I'm convinced that Hultén didn't see it as a sin to swindle money from the merchants, dealers and nouveau riche collectors — groups of people overrepresented in the Andy Warhol market — even if, unlike Robin Hood, he didn't take the money and give it to the poor, but instead made sure to enrich himself and his descendants. One thing is certain: the Brillo deal didn't affect the poor. "Ce n'est pas un pauvre qui paie" ("it's no poor man who pays"), as Hultén said to Andres Pardey about his sales to Hoffmann-La Roche.[130]

What is striking is that in the end, the scandal did not affect anyone at all. Fifteen years after the revelation, no one has lost any major money in connection with the scandal. Neither Ronny Van de Velde, Brian Balfour-Oatts, Sotheby's, the Warhol Foundation, nor anyone else has been sued for damages. The art institutions that received the boxes as gifts, including Moderna Museet, still have them in their collections. Moderna's six infamous Malmö boxes, downgraded to "scenography, props" after the museum's own investigation, were displayed in the fall/winter of 2018/2019 in a place of honor in the museum's small success exhibition in memory of Pontus Hultén's Warhol show in 1968. Together with the signs summarizing the events of the scandal, the boxes were the main attraction of the exhibition. Miniature spectacle boxes were big-selling souvenirs in the museum shop. International art historians, scholars and journalists demanded information about the affair. It could be argued that the Brillo scandal has become another magnet for Moderna Museet and made the museum even better known internationally. It's difficult to speculate on what the six Malmo boxes in the museum's collection might be worth. One market price that has been mentioned is one hundred thousand dollars each.[131]

In the end, the entire Brillo affair became a zero-sum game, or more than that. The scandal has helped to further reinforce the myth and allure of the legendary Andy Warhol — the teflon artist whose value only continues to rise through ruthless exploitation, overexposure and systematic falsification. Isn't that pretty amazing?

No, I don't think Pontus Hultén saw anything immoral in dragging this industry and world by the nose — or kicking it in the ass, to use a more powerful and relevant bodily metaphor — as a farewell to earthly life. In my conversation with Dan Wolgers, he is adamant that Hultén enjoyed exposing the art market and that he truly succeeded in achieving this. I argue that this may be so, but that it was hardly this but the money that was his main incentive. "Well, so what?" says Wolgers. "He still managed to expose how sick the whole thing is. I still think that's pretty damn cool."[132]

Epilog

Although dramatic, it feels sad to have to end this tale with the Brillo story, the tragic final chapter in Pontus Hultén's long life and career.

Pontus Hultén remains a man of controversy even posthumously. Such a legacy is a natural consequence of his work and personality. Hultén never sought to please and befriend everyone. On the contrary, his relentless drive to push all boundaries led to constant conflicts — personal, artistic, political, economic and of all other kinds. Hultén was a pioneer in the true sense of the word, that is, like his parents in Kamchatka in the twenties, he was most comfortable blazing trails in uncharted territory, with no more regard than necessary for rules, order or convention.

It seems inevitable that such a person will acquire opponents and enemies — but also inspire love and loyalty. In my travels around the world, it has been moving to meet so many people from several generations — artists, colleagues, friends, rivals, disciples — whose lives and worldviews have been influenced by Pontus Hultén. It would be no exaggeration to call this group Hultén's global extended family, whose members, even when their words are critical, speak warmly of Pontus, as if he were still personally present so many years after his exit from the living.

Over the past few years, I've been pleased to note that the Brillo affair and other negatives seem to be fading away as the sludge in the wake of the storm. Instead, the bigger picture emerges of his immense, unequivocal importance to the international art history of the twentieth century, and his influence far beyond the territories of art.

A summary of Pontus Hultén's legacy naturally begins in Stockholm, more specifically on Skeppsholmen and Moderna Museet, one of the world's leading museums of modern art. In international rankings, Moderna Museet is usually placed immediately after the giants MoMA, MNAM Centre Pompidou, Tate Modern, Guggenheim and Metropolitan.

We Swedes should appreciate the importance of such a museum in this small, geographically and historically peripheral city, where the main features of modern art history can be read through key works from all the most important movements of young Modernism. There is no equivalent in northern Europe. Only the Stedelijk and Louisiana can even stand comparison.

We can regret that our rulers have far from always understood the importance of this treasure — that for decades after Pontus Hultén's departure, the museum was neglected and underfunded, making it impossible to vigorously develop its invaluable collection. It was an omission that plagued Hultén and which he repeatedly regretted. Let us instead rejoice in a recent, slow awakening that we have nevertheless been able to follow, with a growing realization of the incomparable national resource that Moderna Museet represents.

After the unfortunate era of stagnation following Pontus Hultén's departure, the museum has once again grown bigger, stronger and more international in Rafael Moneo's now more than twenty-year-old museum building, which, despite the lack of any intrusive charisma or magic, no longer appears so unprepossessing in an international comparison. The museum is an arena with boundless potential — as a meeting venue for Stockholmers and visitors, as a source of inspiration for creativity of all kinds, as an educational institution and playground, as an international cultural magnet and image tool for Stockholm and Sweden.

There is no questioning the total importance of Pontus Hultén to Moderna Museet on Skeppsholmen in Stockholm. Remember how combative he was in his convictions already in the mid-fifties about creating not a Swedish but an international modern art museum or rather cultural hub — how he pushed through this vision against a compact provincial resistance, which must be said to have included his own boss, the museum's formal founder Otte Sköld; how Hultén confronted the astonished Stockholm cultural public with a fait accompli of a kind they could never have imagined in their wildest dreams.[1]

A recurring criticism of Pontus Hultén from his enemies, antagonists, colleagues and even some friends is that he was, as Olle Granath put it, "bad at giving credit" — quick to claim for himself what was in fact the merit of others' work. There is certainly truth in this characterization, although there is no shortage of friends or colleagues who take a different, even opposite view. The testimonies are unanimous that Hultén had "big ears," as his long-serving Parisian collaborator Serge Fauchereau put it[2] — that is, he was quick to pick up ideas from co-workers and subordinates and make them his own.

In regular attempts to downplay the contribution and importance of Pontus Hultén, I have been told from various quarters that many of the fundamental ideas behind Moderna Museet were not actually Hultén's, but were alternately the work of Otte Sköld, Oscar Reutersvärd, Hans Nordenström, Ulf Linde, Carlo Derkert and others (yes, all men ...). That may be the case. Yet a distinct impression emerges that behind the saga of this small northern museum looms a main figure without whom this would never have been imaginable: Pontus Hultén, of course, the then very young man who "combined knowledge and deep familiarity with the modern art world with a talent for organization of the kind that usually sets off multinational corporations," to quote the museum's benefactor Roland Pålsson.[3]

Pontus Hultén may have been a hustler, a buffoon, a mythomaniac, a brute, an untrustworthy rascal and other epithets that I have heard used about him. His colleagues and friends, Reutersvärd, Nordenström, Derkert, Linde and others, indeed made invaluable contributions in various fields. Yet there can be no doubt as to who was the engine; who pulled the others with him far beyond the boundaries of the city and the country, out on the hazardous voyage on the oceans of the international art world. Throughout his career, Pontus Hultén was surrounded by talented collaborators, without whom history would not have turned out as it did. Yet, no one needed to question who the leader was.

In Stockholm and Sweden, Moderna Museet exerted influence far beyond the domains of art. The museum influenced social development, public debate, culture and politics to a degree that must be incomprehensible to younger generations who have grown up with the image of art museums as perhaps fantastic but still passive mediators of cultural experiences. Moderna Museet during Pontus Hultén's time was not content with its role as a cultural broker. The museum never hesitated to take a stand, not only artistically but politically, morally and philosophically. The expansive institution intervened in the development of culture and society in every way it could, with the outspoken ambition of helping to change society into something better, more modern. "Imagination to power!" was Pontus Hultén's oft-quoted slogan from the 1968 student revolt in Paris, one of his most beloved mottos.

For more than a decade, Moderna Museet was the only scene to offer the small northern city of Stockholm and the rest of the country's more advanced cultural audience a view of the big world on a larger scale — and how they did it! It was here — not in Paris, London or New York — that it happened during those years. The eyes of the whole world were turned to Stockholm. Moderna Museet was at the time, as proclaimed by the New York Times in 2021, undoubtedly "the coolest museum on the planet."[4] Who can underestimate the magnitude of the achievement of creating something so outstanding with the conditions at hand?

Not even Hultén's and the museum's many sworn political enemies from the time can deny that Moderna Museet contributed more than any other single actor to breaking Stockholm's and Sweden's cultural isolation after the war and the post-war period, and to transforming our capital from a provincial, large small town into an admittedly small but still international metropolis — a destination that has since maintained its manifested position in the geography of the international art world.

Much of what was created during these mythical years has influenced our present day. Remember the text I quoted[5] about how Swedish playgrounds, after-school centers and children's education would not have looked like they do today if it had not been for Moderna Museet and the exhibition *The Model* in 1968, for example. As Pontus Hultén himself pointed out, he and the museum were fortunate to operate at a time of unique success and optimistic dynamism for Sweden, when our country was a leader in a wide range of fields — cultural, political, industrial, economic, social and humanistic; a socio-political experiment unparalleled in world history. The museum was able to benefit from the formidable social spirit as the fruits of half a century of economic growth were reaped, but was also, arguably, one of the most important drivers of this development.

We can even opt to take a stark economic perspective. In their far-sighted, radical ambition to build, against all odds, an international art collection of the highest order, Pontus Hultén and his colleagues seized an opportunity that will never return. The art that the museum's management acquired for the museum during the "heroic years," constantly under fierce political criticism, ridicule and mockery, would in our time be worth surreal amounts if it were even possible to buy. In our time, no money in the world could have acquired these works of art; historical masterpieces that are part of the museum's permanent collection accessible to all Stockholmers and visitors — invaluable attractions for the museum, the city and the nation. The money provided by the Swedish government in the pioneer years of the early 1960s, for which it was vilified by political opponents, seems like a pittance in our time. The grotesque gender imbalance among the artists represented in this collection is another story.[6]

In my interview with the artist Susan Weil, Robert Rauschenberg's ex-wife, she told me that she had once raised the provocative gender imbalance with Pontus Hultén, at the opening of the *Sleeping Beauty* exhibition at the Guggenheim in New York in 1982, featuring contemporary Scandinavian art, curated by Hultén. Weil asked why all ten participating artists were men. "He got angry and said they were judging by quality, not gender," Weil said (Susan Weil, telephone interview, April 13, 2016).

If we then look at the museum and art itself, we can see that Pontus Hultén more than anyone else in the world contributed to revolutionizing the concept of art museums in the sixties, even though there were models primarily in Willem Sandberg's Stedelijk and Alfred Barr's Museum of Modern Art — the institutions that Hultén himself said he wanted to merge on Skeppsholmen in Stockholm[7] — and even though he had influential contemporary colleagues and collaborators in mainly other smaller European cities (Humlebaek/Copenhagen, Brussels, Bern, Düsseldorf, among others).

Most sensational in Pontus Hultén's new approach is the expansion of the realms of art and the concept of the museum, for which Moderna Museet became the most important experimental workshop in the world. Hultén was never satisfied with simply showing art as all museums had done before. His aim was to place art in a wider context, in interaction with other creative expressions such as film, literature, architecture, photography, design, music, dance, fashion and so on, freeing it from the traditional hierarchical museum order in which painting and sculpture had always been elevated above other artistic expressions.

Hultén represented a de-dramatized, extended vision of the mission he was convinced art had to shoulder in a new utopian world order. With these "territorial gains," a radically broader audience was attracted. Previously unimagined crowds of visitors flocked to the remote Skeppsholmen, where they had the privilege of experiencing the best and most experimental of what the international avant-garde had to offer. "Pontus invented a whole new totality in the view of art and the role of art in society, and in the way of producing exhibitions that took a stand in the political and historical debate and showed the audience new contexts," as Germano Celant, the Italian star curator, declared.[8] He called Hultén "the first curator."[9]

Children deserve a special mention. Hultén and his colleagues contributed like few others to broadening the contemporary art museum's audience base also generationally, by inviting children to the museum — as audiences and as artistic participants. Although he himself was very far from a "soccer dad," Pontus Hultén held the child's gaze in high esteem. One of his beautiful slogans was that a mark of a good art exhibition was that it should also be appreciated by a child. Moderna Museet's children's activities from Hultén's era have served as a source of inspiration and a model for museums and other institutions around the world.

Pontus Hultén was not without precedents from other museums and institutions, but he was the first to take the ideas so far, on such a scale and with such radicalism. His realized vision for the modern art museum formed a school. Pontus Hulén's museums were more than art venues. They were cultural centers in the broadest possible definition of that term.

This brings us to Pontus Hultén's international career. MNAM Centre Pompidou became the world's first mega-museum and, in the same way as Moderna Museet in Stockholm, but on a different scale, attracted audiences to modern art that few other than Hultén himself could have envisioned. With its widened perspectives, the Centre Pompidou drew new and broader, younger audiences to art and culture who would never before have thought of visiting a modern art museum. With its unprecedented success, the Centre Pompidou became the great model for other mega-museums and cultural centers around the world; it set the standard for the great modern art museum. In many ways, Moderna Museet in Stockholm can therefore be said to have served as a first experimental prototype for the "modern contemporary art museum" with its expanded, broader function.[10] In the great words of Calvin Tomkins: "Pontus was one of the handful of people[11] who contributed most to transforming art from a small clique phenomenon into a major part of daily life for the broader masses."[12]

In a 2012 profile interview, Tate Modern founder Sir Nicholas Serota says: "The opening of the Centre Pompidou, in 1977, had shown that new ideas for the museum experience could attract a much larger, younger and more diverse audience."

Pontus Hultén was a radical innovator also in terms of working methodology. What contradicts the oft-stated criticism that he stole ideas and failed to give his collaborators the credit they deserved is that, as the New York Times writes in its obituary of Hultén,[13] he is credited in the art world with creating the system that has become commonplace in modern art museums, with teams of young curators assembled to work on different exhibitions with great creative freedom. I have interviewed many of his younger collaborators and all of them, without exception, speak passionately about all they learned from Hultén and how the insights he gave them have influenced not only their careers but also their beliefs and lives.

Another invaluable legacy that Hultén left behind is the collections. He constantly returned to the importance of the collection for a museum, as an encyclopedia and protection against political and economic threats, trends and historical upheavals.

Hultén and his colleagues' achievements in building of the collection in Stockholm is well documented, and thoroughly discussed here. His contributions to the collections in Paris and also in Los Angeles are less widely known. Since Hultén's postings at MNAM in Paris and MOCA in Los Angeles took place later in time, in the seventies and early eighties, access to art historical masterpieces was more scarce than in the early sixties, when Moderna Museet's collection was built with the help of grants to *The Museum of Wishes* and other key purchases and gifts from Hultén's artist friends. The feat that MNAM was able to complete its collection under his leadership, and that he succeeded in laying the foundations for a completely new collection in Los Angeles with the help of his contacts among international collectors and patrons, therefore appear all the greater achievements. Many of the works acquired under Hultén's leadership are cornerstones and crowd-pleasers in these collections. Hultén often regretted that he was unable to convince his patrons in Venice and Bonn to invest in building their own collections — which partly explains why these institutions do not exist as the major international cultural centers that Hultén had the ambition to create.

In her catalog text for the Arcimboldo exhibition at the Centre Pompidou-Metz in 2021, curator Anne Horvath writes beautifully about a core of Hultén's philosophy, the interplay of the present and the past: "When he takes the helm of the Musée National d'Art Moderne, the collection suffers from major shortcomings: Surrealism, Dadaism, as well as American art, are almost entirely absent (...). Since

1974, Pontus Hultén had been working to enrich these collections to bear witness to the great currents of the past while supporting contemporary creation, with the aim of creating an open museum where 'the present is expressed and the past explains itself.'"[14]

Pontus Hultén's lasting contributions to modern art and the museum world are many. His bibliography of art-historically invaluable exhibition catalogs and his seminal work as an art publicist are far from least among these. Nineteen years after Hultén's death, many of his disciples are now influential leaders and key figures in the international art world, where they have carried on his legacy in various ways.

As a museum director and curator, Pontus Hultén made crucial contributions to many individual artists. Jean Tinguely and Niki de Saint Phalle are the obvious names, as their lives and careers were symbiotically intertwined with Hultén's. In international art circles, Hultén is widely recognized for his role in making Robert Rauschenberg and Andy Warhol superstars. Many more names could be listed.

Inevitably, however, there is one artist with whom Pontus Hultén must be associated first, foremost and last: his great hero Marcel Duchamp. The importance that Hultén had in Duchamp's return from oblivion to become the most influential artist of the twentieth century, and still today, is undeniable. Hultén was, in my view, the single most important person behind this powerful Duchamp comeback, which transformed contemporary art. Hultén's efforts helped this enigmatic artist to indirectly fulfill Guillaume Apollinaire's remarkable prophecy of "reuniting art with the people."[15]

Finally, the international perspective that Pontus Hultén adopted from the outset in his vision of art deserves to be emphasized. Hultén is most famous for being the first to introduce Pop Art and other American art to Europe on a larger scale. Less commonly known is his relentless efforts for Russian art — both for the avant-garde legacy and for contemporary art. Overall, Hultén's work as an exhibition maker, culminating in the Pingpong shows in Paris, aimed to clarify international historical connections and how these had propelled the evolution of art — how art had developed not in isolation but in exchange between metropolises. Artists and others have praised how Hultén's exhibitions opened up new global perspectives and made them realize historical connections. A recurrent depiction is that Hultén's mere presence put people and places in the context of international art history.

These epic historical perspectives on art and its role in society and history are neatly summarized by Suzanne Pagé, founding director of the Fondation Louis Vuitton in Paris: "Pontus was very intelligent. He had a unique knowledge and insight into the historical, intellectual and artistic contexts and an equally unique ability to tell this story in his exhibitions. With his broad perspective, he has influenced me more than anyone else."[16]

Over the years, I have become increasingly skeptical of the concept of genius, especially the male genius. I still have to consider Pontus Hultén a genius — in his understanding of art, society and historical movements, but also of the audience, as a communicator and educator. Although Hultén himself chose to abandon the easel and the thinner vapor to use the whole art world as his studio, I think he deserves to be mentioned alongside Marcel Duchamp and other of the greatest artists of the twentieth century.

Using Renoir as an example, Marcel Duchamp theorized that the addictive thinner fumes were one reason why many artists continued to paint and repeat their subjects into advanced old age.

I will let the final word go to one of Hultén's oldest and most longtime collaborators Carlo Derkert, portrayed as almost a punching bag for Pontus Hultén — hounded and, according to some, denied his rightful share of the credit in the construction of Moderna Museet. Troels Andersen in Copenhagen, a good friend of both Pontus Hultén and Carlo Derkert, confided that sometime in the 1980s he asked Derkert in a lunch queue what it had been like to work under Hultén. Andersen assumed that this collaboration could not have been easy, to which Derkert replied: "No, it wasn't. It probably wasn't easy to work with Cézanne either. But I'm very glad that I have done it."[17]

Gratitude

Wow, so many, hundreds of people around the world, to whom I owe thanks for making this story possible.

I must start with Stephan Andreae, artist and curator in Hasenbüchel outside Cologne. I am deeply grateful for Stephan's magnificent generosity in giving me free access to the material he compiled after his many hours of interviews with Pontus Hultén in 1997–1999, for the never-published autobiography that Hultén planned together with Andreae. This coherent life story, which I have quoted so lavishly, has provided a backbone that I could hardly have done without. Thank you Stephan! You played a big part in this book.

In Paris, Pontus Hultén's closest collaborator and successor Jean-Hubert Martin has been absolutely invaluable as a source, guide and support in the story of the culmination of Hultén's career, the so packed, charged, complicated era in Paris. Jean-Hubert has not only been tireless in his answers to a never-ending stream of questions, digitally and in many meetings, but has also put in considerable work of his own to be able to explain in detail particularly complicated processes and correct errors in the text. I and historiography owe a debt of gratitude to Jean-Hubert for having found it worthwhile to invest so much time and energy to make this documentation as true as possible, alongside his own extensive professional activities. Without Jean-Hubert, the story of Pontus in Paris could not have been told.

In Stockholm, Olle Granath has shouldered a similar responsibility, generously offering his time in numerous meetings and incessant correspondence. With his unique first-hand experience of working with Pontus Hultén from early in his career — "the heroic years" of Moderna Museet — and his keen analytical skills, Olle has been invaluable to the story, not only in the initial Swedish part but also as an observer of Hultén's international career at its various stages, when Granath as director of Moderna Museet collaborated with Hultén continuously. Thank you Olle for seeing from the beginning that it is important that this story is told. I especially appreciate that you have always mentioned how much fun it was too.

Daniel Birnbaum has been indispensable from the very beginning as a source, contact provider, inspiration, conversation partner and advisor. Daniel, then Moderna Museet's director, was the first person other than my wife and partner Christina that I told when I decided to embark on this work in the fall of 2013. Especially in the vulnerable initial phase, Daniel contributed many key international contacts which in turn led to so much more. Throughout these years, Daniel has continued to be encouraging and helpful, in the final phase as an important reader, including in his wise advice to carry out a final, laborious and beneficial cutting. Thank you also for introducing me to our now mutual friend Hans Ulrich Obrist, who has provided spiritual support and background with his classic interviews with Pontus Hultén and other contemporary pioneers of the modern museum world.

At La Motte, Pontus Hultén's longtime life partner Marie-Louise von Plessen has been another of my endlessly patient sources, supporters and advisors, in all my visits to La Motte, Marie-Louise's visit here in Sweden, and in uninterrupted correspondence. The constant connection to La Motte, Pontus Hultén's most enduring home, has given the story indispensable anchorage especially in its later parts. My stays at La Motte have deepened my understanding of Pontus Hultén's personality, life and career, on several levels.

Another person who has helped me throughout this long journey is Bloum Cardenas. With generosity, enthusiasm and humor, Bloum has been a constant support, a wonderful inspiration, connector and unique source of knowledge about Pontus Hultén's symbiotic relationship with Jean Tinguely and Niki de Saint Phalle, her grandmother, both of whose legacies Bloum represents — a major part of Hultén's life and career as the story has shown. Jana Shenefield at the Niki Charitable Art Foundation has been an unfailing collaborator with Bloum in responding to my constant stream of inquiries over the years.

In Los Angeles, since our first meeting in 2014, Jerry Sohn has taken on a similar responsibility, tireless in answering questions and contributing materials and contacts. Jerry's efforts and knowledge have been invaluable not only to the story of Los Angeles but to the entire latter part of Hultén's career, during which Jerry was his close friend, collaborator and confidant.

In New York, Julie Martin has been my main source of knowledge from the beginning — and even before — a key person in the knowledge of the New York sixties scene together with her husband Billy Klüver (a huge posthumous thank you to you too!). I have received many testimonies of the couple's standing in the New York art community. Special thanks also to Claes Oldenburg for our unforgettable day and evening together and for his generous help during my further work. Francis M. Neumann deserves great thanks for fruitful conversations and help with important material on Duchamp, another of the main topics of the story. I am deeply indebted to Calvin Tomkins, the great author and art writer with his unique contemporary historical perspective of more than sixty years, for a wonderful meeting, generous follow-up help, and, above all, for a large number of classic texts that form the basis of significant parts of this story.

In Basel, I have had another of my most important sources in Andres Pardey, who has also been patient from start to finish in responding to my requests with his unique knowledge. There have also been many enjoyable meetings!

In Copenhagen, art historian, museum director and Russia expert Troels Andersen has been an invaluable source for the story of Pontus Hultén's entire Russian endeavor, a core emphasis in the whole story. Art collector and dealer Peter Hvidberg was my most important source and interlocutor in the laborious work on the sad concluding chapter on the Brillo affair. Many thanks Peter for all the answers and for so generously giving me free access to your great unfinished research work!

In Paris, I must also pay special tribute to Hultén's colleagues Germain Viatte, also later his successor as director of the MNAM Centre Pompidou, and Jean-Yves Mock (the man, the myth!) for repeated invaluable interviews and recurrent help in correspondence — and for unforgettable meetings! Hultén's assistants Nathalie Meneau and Annick Boisnard were, especially in the early years, fundamental as sources and intermediaries. Perhaps his two closest collaborators over his career, Serge Fauchereau and Stanislas Zadora, have generously contributed key memories and insights. I would also like to express my special thanks to the artist Daniel Buren, colleagues Jean Clair, Jacques Caumont and former MNAM director Bernard Blistène for their recurring contributions, of the utmost importance to the story.

Since our meeting in 2015, Renzo Piano and his collaborator Francesca Bianchi have generously responded to repeated requests and contributed unique material to the book. Claude Mollard has kindly provided insights into the administrative aspects of Hultén's Parisian activities in meetings, conversations and correspondence. I would like to thank Jean-Philippe Arnould, my old friend from Stockholm and Paris, for his valuable help as an intermediary.

In Italy and Venice, Clarenza Catullo has been my most important guide and source of knowledge. In this country, where an important part of Pontus Hultén's life and career took place, I must also give special thanks to his collaborators Ida Gianelli and Germano Celant.

In London, I would like to posthumously thank Sir Richard Rogers, and his associate Jo Murtagh, for an unforgettable meeting and important information during the further work, and Sir Nicholas Serota for valuable conversations and friendly help in correspondence.

In Bonn and Germany, in addition to Stephan Andreae, Karin Weber has been indispensable as a facilitator and source. I would especially like to thank Kasper König, Hultén's colleague from his early career and also later, for our meetings in Cologne and Stockholm. Kay Heymer in Düsseldorf also deserves special thanks as a source and reader. Lutz Jahre in Mannheim has contributed important material and kind hospitality, in addition to his book on Pontus Hultén's printed museum, so important to the story.

In Saint Petersburg, another of these legends, Sergei "Afrika" Bugaev, has been my main entry point, thanks to which my visit to the city became such a memorable experience. The art historians and curators Ekaterina Andreeva and Olesia Turkina have contributed important insights and knowledge. For insights into Pontus Hultén's contributions to Russian art life — a large part of the story — I would also like to give special thanks to Andrei Erofeev, whom I unfortunately did not meet in person but whose text on *Moscow–Paris* enriches this important part of the tale.

Here at home in Stockholm and Sweden, I am also deeply indebted to Kerstin Ehrenberg, Gunilla Palmstierna-Weiss, Anna-Lena Wibom, Felix Hultén and Maj Hultén for important interviews during the initial phase of this work. From start to finish, Tonie Roos has generously offered not only invaluable information and insights but also mental support, love and joy. My old friend Lars Nittve was an important interlocutor long before the idea of this biography arose, during his time as director of Moderna Museet, and has been an irreplaceable source, reader and always kindly encouraging inspirer during the work. Carl Fredrik Hårleman and Dan Wolgers have contributed valuable memories and thoughts, especially from the later part of Hultén's life. Jan Öqvist added new information and energy to an important section. In Värnamo, Karin Lundh has been another patient, generous, inspiring and encouraging main source from Hultén's late career with its remarkable final chapter on the Vandals and Vandalorum. Your warmth has spurred me on!

At Moderna Museet and the Art Library in Stockholm, I owe many thanks. I would especially like to mention Anna Tellgren, Susana Mendoza Brackenhoff, John Peter Nilsson, Kaj Hällqvist, Stefan Ståhle, Teresa Hahr and Gitte Ørskou. Ann-Sofi Noring deserves special thanks for important encouragement and support at a delicate stage in the beginning.

For financial support, many thanks for scholarships from Helge Ax:son Johnson Foundation, Stiftelsen Längsmanska kulturfonden, The Authors' Copy Fund and the Royal Academy of Fine Arts. A very special thank you also to my dear old friend and club comrade Christer Gardell for very much needed, most generous extra support. His twin brother Rickard Gardell, my dear friend, has also contributed support for which I am deeply grateful.

Thanks also to: Daniel Abadie, Igor Antic, Irina Antonova, Richard Armstrong, William Aronowitsch, John Baldessari, Brian Balfour Oatts, Etienne Baulieu, Britta Birnbaum and the old colleagues at the National Museum, Tova Bjurström, Johanna Blomberg, Varis Bokalders, Jeanette Bonnier, Eli Broad, Kerry Brougher, Per Olov Börjeson, Nicola Caracciolo, Rosella Caracciolo, Johan Celsing, Annie Cohen Solal, Greg Colson, Jeff Colson, Furio Colombo, Elsian Cozens, Christina Dave, Yasha David, Carl Johan De Geer, François de Menil, Bernadette Dufrêne, Annagreta Dyring, Nathalie Elemento, Lars Englund, Jacques Faujour, Margot Flatow, Antonio Foscari, Gérard Fromanger, Paul B. Franklin, Frank Gehry, Marie Gispert, Dominique Gonzalez-Foerster, Daria Gorelik, Angela Green, Marina Gregotti, Vittorio Gregotti, Elena Gubanova, Tina Guy/Rauschenberg Estate, Bengt Göransson, Margareta Hellerberg, Sven-Olof Hellström, Ingvar Holm, Christian Holmén, Rebecca Horn, Ann Horvath, Pierre Huyghe, Gunnar Höglund, Louise Hultén, Seppi Imhof, Robert Irwin, Arata Isozaki, Wenzel Jacob, Bengt Jangfeldt, Jasper Johns, Alain Jouffroy, Lyn Kienholtz, Hélène Klein, Richard Koshalek, Rem Koolhaas, Lawrence Kumpf, Calypso Lejeune, Sivert Lindblom, Richard Long, Greg Mahoney, Anna-Stina

Malmborg, Harry Mathews, Paul Matisse, Catherine Matisse Monnier, Malitte Matta, Natascha Milovzorova, Patty Mucha (Oldenburg), Bo Nilsson, Håkan Nilsson, Anna Nordenström, Maja Oeri, Suzanne Osten, Alfred Pacquement, Suzanne Pagé, Giuseppina Panza, Imma Parada, Chiara Parisi, Ad Petersen, Philippe Parreno, Yevgeniya Petrova, Sarah Perry, Alain Pompidou, Mette Prawitz, Rebecca Quaytman, Klaus Rinke, James Rosenquist, Ed Ruscha, Märta Sahlberg, Sarkis, Paul Schimmel, Simone Schmid, Didier Schulmann, Arturo Schwarz, Tom Shannon, Paul Sebes, Eva Seta, Werner Spies, Daniel Spoerri, Björn Springfeldt, Milla Springfeldt, Pär Stolpe, Jan Svenungsson, François Taillade, Sophie Tottie, Xavier Veilhan, Susan Weil, Philippe Vergne, Jacques Villeglé, Marika Wachtmeister, Jerk Olof Werkmäster, Oliver Wolleh, Bill Öhrström, Micke Ölander, Johan Örn.

Too many of the all wonderful people I have met around the world for the story have passed away after our encounters and contacts. Peace and love on all your memories!

This book is not a creation of mine but of a group of amazing people. I would first like to thank Martin Kaunitz, who was my publisher when the work began and gave all the support and encouragement that was so badly needed. My dear current publisher, Sara Nyström, had the questionable pleasure of taking over the responsibility and has led the work superbly, with calm and experience. Elisabeth Watson Straarup, my brilliant editor, deserves special thanks for the copious, masterful work she has put into editing this monstrous manuscript, which was originally probably nearly double the size. Elisabeth has as much to do with this text as I do. Writing was the least of problems. Editing and abridging required considerably more work. As luck would have it, during a critical phase she had great help from Emma Bonnier, who contributed superb editing. Many thanks also to Nina Ulmaja for the splendid design, Tove Falk-Olsson for her work with the images, Maria Ulaner for final edit and Anna-Karin Korpi for communication. In general, I am full of gratitude to my publisher Albert Bonniers Förlag who has understood the importance of this history and invested the considerable efforts and resources required to execute it all without compromise, in a subject that cannot be counted among the broadest. I dare say that this is a cultural achievement.

For this English language edition, in has been an honor and pleasure to collaborate with Verlag der Buchandlung Walther und Franz König, Köln in Germany. A special thank you to Franz König and Walther König, the legendary book dealer. The partnership with König is most natural, based on old alliances. The sadly recently deceased Kasper König, one of Pontus Hultén's most distinguished younger colleagues and a main source in this story, was the brother of Walther König, himself a friend of Hultén's. It feels so satisfying to have done this together for the legacy. Thanks also to Nicole Rankers and Eva Möller. For the design and production of this edition, many thanks to the brilliant Nina Ulmaja, Christina Britton and Maria Ulaner, and to Claire Cahm for the final proof. For the translation, I sincerely thank the young, devilishly handsome stable genius Claes Britton.

My great gratitude also for the generous support of the co-publishers of the edition, the Center of Curatorial Studies at Bard College (CCS Bard) in New York and its executive director Tom Eccles. This institution, which includes the Hessel Museum and the CCS Bard Library and Archives, has made an important contribution to the legacy of Pontus Hultén. As part of the expansion of its Library and Archives with the new Keith Hering Wing, CCS Bard's newest classroom was named the Pontus Hultén Classroom, thanks to a generous contribution by the Marieluise Hessel Foundation. Thanks also to Shane Brennan and Ramona Rosenberg.

I am deeply grateful for the fantastic support in every way from the wonderful Centre Pompidou and its brilliant staff. I want to mention especially president Laurent Le Bon, chief curator Sophie Duplaix and her colleague Rita Cusimano, and director of publishing Guillaume Grandgeorges. Thank you all so very much for appreciating the importance of this story, encouraging me and giving me the honor of contributing in a small way to the great Centre Pompidou exhibition *Niki de Saint Phalle, Jean Tinguely, Pontus Hultén* at the Grand Palais in 2025–2026.

Another thanks also to Christer Gardell, my dear old friend, basketball club mate and protagonist for additional most generous support.

The idea to engage in this mastodon mission was not my own. I have two friends to thank who, in the space of a week in the autumn of 2013, made me realize that this was a calling for me (although, fortunately, I could not have dreamed at the time that it would take up twelve years of my life ...). Art critic Nils Forsberg sparked a notion that was clearly articulated a week later by my young friend Max Schiller, the fashion entrepreneur, who suddenly challenged me to write this biography.

Finally, in my immediate circle, I would like to thank my venerable father Sven Britton, who gave me life, energy and inspiration, and who took us to the Moderna Museet on all the weekends of my childhood, so decisive for me. Dad has been there from the first beginning as a conversation partner, reader and traveling companion, to our common old second hometown Los Angeles, to Uppland and to Saint Petersburg. This feels like my dad's book too!

Above all — endless thanks to my beloved wife, colleague and partner Christina Britton who, from start to finish, has been almost as deeply committed as myself and who has made sacrifices to enable this work. Christina has been my most important advisor and support, of course, far beyond her work on the visuals and supervision for the book — in all its details. Much love! Last but not least, a thank you note to my endlessly beloved soon-to-be-nineteen-year-old Siamese boy Morris, also known as "Groke," for all the thousands of hours of warm and soft companionship on the work sofas and beds over all these years ...

Notes

Preface

1. Maud Jacobsson and Anita Englund.
2. Love Jacobsson and Tom Britton.
3. Anna Tellgren ed., *The History Book. About Moderna Museet 1958–2008*. Moderna Museet/Steidl Verlag, Stockholm, 2008.
4. Max Schiller.

1 Origin

1. Eric Hultén, *Men roligt har det varit*. Generalstabens litografiska anstalts förlag, Stockholm, 1973.
2. Eric Hultén, 1973, p. 31.
3. Stephan Andreae, "Reisen mit Riesen/ Walking With Giants." Transcript of recorded conversations with Pontus Hultén for unpublished autobiography, La Motte, 1997–1999. © Stephan Andreae.
4. Eric Hultén, 1973, p. 98.
5. Eric Hultén, 1973, pp. 228–229.
6. Fredrik Sjöberg, *Flugfällan*, Bonnier Pocket, Stockholm, 2020. Note 4, p. 616.
7. The house was published in the Swedish Tourist Association's annual magazine in 1915.

2 Childhood, youth and education

1. Kerstin Ehrenberg, interview Stockholm, February 18, 2015.
2. Pontus Hultén archive, Moderna Museet, Stockholm. Box 1.3 Childhood and student years, folder 4.
3. Stephan Andreae, "Reisen mit Riesen/ Walking With Giants." Transcript of recorded conversations with Pontus Hultén for unpublished autobiography, La Motte, 1997–1999. © Stephan Andreae.
4. Jerk Olof Werkmäster, telephone interview, November 17, 2014.
5. Maj Hultén, interview Lidingö, February 17, 2015.
6. Maj Hultén, interview 2015.
7. Kerstin Ehrenberg, interview Stockholm, March 21, 2014.
8. 56 Kerstin Ehrenberg, interview 2014.
9. Gunilla Palmstierna-Weiss, interview Stockholm, March 12, 2014.
10. Maj Hultén, interview 2015.
11. Maj Hultén, interview 2015.
12. Maj Hultén, interview 2015.
13. Maj Hultén, interview 2015.
14. Maj Hultén, interview 2015.
15. Felix Hultén, interview Västra Frölunda, June 23, 2014.
16. Andreae, 1997–1999.
17. Pontus Hultén's archive, Box 1.3, Folder 4.
18. Ingvar Holm, interview Vik, June 24, 2014.
19. Ingvar Holm, interview 2014.
20. Ingvar Holm, interview 2014.
21. Andreae, 1997–1999.
22. Andreae, 1997–1999.
23. Ingvar Holm, interview 2014.
24. Andreae, 1997–1999.
25. Ingvar Holm, interview 2014.
26. Ingvar Holm, interview 2014.
27. Peter Kropotkin (1842–1921). Russian philosopher, historian, economist, sociologist, cultural geographer, anarchist and revolutionary.
28. Mikhail Bakunin (1814–1876). Russian anarchist and socialist. Considered one of the founders of the revolutionary socialist and anarchist tradition.
29. Olle Granath, interview Stockholm, February 16, 2015.
30. Maj Hultén, interview 2015.
31. Ingvar Holm, interview 2014.
32. Bernard Blistène, interview Paris, October 29, 2015.
33. Hans Eklund (1922–2019), art historian and museum man, for many years antiquarian at the City Museum in Stockholm.
34. Andreae, 1997–1999.
35. Andreae, 1997–1999.
36. Pontus Hultén archive, Moderna Museet, Stockholm. Box 1.3, folder 4. Childhood and student years.
37. Paul B. Franklin, ed., *Étant donné Marcel Duchamp No.11, Ulf Linde Marcel Duchamp Pontus Hultén en Suède & friends*, l'Association Marcel Duchamp, Paris, 2016, p. 11.
38. The Gattamelata is a 1447–1450 sculpture by Renaissance artist Donatello of the Venetian commander Erasmo da Narni, considered the prototype for equestrian monuments in the Western European tradition.
39. Paul B. Franklin, 2016, p. 11.
40. Certificate signed Erik Wettergren and Carl Nordenfalk, September 7, 1949, Pontus Hultén Archive, Moderna Museet, Stockholm. Box 1.3 Childhood and student years, folder 2.
41. Certificate signed Folke Holmér, March 16, 1950. Box 1.3 Childhood and study period, folder 2.
42. Kerstin Ehrenberg, interview 2014.
43. Kerstin Ehrenberg, interview 2014.
44. Baruch Spinoza, who came from a family of Jewish Portuguese refugees, grew up in Amsterdam where he spent twenty-three years was expelled from the Jewish community for his supposedly blasphemous ideas (the philosopher doubted, among other things, that the Torah scrolls were written by God). He later lived in The Hague. A period in Delft is not usually mentioned in biographical information on Spinoza.

45. Kerstin Ehrenberg, interview Stockholm, February 18, 2015.
46. Kerstin Ehrenberg, interview 2014.
47. Kerstin Ehrenberg, interview 2014.
48. Kerstin Ehrenberg, interview 2015.
49. Kerstin Ehrenberg, interview 2015.
50. Rolf Söderberg, *Mina konstnärsänkor och andra konstminnen*, Carlsson, Stockholm, 1999.
51. Rolf Söderberg, 1999, p. 73.
52. Kerstin Ehrenberg, interview 2015.
53. Anna-Lena Wibom, interview Lidingö, March 21, 2014.
54. Björn Springfeldt, interview Värmdö, March 13, 2014.
55. Gunilla Palmstierna-Weiss, interview Stockholm, March 12, 2014.
56. Kerstin Ehrenberg, interview 2014.

3 The career sets off in Stockholm and Paris

1. Kerstin Ehrenberg, interview Stockholm, February 18, 2015.
2. Pontus Hultén archive, Moderna Museet, Stockholm. Box 1.3, folder 4. Childhood and student years.
3. Stephan Andreae, "Reisen mit Riesen/ Walking With Giants." Transcript of recorded conversation with Pontus Hultén for unpublished autobiography, La Motte, 1997–1999. © Stephan Andreae.
4. Pontus Hultén, *Vermeer et Spinoza*, Éhoppe, Paris, 2002, translation from the Swedish by Lydie Rosseau. Foreword by Bernadette and Thierry Dufrène.
5. Andreae, 1997–1999.
6. Pontus Hultén archive, Moderna Museet, Stockholm. Box 1.3, folder 4. Childhood and student years.
7. Anna-Lena Wibom, interview Lidingö, March 21, 2014.
8. Andreae, 1997–1999.
9. Andreae, 1997–1999.
10. Andreae, 1997–1999.
11. Kerstin Ehrenberg, interview Stockholm, March 21, 2014.
12. Rolf Söderberg, *Mina konstnärsänkor och andra konstminnen*, Carlsson, Stockholm, 1999, p. 77.
13. Andreae, 1997–1999.
14. Pontus Hultén archive, Moderna Museet, Stockholm. Box 1.3 Childhood and student years, folder 5. Economy and family.
15. Stig Claesson, *Om vänskap funnes*, Albert Bonniers Förlag, Stockholm, 1981 / e-book 2013, p. 40.
16. See picture on p. 58.
17. Marcel Duchamp's often used expression 'retinal' meaning that something appeals only to the visual sense, not the brain.
18. Andreae, 1997–1999. The artist friend Hultén refers to is Per-Evert Taube.
19. Andreae, 1997–1999.
20. Andreae, 1997–1999.
21. Andreae, 1997–1999.
22. Description in K.G. Pontus Hultén, *Jean Tinguely Méta*, Moderna Museet/Verlag Ullstein GmbH, Stockholm/Frankfurt/ Berlin/Vienna, 1972, p. 10.
23. Henri Langlois (1914–1977), pioneering film antiquarian and historian. Founded the Cinémathèque française film and theater museum in Paris in 1936 with Georges Franju and Jean Mitry.
24. Andreae, 1997–1999.
25. Hans Ulrich Obrist, *A Brief History of Curating*, JRP-Ringier / Les Presses du Réel, Geneva, 2008, p. 35.
26. Hans Ulrich Obrist, 2008, p. 35.
27. Theodor "Teto" Ahrenberg, Ulla Ahrenberg, Folke Edwards, *Jag har ju ändå ägt en Picasso. Memoarer av Teto Ahrenberg, utmanaren, konstsamlaren, mecenaten.* Wahlström & Widstrand, Stockholm, 1993.
28. Pontus Hultén, interview Stockholm, December 17, 1996.
29. Jeanette Bonnier and William Aronowitsch, interview Stockholm, October 8, 2014.
30. Jeanette Bonnier and William Aronowitsch, interview 2014.
31. Jeanette Bonnier and William Aronowitsch, interview 2014.
32. Rolf Söderberg, 1999, p. 113.
33. *Objects or artifacts. Reality realized.* Galerie Samlaren, Stockholm, February-March, 1954.
34. Among others in Paul B. Franklin, ed., *Given Marcel Duchamp No.11. Ulf Linde Marcel Duchamp Pontus Hultén en Suède & friends*, l'Association Marcel Duchamp, Paris, 2016, p. 14. Also in my own interview with Ulf Linde, Stockholm, October 8, 2008.
35. Ulf Linde, "Reality Realized," Konstrevy, Volume 30, no. 3, 1954, p. 131.
36. Mette Prawitz, interview Stockholm, June 30, 2016.
37. Mette Prawitz, interview 2016.
38. Mette Prawitz, interview 2016.

4 A first breakthrough as exhibition maker

1. Kasper König, interview Cologne, November 30, 2015.
2. Stephan Andreae, "Reisen mit Riesen/ Walking With Giants." Transcript of recorded conversations with Pontus Hultén for unpublished autobiography, La Motte, 1997–1999. © Stephan Andreae.
3. Andreae, 1997–1999.
4. Calvin Tomkins, "Beyond the Machine. A Profile on Jean Tinguely." The New Yorker, February 1962.
5. K.G. Pontus Hultén, *Jean Tinguely Méta*, Moderna Museet/Verlag Ullstein GmbH, Stockholm/Frankfurt/Berlin/Vienna, 1972.
6. K.G. Pontus Hultén, 1972, p. 35.
7. Andreae, 1997–1999.
8. Hans Ulrich Obrist, *A Brief History of Curating*, JRP-Ringier / Les Presses du Réel, Geneva, 2008, p. 34.

9. Andreae, 1997–1999.
10. Pontus Hultén borrowed the Rotoreliefs from Henri-Pierre Roché (1879–1959), an art-trained journalist, writer, art collector and dealer from Paris who was a key figure in avant-garde art circles in both his hometown and New York during the war. Good friends with Picasso, Brancusi, Picabia and many other artists, notably Marcel Duchamp, with whom he moved to New York in 1916 and collaborated with on many projects. Published two novels late in life, *Jules et Jim* (1953) and *Two English Girls* (1956), both adapted for the screen by François Truffaut (1962 and 1971). Also wrote an unpublished novel, *Victor*, with the protagonist modeled on Duchamp (see Chapter 21).
11. Niki de Saint Phalle, "Ein Portrait von Pontus," *Das gedruckte Museum von Pontus Hultén. Kunstausstellungen und ihre Bücher*. Kunst- und Ausstellungshalle der Bundesrepublik Deutschland/Cantz, Bonn, 1996, pp. 102–103.
12. Andreae, 1997–1999.
13. Andreae, 1997–1999.
14. Mats B, interview Pontus Hultén. Moderna Museet (Friends of Moderna Museet magazine), no. 2, 1981.
15. K.G. Pontus Hultén, 1972, p. 35.
16. Hans Nordenström, "Preludes in the 50s." Olle Granath and Monica Nieckels eds., *Moderna Museet 1958–1983*, Moderna Museet, Stockholm, 1983, p. 26.
17. Hans Nordenström, 1983, p. 26.
18. Hans Nordenström, 1983, p. 26.
19. Heidi E. Violand-Hobi, *Jean Tinguely, life and work*, Prestel, Munich/New York, 1995, p. 45.
20. *Museum Tinguely Basel. The Collection*, Museum Tinguely Basel / Kehrer Verlag Heidelberg Berlin, 2012, p. 400.
21. Izvestiya, Moscow, March 1, 1963, p. 2.
22. Hans Nordenström, 1983, p. 26.
23. Among others, Hans Ulrich Obrist, *A Brief History of Curating*, JRP-Ringier / Les Presses du Réel, Geneva, 2008, p. 33.
24. Hans Nordenström, 1983, pp. 22–28.
25. Hans Nordenström, 1983, p. 24.
26. Hans Nordenström, 1983, p. 24.

5 Moderna Museet begins

1. Among others, Hans Ulrich Obrist, *A Brief History of Curating*, JRP-Ringier / Les Presses du Réel, Geneva, 2008, p. 33.
2. Among others, Serge Fauchereau, "Conversation avec Pontus Hultén," Les Cahiers du musée national d'art moderne, no. 141, *Hommage à Pontus Hultén*, Éditions du Centre Pompidou, Paris, fall 2017, pp. 8–29.
3. Calvin Tomkins, *Duchamp: A Biography*, Henry Holt and Company, New York, 1996, p. 227.
4. Tomkins, 1996, p. 226.
5. 69th Regiment Armory, 68 Lexington Avenue, between 25th and 26th Streets, opened in 1906.
6. Société Anonyme Inc. had the subtitle "Museum of Modern Art," predating its hated rival of that name by nine years, when MoMA opened in 1929.
7. Calvin Tomkins, 1996, pp. 312–313.
8. Calvin Tomkins, 1996, pp. 312–313.
9. Yves Klein, through his contacts, had succeeded in hiring these guards, which caused great outrage in conservative circles in Paris.
10. Arman is the stage name of Armand Fernandez (1928–2005), a childhood friend of Yves Klein from their shared hometown of Nice.
11. Christo, soubriquet for Christo Vladimorov Javaneff (1935–2020) was born in Bulgaria. His wife, Jeanne-Claude Denat de Guillebon (1935–2009), was born on the same day as Christo in Morocco. The couple met in Paris in the late fifties. They worked together for a long time under the stage name Christo which they later changed to Christo and Jeanne-Claude.
12. According to information I have received from several sources, this was due to Pontus Hultén's difficulties in cooperating with Yves Klein's widow, the artist Rotraut Klein-Moquay, born Rotraut Uecker and sister of the German artist Günther Uecker.
13. Rolf Söderberg, *Mina konstnärsänkor och andra konstminnen*, Carlsson, Stockholm, 1999, pp. 71–72.
14. Pontus Hultén archive, Moderna Museet, Stockholm. Box 1.3, folder 4. Childhood and student years.
15. A group also called The Young, formed in 1907 by artists mainly from the Swedish Artists' Association's 3rd school of painting, including Isaac Grünewald and the leading figure Birger Simonsson.
16. The Museum of Visual Culture in Moscow, *Muzej zjivopisnoj kultury*, is considered the world's first modern museum, founded in 1919 by leading artists of the Russian avant-garde, including Wassily Kandinsky, Kazimir Malevich, Vladimir Tatlin and Aleksandr Rodchenko. The museum, which operated until 1929, is said to have been built on ideas so radical that some of them have yet to be realized.
17. Otte Sköld (1894–1958) was born to missionary ancestors in Wuchang, China. In addition to his work as an artist, he spent much of his life teaching at art schools, both in Stockholm and Paris. Sköld was a professor at the Royal Institute of Art and director of the National Museum from 1950 until his death in 1958. He is considered the founder of Moderna Museet.
18. Emma Spitzer (1870–1941) was a ceramicist and sculptor.
19. Pontus Hultén, "Fem fragment ur museets

historia. Moderna Museets tillkomst och första år." Olle Granath and Monica Nieckels eds., *Moderna Museet 1958–1983*, Moderna Museet, Stockholm, 1983, p. 30.

20. Pontus Hultén, 1983, p. 30.
21. The New Objectivity, Die Neue Sachlichkeit, an originally German, later international movement in art, literature, architecture, film and music. The term was coined in 1923 to describe German Expressionist artists who, during the interwar period in the Weimar Republic, moved to a more detailed, realistic style.
22. Stephan Andreae, "Reisen mit Riesen/ Walking With Giants." Transcript of recorded conversations with Pontus Hultén for unpublished autobiography, La Motte, 1997–1999. © Stephan Andreae.
23. Rolf Söderberg, *Otte Sköld*, Kungl. Boktryckeriet PA Norstedt & Söner, Stockholm, 1968, pp. 137–150.
24. Rolf Söderberg, 1968, among others s. 167–181.
25. Pontus Hultén, 1983, p. 31.
26. Pontus Hultén, 1983, p. 31.
27. Pontus Hultén, interview Stockholm, December 16, 1996.
28. Pontus Hultén, 1983, p. 31.
29. Pontus Hultén, 1983, p. 31.
30. Pontus Hultén, 1983, p. 31.
31. Pontus Hultén, 1983, p. 31.
32. The year of this never-opened exhibition, usually called *Total Art*, is listed in several sources as 1956. However, Per Olof Ultvedt's son Fredrik Ultvedt claims that this is a recurring mistake and that the exhibition was in fact built in the summer of 1958.
33. Hans Nordenström, 1983, p. 28.
34. Per-Olof Olsson, "Moderna Museet." Olle Granath and Monica Nieckels eds., *Moderna Museet 1958–1983*. Moderna Museet, Stockholm, 1983, p. 17.
35. Per-Olof Olsson, 1983, p. 21.
36. Per-Olof Olsson, 1983, p. 21.
37. Per-Olof Olsson, 1983, p. 21.
38. Pontus Hultén, 1983, p. 31.
39. Pontus Hultén, 1983, p. 31.
40. Anna Tellgren, ed., *Historieboken. Om Moderna Museet 1958–2008*, Moderna Museet/Steidl Verlag, Stockholm, 2008, pp. 374–380.
41. Pontus Hultén, interview Stockholm, December 17, 1996.
42. Öyvind Fahlström, "Moderna Museet — Från pompa och ståt till informationscentrum," Olle Granath and Monika Nieckels eds., *Moderna Museet 1958–1983*. Moderna Museet, Stockholm, 1983, p. 169.
43. Pontus Hultén, 1983, p. 32.
44. Pontus Hultén, 1983, p. 32.
45. Pontus Hultén, 1983, p. 32.
46. Pontus Hultén, 1983, p. 32.
47. Pontus Hultén, 1983, p. 32.
48. Pontus Hultén, 1983, p. 32.
49. Pontus Hultén, 1983, p. 33.
50. Among other things, as director of *A Day in the City* in 1956, together with Hans Nordenström. https://www.filmarkivet.se/movies/en-dag-i-staden-varlden-genom-kameraorat/?jwsource=cl
51. The Terrassen cinema was located on Birger Jarlsgatan, in the premises that have long since become the Church of the Cross, with only the entrance preserved.
52. Pontus Hultén, 1983, p. 33.
53. Pontus Hultén, interview Stockholm, December 16, 1996.
54. Pontus Hultén, interview December 16, 1996.
55. Undated program sheet, Pontus Hultén archive, Box 4.1, folder 23.
56. Viking Eggeling (1880–1925), artist and experimental film director. Internationally associated with both Dadaism, Constructivism and early abstract art. Born in Lund but moved to Germany at the age of sixteen to pursue a career as an artist. Lived alternately in Milan, Zürich, Paris and Berlin. Was originally a Cubist but developed in a more radically experimental direction. Became good friends and collaborator with many of the leading artists and writers of the early twentieth-century avant-garde, including Tristan Tzara, Hans Arp, Richard Huelsenbeck, Sophie Taeuber-Arp, Hannah Höch and Amedeo Modigliani. His 1924 film *Diagonal Symphony* is internationally recognized as one of the most influential abstract works in the history of experimental film.
57. Pontus Hultén, 1983, p. 38.
58. Pontus Hultén, interview December 16, 1996.
59. Pontus Hultén, 1983, p. 34.
60. Pontus Hultén, 1983, p. 32.
61. Carl Nordenfalk (1907–1992) was director of the National Museum from 1958 to 1968. He is considered by many to be one of Sweden's most internationally renowned art historians at the time, noted for his work on medieval writings but also on artists such as Rembrandt and Vincent van Gogh.
62. According to Johan Nordenfalk.
63. Pontus Hultén, 1983, inter alia p. 34.
64. Pontus Hultén, 1983, p. 34.
65. Le Corbusier (1887–1965), pen name of Charles-Édouard Jeanneret.
66. Le Corbusier. Architecture, paintings, sculptures, tapestries, drawings. Moderna Museet August 28–September 28, 1958. In collaboration with the Swiss architects Willy Boesiger and Ello Katzenstein.
67. Pontus Hultén, interview Stockholm, February 16, 1996.
68. Pontus Hultén, interview, February 16, 1996.
69. Pontus Hultén, 1983, p. 34.
70. Anna-Lena Wibom, interview Lidingö, March 21, 2014.
71. Quoted in Knut Bergengren, *När skönheten kom till byn*, Aldus, Stockholm, 1976.
72. Pontus Hultén, 1983, p. 34.
73. Malitte Matta, interview Paris, January 7, 2015.

74. Malitte Matta, interview, January 7, 2015.
75. Pontus Hultén, 1983, p. 34, and interview Pontus Hultén, Stockholm, December 16, 1996.
76. Roberto Matta was introduced at the exhibition as Sebastian Matta. The exhibition was on display from October 24 to November 22.
77. Carl Nordenfalk, *Mest om konst*, Natur och Kultur, Stockholm, 1996 (memoirs published posthumously).
78. Nordenfalk, 1996, pp. 233–235.
79. Nordenfalk, 1996, p. 234.
80. Nordenfalk, 1996, p. 234.

6 The New York Connection

1. Pontus Hultén, "Fem fragment ur museets historia. Moderna Museets tillkomst och första år." Olle Granath and Monika Nieckels eds., *Moderna Museet 1958–1983*. Moderna Museet, Stockholm, 1983, p. 35.
2. Barbro Schultz, "Party for Öyvind," Group Exhibition Catalogue, Schultz Förlag AB, Stockholm, 2021, p. 13.
3. Among others Marianne Hultman, "Our man in New York: An interview with Billy Klüver about the collaboration with Moderna Museet," Anna Tellgren ed., *The History Book. About Moderna Museet 1958–2008*. Moderna Museet/Steidl Verlag, Stockholm, 2008, p. 238.
4. For example, Hultén in Granath and Nieckels, 1983, pp. 35–36.
5. Pontus Hultén, interview Stockholm, December 16, 1996.
6. Olle Granath, e-mail, April 3, 2020.
7. For example, Pontus Hultén, interview Stockholm, December 17, 1996, and Hultén in Granath and Nieckels, 1983, pp. 35–36.
8. Among others Pontus Hultén, interview Stockholm, December 17, 1996.
9. For example, Hultman in Tellgren, 2008, p. 238, and Hultén in Granath and Nieckels, 1983, pp. 35–36.
10. Richard Armstrong, interview New York, September 9, 2014.
11. Billy Klüver, interview Stockholm, probably September 1998.
12. The art form is said to have originated from a mushroom picking walk Allan Kaprow took with John Cage and George Brecht in 1957. He began attending Cage's composition classes in New York and was assigned as homework to compose musical pieces, which he developed into full-scale events he called "happenings." In 1959, Kaprow presented his first major public event, "18 happenings in 6 Parts," at the Reuben Gallery in New York (www.tate.org.uk/art/art-terms/h/happening/happening).
13. Claes Oldenburg, interview New York, September 8, 2014.
14. Claes Oldenburg, interview New York, September 8, 2014.
15. Among others, Ulf Linde, interview Stockholm, October 8, 2008.
16. For example, Hultén in Granath and Nieckels, 1983, pp. 35–36, and Pontus Hultén, interview Stockholm, December 17, 1996.

7 Towards Art in Motion

1. Carl Nordenfalk, *Mest om konst*, Natur och Kultur, Stockholm, 1996, pp. 233–235.
2. Hultén in Granath and Nieckels, 1983, pp. 34–35.
3. Jacques Villon, *Paintings and Prints 1902–1959*. Moderna Museet, Stockholm, March 2–April 3, 1960.
4. Hultén in Granath and Nieckels, 1983, p. 34.
5. Hultén in Granath and Nieckels, 1983, p. 34.
6. *Siri Derkert*, Moderna Museet, Stockholm, April 27–June 7, 1960.
7. Hultén in Granath and Nieckels, 1983, p. 34.
8. Siri Derkert's decoration of Östermalmstorg metro station, carvings in concrete with motifs from the struggle for the women's, environmental and peace movements, was executed in 1961–1965.
9. *Anna Casparsson. Embroidery*. Moderna Museet, Stockholm, October 10–November 13, 1960.
10. Olle Granath, interview Stockholm, October 23, 2015.
11. *Hannah Ryggen. Tapestries 1933–1961*, Moderna Museet, Stockholm, March 3–March 11, 1962.
12. *Sigrid Hjertén 1885–1948, Retrospective*, Moderna Museet, Stockholm, April 18–May 31, 1964. *Barbara Hepworth*. November 20–December 27, 1964.
13. *Sam Francis*, Moderna Museet, Stockholm, September 19-October 30, 1960.
14. Sam Francis, exhibition catalog no. 12, Moderna Museet, Stockholm, 1960.
15. Moderna Museet archive, folder "Art in Motion," 1961.
16. Daniel Spoerri, interview Vienna, December 6, 2014.
17. Édition MAT is short for of *Multiplication d'art transformable* (roughly Multiplication of transformable art).
18. Daniel Spoerri, interview Vienna, December 6, 2014.
19. Andres Pardey, "Curating *Bewogen Beweging*: The Exchange Between Daniel Spoerri, Jean Tinguely, Pontus Hultén and Willem Sandberg." Tiziana Caianiello and Mattijs Visser eds., *The Artist As Curator. Collaborative Initiatives in the International Zeromovement 1957–1967*, Düsseldorf, 2015, pp. 221–235.
20. Pardey, in Caianiello and Visser, 2015, pp. 221–235.
21. Pardey, in Caianiello and Visser, 2015, pp. 221–235.
22. Pardey, in Caianiello and Visser, 2015, pp. 221–235.

23. Pardey, in Caianiello and Visser, 2015, pp. 221–235.
24. Willem Sandberg, letter to Daniel Spoerri, August 15, 1960, Stedelijk Museum archive, Amsterdam, access number 30041, file 3980, Stadsarchief Amsterdam. Archival material for the exhibition *Bewogen Beweging* 1961 is archived in files 3980-3983 in the archives of the Stedelijk Museum, housed in the Stadsarchief Amsterdam, with access number 30041, henceforth Stedelijk archive (from Andres Pardey).
25. Daniel Spoerri, interview Vienna, December 6, 2014.
26. Daniel Spoerri, interview Vienna, December 6, 2014.
27. Letter Daniel Spoerri to Willem Sandberg, August 28, 1960. Stedelijk archive, Amsterdam (Andres Pardey).
28. Pardey, in Caianiello and Visser, 2015, pp. 221–235.
29. Letter Daniel Spoerri to Willem Sandberg, October 4, 1960. Stedelijk archive, Amsterdam (Andres Pardey).
30. Letter Daniel Spoerri to Willem Sandberg, October 4, 1960. Stedelijk archive, Amsterdam (Andres Pardey).
31. Letter Daniel Spoerri to Willem Sandberg, October 4, 1960. Stedelijk archive, Amsterdam (Andres Pardey).
32. Letter Pontus Hultén to Willem Sandberg, October 14, 1960, Stedelijk archive, Amsterdam (Andres Pardey).
33. Letter from Daniel Spoerri, Jean Tinguely and Pontus Hultén to Willem Sandberg, October 19, 1960, Stedelijk archive, Amsterdam (Andres Pardey).
34. Pardey, in Caianiello and Visser, 2015, pp. 221–235.
35. Letter Pontus Hultén to Willem Sandberg, January 11, 1961, Stedelijk archive, Amsterdam (Andres Pardey).
36. Letter Pontus Hultén to Willem Sandberg, January 11, 1961, Stedelijk archive, Amsterdam (Andres Pardey).
37. Pontus Hultén, interview Stockholm, December 16, 1996.
38. Pontus Hultén, interview Stockholm, December 16, 1996.
39. Among others, Daniel Spoerri, interview Vienna, December 6, 2014.
40. Pardey, in Caianiello and Visser, 2015, pp. 221–235.
41. Hultén in Granath and Nieckels, 1983, p. 36.
42. Hultén in Granath and Nieckels, 1983, p. 36.
43. Hultén in Granath and Nieckels, 1983, p. 36.
44. Anna-Lena Wibom, interview Lidingö, March 21, 2014.
45. Alexander Calder, "The Four Elements," 1937/1961. Moderna Museet Stockholm. Donated in 1967 by the artist and Allan Skarne, restored and rebuilt in 2001. NMSK 1966.
46. Robert Rauschenberg, "Money Thrower for Tinguely's H.T.N.Y. (Homage to New York)," 1960. Moderna Museet Stockholm. Donation Pontus Hultén 2005. MOM/2005/585.
47. Program sheet *Homage to New York. A selfconstructing and selfdestroying work of art conceived by Jean Tinguely. The Museum of Modern Art Sculpture Garden, March 17, 1960, 6.30–7 p.m.* The short texts in the program leaflet are signed Peter Sele, Alfred H. Barr Jr, K.G. Hultén, Dore Ashton, Richard Huelsenbeck and Marcel Duchamp.
48. Calvin Tomkins, *Off the Wall. A Portrait of Robert Rauschenberg*. Picador, New York, 1980/2005, p. 155.
49. Tomkins, 1980/2005, p. 155.
50. Daniel Spoerri, interview Vienna, December 6, 2014. Jacques Villeglé, Interview Paris, February 15, 2017.
51. Christiane Weidemann, *Niki de Saint Phalle*, Prestel Verlag, Munich/London/New York, 2014, p. 39.
52. *Tir séanse TV suédoise*, c. May 14, 1961, filmed by Torbjörn Axelman for SVT Film, Sveriges Television on a "courtyard in Stockholm" (probably outside Moderna Museet). *Tir séanse Stockholm*. Stäket's sandy roof, Värmdö, May 23, 1961. Source: Niki Charitable Art Foundation.
53. Niki de Saint Phalle, "Tableau tir," 1961. Donation from the artist in 1972. NMSK 2134.
54. Among others, "Tir de Jasper Johns," 1961, Donation 2005 from Pontus Hultén, MOM 2005/217, and "Martyr nécessaire (Saint Sébastien)," now in private collection.
55. Anna Lundström, "Art in Motion. The different layers of an exhibition." Anna Tellgren, ed., *Pontus Hultén and Moderna Museet. The formative years*, Moderna Museet, Stockholm, 2017, p. 75.
56. Lundström, 2017, pp. 75–78.
57. Niki de Saint Phalle, "Ein Portrait von Pontus," *Das gedruckte Museum von Pontus Hultén. Kunstausstellungen und ihre Bücher*. Kunst- und Ausstellungshalle der Bundesrepublik Deutschland/Cantz, Bonn, 1996, p. 103.
58. Leif Eriksson, *Duchamp in Sweden 1933–1970: A Critical Review*, Malmö, 2000, updated 2019. https://www.toutfait.com/duchamp-in-sweden-1933-1970-a-critical-review/
59. Hans Ulrich Obrist, *A Brief History of Curating*, JRP-Ringier/Les Presses du Réel, Geneva, 2008, p. 38.
60. Obrist, 2008, p. 38.
61. Pontus Hultén, interview Stockholm, December 16, 1996.
62. Now called Cirkus Djurgården.
63. Billy Klüver and Robert Rauschenberg, "Art in Motion — a combined memory." Olle Granath and Monika Nieckels eds., *Moderna Museet 1958–1983*. Moderna Museet, Stockholm, 1983, pp. 143–150.
64. Klüver and Rauschenberg, in Granath and Nieckels, 1983, p. 146.

65. Niki de Saint Phalle and Robert Rauschenberg, "Painting made through dance," acrylic on canvas, 207 x 413.5 centimeters, Moderna Museet Stockholm, Pontus Hultén donation 2005. MOM/2005/592.
66. Björn Springfeldt, interview Värmdö, March 13, 2014.
67. Sven Erixon, "Misplaced exhibition," Dagens Nyheter, August 17, 1961.
68. Hultén in Granath and Nieckels, 1983, p. 36.
69. Bror Hjorth, "Art in Motion," Dagens Nyheter, August 30, 1961.
70. Hultén in Granath and Nieckels, 1983, p. 36.
71. Hultén in Granath and Nieckels, 1983, p. 36.
72. Moderna Museet archive, folder *Art in Motion*.
73. Hultén in Granath and Nieckels, 1983, p. 36.
74. Pontus Hultén, interview Stockholm, December 16, 1996.

8 Marcel Duchamp in Stockholm

1. A source for several international texts is the ambitious English-language chronology of Duchamp's appearances in the Swedish press from thirties onwards published in 2000 by artist Leif Eriksson, founder of The Swedish Archive of Artists' Books in Malmö, entitled *Duchamp in Sweden 1933–1970: A Critical Review*. https://www.toutfait.com/duchamp-in-sweden-1933-1970-a-critical-review/
2. Paul B. Franklin ed., *Étant donné Marcel Duchamp No. 11*, "Marcel Duchamp in Sweden: Ulf Linde, Pontus Hultén & Friends," Association pour L'Étude de Marcel Duchamp, Paris, 2016.
3. Paul B. Franklin, interviews with Ulf Linde 2012-2013, Paul B. Franklin ed., *Étant donné Marcel Duchamp No. 11*, "Marcel Duchamp in Sweden: Ulf Linde, Pontus Hultén & Friends," Association pour L'Étude de Marcel Duchamp, Paris, 2016, pp. 10–43.
4. Franklin, 2016, p. 14.
5. Franklin, 2016, p. 77.
6. For example, *Pontus Hultén's collection ...*, Moderna Museet, Stockholm, 2004, p. 66.
7. Franklin, 2016, p. 96.
8. Pontus Hultén, "Five fragments from the history of the museum. The birth and first years of Moderna Museet." Olle Granath and Monika Nieckels eds., *Moderna Museet 1958–1983*. Moderna Museet, Stockholm, 1983, p. 36.
9. Among others, Stephan Andreae, "Reisen mit Riesen/Walking With Giants." Transcript of recorded conversations with Pontus Hultén for unpublished autobiography, La Motte, 1997–1999. © Stephan Andreae.
10. Kasark no. 4, April 1960, "A work of art has no price."
11. Franklin, 2016, p. 96.
12. Franklin, 2016, p. 96.
13. Marcel Duchamp, *Rotoreliefs*, 1935. Moderna Museet, Stockholm, purchase 1960. NMB 1799.
14. Robert Lebel, *On Marcel Duchamp*, Trianon Press, Paris, 1959.
15. Franklin, 2016, p. 97.
16. Letter Per Olof Ultvedt to Arnold Fawcus, January 18, 1960. Trianon Press Archive, University of California, Santa Cruz.
17. Ulf Linde, Per Olof Ultvedt, "Study for the reconstruction of Marcel Duchamp: La mariée mise à nu par ses célibataires, même," 1915–1923/1959–1960. Moderna Museet, Stockholm. Donation in 2011 from Per Thelander and Louise Lidströmer. REPLY 2.
18. Letter Pontus Hultén to David Sellin, August 3, 1960. Philadelphia Museum of Art Archives, Philadelphia. Reproduced in Franklin, 2016, p. 100.
19. Wall text for "Fresh Widow" in the *Dada* exhibition at the Museum of Modern Art, New York, 2006, moma.org.
20. Ulf Linde, *Marcel Duchamp*, Rabén & Sjögren, Stockholm, 1986, p. 11.
21. Invitation card "Marcel Duchamp," May 1960, Pontus Hultén Archive, Moderna Museet, Stockholm, 4.1 Museums and Art Galleries: 1 A-C. Text reproduced in Franklin, 2016, p. 103.
22. Pontus Hultén, Magnus Wibom, Per Olof Ultvedt, "Marcel Duchamp Rotary Glass Plaques," 1920/1960-61. Moderna Museet, Stockholm. Donation by Pontus Hultén, Magnus Wibom and Per Olof Ultvedt, 1961. Object number NMSK 1790.
23. Olle Granath, interview Stockholm, May 7, 2021.
24. In Marcel Duchamp's original of "The Large Glass," which is in the collection of the Philadelphia Museum of Art, the frame is made not of copper but of aluminum. www.philamuseum.org/collection/object/54149
25. Man Ray, "Dust Breeding," 1920. Among other, Metropolitan Museum of Art, New York. www.metmuseum.org/art/collection/search/271420
26. Calvin Tomkins, *Duchamp: A Biography*, Henry Holt and Company, New York, 1996, pp. 305–308.
27. Pierre Cabanne, *Dialogues With Marcel Duchamp*, Thames and Hudson, London, 1971, p. 75.
28. Tomkins, 1996, pp. 305–308.
29. Letter Marcel Duchamp to Pontus Hultén, August 21, 1960. Private collection.
30. Linde, 1986, p. 26.
31. Pontus Hultén, interview Stockholm, December 17, 1996.
32. *Is everything art? Contributions to the Great Art Debate*. Bonniers, Stockholm, 1963.
33. Rolf Blylods and Eric H. Olson (Franklin, 2016, p. 107).
34. Franklin, 2016, p. 113.
35. Pontus Hultén, interview Stockholm, December 17, 1996.
36. Linde, 1986, p. 32.

37. Linde, 1986, p. 32.
38. Linde, 1986, p. 32.
39. Franklin, 2016, p. 113.
40. Linde, 1986, p. 32.
41. Unpublished memories written down by Oscar Reutersvärd in 1979 and sent to Leif Eriksson. Translated by Jan Hannerz and published in Franklin, 2016, p. 114.
42. Olle Granath, interview Stockholm, September 7, 2016.
43. Pontus Hultén, interview Stockholm, December 17, 1996.
44. Pontus Hultén, interview Stockholm, December 17, 1996.
45. Pontus Hultén, interview Stockholm, December 16, 1996.
46. Pontus Hultén, interview Stockholm, December 16, 1996.
47. Pontus Hultén, interview Stockholm, December 16, 1996.
48. Pontus Hultén, interview Stockholm, December 16, 1996.
49. Pontus Hultén, interview Stockholm, December 16, 1996.
50. Joan Miró, "La Figure rouge," 1927. Purchase 1967 (*The Museum of Wishes*). NM6079.
51. Ulf Linde, "Memoirs," Olle Granath and Monika Nieckels eds., *Moderna Museet 1958–1983*. Moderna Museet, Stockholm, 1983, pp. 61–63.
52. Linde, in Granath and Nieckels, 1983, pp. 61–63.
53. Linde, in Granath and Nieckels, 1983, pp. 61–63.
54. Salvador Dalí "The Enigma of William Tell," 1933. Moderna Museet, Stockholm. Purchase 1967 (*The Museum of Wishes*). NM 6069.
55. Pontus Hultén, interview Stockholm, December 16, 1996.
56. Marianne Hultman, "Our man in New York. An interview with Billy Klüver on the collaboration with Moderna Museet," Anna Tellgren ed., *The History Book. About Moderna Museet 1958–2008*. Moderna Museet/Steidl Verlag, Stockholm, 2008, p. 243.
57. Olle Granath, interview Stockholm, April 23, 2020.
58. Linde, 1986, p. 57.
59. Letter from Marcel Duchamp to Ulf Linde, December 12, 1962, Ulf Linde archive.
60. Franklin, 2016, pp. 115–124.
61. Ulf Linde, *Från kart till fallfrukt*. Albert Bonniers förlag, Stockholm, 2008, p. 114.
62. Linde, 1986, p. 54.
63. Linde, 1986, p. 54.
64. Franklin, 2016, p. 126.
65. Franklin, 2016, p. 126.
66. Franklin, 2016, p. 125.
67. Franklin, 2016, p. 126.
68. Franklin, 2016, p. 126.
69. Arturo Schwarz, interview Milan, April 18, 2016.
70. Franklin, 2016, p. 76.
71. P4 Stockholm, "Disappeared Duchamp sketch worth one million was found in Sweden," May 31, 2018, 09:44. sverigesradio.se/artikel/6966886

9 New York goes Stockholm

1. Pontus Hultén, interview Stockholm, December 16, 1996.
2. *Pull My Daisy* from 1959 is directed by Alfred Leslie and Robert Frank, an adaptation of part of Jack Kerouac's play *Beat Generation*. Kerouac improvises the narration. The cast includes poets Allen Ginsberg and Peter Orlovsky, and artist Larry Rivers.
3. Pontus Hultén, interview Stockholm, December 16, 1996.
4. Pontus Hultén, interview Stockholm, December 16, 1996.
5. Ulf Linde, interview Stockholm, October 8, 2008.
6. Anna-Lena Wibom, interview Lidingö, March 21, 2014.
7. *American Pop Art. 106 forms of love and despair*. Moderna Museet, Stockholm, February 29–April 12, 1964.
8. Pontus Hultén, interview Stockholm, December 16, 1996.
9. *New American Cinema*, Moderna Museet, Stockholm, March 17–April 1, 1964. Films by Ron Rice, Stan Brakhage, Ken Jacobs, Andy Warhol, Jack Smith, Adolfas Mekas, Gregory Markopoulus, George Landow and Kenneth Anger.
10. Pontus Hultén, interview Stockholm, December 16, 1996.
11. Pontus Hultén, "The New York Connection." Olle Granath and Monika Nieckels eds., *Moderna Museet 1958–1983*. Moderna Museet, Stockholm, 1983, p. 57.
12. Among others, Allan Kaprow, *Assemblage, Environments and Happenings*, H.N. Abrams, New York, 1966.
13. *18 Happenings in 6 Parts*, Reuben Gallery, New York, October 1959. Pontus Hultén mentions this in Hultén, in Granath and Nieckels, 1983, p. 52.
14. Robert Rauschenberg disliked the term "happening" and preferred to call his stage performances "events."
15. Hultén, in Granath and Nieckels, 1983, p. 56.
16. *Five New York Evenings*, Moderna Museet, Stockholm, September 8–14, 1964. Program: September 8: Merce Cunningham, "Atlas Eclipticalis." To music by John Cage. September 10: John Cage and David Tudor play various musical pieces. September 11: Yvonne Rainer and Robert Morris, "An Evening of Talking and Dancing." September 13: Alex Hay, "Colorado Plateau." Robert Rauschenberg, "Shotput" and "Elgin Tie." Öyvind Fahlström, from "Mellanöl." Steve Paxton, "I would like to make a phone

call." September 14: Merce Cunningham, "Variations IV." To the music of John Cage.

17. Calvin Tomkins, *Off the Wall. A Portrait of Robert Rauschenberg*. Picador, New York, 1980/2005, p. 211.
18. Tomkins, 1980/2005, p. 211.
19. Anna-Stina Malmborg and Gunnar Höglund, interview Stockholm, January 13, 2016.

10 The Museum of Wishes — a unique chance gives an outstanding collection

1. Calvin Tomkins, interview New York, September 10, 2014.
2. Tonie Roos, telephone call, October 1, 2021.
3. Pontus Hultén, "Five fragments from the history of the museum. The birth and first years of Moderna Museet." Olle Granath and Monika Nieckels eds., *Moderna Museet 1958–1983*, Moderna Museet, Stockholm, 1983, p. 34.
4. Maria Görts, "Routines and choices. The emergence of the Moderna Museet collection." Anna Tellgren, ed., *The History Book. About Moderna Museet 1958–2008*. Moderna Museet/Steidl Verlag, Stockholm, 2008, pp. 9–32.
5. Görts, 2008, pp. 12–14.
6. Görts, 2008, p. 12.
7. https://www.modernamuseet.se/stockholm/wp-content/uploads/sites/3/2018/09/decision-making-restitution-of-oskar-kokoschkas-mlning-bildnis-eines-marquis-joseph-de-montesquiou-fezensac.pdf
8. Görts, 2008, p. 14.
9. Alexander Calder, "The Forest is the Best Place," 1945. Moderna Museet, Stockholm. Donation from the Friends of Moderna Museet 1958. NMSK 1728.
10. Constantin Brancusi, "Le Nouveau Né II" ("The Newborn II"), 1919–1921, purchase 1961 with contributions from the Friends of Moderna Museet, Carina Ari, Gerard Bonnier, Sten Hellner, Charles Nilsson, Hildur Nordin and Ivar Philipson. NMSK 1795.
11. Ulf Linde, "Memoirs," Olle Granath and Monika Nieckels eds., *Moderna Museet 1958–1983*. Moderna Museet, Stockholm, 1983, p. 59.
12. Linde, in Granath and Nieckels, 1983, p. 59.
13. K.G. Hultén, "The artwork has no price," *The Museum of Wishes*, Exhibition catalog no. 36, Moderna Museet, Stockholm, 1963, p. 11.
14. K.G. Hultén, "The artwork has no price," *The Museum of Wishes*, Exhibition catalog no. 36, Moderna Museet, Stockholm, 1963, p. 11.
15. Pontus Hultén, interview Stockholm, December 17, 1996.
16. Åke Meyerson was a museum man who worked at the Royal Armory and the Swedish Museum of Natural History, before becoming the director of Tidens förlag and later Secretary of State at the Ministry of Ecclesiastical Affairs. Meyerson ended his professional career as Superintendent of the Livrust Chamber.
17. Pontus Hultén, interview Stockholm, December 17, 1996.
18. Roland Pålsson, "60-talet 'in nostalgiam,'" Olle Granath and Monika Nieckels eds., *Moderna Museet 1958–1983*. Moderna Museet, Stockholm, 1983, pp. 141–142.
19. In 2022, Moderna Museet has a total of around SEK 20 million in annual funding for art purchases, including government and private funding.
20. Pontus Hultén, interview Stockholm, December 17, 1996.
21. Complete list of works purchased with the one-off grant for *The Museum of Wishes*: sis.modernamuseet.se/en/search/*/objects?filter=collections%3A%C3%96nskemuseet
22. Linde, in Granath and Nieckels, 1983, p. 60.
23. Giorgio de Chirico, "Le Cerveau de l'enfant" ("The Child's Brain"), 1914, Moderna Museet, Stockholm. Purchase 1964 (*The Museum of Wishes*). NM 6068.
24. Salvador Dalí, "L'Énigme de Guillaume Tell" ("The Riddle of William Tell"), 1933. Moderna Museet, Stockholm. Purchase in 1967 (*The Museum of Wishes*). NM 6069.
25. Kurt Schwitters, "Das Arbeiterbild" ("The Workers' Picture"), 1919, Moderna Museet, Stockholm. Donation from the Friends of Moderna Museet in 1964. NM 5853.
26. Philip Sandblom (1903–2001) was a professor of surgery and rector of Lund University. Sandblom was born in the USA and partly raised in Norway. Like his father, he was a prominent sailor and won a bronze medal with his father in the 8-meter class at the 1928 Amsterdam Olympics. Sandblom amassed a significant collection, most of which he donated to Lund University.
27. Kazimir Malevich's groundbreaking "Black and White. Suprematist Composition" was donated to the Moderna Museet collection in 2004 by Bengt and Jelena Jangfeldt. The collection now also includes Malevich's figurative "Portrait of Una" from 1930–1933, donated by George Costakis in 1983. The story of how these priceless paintings (no work by Malevich has ever been sold on the commercial market) came to be included in the Moderna Museet collection is told in Bengt Jangfeldt's book *En rysk historia* (*A Russian History*), Wahlström & Widstrand, Stockholm, 2015. (Kazimir Malevich, "Black and White. Suprematist Composition," 1915, Moderna Museet, Stockholm. Donated in 2004 by Bengt and Jelena Jangfeldt. MOM/2004/97, Kazimir Malevich, "Portrait of Una," 1930–1933. Moderna Museet, Stockholm. Donated by George Costakis in 1983. MOM 280.)

28. Pontus Hultén, interview Stockholm, December 17, 1996.
29. Gerard Bonnier's donation of twenty-three early Modernist masterpieces in 1989 was completed in 2014 when his wife Elisabeth "Peggy" Bonnier donated eight more classical paintings by Pablo Picasso, Juan Gris, Paul Klee, Henri Laurens and Jean Fautrier to the museum. https://www.modernamuseet.se/ stockholm/en/2014/05/31/donation-of-historical-significance-to-the-modern-museum/

11 A Dutch intermezzo

1. Roland Pålsson, "60-talet 'in nostalgiam,'" Olle Granath and Monika Nieckels eds., *Moderna Museet 1958–1983*. Moderna Museet, Stockholm, 1983, p. 141.
2. Willem Sandberg, *Portrait of an Artist*, interviews compiled by Ank Leeuw Marcar, Valiz, Amsterdam, 2013, p. 165.
3. Sandberg, 2013, p. 169.
4. Sandberg, 2013, pp. 108–109. The concept of museion: https://referenceworks.brillonline.com/entries/brill-s-new-pauly/mouseion-e812620
5. Billy Klüver and Robert Rauschenberg, "Art in Motion — a combined memory." Olle Granath and Monika Nieckels eds., *Moderna Museet 1958–1983*. Moderna Museet, Stockholm, 1983, p. 145.
6. Sandberg, 2013, pp. 103–104.
7. Stephan Andreae, "Reisen mit Riesen/Walking With Giants." Transcript of recorded conversations with Pontus Hultén for unpublished autobiography, La Motte, 1997–1999. © Stephan Andreae.
8. Hans Ulrich Obrist, *A Brief History of Curating*, JRP-Ringier/Les Presses du Réel, Geneva, 2008, p. 39.
9. Anna-Lena Wibom, interview Lidingö, March 21, 2014.
10. Anna-Lena Wibom, interview Lidingö, March 21, 2014.
11. Anna-Lena Wibom, interview Lidingö, March 21, 2014.
12. Germano Celant, interview Milan, April 18, 2016. I heard the story told by several people who heard it from Hultén himself.
13. Among others DN, August 9, 1962, Expressen, September 16, 1962, Stockholmstidningen, September 10, 1962 and SvD, February 14, 1963.
14. Ad Petersen used the term "Aldermen," the name of the council that governed the city of Amsterdam at the time.
15. Ad Petersen, interview Amsterdam, February 3, 2017.

12 "The Grobian on the Pea"

1. Birgitta Arvas, "Children at Moderna Museet — VERKSTAN." Olle Granath and Monika Nieckels eds., *Moderna Museet* 1958–1983. Moderna Museet, Stockholm, 1983, p. 187.
2. Björn Springfeldt, interview Värmdö, March 13, 2014.
3. Björn Springfeldt, interview Värmdö, March 13, 2014.
4. Björn Springfeldt, interview Värmdö, March 13, 2014.
5. Olle Granath, interview Stockholm, February 3, 2015.
6. Olle Granath, interview Stockholm, October 23, 2015.
7. Olle Granath, interview Stockholm, November 11, 2021.
8. Mette Prawitz, interview Stockholm, June 30, 2016.
9. Märta Sahlberg, interview Stockholm, March 31, 2014.
10. Märta Sahlberg, interview Stockholm, March 31, 2014.
11. Mette Prawitz, interview Stockholm, June 30, 2016.
12. Olle Granath, interview Stockholm, October 23, 2015.
13. "Bed" from 1955 is one of Robert Rauschenberg's first "combines." It is part of the collection at MoMA in New York.
14. K.G. Hultén, "Enkell's Confusions," *Är allting konst*, Albert Bonniers förlag, Stockholm, 1963, pp. 7–8.
15. Ingemar Hedenius, "The contemporary and the human," *Är allting konst?*, 1963, pp. 74–79.
16. Ingmar Hedenius, "Replik," *Är allting konst?*, 1963, pp. 81–82.
17. Pontus Hultén, "The big role of the small museum." Olle Granath and Monika Nieckels eds., *Moderna Museet 1958–1983*. Moderna Museet, Stockholm, 1983, p. 39.
18. *Moderna Museet in Louisiana*, September 1–October 30, 1960. *Stedelijk Museum Amsterdam visits Moderna Museet*, December 26, 1961–January 27, 1962. *Moderna Museet visits Helsinki*, March 17–April 19, 1964. *Moderna Museet visits Oslo*, November 12–December 11, 1966. *Peggy Guggenheim's collection from Venice*, November 26, 1966–January 8, 1967. *Moderna Museet visits Tampere*, February 9–March 10, 1968.
19. Knut W. Jensen, "Traveling with Pontus," Lutz Jahre, *Das gedruckte Museum von Pontus Hultén. Kunstausstellungen und ihre Bücher*, Kunst- und Ausstellungshalle der Bundesrepublik Deutschland/Cantz, Bonn, 1996, pp. 92–95.
20. Olle Granath, interview Stockholm, October 23, 2015.
21. Pontus Hultén, interview Stockholm, December 17, 1996.

13 The Inner and the Outer Space and she

1. Pontus Hultén, "The big role of the small museum." Olle Granath and Monika Nieckels eds., *Moderna Museet* 1958–1983. Moderna Museet, Stockholm, 1983, p. 40.

2. Hultén, in Granath and Nieckels, 1983, p. 40.
3. Hultén, in Granath and Nieckels, 1983, p. 40.
4. The artist Rotraut Klein-Moquay (born Uecker in 1938) is the younger sister of the German artist Günther Uecker. She met Yves Klein while working as a nanny for his good friend and fellow artist Arman in Nice. The couple married six months before Klein's death. June 6, 1962.
5. Yves Klein, "Monochrome bleu IKB 48," 1956, purchase 1967 (*The Museum of Wishes*). NM 6073. Yves Klein, "Relief éponge/ Bleu RE 17," 1960. Donation 1967 from the Friends of Moderna Museet. NMSK 1971. "Suaire (ANT-SU 2)," 1961. Purchase 1967 (*The Museum of Wishes*). NM 6074.
6. Naum Gabo with Antoine Pevsner, "Realistic Manifesto," 1920.
7. Minimalism was one of the younger movements on which *The Inner and the Outer Space* was based.
8. K.G. Hultén, Karin Bergqvist Lindgren, *Den inre och den yttre rymden*. Exhibition catalog no. 51, Moderna Museet, Stockholm, 1965. The catalog, a classic, was presented in a box with a flap and densely typed, illegible text, without title or other information.
9. Olof Lagercrantz (1911–2002), famous author and legend editor-in-chief of Dagens Nyheter 1960–1975.
10. Troels Andersen, interview Copenhagen, September 28, 2015.
11. For detailed descriptions of the extensive pictorial documentation of *Dylaby*, see *she — a history*. Exhibition catalog no. 45. Moderna Museet, Stockholm, 1967. Typography and layout by K.G. Hultén, John Melin and Anders Österlin, pp. 18–25.
12. *she — a history*, 1967, pp. 18–25.
13. *she — a history*, 1967, p. 19.
14. Billy Klüver and Robert Rauschenberg, "Art in Motion — a combined memory," Olle Granath and Monika Nieckels eds., *Moderna Museet 1958–1983*. Moderna Museet, Stockholm, 1983, p. 145.
15. Calvin Tomkins, *Off the Wall. A Portrait of Robert Rauschenberg*. Picador, New York, 1980/2005, p. 205.
16. *she — a history*, p. 34.
17. *she — a history*, p. 40.
18. Hans Hammarskiöld, K.G. Hultén, Magnus Wibom, Lutfi Özkök.
19. Niki de Saint Phalle, "A Portrait of Pontus." Lutz Jahre, *Das gedruckte Museum von Pontus Hultén. Kunstausstellungen und ihre Bücher*, Kunst- und Ausstellungshalle der Bundesrepublik Deutschland/Cantz, Bonn, 1996, p. 105.
20. *she — a history*, p. 40.
21. For the story of the creation process with amazingly rich pictorial documentation, see *she — a history*.
22. Data on the dimensions of the sculpture vary in different sources, the length between twenty-three and twenty-six meters.
23. *she — a history*, p. 41. In the catalog and elsewhere, the restaurateur Robert Michels and his staff are praised by the participants for their efforts during the production of *she — a cathedral*, "and in particular Georg Ohlert."
24. Time, June 17, 1996. Article printed in *she — a history*.
25. The Times, June 27, 1966.
26. *Nyfiken gul* (*Curious Yellow*), or *Jag är nyfiken gul* (*I am Curious Yellow*) as Vilgot Sjöman's 1968 global scandal film is popularly known, was actually titled *Jag är nyfiken — en film i gult* (*I am Curious — a Film in Yellow*) and was the first of two parts, the second being *I Am Curious — a Film in Blue* from the following year, 1969.
27. Pontus Hultén, interview Stockholm, December 16, 2016.
28. Lars Nittve, interview Stockholm, March 3, 2016.
29. Interview Britta Birnbaum, Erik Topelius, Erik Cornelius, Ann-Sofi Topelius, Ulf Abel and Ulf G Johansson, Stockholm, April 7, 2015.
30. Pontus Hultén, "The big role of the small museum." Olle Granath and Monika Nieckels eds., *Moderna Museet 1958–1983*. Moderna Museet, Stockholm, 1983, p. 42.
31. Claes Oldenburg, interview New York, September 8, 2014.
32. Around thirty thousand visitors.
33. *she — a history*, p. 167.
34. Hultén, in Granath and Nieckels, 1983, p. 44.
35. Hultén, in Granath and Nieckels, 1983, p. 44.
36. Hultén, in Granath and Nieckels, 1983, p. 44.
37. Hultén, in Granath and Nieckels, 1983, p. 46.
38. Hultén, in Granath and Nieckels, 1983, p. 46.
39. Erik Trägårdh memorial text, Dagens Nyheter, July 8, 2000.
40. Moderna Museet archive, folder Paradise.
41. Hultén, in Granath and Nieckels, 1983, p. 46.
42. Olle Granath, interview Stockholm, October 23, 2015.

14 Making art history with Andy Warhol

1. Pontus Hultén, "Five fragments from the history of Moderna Museet." Olle Granath and Monika Nieckels eds., *Moderna Museet 1958–1983*. Moderna Museet, Stockholm, 1983, p. 34.
2. *Les Peintres Cubistes, Méditations Estéthiques* (*The Cubist Painters, Aesthetic Meditations*), first published in 1913 by Eugène Figuière Éditeurs, Collection "Tous Les Arts," Paris, 1913.
3. Olle Granath, interview Stockholm, February 16, 2015.
4. Eva Meyer-Herman ed., *Andy Warhol. A guide to 256 objects in 2 hours and 56*

minutes. Other voices, other rooms. Moderna Museet, Stockholm in collaboration with Stedelijk Museum, Amsterdam, and The Andy Warholm Museum, Pittsburgh. NAi Publishers, Rotterdam, 2008.

5. Andy Warhol, *Other Voices, Other Rooms*. Exhibited at the Stedelijk Museum, Amsterdam, October 12, 2007–January 13, 2008. Moderna Museet, Stockholm, February 9–May 4, 2008.
6. Olle Granath, "With Andy Warhol 1968." Eva Meyer-Herman, ed., *Andy Warhol. A guide to 256 objects in 2 hours and 56 minutes. Other Voices, Other Rooms*. Moderna Museet, Stockholm in collaboration with Stedelijk Museum, Amsterdam, and The Andy Warholm Museum, Pittsburgh. NAi Publishers, Rotterdam, 2008, p. 11.
7. Olle Granath, interview Stockholm, February 16, 2015.
8. Granath, in Meyer-Herman, 2008, p. 11.
9. Kasper König, interview Cologne, November 13, 2015.
10. Granath, in Meyer-Herman, 2008, p. 13.
11. *The Medium is the Massage* (Bantam Books, New York, 1967) is the prophetic book, important for the creative culture of the late sixties, published by media analyst Marshall McLuhan in collaboration with graphic designer Quentin Fiore and which influenced Andy Warhol. Note that the title is a pun — that the media is not the message but the "massage."
12. Granath, in Meyer-Herman, 2008, p. 12.
13. Olle Granath, interview Stockholm, February 16, 2015.
14. Anna-Lena Wibom, interview Lidingö, March 21, 2014.
15. Bill Öhrström, telephone interview, July 6, 2017.
16. Bill Öhrström, telephone interview, July 6, 2017.
17. Olle Granath, telephone interview, August 18, 2017.
18. Bill Öhrström, telephone interview, July 6, 2017.
19. Bo A. Karlsson, *With Warhol from Moderna to Cirkeln*. Publications from the jazz department of the Swedish Song Archive (No 16). Bokförlaget Prisma, Stockholm, 2002, pp. 174–176.
20. Bo A. Karlsson founded Galleri Karlsson on Vidargatan in Stockholm in 1964 with his then wife Eva Karlsson, which became influential in the late sixties, with controversial exhibitions of Carl Johan De Geer, Dick Bengtsson, Kjartan Slettermark, Marie-Louise De Geer and Lars Hillersberg, among others.
21. 24,613 visitors: accounting records in the Moderna Museet archive, Andy Warhol 1968 folder. 30,000 visitors: https://www.modernamuseet.se/stockholm/wp-content/uploads/sites/3/2016/01/mmlararhandledning-warhol-1968.pdf
22. Granath, in Meyer-Herman, 2008, p. 13.
23. Kasper König, interview Stockholm, September 14, 2018.
24. Letter from Leo Castelli on letterhead from Castelli gallery, May 21, 1970. Moderna Museet archive, Andy Warhol folder 1968.
25. John Coplan (1920–2003). Art historian who between 1967 and 1978 was senior curator at the Pasadena Art Museum, where he organized important solo retrospectives with, in addition to Andy Warhol, Roy Lichtenstein, Robert Irwin, Richard Serra, James Turell, Donald Judd and Ellsworth Kelly, among others.
26. Letter from Leo Castelli on letterhead from Castelli gallery, May 21, 1970. Moderna Museet archive, Andy Warhol folder 1968.
27. Letter from Leo Castelli on letterhead from Castelli gallery, June 17, 1970. Moderna Museet archive, Andy Warhol folder 1968.
28. Andy Warhol, "Ten-Foot Flowers," 1967. Moderna Museet, Stockholm. Donation in 1976 from the artist. MOM 57.
29. Kasper König, interview Cologne, November 13, 2015.
30. The exhibition was curated by John Peter Nilsson.
31. Kasper König, interview Stockholm, September 14, 2018.
32. Pontus Hultén, *Pontus Hultén Collection ....* Exhibition catalog no. 321. Moderna Museet, Stockholm, 2004, p. 360.
33. William Middleton *Double Vision. The Unnerring Eye of Art World Avatars Dominique and John de Menil*. Alfred A. Knopf, New York, 2018, p. 567.

15 The Machine

1. A retrospective of Wassily Kandinsky was shown from April 10 to May 30, 1965, but without works on loan from Russia, mainly based on the collection of his widow Nina Kandinsky in Paris.
2. Troels Andersen, interview Copenhagen, September 28, 2015.
3. This year seems uncertain. Andersen has given it as 1963, but some information suggests that it may have been 1961.
4. Stephan Andreae, "Reisen mit Riesen/Walking With Giants." Transcript of recorded conversations with Pontus Hultén for unpublished autobiography, La Motte, 1997–1999. © Stephan Andreae.
5. Troels Andersen, interview Copenhagen, September 28, 2015.
6. Troels Andersen, interview Copenhagen, September 28, 2015.
7. Andreae, 1997–1999.
8. Moderna Museet archive, folder Vladimir Tatlin 1968.
9. "Letatlin," 1932, recorded as purchased 1973, NMSK 2158. "Moon," no year of creation or acquisition inscribed, MOM 2001/179. "Chair," year of acquisition 1968,

MOM 2001/1980. Untitled sculpture, year of acquisition "ca 1968," MOM 2013/92. Untitled sculpture, year of creation "ca 1968," MOM 2013/93.

10. Moderna Museet archive, folder Vladimir Tatlin 1968.
11. Letter from Pontus Hultén to Alfred H. Barr Jr, MoMA, March 22, 1967. Pontus Hultén's archive, Moderna Museet, Stockholm. 4.2 Exhibitions. 54 The Machine 3.
12. Letter from René d'Harnoncourt to Pontus Hultén, December 20, 1965. Pontus Hultén's archive, Moderna Museet, Stockholm. 4.2 Exhibitions. 54 The Machine 3.
13. Letter from Pontus Hultén to René d'Harnoncourt, MoMA, January 13, 1966. Pontus Hultén's archive, Moderna Museet, Stockholm. 4.2 Exhibitions. 54 The Machine 3.
14. Letter from Pontus Hultén to René d'Harnoncourt, January 13, 1966.
15. Press release available on MoMA's website moma.org. https:// www.moma.org/momaorg/shared/pdfs/docs/pressarchives/4149/releases/MOMA1968July-December0081.pdf
16. K.G. Pontus Hultén, catalog *The Machine — as Seen at the End of the Mechanical Age*, Museum of Modern Art, New York, 1968, p. 180.
17. Thomas Shannon, interview New York, September 8, 2014.
18. Hultén, catalog, 1968, p. 3.
19. https://www.moma.org/momaorg/shared/pdfs/docs/pressarchives/4149/releases/MOMA1968July-December0081.pdf
20. Among others for Stephan Andreae.
21. Alex Greenberger, Art News, 30 September, 2019. "9 Stories. MoMA Shows from the 1960s — and What Art News Said at the Time." https://www. artnews.com/art-news/retrospective/moma-1960s-best-shows-jean-tinguely-mark-rothko-13289/ and William Middleton, *Double Vision. The Unnerring Eye of Art World Avatars Dominique and John de Menil*, Alfred A. Knopf, New York, 2018, pp. 458–463.
22. Richard Armstrong, interview New York, September 9, 2014.
23. Marianne Hultman, "Our man in New York. An interview with Billy Klüver about the collaboration with Moderna Museet," Anna Tellgren ed., *The History Book. About Moderna Museet 1958–2008*. Moderna Museet/Steidl Verlag, Stockholm, 2008, p. 239.
24. Richard Armstrong, interview New York, September 9, 2014.
25. Middleton, 2018, pp. 458–463.
26. Middleton, 2018, pp. 458–463.
27. Greenberger, September 30, 2019.
28. Calvin Tomkins, interview New York, September 10, 2014.
29. Calvin Tomkins, "A Good Monster," The New Yorker, January 16, 1978.
30. Calvin Tomkins, January 16, 1978.
31. Conversation with Billy Klüver, Stockholm, fall 1997.
32. Expressen, June 5, 1973. Anna-Lena Wibom, interview Lidingö, March 21, 2014.
33. Julie Martin, interview New York, September 9, 2014.
34. Daniel Birnbaum, conversation Stockholm, April 21, 2015.
35. Björn Springfeldt, interview Värmdö, November 20, 2018.
36. Eli Broad, interview Los Angeles, November 6, 2014.
37. Calvin Tomkins, interview New York, September 10, 2014.

16 The father rebellion in the magma chamber

1. Described by Kasper König, among others in Lutz Jahre, *Das gedruckte Museum von Pontus Hultén. Kunstausstellungen und ihre Bücher*, Kunst- und Ausstellungshalle der Bundesrepublik Deutschland/Cantz, Bonn, 1996, p. 113.
2. Marie-Louise von Plessen, interview La Motte, June 29, 2021.
3. Olle Granath, interview Stockholm, February 16, 2015.
4. Olle Granath, interview Stockholm, February 16, 2015.
5. Pontus Hultén, interview Stockholm, December 17, 1996.
6. Maja Oeri, interview Basel, December 6, 2014.
7. Interview Kjartan Slettemark, DN Sthlm, October 4, 2007.
8. *The language of revolution. Communist posters from around the world*. Moderna Museet, Stockholm, March 23–April 28, 1968.
9. Pontus Hultén, "The big role of the small museum." Olle Granath and Monika Nieckels eds., *Moderna Museet 1958–1983*. Moderna Museet, Stockholm, 1983, p. 42.
10. *The Model. A Model for a Qualitative Society*. Moderna Museet, Stockholm, September 30–October 23, 1968.
11. Hultén, in Granath and Nieckels, 1983, pp. 43–44.
12. Hultén, in Granath and Nieckels, 1983, pp. 43–44.
13. K.G.P. Hultén, "The New Role of Museums," *The Model: A Model for a Qualitative Society*, catalog, Moderna Museet, Stockholm, 1968, p. 32.
14. Anette Göthlund, "Work in Workshop and Zone. Art education at Moderna Museet." Anna Tellgren, ed., *The History Book. About Moderna Museet 1958–2008*. Moderna Museet/Steidl Verlag, Stockholm, 2008, p. 268.
15. *Egyptian youth weaving*, Moderna Museet, Stockholm, December 2, 1960–January 22, 1961. *Egyptian youth Weaving 1961–1966*, November 3–20, 1966.
16. Pär Stolpe, interview Stockholm, November 29, 2015.

17. Pär Stolpe, interview Stockholm, November 29, 2015.
18. The Museum of Architecture had previously been housed in premises on Odengatan 3, in a building owned by the Swedish Association of Architects.
19. *Hej stad*, Moderna Museet, Stockholm (organized by the Museum of Architecture), 2–24 April 1966.
20. Pär Stolpe, interview Stockholm, November 29, 2015.
21. Pär Stolpe, interview Stockholm, November 29, 2015.
22. Pär Stolpe, interview Stockholm, November 29, 2015.
23. Pär Stolpe, interview Stockholm, November 29, 2015.
24. Pontus Hultén, "Moderna Museet and May 1968." Olle Granath and Monika Nieckels eds., *Moderna Museet 1958–1983*. Moderna Museet, Stockholm, 1983, p. 48.
25. Kurt Bergengren, *När skönheten kom till City*, Aldus, Stockholm, 1976.
26. Christopher Grafe, *People's Palaces — Architecture, Culture and Democracy in Post-War Europe*, Architecturea & Natura, Amsterdam, 2014.
27. Kim West, *The Exhibitionary Complex: Exhibition, Apparatus, and Media from Kulturhuset to the Centre Pompidou, 1963–1977*, Södertörn University, 2017.
28. K.G. Hultén, "Moderna Museet in the center," DN, February 17, 1965.
29. K.G. Hultén, "Stockholm's cultural living room," DN, November 29, 1966.
30. Johan Celsing, interview Stockholm, March 26, 2020.
31. Pär Stolpe, interview Stockholm, November 29, 2015.
32. Pär Stolpe, interview Stockholm, November 29, 2015.
33. Pär Stolpe, interview Stockholm, November 29, 2015.
34. Hultén, in Granath and Nieckels, 1983, p. 48.
35. Staffan Olzon, together with Pi Lind, founded Pistolteatern (named after the initials of the founders), located on Mälartorget in Gamla stan 1964–1968, then from 1972–1985 on Torsgatan in Vasastaden. The theater, and its creators, were influential in the cultural life of Stockholm in the 1960s.
36. Pär Stolpe, interview Stockholm, November 29, 2015.
37. Pär Stolpe, interview Stockholm, November 29, 2015.
38. Pär Stolpe, interview Stockholm, November 29, 2015.
39. Pär Stolpe, interview Stockholm, November 29, 2015.
40. Johan Celsing, interview Stockholm, March 26, 2020.
41. Pär Stolpe, interview Stockholm, November 29, 2015.
42. Pär Stolpe, interview Stockholm, November 29, 2015.
43. Olle Granath, interview Stockholm, February 16, 2015.
44. Pär Stolpe, interview Stockholm, November 29, 2015.
45. Hultén, in Granath and Nieckels, 1983, p. 48.
46. Hultén, in Granath and Nieckels, 1983, p. 48.
47. Hultén, in Granath and Nieckels, 1983, p. 48.
48. Hultén, interview Stockholm, December 17, 1996.
49. Pär Stolpe, interview Stockholm, November 29, 2015.
50. Pär Stolpe, interview Stockholm, November 29, 2015.
51. Bror Andersson, Carlo Derkert, K.G. Hultén, Pi Lind, Pär Stolpe, Anna-Lena Thorsell, "Ett kulturhusprogram: Experiment i social samlevnad," DN, May 18, 1969.
52. Pär Stolpe, interview Stockholm, November 29, 2015.
53. Jimmy Nyström, "The Culture House Toilets Cancelled. The museum director issued an ultimatum," SvD, November 5, 1969.
54. Hultén, in Granath and Nieckels, 1983, p. 48.
55. Pär Stolpe, interview Stockholm, November 29, 2015.
56. "Moderna Museet stops. No room in Kulturhuset," SvD, March 1, 1970.
57. Peter Celsing died on March 16, 1974, aged only fifty-four, as a result of a brain tumor. In my 1996 interview, Pontus Hultén claimed that as a consequence of Celsing's illness the creative working group lost considerable power vis-à-vis politicians.
58. Hultén, in Granath and Nieckels, 1983, p. 50.
59. Hultén, in Granath and Nieckels, 1983, p. 50.
60. Pontus Hultén, interview Stockholm, December 17, 1996.
61. Olle Granath, interview Stockholm, February 16, 2015.
62. Olle Granath, interview Stockholm, February 16, 2015.
63. Pär Stolpe, interview Stockholm, November 29, 2015.
64. Olle Granath, interview Stockholm, February 16, 2015.
65. Pär Stolpe, interview Stockholm, November 29, 2015.
66. *Poetry Must Be Made by All! Transform the World*, Moderna Museet, Stockholm, November 15, 1969–January 18, 1970.
67. *After Babel* and *89+: Poetry Will be Made by All!*, group exhibition and event at Moderna Museet June 13–August 30, 2015, curated by Daniel Birnbaum and Hans Ulrich Obrist. The exhibition took as its starting point 1989, seen as a counterpart to 1968 and the beginning of a new era with the fall of the Berlin Wall, the Soviet empire and the invention of the internet. The participating artists included Etel Adnan, Kader Attia, Yael Bartana, Paul Chan, Rivane Neuenscwander, Michelangelo Pistoletti and Haegue Yang. Like the source of inspiration *Poetry Must Be Made by All!* in 1969, *After Babel* was a multimedia exhibition, which also included the poetry event *89+: Poetry*

Will Be Made by All!, featuring poets born after 1989.
68. Solidarity evening for the Black Panthers, Moderna Museet, July 4, 1970.
69. Olle Granath, interview Stockholm, February 16, 2015.
70. Björn Springfeldt, interview Värmdö, March 13, 2014.
71. Björn Springfeldt, interview Värmdö, March 13, 2014.
72. History of the museum. Olle Granath and Monika Nieckels eds., *Moderna Museet 1958–1983*. Moderna Museet, Stockholm, 1983, p. 106.
73. Pär Stolpe, interview Stockholm, November 29, 2015.
74. Pär Stolpe, interview Stockholm, November 29, 2015.
75. History of the museum. Olle Granath and Monika Nieckels eds., *Moderna Museet 1958–1983*. Moderna Museet, Stockholm, 1983, pp. 106–113.
76. Tonie Roos, interview Stockholm, October 22, 2021.
77. Tonie Roos, interview Stockholm, October 22, 2021.
78. Tonie Roos, interview Stockholm, October 22, 2021.
79. Tonie Roos, interview Dalarö, September 8, 2015.
80. Tonie Roos, interview Stockholm, October 22, 2021.
81. Tonie Roos, interview Stockholm, October 22, 2021.
82. According to the testimonies of Tonie Roos and others, these "connections" consisted in practice of friends/contacts in these cities and were only sporadically functional — especially the one in Bombay which never worked properly (Tonie Roos, interview Stockholm, October 22, 2021).
83. Olle Granath, interview Stockholm, February 16, 2015.
84. *Moment — Moki Cherry*. Moderna Museet, Stockholm, April 7, 2016–April 9, 2017. Curated by Fredrik Liew.
85. In connection with an exhibition at the Blank Forms gallery in New York, the book *Organic Music Societies* (Lawrence Kumpf, Naima Karlsson, Magnus Nygren. Blank Forms Editions, New York, 2021) was published, based on many years of extensive and thorough research into the lives and artistic work of Moki and Don Cherry. The book includes many quotes from Moki Cherry's diary entries. The exhibition and book were celebrated with a major article in the New York Times ("A Fresh Look at the 'Organic Music' of Moki and Don Cherry," The New York Times, April 28, 2021).
86. Pontus Hultén, "The big role of the small museum." Olle Granath and Monika Nieckels eds., *Moderna Museet 1958–1983*. Moderna Museet, Stockholm, 1983, p. 44.
87. *Max Ernst. Paintings, Collages, Frottage, Drawings, Prints, Books, Sculptures, 1917–1969*, Moderna Museet, Stockholm, September 13–October 19, 1969. Film series Max Ernst, Seppo Saves, September 27–October 19, 1969.
88. *Surrealism?* Moderna Museet, Stockholm, March 7–April 12, 1970.
89. *Alternative Suédoise/Svenskt alternativ*, Moderna Museet, Stockholm, October 24–November 29, 1970.
90. *Edward Kienholz 11+11 Tableaux*, Moderna Museet, Stockholm, January 17–March 1, 1970.
91. Edward Kienholz, "The State Hospital," 1966. Moderna Museet, Stockholm. Purchase 1971. NMSK 2094.
92. Olle Granath, telephone interview, June 14, 2021.
93. *Joseph Beuys. Aktioner/Aktionen*, Moderna Museet, Stockholm, January 16–February 28, 1971.
94. *Günther Uecker. Pictorial objects 1957–1970*, Moderna Museet, Stockholm, January 1–February 28, 1971.
95. Marie-Louise von Plessen, interview La Motte, July 7, 2018.
96. Moderna Museet archive, Joseph Beuys folder 1971.
97. Pontus Hultén, preface, *Joseph Beuys, Aktioner/Aktionen*, exhibition catalog no. 90, Moderna Museet, Stockholm, 1971, unpaginated.
98. Joseph Beuys "The Pack," installation/assembly, 1969.
99. Joseph Beuys "Das Schweigen von Marcel Duchamp wird überbewertet" ("Marcel Duchamp's silence is overrated"). Action broadcast live on German TV, December 11, 1964.
100. Joseph Beuys, "Unterwasserbuch," sculpture/assemblage, 1972, edition of two.
101. In connection with an exhibition at the Goethe Institute in Stockholm, a two-volume book documenting Joseph Beuys' visit to Stockholm in 1971 was published in 2021: "Joseph Beuys und Lothar Wolleh, 'Das Unterwasserbuch-Project'/'The Unterwasserbuch Project,'" Kerber Verlag, Bielefeld/Berlin, 2021.
102. Information from curator Simone Schmid, who researched Joseph Beuys' exhibition and visit to Stockholm in 1971 for the Goethe Institute's exhibition in Stockholm in the fall of 2021.
103. Olle Granath, "German counterpoint," Dagens Nyheter, January 22, 1971.
104. Olle Granath, telephone interview, June 14, 2021.
105. Pontus Hultén, interview Stockholm, December 17, 1996.
106. Björn Springfeldt, interview Värmdö, March 13, 2014.
107. Pontus Hultén, "Moderna Museet and May 1968." Olle Granath and Monika Nieckels eds., *Moderna Museet 1958–1983*. Moderna Museet, Stockholm, 1983, p. 50.

108. Björn Springfeldt, interview Värmdö, March 13, 2014.
109. Olle Granath, interview Stockholm, February 16, 2015.
110. Pontus Hultén, interview Stockholm, December 17, 1996.
111. Pär Stolpe, interview Stockholm, November 29, 2015.
112. Anna-Stina Malmborg and Gunnar Höglund, interview Stockholm, January 13, 2016.
113. Pontus Hultén, interview Stockholm, December 17, 1996.

17 The New York Collection for Stockholm

1. K.G. Pontus Hultén, *Jean Tinguely Méta*, Moderna Museet/Verlag Ullstein GmbH, Stockholm/Frankfurt/Berlin/Vienna, 1972.
2. On Kawara, "From the series: I Got Up," 1972. Moderna Museet, Stockholm. Pontus Hultén's donation 2005. MOM/2005/436.
3. Olle Granath, interview Stockholm, February 16, 2015.
4. Olle Granath, interview Stockholm, February 16, 2015.
5. Paul Thek, *Pyramid*, Moderna Museet, Stockholm, November 6, 1971–January 9, 1972.
6. *Images of the 1910s. Paintings, drawings, sculptures, posters, films, photographs, newspaper images, texts that make us see, experience.* Moderna Museet, Stockholm, February 5–April 9, 1972.
7. Olle Granath, interview Stockholm, February 16, 2015.
8. Pontus Hultén, interview Stockholm, December 17, 1996.
9. Pontus Hultén, interview Stockholm, December 17, 1996.
10. Robert Whitman, telephone interview, September 4, 2017.
11. Pontus Hultén, interview Stockholm, December 17, 1996.
12. Pontus Hultén, "The New York Connection." Olle Granath and Monika Nieckels eds., *Moderna Museet 1958–1983*. Moderna Museet, Stockholm, 1983, p. 57.
13. Robert Whitman, telephone interview, September 4, 2017.
14. Jeanette Bonnier, interview Stockholm, October 8, 2014.
15. Jeanette Bonnier, interview Stockholm, October 8, 2014.
16. For a complete list of exhibited and acquired works, see Maria Görts, "Routines and choices. The emergence of the Moderna Museet collection," Anna Tellgren ed., *The History Book. About Moderna Museet 1958–2008*. Moderna Museet/Steidl Verlag, Stockholm, 2008. Note 34, p. 31.
17. Ulf Linde, "Memoirs," Olle Granath and Monika Nieckels eds., *Moderna Museet 1958–1983*. Moderna Museet, Stockholm, 1983, p. 65.
18. Hultén, in Granath and Nieckels, 1983, p. 57.
19. Italian Count Giuseppe Panza di Biumo, one of the world's foremost collectors of post-war art, returns in Chapter 29 from Los Angeles.
20. Hultén, in Granath and Nieckels, 1983, p. 57.
21. "Moderna's USA collection becomes one of the world's best," Dagens Nyheter, October 26, 1973.
22. Karl Olov Björk, Margareta Carlstedt, Sten Dunér, Bror Marklund, Per Olof Ultvedt, "What Art do We Want?," Dagens Nyheter, June 16, 1972. Same signatories, "There is a world outside the Paris–New York axis," Dagens Nyheter, June 27, 1972. Bo Ahlsén, Karl Olov Björk, Margareta Carlstedt, Sten Dunér, Pär Stolpe, Per Olof Ultvedt, "Surplus Storage at Moderna Museet," Dagens Nyheter November 23, 1973.
23. Emile de Antonio, documentary film director and producer, a profile in the New York artistic avant-garde of the sixties, was part of the group that worked on *the New York Collection for Stockholm* and who traveled to Stockholm for the opening.
24. Björn Springfeldt, interview Värmdö, March 13, 2014.
25. Olle Granath, interview Stockholm, April 25, 2018.
26. Julie Martin, interview New York, September 9, 2014.
27. Olle Granath, interview Stockholm, April 25, 2018.
28. Björn Springfeldt, interview Värmdö, November 20, 2018.
29. Jean-Hubert Martin, interview Paris, January 12, 2015.
30. Jason Farago, "Niki de Saint Phalle: Nothing More Shocking Than Joy," The New York Times, April 8, 2021.
31. Calvin Tomkins, "Beyond the Machine. A Profile on Jean Tinguely," The New Yorker, February 1962.
32. Calvin Tomkins, interview New York, September 10, 2014.
33. Olle Granath, interview Stockholm, February 16, 2015.
34. *Marc Chagall*, Moderna Museet, Stockholm, September 25, 1982–January 9, 1983. 297,000 visitors.
35. *Henri Matisse*, Moderna Museet, Stockholm, November 3, 1984–January 6, 1985. 180,500 visitors.
36. *Pablo Picasso*, Moderna Museet, Stockholm, October 15, 1988–January 8, 1989. 277,000 visitors.
37. Olle Granath, interview Stockholm, February 16, 2015.
38. Olle Granath, interview Stockholm, February 16, 2015.
39. Monika Nieckels, interview Stockholm, April 26, 2018.
40. *Implosion. A Postmodern Perspective*, Moderna Museet, Stockholm, October 24, 1987–January 10, 1988.

41. Olle Granath, interview Stockholm, April 25, 2018.
42. Björn Springfeldt, interview Värmdö, March 13, 2014.
43. Bengt Göransson, telephone interview, September 21, 2017.
44. Daniel Birnbaum, conversation Stockholm, May 16, 2015.
45. *Ararat. Alternative research in architecture, resources, art and technology*, Moderna Museet, Stockholm, April 2–June 20, 1976.
46. The exhibition is described on the Moderna Museet website as follows: "The *Ararat* exhibition, an acronym for 'Alternative Research in Architecture, Resources, Art and Technology,' was a collaboration between artists, architects, technicians, craftsmen and humanists. The original core group consisted of Kerstin Abram-Nilsson, Valdemar Axelsson, Lars Englund, Bo Hall, Sivert Lindblom, Lennart Mörk, Hans Nordenström and Monica Nordenström. The concept for Ararat began to be formulated in September 1972 and the exhibition was realized by Moderna Museet making premises and resources available to the Ararat group. The then director of the museum, Philip von Schantz appointed Björn Springfeldt as curator, and Per Stolpe organized seminars, programming and printed material. The exhibition was about the future, about a society that worked in balance with the surrounding nature and drew its energy from natural sources. It was intended to stimulate the spread of knowledge and provide impetus and inspiration to action, through the active participation of visitors. The archive includes a longer compilation, a diary, of what each day of the exhibition entailed, as well as material relating to the project's presentation at the Venice Biennale in 1976." https://www.modernamuseet. se/stockholm/en/collection/research/pontus-hulten-and-modern-museum/ visningsmagasinet/
47. "Nutidsgalleriet/Nuet." Unsigned, unpaginated loose leaf. *Ararat. Alternative Reasearch in Art, Research and Technology.* Exhibition catalog 136, Moderna Museet, Stockholm, 1976.
48. Olle Granath, interview Stockholm, April 25, 2018.
49. Jan Öqvist, conversation Stockholm, October 29, 2018.
50. Varis Bokalders, telephone interview, March 9, 2022, Anna Nordenström, telephone interview, March 10, 2022, Milla and Björn Springfeldt, telephone interview, March 11, 2022, Sivert Lindblom, conversation telephone, April 16, 2022.
51. Varis Bokalders, telephone interview, March 9, 2022.
52. Varis Bokalders, telephone interview, March 9, 2022.
53. Milla and Björn Springfeldt, telephone interview, March 11, 2022.

18 A new horizon in Paris

1. The École de Paris is a broad term that is difficult to define. It refers not to any single art movement but primarily to the international influence exerted by immigrant artists in the first half of the twentieth century, when Paris was the world's undisputed sole global art metropolis. At the beginning of the century, the term was used for the foreign influence of Post-Impressionism, Fauvism and Cubism exerted by artists such as Picasso, Chagall, Modigliani and Mondrian, and for "associated" French artists such as Bonnard, Matisse, Metzinger and Gleizes. The term École de Paris was used pejoratively by nationalist art critics, often with racist and antisemitic undertones, and was contrasted with the "French School." After the World War II, the term came to encompass movements such as Dada and Surrealism, with artists such as Brancusi, Míro, Giacometti, Jean Arp and Raoul Dufy. After the Second World War, when nationalist and antisemitic perspectives were less viable, the concept of the "Paris School" came to be set against the increasingly prominent "New York School." École de Paris came to define "Tachisme," the school of abstract painting that was the French equivalent of American Abstract Expressionism, with artists such as Jean Dubuffet, Jean Fautrier, Pierre Soulages and many more.
2. Jean-Hubert Martin, interview Paris, April 23, 2015.
3. Jean-Hubert Martin, interview Paris, July 2, 2021.
4. The early "Les Joueurs d'échecs," "The Chess Players," from 1911, purchase 1954, in the MNAM collection.
5. *August Strindberg. Painting.* Musée national d'art moderne, Paris, May 15–June 10, 1962. *August Strindberg. Paintings 1870–1907.* Moderna Museet, Stockholm, February 27–April 15, 1963.
6. Stephan Andreae, "Reisen mit Riesen/ Walking With Giants." Transcript of recorded conversations with Pontus Hultén for unpublished autobiography, La Motte, 1997–1999. © Stephan Andreae.
7. Largest museum: https://en.wikipedia.org/wiki/List_of_largest_art_museums Largest collection in Europe: https://www.culturepartnership.eu/en/article/top-10-evropeyskih-muzeev-sovremen-nogo-iskusstva
8. Alain Pompidou, interview Paris, February 14, 2017.
9. Pontus Hultén, interview Stockholm, December 17, 1996.
10. Richard Rogers, interview London, May 5, 2016.
11. Founded in 1946 in London by Danish engineer Ove Arup as Ove N. Arup

Consulting Engineers. In 1970 it transformed into Ove Arup & Partners.

12. Rowan Moore, "Pompidou Centre: a 70s French Radical That's Never Gone Out of Fashion," The Guardian, January 8, 2017.
13. The Palm House glass house in Kew Gardens, London, built in 1844–1848, a collaboration between architect Decimus Burton and iron engineer Richard Turner.
14. The Crystal Palace glass building was built for the "Great Exhibition," in Hyde Park London in 1851, in revolutionary glass architecture by Joseph Paxton. After the exhibition, the edifice building was moved to south London, in an area later named after the building, where it remained until it was destroyed by fire in 1936.
15. "'Today is much more an age of greed.' Richard Rogers reflects on 50-year career." Dezeen.com, August 7, 2013.
16. In his article in The New Yorker, Calvin Tomkins states that the "double soccer fields" were something that the project management and the media "never failed to point out."
17. Calvin Tomkins, "The Good Monster," The New Yorker, February 1, 1978.
18. Richard Rogers, interview London, May 5, 2016.
19. "'Today is much more an age of greed.' Richard Rogers reflects on 50-year career." Dezeen.com, August 7, 2013.
20. Kim Willsher, "Pompidou Centre gets a £90m facelift 40 years on." The Guardian, January 15, 2017.
21. Richard Rogers, interview London, May 5, 2016.
22. Mary Blume, "Richard Rogers: Transforming Public Spaces." The New York Times, October 1, 2007.
23. Kim Willsher, "Pompidou Centre gets a £90m facelift 40 years on." The Guardian, January 15, 2017.
24. Philippe Jodebo, *Renzo Piano Building Workshop*, Taschen, 2016.
25. Renzo Piano, interview Paris, January 8, 2015.
26. Mary Blume, "Richard Rogers: Transforming Public Spaces." The New York Times, October 1, 2007.
27. Reyner Banham, "The Pompidou cannot be perceived as anything but a monument." Architectural Review, May 11, 1977.
28. Kim Willsher, "Pompidou Centre gets a £90m facelift 40 years on." The Guardian, January 15, 2017.
29. Jean-Hubert Martin, interview Paris, April 23, 2015.
30. Jean-Yves Mock, interview Paris, January 7, 2015.
31. Claude Mollard, interview Paris, April 24, 2015.
32. Among others, *Pentacle*, exhibited at the Musée des arts décoratifs in Paris from January 18 to March 31, 1968 (Olle Baertling, Öyvind Fahlström, Carl-Fredrik Reuterswärd, Max Walter Svanberg, Per Olof Ultvedt).
33. Claude Mollard, interview Paris, April 24, 2015.
34. Tomkins, February 1, 1978.
35. Claude Mollard, interview Paris, April 24, 2015.
36. Claude Mollard, interview Paris, April 24, 2015.
37. Jacques Caumont, interview Paris, April 2, 2015.
38. Tomkins, February 1, 1978.
39. Andreae, 1997–1999.
40. Robert Bordaz and Renzo Piano, *Entretiens Robert Bordaz Renzo Piano*, Diagonales, Paris, 1997. Olle Granath, interview Stockholm, February 16, 2015.
41. Olle Granath, interview Stockholm, February 16, 2015.
42. Jacques Villeglé, interview Paris, February 15, 2017.
43. Alain Jouffroy, interview Paris, April 22, 2015.
44. Daniel Abadie, interview Paris, October 22, 2015.

19 "Hugely impressive to see him conquer Paris with Picabia"

1. Felix Hultén, interview Västra Frölunda, June 23, 2014.
2. Stephan Andreae, "Reisen mit Riesen/ Walking With Giants." Transcript of recorded conversations with Pontus Hultén for unpublished autobiography, La Motte, 1997–1999. © Stephan Andreae.
3. Andreae, 1997–1999.
4. Andreae, 1997–1999.
5. Andreae, 1997–1999.
6. Annick Boisnard, interview Paris, January 14, 2015.
7. Annick Boisnard, interview Paris, January 14, 2015.
8. Andreae, 1997–1999.
9. Jean-Yves Mock, interview Paris, January 7, 2015.
10. Jean-Yves Mock, interview Paris, January 7, 2015.
11. Near where the Institut du Monde Arabe is now located.
12. Tomkins, February 1, 1978.
13. Tomkins, February 1, 1978.
14. Tomkins, February 1, 1978.
15. Jean-Yves Mock, interview Paris, January 12, 2015.
16. Renzo Piano, interview Paris, January 8, 2015.
17. Andreae, 1997–1999.
18. Andreae, 1997–1999.
19. Jean-Hubert Martin, interview Paris, April 23, 2015.
20. Andreae, 1997–1999.
21. Bernard Blistène, interview Paris, October 29, 2015.
22. Germain Viatte, interview Paris, April 24, 2015.

23. Jean-Hubert Martin, interview Paris, April 23, 2015.
24. Jean-Hubert Martin, interview Paris, January 12, 2015.
25. Jean-Hubert Martin, interview Paris, April 23, 2015.
26. Jean-Hubert Martin, interview Paris, April 23, 2015.
27. Andreae, 1997–1999.
28. Jean-Yves Mock, interview Paris, January 12, 2015.
29. Pontus Hultén, interview Stockholm, December 16, 1996.
30. Pontus Hultén, interview Stockholm, December 16, 1996.
31. Tomkins, February 1, 1978.
32. Richard Rogers, interview London, May 5, 2016.
33. Andreae, 1997–1999.
34. "'Today is much more an age of greed.' Richard Rogers reflects on 50-year career." Dezeen.com, August 7, 2013.
35. "'Today is much more an age of greed.' Richard Rogers reflects on 50-year career." Dezeen.com, August 7, 2013.
36. Archdaily.com, June 11, 2010.
37. Archdaily.com, June 11, 2010.
38. Renzo Piano, interview Paris, January 8, 2015.
39. Pierre Schneider, The New York Times, May 29, 1974.
40. Andreae, 1997–1999.
41. Andreae, 1997–1999.
42. Jean-Hubert Martin, interview Paris, April 23, 2015.
43. Jean-Hubert Martin, interview Paris, April 23, 2015.
44. Giorgio de Chirico "Portrait of Guillaume Apollinaire," 1914, MNAM, Paris, purchase 1975.
45. Bengt Jangfeldt, *A Russian History*, Wahlström & Widstrand, Stockholm, e-book 2015, pp. 349–366.
46. Jean-Hubert Martin, interview Paris, April 23, 2015.
47. Jean-Hubert Martin, interview Paris, April 23, 2015.
48. Jean Clair, interview Paris, April 22, 2015.
49. Andreae, 1997–1999.
50. Mats B, interview Pontus Hultén. Moderna Museet (Friends of Moderna Museet magazine), no. 2, 1981.
51. Andreae, 1997–1999.
52. The *20 Years of Work* exhibition opened at the Moscow Writers' Club in February 1930. Mayakovsky committed suicide by shooting himself on April 14, 1930, a date considered by Pontus Hultén and others to be the end of experimental art in the Soviet Union.
53. Andreae, 1997–1999.
54. Lilya 'Lili' Brik (1891–1978) was born as Lilya Kagan. She came from a wealthy and intellectual Jewish family in Moscow. Pablo Neruda called her "the muse of the Russian avant-garde." She was the elder sister of the writer Elsa Triolet (1896–1970), who first met and fell in love with Mayakovsky and marrying Louis Aragon in 1928.
55. Andreae, 1997–1999.
56. Andreae, 1997–1999.
57. Germain Viatte, e-mail, November 25, 2021.
58. Andreae, 1997–1999.
59. The Grand Palais des Champs-Élysées exhibition center, known simply as the Grand Palais, began construction in 1897 and was inaugurated for the 1900 Paris World Fair. The complex also includes the Petit Palais and spectacular Pont Alexandre bridge. The architects were Henry Deglane, Albert Louvet, Albert Thomas and Charles Girault.
60. Andreae, 1997–1999.
61. *Max Ernst. Paintings, collages, frottage, drawings, prints, books, sculptures 1917–1969*. Moderna Museet, Stockholm, September 13–November 2, 1969.
62. Andreae, 1997–1999.
63. Werner Spies has come under fire since he authenticated a number of what turned out to be forged Max Ernst paintings in the early 2000s, one of which was sold for seven million dollars in New York in 2006. Spies was initially convicted but later acquitted for his role in the counterfeiting scandal (see, among others, Spiegel International, June 13, 2011 and The Art Newspaper, December 9, 2015).
64. Jean-Hubert Martin strongly contradicts Hultén's description to Stephan Andreae of old MNAM as unprofessional in the presentation of exhibitions (e-mail, November 17, 2021).
65. Andreae, 1997–1999.
66. Andreae, 1997–1999.
67. Olle Granath, interview Stockholm, April 25, 2018.
68. Jean-Hubert Martin, e-mail, November 13, 2020.
69. Roberta Smith, "Pontus Hultén, 82, Champion of Contemporary Art, Dies," The New York Times, October 30, 2006.
70. Marie-Louise von Plessen, interview La Motte, June 30, 2021.
71. Hélène Klein, interview Paris, February 13, 2017.
72. Andreae, 1997–1999.
73. *Francis Picabia*, Département des Arts Plastiques du Centre Georges Pompidou, exhibition catalog no. 2, MNAM, Paris, 1976.
74. Gabrielle Buffet-Picabia (1881–1985) was a writer and art critic, well known in Dadaist circles. She was involved in the French Resistance in Paris during the Second World War.
75. Jean-Hubert Martin, interview Paris, April 23, 2015.
76. Jean-Hubert Martin, e-mail, November 13, 2020.
77. The previously mentioned influential Documenta 5 under the artistic direction of Harald Szeemann.

78. Jean-Hubert Martin, interview Paris, April 23, 2015.
79. Andreae, 1997–1999.
80. *The Peggy Guggenheim Collection from Venice*, Moderna Museet, Stockholm, November 26, 1966–January 8, 1967.
81. Andreae, 1997–1999.
82. Pontus Hultén, "Un billet de mille francs enfermé meurt de faim (Picabia)." *Francis Picabia*, Département des Arts Plastiques du Centre Georges Pompidou, exhibition catalog no. 2, MNAM, Paris, 1976, p. 5.
83. Jean-Hubert Martin, "Alle Fragen, die ich Pontus Hultén nicht gestellt habe (All questions I didn't ask Pontus Hultén)," Lutz Jahre, *Das gedruckte Museum von Pontus Hultén. Kunstausstellungen und ihre Bücher*, Kunst- und Ausstellungshalle der Bundesrepublik Deutschland/Cantz, Bonn, 1996, p. 123.
84. Pontus Hultén, "Un billet de mille francs enfermé meurt de faim (Picabia)." *Francis Picabia*, Département des Arts Plastiques du Centre Georges Pompidou, exhibition catalog no. 2, MNAM, Paris, 1976, p. 5.
85. Jean-Hubert Martin, interview Paris, April 23, 2015.
86. Olle Granath, interview Stockholm, February 26, 2015.
87. Jean-Hubert Martin, interview Paris, April 23, 2015.

20 Grand Opening

1. Sven-Olof Hellström, interview Stockholm, May 20, 2014.
2. Calvin Tomkins, "The Good Monster," The New Yorker, February 1, 1978.
3. Stephan Andreae, "Reisen mit Riesen/ Walking With Giants." Transcript of recorded conversations with Pontus Hultén for unpublished autobiography, La Motte, 1997–1999. © Stephan Andreae.
4. Andreae, 1997–1999.
5. Andreae, 1997–1999.
6. Jean-Hubert Martin, e-mail, June 24, 2021.
7. Andreae, 1997–1999.
8. Andreae, 1997–1999.
9. Andreae, 1997–1999.
10. Andreae, 1997–1999.
11. Andreae, 1997–1999.
12. Jean-Yves Mock interview Paris, January 12, 2015.
13. Jean-Yves Mock, interview Paris, January 11, 2015.
14. Jean-Yves Mock, interview Paris, January 11, 2015.
15. Andreae, 1997–1999.
16. Jean-Yves Mock, interview Paris, January 11, 2015.
17. Niki de Saint Phalle, "A Portrait of Pontus," Lutz Jahre, *Das gedruckte Museum von Pontus Hultén. Kunstausstellungen und ihre Bücher*, Kunst- und Ausstellungshalle der Bundesrepublik Deutschland/Cantz, Bonn, 1996, p. 106
18. Tomkins, February 1, 1978.
19. Jean-Hubert Martin confirms this picture of Duchamp's position in Paris at the time (e-mail July 6, 2020).
20. Jean Clair, interview Paris, April 22, 2015.
21. Tomkins, February 1, 1978.
22. Jean Clair, interview Paris, April 22, 2015.
23. Jean Clair, interview Paris, April 22, 2015.
24. Henri-Pierre Roché was a journalist, writer, art collector and dealer — a key figure in avant-garde art circles in both his native Paris and New York during the war, good friend of Picasso, Brancusi, Picabia and many other artists. Roché moved with Marcel Duchamp to New York in 1916 and worked with him on many projects. Late in life he published two novels, *Jules et Jim* (1953) and *Two English Girls* (1956), both adapted for the screen by François Truffaut (1962 and 1971). Also wrote an unpublished novel, *Victor*, with the main character modeled after Duchamp.
25. *Marcel Duchamp*, exhibition catalog no. 8, MNAM Centre Pompidou, Paris, 1977. Volume no. 4.
26. Jean Clair, interview Paris, April 22, 2015.
27. Jacques Caumont, interview Paris, April 24, 2015.
28. Andreae, 1997–1999.
29. Jacques Caumont, interview Paris, April 24, 2015.
30. Andreae, 1997–1999.
31. André Chastel, "L'au-delà de la peinture de Marcel Duchamp." Le Monde, February 3, 1977.
32. Jean Clair, interview Paris, April 22, 2015.
33. Andreae, 1997–1999.
34. Unsurprisingly, there are contradictory accounts.
35. Jean-Hubert Martin, interview Paris, April 23, 2015. Sigmar Polke, "Cameleonardo da Willich," 1979. MNAM Centre Pompidou, Paris, purchase 1980. The painting is intended to be worn as a garment.
36. Ben Vautier, known as Ben, was a French artist born in 1935 in Naples, strongly influenced by Duchamp, who ran his small shop in Nice between 1958 and 1973, a meeting place for Ben's artist friends such as Yves Klein, Armand, Martial Raysse (all from Nice) and others from the Neo-Realist and Fluxus movements. The shop was purchased for the MNAM collection in 1975 and was displayed at the opening in 1977.
37. Jean-Hubert Martin, interview Paris, April 23, 2015.
38. Jean-Hubert Martin, interview Paris, April 23, 2015.
39. Jean-Hubert Martin, interview Paris, April 23, 2015.
40. Jean-Hubert Martin, interview Paris, April 23, 2015.
41. Jean-Yves Mock, interview Paris, January 12, 2015.
42. Daniel Abadie, interview Paris, October 22, 2015.

43. Meeting of the General Assembly of French Artists, Créteil, January 3, 1977.
44. Annick Boisnard, interview Paris, January 14, 2015.
45. Annick Boisnard, interview Paris, January 14, 2015.
46. Jean-Yves Mock, interview Paris, January 12, 2015.
47. Descriptions of the opening by Pontus Hultén for Stephan Andrea and by Calvin Tomkins, "The Good Monster," The New Yorker, February 1, 1978.
48. Andreae, 1997–1999.
49. Tomkins, February 1, 1978.
50. Jean-Yves Mock, interview Paris, January 12, 2015.
51. Andreae, 1997–1999.
52. Rowan Moore, "Pompidou Centre: a 70s French radical that's never gone out of fashion," The Guardian, January 8, 2017.
53. Pontus Hultén himself estimated that the ideas from Kulturhuset "to 60–70 percent" were realized in the Pompidou center (Pontus Hultén, interview with Mats B, Moderna Museet magazine, 1981).
54. Tomkins, February 1, 1978.
55. Tomkins, February 1, 1978.
56. Calvin Tomkins, interview New York, September 10, 2014.
57. Renzo Piano, interview Paris, January 8, 2015.
58. Rowan Moore, "Pompidou Centre: a 70s French radical that's never gone out of fashion," The Guardian, January 8, 2017.
59. Rowan Moore, "Pompidou Centre: a 70s French radical that's never gone out of fashion," The Guardian, January 8, 2017.
60. Renzo Piano, interview Paris, January 8, 2015.

21 Pingpong with the world and art history

1. Stephan Andreae, "Reisen mit Riesen/ Walking With Giants." Transcript of recorded conversations with Pontus Hultén for unpublished autobiography, La Motte, 1997–1999. © Stephan Andreae.
2. Hans Ulrich Obrist, *A Brief History of Curating*, JRP-Ringier/Les Presses du Réel, Geneva, 2008, p. 38.
3. Jean-Hubert Martin, e-mail, April 12, 2020.
4. Jean-Hubert Martin, interview Paris, July 2, 2021.
5. Germain Viatte, e-mail, May 10, 2021.
6. Jean Clair, interview Paris, April 22, 2015.
7. Andreae, 1997–1999.
8. Malitte Matta, interview Paris, February 7, 2015.
9. Hélène Klein (Seckel), interview Paris, February 14, 2017.
10. Hélène Klein (Seckel), interview Paris, February 14, 2017.
11. Serge Fauchereau, interview Paris, January 12, 2015.
12. Daniel Abadie, interview Paris, October 22, 2015.
13. Daniel Abadie, interview Paris, October 22, 2015.
14. Daniel Abadie, interview Paris, October 22, 2015.
15. 2000–2013.
16. Alfred Pacquement, interview Paris, October 27, 2015.
17. Pontus Hultén, "L'art, un style de vie — les échanges," *Paris–New York*. MNAM Pompidou center, exhibition catalog no. 20. MNAM Centre Pompidou, Paris, 1977, pp. 1–3.
18. Jean-Hubert Martin, e-mail, April 17, 2021.
19. Alfred Pacquement, interview Paris, October 27, 2015.
20. Mats B, interview Pontus Hultén, Moderna Museet (Friends of Moderna Museet magazine), no. 2, 1981.
21. Andreae, 1997–1999.
22. Andreae, 1997–1999.
23. John Russell, "'Paris–New York': A Century of Modern Art," The New York Times, June 14, 1977.
24. Jean-Hubert Martin, interview Paris, April 23, 2015.
25. Jean-Hubert Martin, interview Paris, April 23, 2015.
26. Olle Granath, interview Stockholm, October 23, 2015.
27. Richard Armstrong, interview New York, September 9, 2014.
28. Serge Fauchereau, interview Villejuif, October 29, 2015.
29. Stanislas Zadora, interview Paris, October 22, 2015.
30. Stanislas Zadora, interview Paris, October 22, 2015.
31. Sergei "Afrika" Bugaev, interview Saint Petersburg, November 10, 2019.
32. Art historian Irina Antonova joined the Pushkin Museum at the end of the war in 1945. She was its director from 1961 to 2013, when she was dismissed after a political controversy and appointed president of the museum, a ceremonial function. Her 52 years as director make her the world's oldest and longest-serving museum director. Even in 2020, at the age of 98, Antonova was still active, with her own office and secretary at the museum. Antonova is controversial for her ties with the Soviet regime. As a new employee, she witnessed the arrival at the Pushkin Museum of tons of art seized by the Red Army. Antonova defended Russia's right to looted art, as compensation for the Russian cultural treasures looted by Nazi Germany. "Priam's Treasure" is a priceless collection of archaeological finds in gold and other materials excavated in the 1870s in northwestern Turkey, alleged remains of the Homeric city of Troy. The treasure disappeared at the end of the war in 1945 from a bunker in Berlin. The Soviet and the

Russian authorities, represented by Irina Antonova, denied all knowledge of the tax for years, until it was revealed to have been stored in its magazine all along.

33. Irina Antonova, telephone interview, December 7, 2019.
34. Jean-Hubert Martin, e-mail, April 20, 2020.
35. Jean-Hubert Martin, interview Paris, April 23, 2015.
36. Werner Spies, interview Paris, October 28, 2015.
37. Serge Fauchereau, interview Villejuif, October 29, 2015.
38. *Paris–Berlin 1900–1933*, catalog, Centre national d'art et de culture Georges Pompidou, Paris, 1978, p. 7.
39. George Grosz, "Remember Uncle August, the Unhappy Inventor," 1919. MNAM Centre Pompidou, Paris. Purchase 1977.
40. Jean-Hubert Martin, e-mail, September 23, 2021.
41. Richard Huelsenbeck, *En avant Dada: A History of Dadaism*, Paul Steegemann Verlag, Hannover, Leipzig, Vienna, Zürich, 1920.
42. Werner Spies, interview Paris, October 28, 2015.
43. Werner Spies, interview Paris, October 28, 2015.
44. Jean-Hubert Martin, interview Paris, April 23, 2015.
45. Andreae, 1997–1999.
46. Stanislas Zadora, interview Paris, October 22, 2015.
47. Jean-Hubert Martin, interview Paris, April 23, 2015.
48. Jean-Hubert Martin, interview Paris, April 23, 2015.
49. Stanislas Zadora, interview Paris, October 22, 2015.
50. Jean-Hubert Martin, interview Paris, April 23, 2015.
51. Stanislas Zadora, interview Paris, October 22, 2015.
52. Olle Granath, e-mail, September 20, 2021.
53. *Paris–Moscow 1900–1930*. Centre national d'art et de culture Georges Pompidou/ Ministère de la culture de l'URSS, Paris, 1979, p. 7.
54. Jean-Hubert Martin, e-mail, March 14, 2020.
55. Jean-Hubert Martin, interview Paris, April 23, 2015.
56. Jean-Hubert Martin, e-mail, March 13, 2020.
57. *Malevich. Planités and Architectones*. MNAM Centre Pompidou, Paris, April 2–June 2, 1980, catalog, Jean-Hubert Martin, *Malevich. Architectones. Paintings. Drawings*. Collections du musée national d'art moderne, Centre Georges Pompidou, Paris, 1980.
58. Andrei Erofeev is a Russian art historian, curator and critic who was curator of contemporary art at the Tsaritsyno Museum in Moscow from 1989 to 2002, and curator from 2002 to 2008 for contemporary art at the Tretyakov Gallery in Moscow. As a young curator at the Pushkin Museum, he worked with *Moscow–Paris* and became good friends with Pontus Hultén.
59. Andrei Erofeev, *Moscow–Paris*, Isskousstvo, Moscow, spring 2020.
60. Détente — international term for the improvement of relations between East and West during the Cold War.
61. Apparatchik — term for functionaries and bureaucrats of the Soviet Communist Party.
62. Mickhail Matiushin, composer, artist and theorist who formulated a definition of a "fourth dimension" that brought together music and visual arts.
63. Andrei Erofeev, *Moscow–Paris*, Isskousstvo, Moscow, spring 2020.
64. Jean-Hubert Martin, e-mail, August 23, 2021.
65. Olesya Turkina, interview Saint Petersburg, November 10, 2019.
66. Andrei Erofeev, *Moscow–Paris*, Isskousstvo, Moscow, spring 2020.
67. Information on the timing of Brezhnev's visit varies.
68. Olesia Turkina, interview Saint Petersburg, November 10, 2019.
69. Jean-Hubert Martin, interview Paris, April 23, 2015.
70. Irina Antonova, telephone interview, December 7, 2019.
71. Jean-Yves Mock, interview Paris, October 24, 2015.
72. Roman Cieślewicz was a Polish graphic designer living in Paris, a good friend of Pontus Hultén, who designed many catalogs and other materials for MNAM Centre Pompidou. Cieślewicz designed the covers for *Paris–Berlin*, *Paris–Moscow* and *Paris–Paris*.
73. Germain Viatte, interview Paris, November 23, 2017.
74. Andreae, 1997–1999.
75. Jean Clair, interview Paris, April 22, 2015.
76. "Marcel Duchamp, the spiritual godfather of Pop Art," Victor Bockris, *The Life and Death of Andy Warhol*. Bantam Books, New York, 1989, p. 134.
77. Nicholas Serota, telephone interview, March 11, 2015.
78. Germain Viatte, interview Paris, April 21, 2015.
79. Les Cahiers du musée national d'art moderne, no 141, "Hommage à Pontus Hultén," Éditions du Centre Pompidou, Paris, fall 2017. Les Cahiers du musée national d'art moderne hors-series 2019, "Paris–Moscou 40 ans après," Éditions du Centre Pompidou, Paris, 2019.
80. Ben Luke, "The art machine: the Centre Pompidou at 40." The Art Newspaper, New York/London, February 1, 2017.
81. An abbreviation of arkhitektons, the name commonly used for Malevich's abstract architectural sculptures/models.

82. Luke, February 1, 2017.
83. Luke, February 1, 2017.
84. Quote from Swedish Television's documentary film "Pontus Hultén — succéerna och Brilloskandalen," from 2024, directed by Ann-Linn Guillou.
85. Olle Granath, interview Stockholm, October 23, 2015.

22 Pontus in Paris

1. Jean-Yves Mock, interview Paris, January 7, 2015.
2. Jean-Hubert Martin, interview Paris, April 23, 2015.
3. Serge Fauchereau, interview Paris, January 12, 2015.
4. The "Commandery" is a soldier's home for Templars probably from the thirteenth century in the village of Dannemois, near Milly-la-Forêt in Fontainebleau. Jean Tinguely bought the property in 1970. During the 1970s, the Commanderie was a focal point for artists and other members of the Tinguley and Niki de Saint Phalle entourage, as well as the location for several films.
5. Catherine Matisse Monnier, interview New York, September 8, 2014.
6. The unlikely life and work of Ferdinand Cheval — "Le facteur Cheval" — was depicted in the 2018 French blockbuster film *L'Incroyable Histoire du facteur Cheval*.
7. In Sweden, Lars Wilks and his creation "Nimis" can be counted among this category of artworks created over a long period of time by "maverick artists" outside the established art world.
8. Bloum called Tinguely her grandfather, but her real grandfather was Niki de Saint Phalle's first husband, the American writer and poet Harry Mathews.
9. Probably Niki de Saint Phalle's fantastic "Snow White-like" horror saga *Un rêve plus long que la nuit* (A dream longer than night) from 1976, filmed in Fontainebleau, with scenes from "The Commandery" and "The Cycle," with Bloum's mother Laura Duke Condeminas in a memorable role.
10. Bloum Cardenas, interview Milly-la-Forêt, October 23, 2015.
11. CIMAM, Comité internationale des musées d'art modernes, a subdivision of ICOM, a UNESCO-related body. Pontus Hultén was president of the committee from the late seventies. He was succeeded in 1986 by Richard Oldenburg, who in turn was succeeded by Olle Granath.
12. *Öyvind Fahlström*, MNAM Centre Pompidou, Paris, January 23–March 31, 1980. A retrospective exhibition in memory of Fahlström, who died in 1976. Produced in collaboration with Moderna Museet in Stockholm, where it was shown October 13–December 9, 1979.
13. *Ellsworth Kelly*, Centre Pompidou, Paris, April 23–June 15, 1980. Several people claim that Kelly was the only one of the famous Minimalists that appealed to Pontus Hultén's personal taste.
14. Jean-Hubert Martin, interview Paris, January 12, 2015.
15. Joseph Beuys, "Infiltration homogen für Konzertflügel," 1966. MNAM Pompidou center, Paris. Purchase 1976.
16. *Les Realismes 1919–1939*, MNAM Centre Pompidou, Paris, December 17, 1980–February 20, 1981.
17. Jean Clair, interview Paris, April 22, 2015.
18. Jean-Hubert Martin, e-mail, August 23, 2021.
19. Ida Gianelli, interview Milan, November 25, 2015.
20. Alfred Pacquement, interview Paris, October 27, 2015.
21. Stanislas Zadora, interview Paris, October 22, 2015.
22. Gérard Fromanger, interview Paris, April 19, 2015.
23. The one Pontus Hultén mourned was almost certainly Sture Johansson, janitor and handyman at the National Museum, who played a such a key role in the creation and early years of Moderna Museet.
24. Daniel Buren, interview Paris, January 14, 2015.
25. Stephan Andreae, "Reisen mit Riesen/ Walking With Giants." Transcript of recorded conversations with Pontus Hultén for unpublished autobiography, La Motte, 1997–1999. © Stephan Andreae.
26. Andreae, 1997–1999.
27. Andreae, 1997–1999.
28. Andreae, 1997–1999.
29. Calvin Tomkins, interview New York, September 10, 2014.
30. Andreae, 1997–1999.
31. Andreae, 1997–1999.
32. Jean-Hubert Martin, e-mail, August 27, 2021.
33. Germain Viatte, interview Paris, October 28, 2015.
34. Germain Viatte, interview Paris, October 28, 2015.
35. Andreae, 1997–1999.
36. Germain Viatte, interview Paris, October 28, 2015.
37. Andreae, 1997–1999.
38. Jean-Hubert Martin, interview Paris, July 2, 2021.
39. Andreae, 1997–1999.
40. Andreae, 1997–1999.
41. Andreae, 1997–1999.

23 Surrealism's revenge

1. *Paris–Moscow*, MNAM Centre Pompidou, Paris, May 31–November 5, 1979.
2. *Magritte retrospective*, MNAM Centre Pompidou, Paris, January 17–April 9, 1979.
3. Daniel Abadie, interview Paris, 22 October 2015.

4. Daniel Abadie, interview Paris, October 22, 2015.
5. Daniel Abadie, interview Paris, October 22, 2015.
6. Daniel Abadie, interview Paris, October 22, 2015.
7. Daniel Abadie, interview Paris, October 22, 2015.
8. Daniel Abadie, interview Paris, October 22, 2015.
9. "Visage du Grand Masturbateur," 1929. Since 1990 in the collection of the Reina Sofia in Madrid, by donation from the estate of Salvador Dalí.
10. Daniel Abadie, interview Paris, October 22, 2015.
11. Daniel Abadie, interview Paris, October 22, 2015.
12. Bernadette Dufrène, *Centre Pompidou trente ans d'histoire*, Centre Pompidou, Paris, 2007, p. 441.
13. Daniel Abadie, interview Paris, October 22, 2015.
14. Stephan Andreae, "Reisen mit Riesen/ Walking With Giants." Transcript of recorded conversations with Pontus Hultén for unpublished autobiography, La Motte, 1997–1999. © Stephan Andreae.
15. Andreae, 1997–1999.
16. There are various reports about the origins of this strike.
17. Andreae, 1997–1999.
18. Andreae, 1997–1999.
19. Daniel Abadie, interview Paris, October 22, 2015.
20. Dufrène, 2007, p. 587.
21. Daniel Abadie, interview Paris, October 22, 2015.
22. Philippe Vergne, telephone interview, March 13, 2016.

24 Exit Paris

1. In many articles and interviews, including Calvin Tomkins, "The Camel in the Tent," The New Yorker, March 2, 1981.
2. Hélène Arweller.
3. Stephan Andreae, "Reisen mit Riesen/ Walking With Giants." Transcript of recorded conversations with Pontus Hultén for unpublished autobiography, La Motte, 1997–1999. © Stephan Andreae.
4. Among others, Claude Mollard.
5. Andreae, 1997–1999.
6. Claude Mollard, telephone interview, March 17, 2017.
7. Jean-Hubert Martin, interview Paris, April 23, 2015.
8. Jean-Hubert Martin, interview Paris, April 23, 2015.
9. Jean-Hubert Martin was Director of the MNAM Centre Pompidou from 1987 to 1990.
10. Jean-Yves Mock, interview Paris, October 24, 2015.
11. Jean-Hubert Martin, interview Paris, July 3, 2021.
12. Bernard Blistène, interview Paris, October 29, 2015.
13. Centre Pompidou Metz is considered the first major cultural decentralization project in France — a collaboration between the Centre Pompidou and the local authorities of Lorraine in northeastern France, where Metz is the capital. Centre Pompidou Metz is the largest exhibition facility in France outside Paris with over 5000 square meters of exhibition space, inaugurated in 2010 in spectacular architecture by Japanese Shigeru Ban. The institution is neither an annex nor branch of the Centre Pompidou in Paris but rather a sister institution, operating in the spirit of the Centre Pompidou with its own exhibition and research programs, as well as exhibiting the Centre Pompidou's collection of over 100,000 artworks.
14. *Face à Arcimboldo*, Centre Pompidou Metz, May 29–November 22, 2021.
15. Anne Horwath, "L'Effet Pontus Hultén," catalog *Face à Arcimboldo*, Centre Pompidou Metz, 2021, pp. 385–389.
16. *Niki de Saint Phalle, Jean Tingely, Pontus Hultén*. Exhibition by the Centre Pompidou at Grand Palais, Paris, June 20, 2025–January 4, 2026.
17. Quote from Swedish Television's documentary film "Pontus Hultén — succéerna och Brilloskandalen," from 2024, directed by Ann-Linn Guillou.
18. Andreae, 1997–1999.
19. Jean-Hubert Martin, e-mail, February 20, 2021.
20. Jean-Hubert Martin, interview Paris, July 3, 2021.

25 MOCA, Los Angeles, California

1. Connie Bruck, "The Art of the Billionaire," The New Yorker, November 29, 2010.
2. "Hulten of Paris to Head New Museum on Coast," The New York Times, August 20, 1980: https://www.nytimes.com/1980/08/20/archives/hulten-of-paris-to-head-new-museum-on-coast-goals-of-the-museum.html
3. Calvin Tomkins, "The Camel in the Tent," The New Yorker, March 2, 1981.
4. Tomkins, March 2, 1981.
5. An assemblage can be described as a larger-scale, three-dimensional collage, with different two- and three-dimensional components assembled in a three-dimensional whole, often a spatiality.
6. Aurora Garrison, "Irving Blum, Andy Warhol and the LA Art Scene: The Birth of Pop Art on the West Coast," revolverwarholgallery.com, February 2018.
7. Tomkins, March 2, 1981.
8. Connie Bruck, "The Art of the Billionaire," The New Yorker, November 29, 2010.
9. Bruck, November 29, 2010.
10. Bruck, November 29, 2010.

11. Bruck, November 29, 2010.
12. Marcia Weisman is pictured with her husband Fred on David Hockney's classic large double portrait "American Collectors (Fred and Marcia Weisman)" from 1968. The painting is in the collection of the Art Institute of Chicago.
13. Tomkins, March 2, 1981.
14. Tomkins, March 2, 1981.
15. Tomkins, March 2, 1981.
16. Tomkins, March 2, 1981.
17. Eli Broad, interview Los Angeles, November 6, 2014.
18. Tomkins, March 2, 1981.
19. Richard Koshalek, interview Los Angeles, November 10, 2014.
20. Stephan Andreae, "Reisen mit Riesen/ Walking With Giants." Transcript of recorded conversations with Pontus Hultén for unpublished autobiography, La Motte, 1997–1999. © Stephan Andreae.
21. Tomkins, March 2, 1981.
22. Andreae, 1997–1999.
23. Tomkins, March 2, 1981.
24. Andreae, 1997–1999.
25. MOCA's expansion has been debated more or less since the museum opened but has not yet materialized due to lack of funding.
26. Eli Broad, interview Los Angeles, November 6, 2014.
27. Tomkins, March 2, 1981.
28. Bruck, November 29, 2010.
29. Bruck, November 29, 2010.
30. Bruck, November 29, 2010.
31. Eli Broad, interview Los Angeles, November 6, 2014.
32. Richard Koshalek, interview Los Angeles, November 10, 2014.
33. Smithsonian Archives of American Art. Oral history interview by Christopher Knight with Giuseppe Panza di Biumo, April 2–4, 1985, p. 55.
34. Panza di Biumo mentions in the interview that he first met Pontus Hultén during a visit to Stockholm in 1963.
35. Giuseppina Panza, e-mail, March 1 2021.
36. William Middleton, *Double Vision. The Unnerring Eye of Art World Avatars Dominique and John de Menil*, Alfred A. Knopf, New York, 2018, p. 551.
37. Museum and Contemporary Art Los Angeles, *Automobile and Culture*, catalog, Harry N. Abrams Incorporated, New York, 1984.
38. Richard Koshalek, interview Los Angeles, November 10, 2014.
39. Kerry Brougher, interview Los Angeles, November 11, 2014.
40. Gregory Mahoney, telephone interview, February 3, 2021.
41. Ed Ruscha, interview Los Angeles, November 10, 2014.
42. Tomkins, March 2, 1981.
43. Pontus Hultén, interview Stockholm, December 17, 1996.
44. Kerry Brougher, interview Los Angeles, November 11, 2014.
45. Richard Armstrong, interview New York, September 9, 2014.
46. Richard Koshalek, interview Los Angeles, November 10, 2014.
47. Richard Koshalek, interview Los Angeles, November 10, 2014.
48. Andreae, 1997–1999.
49. Richard Koshalek, interview Los Angeles, November 10, 2014.
50. Gregory Mahoney, telephone interview, February 3, 2021.
51. Kerry Brougher, interview Los Angeles, November 11, 2014.
52. Ann Goldstein, telephone interview, October 22, 2014.
53. Jerry Sohn, interview Los Angeles, November 7, 2014.
54. Jerry Sohn, interview Los Angeles, November 7, 2014.
55. Margareta Hellerberg, Interview Stockholm, March 12, 2015.
56. Kerry Brougher, interview Los Angeles, November 11, 2014.
57. Richard Koshalek, interview Los Angeles, November 10, 2014.
58. Richard Koshalek, interview Los Angeles, November 10, 2014.
59. Troels Andersen, interview Copenhagen, September 28, 2015.
60. I have found no evidence that any such plans have been made.
61. Richard Koshalek, interview Los Angeles, November 10, 2014.
62. Eli Broad, interview Los Angeles, November 6, 2014.
63. Ed Ruscha, interview Los Angeles, November 10, 2014.
64. Gregory Mahoney, telephone interview, February 3, 2021.
65. Richard Koshalek, interview Los Angeles, November 10, 2014.
66. Kerry Brougher, interview Los Angeles, November 11, 2014.
67. moca.org/exhibition/hall-of-mirrors-art-and-film-since-1945
68. Kerry Brougher, interview Los Angeles, November 11, 2014.
69. Richard Koshalek was director of the Fort Worth Art Museum in Texas from 1972 to 1976 and then became director of the Hudson River Museum in New York.
70. Robert Irwin, interview Oceanside, November 11, 2014.
71. Connie Bruck, "The Art of the Billionaire," The New Yorker, November 29, 2010.
72. Adam Nagourney, "A Soaring Arts Scene in Los Angeles Confronts a Changing Landscape," The New York Times, May 12, 2021.
73. Connie Bruck, "The Art of the Billionaire," The New Yorker, November 29, 2010.
74. Letter from Richard Long, The Old School, Bristol, April 16, 2015: "Pontus seemed like a giant from a bygone age, when a great curator/museum director was a rare creature. I only met Pontus a few times, so I did not

know him well or during his heyday, but enough to know a charismatic man of great intellect, life experience and knowledge (...) he regaled us with a rich trove of anecdotes, both senseless and insightful, from his long life with artists. He had been at the epicenter of much European art history. (...). He was also a very good writer, with a clear style and always with something original to say. I was staying at a bed & breakfast on Venice Beach the night of the big Los Angeles earthquake; Pontus was staying at a hotel a bit higher up, and he just thought that his female friend had kicked him off the bed (again) and went back to sleep. He liked to drink, he had a great sense of humor and enthusiasm, he had a generous spirit."

75. Jerry Sohn, e-mail, January 11, 2016.
76. Jerry Sohn, e-mail, January 11, 2016.

26 The World Expo that was canceled and became a school

1. Claude Mollard, *Le cinquième pouvoir: le culture et l'État de Malraux à Lang*, Armand Collin. Paris, 1999.
2. Claude Mollard, telephone interview, March 13, 2017.
3. Claude Mollard, telephone interview, March 13, 2017.
4. Mollard, 1999, pp. 271–273.
5. After serving a second term as Prime Minister under opponent François Mitterrand, and after previous attempts in presidential campaigns, Jacques Chirac was elected President in 1995 and re-elected in 2002, when the mandate term of office of the President had been shortened to five years. Chirac served as president until 2007 and died in 2019 in his home in Paris.
6. Claude Mollard, telephone interview, March 13, 2017.
7. Stephan Andreae, "Reisen mit Riesen/ Walking With Giants." Transcript of recorded conversations with Pontus Hultén for unpublished autobiography, La Motte, 1997–1999. © Stephan Andreae.
8. Daniel Buren, interview Paris, January 14, 2015.
9. Daniel Buren, *Passages Pontus Hultén*, memorial texts after Hultén's death. Artforum, New York, February 2007.
10. Annick Boisnard, interview Paris, April 25, 2015.
11. In ancient Greece, symposium (Greek for "drinking together") was the part of the banquet that took place after the meal, when drinking for pleasure was accompanied by music, dancing, readings, or conversation. Among literary works that describe or take place at the Symposium are two of Socrates' dialogs, Plato's Symposium and Xenophon's Symposium (see en.wikipedia.org/wiki/ Symposium).
12. Sarkis, interview Villejuif, October 28, 2015.
13. Meir Eshel, Israeli-French artist known by his pen name Absalon. Died at the age of only twenty-eight from AIDS-related disease at the beginning of a promising career. Since his death, his work has been exhibited in many leading museums and institutions worldwide.
14. Rebecca Quaytman, telephone interview, September 23, 2015.
15. Xavier Veilhan, interview Paris, April 20, 2015.
16. Autumn 1988 and spring 1989.
17. Michael Asher (1943–2012) was a radical American Conceptual artist working in Los Angeles whose works were always temporary and based on the sites where they were created, disposed after the exhibitions.
18. Dominique Gonzalez-Foerster, interview Paris, October 24, 2015.
19. Rebecca Quaytman, telephone interview, September 23, 2015.
20. Dominique Gonzalez-Foerster, interview Paris, October 24, 2015.
21. Jan Svenungsson, telephone interview, September 23, 2018.
22. Jan Svenungsson, telephone interview, September 23, 2018.
23. Jan Svenungsson is certainly referring to the connecting bolts on which the construction of the Centre Pompidou is largely based. Jan Svenungsson, telephone interview, September 23, 2018.
24. Jan Svenungsson, telephone interview, September 23, 2018.
25. Jan Svenungsson, telephone interview, September 23, 2018.
26. Daniel Buren, interview Paris, January 14, 2015.
27. Jan Svenungsson, telephone interview, September 23, 2018.
28. Serge Fauchereau, interview Villejuif, October 29, 2015.
29. Daniel Buren, interview Paris, January 14, 2015.
30. Serge Fauchereau, interview Villejuif, October 29, 2015.
31. *Quand les artistes font école. Vingt-quatre journées des hautes études en arts plastiques 1991–1992, tome III*. Amis de l'institut des hautes études en arts plastiques/Musees de Marseilles/ Éditions du Centre Pompidou, Paris, 2004.
32. Jean-Hubert Martin, e-mail, November 11, 2021.
33. After years of controversy and scandal, the Paris Biennale was formally closed in 2021.
34. Daniel Buren, telephone interview, February 19, 2022.

27 Saint Petersburg

1. Xavier Veilhan, interview Paris, April 20, 2015.
2. In 2020, Yekaterina Andreeva published the essay "Pontus Hultén's museum revolutions

in the territories of Moscow and Saint Petersburg" in The Garage Journal, an academic journal published by the Garage Museum of Contemporary Art in Moscow, the now highly controversial contemporary art museum founded in 2008 by Roman Abramovic and his then wife Dasha Zhukova, who still operates the museum, housed since 2015 in a spectacular building by Rem Koolhaas.

3. Jean-Hubert Martin, e-mail, October 10, 2020.
4. Sergei Bugaev, conversation Saint Petersburg, November 9, 2019.
5. Sergei Bugaev, conversation Saint Petersburg, November 9, 2019.
6. Sergei Bugaev, conversation Saint Petersburg, November 9, 2019.
7. *Assa* is a 1987 Soviet crime film directed by Sergei Solovyov that gained cult status in late Soviet youth culture, mainly because it was the first time that Soviet rock music from the underground culture was played to a mainstream audience.
8. Olesia Turkina, interview Saint Petersburg, November 10, 2019.
9. Sergei Bugaev, interview Saint Petersburg, November 12, 2019.
10. Sergei Bugaev, interview Saint Petersburg, November 9, 2019.
11. Sergei Bugaev, interview Saint Petersburg, November 9, 2019.
12. *The new ones from Leningrad*. Kulturhuset, Stockholm, August 27 to September 25, 1988.
13. Sergei Bugaev, interview Saint Petersburg, November 10, 2019.
14. Olesia Turkina, interview Saint Petersburg, November 10, 2019.
15. Ekaterina Andreeva, interview Saint Petersburg, November 11, 2019.
16. Ekaterina Andreeva, e-mail, June 21, 2021.
17. Elena Gubanova, interview Saint Petersburg, November 10, 2019.
18. Olesia Turkina, interview Saint Petersburg, November 10, 2019.
19. Ekaterina Andreeva, e-mail, June 21, 2021.
20. Elena Gubanova, interview Saint Petersburg, November 10, 2019.
21. Stephan Andreae, "Reisen mit Riesen/Walking With Giants." Transcript of recorded conversations with Pontus Hultén for unpublished autobiography, La Motte, 1997–1999. © Stephan Andreae.
22. Olesia Turkina, interview Saint Petersburg, November 10, 2019.
23. Sophie Tottie, interview Stockholm, December 19, 2019.
24. A project that was part of the so-called "Baltic Sea Billion," a policy initiative at the time intended to stimulate commercial, cultural and other cooperation with the post-communist neighboring countries in the East.
25. Ekaterina Andreeva, interview Saint Petersburg, November 11, 2019.
26. Robert Rauschenberg, "Mud Muse," created in 1968–1971 for an exhibition for Experiments in Art and Technology, E.A.T., Moderna Museet, Stockholm. Donation 1973 (New York Collection). NMSK 2174.
27. Olle Granath, interview Stockholm, February 16, 2015.
28. René Magritte's iconic "La trahison des images (Ceci n'est pas une pipe)," curiously listed with the year of creation "ca 1928–1967."
29. During the second half of the eighties, Pontus Hultén had lived in a relationship with German artist Rebecca Horn.
30. Catalog *Le Territoire de L'Art*, Institut des Hautes Études en Arts Plastiques/Éditions Cercle d'Arts, Paris, 1990. Unpaginated.
31. Bernard Blistène, interview Paris, October 29, 2015.
32. Yevgeniya Petrova, interview Saint Petersburg, November 12, 2019.
33. Yevgeniya Petrova, interview Saint Petersburg, November 12, 2019.
34. Olle Granath remembers correctly.
35. Olle Granath, interview Stockholm, February 16, 2015.
36. Olesia Turkina, interview Saint Petersburg, November 10, 2019.
37. Ekaterina Andreeva, interview Saint Petersburg, November 11, 2019.
38. Rebecca Quaytman, telephone interview, September 23, 2015.
39. Sophie Tottie, interview Stockholm, December 19, 2019.
40. Sophie Tottie, interview Stockholm, December 19, 2019.
41. Yevgeniya Petrova, interview Saint Petersburg, November 12, 2019.
42. Olesia Turkina, interview Saint Petersburg, November 10, 2019.
43. Yevgeniya Petrova, interview Saint Petersburg, November 12, 2019.
44. Yevgeniya Petrova, interview Saint Petersburg, November 12, 2019.
45. For example, in his speech at the symposium "Perestroïka et période post-soviétique" at MNAM Centre Pompidou, September 16, 2016. https://www.centrepompidou.fr/fr/ressources/media/2Cu01Bn
46. Sergei Bugaev, interview Saint Petersburg, November 12, 2019.
47. Ekaterina Andreeva, interview Saint Petersburg, November 11, 2019.
48. Sergei Bugaev, interview Saint Petersburg, November 12, 2019.
49. Elena Gubanova, interview Saint Petersburg, November 10, 2019.
50. Timur Novikov died in 2002.
51. Afrika (Sergei Bugaev), "Forms of Destruction," 1990. Donation 2005 from Pontus Hultén. MOM/2005/129. Timur Novikov, "Solntse (Sun)," 1989. Pontus Hultén's collection ..., Moderna Museet exhibition catalog 321, 2004, p. 232–233.
52. Sergei Bugaev, interview Saint Petersburg, November 12, 2019.

28 A realized dream of Venice?

1. Stephan Andreae, "Reisen mit Riesen/ Walking With Giants." Transcript of recorded conversations with Pontus Hultén for unpublished autobiography, La Motte, 1997–1999. © Stephan Andreae.
2. Vittorio Gregotti claims that no Venice Biennale was organized between 1968 and 1976, but according to the Biennale's own history, one was held in 1972.
3. Vittorio Gregotti, interview Milan, November 24, 2015.
4. Vittorio Gregotti, interview Milan, November 24, 2015.
5. Palazzo Grassi was by definition not a museum but an art gallery and cultural center.
6. Truman Capote, *Breakfast at Tiffany's*, Random House, New York, 1958.
7. See Hamish Bowles, "A Breathtaking New Book Charts the Life of Style Goddess Marella Agnelli," Vogue U.S., October 18, 2014.
8. Niki de Saint Phalle, "A Portrait of Pontus." Lutz Jahre, *Das gedruckte Museum von Pontus Hultén. Kunstausstellungen und ihre Bücher*, Kunst- und Ausstellungshalle der Bundesrepublik Deutschland/Cantz, Bonn, 1996, p. 105.
9. For the story of the Caracciolo family, see Bob Colacello, "Inheritance, Italian Style," Vanity Fair, December 2009. archive.vanityfair.com/article/2009/12/inheritance-italian-style
10. Nicola Caracciolo, interview Garravicchio, November 22, 2015.
11. Germano Celant, interview Milan, April 18, 2016.
12. Germano Celant died in spring 2020 as a result of COVID-19. He was honored in the art media worldwide as one of the great curators of modern and contemporary art.
13. Germano Celant, interview Milan, April 18, 2016.
14. Furio Colombo, interview Rome, November 21, 2015.
15. Furio Colombo, interview Rome, November 21, 2015.
16. Andreae, 1997–1999.
17. Serge Fauchereau, interview Paris, January 12, 2015.
18. Andreae, 1997–1999.
19. Germano Celant, interview Milan, April 18, 2016.
20. Ida Gianelli, interview Milan, September 25, 2015.
21. Germano Celant, interview Milan, April 18, 2016.
22. Ida Gianelli, interview Milan, September 25, 2015.
23. Ida Gianelli, interview Milan, September 25, 2015.
24. Ida Gianelli, interview Milan, September 25, 2015.
25. Antonio Foscari, interview Venice, November 27, 2015.
26. Pastasciutta is a term used for classic Italian pasta dishes with sauces like tomato or ragu.
27. Antonio Foscari, interview Venice, November 27, 2015.
28. Andreae, 1997–1999.
29. Germano Celant, interview Milan, April 18, 2016.
30. *Italian identity. Art in Italy since 1959*. MNAM Centre Pompidou, Paris, June 25–September 7, 1981.
31. Germano Celant, interview Milan, April 18, 2016.
32. Ida Gianelli, interview Milan, September 25, 2015.
33. Germano Celant, interview Milan, April 18, 2016.
34. Olle Granath, interview Stockholm, February 16, 2015.
35. Olle Granath, interview Stockholm, February 16, 2015.
36. Serge Fauchereau, interview Villejuif, October 29, 2015.
37. Catalog *Futurismo & Futurismi* (*Futurism & Futurisms*), Bompiani, Milan, 1986. Pontus Hultén foreword texts pp. 13–21, English edition.
38. *Futurismo & Futurismi*, 1986. Hultén, pp. 13–21.
39. Funding the restoration of works of art is a common form of payment for loans of particularly desirable works between institutions and collectors.
40. Ida Gianelli, interview Milan, September 25, 2015.
41. *Futurismo & Futurismi* (*Futurism & Futurisms*), Bompiani, Milan, 1986.
42. Germano Celant, interview Milan, April 18, 2016.
43. *Futurismo & Futurismi*, 1986. Hultén pp. 13–21.
44. *Futurismo & Futurismi*, 1986. Hultén pp. 13–21.
45. See, for example, newsrnd.com/life/2021-05-16-futurism-comes-out-of-the-closet.SyxA8rQ1FO.html
46. Olle Granath, interview Stockholm, February 16, 2015.
47. Antonio Foscari, interview Venice, November 27, 2015.
48. *Futurismo & Futurismi*, 1986. Hultén pp. 13–21.
49. Serge Fauchereau, "Conversation with Pontus Hultén," *Les Cahiers du musée national d'art moderne*, no. 141, "Hommage à Pontus Hultén," Éditions du Centre Pompidou, Paris, fall 2017. pp. 8–29.
50. Ida Gianelli, interview Milan, September 25, 2015.
51. Letter from Pontus Hultén to Dominique de Menil, April 16, 1969. Pontus Hultén's archive, Moderna Museet, *The Machine*, folder 3.
52. Letter from Dominique de Menil to Pontus Hultén, April 25, 1969. Pontus Hultén's

archive, Moderna Museet, *The Machine*, folder 3.
53. Olle Granath, e-mail, December 22, 2021.
54. *Face à Arcimboldo*, Éditions du Centre Pompidou-Metz, Metz, 2021. May 29–November 22, 2021.
55. Giuseppe Arcimboldo, "The Jurist," 1566.
56. Giuseppe Arcimboldo "The Cook," not dated in the National Museum's list but considered painted in 1566. Gift from the Friends of the National Museum in 1994. NM6897.
57. Olle Granath, interview Stockholm, February 16, 2015.
58. Yasha David, interview Paris, October 22, 2015.
59. Andreae, 1997–1999.
60. Andreae, 1997–1999.
61. Clarenza Catullo, interview Rovereto, November 26, 2015.
62. Andreae, 1997–1999.
63. Germano Celant, interview Milan, April 18, 2016.
64. Andreae, 1997–1999.
65. Chiara Parisi, "1987, 1526, 2021, 1947, 2666. Mettre au monde le monde." Text catalog *Face à Arcimboldo*, Éditions du Centre Pompidou-Metz, 2021, pp. 369–375.
66. Andreae, 1997–1999.
67. Clarenza Catullo, interview Rovereto, November 26, 2015.
68. Andreae, 1997–1999.
69. Renzo Piano, interview Paris, January 8, 2015.
70. A neighboring farm to Jean Tinguely's residence and studio in Neyruz, Switzerland.
71. Seppi Imhof, interview Basel, December 9, 2014.
72. Seppi Imhof, interview Basel, December 9, 2014.
73. Seppi Imhof, interview Basel, December 9, 2014.
74. Andreae, 1997–1999.
75. Pontus Hultén foreword, Pontus Hultén, *A Magic Stronger than Death*, Bompiani, Milan, 1987. Unpaginated page.
76. Clarenza Catullo, interview Rovereto, November 26, 2015.
77. Andreae, 1997–1999.
78. Germano Celant, interview Milan, April 18, 2016.
79. Jean-Hubert Martin, e-mail, July 23, 2020.
80. Several people have used the expression "elder statesman of art" to describe Pontus Hultén, including Kasper König, Germano Celant and Jerry Sohn.
81. Marie-Louise von Plessen, interview La Motte, October 20, 2015.
82. Among others, Jean-Yves Mock, interview Paris, October 24, 2015.
83. Renzo Piano, interview Paris, January 8, 2015.
84. William Middleton, *Double Vision. The Unnerring Eye of Art World Avatars Dominique and John de Menil*, Alfred A. Knopf, New York, 2018, p. 551.
85. Ted Loos, "A Portfolio That Surprises Even Its Creator," The New York Times, October 25, 2013.
86. 1987–1990.
87. Jacques Caumont, interview Paris, April 24, 2015.
88. Pontus Hultén, Natalia Dumitresco, Alexandre Istrati, *Brâncuşi*. Harry N Abrams Inc, New York, 1987.
89. Pontus Hultén, *The Surrealists Look at Art*, Lapis Press, Los Angeles, 1990.
90. Robert Shapazian in Jahre, 1996, pp. 153–154.
91. Ida Gianelli, interview Milan, September 25, 2015.
92. Ida Gianelli, interview Milan, September 25, 2015.
93. Clarenza Catullo, interview Rovereto, November 26, 2015.
94. Andreae, 1997–1999.
95. Vittorio Gregotti, interview Milan, November 24, 2015.
96. Monika Nieckels, interview Stockholm, April 26, 2018.
97. Germano Celant, interview Milan, April 18, 2016.
98. Ida Gianelli, interview Milan, September 25, 2015.
99. Clarenza Catullo, interview Rovereto, November 26, 2015.
100. Rebecca Horn, telephone interview, March 13, 2016.
101. Ida Gianelli, interview Milan, September 25, 2015.
102. Clarenza Catullo, interview Rovereto, November 26, 2015.
103. Andreae, 1997–1999.
104. Calvin Tomkins, *Off the Wall. A Portrait of Robert Rauschenberg*, Picador, New York, 1980/2005, p. 252.
105. Ulf Linde was formally curator of the Thielska Gallery from 1977 to 1997. He was succeeded by his wife Nina Öhman (former curator at Moderna Museet). The couple lived and worked at the Thielska Gallery until 2011.
106. Jacques Caumont, interview Paris, April 24, 2015.
107. Among others, Francis M. Neumann, interview New York, September 11, 2014 and Paul B. Franklin, interview Paris, April 25, 2015.
108. Francis M. Naumann, *The Recurrent, Haunting Ghost*, Ready-made Press, New York, 2012, pp. 293–294.
109. Naumann, 2012, pp. 293–294.
110. Ida Gianelli, interview Milan, September 25, 2015.
111. Jacques Caumont, e-mail, October 12, 2018.
112. Ida Gianelli, interview Milan, September 25, 2015.
113. Clarenza Catullo, interview Rovereto, November 26, 2015.
114. Read Daniel Birnbaum's review of the 1993 Duchamp exhibition at Palazzo Grassi from Dagens Nyheter July 4, 1993: www.dn.se/arkiv/kultur/finalized-finalized-art-of-the-slump-numbered-and-dated/

115. Clarenza Catullo, interview Rovereto, November 26, 2015.
116. Antonio Foscari, interview Venice, November 27, 2015.
117. Germano Celant, interview Milan, April 18, 2016.
118. Ida Gianelli, interview Milan, September 25, 2015.

29 Who would have thought? Pontus sets foot in Germany ...

1. Sarkis, interview Villejuif, October 28, 2015.
2. Among others, Kasper König, interview Cologne, November 30, 2015.
3. Jan Svenungsson, telephone interview, April 17, 2018.
4. Kay Heymer, interview Düsseldorf, December 2, 2015.
5. Wenzel Jacob, interview Bonn, November 29, 2015.
6. Stephan Andreae, "Reisen mit Riesen/ Walking With Giants." Transcript of recorded conversations with Pontus Hultén for unpublished autobiography, La Motte, 1997–1999. © Stephan Andreae.
7. Wenzel Jacob, interview Bonn, November 29, 2015.
8. Wenzel Jacob, interview Bonn, November 29, 2015.
9. Andreae, 1997–1999.
10. Wenzel Jacob, interview Bonn, November 29, 2015.
11. Wenzel Jacob, interview Bonn, November 29, 2015.
12. Wenzel Jacob, interview Bonn, November 29, 2015.
13. See Chapter 19.
14. Andreae, 1997–1999.
15. Andreae, 1997–1999.
16. Wenzel Jacob, interview Bonn, November 29, 2015.
17. Peter Iden, *Territorim Artis*, Frankfurter Rundschau, July 25, 1992.
18. *Territorium Artis*, catalog, Kunst- und Ausstellungshalle der Bundesrepublik Deutschland, Bonn, 1992.
19. Cply (William Copley), "Portrait de l'artiste en jeune marchand de tableaux," *Paris-New York*, catalog, Centre national d'art et de culture Georges Pompidou, Paris, 1977, pp. 88–105.
20. Kay Heymer, interview Düsseldorf, December 2, 2015.
21. Serge Fauchereau, interview Villejuif, October 29, 2015.
22. Andreae, 1997–1999.
23. Olle Granath, interview Stockholm, February 16, 2015.
24. Kay Heymer, interview Düsseldorf, December 2, 2015.
25. Andreae, 1997–1999.
26. *Niki de Saint Phalle*, catalog, Kunst- und Ausstellungshalle der Bundesrepublik Deutschland, Bonn, 1992.
27. Andreae, 1997–1999.
28. Kay Heymer, interview Düsseldorf, December 2, 2015.
29. *Visible and invisible. The New Images of Science*. Moderna Museet, Stockholm, March 17-May 13, 1973.
30. Annagreta Dyring, interview Uppsala, September 7, 2018.
31. Stephan Andreae, interview Hasenbüchel, November 30, 2015.
32. Arved Fuchs, *In Shackleton's Wake*, Dobbs Ferry, New York and Sheridan House, London, 2001.
33. Andreae, 1997–1999.
34. Wenzel Jacob, interview Bonn, November 29, 2015.
35. Karin Weber, interview Bonn, November 30, 2015.
36. Pablo Picasso, "Portrait of Ambroise Vollard," 1910, in the collection of the Pushkin Museum, Moscow.
37. Hans Haacke, "Homage à Marcel Broodthaers," 1982, first shown that year at Documenta 7 in Kassel. In the collection at LACMA in Los Angeles.
38. Kay Heymer, interview Düsseldorf, December 2, 2015.
39. Wenzel Jacob, interview Bonn, November 29, 2015.
40. Wenzel Jacob, interview Bonn, November 29, 2015.
41. Andreae, 1997–1999.
42. Wenzel Jacob, interview Bonn, November 29, 2015.
43. Wenzel Jacob, interview Bonn, November 29, 2015.
44. Kay Heymer, interview Düsseldorf, December 2, 2015.
45. Among others, Serge Fauchereau, *Conversation with Pontus Hultén*, pp. 8–29.
46. Among others, Stephan Andreae.
47. With the exhibition *Le musée sentimental d'Eva Aeppli*, Centre Pompidou-Metz, May 7–November 14, 2022.
48. Eva Aeppli, "La Table," 1965, with thirteen female figures sitting at a table modeled after Michelangelo's "Last Supper." Moderna Museet, Stockholm. Purchase 1969. NMSK 2031: Moderna Museet has an extensive collection of Eva Aeppli's art as a result of a donation from Niki de Saint Phalle in 1993 and one from the artist herself in 1994.
49. Karin Weber, interview Bonn, November 30, 2015.
50. Karin Weber, interview Bonn, November 30, 2015.
51. Yasha David, interview Paris, October 22, 2015.
52. Stephan Andreae, interview Hasenbüchel, November 30, 2015.
53. Gerhard Richter, "Bach 1–4," 1992. Purchased for the Moderna Museet collection in 1994 with the support of the Friends of Moderna Museet. MOM 769 A-D.
54. Björn Springfeldt, interview Värmdö, November 20, 2018.

55. Björn Springfeldt, interview Värmdö, November 20, 2018.
56. Kay Heymer, interview Düsseldorf, December 2, 2015.
57. Chronology compiled in collaboration with Stephan Andreae around 2000.
58. Wenzel Jacob, interview Bonn, November 29, 2015.
59. Wenzel Jacob, interview Bonn, November 29, 2015.
60. The afficionado Picasso was described — and liked to describe himself — as the bull and the bullfighter in the same person.
61. Karin Weber, interview Bonn, November 30, 2015.
62. François Pinault (born 1936) and Bernard Arnault (born 1949) are both among the world's greatest art collectors. Both of them are billionaires in the fashion and luxury industries. Pinault, originally a timber merchant, is the majority owner of the Gucci Group, the Christie's auction house, several leading wine houses, and more. Arnault, originally trained as an engineer, ranked among the world's richest persons, is the largest owner and chairman of the LVMH (Louis Vuitton Moët Hennessey) group, with fashion, jewelry and cosmetics houses such as Dior, Céline and Tiffany's, champagne and wine houses, liquor brands, and more. In addition to Palazzo Grassi, Pinault also owns the new Bourse de commerce in Paris, opened in 2021. Bernard Arnault inaugurated in 2014 the Fondation Louis Vuitton in the Boulogne Forest in Paris, in a spectacular design by Frank Gehry.
63. Lutz Jahre. *Das gedruckte Museum von Pontus Hultén. Kunstausstellungen und ihre Bücher*, Kunst- und Ausstellungshalle der Bundesrepublik Deutschland/Cantz, Bonn, 1996.
64. Lutz Jahre, interview Mannheim, November 28, 2015.
65. Lutz Jahre, "Ein Gespräch mit Pontus Hultén," Jahre, 1996, p. 11.
66. Niki de Saint Phalle, "A Portrait of Pontus," Jahre, 1996, pp. 102–108.
67. Lutz Jahre, interview Mannheim, November 28, 2015.
68. Wenzel Jacob, interview Bonn, November 29, 2015.
69. Pontus Hultén, interview Stockholm, December 1, 1996.
70. Olle Granath, interview Stockholm, February 16, 2015.
71. Karin Weber, interview Bonn, November 30, 2015.

30 Finally a recluse, where to settle down?

1. Marie-Louise von Plessen, interview La Motte, February 11, 2017.
2. Marie-Louise von Plessen, interview La Motte, June 29, 2021.
3. Serge Fauchereau, interview Paris, January 12, 2015.
4. Marie-Louise von Plessen, interview La Motte, October 20, 2015.
5. Marie-Louise von Plessen, interview La Motte, October 20, 2015. Pontus Hultén also recorded the peacocks' sounds, which he used in his Vandal exhibition (Chapter 33).
6. See Chapter 26.
7. The Loire Valley is a vast area. The "chic" parts include the area further west, towards the Atlantic coast.
8. Marie-Louise von Plessen, interview La Motte, February 11, 2017.
9. *The Rhine. The Biography of a European River*, KAH, Bonn, September 9, 2016–January 22, 2017.
10. Marie-Louise von Plessen, interview La Motte, February 11, 2017.
11. Marie-Louise von Plessen, interview La Motte, February 11, 2017.
12. Marie-Louise von Plessen, interview Dalarö, July 29, 2016.
13. Marie-Louise von Plessen, interview Dalarö, July 29, 2016.
14. Daniel Abadie, interview Paris, October 22, 2015.
15. Marie-Louise von Plessen, interview La Motte, June 30, 2021.

31 Finale in the museum world with Jean Tinguely

1. Bloum Cardenas, conversation Paris, November 25, 2017.
2. Jean Tinguely, interview Swiss radio, August 20, 1989. From catalog *Museum Tinguely. The Collection*, English language version, Museum Tinguely, Basel, 2012.
3. Chronology catalog *Museum Tinguely. The Collection*, English language version, Museum Tinguely, Basel, 2012.
4. Department of Applied Arts at the Basel School of Arts and Crafts.
5. Catalog *Museum Tinguely. The Collection*, 2012, p. 396. From interview by Violand Hobi in 1995.
6. Seppi Imhof, interview Basel, December 9, 2014.
7. Seppi Imhof, interview Basel, December 9, 2014.
8. Seppi Imhof, interview Basel, December 9, 2014.
9. Daniel Spoerri, interview Vienna, November 6, 2014.
10. Catalog *Museum Tinguely. The Collection*, 2012, p. 468.
11. "Jean Tinguely Le Cyclop," Centre national des arts plastiques, Paris, 2007, pp. 111–113.
12. "Jean Tinguely Le Cyclop," Centre national des arts plastiques, Paris, 2007, pp. 111–113.
13. Andreae, 1997–1999.
14. Andres Pardey, interview Basel, December 9, 2014.
15. Andreae, 1997–1999.

16. Andres Pardey, interview Basel, December 9, 2014.
17. Andres Pardey, interview Basel, December 9, 2014.
18. Andres Pardey, interview Basel, December 9, 2014.
19. Among others Olle Granath, interview Stockholm, October 18, 2019.
20. Some information suggests that Pontus Hultén also had some form of pension from Palazzo Grassi.
21. Catalog *Museum Tinguely, The Collection*, English language version, Museum Tinguely, Basel, 2012, p. 382.
22. Catalog *Museum Tinguely*, 2012, p. 14.
23. Andreae, 1997–1999.
24. Anna-Lena Wibom, interview Lidingö, March 21, 2014.
25. Seppi Imhof, interview Basel, December 9, 2014.
26. Seppi Imhof, interview Basel, December 9, 2014.
27. Catalog *Museum Tinguely*, 2012, p. 174.
28. Jerry Sohn, interview Los Angeles, November 7, 2014.
29. K.G. Pontus Hultén preface, catalog *The Machine — as seen at the end of the mechanical age*, Museum of Modern Art, New York, 1968, p. 3.
30. Daniel Buren, interview Paris, January 14, 2015.
31. Richard Armstrong, interview New York, September 9, 2014.
32. Daniel Buren, interview Paris, January 14, 2015.

32 My meeting with Pontus

1. Pontus Hultén, interview Stockholm, December 16, 1996.
2. Pontus Hultén, interview Stockholm, December 16, 1996.
3. Pontus Hultén, interview Stockholm, December 17, 1996.
4. Pontus Hultén, interview Stockholm, December 16, 1996.
5. The park area adjacent to the university campus in Frescati, north of Stockholm city center.
6. Pontus Hultén told me this story according to my notes. According to Olle Granath (e-mail August 27, 2021) however, the French kleptomaniac took the small painting attributed to Frans Hals with him to France. According to Granath, he had buried two bronzes by Carl Frisendahl, stolen from Moderna Museet, in Albano, which was what was recovered.
7. The official cost of building the new Moderna Museet is SEK 450 million. The cost of the decontamination, renovation and evacuation of the museum in 2002–2004 officially amounted to SEK 344 million.
8. Pontus Hultén, "Moderna Museet and May 1968." Olle Granath and Monika Nieckels eds., Moderna Museet 1958–1983, Moderna Museet, Stockholm, 1983, p. 48.
9. Pontus Hultén, interview Stockholm, December 17, 1996.
10. Olle Granath, interview Stockholm, February 16, 2015.
11. Moderna Museet was reopened in its new building on February 12, 1998.
12. Claes Britton, *Sår är till för att göra ont!*, E-book Albert Bonniers förlag, Stockholm, 2016. https://www.adlibris.com/se/e-bok/sar-ar-till-att-gora-ont-9789100168018
13. The Greek city of Thessaloniki preceded Stockholm as European Capital of Culture in 1997.
14. Pontus Hultén, telephone interview, March 1998.

33 Vandals, Vandals ...

1. Stephan Andreae, "Reisen mit Riesen/Walking With Giants." Transcript of recorded conversations with Pontus Hultén for unpublished autobiography, La Motte, 1997–1999. © Stephan Andreae.
2. Karin Lundh, interview Värnamo, September 17, 2018.
3. Karin Lundh, interview Värnamo, September 17, 2018.
4. Karin Lundh, interview Värnamo, September 17, 2018.
5. Renzo Piano, interview Paris, January 8, 2015.
6. Andreae, 1997–1999.
7. Pontus Hultén, Marie-Louise von Plessen, *Den sanna historien om vandalerna*. Vandalorum catalog no. 1, Värnamo, 2001.
8. Sam Francis. "Swedish Flag for Pontus," 1987. Moderna Museet Stockholm, Pontus Hultén donation 2005. MOM/2005/355.
9. Öyvind Fahlström's experimental feature film *Du gamla, du fria* was filmed in 1969 but was not released until 1972. The film mixes interviews with documentary and fictional elements, with many scandalous and controversial scenes such as the burning of flags and bundles of money being smeared in feces. The film ran for only two weeks but has gained cult status as a manifesto for the progressive sixties movement.
10. Gunilla Palmstierna-Weiss, interview Stockholm, March 12, 2014.
11. Anna-Lena Wibom, interview Lidingö, March 21, 2014.
12. Jacques Faujour, interview Paris, January 12, 2015.
13. Felix Hultén, interview Västra Frölunda, June 23, 2014.
14. Louise Hultén, interview Stockholm, February 17, 2019.
15. Marie-Louise von Plessen, interview La Motte, February 12, 2017.
16. Karin Lundh, interview Värnamo, September 17, 2018.
17. Troels Andersen, interview Copenhagen, September 28, 2015.

18. Karin Lundh, interview Värnamo, September 17, 2018.
19. Björn Springfeldt, interview Värmdö, November 20, 2018.
20. Hultén, von Plessen, "Preface," 2001, unpaginated.
21. Karin Lundh, interview Värnamo, September 17, 2018.
22. Dick Harrison, review of *Den sanna historien om vandalerna*, SvD, October 7, 2001. The article gave rise to several subsequent articles in which Pontus Hultén, among others, were accused of inappropriateness and murky nationalist aims (Peter Cornell, "The vandal book advocates revisionist ideas," SvD, April 12, 2002).
23. Harrison, October 7, 2001.
24. Karin Lundh, interview Värnamo, September 17, 2018.
25. Hultén, von Plessen, 2001, unpaginated.
26. Monika Nieckels, interview Stockholm, April 26, 2018.
27. Monika Nieckels, interview Stockholm, April 26, 2018.
28. Karin Lundh, interview Värnamo, September 17, 2018.
29. E-mail from Renzo Piano's personal assistant Francesca Bianchi, Renzo Piano Building Workshop, September 27, 2018.
30. Andreae, 1997–1999.

34 Escape from La Motte

1. Marie-Louise von Plessen, interview La Motte, October 21, 2015.
2. Serge Fauchereau, interview Villejuif, October 29, 2015.
3. Thomas M. Messer, Director of the Solomon R. Guggenheim Museum 1961–1988. Named as a candidate for the position of founding director of MNAM Centre Pompidou and thus a rival to Pontus Hultén.
4. Ida Gianelli, interview Milan, November 25, 2015.
5. Marie-Louise von Plessen, interview La Motte, October 21, 2015.
6. Lars Nittve, interview Stockholm, March 3, 2016.
7. Lars Nittve, interview Stockholm, March 3, 2016.
8. Lars Nittve, interview Stockholm, March 3, 2016.
9. Catherine Monnier, interview New York, September 8, 2014.
10. Ronny Van de Velde, e-mail, November 30, 2014.
11. Marie-Louise von Plessen, interview La Motte, June 30, 2021.
12. Pontus Hultén, *Pontus Hultén's collection ...*, Moderna Museet Stockholm, February 14–April 18, 2004.
13. *Pontus Hultén. Artisti di una collezione*, catalog, Arthemisia, Milan, 2006.
14. Marie-Louise von Plessen, interview La Motte, October 21, 2015.
15. Tova Bjurström, interview, September 18, 2017.
16. Marie-Louise von Plessen, interview La Motte, June 30, 2021.
17. Clarenza Catullo, interview Rovereto, November 26, 2015.
18. Lars Nittve e-mail, January 31, 2022.
19. Pontus Hultén, *Pontus Hultén's Collection ...*, Moderna Museet, Stockholm, exhibition catalog no. 321, 2004.
20. Lars Nittve, interview Stockholm, March 3, 2016.
21. *Niki de Saint Phalle in the 1960s*, Menil, Houston. September 10, 2021–January 23, 2022.
22. Michelle White, telephone conversation, March 18, 2021.
23. Carl Fredrik Hårleman, interview Stockholm, April 4, 2016.
24. Calvin Tomkins, *Duchamp, A biography*, Henry Holt and Company, New York, 1996, p. 417.

35 End of the earth life

1. Felix Hultén, interview Västra Frölunda, June 23, 2014.
2. Serge Fauchereau, interview Villejuif, October 29, 2015.
3. Daniel Birnbaum, "Passages Pontus Hultén," Artforum, February 2007.
4. Text from Wikipedia: "The ship grave field in Vendel was a grave field containing fourteen so-called ship graves. It was located in the cemetery, just southeast of Vendels church in Tierp municipality in Uppland. It has now been investigated and removed and is best known for the rich finds that were discovered in the graves. The finds, which are kept at the National Historical Museum, are dated to around 700 AD and have given rise to the name Vendel period, usually relating to the period between the years 550 and 800."
5. Dan Wolgers, interview Stockholm, November 27, 2018.
6. Olle Granath, interview Stockholm, April 25, 2018.
7. Dan Wolgers, interview Stockholm, November 27, 2018.
8. Renzo Piano, interview Paris, January 8, 2015.

36 Brillo — a posthumous global mega-scandal

1. Adrien Levy, Cathy Scott-Clark, "Warhol's box of tricks," The Guardian, August 21, 2010.
2. Thomas Anderberg, *Den stora konstsvindeln*, Atlas, Stockholm, 2010.
3. Thomas Anderberg, "Warhol would have smiled in his heaven," Dagens Nyheter, January 10, 2008.
4. Bernard Blistène, interview Paris, October 29, 2015.

5. Germain Viatte, interview Paris, October 28, 2015.
6. Levy, Scott-Clark, August 21, 2010.
7. Levy, Scott-Clark, August 21, 2010.
8. Bo Nilsson, interview Stockholm, November 10, 2018.
9. Andreas Rydén, interview Stockholm, September 22, 2018.
10. Bo Nilsson, interview Stockholm, November 10, 2018.
11. Micke Ölander, Leo Lagercrantz, Christian Holmén, "Warhol — the mystery of Swedish million-dollar boxes. Museum director Pontus Hultén took the riddle of Andy Warhol's work to his grave," Expressen, May 30, 2007.
12. Björn Springfeldt, interview Värmdö, November 20, 2018.
13. Micke Ölander, telephone interview, October 20, 2018.
14. Micke Ölander, telephone interview, October 20, 2018.
15. Micke Ölander, telephone interview, October 20, 2018.
16. Micke Ölander, telephone interview, October 20, 2018.
17. Ölander, Lagercrantz, Holmén, May 30, 2007.
18. Per-Olov Börjeson, telephone interview, September 23, 2018.
19. Micke Ölander, telephone interview, October 20, 2018.
20. Pontus Hultén's archive, Moderna Museet, Stockholm, 4.1, folders 48–50 Palazzo Grassi.
21. Thomas Anderberg, *Den stora konstsvindeln*, Atlas, Stockholm, 2010, pp. 61–66.
22. Swedish Radio P3 Documentary *Andy Warhol's Brillo boxes*. Produced by Anna Gjöres. First broadcast April 15, 2012.
23. P3 Documentary, April 15, 2012.
24. P3 Documentary, April 15, 2012.
25. *Second Report: The Stockholm type boxes. Prepared by the Andy Warhol Art Authenication Board*. Final Report AWAAB, New York, July 19, 2010.
26. AWAAB final report, July 19, 2010.
27. P3 Documentary, April 15, 2012.
28. P3 Documentary, April 15, 2012.
29. Pontus Hultén, *Pontus Hultén's Collection* ..., Moderna Museet, Stockholm, exhibition catalog no. 321, 2004.
30. Micke Ölander, telephone interview, October 20, 2018.
31. Ölander, Lagercrantz, Holmén, May 30, 2007.
32. Ölander, Lagercrantz, Holmén, May 30, 2007.
33. Ölander, Lagercrantz, Holmén, May 30, 2007.
34. Micke Ölander, Leo Lagercrantz, Christian Holmén, "Jag fick 120 000 kronor för Brilloboxarna," Expressen, June 1, 2007.
35. Ölander, Lagercrantz, Holmén, May 30, 2007.
36. Micke Ölander, telephone interview, October 20, 2018.
37. Ölander, Lagercrantz, Holmén, May 30, 2007.
38. Ölander, Lagercrantz, Holmén, May 30, 2007.
39. Hultén, 2004, pp. 360–367.
40. Hultén, 2004, pp. 360–367.
41. See Chapter 14.
42. Hultén, 2004, pp. 360–367.
43. Bo Nilsson, interview Stockholm, November 10, 2018.
44. Peter Hvidberg, "Why don't you make them over there? The true story about the so-called Brillo scandal." Research work in progress, Copenhagen, 2019. Unpublished.
45. AWAAB Final Report, July 19, 2010, pp. 17–19. This correspondence took place with representatives of the Warhol Estate. AWAAB was formed shortly after, in 1995.
46. Hvidberg, 2019. Unpublished.
47. Many, including Thomas Anderberg in his book, have argued that money was not a motive for Pontus Hultén.
48. P3 Documentary, April 15, 2012.
49. Hultén, 2004, p. 366.
50. Hultén, 2004, p. 366.
51. Olle Granath, interview Stockholm, April 25, 2018.
52. Leo Lagercrantz, Christian Holmén, "Today, art for 100 million Euros can become worthless junk," Expressen, June 14, 2007.
53. Olle Granath, e-mail, August 26, 2021.
54. Anderberg 2010, p. 80.
55. Anderberg 2010, pp. 88–89.
56. Olle Granath, interview Stockholm, April 25, 2018.
57. Björn Springfeldt, interview Värmdö, November 20, 2018.
58. Björn Springfeldt, interview Värmdö, November 20, 2018.
59. P3 Documentary, April 15, 2012.
60. P3 Documentary, April 15, 2012.
61. Christian Holmén, interview Stockholm, November 23, 2018.
62. Ölander, Lagercrantz, Holmén, May 30, 2007.
63. Christian Holmén, interview Stockholm, November 23, 2018.
64. Leo Lagercrantz, Christian Holmén, "Här flyr Warhol-experten från Expressens frågor," Expressen, June 15, 2007.
65. Lagercrantz, Holmén, June 15, 2007.
66. Micke Ölander, "Warhol's manager: 'Andy could not have given permission for that,'" Expressen, June 14, 2007.
67. Ölander, June 14, 2007.
68. Micke Ölander, Leo Lagercrantz, Christian Holmén, "The museum's own investigation shows that the boxes are worthless," Expressen, November 16, 2007.
69. Micke Ölander, telephone interview, October 20, 2018.
70. See *Uppdrag Granskning*, Sveriges Television, May 13, 2015, about the auction house

Lauritz's extensive trade in non-authentic Warhol works in the lower price segments.

71. "Frederick W. Hughes, Andy Warhol's business manager for more than 25 years, died on Sunday at his home in Manhattan. He was 57," New York Times, January 16, 2001.
72. Letter from Olle Granath to Archie Gilles, Warhol Foundation, November 20, 1998. Cited in AWAAB's final report of July 2010, p. 22.
73. Levy, Scott-Clark, August 21, 2010.
74. Ölander, Lagercrantz, Holmén, May 30, 2007.
75. Christian Holmén, interview Stockholm, November 23, 2018.
76. Press release from Moderna Museet dated November 2007, signed by Lars Nittve and Lars Byström. Moderna Museet archive.
76. Press release from Moderna Museet, November 2007.
78. Micke Ölander, Leo Lagercrantz, Christian Holmén, "Silence among the world's art dealers," Expressen, November 16, 2007.
79. Report first addressed as a letter to Lars Nittve, Moderna Museet from AWAAB, New York, December 18, 2007, signed Sally King Nero. Moderna Museet archive.
80. Christian Holmén, interview Stockholm, November 23, 2018.
81. Micke Ölander, Leo Lagercrantz, Christina Holmén, "Andy Warhol Commission: Expressens avslöjande stämmer på samtliga punkter," Expressen, January 8, 2008.
82. Anderberg, 2010.
83. Levy, Scott-Clark, August 21, 2010.
84. P3 Documentary, April 15, 2012.
85. Brian Balfour-Oatts, telephone interview, November 22, 2018.
85. Brian Balfour-Oatts, telephone interview, November 22, 2018.
87. Nathalie Meneau.
88. Brian Balfour-Oatts, telephone interview, November 22, 2018.
89. Anderberg, 2010 p. 88.
90. Anderberg, 2010, pp. 88–89.
91. Holmén, Ölander, October 15, 2010.
92. Holmén, Ölander, October 15, 2010.
93. Holmén, Ölander, October 15, 2010.
94. Natalia Kazmierska, "Thomas Anderberg: *Den stora konstsvindeln* — en Brillobok," Expressen, October 14, 2010.
95. Kazmierska, October 14, 2010.
96. Kay Heymer, telephone interview, August 16, 2018.
97. *Second Report: The Stockholm type boxes. Prepared by the Andy Warhol Art Authenication Board.* AWAAB Final Report, New York, July 19, 2010, pp. 12–13.
98. Hans Ulrich Obrist, "The Hang of It," interview with Pontus Hultén, first published in Artforum, April 1997.
99. Obrist, interview with Pontus Hultén, April 1997.
100. It is unclear whether Björn Springfeldt means *Le Territoire de l'Art* in Leningrad in 1990 or whether he knew in advance that the Brillo boxes would also be shown at the the "full-scale" edition of the *Territorium Artis* exhibition in Bonn in 1992.
101. *Second Report: The Stockholm type boxes. Prepared by the Andy Warhol Art Authenication Board.* Final Report AWAAB, New York, July 19, 2010, p. 6.
102. Hultén, 2004, pp. 360–367.
103. Kasper König, interview Stockholm, September 14, 2018.
104. AWAAB final report, July 19, 2010, p. 3.
105. AWAAB final report, July 19, 2010, p. 6.
106. Neil Printz, conversation with Anna-Lena Wibom, Stockholm, December 16, 2008. Cited in AWAAB final report of July 2010, p. 10.
107. Ölander, Lagercrantz, Holmén, May 30, 2007.
108. AWAAB final report, July 19, 2010, p. 11.
109. AWAAB final report, July 19, 2010, p. 12.
110. AWAAB final report, July 19, 2010, p. 14.
111. Bo Nilsson, interview Stockholm, November 10, 2018.
112. AWAAB final report, July 19, 2010, p. 16.
113. AWAAB final report, July 19, 2010, p. 17.
114. Pontus Hultén *Territorium Aertis*, KAH/Hatje, Bonn/Stuttgart, 1992, pp. 358–359.
115. Brian Balfour-Oatts, telephone interview, November 22, 2018.
116. Olle Granath, telephone conversation, December 5, 2018.
117. Christian Holmén, interview Stockholm, November 23, 2018.
118. Christian Holmén, interview Stockholm, November 23, 2018.
119. Christian Holmén, interview Stockholm, November 23, 2018.
120. Anna-Lena Wibom, interview Lidingö, March 21, 2014.
121. P3 Documentary, April 15, 2012.
122. P3 Documentary, April 15, 2012.
123. Peter Hvidberg, interview with Anna-Lena Wibom, October 9, 2017. Hvidberg, 2019. Unpublished, p. 7.
124. Peter Hvidberg, e-mail, July 3, 2017.
125. Hvidberg, 2019. Unpublished.
126. Peter Hvidberg, e-mail, October 25, 2018.
127. Letter from Waldo Rasmusen/Kynaston L. McShine, MoMA, to Pontus Hultén, Palazzo Grassi, November 3, 1987. Pontus Hultén's archive, Moderna Museet, Stockholm. 4.1, folders 48–50, Palazzo Grassi.
128. Letter from Waldo Rasmusen/Kynaston L. McShine, MoMA, to Pontus Hultén, Palazzo Grassi, November 3, 1987. Pontus Hultén's archive, Moderna Museet, Stockholm. 4.1, folders 48–50, Palazzo Grassi.
129. Jean-Hubert Martin, e-mail, November 29, 2018.
130. Andres Pardey, interview Basel, December 9, 2014.
131. Estimate by Peter Hvidberg, spring 2022.
132. Dan Wolgers, interview Stockholm, November 27, 2018.

Epilogue

1. See Chapter 5.
2. Serge Fauchereau, interview Paris, January 12, 2015.
3. Roland Pålsson, "60s 'in nostalgia,'" Olle Granath and Monika Nieckels eds., *Moderna Museet* 1958–1983. Moderna Museet, Stockholm, 1983, pp. 141–142.
4. Jason Farago, "Niki de Saint Phalle: Nothing More Shocking Than Joy," The New York Times, April 8, 2021.
5. Anette Göthlund, "Work in workshop and zone. Art education at Moderna Museet." Anna Tellgren ed., *The History Book. On Moderna Museet 1958–2008*, Moderna Museet/Steidl Verlag, Stockholm, 2008, p. 268.
6. Susan Weil, telephone interview, November 13, 2016.
7. Lutz Jahre, "A conversation with Pontus Hulten," Lutz Jahre. *Das gedruckte Museum von Pontus Hultén. Kunstausstellungen und ihre Bücher*, Kunst- und Ausstellungshalle der Bundesrepublik Deutschland/Cantz, Bonn, 1996, pp. 10–28.
8. Germano Celant, interview Milan, April 18, 2016.
9. Germano Celant, interview Milan, April 18, 2016.
10. Calvin Tomkins, "The Modern Man," The New Yorker, July 2, 2012.
11. When I asked for names, Calvin Tomkins mentioned Marcel Duchamp, Willem Sandberg and Andy Warhol.
12. Calvin Tomkins, interview New York, September 14, 2014.
13. Roberta Smith, "Pontus Hultén, 82, Champion of Contemporary Art, Dies," The New York Times, October 30, 2006.
14. Anne Horvath, "L'Effet Pontus Hultén," catalog text for the exhibition *Face à Arcimboldo*, Centre Pompidou-Metz, May 5–November 3, 2021.
15. Guillame Apollinaire, *Les Peintres Cubistes, Méditiations Esthéthiques*, Eugène Figuière Éditeurs, "Collection Tous les Arts," Paris, 1913
16. Suzanne Pagé, interview Paris, February 18, 2017.
17. Troels Andersen, interview Copenhagen, September 28, 2016.

Selected literature and other sources

Most of the printed sources in this list are available or can be obtained through the fantastic Art Library of the Moderna Museet/ Nationalmuseum on Skeppsholmen in Stockholm. I am deeply grateful for all their professional help over the years.

www.modernamuseet.se/stockholm/sv/about-the-museum/art-library/

Books:

af Petersen, Magnus, Hahr, Teresa, Widenheim, Cecilia, *Moderna Museet. The book*. Moderna Museet, Stockholm 2004.

Agnelli, Marella, Caracciolo Chia, Marella, *Marella Agnelli: The Last Swan*. Rizzoli, New York 2014.

Anderberg, Thomas, *Den stora konstsvindeln*, Atlas, Stockholm 2010.

Andersen, Troels, *Ude af øje, erindringer 1940–1973(?)*. Forlaget Vandkunsten, Copenhagen 2004.

Apollinaire, Guillaume, *Les Peintres Cubistes*. Collection Savoir/Hr. Savoir Arts, Paris 1913/1980.

Ahrenberg, Teto, Ahrenberg, Ulla, Edwards, Folke, *Jag har ju ändå ägt en Picasso. Memoarer av Teto Ahrenberg, utmanaren, konstsamlaren, mecenaten (?)*. Wahlström & Widstrand, Stockholm 1993.

Bahlenberg, Jan, *Carlo Derkert: porträtt av en konstvisare*. Gidlunds förlag, Stockholm 2005.

Battista Kathy, Forti, Simone, *E.A.T.: Experiments in Art and Technology*. Walther König, Cologne 2016.

Bergengren, Knut, *När skönheten kom till City*, Aldus, Stockholm 1976.

Beuys, Joseph, Wolleh, Lothar, *Das Unter-wasserbuchproject/The Unterwasserbuch Project*.Kerber Verlag, Bielefeld/Berlin 2021.

Birnbaum, Daniel, Noring, Ann-Sofi, *A Plurality of Tongues Giving Direction to the Museum*. Moderna Museet, Stockholm/Koenig Books, London 2015.

Birnbaum, Daniel, *Notes on the Frames of Art*. Verlag der Buchhandlung Walther und Franz König, Cologne 2022.

Björk, Kaj, *En utskälld man. Allan Vougt och hans tid(?)*. Hjalmarsson & Högberg, Stockholm 2007.

Blankert, Albert, *Vermeer of Delft: Complete edition of the paintings*. Phaidon, London 1978.

Bockris, Victor, *The Life and Death of Andy Warhol*, Bantam Books, New York 1989.

Bordaz, Robert, Piano, Renzo, *Entretiens Robert Bordaz Renzo Piano*. Diagonales, Éditions cercle d'art. Paris 1997.

Britton, Claes, *Sår är till för att göra ont!*. Albert Bonniers Förlag/e-book, Stockholm 2016.

Broad, Eli, *The Art of Being Unreasonable. Lessons in Unconventional Thinking*. Wiley, New York 2012.

Brougher, Kerry, Vergne, Philippe, *Yves Klein. With the Void. Full Powers*. Hirshorn Museum and Sculpture Garden, Washington 2010.

Cabanne, Pierre, *Dialogues with Marcel Duchamp*. Thames and Hudson, London 1967/1971.

Caddy, Davinia, *The Ballets Russes and Beyond: Music and Dance in Belle Époque Paris*. Cambridge University Press, Cambridge 2012.

Camfield, William, *Francis Picabia: His Art, Life and Times*. Princeton University Press, Princeton 1979.

Canal, Virginie, *Jean Tinguely Le Cyclop*. Centre national des arts plastiques, Paris 2007.

Capote, Truman, *Breakfast at Tiffany's*, Random House, New York 1958.

Celant, Germano, *Art Povera. Conceptual, Actual or Impossible Art?* Littlehampton Book Services Ltd, Worthing 1969.

Celant, Germano, *Claes Oldenburg Coosje van Bruggen*. Skira editore S.p.A., Milan 1999.

Charbonnier, Georges, *Marcel Duchamp on the radio: interviews with Marcel Duchamp on French radio 1960–1961*. Translation Jan Hannerz, Lars Axel Söderberg. Errata/ Kungliga Akademien för de fria konsternas skriftserie 15, Stockholm 2009.

Chirac, Jacques, *My Life in Politics*. St. Martin's Press, New York 2012.

Claesson, Stig, *Om vänskap funnes*, Albert Bonniers Förlag 1981/e-book, Stockholm 2013.

Clair, Jean, *Duchamp et la fin de l'art*. Gallimard, Paris 2000, English excerpt translated by Sarah Skinner https://www.toutfait.com/issues/issue_3/News/clair/clair.html.

Clair, Jean, *The Winter of Culture*, Café Voltaire/Flammarion, Paris 2011.

Dali, Salvador, *The Secret Life of Salvador Dali*. Bo Cavefors Bokförlag AB, Stockholm 1978.

de Saint Phalle, Niki, *Mon Secret*. La Différence, Paris 1994.

Dufrène, Bernadette, *Centre Pompidou trente ans d'histoire*. Centre Pompidou, Paris 2007.

Gedin, Andreas, *Pontus Hultén, She, a Cathedral & Moderna Museet*. Koenig Books, Cologne 2020.

Gopnik, Blake, *Warhol: A Life as Art*. HarperCollins, New York 2020.

Granath, Olle, *I konstens värld*. Appel Förlag, Stockholm 2024.

Granath, Olle, Nieckels, Monika eds., *Moderna Museet 1958–1983*. Moderna Museet, Stockholm 1983.

Gromark, Stina, *Keep Smiling! The printed universe of Pontus Hultén*. Out Side In, Paris 2025.

Hackman, William, *Out of Sight: The Los Angeles Arts Scene of the Sixties*. Other Press, New York 2015.

Hultén, Eric, *Men roligt har det varit*. Generalstabens litografiska anstalts förlag, Stockholm 1973.

Hultén, Pontus, Dumitresco, Natalia, Istrati, Alexandre, *Brancusi*. Harry N. Abrams, New York 1997.

Hultén, Pontus, Matisse, Paul, *Marcel Duchamp, Notes*. Georges Pompidou Cultural Center, Paris 1980.

Hultén, Pontus, *The Surrealists Look at Art*. Lapis Press, Los Angeles 1990.

Hultén, Pontus, *Vermeer et Spinoza*. L'Échoppe, Paris 2003.

Jahre, Lutz, *Das gedruckte Museum von Pontus Hultén. Kunstausstellungen und ihre Bücher*. Kunst- und Ausstellungshalle der Bundesrepublik Deutschland/Cantz, Bonn 1996.

Jangfeldt, Bengt, *En rysk historia*. Wahlström & Widstrand, e-book Stockholm 2015.

Jangfeldt, Bengt, *Med livet som insats: Berättelsen om Vladimir Majakovskij och hans krets*, Wahlström & Widstrand, Stockholm 2007.

Jodebo, Philippe, *Renzo Piano Building Workshop*. Taschen 2016.

Kaprow, Allan, *Assemblage, Environments and Happenings*. H.N. Abrams, New York 1966.

Karlsson, Bo A., *Med Warhol från Moderna till Cirkeln*. Publications from the Jazz Department of the Swedish Song Archive (no. 16)/Bokförlaget Prisma, Stockholm 2002.

Klüver, Billy, Martin, Julie, *Kiki's Paris: Artists and Lovers 1900–1930*. H. N. Abrams, New York 1989.

Kumpf, Lawrence, Karlsson, Naima, Nygren, Magnus. *Organic Music Societies*. Blank Forms Editions, New York 2021.

Lebel, Robert, *Sur Marcel Duchamp*, Trianon Press, Paris 1959.

Linde, Ulf, *Från kart till fallfrukt*. Albert Bonniers Förlag, Stockholm 2008.

Linde, Ulf, *Marcel Duchamp*. Rabén & Sjögren, Stockholm 1986.

Linde, Ulf, *Scouts*. Bokförlaget Korpen, Stockholm 1984.

Marcadé, Bernard, *Marcel Duchamp, La vie à credit*. Flammarion, Paris 2007.

Masheck, Joseph, *Marcel Duchamp in Perspective*. Da Capo Press, Boston 2002.

Middleton, William, *Double Vision. The Unerring Eye of Art World Avatars Dominique and John de Menil*. Alfred A. Knopf, New York 2018.

Millet, Catherine, *Conversations with Denise René*, Éditions Adam Biró, Paris 2001.

Mink, Janis, *Marcel Duchamp: 1887–1968; Art As AntiArt*. Taschen, London 1978/2000.

Molderings, Herbert, *Duchamp and the Aesthetics of Chance. Art as Experiment*, Columbia University Press, New York 2010.

Mollard, Claude, *Le cinquième pouvoir: le culture et l'État de Malraux à Lang*, Armand Collin, Paris 1999.

Motherwell, Robert, *The Dada Painters and Poets*. Belknab Press, Harvard 1951/1959.

Nordenfalk, Carl, *Mest om konst*, Natur och Kultur, Stockholm 1996.

Näslund, Erik, *Rolf de Maré. Konstsamlare, balletledare, museiskapare*. Bokförlaget Langenskiöld, Stockholm 2008.

Obrist, Hans Ulrich, *A Brief History of Curating*. JRP-Ringier/Les Presses du Réel, Geneva 2008.

Obrist, Hans Ulrich, *Ways of Curating*. Allen Lane/Penguin Books UK, London 2014/2015.

Palmstierna-Weiss, Gunilla, *Minnets spelplats*, Albert Bonniers Förlag, Stockholm 2013.

Petersen, Ad, *Sandberg, Designer and Director of the Stedelijk*. 010 Publishers, Rotterdam 2004.

Philips, Glenn, Kaiser, Philippe, Chon, Doris, Rigolo, Pietro, *Harald Szeemann — Museum of Obsessions*. Getty Publications, Los Angeles 2018.

Restany, Pierre, *Yves Klein*, H.N. Abrams, New York 1982.

Richardson, John, *A Life of Picasso*, vols. 1–4, Penguin/Random House, New York 1991.

Roché, Henri-Pierre, *Victor*. Volume IV, *Marcel Duchamp* catalog, exhibition catalog no. 8, MNAM Centre Pompidou, Paris 1977.

Roussel, Raymond, *Locus Solus*. Riverrun Press, New York 1913/1998.

Roussel, Raymond, *New Impressions of Africa*. Princeton University Press, Princeton 1910/2011.

Sandberg, Willem, *Portrait of an Artist*, interviews compiled by Ank Leeuw Marcar. Valiz, Amsterdam 2013.

Sjöberg, Fredrik, *Flugfällan*. Bonnier Pocket, Stockholm 2020.

Sokalow, Paulina, Malmborg, Anna-Stina ed., *Moderna före Moderna*. Bukowskis, Stockholm 2013.

Spies, Werner, *The Chances of my Life. Memoirs*. Gallimard, Paris 2014.

Spurling, Hillary, *Matisse — the Life*. Penguin Books, New York 2009.

Söderberg, Rolf, *Mina konstnärsänkor och andra konstminnen*. Carlsson, Stockholm 1999.

Söderberg, Rolf, *Otte Sköld*. Kungl. Boktryckeriet PA Norstedt & Söner, Stockholm 1968.

Tellgren, Anna ed., *Pontus Hultén and Moderna Museet. The formative years*, Moderna Museet, Stockholm 2017.

Tellgren, Anna ed., *The History Book. About Moderna Museet 1958–2008*. Moderna Museet/Steidl Verlag, Stockholm 2008.

Tomkins, Calvin, *Duchamp: A Biography*. Henry Holt and Company, New York 1996.

Tomkins, Calvin, *Lives of Artists*, Henry Holt and Company, New York 2008.

Tomkins, Calvin, *Marcel Duchamp: The Afternoon Interviews*. Badlands Unlimited, New York 2013.

Tomkins, Calvin, *The Lives of Artists*, Phaidon, London 2019.

Tomkins, Calvin, *Off the Wall. A Portrait of Robert Rauschenberg*. Picador, New York 1980/2005.

Treisman, Deborah, *The Dream Colony. A Life in Art*. Interviews with Walter Hopps by Anne Doran, edited by Deborah Treisman. Bloomsbury, New York 2017.
Violand-Hobi, Heidi E., *Jean Tinguely, Life and Work*. Prestel, Munich/New York 1995.
Weidemann, Christiane, *Niki de Saint Phalle*. Prestel Verlag, Munich/London/New York 2014.
White, Fredrik H., *The Russian Avant-garde and Radical Modernism*. Academic Studies Press, Boston 2012.
Williams, Charles, *The Last Great Frenchman: A Life of General de Gaulle*. John Wiley & Sons Inc, New York 1997.
Är allting konst? Inlägg i den stora konstdebatten (Is everything art? Contributions to the Great Art Debate). Bonniers, Stockholm 1963.
10. 1992–2002 10 Years of Art and Exhibition Hall of the Federal Republic of Germany," KAH, Bonn 2002.

Catalogs:

Andersen, Troels, Derkert, Carlo, Hultén, K.G, *Vladimir Tatlin*. Exhibition catalog no. 75, Moderna Museet, Stockholm 1968.
Automobile and Culture, Museum of Contemporary Art Los Angeles/Harry N. Abrams Inc, New York 1984.
Bergqvist Lindegren, Karin, *Joseph Beuys*. Exhibition catalog no. 90, Moderna Museet, Stockholm 1971.
Bergqvist Lindegren, Karin, Hultén, K.G., *Den inre och den yttre rymden*. Exhibition catalog no. 51, Moderna Museet, Stockholm 1965.
Bergqvist Lindegren, Karin, Granath, Olle, Hultén, K.G., Linde, Ulf, *Önskemuseet (The Museum of Wishes)*. Exhibition catalog no. 36, Moderna Museet, Stockholm 1963.
Birnbaum, Daniel, Noring, Ann-Sofie, Obrist, Hans Ulrich. *After Babel. Poetry will be made by everyone! 89Plus*. Moderna Museet, Stockholm/Koenig Books, London 2015.
Birnbaum, Daniel, Åman, Jan, *De ou par Marcel Duchamp par Ulf Linde*, Konstakademien/Moderna Museet (exhibition catalog no. 367), Stockholm 2011.
Dali/Duchamp. Royal Academy of Arts, London 2017.
David, Yasha, *The Archimboldo effect, tranformations of the face from the sixtieth to the twentieth century*. Bompiani, Milan 1987.
Derkert, Carlo, Hultén, K.G., Klüver, Billy, O'Konor, Louise, Wibom, Anna-Lena, *American Pop Art*. Exhibition catalog no. 37, Moderna Museet, Stockholm 1964.
Devant, le futur. Institute of Advanced Studies in Plastic Arts, Seoul/Paris 1993.
Francis Picabia. Exhibition catalog no. 2, Département des Arts Plastiques du Centre Georges Pompidou, Paris 1976.
Futurismo & Futurismi (Futurism & Futurisms). Bompiani, Milan 1986.
Granath, Olle, Hultén, Pontus, König, Kasper, Warhol, Andy, *Andy Warhol*. Moderna Museet, Stockholm 1968.
Guernica. Exhibition catalog no. 1, Moderna Museet, Stockholm 1956.
He Was Wrong. Picasso/Duchamp. Moderna Museet, Stockholm 2013.
hon – en historia (she – a history). Exhibition catalog no. 54. Moderna Museet, Stockholm 1967.
Hultén, K.G, *4 Amerikanare (4 Americans): Jasper Johns, Alfred Leslie, Robert Rauschenberg, Richard Stankiewicz*. Exhibition catalog no. 22, Moderna Museet, Stockholm 1962.
Hultén, Karl G., *Apropå Eggeling*. Moderna Museet, Stockholm 1958.
Hultén, Pontus, von Plessen, Marie-Louise, *Den sanna historien om vandalerna*. Vandalorum catalog no. 1, Värnamo 2001.
Hultén, K.G.P., Waldén, Katja, *Edward Kienholz 11 + 11 Tableaux*. Exhibition catalog no. 85, Moderna Museet, Stockholm 1970.
Hultén, K.G Pontus, *Jean Tinguely Méta*. Moderna Museet/Verlag Ullstein GmbH, Stockholm/Frankfurt/Berlin/Vienna 1972.
K.G.H. (Pontus Hultén), *Marcel Duchamp*. Bokkonsum, Stockholm 1960.
Hultén, K.G., *Rörelse i konsten (Art in Motion)*. Exhibition catalog no. 18, Moderna Museet, Stockholm 1961.
Hultén, K.G, Gysin, Brion et al, *Sam Francis*. Exhibition catalog no. 12, Moderna Museet, Stockholm 1960.
Hultén, K.G. Pontus, *The Machine — as seen at the end of the mechanical age*, Museum of Modern Art, New York 1968.
Hultén, Pontus, *Niki de Saint Phalle*. Kunst- und Ausstellungshalle der Bundesrepublik Deutschland, Bonn 1992.
Hultén, Pontus, *Pontus Hultén's Collection ....* Exhibition catalog no. 321, Moderna Museet, Stockholm 2004.
Hultén, Pontus, *Sam Francis*. Kunst- und Ausstellungshalle der Bundesrepublik Deutschland, Bonn 1993.
Hultén, Pontus, *Territory Artis*. Kunst- und Ausstellungshalle der Bundesrepublik Deutschland, Bonn 1992.
Il Corso del Coltello. Mazotta, Milan 1985.
Jackson Pollock. Exhibition catalog no. 27, Moderna Museet, Stockholm 1963.
Jean Tinguely. A Magic Stronger than Death. Bompiani, Milan 1987
Katrib, Ruba, *Niki de Saint Phalle. Structures for Life*. MoMA PS 1, New York 2021.
Le Mouvement. Galerie Denise René, Paris 1955.
Le territoire de l'art. Institut des Hautes Études en Arts Plastiques/Musée Russe/Éditions Cercle d'Arts, Paris 1990.
Malevich. Musée national d'art moderne, Centre Georges Pompidou, Paris 1978.
Marcel Duchamp. Exhibition catalog no. 8, Musée national d'art moderne, Centre Pompidou, Paris 1976.
Marcel Duchamp. Palazzo Grassi, Venice/Bompiani, Milan 1993.

Martin, Jean-Hubert, *Malévitch. Planités et Architectones*. Musée national d'art moderne, Centre Pompidou, Paris 1980.

Meyer-Herman, Eva ed., *Andy Warhol. A guide to 256 objects in 2 hours and 56 minutes. Other Voices, Other Rooms*. NAi Publishers, Rotterdam 2008.

Moderna Museet Stockholm in Bonn, Art and Exhibition Hall of the Federal Republic of Germany, Bonn 1996.

Moscow–Paris. Musée national d'art moderne, Centre Pompidou/Ministry of Culture of the USSR, Moscow 1981.

Mud Muses — A Rant About Technology. Moderna Museet, Stockholm/Koenig Books, London 2019.

Museum Tinguely Basel. *The Collection*. Museum Tinguely Basel/Kehrer Verlag Heidelberg Berlin 2012.

Olof-Ors, Matilda, ed., *Björn Lövin. Den omgivande verkligheten/The surrounding reality*, Moderna Museeet exhibition catalog no. 416. Moderna Museet, Stockholm/Null & Void Books, Lund/Verlag der Buchhandlung Walther und Franz König, Cologne 2022.

Paris–Berlin 1900–1933, Centre national d'art et de culture Georges Pompidou, Paris 1978.

Paris–Moscow 1900–1930, Centre national d'art et de culture Georges Pompidou/Ministère de la culture de l'URSS, Paris 1979.

Paris–New York, exhibition catalog no. 20, Musée national d'art moderne, Centre Georges Pompidou, Paris 1977.

Paris–Paris 1937–1957. Centre Georges Pompidou: Bibliothèque publique d'information, Centre de création industrielle, Insitute de recherche et de coordination acoustique/musique, Musée national d'art moderne, Paris 1981.

Parisi, Chiara, Horvath, Anne, *Face to Arcimboldo*. Centre Pompidou-Metz, 2021.

Poesin måste göra av alla! Förändra världen! (*Poetry must be done by all! Transform the world!*) Exhibition catalog no. 84, Moderna Museet, Stockholm 1969.

Pontus Hultén. Artisti di una collezione, catalog, Arthemisia, Milan 2006.

Roelofs, Pieter, Weber, Gregor J.M., *Vermeer*. Thames & Hudson, London/Rijksmuseum Amsterdam 2023.

Schultz, Barbro, *Party for Öyvind*, Group Exhibition Catalogue, Schultz Förlag AB, Stockholm 2021.

Springfeldt, Björn, *New York Collection for Stockholm*. Moderna Museet, Stockholm 1973.

Utopias & Visions 1871–1981. Exhibition catalog no. 94, Moderna Museet, Stockholm 1971.

Journals:

Blandaren/Boulevard-kartongen Tvångsblandaren, Royal Institute of Technology, Stockholm 1955.

Franklin, Paul ed. Étant donne Marcel Duchamp No. 11. Ulf Linde Marcel Duchamp Pontus Hultén en Suède & friends. l'Association Marcel Duchamp, Paris 2016.

Hultén, Pontus, Reutersvärd, Oscar and others. ed., Kasark, no. 1–4. Stockholm 1954–1960.

Les Cahiers du musée national d'art moderne, no. 141, "Hommage à Pontus Hultén." Special issue published for the fortieth anniversary of the Centre Pompidou, Éditions du Centre Pompidou, Paris, fall 2017.

Les Cahiers du musée national d'art moderne hors-series 2019, "Paris–Moscou 40 ans après." Special issue published for the fortieth anniversary of *Paris–Moscow* 1979. Éditions du Centre Pompidou, Paris 2019.

Websites:

Centrepompidou.fr

(E.A.T.) Monoskop.org/ https://monoskop.org/Experiments_in_Art_and_Technology

(9 Evenings/E.A.T.) www.fondation-langlois.org/html/e/page.php?NumPage=294

Eriksson, Leif, "Duchamp in Sweden 1933–1970: A Critical Review." Malmö, 2000, updated 2019. https://www.toutfait.com/duchamp-in-sweden-1933-1970-a-critical-review/

(Malevich 1978) https://histoiredesexpos.hypotheses.org/tag/architectones

Modernamuseet.se

Moderna Museet's older chronology: www.modernamuseet.se/stockholm/en/collection/history/chronology/

Rauschenberg Research Project, SFMOMA. https://www.sfmoma.org/rauschenberg-research-project/

yvesklein.com

Newspaper articles:

Ahlsén, Bo, Björk, Karl Olov, Carlstedt, Margareta, Dunér, Sten, Stolpe, Pär, Ultvedt, Per Olof, "Restlager på Moderna Museet". Dagens Nyheter, November 23, 1973.

Andersson, Bror, Derkert, Carlo, Hultén, K.G., Lind, Pi, Stolpe, Pär, Thorsell, Anna-Lena, "Ett kulturhusprogram: Experiment i social samlevnad". Dagens Nyheter, May 18, 1969.

Birnbaum, Daniel, "Marcel Duchamps nyckelroll speglas i jätteutställning". Dagens Nyheter, June 15, 2022. www.dn.se/culture/marcel-duchamps-key-role-reflected-in-giant-exhibition/

Birnbaum, Daniel, "Slutgiltigt oavslutat. Slumpens konstnär ordad, numrerad och daterad". Dagens Nyheter, April 7, 1993. https://www.dn.se/arkiv/culture/finally-unfinished-slumpens-konstnar-ordnad-numbered-and-dated/

Björk, Karl Olov, Carlstedt, Margareta, Dunér, Sten, Marklund, Bror, Ultvedt, Per Olof, "Vilken konst ska vi ha?" Dagens Nyheter, June 16, 1972. Same signatories, "Det finns en värld utanför axeln Paris–New York". Dagens Nyheter, June 27, 1972.

Cornell, Peter, "Vandalboken för fram revisionistiska idéer". Svenska Dagbladet, April 12, 2002.

Erixon, Sven, "Felplacerad utställning". Dagens Nyheter, August 17, 1961.

Farago, Jason, "Catch a Rising Star at the Auction House." The New York Times, May 23, 2022.
Farago, Jason, "Germano Celant, Curator Behind Italy's Arte Povera, Dies at 79." The New York Times, April 30, 2020.
Farago, Jason, "Niki de Saint Phalle: Nothing More Shocking Than Joy." The New York Times, April 8, 2021.
Fornoul, Alexis, "Judgement over Max Ernst expert Werner Spies overturned in appeal." The Arts Newspaper, December 9, 2015.
"Frederick W. Hughes, Andy Warhol's business manager for more than 25 years, died on Sunday at his home in Manhattan. He was 57." The New York Times, January 16, 2001.
Granath, Olle, "Tysk kontrapunkt". Dagens Nyheter, January 22, 1971.
Harrison, Dick, "Den sanna historien om vandalerna". Svenska Dagbladet, October 7, 2001.
Hjorth, Bror, "Rörelse i konsten". Dagens Nyheter, August 30, 1961.
Kazmierska, Natalia, "Thomas Anderberg: Den stora konstsvindeln — en Brillobok". Expressen, October 14, 2010.
Levy, Adrien, Scott-Clark, Cathy, "Warhol's box of tricks." The Guardian, August 21, 2010.
Loos, Ted, "A Portfolio That Surprises Even Its Creator." The New York Times, October 25, 2013.
"Modernas USA-samling blir en av världens främsta", ("Moderna's US collection becomes one of the world's best"). Dagens Nyheter, October 26, 1973.
Moore, Rowan, "Pompidou Centre: a 70s French radical that's never gone out of fashion." The Guardian, January 8, 2017.
Nagourney, Adam, "A Soaring Arts Scene in Los Angeles Confronts a Changing Landscape." The New York Times, May 12, 2021.
"Pompidou Centre gets a £90m facelift 40 years on." The Guardian, January 15, 2017.
Russell, John, "'Paris–New York': A Century of Modern Art." The New York Times, June 14, 1977.
Semuels, Alana, "New MOCA director Philippe Vergne plans an artist-enabling museum." Los Angeles Times, January 21, 2014.
Smith, Roberta, "Pontus Hultén, 82, Champion of Contemporary Art, Dies." The New York Times, October 30, 2006. www.nytimes.com/2006/10/30/ arts/30hult.html?fta=y&_r=0
Ölander, Micke, Lagercrantz, Leo, Holmén, Christian, "Andy Warhol — mysteriet med svenska miljonboxar". Expressen, May 30, 2007.
Ölander, Micke, Lagercrantz, Leo, Holmén, Christian, "Tyst bland världens alla konsthandlare" ("Silence among the world's art dealers"). Expressen, November 6, 2007.
Ölander, Micke, Lagercrantz, Leo, Holmén, Christian, "Andy Warhol-kommissionen: Expressens avslöjande stämmer på samtliga punkter". Expressen, January 8, 2008.

Articles journals/web forums:

Allgeier, Wyatt, "Pontus Hultén Game Changer." Gagosian Quartely, Summer Issue, 2020. https://gagosian.com/quarterly/2020/08/17/pontus-hulten-game-changer-essay/
B, Mats, "Interview Pontus Hultén." Moderna Museet (Journal of the Friends of Moderna Museet), no. 2, 1981.
Banham, Renyner, "The Pompidou cannot be perceived as anything but a monument." Architectural Review, May 11, 1977.
Birnbaum, Daniel, "Man and Machine." Artforum, September 2008. http://www.mutualart.com/OpenArticle/Man-and-Machine/47D05DBE3835CBD8
Birnbaum, Daniel, Buren, Daniel, Goldstein, Ann, "Passages Pontus Hultén." Artforum, February 2007. https://www.artforum.com/print/200702/pontus-hulten-12381
Bowles, Hamish, "A Breathtaking New Book Charts the Life of Style Goddess Marella Agnelli." Vogue U.S., October 18, 2014. https://www.vogue.com/article/marella-agnelli-the-last-swan-book
Bruck, Connie, "The Art of the Billionaire." The New Yorker, November 29, 2010
Challiou, Timothée, "Un rencontre avec Jean-Hubert Martin." Profane no. 7, autumn/winter 2018/19. www.revueprofane.com/en/avec-jean-hubert-martin-eternel-curieux
Colacello, Bob, "Inheritance, Italian Style." Vanity Fair, December 2009.
Erofeev, Andrei, "Interview with Jean-Hubert Martin, one of the curators of the exhibitions Paris–Moscow and Moscow–Paris." RAAN (Russian Archive Art Archive), November 18, 2020. russianartarchive.net/en/research/interview-with-jean-hubert-martin-one-of-the-curators-of-the-exhibitions-paris-moscow-and-moscow-paris
Erofeev, Andrei, "Moscow–Paris," Isskuosstvo, Moscow Spring 2020.
Fairs, Marcus, "'Today is much more an age of greed.' Richard Rogers reflects on 50-year career." Dezeen.com, August 7, 2013.
Fauchereau, Serge, "Conversation with Pontus Hultén" (2006). Les Cahiers du musée national d'art modern no. 11, "Hommage à Pontus Hultén." Paris fall 2017.
Freeman, Nate, "Russia's Red-Hot Temple of Contemporary Art, and Its Jet-Setting Cofounder, Are Losing Major Exhibitions." Vanity Fair, March 10, 2022. www. vanityfair.com/culture/2022/03/russias-red-hot-temple-of-contemporary-art-losing-major-exhibitions
Garrison, Aurora, "Irving Blum, Andy Warhol and the LA Art Scene; the Birth of Pop Art on the West Coast." Revolver, February 2018.
"Germano Celant 1940–2020." Artforum, April 29, 2020.
Gispert, Marie, "'Je ne voulais pas seulment documenter, je voulais aussi convaincre' L'Exposition 'Paris–Berlin' au Centre Pompidou, 12 juillet–6 novembre 1978." Les Cahiers du MNAM 148, summer 2019.

Glueck, Grace, "The de Menil family: the Medici of Modern Art." The New York Times Magazine, May 18, 1986.
Greenberger, Alex, Art News, September 30, 2019. "9 Storied MoMA Shows from the 1960s — and What ARTnews Said at the Time." https://www.artnews.com/art-news/retrospective/moma-1960s-best-shows-jean-tinguely-mark-rothko-13289/
Greenberger, Alex, "9 Storied MoMA Shows from the 1960s — and What ARTnews Said at the Time." Art News, September 30, 2019.
Greenberger, Alex, "5 Essential Exhibitions by Germano Celant, Late Curator Who Coined Arte Povera." Art News, April 30, 2020.
Healy, Claire Marie, "The Secret History of MOCA." Dazed Digital, July 7, 2014. https://www.dazeddigital.com/artsand culture/article/20707/1/the-secret-history-of-moca
Kennedy, Randy, "Six decades in the art world: Randy Kennedy sits down with Calvin Tomkins." Ursula, Issue 6, Spring 2020, Hauser & Wirth, hauserwirth.com, https://www.hauserwirth.com/ursula/27463-six-decades-art-world-calvin-tomkins-conversation-randy-kennedy
Leiser, Erwin, "Pontus Hultén." Frankfurter Allgemeine Magazin, April 15, 1988.
Luke, Ben, "The art machine: the Centre Pompidou at 40." The Art Newspaper, New York/London, February 1, 2017.
Naumann, Francis M., "The Recurrent, Haunting Ghost." Readymade Press, New York, 2012.
Obrist, Hans Ulrich, "The Hang of It." Artforum, April 1997. www.artforum.com/print/199704/the-hang-of-it-32879
Pardey, Andres, "Curating *Bewogen Beweging*. The Exchange between Daniel Spoerri, Jean Tinguely, Pontus Hultén and Willem Sandberg." in "The Artist as Curator." p. 221 ff, published by Zero Foundation, Düsseldorf, 2015.
Smolik, Noemi, "The Showman" (Kasper König). Artforum, November 1994.
Strängberg, Ulla, "The question is how to approach a legend? One of Sweden's most internationally renowned cultural figures?" Academics/Saco magazine, no. 4, 2001.
Tomkins, Calvin, "Beyond the Machine. A Profile on Jean Tinguely." The New Yorker, February 1962.
Tomkins, Calvin, "The Camel in the Tent." The New Yorker, March 2, 1981.
Tomkins, Calvin, "The Good Monster." The New Yorker, February 1, 1978.
Tomkins, Calvin, "The Modern Man." The New Yorker, July 2, 2012.
van der Heeg, Erik, Holm, Eva-Lotta, Nilsson, Håkan, "Dominance of star curators harms the art world in the long run. Conversations with curators (4): Pontus Hultén, Kunsthalle Bonn and IHEAP, Paris." Material, Stockholm, 3rd edition, no. 5, 1994.
Zara, Janelle, "Inside the Private World of David Hockney." Architectural Digest, September 12, 2018. https:// www.architecturaldigest.com/story/david-hockney-studio-visit.

Academic work/other forums:

Andersson, Patrik, "Euro-Pop: the mechanical bride stripped bare in Stockholm, even." University of British Columbia, Vancouver, 2001. https://open.library.ubc.ca/soa/cIRcle/collections/ubctheses/831/items/1.0090453
Andreeva, Ekaterina, Понтюс Хюльтен и музейные революции на территориях Москвы и Петербурга Екатерина Андреева Международная ассоциация художественных критиков (AICA), Санкт-Петербург ("Pontus Hultén's museum revolutions in the territories of Moscow and Saint Petersburg"). The Garage Journal. Studies in Art, Museums & Culture, Garage Museum of Contemoprary Art, Moscow 2020.
af Petersens, Magnus, "The exhibitions of Pontus Hultén." Lecture MACBA, October 26, 2009. https://img.macba.cat/public/uploads/20091025/Hulten_eng.pdf
Bydler, Charlotte, Gedin, Andreas, Ringarp, Johanna, "Pontus Hultén at Moderna Museet: Witness Seminar Södertörn University, April 26, 2017." Södertörn University, Stockholm, 2018.
Grafe, Christopher, "People's Palaces Architecture, Culture and Democracy in two European Post-War Cultural Centres." NUR 648 Bouwkunst, architecture, Amsterdam 2010. https://www.academia.edu/8767211/Peoples_Palaces
Oral history interview with Giuseppe Panza di Biumo by Christopher Knight, April 2-4, 1985. Smithsonian Archives https://www.aaa.si.edu/collections/interviews/oral-history-interview-giuseppe-panza-12827
Oral history interview with Julie Martin by Liza Zapol, November 7–8, 2018. Smithsonian Archives. https://www.aaa.si.edu/collections/interviews/oral-history-interview-julie-b-martin-17613#transcript
Paez, Milena, "Kazimir Malevich: retour sur l'exposition homage de 1978." Thesis L'université Paris 8 (EDESTA), 2014. histoiredesexpos.hypotheses.org/tag/architectones
Pettersson, Jimmy, "Film at the Art Museum: The National Museum's encounter with the film medium 1945–1950." Thesis Stockholm University, 2019. Su.diva-portal.org
"Second Report: The Stockholm type boxes." AWAAB final report, New York, July 19, 2010.
The Machine: As Seen at the End of the Mechanical Age, press release. November 35, 1968. https://www.moma.org/momaorg/shared/pdfs/docs/press_archives/4149/releases/MOMA_1968_July-December_0081.pdf

West, Kim, "The Exhibitionary Complex Exhibition, Apparatus, and Media from Kulturhuset to the Centre Pompidou, 1963–1977." Södertörn University, 2017.

Radio/TV/Web postings:

"Andy Warhol's Brillo boxes." Documentary Sveriges Radio P3 Dokumentär, produced by Anna Gjöres, Stockholm, 2012. sverigesradio.se/avsnitt/48002
"Brillo Box and so forth. An interview with Arthur Danto." www.youtube.com/watch?v=gW_QiTvWA20
"Centre Pompidou: Refreshing Reality." www.youtube.com/watch?v=9DOVlROG-lY
"Disappeared Duchamp sketch worth one million found in Sweden." P4 Stockholm, May 31, 2018, 09:44. sverigesradio.se/artikel/6966886
"E.A.T. Experiments in Art and Technology, 1960–2001." Dartmouth College Seminary 2006. www.youtube.com/watch?v=BocoC9CxER4
"Fakes in the Art World." DW Documentary. www.youtube.com/ watch?v=1lNSXB4i4fE
"Jean Tinguely and Niki de Saint Phalle Le Cyclop." www.youtube.com/watch?v=DHF_bXfoThw
"Jo Siffert & Jean Tinguely 1–4." www.youtube.com/watch?v=a2GNcbsWFLY
"Marcel Duchamp interview with Georges Charbonnier 1961." www.youtube.com/watch?v=1gNqeNNPkOs
"Marcel Duchamp (1887–1968): a life, a work." www.youtube.com/ watch?v=EIbe2nyq79A
"Meeting in 1960 with Marcel Duchamp, tutelary figure of 20th century art." www.youtube.com/watch?v=rZOatKrmpxA
"Niki de Saint Phalle — The story of a free woman." https://www.youtube.com/watch?v=tZnQijyAsgU
"Perestroika and the Post-Soviet Period." MNAM Centre Pompidou, September 16, 2016. https://www.centrepompidou.fr/en/resources/media/2Cu01Bn
"Pompidou Center to open at Beaubourg." INA Archive. www.youtube.com/watch?v=sYH3nbvNdL4
"Pontus Hultén: between Stockholm, Amsterdam and Paris (conversation with Jean-Hubert Martin, Ann-Sofi Noring, and others." Festival de l'Histoire de l'art, Fontainebleau, 2019. www.youtube.com/watch?v=mGfddLeOgho
"Pontus Hultén — succéerna och Brilloskandalen". Swedish Television Documentary, 2024, directed by Ann-Linn Guillou.
"The art collector and the disaster" (about Teto Ahrenberg). Swedish Television Documentary, 2017.
"The monster in the forest. Jean Tinguely's Cyclops." www.youtube.com/watch?v=deimrBq1Mvo
"The Story of the Centre Pompidou." www.youtube.com/watch?v=uoZukiuGxVo
"Uppdrag Granskning", Swedish Television, May 13, 2015.

Unpublished works:

Andreae, Stephan, "Reisen mit Riesen/Walking With Giants." Transcript of recorded conversations with Pontus Hultén for unpublished autobiography, La Motte, 1997–1999. © Stephan Andreae.
Hvidberg, Peter, "Why don't you make them over there? The true story about the so-called Brillo scandal." Research in progress, Copenhagen. © Peter Hvidberg.

List of images

Index of persons

Duchamp's typeface! The types in this book are Pyke, sculpted by Sofie Beier, Sélavy by Nina Stössinger, and Whitney by Tobias Frere-Jones (originally created for the Whitney Museum). Sélavy is "loosely based" on the typography used in Marcel Duchamp's "La Boîte verte," "The Green Box," from 1934, an important source of inspiration for Pontus Hultén througout his career. The typeface's name is rendered from Rrose Sélavy, Marcel Duchamp's androgynous alter ego.

First published in Sweden by Albert Bonniers Förlag, 2022.

PUBLISHED BY
Verlag der Buchhandlung Walther & Franz König, Köln

IN COLLABORATION WITH
The Center for Curatorial Studies, Bard College (CCS Bard)

The Center for Curatorial Studies, Bard College (CCS Bard) is the leading institution dedicated to curatorial studies. Through its Graduate Program, Library and Archives, and the Hessel Museum of Art, CCS Bard serves as an incubator for interdisciplinary practices and advances new perspectives in contemporary art. In 2025, CCS Bard expanded its Library and Archives with the Keith Haring Wing, including the dedication of a new classroom, the Pontus Hultén Classroom, made possible through a generous gift from the Marieluise Hessel Foundation.

TRANSLATION Claes Britton
DESIGN Nina Ulmaja
IMAGE EDITOR Christina Sollenberg Britton
LAYOUT & PRODUCTION Maria Ulaner
PRINT Livonia Print, Latvia, 2025
ISBN 978-3-7533-0876-0

Bibliographic information published by the Deutsche Nationalbibliothek
The Deutsche Nationalbibliothek lists this publication in the Deutsche Nationalbibliografie; detailed bibliographic data are available at http://dnb.d-nb.de

DISTRIBUTION EUROPE
Buchhandlung Walther König
Ehrenstraße 4
D – 50672 Köln
TEL +49 (0) 221 / 20 59 6 53
verlag@buchhandlung-walther-koenig.de

DISTRIBUTION OUTSIDE EUROPE
D.A.P./Distributed Art Publishers, Inc.
75 Broad Street, Suite 630
USA – New York, NY 10004
TEL +1 (0) 212 627 1999
orders@dapinc.com

DISTRIBUTION UK & IRELAND
ART DATA
12 Bell Industrial Estate
50 Cunnington Street
London W4 5HB
United Kingdom
TEL +44 (0)208 747 10 61
orders@artdata.co.uk

"There is no solution because there is no problem."

MARCEL DUCHAMP